My Journal of the Council

Yves Congar OP

My Journal of the Council

Yves Congar OP

Translated from French by
Mary John Ronayne OP
Mary Cecily Boulding OP

English Translation Editor
Denis Minns OP

A Michael Glazier Book

LITURGICAL PRESS
Collegeville, Minnesota

www.litpress.org

A Michael Glazier Book published by Liturgical Press

The original edition published in French with the title:
Mon journal du Concile, I et II, tome I : 1960-1963 - tome II : 1964-1966 © Les Éditions du
  Cerf, 2002.

English text copyright © 2012 ATF Press.

The present edition in the English language is jointly published by:
ATF Press (Australia)—Australian, Asian, Pacific, and South American rights
Dominican Publications (Ireland)—European rights
Liturgical Press (USA)—North American rights

Printed in the United States of America.

ISBN 978-0-8146-8029-2

Library of Congress Control Number: 2012904797

Jacket and cover design by David Manahan, OSB.
Cover photo courtesy of Thinkstock/iStockphoto;
photo inset of Yves Congar courtesy of Catholic News Service.
Back flap photo © Archives de la Province Dominicaine de France.

Avec le soutien du

www.centrenationaldulivre.fr

TABLE OF CONTENTS

FOREWORD

DOMINIQUE CONGAR

The appearance of *My Journal of the Council* completes the publication of the three main journals written by Yves Congar, who died on 22 June 1995 in the Invalides in Paris.

May I be allowed to append this somewhat intimate foreword, which would probably not have been disapproved of by this Dominican, who was so attached to his family and to the Ardennes where he was born.

The first journal was his *Journal de la guerre 1914–1918* (Cerf, 1997), the second, his *Journal d'un théologien, 1946–1956* (Cerf, 2000). Here, now, is the third, *Mon Journal du Concile*.

First and foremost, I should like, in my own name and in that of the Congar family, to thank Éditions du Cerf who have completed the difficult task of publishing this *Journal*. My thanks go also to all those who have contributed to this publication.

Yves Congar had not shown to anyone the exercise books in which he had written the journal he kept during the 1914–1918 war, but he often spoke about it. This journal, which had been kept over a period of five years in Sedan, revealed a highly gifted and precocious boy, sensitive and open—already at that age—to world events. Interesting in this regard is Jean-Pierre Jossua's presentation (30 June 1997) as well as the analysis and notes by Stéphane Audoin-Rouzeau.

The second journal covers the years between 1946 and 1956, following on Yves Congar's period in captivity. There is nothing to add to the excellent 'General Introduction' to that book written by Étienne Fouilleux. Everything was said, and well said. In that book we encounter a Congar entangled in the difficulties emanating from ecclesiastical authority. A number of people have found this document exceptional.

Yves Congar had explicitly stated his wish that his journal should not be made public until the year 2000. So the reader will discover that this theologian and expert, faithful to his personal journal technique, wrote day by day during this great event. And that he did this in spite of intense fatigue and an illness which was becoming progressively worse.

As a small boy in 1914, Yves Congar already displayed an alert style in which all the details were noted in a living and precise way; his *Journal of the Council* makes it clear that the theologian was never at a loss for words, nor had he lost his powers of observation.

When startled, perhaps, by somewhat crude personal reflections or comments, the reader should recall that what the 1914–1918 child and the 1946–1956 theologian had written was by no means always innocuous.

There are not many references to his family in his *Journal of the Council*, but they do exist. As before, his beloved mother, Tere, is mentioned. With his older brothers and with his childhood companions in the Fond-de-Givonne (Sedan, Ardennes), Yves Congar spoke the language of a corner tearaway in an Ardennes accent. Then his life as a soldier and his harsh captivity reinforced this tendency to say exactly what he thought.

When he began writing his *Journal of the Council*, Congar had not yet fully recovered from the years during which his life as a teacher, theologian and writer had been forcibly interrupted. In 1962, this Dominican was still a wounded man, no longer in full possession of his physical strength, though his intellectual powers were fully intact.

His *Journal of a Theologian (1946–1956)* ended with the appointment of Yves Congar as a consultor to the Preparatory Theological Commission for the Council.

So here, now, is his *Journal of the Council*, the text of which had been carefully revised by Yves Congar himself, and which he had had typed, and the original of which is carefully preserved in the archives of the Dominican Province of France.

Out of respect for the author's text, I have expressed the wish that there should be no excisions or suppressions, even if some of the things he says are a bit 'sharp'. This, after all, is something which we had grown accustomed to in our uncle over many years!

INTRODUCTION

ÉRIC MAHIEU

Yves Congar's career prior to the Council

Yves Congar[1] was born in 1904 in Sedan where he spent his youth, marked by the First World War.[2] In 1921 he entered the university seminary 'Des Carmes' at the Institut Catholique in Paris. After studying philosophy for three years, and a year's military service, he opted for life as a Dominican, and entered the novitiate of the Province of France in 1925. Having been given the religious name of Marie-Joseph, he then did his theological studies from 1926 to 1931 at the House of Studies of Le Saulchoir which was at that time situated in Kain-la-Tombe in Belgium, due to the expulsion of religious from France at the beginning of the century.

It was there that he made the acquaintance, among the professors, of Fr Marie-Dominique Chenu, OP, a little his senior, who was to have a great influence on him thanks to his theological method[3] and in particular to the attention he paid to the 'relevance of the past for the present and to its reinterrogation by

---

1. For a more detailed biography, *cf* Étienne Fouilloux, 'Frère Yves, Cardinal Congar, dominicain. Itinéraire d'un théologien', in *Revue des Sciences Philosophiques et Théologiques,* 1995: 379–404, and Jean-Pierre Jossua, who presented the life and work of Congar up to and including the Council in *Le Père Congar: la théologie au service du peuple de Dieu* (Paris: Cerf, 1967). Étienne Fouilloux has edited and presented precious fragments of journals or of memoirs written before the Council: *cf* Yves Congar, *Journal d'un théologien (1946–1956)* (Paris: Cerf, 2000). Congar reflected on his ecumenical commitment in 'Appels et cheminements, 1919–1963', preface to Yves M-J Congar, *Chrétiens en dialogue. Contributions catholiques à l'Œcuménisme,* 'Unam Sanctam' 50 (Paris: Cerf, 1964), IX–LXIV, revised and completed ten years later in *Une passion: l'unité. Refléxions et souvenirs 1929–1973,* 'Foi Vivante', 156 (Paris: Cerf, 1974); he reflected once more on his career in *Une vie pour la vérité. Jean Puyo interroge le Père Congar* (Paris: Cerf, Le Centurion, 1975).
2. *Cf* Yves Congar, *Journal de la guerre 1914–1918,* with notes and commentary by the historian Stéphane Audoin-Rouzeau and by Dominique Congar (the author's nephew) (Paris: Cerf, 1997).
3. *Cf* Marie-Dominique Chenu, *Une école de théologie: le Saulchoir* (Paris: Cerf, 1985).

the present'.[4] From 1928 onwards, he directed his work towards ecclesiology and chose the unity of the Church as the subject of his thesis for the lectorate in theology. In preparation for his ordination as a priest, which took place in July 1930, he meditated on chapter 17 of the Gospel of St John, and felt called to work for the unity of all those who believe in Jesus Christ. Later he was to write: 'I have said that I had at that time *recognised* an ecumenical vocation which was, at the same time, an ecclesiological vocation, but the seed had been planted in me several years earlier, no doubt even during my childhood'.[5]

From 1932 onwards, he taught ecclesiology at Le Saulchoir while at the same time taking part in ecumenical research by attending many meetings. These early theological commitments were stimulated by the enquiry into the cause of unbelief conducted by his confrères in *La Vie intellectuelle,* to which he contributed a conclusion in the issue for 25 July 1935. Reflecting on this enquiry, he was to write: 'To the extent to which (…) we ourselves have a responsibility for unbelief, it seemed to me that this was due to the fact that the Church was showing to the world a face that betrayed, rather than expressed, its true nature in accordance with the Gospel and its own profound tradition. The true response, the positive conclusion, consisted in renewing our presentation and, for this reason, first and foremost our own vision of the Church, by going beyond the presentations and the juridical vision that were then predominant, and had been for a long time'.[6] It was in this spirit that, in 1937, he inaugurated, with Éditions du Cerf, the ecclesiological collection 'Unam Sanctam'.

'The aim of the collection was to revive and reinsert into the world of ideas a certain number of profoundly traditional themes and ecclesiological values which had, however, due to the creation of a special treatise on the Church, been more or less forgotten or buried under other themes in the Tradition that were less profound and of lesser value'.[7] He published, as the first volume in this collection, his own first great theological work, *Chrétiens désunis, Principes d'un 'œcumenisme' catholique.* Innovatively, he no longer thought of the reunion of the Churches simply in terms of the return of non-Catholic Christians to the fold, but as the possibility of a qualitative development of Catholicity, the other Churches having managed, at times better than his own, to preserve or develop certain values. This bold position was to occasion, even then, some suspicions concerning the young theologian. Mobilised in 1939, a prisoner of war from 1940 until 1945, Y Congar in this way lost several years of intellectual work, but pursued, in the camps, his tireless activity as a preacher, never hesitating, while doing so, publicly to assail Nazism.

---

4. Jean-Pierre Jossua OP, *op cit,* 19.
5. 'Appels et cheminements, 1919–1963', *op cit,* XI.
6. *Ibid,* XXXIII.
7. *Ibid,* XXXIII–XXXIV.

After the Liberation, Congar resumed his teaching at Le Saulchoir, which had by this time been re-established in France, at Étiolles near Paris. French Catholicism was experiencing at that time an intense vitality, marked by biblical, patristic and liturgical research and by varied community and apostolic initiatives. In 1950, Congar published *Vraie et fausse réforme dans l'Église*,[8] which provided the ecclesiological foundations for this reformist ferment, then in 1953 *Jalons pour une théologie du laïcat*,[9] which reasserted the value of the mission of lay people in the Catholic Church. In the meantime, however, suspicions in Rome began to weigh on his activity and were destined to put a brake on, if not to bring to a complete halt, his plans for further publications and re-editions. As he was to write later: 'As far as I myself am concerned, from the beginning of 1947 until the end of 1956, I have never known anything from that quarter except an uninterrupted stream of denunciations, warnings, restrictive or discriminatory measures and distrustful interventions.'[10] Though he had a share, in 1952, in the creation of the Catholic Conference for Ecumenical Matters, which was launched and animated by J Willebrands, his ecumenical activity thereafter was destined to become more discreet.

He devoted himself to ecclesiological research, with an increasingly marked interest in the history of doctrines.[11] But in February 1954 Roman suspicions about the theological and pastoral ferment in France led the Fr General of the Dominicans to take some draconian steps: he dismissed the three French Provincials and banned Frs Chenu, Boisselot, Féret and Congar from teaching. At his own request, Congar was sent for several months to Jerusalem. Having been summoned to Rome in November of that year by the Holy Office, where he remained for several months, held up by pointless petty annoyances,[12] he was sent to Cambridge in February 1956. It was only at the end of that year that his exile came to an end and he was assigned to the priory in Strasbourg, where the bishop, Mgr Weber, was favourably disposed towards him. From then onwards, his difficulties with the Roman authorities gradually decreased. Certainly, he was still not allowed to hold any teaching position, but he was able to resume his work of publishing and research, of preaching and giving lectures. On 28 October 1958, Giuseppe Roncalli was elected pope and took the name of John XXIII. On 12 January 1959, Yves Congar wrote to his friend, Christophe-Jean Dumont, OP, director of the Istina Centre as follows: 'John XXIII? Such a complete conversion

---

8. 'Unam Sanctam', 20, Cerf.
9. 'Unam Sanctam', 23, Cerf.
10. *Ibid*, XLVI.
11. This historical research, which was still proceeding at the time of the Council, was to bear fruit principally in *L'Église de saint Augustin à l'époque moderne* (Paris: Cerf, 1970): the German version of this work is part of the *Handbuch der Dogmengeschichte* and was to be published in the same year by Éditions Herder, Freiburg im Breisgau.
12. However, Congar was never actually formally condemned, nor yet subjected to a process in good and due form on the part of the Holy Office.

would be needed in Rome! Conversion to no longer laying claim to the control of everything: it was that, under Pius XII, that took on unprecedented dimensions and produced a bottomless paternalism and stupidity'.[13] But then, on 25 January, the new Pope announced his intention to summon an ecumenical Council! Three days later, Congar wrote to his friend, Bernard Dupuy, OP, saying: 'Clearly, something new is in the air. It is very serious'.[14] Of this unforeseen event, he has left us an eye-witness account of inestimable value.

The writing of the Journal *of the Council*

In 1963, Congar wrote that he had not kept a journal except 'from time to time, on two kinds of occasion: when it was given to me to experience something new, to make contact with a new world; when I was involved in historically important events (war, the 1954 crisis, the Council)'.[15] But that amounted to quite a number of journals or fragments of journals kept by Yves Congar all through his life.[16] From an early age, his mother had urged him to record events: '1914! I was ten years old. It was thought that the war would only last for a few months. At the end of July, my mother said to us, my brothers, my sister and myself: "Keep a Journal"'.[17] Of all the diaries that he has left behind him, the most imposing of all for its sheer size is this *Journal of the Council*. It is not an intimate or spiritual journal. As he wrote the day after the death of his mother: 'I am keeping this little journal as a reference. I do not mix it up with the expression of my personal feelings' (26 November 1963). That did not prevent him, then and at other times, from reflecting on his vocation and his life, or recalling 'the mystical history of the Council' (26 November 1963) made up of the prayer and the sufferings of many. However, the personal impressions or judgments that are scattered throughout the *Journal* are above all those of a theologian involved in an adventure of which he wants to keep a record, with the presentiment that it may one day be useful in one way or another. Hence he wrote: 'I am writing, if not for History!! at least so that my witness is recorded' (14 March 1964).

---

13. Istina Centre Archives.
14. Istina Centre Archives.
15. 'Appels et cheminements, 1929–1963', *op cit,* p X.
16. Concerning these journals, *cf* the article by Étienne Fouilloux: 'Congar, témoin de l'Église de son temps', in André Vauchez (editor), *Cardinal Yves Congar,* 71–91; however the list given there is not complete, especially for the post-conciliar period; in particular, Congar had kept journals of his visits to the United States and to Poland in 1966, as a result of contacts and invitations during the Council.
17. 'Enfance sedanaise (1904–1919)', *Le Pays sedanais,* 27.

Could Congar have doubted the immense interest that this *Journal* would have for future historians of Vatican II?[18] He was not, of course, the only one of the experts or Council Fathers to have kept a journal.[19]

However, kept virtually day by day during the Conciliar sessions, but also between the sessions, in particular when the Commissions were meeting, it makes it possible to follow step by step the work of a consultor to the Preparatory Theological Commission, then of a Council expert who regularly took part in meetings of the Doctrinal Commission as well as of a number of other conciliar Commissions, and who was also present at many of the General Congregations of the Council Fathers in St Peter's Basilica. Written without stylistic pretensions, and quite freely, very often at the end of harassing days, its style is hardly elegant, and the author, probably in his concern for historical accuracy, did not wish to revise it, but for this reason it has the advantage of giving us this theologian's immediate reactions and impressions. It may well be felt that Congar was at times fierce or merciless in his assessments, but one must acknowledge that he knew how to be just, when they deserved it, to those who were not theologically on his side. That, in his own foreword, he forbade any public use of the *Journal* before the year 2000 is, moreover, a mark of respect for all the protagonists of the Council.

Congar's participation in the various stages of the Council
The preparations for the Council (from 25 January 1959 to 11 October 1962)
It was when he was named as a consultor to the Preparatory Theological Commission in July 1960 that Congar began writing his *Journal of the Council*.

He began by reflecting on the period that had elapsed since 25 January 1959, the day on which Pope John XXIII had announced the summoning of an ecumenical Council. The long-term aim of the reunion of separated Christians, envisaged by the newly elected Pope, and the corresponding aim of an ecclesiological renewal and a pastoral and missionary opening of the Church had, to begin with, filled him with hope; but the resistance of conservative circles in the Roman Curia which were seeking to control the preparation of the Council, subsequently made him uneasy. So, like his friend, Fr Henri de Lubac SJ, who had been appointed a consultor to the same Commission, he feared that he was no more than

---

18. Borne witness to by the frequent references to the *Journal* in the five volumes of the first comprehensive historical survey of the Council, edited by Giuseppe Alberigo, *Storia del Concilio Vaticano II* (il Mulino, Bologna; Peeters, Leuven), 1995-2001; English translation edited by Joseph A. Komonchak, five volumes (Orbis, Maryknoll; Peeters, Leuven) 1995, 1997, 2000, 2006.
19. On this, see the study by Alberto Melloni, 'Les journaux privés dans l'histoire de Vatican II', as an introduction to the fragmentary journal of Marie-Dominique Chenu, *Notes quotidiennes au Concile* (Paris: Cerf, 1995); since then, the interesting journal of Mgr Charue, vice-president of the Doctrinal Commission, in which he played a major role, has been published: *Carnets conciliaires de l'évêque de Namur A-M Charue*, Cahiers de la Revue Théologique de Louvain 32, Louvain-le-Neuve, 2000.

a hostage, without any real margin for action and bound by the conciliar oath of secrecy that they would both have to swear. This Commission was clearly dominated by the theologians of the Roman universities who were more concerned to defend the pontifical teachings of the most recent popes than to take any account of the theological renewal that was in train. However, it also included some theologians who were more open, such as Gérard Philips, Philippe Delhaye, René Laurentin or Joseph Lécuyer. In the end, Congar decided to commit himself loyally to the work of this Commission in the hope of being useful.

In any case, he had not waited for this nomination in order to contribute to the preparation of the Council. Convinced that public opinion must make itself known and play its part in the Church, he had sought to arouse it by means of articles and lectures. He continued his work within the networks of Catholic theologians involved in the ecumenical movement.[20] He began again on the preparation of a volume on the episcopate, which he had had in mind for several years, in the 'Unam Sanctam' collection that he had inaugurated and that he directed. The bishop of Strasbourg, Mgr Weber, called upon his services for the preparation of his reply to the ante-preparatory consultation. On the other hand, the Catholic Theology Faculty in Strasbourg, which had also been consulted, did not ask for his help.

Immediately after his nomination, Cardinal Ottaviani, Prefect of the Holy Office and President of the Preparatory Theological Commission, asked Congar to indicate which questions he would prefer to deal with. Congar wrote back on 15 August 1960 mentioning Tradition, the theology of the laity and, in general, ecclesiology. Then, in September, he sent to all the members and consultors of the Commission a report on the way he envisaged the proposed preparatory schemas.

It was in November 1960 that the Preparatory Commission officially began its work in Rome. Congar went there, but he quickly perceived that his margin for manoeuvre was very limited. The Secretary of the Commission, Fr Sebastian Tromp, SJ, who had been one of Pius XII's theological experts, directed the work very rigidly. However, having been allocated to the *De ecclesia* sub-commission, Congar had the pleasure of being welcomed there by his confrère, Fr Gagnebet, OP. But he was forced to conclude that the texts that he was being asked to write[21] and the comments that he made on the schemas had little effect in the face of the

---

20. Congar took part in the ecumenical days at the monastery of Chevetogne in 1959 (*cf* Yves M-J Congar, 'Conclusion', in *Le Concile et les conciles. Contribution à l'histoire de la vie conciliaire de l'Église* (Paris: Cerf-Chevetogne, 1960), 285–334, and in 1960 (concerned with the local Church and the universal Church); within the Catholic Conference for Ecumenical Matters, he proposed the writing of a memorandum on the question of the unity of Christians; this was to be widely distributed among the various Roman bodies and those who were to be Council Fathers.

21. Congar prepared four *vota* for the Preparatory Theological Commission: on the laity, on the question of who was or was not a member of the Church, on the episcopate and on ecumenism.

preponderance of the conservative environment. Being only a simple consultor, he was not invited to attend all the meetings of the Commission in which, moreover, he was only rarely called upon to speak.

In August 1961, he received the preparatory schemas in their provisional state, and reading them proved a great disappointment; instead of an overall vision, he found that all the questions had been compartmentalised; instead of a return to sources, there was a florilegium of declarations by recent popes; these schemas were closed to ecumenical questioning; mariological positions were maximalised in them. Only Gérard Philips' text on the laity met with his approval.

In fact, the Preparatory Theological Commission functioned without any collaboration with the other Preparatory Commissions, nor yet with the Secretariat for the Unity of Christians, a body that had been set up by John XXIII to work during the Council on reconciliation with separated Christians. Cardinal Ottaviani and Fr Tromp considered that only the Theological Commission was competent to deal with doctrinal questions, the role of the other Commissions being of a more practical nature. Thus there was no interaction between doctrinal questions and pastoral concerns.

Nevertheless, encouraging signs were gradually appearing. The Central Preparatory Commission, consisting mainly of bishops playing an important role in their own countries, was requiring a more pastoral approach from the various Preparatory Commissions and sent some of the schemas back to be reworked.[22] The atmosphere of the Theological Commission itself began to become more open.

At the beginning of August 1962, two months before the opening of the Council, Congar still had no clear idea about the likely role he was to play in the conciliar Commissions. He offered his services to Mgr Weber, who chose him as his personal expert at the Council and consulted him on the preparatory schemas, which he had just received. It was only on 28 September that his name appeared in the first wave of nominations of official Council experts published in *L'Osservatore Romano*.[23] He would thus be able to attend all the General Congregations in St Peter's Basilica and to participate in the workings of the conciliar Commissions, when invited to do so by one of their members.

The First Session (from 11 October to 8 December 1962)

On 9 October 1962, Congar, with the French bishops, boarded the plane that was to take them to Rome for the First Session. While with them, he championed a plan for an initial message from the Council Fathers to the world, an idea that

---

22. He had direct information about this from Cardinals Liénart and Richaud, and Mgr Hurley.
23. Curiously enough, Congar does not mention this, though it was so important for what followed; he simply mentioned in passing that he had gone to collect his expert's identity card the day after his arrival in Rome.

came from his friend and master, M-D Chenu OP. He also campaigned for the doctrinal schemas to be revised, while his more radical theological colleagues from across the Rhine were advocating their complete rejection.

The postponement of the election of members to the conciliar Commissions, which was secured by Cardinals Liénart and Frings on 13 October, was looked upon by Congar as the first conciliar act; that same day he wrote 'What I foresaw is happening: the Council itself could well be very different from its preparation', adding, the next day, that thanks to the preparation for these elections, collegiality was being launched. The preparation of the message to the world by the conciliar assembly on 20 October, even though the text differed considerably from that prepared with Chenu, portrayed a Church that wanted to renew itself and rejoin the world in a spirit of dialogue and service.

The first text to be examined by the conciliar Fathers was the schema on the liturgy, which incorporated many of the achievements of the liturgical movement. The debate gave the assembly the opportunity to run itself in, so to speak, and to establish the polarities. Congar sought, more or less successfully, to arrange for a Council Father to intervene on the topics that were important to him on the ecclesiological plane: the granting of Communion under both kinds to the laity, the bases of the participation of the laity in the liturgy.

But, at the same time, and principally in conjunction with German, Belgian, Dutch and French theologians, he was preparing the debate on the doctrinal schemas that had been drawn up by the Preparatory Theological Commission. Some of the bishops got things started: Mgr Volk, Bishop of Mainz, formerly a professor of theology, Mgr Elchinger, Coadjutor Bishop of Strasbourg, whom Cardinal Liénart had asked to act as liaison between the German and French bishops, and Cardinal Suenens, Archbishop of Malines-Brussels. Several theologians each prepared his own attempt at an audacious draft foreword to the doctrinal schemas. One of these texts, prepared principally by Karl Rahner and distributed too soon to the Fathers, came to nothing: it reflected too strongly the author's own theological views. As for Congar attempt, it was put to one side.

Eventually, the work of these theologians was aimed more realistically at preparing alternative texts that might serve to replace the schema on the sources of Revelation *(De fontibus)* and the one on the Church. On 18 October, Congar agreed to work as one of an international team led by Gérard Philips in the preparation of a new schema on the Church that had been requested by Cardinal Suenens. On 10 November, at the request of J Daniélou, he took part in the rewriting of the *De fontibus* and thus found himself a member of the 'workshops' that were to organise the French bishops and their experts from that point and throughout the Sessions. It was on these two schemas that the preoccupations of many bishops were centred, and Congar very soon found himself being asked by various groups of bishops for discussions with them, and lectures on these two topics. These encounters made manifest the strong expectation of a schema on the Church that would complete the First Vatican Council on the question of the episcopate.

It was with the opening of the debate on *De fontibus* on 14 November that a conciliar majority and minority clearly appeared in relation to the question of the relationship between Scripture and Tradition: the defenders of a controversialist anti-Protestant attitude against the partisans of theological renewal and openness. Congar recommended the development of a text that would be acceptable to all, and prepared a draft intervention along these lines that was to be used by Mgr Zoa *in aula*. Although the vote on 20 November that rejected the schema did not secure the required two-thirds majority, it led to a legal deadlock that John XXIII cleared the following day by setting up a joint Commission charged with writing anew a schema on Revelation. Congar, who at the time was working on the question of Tradition, regretted not having been called upon to take part in it.

As for the schema *De ecclesia*, it was not distributed to the Fathers until 23 November, although the debate was to begin on 1 December. On 28 November, Congar found himself being made responsible by the French bishops for organising working parties. The debate itself, which did not last long, revealed the assembly's dissatisfaction and need for an extensive revision of the schema. In fact, things were moving in the direction of preparing for the intersession, with the interventions of Cardinals Montini and Suenens each suggesting a veritable programme of conciliar action centred above all on the theme of the Church, and with the setting up, announced on 6 December, of a Co-ordinating Commission charged with supervising the work of the conciliar Commissions until the next Session.

The Session ended on 8 December. Congar quite often had the impression that he was wasting his time. It is true that he had not, up to that date, been called upon by any conciliar Commission, and that the French bishops, still not very well organised, were slow in making use of his abilities.

However, a number of episcopates had asked to meet with him, and the Secretariat for Unity had invited him to attend their meetings with the non-Catholic Observers. In addition, he had been involved in the initial steps taken by the informal grouping of bishops and theologians 'Jesus, the Church and the poor', which was to be active throughout the Council along the lines of an evangelical conversion of the Church and the taking into account of the world of the poor. But, above all, Congar was convinced that the Council had need of this running-in period and, when all is said and done, he recognised that a Council spirit had been created and that the presence of the Observers had a considerable impact.

First intersession (from 8 December 1962 to 29 September 1963)
The first echoes that Congar heard of the Co-ordinating Commission led him to think that the Council had really been released from the grip of the Roman

Curia. It was in this new climate that he gladly took part in the work of repairing the *De Ecclesia*. He made his own contribution to the last revision of the Philips schema sponsored by Cardinal Suenens, but he also met together with the German experts who were preparing another proposal. He sent his first contributions to *Études et documents,* dossiers that the French episcopate was to circulate from then onwards during the Council. These dossiers, intended primarily for the French bishops, were to be widely appreciated well beyond France itself.

When the Doctrinal Commission began the revision of the *De ecclesia* in Rome, many were astonished that Congar was not present, and he was summoned to join the sub-commission responsible for this revision. From then onwards he was to be a more or less permanent expert on the Doctrinal Commission. The Philips schema was adopted as a working basis and its author quickly became the real animator of this revision. Seduced by the efficiency and the good atmosphere of mutual understanding between the Belgian experts, Congar moved into the Belgian College, which was to be from then onwards one of the strategic focal points of the Council. On 13 March he there celebrated the happy conclusion of the *De ecclesia* with those whom he now considered his friends: Gérard Philips, but also the Belgians Charles Moeller and Gustave Thils. After centuries of Roman centralisation, which had reached their culminating point in the pontificate of Pius XII, Congar rejoiced to see episcopal collegiality finding its place in a conciliar schema.

Having returned to Rome for the last chapters of the *De ecclesia*, Congar was also, for the first time, approached by Mgr Garrone, at the time the only French bishop on the Doctrinal Commission, who asked him to work on 'schema XVII' on the Church in the world. This had been put on the agenda in January by the Co-ordinating Commission, which entrusted it to a Joint Commission comprising members of both the Doctrinal Commission and the Commission for the Apostolate of the Laity. Mgr Garrone asked him to help with the chapter on anthropology, and Congar then put in a plea for a true Christian anthropology that would perceive humankind biblically, in the image of God, and not according to scholastic schemes. When he came to look at the other chapters dealing with matters concerning other sectors that interested him (marriage and the family, war and peace, culture), he regretted that the work, somewhat slapdash, had not been based on serious documentation. The uncertainty over who would succeed John XXIII, who had died on 3 June, was done away with on 21 June with the election of Paul VI and the announcement that the Council was to resume. Accordingly, the Co-ordinating Commission met again in July. At that meeting, Cardinal Suenens successfully proposed the insertion of a chapter on the People of God between the first chapter of the *De ecclesia*, on the mystery of the Church, and the chapter on the hierarchy. The rector of the Belgian College, Mgr Prignon, who had first made this suggestion, was later to assure Congar that his theology had played a part in it.[24] Moreover, Congar was invited to Malines as part of the little group asked by the cardinal to develop this chapter: this group was also asked to have another look at the theological basis of schema XVII and produce for it a text of an ecclesiological nature. Even so, Congar was to insist on the importance of retaining the chapter on anthropology that had been prepared in May.

During this year 1963, Congar found himself fully rehabilitated. Paul VI, who consulted him shortly after his election through his personal theologian, Carlo Colombo, made known on several occasions the esteem he had for his work. On 13 March, the Master General of the Dominicans, Aniceto Fernandez, had summoned him in order for the first time to say 'nice things' to him.

Later in the year, the Master General granted the request of the Chapter of the Province of France for Congar to undergo the *Ad gradus* examination and so be declared a Master of Theology in the Dominican Order. The examination took place on 14 September and Congar was to be fêted at Le Saulchoir on 8 December and then in his Priory in Strasbourg on the 16 December.[25] Even so, in the following year he was to write: 'Personally, I have never been, I am still not, free of the fears attached to a man who is suspect, sanctioned, judged, discriminated against' (12 March 1964).

Second Session (from 29 September to 4 December 1963)

The Second Session opened with a great debate on the new schema *De ecclesia*. At the Doctrinal Commission, as with the bishops that he met, Congar campaigned on behalf of the proposed new chapter on the People of God, wishing that the Church be presented in it within the framework of the history of salvation and, in particular, in the context of its relationship with the people of Israel.

But it was the following chapter, on the hierarchy, dealing basically with the episcopate and its relationship with the primacy of the Pope, that resulted in the fiercest clash within the Conciliar assembly. By means of lectures, notes and interventions prepared for the bishops, Congar fought on behalf of the new schema which, though by no means perfect, had the merit of bringing in the collegial responsibility of the bishops. His friends at the Belgian College, who were permanently in touch with Cardinal Suenens, passed on to him information about the conflicts that were rocking the supervisory bodies of the Council as to whether or not there should be a vote of orientation as demanded by the Fathers. In the end, such a vote was taken on 30 October and made it possible for the assembly to declare itself clearly in favour of episcopal collegiality and the restoration of the permanent diaconate. But on the very morning on which the vote took place, Congar was amazed to find that many of the bishops still had not perceived what was at stake doctrinally.

---

24. In a letter to Congar dated 27 September 1973 (Congar Archives).
25. This rehabilitation was to make it possible for Congar to publish his ecumenical autobiography: *cf* 'Appels et cheminements, 1929–1963', *op cit.*

The question of whether or not to insert the schema on Mary into the *De Ecclesia*, only just settled in the affirmative, also provoked a passionate debate.

Our ecclesiologist was all in favour of a balanced mariology and hence wished to see the Virgin Mary situated within the Church and not above it.

A certain number of the Council Fathers wanted to see the ministry of priests further developed in the chapter on the hierarchy. As Congar also shared this point of view, he, together with other experts, prepared a text along these lines for a group of French bishops. But, in the end, it was a text proposed by the German bishops that was used as a basis by the Doctrinal Commission.

In the end, as what was to happen to the schema on Revelation remained unclear, the French bishops asked that the living Tradition be dealt with in the *De Ecclesia*. Thus Congar found himself made responsible, together with his Dominican friends and colleagues, Frs Féret and Liégé, for preparing an amended text. The resumption of work on the *De revelatione*, called for by the Pope at the end of the Session, was to sound the knell to that.

Naturally, it was with emotion that Congar attended the debate on the new schema *De oecumenismo*. He noted that, although many of the Fathers entered well into the perspective of the ecumenical movement, there were others who saw in it nothing more than a simple strategy for promoting the return of Christians separated from Rome. It was only in the following February that Congar was to become involved in the work of the revision of this schema by the Secretariat for Unity.

Following the election of additional members to the Commissions, which was to make possible a better representation of the conciliar majority, Mgr Philips was elected assistant secretary to the Doctrinal Commission. It was an official recognition of the man who had been working on the revision of the new *De ecclesia* since the previous October, and who, *de facto,* had taken on the role of the now somewhat less prominent Fr Tromp. Congar ended up in the sub-commission charged with perfecting the new chapter on the People of God, under the leadership of Mgr Garrone.

Second intersession (from 4 December 1963 to 14 September 1964)
During this period, the Doctrinal Commission continued the work of revising the *De ecclesia* following the conciliar debate in October 1963. If the work of perfecting Chapter II, on the People of God, went well, the same could not be said of Chapter III, on the hierarchy.

In March, the meeting of the Commission led to an agreement that Congar deemed satisfactory. But the balance thus achieved was very fragile and was soon threatened by the pressure that was being brought to bear on a Pope who was scrupulous, and anxious to secure unanimous agreement. Accordingly, in order to satisfy the more conservative wing, in June Paul VI sent to the Doctrinal Commission a list of suggestions in relation to this chapter. Congar reacted then, together with his Belgian friends, in order to restrict the addition of expressions that excessively exalted the primacy of the pope. Alerted by Fr Pierre Duprey, of the Secretariat for Christian Unity, he showed himself on the other hand very sensitive to the obstacles that some sections of Chapters II and III could create for reconcilation with the Orthodox Churches. This concern led him, during the summer, to prepare in conjunction with Frs Duprey and Féret a list of *modi* for the *De ecclesia* that they would distribute widely at the beginning of the Third Session.

Congar also contributed to the writing of the future Chapter VII of *Lumen gentium,* his wish being that it would not be limited to the eschatological vocation of the Church, but that it would locate this within the framework of the eschatological vocation of humanity and of the cosmos.

Finally, in the course of the painful revision of Chapter VIII on the Virgin Mary, he opposed those who were supporting certain mariological developments that, in his view, threatened the unique mediation of Christ.

Congar also came to be involved in the less fraught re-working of the *De revelatione* by the Doctrinal Commission. His personal contribution consisted essentially in a more concrete description of the living Tradition, going beyond the anti-Protestant controversy concerning the respective contents of Scripture and Tradition.

As for schema XVII, which from January onwards became schema XIII, it was taken up again on a new basis after the rejection of the text that had been produced in September in Malines. A group of experts meeting in Zurich in February produced a new text. This 'Zurich text' was submitted to the joint Commission in March. Without being as radical as K Rahner and J Ratzinger, Congar, like his friends G Philips and C Moeller, considered that it was not sufficiently well grounded doctrinally and that it was too naively optimistic in the face of the ambiguity of the world of today.

During this intersession, Congar found himself involved for the first time, though unofficially, in the work of the Secretariat for Unity. Thus it was that he had a share in the revision of the *De oecumenismo* in February, as well as in the revision of the text on the Jews. He felt that, twenty years after Auschwitz, the Church could not keep silent on the subject of the Jewish people. In April, he was called upon by Mgr Willebrands to prepare, with C Moeller, a new text on the Jews and non-Christians. Whereas the previous version, endorsed almost unanimously on this point by the Secretariat for Unity, condemned the naming of the Jewish people a 'deicide' people, the fear of reprisals against Christians in certain Arab countries led Mgr Willebrands to ask them to produce a watered-down text which did not mention this. Congar agreed to this request. From then on, he was to be involved in all the ups and downs this text went through. Though he was in favour of condemning this idea of a 'deicide' people, which would make it possible to condemn out of hand all Christian anti-Semitism, he would nevertheless be anxious to approach the relationship between Jews and Christians in accordance with what was given in the New Testament, in the way that this was viewed by his confrère, the exegete Pierre Benoit, and he would also be vigilant that the future declaration on non-Christian religions should clearly recognise Christ as being the fullness of the truth of salvation.

Third Session (from 14 September to 21 November 1964)
This Session saw the culmination of the schemas *De oecumenismo* and *De ecclesia*. It was with the latter that Congar was particularly concerned. Pleased though he was to see the Doctrinal Commission take into account the *modi* that he had drafted concerning priests, he was at the same time disappointed at the lack of interest shown by G Philips in the *modi* he had suggested in order to keep open the possibility of dialogue with the Orthodox. He was to perceive, by degrees, that Philips, in endeavouring to secure a unanimous vote on the schema, had been obliged to concentrate on the front of the most radical of those opposed to collegiality, and to negotiate whatever concessions were necessary to secure their support, in particular, the *Nota explicativa praevia* in relation to Chapter III of the schema. However, Congar urged the Fathers to approve the final version of the schema, in contrast with some of the more radical experts who did not.

Congar collaborated in the revision of both the *De revelatione* and the schema on non-Christian religious. The author of *Jalons pour une théologie du laïcat* offered his services for the schema on the Apostolate of the Laity, but was turned down. On the other hand, he was to find himself involved in the recasting of two other texts with which the Council Fathers were unhappy, one on priests and the other on the missions. These, shortened considerably, had been reduced to a collection of propositions, following in this the instructions that had been given by the Co-ordinating Commission in January with the aim of bringing the Council to a speedier conclusion. It was at the level of the theological foundations of these propositions that Congar was to make his contribution to these two schemas, following in the wake of the *De ecclesia*. Towards the end of the Council, he was to express his joy at having thus been able to be of service to two causes which were close to his own heart: the ministry of priests and missionary activity.

The schema on priests was very quickly destined to be completely rewritten and, as early as 15 October, Congar had offered his services to Mgr Marty, who was a member of the Commission for the Clergy. He was thus included in the new team of experts charged with rewriting it in conjunction, in particular, with the Frenchmen Joseph Lécuyer, Henri Denis and Gustave Martelet, but also with some Spaniards from Opus Dei such as Julian Herranz and Alvaro del Portillo. From the start, Congar suggested viewing the priesthood in the context of a biblical theology of priesthood, but he settled for a less ambitious project that was more easily acceptable by the Fathers. The team of experts succeeded in completing the text and distributing it before the end of the Session.

As for the Commission on the missions, forestalling unfavourable reactions, it successfully proposed to the conciliar assembly the preparation of a full-scale schema on the missions. In spite of the resistance of his president, Cardinal Agagianian, Mgr Riobé, who was a member of the Commission, succeeded in getting Congar into the sub-commission charged with producing a revised version, so that Congar could contribute to the theological part.

Third intersession (from 21 November 1964 to 14 September 1965)

As soon as he returned to Strasbourg, Congar started work on writing the doctrinal chapter that he had to prepare for the schema on the missions. He did so in conjunction with the missiologists Xavier Seumois and Joseph Glazik. In January, the sub-commission, which met by the shores of Lake Nemi, put the finishing touches to the new text. Congar, who conceived of missionary activity as coextensive with the entire life of the Church, came up against a narrower view, held by the Congregation for Propaganda and some missionary institutes, limiting missionary activity to specific territories. He was thus led to prepare a compromise text situating the missions in the strictly territorial sense in the wider framework of the evangelising action of the Church.

Schema XIII, which had been strongly criticised during the Third Session, was tackled anew by a new team under the leadership of Pierre Haubtmann. Congar was invited in February to the meeting arranged in Ariccia in order to put the finishing touches to this new draft. There he contributed to the first part, which outlined the theological bases, in particular that Christian anthropology called for by the Council Fathers. However, he also contributed to a chapter on the mission of the Church in the world that it was decided to add to the document. Confronted by the combined threats of a conservative wing rejecting the opening to the modern world and some of the German experts who felt that its theological basis was too weak, Congar committed himself from then on to defending the existence of the schema, while at the same time working to improve it, in particular by means of interventions suggested to some of the Council Fathers.

Congar also met up again with the experts of the Secretariat for Unity. Not only did he continue to help with putting the finishing touches to the schema on non-Christian religions, but he also became more deeply involved in the work of revising the Declaration on Religious Freedom. This, to his delight, was to turn its back to the intransigent and negative attitude of Pius IX and the *Syllabus* and was to make possible a real dialogue with the various currents of the contemporary world. But those who were in favour of this right to religious freedom were divided on the question of the basis on which to rest the Declaration. Were they to favour an approach based on Christian Revelation, or instead a more philosophical and rational argumentation? In February, Congar, who was inclined to the first approach, secured agreement to a preamble on education to freedom in the history of salvation. In May, however, he agreed to abandon this approach in order to secure a wider consensus.

Finally, in March and April, Congar was involved in the revision of the schema on priests, on the basis of comments on the schema that had been submitted at the end of the Third Session.

Fourth Session (from 14 September to 8 December 1965)
Congar frequently found himself torn in two during this last Session, owing to
the number of Commissions to which he now belonged. In each one, he worked
towards securing agreement when the schemas being discussed were under
threat. This was the case with the schema on Revelation, in which the minority
would have liked to reintroduce mention of a wider content of revealed truths in
Tradition than in Scripture. A number of *modi* were proposed along these lines,
in particular by the Pope, who hoped to rally this minority and secure a unanimous vote. Congar sought a compromise solution that would retain the possibility of accepting the doctrine of the material sufficiency of Scripture that had
been largely accepted in the Middle Ages. The same was true of the Decree on
Religious Freedom. In this case, Congar worked on the paragraphs dealing with
the basis of this freedom in Revelation. But above all he worked actively in putting the finishing touches to a new preamble that stated from the outset the mission of evangelisation and the duty that everyone has to seek religious truth. This
preamble would also rally the support of all those who feared, as Congar himself
feared, that the decree might favour indifferentism.

Congar was also very involved in the revision of the schemas on the missions
and on priests. He endeavoured to acquit himself scrupulously of the fastidious
task of reading and synthesising the comments submitted by the Council Fathers
so that this revision would in fact meet their wishes. However, this did not prevent him from adopting, in relation to them, the role of advocate in favour of his
own convictions. Thus in the schema on the missions he endeavoured to ensure
that account was taken of the ecumenical dimension. Similarly, in the schema on
priests, he secured acceptance of his idea, based on Romans 15:16, of an apostolic
and pastoral 'priesthood of the Gospel', and not merely a cultic one.

This session also saw the flowering of schema XIII. Congar, who had worked
on the revision of the anthropological chapter, was to regret later that he had not
been called upon by the editorial team that put the finishing touches to the text,
as he would above all have liked to work on the question of the attitude of the
Church to atheism.

But the last Session led the theologians to reflect on their role after the Council. On 30 November, Hans Küng brought a number of them together and an organic collaboration between bishops and theologians was firmly called for. Congar, who was later to be appointed to the International Theological Commission,
was associated, from 1965 onwards, with the implementation of the Council and
in particular with that of the decree *Unitatis redintegratio*. In May, within the Secretariat for Unity, he took part in the development of an ecumenical Directory.

In August, he attended the first official meeting between Catholics and Lutherans since the century of the Reformation, a prelude to the setting up of an
International Catholic/Lutheran Commission in 1967. In November, he took part
in the meeting of the joint working party between the Catholic Church and the
World Council of Churches and then in the work of the Academic Committee

charged with preparing the basis for the future Ecumenical Institute of Theological Research that was to be established at Tantur near Jerusalem.

After the Fourth Session (from 8 December 1965 to 30 September 1966)
It is significant that the *Journal* does not break off at the end of the Council, but, in fact, on 30 September 1966, on the conclusion, in Rome, of the International Congress of Theology on Vatican II. It thus gives us, through Congar's various commitments, an insight into the evolution, so very important in his eyes, of this more trusting collaboration between bishops and theologians that had come into being during the Council. In addition to attending this Congress, he also attended the post-conciliar Commission on the Missions and the new Secretariat for Non-believers. This collaboration was to be facilitated by the appointment to some important posts in the Roman Curia of some of the great Council figures, such as Mgr Garrone,[26] and C Moeller.[27] However, the difficulties encountered in Rome by Y Congar and G Baraúna for the publication of certain works presaged the existence of tensions that would not fail to surface in the course of the implementation of the Council.

Congar and his mission as an expert
Congar had gone to the Council in a spirit of availability which he described as follows:

> 'It is because I have (somehow or other) followed what I believed to be the will and the call of God. It is he who has managed everything, prepared everything. At the Council itself, I have no other rule except to make him direct everything. A fully God-centred ethic, even in small material details. I have taken the following as a general rule: not to undertake anything unless asked to do so by the bishops. It is they who are the Council. However, if an initiative bore the mark of a call from God, I would open myself to it.' (31 October 1962)

This was, in effect, to be his attitude throughout the Council. On the one hand he felt the need to respect fully the mission of the Council Fathers themselves. We thus see him scrupulously going through and classifying their comments on the schemas and bearing them in mind while they were being revised by the Commission. At the same time, however, he did not hesitate to present the results of his own theological research in countless lectures, and to campaign for this or that initiative. At the beginning of the Council, he fought for a message to the world and for a revision of the doctrinal schemas; later, he was to fight for the

---

26. He was appointed Pro-Prefect of the Congregation for Seminaries and Universities.
27. He was appointed sub-secretary of the Congregation for the Doctrine of the Faith.

chapter on the People of God to be written in accordance with the history of salvation in which he included the role of the Jewish people, for schema XIII to be tackled by the Fathers on the basis of an assessment of the state of the world, and also for the Council to produce a new Profession of Faith.

Congar also took part in the intense collaboration that had been established between pastors and theologians. Whereas some of the great theologians such as Scheeben, Döllinger or Newman had not been invited to attend Vatican I, the Fathers of Vatican II were to make considerable use of theologians, who recovered a real freedom of speech[28] and a great many of whom 'exercised a true magisterium' (21 October 1962).[29] Congar would be able to write that 'this Council will have been to a considerable extent that of the theologians' (5 October 1965).

But the relationship between bishops and theologians must not cause us to forget the third partner, which is the People of God. During the Council, this showed itself in the presence of lay Auditors but also, and to a much greater extent, through public opinion. Congar, who deemed the *sensus fidelium* important, did not hesitate to enlighten ecclesial public opinion with his articles.

As an expert, Congar began by experiencing the 'fact of the Council', this assembly involving an unforeseeable element and needing to grow to maturity more or less slowly. He saw therein 'a profound anthropological truth' which should serve to moderate impatience. Nonetheless he was often both impatient and weary at having to attend General Congregations that amounted to a series of interventions instead of a genuine debate. He regretted that the experts who had drafted and then revised the schemas were not allowed to come and present them. But in the end, although such things had hardly been thought of in advance, he noted with astonishment that a spirit of the Council was in fact emerging and that the conciliar schemas were gradually finding their own coherence.

Nevertheless, this did not come about without some painful clashes. Though a conciliar majority and minority emerged, the composition of each could often vary more or less markedly depending on the topic under discussion. Congar clearly understood that Paul VI wanted to secure a large consensus of the Fathers and that that presupposed compromise. It was in this spirit that he himself worked in the Commissions and in relation to the Fathers, accepting that his own ideas could not fully prevail and in this way distancing himself from some of the more intransigent experts. Moreover, someone who has had the experience of being set aside, and viewed with suspicion, practises a kind of intra-ecclesial ecumenism with those who might, in their turn, feel themselves banished from the ecclesial communion after the Council, even while regretting that some showed

---

28. This recovered freedom was to open the way for the plan for an international theological journal to be implemented with the creation of *Concilium*, with which Congar had been associated since 1963.

29. *Cf* Karl Heinz Neufeld, 'Au service du Concile, Évêques et théologiens au deuxième Concile du Vatican', in René Latourelle, *Vatican II, Bilan et perspectives, vingt-cinq ans après (1962–1987)*, Volume I (Montréal, Bellarmine ; Paris, Cerf, 1988), 95–124.

a purely negative spirit while others adopted underhand procedures in the work of the Council.

The various ways in which Congar operated during the Council

Congar's *Journal* bears witness to the variety of ways in which an expert operated at the Council, whether within the various Commissions, in relation to the Fathers, the non-Catholic Observers or else in theological publications and in the press. It also reveals the importance of the more or less informal networks, of conversations at mealtimes or in the corridors, and personal contact.

Among these contacts, there were first and foremost those which Congar had with the other experts. In the Preparatory Theological Commission, which was dominated by theologians based in Rome, Congar counted only a few fellow members who were genuinely open to renewal. On the other hand, in the Secretariat for Christian Unity, he met up again with several friends who were sometimes very close and with whom he had worked in the ecumenical field, in particular within the Catholic Conference for Ecumenical Matters, and who kept him abreast of contacts with the separated brethren. Even though he collaborated only unofficially with the Secretariat during the Council, the relationships which he maintained with its members were for him essential.

During the First Session, Congar, who was already weakened by his illness, felt very isolated at the Angelicum, where he was staying; he was no longer associated with the work of the Theological Commission which, moreover, rarely met. However, he very quickly found himself integrated into that circle of theologians from North Western Europe, in which principally the Germans, the Belgians, the Dutch and the French worked side by side and which was to dominate to a marked degree the theological activity of the Council.

While he admired the ability of K Rahner and appreciated the collaboration of J Ratzinger, he did not share the reforming radicalism of the German experts and proved to be himself much more prepared to compromise. Unlike H Küng, who kept himself out of all the Commissions in order to be freer in his criticism, Y Congar faithfully committed himself to patiently improving the schemas, even though he perceived their limits. In this, he was much closer to the Belgian experts, with whom he got on extremely well. He appreciated their pragmatism and their realism, which led them to look to the possible and not the ideal, according to a tactical method that he was to define as follows: 'come to an understanding in advance, know very precisely what one wants to avoid, what one wants to get passed; prepare a fall-back position; win people round to one's own point of view and neutralise the others' (22 April 1964). It was principally with them that he prepared for many meetings of the Theological Commission or of its various subcommissions. During these meetings, his own interventions were, as he himself recognised, 'rather discreet and rare' (2 June 1964).

This is explained by a reserved temperament, as well by the lack of requests for help coming from the French bishops who were members of this Commission.

However, he was to reach a very positive conclusion concerning the work of this Commission which had, in his view, made possible a real theological encounter between the various schools of thought at the Council. Moreover, it was the model of the Doctrinal Commission that he had in mind when he became progressively more involved in the work of other Commissions and of the Secretariat for Unity.

But over and above the work in the commissions, Congar was at work among the Council Fathers in order to prepare the debates *in aula*. Although he had come to the Council as the personal expert of Mgr Weber, Bishop of Strasbourg, the bishop, who was quite elderly, very rarely called on him. On the other hand, his young Coadjutor, Mgr Elchinger, who was very much up to date with theological and pastoral renewal, and who was responsible for contacts between the French and German episcopates, quickly involved Congar in the 'Conciliar strategy' meetings that he was organising between the bishops and theologians of North Western Europe. However, the French episcopate was in no hurry to make use of the abilities of the theologian. Congar felt this was due both to the still fairly recent suspicions of him in Rome as well as to the hesitation occasioned by his own very poor health. He also expressed regret that the French bishops were less combative at the theological level, and that their interventions, often homiletic in style, took the form of wide-ranging pastoral syntheses with little doctrinal acuity. However, there is no need to minimise the real influence the theologian had on the French bishops. Although he was very infrequently called upon to contribute to the 'workshops' that they had set up in Rome, his lectures had a real impact as did his contributions to the *Études et documents* distributed by the episcopate's secretariat which reached well beyond the country's borders.

Clearly, however, Congar's influence was not restricted to the French bishops. Though he was not often asked to prepare interventions for the conciliar assembly or amendments for the revision of the schemas, though he had relatively few on-going contacts with particular bishops, his *Journal* mentions an impressive number of lectures and talks given to different groups of bishops on the main ecclesiological and ecumenical topics that they were dealing with. In addition, though in the end he did not feel it had been very effective, Congar regularly attended the meetings of the informal group known as 'Jesus, the Church and the poor'.

For Congar, the presence at the Council of the non-Catholic Observers and of the guests invited by the Secretariat for Unity was an extraordinary event and made it possible for the Council to go beyond a mere improvement of what he called the 'system', and to open an era of dialogue with those whom he called the 'Others' (other Christians, but more widely representing other spiritual worlds). The man who had been, in the Catholic world, one of the pioneers of ecumenical contact, thus met up again with old friends in the conciliar *aula* and its surroundings. In particular he was invited several times to attend the working sessions with the Council experts that the Secretariat for Unity organised each week for the Observers and other guests.

Finally, Congar's influence was at work also through his various publications: books, interviews and articles. The bulletins that he wrote for *Informations Catholiques Internationales* or for other periodicals and that were then published on conclusion of each session,[30] make it possible to grasp clearly the profound issues at stake in the conciliar adventure. As for the theological works that Congar published before and during the Council, these had a very deep influence, of which he received many testimonials during the Council sessions. Thus he recorded that the collective volume *L'Épiscopat et l'Église universelle*, which he was working on before the Council and which was published in 1962, prior to the first Session, in the 'Unam Sanctam' collection, had had a 'decisive' impact (22 November 1963), which encouraged him to prepare a work of the same type on the question of poverty.[31] Among the many things published by Congar during the Council, special mention should be made of the influence of his works on Tradition, published in 1960 and 1963.

Congar and his vision of the Council

The reforming and ecumenical purpose of the Council

Although some of the Curia circles saw in the Council an opportunity to condemn what they considered dangerous in theological writings, Congar, for his part, felt that there was no harm in delay and that it was above all the Church that was being put in question by the world 'which was calling on it to rejoin it in order to speak validly of Jesus Christ'.[32] Ever since 1959, at a meeting in Chevetogne, it had seemed to him that 'today the questions are above all those that are being addressed to the Church *by the world* and *by the Others*. They are missionary, ecumenical and pastoral questions'.[33] During the First Session, he noted in his chronicles: 'It seems certain that the Council will be principally apostolic and pastoral. Even the theological formulations should take on this tonality. If there are points of doctrine to be discussed or expressed in a new way, it is those that are concerned with the evangelical and pastoral relationship with others'.[34] Thus the Council would be both doctrinal and pastoral and the relationship between the two aspects would be essential. As he was to write later: 'The pastoral is no less doctrinal, but it is doctrinal in a way that is not content with conceptualising, defining, deducing and anathematising: it seeks to express the saving truth in a way that reaches out to the men and women of today, takes up their difficulties, replies to their questions'.[35] In this regard, he quickly came up against men such

---

30. See the four volumes: *Le Concile au jour le jour* (Paris: Cerf, 1963); *Le Concile au jour le jour. Deuxième session* (Paris: Cerf, 1964); *Le Concile au jour le jour. Troisième session* (Paris: Cerf, 1965; *Le Concile au jour le jour. Quatrième session* (Paris: Cerf, 1966).
31. See *Église et pauvreté*, 'Unam Sanctam', 57 (Paris: Cerf, 1965).
32. Yves M-J Congar, *Le Concile au jour le jour, op cit*, 11.
33. 'Conclusion', in *Le Concile et les conciles, op cit*, 329.
34. Yves M-J Congar, *Le Concile au jour le jour, op cit*, 15.
35. *Le Concile de Vatican II. Son Église peuple de Dieu et corps du Christ*, 'Théologie histo-

as Cardinal Ottaviani or Fr Tromp, for whom the pastoral was, like ecumenism, a purely practical matter, reserved for other organisms.

In investigating the history of doctrines to do with ecclesiology in the years before the Council, Congar had rightly observed the extent to which the Church's contacts *ad extra* had influenced its own inner evolution and in particular her ecclesiology. The Gregorian Reform, in reaction to secular pretensions, the defensive reactions provoked by the putting of things in question by the Protestant Reformation, then the currents of modern thought had led to a progressive concentration of ecclesiastical power in the papacy[36] and, in the same movement, had reduced the treatise on the Church to a narrowly juridical approach.

With the end of Christendom, the new situation of the Church in a world that was now escaping from its tutelage was leading it not only to an *aggiornamento*, as John XXIII called it, but to a genuine ecclesial reform, as Paul VI was later to say. It was not to be simply a question of improving or rendering more flexible what Congar called 'the system', that is to say the institutional organisation and its discourse, but of achieving a true renewal in order to place the Church in a state of mission and of dialogue with this modern world. This renewal comes by means of a thoroughgoing return to sources in both Scripture and Tradition. Since writing his book *Vraie et fausse réforme dans l'Église*, in order to define what form an ecclesial reform might take, he had adopted the words of Charles Péguy: 'an appeal from a less perfect tradition to one that is more perfect, an appeal from a less profound tradition to one that is more so, an extension of tradition, a going deeper: a search for the deeper sources; in the literal sense of the world, a resource.'[37] In order to make progress in this direction, the presence of the representatives of other Churches and of Eastern Catholics played, for Congar, a vital role.

It is at this point that the dynamic of the Council fuses in an astonishing way with the ecumenical and ecclesiological vocation that Congar had recognised to be his since 1930, when he reflected on John 17. In fact, Congar saw from the beginning the reunion of Christians as the ultimate aim of the Council. From John XXIII onwards, the Catholic Church became fully involved in the ecumenical movement. From then on, ecumenism was no longer to be a particular discipline, but 'a dimension of everything that is done in the Church.'[38] As early as the opening of the Council, Congar recorded with realism: 'It would be fanciful to be hoping for decisions to unite; but it is not fanciful to hope for the establishment of a relationship of dialogue that could pave the way for decisive reconciliation on certain points.'[39] In fact, the ecumenical opening was to surpass all others by the reintegration of values that had become blurred in the Catholic Church and that the other Churches had known better how to develop; hence the decisive role of

---

rique', 71 (Beauchesne, 1984) 64.
36. He noted in his *Journal* in July 1960 that 'by 1950, it was perfect'.
37. Foreword to *Cahiers de la Quinzaine*, 1 March, 1904.
38. Yves M-J Congar, *Le Concile au jour le jour. Deuxième session, op cit*, 105.
39. Yves M-J Congar, *Le Concile au jour le jour, op cit*, 14.

a good *De revelatione* and a good *De ecclesia*: hence also the real recognition of the Eastern tradition in the Catholic Church (25 October 1963), a tradition that had been better able to preserve and develop certain values than had the Latin tradition.[40]

For a Church refreshed from its sources

When he began his *Journal*, Congar felt that the Council had come too soon: only the youngest bishops had been able to enter into that return to the biblical, patristic and liturgical sources that was essential for a genuine reform of the Church. In his chronicles, he drew a distinction between those who were 'resourced' and those who were 'un-resourced'[41] and opted, himself, in favour of a Catholicism that was refreshed from its sources, 'that is, at the same time, a Catholicism centred once more on Christ, and that is at one and the same time biblical, liturgical, paschal, community-centred, ecumenical and missionary.'[42]

In this theological movement of the Council, setting oneself to listen to the Word of God is essential. Congar noted that in the texts of the Preparatory Theological Commission, 'the SOURCE is not the Word of God: it is the Church itself, and even the Church reduced to the Pope, which is VERY serious' (24 August 1961). He added that: 'all the work has been done as if the encyclicals were THE necessary and sufficient source. It is a NOVELTY in the technical sense this word has in theology' *(ibid).*

During the Second Session, he further commented: 'For years I have realised that at no time has the Word of God been encountered in an entirely new and fresh way. There has not been a REAL return to the sources[...] Exegetes have played almost no part in the work: those from Jerusalem and the Biblical Institute have been set aside' (12 October 1963).

This source, which is the Word of God, is given to us through Scripture and Tradition, and it ought to be listened to by the pope, the bishops and the Church as a whole, hence the importance, for Congar, of the *De revelatione*: 'a text that ought to provide the basis for a renewal in theology and preaching, as well as the basis for ecumenical dialogue for several decades to come.'[43]

In Congar's view, the return to Scripture went hand in hand with the great importance he attached to the category of the history of salvation. It was on the occasion of a meeting of Paul VI with the Observers that Congar drew attention to the importance of specific teaching relating to it, picking up the idea expressed by Paul VI: 'it would be extremely important that there should be, in every Catho-

---

40. See in particular his meetings with the Melkite bishops on 27 October 1962 and 10 October 1963.
41. *Le Concile au jour le jour, op cit,* 45.
42. *Le Concile au jour le jour. Deuxième session, op cit,* 111.
43. *Le Concile au jour le jour. Quatrième session, op cit,* 20.

lic university centre, a chair of the theology of the history of salvation, where the divine economy in the history of the People of God would be studied'.[44]

Even more radically, however, one can say that the return to the Word of God made possible through the history of salvation required a deepening of the theology of the Trinity, the movement of the Son and the Spirit in the world itself drawing its dynamism from the life of the Trinity *ad intra*. At its very root, the Church is *Ecclesia de Trinitate,* it is People of God, Body of Christ and Temple of the Spirit. Congar was to conclude later that Vatican II had done nothing more than undertake a deepening of ecclesiology based on 'a trinitarian *theo*-logy'.[45]

Towards a renewed ecclesiology

This refocusing on the Word, on the history of salvation and, more profoundly, on the mystery of the Trinity is at the root of a new vision of the Church that became progressively clearer as the Council was in progress. It is characterised by the transition from an essentially juridical vision to a sacramental one that places what he calls a Christian ontology, the ontology of grace ahead of ministerial structures.

It is Christian existence, the quality of the disciple that is primary, founded on the sacraments of initiation. Congar regretted that 'an ecclesiology that did not include an anthropology'[46] (CJJ II, 108) had been constructed, and he agreed with his Orthodox friends, A Schmemann and N Nissiotis, in judging that 'the best ecclesiology would be, in the *De populo Dei,* a development on the Christian human being' (17 October 1963). Thus, in connection with the chapter on the laity, his wish was that, in virtue of the primacy given to 'Christian ontology or to the spiritual reality of the Christian human being over the structures of service and commandment', the Council would not be content with 'describing the condition of lay people in the Church, but give us a chapter that was dense and full of Biblical vigour about what a Christian human being is!'[47]

This explains the importance that Congar attached to certain results of the Council. He insisted in particular on the decisive nature, for a renewal of the whole of ecclesiology, of the insertion of a chapter on the People of God ahead of the one on the hierarchy in the Constitution *Lumen gentium.* But he also welcomed the expounding of the notion of living Tradition, borne by this Christian People, the sketch of a Christian anthropology in *Gaudium et spes,* as well as the integration of the chapter on Mary into the schema on the Church.

As for the ministerial structures, they are above all at the service of this Christian existence and they too are viewed in the light of their sacramental basis: this is particularly true of the episcopate and of the restored permanent diaconate.

---

44. *Le Concile au jour le jour. Deuxième session, op cit,* 103–104.
45. *Le Concile de Vatican II. Son Église peuple de Dieu et corps du Christ, op cit,* 82.
46. *Le Concile au jour le jour. Deuxième session, op cit,* 108.
47. *Ibid.*

This Christian ontology is very profoundly an ontology of communion, modelled on the Trinity. In the audience Paul VI gave him on 8 June 1964, Congar ventured to say to him that his ecumenical gestures 'indicate (. . .) an ecclesiology that has not yet been worked out: an ecclesiology of Communion, in which the Church is seen as a Communion of Churches'. Moreover, it was in this ontology of communion that a theology of episcopal collegiality could sink its roots.[48]

In this return to the primary character of Christian ontology and Christian existence, the eschatological dimension, which had been brought back to light by biblical exegesis, could not be under-estimated. Situated between the Incarnation and the Parousia, the Church rediscovers her proper place in the midst of humanity and of the cosmos: it is not the Kingdom of God already attained, but the 'sacrament of salvation'. This expression, which was taken up by the Council, expresses well, in Congar's view, the mission of the Church: People of God inserted into the history of humankind. The Church must no longer look upon itself as a citadel, obsessed with the battle against enemy forces. It is called to enter into a true dialogue with the contemporary world, a dialogue that Congar did not envisage naively, as being without confrontations and arguments between the parties, but one in which both partners would enrich each other, the Church having the mission to proclaim the Gospel and to serve the world in accordance with this Gospel, the world leading the Church to question the Gospel anew, to purify itself continually and to develop its catholicity by welcoming new values. This Church 'servant and poor', aware of its weaknesses and of its deficiencies throughout history, must show itself to be in solidarity with the world in its pilgrimage towards the Kingdom.

A stage on the Church's way

This renewal of ecclesiology that Congar hoped and prayed for was realised only gradually and partially during the Council. To begin with, it was marked by the clash between the conciliar majority and minority. But Congar did not have a Manichaean view it. He considered that the activity of the experts on the minority side, most of whom were men of the Curia and of the Holy Office, had forced the conciliar majority to clarify their own ideas.[49] He even hoped that the options put forward in the concilar schemas might be clearly explained to the Fathers:[50]

---

48. In 'La mission dans la théologie de l'Église', *Repenser la Mission. Rapports et compte-rendu de la XXXV semaine de Missiologie de Louvain* (Paris: Desclée de Brouwer, 1965) 61, Congar wrote: 'Collegiality (. . .) affects the deep nature of the episcopate and of the Church; it expresses its nature, in which there is a mystery of communion. More and more, where collegiality is concerned, recourse is had to the model of the Three Divine Persons who are one... There are still many things to be made deeper and worked out in the theology of collegiality.'
49. *Cf Une vie pour la vérité, op cit,* 141.
50. Congar regretted that the rapporteur of a text was not able to defend his text after having presented it to the Fathers, as had been the case at Vatican I (*Le Concile au jour le*

whether this was concerning collegiality, where the *De Beata Maria* should be placed, or the matter of a 'deicide' people.

In the same spirit, he thought it preferable to take the time to clarify the question of religious freedom and not have a text voted on with headlong haste. He even considered that one should try to reach unanimity,[51] and he did not hesitate to meet an adversary of collegiality such as R Dulac, of *Pensée catholique,* in the hope of showing him that the declarations of Vatican I were not being put in danger (18 September 1964). For him, the *Nota praevia explicativa* ought to play 'the role that Zinelli's speech had played at Vatican I' (16 November 1964). Congar, in fact, and in this he was completely traditional, considered that a Council did not have the objective of securing victory for one theological school of thought. At the end of the last Session, he wrote:

> 'However, the Council has been very careful not to seek the victory of one particular school of theology over another. On several important points, its formulas do not settle the debates between theological schools. We ourselves, who have worked in several Commissions, can bear witness to the care that was taken in this regard. We should also like to say that, often, the opposition of the minority made a contribution that was, all in all, felicitous and positive. Of course, it was sometimes irritating. It made it necessary to dig deeper, to introduce nuances or to attain greater clarity, to recognise other aspects.'[52]

Moreover, the conciliar dynamic relativises a static vision of the majority and the minority: even during the First Session, Congar perceived the evolution of whole episcopates 'under the action, not so much, perhaps, of the arguments put forward as of the general atmosphere and the contact with other episcopates, coming from other continents and other horizons.'[53] Comparing himself with Hans

---

jour, op cit, 81); he even suggested that 'perhaps the debates would be better focused if the Commission concerned were to intervene in them at the beginning, and at least once or twice in the course of the discussion, in order to state clearly the meaning or the intention of the text that it was proposing, and so prevent people losing their way unnecessarily' (*Le Concile au jour le jour. Deuxième session, op cit,* 118).

51. See *Le Concile au jour le jour. Deuxième session, op cit,* 141; during the fourth session, he wrote: 'Vatican II has been incomparably more patient and more generous towards its minority than Vatican I had been for its minority' (*Le Concile au jour le jour. Quatrième session, op cit,* 23); later, when Mgr Marcel Lefebvre began to call the Council into question, Congar was to recall that, at the request of Paul VI, the widest possible unanimity had been sought during it; Yves Congar, *La Crise dans l'Église et Mgr Lefebvre* (Paris: Cerf, 1976) 17.

52. *Le Concile au jour le jour. Quatrième session, op cit,* 124.

53. *Le Concile au jour le jour, op cit,* 46.

Küng, he was aware of his own acute perception 'that some time-lags are necessary and that an active patience has strength' (12 October 1963). At the time of the First Session he estimated that it would take two or three years for the conciliar assembly to reach real maturity, as much at the level of a collegial pastoral awareness as at that of a theological deepening,[54] and at a later date he was to regret that Cardinal Döpfner, who was responsible for a draconian plan designed to make it possible to complete the work of the Council more speedily, could not see that 'the primary aim of the Council is not to vote on texts but to create a new spirit and a new awareness, and THAT THAT REQUIRED TIME' (1 February 1964).

In any case, Congar had never thought that Vatican II could fully endorse the theological renewal that was taking place at the time. Some happenings even seemed to him, at the end of the Council, unimaginable five years earlier, such as the ecumenical celebration in St Paul outside the Walls on 4 December 1965. Ten years later, he was to note that the Council had 'stopped half-way on many questions. It began a task that is not completed, whether it is a question of collegiality, of the role of the laity, of the missions and even of ecumenism.'[55] In 1966, in concluding his two volumes of commentary on *Lumen gentium,* and reverting to the image of the seed that was so dear to him, he wrote: 'The studies contained in this collection will make it possible for many of the seeds scattered throughout the sixty-nine Numbers of the Constitution *Lumen gentium* to bear fruit.'[56]

Finally, the experience of the Council of Trent had shown Congar that decisions even of a Council need time before they can take shape in the ecclesial reality.[57] Alongside further theological research, the period after the Council was to be the time for putting the conciliar decisions into effect.

Congar proved attentive to the institutional implementation of the ecclesiology of the Council, and in particular of collegiality. But it was not to be a question of merely putting things into practice: what he thought about the future of collegiality can be extended to other fields such as the re-introduction of the permanent diaconate,[58] or involvement in the ecumenical movement: 'The Council contented itself with a declaration. Soon, concrete collegial structures will be put in place. There will be some coming and going between practice, theological reflection and historical research.'[59] In this connection, Congar noted that he had seen 'for a long time that one of the major problems after the Council would be that of preserving that organic cooperation—which alone had made the Council possible—between bishops and theologians' (5 February 1966). He was to partici-

---

54. *Ibid,* 68.
55. *Une vie pour la vérité, op cit,* 131; *cf* also 149.
56. *L'Église de Vatican II,* 'Unam Sanctam', 51 (Paris: Cerf, 1966), 1369.
57. See *Le Concile au jour le jour. Deuxième session,op cit,* 125.
58. On the diaconate, *cf* Yves M-J Congar, 'Le diaconat dans la théologie des ministéres', in *Le diacre dans l'Église et le monde d'aujourd'hui,* 'Unam Sanctam', 59 (Paris: Cerf, 1966), 121–141.
59. *L'Église du Vatican II,* 'Unam Sanctam', 51 c, *op cit,* 1371.

pate vigorously in this reception of the Council, in particular by his commentaries on the Council documents, which were to be published under his direction in the 'Unam Sanctam' collection.[60]

The Council and the work of the theologian

Although the influence of the theologian's work on the Council was undeniable, it nevertheless remains difficult to evaluate. One might be tempted to focus on what the final drafting of the Conciliar documents owes to him. In fact, at the end of his *Journal* (7 December 1965), Congar lists those paragraphs of which he had produced the first draft. Generally speaking, they were passages giving doctrinal foundations and dealing with his favourite themes: Tradition, the People of God, ecumenism, priests and priesthood, Christian anthropology, the missionary nature of the Church, the relationship between the Church and the world, the salvation of non-Christians. Of course, these passages necessarily bear more or less clearly the style of the author, his vocabulary, even his theology, and his young confrere Fr Liégé was even able to recognise it: 'I have greatly appreciated your contributions to the schemas on the missions and on Priests, which are easily recognisable.'[61] But, on the one hand, Congar was functioning as an expert and he was required, in what he wrote, to take into account the *desiderata* of the Fathers rather than to express his own personal ideas, and, on the other hand, these texts were subsequently, to a greater or lesser extent, amended.

In fact, Congar's influence went beyond the texts that he drafted. He did not collaborate in the writing of the texts relating to the laity, nor on that of the schema on the Apostolate of the Laity, even though he was one of the architects of a theology of the laity. Similarly, he had very little hand in the writing of the schema on ecumenism or of the texts concerning episcopal collegiality. As we have seen above, the ways in which Congar operated at the Council were manifold and went well beyond the writing or even the amendment of texts. In all of his activity, he theologically accompanied the actual movement of the Council with an astonishing matching of his own vocation, which was both ecclesiological and ecumenical, with the intentions of John XXIII who had wanted the Council and 'had given it these two purposes, which he linked together: the internal renewal of the Catholic Church and the service of the cause of Christian unity.'[62] The Council themes frequently coincided with those on which Congar had worked[63] and the

---

60. Commentaries on thirteen of the sixteen conciliar texts were to be published in this collection between 1966 and 1970.
61. Letter from Pierre-André Liégé, OP, to Yves Congar, 18 October 1965 (Congar Archives).
62. Yves M-J Congar, *Concile œcuménique Vatican II: L'Église, l'œcuménisme, les Églises orientales* (Paris, Le Centurion, 1965), 165.
63. On 12 January 1963, Fr Liégé, OP, had written to him as follows: 'I was so glad to see during the past year how the Council has, in fact, endorsed each one of the theological sectors which you have endeavoured to renew and with which you have familiarised

Council was for him the opportunity to present the results widely among the Council Fathers. As he was to write in 1973: 'The great causes I have tried to serve surfaced in the Council: renewal of ecclesiology, Tradition, reformism, ecumenism, laity, mission, ministries...'[64]

Congar's contribution to the Council, then, is to be found above all in his theological work. Throughout the Council, he received numerous testimonials to his influence, coming from all parts of the world. So it is not to be wondered at that a number of bishops came to congratulate him on 21 November 1962, when the schema on the two sources of Revelation was sent back to be rewritten, even though he had been so discreet during those early days of the Council. But, as he wrote to a colleague in Strasbourg during this Session: 'As for me, I am there because it is my duty, but I consider that my usual work is not only more interesting, but more important. Because the Council is but one outcome in the life of the Church. Progress has been made in those places where the work has been done. The points at which there is no progress, or too little, are those on which the work has not been taken sufficiently forward. Conclusion: work is the deciding factor. We would still be at the stage of the Syllabus if no work had been done!'[65]

There can be no doubt that the works published by Congar on the living Tradition played a role at the Council; but his earlier works also opened new avenues: *Chrétiens désunis* in opening the Catholic Church to the ecumenical movement, *Vraie et fausse réforme dans l'Église* in providing a basis for the reforming currents that were at work in it, *Jalons pour une théologie du laïcat* for reasserting the value of the mission of the laity by situating them in a People of God that was wholly priestly, royal and prophetic. On the other hand, in spite of quite a few articles, his theology of ministries was in need of distinctly more advanced research. Congar recognised this throughout the Council in connection with episcopal collegiality, a central theme. As early as July 1960 he spoke of 'a certain number of works to be done, here and there. I am thinking of work on the jurisdiction of bishops, on episcopal collegiality, on the law of the Eastern Churches, etc'. On 3 December 1963, towards the end of the Second Session, he agreed with his friends G Dossetti and G Alberigo that: 'what is most important, most decisive, is the basic groundwork. Things have advanced well where such work has already been done: on the liturgy for example. So one has to work. On this question of the episcopate, no work has been done'.

Well aware of this problem, which those who were against collegiality were endeavouring to exploit in order to overthrow Chapter III of *Lumen gentium*, Congar, from the beginning to the end of the Council, fought to prevent precipitate conclusions being reached on questions that were still being debated among

---

us: Word of God, Tradition, collegiality, priesthood, mission, etc. That must be for you a source of reassurance: you have worked the good seams and prepared the renewal' (Congar Archive).

64. *Cf Une passion: l'unité. Réflexions et souvenirs 1929–1973, op cit,* 90.
65. Letter dated 12 November 1962 (Congar Archive).

My Journal of the Council

theologians. As for the priestly ministry, which some were to consider the poor relation of ministries at the Council, Congar sought to free it from a vision that was narrowly restricted to cult, but he was to reach the conclusion, not long after the Council, that 'Presbyterorum Ordinis was full of good things, but it has been adversely affected by the radicality of the questions that have been asked since: it came before the crisis in ministry and the burgeoning of ministries'.[66] During the Council, Congar was also interested in the restoration of the ministry of deacon, for which he had campaigned, and he took part in the Congress on the Diaconate in Rome in October 1965.[67] He viewed this ministry within the wider context of a renewal of ministries that the Council had no more than sketched out. However, it was not until 1971, in his *Ministères et communion ecclésiale,* that Congar was to outline real foundations for this theology of ministries which he was to see closely connected with an ecclesiology of communion, another theme that had been initiated by the Council. This was because, in fact, the great intuitions and rediscoveries endorsed by the Council, which in many cases he had himself foreseen and proclaimed, called for a deepening and even a new start at the heart of these questions on the ministries. As he was to write: 'The Council has left to historians and theologians the task of developing a theology of the Church, "we" Christians, a communion of disciples built up on a sacramental foundation of which the law specifies the conditions, a theology of local or particular churches, a theology of ministries, of the place of women in the whole life of the Church, a theology of the exact status of the primatial power of the Bishop of Rome with regard to the communion of churches and to collegiality . . . '[68] But the Council also raised new questions concerning the mission of the Church in the world: Gospel and human liberations, a theology of non-Christian religions, a new approach to missionary activity, etc.

Hence, as well as being a culmination or a consecration, the Council was also the catalyst or the taking-off point for new research for the theologian. Aware as he was of the disappointment of the other Churches, he noted also, at the end of the Third Session:

> 'I ask myself what is to be done. I know that, whatever I tell myself, there will be only one conclusion for me: the work has to be done. The check we have come up against indicates the limit of what our work has achieved. But overburdened, literally crushed, living constantly way beyond my strength, I ask myself what is it better to do, to what should I bend my efforts by way of priority? I am overloaded with a heap of things. Otherwise, I think that the

---

66. *Le Concile de Vatican II. Son Église peuple de Dieu et corps du Christ, op cit,* 104.
67. The papers were published in: Paul Winninger and Yves Congar (editors), *Le Diacre dans l'Église et le monde d'aujourd'hui,* 'Unam Sanctam', 59 (Paris: Cerf, 1966).
68. *Le Concile de Vatican II. Son Église peuple de Dieu et corps du Christ, op cit,* 81–82.

History of Ecclesiology should have first priority. It alone will break the deadlock for certain questions, by showing where this or the other position comes from.' (22 November 1964)

Side by side with his historical research, to which he was to continue to devote a great deal of time and interest,[69] a work of more systematic reconstruction was to prove necessary, starting from the great ecclesiological intuitions that had been brought back into currency by the Council. Though Congar undoubtedly made his contribution to that,[70] he was, above all, to play the role of trail-blazer, indicating new fields to explore but in general leaving to another generation the task of working out new models. As he said at the time of the homage paid to him in December 1963, evoking the figure of St John the Baptist, the friend of the messianic Bridegroom, 'each one has his vocation, and for each one, it is that vocation that is the best'.[71]

---

69. They were to bear fruit, in particular, in *L'Église de saint Augustin à l'époque moderne, op cit*, a book that had been in preparation since 1954.
70. *Cf* in particular Yves Congar, *Ministères et communion ecclésiale* (Paris: Cerf, 1971).
71. *Cf* Jean-Pierre Jossua, *Le Père Congar: la théologie au service du peuple de Dieu, op cit*, 49.

CONGAR AT THE SECOND VATICAN COUNCIL
MARY CECILY BOULDING OP

The French Dominican priest, Yves Congar, accompanied his bishop to the Second Vatican Council in the capacity of expert theological adviser. From the time of its first announcement until a year after its conclusion he kept a journal, in a tone of such uninhibited and brutal frankness that its publication was embargoed until the year 2000.

It is a remarkable historical record, documenting in a wealth of detail the 'human' aspect of the Council: the personalities with all their foibles, faults and failings: 'Cardinal Jaeger . . . He is a much weakened man. He is not there; he falls asleep, he is incapable of putting a precise question at the appropriate moment and directing the discussion, which follows its course whether he is presiding or whether he is absent' [1 March 1965] and, occasionally, their strengths and virtues: 'Philips has been crucial. Without him the work of the Theological Commission would never have been what it has been' [3 April 1965]; ' Prignon . . . He too, in his own way, holds together a collection of qualities that are themselves rare enough. He has, at once, a theological sense, a practical sense and a sense of tactics' [27 April 1964]; the rows and arguments, the strategies and manoeuvrings employed by individuals, cliques and national groupings to secure their particular aims, which of course they believed to be essential to the good of the Church.

So too the endless hours of very hard work, all too often having to be repeated several times, to secure the aims gradually elaborated and approved by the discussion and votes of the bishops: 'We went over again with the whole group what had been done this morning at the Belgian College. But this was not without value: agreement and some very valuable refinements were progressively achieved in this way. Work like this is very burdensome and tiring. It takes days of meetings to reach a result, but that is the nature of the case' [12 September 1964]. 'And since I am exhausted by the dreadful work of these pernickety discussions, and the meticulous revision I have been doing non-stop since 22 March, I would like to send the whole lot packing' [31 March 1965].

The *Journal* makes it possible to trace the evolution of the more significant documents and so, in a sense actually to observe the Church changing its mind, and arriving at the formal, and almost universal agreement to discard definitively what Congar dubbed the '[W]e are stuck with a Denzinger point of view: one of the deadliest of books in spite of its great usefulness' [28 September 1961].

The Tridentine style of theology found in the manuals used in seminaries and official departments—and offering a positive welcome to the influence of contemporary human culture, as well as the experience of other christian churches, and indeed other religions.

On 25 January 1959 Pope John XXIII stunned the Church and surprised the world with the announcement that he intended to convoke a General Council. The previous one had taken place nearly a hundred years earlier—Vatican I, 1869–70—and had among other things, defined—in strictly limited terms—the primacy and infallibility of the papacy. Since earlier councils had generally been convoked to deal with some doctrinal or moral crisis, there was widespread discussion about the reason for this one. Pope John answered this in his opening speech on 11 October 1962:

> The problem confronting the Church after 2000 years remains unchanged . . . Christ is ever resplendent as the centre of history and of life: men are either with him and with his Church, and enjoy light, goodness, order and peace; or against him, so giving rise to confusion and bitterness in human relations and the constant danger of fratricidal wars . . . In the exercise of our pastoral office we sometimes have to listen—much to our regret—to persons who, though burning with zeal, are not endowed with too much sense of discretion and measure . . . In these modern times they see nothing but prevarication and ruin . . . we feel we must disagree with these prophets of gloom . . . from tranquil adherence to the teaching of the Church the apostolic spirit of the whole world expects a step towards a doctrinal presentation, in conformity with authentic doctrine, studied and expounded through the methods of research and the literary forms of modern thought: the substance of the ancient doctrine of the faith is one thing: the way in which it is presented is another. [*Documents of Vatican II*, translated by Abbott (London: Chapman 1966), 715]

The logistics of a Council in the late twentieth century were something of a nightmare: Vatican I had mustered some 750 delegates: Vatican II mustered more than 3000. At one stage it was suggested that the debating chamber should be a marquee erected within the Vatican [7 November 1965], but it soon became clear that nothing less than St Peter's Basilica would be adequate, not only for the episcopal members, but also the invited Observers, secretaries, ancillary staff and others who would, for various reasons, be present at the debates. Congar records a conversation with the official treasurer responsible for the budget who told him that the cost amounted to 1,4000, 000, 000 Italian lira each year [28 September 1964].

Preparation of the agenda started in 1959: suggestions were invited from all bishops and from Catholic universities, to be submitted by June 1960, to the ten preparatory commissions created for the purpose. From these, 'schema' or draft texts, would be drawn up by three secretariats and circulated to all bishops, with instructions to study them carefully before the opening of the Council on 11 October 1962.

On the first announcement of the Council Congar had tentatively offered his services to his bishop, but these were casually dismissed on a postcard. When the bishop found himself confronted with thirty-two schemas to be studied in detail by the opening of the Council he changed his tune, and offered Congar the hospitality of the St Sulpice Hostel in Rome for the duration of the Council, to avoid—Congar cynically suggests—having himself to pay for Congar`s lodgings [5 August 1962].

The Council ultimately promulgated sixteen official documents. There were three Dogmatic Constitutions: on the Church, on Divine Revelation, which finally settled the question of 'Scripture versus Tradition' by solemnly asserting that Revelation is transmitted by both [18 November 1965] and the Latin Liturgy. Another document, officially designated 'The Pastoral Constitution on the Church in the Modern World', attempted to express directly the changed and positive attitude of the Church towards that secular, human culture in which Catholic Christians live out their lives alongside all other human beings. Congar rejoiced at this: 'a veritable declaration of the complete acceptance of the modern human being and of the primacy of anthropology. (The Holy Father's speech was remarkable: he gave expression to the fundamental intention of schema XIII: to renew contact with humanity, to re-introduce the consideration of humankind into theology)' [7 December 1965].

Another nine documents described as 'Decrees' dealt with the Means of Social Communication, the Oriental Churches in Communion with Rome, Ecumenism, the Pastoral Office of Bishops, the Training and the Life and Ministry of Priests, Consecrated Religious Life, the Apostolate of the Laity, and the Church's Missionary Activity. There were also three 'Declarations': on Christian Education, Non-Christian Religions, and Religious Freedom. Theoretical differences between these categories were not, however, particularly clear or rigid, since every topic had some theological basis, and every position adopted implied theological presuppositions. Officially the term 'constitution' indicated direct concern with doctrine while 'decrees' referred to specific activities in the on-going life of the Church. 'Declarations' stated the official position of the contemporary Church on the topics concerned: the Declarations on Religious Freedom and on Non-christian Religions were among the most radical and controversial products of the Council, causing anxious and passionate debate well beyond the limits of Rome.

To his surprise Congar was appointed a consultor to the Preparatory Theological Commission in 1960, at the personal instigation of the Pope as he later discovered. At the time he was sceptical about how much influence mere 'consultors' would have, and described his appointment (together with that of the Jesuit Henri de Lubac) as 'mere window-dressing', but he did later recognise it as a long-delayed rehabilitation, since both men had been censured and silenced by Rome in 1950s [July 1960].[1]

His pessimism was not, however, justified: during the years of the Council he was consulted not only by bishops, but also by literally hundreds of people of every rank in the Church and from all quarters of the globe [cf 28 February 1962; 5 March 1962], and was in constant demand for lectures, talks, courses of instruction, written articles and books, to an extent which led him to complain, frequently, about the unrealism and lack of consideration shown by the people who came and asked him for contributions: 'I have agreed to give a lecture to the Salesians. But neither they nor anyone else has the least idea what my life is like and what five minutes means to me . . . It is the same people who are constantly asking me: 'What are you working on at the moment?', 'When will your commentary on *Lumen Gentium* appear?' who prevent me from working' [23 November 1965].

As a member of the Preparatory Theological Commission he had some influence on several initial schemas; as an expert during the Council he was most interested in, and involved with, the documents on the Church and Ecumenism. He was involved, to a lesser extent, with the documents on Religious Freedom, Non-Christian Religions, the Lay Apostolate, the Life and Ministry of Priests as well as On Missions, and the Church in the Modern World. [*Cf* his own list given in the *Journal*, 7 December 1965].

The Dogmatic Constitution on the Church (commonly known by its opening words in Latin, *Lumen gentium*, or just as *LG*, became the foundational document of the Council: not only did it formulate the post-conciliar programme for renewal in the Church but, to a large extent, already enshrined the attitude of some of those most actively involved in the Council and the principles at work in the compilation of the other major documents—the attitude which had led Pope John to convoke the Council in the first place.

Since the sixteenth century Reformation, when many Christians had felt compelled to reject much of the outward structure of the medieval European Church—its liturgy and sacraments, its hierarchical and papal constitution—popular Catholic belief had in fact come to conceive of the Church in terms precisely of those visible and external features. In contrast Vatican II's Dogmatic Constitution on the Church opened with a chapter on 'The Mystery of the Church' which was programmatic not only for the rest of that text, but also for the ensuing documents on Bishops, Priesthood, Lay Apostolate, Missions, Ecumenism and Religious Freedom.

---

1. *Cf*: 'Letter from Fr Yves Congar OP', translated by Ronald John Zamilla, *Theology Digest* 32 (1985): 213–6].

'Mystery' here translates the Greek word *mysterion* which is roughly equivalent to *sacrament* in common Catholic usage—the word which appears in the very first paragraph of the document: 'The Church, in Christ, is in the nature of a sacrament, a sign and instrument of communion with God and of unity among all human beings'. This concept underlies all that is further said about the ordained and lay members of the Church, about the Church`s relations with other Christians, with all human beings and with the secular and material world in which we live.

Chapter II makes clear that the primary visible manifestation of this 'sign' is not any ceremony or sacred object, but the very 'People of God' themselves— ordained and lay, of all ranks, races and character. Only after having established this inclusive framework are the specific characteristics of clergy and laity, Roman Catholics and other Christians, and humankind in general considered in Chapters III and IV. Chapters V and VI offer further development of I and II, examining in more detail what it means for the various groups of people who make up the Church to live out in practice the divine life they share through their communion with God in Christ, while Chapter VII tries to sketch out what will be the final, glorious consummation, the *eschaton* of that relationship. Congar was reasonably satisfied with this inclusive approach, though he did stigmatise it as 'very much in the scholastic mode', and 'a summary of papal documents over the past century' [24 August 1961].

It was not achieved without prolonged debate and some in-fighting over three sessions of the Council. At the time of its final promulgation Congar records that, a year earlier, when two principal draft texts were still under discussion as well as various other drafts, a small commission meeting was convened at the Holy Office, designed to influence the choice in favour of the more 'conservative' version. The following day, when the 'officially' preferred text was presented to the bishops as that of the Theology Commission, a member of the previous day's meeting pointedly reminded the speaker—Cardinal Ottaviani, that a vote had been taken resulting in preference for the other text [19 November 1964].

The inclusive approach of *LG* in chapter 8, where the Blessed Virgin Mother of God is treated not as Queen high above all else but as a member within the Church, albeit the most exalted member, was only achieved after bitter, acrimonious and even violent debate: 'Fenton was absolutley against it. . . . He makes use of every single WORD which he thinks conatians something that might favour a little opennes in order to charge at it like a bull at a red rag' [8 March 1962]. 'Fr Balić, alas, had the floor. He made a voluble sales-pitch. I leaned towards my neighbour, Mgr Philips, and asked him: is he selling braces or socks? Fr Balić is pure passion' [21 September 1961].

Congar`s comments on the extravagant positions to which unintelligent devotion leads some 'Mariologues' are biting and sarcastic throughout the three years it took the Council to achieve agreement on the text: 'François Bussini[2] tells me that Mgr Dubois, Archbishop of Besançon, and a member of the Theological Commission, declared, at the Besançon Major Seminary, that he ventured to say that, in a certain way, Jesus PRAYS to Mary' [26 October 1960], *IDIOCIES:* a combination of verbalism, abstract dialectic and sentimentalism' [18 September 1964]. He did however express satisfaction with the final text: 'A wholly biblical exposition of the mystery of Mary, along the lines of 'virgin daughter of Sion' [3 June 1964 & 22 September 1964]. The result of the vote taken on whether to include the text on the Blessed Virgin in the Document on the Church was the closest of all those taken during the Council, with a difference of only forty votes between those in favour and those against, out of a total of over 2000.

Chapter III of *LG*, entitled 'The Hierarchical Structure of the Church, with special reference to the Episcopate' provided the point of departure for the documents: 'On the Pastoral Office of Bishops', 'On the Training of Priests' and 'On the Life and Ministry of Priests'. The question of whether episcopal consecration is part of the sacrament of Holy Order was settled, in the affirmative, relatively easily, but bitter dispute raged over the questions of 'Collegiality' [4 February 1964 to 2 June 1964]. Chapter III of the text asserted that 'Bishops form a collegial body empowered with its own supreme authority over the whole Church, exercised in a solemn way through an Eucmenical Council' [22 September 1964].

The bishops and many of the experts became sharply divided between 'collegialists' and 'anti-collegialists', the latter seeing in this assertion an attack on the authority of the pope as defined by Vatican I [12–27 September 1964 and 27 February 1965]. The actual object of much of the criticism was rather the various offices of the Roman Curia whose very extensive influence now came under threat. Bishops who—isolated in their own dioceses around the world—had generally bowed to instructions and regulations 'from Rome', now gathered in Council as a corporate body were enjoying the realisation of their own power and authority to carry out their functions according to their own wisdom and discretion, without the constant influence and supervision of uninformed bureaucrats in Rome [22 February 1965]. A more evenhanded commentator pointed out that 'Bureaucracy usurps the function of both the petrine and the episcopal office'.

As with some other topics, the issue became acutely polarised and emotional, the anti-collegialists accusing the collegialists of 'disloyalty to the Holy Father' [17–22 September 1964]. They evoked some of Congar's severest criticism, largely aimed at the civil servants who presided over the various Roman Congregations, whose age and abilities he describes with savage sarcasm: "'Is this the sign that we

---

2. François Bussini was at that time a seminarian of the diocese of Besançon at the International Seminary in Strasbourg. He was later to teach at the Catholic Faculty of Theology in Strasbourg, before becoming Auxiliary Bishop in Grenoble and, finally, Bishop of Amiens.

are getting away from the regime of Pizzardo and the other cretins"?' [1 October 1964, 8 October 1964, 17 November 1964, 27 February 1964].

The final vote on the chapter on the hierarchy was taken only during the third session in November 1964, after a 'Preliminary Note' had been appended to the text, mandated by 'Higher Authority', setting out, with sophisticated finesse and diplomacy, the relationship between the authority of the College of Bishops and that of the Papacy. The bishops felt that, after this vote, a corner had been turned: 'Vatican I has received its necessary complement' [23 September 1964].

The Decree on the Pastoral Office of Bishops was, thereafter, relatively uncontroversial: the need was recognised for a more contemporary understanding of the bishop's role for the overall good of the Church in the modern world, and the consequent need for good fraternal relationships. It also provided for the creation of a permanent synod of bishops to meet regularly in Rome, intended to bear witness to the participation of all bishops in the care of the whole Church [21 September 1964 ,4 April 1965, 15 September 1965].

The Decree on the Training of Priests offered only general regulations, recognising the need for adaptation to various countries and cultures, thereby putting an end to the rigid system inherited from the Council of Trent. The need for major seminaries was re-asserted, but all elements of training should be co-ordinated with the pastoral aim that priests should win people to Christ by becoming servants of all: philosophical and theological studies should be integrated more closely with pastoral training and experience. Congar was not the only one to rejoice in the abandonment of the 'Denzinger mentality' and the era of the Manuals, and commented that bishops had too easily replaced intellectual formation with piety and spirituality [9 November 1964, 25 October 1965, 5 March 1966.]

The Decree on the Life and Ministry of Priests recognised that conciliar renewal asserted an increasingly important and difficult role for them. It considered priesthood itself in the contemporary world, defined as the ministry of word and sacrament, within the framework of Christ's threefold office of prophet, priest and king [13–15 October 1964 and 20 October 1965]. Attention was given to their relationship with other categories in the Church, and the demand for holiness of life. In the Latin church this included celibacy—the focus of some debate, curtailed however,by Pope Paul VI`s statement that celibacy was not up for discussion [11–12 October 1965 and 20 October 1965]. This absolute prohibition evoked protest from some oriental bishops who felt that it implied criticism of their own, legitimate, practice of ordaining married men.

For Congar and others, discussion centred not so much on celibacy as on the wider concept of priestly dedication. Two extremes of the spectrum were seen in the quasi-monastic concept of consecrated life inherited from the medieval Church, and the currently controversial 'worker-priest' movement, increasingly widespread in Belgium and Northern France.

The Decree on the Apostolate of the Laity also had its basis in the Constitution on the Church, where Chapter 4 states that: 'Because of their situation and mission certain things pertain particularly to the Laity, both men and women'. It further states that 'the pastors indeed know that they themselves are not established by Christ to undertake alone the whole salvific mission of the Church in the world...'—a marked contrast with the assertion of Pius X in 1906: 'The Church is essentially an unequal society . . . of two categories, the pastors and the flock . . . so distinct . . . that with the pastoral body only rests the necessary right and authority for promoting the end of the society and directing the members to that end: the one duty of the multitude is to allow itself to be led and like a docile flock, to follow the pastors' [*Vehementer nos*, 1906].

The Laity are defined by their specifically secular vocation, which is also developed in terms of Christ's three-fold office of prophet, priest and king, while their rights as well as their duties are clearly defined. The Decree goes on to consider in some detail the role of the family, modern forms of lay training and organisation, as well as the need for a specifically lay spirituality, again to be clearly distinguished from inherited monastic models. The reforms embodied in the Constitution on the Liturgy were also largely intended to enable the laity to play their full part there.

The other main shift in position promoted by Vatican II concerned the relationship of the Church with other groups beyond her own membership: other Christians, Non-Christian religions, the protagonists of complete religious freedom and the secular world at large.

Building on paragraph 16 of *LG*, the Decree on Ecumenism analysed the various modes of relationship of the Church with other Christians and, contrary to the stance of the past four hundred years, recommended and encouraged appropriate contact and co-operation. The compilation of an 'Ecumenical Directory' was initiated to facilitate this [25 November 1963, 24 September 1966].

The Declaration of the Relationship of the Church to Non-Christian Religions, on the other hand, was fraught with controversy. The Council's original intention had been to recognise the Church's own origin in pre-Christian Judaism and to honour the monotheistic faith of Moslems. Social and political factors in the Near and Middle East made this impossible however [11 October 1963]. Bishops from those regions pointed out that any such statement would be interpreted by both Jews and Moslems as hostile to themselves and favouring the other, while Israel was inclined to interpret any favouring of the Arab point of view as an encouragement to terrorism [25 April 1964, 25 October 1964, 26 February 1965, 3 April 1965; 25 October 1965].

So serious was the situation that various bishops from Arab regions insisted that any apparent gesture of goodwill towards the Jews would unleash real persecution in their territories, with mob-violence, killings and burning of their churches. Discussion of the document was consequently long drawn-out and very complex, concluding at one point that it would be impossible to promulgate any such document at all, even with widely disseminated disclaimers and statements of intent [28 September 1964].

Eventually such measures, addressed in particular to Arab governments, persuaded most of the bishops concerned to tolerate the document, while those whose efforts had been concentrated on banishing the word 'deicide' from Christian vocabulary got their way [12.11.64 & 15.10.65]. Even so the text was only approved for promulgation by 1763 against 260. A significant number of bishops sought to safeguard their position by abstaining from the vote.

The Declaration on Religious Freedom had its basis in the opening words of the text: *Dignitatis humanae* [9 March 1964, 23–4 March 1964, 28 November 1965] and elaborated the belief that human beings, of their very nature, enjoy responsible freedom in activity and decision making; consequently they should be influenced not by coercion, but by conviction, by a sense of duty and a consciousness of spiritual values. Development in sociological and psychological studies emphasises this, but the document sought, not without controversy, to assert the inherent moral obligation to embrace truth when it is found, and the conviction that ultimate human fulfilment is found only in Christ, an aspect developed more fully in the Council's document on *Divine Revelation*. The Declaration extends this personal right and obligation to natural, social and political groupings, and recognises the historical fact that the Church itself has not always respected it. Its relevance to missionary work, and to relations with adherents of other religions is also noted.

The Decree on the Church's Missionary Activity was largely concerned with the distinction between the Church's fundamental mission to preach the Gospel to all people, and the particular manner in which this is carried out by specific groups within the Church [30 October 1963 and 31 March 1965].

The Pastoral Constitution on the Church in the Modern World originated in the desire to dismantle the 'fortress mentality' engendered by the Council of Trent in the sixteenth century, and to harmonise awareness of the natural goodness inherent in creation and human life with the supernatural life proclaimed by revelation, and made accessible through the Incarnation [26 October 1964].

The point of departure was the question of how far, and in what manner, the Council intended to address the world in general outside the boundaries of the Catholic Church [8 October 1964]. Congar asked, doubtfully, 'Has the Church found the language with which to address the world?' [5 October 1965].

The text had a chequered history: originally identified as 'schema XVII' it was later promoted to 'schema XIII' as other schemas were abandoned or combined. [3-4 March 1964]. The final title, 'Pastoral Constitution' indicates the ambiguity of its character and target audience [8 October 1964]. One English bishop subsequently described it as 'the rag-bag containing all those things that bishops wanted to say which did not fit in anywhere else.' Congar described it, originally, as a poultice [9 February 1965].

Diverse attitudes were apparent about the inclusion of such items as the explicit condemnation of Communist political regimes—there was a press campaign in Italy in favour of this [24 October 1965]—nuclear weapons and a more nuanced position with regard to artificial birth control: In short the Englsh bishops do not want to hear mention at the Council of either the pill or the bomb' [22 October 1964].

General agreement was eventually reached on a more positive survey and commendation of the contemporary human situation, and recognition of some of the ways in which the Church could appreciate, co-operate with and promote the goods of human civilisation [7 December 1965].

Congar was an inveterate grumbler: the *Journal* is laced throughout with a stream of criticisms and complaints, but occasionally a more attractive attitude becomes apparent, as for instance, when he reflects on the death of his mother [26 November 1963, 29 March 1965, 26 November 1965] and ponders how much her sufferings and prayers may have contributed to his own work. He was deeply moved and genuinely thrilled to be present, on 7 December 1965, at the mutual lifting by Rome and Constantinople of the anathemas pronounced against each other in 1054, conscious of being part of a truly historic event, but, predictably, less enthusiastic about the elaborate closing ceremonial of the Council. This included the reading out of 'messages' addressed to various categories of people: diplomats, intellectuals, artists, women, workers, the poor, the sick and the young. During the reading of the message to 'the young', the Pope was surrounded by a crowd of little boys, 'even one still in short trousers'. 'But why', asked Congar, 'were there no little girls?' [8 December 1965].

CONGAR'S ECCLESIASTICAL SUBTEXT: INTRANSIGENT CONSERVATISM
PAUL PHILIBERT OP

For most Catholics the events of the Second Vatican Council are a thing of the past. The liturgy they have known for their lifetime, a product of the Council and its reforms, is the only one they can remember. Using the vernacular for common prayer, as they have done all their lives, makes perfect sense; why would anyone want to use a language people don't understand? The active participation of lay ministers in the pastoral life of the parish and in the administration of the diocese is so widespread that it seems completely normal. Yet all of these elements, and much more, flowed out of the pastoral renewal of the Council and were bitterly contested at the time. Why would that have been the case?

It is a question worth asking, especially since an important and powerful minority in the church today is inclined to reverse changes of this sort. This council journal of Yves Congar is revealing in portraying the attitudes and the mechanisms of an ecclesiastical mentality that is crucial to understand, if we are to comprehend present transitions in the life of the church. Congar generally referred to this mentality as '*intégrisme*', a French word that cannot easily be translated directly into English, although many translators have simply transliterated it as 'integralism'. From time to time in this journal, Congar characterises certain figures as '*intégristes*', meaning a camp of ultramontane, authoritarian, and clericalised ecclesiastics who wanted to control everything and did not want to see anything change, but rather remain integrally or exactly the same as they had always known it to be.

To eyes unfamiliar with Catholic history, these differences might appear to be relatively unimportant, if bitter, ideological skirmishes between liberals and conservatives. In fact, a great deal is at stake. Congar's whole life work was put on the line at Vatican II in his personal combat to make the case for an understanding of the church that is grounded in the Holy Scriptures, expressed in the lives of all the baptised, oriented toward the mission of the kingdom of God in the world, and a vocation to freedom under the guidance of the Holy Spirit. He knew that the church had to be a living organism, as opposed to a church that was merely a museum of past spiritual treasures.

For his whole adult life, Congar fought to develop and articulate a new ecclesiology suited for his time which was, in fact, the ancient one of the church's origins. As Éric Mahieu's superb introduction makes clear, Yves Congar arrived at the Council with a theological maturity and an international and ecumenical network of relationships that made it possible for him to profoundly influence the direction of the council's documents, particularly at crucial moments of controversy among those drafting the texts. Along with Henri de Lubac and some others, he was a skilled exponent of the 'return to the sources' approach that rendered the pastoral teachings of the early centuries apt and lucid resources for the contemporary church. In addition, from the beginning of his theological career, Congar was devoted to church reunion and was steeped in the theological insights of both Orthodox and Protestant traditions. Above all, drawing from the vision of the Scriptures and the early church Fathers, Congar had a passionate commitment to communicate to all the laity their vocation both to holiness and to apostolic fruitfulness. As someone systematically trained in the theology of St Thomas Aquinas, Congar possessed a capacity for synthetic thinking that allowed him to honor the irreplaceable foundations of the faith and still integrate what was new and creative. Given that, Congar's ecclesiology was essentially biblical, patristic, ecumenical, apostolic, and practical.

Congar had published theological writings for more than thirty years before Vatican II. In them, these principles became the foundation for his ground-breaking work in ecumenism, biblical theology, theology of the laity, and ecclesiology. Although Congar's insights would eventually be endorsed by the council, before Pope John XXIII they did not win him friends in Rome. Indeed, in the eyes of the principal exponents of Roman integralism, Congar remained the quintessential symbolic enemy of what they considered tradition to be. Congar's perspective was so foreign to the Roman Curia that he was ruthlessly ostracised and penalised by them for being a threat to their worldview.

The infallibility of the pope had not been defined until 1870 at the First Vatican Council, and in the minds of the integralists that was the high point of Catholic tradition. Consequently, for them, all the ecclesiastical customs of that period, including a suffocating clericalism, became symbolic of the church's tradition. The pageantry of an imperial court, including taken for granted deference to those invested with roles of power, was an essential part of this nineteenth century Vatican structure. By going back to the early sources, Congar and others represented a risk for the power structure that conceived the papal office as a monarchy supported by a dictatorial Roman Curia and always inclined to consider anything done in the Vatican as sharing in the infallibility of the pope.

This battle for a living church, exemplified again and again in confrontations over texts and principles, is the underlying story of Congar's council journal. Before 1962, Congar had lived many years under the shadow of the Roman Curia. Rome sanctioned him for his writings, expelled him from his professorship, and exiled him from his home for having articulated a theological tendency that would be firmly embraced by Vatican II. In 1960, Pope John XXIII rehabilitated him by naming him to the preparatory commission of the Council and appointing him a *peritus* (expert) to assist the leadership of the council. Further, Pope John officially opened the council with an inaugural speech that echoed some of the themes of Congar's great work, *True and False Reform in the Church.*

Accordingly, the Council's great aim was to update the church's doctrinal expressions so as to make them potent in a changed world, to invite all Christians into a common search for the unity desired by Christ for his church, and to reform the church's way of being in the world. This meant especially its sacramental and ritual life, so that people could enter and understand the rites as agents of liturgical prayer rather than observers of solemn ceremonies. Despite Pope John's clear directives for the Council, so redolent of Congar's theological agenda, Congar never lost his fear of being suspect in the eyes of the Roman Curia and would later castigate himself for being too timid in expressing his ideas while at the Council.[1] What is astonishing, therefore, given what he had suffered for years from the church's highest administration, is the unbounded generosity of his investment in the Council, to the point of exhausting himself and pouring himself out in the midst of chronic fatigue and physical pain.

It can help us to gain some perspective on the way Congar saw things, I think, to turn to an essay that he published in 1950 as Appendix III to the first edition of *True and False Reform in the Church.* It is a brief sketch of what he calls the 'mentality of the right' and in which he describes what he means by '*intégrisme*'.[2] To begin, he insists that he is talking about a 'mentality,' by which he means a worldview or perspective that governs or controls the way someone *sees* things. He explains that *intégristes* are emotionally attached to the idea of a Christendom invested with a glorious past of kings and bishops working hand-in-hand with the pope—all of them enjoying the authority to impose their views. This is, says Congar, a fatal nostalgia which ultimately led 'loyal' Catholics in the nineteenth century to be opposed to anything modern, to be repelled by the aims of the French Revolution, and to yearn for the restoration of monarchy. Thus positioned, the Catholic Church in France became a caricature of everything old-fashioned and authoritarian. It is not by chance that the enemies of Modernism (a grab bag of 'heresies' that was named by a disapproving Pope Pius X) supported the right wing *Action Française* and opposed any efforts to reconcile Catholic faith with modern culture.

---

1. December 7, 1965—II 510.
2. 'Appendice III: Mentalité 'de droite' et Intégrisme en France', in Yves M-J Congar, *Vraie et fausse réforme dans l'Église*, first edition (Paris: Editions du Cerf, 1950), 604–622. In the second edition of this work, Congar removed the 18 pages of appendix 3, saying, 'This constitutes on my part neither a change of heart nor a retraction; it is just a fraternal gesture inspired by my desire to contribute to the peace and mutual understanding among the Catholics of France, something much to be desired' (*True and False Reform*, second edition [1968], 7).

The affinity of traditionalist Catholicism for the political right is grounded in its dream of restoring a monarchical order or, at least, a fundamentally authoritarian one. Congar quotes an old saying that those on the right prefer order to justice,[3] explaining that order appeals to them because it is assured of its rectitude from on high through precepts and authority. Those on the right place little trust in human instincts and have little interest in new ideas. Their attitude is typically a refusal or a condemnation of anything new and a condescension before any expression of grassroots hopes or desires. They instinctively see things from the perspective of authority, from a hierarchical point of view. This goes along, of course, with their inexpressibly vulgar tendency to spy on others and turn them in to the ecclesiastical authorities for judgment and punishment.

To understand *intégrisme*, then, we have to understand it as a mentality that identifies itself completely with what is old-fashioned and that appeals to hierarchical authority as the justification for its point of view. It is an instinct to choose what was done before over what is struggling for new expression. It has little respect for anything that comes from below, but is deeply attached to what comes down from on high. When it is a question of expressing this attitude in religious matters, there are certain characteristic positions typical of this mentality. Congar gives eight examples in his essay.

First, *intégrisme* is usually pessimistic. It insists upon fallen nature, original sin, and the evil of the world. It has a strong inclination to condemn things that are in themselves inoffensive (like the Scout movement in Congar's time or new movements of lay solidarity in our time). It is inclined to emphasise whatever is most contrary to spontaneous human desires, to make life difficult. No pain, no gain.

Second, it believes in ruling with a firm hand, imposing its point of view through the exercise of authority and an appeal to hierarchical powers. As a consequence, it feels no need to justify the positions that it takes or to explain itself. It considers it perfectly legitimate to conduct its investigations of suspect doctrines or persons in secret, since, from its point of view, those in error have no rights. (Congar himself was never allowed to see the dossier of complaints and condemnations that the Holy Office created about him in the 1950s, when he became officially *persona non grata* in Rome.)

Third, this mentality is horrified by the very idea of evolution and mistrustful of the notion of development. Things are what they are. Every time someone speaks about 'life' or 'experience', *intégristes* frown. Such talk suggests relativism, exceptions to the rule, and the possibility of change.

Fourth, *intégrisme* has a distaste for any attempt to facilitate the access of others to the Catholic community—a horror of making things too easy for them. Its inclination is to insist on every jot and tittle of the law, even to maximise the demands of what it means to be Catholic.[4]

---

3. *Ibid*, 612.
4. The dramatic exception of facilitating Anglicans to enter the Catholic communion as

Fifth, this mentality is deeply attached to the idea of faith being an *intellectual* assent, insisting strongly on the objective component of the faith (*fides quae creditur*—the subject matter believed). It emphasises the dogmatic formula proposed to the believer in a defined fashion, and it has no interest in considering the subjective reality of faith (*fides qua creditur*—the inner working of belief in the person) and the ways in which it develops.

Sixth, *intégrisme* places great value on the role of reason and on demonstrating conclusions through a rational process. It has a passion for deduction and little interest in inductive thinking or in any appeal to experience, to personal witness, or to the internal workings of conscience. It is deeply attached to the kind of neo-scholasticism that developed at the end of the nineteenth century, to such a degree that it is practically incapable of imagining problems that cannot be addressed through rational demonstration by weighing up premises and conclusions. Their world is completely defined.

Seventh, with respect to the church, it accentuates the strict, authoritarian side of things. It maximises the authority to be given to any words coming from Rome, slipping easily into considering any directive from the hierarchy as definitive. In general, they cannot imagine the truth as a fullness that arises out of a communion of believers who are all filled with spiritual gifts. Rather, the truth has to be arrived at in a linear fashion by the logical exploitation of received doctrines. As Congar puts it, 'These people sniff out heresy anywhere they find someone searching seriously for the expression of the truth or in dialogue with contemporary problems'.[5] For them, there are only conclusions, not problems.

Eighth, and finally, a certain kind of ecclesiology corresponds to these attitudes. They understand the church as a mystery of grace, of course; and they clearly affirm the mystical dimension of the church. *Intégristes* are very positive about the spiritual life and about the fact that God works within souls. But that sort of thing remains confined to the order of one's personal life in the Church. When it comes to ecclesiology, the church itself is considered only according to the structure of authority, something exterior to the religious subject, and in such a fashion that everything is imagined as coming from on high. From one end of the spectrum to the other, *intégrisme* emphasises what *was*, what is *given*, what is *commanded*.

Congar goes on to remark that these thinkers of the right are still able to talk about reform in the church, even if they like to see everything settled from on high and imposed as precepts. *Intégristes* don't just love formalism or dislike the interior life; but when it comes to reforming the church, they are inclined to reduce every question to one of morality and to claim that each person must

---

intact diocesan communities or parochial bodies can be explained by the deep ideological affinity between the Roman position on ordination of women and the similar position of the break-off Anglican groups.

5. *Ibid*, 618.

reform himself or herself—become more pure, more zealous, more committed —and that will suffice. In that way, reforming the church boils down to returning to fixed regulations determined from on high, and so solving problems by getting everyone in line with the regulations given by the authorities.

Intégristes have no idea that a reform might involve adapting the life of the church to the transformations taking place in the world. To the degree that they see changes taking place around them, their inclination is to judge them as deviations from what is 'traditional'. They consider all kinds of newness (inventions, discoveries, technologies) an offence against the perennial understanding of the truth. Congar concludes this list characterising the *intégriste* tendency by saying, 'If my interpretation of all this is on the mark, you can understand why such an attitude has the terrible inclination to see everything that has happened since the Middle Ages or since 1789 as a conspiracy of errors, and to think that anything that proposes something new is going to lead to mistakes.'[6]

So, twelve years after writing this essay, Congar found himself at Vatican II feeling like Don Quixote in a landscape controlled by such people. Early on, reflecting on his work with the Preparatory Commission, he remarked on 24 September 1961, that 'these "Romans" don't take the Tradition seriously; they look only at what the popes say. That's where the big fight is going to be. But the truth will prevail.' Then he observes that he has studied the development of ecclesiology and the growth of papal authority through the centuries. Roman theologians have long been inclined to build a huge superstructure on a few lines of Scripture, whether the case is '*Tu es Petrus*—You are Peter', on the one hand, or '*gratia plena*—full of grace', on the other. In either case, whether about papal primacy or Mariology, these Roman theologians pursue just one idea—to maximise, to push to its fullest expression, either a power or a glory. Such people are willing to 'utilise anything.'[7]

In November 1962, in the midst of an incredible multitude of projects for the Council, Congar accepted an invitation to lecture at the seminary known as the Capranica for about forty Roman seminarians. He was invited to speak on ecumenism, but he was obliged to give his talk in Latin, which he found difficult and limiting. Toward the end of his conference, three bishops came into the room, including the bishop of Benevento. During the question period, this bishop violently attacked Congar insisting that Catholic doctrine has been perfectly expressed in the manuals taught in the seminaries, that they are not superficial (as Congar had claimed), nor ambiguous. 'What determines everything', the bishop added, 'is the magisterium. You talk about the presence of Christ in the church: there is only *one* presence—it is the magisterium!'[8] Congar replied that in the church there is an experience of the mystery of Christ, to which the bishop

---

6. *Ibid*, 620.
7. 24 September 1961.
8. 22 November 1962.

bellowed: 'Experience! People talked about that at the beginning of the century – that's Modernism!!!'[9]

At the end of November, Cardinal Ottaviani invited Congar to meet with him at the Holy Office where, among other remarks, the cardinal blamed Congar for producing only negative criticism of the schemas presented to the Council and then added, 'Since you are so much under surveillance and so suspect, you ought to be all the more careful to refer everything to the authentic magisterium'. Congar remarks in his journal, 'I perceive that I am once and for all and for ever under suspicion. That will not prevent me from working. My work displeases them because they realise very well that its whole aim is to bring back into circulation certain ideas, certain things that they have been endeavouring to shut out for four hundred years, and above all for the past hundred years. But that is my vocation and my service in the name of the Gospel and of the Traditon.'[10]

Two years and much enormous effort later, the Council began its discussion of what eventually became its Constitution on the Church in the Modern World. Congar reacts to the criticisms of the document by Cardinal Ruffini, one of the stalwarts of the curial *intégristes*: 'He is perfectly consistent with himself and with his attitude of rejecting real openings. *Ut schema funditus reficatur* [the schema should be fundamentally remade] in line with the encyclicals of recent popes'.[11] In November, Congar is working on the *modi* (suggestions for revision) for the decree on bishops and comes across the revisions suggested by Cardinals Ruffini, Siri, Browne and some others. Referring to them, he says, 'It is truly a hatred of all 'democratic' spirit, and an expression of integrism, just as I described it in *Vrai et fausse Réforme* [*True and False Reform*]'.[12]

In February 1965, Congar reads an article in the Italian newspaper, *Il Messaggero*, that claims that he and Chenu are behind a Marxist plot to influence the French bishops, an insinuation of the French Catholic right.[13] Meanwhile, he is working full time producing texts and critically appraising sections of *De Revelatione*, the beginnings of *Gaudium et spes*, and *Presbyterorum ordinis*. Where does his energy come from? That is the marvel here.

At the very end of the Council, following the closing Mass, Congar remarks that as wonderful as that closing celebration was, from the point of view of ecclesiology and ecumenism there was something wrong. It was all about the pope. It gave the impression the pope was *above* the church rather than *in* it. Perhaps this remark helps us to assess better what Congar really wanted from the Council. As he himself says in many places, the Council planted the seeds of a new ecclesiology—a new church. But the obstructionism of the Roman Curia and of

---

9. *Ibid*, 255.
10. 30 November 1962.
11. 20 October 1964.
12. 3 November 1964.
13. 8 February 1965.

the forces of the right led to too many essential points being expressed as compromises (as, for example, the introduction of the *Nota Praevia* to *Lumen gentium* to underscore papal privilege in a document about the People of God). It is true, perhaps, that the influence of the Council's minority forced the majority to be more articulate and precise.[14] But it is also true that the ambiguities forced upon the texts by controversies opened the possibility for regressive interpretations of what are genuine developments in the Council's documents for theology and pastoral life. In too many places, the impression is still given that the church is essentially about the pope or the hierarchy. In the light of this ambiguity, I am reminded of an extraordinary passage in Congar's essay on the structure of Christian priesthood.[15]

Christ's priesthood was not about liturgy but about life. He came to inaugurate a new creation. Referring to the theology of the Book of Revelation, Congar speaks of Christ as the principle or the Alpha of everything, as well as the end or the Omega, as well. But Christ is also the *way* from the beginning to the end and will remain that as long as the Alpha is not completely transformed into the Omega. Referring to 1 Corinthians 15:28: 'When all things are subjected to him, then the Son himself will also be subjected to the one who put all things in subjection under him, so that God may be all in all', Congar points out the essential importance of the faithful entering knowingly and willingly into the mystery of Christ, being 'subjected to him'. As long as our transformation by the grace of Christ's resurrection is incomplete, this plenitude or fullness of Christ will not yet be achieved.[16]

This movement from Christ as Alpha to Christ as Omega is a very powerful image. The first is Christ's unique divine initiative in the incarnation, and the second is the plenitude of the Body of Christ incorporating the lives and sacrifices of all his members. Congar explains that Christ can be the Alpha of the new creation without us, but he cannot be its Omega without our contributing to its plenitude. The church celebrates in the sacraments, especially in the Eucharist, Jesus's passing over to his Father. 'The role of the sacraments is to reproduce in a particular mode of being [as sign] . . . what Jesus did for us in the days of his flesh. This allows the root to bear its fruits—to make the Christ Alpha produce within us over time the reality of life in such a way as to form the Christ Omega.'[17] Consequently the participation of the faithful in the church's sacramental life cannot be that of observers or of mere recipients. We are baptised into a common priesthood that makes us participants in the celebration of the body and blood of the Lord. Christ's priesthood exists in the members of his body to stimulate their

---

14. *Cf* LVI.
15. 'The Structure of Christian Priesthood' in Yves Congar, *At the Heart of Christian Worship: Liturgical Essays of Yves Congar*, Translated by Paul Philibert (Collegeville: Liturgical Press, 2010), 69°105.
16. *Ibid*, 83.
17. *Ibid*, 85.

participation in his own sacrifice, bringing about the willing sacrifice of human persons united to the sacrifice of Jesus Christ. 'In this way the faithful accomplish and fill up the sacrifice of Jesus, their Alpha (their source).'[18]

Naturally, Congar insists upon the role of the hierarchical powers in the church; they assure that the church maintains its structure. However, the church lives in all the people. By baptismal consecration, all the faithful are constituted as legitimate co-celebrants in the sacrifice of Christ. 'The church develops and makes actual the offering which Christ made of her on the cross. The church fulfills in the body what had already been offered by the head.'[19] The faithful, by voluntarily offering their own lives in union with the self-offering of Christ their head, expand the outreach of the new creation of grace in space and time. This is how the body of Christ experiences and contributes to the growth of the one who, having achieved everything fully in himself, now desires that we join him in doing the same. Thus the mystery of Christ's passover becomes the mystery of our own passover. In this way the identity of the Omega with the Alpha is the real filling up of the resurrected Christ with the transformed lives of the members of his body.

This essentially mystical vision of the church was at the heart of Congar's theological agenda. It had ramifications for practically every theological question undertaken by Vatican II. He accommodated this fundamental ecclesial vision to the various projects of the Council. Without Congar's participation, it is hard to imagine that the Council would have articulated as it did in the Constitution on the Church its extraordinary account of biblical images of the church (*LG* 4-6), its rich development of the theme of the people of God, and its critically important use of the theology of baptismal priesthood (*LG* 10, 34). Likewise, in the Constitution on Divine Revelation, Congar's contribution of chapter 2, especially note 10, is the key to the theology of the entire document. His central role in drafting the Decree on Ecumenism had to be one of the most gratifying moments for him, given his lifelong commitment to Christian unity. In n. 11, the decree articulates that in Catholic doctrine there exists 'an order or hierarchy of truths, since they vary in their relation to the foundation of the Christian faith. Thus the way will be opened whereby [a] kind of friendly rivalry will incite all to a deeper realisation and a clearer expression of the unfathomable riches of Christ'. This profoundly fraternal image of a rivalry among friends expresses deep respect for the theological and spiritual life of the reformed churches. In all these ways, Congar consolidated the theological riches of the patristic age with an eye always fixed upon the goal of future unity.

In a number of places throughout the journal, Congar remarks upon the transformation taking place among the bishops of the world because of their participation in the Council. This represented nothing less than a veritable conver-

---

18. *Ibid*, 95.
19. *Ibid*, 105.

sion of perspective on their part. In addition to all the technical work he did in writing documents and assisting the commissions of the Council, Congar was also indefatigable in offering lectures, seminars, and dialogues with groups of bishops, with students, with journalists, and with the non-Catholic Observers. He was convinced that if people could only *see*, their hearts would change. Clearly, though, he never succeeded in changing the hearts of the curial leaders—Ottaviani, Ruffini, Browne, and so many others. They, who had their day before the Council, would also have too strong an influence upon the implementation of the Council's work afterwards. For that reason, it is important to grasp the subtext of the many confrontations described by Congar in this journal.

In ending his essay from 1950 cited above, Congar talks about how Newman described the forces of the right that caused him so much pain and frustration. In Newman's words, 'They set up a church within a church… turning their own point of view into dogmas. I defend myself not against their positions, but against what I have to call their schismatic spirit.'[20] Then Congar goes on to say that the tendency in Catholicism to exaggerate the role of authority in solving questions goes along with an equally strong inclination to judge and condemn any openness, any real spirit of research, or any questioning of received ideas. It also tends to judge someone's orthodoxy by whether or not they find others heterodox. In so doing, these people put their judgment above that of the church and they arrogate to themselves the right to judge what is Catholic in terms of their own narrowness, if not their own ignorance. What *intégrisme* really lacks is a genuine confidence in the truth, a genuine love of the truth, which can respect and honour the truth even in its developing expressions. Congar ends by citing the prayer of St Catherine of Siena, 'Lord, open up my heart'.[21]

To the degree that the tendency to restorationism in today's church replicates the spirit of the European *intégrisme* of the nineteenth century or of the curial *intégrisme* of the pre-Vatican II world, Congar's journal offers useful lessons. It also, thank God, shows us how profound theological training, immense hard work, and a trust in divine providence can overcome the divisive spirit of the *intégrisme* of any age.

---

20. 'Appendice III', 621.
21. *Ibid*, 622.

EDITORIAL NOTE
ÉRIC MAHIEU
(with some alterations and additions respecting the English edition)

The manuscript text of *My Journal of the Council* comprises nine exercise books into which have been inserted a certain number of documents. Shortly after the Council, Congar had it typed in triplicate by Delphine Guillou, his secretary at that time. Two copies were deposited with the original manuscript in the archives of the Dominican Province of France at the library of Le Saulchoir. The third copy was sent to the library of the Faculty of Theology in Leuven (Belgium). Congar had re-read, corrected and signed the typed version of his *Journal* and it is this that has been used as a basis for this edition. However, the manuscript text has been compared with the typed one in order to discover any words or passages that might have been forgotten or omitted from the typescript. These are few in number and have been incorporated in this edition between double square brackets. (The passages in single brackets, round or square, were included by Congar himself. For the English translation, single square brackets have also been used when giving the English translation of text in another language. As these always follow the non-English text, they should not cause confusion. Braces, or curly brackets, in the text are original. In the footnotes they indicate a footnote not found in the French edition). Italicised square brackets around a blank space indicate a blank space in the manuscript. When re-reading the typescript, Congar made, besides some orthographic corrections, some handwritten additions. In the French edition, these were indicated by asterisks. In the English translation, they have been incorporated into the footnotes. The correction of simple mistakes in spelling has not been noted. As for the documents attached to the *Journal*, which are of very different types (ranging from an invitation to the rough draft of a lecture, from a text given to him to read by a bishop to correspondence), we have briefly described in the notes those that are of direct historical interest in relation to the Council.

As far as possible, the layout and the paragraph divisions of the original have been respected. In the French edition, the often chaotic style and punctuation of the *Journal* were left as they were. Moreover, Congar made much use of underlining. In order to assist the ease of reading, words or phrases that were underlined once have here been given in capitals, those that were underlined twice have here been given in italic capitals, and those that were underlined three times or more have here been given in underlined italic capitals. The results of the voting in the Conciliar assembly are given here as they were recorded by Congar (they can be checked against those given in the official Acta). On the other hand, the spelling of the names of persons, places, books or journals has been checked and, where necessary, corrected. However, some personal names have been left as they were when their identification was doubtful or when they differed phonetically from the correct name. In these rare cases, the correct or probable name is indicated in the notes. In order to make reading easier, the summary of the interventions *in aula* has been slightly offset. The references for these interventions in the *Acta Synodalia*, the official Acts of the Council, are given in the footnotes.

The people involved have nearly all been identified, by means, in particular, of consultation of the Congar archives. When they are first mentioned in the *Journal*, a brief introductory note has been provided, normally restricted to the offices held by those persons at the various moments when they are mentioned in the *Journal*. In some cases, it has seemed useful to mention also the important responsibilities later assumed by them, whether internationally (Roman organisms, Catholic episcopates, Catholic universities, World Council of Churches) or in the French ecclesiastical world.

In the French edition, a translation of words or passages in Latin or in other languages was given in the notes. In the English translation, these have been included in the text, following the words or passages concerned, in square brackets. The occasional barbarisms in Congar's Latin have been corrected. Words and expressions that occur frequently have been translated only at the first occurrence; they and their translation will also be found among the appendices at the end of Volume II.

Amongst these appendices there is a glossary of the principal technical terms used in the *Journal*, tables of the different names used by Congar to designate the schemas and the conciliar Commissions, and a map of Rome indicating the principal places of residence and work frequented by Congar.

To enable the reader to follow more easily his conciliar activity, the 'Points of reference' which Congar himself had published in his four volumes of Chronicles of the Council (*Le Concile au jour le jour, Cerf, 1963 to 1966*) have been completed and reprinted here, together with chronological tables showing his participation in the drafting of the various schemas.

We wish to thank Fr Éric de Clermont-Tonnerre who, as Prior Provincial of the Province of France, authorised the publication of this *Journal*, Fr André Duval OP who, as archivist of the Dominican Province of France, received us so cordially and gave us access to the Congar archives, and Fr Nicolas-Jean Sed, general manager of Éditions du Cerf. Our thanks go also to all those who have contributed to the publication of this edition, in particular Br Saulius Rumšas OP, Fr Hervé Legrand OP; Andrée Thomas, of Éditions du Cerf; Sr Borromée OP, Sr Marie-Clotilde OCBE, Hubert Le Bourdellès and Yves-Marie Hilaire; and also, naturally, Dominique Congar, the nephew of Fr Congar, for the information he was able to give us about his family, and for his careful monitoring of our work.

PUBLISHERS' ACKNOWLEDGEMENTS

Many people have been involved in this Congar project along the years.

Discussion between Editions du Cerf and ATF Press began at Frankfurt Book Fair in 2006. Discussions were held by ATF Press with Ms Laurence Rodinet, Frs Nicolas-Jean Sed OP and Eric de Clermont-Tonnerre OP of Cerf. A number of other English language publishers had looked at translating Congar's work from the Second Vatican Council but did not proceed. A Spanish translation has appeared. English publishers may well have been put off by the length and the difficulties involved in such a task. This in part is due to Congar's French style in the journal, shorthand, a type of note-taking on the run, which had been faithfully rendered by Cerf from the original hand-written, later typed, notebooks.

ATF Press undertook full translation of both volumes of the French text and it soon became an international project. Translators were found in Europe: Sr Mary John Ronayne OP (Lisbon, Portugal) undertook Volume I (in this volume pages 1 to 469)and Sr Mary Cecily Boulding OP (Stone, United Kingdom) translated Volume II (in this volume pages 471 to 931). Dominican Publications from Ireland and Liturgical Press from the USA agreed to work with ATF Press as international publishing partners.

Once the two sisters completed their work, ATF Press had assistance from Cerf's Frs Gilles-Hervé Masson OP and Eric de Clermont-Tonnerre OP who came to Australia in early 2011 to work with ATF Press on a number of projects. Frs Bruno-Dominique la Fille OP and Jérôme Rousse-Lacordaire OP of Cerf enabled invaluable access to the photographs of Congar held by Cerf and to the Saulchoir Library. Fr Jean-Michel Potin OP of the French Province, from the Saulchoir Library, gave permission to access the original note-books which are held in the Library.

From the Australian Dominican Province, Dr Denis Minns OP, undertook an editorial review of the translation. In this work he consulted with Dr Helen Frank, of the Australian Dominican Studium Library in Melbourne and an Honorary Research Fellow (French Studies) at the University of Melbourne, and also with

Fr Bob Wilkinson of Adelaide, who had edited an Australian Catholic newspaper throughout the Vatican Council.

Fr Minns also expanded the French glossary for an English readership. While Australian English spelling has been used throughout, the translation of Congar's French colloquialisms kept in mind a readership wider than Australian.

ATF Press was assisted by members of Cerf in a number of fascinating translation decisions. The project is indebted to the French literary agency, CNL, for its contribution to the translation costs. Very useful correspondence was also had between the publisher of ATF Press and Congar's nephew, M Dominique Congar.

The partnership with Dominican Publications and Liturgical Press has always been fraternal and decisions have been made jointly wherever possible. Fr Bernard Treacy OP and his editorial staff at Dominican Publications and Mr Hans Christoffersen and Mr Peter Dywer and others at Liturgical Press have followed this project from the start. Meetings at different places around the world planned and monitored the project over the five years.

Thanks are due to the Dominican Sisters in Stone and the Monastery of Dominican Nuns in Lisbon for their hospitality to the publisher of ATF Press over the five-year period.

Liturgical Press undertook the cover art work and obtained the services of Fr Paul Philibert OP, from the USA, to contribute introductory pages. ATF Press provided layout for the combined publication.

The French edition was in the two volumes which now appear in English as one volume in hard back. Congar was not consistent in the way he named conciliar documents in Latin or in French. In the English translation we have not attempted to standardise his usage. Neither was this done in the French edition, which was assembled from the typewritten text which had been taken directly from his notebooks, written each day during the Council. The French edition had two indices of names which were at the back of Volume II. The English edition has both indices. Responsibility for these indices lies with Hilary Regan.

When the idea of translating Congar's journal from the Second Vatican Council arose, it was seen that it could contribute to events surrounding the fiftieth anniversary of the Council. In launching the English translation in 2012, this aim will have been accomplished.

I wish to express my personal thanks also to the many others in each of the four publishing houses who have supplied information or assisted in any way. My thanks to you all.

Hilary Regan
ATF Press
Adelaide
February 2012

ABBREVIATIONS

AD	*Acta et Documenta Concilio Oecumenico Vaticano apparando*
AS	*Acta Synodalia Sacrosancti Concilii Oecumenici Vaticani II*
CCIF	Catholic Centre for French Intellectuals
CELAM	Episcopal Conference of the Bishops of Latin America
DO-C	Dutch Centre for Council Documentation
ICI	International Catholic Information
NT	New Testament
OT	Old Testament
TC	Témoignage chrétien (Christian Witness): an independent weekly journal of social, political, cultural and religious affairs, founded in France in 1941 in resistance to Nazism.
WCC	World Council of Churches

In order to make this journal more intelligible, I begin with a few preliminary remarks.

During the First and Second Sessions, I lived at the Angelicum.[1] While there, I had very little contact with the Conciliar Fathers, being cut off from everything and living there the life of a religious community.

During the Third and Fourth sessions, I lived at the French Seminary,[2] as did about forty of the bishops. A number of 'workshops'[3] were also held there, and it was more in the centre of Rome. Moreover, whereas at the Angelicum I never had the remotest chance of a car (I used to go to and from St Peter's in the coach that collected the bishops), at the French Seminary I had the chance of a car and other kinds of help fairly frequently.

During the meetings of the Commission, whenever possible I stayed at the Belgian College[4] where the Theological Commission had its working centre. While the Council was in session, however, the few available rooms were occupied by the Belgian bishops and I was not able to stay there.

Throughout this journal, the expression 'at St Peter's' means the General Congregations; 'at the Vatican' means meetings of the Theological Commission or, at times, of the Joint Commission (theology and lay apostolate) for schema XIII: these meetings were held in the room known as the 'Hall of the Congregations'. The expression 'at St Martha's' denotes the pilgrim hostel at the Vatican where nearly all the various conciliar Commissions had their secretariats. These

1. The Angelicum, where the Dominican ecclesiastical faculties in Rome are based, became a Pontifical University in 1963.
2. The 'Séminaire Français' in Rome, which is run by the Holy Ghost Fathers, trains students for the priesthood destined mainly for French dioceses.
3. Working groups set up by the French bishops in Rome during the Council.
4. The seminary for the formation of students for the priesthood for the dioceses of Belgium.

1

meetings were sometimes held in a kind of passageway, sometimes in the large room downstairs, sometimes in a parlour, and sometimes in other rooms that were more or less suitable, and mostly rather less than more! The expression 'at the Secretariat' refers to the Secretariat for Christian Unity which, to begin with, was at 64 Via dei Corridori, and later, during the Fourth Session, in the larger premises at 1 Via dell'Erba.

The names of the Conciliar Fathers who spoke *in aula* were written down as heard and may not always be quite correct. However, in most cases, the spelling was checked by Mlle Guillou[1] from the official *elenchi* [lists].

I have personally checked this copy.[2]

Strasbourg, 6 July 1967
(autograph signature)
f Yves MJ Congar

---

1. Delphine Guillou became Congar's secretary towards the end of the Council, and continued to be so for several years thereafter. It was she whom he asked to type the manuscript of his journal.
2. The second copy of the typescript does not include this phrase. On the top copy of the typescript, Fr Congar added the following hand-written note: 'on account of the people who are mentioned in this journal, I forbid any public use of it before the year 2000.' On the second copy he wrote: 'I forbid any PUBLIC use of this journal before the year 2000.'
    A hand-written sheet glued to the fly leaf of the top copy reads as follows: 'This is a transcription of my personal journal of the Council revised by myself. I want this copy to be deposited in the Provincial Archives. As I have already written above, no use is to be made of it before the year 2000.'
    24.2.68
    f Y Congar

My Journal of the Council
'I walk so that the Church may go forward!' [1]

This journal cannot begin here and now at the end of July 1960, which is when I learned of my appointment as Consultor to the Theological Commission.[2] It must begin further back. I shall undoubtedly have subsequent impressions to record here later on. But I do not begin today from scratch, with a *tabula rasa*. The decision to hold a Council was announced a year and a half ago, and I have clearly had time to develop a certain number of ideas. It is worthwhile putting them on paper before, perhaps, they are contradicted and replaced by others. Moreover, I have already stated in public a number of my reactions. I have not written much in letters—I don't like that—but I have said quite a lot in lectures and articles:

- *Informations Catholiques Internationales* 15 February 1959:[3]
- the two studies which I included in my *Le Concile et les conciles*;[4]

1. In *Une vie pour la vérité* (Paris: Le Centurion, 1975), 154, Congar explained that he had adopted and modified the words of St Thérèse of the Child Jesus who, in obedience to her infirmarian, forced herself to walk in the garden of her Carmel, at the cost of intense fatigue: 'I walk for a missionary'. He must have come across the phrase while reading Chapter 12 of *Histoire d'une âme* (page 177 in the 1953 edition published by the Office Central de Lisieux).
2. The reference is to the Preparatory Theological Commission, one of the various Preparatory Commissions appointed by the Pope to prepare the Conciliar schemas; it was responsible for the doctrinal schemas. On 16 July 1960 *L'Osservatore Romano* published a preliminary, and not yet complete, list of the members and consultors of the Commission.
3. 'Les Conciles dans la vie de l Église', *Informations catholiques internationales*, No. 80, 15 February 1960: 17–26.
4. Yves Congar, 'La Primauté des quatre premiers conciles œcumeniques. Origine, destin, sens et portée d'un thème traditionnel', and 'Conclusion' in *Le Concile et les conciles, Contribution à l'histoire de la vie conciliaire de l'Église* (Chevetogne-Cerf, 1960), 75–123 and 285–334.

-   article in the January 1960 issue of *Lumière et Vie*,[1] reprinted in *Trierer Theologische Zeitschrift*,[2] and, somewhat differently, in ten or more lectures;
-   article in the 16 June 1960 issue of *Témoignage Chrétien*, reprinted in *Herder Korrespondenz*.[3]

A number of us at once saw in the Council an opening for the cause, not only of unionism,[4] but also of ecclesiology. We saw in it an opportunity, which needed to be exploited to the maximum, of hastening the recovery of the values of episcopacy and *Ecclesia*[5] in ecclesiology, and of making substantial progress from the point of view of ecumenism. Personally, I have endeavoured to urge public opinion to expect and to ask for a great deal. I have kept saying everywhere that it would pass perhaps no more than five per cent of what we wanted. All the more reason, therefore, to maximise our requests. Christian public opinion must force the Council to exist in fact, and to achieve something.

From the theological point of view, and above all from that of ecumenism, it would seem that the Council has come twenty-five years too soon. In fact, things have not been moving long enough. Quite a few ideas have already changed. But in twenty years time, we might have had an episcopate comprised of men who had grown up in ideas rooted in the Bible and in tradition, in a realistic pastoral and missionary outlook. We have not reached that point yet. However, a number of ideas have already come a long way, and the very announcement of the Council, with its long-term ecumenical aim, in the more humane and more Christian climate of the pontificate of John XXIII[6] might well accelerate this process. A number of bishops, who up to then had been against it, would undoubtedly become open to the idea of ecumenism, because Rome was now in favour. In the space of two years, things have become 'good ideas' which had been barely tolerated for the previous twenty: except that nothing would now be in favour with the authorities that had not been struggled for and sown in tears.

---

1. It was in fact the November/December 1959 issue: cf Yves Congar, 'Le Concile, l'Église et . . . les autres', *Lumière et Vie,* No. 45, 1959: 69–92.
2. Yves Congar, 'Konzil und Ökumene', *Trierer Theologische Zeitschrift,* year 69, cahier 3, 1960: 129–147.
3. *Herder Korrespondenz,* July 1960, where we find, in fact, a summary of the article in *Trierer Theologische Zeitschrift.*
4. This word (l'unionisme) was used before the last Council to indicate the activity of Catholics who were in favour of Christian unity: Vatican II came to prefer the term 'ecumenism', specifying its meaning in the Decree *Unitatis Redintegratio.*
5. *Church.* When Congar uses this Latin word, he is looking at the Church as an integral Christian community.
6. Angelo G Roncalli was elected pope on 28 October 1958. He had been Nuncio in Paris from 1944 to 1953, and then Patriarch of Venice. He died on 3 June 1963, and was beatified by Pope John Paul II in the year 2000.

The announcement of the Council aroused great interest and great hope. It seemed that, after the stifling regime of Pius XII,[1] the windows were at last being opened; one could breathe. The Church was being given its chance. One was becoming open to dialogue.

Little by little, these hopes became shrouded in a fine film of dust. There was a long silence, a sort of blackout, interrupted only by this or that encouraging announcement from the Pope. But even these were rather vague, and they seemed to some extent to have gone backwards as compared with the original announcement. This impression came from a number of sources. The Pope himself declared publicly that he had not changed his mind. But in a conversation with Fr Liégé,[2] he admitted that his original idea had been a genuine conversation with the Others.[3]

One had the impression—confirmed by people coming from Rome with the latest gossip from 'that miserable court'—that in Rome a whole team of people was applying itself to sabotaging the Pope's project. It was even being said that the Pope knew what was going on and had spoken about it in confidence (something which continues to surprise me and makes me rather sceptical: a pope does not divulge such confidences).

Personally, I very quickly and repeatedly felt deceived because, although Pope John XXIII spoke and acted extremely sympathetically, his decisions, his government, belied much of what had aroused hope. His human style was warm and friendly, Christian. Everything connected with him personally had rescued us from the horrible satrapism of Pius XII. However, he had retained almost all of his predecessor's personnel: not the Jesuit brains trust which, however, had been remarkably effective; not Sr Pasqualina;[4] not all of the prelates. But all the others: Cardinals Tardini[5] and Ottaviani[6] were his close advisers. The Pope had recalled Mgr Parente[7] to Rome and had given him an important job at the 'Holy Office':

---

1. Pius XII (Eugenio Pacelli) had been Pope from 1939 until his death in October 1958.
2. Pierre-André Liégé, OP, of the Province of France, was Professor of Fundamental and Pastoral Theology at the Institut Catholique in Paris, and at the Dominican faculties at Le Saulchoir. He was to be personal adviser to Mgr Elchinger and Mgr Schmidt at the Council. Later he became Dean of the Faculty of Theology at the Institut Catholique in Paris.
3. Congar's way of referring to non-Catholic Christians.
4. Pasqualina Lehnert, a Bavarian religious who entered the future Pius XII's service when he was Nuncio in Munich.
5. Almost as soon as he was elected, John XXIII had appointed Pius XII's Pro-Secretary of State, Domenico Tardini, as Secretary of State. He was to die in July 1961.
6. Alfredo Ottaviani continued to be head of the Holy Office, of which he had been appointed Secretary in October 1959. He was to be President of the Preparatory Theological Commission and then, during the Council, of the Doctrinal Commission. In 1965, he was to be appointed Pro-Prefect of the new Congregation for the Doctrine of the Faith which replaced the Holy Office.
7. Having been Archbishop of Perugia since 1955, Pietro Parente returned to Rome as

Parente, the man who condemned P Chenu,[1] the fascist, the monophysite.

I met Miss Christine Mohrmann[2] on her return from a six-week stay in Rome, in April and May 1959.[3] She goes to Rome fairly frequently, perhaps every year. She has a number of contacts and 'antennae' there. Her feminine and humanist finesse perceives many things. I told her how I felt, my astonishment and my fears. She replied with an optimism which appeared to me to be excessive. According to her, the Pope knows very well what he is doing and where he is going. He is well aware that he is surrounded by men with a totally different outlook on things, even a totally contrary outlook. In time, he will neutralise them, but little by little. He does not want to rush things, but to proceed very gently, etc. It did not seem to me that these conclusions were borne out by the facts.

It seemed to me that the entire 'old guard' had remained in office. What difference would the resignation of Cardinal Tisserant[4] in the autumn of 1959

---

assessor at the Holy Office in 1959. He was to be appointed member of the Doctrinal Commission at the end of the First Session of the Council. During Vatican II, Congar came to know him better and to recognise his capacity for doctrinal reflection which was to result, for example, in Archbishop Parente writing publicly in favour of collegiality in *Avvenire d'Italia* on 21 January 1965. Contradicting his earlier rather insulting opinion, Congar later honoured him publicly by contributing an important essay to Mélanges Parente: 'La consécration épiscopale et la succession apostolique constituent-elles chef d'une Église locale ou membre du college?' (Rome: 1967), 29–40, which was subsequently reprinted in his *Ministères et communion ecclésiale* (Paris: Cerf, 1971), 123–140.

1. Marie-Dominique Chenu, OP, of the Province of France. In 1937, as Regent of Studies for his Province, he had distributed, in brochure form, a text entitled *Une école de théologie. Le Saulchoir,* outlining a new approach to theology. This text had been put on the Index in 1942 and it was Parente who had written the article in *L'Osservatore Romano* justifying this decision. During the Council, Chenu was to be the personal adviser of one of his former pupils, Claude Rolland, a La Salette missionary, and Bishop of Antsirabé (Madagascar). Cf Marie-Dominique Chenu, *Notes quotidiennes au Concile. Journal de Vatican II, 1962–1963,* critical edition and introduction by Alberto Melloni (Paris: Cerf, 1995).

2. Philologist and professor at the Catholic University of Nijmegen, known in particular for her four volume *Études sur le latin des chrétiens* (Rome: 1958, 1961, 1965, 1977).

3. The Congar Archives contain notes of a conversation with Christine Mohrmann which took place on 22 April 1959, on her return from a stay in Rome. In particular, Congar recorded the following: 'The Pope DOES NOT WANT to carry on like his predecessor. But he does not want to start revolutions. That is why he does not change the people in office all at once. Moreover, he wants to watch in order to avoid appointing people who might, in fact, try to counteract his policy [. . .] His plan for a Council is being resolutely fought against and sabotaged by those appointed during the previous regime who are still in office. The Pope seems to know this. He is very observant and is fully aware of what is going on.'

4. Specialist in ancient semitic languages and expert in Eastern Christianity, Cardinal Eugène Tisserant had just resigned from the position of Secretary of the Congregation

actually make? I asked several people about this and did not get a satisfactory answer; rather, a variety of differing, even divergent opinions. It doesn't much matter. I never hoped for great things from that quarter. But one had a clear impression that in Rome, the 'old guard' in the Curia felt it was in danger and was doing all in its power to avoid it, while at the same time playing along with the new pontificate since a NEW pontificate was what they were faced with. The danger was that some of the reins of government were slipping away from them.

I am beginning to know the history of ecclesiology quite well. For more than fifteen centuries now, Rome has striven to monopolise—yes to monopolise—all the lines of direction and control. And has succeeded! One can say that by 1950, it was perfect. And now, here we have a pope who threatens to surrender some of these positions. The Church was going to have its say. There was some talk of the bishops being given more independence. Whereas before, the small team of co-opted Roman theologians had imposed its ideas on the rest, there was talk now of giving that 'rest' its own opportunity. It seemed to me that what was happening was that the Curia of Pius XII was still in place; that it was well aware of the danger; that it would give way when necessary but would not break, would, in fact, do all in its power to minimise the damage being done to the system.

This had been my very clear impression since Easter 1959, and was confirmed by a conversation I had with Pastor Roger Schutz[1] on 20 June 1960. Schutz told me, though with the greatest of discretion, about the audience, arranged for him by Cardinal Gerlier,[2] that he had had with John XXIII on the evening of, or the morning after, his consecration. According to Schutz, the Pope had said some very incredible, even downright heretical, things to him, such as: the Catholic Church does not possess the whole truth; we should search together . . . I think that the leading members of the Curia very quickly realised that, with John XXIII and his plan for a Council, they might be in for a very strange adventure, that they needed to erect fences, regain control as far as possible, and limit any possible damage.

A number of indications, the internal logic of the reactions of the Curia as they appeared to me, very quickly made me think what I am going to write down here, in this month of July 1960, in order to keep a dated record, whatever happens: whether or not the future confirms or belies what I now think. I was afraid, it

---

for the Eastern Church which he had occupied since 1937. He remained on as Vatican Librarian and Archivist. He was to be the Dean of the Council of Presidents for the Council.

1. Pastor Roger Schutz was the co-founder and Prior of the ecumenical community of Taizé; during the Council he was to be one of the guests of the Secretariat for Christian Unity. Congar had stayed in Taizé on 19 and 20 June 1959 (account in Congar Archives).
2. Pierre Gerlier, Archbishop of Lyons since 1937; he was to die in January, 1965. In the account he left in the Archives, Congar speaks of Gerlier's intervention as no more than a strong presumption.

seemed to me, that the Curia would restrict the working of the actual Council as far as possible. The Council is an effective meeting of bishops, in which they discuss freely, and then come to a decision. My fear was that this effective meeting of bishops would be reduced to a final stage, and that the work would be done through texts fully elaborated by commissions controlled by Rome, if not actually composed in Rome, to which the bishops would be asked to give their reactions in writing. These reactions, if any, might or might not be taken into account in a final text which could not but be overwhelmingly approved in the course of the actual Council session, which would last only a few weeks.

This procedure, if it really is put into effect, can be justified from some points of view. It is certain that a discussion from A to Z has become virtually impossible. The work will have to be well advanced before the bishops actually assemble in Council. But what a risk! The great risk is that the Council will prove to have been prefabricated in Rome or under Roman direction. A great many of the bishops are incapable of having an overall view of things, particularly of their ideological or theological aspects. They are coping with their own immediate pastoral problems. Moreover, to a considerable extent, they have lost the habit of study and of deciding things for themselves! They have become accustomed to accepting decisions from Rome even when these suppress or overturn arrangements which they themselves thought good (cf the worker priest movement,[3] the Catechism[4]). I am afraid that many of them, when they receive a document, will skim through it and will find only a few editorial details to comment on, and that is how the texts will be produced . . .

This would be a betrayal of the Council. Theology makes a careful distinction between the dispersed and assembled episcopate. Only the latter forms a Council. The idea and the expression 'a kind of Council in writing' which were used in connection with the barely half-real consultation of the episcopate that preceded the declarations of 1854 and 1950 were a betrayal of what a Council really is. This is because, in fact, there is no such thing as a Council in such a procedure. There is no Council except in the effective meeting of the bishops, involving free discussion and decision-making. Moreover, psychologically, morally, anthropologically, the episcopate when assembled is quite different from bishops on their own. Assembled, they become aware of their episcopacy and their right. As some of them speak, react, awaken echoes in others, they come to form a group which has its own density, which becomes a bloc. Dispersed, they hardly exist; they can only express isolated, unplanned reactions, which will be received

---

3. Rome put an end to the worker-priest experiment in 1954.
4. Canon Joseph Colomb, principal instigator of the French catechetical movement, was dismissed in 1957 from his position as Director of the *Centre national de l'enseignement religieux* [National Religious Education Centre] and his works were censured.

and doctored by a Roman commission or one controlled by Rome, which will do what it likes with them. Being unaware of the reactions of others, the bishops will not even realise that they have been tricked.

This dispersion, this atomisation, of the episcopate is the perfect example of *'Divide ut imperes'* [divide and rule]. How can it be avoided?

If I remember correctly, in April or May 1960, though it may have been earlier, I saw Schmidthüs[1] here. He spoke to me of a scheme which seemed to me interesting in itself, but was unrealisable in practice. The idea was to set up a sort of central secretariat for information that was well-geared for the bishops and for co-ordinating efforts or work such as my own, (and that of several others also), which all point in a certain direction. Maison Herder[2] or *Herder Korrespondenz* would finance the project and would provide office space and a secretary . . . (it had been Schmidthüs' idea . . .). We discussed WHO could perform such a task. I suggested Fr Baum,[3] Küng,[4] and someone else, a Dutchman. But, as far as I know, the idea went no further. Moreover, I do not see how one might have proceeded. In fact, a certain understanding existed between a few isolated individual workers: it was virtual, implicit, but real, and little would be needed to make it active. However, I have little faith in directed work. I believe in PEOPLE, in personal initiative. But it is true that, if the thing had been possible, one would have derived great benefit from mutual agreement on the need to arrange for a certain number of works to be undertaken here and there. I am thinking of works on the jurisdiction of bishops, on episcopal collegiality, on the law of the Eastern Churches, etc. An understanding between existing Centres (but their existence is not very stable!) such as the Möhler Institute,[5] the Catholic Conference for

---

1. Karlheinz Schmidthüs, editor-in-chief of *Herder Korrespondenz*.
2. Catholic publisher based in Freiburg im Breisgau (Germany).
3. Gregory Baum, OSA, defended his doctoral thesis in theology in Fribourg in 1956; it was published in 1958: cf *That they may be one. A Study of papal Doctrine (Leo XIII-Pius XII)* (London: 1958). Congar had it translated in the 'Unam Sanctam' Collection which he himself directed: *L'Unité chrétienne d'après la doctrine des Papes de Léon XIII à Pie XII* (Paris: Cerf, 1961). Shortly afterwards, Baum went to teach theology at St Michael's College (Toronto), where he founded a Centre of Ecumenical Studies in 1963. He was appointed consultor of the Secretariat for Christian Unity in 1960, and then an expert at the Council during the First Session.
4. Hans Küng, Swiss priest and theologian, was at this time 'Assistant' at the University of Münster. From 1960 onwards, he was professor at the University of Tübingen where, in 1963, he became Director of the Institute for Ecumenical Research: he was appointed an expert at the Council during the First Session.
5. Centre of ecumenical research founded by Cardinal Jäger in Paderborn in 1957, and oriented towards the Protestant world.

Ecumenical Matters,[1] Istina,[2] Chevetogne,[3] (Liguge),[4] etc, would be quite possible and desirable. One could perhaps come back to this question.

On 4 April 1959, at the request of Mgr Weber,[5] I had prepared for him a draft reply to the request sent to all the bishops asking for topics to be discussed at the Council.[6] Mgr Weber made considerable use of my outline.[7] He had also asked Fr Durrwell, CSSR,[8] and invited us both to lunch. I also wrote a paper for Mgr Elchinger[9] for his own reply. It had been agreed that he would insist on the biblical notion of Faith, which is so important. See special file on this question.

The Catholic Faculty of Theology[10] had also been consulted[11] but was in no hurry to reply. I tried to discover, through Dean Nédoncelle,[12] the line that the Faculty would take. He told me that they were waiting for the Colloquium on

---

1. Working party of Catholic ecumenists set up on the initiative of two Dutch priests, Jan Willebrands and Franz Thijssen in the early 1950's. Congar took a very active part in it from its inception, and quite a number of the members of the future Secretariat for Christian Unity came from its ranks.
2. Centre of ecumenical research founded by the Dominicans of the Province of France in Lille in 1923, and transferred to Boulogne-sur-Seine in 1946. Fr Christophe-Jean Dumont, OP, who was an active member of the Catholic Conference for Ecumenical Matters (cf previous note) and a close friend of Congar's, was in charge of it. The journal *Istina* had been published by the Centre from 1954 onward and, broadening out to embrace the whole range of ecumenism, also took over *Russie et chrétienté* [Russia and Christendom] which had been founded in 1934.
3. Benedictine abbey in Belgium founded by Dom Lambert Beauduin, initially in Amay-sur-Meuse; its special vocation was reconciliation with Eastern Christians; in particular it had published *Irénikon* since 1926.
4. French Benedictine abbey founded by St Martin. In 1959, it had been chosen by the Benedictine abbots as the ecumenical centre for France.
5. Jean-Julien Weber, Sulpician, Bishop of Strasbourg since 1945. He had welcomed Congar to his diocese in 1956.
6. The reference is to the pre-preparatory consultation of all the Catholic bishops, but, more widely, of all the future Fathers of the Council. A circular had been sent to them on 18 June, 1959.
7. Yves Congar, Report on what it seems desirable to envisage for the Council, 4–6 August 1959 (Congar Archives). This document is probably the one to which Congar refers here. It is in two parts: pastoral matters and the question of ecumenism.
8. The Redemptorist François-Xavier Durrwell. He taught Sacred Scripture at the Redemptorist Fathers' scholasticate until he was elected Provincial of their Strasbourg Province, an office he held from 1952 until 1962.
9. Léon-Arthur Elchinger, Coadjutor Bishop of Strasbourg. He was to succeed Mgr J-J Weber when the latter resigned in December 1966.
10. In Strasbourg.
11. On 18 July 1960, a second circular had extended the consultation to the Universities.
12. Maurice Nédoncelle, Professor of Fundamental Theology at the Faculty of Catholic Theology at the University of Strasbourg had been Dean of the Faculty since 1956.

Ecclesiology in the nineteenth century[1] which they were organising for the end of November, 1959 (in the organisation of which I, too, had had some part), and that they would base their replies on the conclusions reached by the Colloquium.

I have heard nothing since then and I do not know what the Faculty actually said, as I have been out of touch with what it has been doing.

In June 1960 (*La Croix* for 8 June), the first fruits of the consultation of the bishops were announced. There were to be ten preparatory commissions, plus two secretariats[2] and a central commission.[3] But, with the exception of the Secretariat for Christian Unity, which is a new creation uncluttered by precedent, the President of each Commission was to be the cardinal in charge of the corresponding Roman dicastery.[4]

This news depressed me enormously. I could see it all: the machine which Rome had so carefully put together was taking into its iron grip this tiny infant Council which had only just been born and sought to live. Within those arms of steel, it would not be allowed to move, speak, or even breathe except as they directed. Everything would be under the control and direction of the Curia. The Council was to be mastered, dominated, emasculated, as soon as it had been born and before it had even lived.

I wrote the two letters and the reply about all this in the 16 June issue of *Témoignage chrétien*.[5] I could have written a single article under a pseudonym. I was reluctant to do so. I have only twice written under a pseudonym, in *Sept*,[6] about the situation of Catholics in Hitler's Reich. I wanted to write the truth, but it could have backfired in Germany . . . On the other hand, I thought I did not have the right to handicap or spoil the chance of my being sought out and used in some way in the preparation for the Council. I knew that our Fr General[7] had given my

---

1. This Colloquium was held from 26–28 November 1959 on the theme 'Ecclesiology in the nineteenth Century'. Its acts were published in 1960 in the *Revue des Sciences Religieuses,* and also as No. 34 of the 'Unam Sanctam' collection edited by Congar.
2. The Secretariat for Christian Unity and the Secretariat for the Press and the Communication Media.
3. The Central Preparatory Commission, charged with co-ordinating the working of the various Commissions and revising their work.
4. Another name for the various Roman congregations that are at the service of the pope.
5. Congar had included this article in the earlier list of his public reactions to the Council (cf Volume I, page 4).
6. Under the pseudonym 'Ober' he wrote '*Anxiété des catholiques allemands*' [Anxiety of German Catholics] in *Sept* for 8 September 1934, page 7, and 15 September 1934, pages 6–7.
7. The Master of the Dominican Order at that time was Michael Browne. An Irishman, he had taught at the Angelicum and was a former Master of the Sacred Palace. He was Master General from 1955 until March 1962, when he was created cardinal. Being a member of the Holy Office, he was appointed to the Doctrinal Commission, where he was Vice-President from the end of the First Session onwards.

name.[1] At the time, I had no indication that I would, in fact, be called upon, but I felt obliged to bear in mind the possibility.

That is why I took the not very glorious middle way of writing those two letters clearly asking the question, and a reply which, while to some extent moderating my criticism, did not eliminate it entirely, indeed recognised its underlying validity. All the same, it was necessary to sound some sort of alarm, and above all to enlighten and guide public opinion. Experience and history have taught me that one must ALWAYS protest when one feels in conscience or by conviction that there are grounds for doing so. Of course, one thereby makes trouble for oneself, but something positive is nevertheless achieved.

I took my usual week's holiday in Sedan[2] after the 'Social Week',[3] and the meeting of the 'Équipes enseignantes' [teaching teams].[4] One day, while I was in Sedan, I received a congratulatory note from l'abbé Poupard[5] (I had been interested in his thesis on Bautain[6]), then, the next day, another from Fr Dumont.[7] I knew nothing. I got hold of *La Croix* and saw that I had been appointed as consultor of the Theological Commission.

---

1. On 17 February, 1959, Fr Jerome Hamer, OP, of the Belgian Province, had told Fr Congar that the Master General, whom he had met in Rome, intended to submit both their names for the Preparatory Commissions (Congar Archives).

2. Yves Congar was a native of Sedan (Ardennes) where his parents lived in a large family property in Fond-de-Givonne, one of the suburbs of Sedan.

3. From 1904 onwards, the 'Semaines Sociales de France' had brought together a number of Catholics involved in the social field. Fr Congar attended the one that was held in 1960 and gave a lecture on 15 July: cf Yves M-J Congar, 'Perspectives chrétiennes sur la vie personnelle et la vie collective' in *Socialisation et personne humaine—Semaines sociales de France—47ième Session* (Lyons: Chronique sociale de France, 1961), 195–221.

4. The 'Équipes enseignantes' brought together Catholic primary school teachers in public schools. Fr Congar attended the end of one such meeting which was held at Fontcouverte-Toussuire, in Savoy, from 5 to 18 July.

5. Paul Poupard, of the diocese of Angers, had been attaché of the Secretariat of State since 1959; he was to become head of the French section in 1966. Later he became Rector of the Institute Catholique in Paris. He was appointed bishop in 1979, and was later made a cardinal when he became President of the Secretariat for Non-Christians and then President of the Pontifical Council for Culture.

6. Poupard had defended his doctoral thesis in theology in February 1959 at the Université Catholique de l'Ouest: cf Paul Poupard, *Un essai de philosophie chrétienne au XIXième siècle. L'abbé Louis Bautain* (Paris: Tournai, Desclée, 1961).

7. Christophe-Jean Dumont, OP, of the Province of France, Director of the Istina Institute and a friend of Congar's. He was appointed consultor to the Secretariat for Unity in 1960 and an expert at the Council in 1962. When Congar refers to 'P[ère] Dumont', it is to this man that he is referring and not his namesake, Pierre Dumont OSB.

A few days later, I received the official notification, via Santa Sabina[1] and Strasbourg. I sent my reply from Sedan on 25 July, addressing it to Cardinal Tardini, by whom the document had been signed.[2]

I hesitated before doing so.

In fact, all that I had heard largely confirmed my fears and plunged me back into a deep depression. This Theological Commission seemed to me to be too much pointed in a conservative direction. We were faced with two different things: the actual members of the Commission, and the consultors. It was the members who would do the work. The consultors would have nothing to say unless they were consulted. But would they be? Fr Allo told me, shortly before the war[3] that he had been appointed as consultor to the Biblical Commission but had never been consulted . . .

Now: Mgr Dubois,[4] Archbishop of Besançon, was the French bishop on the Commission. I had never met him, but I had heard quite a lot about him. He does not like us. When asked to renew the faculties for hearing confessions for the [Dominican] fathers in Dijon and Strasbourg, in his diocese, he replied that not only would he not grant faculties to any new fathers, but that he would withdraw them or not renew them in the case of those to whom they had already been granted . . . Among his clergy, he had the reputation of being a good man but a timid one and, for this reason, tended to be rather authoritarian. I know an archpriest's house in his diocese where his confirmation sermons have been taped and where people listen to the tape when they want a bit of fun . . . His theology? I know he has published a little book that is ultra-mariological.[5] Mgr Weber has told me about him; he finds him domineering.

---

1. Headquarters of the Dominican Order in Rome.
2. The letter from Cardinal Tardini was dated 12 July 1960.
3. It was in fact in the year 1941 that Ernest Allo, OP, Professor of Exegesis in Fribourg until 1938, when he left for Le Saulchoir, had been appointed consultor to the Pontifical Biblical Commission.
4. Marcel-M Dubois, ordained bishop in 1948, he became Archbishop of Besançon in 1954.
5. Marcel-Marie Dubois, *Petite somme mariale* (Paris: Bonne Presse, 1957); a second volume was to be published in 1961.

Of course, the theologian members of the Commission included Mgr Cerfaux,[1] Mgr G Philips,[2] Mgr M Schmaus.[3] But there was also Fenton,[4] an ultra-papist and possibly also an 'integrist'; Mgr Journet,[5] of a different stamp, indeed, but very limited in his views and in his ability to share . . . Then, there is also Balić[6] who thinks of nothing except super-exalting Mary in order to promote the 'cause' of Scotus;[7] Albert Michel . . . ,[8] Rosaire Gagnebet.[9]. . .

It really is very slanted in one direction.

---

1. The exegete Lucien Cerfaux, of the diocese of Tournai, had long held the chair of New Testament Exegesis at the University of Louvain; he was appointed an expert at the Council in 1962.
2. Gérard Philips, of the diocese of Liège, was Professor of Dogmatic Theology at the University of Louvain and a member of the Belgian Senate. Having been appointed a Council expert in 1962, he was elected secretary of the Doctrinal Commission in December 1963.
3. Michael Schmaus, of the diocese of Munich, was Professor of Dogmatic Theology at the University of Munich until he retired in 1965. He was appointed a Council expert in 1962.
4. Joseph Fenton was Professor of Theology at the Catholic University in Washington until 1963, then a parish priest. He was appointed a Council expert in 1962.
5. Charles Journet was professor at the major seminary in Fribourg, Switzerland, and director of the journal *Nova et Vetera* which he had founded with Mgr Charrière. He was created cardinal in February 1965.
6. The Croatian Charles Balić OFM, theologian and Professor of Dogmatic and Marian Theology at the Antonianum and, from 1961 onwards, at the Lateran. He was also consultor to the Congregation of the Holy Office and founder and President of the Pontifical International Marian Academy; he was appointed a Council expert in 1962.
7. The cause of the beatification of Duns Scotus, which took place in 1991.
8. Albert Michel, priest of the diocese of Saint-Dié, who had taught dogmatic theology at the Catholic Faculties in Lille and had been deeply involved in the anti-Modernist battle, and was now a parish priest, while continuing to write for *L'Ami du Clergé*.
9. Rosaire Gagnebet, OP, of the Province of Toulouse, who taught theology at the Angelicum and became first an assessor and then a consultor to the Congregation of the Holy Office; he was appointed a Council expert in 1962.

There are some attractive names among the consultors: Jouassard,[1] Häring,[2] Lécuyer,[3] Backes,[4] Delhaye.[5] But there is also Labourdette,[6] Salaverri,[7] Witte,[8] Laurentin[9]—whose name makes me fear that there will be Marian doctrines on the agenda.

Then there was Lubac[10] and myself. Undoubtedly, this re-instates us in Catholic opinion, at least in official circles—for its truly alive and active levels had never heeded the repeated discrediting signals from Rome. Official circles had been rather more inclined to do so. This is a valid point, and I do not want to minimise its importance. But then? We are both *hapax* [11] in a text the context of which seems to me so slanted in a conservative direction. To name us as consultors is also a way of keeping us away from the actual work, which will be done by the members of the Commission. I see myself, in effect, as having been marginalised . . . I see things developing in a clearly Rome-ward direction. It is Rome that nominates and, though she may ease her conscience or feel she deserves to be well thought

1. Georges Jouassard, of the diocese of Lyons, was Dean of the Faculty of Theology at the Catholic Faculties in Lyons.

2. The German Redemptorist Bernhard Häring was one of the great post-war moral theologians. He taught at the Redemptorist studentate in Bavaria, but also in Rome at the Alphonsian Academy and at the Lateran. He was appointed a Council expert in 1962.

3. Joseph Lécuyer, a Holy Ghost Father, was Director of the French seminary in Rome and taught at the Lateran. He was appointed a Council expert in 1962 and, in 1968, succeeded Marcel Lefebvre as leader of the Congregation of the Holy Ghost Fathers.

4. Ignaz Backes was Professor of Dogmatics at the Faculty of Theology in Trèves.

5. Philippe Delhaye, priest of the diocese of Namur, was at the time Professor of Moral Theology at the Faculty of Theology in Lille. He was to be a Council expert from the Second Session onwards. Later he was to become Dean of the Faculty of Theology at Louvain-la-Neuve and secretary of the International Theology Commission.

6. Michel Labourdette, OP, of the Province of Toulouse taught moral theology at the Dominican *studium* in Toulouse; he was to be appointed expert to the Council in 1962.

7. Joaquín Salaverri, SJ, was Professor of Theology at the Pontifical University of Comillas (Spain); he was to be appointed a Council expert in 1962.

8. The Dutch Jesuit, Jan Witte, occupied the chair of Ecumenical Theology at the Gregorianum and was to be appointed a Council expert in 1962.

9. The mariologist René Laurentin, priest of the diocese of Angers, was Professor of Theology at the Catholic University of Angers; he was appointed a Council expert during the First Session and was to cover the Council for *Le Figaro* from June 1963 onwards. He has published four volumes of chronicles of the Council: *Bilan de la première session; Bilan de la deuxième session; Bilan de la troisième session* and *Bilan du Concile* (Paris: Éditions du Seuil, 1963 to 1966).

10. Henri de Lubac, SJ, one of the leading theologians of the twentieth century. He taught in the Jesuit scholasticate in Lyons-Fourvière and at the Catholic Faculties in Lyons. Like Congar, whose friend he was, he had endured the trial of being discredited, having been forbidden to teach by the authorities in Rome from 1950 to 1958. He was appointed a Council expert in 1962.

11. The term used in exegesis for a word that only occurs once in the Bible.

of for having broadened the range, her precautions have been taken, and very effectively taken, to ensure that there is no risk involved. Have not Lubac and I been put there as a form of WINDOW DRESSING?

In the Church there is always window-dressing—put there to attract—and the warehouse. The window dressing highlights Lubac, but the warehouse contains Gagnebet.

That is why I felt so profoundly depressed.

That is also why I hesitated for a while before accepting. Would it not be better to remain FREE for a more difficult, thwarted, isolated service, rather than to let myself be tied, however tenuously, to the system?

Realism—which is not 'shrewdness' but 'truth' and intelligence—prompted me to accept and to try my best to be useful, if in fact they did use me . . . Free to ask to regain my liberty if I came to feel that what was being done, and what I was, in fact, collaborating in doing, was a work that amounted to the negation of what I believe to be true. I never wanted to collaborate with Fr Boyer's *Unitas*[1] as it was something QUITE OTHER than ecumenism. If I found myself being asked to do something that contradicted ecumenism, I would have to resign. For the moment, nothing of this kind is being asked of me.

There was something else that made me uneasy: the fact that all these Roman things demand secrecy. I am asked to swear secrecy, except with the members of the Commission. I could see the need for secrecy from some points of view: the indiscretion of the press and public opinion is catastrophic. But secrecy is also a means of isolating people and neutralising all opposition. It reduces us, in effect, to the status of men who have direct contact only with Rome, but not with one another; it amounts, in practice, to destroying horizontal Catholicity for the sole benefit of the vertical one. Moreover, assuming that we are actually consulted, and that we have given our reactions, these will remain secret; they will be received in Rome which can pass them over in silence and, with impunity, take no account of them whatsoever.

On the other hand, the members of the Commission who work together in Rome, at least from time to time, can talk about their reactions among themselves. The result will be to create a sort of isolated, atomised, non-Roman world which would be bound to secrecy, and also a Roman body forming a group and free to express itself.

Shortly after I returned to Strasbourg, I received, in reply to the letter of acceptance which I had sent from Sedan to Cardinal Tardini,[2] a second official

---

1. Charles Boyer, SJ, was Professor of Theology at the Gregorianum until 1962. In 1946, he had founded the *Unitas* Centre and the journal of the same name, both of which were official organs of the Roman 'unionism' of Pius XII, which advocated the return of the separated brethren to the bosom of the Catholic Church. He was appointed a member of the Secretariat for Christian Unity in 1960 and then a Council expert in 1962.

2. Congar's letter was dated 25 July 1960 (Congar Archives).

document signed, this time, by Cardinal Ottaviani, outlining the conditions under which the consultors would be working and asking on which topics I felt I was most qualified to collaborate, and also if I had any further comments and suggestions, etc.

I acknowledged this on 15 August.[1]

I asked myself a question. I would have a lot of things to say, remarks to make, criticisms or warnings to express. Would I do that, or would I refrain from doing so?

I thought. I prayed. In the end I decided to tell Cardinal Ottaviani that I would reply shortly. I shall begin preparing that reply now. I shall work out or review my conclusions and intentions when I have spoken to the various friends that I shall be meeting in Milan[2] or Chevetogne[3] next September. I will try to meet up with Fr de Lubac in Lyons when I return from Pradines[4] on the 5 September.

After all, I have nothing to lose, and I must do my duty. It is always necessary to say what one knows or believes to be true. So I shall be frank and will try to be evangelical.

The grace of the Lord will do the rest—Indeed it will!

I want to offer myself faithfully to serve, to the best of my ability, in the context of the Council which has been opened up by John XXIII under the impulse of the Holy Spirit. I shall avoid flattery or compromise, but state that I wish to cooperate loyally and humbly with this great enterprise. I pray every day that I may offer myself in this way, that God will not allow lying men or power-seekers to hijack it, and that he will safeguard and strengthen Pope John.

If I have felt it necessary to record my critical reactions and my fears here, it is not in order to be negative or in order, by accusing others, to clothe myself in a justice which I do not possess. It is in order to serve the truth. I wish to serve the truth. Sincerely and humbly I will try to do just this in this opportunity which has been given to me and which I have done nothing to secure.

6 September 1960

On my way back from Pradines, I stopped in Lyons in order to see Fr de Lubac. He was waiting for me at the station: stooped, holding his back, in pain, aged—except for his eyes, always wonderfully bright, clear, and questioning. He has pain all down one side and told me that he can no longer do anything. He is not even sure that he will be able to complete his *Exégèse au moyen âge*.[5]

---

1. In his reply (Congar Archives), Congar spoke of his work on tradition, ecclesiology and the apostolate of the laity.
2. The Catholic Conference for Ecumenical Matters met in Gazzada, near Milan, in September 1960.
3. The Benedictine abbey of Chevetogne, founded with the aim of working towards reconciliation between Western and Eastern Christians, organised an ecumenical colloquium every year.
4. Benedictine abbey where his sister and one of his nieces were nuns.
5. Henri De Lubac, *Exégèse médiévale. Les quatre sens de l'Écriture* (Paris: Aubier,

That is also why, as far as the Council is concerned, he will do nothing beyond a few written interventions. But he would like these interventions to point in the same direction as anything that I might say. For this reason he asked me to keep him abreast of what I was doing, and he also asked about my current reactions and intentions.

We are very much in agreement as to the orientation that seems to have been behind the composition of the Theological Commission. Fr de Lubac stressed the weight of the ROMAN professors as such. They always tend to want to dogmatise their personal views, or even to win a victory over a colleague or the objections of their students by getting their ideas incorporated in an official text. The case of Fr Hürth[1] (Congress of Assisi[2]). Fr de Lubac fears the systematic and stubborn spirit of Fr Dhanis.[3] We also discussed several other members or consultors.

Fr de Lubac thinks that our two names have been added as a way of indicating that the 'French problems'[4] are now things of the past. Somebody had pointed out to him that there were twenty-seven members of the Commission but the number of consultors was twenty-seven + two . . .

He was very keen that I should do my best to meet personally with the members of the Commission, and to prepare a paper for Rome. A door has been opened to us, we must take advantage of it. This is exactly what I had decided to do. But it seemed to me that Fr de Lubac was being optimistic in thinking that we would not be upset, in Rome, by finding the work DONE and that, if we sent something well-prepared and ready to be used, it would have its effect sooner or later. However, he himself feels he has neither the strength nor the necessary preparation to do this usefully.

He said that as far as he himself was concerned all has not been settled. His *Exégèse* was passed for publication because that counts as history; but his THEOLOGICAL texts are all held up, or have been. He is still under a Roman Jesuit censure.

We spoke of Fr Chenu, of Gilson and Bergson, of my own work, of R Jolivet's candidature for the Académie. Fr de Lubac considers it ridiculous and pathetic.

1959/1964); the third volume had already received its *Nihil obstat* and was to be published in 1961; but the fourth and last volume did not appear until 1964.

1. The German moral theologian Franz X Hürth SJ, who had been one of Pius XII's advisers and taught at the Gregorianum. He was a member of the Preparatory Theological Commission and was appointed a Council expert in 1962. He died in May 1963.
2. International pastoral liturgy congress held in Assisi in September 1956.
3. The Belgian Jesuit Édouard Dhanis was Professor of Theology at the Gregorianum, where he was Prefect of Studies and later Rector. He was a member of the Preparatory Theological Commission, was appointed a Council expert in 1962 and a consultor of the Congregation of the Holy Office in 1963.
4. H de Lubac was referring here to the various crises in theological and pastoral matters that arose during the 1950's between Rome and the French Church, crises in which Congar and he himself had been involved.

The priests do not realise ... There is also a Canon being put forward as candidate: Renaud[1] ... Another is Mgr Blanchet,[2] strongly supported by Cardinal Feltin[3] and several other bishops. It looks as if that will go through but that, given his scholarly credentials, the Academy will balance it out by electing someone worthwhile!

We also spoke of Laurentin (WILL there be a mariological move at the Council? Fr de Lubac says that Fr Balić dreams of nothing else. He would like to see Mary defined as the *socia* [associate][4] of Christ ...) – of Mgr Jouassard, of the Instituts Catholiques. Fr de Lubac thinks that Lyons is slowing down: the bishops do too little to support intellectual work, having themselves very little in the way of an overall view of the situation in the world. In his view, Mgr Jouassard is an example of what he frequently sees happen among Catholics. They leave to one side the real questions and juxtapose good technical competence on periferal points of erudition with a rather backward-looking intellectual conformism ...

17 and 18 September 1960

I am more or less free for forty-eight hours. I am going to use them to prepare a preliminary draft of the report which I plan to send to the Theological Commission and in which I have decided to say what I believe, in conscience, must be said. I am also praying about this work. I will come back to it, finish it and type it when I return from the Conference in Milan, where I shall meet a certain number of people, and perhaps even a few VIPs.[5]

26 October 1960

François Bussini[6] tells me that Mgr Dubois, Archbishop of Besançon, and a member of the Theological Commission, declared, at the Besançon Major Seminary, that he ventured to say that, in a certain way, Jesus PRAYS to Mary.

He is the author of a book on Mary which Mgr Weber told me he found exaggerated.

---

1. Ferdinand Renaud, at that time parish priest of Saint-Charles-de Monceau in Paris.
2. Émile Blanchet, titular archbishop, was Rector of the Institut Catholique in Paris. He was a member of the Preparatory Commission on Studies and Seminaries and was elected as a member of the Commission on Seminaries, Studies and Catholic Education during the First Session of the Council.
3. Maurice Feltin, Archbishop of Paris.
4. This title is not much better than that of *co-redemptrix* in showing the subordinate nature of Mary's co-operation in salvation.
5. Congar was to type his report on 24 September 1960 and send it on 3 October 1960. The meeting in Gazzada, near Milan, was attended in particular by Cardinals Augustin Bea and Giovanni Battista Montini.
6. François Bussini was at that time a seminarian of the diocese of Besançon at the International Seminary in Strasbourg. He was later to teach at the Catholic Faculty of Theology in Strasbourg, before becoming Auxiliary Bishop in Grenoble and, finally, Bishop of Amiens.

He is made fun of in his diocese. At the Major Seminary, the priests have taped his confirmation sermons and they play the tape when they want a bit of fun.

Moreover, another member of the Theological Commission, Fr Domenico Berretto[1] has written the following on page 90 of his *Meditazioni su 'San Giovanni Bosco'* [Meditations on St John Bosco]:[2]

The pope is God on earth.

Jesus has placed the pope:

> *a)   above the prophets, because these announced Christ, whereas the pope is the voice of Jesus;*
>
> *b)   above the Forerunner, because John the Baptist used to say: 'I am not worthy to untie his sandals', whereas the pope must say 'God speaks through us'.*
>
> *c)   Above the Angels – to which of the Angels did he say: 'Sit on my right'? But to St Peter and the apostles he said: 'You will sit and judge the twelve tribes of Israel'?*
>
> *d)   Jesus has placed the pope on the same level as God. In fact, he said to Peter and his successors: 'He who hears you hears me, and he who rejects you rejects me, and he who rejects me rejects him who sent me'.*[3]

L'Arbresle 29.10—2.11.1960[4]

Fr Le Guillou[5] gave me some news about Fr Dumont's trip to Rome. He was received personally by the Pope who told him that he fully agreed with all that Fr Dumont said concerning relationship with the Orthodox.

Cardinal Bea[6] wants to be put in charge of the whole field of these relationships.[7]

Fr Gerlaud,[8] who had been to Rome recently, told me he had seen someone in

---

1. Domenico Berretto, SDB, Professor of Theology at the Pontifical Salesian Athenaeum, was consultor of the Preparatory Theological Commission.
2. The correct title is: *San Giovanni Bosco—Meditazioni per la novena, le commemorazioni mensili e la formazione salesiana*, 1955.
3. {Congar quotes the Italian original at this point}.
4. An inter-provincial meeting of teachers from French-speaking Dominican provinces on fundamental theology and the treatise on the Church. At that time l'Arbresle was the house of studies for the Province of Lyons.
5. Marie-Joseph Le Guillou, OP, of the Province of France, belonged to the Istina Study Centre and taught Eastern theology at the Dominican Faculties at Le Saulchoir. At the Council he was to be the personal expert of Mgr Rougé, Bishop of Nîmes. Later he was to become the first Director of the Higher Institute of Ecumenical Studies (ISEO) at the Institut Catholique in Paris.
6. Augustin Bea, SJ, a biblical scholar by training, had been Rector of the Pontifical Biblical Institute and confessor to Pius XII. John XXIII had just made him a cardinal and had named him President of the Secretariat for Christian Unity.
7. Field normally entrusted to the Eastern Congregation.
8. Marie-Joseph Gerlaud OP, of the Province of Lyons was Professor of Moral Theology at the Catholic Faculties in Angers.

the Secretariat of State who had asked him: 'What did they think in France of the appointment of Fr de Lubac and Fr Congar as consultors?' Fr Gerlaud had replied that it was thought the nomination had come personally from the Pope. 'They are right', the Monsignor replied.

Other minor matters were also discussed. There were comments concerning some of the appointments which seemed somewhat strange. It would seem that the appointment of Mgr Calewaert[1] to the Liturgical Commission was the result of mistaken identity. He had been confused with the liturgist of the same name who has already died.[2]

Fr Christophe Dumont had received, at Istina, the papers intended for Fr Pierre Dumont,[3] superior of the Greek College.[4]

Minor running-in problems.

Journey to Rome 13—17 November 1960
Written at the time, in Rome.

Train from Strasbourg during the night of 12–13 November; departed at 0.35 am on Sunday, 13 November 1960. Italy shrouded in mist; more precisely in—clouds. Arrived in Rome at 4.30 pm. As I approached S Louis-des-Français,[5] I met Mgr Baron,[6] accompanied by Mgr Blanchet, Mgr Mazerat,[7] Mgr Jenny,[8]

---

1. Karel J Calewaert, Bishop of Gand, member of the Preparatory Commission on the Liturgy.
2. Camille Callewaert, who died in 1943.
3. Pierre Dumont, OSB, was a monk at Chevetogne.
4. The Pontifical Greek College located in Rome.
5. National church for the French, and residence for priests studying or working in Rome.
6. André Baron, of the diocese of Bourges, was the Rector of Saint-Louis-des-Français until 1962; in 1960 he was appointed consultor to the Preparatory Commission on Religious.
7. Henri Mazerat, Bishop of Fréjus et Toulon, was a member of the Preparatory Commission on the Discipline of the Clergy and of the Christian People. He was to become Bishop of Angers in December 1961. From the First Session of the Council onwards he was a member of the Commission on the Discipline of the Clergy and of the Christian People.
8. Henri Jenny, Auxiliary Bishop of Cambrai and member of the Preparatory Commission on the Liturgy. He was to become a member of the Commission on the Liturgy at the Council.

Canon Boulard,[1] and M Chavasse.[2] They told me they were going to the Embassy[3] where a reception was being held in our honour. It would be an opportunity to see all the French members of the Commissions. But I was extremely tired.[4] Also I wished to celebrate Mass. In principle this is impossible as one is not allowed to celebrate Mass in the evening in Rome unless one has a congregation of at least 50 pilgrims. So I stayed behind and said Mass. Then I went to Santa Sabina to greet Fr General.[5]

He had just returned, but was tired so I did not see him. I myself could hardly stand. The last few days in Strasbourg have been exhausting. I was at the end of my tether.

In the evening, supper at Saint-Louis.

Preliminary gossip. The pretensions of the Faculties of the Lateran, which the Pope has recently raised to the status of a university. At the opening session, Mgr Piolanti[6] declared that just as the Church of St John Lateran is the mother of all the churches, so the Lateran University should be the first of all universities.

But these things cannot come about by decree. Any more than one can create a poet by consular decree.

Great importance of Fr Gagnebet, who is very much in with Cardinal Ottaviani, who himself holds a key position.

The Lateran professors, Piolanti and Garofalo[7] would like to be accorded a kind of magisterium of orthodoxy, judging everything. According to Mgr Baron,

---

1. Fernand Boulard of the diocese of Versailles was an expert of world-wide renown in sociology of religion and taught at the Institut Catholique in Paris. He was a member of the Preparatory Commission on Bishops and the Government of Dioceses and was to be appointed a Council expert during the First Session.
2. Antoine Chavasse, priest of the diocese of Chambéry, was Professor at the Faculty of Catholic Theology of the University of Strasbourg; having been a member of the Preparatory Commission on the Liturgy, he was to be appointed a Council expert in 1962.
3. The French Embassy to the Holy See.
4. Congar added to the typescript: 'I can see myself now dragging my case from the Sant'Andrea della Valle bus station to Saint-Louis. It is not far, but I was at the end of my tether. I could hardly put one foot in front of the other. I am convinced that my hemiplegic-type neurological disease was already developing. In fact it had been doing so since the month of April when I gave a series of lectures in Barcelona and was dragging my leg in climbing the stairs and at night was well-nigh exhausted. The first signs go back to 1950.
5. Michael Browne, OP.
6. Antonio Piolanti, of the diocese of Rome, was Rector of the Lateran and consultor of the Congregation of the Holy Office; he was also a member of the Preparatory Theological Commission and was to be appointed a Council expert in 1962.
7. Salvatore Garofalo, priest of the diocese of Naples, exegete, Professor at the Lateran and later Rector of the Urbanianum; member of the Preparatory Theological Commission, he was named a Council expert in 1962.

Piolanti said of me that I was the wisest of the theologians but there were three heresies on every page.

Mgr Journet will not come: 'I am deaf', he says . . .

L'abbé R Laurentin called to see me. He has been here for three days and has already been everywhere, seen everyone. He told me that he had been through the Bishops' *Postulata*[1] which have been printed in volumes and can be read at the headquarters of each Commission. It would seem that a great majority of the bishops call for doctrinal developments in mariology. Cardinal Richaud[2] asked for the mediation and co-redemption to be proclaimed as dogmas . . . But the Commission would not lean too much in this direction. However, one cannot avoid doing something along these lines. The best—and this would be the inclination of Fr Tromp[3]—would be to produce a synthetic declaration linking Mary to Christ and the Church.

According to Laurentin, my Report had not aroused the bad impression that he had feared on the grounds, he said, that it had the misfortune 1) of being in French; 2) of not being diplomatic enough; 3) of saying at the end things that it would have been better to have put somewhere else and to have toned down.

Dinner, after which I saw Mgr Blanchet for a while; he was bursting with health and very positive. It is essential, he said, not to allow some things to be stifled. All the bishops have called for a change in the way the Curia works. The role of the consultors and of the members of the Commission is to bring up these matters, *importune opportune* [in season, out of season (2 Tim 4:2)].

I am dead tired.

Monday 14 November 1960

Mass, after which I served one. Very tired, from morning onwards. I went to the Secretariat for Christian Unity. It is the apartment left by the former parish priest of the Pantheon, and has two bathrooms. There are just five offices and space to create a small library, but so far there is neither a single file nor a single set of journals. It is very very simple. Arrighi[4] is always very enthusiastic about the work

---

1. Replies to the pre-preparatory consultation. They are to be found in AD I/II: Consilia et vota Episcoporum ac Praelatorum. The first seven volumes contain the bishops' replies.
2. Paul M Richaud, Archbishop of Bordeaux. He was a member of the Central Preparatory Commission. During the Council, he was to be a member of the Technical and Organisational Commission.
3. The Dutch Jesuit, Sebastian Tromp, was Professor of Theology at the Gregorianum and consultor at the Holy Office; he was secretary of the Preparatory Theological Commission and later secretary of the Doctrinal Commission at the Council itself.
4. Jean-François Arrighi, of the diocese of Ajaccio, worked for the Congregation for the Eastern Church; he was *minutante* (minute-taker) at the Secretariat for Unity where, in 1963, he was appointed sub-secretary for relations with Protestants; he was to be appointed a Council expert from the Second Session onwards.

to be done, and what he has already done or is doing. I saw Mgr Willebrands[1] who told me in detail how the visit of Mgr Fisher[2] Archbishop of Canterbury had been organised and what the background to it might be. Mgr Fisher would undoubtedly like it to result in a welcoming attitude on the part of the Catholic hierarchy in England. But it would be necessary to take care that this visit does not arouse reactions in the Catholic hierarchy that turn out, instead, to be very negative.

From there I went to the 'Holy Office'. Memories. I saw Fr Leclerq,[3] a very likeable Oblate who is Fr Tromp's secretary. When I told him that the problem for me was to be USEFUL, he replied: all you need to do for that is to take initiatives such as you have taken. I met Mgr Backes. I began to read the *Postulata* of the bishops. Stupidly: that is to say, from the beginning. *Anglia.*[4] I made a few notes. It is VERY interesting. Almost no doctrinal horizon, but practical questions. Several English bishops say categorically: no new mariological dogmas (thus Leeds,[5] Liverpool,[6] Westminster[7]); on the other hand, the Archbishop of Armagh[8] (Ireland) requests that Mary be declared the centre of devotion from the psychological and practical point of view, Christ remaining so only '*de iure*'. (Actually, no. I had misread the text and am not the only one to have understood it in this sense. It has been badly written. The Archbishop was in fact protesting against the view that would preserve Christ's place at the centre *de iure,* while at the same time placing Mary at the centre *de facto.*) In his copy, Fr Tromp put an exclamation mark in the margin.

---

1. Jan Willebrands, of the diocese of Harlem (Netherlands) had been Professor of Philosophy at the Warmond Major Seminary of which he became Director in 1945; he founded and ran the Catholic Conference for Ecumenical Questions (CCQO) and in 1960 was appointed Secretary to the Secretariat for Christian Unity and was to become a bishop in 1964. Later he became President of the Secretariat for Christian Unity, which later became the Pontifical Council for the Promotion of Christian Unity, and also a cardinal and Archbishop of Utrecht.
2. Geoffrey F Fisher, had been the Archbishop of Canterbury since 1945; he was one of the presidents of the World Council of Churches (WCC) from 1948 to 1954.
3. Michel Leclercq, OMI, was a *scrittore* in the censorship of books section of the Congregation of the Holy Office and a *minutante* for the Preparatory Theological Commission.
4. England. See AD I/II, 1, 1–57.
5. George P Dwyer, Bishop of Leeds, member of the Preparatory Commission on Bishops and the Government of Dioceses. He continued his work in the Commission on Bishops and the Government of Dioceses from the First Session onwards.
6. John C Heenan, Archbishop of Liverpool and member of the Secretariat for Christian Unity; he was to become Archbishop of Westminster in 1963 and cardinal in 1965.
7. Cardinal William Godfrey was Archbishop of Westminster.
8. Cardinal John d'Alton was at that time Archbishop of Armagh (Ireland) and a member of the Central Preparatory Commission. See AD I/II, 1, 1–57.

Fr Tromp came in. He was cordial with me. He wants us to go to St Peter's for the audience at 10 am! An hour away. So we went. What a performance! Papal gendarmes or Swiss guards in full uniform everywhere. The actual arrangements were impeccable. But what ceremonial, what a display of pomp! We were shown into a tribune, where I went and sat beside Fr de Lubac. The whole length of St Peter's has been fitted out with tribunes, armchairs. A fantastic equipage of fellows in crimson uniforms, Swiss guards in helmets, holding their halberds with proud bearing. All the colleges in Rome have been mobilised and there were certainly a good ten thousand people present. Why? What a waste of time! Little by little, the place filled up. Costumes of all kinds, a great many young faces of priests from the colleges; some (not many) frightful Dreyer[1]-like faces. Forty or so cardinals took their places in the armchairs: behind them, in the tribunes, bishops and archbishops.

At about ten minutes past eleven, the *Credo* was intoned and the Pope came in on foot. It was a good moment. But then the Sistine choir sang a theatrical *'Tu es Petrus'*: mediocre opera. The 10,000 people, the forty cardinals, the 250 or 300 bishops, said nothing. One only will have the right to speak. As for the Christian people, they are there neither by right nor in fact. I sensed the blind door of the underlying ecclesiology. It is the ostentatious ceremonial of a monarchical power.

The Pope read a text in Italian which I did not fully understand, but which seemed to me very banal. He was speaking about the separated brethren. One hopes that they will send representatives (if I understood correctly). However, the Council is a matter for the Catholic Church and only afterwards will one embark on dialogue with the separated brethren.

Alas! After giving his blessing (alone, always alone, to the 10,000, the 300, the 40 . . .), the Pope got up and departed, enthroned on the *sedia*;[2] stupid applause. The Pope made a gesture as if to say: alas, I can do nothing about it . . .

---

1. Carl Dreyer, Danish film-maker.
2. The *sedia gestatoria*: the portable throne used by the popes.

On the way out I saw Fr General, Fr de Lubac, Fr Gagnebet, the group of liturgists (Gy,[1] Jounel,[2] Martimort,[3] Chavasse), D Rousseau,[4] Fr Hamer,[5] Fr Witte, Dubois-Dumée[6] (at last—a Christian!), Mgr Charrière,[7] Mgr de Provenchères.[8]

I came back here and got a bit lost in making my way through the working-class and populous areas; very narrow streets with no pavement, washing hanging from the windows, craft stalls, banners inviting one to vote communist . . . And I told myself that what I had just seen, what we had 'done' at St Peter's, had NOTHING AT ALL to do with THIS OTHER world I was passing through. They haven't even a square millimetre in common. All the same!

There is an apparatus known as 'Church' which functions by itself, without any contact with ordinary men and women.

I was dead tired and had difficulty climbing the stairs.

---

1. Pierre-Marie Gy, OP, of the Province of France, professor at the Dominican Faculties of Le Saulchoir, was Sub-Director of the Institut Supérieur de Liturgie at the Institut Catholique in Paris, and was to become its Director in 1964; he was a consultor to the Preparatory Liturgical Commission.

2. Pierre Jounel, priest of the diocese of Nantes, was professor at the Institut Supérieur de Liturgie at the Institut Catholique in Paris; he was a consultor to the Preparatory Liturgical Commission.

3. Aimé-Georges Martimort, Professor of Liturgical History at the Faculty of Theology in Toulouse, was Co-Director of the Pastoral Liturgical Centre until 1964: he was a consultor to the Preparatory Liturgical Commission and then a Council expert in 1962.

4. Dom Olivier Rousseau, OSB, monk of Chevetogne, was director of the journal *Irénikon* and worked in the fields of liturgy, ecumenism and the monastic life.

5. Jérôme Hamer, OP, of the Province of Belgium, was Rector of the Dominican Faculties at Le Saulchoir until 1962, when he became Assistant to the Master General for the French-speaking provinces and Secretary General of Studies for the Dominican Order; he was a consultor to the Secretariat for Unity of which he was to be named Assistant Secretary in 1966; he was appointed a Council expert in 1962. Later he was to become Secretary of the Congregation for the Doctrine of the Faith, then Pro-Prefect of the Congregation for Religious and Secular Institutes, and created cardinal.

6. Jean-Pierre Dubois-Dumée was assistant director of *Informations catholiques internationales* (International Catholic Information) and *La Vie catholique illustrée* (Illustrated Catholic Life), {and the only layman mentioned in this group}.

7. François Charrière, Bishop of Fribourg (Switzerland), member of the Secretariat for Christian Unity.

8. Charles de Provenchères, Archbishop of Aix-en-Provence, member of the Preparatory Commission on the Discipline of the Clergy and of the Christian People, member of the Commission on the Eastern Churches from the Second Session onwards.

Lunch with four cardinals (Tisserant, Liénart,[1] Marella,[2] Valeri[3]) and the French bishops present. I saw in particular Mgr Marty,[4] with his simple and warm southern cordiality; Mgr Mercier,[5] whom I had not seen since 1921; Mgr Veuillot,[6] Mgr de Bazelaire;[7] Mgr Guerry,[8] who is very cordial and speaks openly; Mgr Garrone[9] for a brief moment; also, very briefly, the North African bishops (Algiers, Carthage, Oran, Constantine[10]), a good exchange with Mgr Martin,[11] who told me that ecumenism is for him a revelation and an unexpected enrichment.

The bishops are all confident and simple.

But how difficult it is to arrange useful meetings. Fr General has put me off until Wednesday, Gagnebet to later on; I telephoned Fr Paul Philippe[12] twice to no avail. I feel I am wasting my time.

---

1. Achille Liénart, Bishop of Lille, President of the Assembly of Cardinals and Archbishops of France. Member of the Central Preparatory Commission, he was to belong, during the Council, to the Co-ordinating Commission and to the Council of Presidents.
2. Paolo Marella, former Apostolic Nuncio to Paris (from 1953 to February 1960). He was to be President of the Preparatory and then of the Conciliar Commission on Bishops and the Government of Dioceses.
3. Valerio Valeri, Prefect of the Congregation for Religious, had been Apostolic Nuncio in Paris from 1936 until December 1944.
4. François Marty, Archbishop of Rheims, consultor to the Preparatory Commission on Studies and Seminaries. At the First Session, he was elected a member of the Commission on the Discipline of the Clergy and of the Christian People.
5. Georges Mercier, bishop of Laghouat (Algeria); originally of the diocese of Rheims and a former student at the minor seminary of Rheims where Congar also was from 1919 to 1921.
6. Pierre Veuillot, a native of Paris, was Bishop of Angers; he was to be appointed Coadjutor of the Archbishop of Paris in 1961. At the time of the First Session, he was elected a member of the Commission on Bishops and the Government of Dioceses.
7. Louis MF de Bazelaire de Ruppierre, Archbishop of Chambéry, member of the Preparatory Commission on Studies and Seminaries.
8. Émile Guerry, Archbishop of Cambrai, member of the Preparatory Commission on Bishops and the Government of Dioceses. He continued to work in the Commission on Bishops and the Government of Dioceses, of which he was a member from the First Session onwards.
9. Gabriel-M Garrone, Archbishop of Toulouse, member of the Doctrinal Commission from the First Session onwards; at the beginning of 1966, he was to be appointed Pro-Prefect of the Congregation for Seminaries and Universities.
10. Respectively Léon-Étienne Duval (who was to be created cardinal in February 1965), Maurice Perrin, Bertrand Lacaste and Paul P Pinier.
11. Joseph-M Martin, Archbishop of Rouen, member of the Secretariat for Christian Unity; he was to be created cardinal in February 1966. Unless otherwise indicated, when Congar mentions Martin or Mgr Martin in the *Journal*, he is usually referring to Joseph-M Martin, Archbishop of Rouen.
12. Paul Philippe, OP, of the Province of France, was Secretary of the Congregation for Religious; he was to become a bishop in 1962 and be elected a member of the Commission on Religious at the First Session; he was later to be appointed Prefect of the

I called in to see Fr Lécuyer at the French Seminary; I went to the Angelicum to order some books and do a bit of work. I am finding it difficult to put one foot in front of the other, I am so tired, exhausted.

Tuesday 15 November 1960

There was a meeting of the Theological Commission at the 'Holy Office' at 9 am. As the large meeting hall was occupied, our meeting was held in Cardinal Ottaviani's audience hall. Room very warm, chandelier lit, curtains drawn. Anthropological bearing of those present: mixture of honest old Religious, fairly young prelates, rather off-putting heads. The cardinal has a kind of double chin which has a look of goitre about it.

The proceedings began with those members who had not yet done so taking the oath. I did not actually say the word '*iuro*' [I swear] in the formula, but I signed my name to it in the pre-printed form complete with the name of each one which were handed out to us. May God forgive me!

Speech in Latin by Cardinal Ottaviani.

The Commission has divided up into sub-commissions: the first was to study '*quid faciendum quoad ordinationem materiae*' [what is to be done in relation to arranging the material] and the other four the four proposed schemas.[1]

We will be told what the members of the Commission have said and we may express our opinion, but it is not a question of writing a treatise. We must confine ourselves to specific and necessary points.

Speech in Latin by Fr Tromp.

Before the summer break, a kind of preparatory commission with a dozen or so members had determined '*de quo agendum*' [what was to be dealt with], not *a priori* but *a posteriori*, according to the *vota*[2] by the bishops, congregations, universities, etc, and the Pope's own comments.

On 27 October and subsequent days, the Commission twice held three work sessions. There was a fairly animated discussion on the *ordo materiae* [order of subjects]. Fr Tromp was in favour of two schemas; 1) *de Ecclesia* [on the Church]; 2) *de Ecclesia quatenus curat ad sanitatem de fide et moribus* [on the Church as regards its care for faith and morals].

(I thought to myself that there was a unity embracing both of these:
- God's plan
- the covenant relationship offered to humanity.)

The subject will be re-opened in January but '*auditis omnibus consultoribus*' [after listening to what all the consultors have to say]: these are to state their opinion '*lingua latina*' [in Latin] and do so both briefly and succinctly.

Congregation for Eastern Churches, and created cardinal.

1. These were the documents *On the Sources of Revelation, On the Church, on the Moral and Social Order* and *On the Deposit of the Faith.*
2. Written requests (these are the *postulata*: cf above, page 23, No. 1)

ENTER TO LEARN
LEAVE TO SERVE

Tribute to the Brothers
135 Years in Sacramento
May 15, 2011

"MAKE

YOURSELF

RESPONSIVE

TO

WHATEVER

GOD ASKS

OF YOU."

ST. JOHN BAPTIST
DE LA SALLE

We are dealing with *rebus non definitis* [matters that have not been defined], that is, free. Moreover, there are many ways in which they can be put forward, but one must stick to ONE and eschew personal ideas.

There will be sub-commissions, to be constituted as follows, though nothing is as yet definite: (The name of the President of each sub-commission is in italics in this list).

De Ecclesia: Mgr Dubois . . . , Piolanti, Fenton, Philips, Colombo,[1] Schauf,[2] Lécuyer, *Gagnebet* . . .

De fontibus: Schröffer,[3] Hermaniuk,[4] *Garofalo*, Cerfaux, van den Eynde.[5]

De deposito fidei: . . . Carpino,[6] *Ciappi*,[7] Ramirez,[8] Dhanis . . . Kerrigan.[9]

De re morali individuali [*on matters of personal morality*]: . . . Frs *Philippe*, Hürth, Gillon.[10]

---

1. Carlo Colombo of the diocese of Milan, Professor of Dogmatics at the seminary of Milan, was a member of the Preparatory Theological Commission; he was to be appointed a Council expert in 1962; during the First Session he was personal expert to Cardinal Montini. When the latter became pope, he made Colombo a titular bishop in March 1964; he later became President of the Faculty of Theology of Northern Italy and Auxiliary Bishop of Milan.

2. Heribert Schauf, priest of the diocese of Aix-la-Chapelle, was Professor of Canon Law at the diocesan seminary; consultor to the Preparatory Theological Commission, he was to be appointed a Council expert in 1962.

3. Joseph Schröffer, Bishop of Eichstätt (Germany) and member of the Preparatory Theological Commission; he was to become a member of the Doctrinal Commission in 1962.

4. Maxim Hermaniuk, Archbishop of the Catholic Ukrainians in Winnipeg (Canada) and a member of the Preparatory Theological Commission. He was elected a member of the Secretariat for Christian Unity during the Second Session.

5. The Belgian Franciscan Damien van den Eynde was Rector of the Antonianum; he was a member of the Preparatory Theological Commission and was appointed a Council expert in 1962.

6. Francesco Carpino, titular archbishop, assessor of the Consistorial Congregation.

7. Luigi Ciappi, OP, of the Roman Province, was Master of the Sacred Palace and consultor to the Congregation of the Holy Office; he was a member of the Preparatory Theological Commission, and was to be appointed a Council expert in 1962 and later created cardinal.

8. Santiago Ramirez Dulanto, OP, of the Province of Spain, was Professor of Theology at the Pontifical University of Salamanca, Regent of Studies for his Province and President of the Dominican Faculty of Salamanca; he was a member of the Preparatory Theological Commission and was to be appointed a Council expert in 1962.

9. Alexander Kerrigan, OFM, exegete, consultor to the Pontifical Biblical Commission, taught at the Antonianum; he was a consultor to the Preparatory Theological Commission and was appointed a Council expert in 1962.

10. The theologian Louis-Bertrand Gillon, OP, of the Province of Toulouse, was Rector of the Angelicum until 1961, then Dean of the Faculty of Theology from 1963 onwards: he was a member of the Preparatory Theological Commission, and later a Council

De re morali sociali [*on matters of social morality*]: *nondum est facta commissio* [no commission has yet been established].

The law of secrecy was explained to us: it applies to everybody, including the members of other Commissions, except when there is an OFFICIAL joint meeting. One can ask for such a meeting to be held. Freedom with regard to the members and consultors of our own Commission. One may use secretaries and typists provided these too are sworn to secrecy.

One can consult the *Acta antepraeparatoria*[1] at the Holy Office, but they must not leave Rome. Only the first volume (papal documents) is on sale to the public.

Cardinal Ottaviani spoke once more: we can ask questions but only in order to ask for explanations. We may produce a joint *votum*.

Nobody asked to speak. The meeting was over. Cardinal Ottaviani said: *Agimus tibi gratias.*

Fidelium animae . . . in pace.[2]

These were the last words that were spoken.

I spoke to some of the members then. Unfortunately, while you are speaking to two or three, the others leave . . . I saw Fr Kerrigan, Fr van den Eynde, who was very cordial, and to whom I gave a copy of my *Tradition*;[3] also to Mgr Garofalo, who was very gratified by this; Frs Häring and Lio[4] with whom I raised the question of the need for a solemn condemnation of war and of the atomic bomb; Mgr Cerfaux; quite a long talk with Fr Lécuyer and Fr Leclercq, and another equally long one with Fr Paul Philippe. With these three I spoke openly and from my heart. I criticised what I had seen of the preparatory work and of the draft of the schema = in the mold of scholasticism, a summary of all the condemnations of the past twenty-five years. That is not what is needed. What is needed is a broad declaration of the faith of the Church, dynamic and kerygmatic, rooted in God's plan.

I waited (quite a long time) for Cardinal Ottaviani in order to talk to him (for the first time). Alas, the conversation was rather tense: eye to eye, knee to knee . . .

---

expert.

1. Pre-preparatory documents: these were published, together with the preparatory documents under the title *Acta et Documenta concilio œcumenico Vaticano II apparando;* the first series *(Series I)* which contained the pre-preparatory documents, was published in 1960 and 1961; the first volume contained the papal documents: *AD,* I/I.

2. We give you thanks . . . May the souls of the faithful departed . . . rest in peace.

3. The reference is to the first volume of Congar's work on tradition: *La Tradition et les traditions. Essai historique* (Paris: Fayard, 1960). [*Tradition and Traditions. An Historical Essay and A Theological Essay* (London: Burns and Oates, 1966).]

4. Ermenegildo Lio, OFM, Professor of Moral Theology at the Antonianum, worked at the Congregation of the Holy Office as a defender of the bond, then as consultor; he was a consultor to the Preparatory Theological Commission and was to be appointed a Council expert in 1962.

The cardinal said at once that my report had provoked criticism: why could I not 'keep in line'. I was intelligent, learned: in my book (*Réforme*[1]) there were some very fine pages, but others which contradicted them. Why must one always point out the weaknesses of the Church? By doing so one undermines confidence in the hierarchy and the Magisterium.

One speaks as if everything was fine with the others and everything was wrong with ourselves.

I asked if I had done that?

The cardinal replied that he was speaking in general. I said that I had no intention of undermining confidence in the hierarchy, but that the Church ought at least to think about herself; if she were giving herself completely to the service of the Gospel, all her authority would to her come of its own accord. The cardinal: but the Congregations, the bishops, the priests, the professors in the seminaries, do nothing but serve . . .

I said that I had noticed, and deplored, a kind of breach between the theology that one expresses and the Christian people. I referred to my experience of the day before: what was there in common between our (magnificent) ceremony and the good people in the narrow, insalubrious streets through which I had walked. The Church is FOR PEOPLE.

The cardinal: it's a question of pastoral care. There is a commission on pastoral care, which must find ways of adapting. We, we must set forth the Faith. And the cardinal attacked those who seek to adapt religion. They are committing afresh the error committed by Action Française: politics first. What they are offering people is nothing more than ways and means to a better human life . . .

The cardinal spoke of catechism, but I could not quite see what he was trying to say and what he is looking for.

This conversation left me somewhat dismayed. There is a total *quiproquo*. Or two totally opposed *Denkformen* [ways of thinking]. The cardinal seems to have created a coherent, flawless synthesis of errors to which he seems to think I am party, and which he cleaves in two as in a waking dream. He is slaying the dragon.[2]

I saw Fr Paul Philippe for a moment. We spoke of his approaching consecration as bishop.[3] He told me that the Angelicum is slowing down and that Fr General[4]

---

1. *Vraie et fausse réforme dans l'Église*, 'Unam Sanctam', 20 (Paris: Cerf, 1950).
2. {The French word used here is *tarasque*}. In connection with the difficulties which Congar, de Lubac and others had to endure during the second half of the pontificate of Pius XII, Congar was to write later: 'I had prepared a defence dossier which I called *La tarasque!* This is a very dangerous animal . . . but an imaginary one! In my view, the dangers which Rome tended to see everywhere were not real' (*Une vie pour la vérité* [Paris: Le Centurion, 1975], 99).
3. Paul Philippe was to be consecrated bishop in September 1962.
4. Michael Browne, Master General of the Dominicans.

has none of the kind of initiative and drive that is needed. The Generals of the Franciscans[1] and the Carmelites[2] are quite different, he said.

After a walk round the Vatican Gardens and a visit to the library, I went to lunch at St Jerome,[3] which had been so welcoming when I stayed at the time of my disgrace. There I met Mgr Suhr.[4] Dom Leclercq[5] told me that Mgr Felici[6] had told a Benedictine that the Council would only last for a few weeks as a meeting of bishops; that as much as possible would need to be done by correspondence.

I tried to go and read the *Vota*[7] of the bishops at the Secretariat for Unity. The caretaker was unpleasant and told me that it would not be open until tomorrow. That will give me only forty minutes in all in order to have a preliminary look at these extremely interesting documents. It is far too little. One would need four days, working ten or twelve hours per day.

I went to the Gregorianum[8] to see Fr Hürth, in order to intone for him too the refrain about the condemnation of war. He thinks that everybody agrees in principle, but that no-one will be willing to condemn legitimate armed defence, or to condemn atomic weapons if this would mean making things difficult for the free nations but not at all for the USSR. Fr Tromp had rung exactly the same changes, only more emphatically: he is only sixty-two years of age, whereas Fr Hürth is an old man who keeps his room at a tropical temperature . . . Fr Hürth gave me a lecture on the foundations of the moral order. It is his great concern. It is THAT that he is looking for in the Council schema. According to Fr Hürth, if Fr Tromp has not yet named the sub-commission *de re morali sociali* [on matters of social morality], this is because the Pope is preparing an encyclical for the anniversary of *Rerum Novarum*.[9] So we will have to wait until May of 1961!

I then saw Fr Dhanis, and we spoke about many things. Then I went back to the Biblicum[10] to see Fr de Lubac and tell him my impressions.

From there I went to the Angelicum to see Fr Gagnebet. Quite open and friendly. He has been studying the Vatican Council for the past two years, and

---

1. At the time, the Minister General of the Friars Minor (OFM) was Agostino Sépinski, who was to become a member of the Commission on Religious in 1962.
2. The reference must be to the Superior General of the Discalced Carmelites, Anastasio del S Rosario.
3. Benedictine abbey founded by Pope Pius XI in 1933 for the revision of the Vulgate.
4. Johannes T Suhr, Benedictine, Bishop of Copenhagen and a member of the Central Preparatory Commission.
5. Dom Jean Leclercq OSB, of the Abbey of St Maurice in Clervaux (Luxembourg) was a specialist in monastic history and spirituality in the Middle Ages.
6. Pericle Felici, titular archbishop, was general secretary of the Central Preparatory Commission, and was later to become Secretary General of the Council.
7. As before, the reference is to the replies to the pre-preparatory consultation.
8. The Pontifical Gregorian University was run by the Jesuits.
9. Leo XIII's social encyclical, published on 15 May 1891.
10. The Pontifical Biblical Institute, run by the Jesuits.

his studies have helped to elucidate some points for which the 1869 Council had indicated legal precedent: for example that the Presidents of Roman dicasteries should be Presidents of the Commissions; that the secretaries of Congregations should not belong to the corresponding Commission . . . He told me that the consultors had been chosen from the lists drawn up by the nuncios. We spoke about a few things. Then about Fr Thomas Philippe,[1] whom he made me promise to go and see as he was at Santa Sabina.

I then saw Fr Gillon for a few minutes. A little caustic, as always. He told me that it is the German bishops who have asked for an overall doctrinal synthesis covering statements about God.

Wednesday 16 November 1960

I went to see Fr Gregory Baum at Bea's Secretariat.[2] Then Fr Tromp at the 'Holy Office'. He was extremely cordial and almost pally, I mean friendly. Very concerned about the crisis of authority, which he blames to a considerable extent on the wartime Resistance. He is right. I intoned for him my refrain against war and the bomb. He had the same reaction as Fr Hürth, only even more passionate. If he had not appointed members to a *sub-commissio de re morali sociali* [sub-commission on matters of social morality], this was because the Pope had himself appointed a commission to prepare an encyclical and it was necessary to wait for the results of this, maybe even take over THIS commission as a sub-commission of our own.

It will be necessary to prepare everything in Latin FROM THE WORD GO, otherwise one will never be able to give a precise meaning to the words used. He told me, in confidence, the history of the encyclical *Quadragesimo*,[3] which three different authors had prepared in different languages.[4] Moreover, they did not agree about everything, and each one stuck to his own point of view. The translator, Mgr Parenti[5] had suffered a veritable purgatory in his efforts to produce a single version.

---

1. Thomas Philippe, OP, of the Province of France, became Regent of Studies at Le Saulchoir after Chenu had been put on the Index in 1942: he had been responsible for *Eau Vive* (Living Water) the International Centre of Spiritual and Doctrinal Formation that had been founded alongside Le Saulchoir in 1948. He was dismissed from it in 1952 and canonically sanctioned by the Holy Office in 1954, a sanction which had been lifted ten years later. From 1963 onwards, he worked with handicapped people in conjunction with Jean Vanier, formerly of Eau Vive, who was to found the Arche communities.
2. The Secretariat for Christian Unity of which Cardinal Bea was President.
3. Pius XI's *Quadragesimo anno*, published in 1931.
4. The encyclical had been prepared with the cooperation of German and French-speaking experts.
5. The reference is probably to Pietro Parente.

He spoke to me about Fenton, who is very nervy and had abusively accused Tromp of having wronged him. Tromp told me that he had not pressed him because Fenton might have an attack. For my part, having been beside him at the ceremony in St Peter's, I had noticed that he burst out laughing like a child, immoderately . . . I told Tromp that Fenton was of no account in the USA. I know that, he said. For my part, I know that he is there as a personal friend of Cardinal Ottaviani. Fr Tromp had on his table the issue of the *RSPT* containing Hamer's article on Bolgeni.[1] That is going to be a point for discussion . . .

I suggested to Fr Tromp that for the various chapters that we are to write, it would be necessary to be in contact with Bea's Secretariat. He saw no point in that. For him, we need only refer to that Secretariat in relation to the paragraph concerning the relationship with separated Christians and, an even more delicate matter, with 'separated communities'. Always the same atomising and separating structure. They distribute all the chapters SEPARATELY, and do not see that pastoral care on the one hand and ecumenism on the other must be present as matters of question and of concern, therefore also of information, throughout both the study and the setting forth of doctrine.

In a similar way, Fr Tromp completely rejected my idea that it is important to decide now on the order in which to set matters forth, which I would like to be one that is dynamic and proclaims salvation. For him, what is needed is for THESES to be worked out; then one will see in which order to present them. Whereas for me, the over-all order in which they are treated makes a difference to the way the unity of the Church, Scripture and Tradition, the laity, etc. are understood.

Similarly, again, for Fr Tromp, Catholic Action and the laity are almost entirely PRACTICAL questions to be dealt with by a non-doctrinal commission created *ad hoc*.

No agreement.

Fr Tromp also told me a few other things. For example: the absurd things that are being written. A German journal for the formation of the laity had written that one can no longer say that our Church is the one Church of Christ . . .

Strasbourg 17 November 1960
Evening. From the 'Holy Office' I took a taxi in order to arrive in time at Santa Sabina, where I had an appointment with Fr General at 10.30 a.m. I saw him at 11 am. He is very well. He has had no sign of pains in his heart for a month. In fact he looked completely rested. He told me that it was HE, not the 'Holy Office', who had sent me to Cambridge,[2] in the belief that I would be all right there, as there was a good library and I was interested in Anglicans . . .

---

1. Jérôme Hamer, 'Note sur la collégialité épiscopale' , *Revue des Sciences Philosophiques et Théologiques*, 1960: 40–50; the reference is to the theologian Giovanni V Bolgeni, SJ (1733–1811).
2. In 1956, Congar had spent nearly a year in Cambridge without any kind of ministry, away from the teaching of theology due to suspicions in Rome.

He asked me if I would be bringing out my book on the 'primacy of the Holy See',[1] and, as I was very doubtful, indeed inclined to say no to this, he asked me why. He spoke highly of Scott's work on *The Eastern Churches*[2] . . . He really only thinks about that . . .

He said he had begun to look at *Le concile et les conciles*.[3] But he could not accept that, like Dom O Rousseau, one should speak of 'hardening'.[4] That would imply, he said, that dogma began by being 'soft', and then became hard . . .

I spent quite a long time with poor Fr T Philippe, whom I had not seen since 1953 or thereabouts. The poor Father. He is very deaf. He outlined his thinking for me.

He exaggerated enormously his faults. He spoke in a monologue, punctuating what he said with 'No?', 'You see what I am saying?', 'Don't you agree?'. In what he says there are some keen and interesting ideas, but trapped in a very personal construction, reduced to 'principles' which are both rigorous and fuzzy. It is very difficult to follow, rather painful and tiring also.

But I sincerely pity him. The way he was treated is truly dreadful. He speaks of his 'trial' as a grace . . .

After that I went to bring Fr Hamer up to date with some of my impressions.

In the afternoon, conversation with Chavasse. What good sense and what a clear, solid spirit!

With Mgr Baron. He spoke to me a bit about the atmosphere. He is no longer on the laity commission but on the one for Religious. He told me that Opus Dei, which is spreading fantastically, is also spreading its own view that only the members of secular institutes are the true laity!!!!

He spoke very highly of Cardinal Marella, who had well understood and defended French concerns.

He said that if Maritain[5] were to die, *Humanisme intégral*[6] could well be condemned. Certain South American bishops have asked that the Council pronounce such a condemnation . . . According to him, the background is this: Maritain is blamed for having maintained that the Church's action rests on the

---

1. On 9 December 1955, in his interview with the then Master of the Order, Congar had spoken of his study on the primacy of Peter in the New Testament, which he had written in Jerusalem in 1954.
2. S Herbert Scott, *The Eastern Churches and the Papacy* (London: 1928).
3. *Le Concile et les conciles. Contribution à l'histoire de la vie conciliare de l'Église* (Paris: Éditions de Chevetogne et du Cerf, 1960): the acts of an ecumenical colloquium held at Chevetogne.
4. Cf Olivier Rousseau, 'Introduction', pages IX–XIX; in particular, he wrote: 'Every dogmatic definition involves in itself a certain hardening' (X).
5. The Catholic philosopher Jacques Maritain, one of the masters of neo-Thomism in the twentieth century; born in 1882, he withdrew to the Little Brothers of Charles de Foucauld after the death of his wife Raïssa in 1960.
6. *Humanisme intégral*, Paris, 1936.

holiness of Christians. One needs to rely on system and on Power in order to have religion. (Even in Rome, people were worried above all by the resurgence of Maritain's theses IN ITALY; for example, the journal *Adesso* in Milan). Even Cardinal Tardini thinks along these lines. He is very pastoral in the charitable work in which he is involved: but, apart from that, he thinks that good elections would settle matters.

- Always the same lamentable cleavage between pastoral work and ecclesiology.

The underlying question is always: *'Quid sit Ecclesia?'* [What is the Church?]. Is it the machine, the authority, or is it the faithful community with people who are Christians or are endeavouring to be such?

Cardinal Montini,[1] on the other hand, thought along the lines of Maritain.

I then saw a Basque priest who asked me to suggest a topic for an ecclesiological and ecumenical thesis. I said: reform and renewal. The holiness and imperfection of the Church in the light of the relationship of Church to Kingdom and of the eschatological perspective.

I spent the rest of the evening at the Angelicum, where I read some journals that we have not got here.

Train at 8.40 pm. I am at my desk in Strasbourg (where it is raining heavily) at 4 pm on Thursday, 17 November. I have found thirty-nine letters and seven parcels of books waiting for me . . . !

2 January 1961
Dined and conversed with l'abbé Caffarel,[2] consultor to the Commission on the Laity. He wanted to show me a text he has prepared and a number of questions with ecclesiological implications.

23 January 1961
Saw Mgr Larraín, Bishop of Talca (Chile), in the presbytery at St Sulpice[3] where I had arranged to meet him. He is also on the Commission on the Laity and was on his way to Rome. He, too, wanted my advice on a certain number of points, in particular the definition of a lay person, of Mission, of Catholic Action. He wants to ask that, before going any further, his Commission makes sure that it is in agreement with the Theological Commission on the theological ideas which it is to discuss. I urged him to do that, and to demand a greater degree of working together. He read to me (unfortunately too fast and with an accent which made it difficult for me to grasp the precise meaning of the words) a Latin text which they

1. Formerly 'substitute' in the Secretariat of State, Giovanni Battista Montini was Archbishop of Milan; he was to succeed John XXIII in June 1963 under the name of Paul VI.
2. Henri Caffarel, founder of the Équipes de Notre Dame (Teams of Our Lady).
3. Parish of Saint-Sulpice in Paris.

had been given and which seemed to me to be canonico-scholastic. I laid stress on the apostolic and pastoral aspect.

This bishop from Chile is 100% in our ideas or in good ideas, as Dom Beauduin[1] would have said. He told me he had read *Chrétiens désunis*[2] as soon as it appeared and, since then, nearly all my books. He also told me that I am very well known in Chile, and that people refer to me, follow my ideas. Moreover, as a nuncio or an apostolic visitator, or the Spanish bishop once said: 'in Chile, they speak in Spanish, but they think in French.' Lay people there are very keen to assume their responsibilities in the Church. We spoke of Cardinal Caggiano's[3] incredible report to the first Lay Apostolate Congress. Mgr Larraín told me that Caggiano had been a student of Civardi[4] and that they both regarded the Catholic Action organisation as a kind of replica of Fascism: disciplined and spectacular organisations. He had himself heard one or other of these prelates, or perhaps some other prelate, say that the priority for Catholic Action was to have a flag and to march out with it, playing a fanfare. He told me that, alas, Argentina is very much under Italian influence and rather 'integrist'. There are people there who are against Maritain and seek to have him condemned at all costs, even by the Council.

I spoke to Mgr Larraín about Protestant propaganda in South America and especially in Chile. I asked him whether it was the apostolate that predominated or propaganda: the latter, surely? He replied that it was most definitely the apostolate, and that it was authentic. They preach the kerygma, he said: Jesus the Saviour, repentance and dedication to Him.

This good hour of conversation was extraordinary. We were at one on all points: on the laity, on the people involved, on the ideal of and the need for openness . . .

1. Dom Lambert Beauduin (1873–1960): first a priest of the diocese of Liège, then a Benedictine at Mont-César in Louvain. With a view to the meeting between the Christian East and the Christian West, he had then founded the monastery of Amay-Chevetogne, and created the journal *Irénikon*. As a pioneer of liturgical renewal, he had played a part, too, in the founding of the CPL (Pastoral Liturgical Centre) in Paris.
2. Yves Congar, *Chrétiens désunis. Principes d'un 'œcuménisme' catholique*, 'Unam Sanctam', 1 (Paris: Cerf, 1937).
3. Cardinal Antonio Caggiano, Archbishop of Buenos Aires, had given a report on the doctrinal basis of the lay apostolate. It was published in *Actes du 1er Congrès mondial pour l'apostolat des laïcs*, edited by the Permanent Committee of International Congresses for the Lay Apostolate, volume I, 1952: 196–229.
4. At the time of the Congress, Luigi Civardi had been national ecclesiastical assistant for Italian Christian workers' associations. He became a titular bishop in 1962 and was to be a member of the Lay Apostolate Commission at the First Session of the Council.

Thursday 26 January 1961

On my way back from Ligugé to Strasbourg I had lunch at the CCIF [Catholic Centre for French Intellectuals]. L'abbé Biard[1] had invited me because the nuncio[2] and Mgr Gouet,[3] secretary to the episcopate, were to be there.

The latter (who came late) is a native of Le Mans. He is a man who is very much a secretary, that is to say he is a bit secretive, gives nothing away and wraps his silence in a sheath of amiability.

The Nuncio, Mgr Bertoli, is a very different kind of man. With him, too, I am very much at one. He is intelligent, he cracks jokes, he treats men as men, indeed as brothers. He is interested in the priestly and pastoral aspect of things. He could be taken for a Frenchman, his outlook is so French. He is decidedly ecumenical even though his postings to Constantinople and to Beirut were both very brief.

I must see him again on his own.

21 February 1961

A letter from Fr de Lubac tells me that there has been a meeting of the Theological Commission. I knew nothing about it. There are two possibilities. Either, in Rome, this meeting was deemed to have been fixed last November and we were invited to it in principle. But I don't remember that anything SPECIFIC was said. Or they did not want to invite me. It is also possible that only those consultors were invited who had been asked for a *votum* which was to be discussed at this meeting.[4] But it is equally possible that they intentionally failed to invite me because the subject of discussion was the Church, and Fr Gagnebet had told me that I had been assigned to the sub-commission on the Church.

That puts me in the dumps. It seems quite clear to me that I would not be able to make my voice heard. I am afraid that what they prepare will be rather bad, that I won't be able to do anything, and that I will be allowing my name to be linked with theses that I do not share.

What should I do?

In any case, Mgr Dubois wants a little meeting at his place with de Lubac, myself, and perhaps Laurentin and Bride.[5] I will see then what to do.

---

1. Pierre Biard, priest of the diocese of Paris, was at that time ecclesiastical assistant to the CCIF.
2. Paolo Bertoli was Apostolic Nuncio to Paris from April 1960 onwards after having been successively Apostolic Delegate in Turkey and Apostolic Nuncio in Colombia and then in the Lebanon. He was later to become a cardinal and Prefect of the Congregation for the Causes of Saints.
3. Julien Gouet, of the diocese of Le Mans, was Director of the General Secretariat of the French bishops; he was later to become Auxiliary Bishop in Paris.
4. This, at any rate, was the reason that he was given later by Gagnebet and Tromp.
5. André Bride, of the diocese of Saint-Claude, Dean of the Faculty of Canon Law at the Catholic Faculties of Lyons, was a consultor on the Preparatory Theological Commission.

3–4 March 1961

I have just returned from lecturing in Brussels and Louvain. I managed to see Mgr Philips for thirty-five to forty minutes between my lecture and the moment when he had to return to Brussels. I asked him what had happened at the recent meeting of the Commission. This is what he told me.

There is a schema *De Ecclesia*[1] prepared by Mgr Lattanzi,[2] Professor of Fundamental Theology at the Lateran. He had prepared three successive drafts, all of which were distributed to the members of the Commission. But they only received the papers on the Sunday, the day before the day (13 February, I think) on which the meeting was to be held. As a result, neither the members nor the consultors were able to read all the (numerous) papers they had been given. Philips told me that this schema is not very satisfactory. Moreover he, Philips, had suggested that they should adopt the idea of the 'People of God', which would have the advantage of showing the historic link between Israel, Christ and the Church.

But, he said, Fr Tromp had said that, in his view, this historical idea was of no interest.

Tromp had been dropped from the preparation of this schema thanks to the influence of Fenton, working on Ottaviani.

I find all that deplorable and it fills me with deep sadness.

There was a discussion on the membership of the Church and the situation of non-Catholic Christians. Ways of expressing their situation were looked at: *voto, ordinati ad*[3] ... Fr Tromp would very much like to return to the distinction between *Communio sanctorum* [communion of saints] and *communio sacramentorum* [communion of sacraments]. Philips told me he supported this: not because he thought this a perfect distinction, but in order to keep the question open. Non-Catholics would possibly belong to the *communio sanctorum*. I myself am convinced that the problem cannot be solved without reference to eschatology, to eschatological salvation.

Mgr Journet intervened strongly in order to say that one cannot call the Protestants of today 'heretics'. He intervened at another point in the discussion to ask whether there would be reference to the ROMAN Church. In Journet's view, this is a name of humility, like 'Nazarene' for Christ ... !!! How out of touch with reality can you be?!

The question of whether it is possible to demonstrate the existence of God was also discussed. The text had been prepared by Fr Ciappi. It seems like a chapter on philosophy of fifty years ago, with a quotation from Zigliara.[4] The

---

1. More precisely, the reference is to the first chapter of the schema *De Ecclesiae militantis natura* (On the nature of the Church militant).
2. Ugo Lattanzi, Dean of the Faculty of Theology at the Lateran, consultor to the Preparatory Theological Commission; he was to be appointed a Council expert in 1962.
3. {Members of the church} 'by desire', 'are aligned to {the Church}.
4. Tommaso Zigliara, OP, (1833–1893), author of several works on neo-Thomistic phi-

majority declared themselves in favour of the view that it was possible to have a DEMONSTRATION that was rational in the strict sense of the word. Because, they said, we have professed this scores of times when we swore the anti-Modernist oath.[1] Philips intervened in order to say, with reference to Max Scheler, that there can be an INTELLECTUAL apprehension of the existence of God which is not a logical demonstration.

He had also suggested that one should speak first of all of truth, and do so in BIBLICAL terms. He would like the truth to be shown as having its absolute basis in 'God', communicating himself to Christ and in Christ, then from Christ to the Church, the pillar and support of the truth. But Fr Gillon, who was sitting beside Philips, said to him that in his view the Bible views the truth in terms of a true judgement, therefore philosophically . . .

The Commission arranged its next meeting for 18 September; and then for 20 November.

Philips told me that he had been asked for a *'votum'* regarding *De laicis* [on the Laity], as a separate chapter of the schema *De Ecclesia*. He did not know—it was I who told him—that Fr Tromp had asked me for one two months ago.[2]

What does all this mean? Was Tromp proceeding *motu proprio* [of his own accord]? Was he thinking, at this moment, of drawing up the schema *De Ecclesia*? What I have done is as if it did not exist.

It looks as if an obscurantist clique (Fenton—Ottaviani—the Lateran) wants to monopolise the whole thing.

I am very downcast, not to say crushed, by all that. But what to do about it?

On returning to Strasbourg from Brussels (3 March) I had a brief meeting with Fr de La Potterie,[3] who was going to Rome, where he teaches one semester. He gave me new information about the 'integrist' campaign being conducted by Piolanti and the Lateran. In particular, he told me in detail the story of the attacks by the Lateran, in *Divinitas*[4] on: 1) The *Introduction à l'Écriture Sainte*, with a preface by Mgr Weber;[5] 2) the Biblical Institute in Rome. It was the same Mgr Romeo[6]

---

losophy; created cardinal by Leo XIII.

1. An oath, still in force at the time of the Council, imposed upon priests by Pius X in order to combat Modernism.

2. Tromp had asked Congar for this *votum* on 26 November 1960, and Congar had sent him a text on the following 10 December.

3. The Belgian Jesuit Ignace de la Potterie was an exegete and taught at the Pontifical Biblical Institute.

4. Cf A Romeo, 'L'Enciclica "Divino afflante spiritu" e le "Opiniones Novas"', *Divinitas*, December 1960.

5. A Robert and A Feuillet (editors), *Introduction à la Bible* (Paris: Tournai, Desclée & Cie, 1957–1959): volume I, delated to the Holy Office, reappeared in 1959 in a new edition which contained only a few modifications but no basic alterations. Volume II appeared without any obstacles in 1959.

6. The biblical scholar Antonino Romeo, of the diocese of Reggio Calabria, worked at the Congregation for Seminaries and Universities.

who led the attack. The Biblical Institute had asked Piolanti for a correction in *Divinitas*. When Piolanti refused, the Biblical Institute had published a collective article in *Verbum Domini*.[1]

The Pope had let the Biblical Institute know that he disapproved of this campaign. But he leaves the men in place. He will end by seeing all his plans betrayed.

What a wretched business it all is!

One person in four is Chinese; one in three lives under a Communist regime: one Christian in every two is non-Catholic.

On March 4 I had a telephone call from Mgr Elchinger. With reference to the Romeo attack, he told me that Mgr Weber had written to Cardinal Bea (as he had told me he wished to do). He had received a reply from the cardinal acknowledging that the matter was serious. It would be useless to write to Cardinal Tisserant as he is a party to the matter. One must write directly to the Pope, which is what Mgr Weber was in the process of doing.

IN *LA CROIX* FOR MARCH 7, AN INTERVIEW WITH CARDINAL KÖNIG.[2] HE STATES THE TRUTH WITH AUTHORITY AND COURAGE.

12 March 1961

Two or three weeks ago I saw Fr Bouyer[3] who had only just returned from Rome and Italy. He gave me some information: to begin with concerning *Divinitas* and Romeo's article, but also concerning the Studies Commission for which he is a consultor. In this Commission there is a *votum* from the Congregation of Seminaries and Universities asking in particular: 1) for the suppression of co-education in Catholic Universities; and 2) for the withdrawal of all concessions regarding the use of modern languages in teaching.

Once again, what world do they live in? In none, except their own, which consists entirely of fictions and a desire for authority.

Now, on Friday evening (10 March) I received a letter from Tollu[4] informing me that, in a letter dated 15 February to the Superior General of St Sulpice,

---

1. 'Pontificium Institutum Biblicum et recens libellus Reverendissimi Domini A Romeo', in *Verbum Domini*, 1961: 3–17.
2. Cardinal Franz König was Archbishop of Vienna. He was a member of the Doctrinal Commission from the First Session of the Council onwards.
3. The theologian Louis Bouyer, from a Protestant family, had been a minister of religion before joining the Catholic Church. Having been ordained a priest of the Oratory, he taught at the Faculty of Theology of the Institut Catholique in Paris. He was consultor to the Preparatory Commission on Studies and Seminaries.
4. François Tollu, PSS, superior of the Séminaire des Carmes (Seminary of the Institut Catholique in Paris); the reference is probably to the circular letter from Tollu and C Bouchaud dated 8 March 1961 and addressed to all the collaborators of the proposed manual which said: 'A letter from His Eminence Cardinal Pizzardo sent on 15 Febru-ary to the Superior General of Saint Sulpice forbade the publication of a manual writ-

Pizzardo[1] had forbidden the publication of a manual written in the vernacular intended for the use of seminaries. Cf my file on the matter: 'Manuel Dogme St-Sulpice' [St-Sulpice Dogmatic Manual].[2]

On 11 March I went to see Mgr Weber to talk to him in confidence about that and the Lateran-Romeo integrist offensive, etc. He knows about the manual question and even told me that there is more to it than Tollu had actually said: 1) it is said that the Congregation is forbidding the publication of this manual for other reasons also; 2) that even if it were to be published, not as a manual but as an auxiliary book (reference to the *Introduction à la Bible*), there would be difficulties.

I am absolutely disgusted by this appalling abuse of power. IN THE NAME OF WHAT DOES Pizzardo, who is an idiot and known to be such by all, utter these threats? He is only strong because one submits to all these blows. The French bishops, who have divine right on their side, ought to take no notice of steps of this sort. Truth and theology do not belong to Pizzardo or to a Roman Congregation of Seminaries and Universities.

I said all this to Mgr Weber, but he did not seem to be at all prepared to recover a freedom which had been purely and simply stolen from us. Nevertheless, once again he spoke against 'integrism' to me and told me about the Brassac affair.[3] Brassac had been told that all was well and that he would receive approval of his excellent manual in two weeks' time. But what the newspapers reported was that it had been put on the Index. And in odious conditions, Mgr Weber told me. A condemnation had to be read before all the assembled students, in which it was stated that the manual was filled from end to end and in all its parts with the spirit of Modernism and that it was not even possible for it to be corrected!!!

Mgr Weber read me the reply that Cardinal Bea had sent him concerning the attacks of Romeo. In it he said simply that Cardinal Tisserant knew about the situation. He also read me his letter to the Pope, very firm, reminding him,

---

ten in the vernacular intended for the use of seminaries. The ecclesiastical authorities in France have approached the Sacred Congregation for Seminaries with a view to securing the withdrawal of the decision which affects us.' Tollu added a written note to Congar to say that Cardinal Feltin intended to appeal directly to the Pope.

1. Cardinal Giuseppe Pizzardo was Prefect of the Congregation for Seminaries and Universities and President of the Preparatory Commission on Studies and Seminaries; he would later be President of the conciliar Commission on Seminaries, Studies, and Catholic Education.
2. A compromise was reached, requiring that the theses maintained in the different volumes of this manual be translated into Latin. Congar would inaugurate the collection entitled 'The Christian Mystery' with *La Foi et la Théologie* (Tournai: Desclee, 1962), written from 1958-1959.
3. Auguste Brassac, who had brought out several issues of the *Manuel biblique* (Biblical Manual) by Louis Bacuez and Fulcran Vigouroux, saw one of them put on the Index by the Holy Office in 1923; cf Bernard Montagnes, OP, *Le Père Lagrange* (Paris: Cerf, 1995).

without mentioning the name, of the time of the Sapinière,[1] and adding that, when he came to Rome at the end of May, he would talk to him about the whole affair. And in fact, that is what he wishes to do.

I sent a very forcible reply to Tollu.[2] I really think that the French bishops ought to go ahead and ignore the senile threats of an idiot. But they will never have the unanimity of feeling among themselves that would give them the courage to do that.

At the invitation of Mgr Dubois, Archbishop of Besançon, I went to Besançon on 27/28 March. Mgr Dubois wished to bring together some members of the Theological Commission in order 'to survey the situation'. He had invited Fr de Lubac (who had insisted to me that I should go too), Mgr Bride, l'abbé Laurentin and myself. Unfortunately, Fr de Lubac was ill in bed and unable to come.

We were welcomed with great charm and cordiality. But one cannot say that there was much substance to the meeting. Mgr Dubois is not very theologically minded. Why is he the French bishop on this Commission? That is the question everybody is asking, including his fellow bishops, but nobody knows the answer. Is it due to the protection of Mgr Grente?[3] He did not say much to us and, even at the level of information, I learnt less in a day than in twenty-five minutes' conversation with Mgr Philips. By the evening of Monday 27 it was all over, and Laurentin had gone, not wishing to interrupt his current piece of work . . . I remained in Besançon as Mgr Dubois' guest all day Tuesday in order to go through the volumes of the *vota* of which he had nearly the whole set. I did a lot of work and did not regret the effort, even though I could not finish. I made a note of the place where I stopped and will try to continue at the Ascension.

Mgr Bride, Dean of the Faculty of Canon Law in Lyons, is a charming man, very informed and very efficient in canon law, but frightfully positivist in juridical matters. For him, the pope is the Vicar of Christ, in the sense that, after Christ, he

---

1. An integrist network at the beginning of the century.
2. In fact, on that same day (12 March, 1961), Congar wrote as follows to Tollu (Congar Archives): 'I think that it is all part of a wider whole: a reaction, in the most specific and almost political meaning of the word: a reaction of people who seek to cling to certain structures of influence, of which they occupy the key posts. Latin is one of these structures: it will be retained for as long as possible. As Mgr Weber was saying to me yesterday: it makes it possible not to think. There is now, in the climate of the pontificate of John XXIII that is so attractive from a human and Christian point of view, a reactionary and stupidly narrow clique which is showing itself in various ways and is endeavouring to keep the windows closed.' He then evoked, in contrast, the challenges of evangelisation and ended by describing the attitude to take: 'However, I find that the French Bishops could totally disregard certain threats. They are the ones of divine right . . . And in the name of what are these threats being made? Who or what entitles them to do so? All the same it is a question that one could certainly ask. There is no sin in recovering a freedom that has been stolen.'
3. A priest of the diocese of Le Mans, Marcel-M Dubois had been the disciple and friend of Cardinal George Grente, his bishop, who died in 1959.

truly has the powers of Christ himself, for example over the Sacraments. I have never met anyone else who went so far in this sense, except among the canonists of Gregory VII, in the thirteen and beginning of the fourteenth centuries. I contradicted him calmly but firmly.

From 6 to 9 April, christological colloquium in Évreux.[1] There I met Fr K Rahner.[2] Cardinal Ottaviani is against him, having recently summed up Rahner's position on the Mass as follows: for Rahner one devout Mass is worth more than one hundred Masses that are not devout . . . So he is blocking him. But Cardinal König and two or three other bishops have insisted that he should be appointed to a Council Commission. He has just been appointed consultor to the Commission on the Sacraments . . . He himself considers it laughable.

Mgr Marty, Archbishop of Rheims, was present throughout the colloquium. The bishop resident at Saint-Étienne[3] was there for part of it. Cardinal Gerlier and Mgr Villot[4] were there for my own presentation. I spoke to Mgr Marty. He told me that when he went to Rome as a member of the Studies Commission, Cardinal Pizzardo knelt before him and asked for his blessing! Mgr Marty, refusing to bless a cardinal, himself went on his knees. So there they both were, face to face, on their knees, rather ridiculously, he said. He also told me—which is more serious—that in the Commission there is unanimity of all the other members against the members who are from the Congregation for Seminaries and Universities. According to what I am hearing everywhere, this is what is happening in nearly all the Commissions.

Mgr Marty said: something will come of it. The bishops are beginning to like seeing one another, talking to one another. A lot has been lost, in recent decades, in not meeting with one another. There ought to be regular meetings. And Mgr Marty thinks that we are on the threshold of a conciliar era.

---

1. At L'Arbresle, at the time the house of studies for the Province of Lyons. The acts of this Colloquium have been published: H Bouëssé and J-J Latour (editors), *Problèmes actuels de christologie. Travaux du symposium de l'Arbresle 1961* (Bruges: 1965).
2. Karl Rahner, SJ, was one of the leading theologians of the twentieth century. He taught at Innsbruck, then, from 1964 onwards, in Munich; he was a consultor on the Preparatory Commission on the Discipline of the Sacraments, and was to be appointed a Council expert in 1962.
3. Marius Maziers, Auxiliary Bishop of Lyons.
4. Jean Villot, Coadjutor Archbishop of Lyons: on the death of Cardinal Gerlier in January 1965, he was to succeed him as Archbishop of Lyons and was created cardinal a month later; he was to be sub-secretary to the Council during the first three Sessions. He was later to be Prefect of the Congregation for Clergy, then Secretary of State to Pope Paul VI. The *Avant-Propos* of H Bouëssé adds that he took Cardinal Gerlier along to Congar's lecture (p 10).

After Évreux, I went to a Franco-British colloquium on authority at the abbey of Bec.[1] Mgr Martin came there one day, accompanied by his auxiliary.[2] In addition, Mgr Roberts[3] was there for the whole of the Colloquium. He told me (and he told others . . .) that he had had problems over his *Black Popes[4]* and the French translation. If I understood correctly, there was a process before the 'Holy Office'. He was asked to suppress, in any future edition, two historical chapters in which he had stated that there had been abuses, faults, and bad popes: in short, he was to suppress everything that might in any way derogate from the 'prestige of the Church' or the honour of the Holy See.

Always the same thing, the same faking, relating to the same points.

Mgr Roberts reacted: he saw the Pope, and wrote to him. Moreover, he has not been asked to remove the pages of criticism of the PRESENT exercise of authority: and those are the pages to which he himself is most attached . . .

12 July 1961

I saw Mgr Willebrands. The atmosphere in Rome does not seem to be very interesting. He sees it dominated by two great concerns, psychologically speaking:

1) 'Do not lean out of the window': *Pericoloso di sporgersi! Nicht hinauslehnen!*

2) A willingness for *tenderezza,* for gentleness. Not to upset anyone; that is why one says YES to everyone, without adopting a clear position, and then one arranges things either by means of a compromise or by a mutual cancelling out.

I wrote to the Holy Father, c/o the Nuncio. (cf here: copy[5])

---

1. The Benedictine Abbey of Bec-Hellouin in Normandy, Congar was to publish the act of this colloquim as *Problèmes de l'Autorité*, in 'Unam Sanctam', 38 (Paris: Cerf, 1962).
2. Joseph-M Martin, Archbishop of Rouen, and André Pailler, his Auxiliary, who was to become his Coadjutor in 1964.
3. Thomas Roberts, Jesuit, former Archbishop of Bombay.
4. Thomas Roberts, *Black Popes, Authority: its Use and Abuse* (London: 1954): French translation: Thomas Roberts, *Réflexions sur l'exercice de l'autorité* (Paris: Cerf, 1956).
5. In his letter to the Pope, dated 12 July, Congar wrote:
   'Most Holy Father,
   One of your sons comes to tell you of his anguish and his suffering.
   Called, by an interior vocation, in 1929, to work for ecumenism, I am a consultor of the Theological Commission for the forthcoming Council. Your Holiness has stated repeatedly that the Council is an internal matter for the Catholic Church, but that it ought to be aiming at, and arranging everything in such a way as ultimately to serve the cause of Christian unity.
   Your Holiness knows what intense interest and immense hopes the Council has aroused in the hearts of people throughout the world. This interest, these hopes, are above all linked to the prospect of reunion that has thus been opened.
   So that this long-term aim of the Council can be achieved, it will need to be present in all the preparatory work of the Council and at the Council itself: in everything that is done this intention and all the demands that it implies will need to be borne in mind.
   Now, what I see from the working of my own Commission, what I have been able to

24 August 1961

Catholic Conference for ecumenical matters.[1]

Fr Dumont told me that, when the Secretariat for Unity asked for a joint commission in conjunction with the Theological Commission, the answer was that there were no joint commissions except between actual Commissions and that, if the Theological Commission held a meeting with the Secretariat, the Commission would retain full freedom of judgement: IT would make the decisions, whereas, in the case of a truly joint commission, the decision would be taken by this joint commission itself.

Thus when, last November, I let fall the word 'commission' when speaking of Bea's Secretariat, Fr Tromp pointed out to me that it was not a commission but a secretariat. And this was already known because it had already been decided, because this was how they wanted things to be, that the Secretariat for Unity would not really take an active part in the preparatory work.

The further I go, the more I find that defect number 1 in the way things are organised in Rome is the partitioning off of things. Everything has its special place. That is all right when it is a question of administration and it is a question of knowing which office deals with what. It is a good administrative principle. But it is not a working principle for an intelligence seeking to attain reality, nor a pastoral principle.

In the past few days, I have read very attentively the Theological Commission's final texts. They contain some good things. The chapter *De Laicis* [on the Laity] expresses fairly closely my ideas and my own paper. It was prepared by Mgr Philips. However, in my view, the text as a whole has three major defects:

---

learn or hear about the work done by the others, with the exception of the Secretariat for Unity, makes me think that none of this is happening. Everything, or nearly everything, is being done as if the Council did not have this ultimate aim. The Secretariat for Unity is working very well, but the work it is doing is not having an effect on the work of the Commissions. When, at the end, it presents a certain number of reports to them, it will be too late: the work will have been done and there will be no beginning again. Moreover, often, the men who are working for the Council do not possess either the ecumenical spirit or the formation or information that would turn them into workers for ecumenism, and that requires 1) a specific vocation and 2) long years of work.

Most Holy Father, if the hopes aroused in so many hearts were to be deceived! If the exceptional opportunity of the Council were to be lost! This is my anguish, my suffering!

I pray every day for Your Holiness, for the Council, for the members of the Roman Curia and of the Commissions. And for all Catholic intentions.

It is in these sentiments and in the love of Christ that I am the most humble and most obedient servant of Your Holiness.

Fr Yves Marie Joseph CONGAR

of the Friars Preachers.'

1. It was held in Strasbourg on the theme: 'Renewal in the Church'.

1. It is very much in the scholastic mode, and also very scholarly. More than anything else, it is a series of chapters from a good manual. Some chapters are purely philosophical: in particular *De ordine sociali* [on the social order], which must have been written by an Italian.

2. It is a summary of papal documents over the past century: a sort of *syllabus* of these documents, including the ADDRESSES of Pius XII. That has the disadvantage of highlighting the errors which these documents have successively denounced. At times, errors of long ago. A Modernism which is already dead is slain yet again . . . There are strong words against interrupted sexual intercourse.[1] But above all the SOURCE is never the Word of God: it is the Church herself, and even the Church reduced to the pope, which is VERY serious.

3. There is NOTHING ecumenical. The only ecumenical reference is in the chapter on the Virgin Mary, in order to say that the Mother of God brings about, is an agent of, reunion between Christians. This does no more than state a very remote and theoretical truth, if it is not actually a fiction and, from the immediately concrete point of view, a counter-truth. I think that, if I were to make this remark to the people in Rome, they would reply that there will be a chapter on ecumenism. And in fact, there will be one, prepared by Fr Witte, but I have not yet received it. Once again, one comes back to compartmentalising: ecumenism is not to intervene in the theological work—on Scripture and Tradition, for example—it is a separate office, it has its own specialist . . .

Don Colombo told me that same day that it comes from Cardinal Ottaviani; that because he had so decided, the Theological Commission had so far not agreed to discuss anything with anyone, not even with the other official Commissions such as the Commission on the Liturgy. But, he added, it was not certain that this attitude would be maintained in the future. In the end, the question will be settled by the Pope.

It seems that Fr Tromp gave people to understand that, after the Commissions had done their work, when the texts had been produced in their final form, there would be a moment of contact between the Commissions.

When all is said and done, Cardinal Ottaviani has really thought of these things as an extension of the Holy Office, the 'Supreme Congregation'.

The drafts of 'Constitutions' which I have received are clearly serious pieces of work. However, I see three major flaws in them. I have hesitated to write an overall critique in the sense of what I write here. In the end, I have not done

---

1. In 1952, the Holy-Office had disapproved of this method of birth control, which had been defended in particular by Dr Paul Chanson, with the support of Henri Féret, OP, a close friend of Congar's. Cf the sixth chapter in the book by Martine Sevegrand, *Les Enfants du bon Dieu. Les catholiques français et la procréation au XXième siècle* (Paris: Albin Michel, 1995).

so because the work I have been asked to do has its rules. It calls for specific comments on each document, which the curial staff will then distribute to the various sub-commissions. To WHOM would one address general remarks which would, in the end, be the business of the Curia and its staff?

But my three criticisms are not unconnected:

1) It is very scholastic. You would think you had in your hands an extract from a good theological manual, or sometimes a philosophical one. Because it is also very philosophical. The *De ordine sociali* [on the social order] is a course in natural law or theoretical sociology. It contains little that is specifically Christian.

2) There is no trace of an ecumenical perspective or concern. The only mention in this sense is the reference Fr Balić makes at the end of his chapter on Our Lady. And then only in order to say that Mary will unite all Christians. At the same time his chapter, which is relatively moderate, will be a new cause of alienation, not only of Protestants but also of the Orthodox. Everything goes on as if promoting the reunion of Christians was not the ultimate aim of the Council.

3) It is not very biblical—except for the *De laicis* and some bits in *De Ordine Morali*. Scripture is almost never quoted except as a kind of ornamentation, conferring a kind of solemnity of style and in keeping with the literary genre. There has been no attempt to SEEK OUT scriptural formulations as forming the basis of all   formulations claiming to be normative. Formulations are adopted, and they are adopted as they are to be found in the various encyclicals, speeches and other utterances of the popes, from Pius IX to Pius XII. THE source is the Church. I see there the tragic outcome of the movement of which I traced the history in my *Tradition and Traditions*. There is now a veritable duality in the way things are done in Rome. On the one hand, the popes proclaim that Scripture and Tradition constitute the source and rule of everything, and that all they do is to guard and protect it. But, on the other hand, they behave, and they want everyone to behave—and they do all that they can, with an implacable power, to make sure that everyone does behave—as if the popes themselves were the source.

Fr Colombo said to me that, for Fr Tromp, an encyclical takes precedence over a clear text of Scripture.

All the work has been done as if the encyclicals were THE necessary and sufficient source.

It is a *novitas* [novelty], in the technical sense this word has in theology.

What can be done? I have criticised specific points as best I could. How to express a thorough and general criticism? I think that I shall find myself doing it *viva voce* in Rome, if there is a response to my criticisms, especially in mariology, that invokes papal utterances. It is extremely serious.

Visit to Rome in September 1961. I don't want to take this notebook with me. I shall take another, and insert the pages in this one when I return.

The same applies to November 1961. Summoned by Fr Gagnebet for the discussion of the sub-commission on ecumenism (concerning which I had submitted a *votum* at the beginning of October[1]), I will take the other notebook.

Sunday 17 September 1961
Take-off at 7.30 am or 7.40 am. We did nothing but fly over mountains: Vosges, Jurals, Alps. We flew over the West side of the lake of Geneva and directly over Grenoble.

An hour's stopover in Nice. What sun! Caravelle.

Landed in Rome at 12.50 pm. But the airport is ridiculously far from the city. I arrived at the Angelicum at 1.30 pm.

Conversation with Fr Witte, who said that I should come and stay in Rome to support him in ecumenical matters before the Council. He told me about a number of discussions he had had.

Paid a visit to Fr de Lubac and Fr S Lyonnet.[2]

Also paid visits to Frs Gillon, Labourdette, Gagnebet and the new rector of the Angelicum, Fr Sigmond.[3]

Monday 18 September 1961
Meeting at 9.30 am at the Cancelleria. People greeted one another, met again, introduced themselves to one another. All were not present, as that would be a great many: nearly sixty people. In the room, a room in a Roman palace with a high ceiling, the members were seated around a very long rectangular table. The consultors were seated behind them on plain armchairs the right arm of which ended in the form of a very practical little table. It was understood that the members could speak as they wished and vote or decide on their own. The consultors did not speak unless asked to do so. None of them spoke this morning. On the other hand, their written remarks were taken into consideration.

---

1. This written proposition, completed on 18 October, was printed on 27 October by the Preparatory Theological Commission.
2. Stanislas Lyonnet, SJ, Professor of New Testament Exegesis and Dean of the Biblical Faculty of the Pontifical Biblical Institute; he was to be debarred from teaching from 1962 to 1964.
3. Raymond Sigmond, OP, of the Province of Hungary, a sociologist, was President of the Institute of Social Sciences at the Angelicum of which he was also Rector until 1964; he was also a consultor to the Preparatory Theological Commission and then a Council expert in 1962; he was to be appointed a member of the Commission on the Study of the Problems of Population, the Family, and Birth Control in 1965, and then consultor to the Secretariat for Non-believers in 1966.

After an opening speech by Cardinal Ottaviani and a report by Fr Tromp, work began on the text of the new Profession of Faith.[1] For each phrase, the rapporteur—in the present instance Fr Tromp—read the phrase, indicated the principal comments that had been made concerning it, then briefly explained why and how one had, or had not, taken it into account. Fr Tromp did this with great skill, in a Latin that was clear, precise and comprehensible. It was principally the Bishop of Eichstätt,[2] Fr Ciappi, and Fr Dhanis (who seemed to be much heeded), who intervened; Cardinal Ottaviani played a purely presidential role, inviting people to speak, drawing particular discussions to a close, moving on to the next point.

None of the consultors intervened. I spoke to several of the bishops, in particular the Bishop of Eichstätt, and Don Colombo, in order to persuade them to ask for a change in the text. As it stands, it refers only to Peter and his successors as the shepherds to whom Christ had entrusted his Church. I myself prepared a memorandum on this point which I gave to Fr Ciappi, who is the President of the sub-commission *De Deposito fidei* [On the Deposit of the Faith], which is responsible for the Profession of Faith. The next day, the Bishop of Eichstätt showed me the text he had produced which calls, more fully, for a less JURIDICAL formulation of the way the faith is given expression in the Church. Don Colombo told me that he had done something along the lines I had suggested: his text, which is shorter than mine, has a chance of being accepted and would be a real improvement.

In the afternoon, I rested (siesta and prayer) and worked. I am very tired. I am having difficulty in walking and going upstairs. I have no strength and my arms droop, weak.

Tuesday 19 September 1961
Plenary session at 9.30 am *On the Sources of Revelation*. The rapporteur was Mgr Garofalo, President of the sub-commission. Like all Italians, he spoke a voluble, strongly accented Latin, which was difficult to understand. A very lively discussion
arose following an intervention by Fr Tromp drawing attention to a text of Pius XII's in a speech at the Gregorianum saying that '*Ecclesia ipsa sibi est FONS*' [The Church is herself her own SOURCE]. Fr Tromp sought to make Tradition and Magisterium, or rather Tradition and the preaching of the Magisterium, identical. Fortunately, one member, whom I later learned was Mgr Piolanti, contradicted him vigorously (in an Italian-like Latin); then Fr Balić. Fr Gagnebet asked the cardinal to ask the consultors what they thought, in order to give me an opportunity to speak (he signalled to me). Fr Salaverri was then called upon

---

1. The Pope had asked the Preparatory Theological Commission to prepare a new Profession of Faith in view of the Council.
2. Joseph Schröffer, Bishop of Eichstätt (Germany).

(fluent Latin, but fast: he spoke at length, and I had difficulty in understanding, but fortunately it calmed the very great excitement aroused by the discussion), then I myself, followed by Mgr Lattanzi.

I said that for one text of Pius XI there are thirty or forty from Vatican Council I and from the popes since Pius IX which distinguish between tradition as a deposit or objective norm, and the magisterium which is an agency equipped to preserve and explain it. Moreover, even the text we were dealing with spoke of *'Fontibus'* [sources] in this way.

The cardinal said that the question would be taken up again by the sub-commission. Afterwards, I went to see Mgr Piolanti who spoke to me at length in ultra-voluble Italian from which I understood him to say that, as he saw it, we were faced here with a thesis from the GREGORIANUM, proclaimed by Pius XII AT THE GREGORIANUM = a Jesuit trick in the legendary sense of the word. In short, a question of ecclesiastical politics.

That afternoon. Fr Gagnebet organised a meeting of the sub-commission for *De Ecclesia* at the Angelicum, in order to make headway with the discussion on the constitution *De Ecclesia* and to give more opportunity to the consultors. The meeting was not official. We discussed the chapter *De laicis*. Mgr Philips had both written the text and acted as rapporteur. I made the acquaintance of Mgr Griffiths,[1] Cardinal Spellman's auxiliary,[2] who asked me twice to lay stress on the liturgy.

20 September 1961

Plenary session: Work on *De fontibus revelationis* [on the sources of revelation] was completed. Before the meeting began, I saw Mgr Garofalo. I realised that he had not understood the point in my request to retain the Council of Trent's use of 'Gospel'.[3] I explained the point to him. Fr Salaverri intervened and suggested a double application of the idea of *'Fons'*: 1) *fons principium* [source as origin]; 2) *fons in quo hauritur* [source as that from which one draws]. In the first sense, the source is only Christ and the preached Gospel; in the second sense, the source is *depositum scriptum et depositum non scriptum* [the written and unwritten deposit].

Mgr Garofalo asked us to write a brief paragraph which he would insert into the text submitted to the Central Commission because, he said, there are friends there . . .

---

1. James H Griffiths, Auxiliary Bishop of New York, member of the Preparatory Theological Commission, then member of the Doctrinal Commission. He was to die in February 1964.
2. Cardinal Francis Spellman, Archbishop of New York. He was to become a member of the Council of Presidents and of the Co-ordinating Commission.
3. Congar was to note, in a letter to Carlo Colombo on 27 April 1962, that the Council of Trent spoke of only one source, the Gospel, which comes to us in two complementary ways, Scripture and Tradition.

If this were done, I would be pleased to have gained this point. I wrote the text and gave it to him; later on, I referred Mgr Garofalo to the Biblical Institute's excellent *votum*: Acta et Doc IV Fac et Univ Pars I, R 1961, p 125-26.[1]

Rather a heavy discussion on exegetes and theologians. The cardinal asked the consultors to prepare a text on this point.

In the afternoon, at the Angelicum: meeting of the sub-commission *De Ecclesia*. Only Chapter 2 *De Episcopatu* [on the Episcopate] was discussed. I had not imagined that it would elicit so many detailed comments. Mgr Bride once again displayed the utter positivism of a canonist.

21 September 1961

In the morning, we began examining the Constitution *De ordine morali* [on the moral order]. Rapporteur: Fr Tromp in the absence of Fr Hürth, who is more than half dead. It is a strong text, which responds well to today's errors. I approved it, while at the same time regretting that the specifically Christian note was not sufficiently marked. But it would have been necessary to re-do it and write it differently.

Generally speaking, I had understood that the texts we had been given to study were fixed and substantially unchangeable. That is why I settled for making a few remarks on the text as it stood. Canon Delhaye, who was next to me, was very unhappy. He told me that at the sub-commission *De re morali*, Fr Gillon had been odious; that no notice had been taken of his remarks, even when his *votum* was read out (Mgr Philips confirmed that this was so). Delhaye, too, instead of intervening even when the cardinal invited the consultors to do so, retires to his tent and grumbles under his breath.

In the afternoon, at the Franciscans, at the Marian Academy Centre, a meeting dedicated to the chapter *De Beata Maria Virgine*. And first of all on general and preliminary matters. Fr Balić, alas, had the floor. He made a voluble sales-pitch. I leaned towards my neighbour, Mgr Philips, and asked him: is he selling braces or socks? Fr Balić is pure passion. He cannot bear to be contradicted; often, he does not even let the other speak. At one point, the discussion reached an ultra-high pitch between Fr Balić and Fr Salaverri. Having kept himself under control, the latter exploded. He shouted in order to be heard in spite of the fact that Balić too was shouting. Salaverri wanted to assert that a Conciliar Constitution was above a papal encyclical.

Two preliminary and general questions were looked at:

1. Should the chapter be kept in the Constitution *De Ecclesia*, or should it be transferred to the Constitution *De Deposito Fidei pure Custodiendo* [On keeping pure the Deposit of the Faith] ? Each one gave his opinion. Most were in favour of keeping it where it was, but then it would be necessary for the relationship between Mary and the Church to be better formulated.

---

1. AD I/IV, 1/2, 123–136

2. Should one, for the sake of non-Catholics, tone down certain expressions and even not go quite as far (!) as some papal utterances. Fr García,[1] animator of the Spanish Marian Weeks, came out very strongly against any toning down. Fr Philippe de la Trinité[2] too, but less forcefully. I spoke along the following lines:

    a. The only question to be answered is what God is asking of us and the Church. He is asking the Church to be faithful. Faithful to the deposit, which is primarily Sacred Scripture. In our day, when a growing number of the faithful are nourishing themselves at the biblical sources, when, in many countries (I mentioned Brazil), Catholics cannot avoid the questions being asked by Protestants, we must not indulge in imaginative and pious exaggerations but rely on Scripture.

    b. The Church must declare its faith. She should do so frankly, without diminution, by means of a profession of faith, and BY EXPLAINING the reasons for her faith, how she has arrived at that point and must stick there in order to be faithful. She should say: I, the Church, I was at Calvary, I was in the Upper Room, I was at the Council of Ephesus . . . Down through the centuries I have come to understand this and that. Ecumenism is also a will of God for his Church, in the twentieth century. And taking it into account belongs to the fidelity of the Church.

L'abbé Laurentin spoke strongly and courageously in the sense of doing our utmost to: 1) declare FIRST OF ALL what we hold in common, at all events, what we hold in common with the Orthodox; 2) then develop. And do so as far as possible in terms of the Bible and tradition, avoiding all that does not have serious and ancient roots in tradition.

Fr Balić, with good humour, to some extent combined with a kind of clowning, reproached Laurentin, whom he had had appointed to the Commission (Fr Gagnebet told me that he had done all he could to bring into the Commission as many mariologists as he could), for giving in to ecumenism—in which, judging by the evidence, Balić himself does not believe.

It seems that a non-minimising, but very eirenical declaration will be made, explaining '*modo pacato*' [peacefully] (Mgr Philips) the faith of the Church and the reasons for it.

A third point was tackled, which set Fr Balić off once again: the question of the DEATH of Our Lady. The Council would like to declare the fact of this death. As

---

1. The Claretian, Narciso García Garcés was the founder of the Spanish Mariological Centre and also of the journal *Ephemerides Mariologicae*; consultor of the Preparatory Theological Commission, he was also consultor to the Spanish bishops at the Council.
2. Jean Rambaud, in religion Philippe de la Trinité, OCD, taught at the Discalced Carmelite Theology Faculty in Rome. He was President of this Faculty until 1963; he was also a consultor on the Preparatory Theological Commission.

the immortalists[1] have appealed a great deal to Pius XII, Fr Balić told us, under the secret of the Holy Office, that Pius XII was personally convinced of her death. He told us a lot about the drawing up of the Constitution *Munificentissimus*[2]. But I am not able to summon up interest in these intrigues that our Dalmatian street vendor likes so much.

22 September 1961

I tried to do some work, because one must prepare the discussion, read the comments . . . Moreover, I keep being asked for my opinion concerning various texts:

Laurentin on a text in place of the *De BVM*;

Don Colombo on his chapter *De Magisterio* [on the Magisterium];

Fr Gagnebet on the draft chapter *De œcumenismo*, prepared by Fr Witte. He has asked me to prepare a *votum* about this.

The state of my health is very worrying. I can hardly walk; the first two or three fingers of the right hand opposite the thumb are almost dead or paralysed. I have no strength!

This morning, we went on examining *De ordine morali*. I saw Mgr Janssen (from Louvain), Canon Delhaye and Fr de Lubac. They were fairly despondent and embittered. No notice has been taken, or is being taken, of their opinions. Those based in Rome take care of everything among themselves. 'We are nothing but hostages'. And they are totally dissatisfied with the draft of the Constitution *De ordine morali*.

In the evening, at the Antonianum (Hall of Promotions), discussion of the actual text of the Chapter *De B Maria V*. I saw there the drama which I have experienced all my life. The need to fight, in the name of the Gospel and of apostolic faith, against a development, a Mediterranean and Irish proliferation, of a mariology which does not come from Revelation, but is backed up by pontifical texts. Several times, I was told that the rule of faith is not Scripture but the living Magisterium; what do you make of the papal pronouncements? I understand better the way Luther reacted, for *this* was the reply he, too, was given. He threw overboard all texts and all ecclesiastical authority in order to hold fast to Scripture alone.

At first, the discussion was quite tough going. Fortunately, Laurentin is brave, measured and knowledgeable. He fights the anti-maximalist battle. We tell each other that we must not be TOO antagonistic, for fear of bringing about worse than what we are anxious to avoid. Two things are certain, about which we can do nothing: 1) the existence of the pontifical texts and of mariological currents; 2) the existence of more than 450 requests from bishops in the *vota*. What we can

---

1. Those who believe that the Virgin Mary did not know death before her glorification.
2. The Apostolic Constitution *Munificentissumus Deus* proclaimed the dogma of the Assumption of Mary.

do is to work towards achieving a relatively cautious text by seeking to tone down some turns of phrase which the maximalists would take advantage of in order to go even further.

On the whole, things did not go too badly. On one hand, I accept quite a lot of positive Marian thinking. On the other hand, Fr Gagnebet, Fr Balić and the others are patient and objective in their approach. But I don't think we can take our opposition any further, and we have achieved some considerable improvements.

23 September 1961

In the morning, the chapter *De Matrimonio*. Numerous and courageous interventions by Fr Häring. Fr Lio, who drafted the text, defended it at length and vehemently. Fr Tromp, too, was also quite intractable. However, the discussion secured something, and at least a promise of improvement on two very important points: 1) birth control, which was referred back, in general terms, to the Holy Office text.[1] 2) the ends of marriage. Fr Lio defended, as being a precious dogma, the idea of children being the primary, principal and sole specific end of marriage. Fr Hürth also came to his aid by saying that it is THE *finis operis* [the purpose of the action], THE end wished by God when he instituted marriage, even though mutual aid, and living together, are often primary in the order of the *finis operantis* [the end sought by the one performing the action]. That seems to me insufficient, even from the point of view of divine institution.

Mgr Janssen, from Louvain, intervened with great courage and perseverance. And HE SECURED SOMETHING. I congratulated him and thanked him.

The whole of this week has taught me a lesson concerning the psychology of meetings which will probably apply also to the Council: 1) When one persists in one's objection or criticism, one always ends up by gaining something; 2) when there is discussion and opposition, the person who calmly suggests a formula has a good chance of being listened to. This often happens with Mgr Philips.

The consultors are complaining of being treated as unimportant. Normally, they do not attend the meetings of their sub-commissions except when they are formally invited to do so. I was told that Mgr Janssen calmly went to the meeting of the one *De re morali*. Fr Tromp told him that he ought not to be there. But he was there, and there he remained. He even intervened in the discussion. Some people protested at this, but he calmly went on . . .

I gave Don Colombo three pages of comments on his chapter *De Magisterio*.

Afternoon: Discussion of the chapter *De Episcopis* with the man who had written it, Schauf. I tried to speak on behalf of the Easterners who were not present. I was told that there is an Eastern Commission . . . (always the same dividing up into compartments)—and that it had acknowledged that the powers of the patriarchs which, in any case, are of ecclesiastical law, are granted to them by the pope . . .

---

1. The Holy Office had published a *Monitum* on 30 June, 1952.

A visit from Mlle Yvonne Batard,[1] from Fr Féret's group.[2] She wants to put a taxi at our disposal tomorrow for an outing of about 120 km: we will pay anything over and above the initial down payment.

I am told that Mgr Journet has gone. He understands almost nothing and can neither follow what is said nor intervene. Moreover, they say that when he does intervene, all he does is to repeat his own opinions without ever entering into the question or the problem as stated by the others. What a shame! Because he could have introduced a THEOlogical and spiritual tone, which is greatly lacking. Everything is formulated very juridically. This is clear in the case of Schauf too, who is Tromp's creature. The liturgical and mystical aspect of the episcopate passes him by completely, or rather he is not interested in it.

As for Fr Tromp, he plays a decisive role: he dominates the Commission, in both senses of the word 'dominate'. On the one hand, for the intellectual worth, the force, clarity, vigour of his vision of things and of his statements. He has the gift of stripping the matter in hand down to its essentials from the point of view of clarity, and of stating them forcefully. On the other hand, he has a fascist temperament. Clearly, for him, the less parliament there is, the better. He behaves like a dictator, he speaks in a loud voice, bangs his fist on the table, storms at those who oppose him. However, he does allow people to object and, if his opponent manages to withstand the first onslaught, is even able to give way and side with him.

Fortunately, Fr Tromp has not been coming to our private meetings. We could not have said the things we did say. Fr Gagnebet has behaved with fraternity and humility in arranging these meetings, and in conducting them as he has done. He really wants everyone to have the opportunity to say what they want to say.

Sunday 24 September 1961

We left at 10 am with Frs Labourdette and Laurentin. First Anagni. It is a small very populous town on a peak in the middle of a wide and grandiose landscape at the foot of the mountains. The narrow road leading to it was crowded with people. It reminded me of the atmosphere in the East. Frequently, today, I found myself recalling scenes in the Holy Land. The cathedral, on the side of which (Innocent III Square) a statue of Boniface VIII was enthroned, is a monastic type building, bare and noble. Not a bit like the baroque Rome of St Peter's. As it was nearly noon, a Mass was about to begin at the top of a nave which was nearly empty. What a contrast between this semi-death and the street outside teeming

---

1. Specialist in comparative literature.
2. Henri-Marie Féret, OP, of the Province of France, involved in liturgical renewal, and in studying the biblical sources of theology. Like Chenu and Congar, he had been dismissed from the teaching staff of Le Saulchoir due to the pressure of Roman suspicions. In 1941 he had founded the 'Evangelical Group' comprising laypeople anxious to deepen their faith. Prior of the Priory in Dijon until 1964, during the Council he was to be personal expert to Mgr Flusin, Bishop of Saint-Claude.

with life! We had to wait before we could visit the cathedral. We took advantage of the wait to go and find some bread and pieces of fruit. Which we did with some difficulty.

At one pm the cathedral was empty.

Nave dating from the eleventh or twelfth century, bare and noble. Crypt with extraordinarily interesting paintings. I understand that Mlle Batard found there material for studying both iconography and the history of art. A second crypt is clearly an ancient pagan temple and closely resembles the Mythraeum located below the Basilica of San Clemente. There, too, paintings that would need to be studied in detail, with the necessary technique.

Once again, the grandiose landscape encircled by mountains with strange shapes. I had another look at Boniface VIII and reconstructed Nogaret's surprise attack.

The street urchins came begging. Some hunters had left a fox cub they had just killed in the middle of the square . . .

Subiaco. Mountains, valleys and passes. The valley of St Benedict's grotto is quite narrow and deep (the grotto is from 650 to 660 metres deep) richly wooded with fine very green trees with large twisted trunks. The place was filled with a silence that I savoured greedily to the full. It is extremely beautiful. It was from here that religious and moral education spread throughout the West. I prayed my Benedictine intentions. I sent to Pradines[1] some feathers from three crows that the Fathers keep in an aviary.

Return journey through a very beautiful long valley, which the young Benedict must have traversed when he left Rome for the solitary life.

Tivoli, Villa d'Este. Crowd of silly, noisy human beings, whose body odour was scarcely endurable.

Back once more in the busy, stupid city.

Long live silence!

Laurentin told me a lot about his remarks and interventions. Those that he made in relation to *De ordine morali* upset Fr Tromp, he thinks. He had reacted to a point that, stupidly, I had completely missed. I regret this, as I would have reacted as Laurentin did. It concerns the presentation of ownership in the exclusive or predominant sense of private ownership. In reacting, Laurentin used the thesis of Gilles Couvreur[2] who had been warmly supported at the Gregorianum by Fr Jarlot.[3] Laurentin had seen this Father. Although in no way connected with

---

1. {Benedictine monastery where his sister and niece were nuns}.
2. Gilles Couvreur, *Les pauvres ont-ils des droits? Recherches sur le vol en cas d'extrême nécessité depuis la Concordia de Gratien (1140) jusqu'à Guillaume d'Auxerre (+ 1231)* (Paris-Rome, 1961). Gilles Couvreur, Mission de France priest, was at that time teaching at the Mission de France seminary in Pontigny.
3. Georges Jarlot, SJ, Professor of Social Doctrine at the Gregorianum, member of the Preparatory Commission on the Lay Apostolate, had written a highly laudatory preface to Gilles Couvreur's thesis.

the Commission, it was this Father who, at Fr Tromp's request, had written the paragraph on property. And he declared to Laurentin that, though he thought like Gilles Couvreur and like Laurentin himself did (I add: like the Tradition does), he had nonetheless written his text in favour of private property only, because he had been asked to do so!

The contempt for the Tradition, this masking of the truth, are sickening and despicable. But the truth will prevail.

These Rome-based theologians have no respect for the Tradition. All they can see are papal utterances. That is where the great battle will continue to be waged. The truth will prevail.

I have studied extensively the history of ecclesiological ideas and of the growth in papal authority. I am very struck to see a process similar to the one that took place there being applied in our own day to mariology. It is the same way of behaving, the same process. In both cases, an enormous outgrowth resting on two or three texts, with no certainty that these texts meant originally what they are now being taken to mean, and in which the ancient tradition had not seen all that is now seen in them, even if, sometimes, it had not understood the opposite. They go on repeating, here *'Tu es Petrus'* [You are Peter (Mt 16:18)], there *'gratia plena'* [full of grace (Lk 1:28)], *'stabat'* [She stood (by the foot of the cross)(Jn 19:25)], *'conteret caput tuum'* [She will crush your head (Gen 3:15)], etc. In each case, tirelessly, patiently, across the centuries, little steps forward are constantly being taken which, at the time, seem of little account. One is not too happy, perhaps, indeed, one does not agree; but one will not create a schism over that, one will not even maintain simple resistance over such a trifle. In each case, there is ONE idea only: to increase, to take as far as possible either a power or a glory. In each case, there is only one aim, and advantage is taken of everything for the sake of that. EVERYTHING IS MADE USE OF. In each case you are told, it is pointed out to you that, having granted such and such, you cannot refuse such other; that having gone as far as three, you cannot not agree to go as far as ten . . . In each case, a point gained is never let go of, they just go on adding to it.

At 9.30 pm, arrival of a group of provincials and their *socii* [1] from the General Chapter in Bologna for an audience with the Pope. Fr Kopf [2] is at Santa Sabina and his *socius* [3] has already left.

Monday 25 September 1961
I had a brief word with the Provincial of Brazil, [4] who wanted to talk to me. He told me 1) how bitterly disappointed he was in the General Chapter. It was extremely banal and brief. Fr Browne himself is just that. He ought to resign. 2) His anxiety

---

1. Companions: at General Chapters each provincial is accompanied by a companion (*socius*) delegated by his Province.
2. Joseph Kopf, OP, was the Provincial of France.
3. Pierre-Léopold Grégoire, OP, of the Province of France.
4. Mateus Rocha, OP.

about Brazil. The young people are all left-wing. People are looking to Fidel Castro. The Americans are detested. They need men. The government wants to found a faculty of theology in Brasilia. Would I agree to come? At least to give a series of courses?

I replied that unfortunately I was too old, too tired. And too involved in a hundred and one things. Younger people would be needed for such a task. Moreover, I am afraid that people put a label on me and then interpret what I might say in a particular sense . . .

At the Commission meeting, we plunged fairly quickly into *De deposito fidei* [on the deposit of faith]. This was Fr Ciappi assisted by Fr Dhanis. Quite a few people were missing (we were thirty-seven in all) and the room was stifling. I see a great lassitude in the consultors; one does nothing, no account is taken of what we say; the whole thing is confined to those based in Rome.

When I read the texts and wrote my comments a month ago, I thought these texts were definitive and that only comments on minor details were in order. Even then it seemed to me that, taken individually and together, they ought to be written DIFFERENTLY. This is even clearer to me today. Everything is viewed 1) from a natural point of view: natural law, reason, rational proofs concerning God; 2) juridically; 3) whenever there is question of the life of human beings and a bit of initiative, this is viewed negatively by way of concessions that concede as little as possible, and that reluctantly.

The God we are dealing with here, knowledge of whom is the subject of our discussion, is almost exclusively the God whose existence can be demonstrated by reason. Everything which might sound Christian and evangelical has been excluded. Fr de Lubac intervened at one point to make this point. People listened to him and he was asked to propose a text.

This was good. But it is the whole thing that needs to be rewritten!

Laurentin made a number of comments along the same lines on the subject of morality. As far as possible, it was the legal aspect that had been emphasised, the most Christian statements having been excluded.

I lunched with Canon Delhaye. He was extremely disappointed and embittered. He is thinking of making a stir by resigning. He told me that, once he was back in France, he would make known as far as possible how things are going, how little notice is being taken of us, of him. He told me that at the sub-commission *De ordine morali*, Fr Tromp had systematically eliminated everything that is Christian and that speaks of charity. According to him, morality is principally a matter of commandments and PROHIBITIONS. Fr Hürth had said that Our Lord had only spoken of charity '*per transenam*' [in passing], when replying to a question put to Him by one of the Pharisees . . . As Delhaye sees it, everything is managed by the Holy Office, which wants to secure a kind of *syllabus* of modern condemnations.

Delhaye spoke to me critically of Laurentin and of the way he behaved at his little meeting in Paris to which he had invited me. According to Delhaye, he took advantage of what all the others said in order to prepare his own remarks. It could be true. But it does not matter by whom a thing is discovered and said. The essential is that it should be said.

On the other hand, Laurentin has been brave, though a bit naïve perhaps in what he says. He has committed himself.

Before coming here, I, too had thought of resigning in order to make a gesture which would alert public opinion and the bishops. I spoke of the idea to Fr de Lubac, who expressly advised me against it. I very much agree with Delhaye on the basics: Rome is only interested in its own authority, not in the Gospel. But I would certainly not like to hitch my wagon to Delhaye's tractor. There is a truly irritating personal and passionate factor in his reactions. I have the impression that we are far from singing in the same key.

In the afternoon I was free, as Fr Gagnebet had told me specifically not to come to the formal meetings of the sub-commission (but Fr Labourdette has been invited to those of his sub-commission).

I wrote some letters and had a short talk with Fr Trémel,[1] *socius* from Lyons at the General Chapter. He told me that this Chapter was lamentable and that Fr Browne is an old fogey; counting Fr Gomez[2] and the *socii*, that makes five old fogies in all, he told me. It is a void, nothingness. He also told me that the Chapter had rejected a *ratio studiorum* [programme of studies] prepared by Santa Sabina[3] which the Congregation for Religious had itself declared unsatisfactory. He had the feeling that provinces thinking along our lines were a tiny minority in an Italian, Spanish and American world that is very different. Fr Léonard[4] said the same thing to me, only more discreetly.

As I had some time, I read the *vota* of the Universities. Or, rather, I began to read them: those from the ROMAN faculties alone occupy two enormous volumes. Those from the Gregorianum: fine. Those from the Biblical Institute: excellent.

Propaganda[5] and above all the Lateran did not submit *vota* but lengthy dissertations. Who will read all that?

It was I who shortened Fr Gagnebet's text.

Tuesday 26 September 1961

I continued reading the *vota*. The one from the Angelicum is staggering in its poverty, its negativity, its sorry narrowness.

Sacra Doctrina!

---

1. Yves-Bernard Trémel, OP, exegete, of the Province of Lyons.
2. Esteban Gómez, OP, of the Province of Spain, *socius* of the Master General for the Spanish provinces. The Master General was assisted by several such *socii*.
3. That is, by the General Curia resident at Santa Sabina.
4. Augustin Léonard, OP, of the Southern Belgium Province, who attended the Chapter as *socius* of this Province.
5. The Congregation of Propaganda.

The *votum* submitted by the Salesians is far more serious and realistic. But it is in effect a whole book: forty-eight *vota*, explained and defended, concerning the entire life of the Church . . .

Wednesday 27 September 1961

This morning I gave my talk at the Biblical Week[1] in honour of St Paul. Quite a large and very responsive audience. Some friends: Fr Gribomont,[2] J Dupont;[3] some well-known people: Mgr Jenny, Mgr Pellegrino,[4] Coppens,[5] Fr Levie,[6] Fr Raes,[7] Fr Prümm, SJ.[8] The latter told me to criticise Fr Gaechter,[9] who exaggerates . . .

I arrived very late for the Commission. They were still discussing '*In quo omnes peccaverunt*'.[10] Fr de Lubac told me that the discussion had been going on for half an hour. There followed a fairly tense discussion on a chapter condemning polygenism. Fr Labourdette in a few words, Mgr Philips defending himself at length and step by step, both wanted nothing added to what was said in *Humani Generis*.[11] But the Commission wants to go further. Fr Tromp asked: Do you think that the condemnation of polygenism as it has been formulated (that is, saying more than in *Humani Generis*) is CONTAINED in the Biblical texts and in the text of the Council of Trent concerning Original Sin?—Embarrassed silence: this silence ended in an overwhelming majority in the affirmative.

---

1. The Acts were published by the Pontifical Biblical Institute: see *Studiorum paulinorum congressus internationalis catholicus 1961,* Rome, 1963; Congar gave a talk on 'Saint Paul and the authority of the Roman Church according to the tradition'.
2. Jean Gribomont, OSB, monk of the Abbey of Clervaux (Luxemburg), later sent to the Abbey of St Jerome in Rome, Director of the critical edition of the Vulgate.
3. Jacques Dupont, OSB, of the Abbey of Saint Andrew in Bruges, where he taught Sacred Scripture.
4. Michele Pellegrino, specialist in the Fathers of the Church, and in particular in St Augustine, taught at the University of Turin; he was to be appointed Archbishop of Turin in September 1965.
5. Josef Coppens, priest of the diocese of Gand, exegete and professor at the University of Louvain.
6. Jean Levie, SJ, New Testament specialist and professor at the Jesuit Theological College at Eegenhoven-Louvain (Belgium).
7. The Belgian Jesuit Alphonse Raes, Professor of Eastern Liturgy and President of the Pontifical Oriental Institute, until he became Prefect of the Vatican Apostolic Library in 1962; having been appointed a Council expert in 1962, he became a member of the Secretariat for Unity in 1963.
8. Karl Prümm, SJ, Professor of Exegesis at the Pontifical Biblical Institute.
9. Paul Gaechter, SJ, Professor of Exegesis at Innsbruck; in his communication to the Congress, Congar referred in a footnote to P Gaechter, *Petrus und seine Zeit. Neutestamentliche Studien* (Innsbruck-Vienna-Munich, 1958).
10. 'In whom all have sinned' (Rom 5:12): but there are problems with the translation and interpretation of the verse.
11. Encyclical published by Pope Pius XII in 1950.

However, the embarrassment was so palpable that I do not think things will be left thus. I said something about it to the rapporteur, Fr Trapè,[1] and tomorrow morning I will intervene—unless the thing, absolutely decided and concluded, is not brought up again for discussion in any way.

That evening, I dined with Mgr Arrighi. Mgr Gouet, secretary to the bishops was also there. We spoke mainly about the Little Church,[2] and Fr Gagnebet told me that the Holy See had made approaches towards it: the Pope had written personally a very fine letter; a bishop, a former missionary in China,[3] had been appointed with personal jurisdiction. It would be acknowledged, if they return to the Catholic Church that, for two generations, they would be under the jurisdiction of their own bishop with personal jurisdiction. Mgr Gouet, who does not seem to have known about these arrangements, promised to do something. It would seem that what had been agreed under Pius XII in 1950 had come unstuck, owing to the group in Lyons. This is the group that needs to be won over; otherwise what would be accomplished in Deux-Sèvres would be as nil.

28 September 1961

This morning I returned a text on monogenism to Fr Ciappi. I discussed the matter again with Fr Labourdette who is entirely of my opinion. He has been told the following by Fr Dhanis: 1) it is Fr Tromp who wants to go further than Pius XII; 2) at the time of *Humani Generis*, Fr Bea had tried to persuade Pius XII to move in the same direction. But Pius XII had resisted and deliberately stuck to the formula which we, too, would still like to see retained.

The question of monogenism was not re-opened. I put away my memorandum. Instead, much discussion concerning the fate of children who die unbaptised.

At 12.30 pm, I encountered a closed door at the Museum of the Baths of Diocletian.

The next session is set for February or March 1962 . . .!!!!

I read the *vota* from the bishops of Africa. Mgr Marcel Lefebvre[4] Archbishop of Dakar (*Acta et Doc.* Sn I (*anteprep*) vol I pars V. R. 1960, p 48):[5] 'Against the

---

1. Agostino Trapè, OSA, specialist in St Augustine, taught at the Lateran; member of the Preparatory Theological Commission, he was to be appointed a Council expert in 1962.
2. Church born of the rejection of the Concordat between Pius VII and Bonaparte in 1801.
3. Alexandre Derouineau, of Missions Étrangères de Paris, former Bishop of Kunming (China) had been sent by Pius XII on a mission to Poitou after his expulsion from the People's Republic of China.
4. The Holy Ghost Father Marcel Lefebvre was a member of the Central Preparatory Commission. Transferred, in January 1962, to the episcopal see of Tulle, he was elected Superior General of the Holy Ghost Fathers in June 1962.
5. *AD* 1/II, 5, 48.

errors of Fr Congar in his book *Essai d'une théologie pour le laïcat*.[1] Define the value of the Holy Sacrifice of the Mass, the extension of its graces even to pagans and unbelievers. Specify the place of the laity in the Church and give precise notions concerning Catholic Action. Fortunately, the latest encyclicals have already clarified some issues, but it is very opportune to deny definitively some erroneous ideas which have caused considerable damage.'

Request that there be a definition or statement that the Blessed Virgin Mary is the mediatrix of all graces . . .

In the afternoon, paid a visit to Fr de Lubac at the Gregorianum. He is very fed up, very crushed. He is convinced that Fr Dhanis has inserted into the document *De Deposito* [On the Deposit of the Faith] a No. 22 against himself. Fr de Lubac has in fact found there EXACTLY what Fr Dhanis had imputed to him in the troubles that Fr de Lubac has experienced since 1950. Fr Dhanis knew Fr Janssens,[2] current General of the Society, who brought him to Rome and has to some extent made him his theologian. It is Dhanis who, from the Jesuit side in Rome, handled matters concerning Fr de Lubac. The latter is convinced that Fr Dhanis is taking advantage of the Council and of the quite important part he is playing in it, to justify his attacks against de Lubac and Teilhard de Chardin, and that, when he has his text, he will say: they are condemned in these paragraphs.

Fr de Lubac has seen Fr Dhanis and has asked him whom he had in mind by the phrase '*qui sentient*' [who think that] . . . Dhanis refused to give him an answer and when de Lubac insisted, Dhanis said to him: I have my reasons.

Fr de Lubac has decided to write a letter to Fr Tromp in order to ask for clear explanations and remove the ambiguity. If he gets no satisfaction, or if he is told that it is in fact himself who is being referred to, he will offer his resignation to the Pope. He thinks that the threat of this resignation will instil fear into the 'Romans' who would be embarrassed by it.

I told Fr de Lubac that when I returned to Strasbourg, I would write a few comments on this No. 22 and send them.[3] What else can one do? There is nothing to be done. It is a question of attitude. One reacts to things in one way or another. The 'Romans' take no part in the stream of living thought. They are hardly even aware of it. None of the interesting things that have been written concerning such questions as sexual morality, marriage, original sin, has been taken into consideration. We are stuck with a Denzinger point of view:[4] one of the deadliest of books in spite of its great usefulness.

---

1. The correct reference is *Jalons pour une théologie du laïcat*, 'Unam Sanctam', 23 (Paris: Cerf, 1953).
2. Jean Baptiste Janssens, Superior General of the Society of Jesus.
3. He did so on 12 October 1961 (Congar Archives).
4. A well-known collection of documents of the Magisterium (principally Conciliar and Papal) known traditionally by the name of the first editor; cf Congar, 'Du bon usage de Denzinger', in *L'Ami du Clergé*, 23 May 1963. Congar reprinted this article in his *Situation et tâches présentes de la théologie* (Paris: Cerf, 1967), 111–133.

After 5 pm, I attended the reception given at the Gregorianum for the rapporteurs of the Pauline Week. Fr Häring, who was there, told me once again of his dissatisfaction and his deep anxiety as regards our work. He finds everything too juridical, neither kerygmatic nor pastoral, very far from, and very inferior to, what is being said and written in our own countries. He would like to utter a cry of alarm because, according to him, we are on a false trail. THIS is not what the Church is waiting for, nor WHAT it needs. What to do? I told him I would be party to a letter addressed to the Holy Father. Because I do not see that there is any possibility of making any impression on the President or the Secretary of our Commission.

Fr Häring is speaking on behalf of a vast pastoral, catechetical experience. He takes things very tragically. But deep down, I agree with him. The problem is that my extreme physical weakness means that I have not the energy to be indignant and to react. Except for the approach I made to the Holy Father last July.

I did not manage to see those I wanted to see at this reception: people were accosting me and each one wanted to discuss his own particular hobby horse with me. I was asked my opinion about this, that and the other. I saw Feuillet,[1] a professor from Poland, a monsignor from the Ambrosianum, and above all Mgr Oesterreicher,[2] who wants me to take part in a congress on Israel restricted to biblical scholars and theologians.

Friday 29 September 1960 St Michael

I wrote a text concerning infants who die unbaptised, but I have no access to a machine on which to type it. The rough draft is here.[3]

---

1. One of those who had attended the Pauline Congress was, in fact, André Feuillet, PSS, Professor of Sacred Scripture at the Institut Catholique in Paris.
2. Of Jewish origin, John Oesterreicher, of the diocese of Vienna (Austria), had founded and directed the Institute of Judeo-Christian Studies at the University of Seton Hall (United States); being a consultor to the Secretariat for Christian Unity, he belonged to the sub-committee responsible for preparing a text concerning the relationship between the Church and the Jewish People. Theological problems connected with this text were beginning to surface at this point. At the Pauline Congress, he had presented a paper on the stumbling and fall of Israel in Romans 9–11.
3. Congar, who later made a note on this draft to the effect that, at that time, the question was discussed 'in a very rigid and negative manner', was of the opinion that there was no need for a special chapter on this question, simply a paragraph in the chapter on original sin. Such a chapter needed to deal with the matter from a christological and soteriological point of view, along the lines used by Saint Paul in his letter to the Romans. One should state firmly what has been revealed in the Word of God but be careful not to go beyond what is definitely known.

November 1961[1]

Left Strasbourg on Saturday evening, 18 November 1961 at 11.23 pm. Sunday 19: Mass at Notre Dame des Champs.[2] I met up with good Fr Lamothe[3] whom I had helped in the past.

Baptism of Sabine Congar[4] in Le Mans.

Went to Istina that evening at 9 pm. I saw Fr Dumont (and later Fr Hamer) who told me about his contacts in Rhodes.[5] Istina is now a dynamic and much patronised house. What progress has been made over the past thirty years. What a splendid work Fr Dumont has accomplished!

Monday 20 November 1961

Left Orly at 10.35 am. Very quickly we were above an immense white blanket, smooth and cottonnish. For a long time we flew over the Alps from NW to SE. Below us, mountains covered with snow and valleys filled with clouds like cotton wool in an ear. Blue sky above us.

The temperature in Rome was 17C! Bus, then taxi from St Peter's. Domus Mariae, where the sub-commission has its headquarters, is a very large and quite new building in the centre of an immense newly built area, where all the large buildings are for ecclesiastical purposes. From my window, I can see the Abbey of St Jerome.

Working session at 4.15 pm: end of the text *De Laicis* [On the Laity] (Mgr Philips) and beginning of *De Ecclesia et Statu* [On Church and State] (Fr Gagnebet). The text reproduces the theses of Cardinal Ottaviani's Treatise on Public Law. The State is treated as if it were a *potestas regalis* [royal power] charged with seeking the well-being of the citizens and obliged to offer public worship to the true God . . . What kind of connection is there with the reality of things? We managed all the same to change some formulae, but what will the bishops say when they have this text in their hands?

The following were present at the meeting: Frs Tromp, Gagnebet, Witte, Balić, Mgr Colombo, Mgr Philips (not well), Fr Lécuyer, Fr Betti OFM[6] who wrote a study on the Constitution *Pastor aeternus*,[7] and who, for this reason, has recently

---

1. Congar added this heading to the typescript.
2. Parish in Paris.
3. Franck Lamothe, then at Notre-Dame-des-Champs. He had first been ordained priest in the Orthodox Church and Congar had helped him when, having been received into the Catholic Church, he had asked to be recognised as a priest.
4. Congar's great niece.
5. The first pan-Orthodox Rhodes Conference took place in September 1961.
6. Umberto Betti, OFM, was Professor of Theology at the Antonianum; a consultor to the Preparatory Theological Commission, he was appointed a Council expert in 1963, and was later to become Rector of the Lateran.
7. Umberto Betti, *La costituzione dommatica 'Pastor aeternus' del concilio Vaticano I* (Rome, 1961).

been brought into the Commission. Mgr Journet did not come. Fr Laberge[1] acted as secretary.

Tuesday 21 November 1961

In the morning we finished studying Fr Gagnebet's text *De Ecclesia et Statu*. A discussion about toleration.

In the afternoon, we began work on Fr Witte's text on ecumenism. It is much too long.

Fr Balić violently attacked the entire document, so much so that, for quite some time, the atmosphere created by his intervention weighed on the discussion. All the more so in that Fr Tromp, too, is very negative. He brings everything under his one thesis: *Ecclesia catholica est sola Ecclesia; est Corpus Christi mysticum* [The Catholic Church is the only Church; she is the Mystical Body of Christ].

The discussion of the question what non-Catholic communities, as such, intrinsically are, was left hanging.

During the intervals and at lunch, conversed with Fr Witte, Mgr Philips, Schauf (I spoke to him about Küng). Schauf, who has remained here since September and who clings to Fr Tromp, clearly plays quite an important role. He has the necessary qualities for this type of work: scholastic precision, a fairly juridical mentality.

Discussed the Council itself, briefly, with Fr Gagnebet; the composition of the sub-commissions (the preparatory ones which have been turned into Consultative Conciliar Commissions), etc.

Wednesday 22 November 1961

Continuation of the Constitution on Ecumenism. A DOGMATIC Constitution of this kind cannot but be a disappointment from the ecumenical point of view. On the one hand, all it can do is to proclaim general principles, which are always valid, whereas ecumenism is a fact, a movement, entirely dependent on the will of God recognised as such in our own day; on the other hand, at the level of dogmatic principles, one can hardly find anything other than very rigid statements about the oneness of the Church and warnings against indifferentism, against *communicatio in sacris* [sharing in the sacraments], against false irenicism . . . I asked for the Constitution to express its own proper limits and that it should refer specifically to more positive pastoral and practical indications to be supplied either by the Secretariat or by the Congregation for the Eastern Churches. I was told that: 1) that would happen of its own accord when THIS constitution came to be published TOGETHER WITH all the other documents; 2) when all the documents were about to be published would be the time for inserting something along the lines I was suggesting.

---

1.   Léon Laberge, OMI, *scrittore* on the Preparatory Theological Commission.

Our group is very much dominated by Fr Tromp on account of his prestige, his knowledge, the clarity of what he says, backed up by extremely good knowledge of Latin, his capacity for stating things, and the fact that he is accustomed to being listened to. Practically speaking, he dominates everything. With him, inseparable from him, there is Mgr Schauf, who has a markedly juridical spirit, but who also has the gift of stating things clearly. I feel myself personally dominated by people like this who are PERFECTLY at ease in this kind of work. They were born to write and comment on Denzinger. But neither of them possesses an ecumenical spirit. They both know only a world of thought and declaration formed by the most logically consistent applications of their basic principle: the Catholic Church is the Mystical Body of Christ and it is the only Church and Mystical Body. One is completely disarmed, transported as one is to a terrain where ecumenism can no more survive than a plant transplanted to a slab of concrete. For example, in order to combat the idea that the Orthodox Churches are truly local Churches, such as I maintain they are in view of their possessing the priesthood and therefore sacramental power, Fr Tromp says: even an apostate can validly celebrate the Eucharist . . . In his view, the Orthodox Churches are no more than a social product of apostasy. That bears NO RELATION WHATSOEVER to the concrete and historical reality of things.

Frs Tromp and Schauf reason like this about everything. The ecumenical plant cannot find either soil or air in this kind of thinking.

All the same, Tromp does, in the end, allow or say some things because his duties in the 'Holy Office' have brought them to his awareness. A true canonist cannot be entirely narrow-minded.

It is Fr Lécuyer, Mgr Philips and Mgr Colombo who, astutely and delicately, secure the best hearing for good ideas or who, without seeming to do so, tone down the formulae to the point of making them inoffensive. We owe them a great deal.

Towards the end of the evening session, we began work on the Constitution *De Beata Maria Virgine*, which has been much altered as compared with the version we studied in September. Obviously, I dislike much of what it says. Several times, beneath very general formulae which seem harmless, there is insinuated, or it is possible to insinuate, the worst theses concerning objective co-redemption. Generally speaking, I find the idea of 'Mother of the Mystical Body' very ambiguous. However, I must confess: 1) that this new text contains several very strong statements on the unicity of the redemption and of the mediation of Christ; 2) that the MINIMUM possible is said concretely, given that so many bishops have even called for the DEFINITION of the co-redemption, of Mary Mediatrix, Mary Queen, etc!!! Fr Balić's text consists mainly of generalities and is geared mainly to devotion to the Virgin Mary. One can even doubt whether the bishops will be content with it.

Thursday 23 November 1961

We completed work on the Constitution on the Blessed Virgin Mary.

Don Colombo asked whether we could have a joint commission with the Secretariat on the question of ecumenism. Fr Tromp sulked at once like a bad-tempered dog and refused categorically. Reasons: 1) that would lead to our having to create other joint commissions, there would be no end to them; 2) we alone have the doctrinal competence, the other Commissions or Secretariats are purely disciplinary bodies and have nothing to give to us.

I pointed out that even so it was a pity that we had not worked together. When the Secretariat produces its texts (apparently they are preparing one on Mary among the Protestants) it will be too late; that will not be of any use.

I had already seen this, and said it, eighteen months ago! I put it in my letter to the Holy Father . . .

Fr Tromp sulks quite easily. He seems not to like it when I intervene, no matter how (very) timidly I do so. He has a way of shrugging his shoulders and showing his disapproval, or even his contempt, which does not make it easy to express what one wants to say. But one says it just the same, of course.

He told me that Don Colombo's text *De Magisterio* is unsatisfactory; it is neither clear nor vigorous, resembling more a scholastic course than a constitution. Tromp said: Colombo is incapable of doing anything else.

There was in any case no time to see this text of Colombo's, and Fr Gagnebet asked for it to be sent to him within the eight days allowed for the submission of written comments.

At 1.15 pm, grand lunch with Cardinal Ottaviani. The house did things well—and in any case this house, built by Italian Women's Catholic Action (not, assuredly, without substantial help from the Holy See), is a remarkable achievement: four hundred rooms or beds, meeting rooms, dining rooms, lecture rooms, etc. I do not see that France, a 'rich' country, could afford that!

We went back down to Rome at 4.00 pm. I left my luggage at the Angelicum and went immediately to San Clemente[1] where Fr General was supposed to be. My right leg has never been so bad. It feels dead below the calf, and only works by being moved by its own weight. Still no news from Fr Maillard[2] who was to make an appointment for me to see a good doctor in Paris tomorrow, Friday, afternoon. Without that possibility, I would have gone to Paris this evening and taken the night train for Strasbourg or for St-Avold.

Fr General had already left San Clemente. So I went to Santa Sabina. It took me twenty-five minutes to climb the hill, and it began to rain. What could I do? I saw Fr General for a few minutes. He looked younger and seemed to be in very good spirits. I had gone to see him concerning the question of the green light

---

1. A Dominican priory in Rome.
2. Philippe Maillard, OP, of the Province of France, Prior of the priory in Strasbourg where Congar was in residence.

from the Holy Office for my contribution to Mélanges Visser't Hooft.[1] This has been brewing for two months; Fr Leclercq (Holy Office) had said to me: go and see your Fr General, he should have a reply for you. But Fr General had heard nothing.

But he took advantage of my visit to say to me—entirely in his own name, he said . . . —that he did not like my article about Hernegger's book[2] in *Signes du temps*,[3] 'a very dangerous book', he added.

That article appeared in June 1960. What a memory Fr General has. I have never seen him except for disagreeable things, though always wrapped in kind words.

I returned to the Angelicum almost on my hands and knees. There I saw Fr de La Brosse,[4] who had been there for three weeks.

VERY fraternal welcome from the Prior,[5] and the Sub-Prior (Fr Perreault,[6] a Canadian and psychologist).

Return journey by plane on Friday 24: (weather pretty bad); lunch at Éditions Cerf;[7] appointment with Dr Bricaire;[8] 'European' extremely crowded, standing as far as Bar-le-Duc. (Dr Bricaire, 16 rue Assomption).

28 February 1962

Left Strasbourg at 7.20 am, *via* Orly. Arrived at Rome-Termini at 1.30 pm. In Orly, I met up with Fr Bouyer. Who would have said, back in 1932, when I first

---

1. In the end, Congar was able to publish his contribution: 'Ecumenical experience and conversion: a personal testimony', in Robert C Mackie and Charles C West, *The Sufficiency of God. Essays on the Ecumenical Hope in Honour of WA Visser't Hooft, Doctor of Divinity, First General Secretary of the World Council of Churches* (London, 1963); the Dutch Protestant Willem Visser't Hooft had been the General Secretary of the WCC since its inception.
2. Rudolf Hernegger, *Volkskirche oder Kirche der Glaübigen? (Ideologie und Glaube. Eine christliche Ideologienkritik, 1)* (Nuremberg, 1959).
3. Yves Congar, 'Pour que l'Église soit l'Église!', *Signes du temps*, June,1960.
4. Olivier de La Brosse, OP, of the Province of France, lived for two years at the Angelicum, where he was preparing his thesis for the lectorate in theology, which he presented in June 1962, and his thesis for the doctorate in theology, which Congar was to publish: *Le Pape et le Concile. La comparaison de leurs pouvoirs à la veille de la Réforme*, 'Unam Sanctam', 58 (Paris: Cerf, 1965).
5. Raymond Sigmond (see above).
6. Aimon-Marie Perreault, OP, of the Province of Canada, psychologist, and Professor in the Faculty of Philosophy at the Angelicum.
7. Les Éditions du Cerf in Paris, founded and directed by Congar's Dominican colleagues.
8. Henri Bricaire, doctor specialising in endocrinology.

met him in the Faculty of Protestant Theology,[1] that we would one day be going TOGETHER as consultors for a Council?

After a short siesta, my LEFT leg (the 'good' one!) was completely dead. Is that because I carried a heavy package (8 kg) in my left hand!

Extremely cordial and fraternal welcome everywhere: at the Angelicum and at the Gregorianum, where I go to work in the library.

Fr Gagnebet told me that it was he who had written the chapter *De missionibus* [On the Missions] which I had found very inadequate and even bad. He had in his mind everything that I had said in my comments, he told me. But at the sub-commission he was told that that had all been said in the chapter *De Ecclesiae natura*; what was needed was not to repeat things but to add the law. I do not agree. 1) This was not said truthfully 2) it would indeed have been a good thing to speak of the missions precisely in the chapter on the Church. The best solution would be to develop this point, only more clearly, and simply to add a few lines concerning the LEGAL aspect.

As for the chapter *De Ecclesiae natura* [on the nature of the Church], Fr Gagnebet said that Lattanzi had written it and that there had been sharp differences of opinion between Lattanzi, representing the Lateran, and Tromp, representing the Gregorianum. It should have been a matter for the Lateran! The wretches!

Sunday 4 March 1962

Six large and heavy working sessions in the Hall of the 'Holy Office' where the cardinals meet. The climate is very different from what it was a year ago. The consultors intervene like the others, the discussion is free and fruitful. The exercise was absolutely straightforward: the comments of those who are not there are almost never taken into account, except when they are either very brief and precise (a minimum change of words) or very important and well presented. On the other hand, by intervening directly, one is often able, without great difficulty, to put one's idea across. I did so with reference to several points.

Grand lunch at the Canadian College: fifty-four students, all priests. Atmosphere both festive (not exactly solemn) and unhurried: each one serves himself from what is there on the table without taking too much notice of others. Very little active curiosity.

Evening of Sunday 4 [of March]: I went to the Oblates of Mary Immaculate. Huge house, and another one is going to be built. All of it completed, covered in marble, clean. I thought of Le Saulchoir, not yet finished and unfinishable, given our lack of means.

---

1. In Paris. Congar had followed several courses there and Bouyer, still a Protestant at the time, was preparing to be a minister.

Very friendly men. I spoke to Frs Perbal[1] and Seumois.[2] I gave a talk by way of replying to thirteen 'little' questions that their students had put to me. Whenever I speak, I always have the odd impression of a new vibration and resonance such as I had at Saint-Odile last Tuesday, after the chiropractic session.

After supper, conversation-cum-lecture with the Fathers (but not the scholastics) on ecumenism and above all on the East.

Monday 5 March 1962

Fr Gagnebet told me that the idea of producing a text *De ordine morali SOCIALI* [on the SOCIAL moral order] had been abandoned: there was implacable opposition between Fr Gundlach[3] and Mgr Pavan.[4] But the bishops are calling for such a text! All that is needed is to appoint another Commission . . .

9.30 am: Plenary Session of the Commission in the Hall of the Congregations in the Vatican. Gendarmes, gentlemen ushers everywhere. Very fine room, completely redone, with lovely tapestries. Cardinal Ottaviani began by briefly telling us the Central Commission's reaction to our texts. It had made some changes to the Profession of Faith, inserting, with reference to Christ, the words *'unicus mediator'* [one and only mediator]; it is not yet known whether this Profession of Faith will be proclaimed before or after the Council. In the Constitution *De deposito* [on the deposit of the Faith], which the Central Council had deemed *'nimis defensiva'* [too defensive], a number of changes had been called for in relation to the historicity of the Gospels. The Central Commission was astonished that the Constitution *De re morali* [on moral matters] had not dealt with any virtue, apart from chastity.

In conclusion, it had found all our texts too professorial [*'nimis cathedraticum'*]. What was needed was something more pastoral, and also more scriptural. And, finally, the Latin at times leaves something to be desired.

After that, Fr Tromp gave an account of what the Commission had been doing since the last general session. He gave the figure for the number of pages of remarks made by the Central Commission and of the replies submitted by a

---

1. Albert Perbal, OMI, had for many years been Professor of Missiology at the Institute of Missionary Sciences at the Urbanianum: he was consultor to the Congregation of Propaganda.
2. André Seumois, OMI, was Professor of Missiology at the Urbanianum and consultor to the Congregation of Propaganda; consultor also to the Preparatory Commission on the Missions, he was to be appointed a Council expert in 1962.
3. The German Jesuit Gustav Gundlach, who had been Pius XII's trusted adviser in social matters, taught social ethics at the Gregorianum, and was consultor to the Preparatory Theological Commission. He died in June 1963.
4. Pietro Pavan, of the diocese of Treviso, specialised in the Church's social doctrine, and was a professor at the Lateran. He was a member of the Preparatory Theological Commission and of that for the Apostolate of the Laity. He was appointed a Council expert in 1962 and was to become Rector of the Lateran in 1969, then cardinal in 1985.

sub-commission on these remarks. The Central Commission had also asked for a clearer statement of the propositions in our text, adding that these dogmatic Constitutions should not contain anything other than things that were *absolute certae* [absolutely certain].

In fact, nearly all the propositions are taken from theological courses and mix non-dogmatic considerations in with what is truly dogmatic. What a low level as compared with the chapters from the Council of Trent! All in all, the Central Commission anticipates what I hope will be the bishops' reaction: it wants something that matches more closely what Christians in fact need. But this Theological Commission has worked entirely in the atmosphere of the 'Holy Office' as well as being under orders to prepare a sort of 'Summa' of papal teaching since Pius XI, the references being entirely to encyclicals and papal discourses. The worst of it is that there is nothing one can do, or, if one can do a little, it cannot be more than an addition to or a correction of some detail; but EVERYTHING should have been conceived differently, and that *a principio* [from the very beginning].

Fr de Lubac told me that the Central Commission passes its comments on to a sub-commission drawn from ours, which does more or less as it likes, and has its replies or alterations ratified by a group of five cardinals.

Fr Balić presented his text *De Beata Maria Virgine*. What a talent and what cunning he has! He does what he wants, playing on all strings, with incredible skill and glibness.

Endless discussion about *mediatrix*. Balić told us that Pius XII had deleted the word *Coredemptrix* in all the documents bearing this title and had replaced it by 'Socia Christi Redemptoris' [Associate of Christ the Redeemer].

Balić finished quickly in the afternoon and Fr Gagnebet began his *De Ecclesia et Statu, deque Tolerantia* [on Church and State, and on tolerance]. He spoke quickly in order to get finished this evening. Yet another text that I would have written quite differently. I did not stay till the end of the session. Mgr Philips and Fr de Lubac told me later that there was tense discussion, that Cardinal Ottaviani and Frs Dhanis and Balić wanted a tougher text, but that even so several of the expressions had been either toned down or broadened.

I left the meeting at 5.35 pm because I had an audience with Cardinal Bea at 6.00 pm. He received me in a very friendly and open fashion. He said he was pleased to meet me personally at last. I felt I was back in an open world where one could breathe. He touched on the following points :

- Cerf to publish his articles and speeches. Yes, in principle;
- the question of my contributing to the Visser't Hooft volume and a German Protestant publication in Berlin;

- The publication of the Chevetogne texts on infallibility;[1]
- The reactions of the Central Commission. The cardinal told me that the texts of the Theological Commission are the least satisfactory, that there is nothing biblical about them; that the text on Scripture and Tradition is short and inadequate.

I shared my own anxiety with him. This Council, which ought to be a step towards unity, is in no way animated by this idea; it hardly ever occurs in our Commission, or if it does, only in order to avoid such and such a word. This Commission, moreover, is entirely 'Latin', and the Eastern point of view is NEVER put forward. I told him that I had written to the Pope who, the cardinal told me, was amazed to hear that there had never been a joint commission comprising the Secretariat and the Theological Commission.

The Cardinal also told me that when he was preparing the statutes for the Secretariat, he had written 'the Commission'. It was the Pope who had told him to keep the word 'secretariat', in order to be freer. He also said that the Pope had informed those who needed to know that for all ecumenical matters, it was Cardinal Bea's Secretariat which was the competent authority. After the Council, he said, the responsibilities of the Secretariat will have to be well defined, and that he was responsible for all matters affecting the relationship with the separated brethren.

I asked the cardinal how he had come to know about ecumenism: because it was not generally known that he was in the picture and, when he had been appointed to this position, people had almost been astonished to hear it . . . He told me that he had been in touch with Protestants for almost the whole of his life. In Bade, where he was born, at school; then, later on, during his biblical studies. In 1935, he had been invited to a Biblical Congress at Göttingen as President of the Pontifical Biblical Institute. He had asked Pius XI about this, and the Pope had told him to go. Finally, he had even presided at the last meeting of the Congress. Thereafter, he had remained in contact with Protestant exegetes and, when one or other of them came to Rome, he always received them. But it was true that, apart from that, he had no other preparation. And he confessed that, to begin with, he knew nothing about the East apart from visits to the Holy Land (where he had established contact with Fr Lagrange,[2] in order to put an end to the stand-off between the *École Biblique* and the Biblical Institute).

In the tram on the way back I met Mgr Philips and Fr de Lubac; they told me how the discussion had gone.

---

1. *L'Infaillibilité de l'Église. Journées œcuméniques de Chevetogne 25-29 septembre 1961* (Éditions de Chevetogne, 1963).
2. Marie-Joseph Lagrange, OP, founder of the French Biblical and Archeological School in Jerusalem.

(Shrove) Tuesday 6 March 1962

Fr Balić is going to each of the members of the sub-commission in turn in order to intone for them his refrain about adding a paragraph on the mediation of Mary.

Speedy end to the discussion of Fr Gagnebet's Constitution on Church and State.

Constitution *De Magisterio* [*on the Magisterium*] (Colombo). Piolanti, who seeks every possible opportunity to push his points in the narrowest possible 'Roman' direction, and who at every possible occasion makes jokes from allusions to trivial current events, would like the bishops assembled in Council to rely on the pope *fontaliter* [as the source]. This is also Fr Gagnebet's position, but he has stated clearly that he does not want the idea to be expressed in the Constitution. On the other hand, Mgr Hermaniuk put forward, firmly and calmly, a point of view which he rightly believes would amount to extending a hand to some of the Orthodox. I saw Mgr Hermaniuk afterwards and told him that I would like to prepare a text along the lines he is advocating. He said that he would come to the sub-commission, even though he does not belong to it.

At noon (or rather at 2 pm!!!) lunch at Saint-Louis des Français with the Senegalese Ambassador to the Quirinal,[1] and M Alioun Diop.[2] I spoke a great deal to both of them. I found myself in the presence of highly cultured men. And their culture was French. It is clear that Africa will have a lot to say in the future. It will not happen tomorrow, but it will happen.

After the afternoon meeting, Fr Leclercq spoke to me again about the commissions of experts that will be operating during the Council. He said that he is doing his best to ensure that I am involved because, he said, there will be a need for theologians who will produce alternative texts, as Kleutgen[3] had done during the First Vatican Council.

Wednesday 7 March 1962

Fr General had asked to see me. The time had been changed by telephone, so it was this morning at 8.30 am that I was to see him. I had said beforehand to Fr Labourdette: this must be for something disagreeable, because I have never seen him for anything else. And I was right. He told me that he wanted to 'have another chat about THAT book . . . ' I did not understand what he was referring to. In the end, it was this: he had been asked by the 'Holy Office' (which he never refers to by name, saying only 'the higher ups') to reprimand me for my little piece

---

1. At that time the Senegalese Ambassador in Italy was Colonel Claude Mademba Sy.
2. This Senegalese intellectual, a Moslem who had become a Catholic, had founded the review *Présence africaine* in 1947.
3. Joseph Kleutgen, SJ, a German theologian. At Vatican I, he was one of those who re-cast what would become the Constitution *Dei Filius* and found himself entrusted with recasting the schema *De Ecclesia Christi* which, however, could not be discussed by the Fathers.

on Hernegger in *Signes du Temps*. He said he had read this book (???) and found it very false.

Poor man, totally imprisoned in the system, without the least idea of what the asking of questions might involve. I have been told on good authority that his cardinalate—to which I did not refer—has come to him from the bishops on the Central Commission, WHO WANTED TO HAVE A THEOLOGIAN AMONGST THEM . . .!!!¹

We received our ashes in the Pauline Chapel in the Vatican. I said my prayers while I waited. But on entering the Chapel I could not but notice the spiritual atmosphere of the place: that of Paul IV. Above the altar, very high up, there is a TINY medallion representing the Lamb. Below is the inscription '*Ego sum via, veritas et vita*' [I am the way, the truth and the life]. Thus, while making use of these words of Christ, the Lamb is made to preside over an order which makes no further reference to the Gospel. In the corners, statues of the splendid bodies of young men showing off their legs. The atmosphere is one of a combination of rigour and latent sensuality.

Meeting on *De laicis* [On the laity]. Mgr Philips' admirable temperament, helped by his perfect command of Latin. He is very gracious, extremely affable, based on an interior respect for others and for the truth. If everything were in his image, how well everything would go! Outbursts by Balić, who feels too much has been given to lay people and, in a menacing voice, foretells future disasters on this account.

De statibus perfectionis [on the states of perfection] no difficulty.

Problem with the airline; the Nice-Strasbourg connection will not run on Sunday (the plane comes from Oran). I had to go to Air France to see what other possibilities there were. I decided to cancel my return flight and go by train on Saturday evening.

Brisk meeting *De Matrimonio* [on marriage]: a monster Constitution, spelling out all the duties of married people!!

These days, I have often been beside Fr Gundlach. He does not like any of these texts. But I am told that he is never satisfied. I confess that, for my part, I am a little indifferent to all the excessive paternalism in these texts because I am so convinced that they will change nothing and that life will go on in spite of everything! Moreover, the documents contain a great many excellent principles which I fully endorse.

Thursday 8 March 1962 *St Thomas (transferred)*. Before leaving, I typed a paper on collegiality: not a TEXT as such, but a *votum* designed to introduce the question and prevent it from being ignored. This question MUST be taken

---

1. Michael Browne was created cardinal at the Consistory held on 19 March 1962, and consecrated bishop on the following 19 April. He was already a member of the Central Preparatory Commission.

up again, with calm deliberation. But that presupposes a NEW version of THE WHOLE of the Constitution *De Magisterio*. But will there be such a thing? It cannot happen except in a new session, as this one is already over-loaded.

The day was spent at the meeting of the sub-commission *De Ecclesia*, at the 'Holy Office'. In the morning, a brief look at public opinion in the Church (where Mgr Philips was excellent: he maintains that public opinion, as such, is always good and that even when it goes too far or is wrong, there is SOMETHING GOOD in it), followed by *De Ecclesiae natura* [on the nature of the Church] presented by Mgr Lattanzi. This text has a story attached to it. Ever since the beginning (November 1960), Lattanzi has been impossible, verbose, confused. Fr Gagnebet had wanted to relieve him of his role as the one responsible for the drafting of this chapter, but Lattanzi had gone to see the Pope and had maintained that the honour of the Lateran was at stake. It was all a question of competition. The Lateran had to produce a dogmatic text . . . Three months had been wasted in this way, Fr Gagnebet told me. In the end, Fr Tromp produced a text of which Lattanzi retained the outline and the ideas, but putting it all into his Latin and his pathos.

His text is impossible. In the first place, it is a Niagara of words, poured out at full speed. One can only just understand it. Moreover he had altered a great deal, added some things and removed others, to the extent that one is now dealing with a new text and it is impossible to know where one is. When the Latin is not enough for him, Lattanzi starts to use Greek. It is chaotic. Very tiresome and tiring. Finally, he does not understand the questions. Neither does Fr Tromp, who is deaf. For this reason it was in vain that I repeated the question concerning the meaning of σῶμα, *corpus* [body]. Fr Tromp believes he can satisfy everything by the sociological and ABOVE ALL BIOLOGICAL meaning. He does not know any recent exegetical studies. So I have warned the exegetes, Mgr Cerfaux and Fr Kerrigan.

A lunch with all the stops out at the Angelicum: two cardinals, Fr General, Fr Philippe, the superiors who send their students to the Angelicum, and some members of our Commission (Tromp, Philips, Fenton).

Afterwards I went to change some money and buy my train ticket.

In the afternoon, *De œcumenismo*. Fr Witte is ill so it was Fr Lécuyer who, bravely and sportingly, undertook to present this difficult text. From the very beginning, Fenton was absolutely against it. He did not for a moment attempt to understand the question, still less to enter into the others' points of view. He makes use of every single WORD which he thinks contains something that might favour a little openness in order to charge at it like a bull at a red rag. His attitude is absolutely CHILDISH. He has built a fortress around a SINGLE point to which he tries to link everything, without, however, really understanding the overall theology *De Ecclesia*: the Church is visible; the Church is the Roman Catholic Church; there is no salvation except in this Church, taken in the narrowest possible confessional meaning of the word. After a number of charges by the bull, foaming and trembling with nervous excitement (I was beside him), Fr Tromp announced that we were discussing a SINGLE TEXT, in order to improve it. If the text itself and its subject matter is rejected, then our meeting is pointless. We must vote on this: to improve the text or to reject it totally. FENTON is the only one who wishes to reject it. There was a great squabble with Tromp over Bellarmine's[1] position, because, according to Fenton, the Council would be condemning Bellarmine and that would be the greatest scandal in the entire history of the Church.

I did not intervene at all throughout this debate because ecumenism is defended (and well defended) by Fr Tromp and Mgr Dubois, not to mention Frs Lécuyer and Salaverri. Thereafter, Tromp held his peace, or withdrew, and I intervened several times. After some time, Fenton was so hateful, so obstinately negative, so aggressive, so utterly senseless, that Mgr Philips got up and said, with emotion, but forcefully and calmly: it is impossible to work in these conditions and I am leaving. Because (turning to Fenton) you accuse everyone of heresy. It is impossible to work unless one respects others and their points of view.

Fenton was quiet for a while and then began again. He is out of his senses and beyond all reasonable control.

We did not finish until 7.35 pm. Or rather, we broke up without finishing. Everybody was tired, marking time, lacking the minimum of freshness needed in order to pay full attention and find solutions. It was decided to hold a further meeting of the sub-commission on the following afternoon.

In the evening, supper with Laurentin.

Friday 9 March 1962
Conversation with Fr Hamer about the Secretariat for Christian Unity. Meeting on the *De Familia* [On the family]. Great discussion about over-population. In the end a Passionist bishop aged eighty-six[2] declared that he had been scandalised by the carnal spirit of many of the members. He read the text:

> '*Ne solliciti sitis*' [Do not be anxious . . . (Mt 6:25)]. But, during the discussion, he professed a fairly facile kind of liberalism: if there are too many people, some will die, so there will never be too many.

It is *FACILE* to invoke the Gospel and leave insoluble problems to others. This Archbishop of Agrigento—the Infant of Agrigento is eighty-six years of age![3]—

---

1. St Robert Bellarmine (1542–1621), SJ, major Counter Reformation theologian.
2. Giovanni Battista Peruzzo, Archbishop-Bishop of Agrigento (Italy), member of the Preparatory Theological Commission. At the Council, he was a member of the Doctrinal Commission.
3. {A reference to the whimsical title of a collection of essays on aspects of ancient Greek and Roman culture} by André-Jean Festugière, OP, of the Province of France: *L'enfant d'Agrigente* (Paris: Cerf, 1941). {In the sanctuary of Castor and Pollux at Agrigento,

was brought into the Commission recently. The few interventions he has made are always extremely pious, very 'integrist', the least open, the most *'vom katholischen her'* [from the Catholic point of view]. The choice of members is indeed significant . . . !

Lunch at Mgr Arrighi's with Bouyer, Peri[1] and Mgr Colombo. But wherever I go, I arrive dead tired and worn out whenever I have had to walk a little.

In the afternoon, at the 'Holy Office', meeting of the sub-commission on the Constitution on the Preaching of the Bishop and an examination of Mgr Hermaniuk's proposition. Immense joy for me: it was accepted.

That evening, supper and lecture on ecumenism at the Canadian College.

Saturday 10 March 1962

My last day here. Chapter *De natura Ecclesiae* [On the Nature of the Church]. Once again Fr Tromp was not in the least interested in any exegesis other than his own, in relation to St Paul's texts concerning the Body of Christ. Moreover, his complaint against Lattanzi's text is that it makes reference to hardly anything other than Sacred Scripture: IT IS ESSENTIAL, he says, to insert notes giving references to texts of the Magisterium. From beginning to end, this insistence has weighed on the work and on the texts produced by the Commission. It is very serious. The source of knowledge, for them, is not Holy Scripture and Tradition under the direction of the Magisterium: it is the Magisterium itself.

As yesterday in the sub-commission, major discussion on how to express the bishops' obligation to preach to 'unbelievers'. Our Constitution *De officio praedicandi* [On the office of preaching] is concerned ONLY with *'gentes'*;[2] it has the great advantage of making a distinction between the Mission to pagans and the Mission to those who have already been (imperfectly) evangelised.

Grand lunch at Domus Mariae; at the centre of the table Cardinal Ottaviani (who has several times treated me very coldly: but Fr Tromp not at all . . .), Mgr Parente, Mgr Felici, Mgr Scicca,[3] (Secretary to the Congregation for Studies).

At 4 pm, meeting for the additions on mediation made by Fr Balić to his text on *B M Virgine*. Not too bad.

At the end, Fr Hürth read a paper claiming that Pius XII and John XXIII, in spite of opposition from Mgr (Cardinal) Larraona, had said that not only secular institutes, but even private vows established the same state of perfection as public vows. The Supreme Pontiff, he declared, has thus CREATED a doctrine by making even private vows have the same effect as solemn vows. This is to deny

---

Festugière had encountered a shepherd boy whom he took to be emblematic of the allure and the otherness of the Graeco-Roman world.}

1. Vittorio Peri, *scrittore* at the Vatican Apostolic Library, specialist on the Christian East.
2. 'Nations': here meaning peoples not yet evangelised.
3. This name does not appear in the *Annuario Pontificio* for 1962; at that time, Dino Staffa was Secretary to the Congregation for Seminaries and Universities.

the very principle of the 'STATES' of perfection which imply solemnity (being made in public). The matter will be submitted to us.

So we broke up without having finished. There remain not only the social questions on which it was impossible to reach agreement, but ecumenism, Mgr Hermaniuk's proposition and one or two minor points. For ecumenism, Fenton has secured this result: that we have not finished and that a chapter on ecumenism cannot be presented in the Constitution *De Ecclesia*.

We were told that SUCH MEMBERS of the sub-commission, AS CAN MEET IN ROME, will decide on this text. Or that, perhaps, these things will be discussed during the first session of the Council in October.

Return journey by train. From Como onwards, with some nice Italians who were going in search of work in Germany or Holland. What likeable people they were! In their bread (large coarse 'ordinary' bread) they ate sausage, cheese, bananas, enough to keep me going for a full two days. They are cheerful, they laugh at everything. They have a realist philosophy. They show me photos of their wives and children. One has to share with them. And their outlook on politics: 'Russia wants this; America wants that; it's all shit!'

What a dose of true uncomplicated humanity. How far removed from our Roman and clerical concerns!

On or about 5 or 6 August 1962

I wrote to Mgr Weber to say that, since nothing certain was known about whether or not there were to be conciliar Commissions, I offered to be his man, as he had said to me from the beginning that he would take me as his theologian.

I received in reply a letter from him which both surprised and upset me and which, for this reason, I tore up. He was not sure, he wrote, whether or not he needed anyone. It seemed to me that, for all his kindness towards me, and for all my own little standing, he does not see how important it is for ME to be in Rome during the Council.

A few days later I received a second letter from him. He had just (17 August) received the first volume of *schemata*.[1] Some things came within my field of competence. So he had decided to take me with him, and even offered to arrange for me to stay at Saint-Sulpice,[2] and would give my name to Mgr Gouet, the bishops' secretary.

I came to the conclusion that Mgr Weber had been under the impression that he would have to defray his theologian's living expenses and that, to begin with, he had wished to avoid this expense.

When I returned to Strasbourg on 30 August, I found a telephone message from Mgr Weber, saying he was anxious to see me as soon as possible. I went to

---

1. *Schemata Constitutionum et Decretorum de quibus disceptabitur in Concilii sessionibus.* Series prima, 13 July, 1962 (Congar Archives).
2. The Procure de Saint-Sulpice in Rome.

see him the very next morning and lunched with him. He gave me the volume of *schemata* which he had received on 17 August, his reactions to which he was required to send to Rome by the middle of September. (It was a bit rushed!!). He told me his comments, then gave me the volume with his own comments and also the (excellent) comments of Fr Durrwell, whom he had already contacted.

In spite of the enormous pile of correspondence that I found waiting for me, in spite of a number of urgent matters awaiting my attention, in spite of my *Tradition*[1] interrupted yet again, and catastrophically, I must now go back to the tedious task of rereading these texts and once again preparing the comments on them which I have already made.

Our theological schemas have remained more or less the same: however, on the points that aroused most discussion, improvements have been made, or a less aggressive text has been reverted to. This is so on the question of the place of charity in the moral life, on Limbo, and on polygenism. However, there are some texts which are too 'Roman', too reactionary, too 'Holy Office'. Mgr Weber has spotted it, and Fr Durrwell even more so.

The text on the liturgy is good; it is much closer to the level of current thinking.

Who wrote the text on unity? I am inclined to see Vodopivec's[2] hand in it. It is in the spirit of John XXIII. Without tackling theological principles directly, in an atmosphere of love and irenicism, it makes far-reaching statements which are capable of leading to important theological consequences. But it concentrates exclusively on the Orthodox. It proceeds without any reference whatsoever to the ecumenical perspective, and as if the World Council of Churches did not exist, as if the Orthodox did not belong to it. The World Council of Churches will resent it as a move designed to secure union with the Orthodox, independently of any approach to the World Council of Churches and the Protestants; therefore, as a move against them. I have written to Mgr Willebrands,[3] because this is a very serious matter.

---

1. The reference is probably to Congar's *La Tradition et les traditions. Essai théologique* (Paris: Fayard, 1963); but Congar was also preparing the publication of *La Tradition et la vie de l'Église* (Paris: Fayard, 1963).
2. Janez Vodopivec, professor at the Lateran, was a consultor to the Secretariat for Unity.
3. Letter dated 4 September 1962 (Congar Archives); on 8 September 1962, Willebrands replied to Congar's letter (Congar Archives) and told him that, if the text did indeed come from the Congregation for the Eastern Church, it was not by Vodopivec, who did not belong to it; he said that he, too, realised that the text made no reference to the ecumenical movement, to which the Orthodox, too, belonged, and informed Congar of his intention to speak to Cardinal Bea about the whole document.

On 16 or 17 September 1962

I received from Fr Chenu the draft of a preliminary declaration.[1] It seemed to me there and then that this initiative was INSPIRED, that it was *THIS* that was NEEDED! Though I did find Fr Chenu's text a little sociological, too human. Of course it is a message addressed to humankind. But I would have liked there to have been a stronger reference to the fact of Jesus Christ and the offer of the Covenant. Also, I wanted to support Fr Chenu's initiative effectively. So I sent his text, with a note of my own, to Cardinals Liénart, Alfrink,[2] König, Döpfner,[3] and Montini; also to Frings[4] and Suenens;[5] to the archbishops of Rheims[6] and Durban (Hurley);[7] to Mgr Charue,[8] Mgr Weber, Mgr Ghattas (Coptic bishop of Thebes),[9] and to Mgr Volk.[10]

I received a very favourable reply from several of them, especially from Cardinals Liénart, Alfrink and Döpfner. I wrote to tell Fr Chenu what they had said. Cardinal Liénart's reply suggested that it would be good to prepare A TEXT. Fr Chenu had drafted one in French which I corrected and added to as regards the paragraph concerning ecumenism, which was a little too short as originally drafted.

I typed this text and sent it on to Küng, so that he could translate it into German. Küng telephoned me on the morning of 27 September asking to see me. He came to Tübingen for this purpose that same day. He, together with several other German theologians, especially Möller[11] from Tübingen, feels that the four dogmatic *schemata* are not good: they must not be amended but rejected. Even if amended, they would remain substantially what they are. As they stand, they present a school theology, that of the Roman schools. For the public, and even in

---

1. For the background to this declaration, cf André Duval, 'Le message au monde', in *Vatican II commence . . . Approches francophones* (Leuven, 1993), 105–118.
2. Cardinal Bernard J Alfrink, Archbishop of Utrecht, future member of the Council of Presidents.
3. Cardinal Julius Döpfner, Archbishop of Munich and Freising, future member of the Co-ordinating Commission and future Moderator of the Council.
4. Cardinal Joseph Frings, Archbishop of Cologne, and future member of the Council of Presidents.
5. Cardinal Léon-J Suenens, Archbishop of Malines-Brussels, future member of the Co-ordinating Commission and future Moderator of the Council.
6. François Marty.
7. Denis E Hurley, Archbishop of Durban (South Africa), future member of the Commission on Seminaries, Study and Catholic Education.
8. André Charue, Bishop of Namur. During the First Session, he was to be a member of the Doctrinal Commission of which he was to become the second Vice-President at the end of the Second Session.
9. Isaac Ghattas, Catholic Coptic Bishop of Luxor (ancient Thebes).
10. Hermann Volk was a theologian and member of the Secretariat for Unity. He became Bishop of Mainz in the spring of 1962. He was elected as a member of the Doctrinal Commission during the First Session of the Council.
11. .Joseph Möller, professor at the Faculty of Catholic Theology in Tübingen.

practice for the average clergy, these Constitutions will be regarded as definitions of faith. This will result in a further hardening in a direction that offers no real possibility of dialogue with the thinking of the men and women of today.

According to Küng, in order to make it easier for them to be rejected, it will be necessary to prevent these dogmatic *schemata* from being THE FIRST to be presented, because they would then be in danger of being tackled in adverse conditions, in a hurry. Hence the need to ensure that the Council begins by tackling schemas dealing with more practical matters.

We mulled over ways in which this might be brought about. It seems to me that we can only appeal to the BISHOPS. Küng and I together drew up a text in this sense, of which he sent me a copy in Latin two days later. We will get it signed by a certain number of well-known theologians.

However, I drew Küng's attention to the danger, and the undesirability, of creating the impression of a para-council of theologians, seeking to influence the true Council of bishops. Küng would have liked to hold a meeting of theologians in Rome. I strongly advised against such a move, saying that, for my part, I would not attend such a meeting, or that I would at least insist that theologians of an integrist cast should also take part. Otherwise, we would create the impression: 1) that some theologians wanted to dictate to the Council the line it should take. Such a move would bring back awkward memories of Döllinger;[1] 2) that we were scheming. Now, every action provokes a reaction. Our action would result in a further hardening of those steeped in scholasticism and opposed to change, who perhaps represent the majority. One must always think about the reaction one risks arousing when planning to do something.

Here is what I received from Küng on 29 September.[2]

1 October 1962

I received the LATIN text from Fr Chenu. I at once sent it to Cardinals Liénart, Suenens, Döpfner and Alfrink, who, in their replies, had shown themselves most favourable to the idea.

2 October 1962

I saw Mgr Weber and brought him Fr Chenu's two texts (Latin and French). He told me that, in conjunction with Mgr Elchinger, he had sent direct to Cardinal Cicognani a request for a step of the kind indicated by Fr Chenu.[3]

Something of this kind MUST be done!

---

1. Johann Josef Ignaz Döllinger (1793–1890): this famous theologian and historian of the University of Munich, implacable opponent of the dogma of papal infallibility, was in the end excommunicated.
2. Küng informed Congar that he had been in touch with K. Rahner; they had translated the text written in Strasbourg into Latin; they thought it advisable to consult Cardinals Döpfner and König about it before collecting the signatures of theologians.
3. Cardinal Amleto Cicognani, Secretary of the Congregation for the Eastern Church from 1960 to 1961, had been appointed Secretary of State on the death of Cardinal Tardini. He was to become President of the Co-ordinating Commission and of the Conciliar Commission on the Eastern Churches.

3 October 1962

Visit from Mgr Elchinger who had asked me, by telephone, to suggest the names of bishops to vote for in the ten episcopal commissions of twenty four members (sixteen of whom were to be elected by the bishops themselves). I had prepared a list and I suggested to him: for France, Mgrs Marty, Guerry, Guyot,[1] Villot, Blanchet, Le Cordier,[2] and himself.

Apart from France,
Mgr Heenan, Liverpool
Mgr Hurley, Durban
Mgr Ghattas, Coptic Bishop of Thebes (Egypt)
Mgr Larraín, Bishop of Talca (Chile)
Mgr Maury,[3] Apostolic Delegate in Dakar
Mgr Schoemaker,[4] Vicar Apostolic of Purwokerto (Indonesia)
Mgr Van Bekkum,[5] Vicar Apostolic of Ruteng (Indonesia)
Mgr Volk, Mainz
Mgr Hermaniuk (CSSR, Ruthenians, Canada)
Mgr Jaeger,[6] Paderborn
Mgr Charue, Namur
Mgr Suhr, Copenhagen.

I added that the following had expressed themselves in favour of the rights of bishops in their pre-preparatory *Votum*:

Mgr Von Streng,[7] Basle and Lugano
Mgr NJ Arnau,[8] Auxiliary Bishop of Barcelona
AH Ibáñez,[9] Bishop of Jaca (Spain)

---

1. Louis Guyot, Bishop of Coutances.
2. Jacques Le Cordier, Auxiliary Bishop of Paris. He was to be appointed sub-secretary of the Council at the beginning of 1965.
3. Jean-Baptiste Maury, Apostolic Delegate in Dakar for West Africa.
4. Willem Schoemaker was in fact Bishop of Purwokerto, an episcopal see since January 1961.
5. Willem van Bekkum, Bishop of Ruteng (Indonesia), member of the Preparatory Commission on the Liturgy, then member of the Conciliar Commission on the Liturgy.
6. Lorenz Jaeger, archbishop of Paderborn (Germany), member of the Secretariat for Unity, created cardinal in February 1965.
7. Franz von Streng, Bishop of Basle and Lugano, member of the Preparatory Commission on the Discipline of the Sacraments.
8. Narcisio Jubany Arnau, Auxiliary bishop of Barcelona, consultor to the Preparatory Commission on Bishops and the Government of Dioceses. During the Council, he was to be a member of the Commission on Bishops and the Government of Dioceses.
9. Angel Hidalgo Ibáñez, Bishop of Jaca (Spain).

Leopoldo Garay,[1] Madrid

+ (Van Roey[2]), Guerry, Cardinal O'Hara[3] (Philadelphia)

and, to secure greater internationalisation of the Roman Curia:

NJ Geise,[4] Prefect Apostolic of Sukabumi, Indonesia, Cardinal Alfrink, who had actually suggested that the Curia should become a simple organ of EXECUTION, the decisions to be made by a permanent synod established along the lines of the Central Commission and meeting once a year.

English-speaking bishops to counter a surfeit of mariology:

Archbishop of Armagh[5]

Bishop of Leeds[6]

Cardinal Godfrey, (Westminster) (but he is not a great ecumenist. When Cardinal Bea went to London [[a few months ago]], he left for his house in the country and did not receive the cardinal either in London or at his country residence.)

9 October 1962

The bishops' plane: took off at 4.45 pm from Orly. Great fuss and commotion, lounge, etc. I saw a number of the bishops and intoned for them my two refrains:

      1)   The message to the world

      2)   The revision of the doctrinal *schemata*.

Mgr Marty, Mgr Guerry, Mgr the Auxiliary Bishop of Angoulême,[7] whom I sat beside during the journey, are all very much in favour of the Message.

10 October 1962

In the morning, at 9 am, went with Fr Camelot to the secretariat[8] bringing two photographs in order to be given an expert's identity card. Both there and on the other side where the press rooms are located, and where the bishops were gathered in their hundreds in order to collect their documentation, there was a lot of unpreparedness. Behind the papers with attractive headings, there is little substance. I met some journalists there, especially Pélissier[9] from *La Croix* and

---

1. Leopoldo Eijo y Garay, Bishop of Madrid.
2. Cardinal Josef van Roey, Archbishop of Malines had died in August 1961.
3. Cardinal John F O'Hara, Archbishop of Philadelphia, who had died on 28 August, 1960.
4. The Franciscan Paternus NJ Geise, who became Bishop of Bogor (Indonesia) in 1961.
5. Cardinal John d'Alton.
6. George P Dwyer.
7. René Kérautret, Coadjutor Bishop of Angoulême.
8. Pierre-Thomas Camelot, OP, of the Province of France, taught patristics and the history of dogma at the Faculties of Le Saulchoir: he became a Council expert.
9. Jean Pélissier was the chief religious correspondent for *La Croix*.

Mayor[1] of *ICI*. They told me that there are seven hundred journalists here and they are furious because the rooms made available to them are wonderful, with very up-to-date equipment, but no-one tells them ANYTHING. They have elected a sort of Committee to get something done and, if this situation continues, they are prepared to make a fuss.

We called in to the Secretariat for Unity where we met Fr Stransky,[2] Mgr Arrighi, Mgr Willebrands. They were engaged in showing round a number of Observers,[3] or Protestant ministers who had come as journalists. Arrighi told me that at this juncture, only a few hours before the opening session, it was still not known where the Observers were to be located in St Peter's. Nothing has been planned for them . . .

Lunch at Santa Sabina. I saw Fr Hamer and Fr General.[4] The Priory is lovely, but this lunch seemed to me very dull.

I had a visit from Laurentin who seemed to me to have become impossible: buzzing about like a bee in a bottle, planning tricks, pouncing on everything that he could make use of, everything that he can turn to his own advantage. If I did not know him, I would say: a schemer.

11 October 1962

I have just come back from the opening ceremony. Left here at 7 am with Fr Camelot. We entered by the Bronze Door and the great staircase, then in front of the Pauline Chapel, we wandered by mistake into the places reserved for the bishops (saw Mgr Guerry, who is entirely in favour of the idea of a Message to the World); we were ejected from there by a huge gendarme in a bearskin, like an ogre in a puppet show: one would hardly know how to invent such a complete bogeyman. We wandered about in search of somewhere where we would be admitted. We encountered Fr Salaverri, Mgr Schmaus, Mgr Fenton and some other American prelates who were talking rather loudly, Mgr Colombo, Fr Tascon,[5] etc. In the end, we were admitted to a tribune, on condition that we

---

1. Francis Mayor, journalist for *Informations catholiques internationales,* appointed to cover the Council.
2. The American Paulist, Thomas F Stransky, was *scrittore-archivista* (writer-archivist) and, later, from 1963 onwards, *minutante* (note-taker) at the Secretariat for Unity.
3. The non-Catholic Observers were appointed by their respective Churches to represent them at the Council; they were looked after by the Secretariat for Christian Unity.
4. At that time, the Spaniard Aniceto Fernandez, who was elected on 22 July 1962 at the General Chapter held in Toulouse. Master of Theology and professor at the Angelicum, he had been Vicar General of the Order, then Provincial of the Spanish Province; he was to be appointed member of the Doctrinal Commission by the Pope during the First Session; with rare exceptions, it is to him that Congar refers when he speaks of 'Fernandez'.
5. Tomás Tascón, OP, of the Province of the Philippines, Secretary General of the Dominican Order and a Council expert.

eventually moved back from the front rows in favour of the Council Fathers (they would be the Superiors of Congregations). I tried to absorb the *genius loci* [spirit of the place]. St Peter's was made for this kind of thing. It is an enchanting display of colours, in which gold and red predominate. The nave is entirely filled with 2,500 tiered seats: in front of the Altar of the Confession, and actually on the Confession, stood the papal throne: *Petrus ipse* [Peter himself]. On the right-hand side, the statue of St Peter dressed as though Boniface VIII; right beside it, like a barrel, the ambo for the speakers. The nearest places, draped in red, are for the cardinals; the others, draped in green, for the archbishops and bishops, stretching as far as the eye can see. The tribunes are draped in red velvet and tapestries. It all gleams, shines, sings under the spotlights. Solemnity, but with a rather cold air about it all. A decorative scheme inspired, as it were, by the theatre of the Baroque. Between the tribunes, the huge statues of the founders of Orders, in their niches. I could only identify St Ignatius of Loyola, throwing impiety to the ground. I wish these statues could speak! What would they say? I imagine what they might say as men of God, consumed by the fire of the Gospel.

At 8.35 am we heard over the loudspeaker the far-away sound of a sort of military march. Then the *Credo* was sung. I have come here *IN ORDER TO PRAY*, to pray WITH, to pray IN. I did in fact pray a lot. However, in order to pass the time, a choir sang in succession anything and everything. The best known chants: *Credo, Magnificat, Adoro Te, Salve Regina, Veni Sancte Spiritus, Inviolata, Benedictus* . . . To begin with, one sang with them, but then got tired.

The most curious pushed to the front and stood up on the chairs. We were overwhelmed by young clerics of all colours. I refused to give way to this unrestrained and ill-mannered behaviour, with the result that I was pushed to the back of the tribune and did not even see the Pope. Little by little, but very slowly, the bishops came in, in cope and mitre, from the lower end of their tribunes. They seemed dead with fatigue and overcome with heat. They removed their mitres and mopped their foreheads. The superiors of the Congregations arrived and took up their seats in the front rows of the tribune. Hoary ecclesiastical heads, their appearance etched by the regularity of their pious exercises and their prudent and edifying behaviour. Some were trembling and seemed ready to collapse. Others were fine and strong.

My God, who have brought me here by ways that I did not choose, I offer myself to you to be, if you will, the instrument of your Gospel in this event in the life of the Church, which I love, but would like to be less 'Renaissance'! less Constantinian . . .

We heard clapping in St Peter's Square. The Pope must be coming. He must have come in. I saw nothing, behind six or seven rows of soutanes standing up on chairs. From time to time, there was clapping in the Basilica, but no shouting and no words.

The *Veni Creator* was sung, alternately with the Sistine Choir, which is nothing but an opera chorus. DELENDA [to be suppressed]. The Pope sang the versicles and the prayers in a firm voice.

The Mass began, sung entirely by the Sistine choir: a few bits of Gregorian (?) and some polyphony. The liturgical movement has not yet reached the Roman Curia. This immense assembly says nothing, sings nothing.

It is said that the Jews are the people of hearing, the Greeks of sight. There is nothing here except for the eye and the musical ear: no liturgy of the Word. No spiritual word. I know that in a few minutes a Bible will be placed on a throne in order to preside over the Council. BUT WILL IT SPEAK? Will it be listened to? Will there be a moment for the Word of God?

After the epistle, I left the tribune. In any case, I could not take any more. And then, I was overcome by this seigneurial, Renaissance set-up. I paused for a moment underneath our tribune. From directly behind the bishops and above their tiers of seats, one could see the whole of the immense white assembly of copes and mitres, in which the Eastern bishops stood out on account of their multi-coloured costumes and headgear. Five or ten minutes later I was ejected by a gendarme in a bearskin.

I tried to get out of the basilica. It was not easy. The unused side aisles and the ends of the transepts were crammed with crowds of young clerics moving around, endeavouring to squeeze into somewhere where they could SEE. All people want is to SEE.

I got out through the Vatican. In St Peter's Square, under the colonnades, crowds of people. The loudspeakers were transmitting the rest of the Mass. From the Square and from the street I thus heard the Preface, the *Sanctus,* the *Pater Noster* and the *Agnus Dei.* I returned, exhausted, by bus to the Angelicum. After about half an hour during which my hand was unable to hold a pen, I wrote these notes. I unfortunately saw far too little of the wonderful sight of the senate of bishops in session. I only saw them for the five or ten minutes during which I was able to stand in the doorway leading downwards, and above the tiers of bishops. The whole Church was there, embodied in its pastors. But I regret that a style of celebration was employed that was so alien to the reality of things. What would it have been if those 2,500 voices had together sung at least the *Credo,* if not all the chants of the Mass, instead of that elegant crooning by paid professionals? I returned with an immensely stronger desire: 1) to be evangelical, to aim at being a *homo plene evangelicus* [human being fully dedicated to the Gospel]; 2) to WORK. THAT produces results. THAT remains. That will prepare, for the next Council, a state of things where what is missing today will be taken for granted.

Afternoon. Fr De la Brosse, who saw it all on TV (until 12.30 pm), told me that it was splendid, very well photographed, transmitted and explained. And to think that with Telstar, the whole world could see it all, at the very moment at which things were happening . . . ! (No: the direct link was restricted to Europe only).

I thought more about this morning's ceremony. Its pomp implies two things: in addition to the fact, not only inevitable, but normal and good, that there must be order, solemnity and beauty; that it is impossible to have an inauguration involving more than 3,000 people without organising some kind of display, a certain ceremonial. That is entirely good and noble. Over and above this state of things, I see how Eastern the Church is. The Reformation was not at all such at its birth: it may win members in the East, but it was not in any way or to any degree Eastern in its creators, in its origins, in its native and formative shape. On top of that, I see the weight, that has never been renounced, of the period when the Church behaved as a feudal lord, when it had temporal power, when popes and bishops were lords who had a court, gave patronage to artists and sought a pomp equal to that of the Caesars. That, the Church has never repudiated in Rome. To emerge from the Constantinian era has never been part of its programme. Poor Pius IX, who understood nothing about the movement of history, who buried French Catholicism in a sterile attitude of opposition, of conservatism, of Restorationist sentiment . . . was called by God to listen to the lesson of events, those masters which he gives us with his own hands, and to free the Church from the wretched logic of the 'Donation of Constantine', and convert it to an evangelical attitude which would have enabled it to be less OF the world and more FOR the world. He did exactly the opposite. A catastrophic man who did not know what the ECCLESIA was, nor yet what Tradition was; he oriented the Church to be always OF the world and not yet FOR the world, which nevertheless stood in need of it.

And Pius IX still reigns. Boniface VIII still reigns; he has been superimposed on Simon Peter, the humble fisher of men!

As they left this morning's ceremony, each of the bishops was given a folder containing the voting papers for them to elect sixteen bishops from among themselves for each of the ten Commissions; a booklet containing a complete and fully up-to-date list of the bishops of the Church; a list, for each Commission, and in the format of a voting paper, of the bishops who were already members of the various Preparatory Commissions. It amounted to an invitation to elect these . . . Yet, a certain continuity between the work of the Council and that of the Preparatory Commissions is desirable. But it is also desirable to do now something both different and better than what has been prepared: something pastoral, less scholastic. Nearly all the bishops that I have spoken to and whose opinion I have been told about, deemed the four dogmatic *schemata* much too academic and philosophical. A Council, they say, does not need to argue by syllogisms, to speak of the principle of sufficient reason, etc.

Basically, scholasticism has penetrated the government of the Roman Curia. The Preparatory Commissions reflected this state of affairs, both because they wanted to produce a *summa* of papal addresses and utterances, and also because most of them (at any rate almost all those who drafted the schemata) were made up of professors in the Roman colleges. But scholasticism hardly has a place in the pastoral government of dioceses, and it is this that now has the floor.

Friday 12 October 1962

Moscow is sending two Observers. Two bishops: one who lives in Geneva and the other in Jerusalem.[1] This will undoubtedly lead to the other Orthodox Churches doing likewise.

This morning I dragged myself over to the Procure de St Sulpice in order to see Mgr Weber and Mgr Marty, 'my' bishops.[2] Unfortunately, they had gone out, like all the other bishops, 'with a satchel, like schoolboys'. They had undoubtedly gone to the meeting to choose the members of the Commissions. I was very sorry not to have found anyone, and went back almost on my hands and knees. Fortunately, at the end of the morning I had a visit from Cardinal Feltin's[3] and Cardinal Gerlier's[4] secretaries. I was able to say to them one of the things I had wanted to suggest to the bishops themselves: contact with the Observers. They told me how very critical their bishops had been of the draft *schemata* they had received. I added to what they had said.[5]

At 2 pm, RAI (Italian radio) recorded a three-way dialogue on the Council to be broadcast on French radio on Friday next, between Laurentin, Dubois-Dumée and myself.

A little before 5 pm, visit from Mgr Young,[6] an Australian bishop, young, mixture of straight-talking and solemnity. He has fed on Congar for twenty years. He told me how terribly disappointed he was in the schemata and in the ceremony

---

1. In fact, two priests: the first, Archpriest Vitalij Borovoj, was a professor of theology; having been made responsible for preparing the entry of his Church into the WCC in 1961, he then represented it in Geneva; he was to be the Observer appointed by the Patriarchate of Moscow throughout the Council; the second, Archimandrite Vladimir Kotliarov, was vice-superior of the Russian religious Mission in Jerusalem.
2. Congar's diocese of origin was Rheims, of which Mgr Marty was Bishop.
3. Jean Diot, CSSp.
4. Henri Denis, priest of the diocese of Lyons, was a professor at the Séminaire Saint Iré-née in Lyons. He became Episcopal Vicar of his diocese in 1964, and was put in charge of on-going formation and sacramental ministry. Having been brought to the Council by Cardinal Gerlier to act as his secretary, he was appointed a Council expert at the end of the First Session.
5. Concerning this conversation, cf Henri Denis, *Église, qu'as-tu fait de ton concile?* (Paris: Le Centurion, 1985), 25: 'Went to the Angelicum where we met Fr Congar, as serene as he was exhausted by his illness. Good conversation displaying a wise prudence. One must not antagonise the Romans by a frontal attack. What are needed are *via media* men. In his view, three things are essential for the moment: 1) What has become of the comments submitted by the bishops on the various draft schemas? 2) What contact have the French bishops got with the 'foreigners'? 3) How do the bishops feel about the Observers? They ought to be sent invitations and engaged in dialogue.'
6. Guilford C Young, born in 1916, Archbishop of Hobart (Australia).

in St Peter's, indeed almost to the point of being scandalised. We preach to the laity about participation, and look at the example they are given! He asked me to suggest the names of bishops for the voting for the Commissions tomorrow. We chatted. We will meet again.

Taxi in order to go to the reception at the embassy. I had not yet received the invitation and I was told that it was at 5 pm. As a result, I arrived much too early. I went to see Fr Delos[1] in order to kill time. I was glad to have the opportunity to meet quite a large number of bishops. (Protocol at these receptions requires that, as soon as they arrive, the cardinals are shown into a separate room, where they have their own buffet. IN THIS WAY THEY ARE KEPT APART AND CAN DIALOGUE ONLY AMONG THEMSELVES. It is only by a kind of breaking and entering that one can reach them.) They are all very dissatisfied with yesterday's ceremony. They are all unhappy with the doctrinal *schemata*. They all tell me that they are pleased to see me there and that they are counting on me. I tell them all that all I want is to work, but cannot do so unless the bishops give me work to do. Cullmann[2] was there, H Roux,[3] Thurian[4] and Schutz. I kissed them all on both cheeks. The first two were devastated by the *schemata*: 'it's as if nothing had been achieved during the last fifty years', 'it amounts to going even further back than the Council of Trent. . . ' Cullmann also said, à propos of Thursday's ceremony: 'Is that what your liturgical movement is?' Alas! It has not yet got through the Bronze Door! All four of them said how pleased they were to see me there, and we promised to meet again.

I introduced Roux and Cullmann to some of the bishops. To a good number of them I intoned my refrain: they need to meet the Observers, to encourage them, to discuss things with them. I'll have to speak to them again about this. If only God would give me back the use of my legs!!!

I learned from Mgr Jenny that the French bishops have voted only for Frenchmen in the Commissions. Unfortunately, those competent in several areas were elected onto several Commissions, with the result that their names did not appear in the end: this happened to Mgr Marty and Mgr Blanchet. It is a great pity.

---

1. Thomas Delos, OP, of the Province of France, was canonical counsellor at the French Embassy to the Holy See and Professor of Public Law at the Angelicum.
2. The Protestant theologian Oscar Cullmann was professor at the Sorbonne and at the University of Basle; he was the guest of the Secretariat for Unity.
3. Hébert Roux, a pastor of the Reformed Church of France, was an Observer appointed by the World Presbyterian Alliance at the first two Sessions, then official Observer for the Protestant Federation of France during the last Session.
4. Max Thurian, reformed pastor and theologian, was sub-prior of Taizé; he was the guest of the Secretariat for Unity during the Council. He was later to pursue his commitment to the ecumenical movement and eventually joined the Catholic Church in which he was ordained priest in 1986.

I saw Cardinal Liénart regarding the Message to the World. He told me that, as this was not included in the programme, it ought to be submitted to Cardinal Cicognani, but that the cardinal (to whom it seems he had already spoken) was inclined to approve of it. The cardinal also told me that I ought to speak to Cardinal Lefebvre[1] and Mgr Garrone. The latter did not come to the reception, but I saw Cardinal Lefebvre, whom I had never met. He was very pleasant, seemed frank and direct. We agreed that we would need a slightly shorter text and one in which it was more clearly stated that it is Jesus Christ who saves humankind from its wretchedness. But he seemed in favour of the idea of doing something in this sense.

I saw Fr M Villain,[2] Fr de Lubac, Fr Daniélou,[3] Jean Guitton,[4] the *TC* team, G Suffert,[5] a great many bishops. Made the acquaintance of Mgr Flusin[6] and others.

Prayer is very badly needed! I believe in prayer. *I HOPE.*

Saturday 13 October 1962

In St Peter's at 9 am, in the tribune. This time, the bishops were all in purple *mantelette*, but those belonging to religious orders had their own specific colour: white, black, grey, and the Eastern Rite bishops had their own particular costume.

Mass of the Holy Spirit, a low Mass and with dialogue. But the responses from 2,500 breasts was rushed and chaotic. It was quite difficult to follow.

The secretary[7] went up into the ambo and announced that the bishops were invited to fill in the sixteen spaces with sixteen names from among themselves for each of the ten Commissions. Many of them started at once to write names. How-

---

1. Joseph Lefebvre, Archbishop of Bourges.
2. The Marist Maurice Villain, after having been a professor at the Séminaire des Missions d'Océanie near Lyons, devoted himself entirely to ecumenical activity, especially by running the 'Groupe des Dombes'; personal expert of a Marist bishop from Oceania, he was also following the Council on behalf of the magazine *Rhythmes du monde*.
3. Jean Daniélou, SJ, patrologist and specialist in the origins of Christianity, had contributed to the patristic renewal, in particular by founding, with Henri de Lubac, the 'Sources chrétiennes' collection; Dean of the Faculty of Theology at the Institut Catholique in Paris, he was a Council expert and the personal expert of Mgr Veuillot; Paul VI was to make him a cardinal in 1969.
4. The philosopher Jean Guitton was a professor at the Sorbonne and a member of the Académie Française; he had been a comrade in captivity with Congar; being also a friend of Cardinal Montini, and connected with the ecumenical movement, he was to be allowed, in November 1962, to sit with the non-Catholic Observers; from the Second Session onwards, he was to sit with the lay Auditors.
5. Georges Suffert, formerly chief editor of *Témoignage chrétien,* was following the Council on behalf of *France Observateur.*
6. Claude Flusin, Bishop of Saint-Claude.
7. Pericle Felici, Secretary General of the Council, *AS* I/I, 207.

ever, after some silence, Cardinal Liénart[1] (at the *presidium*[2] immediately to the right of the first President, Cardinal Tisserant), stood up and read a paper asking for this election to be delayed until Monday or Tuesday, in order to give the bishops time to get to know one another from country to country. This would ensure greater cordiality, greater freedom and confidence, and above all a better selection of names for these Commissions, which were very important. He even suggested a form of procedure: since bishops' conferences exist in forty-two countries, each of these conferences should suggest a certain number of names, with an indication of the number of dioceses that they encompass. (The paper read by Cardinal Liénart on the first day of the First Session had been written by Mgr Garrone, whose idea it had been. Cardinal Liénart did no more than read it.)

This double suggestion was warmly applauded. A little later, Cardinal Frings[3] stood up to say that he seconded this recommendation in the name of the German and Austrian cardinals.

After a brief pause, the Secretary of the Council announced that he concurred with this recommendation and that the elections would take place on the following Tuesday.

This little point was important. To begin with, all points of procedure are important: they involve the work of a group. In this case, the principal importance rests in the fact that THIS IS THE FIRST *CONCILIAR* ACT, a refusal to accept even the possibility of a prefabrication. The bishops had been given, in the same format as the voting papers, a list of those who had been members of the Preparatory PONTIFICAL Commissions: it is likely that many would, to a considerable extent, have copied this list. We would thus have been faced with the same men who had prepared these texts with which the bishops are dissatisfied. Cardinal Liénart's proposal recognised the importance of the Commissions in which the texts will be drawn up. It revealed the bishops' desire to be free to discuss things, without accepting something that had been prepared in advance by the Curia and its people. It means that the bishops intend to talk and discuss things. Moreover, Cardinal Liénart has suggested a procedure which gives reality and importance to the intermediate bodies. Between the supreme head (and his Curia) and the individual bishops, there are intermediate groupings. One of the results of the Council ought to be that of giving them more power and independence. The importance of this was demonstrated on the very first day.

What I foresaw is happening: the Council itself could well be very different from its preparation.

---

1. *AS* I/I, 207–208.
2. The Council of Presidents, consisting of ten Cardinals, was responsible for chairing the Council meetings.
3. *AS* I/I, 208.

Sunday 14 October 1962

I was told that the 'Holy Office' (Parente) has distributed a list of bishops to be elected to the Theological Commission. It has been distributed to the Italian and Spanish bishops and to the English-speaking ones (Irish); and possibly also to others, but not to the French, the Germans or the Dutch . . .

If this is true, it would give notice of the inevitable conflict between the Curia and the *ecclesia*. Two Churches within a single framework!

Visit from Jean Guitton, who has got himself sent here on behalf both of *Le Figaro* and of the Academy. Being himself an Academician, he is well received and honoured! He has lines of approach to Cardinal Montini. He told me that the beatification of Pius IX is in fact being seriously considered: the Pope would like it, in order to link Vatican II with Vatican I.

The further I go the more I find Pius IX puny and catastrophic. He was primarily responsible for the unfortunate orientation that has weighed on French Catholicism for the past sixty years. Precisely when he was being called upon by events to leave behind the frightful lie of the 'Donation of Constantine'[1] and at last adopt an evangelical attitude, he perceived nothing of this summons, and sank the Church even deeper into its insistence on temporal power.

This temporal demeanor is still crushing the Church of today with all its weight. All this heavy and costly apparatus, prestigious and infatuated with itself, imprisoned in its own myth of seigneurial grandeur, belongs to the non-Christian part of the Roman Church and it is this that conditions, or rather prevents, its opening out to a fully evangelical and prophetic task: all of this comes from the lie of the Donation of Constantine. I see it clearly in these present days. Nothing decisive can be done until the Roman Church has emerged *COMPLETELY* from its seigneurial and temporal pretensions. *ALL OF THAT* must be **DONE AWAY WITH**; AND IT WILL BE!

Of course, there must be order: positions of superiority must be given external expression by marks of dignity. But all of that must be limited simply to the function. Those that exist in Rome have been borrowed directly from a world of TEMPORAL POWER which is not even that of the contemporary world but rather that of the Byzantine empire, that of the sumptuous princes of the Renaissance, that of the period of the Restoration and of the Holy Alliance. What is needed is to turn one's back on all that and to discover something else, something which is both modern and evangelical, communitarian too, and not satrapic.

I have read the little speech the Pope made to the Observers whom he received in audience. Some people found it very inadequate. That is not my opinion. It is true that he said nothing on the theological or historical level. But that does not matter very much. He was cordial, very simple, Christian. And then, whatever he

---

1. According to which the emperor Constantine is said to have been baptised by Pope Sylvester and to have given him the city of Rome and a certain number of other territories; it has been criticised and denounced by scholars since the fifteenth century.

is, the monumental fact is that a speech was made, that there are Observers, that the Pope has received them, that there is a Council. Such facts have their own weight, and that is enough. Who would have thought that all this would have happened before I reach my sixtieth year?

Monday 15 October 1962

At 4 pm. I called in to the Biblical Institute where I met Fr Lyonnet who confirmed that that there was, in fact, a list of bishops for the Theological Commission, drawn up by the Holy Office AND MARKED WITH ITS STAMP. He told me that Mgr Spadafora[1] had produced a separate brochure containing his articles against the Biblical Institute, and had distributed it to a great many: at a meeting that they held yesterday, each Italian bishop had found a copy in his place. He showed me the brochure and promised to give me a copy. I think that will contribute to the confusion of the imbeciles.

I went to the reception organised by the Secretariat in honour of the Observers and others invited. Conversation with Fr Pierre Duprey.[2] Cardinal Alfrink's scheme for a kind of *synodos endêmousa*[3] composed of the heads of the bishops' conferences that, by reducing the Curia's role to an executive one, should make it possible for the Eastern patriarchs to become *ipso facto* cardinals, since the heads of the conferences are all cardinals.

Speech by Cardinal Bea (in French, text here); fairly long reply in German by Schlink[4] and in English (Canon Pawley[5]). One went from one to the other.

---

1. Francesco Spadafora, of the diocese of Cosenza, was Professor of Exegesis in the Faculty of Theology at the Lateran; he had been a member of the Preparatory Commission on Studies and Seminaries.

2. Pierre Duprey, White Father, Professor of Dogmatic Theology and the History of Dogma at the Saint-Anne Seminary in Jerusalem until 1963. Congar had met him for the first time when he went to the East on an ecumenical tour in 1954, and had recognised his worth. Very involved in ecumenical contacts, he participated in the First Session of the Council as theological interpreter for the Orthodox Observers. In 1963 he was to be appointed sub-secretary of the completely new section of the Secretariat for Unity responsible for contacts with the Eastern Churches. He was later to become Secretary of the Pontifical Council for the Unity of Christians and a titular bishop.

3. Permanent synod. In the Byzantine Church this synod is formed of bishops who remain with the Patriarch and are regularly consulted by him. Alfrink's proposal was rather different, and drew its inspiration from the experience of the Central Preparatory Commission.

4. Edmund Schlink, Professor of Systematic Theology and Director of the Institute for Ecumenical Research which he had founded at the University of Heidelberg; he also helped with the work of the Faith and Order section of the World Council of Churches; Observer appointed by the Evangelical Church of Germany.

5. Canon Bernard Pawley, of Ely Cathedral (England), was an Observer appointed by the Anglican Communion; he arrived in Rome before the opening of the Council and represented the Archbishops of Canterbury and York during the first three Sessions.

Conversations with Schlink, the two Russians from Moscow, the Russians not attached to Moscow[1] (who were seated apart and to whom the servants were bringing plates of cakes), Roux, Canon Maan[2] (Old Catholic). Bishop Moorman,[3] Skydsgaard,[4] Lukas Vischer,[5] Bishop Corson[6] (Methodist), etc; Mgr Davis,[7] Mgr Volk, Mgr Heenan, Mgr De Smedt,[8] etc.

It has HAPPENED. 'They' are in Rome, and have been received by a cardinal and an organisation dedicated to dialogue; and *Chrétiens désunis*[9] appeared twenty-five years ago.

I was barely able to walk on my way back and I wonder will I be able to keep going until the end of the Council. Since we came, the weather has been unpleasantly stormy.

Mgr Martin told me that the meetings between the conferences of bishops promise to be very interesting. The French bishops are going to set up a sort of permanent arrangement, or regular meetings on a fixed day, to facilitate them and make them as inclusive as possible. ONE OF THE RESULTS OF THE COUNCIL COULD WELL BE THE BIRTH OF AN ORGANISED AND STRUCTURED WORLD-WIDE EPISCOPAL COLLEGIALITY.

---

1. The Observers appointed by the Russian Church in exile were Mgr Antoine (Bartasevic), Bishop of Geneva, and Archpriest Igor Troyanoff, Rector of the Orthodox Churches of Lausanne and Vevey.
2. Canon Peter J Maan, Observer appointed by the Old Catholic Church, was Professor of Holy Scripture at the Amersfoort seminary (Netherlands) and in 1964 became Rector of the Old Catholic Cathedral of Utrecht.
3. John Moorman, Bishop of Ripon (England) was an Observer appointed by the Anglican Communion.
4. Pastor Kristen E Skydsgaard, Professor of Systematic Theology and Director of the Ecumenical Institute at the University of Copenhagen (Denmark), was an Observer appointed by the World Lutheran Federation.
5. Lukas Vischer, pastor of the Swiss Reformed Church, was secretary of the Faith and Order section of the WCC; he was an Observer appointed by the WCC.
6. Fred P Corson, Methodist bishop, President of the World Council of Methodists for which he was one of the official Observers.
7. Henry F Davis, of the diocese of Birmingham (England), was Professor of Theology at the University of Birmingham and a member of the CCEQ [Catholic Conference for Ecumenical Questions]; he was an expert at the Council and consultor to the Secretariat for Unity.
8. Émile De Smedt, Bishop of Bruges, member of the Secretariat for Unity, of which he later became a Vice-President.
9. Yves Congar, *Chrétiens désunis. Principes d'un «oecuménisme» catholique,* 'Unam Sanctam', 1 (Paris: Cerf, 1937).

Tuesday 16 October 1962

General session for the elections to the Commissions. Each of the bishops was given a printed booklet containing the proposals made by the various bishops' conferences. It is enormous and the proposals are still very diverse.

The names of four general sub-secretaries were announced: a German,[1] a Dutchman,[2] an American,[3] and a Frenchman (Mgr Villot).[4] Good.

Cardinal Ottaviani proposed that it be sufficient to obtain a relative majority by adding up all the votes that each person had received, and that a person with such a majority be appointed to the Commission for which he had received the greatest number of votes. This proposal evoked criticism from Cardinal Roberti[5] (juridical question) and from Cardinal Ruffini[6] who said that one cannot change the rules without the Pope's approval. The *praesidium* [Council of Presidents] was of the same opinion.

The bishops were invited to prepare their list and to hand it in to the secretariat either at once or before 6 pm. End of meeting. Enormous waste of time! Having left before 8 am, I returned at 11.15 am . . . Work.

Headline in *France-Soir*, a French newspaper: 'Rebellion of the French Bishops.' What rubbish. How dishonest!!!

17 October 1962

Mayor, of *Informations Catholiques Internationales*, told me that this ridiculous headline came from the editors in Paris, not from the publication's representative in Rome,[7] which is serious. He added, quite rightly: they would never allow themselves to do that in a report on a UN meeting; but because it is about religion, they allow themselves to do almost anything.

Mayor also told me: 1) that the editor of *Civiltà* is very good; he is a friend. 2) that the Pope reads *Civiltà* very carefully. (So I gave him my article[8] that was published in *L'Ami du Clergé* on the *Épiscopat*[9] volume, so that they can translate it . . .)

---

1. Wilhelm Kempf, Bishop of Limburg (Germany), *AS*/I/I, 213.
2. In fact, it was Casimiro Morcillo González, Archbishop of Saragossa (Spain); he was to become Archbishop of Madrid in March 1964. *AS* I/I, 213.
3. John J Krol, Archbishop of Philadelphia, *AS* I/I, 213.
4. *AS* I/I, 213.
5. Cardinal Francesco Roberti, Prefect of the Supreme Tribunal of the Apostolic Signatura, and future member of the Co-ordination Commission.
6. Cardinal Ernesto Ruffini, Archbishop of Palermo, member of the Council of Presidents.
7. Jean Neuvecelle.
8. 'L'Episcopat et l'Église universelle', in *L'Ami du Clergé*, 9 August 1962: 508–511.
9. *L'Épiscopat et l'Église universelle*, 'Unam Sanctam', 39 (Paris: Cerf, 1962).

18 October 1962

I had a number of visitors this morning, including Mgr Philips. Cardinal Suenens has asked him to go over (to complete and correct) with Fr Rahner and one or two others all the texts on the Church. I wonder whether this work is not somewhat premature, as these texts will not be discussed until the Second Session. I also wonder whether, even before this, it will not be necessary to raise the question of an overall plan and orientation with respect to all the doctrinal *schemata*, in the spirit of a synthesis that is kerygmatic in presentation. But I replied very explicitly that I would be ready to share in such a re-working with Rahner, Lécuyer and Lubac.

Mgr Philips envisages the chapters of *De Ecclesia* as follows:
1) The Church as People of God, Mystery, Mystical Body
   (introduce the power of the bishops into the Lattanzi schema[1] which does not mention it).
   I myself would like to see the idea of the Church as missionary in this first chapter: an ever-widening unity.
2) *De membris* [On its membership]. Need for the Church. Adapt Tromp's schema.
3) The bishops. Present them as successors of the college of apostles, as follows:

   PETER   =   POPE
      the other apostles   the bishops

   This chapter would contain the following paragraphs:
   - The bishops as successors of the apostles
   - episcopate as sacrament
   - powers of diocesan bishops
     teaching: their infallibility   -when assembled in Council
                                       -when dispersed
     insert here sections of the chapter *De Magisterio* and an explanation of the expression *ex sese*[2]
   - government (rework Pius IX's text, 1875[3]) cultural power
   — their relationship with the primacy
   — collegial responsibility of the bishops

---

1. The reference is to chapter 1 of the schema on the Church; cf above, page 39, note 1.
2. The expression *ex sese* (by themselves) had been used by Vatican Council I to stipulate that irreformable definitions promulgated by the pope are so of themselves and without the juridical necessity of subsequent approval by the Church.
3. The reference is to the letter of Pius IX to the German bishops dated 2 March 1875 approving these bishops' reaction to Bismarck's claim that the Council had reduced the bishops to simple instruments. Cf Olivier Rousseau, 'La vraie valeur de l'épiscopat dans l'Église d'après d'importants documents de 1875', *Irénikon*, 1956: 121–150. This article was reprinted in *L'Épiscopat et l'Église universelle*, 'Unam Sanctam', 39 (Paris: Cerf, 1962), 709–736.

4) The laity
5) Evangelical perfection (addressed to ALL Christians). Religious
6) Ecumenism

Only after these chapters, which deal with being Christian, the 'within' of Christianity, the prepared chapters on Church and State, tolerance, etc.

I spoke once more to Mgr Philips about the Message to the World, which Cardinal Suenens had already mentioned to him, he told me.

Lunch at the Biblical Institute with Mgr Weber and a Japanese archbishop. The Fathers are quite concerned about what the Council might say as regards Scripture: on the one hand, the poor quality and narrowness or rigidity of the schema on Tradition and on Scripture, and on the other hand, a renewed attack by the Lateran.

In the afternoon, a good visit from Fr Chenu, who sees a great many people: journalists, African bishops, etc.

Friday 19 October 1962
Visit from Dom O Rousseau. He is well known, mixes a lot, sees a lot of people, goes from one to another bringing the good news. He is right. I reproach myself for being a stay-at-home. Perhaps, instead of living here at the Angelicum, I ought to have taken up residence among the bishops, at Saint-Louis des Français, or the French Seminary, or at the Procure de Saint-Sulpice. Here, I am very isolated. I see almost no-one except those who come here to see me. It is a very regular Priory. Above all, I am very restricted by my legs. As I walk with great difficulty and at the cost of great exhaustion, I restrict my outings to those that are a MUST, for things that are official. Many of the bishops, observers, theologians, or priests have said to me: you must come and speak to us, we must have a meeting, you must come to lunch . . . I have said YES to ALL. These invitations have not been followed up.

I do understand this activity, fairly fruitless, even if it is not useless, since it helps to fashion opinion, to channel ideas. I do not want to contribute to this; I cannot do it, in fact, and I have other things to do. But I reproach myself for not mixing enough with people, for not speaking out more often. Perhaps I am failing in my duty as defined by this special occasion. Perhaps I am very far from doing what I ought to do? What to do? I told Mgr Weber that I was prepared to go and live among the bishops, close to them. So far nothing has been asked of me. I have said to all the bishops that I have met that I was at their service for any work they might want me to do. I wait.

I am working as hard as I can on my *Tradition*, though I am being constantly and frequently interrupted. Up to now, I believe this is my duty. I am ready to do something else instead of this as soon as I can see clearly where my duty lies.

Meeting at 4 pm in Maison Mater Dei, 10 Via delle Mura Aurelie, of a number of German bishops and some French ones, some German and French theologians, organised by Mgr Volk. Those present: Mgr Volk, Mgr Reuss,[1] Mgr Bengsch[2] (Berlin), Mgr Elchinger, Mgr Weber, Mgr Schmitt,[3] Mgr Garrone, Mgr Guerry, Mgr Ancel,[4] Frs Rahner, Lubac, Daniélou, Grillmeier,[5] Semmelroth,[6] Rondet,[7] Labourdette, Congar, Chenu, Schillebeeckx,[8] Feiner,[9] Ratzinger,[10] Mgr Philips, Fransen,[11] Küng.

Purpose of the meeting: to discuss and decide on a tactic in relation to the theological schemas. In a discussion lasting nearly three hours, it became clear that all sorts of nuances were involved. Mgr Volk opened the meeting by reading a kind of draft declaration describing the situation of the Christian in the world today and a view of the history of salvation centred on Christ, in its anthropological, social and cosmological dimensions.

On the whole, the Germans were of the opinion: 1) that the dogmatic schemas as presented should be rejected *simpliciter* [without qualification] (but this would apply only to the texts that have been distributed, not to those relating to *De Ecclesia*); 2) that a *proemium* [foreword] be prepared that was kerygmatic in content and style, along the lines of that suggested by Mgr Volk; 3) that this be submitted through the Secretariat for Extraordinary Affairs.[12]

The French (Garrone, Guerry, Ancel) were more inclined to the view: 1) that very forceful interventions by bishops from the principal countries enable

---

1. Joseph Reuss, Auxiliary Bishop of Mainz.
2. Alfred Bengsch, Archbishop of Berlin.
3. Paul-J Schmitt, Bishop of Metz.
4. Alfred Ancel, Auxiliary Bishop of Lyons, superior general of the {Association des Prêtres du} Prado; he was to be elected a member of the Doctrinal Commission during the Second Session of the Council.
5. Alois Grillmeier, SJ, Professor of Dogmatics and Dean of the Faculty of Theology at the Sankt-Georgen Jesuit scholasticate in Frankfurt; he was to be a Council expert from the Second Session onwards and created cardinal in 1994.
6. Otto Semmelroth, SJ, Professor of Dogmatics at the Sankt-Georgen Jesuit scholasticate in Frankfurt, Council expert from the Third Session onwards.
7. Henri Rondet, SJ, having been removed from teaching theology in 1951, he returned to it in 1960 at the Catholic Faculties in Lyons: personal expert for the bishops of Chad.
8. Edward Schillebeeckx, OP, of the Province of Flanders, Professor of Dogmatics at the University of Nijmegen, was personal expert to the Dutch bishops.
9. Johannes Feiner, priest of the diocese of Coire (Switzerland), where he taught theology in the diocesan seminary until 1965; as a member of the Catholic Conference for Ecumenical Matters, he was a consultor to the Secretariat for Unity and was to be co-editor of the compendium of dogmatic theology entitled *Mysterium Salutis*.
10. Joseph Ratzinger, professor of fundamental theology in Bonn, then in Münster in 1963; personal expert of Cardinal Frings: he was to be a Council expert from the Second Session onwards. He later became Archbishop of Munich and cardinal, then Prefect of the Congregation for the Doctrine of the Faith. He was elected Pope in 2005.
11. Probably Piet Fransen, SJ, Professor of Theology at the Jesuit Theological Faculty in Louvain-Heverlee.
12. This Secretariat was established by the Pope to serve as a mediating body.

the assembly to see that the schemas in no way match the pastoral aim of the Council as defined by the Pope once again in his opening discourse, which should be looked upon as the charter for the Council; 2) following from this, that the existing schemas be reworked in a kerygmatic and pastoral perspective. It would be good to have a text to propose.

For my part, I think that something along the lines of this second point is what is needed: the worth-while substance of the *De Ecclesia* schemas should be taken up IN A GENERAL WAY: those on Tradition and Scripture could be set aside, and that on Christ's making satisfaction should be entirely reworked in a paschal perspective. In fact, my reaction since day one goes to the heart of the matter: what is lacking in Rome is a synthesis, vision, the sense of the Christian mystery. In Rome, everything is broken up into separate juridical interventions. The only principle of synthesis that they possess is that of their own power.

Incidentally, I learnt (from Cardinals Döpfner and Frings) that several times, at the Central Commission, Cardinal Ottaviani had expressed himself in favour of the schemas the bishops were discussing, saying that Fr Congar and Fr de Lubac had approved them.

Fr Daniélou, too, has prepared a draft text very similar to that of Mgr Volk. He read it. In the end, it was decided that it was important to be able to present a *proemium* of a *Heilsgeschichtlich-kerygmatisch* kind ([that was kerygmatic and dealt with the history of salvation].

A small group will prepare such a text: K Rahner, Daniélou, Ratzinger, Congar. At the last minute, Rahner also invited Labourdette.

My left leg is as if it were dead from the middle of the calf downwards. I had great difficulty in getting back here.

Saturday 20 October 1962

Large General Congregation.[1] Good news to begin with. Fr Dumont informed me that the Secretariat for Unity has been raised to the status of a Commission.[2] As such, it will hold regular working meetings. This seems to me to be extremely important. Up to now, the texts produced by the Secretariat have not been taken into consideration. They will be from now on. If the Council has to deal with matters connected with Christian unity, these will be sent for further study in commission, not to the Commission *de fide et moralibus* [on faith and morals][3] where, it is to be feared, the tyranny of Fr Tromp reigns supreme, but instead to

---

1. 'General Congregations' is the description used for working meetings of the Council Fathers (they are numbered).
2. The Pope had decided this on 19 October and the decision was announced *in aula* on 22 October.
3. In other words, to the Doctrinal Commission.

the Secretariat which has now become a Commission; or else to both. In any case, Tromp and company no longer have a monopoly.

We were told that the Pope endorses the elections on the basis of a relative majority: not quite according to the system proposed by Cardinal Ottaviani, which took the one hundred and sixty bishops who had obtained the most votes or *quoque modo* [in one way or another], and allocated them to the Commission for which they had received the most votes, but simply taking as having been elected the first sixteen bishops that obtained the most votes in each of the Commissions. We were given the names of the bishops elected to the first seven Commissions;[1] those elected to the other three Commissions will be announced on Monday. I noted down a good number of the names as they were read out, but will not record them here, as they are given in this evening's edition of *L'Osservatore Romano*. It is quite good. Immediately afterwards, the names were also given of the eight prelates[2] whom the Pope has appointed in order to make up the numbers in the Liturgical Commission. They are the names of men from the Curia and men who are very conservative.

After that, the secretary announced that he was going to read a '*Nuntium ad universos homines mittendum*'[3] [a message to be sent to all people]. I listened to this text which I had had a hand in drafting. I record here, as I wrote them, the few remarks I scribbled at the time: it has more of dogma than Chenu's draft; but at least a sort of Christian kerygma has been inserted before the social section; it has been made more ecclesiastical, more biblical. It is too long. Its interest in humankind is expressed somewhat in terms of solicitude. There is a happy insistence on the renewal of the Church and of the Christian life, so that they might be more conformed to Christ.

After the document had been read, the text was distributed (cf *hic*) and a quarter of an hour for reflection and prayer was announced (it will be more than that in fact). After that, whoever wished to speak would be free to do so.

The following then spoke (briefly and clearly. But it was not always possible to catch the names of the speakers as they were announced by the President, Cardinal Liénart):

> Cardinal Bacci:[4] suggested *adhuc* [again] instead of *semper* [always] at the end.

---

1. *AS* I/I, 225–229.
2. *AS* I/I, 213.
3. *AS* I/I, 230-232; *La Documentation Catholique*, 1962, col 1407 -1410.
4. Antonio Bacci, from the Curia, *AS* I/I, 234.

Cardinal Wyszyński:[1] would like the document to be addressed in particular to FAMILIES.Cardinal G Ferretto:[2] would like something for those who suffer persecution.

Mgr ? . . . bishop of Prato:[3] *ditto.*

Cardinal Cicognani:[4] suggested a change in the last paragraph to avoid seeming to condemn progress.

Cardinal Léger:[5] spoke affectionately of the Pope and asked the Cardinal Secretary of State to convey his remarks to the Pope.

Ferrero dei Cavallerleone:[6] asked for Mary to be mentioned: the first announcement of humanity's salvation was made to her and he suggested that something to this effect be added at the end of page 3.

Heenan[7] (who had understood nothing about the significance of this Message) said: this is not the moment. The Council has not yet got anything to say; it should wait until it has got something to say. If this text is made public, the papers will not mention it (sic!). Also, something should be added to console those suffering persecution.

Mgr Compagnone[8] (Anagni):

1) at the bottom of page 2: put the verbs in the indicative, as elsewhere;

2) at the end: be careful not to condemn progress. Instead of *minas* [threats], say *ex malo usu* [due to misuse].

Hurley:[9] the paragraph which begins '*hac de causa*' [for this reason] should be deleted. Because this message is addressed to non-Catholics, and even to non-Christians. Remember that when the Pope received the Observers, he chose not to sit on his throne.

Peruzzo,[10] of Agrigento (the man who, at the Preparatory Theological Commission said cheerfully: if there are too many people, they will die, and there will no longer be too many . . . !): mention '*Maria Sanctissima*' [the most holy Mary]. At the end, mention her intercession.

---

1. Stefan Wyszyński, Archbishop of Gniezno and Warsaw, member of the Council of Presidents, *AS* I/I, 235.
2. Giuseppe Ferretto, Bishop of Sabina and Poggio Mirteto (Italy), *AS* I/I, 235.
3. Pietro Fiordelli, Bishop of Prato (Italy), *AS* I/I, 235.
4. Amleto Cicognani, *AS* I/I, 235.
5. Paul-Émile Léger, Sulpician, Archbishop of Montréal; he was to be a member of the Doctrinal Commission, *AS* I/I, 236.
6. Archbishop Carlo A Ferrero di Cavallerleone was a prelate of the Grand Master of the Sovereign Order of Malta, *AS* I/I, 236.
7. *AS* I/I, 237.
8. Enrico Compagnoni, Bishop of Anagni (Italy), *AS* I/I, 237.
9. *AS* I/I, 238.
10. *AS* I/I, 238.

Costantini:[1] the whole thing sounds a bit like an exhortation TO THE BISHOPS!

Parente:[2] there is no mention of the doctrinal theme . . .! It should be expressed!

Lefebvre[3] (Superior of the Holy Ghost Fathers): this text *'respicit bona humana, civitatem terrenam, non satis coelestia'* [discusses human affairs, the earthly city, and not enough the things of heaven].

van Cauwelaert:[4] say more about the union of the Churches.

Hermaniuk:[5] enlarge on the Catholic doctrine of social justice. Mention the Church of silence.

Alba Palacios[6] (Mexico): not enough has been said about the separated brethren. At the beginning, add: *'cuius caput VISIBILE EST'* [the visible head of which is]. . . page 2, bottom half: change the phrasing because the Council cannot secure these human goods, and is not required to do so.

Malula[7] (black, Léopoldville): pay special attention to those Christians who are already in the Church and who are *testes Christi* [Christ's witnesses]. Mention the responsibility of Christians for the work of the reconciliation of the world.

Episcopus Csanadiensis[8] (Hungary); do not mention 'persecution' at all, things seem to be improving.

Episcopus Ambatensis:[9] approve the text as it stands, except for a few stylistic corrections.

Mgr Maalouf,[10] Baalbek, in French: give time for reflection. Wait until the comments have been submitted in writing to the secretariat.

Pereira da Costa:[11] question of doctrine? That is neither the aim of this document, nor in keeping with the kind of document it is. There is a reference to truth. That is enough for this kind of document.

D'Agostino:[12] very good idea. There should be a mention of our priests.

---

1. Vittorio M Costantini, Bishop of Sessa Aurunca (Italy), *AS* I/I, 239.
2. *AS* I/I, 230–240.
3. Marcel Lefebvre, *AS* I/I, 240.
4. Jean van Cauwelaert, Bishop of Inongo (Congo), who was to be a member of the Commission on the Discipline of the Sacraments, *AS* I/I, 241.
5. *AS* I/I, 241.
6. José de Jesus Alba Palacios, Bishop of Tehuantepec (Mexico), *AS* I/I, 241–242.
7. Joseph Malula, Auxiliary Bishop of Léopoldville; he was to become Archbishop of Léopoldville in July 1964; *AS* I/I, 242.
8. Endre Hamvas, Bishop of Csanád (Hungary), *AS* I/I, 242–243.
9. Bernardino Echeverria Ruiz, Bishop of Ambato (Ecuador), *AS* I/I, 243.
10. Joseph Maalouf, Melkite Bishop of Baalbek (Lebanon), *AS* I/I, 243–244.
11. Manuel Pereira da Costa, Bishop of Campina Grande, (Brazil), *AS* I/I, 244.
12. Biagio D'Agostino, Bishop of Vallo della Lucania (Italy), *AS* I/I, 244.

Ancel:[1] where to put a reference to the Virgin Mary? On page 2: after *'apostolorum successores'* [successors of the apostles], in the following form: *'unanimiter cum Maria Matre Jesu orantes'* [united in prayer with Mary the mother of Jesus].

(I learnt later that this had come from Martimort who, realising that a mention of the Virgin Mary would have to be included, slipped quietly from one side of the nave to the other in order to give this to Mgr Ancel.)

Schröffer:[2] who is speaking in this document? The Council appears to be distinguishing between itself and the Pope. If it is only the Council Fathers, one could correct the reference on page 3 to *'cum S Pontifice'* [together with the Supreme Pontiff].

(This point was important. At the end of the Congregation, Mgr Felici specified, in passing, without stressing the point, that the document was from THE FATHERS, not from the Council as such.)

Page 2, before *'caritas Christi'* [the love of Christ]: do not give the impression that technical progress would be brought about directly by the Council.

Carraro[3] (Verona): It is very good. Would like it to be stated more explicitly that: 1) we are assembled *'in primis in servitium veritatis'* [primarily for the service of truth] (the Council is the organ of the extraordinary magisterium), 2) page 2: spiritual renewal: *'purificatio et renovatio morum'* [purification and renewal of morals].

Kandela:[4] Archbishop of Seleucia: page 3, line 12: add to the Roman Pontiff a mention of the Churches of East and West.

Mgr Zoghby[5] (Egypt). He began by addressing: *'Beatitudines, Eminentissimi'* [Your Beatitudes, your Eminences] . . . Page 3, line 12: mention *'et omnium episcoporum voce'* [by the voice of all the bishops], thereby including also the voice of the non-Catholic bishops.

Morrow[6] (?) Krishnagar(?): This is meant to be a *'salutationis nuntium'* a message of greeting. At the end of the Council we can speak of doctrine!!!

It is meant to be addressed TO HUMANKIND as such, not to Christians. Hence, omit mention of the Virgin Mary.

Shorten the first two pages and move straight on to page 3.

Maximus IV:[7] (in French): we are preparing a message. So it must be short. But this can be accepted AS IT IS. The *praesidium* [Council of Presidents]

---

1. *AS* I/I, 244–245.
2. *AS* I/I, 245.
3. Giuseppe Carraro, Bishop of Verona (Italy), *AS* I/I, 245–246.
4. Jules G Kandela, Auxiliary Archbishop of the Patriarch of Syrian Antioch, *AS* I/I, 246.
5. The Melkite Archbishop Elias Zoghby, Patriarchal Vicar for Egypt, *AS* I/I, 246.
6. Louis La Ravoire Morrow, Bishop of Krishnagar (India), *AS* I/I, 247.
7. Maximos IV Saigh, Melkite Patriarch of Antioch, member of the Commission on the Eastern Churches, he was to become a cardinal in February 1965, *AS* I/I, 247.

should put an end to this 'tournament'. He added some very warm remarks concerning the Pope, who has brought a new spirit into the Catholic Church (applause).

Episcopus Monopolitanus.[1] *'Nuntius est nuntius et non professio fidei sive constitutio'* [a message is a message and not a profession of faith or a constitution]. So, leave the text as it is, *'paucis verbis mutatis'* [changing just a few words].

Mgr Venezia:[2] add a word of gratitude to all those who have done something for the Council: the sick, CHILDREN . . . (!)

Rabban[3] (Chaldean): title: insert *'Ad omnes christianos'* [To all Christians], because the text contains many things that non-Christians would neither accept nor understand.

Guano[4] (Livorno): this message must be widely distributed and easy to read and to understand. It is too long and too complex, and it is formulated as a message TO CHRISTIANS.

Béjot[5] (Rheims): page 1) say *'verum propositum Dei vivi'* [true plan of the living God] instead of *'integram et puram veritatem'* [pure and complete truth].

Trindade, *Eborensis*:[6] it must be sober, brief, deep, precise. *'Denuo redigatur'* [It should be re-written]!

Arrieta[7] (*Pluviensis*): do not mention the Church of silence. This could do them harm. One cannot say everything. The text should be approved as it is *'cum paucis emendationibus'* [with a few corrections] mainly of style.

The end. Mgr Felici asked for a vote—by remaining seated or standing—on the text as it stood, except for two small alterations that he indicated (and that were translated into French, Spanish, English, German and Arabic):

> to add *'unanimiter cum Maria Matre Jesu orantes'* [united in prayer with Mary the Mother of Jesus].
> in the last paragraph: see my copy.

1. Carlo Ferrari, Bishop of Monopoli (Italy), *AS* I/I, 248.
2. Pasquale Venezia, Bishop of Ariano (Italy), *AS* I/I, 248.
3. Raphael Rabban, born in Mosul, Chaldean Archbishop of Kirkuk (Iraq), *AS* I/I, 248.
4. Emilio Guano, Bishop of Livorno, member of the Commission on the Apostolate of the Laity appointed by the Pope at the end of the First Session, *AS* I/I, 249.
5. Georges Béjot, Auxiliary Bishop of Rheims, *AS* I/I, 249.
6. Manuel Trindade Salgueiro, Archbishop of Evora, (Portugal), *AS* I/I, 249–50.
7. Roman Arrieta Villalobos, Bishop of Tilarán (Costa Rica), *AS* I/I, 250.

A count was taken of those who had stood up. Very few remained seated, perhaps not more than twenty. So the text was adopted.[1]

Left St Peter's at 1 pm. Went in the bishops' coach. It took a quarter of an hour to get out of St Peter's Square, because there were a good fifty bishops' coaches to leave at the same time. We reached the Angelicum at 1.50 pm.

At 2 pm, visit from Pastor Rilliet,[2] journalist for the *Tribune de Genève*. I left at 3 pm, having been urged to visit His Beatitude Maximos IV at 3.45 pm; but it was a long way. After taking the wrong tram, I got a taxi.

I was happy to see this old Patriarch,[3] so lively, so resolute, and holding such resolute positions.

He would like the chapter on the bishops to be tackled by the Council straightaway because, for him, it is the key to a balanced ecclesiology and provides a basis for a satisfactory handling of the problems of union. He told me that he had sent a letter to Pius XII when there was talk of beatifying Pius IX. In it he had described in particular how, at the end of the first Vatican Council, when Patriarch Gregory Youssef[4] came, behind all the other bishops, to kiss the pope's feet, Pius IX had put his foot on his neck saying: 'this hard head'!—because the Patriarch had remained to the end opposed to the definition of infallibility. The Patriarch had then got up and left the hall without a word. For more than twenty years he never returned to Rome and had never had any but the most strictly necessary administrative contacts with Rome. It had been Leo XIII who had sought him out and effected a reconciliation. This was the specific context for the encyclical *Orientalium dignitas*.[5]

At about 4.30 pm, the patriarch escorted me to the weekly meeting of the Melkite bishops. He put me sitting on his left. There I once again met Mgr Hakim,[6] Mgr Edelby,[7] the Archbishop of Beirut[8] (who is sub-secretary to the Council: it is he who translates the announcements into Arabic). There were about twenty-five bishops there, sitting in armchairs, forming a large rectangle of which the patriarch occupied one of the short sides. Here, once again, I found that atmosphere of paternal familiarity that struck me in the East in relationships with the bishops. These bishops (who all speak French, often even among themselves) asked me

---

1. *AS* I/I 254–256.
2. Pastor Jean Rilliet, who worked for the *Tribune de Genève*, was to follow the first two Sessions of the Council for that newspaper.
3. He had been born in 1878.
4. The Melkite patriarch at that time.
5. It was in fact an Apostolic Letter of Leo XIII published in 1894.
6. George Hakim, Melkite Bishop of Saint John of Acre (Israel). In 1967, he was to succeed Maximos IV under the name of Maximos V.
7. Neophytos Edelby, Melkite bishop and patriarchal counsellor of the Melkites of Antioch. During the First Session, he was elected a member of the Commission on Eastern Churches. His journal of the Council has been published in Italian: Neophytos Edelby, *Il Vaticano nel diario di un vescovo arabo*, (Milan: 1996).
8. Philippe Nabaa, Melkite Archbishop of Beirut.

about the currents in the Council, what needs to be done, what to think about the schemas. For their part, they told me that, for them, there exists only one Church in the East, which is the Church of their country in the East. There have been quarrels, nothing more. One cannot look upon the Orthodox as being outside the Church, as not being the Church. Fr Oreste Kéramé,[1] who was at the end of the room and said nothing, explained to me afterwards—because I objected that the papacy is now a dogma—that one cannot impute to the Orthodox a fault committed in relation to a doctrine which they were not present to accept and which had not been presented to them in a sufficiently authentic manner. This intrusion of historical and psychological considerations into a dogmatic and canonical matter is clearly totally foreign to the Romans. I cannot say that, in my own eyes, Fr Kéramé's points carry weight. In any case, these bishops insist on the need to have a special schema *de unione* [on union] for the Easterners. It is ecclesiologically necessary. The problem is not the same for them as for Protestants. For them, all purely canonical interdicts prohibiting *communicatio in sacris* should be suppressed, retaining only what is required by divine law, namely prohibition where there is question of belonging to a different faith. In addition, these Melkite bishops would like a general schema *De Œcumenismo* [On ecumenism] followed by a special schema concerning the East. Before that, beginning in this Session, a grappling with the matter of the episcopacy. They have signed a petition to this effect.

Mgr Edelby really stands out in this assembly: young, strong, alive, sharp. He is certainly very capable. He has the quality of a leader.

Sunday 21 October 1962

Very full day. At 10 am at Mgr Volk's on the Janiculum, meeting with Rahner, Ratzinger, Semmelroth, Daniélou and Labourdette. I had prepared a schema of the *'proemium'* which I submitted. We discussed whether to adopt Mgr Volk's text, Fr Daniélou's or mine. In the end, mine was chosen and I was asked to rewrite it in fifteen pages between now and next Sunday. For their part, Frs Ratzinger and Rahner are re-writing the subject matter (*Die Thematik*) of the four doctrinal schemas on behalf of Cardinal König, while Fr Daniélou is doing so on behalf of Mgr Veuillot.

At 12.30 pm, Fr Chalencon,[2] of the La Salette Fathers, came to collect myself and Fr Chenu to have lunch with them. During the conversation, Fr Chenu spoke of the pain he felt that there was no one from the East among the members elected to the Theological Commission. I know, for my part, that the Maronites are hurt that none of them has been elected to the Commissions, and that the Melkites

---

1. Archimandrite Oreste Kéramé was the personal expert and Referendary of Patriarch Maximos at the Council.
2. Jean Chalencon, sixth counsellor and Secretary General of the la Salette Missionaries: M-D Chenu was staying with the Missionary Fathers of la Salette, who, at that time, were sending their students to study at Le Saulchoir.

occupy all the places. At the Preparatory Commission I myself had said several times that it was necessary to hear the Eastern point of view. Nothing had been done, and the presence of Mgr Hermaniuk had not been enough to fill this void. It seems to me that we must use the last chance we have: that the Pope should appoint someone from the East (a Maronite?) among the eight theologians that he is to appoint to complete the Commission *de fide et moribus* [the Doctrinal Commission]. We reached a decision: to arrange for a cardinal to speak to the Pope. We thought of Cardinal Suenens who had said, in an interview, that he had been concerned, at the Central Commission, about the Eastern point of view. We went, at once, by car, to the Belgian College. The cardinal had withdrawn for three or four days to *somewhere*[1] in Rome. So, I saw Mgr De Smedt, Bishop of Bruges, who is a member of the Secretariat. I had my name announced. He was having his siesta, he had left the table. But he came. Excellent welcome. He felt we should approach Cardinal Bea, and he authorised us to present ourselves to the cardinal in his name. Off we went! We dropped off Fr Chenu on the way as he had an appointment. We were lucky. When we reached the Brazilian College where the cardinal was staying, we were told that he would be coming down, as he was going out. In fact, the car was waiting for him.

He appeared after about twenty minutes. In two minutes, I had explained to him the purpose of my visit. I made the point (it seemed to find its mark) that the Easterners would very much appreciate the fact that the POPE had appointed one of them. Luckily, the cardinal is going this evening to a reception given by Cardinal Agagianian[2] at which Cardinal Cicognani would also be present. He promised to raise the matter with both of them.

On the way out, I was recognised by some Brazilian seminarians who had seen me on Italian TV. They surrounded me affectionately. I asked where their bishops were: they are all close by, at Domus Mariae. I went there. In fact, ninety-eight bishops live there, including seventy-five Brazilians. In a short space of time, I saw about ten bishops, then Mgr Helder,[3] secretary of CELAM, arrived. It is extraordinary: only today, at lunch-time, they had spoken of me and had said that they ought to bring me to see them. After chatting for a while, we went into a room where about a dozen young bishops joined us. They asked me questions. Mgr Helder led: not only is he a very open man, but he is full of ideas, of IMAGI-NATION and enthusiasm. This is what is lacking in Rome: 'vision'.

---

1. {English in the original}.
2. The Armenian Gregory P Agagianian, Prefect of the Congregation of Propaganda. President of the Commission on the Missions, he was to become a member of the Co-ordinating Commission, and one of the four Moderators of the Council.
3. Helder Pessôa Câmara, Auxiliary Bishop of Rio de Janeiro. He was in fact the first Vice-president of CELAM (Conference of Latin American Bishops). He was to be elected a member of the Commission on the Apostolate of the Laity during the Second Session of the Council, and was to become Archbishop of Olinda and Recife in March 1964.

The Brazilian bishops, and a large proportion of the South American episcopacy, would like to reject the doctrinal schemas. They would like to make a start on the texts *De episcopis*[1] [on bishops] after dealing with the *De Liturgia*. If this is not done now, they say, it will never be done. If it is postponed until the April 1963 session, many of the bishops will not come to this session. This schema is necessary to balance Vatican I. Moreover, it is called for by the schemas on the liturgy and on ecumenism.

They asked me if I could produce a schema that was wide-ranging and would address their concerns. I said I could, with Frs Lécuyer, Rahner, Ratzinger and Colombo.

But I see that I am taking some crushing burdens on my shoulders. All the more so in that the Brazilian bishops want me to give them lectures. Mgr Helder has also asked me to prepare a bibliography of good books (French, English, German) on the most important questions today's Church is facing: simple and easy enough for bishops who can neither buy nor read very heavy books. Questions of theology, sociology, philosophy, psychology, etc.

What I really need is a secretary!

I tried to meet up with Fr Lécuyer. I did not know where to find him and did not succeed. I returned here at 6 p.m.

Veni Sancte Spiritus! Ad robur! [Come Holy Spirit! Help me!]

I record here also that Mgr Helder told me about the three personal conversations he had had with the Pope. He had suggested to the Pope some things that would have been significant gestures: on behalf of the President of the Republic of Brazil, he invited him to come for the inauguration of Brasilia; he suggested to him the idea of a Catholic Bandung[2], etc. Each time the Pope said: Yes, I would like to, BUT I AM A PRISONER. He had also once said to the Pope: isn't it true, Holy Father, that communism is not the worst enemy? And the Pope had replied: Yes, you are right.

I have also been struck, these past few days, by the role played by the theologians. At the First Vatican Council, they played almost no role at all. Those who could have done so were not invited or did not go: Döllinger, Newman,[3] (even Scheeben[4]!). From the point of view of theologians, it all happened among the people in Rome, or almost. It is true that quite a few of the bishops did their own theology. This time, the bishops are much more shepherds than theologians.

---

1. From now on, this expression refers in general both to the three chapters dedicated to the bishops in *De Ecclesia*, and also to the single chapter being called for by many and of which a first draft occurs in a chapter of the schema prepared by Philips with the assistance of Congar and others.
2. {A meeting of representatives of the Third World was held at Bandung, Indonesia, from 18-24 April 1955.}
3. Cardinal John Henry Newman (1801–1890), famous English theologian.
4. Matthias-Josef Scheeben (1835–1888), German neo-scholastic theologian.

On the other hand, there is in the Church a large group of theologians who are alive and who do not confine themselves to the completed chapters of scholastic theology but try to think about and to explain the facts of the life of the Church. There are quite a few of these theologians. They are very far from being all in Rome, but, speaking only about Rome, I see: Chenu, Colson,[1] Chavasse,[2] Ratzinger, Rahner, Semmelroth, Lubac, Rondet, Daniélou, Schillebeeckx, etc., etc. These theologians exercise a true magisterium. This is what Pius IX would have wished to avoid, at the risk of highlighting Döllinger I presume! Moreover, Pius IX was defeated all along the line, he who chose not to understand the truth of history:

> the Christian Democrats are displaying their motto on the walls: *Libertas* [liberty].
> Last Saturday's appeal to all humankind, as compared with the *Syllabus*,[3] and its last injunction;
> the temporal power (of which vestiges still remain, however); conciliarity reinstated.

Monday 22 October 1962

Telephone call from Cardinal Bea's secretary[4] to say that the step has been taken; that in fact it had already been taken by others and that the Maronites had themselves intervened directly.

Fr Schmidt also said to me: the next time, telephone the cardinal *beforehand* (one does not accost a cardinal on his way out like that, without previous warning !!!).

General Congregation:

To begin with, the names of those who had been elected to the remaining three Commissions were announced.[5]

The Pope's decision to extend the Secretariat for the duration of the Council and to raise it effectively to the level of a Commission was then read. A start was then made on the schema *De liturgia*,[6] beginning with a very clear presentation of the schema. There followed comments on the schema *in genere* [as a whole], of which there were twenty-five:

---

1. Jean Colson, priest of the diocese of Saint-Dié, Professor of the History of the Origins of Christianity at the Catholic University of Angers, and director of the studies/charity section of Secours Catholique in Paris. He was the personal expert of the Bishop of Saint-Dié.
2. Congar added to the typescript 'Chavasse?? no longer came'.
3. Accompanying the encyclical *Quanta cura* published by Pope Pius IX in 1864, the *Syllabus errorum* was a catalogue of eighty errors considered dangerous to Catholicism in modern society.
4. Stjepan Schmidt SJ.
5. *AS* I/I, 259-261.
6. *AS* I/I, 262-303.

Cardinal Frings:[1] this schema is like the last will and testament of Pius XII.
He praised it and then asked:
that the schema be reprinted WITH THE STATEMENTS MADE TO
THE CENTRAL COMMISSION;
that the statements concerning the use of the vernacular be inserted,
that the note on page 155 be deleted as it is not included in the text
approved by the Central Commission, and that the original text
concerning the use of the vernacular be restored, as it had referred the
matter to the episcopal conferences in each country.
Music in the vernacular: the bishops should seek to instruct the faithful
in the use of Gregorian chant so that God can be praised *una voce*
[with one voice] on those occasions when the faithful from several
countries meet together.

Cardinal Ruffini:[2] '*parcite mihi si canam extra chorum*' [forgive me if I sing
apart from the choir]. Against the restriction of the schema to the
Roman liturgy, it should apply to all rites. If particular rites need special
regulations, these should be introduced by special *ad hoc* bodies.

Cardinal Lercaro[3] (quite dull): praise for the clarity, pastoral orientation,
theological basis; progressive wisdom.

Cardinal Montini:[4] expressed approval. Neither anarchical innovations nor
immutability. In favour of a commission, after the Council, composed
of pastoral bishops.
  − Latin for the sacramental, specifically priestly, parts.
  − Vernacular for the didactic sections and the prayer of the faithful
  (quoted I Cor: reply Amen):
  THE FAITHFUL SHOULD UNDERSTAND!!
  − and aim for simplicity, brevity; avoid repetitions.

Cardinal Spellman[5] (not very clear): not too many changes! Benefits of
uniformity. Question of language: for the Eucharist: Latin; for the other
Sacraments and ceremonies, extensive sections in the vernacular.

Cardinal Döpfner:[6] praise for the schema.
The declarations prepared by the Preparatory Commission should be
given.

---

1. *AS* I/I, 309–310.
2. *AS* I/I, 310–311.
3. Giacomo Lercaro, Archbishop of Bologna, member of the Liturgical Commission. In
1963 Paul VI was to appoint him to the Co-ordinating Commission as one of the four
Moderators of the Council, *AS* I/I, 311–313.
4. *AS* I/I, 313–315.
5. *AS* I/I, 316–319.
6. *AS* I/I, 319–321.

Delete the note on page 155, which was not submitted to the Central Commission.

Do not be content with general principles.

A commission should be set up to prepare, within a few years, new liturgical books.

Language: remember that the liturgy is often the only source of life for the faithful. It should be clear! Would like the vernacular to be used also by the celebrant where the good of the faithful calls for it.

The Commission's text authorising the bishops' conferences to prepare regulations governing the use of the vernacular should be restored.

Japanese Cardinal:[1] In favour of adaptation for the peoples of the Far East. The bishops' conferences should have more freedom of movement, more power to arrange matters.

Chilean Cardinal:[2] general praise.

Delete the minimisation of the extraordinary magisterium in the first sentence. Primacy of charity. Avoid formalism.

In favour of a biblical and patristic doctrine of the priesthood of the faithful.

Give authority to the bishops' conferences concerning the use of the vernacular. Words are not made for hiding things, but as a means of expression.

Chaldean Patriarch:[3] most of this schema should be made to apply also to the Eastern Churches.

Vagnozzi:[4] Apostolic Delegate in Washington(!!!): this schema is verbose, 'ascetic'. Its theology is vague, at times inaccurate. Example: it says that the liturgy is the *culmen et fons* [summit and source] of the Christian life: now only God is that.

It should be submitted to the Commission *de fide* [Doctrinal Commission].

All that is needed is for the Council to re-visit the encyclical *Mediator*![5]

Hurley:[6] No longer wished to speak. What he had wanted to say had been very well said by the previous speakers, except the immediately preceding one.

---

1. Peter Tatsuo Doi, Archbishop of Tokyo, *AS* I/I, 323.
2. Raul Silva Henríquez, Archbishop of Santiago, President of the Chilean Bishops' Conference and Vice-President of the Commission on the Apostolate of the Laity, *AS* I/I, 323–325.
3. Paul II Cheikho, Patriarch of Babylon of the Chaldeans (Iraq), *AS* I/I, 325.
4. Egidio Vagnozzi, titular archbishop, Apostolic Delegate in the United States, *AS* I/I, 335–326.
5. The encyclical *Mediator Dei* on the liturgy published by Pius XII in 1947.
6. *AS* I/I, 327

Japanese bishop:[1] all the necessary praise has already been expressed. He, too, no longer wished to speak.

Del Rosario:[2] 1) What is the difference between constitutions, decrees and canons? 2) What canonical regulations would be abrogated by this Constitution? Specify! What MUST one observe?

Lebanese bishop:[3] *unam tantum dicam* [I shall say only one thing]: the text does not distinguish clearly between 'rite' in the purely ceremonial sense and 'rite' in the comprehensive sense of the customs of a community. This needs to be clarified in the *proemium*.

Dante:[4] *Non placet*:

1) The Council should only give general principles.

2) Approval of changes should be reserved to the Holy See.

AS REGARDS THE USE OF LATIN: use of the vernacular should be restricted to preaching.

Against the idea of concelebration, above all for private Masses.

Preserve the Office, the obligation of saying it in Latin.

Condemned certain omissions.

García:[5] (very slow): the schema should be shorter.

Doubtful relics should be done away with. He referred, among other things, to Aaron's rod and the milk of the Virgin. *'Reverenter sepeliantur'* [They should be given a decent burial].

Bishop of Limburg:[6] Two general wishes: take into consideration the conditions of social life today; adopt legitimate ecumenical trends.

Cardinal Rugambwa,[7] from Tanganyika: it is what people are looking for. In favour of adaptations by the bishops' conferences with the pope's approval.

A Franciscan bishop:[8] he spoke of ALL the schemas and found them excellent. Don't waste time DISCUSSING things that express common Catholic doctrine and which are perfect. Accept them as they are and concentrate on concrete, pastoral, matters.

---

1. In fact, it was Guildford C Young, Archbishop of Hobart (Australia), whom Congar had met on 12 October, *AS* I/I, 328.
2. Luis del Rosario, Bishop of Zamboanga (Philippines), *AS* I/I, 328–329.
3. Giovanni B Scapinelli di Léguigno, Assessor of the Congregation for the Eastern Church, *AS* I/I 329–330.
4. Archbishop Enrico Dante, Secretary of the Congregation of Rites, *AS* I/I, 330–331.
5. Fidel García Martinez, Spanish titular bishop, *AS* I/I, 332.
6. Wilhelm Kempf, Bishop of Limburg (Germany), *AS* I/I, 332–333.
7. Cardinal Laurean Rugambwa, Bishop of Bukoba (Tanzania), member of the Commission on the Missions, *AS* I/I, 333–334.
8. Carlos E Saboia Bandeira de Méllo, Bishop of Palmas (Brazil), *AS* I/I, 334–335.

Ungarelli:[1] Why not deal with the Eastern rites?

> Against the uniformity of Latin, which is contrary to the *unum sint* ['let them be one']. Protestants use the vernacular and would return more easily if it were not for the obstacle of Latin.
>
> IN FAVOUR OF NEW LITURGIES, and not only the Latin one!
>
> Completely in favour of languages spoken by the people. The *gentes* [non-Christian peoples] are obliged to accept only the faith, not Western culture!
>
> Latin damages the missions. It should be restricted to those who are true Westerners. That would also facilitate the recruitment of priests.

The President said: *'Satis'* ! [Enough] Has the speaker not had his ten minutes?

> A ten minute limit is not absolutely mandatory, but . . .

X?:[2] found the schema excellent.

It ended at midday.

In the afternoon, for duty's sake, I began work on the *proemium*. I couldn't get on with it. Admittedly, I was interrupted (visit from Fr Cottier,[3] Mgr de Provenchères' theologian; also a young French couple on their honeymoon who did not know where to stay), but I am not in the mood. Between 2 pm and 5.30 pm. I managed to write only six or seven lines!!! What a chore!

Tuesday 23 October 1962

I didn't sleep. I was thinking about it all. I realise the mistake I made in coming to the Angelicum, where I have no contact with the bishops and am in a fairly heavy, though friendly, atmosphere, remote from the Council; where the meals are without conversation, whereas mealtimes are normally a time when 'one talks' (about it all). Mgr Elchinger did in fact offer me a room where he is; but: 1) there are only four French bishops there; 2) I must have reasonable communication, as I have at the Angelicum.

Moreover, at the Angelicum, it is virtually impossible for me to invite the Observers: the community is too heavy, too solemn, too little homogeneous in the French sense. Only ecclesiastics are invited here, in accordance with the rules and a fairly rigid set of customs. I reproach myself for having had so little contact with the Observers, apart from the official meetings. What to do about it?

---

1. Alfonso M Ungarelli, prelate *nullius* from Pinheiro (Brazil), member of the Commission on the Missions elected at the end of the First Session, *AS* I/I, 336–338.
2. Juan Hervás y Benet, prelate *nullius* from Ciudad Real (Spain), *AS* I/I, 339.
3. Georges Cottier, OP, from the Swiss Province, Prior of the Saint Thomas Centre in Geneva, editorial secretary for the journal *Nova et Vetera* founded and directed by Journet; he was to be a Council expert for the Fourth Session. Later he was to become Theologian of the Papal Household.

This morning I did not go to the General Congregation, in order to work on the *proemium* which I have to present on Sunday. I was told that the open thesis (use of the vernacular) supported by Maximos IV,[1] Cardinal Feltin,[2] and Cardinal Léger[3] collided with the closed thesis: Cardinal Ruffini,[4] Cardinal McIntyre,[5] (very violent and very rigid), Cardinal Ottaviani,[6] who asked for the schema to be submitted to some REAL theologians.

In the afternoon from 3 pm to 5 pm, Mgr Elchinger. I asked him to intervene in the schema *De Liturgia* in order to ask for a better presentation of the fact that the basis of the participation of the laity in the liturgy is their priesthood. We prepared a brief schema along these lines.

I also spoke to Mgr Elchinger about a project which I would like to see taken up. People are certainly expecting from the Council something about simplification and poverty. I want it too. But it is very difficult to put something reasonable concretely into words. It would be necessary to bring together some bishops and theologians (I suggested a list to Mgr Elchinger) in order to get something ready. For my part, the important thing seems to me to be, not the details, but the ecclesiological aspect. This covers three points: a) a renunciation, a rejection of the SEIGNEURIAL, the *dominium* [dominion], all that is related to the temporal, and to the pretension of temporal prestige; b) the creation of possibilities of real contact with people, so that priests and members of the hierarchy are not cut off from them; c) to be and appear to be much more a Church of the poor.

He plans to speak on behalf of the double breviary, a breviary in one's native language; I asked him to put himself down to speak about communion under both kinds. I am going to see Mgr Charue to try and persuade him to do it, but if I do not find him, or if he refuses, someone would be down to speak. I had thought of Mgr Weber, but it seems that he reads a text rather badly.

From 5 pm to 6 pm, visit from M [*J*[7] , Brazilian writer and leader of Catholic opinion, and M Murilo Mendes, well-known Brazilian poet, who has a Chair of Portuguese at the University of Rome.

I then went to see Mgr Charue and was lucky to meet him just as he was leaving the Belgian College. I explained to him what I wanted. He will allow me to prepare a text for him, but he is hesitant because the Belgian bishops are not in favour of communion under both kinds.

From there, because of the closeness of one place to the other, I went to see Mgr Weber. I was joined in his anteroom by Fr Gy, who had come on behalf of

---

1. *AS* I/I, 377–379.
2. *AS* I/I, 367–369.
3. *AS* I/I, 371–373.
4. *AS* I/I, 364–367.
5. James McIntyre, Archbishop of Los Angeles, Vice-president of the Commission of Bishops and for the Government of Dioceses, *AS* I/I, 369–371.
6. *AS* I/I, 349–350.
7. Alceu Amoroso Lima (according to Oscar Beozzo).

Mgr Martin[1] and the liturgists to ask Mgr Weber to speak on this article of communion under both kinds.

Curious coincidence!

Fr Gy has been asked by the French members of the Liturgical Commission to sound out and to try to influence the Anglo-Saxon bishops in favour of this. He is more than ever into his role as a negotiator. He told me that the atmosphere of the Council is working: some groups of bishops (the US bishops for example or the South Africans) had already changed considerably in just two weeks.

In fact, I myself realise here the immense influence of the milieu. Human beings are profoundly affected by their milieu. My own reactions, for example, are not, on all points, quite the same today as they were during the work of the Theological Commission. True, they are basically the same, above all as regards their strictly intellectual significance. In speech or in writing, I have uttered (too timidly) most of the comments or criticisms that are being expressed today. But my reactions were to some extent conditioned by the milieu of that time. Today, they are free to develop and be expressed in a totally different milieu. But there is more: they RECEIVE from this milieu and from the free and wide-ranging exchanges for which the normal locus is the Council, not only confirmation, but enriching support. I realise in an almost physical way the contribution being made by the assembly as such. It is yet another argument against the idea of a 'Council by correspondence' put forward in connection with the consultations relating to the Immaculate Conception and the Assumption. I also realise, once again, how very Macchiavellian and depressing is the discipline of secrecy, obtained and sanctioned by an oath, which Rome imposes on all those who work with her. This prevents each of the participants from resuming contact with his natural milieu. Not being allowed to speak except to the selected members of the small group, all of whom have been obliged to swear the same oath, each one is cut off from every other milieu, isolated, walled up in his own problem, in contact only, and in a very formalistic way, with those who are bound by the same oath. This works catastrophically by producing groups cut off from real life, partitioned off, jealous, if not actually distrustful. It is contrary to human nature and to the nature of intelligence, which is DIALOGICAL. At the Council, the Church has been placed in a state of dialogue, at least internally. She feels herself alive from the fact of the enriching contact with others and with an environment vowed to free discussion, marked by the seal of questioning and of freedom.

24 October 1962

Seriously threatening situation concerning Cuba. Nuclear war COULD break out from one day to the next. *Da pacem!* [Grant us peace].

General Congregation. Eastern rite Mass. This too, for the East, is a way of speaking to the Council. Once again, it speaks through its liturgy.

---

1.   Joseph-M Martin was President of the French Liturgical Commission.

Brief commentary in Latin; some prayers were translated at the microphone into FRENCH. French is the lingua franca of the Catholic East.

A bishop has just died in the vestibule of St Peter's; he was on his way into the Basilica for the session. He is the fifth to have died since the Council began!

The cardinal of Toledo[1] presiding. It is very difficult to understand him.

The discussion, or rather the continuation of the discussion, did not begin until 10.15 am; the bishops are already tired from so much standing up and sitting down.

> Cardinal Tisserant:[2] Cyril and Methodius.[3] Other historical and CONTEMPORARY facts: only recently, under Pius XII, the Missal has been translated into a local language (Dalmatian). History tells us: there is no objection to translation into the vernacular.
>
> Cardinal Gracias[4] (India): VERY FINE and quite long intervention. The best is the enemy of the good. *Festinare lente* [hasten slowly], but avoid resistance to change. In India, there are fourteen official languages, each one of which is used by a population equivalent in size to a country in the West.
>
> The bishops' conferences should be granted the faculty to experiment, the final decision being reserved to the Holy See. But they should receive a prompt reply! This needs to be stipulated. The schema is not clear on this point.
>
> He proposed some wide-ranging changes.
>
> A word about concelebration, of which we have just had a fine example.
>
> A word about the simplicity of vestments.

I note that throughout this session, and, according to what I have been told, yesterday, too, the remarks concerning the vernacular have all been on the pragmatic level. NO THEOLOGY UNDERLYING THE QUESTION. In general, the liturgical movements have not provided themselves with the ECCLESIOLOGICAL basis that they ought to have. In this case, the fundamental theological question, which has not been asked, is: who or what is the subject of the liturgical action?! It is the mystical, organic Body, to which the *plebs sancta* [holy people] belongs.

---

1. Enrique Pla y Deniel, Archbishop of Toledo.
2. *AS* I/I, 399–400.
3. In the ninth century, Saints Cyril and Methodius, with the pope's support, translated the Scriptures and the liturgical texts for the Slav peoples.
4. Valerian Gracias, Archbishop of Bombay, *AS* I/I, 400–404.

Cardinal Bea:[1] *De coadunandis schematibus tractantibus de eadem re!* [the schemas dealing with the same questions should be studied together] by joint commissions.

De novis ritibus [concerning new rites]. Avoid prejudging the future. Do not close any doors. Things are moving. There is also the ecumenical movement and it may be that this will affect the liturgical question. Avoid deciding NOW.

Cardinal Bacci:[2] with a very affected diction. A true Diafoirus.[3]

1) No vernacular languages in the Mass. Rosmini[4] was censured.

2) Danger that certain texts would be understood in the vernacular (e.g. the story of Susanna).

3) Solution: catechesis, homily. Translation of the Missals and *annuntiator quidam probatus* [an approved reader] reading the texts.

4) What is envisaged may lead to conflicts and difficulties in multi-lingual countries, such as Canada, Switzerland, Belgium. Unity!

5) In the administration of the sacraments where a relationship is established between the priest and ONE member or a SMALL GROUP of the faithful, use the local language.

'*Statuatur modo unitario pro universa Ecclesia ab Apostolica sede*' [it should be determined uniformly for the universal Church by the Apostolic See]. No intervention on the part of the bishops' conferences.

Cardinal Meyer[5] (Chicago): Cardinal Gracias has spoken well. Two additional remarks:

find a *via media*. This is what the schema has done.

No. 24 on page 170 should be better expressed. Too much is being given away in granting *moderamen* [direction] to the national commission. Each bishop must remain judge in his own diocese.

(Mgr McGrath[6] told me this evening that Cardinal Meyer had spoken because, he said, he was ashamed that his country had been represented yesterday by Cardinal McIntyre.)

Van Lierde:[7] Paragraph 1 of *De Liturgiae natura* [On the nature of the Liturgy]: unsatisfactory. It speaks a bit about everything, including sacristans.

---

1. *AS* I/I, 407–408.
2. *AS* I/I, 408–410.
3. {Characters in Molière's *Le Malade Imaginaire,* both doctors and both ignorant and pretentious.}
4. Antonio Rosmini (1797–1855), Italian priest, theologian and philosopher, had advocated an *aggiornamento* of the Church.
5. Albert G Meyer, Archbishop of Chicago, *AS* I/I, 411–412.
6. Marcos McGrath, Auxiliary Bishop of Panama, member of the Doctrinal Commission elected at the First Session; he was to become Bishop of Santiago Veraguas (Panama) in 1964.
7. The Belgian Pierre Canisius van Lierde, titular archbishop. Sacristan to His Holiness

Ecumenical perspective. Christians should endeavour TOGETHER to introduce the same feasts in civilian life. For example, the Protestants' Good Friday and the Catholics' Thursday of *Corpus Christi.*

Archbishop of Dublin:[1] The people understand nothing of the ancient rites. The bishops of Ireland propose that it should be added to paragraph 27 that in no way is the Rosary being disparaged, etc.

Bishop of Smyrna:[2] paragraph 24: in favour *pro ampliatione maiore facultatum iam concessarum* [of widening even further the faculties already granted], as well as widespread use of the vernacular, bearing in mind the development of the world. Authorisation by the bishops (and not solely by bishops' conferences). He quoted many examples of Eastern liturgies, in which even the words of consecration . . .

(?)[3] (a Spaniard!) very long-winded. Dissertation on the humanity of Christ being the INSTRUMENTAL cause of salvation (with a quotation from St Thomas): clarify along these lines what has been said.

Distinguish the teaching role (for which use the vernacular) from the ministerial.

(Often, especially among those who are conservative, a distinction has been drawn between the DIDACTIC parts of the liturgy, for which the vernacular could be used, and the sacramental or priestly parts. Always the same vice of SEPARATING, of turning abstraction into a category of the real.) Blondel was right (cf his *Monophorisme*[4]).

Archbishop of Madagascar,[5] speaking in the name of three hundred bishops of Africa and Madagascar: in favour of a very international liturgical commission, reflecting ALL cultures.

A Polish bishop,[6] bishop in Northern Rhodesia: with reference to article III of Chapter I: stipulate the various modes of the presence of Christ which are mentioned. Take over the expressions used in *Mediator,* Article 24: thanks to Tisserant and to Bea. *Ne porta claudatur* [the door should not be closed].

Some people have said that Latin is THE language of the Church. But it is not the only one. '*Ne pondus argumenti unitatis exaggeretur!*"

---

and Vicar General for Vatican City, *AS* I/I, 412–413.

1. John C McQuaid, Archbishop of Dublin, *AS* I/I, 414.
2. Joseph Descuffi, Archbishop of Ismir (formerly Smyrna) (Turkey), *AS* I/I, 414-416.
3. In fact, a Brazilian, Alexandre Gonçalves do Amaral, Archbishop of Uberaba (Brazil), *AS* I/I, 417–419.
4. Maurice Blondel, *Catholicisme social et monophorisme* (Paris: Bloud & Gay, 1910).
5. Gilbert Ramanantoanina, Archbishop of Fianarantsoa, member of the Secretariat for Unity from the Second Session of the Council onwards, *AS* I/I, 419–420.
6. Adam Kozłowiecki, SJ, Archbishop of Lusaka (Northern Rhodesia), *AS* I/I, 421–423.

[the weight of the argument from unity should not be exaggerated]. Unity is a matter for the mind and the heart, and goes well beyond the question of language: *Ut facultas daretur conferentiis episcopalibus* [the faculty should be given to the bishops' conferences].

No PRIVILEGED position for Latin. He quoted Acts 15: '*Nihil ultra imponere quam haec necessaria*' [Lay no greater burden than these necessary things]. It is being said: The *Sedes Apostolica* [Apostolic See] should decide . . . In fact, it is the departments that do so: '*Ego sum fortasse successor Bartholomei*' [I am, perhaps, Bartholomew's successor . . .].

Mgr Zanini:[1] no longer wished to speak.

Parente:[2] will use any kind of argument in order to discredit the schema. He said: *Laborat verbositate et levitate* [It is afflicted by wordiness and lack of weight]. It contains things that are at times incoherent; its style is hardly worthy of a Council.

Remarks on some expressions that are not theologically correct . . .

Praise of the Holy Office (the way he went on, you would think they were martyrs!) which has *plura concessisse* [already given way on many things].

The Holy See proceeds prudently and what it does is sufficient.

Mgr Staffa:[3] wholesale attack on the use of the vernacular. Logically, it would need to be used even for the Canon and the Consecration . . .

What is being suggested would be useless for the faith. We would be creating divisions at a time when the world is uniting . . . PRESERVE UNITY. *Ne quid detrahatur iuris Romani Pontificis* [nothing should be taken away from the right of the Roman Pontiff]. He ALONE is able . . . He asked that a vote be taken on this: that the schema be sent back to a joint commission of Theology, Liturgy and the Discipline of the Sacraments.

Archbishop of Colombo[4] (Ceylon) . . . too long. He was told to stop.

The Congregation ended at 12.30 pm. On the way out I saw Hébert Roux. I went to the Procure Saint-Sulpice and to the Belgian College to deliver the text which

---

1. Lino Zanini, apostolic nuncio without appointment. His declining to speak is not mentioned in the *Acta*.
2. *AS* I/I, 423–426.
3. Dino Staffa, titular bishop and Secretary of the Congregation for Seminaries and Universities; at the First Session he was appointed by the Pope as a member of the Commission on Seminaries, Studies and Catholic Education of which he was to become one of the Vice-Presidents, *AS* I/I, 428–429.
4. Thomas B Cooray, appointed a member of the Commission on the Discipline of the Clergy and of the Christian People from the First Session, created cardinal in February 1965, *AS* I/I, 430–432.

I had prepared on communion under both kinds. Tremendous effort to walk!

I went to a meeting of the French bishops at 6.30 pm. To be noted:

The Pope wants the pastoral point of view to predominate.

He wants the discussion to be based on the schemas proposed.

He asks that there be no references to politics at all, *dicit* [so says] Cardinal Feltin.

Mgr Villot, who is very different, said: there is no provision for a preliminary vote on whether or not to accept a schema.

Mgr Jenny spoke of the work of the Liturgical Commission. The bishops do not know one another. Cardinal Larraona seems rather confused; there is no working method. He had asked the question as to whether one could (ought) to take into consideration the written comments made by the bishops prior to 15 September. The cardinal replied saying that they were not conciliar acts ... Then, do the bishops have to repeat orally in a General Congregation what they had already written? No!—Then, *quid* [what]?

Fr Daniélou gave a talk about the matters being raised concerning the episcopate. Very superficial and banal. Fr Daniélou moves about a lot. He has to some extent made himself, or been made, counsellor to the bishops.

After him, Fr Lécuyer described the contents of the schemas prepared on the question of the episcopate. And he added his own comments or suggestions. Excellent.

I returned at 6.30 pm in order to welcome Mgr Philips. At the request of the Belgian bishops, he had prepared a text *De episcopis* [on the bishops] making use of the texts that had already been prepared, but from a different perspective. I typed his text so that he can use it as a basis at tomorrow's meeting.

At 7.30 pm, I had a visit from Mgr McGrath, Auxiliary Bishop of Panama. He reminded me that we had met at Saint-Sébastien, and that we had gone swimming together. In fact I remember very well; it was in '51 or '52. He belongs to the Theological Commission. He is very good. He consulted me on a number of matters: he wanted, in particular, to speak against the idea, put forward by Ottaviani, Parente, Staffa, of submitting the liturgical schema to the Theological Commission. All the Commissions are composed of bishops who also have doctorates. In reality, this is a tactic on the part of Ottaviani and the Holy Office. Mgr McGrath told me that Ottaviani has brought his theologians together, especially Fenton, who has written fifty pages against the expression 'invisible Church' that had been used in the schema *De liturgia*.

He told me that the South American episcopate (nearly six hundred bishops) has been changing considerably for the better over the past ten to twenty years. It is Chile which is leading Spanish-speaking America: it has a CULTIVATED clergy. He told me a little of how and through whom this had come about (Fr Weigel,[1]

---

1. The American Gustave Weigel, SJ, Professor of Theology at the Jesuit College at Woodstock (Maryland), had taught and been Dean of the Theology Faculty in Santiago

Mgr Larraín, etc). These bishops are very anxious to secure a good schema *De episcopis* [on the bishops].

I told him a bit about what is being prepared, what people are thinking, looking for, in the circles in which I move, and I invited him to our meeting tomorrow on the episcopate. There will be rather a lot of people, but that can't be helped. It is essential for there to be communication between the various groups.

Thursday 25 October 1962
From 3 pm until 4.45 pm, meeting here with Rahner, Semmelroth, Ratzinger, Lécuyer, Colombo, Mgr Philips, Mgr McGrath. We read and discussed Philips' text *De episcopis* which in fact covers, at least according to the plan, all the schemas *De Ecclesia*.

Visit from Laurentin. Various telephone calls, as late as 10.00 pm!!

Friday 26 October 1962 – I did not go to the Congregation, in order to work on my laborious 'proemium'.

It seems that the discussion for and against Latin continued. Excellent interventions by the bishop of Bois-le-Duc[1] in the name of the Dutch bishops, by Mgr Ancel,[2] impassioned: *'adiuro vos'* [I adjure you] . . .

On the other hand, Mgr Calewaert,[3] Bishop of Gand (appointed to the preparatory Liturgical Commission in error, due to his name being the same as that of the deceased liturgist), made a declaration in favour of Latin. Evidently, in Belgium, the use of the vernacular would create difficult problems TEMPORARILY, but the question is wider than that relating to the use of Flemish . . .

At 5 pm, lecture on Tradition to the bishops at the French Seminary. The bishops were touchingly kind. Afterwards, I dined at the table of Cardinal Roques[4] and Cardinal Lefebvre. Very trivial conversation. Laurentin was there. Fr Gy went from one to another, came in, went out, made telephone calls . . . He plays the game, which is good. But he is worth more than this game.

Saturday 27 October 1962
Once again I did not go to the General Congregation. I only had the morning in which to work on this *proemium* chore, which is my current duty. In any case, it just went on and on and got nowhere, according to what I have been told. On and on about Latin. Fr General[5] spoke in favour of Latin for the clergy, but was open

---

(Chile); consultor to the Secretariat for Unity; he died in January 1964.
1. Willem Bekkers, *AS* I/I, 441–443.
2. *AS* I/I, 449–450.
3. *AS* I/I, 474–476.
4. Clément Roques, Archbishop of Rennes.
5. Aniceto Fernandez, OP, *AS* I/I, 509.

to the use of the mother tongue for the laity. Mgr Calewaert[1] spoke for nine minutes in favour of Latin but then added a phrase in which he said he accepted the schema. It was thought that he represented the position of the Belgian bishops, whom the language question places in a difficult position. He does not. The truth is that he only gave the first part of his speech, which spoke of Latin, and not the second, which dealt with the use of the vernacular. Cut short, all he did was to add his concluding phrase to the first part of his speech. The Belgian bishops are very unhappy at the way it all happened. (*Dixit* [so said] Mgr Philips.)

Those who are in favour of Latin seem to believe that the others want to do away with Latin entirely, even for the clergy. It is true that the breach in the use of Latin will inevitably widen: already many young priests, including our own, do not know enough Latin to be able to follow the Office properly and they do not seem to be aware of their serious professional obligation to learn Latin . . .

At 1.15 pm, interview (not recorded) with Miss Echegoyez who works both for the BBC, for de la Bedoyère's 'Research'[2] and for a (progressive???) paper in Uruguay.

At 4.30 pm, lecture to the Melkites on Tradition. Their outlook on the question is quite different from that of the French bishops, and several of them asked me very penetrating questions, which were enriching for myself too, but fairly remote from academic and scholastic analytical questions; not very 'usable', in fact. So, authentically Eastern. That makes me glad.

At 6 pm, lecture to the La Salette missionaries (on adult faith), followed by Benediction (including the Rosary) lasting thirty-five minutes, then supper with them and with Fr Chenu.

Sunday 28 October 1962

In France, the referendum on the election of the President of the Republic. I have done all I could to vote: I wrote, on 17 or 18 October, to the Strasbourg City Council. I received the necessary documentation only at 12.30 pm on Friday 26 October. I went to the post office at 1.30 pm: they told me that even by airmail there was no possibility of it arriving on Saturday, as stipulated in the rules. So I was unable to vote. I had put a NO in my envelope. I had voted NO to the 1958 Constitution, which had been fashioned entirely to suit just one man, and which did not give France any political structure:

Between the Man Who Leads and a people which thinks only of watching telly and exposing their bellies to the sun, there was no structure for political life.

---

1. According to the *Acta* (I/I, 493–556), and *La Documentation Catholique* 1962, col 1478–1480, Karel Calewaert did not speak at the eighth General Congregation on 27 October. The reference may be to his intervention on the previous day. Cf *AS* I/I 474–476.
2. The English layman Michael de la Bedoyère was the founder and editor of the *Search Newsletter*, a progressively and ecumenically inclined English Catholic review.

The use which de Gaulle[1] has made of power, excellent in many of its outcomes, has only accentuated this political void. He is asking us to approve a further extension of something which I have not accepted. I cannot do so. Moreover, I attach importance to the violation of the Constitution which too many people, even well-meaning people, perpetrate saying: we must put reality above the letter. It is very serious. If one alters the Constitution as one shapes a piece of wax, there is no longer any fundamental charter. The direct recourse to the people brings nothing but a mendacious justification, because the people are led at will, and the personal prestige of de Gaulle takes the place of reason. Now that, of itself, is unhealthy. Moreover, WHO, could emerge then as a winner, without having been sullied and wounded in the process, from an election with universal suffrage in which there are no organised parties. I can already see the shit that the enemies of a candidate will through at him or her by way of the most vile disparagements. French public morality is too debased to manage such choices successfully. The country would be divided, indifferent, as regards the very thing one would want constituted as the pure and shock-proof framework of its government. It is to open the way to hazardous possibilities. The most extreme of people would take advantage of it.

Of course, it is serious, very serious, to make a move that would result in the departure of de Gaulle: for he ensures the success of the policy of decolonisation, followed by association, of which he has been the author. But it is equally serious to bind oneself to a man (now elderly and at the same time so threatened), instead of working for the structure of the country and the exercise of its political will. With the referendum system, in spite of appearances, there is only one political SUBJECT, the One who has been elected, the Leader. Everyone else is no more than an applauding beneficiary and spectator: not in fact a thinking and deciding subject.

At 11 am, visit from Mgr Philips: he told me that the *De Ecclesia* text (= *De episcopis*) which we corrected last Thursday, has been presented to Bea's Secretariat, which has made only minor corrections of detail. Mgr Suenens has undertaken to be responsible for it beyond that. I am inclined to wonder how? Mgr Philips has told me that, as regards the chapter *De membris* which the obstinacy of Fr Tromp will block, the Secretariat feels that it is better not to speak of MEMBERS and to settle for giving an entirely positive description, in descending order, of the various ways of sharing in the life of the Church: in full, and on all counts, in the case of holy Catholics, incomplete in the case of Catholics who are sinners, etc. Mgr Philips told me that Cardinal Suenens is very isolated among the Belgian bishops on account of his ideas on the lay apostolate: he wants to entrust the direction of the women's Catholic Action TO FEMALE RELIGIOUS.[2] SIC !!!!!!!!!!!!!!!!

---

1. Charles de Gaulle.
2. Cf Léon-Joseph Suenens, *Promotion apostolique de la religieuse* (Bruges-Paris: Desclée de Brouwer, 1962).

Lunch at Santa Sabina, where Fr General had brought together all the Dominican experts, both official and private. Fr Schillebeeckx told me that what had caused the withdrawal of the translation into Italian of the letter from the Dutch Episcopate of which he was the author[1] was: 1) the concept of revelation; 2) the way of speaking about the laity. Cardinal Alfrink has not yet got the measure of the 'Holy Office' except through what is said in the Press.

Fr Gy told me that he had heard from Mgr Griffiths that sixty per cent of the US bishops will vote for the schema *De liturgia*. He has seen an Irish bishop who is in favour of the schema because whether or not to use the local language is left to the judgment of the local Ordinary. But he had not understood that.

At 5 pm, meeting of our little group at Mgr Volk's on the Janiculum. I presented the *Proemium*, the plan for which had been approved last Sunday. Rahner then read the text he had prepared, with Ratzinger, to replace the four unsatisfactory doctrinal schemas.[2] It is very good, especially on Church-Scripture-Tradition, which are well linked together. Some sections will probably not be approved, above all where it is a question of the relationship between revealed religion and the other religions. At all events, by what means and with what probability of success, can we present these new texts? We discussed this point. I recognise that it is necessary to prepare alternative solutions, at the risk of ending up doing a task that will be of no use. But it seems to me practically impossible to take so little account of the work already done and in which there is material that is both good and useful. We are playing at Perrette and the Can of Milk[3]… Daniélou, who is preparing other schemas and is, to some extent, re-doing the entire Council, thinks as I do on this point. He sees everyone, speaks everywhere, says he is working at the request of four or five bishops. *Quid?* [what then?] At the request of Cardinal Döpfner, Fritz Hofmann is to join our little group;[4] Fr Cottier, too, at the request of Mgr de Provenchères.

Monday 29 October 1962

Yesterday, things went OK; this morning, not at all. I went to have my blood pressure taken at the Council's medical centre: 110. That's low, they told me.

Conversation with Canon Boulard. He had been on the Commission on the Bishops. He told me that, on that Commission, the votes grouped the members virtually by nation, because that is how their attitudes grouped them. One of the results of the Council, he believes, will be the emergence of a new kind of bishop.

---

1. Cf the French translation of this pastoral letter, published by the Dutch bishops at the end of 1960: *Le Sens du Concile. Une réforme intérieure de la vie chrétienne* (Bruges: Desclée de Brouwer, 1961); the Italian translation had appeared much later, in the spring of 1962, but was withdrawn from sale.
2. French translation in Bernard-D Dupuy (editor), *La Révélation divine*, 'Unam Sanctam', 70b (Paris: Cerf, 1968), 577–587.
3. {Cf *Fables of La Fontaine*, Book VII, Fable 10.}
4. Fritz Hofmann, Professor of Theology at the University of Würzburg.

Just as after Trent a new type of bishop emerged, more pastoral than feudal, so now, in the middle of the twentieth century. This new kind of bishop will be characterised by the presence of the Church to the world. Not only in creating structures for parishes and other works, but, in addition to these structures, ensuring that the bishop is in touch with the problems of the world, together with his priests, who will keep him informed and whom he will inform, organise, animate, supervise and encourage.

But, once again, that all seems to me to depend on the country, and on the relationship between the Church and the world in each country. For a start, that supposes that one has acknowledged the existence of the world at large. This in turn implies 1) the existence of a mature laity; 2) the presence of the Church, not in the form of clerical authority but in the form of a prophetic awareness of what it means to be human.

I saw Mgr Elchinger for a few seconds. He told me he had seen Cardinal Tisserant yesterday, together with some bishops. Cardinal Tisserant has complained to the Pope about the way in which the elections for the Commissions were conducted. Ottaviani had made a list, supported by the authority of the Holy Office. This list reappeared in the votes of the Fathers to such an extent that it accounted for one third of the members of each Commission. Hence the Commissions can block any amendments which are not to the Holy Office's liking.

Mass celebrated by the Bishop of Nagasaki:[1] said very badly, very fast. The celebrants do not seem to realise the demands imposed by a congregation of 2,500 people and the rhythm that is called for in responding appropriately to such a Mass.

The *Adsumus*[2] was recited, no longer by the President alone, but by the whole assembly.

To begin with, Mgr Felici read out the list of the members chosen by the Pope for the Commissions, the number of which has been increased to nine.[3] On the *De fide et moribus* [Doctrinal] Commission, Cardinal Browne, Parente, Franić,[4] and Fr Fernandez. Once again, that seems somewhat conservative.

The Pope has appointed nine members to each Commission and not eight, as envisaged in the regulations, because, it is said, there had been complaints when the Secretary to the Congregation for Rites had been omitted from the Liturgical Commission. In order to get him back in, it would seem that the Pope added him

---

1. Paul A Yamaguchi, Archbishop of Nagasaki.
2. Latin prayer recited at the beginning of each General Congregation: 'We have come before you, Lord, Holy Spirit, hampered indeed by our many and grievous sins, and yet gathered together in your name. Come to us. Help us. Be pleased to enter our hearts, and teach us what we are to do.'
3. *AS* I/I, 559–562.
4. Franjo Franić, Bishop of Split and Makarska (Yugoslavia). The Pope had appointed him to the Doctrinal Commission.

on as a ninth member and then added a ninth member all round to make things even.

Mgr Felici said that enough had been said about the use of Latin! In fact, the discussion to follow was to be about hardly anything else. I have not noted down everything, as it is very tedious. Moreover, before long I was to count at least a quarter of the places empty: the bishops were crowding into the bars!

An Italian bishop:[1] 1) mention Mary in the schema; 2) ensure agreement between the bishops of neighbouring episcopal conferences; 3) in favour of Latin!

A Chinese bishop:[2]

Franić:[3] in Dalmatia, the Roman liturgy is celebrated in a Slavic language.

An Italian bishop:[4] proposed three PRINCIPLES: 1) the purpose of the liturgy is first the glory of God, and secondly the salvation of souls, which is subordinate to the primary purpose; 2) Christ committed the deposit of faith to the Apostles alone, and to their successors; 3) Peter's mission is to confirm. Conclusion: have recourse to his magisterium. —What ecclesiology!

A German bishop from East Germany:[5] Atheism has access to not only enormous means of propagation (reserved exclusively for its own use), but a veritable liturgy which takes the place of our sacraments by copying them, and which is very effective. Remedy: a liturgy adapted to educating people.

A bishop from Asunción (Paraguay):[6] adaptation to the mentality of today. Many rites relate to the mentality of ages long past.

After a mind-numbing Spanish bishop,[7] a Coptic bishop[8] (Candal?) suggested the example of the Copts who have not retained the Coptic language (which no-one understands today) except for the Consecration, using Arabic for the rest.

An auxiliary bishop from São Paulo:[9] barely able to read his paper, written in a Latin worthy of the Merovingian era; he stuttered in places.

---

1. Giuseppe Battaglia, Bishop of Faenza, *AS* I/I, 565–566.
2. Frederick Melandro, Archbishop of Anking, *AS* I/I, 566–567.
3. *AS* I/I, 568-570.
4. Enrico Nicodemo, Archbishop of Bari, *AS* I/I, 574–575.
5. Otto Spülbeck, Bishop of Meissen, *AS* I/I, 576–577.
6. Felipe Santiago Benítez Avalos, Auxiliary of Asunción, *AS* I/I, 577–578.
7. F García Martinez, *AS* I/I, 579–580.
8. Alexandros Scandar, Coptic-Catholic Bishop of Assiut (Egypt), *AS* I/I, 580–581.
9. Salomão Ferraz, *AS* I/I, 581–583.

A Spanish bishop:[1] *Veterum Sapientia*[2] deals with clerical studies and does not forbid adaptation. In favour of a *via media*. But everything through the Holy See: nothing through the episcopal conferences.

Mgr Simons[3] (India): Look at the present state of the use of Latin! Priests never speak it; the Pope speaks in Italian or French; like international conferences, the Council itself could have used the major modern languages. They are used even in communications with the Holy See. Official translations of encyclicals are published; theologians publish their work in the vernacular. A word about regions with mixed languages. Far from being a factor of unity, Latin is rather one of division.

A Carmelite bishop[4] called for devotions to be included in the *De liturgia*, including the scapular of Our Lady of Mount Carmel (I may not be recording this in the right place).

Mgr Kandela,[5] Auxiliary of the Patriarch of Antioch: in their case, they have sacrificed the use of Syriac, the language spoken by Our Lord and his Mother, in favour of Arabic, the language of the Koran!

Several bishops said they no longer wished to speak.

The Infant from Agrigento, the pitiable Mgr Peruzzo[6] spoke again with his hateful 'quaver' and his great tones of solemn entreaty: *civis Romanus sum:*[7] all holy bishops have been in favour of Latin, etc. Wretched creature, as full of piosity as he is limited in outlook.

A beginning was made on Chapter II: the celebration of the Eucharist.

Cardinal Spellman:[8] against communion under both kinds and concelebration.

Ruffini:[9] against communion under both kinds; the Council of Constance, the condemnation of Luther and the Council of Trent all condemned it . . . and confirmed the change of rite with reference to that of the early Church.

Trent reserved the matter to the pope.

---

1. Pablo Barrachina Estevan, Bishop of Orihuela-Alicante (Spain), *AS* I/I, 583–585.
2. *Veterum Sapientia,* Apostolic Constitution of 22 February 1962, which made the use of Latin compulsory in the training of clerics.
3. Francis Simons was Bishop of Indore (India), *AS* I/I, 586–587.
4. Tarcisio V Benedetti, Bishop of Lodi (Italy), *AS* I/I, 591–593. His intervention took place after those of Kandela and D'Agostino whom Congar does not mention.
5. Jules Georges Kandela, *AS* I/I, 587–589.
6. *AS* I/I, 594–595.
7. 'I am a Roman citizen' (expression attributed by Cicero to a Sicilian in one of his speeches against Verres).
8. *AS* I/I, 598–599.
9. *AS* I/I, 600–602.

There are other disadvantages: the number of communicants
matters of hygiene.

'*Fortasse concedi posset in sacerdotali ordinatione et in aliqua
extraordinaria occasione, praevia concessione S Sedis . . .*' [perhaps it
could be allowed for priestly ordinations and other special occasions,
with the prior permission of the Holy See].

Against concelebration: When there is a large number of priests (such
as pilgrimages, '*in coetibus ecclesiasticis*' [in meetings of clergy], and
there is a shortage of altars, each priest should celebrate every other
day and simply receive communion on the day between.

Cardinal Léger:[1] (made a great impression by his moderation and his
tone which breathed honesty and peace): in favour of *amplificatio*
[extending] the use of concelebration. He asked for the text to be
altered, as it seems only to CONCEDE it, in the absence of anything
better. State the fact in positive terms giving the following reasons: '*Ex
eo quod natura sua concelebratio pietatem sacerdotum fovet et unitatem
manifestat*' [due to the fact that, of its nature, concelebration promotes
the piety of the priests and expresses their unity].

Heavy afternoon:

At 2 pm: Fr Cottier.

At 3.20 pm, M and Mme Goss-Mayr[2] who are tenaciously pursuing, in Rome,
their campaign for total world peace and the abolition of atomic weapons. Clearly,
I am not entirely in favour of his facile exaggeration (which she tones down), but I
do think their cause is a good one and I want to do something for her. They have
contacted some of the cardinals (including Ottaviani who said to them: there is
something to be learned from Gandhi). I told them that there is not the remotest
possibility of getting something useful introduced into the Council unless one
can present a text (in Latin) which is couched in the literary style, and meets the
norms or requirements of conciliar texts. It would be necessary to bring together
a small group of theologians, of which I agreed to be one, to draw up such a text.
I think that Fr Häring could be the central figure and play a key role. I mentioned
some other names.

In the evening, I mentioned the matter to Fr Sigmond. He told me that if
nothing had been envisaged or prepared by the Theological Commission, the
Pope had asked, in May, for a schema on international order and peace. A small
commission of people based in Rome had set to work and had produced a text

1. AS I/I, 602–603.
2. Jean Goss, President of the International Movement for Reconciliation, and his wife
Hildegard Goss-Mayr, both of whom were tirelessly travelling the world in the service
of non-violence, and had already become friends of Congar's, who had encouraged
them. Hildegard described their battles in *Oser le combat non violent. Aux côtés de Jean
Goss* (Paris: Cerf, 1998), which is a translation of *Wie Feinde Freunde werden*, 1996.

(of which Fr Sigmond had prepared the paragraph which would interest me). He brought the text to me on Tuesday morning, in the brochure printed by the Central Commission. In fact, there are two paragraphs, which seem to me sufficient: one against the arms race, especially nuclear arms, the other against the use of nuclear arms with uncontrollable effects, which go beyond what reason might allow (this says nothing, then, against the use of 'modified' nuclear arms).

At 4 pm: Dom Lanne,[1] who joined our conversation at the end.

At 4.20 pm: a whole group of bishops' experts, including Laurentin, Moubarac,[2] Fr Anawati,[3] Fr Dupuy,[4] l'abbé Denis. They are entitled to hear things covered by the vow of secrecy. I shared a little with them about things, with a few theological slants on their meaning.

At 5.15 pm, I had to leave, with Mayor and Fesquet,[5] for a meeting with journalists at Saint-Louis des Français. Impossible to find a taxi (it was raining) so I was obliged to walk.

Tuesday 30 October 1962

At St Peter's. Conversation with Jedin,[6] who arrived yesterday. He is particularly interested, and interests the German bishops, in the *Geschäftsordnung*.[7] He is afraid that discussion of *De Liturgia* will be dragged out in order to wear people out and so induce them in the end to hand the texts over to the Commis-

---

1. Emmanuel Lanne, OSB, from the Monastery of Chevetogne; Rector of the Greek College, and Professor of Eastern Theology and Liturgy, he taught at Sant'Anselmo and the Pontifical Liturgical Institute; having also acted as interpreter for the Observers during the First Session of the Council, he was appointed a member of the Secretariat for Unity in 1963.

2. Youakim Moubarac, a Maronite priest; professor at the Institut Catholique in Paris; involved in Islamo-Christian dialogue, in the steps of Massignon, and also in the search for the unity of the Antiochian Churches.

3. Georges Anawati, OP, of the Province of France, Director of the Dominican Institute for Oriental Studies in Cairo; he was appointed a member of the Secretariat for Unity in 1963 and later, in 1965, as consultor to the Secretariat for Non-Christians.

4. Bernard-Dominique Dupuy, OP, of the Province of France, Professor of Fundamental Theology and Ecclesiology at the Dominican Faculties in Le Saulchoir; being already involved in the ecumenical movement, in 1967 he was to become Director of the Istina Study Centre; he was the personal expert of the bishop of Laval at the Council.

5. Henri Fesquet, a comrade in captivity with Congar, and religious reporter for the newspaper *Le Monde* which had sent him to follow the Council; his articles on the Council were published in *Le Journal du Concile,* edited by Robert Morel (Forcalquier: 1966).

6. Hubert Jedin, priest of the diocese of Cologne, Professor of Church History at Bonn University, specialist in the Council of Trent, of which he wrote the history; Council expert.

7. Cf Hubert Jedin, 'Die Geschäftsordnungen der beiden letzten ökumenischen Konzilien in ekklesiologischer Sicht', *Catholica* 14, 1960: 105–118.

sions which will do what they like, and what their Presidents like, with them. It is important not to let the Council (the *'plenum'*) be dispossessed in favour of the Commissions: in the *'plenum'*, that is, in the full assembly, the conservatives are neutralised, whereas they will recover their reactionary effectiveness in the Commissions.

Mass celebrated by the bishop of Oslo.[1] President: Cardinal Alfrink. Thirty-one people due to speak.

> Cardinal Godfrey:[2] Nos. 39 and 40: homily: *'ubi commode fieri possit'* [where it can conveniently be given], because the Mass must not last more than forty-five minutes.
>> Communion under both kinds: there is a doctrinal difficulty, because some people protest against our practice and would interpret a change as a disavowal of our practice, an avowal of error on our part.
>> Moreover, there are questions of hygiene: *quid* [what] about children, women (the use of lipstick), teetotalers.
>> The expression 'liturgy of the word' is new.
>> Concelebration: not against it. But there are difficulties: the question of Mass stipends.
> Cardinal Gracias:[3] Our discussion is not logical. It should have been organised.
>> Stipulate the role of the episcopal conferences. Concelebration: do not restrict the text too much.
> The seventy Indian bishops are in anguish over the situation which is affecting their country. They are asking themselves whether their place is here or with their people. The Chinese Communist invasion represents a question of life or death, even for the Church in India. Two bishops have already left as their dioceses have been invaded.
>> He asked all the Council Fathers for their prayers.
> (The departure of the seventy Indian bishops would be a serious loss to the Council.)
> Cardinal of Seville:[4] agrees with Ruffini as regards communion under both kinds. Agrees with Léger concerning concelebration. Extend the faculty of celebrating Mass at any hour of the day (in his country life is lived more in the evening than in the morning . . .).

---

1. Jacques Mangers.
2. *AS* I/II, 10–11.
3. *AS* I/II, 12–14.
4. José M Bueno y Monreal, Archbishop of Seville, *AS* I/II, 14–16.

Cardinal Alfrink:[1] (not as President, but as a Council Father). He will speak
about communion under both kinds not from the dogmatic, historical
or practical point of view but from that of the Bible.

The sacrifice, *epulae sacrificiales* [sacrificial banquets] = as in all
banquets: *manducate, bibite* [eat, drink].

The sacrament is of course complete under one species, but not as
regards its exterior form.

The great number of communicants makes it impossible to introduce
communion under both kinds universally, but it is desirable that this
complete form should be seen more often in the Church: that the
intentio Christi Domini [the intention of Christ the Lord] should be
displayed more often.

Therefore, allow it in certain specific cases; leave it to the judgement
of the Holy See to determine these cases, and to the judgement of the
bishops to decide if such a case exists. Bear in mind also the ecumenical
aspect.

Cardinal Ottaviani:[2] No. 37: As Spellman has said, this would be a revolution!
One cannot approach the Mass except by taking off one's shoes like
Moses at the Burning Bush . . . No. 42 (Communion under both kinds):
Miror [I am astonished] . . . Whereas the Central Commission had
almost unanimously rejected it (someone must have protested because
he stopped and then said: a great majority). It would be *periculosum*
[dangerous], because of false interpretations, practical difficulties.

The vernacular: reference has been made to Pius XII, but there are the
very strong words he used in his allocution to the Liturgical Congress
in Assisi[3] (he cited the passage in French).

No. 44: concelebration. Danger of error, of believing that a
concelebrated Mass gives greater glory to God and obtains more grace.
Concelebration would deprive the faithful of Masses . . . There is also
the question of stipends.

Cardinal Alfrink, President, cut him off: he had been speaking for more
than fifteen minutes. There was mounting applause, equivalent to an
expression of hostility to Ottaviani.

Cardinal Bea:[4] *quae in cap 2 practice dicuntur, omnino admittenda*
[all that is effectively said in Chapter 2 should be accepted]. But a good
number of comments concerning the wording. The *proemium* speaks
of 'Pasch' and dwells too much on the sacrificial aspect.

(One sees here something that will be even clearer elsewhere: the idea

---

1. *AS* I/II, 16–17.
2. *AS* I/II, 18–20.
3. Cf above, page 21, note 3.
4. *AS* I/II, 22–24.

of the 'paschal mystery' as including, inseparably, both the Passion and the Resurrection, is not universally known. Many people still understand by 'Pasch' only the Resurrection.

I am told that Cardinal Ottaviani, in an intervention which I did not hear, even maintained that the Resurrection was, as it were, external to the Redemption, which consists in the passion and death of Christ; we have the proof in that the good thief was admitted to heaven before the 'Pasch'[1]).

No. 39: *homilia PRAESCRIBATUR* [the homily should be made compulsory].

No. 44: *rationes concelebrationis melius explicentur* [the basis for concelebration should be better explained].

Communion under both kinds: the question is a disciplinary one, not doctrinal. Therefore *mutare licet* [change is allowable]. (I would be inclined to say the opposite: it is of divine right. It is doctrinal. *Mutare non licebat* [change should not have been allowed]!)

This according to the Council of Trent itself. Moreover, two years after Trent, Pius IV authorised the use of the chalice in some dioceses in Germany.

Nothing contrary to the teaching of Trent is being done by reviving the whole question today.

Constance[2] spoke against I Ius.[3]

Omnino placet: casibus determinatis a S Sede, auditis Conferentiis episcoporum [I am fully in favour: in those cases determined by the Holy See, after consulting the episcopal conferences].

Moreover, there is the ecumenical point of view.

Cardinal Browne:[4] Spoke very badly. Many of the bishops left for the bar.

Suggested corrections of wording.

Proemium: sacrificial value. the Eucharist = *Christus passus (sed regnans! non patiens)* [Christ having suffered (but reigning! no longer suffering!].

Similarly, *sacrificium laudis* [sacrifice of praise] is too vague.

Florit [5] (Florence): the sacrificial aspect, the cross, is being omitted.

No. 42: difficult with unleavened bread; and the time it would take! Restrict communion under both kinds to concelebration, and to the celebrants.

---

1. The reference is to Cardinal Ottaviani's intervention during the fifth General Congregation (23 October 1962), at which Congar was not present. *AS* I/I, 349–350.
2. The Council of Constance.
3. Jan Hus.
4. *AS* I/II, 26–27.
5. Ermenegildo Florit, Archbishop of Florence, member of the Doctrinal Commission, created cardinal in February 1965, *AS* I/II, 28–29.

No. 43: be careful! Word it in such a way as not to make invalid the attendance of those who only arrive in time for the Offertory.

Melendro[1] (China). A great many corrections.

Pereira,[2] Archbishop from Mozambique: restrict the reception of communion under both kinds to priestly ordinations.

> Bishop from China:[3] need for simplification. For example, the rites of baptism.

Rusch[4] (administrator, Innsbruck): great fruits of the liturgical movement. One can go further.

> In favour of real offerings at Mass.
>
> In favour of Bible readings making it possible to have an overall view of the Bible.
>
> In favour of episcopal conferences.

G Dwyer[5] (English) impressed by what the bishops from the Church of silence have said.

> Hence, '*fiat nova ordinatio missae*' [there should be a new rite of Mass]. But there would need to be clear instructions and limitations: restrict any changes to the Mass of the Catechumens, in order to retain one section which is identical and common to all.

Bishop from Portugal.[6]

Bishop from Yugoslavia.[7]

> (I went to the WC. I saw Mgr Roberts and we chatted. A great number of the bishops were in the bar, or chatting, or walking about in the rest of the Basilica. Some were praying in a chapel. When I returned to the tribune, the Archbishop of Dublin[8] was speaking in the name of the bishops of Ireland. He is against communion under both kinds: there would be *periculum fidei* [danger to faith]. He is against extending the possibility of concelebration.)

Fernandes:[9] No. 39. Stress further the requirement of a homily.

An American bishop chose not to speak.[10]

---

1. *AS* I/II, 30–32.
2. Custodio Alvim Pereira, Archbishop of Lorenzo Marques, *AS* I/II, 32–33.
3. Stanislas Lokuang, Bishop of Tainan (Nationalist China), member and, later, Vice-President of the Commission on the Missions, *AS* I/II, 33–34.
4. Paulus Rusch, Apostolic Administrator of Innsbruck-Feldkirch, then, in September 1964, bishop of the see, *AS* I/II, 35–36.
5. *AS* I/II, 37–39.
6. M Trindade Salgueiro, Archbishop of Evora, *AS* I/II, 39–41.
7. C Zazinović, Auxiliary Bishop of Krk, *AS* I/II, 41–42.
8. JC McQuaid, *AS* I/II, 44.
9. Angelo Fernandes, Coadjutor Archbishop of Delhi (India), *AS* I/II, 45.
10. C Helmsing, Bishop of Kansas City, *AS* I/II, 45.

Ddungu,[1] Uganda: Allow priests, when they are binating or trinating, to have a drink at any time (and something other than water! Laughter).

Kleiner[2] Cistercian Abbot General. Very fine intervention, calm and serene, very well spoken. Many people impressed. He spoke in the name of the Cistercian abbots. Listen to a monk on the question of concelebration. The monks who are priests are obliged by their rule to attend the conventual Mass. The Cistercian rules are that one attends the Mass or one serves Mass, according to one's station: an acolyte as an acolyte, a deacon as a deacon. Hence, priests as priests. They should concelebrate! Restore the wording of the text as submitted to the Central Commission.

Nemo cogetur. Nemo reprobetur [No one should be forced. No one should be forbidden.]

B Stein[3] (Auxiliary of Trèves): Very fine intervention on Nos. 38–39: not merely a *mensa Eucharistiae* [table of the Eucharist], but a *mensa Verbi Dei* [table of the Word of God]. (That goes beyond the question of the biblical readings in order to include the whole force of 'the Word of God' in the liturgy.)

Sansierra [4] (Argentina) addressed himself also to the Observers.

The name of St Joseph should be inserted into the Canon of the Mass. He proposed a form for the conclusion of the Mass (eliminating the Gospel of St John and the three Hail Marys).

After No. 41, there should be a paragraph about the time of the celebration: at ANY hour.

No. 42: communion under both kinds at least on Holy Thursday.

No. 44: *ampliatio concelebrationis: laudanda* [in favour of extending concelebration]: *in concilio provinciali* [at provincial Councils], *in concilio œcumenico* [at ecumenical councils]!!!

After this long morning, Mgrs Elchinger and Schmitt took me off to lunch with them.

We chatted. I also saw there a dozen Italian bishops, about ten English and above all SCOTTISH bishops, and four or five Ruthenian bishops (from America): these stopped speaking to the four French bishops after the latter invited the two Russian Observers to join them at table.

These bishops told me that one of the benefits of the Council is that one sees the Curia close up and can see how small-minded it is: that is all!

Immediately on my return, a visit from Fr Chenu. We chatted.

---

1. H Ddungu, Bishop of Masaka, *AS* I/II, 46–47.
2. S Kleiner, *AS* I/II, 47–48.
3. Bernhard Stein, Auxiliary Bishop of Trèves, *AS* I/II, 49–51.
4. Ildefonso M Sansierra, Auxiliary Bishop of San Juan de Cuyo, *AS* I/II, 51–52.

After that, a visit from Poupard, who is at the Secretariat of State. I got him to explain his work to me. John XXIII has only a personal secretary: he has no *brains trust* like the one Pius XII had. The work is prepared by Cardinal Dell'Acqua[5], with whom John XXIII has been close for thirty-five years. Also the presence of the French *Minutanti*[6] is important. They prepare the documentation which the Pope himself studies and which is considerable. Poupard feels that there really is a group of people who are seeking to drag out the discussion in order to prove that the Council is powerless and unworkable. And then, everything to be taken up by the Commissions, in which they would do what they liked and would reinstate the Curia.

He told me that the Pope receives a lot of money every day for the Council, including contributions from poor people—really the widow's mite—who write to him. You are running a Council. I am praying for that. It must cost a lot of money. I had 10,000 francs left over, here they are!

It is the evangelism of the poor who, today as with Dominic and Francis under Innocent III, are supporting the Church.

I just had time to write up these notes before going to supper at the Procure de Saint-Sulpice at 7.30 pm. One has time for nothing! But there is fellowship . . . Here, one does not eat at the bishops' table. After the meal, I had a conversation with Cardinal Gerlier, Cardinal Liénart and Mgr Weber. Cardinal Liénart is the only one to have class, Cardinal Gerlier being now just an old man.

Wednesday 31 October 1962

Before the opening, I went to see the Observers. The Copt[7] said to me: there is unity in so many Fathers who have come from all over the world in order to confess Jesus Christ.

Mass according to the Dominican rite, which somewhat perplexed those attending.[8]

Mgr Felici began with an announcement: *Non distribuere circulares privatas* [private circulars are not to be distributed] in the Council precinct and during the sessions. Someone told me that Cardinal Larraona had circulated a paper among the Italian bishops inviting them to vote against the schema. That seems to me very unlikely: 1) a Commission President could not do such a thing without bringing discredit on himself; 2) such a paper would be known about and in ten minutes would come into the hands of 'others' who would be very interested in it for quite different reasons. However, it remains true that Cardinal Larraona is against the schema *De Liturgia* and that Mgr Staffa, a great defender of Latin, is

---

5. In fact, Angelo Dell'Acqua, from Milan, Substitute for Ordinary Affairs of the Secretariat of State, was a titular archbishop, and was not to be created cardinal until 1967.
6. Employees of the Roman Congregations responsible for studying dossiers and advising how they be dealt with.
7. There were two Coptic Observers at the First Session.
8. The Mass was celebrated by Marie-Joseph Lemieux, OP, Archbishop of Ottawa.

his secretary. Larraona has asked the Spanish bishops to speak against the schema 'in order to defend the Holy See and Christian piety'.

Cardinal Lercaro:[1] suggested the *oratio fidelium*[2] after the homily: he referred to St Justin (which happened three times during the morning): it is the prayer of the assembled community, for the world, for the poor . . .

Concerning No. 43: The term 'Mass' denotes BOTH the didactic and sacrificial parts of the Mass. Do not sacrifice the *mensa divini Verbi* [table of the divine Word].

Cardinal König:[3] *Placet*, in spite of the fact that the comments submitted to the Central Commission have been omitted. As regards communion under both kinds and concelebration: *ne claudatur porta* [do not shut the door].

Cambiaghi[4] (from Crema): No. 39: *homilia non tantum commendanda sed imponenda* [the homily should not only be recommended but made obligatory].

No. 42: restrict communion under both kinds to the ordination of PRIESTS.

Concelebration: On Holy Thursday and at Congresses of Priests for priests who are sick. But one would need to STIPULATE quite what is understood by these congresses of priests.

Jop[5] (Polish) No. 39: *commendetur* [to be recommended] is not enough. *Semper nuntiari debet* [It should always be given].

No. 42: communion under both kinds: *Magna practica difficultas* [great practical difficulty], even for ordinations!

Iglesias[6] (Urgel): No. 42: *Nulla immutatio* [Nothing should be changed]. Restrict it to priests on their ordination. Christ only gave both kinds TO PRIESTS. He listed four reasons against it.

No. 44: there is no adequate reason for a wider use of concelebration.

Nuer[7] (Egypt) addressed his remarks to the Observers as well. Allow the use of ordinary bread.

Auxiliary from Barcelona:[8] spoke very fast, like a machine gun, and for too long, so he was cut off. Many bishops left for the bar.

---

1. *AS* I/II, 56–58.
2. Prayer of the Faithful.
3. *AS* I/II, 58.
4. Placido M Cambiaghi, Bishop of Crema and, later, of Novara (Italy) in February 1963, *AS* I/II, 59–60.
5. Franciszek Jop, titular bishop, living in Opole (Poland), *AS* I/II, 60–61.
6. Ramón Iglesias Navarri, Bishop of Urgel (Spain), *AS* I/II, 61–63.
7. Youhanna Nuer, OFM, Auxiliary Bishop of Luxor of the Copts (formerly Thebes), *AS* I/II, 64.
8. N Jubany Arnau, *AS* I/II, 64-68.

No. 42: it is not a question of introducing communion under both kinds indiscriminately for all, but in particular cases. He gave reasons in favour of this: special incorporation into Christ.

No. 44: in favour of concelebration in certain circumstances.

Cistek?[1] (bishop *Januarius*): Nos. 42 and 44 are the fruit of the very life of the liturgical movement.

Pius X prepared the way for No. 42 by deciding that members of the Latin Church could receive communion in the eastern rite under both kinds. That would express the unity of the faith. *Porta re-aperiatur* [The door should be re-opened]! There is no longer any danger for the faith.

Devoto[2] (Argentina)

I went to the WC. The bar was crowded. There is only one thing on everyone's lips: it is going on for too long.

Archbishop of Atlanta[3] (USA): in favour of adaptations (good).

Jaeger[4] (Paderborn) No. 42: in specified cases: ordinations, solemn professions; the bride and groom at their Nuptial Mass; the baptism of adults and the reception of a convert.

Force of representation more complete.

Brazilian Bishop:[5] delete *tum laicis* [including lay people] in No. 42, 1.11 *celebratio versu populum* [celebration facing the people]: only at the discretion of the Ordinary.

Mgr Weber:[6] 1) it is *absque fidei periculo* [without danger to the faith], so delete the words *sublato fidei periculo* [danger to the faith having been removed].

2) *iudicio episcoporum* [at the discretion of the bishops] and in the cases stipulated by the pope. Thus it is without danger and *libertas episcoporum integra manet* [the freedom of bishops remains undiminished].

3) *quae rationes?* [which reasons?] Ecumenical, pastoral: to show the people the great value of the acts for which it is to be re-introduced.

Mgr Elchinger[7] spoke in the name of young people. He read his text eloquently with, at times, very studied effects, which was not really appropriate. But he was listened to and even, at the end, applauded.

---

1. J-B Przyklenk, Bishop of Januária (Brazil), *AS* I/II, 68–70.
2. Alberto Devoto, Bishop of Goya, *AS* I/II, 71–72.
3. Paul J Hallinan, Archbishop of Atlanta, *AS* I/II, 75–76.
4. *AS* I/II, 76–77.
5. Luis G Da Cunha Marelim, Bishop of Caxias do Maranhão, *AS* I/II, 78.
6. *AS* I/II, 79–80.
7. *AS* I/II, 80–82.

Khoury,[1] Maronite. He also addressed himself to *Carissimi Observatores* [very dear Observers].

Very good intervention.

Concelebration: the Commission's text has been truncated. Why limit it? Extend it to include: Holy Thursday, all meetings of priests, conventual Mass.

Doctrinal basis: the Eucharistic celebration is an act of the community, the act, not alone of the priest but of the *presbyterium* (St Ignatius). Religious eat from a common table, except that of the Lord. He suggested a text saying all that. The Council ought to set an example.

Edelby[2] (very good Latin: very clear; very well presented): he wishes to make the voice of the East heard *in restauranda liturgia latina* [in the restoration of the Latin liturgy].

He agreed with Khoury's remarks concerning concelebration.

Two kinds: *Bibite ex eo omnes* [Drink from it, all of you]. It is the *praxis evangelica, apostolica, normalis. Non privilegium vel concessio* [It is the evangelical, apostolic, normal practice. It is neither a privilege nor a concession]. Communion under only one kind is *praxis exceptionalis* [the exceptional practice]. Moreover, *res mere disciplinaris* [it is only a disciplinary ruling].

The reasons for the hierarchy's opposition are psychological: a complex. They do not want to seem to go back on a decision, to be imitating Protestants and the Orthodox. They should get rid of this complex. Do not exaggerate the practical difficulties (Cardinal Godfrey's reference to the use of lipstick[3]).

Non in uno actu et statim concedenda [not to be granted immediately, and all together].

Aramburu[4] (Tucumán): in favour of a Eucharistic fast of two hours. Inclined to be against communion under both kinds.

Bishop from Formosa[5] [ ]

Mgr Himmer[6] (Tournai): No. 39: the homily is part of the liturgy.

No. 40: very much in favour of the *oratio fidelium* [prayer of the faithful]: a short litany of intercession; in favour of the Eucharistic fast being reduced to one hour?

Van Cauwelaert[7] (Congo). Possibly the finest intervention of the morning. Made with emphasis in the name of 260 bishops of Africa and

1. J Khoury, Maronite Archbishop of Tyre (Lebanon), *AS* I/II, 83–85.
2. *AS* I/II, 85–87.
3. Already mentioned by Congar. Cf the tenth General Congregation, *AS* I/II, 10–11.
4. Juan Carlos Aramburu, Archbishop of Tucumán (Argentina), *AS* I/II, 88–90.
5. P Tou Pao Zin, Bishop of Hsinchu (Taiwan), *AS* I/II, 90–91.
6. Charles Himmer, Bishop of Tournai, *AS* I/II, 92–93.
7. *AS* I/II, 94–95.

Madagascar who are UNANIMOUS.

Stuporem meum omittere non possum [I cannot hide my amazement] that there are some who wish to delete the *'paschale convivium'* [Paschal Meal] from the *proemium*. Saint Paul; Saint Thomas! Concelebration: the 260 bishops are unanimously in favour and endorse the words of Cardinal Léger.

The people will understand from this, more than from the spoken word, the unity of the priesthood and the uniqueness of the priest.

If some regions do not see the usefulness of certain innovations, they should not interfere with those where the bishops are unanimous in considering them necessary; they should not quench the Spirit.

Example of the welcome given to Paul and Barnabas at the Synod of Jerusalem. We should open the Church to all the peoples!

Applause.

Cyril Zohrabian[1] Armenian [ ]

Auxiliary bishop of Verdun: Boillon:[2] Communion for the sick under one kind only, the wine.

De Vito[3] (India): against concelebration for the Chrism Mass but in favour of it for the evening Mass of Holy Thursday. No restriction on the time of celebration.

Melas[4] (Italy): against communion under both kinds for the people.

In the afternoon, a good visit from Fr de Lubac. He told me that last week's *L'Espresso* spoke of one school (Lubac, Congar, Chenu) against the Ottaviani-Parente school . . . He also told me that he had heard that, during a lecture, Piolanti had said that some people had been invited to the Council so that they would not do what Döllinger did in 1870; peeved at not having been invited to the Council he caused a schism. They had been invited in order to keep them in the Church.

We also spoke about the fact that our French bishops were not using their theologians. They do not ask them to work for them and do not work with them. There are a great many lectures in order to give information, to which Mgr Garrone is anxious to invite all and sundry, but there are no working sessions. The situation is very different among the Spaniards, the Germans and the Dutch. The latter have a lecture every evening, given by Fr Schillebeeckx; the Germans hold regular working meetings and were doing so even before the Council. Their cardinals and their bishops consult Rahner, Ratzinger, Häring, Jedin. I have several times heard news of these meetings from them. Our bishops: nothing. It has got

---

1. C G Zohrabian, OFM cap, titular bishop resident in Rome, *AS* I/II, 96.
2. Pierre Boillon was in fact Coadjutor Bishop of Verdun. It was in August 1963 that he was to become bishop of the see. *AS* I/II 97.
3. Albert De Vito, Bishop of Lucknow (India), *AS* I/II 97–99.
4. Giuseppe Melas, Bishop of Nuoro, *AS* I/II 100–101.

to the point where I wonder whether or not I shall return for a Second Session: for there is so much useful and effective work to be done!

Then a visit from Fr Cottier, who suggested some good *emendationes* [alterations] to the Latin of my *proemium*. He told me that Mgr de Provenchères had heard it said that the Pope had rejected the *De episcopis* [on the bishops] that had been prepared. That seems to me a very strange and, I am sure, unreliable tip.

Visit from Fr Prete,[1] Regent of Studies in Bologna, who wants to see me; then Fr Mongillo,[2] Professor of Moral Theology at our *studium* in Naples. He would like me to come to Naples to speak to the fathers 1) on ecclesiology; 2) on the orientation and basis to be given to their journal: *Temi di Predicazione* [Themes for Preaching].

Fr Mongillo drew an advance on this, talking to me about the work he is doing just now, for which, he said, he had found my *Pentecôte* enlightening:[3] *principalissimum in lege nova, est gratia Spiritus Sancti* [the grace of the Holy Spirit is the principal reality of the new law].

I am overcome by the crazy respect there is for me everywhere. People keep on approaching me, even in St Peter's. I hardly dare to say who I am, because mentioning my name sets off these declarations of affection and respect. If I have done something, it is not thanks to my own personal worth, which is puny. It is because I have (come what may) followed what I believed to be the will and the call of God. It is he who has managed everything, prepared everything. At the Council itself, I have no other rule except to make him direct everything. A fully God-centred ethic, even in small material details. I have taken the following as a rule of practice: not to undertake anything unless asked to do so by the bishops. IT IS THEY who are the Council. However, if an initiative bore the mark of a call from God, I would open myself to it.

But above all I wish to note here my feeling about our Italian Fathers (I have also seen Fr Grion[4]). THEY HAVE MADE A GOOD BEGINNING. They are recruiting well. Over the next thirty years, they would be very capable of doing for Italy what we have done for France: provide an ideological animation of a renewal of the Church by means of an authentic return to our sources. That is why I have more or less promised to go to Naples. I want to help them, in so far as I can, to turn this corner. Oh! If only I knew Italian, or if only everybody spoke French!

Thursday 1 November 1962
Three weeks have already elapsed!

At the end of the morning, a visit from three Spanish priests, two from Saragossa and the third from Bilbao: Antero Hombría,[5] Tomás Domingo,[6] Teodoro

---

1. Benedetto Prete, OP, an exegete, of the Province of Lombardy,
2. Antonio D Mongillo, OP, of the Province of Naples.
3. Yves Congar, *La Pentecôte – Chartres, 1956* (Paris: Cerf, 1956).
4. Alvaro Grion, OP, of the Province of Lombardy.
5. Antero Humbría Tortajada, theologian, professor at the seminary of Saragossa, consultor to the Spanish bishops at the Council.
6. Tomás Domingo Pérez, historian, professor at the seminary of Saragossa and consultor

Jimenez-Urresti.[1] The Spanish bishops have collectively appointed fifty theologians and, this time, have brought with them twenty of them: they include historians, teachers of dogmatics, spirituality and canon law. These theologians live together and meet every week. The bishops make them study and then expound the points, and also prepare the text of any amendments. These three were very nice. They declared they were my disciples and are looking to me to suggest a line of approach. I was happy to see that they already had more or less the same reactions as I have myself.

From 3.00 pm to 4.30 pm, a brief outing with Fr Camelot, my first. In the evening, a visit from Mgr Jacq, from the OP Province of Lyons, who is a bishop in Vietnam.[2] The Vietnamese bishops are together in a hotel. I plan to go and see them.

Friday 2 November 1962

Visit from Fr Häring (about a text against thermo-nuclear weapons and against the arms race).

Visit from Fr Gy: he talked to me about the Liturgical Commission's working methods and about what is most likely to get through: *per prius* [most likely] are the written AMENDMENTS; much less likely are general considerations and ideological stances. It is a pity.

Saturday 3 November 1962

The cold has come. But what lovely light, sparkling and soft, golden and young . . .

Visit in the afternoon from l'abbé Houtart.[3] He is fully involved with CELAM. He told me that the Vatican (Secretariat of State) is not very keen on CELAM, even though it was set up by Pius XII; so it [the Secretariat] is constantly putting spokes in its wheels in all kinds of ways. L'abbé Houtart himself gave as a lecture the text which he had published in *L'Épiscopat et l'Église universelle*. This lecture was then published (unknown to him) in the roneoed Bulletin of two Italian bishops conferences. In consequence, he had received requests for explanations and corrections (of details). Clearly, when the bishops are organised in conferences, it is a little as if they had formed a bishops' trade union: they represent a power which will have to be taken into account.

All this is all the more striking in that it was the nuncios who, to a great and decisive extent, were responsible for the creation of CELAM. Not so much in promoting it, as in creating the need for it, despite themselves, on account of

---

to the Spanish bishops at the Council.
1. Teodoro Jimenez-Urresti, of the diocese of Bilbao, where he taught theology at the diocesan seminary.
2. André R Jacq, OP, was a missionary bishop in Vietnam.
3. François Houtart, of the diocese of Malines-Brussels; he was Director of the Centre for Socio-Religious Research which he had founded in Brussels in 1956.

their own stupidity. It seems that in South America the nuncios intervene in everything, reprimand the bishops, forbid things. For example, not very long ago, the Nuncio in Montevideo[1] forbade attendance at a Pax Romana[2] congress on the social responsibilities of the university. He said that it was communist!!!! I have been told of similar things having been done by the Apostolic Delegate in Washington,[3] the man we have heard express at the Council the most solemn integrist nonsense. It has come to the point where the bishops (of Bolivia?) put pressure on the government to get rid of the country's Nuncio, Mgr Samorè.[4] He has gone, but it is he, now, who is responsible for South American affairs in the Secretariat of State. He passes for competent, bearing out the truth that in the kingdom of the blind, one-eyed people are kings: all the more so in that, among the personnel dealing with Latin America in the Secretariat of State, he is the only one who has actually lived in the country. But he understands very little. Even here, in Rome, at the Council, without actually forbidding the South American bishops to meet, such meetings are curbed or impeded.

Thus, my intuition about the history of ecclesiological doctrines, of the tension between the PAPA pole and the ECCLESIA pole, is closer to the truth than I realised. This tension is latent in the Council and it is more than likely that one day it will come out into the open. The Curia understands nothing. The Curia is full of Italians who, being kept in ignorance of the reality of things, in POLITICAL SUBJECTION, in a simplistic and false ecclesiology according to which everything is derived from the pope, see the Church only as a vast centralised administration of which they themselves form the centre. During these days, I have been compiling notes about the Italians and the Church, the ecclesiology of the Italians . . . Ultra-montanism really does exist. Victorious THEORETICALLY in the official ecclesiology, it exists and is powerfully at work at the level of piety, of religious representations and of the corresponding anthropology. The colleges, the universities and scholasticates of Rome distil all that to varying degrees, the maximum, indeed well-nigh fatal, dose being currently administered at the Lateran.

I will study all that. I must feed my dossier.

At 15.05, arrival of a small group of bishops' theologians: Laurentin, a Maronite and, this time, Colson, who is impressive. He has matured. His reactions are excellent. They got me to talk a little bit about everything, for about two hours. Laurentin took notes, asked questions, made me repeat what I had said so that he

---

1. The reference is probably to the Swiss archbishop Raffaele Forni, who was appointed Nuncio to Montevideo (Uruguay) in 1960.
2. International Movement of Catholic Intellectuals.
3. E Vagnozzi.
4. To be exact, the Italian archbishop Antonio Samorè had been Apostolic Nuncio to Colombia from 1950 to 1953. During the First Session of the Council he was appointed a member of the Commission on the Apostolate of the Laity. He was later to become President of the Pontifical Commission on Latin America and created cardinal.

could note it down better. Is he preparing a book? Why does he make such an effort to get people to talk and make notes of what they say? The Maronite said that the Maronite thesis is as follows: do away with the duplication of canon law and organisation between East and West by granting many more powers to the episcopal conferences, so that they can ensure considerable local pluralism within a single unified Church.

My initial reaction was very negative. That seems to me to forget that the East and the West cannot call their history into question, since it has made them what they are. I believe that the difference forms part of the historical character of the Church.

That evening supper at Laurentin's, well organised for work. He always brings his secretary with him.

Health: Not very good. My arms get even more tired than my legs. Sleepless night during which I see all the passivity, the inadequacy, the failure of my life, especially of my life here at the Council.

Sunday 4 November 1962

At 5 pm, meeting of the Rahner, Ratzinger, Semmelroth, Labourdette, Daniélou group at Domus Mariae. Fr Cottier OP and Müller,[1] from Erfurt, have been added to the group. We floundered about a bit. Daniélou speaks of everything and mixes everything up. He would like to turn the *Proemium* I had been asked for into a dogmatic Constitution discussing, in particular, man in the image of God, and original sin.

I find rather naïve the idea that one could SUBSTITUTE the schemas prepared by Rahner and Daniélou for those prepared by the Theological Commission. I detect something of a spirit of revenge on the part of these theologians who did not belong to the Preparatory Theological Commission. It is true that the schemas that were produced are superficial, scholastic, too philosophical and too negative: it is as if the past forty years of biblical, theological and liturgical work had not taken place. I believe that easily two fifths, or even three fifths, of the Council assembly would be in favour of rejecting them. But I am afraid that the question would then simply be returned to the Commission: in other words, that Brutus would be asked to correct Brutus . . .

I am amazed, now, that I myself was not more critical[2] of the texts that came from the Central Commission, even though I considered them mediocre and, at some points, simply bad. I account for my reaction by the following points:

1) I was under the impression that the texts given to me to study were more or less definitive and that one could do no more than offer criticism of details;

2) I did not attach enough importance to these texts, as I was convinced that what forms opinion in every case of everything that is truly alive, is not the of-

---

1.   Orfried Müller, priest and Professor of Dogmatics at the Theological College in Erfurt.

2.   Congar added to the margin of the typescript: 'theologically?'

ficial texts, but living thought. I still think that, and that makes me at the same time both too tolerant and a little skeptical about the texts: but I now recognise more clearly the importance of texts which, nonetheless, point the way for teaching and which may possibly either prevent or stand in the way of better things, of progress.

3) There was nothing one could do. The consultors were not much more than 'extras'. They expressed, by and large, the criticisms that are being made today, and to some extent I did so myself. But in vain. What was the use of the *vota* that I was asked for and produced (*De episcopis, De laicis; De œcumenismo*)? It was not Lubac, or myself, or Häring or Delhaye who were asked to prepare the texts. We were barely allowed to speak (except in the sub-commission which Fr Gagnebet arranged for me come to), and we did not vote. Häring, Lubac and Laurentin all say the same.

4) Everything was dominated by the tyranny of Fr Tromp. It was almost impossible not to go in the direction he himself wanted.

5) The general atmosphere means a lot. Today it is the atmosphere of the Council: a pastoral climate, a climate of freedom and dialogue and openness. Back then, it was the climate of the 'Holy Office' and of the professorships of the Roman Colleges. One was neutralised by a tacit but powerful code, by very strong social pressure against which one did not push back to the point where it would have been necessary to put everything in question.

Today, a ceremony to celebrate the fourth anniversary of the coronation of the Pope. In honour of St Charles, pontifical Mass in the Ambrosian rite. I am told that the Pope preached a homily. He began in Latin, then changed to Italian. He praised the pastoral outlook of St Charles. He extolled the variety of rites. Some see in all that discreet hints to the Council. It is possible.

Health: this evening of 4 November, very bad. My feet feel lifeless below the ankle, and my hands are almost in cramp. What has happened? Until 1, or even 2 November, things were OK: I had the impression that an improvement was taking place. Could it be the cold? In fact, I am cold, especially my feet and my right hand: the parts of me that are not working. Excessive heat saps my energy; cold gives me cramp. Where to go? What to do? I am taking my medications. I thought they were going to do me good, and now look at me: as on one of my worst days!

Monday 5 November 1962

Mass in the Maronite rite. This example of Eastern liturgies will influence the Council far more than speeches. It is, in itself, a demonstration of an adaptation of the liturgy for the people.

Cardinal Confalonieri[1] made clear what had been the contributions of the Central Commission and of the sub-commission *de Emendationibus*

---

1. Carlo Confalonieri, Secretary of the Consistorial Congregation, President of the

[on amendments][1] in order, seemingly, to scotch the argument of those who were appealing to the wishes of the Central Commission.

(I was told later that this was intended as a reply to Cardinal Ottaviani, who had invoked the authority of the Central Commission. It was an Italian Monsignor from the Secretariat of State, Mgr. Luigi Valentini,[2] who told me this.)

> The Martyrology, being one of the liturgical books, must, like them, *recognosci* [be revised].
>
> Cardinal McIntyre[3] (mumbled presentation): against the vernacular (except for the reading of the Epistle and Gospel by a priest other than the celebrant). '*Summus Pontifex locutus est*' [The Supreme Pontiff has spoken].
>
> Surban, Philippines:[4] there have already been many changes. '*Redeatur ad primam et originalem missam*' [We should return to the early and original form of the Mass]: Christ celebrated facing the people and out loud, in the vernacular.
>
> And Christ's actual words should be inserted into the Mass: '*Ego sum vitis vera . . . Ut sint unum*' [I am the true vine . . . That they may all be one . . .].
>
> An ecumenical rite! A *Missa Orbis* [Mass for the World]! This would be a seed of unity!
>
> László,[5] Austria: No. 37: the reform has begun and in accordance with the norms that are invoked today in order to continue it. Let it continue! Let us have the *fortitudo apostolica* [apostolic courage] for that.
>
> Ferrari[6] *Monopolitanus* (Italy). The schema is attractive on account of its doctrinal discretion and pastoral concern. Add to it a brief formulation of the dogmatic basis for the participation of the faithful in the sacrifice. No. 37: between a low Mass and a high Mass, there should be a form better adapted to the COMMUNITY, and its participation.

Pontifical Commission on Latin America. He had been a member of the Central Preparatory Commission and President of the Sub-commission on Amendments. He was to be a member of the Coordinating Commission. *AS* I/II, 106–108.

1. The Sub-commission on Amendments had been made responsible for revising the preparatory schemas in accordance with the wishes expressed by the Central Preparatory Commission.
2. *Minutante* at the Secretariat of State.
3. *AS* I/II, 108–109.
4. In fact, Epifanio Surban Belmonte was the Bishop of Dumaguete (Philippines). However, the reference here is to the intervention of Bishop William I Duschak, Vicar Apostolic of Calapan (Philippines), *AS* I/II, 109–112.
5. Štefan László, Bishop of Eisenstadt, member of the Commission on the Apostolate of the Laity from the First Session onwards, *AS* I/II, 112–114.
6. *AS* I/II, 115–116.

Fares [1] (Italy): Bear in mind the Council of Trent! Do not touch the Canon!
No. 42: Change nothing;
No. 44: concelebration above all for those living in community.

Bandeira[2] (Brazil): No. 37: do not touch the Roman rite which was instituted by St Peter himself!

Another Brazilian said he no longer wished to speak.[3]

Cousineau[4] (Haïti): No. 44: it is in accordance with what Cardinal Léger said as regards the communitarian aspect, sacrificial unity.
No. 37: St Joseph should be mentioned every time there is a reference to Mary.

Jenny:[5] concerning No. 37: the obscurity is due to the removal of the Preparatory Commission's declaration: it is not clear what is meant by the changes envisaged.
He gave a list of the principal points (he was listened to very attentively).

Archbishop of Rwanda:[6] The Liturgy of the Word should teach all doctrine.
Introduce biblical texts covering the whole history of salvation.
No. 42: delete *'sublato fidei periculo'* [danger to the faith having been removed], which is offensive to Christ and to those who follow him in this.
No. 44: supports Cardinal Léger. Make it clear that each concelebrant may receive a stipend.

A Spaniard[7] . . .

I went to the WC and, for the first time, had a coffee at the bar. There I saw Cullmann and the two Brothers from Taizé, and also Mgr Leclercq[8] and Mgr Rolland.[9]

When I returned, the Benedictine Abbot General, Gut,[10] was speaking in favour of Communion under both kinds.

Bishop of Nankin:[11] in favour of *lingua vernacula in omnibus partibus missae celebratae pro populo* [the vernacular in all parts of the Mass celebrated

---

1. Armando Fares, Archbishop of Catanzaro, *AS* I/II, 116–117.
2. CE Saboia Bandeira de Méllo, OFM, Bishop of Palmas, *AS* I/II, 117–118.
3. João Batista da Mota e Albuquerque, Archbishop of Vitória.
4. Albert Cousineau, Bishop of Cap-Haïtien, *AS* I/II, 119–120.
5. *AS* I/II, 121–122.
6. André Perraudin, Archbishop of Kabgayi (Rwanda), *AS* I/II 121–123.
7. P Barrachina Estevan, Bishop of Orihuela-Alicante (Spain).
8. Georges Leclercq, of the diocese of Lille, Rector of the Catholic Faculties in Lille.
9. Claude Rolland, Bishop of Antsirabé (Madagascar). Former pupil of M-D Chenu, OP, at Le Saulchoir; he had asked his former teacher to be his theologian and to help him in the works of the Council.
10. *AS* I/II, 127.
11. Paul Yü Pin, Archbishop of Nankin (China), elected member of the Commission on

for the people] (Sundays and feastdays), *incluso canone* [including the Canon]. He was speaking on behalf of two thirds of humanity.

Bekkers:[1] speaking in the name of the bishops of Holland and of Indonesia. Communion under both kinds is an authentic extension of the liturgical movement. Concelebration is in accordance with the nature of the Sacrament and in the interests of ecumenism.

Bishop from Chile,[2] in the name of the episcopal conference comprising thirty-five bishops. The Liturgy of the Word! Use of the vernacular at least for the sections that include instruction. We have met together, the Pope has said, in order to introduce '*opportunas mutationes*' [appropriate changes]. It is a unique opportunity. We should not forget the words *Misereor super turbam* [I have compassion on the crowd (Mk 8:2)].

Seitz [3] (Vietnam), Full agreement to Nos. 42 and 44.

For the people in his area, who are very communitarian, attached to centuries-old rites, and who reject Latin on the one hand and successions of private Masses on the other, he asks: '*ut aperiatur porta . . . ut divulgetur Evangelium Dei*' [that the door be opened . . . that God's Good News be proclaimed]; agrees with Cardinal Léger and Mgr Bekkers.

Thomas Muldoon:[4] need for theological precision in the statements in chapter 2 of the *proemium,* where there is confusion between sacrament and sacrifice: clarify the relationship between the Mass and the Cross. Explain the word '*repraesentare*' [represent]. Do not speak of the offering of the lay people. The faithful do not offer!

Communion under both kinds: suggested a new formulation, without changing the basic meaning.

Georges Xenopulos[5] (the name is Greek, but his pronunciation of Latin was typically and entirely Italian). He raised difficulties over communion under both kinds, whether one drinks from the chalice: then the question of hygiene, lipstick . . . or . . . He is thinking of the communion of hundreds of people . . .

---

the Apostolate of the Laity from the First Session of the Council onwards, *AS* I/II, 128–129.

1. *AS* I/II, 129–130.
2. Eladio Vicuña Aránguiz, Bishop of Chillán, *AS* I/II, 130–131.
3. Paul Seitz, of Missions étrangères de Paris, Bishop of Kontum (Vietnam), *AS* I/II, 133–134.
4. Thomas W Muldoon, Auxiliary of Sydney (Australia), *AS* I/II, 135–137.
5. Georges Xenopulos, SJ, Bishop of Syra and Administrator of Candia (Greece), *AS* I/II, 137–138.

The President, Cardinal Liénart, cut him off: he was not *ad rem* [to the point]. He did not seem to understand the catastrophe that had happened to him.

> Mgr Théas[1] (listened to with great attention). IN FAVOUR of concelebration: basing his reasoning on the situation in Lourdes. He has already asked the Holy See for it several times for solemn occasions and has always received the reply *non expedire* [it is not expedient].
> Asks for it to be possible to receive Communion on Easter Day even if one has received Communion at the Vigil.
> Bishop from Ecuador[2] in the name of other bishops: 1) abrogate the Mass *pro populo* [for the people]; 2) in cases of necessity, allow the bishop to authorise priests to binate on weekdays.
> Archbishop of Barcelona:[3] No. 39: homily. So that, over a few years, one will have covered the whole of Christian doctrine (richer passages from the Bible). That would remove some of the reasons for the use of the vernacular. No. 42: against communion under both kinds, because the faithful would believe that it imparts more grace . . . Moreover, since the principle to follow is that of simplicity, leave things as they are! No. 44: against concelebration, because there would not be enough priests left to provide Masses for the faithful!
> Joseph D'Avack(?):[4] this will be the last. So, while he was talking in a very strong Italian accent, the Fathers were tidying away their things in preparation for leaving.
> Fr Gillon thinks that all this smacks of Protestantism. What world does he live in?

Tuesday 6 November 1962

I did not go to St Peter's, in order to finish work on my *Proemium*.

I was told that there were seven or eight interventions to begin with, including one from the bishop of Linz[5] giving, with supporting figures, a very positive picture of the results of the liturgical movement in his diocese. Then Mgr Felici read a text from the Pope[6] authorising the Council of Presidents, when they felt that a question or a chapter had been sufficiently discussed, to ask the assembly to vote, by either remaining seated or by standing up, on whether or not the debate should be deemed closed and the next point on the agenda be taken up.

---

1. Pierre Théas, Bishop of Tarbes and Lourdes (France), *AS* I/II, 139–140.
2. CA Mosquera Corral, Archbishop of Guayaquil, *AS* I/II, 140–141.
3. G Modrego y Casáus, member of the Commission on Studies and Seminaries and Catholic Education appointed by the Pope during the First Session of the Council, *AS* I/II, 141–143.
4. Giuseppe D'Avack, Archbishop of Camerino (Italy), *AS* I/II, 145–146.
5. Franz Zauner, *AS* I/II, 151–153.
6. *AS* I/II, 159.

Everybody stood up. A start was then made on Chapter III of the schema. I will see that tomorrow.

I spent twenty-five minutes (at 5.10 pm) at Saint-Louis: first Tuesday: meeting of the French. I saw quite a few bishops and others: Fr de Baciocchi,[1] Villain, etc. I also met Laurentin who told me he had been appointed a Council expert. Has he been working FOR THAT throughout the month that he has been in Rome?

I called in to the Foyer Unitas[2] for a moment.

At 6 pm, I called on Cardinal Frings (at the German Church dell'Anima): he had asked me to come. Ratzinger, Jedin and Rahner were there too. Purpose of the meeting: to see how to go about proposing the Rahner-Ratzinger texts in place of the existing dogmatic schemas. We floundered about and got nowhere. We know nothing and, seemingly, nobody else knows anything, about how the Council will proceed. Cardinal Tisserant, whom Cardinal Frings saw yesterday, knows nothing. What will the Council begin considering after the *De Liturgia*? A mystery! In the meantime, the Liturgical Commission has divided up into sub-commissions which are working hard on the two thousand amendments submitted with reference to the Introduction and the first two chapters. A certain number are not relevant to the Liturgical Commission and one of the sub-commissions will send them back to where they belong. All that clears the ground, but does not move the Council forward . . . I have been asked to find out how the Belgian bishops plan to go about substituting Philips' text *De Ecclesia* for the official text. That is why, on the way out from that meeting, I went to the Belgian College where I saw Cardinal Suenens. He had just returned from Belgium and knew NOTHING. Nobody knows anything. He is thinking of introducing the revised text together with the official text through the Commission for Extraordinary Affairs. This commission, composed of four Italian Cardinals (including Siri[3] and Confalonieri) and four non-Italians, exists in theory to function, at least at the level of consultation, as the body responsible for directing the progress of the Council. But so far there is no evidence that it has been very effective. To put it in a nutshell, I am very disappointed.

The Germans are counting on the French bishops and theologians. But which? There are hardly any. They have more or less asked me to look into that, but I find myself faced with some very doubtful possibilities.[4]

---

1. Joseph Baciocchi, SM, Professor of Theology at the Catholic Faculties in Lyons, personal expert for the Marist missionary bishops.
2. The Foyer Unitas, at 30, Via S Maria dell'Anima, run by the Dutch community of the Dames de Béthanie, was the headquarters of the Centre Unitas (cf page 16, note 1).
3. Giuseppe Siri, Archbishop of Genoa, and member of the Council of Presidents.
4. On 8 November, Congar wrote to Garrone, reporting to him the meetings he had had on 6 November with Frings and Suenens; he informed him of the Germans' hopes, and offered his services to the French bishops. He also added that the German bishops were holding frequent meetings with their theologians (Congar Archives).

Wednesday 7 November 1962

We were officially informed that the schema *De fontibus revelationis* [on the sources of revelation] would follow immediately on *De Liturgia*.

Mgr Rougé,[1] conspicuously the spokesman for the CPL [French Centre for Pastoral Liturgy], replied to the objections to the text relating to the anointing of the sick and the change of name (formerly Extreme Unction).

Angelini:[2] in favour of extending the administration of this Sacrament, for example before a serious operation. And for the anointing of only the forehead and the hands.

Bishop from Brazil[3] *De ritu confirmationis* [on the rite of confirmation]: the bishops are the ones to judge whether or not to celebrate this sacrament during Mass.

Sansierra[4] (Argentina) spoke also to the Observers. In favour of the schema as it stands.

Marriage Ritual: in favour of developing a whole dialogue in which the couple getting married would express the great values of Christian marriage.

Against the use of black for burials: it is pagan.

Faveri[5] (Italian) made people laugh with very serious tales of baptismal water going stagnant and of babies vomiting. Hygiene! Pure clean water: simplify the rites; no breathing on the one being baptised (and what if the priest were tubercular?).

(I went to the WC. I met a lot of people as a lot of people were walking around, going to the bar, chatting in small groups in the side-aisles. In this way I met Jedin, Thils,[6] Mgr Khoury, who invited me to come to visit the Maronites . . . ; the Bishop of Orléans, Picard de la Vacquerie:[7] 'I am the big mouth of the Episcopate . . . I told Ottaviani that there is no longer any Holy Office, it is the bishops' turn to speak', etc; three young bishops from Brazil who insisted that they want a *de*

---

1. Pierre Rougé, Coadjutor of Nîmes: he was to become Bishop of Nîmes in July 1963, *AS* I/II, 292–293.
2. Fiorenzo Angelini, titular bishop, Chaplain General of hospitals in Italy, *AS* I/II, 242–296.
3. Clemente JC Isnard, Bishop of Nova Friburgo, *AS* I/II, 300–301.
4. *AS* I/II, 301–302.
5. Luigi Faveri, Bishop of Tivoli (Italy), *AS* I/II, 302–305.
6. Gustave Thils, Professor of Fundamental Theology at the University of Louvain and involved in the ecumenical movement; he was a member of the Secretariat for Unity and a Council expert.
7. Robert Picard de la Vacquerie, Bishop of Orléans, *AS* I/II, 313–314.

episcopis at THIS Session and that they will not be coming back for the Second Session;

a bishop from Venezuela who wants a lecture

a bishop from Canada

a bishop from Mexico who wants a lecture.

Schmaus, who thinks that the *de fontibus* [on the sources of revelation] leaves the doors open and would be easily alterable. He prevented me from hearing the interventions of Mgr Bekkers, a Polish bishop,[1] and Mgr van Bekkum,[2] of whose intervention I heard only snatches. Why can we not do what St Ambrose did (create a rite)? He repeated the words of St Ambrose quoted by the Pope last Sunday. We too are human beings and we are intelligent!)

I met Laurentin who goes from tribune to tribune. Before returning to my own (I had gone to deliver the corrected version of *De episcopis* to Mgr Colombo) I heard applause. It was Mgr D'Souza,[3] who had just said: one writes to Rome to request a permission, an 'indult' concerning a matter which for us is pastorally important. One receives a bit of paper written by some *minutante* or other from one of the offices with a brief *Non expedit* [not appropriate]! In the different speeches, the speakers are demanding that the bishops' conferences be given the right to authorise extensive adaptations for their people, who need to express themselves in accordance with their own genius and their own culture.

This is also what was said by a bishop from the Congo,[4] who quoted the encyclical *Evangelii Praecones*[5] in favour of a consecration of cultures by their being used in the Church. We now have an opportunity to implement that, he said.

Applause from the younger bishops.

Two or three more bishops. Then, at 11.50 am, the discussion moved on to chapter IV. The following spoke on the subject of the Divine Office:

Cardinal Frings:[6] 1) in favour of a version of the psalms which matches the language of the Fathers: not to depart from the Vulgate, except when the text is obscure or false, and then in favour of the psalter of St Jerome: he gave the example of the Dom Weber[7] psalter.

---

1. This was Karol Wojtyła, the future Pope John Paul II, who at that time was Auxiliary Bishop and Vicar Capitular of Cracow, of which he was to become Archbishop in January 1964, *AS* I/II, 314–315.
2. Bishop of Ruteng (Indonesia), *AS* I/II, 316–317.
3. E D'Souza, Archbishop of Nagpur (India), then of Bhopal (India) in 1963, member of the Commission on the Missions elected during the Second Session of the Council, *AS* I/II, 317–319.
4. Malula, *AS* I/II, 323–324.
5. Published by Pius XII on the missions.
6. *AS* I/II, 327–328.
7. Dom Robert Weber (from the Pontifical Abbey of Saint Jerome in Rome), *Le Psautier romain et les autres anciens psautiers latins,* Collectanea Biblica Latina (Abbaye Saint-Jérôme/Libreria Vaticana, 1953).

2) in favour of greater use of the treasures of Scripture and of the Fathers

3) balance between the psalms and scriptural texts

4) in the name of the German-speaking bishops, that the bishop be given the power to dispense from reciting the Office in Latin.

Cardinal Ruffini:[1] when his name was announced there was a murmur. Now he was speaking of the psalms, he even quoted Luther on them. But in favour of eliminating the imprecatory psalms and some others (those which seem to express doubts about eternal life).

On No. 74: *oratio publica fit a solo sacerdote; orationes fidelium sunt privatae* [public prayer to be made only by the priest; the prayers of the faithful are private].

Cardinal Valeri:[2] in favour of various details. Reduce the obligation [of reciting the Office] to Lauds and Vespers.

Cardinal Archbishop of Compostella:[3] he suggested some changes.

Cardinal Léger:[4] Once again, very much listened to. He certainly expressed the general feeling of the Fathers. I think he ought to be one of those guiding the Council. Concern for our priests . . . That, for those who are not bound to choir, the obligation be restricted to Lauds, Vespers and a *Lectio divina* [meditative reading of the Bible] for about twenty minutes, to be done at any hour of the day.

Criticised the idea of sanctifying the various hours of the day, which leads to formalism.

Language: that the bishops be authorised to allow the use of the vernacular, so that the prayer can be truly prayer, *ut mente intelligent quod labiis pronuntiant* [that they understand with their minds what they say with their lips].

He was applauded.

End of session.

I went to lunch with Schlink, his assistant[5] and Lukas Vischer, at the German Deaconesses' place, where they are living. They asked me a lot of questions and we spoke about everything. At the end of more than two-and-half hours of conversation in German, I was dead. At 3.10 pm, I had a visit from Fesquet. I thanked him for not having seen me earlier: in that way I am freed from any indiscretion. He too asked me a lot of questions and made me talk a bit: he took notes. For my part, I asked him to say two things: 1) that many of the bishops who have come

---

1. *AS* I/II, 328–330.
2. *AS* I/II, 330–331.
3. Fernando Quiroga y Palacios, *AS* I/II, 332–333.
4. *AS* I/II, 334–336.
5. Reinhard Slenczka.

from far away do not want to return for a Second Session (even though their vow of consecration obliges them to attend the Council): this would risk changing, indeed seriously altering the composition of the assembly in discussing the schemas *De Ecclesia* and *De Episcopis*; 2) that in the absence of any programme, it is being asked whether certain matters of importance for humanity will be tackled by the Council: peace, the bomb, hunger.

At 4.30 pm, lecture to the French-speaking bishops of Africa. Very remarkable secretary of this group, Mgr Zoa.[1]

After my lecture (on Tradition), followed by quite a lot of questions, I chatted for a while with Frs Chenu, de Lubac and Martelet.[2] We must speed up the preparation of the battle over the dogmatic schemas on the part of the African and the French bishops. We agree that Martelet will see Karl Rahner and Cardinal Liénart.

I personally find that our French bishops are very kind, very amenable, but slack. They do not work with their theologians. Mgr Garrone actually seems to dislike having recourse to them. He is kind, friendly, but appears not to want to owe them anything and to show that he has no need of them. Now it is he who is the theological representative of the French episcopate. I would be much happier working with Cardinal Liénart or Mgr Villot.[3]

Martelet repeated what I had already heard said twice, that the Pope would not be happy with the chapters *De episcopis*. What is the truth of the matter? How to find out?

I came back here at 7.20 pm, having been out for nearly twelve hours. The days go by without one having time to do anything, least of all to work!

On other hand, on this day alone, I have been asked for five lectures.

Thursday 8 November 1962

Abominable Roman winter weather: rain in a Mediterranean temperature; a kind of tepid sauna. Wind and rain from the South. From 3 am onwards, one is all sweaty and cannot sleep. Storms all the time. This is what I experienced in 1954–1955 and that I suspected were the worst conditions for my neurological well-being.

In the afternoon, a long visit from Mr Sencourt,[4] an English critic. We spoke a little about everything. He knows a lot. He, too, thinks that the pontificates of

1. Jean Baptiste Zoa, Archbishop of Yaoundé, member of the Commission on the Missions.
2. Gustave Martelet, SJ, Professor of Dogmatics at the Jesuit Theology Faculty in Lyons-Fourvière: having come to the Council as expert for Mgr Henry Veniat, Bishop of Fort-Archambault (Chad), he quickly found himself being made secretary of the group of bishops from equatorial Africa, and theological counsellor for the French-speaking African bishops.
3. Neither of these was a member of the Conciliar Commissions.
4. The writer Robert Sencourt, was a Catholic, originally Anglican, with ecumenical con-

Pius IX and Pius XII were catastrophic. He explains Pius XII to a considerable extent as being in reaction against his own personal temperament, which would have been sensual and inclined towards women. A total reaction, which sublimated the tendency by an extraordinary Marianism. Sencourt has been told by a Gentleman Attendant on the pope that Pius XII attributed his devotion to Our Lady and the definition of the Assumption to visions of the Blessed Virgin. At all events, with Pius XII the Church was stifled. John XXIII has done the opposite.

Sencourt lives a lot of the time in Italy: he speaks Italian well. According to him, the Italians, (and the French) are inclined to DEFINE things. However, once defined, they think that is the end of it. The Romans impose laws, for example the obligation to Sunday Mass, or the prohibition of contraception. But once the law has been defined, one does what one likes, each person recovers his or her freedom. The law is not kept, because the feeling of obligation is outside one's conscience.

Sencourt sees quite a few bishops and cardinals: BEA. He told me that it is the secretary, Schmidt, who does things and writes the speeches. CARDINAL GILROY[1] (Australia): in Australia everyone is praying for the Council, including the Protestants. This ecumenism of calling on the Holy Spirit is a sensational spiritual fact. And, in fact, the Holy Spirit responds. Gilroy has said: it is extraordinary how the Australian episcopate has changed during the past month.

Then, a visit from Fr Daniélou. He, too, is disturbed to see that, among the French, nothing is organised for effective work. He has more or less the same impression as I do as regards Mgr Garrone. He would like texts to be prepared on Scripture and Tradition, the historicity of the Gospels, etc. He told me (what I did not know) that the Bea Secretariat has a very good text (prepared mainly by Feiner) on Scripture and Tradition.[2] He invited me to a meeting to be held at the Biblicum at 6.30 pm.

I went to this meeting: Daniélou, Thils, Lyonnet, Vogt[3] (Rector of the Biblicum), Feiner, two Jesuits, de la Potterie, then Mgr Charue and his Auxiliary Mgr Musty.[4] What to do with the schema *De fontibus*? We made a sort of list of all the reactions that are brewing or that could be stirred up. I was told that Fr Salaverri gave a lecture yesterday to the Spanish bishops on *De fontibus*, during which he said: 'This text is perfect. Moreover, Fr Congar and Fr de Lubac have fully approved it.' Mgr Charue read out a very strong text that he will read. It even includes some expressions that are too strong, as, for instance, when he expressed

---

nections.

1. Norman Thomas Gilroy was Archbishop of Sydney.
2. There is a copy in the Congar Archive, accompanied by a letter from Feiner telling him that he will see that his own work on Tradition has been taken into account.
3. The Swiss Ernst Vogt, SJ, was Rector of the Pontifical Biblical Institute until 1963; he had been appointed consultor to the Preparatory Theological Commission at the beginning of 1961.
4. Jean-Baptiste Musty was Auxiliary Bishop of Namur.

the wish that the section on *De duplici fonte* [the twofold source][1] could be replaced by a text more closely in accord with the correctness of the faith . . .

We discussed what it would be good to say to the bishops if reports were made for them on the historicity of the gospels.

But all the little meetings of this kind, which are interesting and no doubt necessary, are rather disappointing and always end on a rather vague note.

At 8 pm, supper with the four Brothers from Taizé.[2] They have created their own atmosphere in the apartment where they live. We talked a lot. I myself most of all, perhaps. They have many guests. There is almost no meal at which there are no guests, sometimes as many as five or six bishops. In this way, there comes into being on such occasions something of a council of consultations and friendships, which help to create the climate of the Council properly so called. They told me that Lucas Vischer is in a great state of agitation: Mass every morning, etc. These are not good dispositions for understanding . . . On the other hand, the editor of *Réforme*,[3] who had spent two weeks in Rome and who had written an earlier article that was aggressive, was subsequently 'converted' and had written a second article that was irenic and open. The view of the Brothers of Taizé is this: one must take the risk, WITH the Pope and with Cardinal Bea, that they have so courageously taken in thus opening the Council to the Observers.

Friday 9 November 1962

I did not go to St Peter's, in order to work. It seems that nothing very interesting happened there. Several of the bishops adopted stances against Cardinal Léger's proposal concerning the Office: Cardinal Wyszyński,[4] Cardinal Lefebvre.[5]

Cardinal Bea agrees on the need to revise the breviary that is attributed to him: a commission is working on it. He praised Dom Weber's *Psalter*.

Mgr Weber[6] spoke.

After lunch, visit from l'abbé Jorge Mejía,[7] who came to talk to me about the lecture I am to give next Wednesday.

---

1. The reference is to chapter 1 of the schema.
2. During the Council, Roger Schultz and Max Thurian were accompanied by other brothers from Taizé with whom they formed a little community which received many guests.
3. Pastor Georges Richard-Molard followed the Council as Director of the Press and Information Service of the Protestant Federation of France and was assistant editor of the Protestant weekly *Réforme*.
4. *AS* I/II, 392–394.
5. *AS* I/II, 396–397.
6. *AS* I/II, 418–420.
7. Jorge M Mejía was Professor of Scripture at the Faculty of Theology at the Catholic University of Argentina, and editor of the journal *Criterio*. He later became Vice-President of the Pontifical Council for Justice and Peace, Secretary of the Congregation for Bishops, and then responsible for the Vatican Archives and Vatican Apostolic Library;

He told me that I shall need to be very elementary, and also very clear, very straightforward. It is true that many of the bishops are well educated and quite up to date. But a great many of them live in very remote countries and never see a book. The attitude of quite a few of them is: the Holy Father has prepared the Council, therefore the texts are excellent and all we have to do is to say: Amen. Many have a simplistic ecclesiology: the pope studies things and says what needs to be said, all we have to do is to follow him. For people like them, there is no point in the Council. Moreover, their feeling that the schemas are very good can be confirmed. Mgr Spadafora came to give them a lecture and his brochure against the Biblical Institute has been quite successful.

At 2.55 pm, a telephone call from Mgr Garrone in reply to my letter. He thinks that we are in a complete mess and that the Germans are deceiving themselves. He also said that he did not know that Rahner had prepared a text. He does not much like Rahner and thinks, in any case, that he is too problematical and too personal to prepare a conciliar text. He added that he would be seeing Cardinal König.

At 3.20 pm, visit from Vogel,[1] from *ICI*.

At 4 p.m. at the Canadian College, where I had an appointment with Cardinal Léger. The man is not as attractive as I imagined him to be from his interventions. To the extent that they are calm, the man himself is highly strung. He is continuously making strange faces. From time to time, his fingers drum nervously. Having heard him speak, I had thought that he could be a leader of the Council. I am less inclined to this view after having seen him: 1) he is too impulsive; 2) he is too isolated and will remain so, both by preference, and by choice in accord with his preferences. He follows HIS path without bothering about whether or not others agree.

We spoke a little about everything: about his diocese, Montréal, where the situation is difficult because, in circles which are still traditional, there is an upsurge of contradictory tendencies. There are some fairly lively lay movements. They have influenced the cardinal because, when he was Rector of the Canadian College in Rome, and at the beginning of his episcopate, he was rather conservative. The turn-around came about as a result of the following circumstance (according to Fr Perreault OP): when Mgr Léger was created cardinal, he believed himself to be in fact a 'Prince'. His episcopal city welcomed him with tremendous manifestations: illuminations, etc. In his numerous speeches (he speaks a lot), he kept on saying: My city has made itself beautiful in order to welcome its prince. But some lively LAY groups pointed out to him that that would not do. He saw them, and entered to a considerable extent into their points of view. Here we have the roots

he was to become a bishop and, later, a cardinal.

1. Jean Vogel, Council correspondent for *Informations catholiques internationales* to which Congar regularly contributed his 'Notes on the Council'.

of his kind of conversion. But there is a very strong 'Cité Catholique' movement,[1] SUPPORTED FROM ROME, he added. Several bishops from his province are patrons of the Cité Catholique movement and have asked their parish priests to establish it in their parishes . . .

The situation of the Church in America: French-speaking Canada is enclosed in the enormous American milieu. The kingdom of Business and the Dollar. Now, the French Canadians, Catholics, are poor. The large businesses, the large fortunes, belong to the Protestants. In this context, for example, *Mater et Magistra*[2] is irrelevant . . . According to the cardinal, the American bishops, those from the USA, are men simply of financial organisation. Cardinal Cushing[3] had left the Council saying: I am wasting my time here; I am going home to work. To work, that is, to collect $25,000 per day. That is all they do. They do not even know the names of their parish priests. As for the idea of the presence of the Church in the world, it does not even enter their heads.

The Council: the cardinal is very scathing about the doctrinal schemas and is determined to get them put aside purely and simply. He told me that Cardinal Bea is even more determined about this: he is prepared to risk his life and his purple to this end.

He knows that Garofalo is the editor of the first Chapter of *de Duplici fonte* [On the twofold source of revelation]. The cardinal told me that several Canadian bishops cannot see this, because they were fellow students of his at the Biblicum and say they have positive proof that he cheated in his exams . . . !!!

Cardinal Léger said that, humanly speaking, he was pessimistic about the outcome of the Council, even about the schema *De liturgia*. Cardinal Larraona, who is President of the Commission, is against the schema and has said so publicly to the Spanish bishops. Cardinal Léger cannot see where we are going or what will be the state of the Church if all the changes that are being envisaged are brought to bear on it . . .

After more than an hour's conversation with Cardinal Léger, I took advantage of Mgr Weber being close by to call on him. I had left a man of drama, full of anguish. I found a man who told me he had slept for an hour after lunch and who left me saying to me: Now that I am up, I must go to the end of the corridor . . .

I am told this evening that Fr Liégé has arrived. It was Mgr Elchinger's and Mgr Schmitt's idea to get him to come.

Saturday 10 November 1962
Heavy day. Climate to begin with; irritation; painful session: uncertainties and indecision . . .

---

1. An integrist movement founded by Jean Ousset.
2. Social encyclical of John XXIII, published on 15 May 1961.
3. Cardinal Richard J Cushing, Archbishop of Boston.

Ruffini presiding.[1] He had a friendly word for the Observers; he then spoke against applause. If applause is to be permitted, then one would also have to allow signs of disapproval, which would destroy what should be an atmosphere of respect and confidence. On this subject, by I know not what mysterious transition, he spoke in praise of the Curia: it should not be attacked. It does nothing other than follow and serve in docile fashion the intentions of the Pope. I wonder whether these words were a kind of compensation offered to Cardinal Ottaviani, who has not attended any of the sessions for the past five or six days, perhaps because he believes he has been offended.

I listened to the speeches for a while, but it was so boring that I left the tribune. Each one speaks from his own idea of the Breviary: they should put all that to a commission composed of competent people!

In the bar, no bishops as yet, the staff (emergency crews, ushers and clerics) were literally stuffing themselves before the rush of the Council Fathers . . . It is amusing.

I went to see the Observers. Had a conversation with Cullmann. He is working on a commentary on St John[2] and on a theology of the history of salvation.[3] I told him that I am waiting for him to produce a study of the Holy Spirit and its relationship with the Church.

I met Mgr van Cauwelaert, Mgr Schmitt, and then my Brazilian friends. They told me that they are to have a meeting on Tuesday as a follow-up to one they have already had, and that after it they hope to collect the signatures of 1500 bishops requesting the replacement of the first three (or four?) dogmatic schemas by just one. THIS schema would be ready, they told me! In that case, there would be four or five: what a mess! This upset me a bit. These Brazilian bishops seem to know nothing about the work of Rahner and Ratzinger. I referred them to Mgr Volk.

I also met a group of French bishops with Mgr Marty and Mgr Pailler. They think that we must get out of this present dream world of lack of organisation and inefficiency. Cardinal Feltin directs nothing: when he attends meetings, he spends all the time looking at his watch. I said that he ought to delegate the organisation to a vicar or to an efficient secretary. Mgr Marty has an idea, which he will put forward this evening, of organising the bishops into commissions, which would be open to all who wish to take part and which would study specific points and prepare the interventions with the experts.

Everywhere, one sees lassitude and boredom because of the vagueness, the lack of direction and method. A whole month was needed to reach this point!

---

1. *AS* I/II, 435–436.
2. The reference must be to *Der johanneische Kreis. Zum Ursprung des Johannesevangeliums* (Tübingen, 1975); *Le Milieu johannique. Étude sur l'origine de l'évangile de Jean* (Neuchâtel-Paris: Delachaux & Niestlé, 1976).
3. Oscar Cullmann, *Heil als Geschichte. Heilsgeschichtliche Existenz im Neuen Testament* (Tübingen, 1965); *Le Salut dans l'histoire. L'existence chrétienne selon le Nouveau Testament* (Neuchâtel-Paris: Delachaux & Niestlé, 1966).

I saw Fr Liégé, who was brought here by Mgr Elchinger and has been granted permission to attend the sessions by Cardinal Marella. He told me that in France the Message to the World did not create a great stir: it was too abstract. On the other hand, the Pope's opening speech was regarded as a real programme, open, and clearly against conservatism and even more so against integrism. Liégé asked me all sorts of questions, with his attention extraordinarily PRESENT to everything.

Towards the end of the session, a bishop (Costantini?) spoke in particular about devotion to St Joseph, in connection with the Liturgical Year.[1] Martimort is in despair: twenty years work for nothing! But Cardinal Ruffini brought this bishop back to the point, saying that the bishops are preachers and like all those who preach, do not themselves like listening to sermons. Ruffini was to conclude the session by adding to the customary prayers (to which he adds a prayer to one's Angel Guardian, etc.) a ringing and somewhat humorous *Holy St Joseph*.

It is clear that the Council has no working method. It would have been necessary for it to be prepared for, not only by the Commissions in Rome, but BY THE BISHOPS meeting in conferences. Without this preparation, we are faced with 2,400 people starting from scratch who have to do their apprenticeships and their trial exercises at the cost of precious weeks.

I had lunch at St Martha's in Vatican City, where some twenty of the French bishops are staying. A long wait. Rather dreary meal: a guest table of old bachelors. In spite of the extreme kindness of Mgr Béjot who had invited me.

After the meal, a meeting. Mgr de Provenchères read a paper which he wants to present in a few moments at the meeting of the heads of Houses and also at the one immediately afterwards, of the French bishops. In it he sets out the reasons for REJECTING the schema *De fontibus*. It is very good, it summarises exactly the reasons that one hears being expressed more or less everywhere. After that, I was asked questions about different points and I said what I knew about the attitude of the other episcopates.

I got lost in the Vatican. I waited twenty-five minutes for a bus. Having just got in at 3.30 pm, I had a visit from Fr Daniélou. He was sickened by the mess this morning (I had seen him in St Peter's), and spoke of leaving Rome. He said (after having seen Mgr Veuillot): we must give up this secret diplomacy and settle on a possible text, the fruit of widespread collaboration. There is no chance of the Rahner-Ratzinger schema being accepted: it is too personal. Moreover, it covers the entire material contained in the dogmatic schemas, whereas what is supposed to be under discussion is just the *De Fontibus*. So what is needed is to produce a less personal text dealing only with the subject matter of the *De Fontibus*. He would help with it it, with Lyonnet and Alonso[2] from the Biblicum, and in do-

---

1. The reference is, in fact, to Antonio Tedde, Bishop of Ales and Terralba (Italy), *AS* I/II, 481–483.
2. Luis Alonso-Schökel, SJ, was Professor of Old Testament Exegesis at the Pontifical Bib-

ing so make as much use as possible of earlier texts. He asked me, on behalf of Mgr Veuillot, whether I would agree to write Chapter I on Tradition and its relationship with Scripture. I agreed to try. That will have to be done for tomorrow night. Then, we will together see Mgr Garrone. Daniélou thinks, and I agree with him, that one cannot purely and simply discard the schemas because the Council MUST, in order to serve the people of our time according to the truth of God, say something positive, specific and strong about Sacred Scripture, inspiration, the historicity of the New Testament.

I began work that evening.

Sunday 11 November 1962

I worked on my chapter *De Traditione*. At noon, Cardinal Browne and Mgr Paul Philippe to lunch.

At 5 pm, meeting with the Germans at Mgr Volk's place. They introduced the counsellor for the Japanese bishops.[1] They gave us all duplicated copies of the Rahner-Ratzinger schema. I learnt that they had made 3,000 copies and distributed them widely. On the other hand, they have not made copies of my *Proemium*.

We read together Fr Schillebeeckx's comments on the *De fontibus Revelationis*. These had been translated into Japanese, English and, I think, Yugoslav. Rahner, too, had made some comments which had been duplicated and copies were distributed to us.

We learnt only a few details. Apparently Cardinal Bea intends to say that mixed questions like those concerning Tradition and Scripture concern the Secretariat and ought to be entrusted to joint commissions, such as Theology and the Secretariat . . . If that were to be approved it would change the outlook substantially . . .

During the preparatory stage, I had greatly regretted that the work of the Secretariat was not producing results and that the Theological Commission, in particular, did not collaborate with it. I had said this, the very first day, to Fr Tromp. I was so concerned about it that in June 1961 I wrote to the Pope, and made sure he personally received my letter. I would therefore be delighted if NOW (*sero* [however late]!!!) the Secretariat were to contribute to the work of the Council. However, I ask myself whether the isolation was due solely to the pride, self-sufficiency, lack of open-mindedness of the Theological Commission.

The Secretariat itself seems to me to isolate itself. It is a bit like a hunting preserve. They do their work, they are very proud to do it, and are not very keen on the idea of opening the closed garden to others.

The Italians are afraid of Cardinal Siri. They do not speak freely because of that.

---

lical Institute.
1. Probably Jean K Sawada.

Fr Daniélou and I went to see Mgr Garrone who was dismayed and very disconcerted. Not only had the Germans distributed the Rahner-Ratzinger schema, but they had added an introductory paragraph saying that it was being presented in the name of the Presidents of the Episcopal Conferences of Austria, Germany, Holland, Belgium and France. However, the French bishops have in no way been consulted. There and then, Mgr Garrone telephoned Cardinal Liénart. It was Mgr Glorieux[1] who answered the telephone. Here are the facts: the Germans had distributed the text BEFORE obtaining Cardinal Liénart's agreement, but this morning the Cardinal in fact agreed but still without consulting the French bishops, not even Mgr Garrone who is their leading theologian. That is a careless act on the part of Cardinal Liénart which astonishes me exceedingly. If the French bishops do not agree, he ought to specify that he did that in his capacity as *praeses* [President] of the Conference *'materialiter'* [materially], but not *'formaliter, ut sic'* [formally, as such]. In any case, we are faced with a *fait accompli*. It is to some extent the way the Germans do things. They rush ahead without bothering about others. That is going to turn out to be a serious blunder. In spite of the fact that the Rahner-Ratzinger text contains some EXCELLENT things, 1) it is nonetheless very personal, not very conciliar; 2) moreover, it does not cover ALL the questions raised in the *De Fontibus*, in particular the doctrinally and pastorally extremely important one of the historicity of the gospels, and yet it goes well beyond the ground covered by the *De Fontibus*. It would be quite easy to say that it deals with things that are not relevant. For these reasons, there is very little chance of its being accepted as a conciliar text. All the more so since it will be necessary, sooner or later and in one way or another, to get it through the *De fide et moribus* [Doctrinal] Commission. That will be a dismal mess.

But perhaps things will work out more quickly and better than one imagines. It may well be that putting another text before the Fathers will help them to realise how inadequate the official schema is, and what really needs to be said.

Mgr Garrone, who knew nothing about Daniélou's project (about which he came to see me yesterday, and which is entirely his own idea), nevertheless expressly agrees that we should go ahead with it. That COULD perhaps work ???

The Theological Commission meets on TUESDAY. That means that discussion of the *De Fontibus* schema will not begin before Wednesday because, according to the Regulations, it has first to be submitted to the Commission, together with the document presenting it.

Fr Gagnebet told me that it is being said, and that even the newspapers have reported, that Fr de Lubac and I were prevented from speaking at the Preparatory Commission. That is not true, as it is equally untrue to say that we have approved the schemas, as Cardinal Ottaviani told the Central Commission and Fr Salaverri the Spanish bishops.

---

1. Palémon Glorieux, from the diocese of Lille: having taught theology at the Catholic Faculties in Lille and been Rector of these Faculties, he became Cardinal Liénart's private secretary.

Monday 12 November 1962

I did not go to St Peter's. There it was announced that the Second Session of the Council would take place from 12 May to 29 June of 1963 and that, in the interval, the Commissions would be working. What a strange thing this Council is, it has no programme and is not being 'led'. Does the Pope look upon it as a period of transition between the reign of the Curia and a collegial government?

I was subsequently told that one reason for this delayed date might be that the Italian elections take place in May. Just as, at the wish of the Pope, the Italian socialist party brought forward its national congress in order not to clash with the opening of the Council, and just as it is the custom for the UN sessions not to coincide with the American elections, in the same way . . . ???

I wonder whether I shall come back for this Second Session. The next few weeks will tell me whether or not I can do any useful work.

At 2 pm, visit from l'abbé Bissonnette,[1] a Canadian, who wants to write a thesis on *'Cooperator ordinis nostri'*.[2] His bishop, Mgr Coderre,[3] came to collect him at 3 pm.

At 5 pm, lecture for the South American bishops. Some of them had heard Mgr Spadafora's lecture (against the Biblical Institute). Some bishops are well trained and well informed. Others are wedded to Biblical literalism and are a little lost when confronted by the problems encountered in present-day exegesis.

I left at 4 pm (it is a long way) under a fierce storm, which lasted several hours, with torrential rain. Poor lecture, badly prepared (subject matter ill-defined), on the schemas. On the way back, it took us twenty minutes by car to travel the 300 metres between Piazza Venezia and the Angelicum.

Yesterday's papers ran the story of the Ottaviani incident. It is some time since he appeared at the Council. He is said to be furious at having been cut off by Cardinal Alfrink, and at the applause that this evoked. A small sign, clearly, of a fairly deep tension and malaise.

Before supper, visit from the adviser ('assistant') to the Indian bishops. He will come back tomorrow. During supper, telephone call about a thesis on the theology of the ministry according to Calvin.[4] Almost no day goes by without a student coming to see me with reference to his work or his thesis.

---

1. Jean-Guy Bissonnette, from the diocese of Saint-Jean de Québec.
2. 'Cooperator of our order' (a very old expression which appears in the preface for the ordination of priests).
3. Gérard-M Coderre, Bishop of Saint-Jean de Québec.
4. Later (page 172), it will become clear that the caller was Alexandre Ganoczy, a priest of Hungarian origin; Congar was to publish his thesis, which he defended at the Gregorianum in 1963 (*Calvin théologien de l'Église et du ministère*, 'Unam Sanctam' 48, [Paris: Cerf, 1964]): he was later to teach at the Institut Catholique in Paris and then in Würzburg.

Tuesday 13 November *1962*

I did not go to St Peter's. I finished my chapter on Tradition for a schema that may well be proposed as a replacement for the official one. Visit from a Spanish priest for a translation of *Aspects de l'œcuménisme.*[1] At 1.45 pm, a visit from Fr [ ], a Canadian Jesuit, anxious about a subject for an ecclesiological thesis. As he had done some medieval studies, I pointed him in the direction of ecclesiology (critique of the 'seigneurial' and temporal aspects in the Church) in the spiritual sects of the twelfth century, or the ecclesiological aspects of the Catholic reactions. I gave him some bibliographical pointers. But one would need to have a real brain to handle such a splendid subject WELL.

At 3 pm, visit from l'abbé Boillat,[2] professor of philosophy at a small college in Porrentruy, chaplain to Catholic Action for French-speaking Switzerland and adviser here for the Indian bishops. A man of great culture, reflection, and real originality of thought. He would like the Council to say something about the unity of humanity (against racism) and the salvation of non-Catholics.

At about 5 pm, a visit from two American priests from Boston (Quint ???); they asked me about the situation of non-Catholics.

That evening, a visit from a very fine young Spanish Father, José Fernandez. He is to go next year to Jerusalem. This year, he is doing a thesis on the membership of the Church: but in the purely dialectic, systematic spirit of Dominican students during their studies. However, I see better things for him later on. Also a Portuguese who wanted my advice about the thesis of one of his confrères, written in Germany, viewing the Council as a sacrament. I tried to dissuade him from taking an interest in this thesis. Several students quite strongly criticise the teaching at the Angelicum, which seems to be lacking in freshness and creativity. The idea here is to earn prestige for the place by inviting a number of bishops and, if possible, several cardinals, to a huge demonstration. I do not agree. That serves as nothing more than decoration. A house is worthwhile if it produces something worthwhile, if the teachers have done something worthwhile, each in his own field. I am careful not to express any criticism of the House. What is more, I hardly know it. I am a passing guest here, and well looked after. That is all. As for the Spaniards, who must represent a good half of the establishment, they appear to be very capable of good things: they are open, and very intelligent. So they must be converted to a true theology, well resourced, dealing with humanity's problems.

Fr Daniélou came to collect my chapter on Tradition.[3]

---

1. Yves Congar, *Aspects de l'œcuménisme* (Brussels: Éditions de la Pensée Catholique, 1962); the work was to be translated into Spanish in 1965.
2. Fernand Boillat was the Chaplain General to Catholic Action in French-speaking Switzerland; secretary to the Swiss bishops at the Council and a Council expert.
3. The Latin text and its translation have been published: cf Yves Congar, 'Tradition et Écriture', in B-D Dupuy (editors), *La Révélation divine,* vol II, 'Unam Sanctam', 70 b (Paris: Cerf, 1968), 589–598.

This morning, at St Peter's, a not very glorious end to the schema on the Liturgy. The discussion was brought to a close well before all those wishing to speak had done so. A decision of the Pope was read out stating that, in response to the request of four hundred bishops, St Joseph was to be inserted into the Canon of the Mass, as from 8 December. It seems the French bishops were very unhappy about it. The Observers were appalled. The problem is not the fact of having put St Joseph into the Canon: he is worth far more than Saints Chrysogonus and John and Paul, who may not even have existed. The problem is rather that, while the Council is in session, and when that Council is discussing the liturgy, the Pope, on his own authority, decides something (the appropriateness of which is at least questionable). Good John XXIII keeps on combining some lovely gestures with others that are regrettable or retrograde.

Wednesday 14 November 1962

Long day under incessant rain and a grey sky. I saw Mgr Garrone before the session. He told me about the meeting of the Theological Commission yesterday. Fr Tromp proposed a text of the report that was to be read this morning in order to present the schema. It was depressing in its negative narrowness. Taking the reactions received from the bishops on 15 September as his starting point, he rejected them all. There is talk of modern man: he does not exist! People are wanting to be pastoral. But the primary pastoral duty is doctrine. Afterwards let the parish priests do the adapting.

There is talk of ecumenism. There is a great danger of minimalism.

Mgr Parente announced that he was circulating two alternative draft schemas: one, by the presidents of some of the episcopal conferences, written in German, which contained a number of theological errors, the other in English, but written by a Frenchman: that shows he wants to argue from circumstance, not from principle.

Mgr Garrone was devastated by the atmosphere at the meeting which he said was frightful. He had declared: 1) I do not accept this schema; 2) I do not subscribe to the introductory report. One member present (was it a bishop? a *peritus*[1]? It seems that there were four or five *periti* at the meeting? Which? Those who had prepared the schema??) had thanked him afterwards saying: 'You have set me free' . . .

I heard some more details about this meeting of the Commission from Mgr McGrath. It was frightful. Ottaviani spoke for twenty minutes, Tromp for forty-five minutes, Parente for twenty minutes. Parente spoke of a German schema and one in English, probably written by a Frenchman at the Angelicum. (He apparently mentioned my name to someone else). This schema in English is in fact Fr Schillebeeckx's *Animadversiones* [Comments] translated into English. Ottaviani

---

1. This word is used in the *Journal* to indicate the experts officially named by the Pope and who were able to participate in the work of the Concilar Commissions.

said that the role of the Commission was to defend the schema before the Council. Cardinal Léger then said: Does my position as a member of the Commission deprive me of my freedom to speak to the Council? In that case, I shall resign from the Commission at once. Cardinal Léger also said: I thought I was joining a Commission as a co-worker; now I find myself before a tribunal of judges . . .

Peruzzo, the old Infant of Agrigento,[1] that outraged figure of piosity, declared that sometimes, at the Council, he felt he was in a mad house: there is a way of dealing with mad men, lock them up . . .

I later learnt from another source that Cardinal Ottaviani had asked Cardinal Browne to make a SUMMARY of the schemas. But an apple tree produces apples, a pear tree pears. Cardinal Browne CANNOT produce a statement for our time. The basic question is a question of personnel, of a team.

I also learnt elsewhere that the press is talking about a schema produced by the presidents of episcopal conferences (=Rahner-Ratzinger). It was inevitable: 3,000 copies have been distributed. This morning's *Tempo* reports yet again that Lubac and I have not been listened to. That is both true and false. But how to re-establish the truth without: 1) telling the whole story, which is bound by secrecy; 2) attempting to explain things that cannot be understood unless one has been involved in them; 3) giving to the matter and to myself more importance than they warrant? I must talk it over with Fr de Lubac.

I saw Cullmann for a moment. Every Tuesday, therefore yesterday, the Observers have a meeting organised by the Secretariat. It was I who was to speak yesterday about the priesthood. At the last minute, I was replaced by Fr Kerrigan on tradition. Cullmann told me that it was very basic. He also spoke to me about St Joseph. He was astonished that the Pope did that when the Council was actually discussing the liturgy. One of the Observers had said to him: You have written a Christology.[2] What you need to do now is to write a Josephology! Cullmann replied: No point, it has already been done. I saw the book at the Gregorianum . . .

A rushed low Mass recited at top speed. Cardinal Tisserant, as President, did the same with the splendid *Adsumus*.

The President suggested that there should be a vote on the following two propositions: 1) approval of the guiding criteria for the schema *De Liturgia*; 2) and that the amendments be considered one by one after the work by the Commission. Repeating this in the five languages took a long time.

The result, announced before the end of the Congregation, was as follows: out of 2,215 voters, 2,162 *placet*, 46 *non placet*, and 7 spoiled votes.

Cardinal Ottaviani began reading the report, which he then passed to Mgr Garofalo to finish reading because of his poor eyesight.[3]

---

1. See footnote 1 page 96.
2. Oscar Cullmann, *Christologie du Nouveau Testament* (Neuchâtel-Paris: Delachaux & Niestlé, 1958).
3. *AS* I/III, 27–32.

1) He distributed replacement schemas. This is against canon 222 §2 (if I have understood it) which reserves the presentation of new texts to the Pope. One may propose corrections, but the discussion must be of THIS schema. 2) People had complained to him of the lack of a pastoral tone. But pastors are required first and foremost to teach: *docete*. Afterwards, others can adapt (it is the false reply that he had given on the very first day in reply to my own remark two years ago . . .). The Council must not speak *'ad modum praedicationis'* [as if it were preaching]; 3) It has been said that the schema lacks *afflatum novae theologiae* [the breath of the new theology] But *debet esse aflatum saeculorum* [it must breathe the breath of the ages].

4) One must bear in mind the hard work of the past two years. At this point, the cardinal's voice, which had been soft, became almost wheedling . . .

From this point on, Garofalo read the rest of the text.

The primary purpose of the Council is doctrinal: to protect doctrine, the deposit. A doctrine which is *integra, non diminuta* [complete, not diminished]. There is no need for homilies and exhortations. The teaching of the extraordinary magisterium is infallible. We must not renounce the exclusion of errors.—The schema has been produced in accordance with the wishes of the BISHOPS and by a commission of BISHOPS assisted by *periti*. The text has then been reviewed by the Central Commission. He gave, briskly, the plan of the schema and its aims. As for the separated brethren, it is necessary to show them Catholic doctrine. One ought to describe this text as a pastoral one because to defend the faith belongs primarily to the pastoral office.

> Cardinal Liénart:[1] Text inadequate for the matters that it is dealing with.
> 1) Scripture and Tradition are means. But nothing is said about the deepest and unique source, the Word of God, the Gospel (cf Denzinger 783).
> 2) It is expressed *modo frigido, nimis scholastico* [in a cold, exceedingly scholastic manner] though it is dealing with the primary gift of God.
> The Council ought to exalt the Word of God, above all in the presence of our separated brethren who love it so much. And it ought also to exalt its effectiveness. The cardinal deplored the absence of all that and of a statement which would be more nourishing than the condemnation of errors. Too scholastic and too much reasoning. Conclusion: *ut recognoscatur penitus* [it needs to be completely revised].
> Cardinal Frings:[2] 1) the question of language. The first duty of the bishops is to preach, but in an attractive way. It is the tone which makes the song. The first Vatican Council rejected the Franzelin[3] schema because it was

---

1. *AS* I/III, 32–34.
2. *AS* I/III, 34–36.
3. Johannes Baptist Franzelin, SJ, professor at the Gregorianum, had prepared a

too scholastic. What we have here is not the *vox Matris et Magistrae* [voice of the Mother and Teacher],[1] the *vox boni pastoris* [voice of the good shepherd].

2) *de duobus fontibus* [on the two sources]: not a good way of expressing the idea, IT IS NOT TRADITIONAL, but recent, from the age of historicism. That is all right FOR US, '*in ordine cognitionis*' [in the order of knowledge], but in reality there is only one source, the Word of God. And this wounds our separated brethren RIGHT from the first line.

3) *De inspiratione et inerrantia: nimis coarctatur libertas scientiae et appropinquat ad doctrinam inspirationis verbalis* [on inspiration and inerrancy: the text limits scientific freedom unduly and comes close to the doctrine of verbal inspiration]. There are two currents among Catholic theologians. Councils do not settle questions that are disputed among reputable theologians.

4) *Non placet propter nimiam amplitudinem* [Not acceptable because the text is too long]. The Commissions have proposed seventy schemas. That makes 1,000 pages. The last edition of ALL the ecumenical Councils contains eight hundred pages . . . The first two schemas must be reduced to one, as the project submitted by the Presidents (=the Rahner text) has done.

Cardinal Ruffini:[2] Extreme importance of the question. *Placet.* It has been done and approved. It would be dangerous if a storm were to knock down a well-built house. The Pope has given us this schema . . . If another schema is put in its place, it would have to be discussed. And if that text were to be rejected in its turn . . .

Basically, Ruffini spoke in such a way as to make it inevitable for there to be a prior vote on whether or not to accept the schema.

Cardinal Siri:[3] The schema needs to be amended but it must be submitted for discussion. There are still echoes of Modernism; there are questions concerning the interpretation of Scripture; about the relationship between Tradition and Scripture.

He made the following comments: lack of balance between what is said about Scripture and what is said about Tradition: it is not clearly shown how the theological criteria for the interpretation of Scripture have pride of place over *human* criteria.

Constitution *De fide catholica* the form of which the Fathers of Vatican I did not like and it was entirely rewritten.

1. An allusion to the encyclical *Mater et Magistra* published by John XXIII on 15 May 1961.
2. *AS* I/III, 37–38.
3. *AS* I/III, 38–39.

Quiroga,[1] Compostela. This schema must be discussed (in this way he, too, asks the question). One could adapt the style in order to make it easier for the separated brethren to understand. He suggested a few corrections concerning inspiration, the historicity of the gospels.

Cardinal Léger:[2] *Ut tota praesens Constitutio recognoscatur* [the whole of the present schema should be revised].

One was hoping for a schema which would enlighten the work positively. In its present form, it would not help at all, because 1) it is imprudent to speak so peremptorily of such highly disputed questions, above all on the relationship between Scripture and Tradition; 2) it seems to speak of work on the Scriptures with mistrust; it promotes mistrust amongst exegetes in the Church: this is not the Pope's spirit 3) There is a reference to *'serpentes errores'* [creeping errors]; that denotes fear of error. It is necessary to speak more positively. 4) Do not substitute a single theological school in place of variety. The schema expresses only one line of thinking. Therefore, return it to a team of men who represent both the traditional and the modern outlook.

Cardinal König:[3] Words of praise. But 1) on the question of the relationship between Scripture and Tradition, he spoke out against allowing just one school of thought; 2) as regards inerrancy, the text says more than a Council can define; it ignores literary genres; it is regressive with respect to *Divino afflante*;[4] 3) nowhere is there any specification of the theological notes.

For example, concerning the author of the Fourth Gospel. *Non placet*.

Cardinal Alfrink:[5] The text is not in accordance with the spirit of the Pope's opening speech. That is, not to repeat what has already been defined . . . But the schema repeats what is contained in all the manuals. The Pope declared that the purpose of the Council was to formulate doctrine in a way suited to our time. Moreover, the schema sheds no light on the matters discussed in recent theology such as the notion of Revelation, Tradition and Magisterium, Two sources.

This is all the more regrettable in that we ought to be serving the cause of unity.

He replied to his former colleague in the study of Syriac, Cardinal Ruffini: the Pope has proposed the schemas for our free discussion, without any restriction; therefore one can pose the question of its being rejected completely.

---

1. *AS* I/III, 39–41.
2. *AS* I/III, 41–42.
3. *AS* I/III, 42–43.
4. The encyclical *Divino afflante Spiritu* was published by Pope Pius XII on 30 September 1943.
5. AS I/III, 43–45.

(In my opinion, in view of the fact that the Pope's wishes have been invoked and used as an argument by both sides in the discussion, he ought to say something. Without leaning on the Council, he ought to make known his point of view, or indicate a way forward.)

Cardinal Suenens:[1] Agreed with the criticisms already made. The other schemas produced by the same Commission please him even less.

But he wished above all to propose a speedier and more efficient way of working. Without this, one is heading for a second Council of Trent.

1) The working method must be reviewed. He suggested:

a) after discussion of the schema as a whole, a vote on whether or not to accept the schema as such;

b) it may well turn out that correcting the schema is not sufficient and it will be necessary to reject it;

c) a great many people speak, but the Council as such, and as a whole, is not expressing an opinion. It needs to vote.

2) After the vote on the schema *in genere* [in general], the Fathers should submit their detailed comments IN WRITING. The Commission would then classify them, examine them, and let its opinion be known. If it accepts an amendment, the person suggesting it would have nothing further to say. If it rejects an amendment, the person suggesting it would have the right to defend it.

3) The Commissions should begin their work at once, seeking to abbreviate, in order to finish up with what is essential.

4) Post-conciliar Commissions should be established in order to ensure the effective implementation of the decisions reached.

5) Cease publishing the names of those who have spoken: it is only an incitement to speak. Shorten the titles *'Reverendissimus'* [Most Reverend] etc. (applause).

Cardinal Ritter:[2] *Reiciendum* [to be rejected].

1) it serves no purpose;

2) ambiguous: negative outlook; against New Testament exegetes. It will not support the faithful and the learned, but will spread suspicion.

Cardinal Bea:[3] No. Because 1) it does not meet the purpose of the Council proposed by the Pope, namely: SIC *proferre Doctrinam* [to express doctrine in SUCH a way]. . . that it meets the needs of our time; 2) it equally does not correspond to what the Council itself declared it wishes to do, in its message to humankind: *Studebimus* [We will endeavour . . .].

---

1. *AS* I/III, 45–47.
2. Cardinal Joseph E Ritter, Archbishop of St Louis (Missouri USA), *AS* I/III, 47–48.
3. *AS* I/III, 48–51.

Doctrine is fundamental, agreed, but a Manual is not a pastoral expression of doctrine.

In some cases, a paragraph has been devoted to rebutting A SINGLE theologian.

Nothing is said about the FACT of Revelation before speaking of the *fontes Revelationis*. There are references to things which the Council itself has not mentioned: the authors of the Gospels, the Vulgate, personal and collective inspiration (on this point, the question is not to know whether or not the community was inspired, but HOW THE COMMUNITY INFLUENCED THE AUTHORS).

Finally, the question of unity has not been taken into consideration. A lot is said about exegetes but, except once and in a few words, their immense work has not been taken into consideration. We are under the sign of fear and of suspicion.

Maximos IV[1] (in French, speaking jerkily and rather breathlessly): Lack of pastoral and ecumenical considerations. A Council deals with matters bound up with the life of the Church. What is the point of discussing these things from an angle that is restricted, negative and polemical? There is no need for a doctrinal declaration which would harden matters which are fully open to debate. Some parts of the schema repeat traditional teaching, but express it negatively. From the ecumenical standpoint, there is no attempt to pave the way for dialogue, but a restatement of Counter Reformation and anti-Modernist formulae. We must purely and simply abandon the examination of this text. In this Council, we have not yet broached the most vital questions: the constitution of the Church. The first Vatican Council had a partial vision. It enlarged the head, but the body of the Church (hierarchy and faithful) remained a dwarf. We must re-establish the proportions between the head and the body. In addition, he reiterated the request that he had already made that the schemas *De Ecclesia, De Sacra hierarchia* [*on the sacred hierarchy*][2] and pastoral and social questions be submitted to the Council Fathers for discussion.

Mgr Felici,[3] secretary: the schema *De Ecclesia* will be distributed at the end of the week or at the beginning of the following week.

He announced the result of the vote on the schema *De S Liturgia*.

Mgr Manek,[4] speaking in the name of the bishops of Indonesia:

Nisi funditus emendetur, non tradatur in concilio [unless the schema is completely revised, it should not be dealt with by the Council]! And

---

1. *AS* I/III, 53–54.
2. Like *De Episcopis*, this seems to refer to the chapter or chapters on the episcopate.
3. *AS* I/III, 55.
4. Gabriel Manek, Archbishop of Endeh (Indonesia), *AS* I/III, 55–57.

that for pastoral and theological reasons; and also for general reasons:
a) . . . (I have his text here).
An archbishop, speaking for the bishops of the other Indonesia:[1] rejection.
Mgr Morcillo,[2] bishop of Saragossa, speaking on behalf of a number of
    bishops: the text should be amended, but the schema should be
    discussed.

I left before the end, which must not have been long afterwards. It seems that the
bishops were asked to vote on three canonisations.[3] (????).
A cold air was falling down from the overhead windows. I already had the
beginnings of a cold since my drenching on Monday in the rain and the storm. I
had several quite strong attacks of neuralgia this morning.
    Got back here at 1.10 pm. At 1.40 pm. visit from l'abbé G Gánóczy (Hun-
garian), in connection with his thesis on the ministry according to Calvin. That
might perhaps result in a volume for *Unam Sanctam*?
    Then a visit from Fr de la Potterie.
    Then a visit from three students from the Capranica[4] (asking for a lecture).
    Then a visit from Fr Gy, who is leaving on Friday.
    Then a visit from Vogel (*ICI*).
    Mgr Garrone had invited me to the bishops' meeting at 4.30 pm, but I had a
lecture myself to the bishops of Argentina . . . It took almost an hour by car, in
pouring rain and a storm (which goes on and on) to travel the 1,800 metres or 2
kilometres from the Angelicum to via Marsala. Lecture on Tradition, in Latin. An
American (USA) priest asked me for a lecture for their college . . .
    Fr Camelot told me this evening about the meeting that I had asked him to at-
tend.[5] To begin with, Mgr Veuillot reported on the various contacts which he had
made;[6] Mgr Ancel reported on a meeting with Mgr Himmer, Bishop of Tournai,
on the Church of the Poor.[7] So that the Council can discuss these matters; and

---

1. Albert Soegijapranata, SJ, Archbishop of Samarang (Java, Indonesia), *AS* I/III, 58–59.
2. *AS* I/III, 59–62.
3. Cf *AS* I/III, 62.
4. Roman college mainly catering for Italian priests and seminarians in formation.
5. The meeting of the French bishops.
6. The reference is to the beginnings of the future Conference of Delegates of Bishops'
    Conferences, also known as the 'Conference of Twenty-two', which was to play an im-
    portant role in the development of the Council: on its genesis, cf Jan Grootaers, 'Une
    concertation épiscopale au concile: la Conférence des vingt-deux (1962–1963)', in his
    book: *Actes et acteurs à Vatican II* (Leuven, 1998), 133–165; for a general overview of
    its activity, cf Pierre Noël, 'Gli encontri delle conferenze episcopali durante il concilio.
    Il "gruppo della Domus Mariae"', in Maria Teresa Fattori, and Alberto Melloni (edi-
    tors), *L'evento e le decisioni* (Bologna, 1997).
7. The reference is to the group known as 'Jésus, l'Église et les pauvres', to which Congar
    later belonged; cf Denis Pelletier, 'Une marginalité engagée: le groupe "Jésus, l'Église et

why not create a secretariat for external relations (*ad extra*), in the same way as there is one for unity?

Fr Daniélou proposed the draft of the schema, and the bishops were asked to divide themselves into groups so that they could work with the theologians on the various chapters. There will be an additional chapter at the beginning on the Word of God.

I very much regret not having been able to attend that meeting, as many of the matters discussed remain unclear to me.

Thursday 15 November 1962 Saint Albert

Morning: went to see Fr Daniélou in search of clarification. Contrary to what I had understood, there is no question of 'preparing a schema', but of WORKING PARTIES which would nonetheless result, in the end, in a text that would be sober and less impersonal than mine. I urged that this distinction should be very clear: what is at stake is that bishops who are interested in doing so should WORK with the theologians on matters to be discussed at the Council. Fr Daniélou thinks that it would be good to have a few foreign theologians. I will ask Canon Thils. I went to the Belgian College, thinking that that was where he was living, but he is not. I will see him tomorrow.

Daniélou told me that yesterday, before the general meeting of the bishops, there was, as usual, the meeting of those representing groups. They complained emphatically at the lack of organisation and the ineffectiveness of the French bishops. So it was decided to react and do something about it. In fact, the French bishops are very poorly organised: it is all happy-go-lucky . . .

At noon, visit from an Italian priest belonging to Italian Foreign missions. A good pleasant type, but who began as follows: I would like to do some work on the Church . . . What? Anything. He mentioned four or five major themes in succession. Something. IT DOES NOT MATTER WHAT!

Afternoon: Visit from an Irish priest, Daly.[1] Expert for a bishop, who asked me what I thought of the schemas. An intelligent man. Visit from l'abbé Boillat, who asked me for some ideas to propose to the Indian bishops who wish to draw the attention of the Council to the following three points:

1) rights of the human person;

2) the UNESCO Declaration, completed with a declaration of belief in God;

3) combating nationalism, racism, contemporary colonialism.

At 5 pm, inaugural session (Saint Albert the Great) in the *Aula Magna*. Eight cardinals and some seventy bishops(?): the Gregorianum 'had had' thirty-two of

---

les pauvres'" in M Lamberigts, C Soetens and J Grootaers (editors), *Les Commissions conciliares à Vatican II* (Leuven, 1996).

1. Cahal B Daly, Professor of Philosophy at Queen's University, Belfast; private expert for an Irish bishop, he was to become a Council expert during the Third Session; later still he was to become Archbishop of Armagh (Ireland) and a cardinal.

the former and three hundred of the latter . . . In his speech, Fr Sigmond spoke of the academic degrees granted in this house as emanating from the Magisterium of the Holy See.

I find that idea unbelievable and absolutely false. I do not know whether Fr Sigmond believes it or whether he said that for the benefit of the gallery. Either way, it is serious. If it is the former, it is the very negation of science, quite contrary to the spirit of Albert the Great (which Mgr Graber,[1] his present successor in the see of Ratisbon, presents in his ecclesiological thought). I spoke about all this to Fr Sigmond this evening. He said he had spoken only in the sense that the Angelicum is an institute of the Holy See, dependent on the authority of the Holy See.

The children from the Sistine Chapel choir (twenty to twenty-three of them) sang magnificently. (Rossini: *La Fede, la Speranza, la Carità*). At times they WERE music and rhythm. The music flowed out of them as if from a spring, sparkling, free, strong, sure. They were less hurried and at least as artistic as the Little Singers of Vienna.

Afterwards, I saw Fr Schillebeeckx for a while; he is delighted with the completely unanimous atmosphere among the Dutch bishops. ALL the Dutch bishops but one are members of one or other of the Commissions. This means that if the Commissions were to remain in Rome in order to work, Holland would be deprived of bishops.

Friday 16 November 1962

The voting on the four points of the revised text of the schema *De Liturgia*, which was distributed, will take place tomorrow.

The names of those down to speak were announced. The cardinals may speak before anyone else and without registering beforehand; this means that they take up quite a lot of the time of the session and that many bishops are not able to speak. This time, Ottaviani must have recruited a good number to speak in favour of the schema.

> Cardinal Tisserant[2] (addressed himself to the Observers): spoke briefly about the genesis of *Divino afflante* and the letter to Cardinal Suhard.[3] It seems that, from the biblical point of view, he is against approval of the schema *sicuti est* [as it stands].

---

1. Rudolf Graber had taught theology before becoming Bishop of Ratisbon (Regensburg) in June 1962.
2. *AS* I/III, 66.
3. The reference is to a letter from the Secretary of the Pontifical Biblical Commission to Cardinal Suhard, Archbishop of Paris, written in 1948 and approved by Pope Pius XII.

Cardinal Cerejeira:[1] Pastoral and ecumenical considerations require the clarity of the fullness of doctrine. Therefore, take the schema as it stands as a basis for discussion. Regretted the indiscretion of the newspapers.

Câmara[2] (Brazil): If this schema is rejected, why not the other one?

McIntyre:[3] Doctrine is necessary.

Charity towards non-Catholics, but an unambiguous statement of Catholic doctrine.

Caggiano:[4] the reasons given for rejecting the schema are insufficient. The text has been prepared by ... and revised by ... He replied to objections.

The question which is causing division = the concept of the two sources; that is a matter which is not open to discussion between Catholics. (All those who are in favour of the schema believe that by speaking against the expression 'two sources', we are denying the tradition!!!) *Placet iuxta modum.*

He acknowledged that the text lacked a pastoral character.

Lefebvre[5] (Bourges): the schemas are not in accordance with the Pope's intentions as expressed in his inaugural address:

1) they are too negative, arid, scholastic in form;

2) they are not expressed in attractive terms;

3) there is too little pastoral concern.

These schemas need to be substantially and fundamentally revised.

Santos[6] (Philippines): the schemas can be discussed freely. Summary of the objections made. It is up to the pastors to present doctrine pastorally; therefore the objection to the lack of a pastoral outlook is not valid. The schema settles controversial questions; but if this were not done, a Council would never define anything.

Patriarch of Venice:[7] *Placet* subject to amendments designed to respond better to ecumenism and present-day problems. But it contains useful things that respond well to the questions being asked.

Cardinal Silva[8] (Santiago, Chile): speaking in the name of a number of South American bishops. What is required is:

1) a more pastoral spirit. This is missing. Only one school of thought is

1. Manuel Gonçalves Cerejeira, Patriarch of Lisbon (Portugal), *AS* I/III, 67–68.
2. Cardinal Jaime de Barros Câmara, Archbishop of Rio de Janeiro, President of the Brazilian Bishops' Conference, *AS* I/III, 68.
3. James McIntyre, *AS* I/III, 70–71.
4. Cardinal Antonio Caggiano, Archbishop of Buenos Aires, *AS* I/III, 71–74.
5. Joseph Lefebvre, *AS* I/III, 74–75.
6. Cardinal Rufino J Santos, Archbishop of Manila, who became a member of the Doctrinal Commission during the First Session, *AS* I/III, 76–78.
7. Cardinal Giovanni Urbani, *AS* I/III, 79–80.
8. *AS* I/III, 81–82.

represented. One senses professional idiosyncrasy.

2) a more positive statement of doctrine is more effective.

3) it contains matters that are very useful today (the historicity of Scripture), but what is needed is a commission of *periti* representing the various schools of thought to rewrite the schema.

Cardinal Browne:[1] there are eleven objections. He will deal only with the first few.

1) The doctrine of the two sources is traditional. He quoted St Thomas.

2) It is not ecumenical. But everything is covered by charity *in agendo cum ipsis* [when working with them].

3) Not pastoral.

4) Too scholastic.

5) pessimistic.

6) Too negative.

7) *Repetit plura iam agnita* [It repeats many things that are already acknowledged].

8) Too rigid on the subject of inspiration.

9) Suspicious of the work of exegetes.

10) Nothing is said against atheism.

I lost one objection . . .

Fr Browne is a mule.

Mgr Fares,[2] Italian. *[ ]*

Mgr Bengsch,[3] East Berlin. Very calm. Arguments against the schema. He spoke in the name of his situation. At the end, he urged the Fathers of the regions where the faith is not in danger to bear in mind this situation. He could not go back to his children bringing them a stone instead of bread! [cf Matt: 7:9; Lk 11:11]

Spain:[4] praised the schema, argued against the objections. Charity, but in truth.

Mgr Reuss.[5] One cannot go on discussing for months. The Council should ask the Pope that, in place of this schema, we begin to discuss *De verbo Dei revelato* [On the revealed Word of God],[6] *De Ecclesia*, *De Episcopis*, *De unitate Ecclesiae* [On the unity of the Church].[7] This is the most urgent and, if one did nothing else, one would have done the essential.

---

1. *AS* I/III, 82–84.
2. *AS* I/III, 85–86.
3. *AS* I/III, 87–89.
4. Arturo Tabera Araoz, Bishop of Albacete, *AS* I/III, 89–91.
5. *AS* I/III, 91–92.
6. The reference is to the schema *De Verbo Dei* prepared by the Secretariat for Unity.
7. This is the schema on the unity of the Church prepared by the Preparatory Commission on the Eastern Churches, *De Ecclesiae unitate*.

Gargitter of Brixen:[1]1) produce a single shorter schema out of the first two. Keep only the essential; 2) the new text should be pastoral and positive, 3) as regards the exegetes: add something new on the pastoral aspect of SCIENTIFIC researches, bearing in mind the difficulties they encounter and their freedom of research. Do not assert vigilance only, but acknowledge the work they do.

Hien,[2] Vietnam. The message to the world was well received and in it the things in which men and women are interested were said in a language accessible to all: *'linguam nostrum in qua nati sumus'* [our language in which we were born] . . . Affirm the unity of all humanity!

(He had to be reminded to keep to the point, and then was cut off.)

Battaglia[3] (Italian) expressed his astonishment and sadness at the arguments adduced against the schema: *fallacia et inania* [false and empty], lacking in respect for the Commission and for the Pope who had proposed the schema. He replied to the objections.

(An example of the miserable result of teaching from Latin manuals in which the objections are magnificently refuted.)

Mgr Guerry.[4] Read his paper badly with a frightful French accent; but very vehement, and earnestly listened to.

In the name of all the French bishops, he spoke against the idea of setting the doctrinal and the pastoral in opposition. What is missing is a *proemium* outlining the history of salvation.

. . .

Mgr Florit[5] (Florence): Had not been down to speak, and was not announced. Some people are allowed to get away with things . . . However, he was listened to with great attention. In fact, he is a splendid advocate.

In favour of the two *fontes* [sources], going back to the Council of Trent. One knows that the one source = *verbum Dei* [the Word of God]. One could shorten the text, which he praises, and make clearer what it says, make the schema more attractive(!!!).

Against *Formgeschichte*.[6]

Bishop from Mexico[7] (addressed himself to the Observers): he spoke of the first two schemas. They repeat the decrees of previous Councils and in addition take positions on matters which are not as yet mature and are still under discussion. A NEW terminology has been introduced, that of two sources. In biblical matters, more restrictive expressions have

1. Joseph Gargitter, Bishop of Bressanone (Brixen), in Italy, *AS* I/III, 92–94.
2. Simon Hoa Nguyen-van Hien, Bishop of Dalat, *AS* I/III, 94–95.
3. *AS* I/III, 97–99.
4. *AS* I/III, 99–101.
5. *AS* I/III, 101–103.
6. History of forms (exegetical method).
7. J Alba Palacios, Bishop of Tehuantepec, *AS* I/III, 104–106.

been added to what Pius XII said. The ordinary magisterium should
be enough: pope, Biblical Commission joined by the Pontifical Biblical
Institute.

Recognoscatur! [It should be revised].

(I detected in this intervention echoes of the lecture I gave the other
day).

Dom Butler,[8] Abbot of Downside. He spoke of his past experience as an
exegete. He was not happy with the tenor of the schema from the
point of view of the future of biblical studies. *Non placet.* He expressed
agreement with those who were saying that the schema is not in
accordance with the intentions of the Pope and the Council, who wish
to bring '*bonum nuntium*' [good news] to the world.

Concerning inspiration and inerrancy, the schema goes beyond
common teaching.

It has been said: it will be corrected. But the schema does not have only
a few thorns that can be removed: it goes deeper than that.

In a doctrinal schema, above all in this first one, one needs unanimity.
Many of the Fathers cannot say *Placet*, even if some corrections are
made. What is needed is for a small group, representing both schools
of thought, to produce something that will please everyone. Or else we
will have to move on to another schema.

(A really excellent intervention. Unfortunately the English accent will
have made it difficult for many ears to understand. This very English
idea of a *Joint Committee*).

In the afternoon, first a visit from Frs Rouquette[9] and Bréchet.[10]

From 4.30 pm until 7.30 pm, working session on tradition with a group of
bishops.

Then, until supper, Fr Liégé. We spoke about many things. His gift of awareness of the essence of things, and, within that, his awareness of the exigencies of
what is essential . . .

---

8. Basil C Butler, OSB, President of the English Benedictine Congregation, elected as
    member of the Doctrinal Commission from the Second Session onwards. He was later
    to become an Auxiliary Bishop of Westminster, *AS* I/III, 107–108.

9. Robert Rouquette, SJ, was a member of the editorial committee for *Études,* a journal
    published by the French Jesuits: a religious journalist, he was interested in the ecumen-
    ical movement; in Rome he was following the unfolding of Council and his reports for
    Études were to be published by Congar: *La Fin d'une chrétienté,* 'Unam Sanctam', 69 a
    and b (Paris: Cerf, 1968).

10. Raymond Bréchet, SJ, trained as an exegete, editor of *Choisir,* a journal published by
    the Jesuits in Geneva, for which he was following the Council.

Saturday 17 November 1962

Before the Congregation, I saw Mgr Elchinger. He invited me to a meeting with Mgr Volk tomorrow on 'Council strategy'. I refused, as I have too much urgent work that is overdue. Mgr Volk was not happy at the way the Ratzinger-Rahner text had been distributed, about which he had not been consulted by Cardinal Frings.

I saw Fr Lécuyer who told me that Cardinal Ottaviani had already summoned two experts: Fenton and another whose name he could not remember.

Mgr Felici[1] read the revised text of the *Proemium*. Then a report by Cardinal Lercaro[2] on the work done, and an excellent statement (very clear) by Mgr Martin[3] (bishop from Canada), on the various amendments.

There will be a separate vote on each of the four numbers.

The result of this vote, announced at the end of the session, was as follows:

Item no	Number of Voters	Placet	Non Placet	Void
1	2,206	2,181	14	11
2	2,202	2,175	26	1
3	2,203	2,175	21	7
4	2,204	2,191	10	3

It is a magnificent success for the liturgy!

> Cardinal de la Torre[4] (Ecuador). The reasons against rejection have been clearly expressed; there is no need to repeat them. It had been stated that Latin America was in favour of replacing this schema by another one. Now the opinion of the bishops is: *placet iuxta modum*.
> Cardinal Garibi[5] (Mexico). Spoke in defence of the schema.
> The Council must leave people free to have opinions, but it is up to the Council to say whether or not a given proposition is an opinion or not. The Council of Trent was most certainly pastoral, but it was primarily doctrinal!
> Cardinal Döpfner:[6] remarks on Cardinal Ottaviani's presentation, who had spoken as if the schema had been prepared in agreement and peacefully during two years' work. But: in the Preparatory Theological Commission, there had been pressure from one side, a spirit 'against';

---

1. *AS* I/III, 114–115.
2. *AS* I/III, 116–118.
3. Joseph-Albert Martin, Bishop of Nicolet, member of the Liturgical Commission, *AS* I/III, 119–121.
4. Carlos María de la Torre, Archbishop of Quito, *AS* I/III, 121–122.
5. José Garibi y Rivera, Archbishop of Guadalajara, *AS* I/III, 122–124.
6. *AS* I/III, 125–126.

no regard for the Secretariat, rejection of the idea of a joint commission; the Central Commission had called for changes which had not been taken into consideration; there had been a block vote, taken without precision, with the result that, inevitably, the same comments were destined to re-appear in the Council. Agreement must be reached.

There is no lack of respect for the Pope to be discussed . . .

After the general remarks, there should be a vote on the schema as a whole.

Cardinal Ottaviani should listen to *periti* from other schools of thought and due account must be taken of the comments made by the Fathers, by the Secretariat.

It would take a long time? But such an important Constitution must be perfect: it would be better to do away with some of the other schemas!

He said all that in the name of the German-speaking bishops.

Cardinal Della [[Conqua(?)]]:[1] astonished that there has been criticism of a schema presented by the Pope.

(I went to the WC and missed Cardinal Bacci's intervention.[2])

Mgr Schmitt[3] (Metz). Along Liégé lines,[4] but much too long (he was cut off), with great conviction.

Trent = the Gospel, source

Vatican I = objective aspect, dogmatic nature of Christian doctrine. Now it is necessary to show other aspects linked with biblical, liturgical and catechetical renewal.

Three points:

1. All revelation consists in the person of Christ: the entire life and person of Christ are revelation.

2. The entire Christian revelation is the Gospel, that is to say the Economy of SALVATION. To reduce it to pure *'doctrinas theologicas'* [theological doctrines] leads to a drying up and diminution of the faith.

3. This Gospel of Salvation meets perfectly the needs of the world of today. But many of the faithful have some truths in their minds, but have never met Christ.

(I see clearly where these ideas are going, which are fairly familiar to myself as well. They aim to take the debate to the most radical and decisive level of the very idea of Revelation and Faith. But, from the point of view of the audience and of the way the debate was going, they were, to my mind, too alien, they came too much from another world for them to be accepted. Moreover, obliged, for this reason, to

---

1.   Luis Concha, Archbishop of Bogota (Colombia), *AS* I/III, 126–127.
2.   *AS* I/III, 127–128.
3.   *AS* I/III, 128–130.
4.   {Pierre-André Liégé, OP, was personal expert to Mgr Schmitt and Mgr Elchinger, cf page 5, note 2.}

EXPLAIN things thought to be unfamiliar, Mgr Schmitt spoke for too long and had to break off.)

Cardinal Ottaviani[1] replied at this point to Cardinal Döpfner, who had said some things that were not correct: 1) in the sub-commission *De re biblica* [on Biblical matters], there had been discussion and opposed positions. Several votes were taken and the minority had, of course, to give way. It is not true to say that there was only one point of view: there were exegetes present: Cerfaux and Fr Vogt . . . (!!!)[2] 2) At the Central Commission, all were able to speak. The Commission for Amendments and the Theological Commission had seen the recommendations.

The President, Cardinal Gilroy,[3] then said that a Council Father had just sent him a note reminding the Fathers of canon 303, according to which the Fathers may freely decide *de reiiciendo vel acceptando* [whether to reject or accept]. And, added the President, *reiiciendo* [to reject] was underlined.

Parente.[4] Not speaking as an assessor of the 'Holy Office' but as Bishop of Ptolemais in the Thebaid[5] (then let him go and live in his diocese!!!).

He suggested a vote, section by section, on the existing text after it has been modified to make it more acceptable and more pastoral. (He spoke of the *forma* [form] and the *substantia* [substance]: as if the living spirit intervened only in the case of the former and not for the perception and preparation of the latter!!!).

He began to discuss the Trent text and the question of *partim, partim* [partly . . . , partly . . .],[6] by referring to the articles of Lennerz. [7]

He was cut off.

Bishop from Yugoslavia:[8] one ought to speak at greater length of Tradition; he made a few suggestions.

---

1. *AS* I/III, 131–132.
2. Vogt had only been a consultor and had been appointed at a late date; as for Cerfaux, he was nearly eighty.
3. *AS* I/III, 132.
4. *AS* I/III, 132–135.
5. Pietro Parente was titular Archbishop of Ptolemais (Egypt).
6. The formula 'partim . . . partim . . . ' was considered, then rejected by the Fathers at the Council of Trent as a way of speaking of truths of the Faith contained both in Scripture and in Tradition.
7. H Lennerz, SJ, who died in 1961, in an article published in the Jesuit journal *Gregorianum* in 1959, opposed the position of Joseph R Geiselmann, a teacher of dogmatics at the University of Tübingen, on the question of the relationship between Scripture and Tradition at the Council of Trent: Geiselmann had sought to show that by rejecting the expression '*partim . . . partim*', that Council had sought to leave open the question of the material sufficiency of Scripture (are the truths of the Faith contained in full in Scripture?).
8. Pavao Butorac, Bishop of Dubrovnik, *AS* I/III, 137–138.

Cardinal Frings:[1] Replying to Parente, had no doubt that Revelation must
  be taken from Scripture AND Tradition, *in ordine cognoscendi* [in the
  order of knowledge]. But, *in ordine essendi* [in the order of being],
  there is only one source which flows in two streams. He had omitted
  to say this the other day because, being unable to read, he had spoken
  from memory.

Simons[2] (India): Spoke of *inerrantia* [inerrancy] being restricted to '*quae
  auctor humanus reapse et absolute intendit*' [that which the human
  author really and absolutely intended].

  He was asked to keep to the point under discussion: the schema IN
  GENERAL. He then added that one should avoid the appearance of
  vainglory in speaking of the magisterium.

Mgr Charue:[3] delivered remarkably well an extremely dense discourse. He
  spoke in the name of all the Belgian bishops and of Belgian bishops
  who were missionaries.

  The schema lacks serenity, and is neither positive, pastoral, biblical nor
  ecumenical. It must be entirely redone. Also, ordinary magisterium
  and extraordinary magisterium should be more clearly distinguished.
  Our conciliar declaration will have great value for a long time to come.
  Therefore, *caute procedatur* [proceed with prudence] when dealing
  with difficult questions, above all where history must speak.

  There are problems: for example, the authors of the Gospels.
  Formgeschichte: distinguish between rationalist presuppositions and
  the historical and philosophical method, which can *nullo modo* [in no
  way] be condemned.

  He referred to the article by Mgr Weber in the *Bulletin de Strasbourg.*[4]
  Be aware of the difficulties faced by exegetes. Let the case of Galileo's
  suffice!

  There is talk of the Modernist danger, but the remedy is not to impose
  impedimenta [barriers], it is to work. This is where the authority of
  Louvain comes from. Rivière[5] said that if there were no Modernists in
  Belgium, this was due to Louvain.

  It is also being said that the previous twenty Councils all condemned

---

1. *AS* I/III, 139.
2. Francis Simons, Bishop of Indore, *AS* I/III, 139-140.
3. *AS* I/III, 143–145.
4. 'Orientations actuelles des études exégétiques sur la vie du Christ', in the *Bulletin ec-
    clésiastique du diocèse de Strasbourg,* 1–15 October, 1962; distributed at the Council
    by the Pontifical Biblical Institute, it was later published, completed and revised, in *La
    Documentation Catholique,* 1963, col 203–212.
5. L'abbé Jean Rivière, Professor of Fundamental Theology at Strasbourg, who died
    in 1946. He had published *Le Modernisme dans l'Église. Étude d'histoire religieuse
    comtemporaine* (Paris: Letouzey et Ané, 1929).

errors. But ours must imitate the Council of Jerusalem, or Peter: not impose more than is necessary. We should apply that to our separated brethren and to *gentes* [non-Christians]. We bear the future for several centuries.

Mgr [[De Minio??]][1] (addressed the Patriarchs and the Observers). The pastoral approach = the problems people are dealing with. This is not the same as following the current fashion. *In re potius quam in forma est ponendum* [This must be established in reality, rather than in appearance].

Don't make it a philosophical text. Nevertheless, a tempered scholastic form is the best.

As for the content, there is no reference to the living tradition, the *sensus fidelium* . . .

(he was cut off: the President has a rather narrow view of the discussion of the schema *in genere* [in general]).

Mgr Zoa:[2] 1) In the name of several bishops in Africa, Madagascar and the Islands: agrees with Cardinals Alfrink, Bea, Frings, Lefebvre, etc. They have given their comments to the Secretariat. *Non placet.*

2) Speaking in his own name: he read a paper expressing three points which I had given him this morning before the session. Agrees with Butler, namely:

a) there must be at least moral unanimity;

b) the opposition of schools of thought is being exaggerated. *All* acknowledge the existence of Tradition: all acknowledge the sovereign nature of Scripture: all acknowledge both Trent and Vatican I.

c) Within the framework of the Theological Commission, a team of *periti* representing the different schools of thought should be established, and it should prepare for the Commission a text acceptable to all.

Mgr Pourchet[3] (Saint-Flour). OUR RESPONSABILITIES. It is very serious. First that of leaving open what Trent has left open and not defining disputed opinions. Then: after Trent, we were dominated by the anti-Protestant polemic and the importance of Scripture was diminished. Now . . . ecumenism, which must be taken into consideration, does not consist in a false irenicism, but in not multiplying obstacles.

Responsibility with respect to exegesis: cf Charue. The discussion over these past three days shows that these schemas arouse no enthusiasm. Those in favour of them recognise the need for amendments. But it would take weeks. Also in favour of the Butler proposal.

---

1. Angel Temiño Saiz, Bishop of Orense, (Spain), *AS* I/III, 146–147.
2. *AS* I/III, 148.
3. Maurice Pourchet, Bishop of Saint-Flour (France), *AS* I/III, 149–151.

Mgr Hakim[1] (*Beatitudines* [Your Beatitudes] . . . dear Observers). In French.
Outstanding. But what he said must have been lost on a great many. He
sought to make the voice of the East and of its patristic tradition heard.
The schemas are foreign to him in their orientation, their structure
and their conceptualisation. It is purely Latin. He expressed regret that,
not knowing the catechesis and theology of the East, those who had
drafted it had monopolised the universal faith for the benefit of their
particular theology.

In Eastern theology, in which the liturgy is the place where the
transmission of the faith actually occurs, the mystery of Christ is
put forward as an economy unfolding in the course of history. The
concrete nature of the Word of God manifests the presence of this in
the world. Every disjunction, even if only apparent, between Scripture
and Tradition will be deemed a violence done to the unity of the paths
of transmission.

Eastern theology gives full importance to the idea of humankind in the
image of God. This leads to consequences of which the following are
two examples:

1) A different way of conceiving nature-grace and the relationship
between God and humankind, including in Revelation;

2) Easter = the unity of the death and resurrection, whereas for Latins,
it is above all the idea of satisfaction.

'I feel myself an alien to the text and to the structure of the schemas put
before us.'

A bishop from the Philippines.[2] [ ]

Mgr Rosales[3] speaking for the majority of the Conference of Bishops of the
Philippines, of which he is the President.

Placet quamvis . . . [In favour although] The objections are insufficient.
The schema is pastoral and it is ecumenical. The Pope has approved it
. . .

Really and truly, there is the Church that has rediscovered its sources and the
Church that has not. The latter, re-encountering the theology that it learnt from
the manuals, is satisfied with that . . .

On the way out, Mgr Blanchet: 'I am campaigning for Butler's idea'.

Most of all, I saw Fr Tucci, editor-in-chief of *Civiltà cattolica*, where he experiences a great deal of difficulty with some who have not gone back to the sources.
He spoke to me about the text that I had asked Mayor to pass on to him. He

---

1. George Hakim, *AS* I/III, 152–153.
2. In fact, it was Jacinto Argaya Goicoechea, Bishop of Mondoñedo-Ferrol (Spain), *AS* I/
III, 153–154.
3. Julio Rosales, Archbishop of Cebù, *AS* I/III, 155–156.

had never received it. If he had received it, he could not have printed it, because there is a ruling at *Civiltà cattolica* not to print anything that has not come from the editorial team. The ruling is necessary, he told, me, because otherwise every little Monsignor would be nagging them to print his prose. Moreover, no article is printed unless it has been passed by two thirds of the members of the editorial council. Finally, to complete the picture of the liberties of this publication, each issue has to be submitted to the Secretariat of State before being sent to the printers.

Fr Tucci is marvellous. Open, intelligent. He sees the Pope regularly. I asked him if it was true that the Pope is not satisfied with the schemas. He told me that, on one occasion, the Pope, who had in front of him a moral schema, told him that he did not agree with it. But the Pope is not a theologian . . . he has intuitions. He is more likely to see a theologian as an enemy . . . He has no means of defence and he has no-one to defend him. He is attacked from different sides and, to keep the peace, he yields on some points. He hardly knows how to say 'no'.

My impression of the point which we have reached in the Council is clear: it is an impasse. We will never secure the necessary majority for a text expressing either school of thought. Hence, the Butler—Zoa (Congar)—Pourchet solution.

That evening, I saw Fr Cottier. He is living with some Italian bishops. They received a paper, IN THE NAME OF THE CONFERENCE OF THE BISHOPS OF ITALY, prepared by the *periti* of this Conference, which reinforced even more the scholastic and negative positions adopted in the schema.

Moreover, Fr Labourdette told me that he had been told, *sub secreto* [in confidence], by Fr Gagnebet that he had asked for there to be Scripture scholars from Jerusalem[1] and the Biblicum on the Commission. Their inclusion was not wanted. So they chose to initiate proceedings against them! A (brave) paper by Laurentin contains a number of details concerning the work of the Preparatory Theological Commission. It is certain that the Commission was being manipulated knowingly and profoundly. Some outside consultors were invited, but everything had been arranged without them. They were seated on chairs along the walls, while the members of the Commission were in the middle, seated around a table. The consultors could only speak if called upon, or by asking to be questioned. They did not attend the sub-commissions, where the work was being prepared. If Fr Gagnebet invited me/us to the *De Ecclesia* sub-commission, he did so on his own initiative: Mgr Janssen and Fr Häring got themselves thrown out of the sub-commission on morals, if not physically, no less really. The non-Roman consultors did not come to Rome very often. I came here three times in all. They were frequently sent the papers at the last moment: not intentionally, no doubt, but rather because the papers were not ready earlier, but the fact remains. The papers which we did receive were often the fifth or sixth version of a text which had been prepared by the Romans at weekly meetings entirely without us.

---

1. The École biblique et archéologique française in Jerusalem.

Moreover, our comments, which we could neither express nor defend verbally when we were present, were not taken into consideration to any great extent. It is true that we managed to secure a few small improvements by deletions, additions or changes. But what happened to the memoranda by Delhaye and Laurentin? What was the effect of my own memoranda on *De Episcopis, De modo exprimendi habitudinem non catholicorum ad ecclesiam, De œcumenismo* [on bishops, on the way of expressing the relationship of non-Catholics to the Church, on ecumenism]? I did intervene on the question of Tradition: both against the idea of the two sources, and against the attribution of the preservation of the Tradition to the Magisterium alone. I submitted a paper to Mgr Garofalo on the first point. It served no purpose.

It is true that I was too timid, that I was not sufficiently worried, nor did I argue[1] strongly enough. I should have been stubbornly importunate. What in fact happened was that one chose to tone down one's intervention, too sure of the result if, the other school of thought having taken the thing to heart, it came to a vote. Every increase in the authority of the 'Magisterium' was accepted, to the point of it becoming ridiculous, and it began to be commented on. Every warning against errors or dangers, however remote, was accepted. Every broadening of the horizon was reduced to a presence that was little more than symbolic. I also said, several times, that there were not enough Scripture scholars amongst us, nor Easterners: that our theology was purely Latin. But I am accustomed: 1) to do no more than state the truth, it being up to each one to pay attention to it; 2) not to vaunt my merchandise, not to repeat things. I should have done so to the point of importunity. I did not.

Sunday 18 November 1962

A bad day: storms most of the night and this morning. Rain, warm and humid weather. My nose bled. That happened again the whole evening and until 2 am. I am sleeping very little these days.

At 5 pm, at the Gregorianum, reception for *periti* and theologians. Opportunity to see MANY people. I also saw the President of the Gregorianum Students' Association, a Spaniard. He complained of the total lack of freedom. There are 3,300 students there from many countries: it would be marvellous to give them a common awareness, but the Curia wants that least of all! So it puts a multiplicity of obstacles in their path, in ways that are never clear. For example, recently they were to receive some Observers (the Brothers from Taizé, I think). The Rector of the Gregorianum was agreeable. Two days before they were due, the whole thing was forbidden by an intervention from X = the Curia.

At noon, I also spoke to a [Polish] professor at the Angelicum, Fr [ ]. He told me that, here research is absolutely impossible. As soon as a professor says, in a course, a single word that goes beyond the manuals, it is reported to the

---

1. battu'. The typescript has 'débattu'—'struggle'.

Curia and one way or another the consequences are disagreeable. It would be impossible, here, for there to be teaching, informed by the sources, that, however partially, touched on the real questions facing humanity. One cannot 'get ahead' except by taking up old School quarrels, as Fr Garrigou had done.[1]

Conversation with Fr de Lubac. He has been given the following secret information directly: Ottaviani has informed some of the bishops that the 'Holy Office' both controlled and judged the Central Commission. The claim of the 'Holy Office' is to control and judge the Council. Now this is the reverse of what is laid down. The conflict will have to come out into the open one day at the Council.

Lubac also told me that Ottaviani has summoned Fenton, Schauf and Lio as experts: that is to say, HIS OWN men. So the comedy continues, from a so-called opening-up, of which Lubac and I were the emblems, but in fact the hostages.

I brought Fr de Lubac to dine with Mgr Elchinger and the three other French bishops.

Mgr Elchinger gave me news of some of the recent meetings: Saturday evening (yesterday), Cardinals Liénart and Ruffini: it really will be necessary to smooth things over and come closer to one another!

Sunday (today) morning, at Mgr Volk's, a meeting like the first one to which I was invited but did not go: Volk thinks that it would be necessary to clear up the misunderstandings about the pastoral approach and doctrine; scholasticism; Revelation; ecumenism—and declare that the 'Holy Office' is not the judge of the Council, but the opposite; the 'Holy Office' will only be at the service of the consequences of the Council. We must make an effort to understand one another.

Rahner thinks that before entering into dialogue with the other school of thought it will be necessary to define a number of positive and precise points on which we will declare that we would never want to give way.

There are many pressures from the 'Holy Office', that is to say Ottaviani and Tromp, who have even presumed to make changes in the text approved by the Theological Commission or by the Central Commission: always in the direction either of a toughening up, or of emphasising caution and authority.

I was also told that Cardinal Siri has brought the Italian bishops together and that, since then, they are avoiding contact with the four French bishops in the *pensione* where they are all living.

Finally, Mgr Elchinger told me that the question of the theological note, so dear to the Germans, will be put to Cardinal Ottaviani. If he replies: of faith,[2] he will have been made to contradict himself and what he said to the Central Commission.

---

1. The neo-Thomist Réginald Garrigou-Lagrange, OP, of the Province of France, Professor of Theology at the Angelicum until 1960, had strongly influenced several generations of students.

2. {A theological note 'de fide' would mean a proposition so qualified required assent by the faithful.}

Monday 19 November

My nose bled until 2 am. Atrocious weather: tepid rain, storm, low pressure. I have difficulty in putting one foot in front of the other.

Spellman presiding. One cannot understand a word he says. The general discussion continued.

Cardinal of Tarragona[1] the schema is opportune *contra serpentes errores* [against creeping errors]. He recalled the warnings of the popes.

Gilroy[2] in favour of mutual tolerance. Praise for the schema, the Commission, its work. In favour of its consideration.

Cardinal Gracias:[3] one is hoping for a constitution WHICH WILL BE HELPFUL. There will not be a sufficient majority for this. Those who are in favour of the scheme are prepared to accept *amendments.* So many will need to be made that it will amount to producing a new text, with the views of both sides represented. As it stands, *schema non satisfacit* [the schema is unsatisfactory]. This is not a reflection on the honour of the Theological Commission, but its members did not have the benefit of help, as the Council has . . .

Cardinal Meyer[4] (Chicago): the conflict that we are experiencing is not in accordance with the aim of the Council. There can be no unanimity with THIS text. He supported the suggestion put forward by Butler and Gracias. And one should express one's confidence in the exegetes, while recommending their docility to the rules laid down.

Cardinal-Archbishop of Lima:[5] replied to the objections raised against the schema. But the points of view are not so very contrary . . . *Placet iuxta modum.* The discussion of each paragraph will go on for ever. Everything has been said. We must move on . . .

Cardinal Rugambwa:[6] a two-thirds majority is needed . . . ! The Presidents should ask the Pope to allow the schema to be held over until the Second Session and from now until then it should be re-examined by theologians, exegetes and ecumenists.

Bishop from New Caledonia[7] (French. Accent!) Supported the arguments against. Added this reason: the schema makes a distinction between *doctrinam de Christo et factum Christi* [doctrine about Christ and the fact of Christ], whereas the perfect revelation is Christ. He is not

1. Cardinal Benjamín de Arriba y Castro, Archbishop of Tarragona (Spain), *AS* I/III, 162–164.
2. *AS* I/III 164–165.
3. *AS* I/III 166–168.
4. *AS* I/III 169-170.
5. Cardinal Juan Landázuri Ricketts (Peru), *AS* I/III, 170-171.
6. *AS* I/III, 172.
7. Pierre Martin was Vicar Apostolic in New Caledonia (Oceania), *AS* I/III, 174–175.

being given his absolute primacy. At least let the title be: *De Scriptura secundum Traditionem Ecclesiae legenda* [on the need to read Scripture according to the Church's tradition]. And omit declarations that are already accepted, by referring to past documents. The first two schemas should be combined into one.

Henríquez (Venezuela),[1] speaking in the name of the Conference of Bishops of Venezuela. *Ut sic est, non admittatur schema* [The schema should not be agreed to as it stands]. Another one should be prepared in collaboration with the Biblical Commission. It lacks ecumenical spirit, which does not imply a diminution of the truth! He replied to the objections made against a major revision of the text, in relation either to the Pope or to the work of the Theological Commission.

Griffiths[2] (Auxiliary, New York). Humour. But too long. *'Per totam noctem laboravimus et nihil cepimus. Sed in verbo tuo laxabo rete'* [we have laboured all night and taken nothing. But at your word I will let down the nets (Luke 5:5)]. All the questions should be taken up by *periti* from both sides, while retaining what is good in the original text.

Mgr De Smedt,[3] Bruges, in the name of the Secretariat. His text very well given, listened to intently. Fairly strong note of emotion coming not from sentimentality but from the entrails of truth.

He wished to state *ex quo praecise consistat œcumenicitas* [what precisely ecumenism consists in], both as a doctrine and in its style. All Christians acknowledge Jesus Christ, but they do not agree on the means of approaching him. For centuries, Catholics and the others have deemed it sufficient for each side to explain its doctrine clearly, but each did so in its own categories, which the other did not understand. That has led to NOTHING. For some time, another method has come to be used: ecumenical DIALOGUE. This consists in the importance one gives to the WAY in which the doctrine is expounded, in order to make it understandable to the other. This is not an attempt to negotiate unity, it is not an attempt to secure a conversion; rather, on each side, the giving of a clear witness, taking the other side into account. Our texts must be responsive to this. It is not easy! There must not be any watering down which would deceive the others.

Nine conditions are required of which, for the sake of brevity, he listed only the first four: 1) *quid sit doctrina hodierna Orthodoxorum et protestantium* [what is the contemporary teaching of the Orthodox and of Protestants]?

---

1. Luiz E Henríquez Jimenez, Auxiliary Bishop of Caracas. He was to be elected a member of the Doctrinal Commission during the Second Session of the Council, *AS* I/III, 178–180.
2. *AS* I/III, 181–183.
3. *AS* I/III, 184–186.

2) What idea have they of OUR doctrine?

3) What has not yet been well enough developed in Catholic doctrine?

4) Is Catholic doctrine put forward in the way that it needs to be? Scholasticism will not do. What is required is a biblical and patristic approach. But it is not enough to express 'the truth' for a text to be ecumenical.

The members of the Secretariat have offered their assistance to the Theological Commission, they have suggested a joint commission. But the Theological Commission has turned down their offer.

Those who live amongst Protestants or the Orthodox have told us that the schema is devoid of ecumenical spirit.

Velint examinare utrum sufficienter consideraverint [would the Council Fathers examine whether they have sufficiently considered] if the method adopted is a good one? The Secretariat, for its part, finds the schema *notabiliter deficit in œcumenicitate* [seriously lacking in an ecumenical spirit]. It does not represent a *progressus* [step forward], but a *regressus* [step backwards]. It will be an *impedimentum et nocumentum* [impediment and occasion of harm]. The new method has borne its fruits: as is evidenced by the presence of the Observers. If the schema is not rewritten, it will be our fault that the Vatican Council will have disappointed an immense hope (warm applause from the bishops; the archbishops did not join in).

De Sousa[1] (long-winded!): five points need to be improved.

Garrone[2] (emotional, sermonising, sentimental, vague. That does not PRESENT anything firm and clear for people's minds . . .).

Two kinds of reconciliation. It is not a message to humankind, there should be a *proemium*. It should be rewritten *integre* [completely]. It should be sent back to the Commission and the Commission should collaborate with the Secretariat.

I went to the WC. While I was away, a French bishop[3] said: we must discuss this schema. Otherwise, what will we do?

Del Pino,[4] Spain [ ]

? (an English speaker) 'Carol'? I think the surname was Hurley.[5]

The schema prepared by the Secretariat *De verbo Dei* [On the Word of God] should be distributed to the Fathers.

---

1. David de Sousa, Bishop of Funchal (Portugal), *AS* I/III 187–189.
2. *AS* I/III 189–191.
3. It was in fact an Italian, Giuseppe D'Avack, Archbishop of Camerino, *AS* I/III 192–193.
4. Aurelio Del Pino Gómez, Bishop of Lérida, *AS* I/III 194–196.
5. It was in fact Denis E Hurley, *AS* I/III 198–200.

In favour of a *coetus bipartitus* [a group from both sides].

The current differences of opinion go beyond the first schema. They will keep on reappearing. Even the Central Commission did not have a clear idea of the pastoral aim of the Council. This point needs to be made clear, and then, in the interval between the First and Second Sessions, a commission can revise the schemas in the light of it.

? (an Italian).[1] It is clear that two points of view are in collision. He, too, was in favour of an honourable compromise.

A *proemium* should be written, to be placed in front of all the schemas: *'ampla panoramica et serena recapitulatio totius historiae salutis'* [giving a wide-ranging, panoramic and serene overview of the entire history of salvation]—of which he listed some elements—to be presented to the Council at once.

In the meantime, discuss in detail the two schemas before the Fathers, in order to improve the style! and bring out the points on which there is agreement.

Mgr Ancel:[2] tried to accentuate clearly, which the French rarely do well. Agreement is deeper than one might think. However, the practical solution is difficult. Even if amended, the schema will not secure a two-thirds majority. And the same will be true of a new schema, if the Pope agrees that one should be produced. What is needed is a *renovatio* [rewriting] of the texts, and not by the people who have produced this one.

Solution: 1) at the Council, there is no need either for winners or losers, what is needed is to secure moral unanimity; 2) one cannot purely and simply reject the work of the Theological Commission; therefore retain those parts of the Commission's text that are acceptable to all.

3) re-do a text incorporating parts of the present text but responding to the demands expressed and, in order to do this, *'salvo iure Commissionis theologicae, novos peritos ad diversas theologiae scholas pertinentes'* [while preserving the rights of the Doctrinal Commission, there should be fresh *periti* belonging to the different theological schools].

A bishop from Vietnam[3] (with French pronunciation): critical comments on the biblical sections of the schema. It needs to be said that the Magisterium is subject to Scripture and Tradition. One cannot tie the present and the future to the theology of the manuals. The schema needs to be revised.

---

1. Giuseppe Ruotolo, Bishop of Ugento-S Maria di Leuca, *AS* I/III 201–203.
2. *AS* I/III 203–204.
3. Paul Seitz, *AS* I/III 205–206.

That evening, conference on the laity of today at the Holy Cross Fathers'. There I met the marvellous Mgr McGrath. Like myself, he had tears in his eyes while Mgr De Smedt was speaking this morning. Cardinal Silva from Chile told him that he had wept, the whole thing had moved him to the depths. Tears of the Holy Spirit, such as I wish for those who are hardened in their dogmatic righteousness!

Tuesday 20 November 1962

(Notes taken directly during the session). Yesterday, at the meeting of Presidents, Cardinal Tisserant was AGAINST terminating the discussion and sending the schema to a commission. Because 'what would be done at the Council?'

Cardinal Lefebvre[1] had seen Cardinal Ottaviani. He would be in favour of making concessions.

In St Peter's, everyone is expecting 'something'. For now, discussion of the general principles of the schema resumed. Lassitude and disappointment.

Mgr Cabana[2] (Canada): against false irenicism; quoted *Humani Generis*. Accordingly, *placet*, and the different chapters of the schema should be presented for discussion as soon as possible.

Echeverria[3] (Ecuador): in recent years, many opinions concerning Scripture have been expressed, many of which are false. The Council must weed out the errors and be vigilant about the integrity of the deposit. Praise for the text (He was cut off).

García[4] (Spain): acknowledged the existence of conflicting opinions.
Ut commissio formetur non valde numerosa [a small commission should be set up] (of bishops) to prepare a new text, and we should move on to discussing the schema *De Ecclesiae unitate*,[5] which is very much in accordance with the ecumenical purpose of the Council.

Polish Bishop:[6] A *proemium* should be prepared. The title is not good: it is God who is the source.
De revelationis deposito vel testimonia [on the deposit or the witness of Revelation].
Better to say that the Scripture must be read IN THE CHURCH.
Efficacitas salutaris Verbi Dei [the saving efficacy of the Word of God] and he made a series of remarks concerning biblical matters.

---

1. Joseph Lefebvre.
2. Georges Cabana, Archbishop of Sherbrooke, *AS* I/III, 209–210.
3. B Echeverria Ruiz, *AS* I/III, 210–211.
4. F Garcia Martinez, *AS* I/III, 213–215.
5. On the unity of the Church: the reference is to the schema prepared by the Preparatory Commission on the Eastern Churches.
6. Michel Klepacz, Bishop of Łódź, *AS* I/III, 215–218.

Nicodemo[1] (Bari, Italy): For the schema to be REJECTED it would need to contain some error. This is not the case. Moreover, a second schema has been distributed. Why do they not propose others?

In brief, the schema needs to be discussed. How to improve it? . . . (A torrent of words with different clichés, he is ripe for the Roman Congregations.)

Mgr Felici,[2] Secretary General, read the following proposal: on conclusion of the general discussion, we are due to move to discussion of *singulis schematis capitibus* [the individual chapters of the schema]. However, as some of the Fathers do not agree, the Council of Presidents puts the following proposition to the vote: *An disceptatio de Schemate Constitutionis dogmaticae de fontibus revelationis interrumpenda sit* [Should the debate on the Schema of the dogmatic Constitution on the sources of revelation be adjourned]?' (after a quarter of an hour of twaddle he added *sine die* [indefinitely]). By secret vote: *placet, non placet*.

Cardinal Frings[3] accepted this proposal (which amounts to a burying of the schema) even though it did not satisfy him completely.

Cardinal Ruffini[4] clarified the quite obscure meaning of this vote: to vote *placet* to the proposal meant to vote in favour of adjourning discussion (in favour of a revised schema). To vote *non placet* was to indicate acceptance of the schema (at least *iuxta modum*) and it would be necessary to take up discussion of the text chapter by chapter.

An American conducted a *Gallup poll* on the outcome of the vote.

Fr Tucci told me that this proposal had come from Cardinal Ruffini. It will reveal the proportion of those who are in favour of rejecting the schema. A TWO THIRDS MAJORITY IS REQUIRED FOR THE SCHEMA TO BE REJECTED. He told me that if the proposal had been simply 'do you want to continue the discussion?' there would have been a quite different majority. Hence the way the proposal is worded is slanted towards the desired proof that only very few of the Fathers are against the schema.

But I am convinced that a great many of the Fathers will not understand the meaning of the vote they are being asked for and will vote in this state of semi-ignorance.

---

1. Enrico Nicodemo, Archbishop of Bari, member of the Commission on the Discipline of the Clergy, *AS* I/III, 218–220.
2. *AS* I/III, 220.
3. President of this particular General Congregation, *AS* I/III, 220.
4. *AS* I/III, 223.

The general discussion continued. The one next called upon to speak was not there.[1]

Sigaud[2] (Brazil): *schema placet. Perficiendum* [needs to be improved]. It contains relics of Modernism etc. Very tedious. Not much listened to. Many of the Fathers no longer in their places.

Quarracino[3] (who came back at that moment): *non placet,* and in favour of the Ancel proposal.

Cardinal Frings[4] explained at this point, but it was too late, now the voting had taken place, that a *placet* vote means that the discussion will be interrupted UNTIL A NEW TEXT HAS BEEN SUBMITTED TO THE COUNCIL.

Carli:[5] the schemas presented by the Pope should be discussed chapter by chapter. One can only reject the schema by rejecting each one of its articles. The schema presented by the Pope is on the table [ ]. And he pointed out that rejection would be contravening several articles of the regulations.

Mgr Costantini[6] replied yet again to the criticisms made of the schema. But he opted for the formula: a single source coming to us by means of two streams.

Fr Fernandez, OP:[7] commented on the pastoral and ecumenical character of the text (VERY tedious). Priority of clarity of doctrine.

Barbetta[8] (Italian): it is impossible that the schema reflects the thinking of only one school when one thinks of the composition of the Commission and the discussions of the Central Commission. Praise for the schema. (Listened to, though very tedious and very long-winded).

Ferro:[9] (*Rheginensis,* Italian): if a few corrections are made, and with a pastoral *proemium, placet.* Primacy of the truth. He quoted *Humani generis* against irenicism. Critical of the idea of a replacement schema: oratorical, speaking of the salvation of all human beings. Perfect example of the Italian outlook on things.

---

1. It was Antonio Quarrracino, Bishop of Nueve de Julio (Argentina).
2. Geraldo de Proença Sigaud, Archbishop of Diamantina (Brazil), *AS* I/III, 224–227.
3. *AS* I/III, 230-231.
4. Neither the *Acta* nor Giovanni Caprile, SJ, in *Il concilio Vaticano II, Il primo periodo 1962–1963* (Rome, 1968), 175–179, mention this intervention by the President of the General Congregation.
5. Luigi Carli, Bishop of Segni, (Italy), appointed member of the Commission on Bishops and the Government of Dioceses at the end of the First Session, *AS* I/III, 231–232.
6. *AS* I/III, 234–235.
7. *AS* I/III, 236–237.
8. Giulio Barbetta, titular bishop, *AS* I/III, 241–242.
9. Giovanni Ferro, Archbishop of Reggio-Calabria (Italy), *AS* I/III, 242–244.

Franić[1] (Split): *placet iuxta modum*. Against mention of ecumenism: this Council is not a Council of union. We must not be content with positively proclaiming the truth but also point out errors.

It has been said that the schema is contrary to the Eastern mentality. But the seven Councils condemned errors. We are the *teaching* Church. There should be a pastoral *proemium* and some emendations of detail.

Felici,[2] General Secretary: the result of the voting will be announced tomorrow. In the meantime, we will discuss Chapter I of the schema. If the vote turns out to have been to reject the schema, discussion of the means of communication will commence on Friday.

Discussion of Chapter I began at once. A list was given of those registered to speak.

Tisserant:[3] there is much confusion in Chapter 1. He made, very quickly, a series of remarks and criticisms of detail, often in the form of questions.

Ruffini:[4] why does it not begin with a definition of Revelation? He defended the *duo fontes* [two sources] in paragraph 4 because to say that we can find revelation either in Scripture or in Tradition, amounts to saying that there are two sources of Revelation. The magisterium *IS* the *regula regulans* [the rule that rules], to which we give our faith, it is not the *regula regulata (a Scriptura)* [the rule that is ruled (by Scripture)]. He quoted St Augustine's *Ego Evangelio non crederem* . . .[5]

Mgr Jacono[6] (Padua, I think): No. 5, paragraph 10–11. He quoted *Humani Generis*. Hardly anyone was listening.

A Monsignor from the Rota, my neighbour, told me about the vote: more than half had voted against the schema, but not the [required] two-thirds. They want to have recourse to the Pope. That is why the results have not been announced.

But, just when everyone was packing up to go, the results of the vote were announced:[7]

Number of Voters	Placet (hence in favour of rejection)	Non placet	Void
2,209	1,368	822	19

I would never have believed that.

1. *AS* I/III, 244–246.
2. *AS* I/III, 248.
3. *AS* I/III, 248–249.
4. *AS* I/III, 249–251.
5. The *Acta* cite the full phrase: '*Ego Evangelio non crederem nisi me catholicae Ecclesiae commoverert auctoritas*' (I would not believe in the Gospel unless the authority of the Church forced me to do so).
6. Vincenzo M Jacono, Italian titular bishop, *AS* I/III, 252–254.
7. *AS* I/III, 254–255.

Mgr Guerry told me that a number of bishops had voted *non placet* believing that to vote *placet* meant deferring discussion of the schema *sine die* [indefinitely], that is to say burying it. They would have voted differently if it had been explained to begin with that *non placet* meant that a revised schema would be presented, when ready.

'It can be said that with this vote on 20 November, the age of the Counter Reformation came to an end and that a new age, with unforeseeable consequences, was beginning for Christendom' Please God! (R Rouquette, Bilan du Concile, *Etudes*, January, 1963: 94–111, 104).

3 pm that afternoon, meeting of the French bishops from the group studying tradition. We prepared: 1) an appeal to the Council's administrative tribunal, because this morning's vote has some aspects that were very doubtful, if not actually contrary to the regulation. It had been said at first that *placet* meant '*interrumpenda discussio*' [the discussion is to be adjourned], then, according to Mgr Felici, '*interrumpenda sine die*' [to be adjourned indefinitely]; the meaning of the vote had then been explained by Cardinal Ruffini. Later, AFTER THE VOTING HAD TAKEN PLACE, Cardinal Frings, who was presiding, had explained that the vote meant '*interrumpenda donec textus noviter conficiatur*' [the discussion is to be adjourned until a new text has been produced]. By then, many people had already voted who would have voted differently had this explanation been given earlier.

2) These were some of the interventions in the discussion:

Mgr Pourchet on the idea of two sources (against).
Mgr Desmazières[1] calling for a mention of the living Tradition (I prepared his text).
Mgr Maziers on the magisterium as BOUND to the norms and deposit and as a servant.
Mgr Boillon on the role of the faithful in the preservation and development of the Tradition.

At 5 pm, I went to the weekly meeting of the Observers in the Hotel Columbus. I explained to them with total frankness but, I hope, with discretion and delicacy, what is behind the tension that they have perceived over the past five days at the Council.

Mgr Heenan did not fully agree. I am very disappointed in him.

Mgr Willebrands explained why the Theological Commission had refused the idea of a joint commission: it is because it is concerned with PRINCIPLES, whereas the Secretariat is concerned with PRACTICAL questions.

Always this false distinction between categories which I perceived from the very first day as *THE* most decisive vice of the institution.

1.　Stéphane Desmazières, Auxiliary Bishop of Bordeaux.

Wednesday 21 November 1962
Before the session, Mgr Vial [1] (Auxiliary in Nevers) gave me a document which had been distributed yesterday morning to all the Italian bishops and which, in four closely written pages, clarified the two following points:

1) *Super duos fontes revelationis est unica origo, scilicet Verbum Dei* [*above the two sources of revelation there is only one origin, namely the Word of God*] because the Word of God is known only through Scripture if one regards it as inspired, which the Church does.

2) *Est evolutio in doctrina Pontificum ab encyclica* Providentissimus Deus *ad aliam* Divino Afflante Spiritu [there is a development in the teaching of the popes from the encyclical *Providentissimus Deus* to the encyclical *Divino Afflante Spiritu*] (history of Roman interventions, with an attack on the current dangers in exegesis, which threaten to undermine the absolute inerrancy of Scripture).

The General Secretary, Mgr Felici,[2] *de mandato* [at the command of] the Secretary of State:[3] yesterday's vote has left some uncertainty . . . It will first be necessary to correct the schema and its deficiencies. The Pope has decided to entrust the work to a commission of cardinals and members of the Theological Commission and of the Secretariat. The schema will then be presented to the Council again. In the meantime, the Council can start work on another schema: work on the schema on the means of communication will begin on Friday.

> Mgr Guano[4] (Italy): the following points should be better expressed in the Introduction:
> 1) *Deus hominibus loquitur per suam Verbum* [God speaks to human beings through his Word], above all through Christ.
> 2) Christ is *imago et vox Patris, unicus magister et via ad Patrem* [the image and voice of the Father, the one teacher and way to the Father] (through his whole person and all his deeds).
> 3) *Deus Verbum suum loqui vult* [God wishes to utter his Word], not to some human beings but to the whole of humanity. Through the Prophets, transmitted by the Church to all humanity.
> 4) *Plurimis viis fit: per vocem prophetarum*
> *per totam vitam Ecclesiae*
> [This is done in various ways: through the voice of the Prophets, through the whole life of the Church]
> but among these ways, Scripture has pride of place.
> 5) *Hominibus patefacere via salutis* [To open to human beings the way of salvation].

---

1. Michel Vial, Coadjutor of Nevers, then Bishop of Nevers in December 1963.
2. *AS* I/III, 259–260.
3. Cicognani.
4. *AS* I/III, 260–261.

6) *Tota vita Christiana*

   Tota vita Ecclesiae de Verbo Dei vivunt

in servitium Verbi Dei positae sunt. [The whole of the Christian life and the whole life of the Church have life from the Word of God: they are established to serve the Word of God].

7) *Munus episcoporum* [the bishops' office] does not diminish the role of the exegetes . . .

Martínez[1] (Zamora): on Chapter 1.

1) What is needed is a general introduction to all the dogmatic constitutions, stating in what sense the Council is proclaiming these constitutions: a pastoral intention. The Council is addressing the people of our own time. Specify the theological note.

2) The title *De fontibus* is not good. It does not cover the entire contents of the chapter. These words do not belong to the conciliar vocabulary. They are contrary to the ecumenical purpose of the Council.

Suggests: *De Revelatione eiusque transmissione* [on Revelation and its transmission].

3) Begin with the idea of Revelation, and not in purely intellectual terms.

4) He proposed an alternative text for No. 1 of the chapter, which is too dry.

5) Concerning No. 2.

Dom Butler OSB:[2] agreed with what was said yesterday by Ruffini: state first the idea of Revelation (along the lines suggested by Mgr Guano).

This schema *'non adequate redolet consensum scholarum catholicarum'* [does not sufficiently reflect the consensus among Catholic schools of thought] nor does it reflect the Eastern Tradition. And this is a deeper question than that of style or some pastoral ornamentation. Moreover, it touches matters which are being legitimately discussed. We must not simply substitute the declarations of a different school of thought, but rather produce something acceptable to all.

Change the title to: *De revelatione et transmissione eius* [on Revelation and its transmission].

And for Chapter 1: *De Traditione et Sacra Scriptura* [on Tradition and Sacred Scripture].

Page 9, No. 4, I. 16 ff: substitute a text (which he provided) which makes room for revelation through the LIFE of Christ, because the incarnate Christ IS the Word of God.

---

1. Eduardo Martínez Gonzáles, Bishop of Zamora (Spain), *AS* I/III, 261–263.
2. *AS* I/III, 264–265.

There was a reference yesterday to Catholic exegetes. He expressed his indignation at the suspicion manifested concerning them, and referred to the Biblical Institute and Biblical School in Jerusalem.

Tso-Huan[1]? (also: *observatores* [included the Observers in his address]): There must be a reference to the original Revelation or *Protorevelatio*: before Abraham. He suggested a formula and explained AT GREAT LENGTH the significance of his suggestion. Tiring to listen to.

Hermaniuk:[2] 1) the title will not do: it does not refer to the sole author of this revelation, who is thus the *unicus fons* [single source]. Say only *De Revelatione divina*, and start by explaining the concept of Revelation; 2) in No. 3, line 17: there should be a reference to the living proclamation BEFORE it was written down. Provided a text; 3) No. 4, line 31; 4) page 10, line [ ] (paper prepared for the discussion of the schema section by section; but there is no longer question of that!!!).

Mgr Rupp,[3] *nomine proprio* [speaking in his own name]! Approved three things: THE DISTINCTION BETWEEN TRADITION AND THE MAGISTERIUM.

the mention of *praxis Ecclesiae* [the practice of the Church]

textus rationem habet genuinae naturae theologiae[4] *modus loquendi longe differt a virili stylo* [the text is couched in an authentically theological style; the way it is written differs greatly from the vigorous style] of the Council of Trent and Vatican I.

Do not claim that the bishops have always preached the pure Gospel. And he suggested two corrections of detail. Quote from Melchior Cano.[5] He would like a quotation from, or a mention of, Vincent of Lerins.[6]

Mgr Marty:[7] made some remarks for the revised version of the schema in relation to Nos. 4, 5, and 6.

Express the content of the entire chapter in the light of the mystery of the Church which is 'Christ made widely known and communicated'. The Church IS the Tradition (handing on} OF CHRIST himself, and not only of his teaching. Holy Scripture bears witness to this Tradition, which transmits the same reality as the Apostles did. This tradition,

---

1. Vito Chang Tso-Huan, titular bishop, *AS* I/III, 267–269.
2. *AS* I/III, 269–270.
3. Jean Rupp, Bishop of Monaco, *AS* I/III, 271.
4. Congar had written *geminae scientiae theologia*; the text is that given in the *Acta* of the Council.
5. Spanish Dominican theologian (1509–1560).
6. Fifth century monk and theologian.
7. *AS* I/III, 273–274.

under the impulse of the Holy Spirit, is the work of the whole Church. (He made an effort to give his paper slowly and clearly: but his manner of speaking was very artificial.)

This presentation sought to be be ecumenical and pastoral.

I took a walk round the side aisles. Many of the bishops were there. All those I saw were looking pleased and approached me to congratulate me as if the victory were mine personally. A relaxed atmosphere everywhere (among those I actually saw).

I heard several interventions (Mgr Veuillot[1] on the necessity for a paragraph on Revelation and the Word of God). But I was not listening attentively, indeed was quite distracted. Many bishops were doing the same.

The meeting ended shortly after midday. Friday, discussion of the schema on the means of communication. I shall not go, but I am going to prepare a paper which Mgr de Provenchères has agreed to read.

I had my blood pressure taken: 10/7. *'Bassa'* [low].

Brother Clément de Bourmont,[2] a Trappist, had organised a lunch for former inmates of IV D[3] = eight bishops and Guitton, who has returned, having got himself appointed by the Académie (more or less) and, here, aggregated to the Observers.[4]

Visit from an American Sulpician, Brown.[5] The same name, which is very common, denotes men who are very different. This man, who is an exegete and Vice-President of the Catholic Biblical Society of the USA, is very open. He is overjoyed at what has happened. He told me that the bishops, not only those from the USA but all the English-speaking bishops, have greatly changed their ideas in the past few days. Before, they had, on the whole, no idea of Scripture and of current biblical studies. In the past few weeks they have attended a number of lectures, some of which were on biblical matters. They glimpse the situation and are interested in it.

Something of the kind is also true, to some degree, of some of the French bishops. Fr Daniélou, who has a lively sense of great things coming to pass, does not want to let this moment and this opportunity pass us by.

He envisages in this sense the work that we are doing with the bishops in small groups, and would like to continue it in one way or another in France, after the Council. Interesting idea, and possibly a fertile one.

---

1. *AS* I/III, 285–286.
2. A monk from the Cistercian abbey of Bellefontaine (Maine-et-Loire); secretary to the Abbot General of the Cistercians, he was living at the abbey of Tre-Fontane.
3. Congar had been a prisoner at Oflag IV D.
4. Congar added to the typescript 'likeable'.
5. Raymond E Brown, a specialist in St John: he was later a member of the Pontifical Biblical Commission.

There can be no doubt that the Council will have had this effect of forcing Rome to discover catholicity (cf *ICI*, 15, XI 1962: 8); and forcing the bishops to discover many things, ideas, currents of thought.

At 4 pm, I took a taxi to go to RAI (the Italian Radio station) where I was to prepare the broadcast for Sunday with some of the Observers. There was a mistake, perhaps on my own part? I found no-one there and returned here.

This evening, at 9 pm, at *Civiltà Cattolica*, at the invitation of Frs Tucci, Rouquette and Bréchet. A few bits and pieces, details about this and that, about some incident or other. Nothing very much.

Fr Fransen showed me, at *Civiltà Cattolica*, (21.IX.62), the issue of *La Libre Belgique* for 16 November 1962, where the leading article is by Fr Stiernon, AA, (from the Lateran):[1] an article against the Geiselmann-Rahner-Holstein position in which I too am implicated. So, there really is an offensive in favour of the two sources and of the old *partim-partim* position.[2]

Thursday 22 November 1962

I spent most of the morning preparing the lecture that I have to give IN LATIN in the Capranica seminary. To prepare it in French would have taken me about ten minutes: to do it in Latin, I needed more than three hours. When I have so much to do and the days keep going by without my making any progress.

It is being said on various sides that Cardinal Ottaviani has offered his resignation to the Pope, who has refused it. The rumour seems to be quite well founded. It is also said, but this seems less reliable, that Cardinal Ottaviani has asked for Karl Rahner to be sent away from Rome.

From 10.45 am to 12.30 pm at the Waldensian Faculty with H Roux, Míguez,[3] Thurian and, briefly, Cullmann. Continuation of Tuesday evening on Tradition, Revelation, Faith, natural knowledge, Magisterium. It does one good to talk theology!

Afternoon, Fr Rieber Mohn[4] (interview for Northern newspapers).

At 5 pm at the Gregorianum for a solemn defence of a doctoral thesis for the Biblical Institute: Fr Lohfink.[5] The Biblical Institute turned it into a display of support for him. Great number of people there, a large number of cardinals and quite a few bishops. It is a new victory for Cardinal Bea. The Council is Cardinal

---

1. Daniel Stiernon, AA, Professor of Eastern Theology at the Lateran, but also teaching at the Urbanianum: collaborator of Boyer for the journal *Unitas*.
2. See page 181, note 7.
3. Pastor José Míguez Bonino, Rector of the Evangelical Faculty of Theology in Buenos Aires, was an Observer appointed by the World Council of Methodists: he was later to become Secretary General of the World Council of Churches.
4. The Norwegian Hallvard Rieber Mohn, OP, of the Province of France; his apostolate was in the world of the media in Oslo.
5. Norbert Lohfink, SJ, was subsequently to teach Old Testament exegesis at the Sankt Georgen Jesuit Faculty of Theology in Frankfurt and at the Pontifical Biblical Institute.

Bea's Council! I left the session at 5.50 pm as I was due to give my lecture at the Capranica at 6 pm. The Capranica is one of the two seminaries for Rome: about forty seminarians. I spoke about ecumenism, in Latin. Latin cramps my ability to express nuances; it does not lend itself to nuance, even for those whose know it better than I do. Certainly also, in spite of my careful preparation, I had devoted all my effort and my time to preparing the material, and had no time or effort left to revise it from the psychological point of view, with the result that I am not sure that I managed to do this evening what I generally try to do in a sermon or a lecture: to meet the audience where they are from the point of view of ideas and outlook, and to lead them where I want them to go. My lecture was too abrupt, perhaps too allusive, although I did quote concrete examples and instances.

About two thirds of the way through my lecture, three bishops came in, perhaps having come from the Gregorianum. One of them took the floor after I had finished. I later learned that it was the bishop of Benevento[1] in Italy. In a stentorian voice, made all the louder by passion, hammering out his words, shouting in a violent paroxysm, he attacked my lecture. All that is vague and amounts to nothing, he said. Only one thing is true: the affirmation of doctrine in all its force and intransigence. The manuals are perfect, not superficial: they contain what is needed: clear, cut and dried, unambiguous formulas. This is what determines everything, this is the Magisterium. The Angel of Benevento said: one speaks of a presence of Christ in the Church. There is only one, it is the Magisterium. And when I replied that there is in the Church an experience of the mystery of Christ, he bellowed: Experience! That was talked about at the beginning of the century, it is Modernism!!! With what result? Between the Protestants or the Orthodox and ourselves there is a 'magnum chaos' [great chasm][2] which is absolutely impassable. Moreover, what have these ecumenists achieved? And the Bishop of Benevento challenged me to give one example of expositions written in the spirit which I had advocated, on inerrancy, historicity, etc.

To begin with, I replied as calmly as I could, and to the extent that the shouter did not drown my voice by his growling. Then I started to attack, and, in my turn, I challenged him to give a single case where I had watered down the truth. He said nothing. There was thunderous applause, which lasted several minutes. Then the questions resumed. I perceived that they were prompted mostly by a scholastic and not very well informed spirit. One of the directors of the house seemed to me to be very close to the bishop of Benevento. Moreover, he clings absolutely to the idea, which I know and say to be false, according to which Protestants might join us today on account of their fear of communism: we are resisting communism; they know we are strong and want to take advantage of our strength.

The seminarians displayed their opposition to the Bishop of Benevento by applauding me enthusiastically. But I was not satisfied and was left with a bad

---

1. Raffaele Calabria, Archbishop of Benevento; Congar added to the typescript 'Calabria'
2. Luke 16:26.

impression. I knew, in accepting the invitation, that I was taking a risk. I thought I could do so in the present climate. Moreover, I think that one has to take risks. The cause is well worth it. It is worthwhile to endure some unpleasantness in order to bring the ecumenical word to an audience which is a seed-bed of future members of the Roman bureaucracies. I am quite willing to endure even more such unpleasantness for the holy cause of reunion. The Italians, moreover, are not disturbed. They content themselves with saying of the bishop of Benevento, that he is from the south, that is what they are like down there, always violent…

Friday, 23rd November: Saint Clement.

Friday, 23rd November: Saint Clement.

I did not go to St Peter's. I sent Mgr de Provenchères a paper which I had prepared for him on the schema on the Means of Communication. The meeting had not been been very interesting. Everyone finds the proposed text too long. It has been announced that the next text to be discussed would be the *De Beata Virgine Maria*, and then the *De unitate Ecclesiae* [on the unity of the Church]. These texts were distributed. But, as regards the *De unitate*, the Eastern Commission itself, which had prepared the text, acknowledged that the Secretariat for Unity would have to bring it into harmony with the text prepared by the Secretariat. There is even a third text, the one produced by the Theological Commission on Ecumenism. The further I go, the more I find that the preparation of the Council has been totally haphazard, not to say hopelessly inadequate, and that in matters or aspects that could easily have been foreseen. How is it that that the things that one is having to do now were not done BEFORE the Council? One would not have acted differently if one had WANTED to display the faults in the system by their results: because it has been clear to me from the very first day that there would be several projects on the same subject, thanks to the lack of co-operation between the different Commissions!

At 3 pm, working session with the group of bishops: at the Biblicum, as Fr General does not want any meetings held at the Angelicum: on account of what Parente said to the Theological Commission (see above, 14 November).

In the evening, visit from Mr Sencourt, who has nothing to do except visit people . . .

Saturday 24th November

Saturday 24th November

I did not go to St Peter's and tried to type some pages of my *Tradition*.[1] The Congregation at St Peter's had not been interesting. Cardinal Léger[2] said, however, that one must not speak of the RIGHTS of the Church, but of its service. The Africans also insisted on being of service to men and women.

---

1. See above, p 99, note 1.
2. *AS* I/III, 460–462.

Visit from Mr Noel Howard Salter[1] an Englishman working as assistant secretary general in the European organisations. A Congregationalist, 'converted' at Taizé, where he has his spiritual home, he devotes himself to Christian action, what we would call Catholic Action, among the European functionaries working in Paris (about two thousand people). What a lovely person. Yesterday he dined with several French bishops at the lodgings of the Brothers of Taizé. He told me: if my compatriots were to see and hear what I am seeing and hearing, unity would soon come about.

O my God, who have shown me since 1929–1930 that if the Church were to change her face, if she were simply to show her TRUE face, if she were quite simply the Church, everything would become possible on the road to unity: raise up effective workers, pure and courageous, for this work which you have undertaken and which I beg you not to abandon!

Cullmann Press Conference yesterday evening. The English text *hic* [attached].[2]

Sunday 25 November *1962*

In the morning, French television with the Observers.[3] Programme attached.[4] We were in direct contact with the people in Paris, who asked us questions to which we replied there and then, the viewers seeing all this in front of them at the very same time. All the same it is quite sensational! Our great nephews and nieces will see things even more sensational!

At 1 pm, lunch with His Beatitude Maximos IV, Mgr Edelby, Mgr the Melkite Archbishop of Beirut.[5] I did not learn much. Above all that Cardinal Ottaviani is not attending the general Congregations. EVERYONE speaks of him as being the one chiefly under accusation, and the one chiefly defeated at the Council which, by contrast, is being described as turning into Cardinal Bea's Council.

Afterwards, conversation with two American priests, bishops' theologians. They asked me questions, mostly about the membership of the Church.

Fenton does not represent the generality of American theologians. He has few disciples. He is to speak tomorrow to the USA bishops: so much the better, the two priests said to me: they will see what a pathetic person he is! He is VERY close to Cardinal Ottaviani (again: both accused and victim) and also to the Apostolic Delegate, Mgr Vagnozzi, who is very narrow, keeps the American bishops under surveillance, intervenes all over the place and tries to point everything along

---

1. Noel H Salter, who worked for the Western European Union Assembly in Paris, organised a conference in which Congar was to take part on the following 22 January (cf page 253 below) with Roger Schutz.
2. Cf The French text in *La Documentation Catholique*, 16 December 1962, col 1619-1626.
3. This broadcast proved quite a sensation, and the Pope asked to see it.
4. Questions on the Missions were addressed to Congar and to H Roux.
5. Philippe Nabaa, who was also sub-secretary to the Council.

'Holy Office' lines. Here in Rome, he does not give the American bishops an inch of slack, and continues to watch what they do.

The American bishops are intimidated. They dare not speak. They feel inadequate as theologians.

They have developed a lot here, above all in biblical matters, thanks to the lectures of a Passionist Father.[1]

In the evening, dinner at Laurentin's place with l'abbé Poupard. The latter gave us a lot of information concerning:

1) The Italian episcopate, which is systematically kept in a state of fragmentation, in a siege mentality: the Germans and the French are placing 'the faith', 'doctrine' in danger: the Italians must protect it, with the Pope.

2) Ottaviani-Tromp. Fr Tromp is saying that once the Council fever has abated, it will be necessary to put everything back in order. For him, for Ruffini, to reject the schemas of the Theological Commission is to abandon the Church to chaos.

L'abbé Poupard also told me this, which he heard from the person concerned, a black bishop.[2] Mgr Parente met this black bishop after the vote and said to him: when you were a student in Rome, you did not have these ideas. But now you are under the thumb of the 'wicked' French theologians, you are not free. The black bishop replied: when I was a student in Rome, I was under the influence of the good Italian theologians. I was not free. I was not myself.

Laurentin has seen (and partly copied) the record of meeting of the Central Commission. It begins with a declaration by Ottaviani stating that the Central Commission has no doctrinal authority; it is the Theological Commission (= the 'Holy Office') which judges doctrine: that is why it has nothing to receive from the other Commissions, still less from the Secretariat,[3] but it must appraise their teaching.

Really and truly, it is a battle between the almighty reign of the 'Holy Office' and the Church, which is alive and is in apostolic contact with the world.

Monday 26 November 1962

Although I knew that there was a danger of not getting beyond discussion of the cinema and radio (in spite of what Patriarch Maximos IV had told me yesterday), I went to St Peter's in order to resume contact with some of the bishops and *periti*.

Health, ability to walk: not at all good.

I also saw the Observers for a moment, then Thils, Mgr McGrath, Feiner, Lubac, Mgr Philips. The latter is fairly optimistic. He thinks that there is a possibility that his revision of the schema *De Ecclesia* will be taken into consideration. The

---

1. The exegete Barnabas Ahern: appointed a Council expert during the First Session. He was also to collaborate with the Secretariat for Unity.
2. Congar added to the typescript 'Zoa'.
3. Congar added to the typescript 'Bea'.

Ottaviani party know about it and have photocopied it. But he would say that it is possible that the schema will be amended in this sense. By contrast, the other people I spoke to were very uneasy:

1) The Joint Commission of the Theology Commission and the Secretariat met yesterday. Cardinal Bea spoke very little; Cardinal Ottaviani was in charge. In the space of an hour, he secured agreement on the principles according to which one will work: it was all done very quickly. Cardinal Ottaviani secured agreement for the idea of simply working on the basis of the framework of the five chapters of the official schema, that is, the same framework as that schema. His idea is simply to make some amendments to that. That would not do and, if that is what is done, the Council would have to REJECT it a second time!

However, with Canon Thils, we went to see Mgr Garrone at about 10.15 am: he was not in St Peter's this morning, as he was working on a text *De Revelatione*[1] for one of the sub-commissions of the Joint Commission. He is less pessimistic. He believes that it is in the sub-commissions that the work will be done and that there are in these some strong-minded bishops; it will be possible to get accepted what must be accepted.

There were seven *periti* from the Theological Commission at yesterday's meeting: Fenton, Balić, van den Eynde, Kerrigan and three others whose names they could not give me. So I have been eliminated by this Commission, which is not without significance. But the bishops on the sub-commission are at liberty to consult the *periti*.

Before I left St Peter's, I heard Mgr Felici[2] announce:

1) Tomorrow there will be a vote on the schema on radio-cinema, on a text which will be distributed.

2) Immediately afterwards the general discussion of the schema *Ut sint unum*[3] will commence. However, this text needs to be combined with the text produced by the Secretariat which has not yet been distributed.

3) At the request of a number of the Fathers, the discussion *De Ecclesia* will begin soon. Those who wish to speak should put their names down. The constitution on the Virgin Mary will be treated as one of the chapters of *De Ecclesia*, '*quia est membrum corporis mystici*' [because she is a member of the Mystical Body] (*sic!*).

The whole thing represents an inconceivable incoherence and casualness of procedure. Incoherence: different things are announced one after another, there is no agenda. The preparation had also been done in an incoherent manner: it was quite well known that there were three different texts concerning unity: they have not managed to harmonise them. Incoherence and casualness yet again: the

---

1. He was preparing a foreword for the new schema on Revelation.
2. *AS* I/III, 501–502.
3. 'That they may be one': this is the schema *De Ecclesiae unitate* [on the unity of the Church] prepared by the Preparatory Commission on the Eastern Churches, also entitled, from the opening words of the text, *Ut omnes unum sint* [that all might be one].

bishops are called upon to discuss from tomorrow onwards texts which were only distributed to them three days ago and which they simply have not had the time to study.

Fr de Lubac thinks that this is all deliberate: THEY DO NOT WANT the bishops to have the time to study the texts seriously with the theologians. Fr de Lubac also fears that, between the first Session and the next, the people in Rome will claim to revise the texts, in appearance making some concessions to what the Council has called for, but in fact in accordance with the Curia's wishes. I have been told by several people that Fr Tromp has said that, as regards *De fontibus*, a new text would be produced which would be the twin of the first one.

Lubac thinks that a CONCILIAR organism should be created which, between the First and Second Sessions, will keep an eye on the Commissions in the course of the work in Commission which will be done in Rome, so as to preserve the spirit of the First Session, and inform or even warn the bishops about what is being done, about whether things are being done in fidelity to their will or in betrayal of it.

Yes, but 1) nothing like this is envisaged.

2) Who will be both strong enough and clear-minded enough, have the time, and be approved of by both sides, in order to perform such a task?

We are all at sea.

But I see that a Council goes through phases of shadow and sunlight. I believe in the Holy Spirit. He makes use of people.

An attempt is to be made to do, in a few days, a job that would require weeks to do. 'Our help is in the name of the Lord, who made heaven and earth' [Ps 123:8].

I left the Council shortly after 10.00 am. I have been told that the series of interventions on the means of communication was broken off and that a start was made on *De Unitate*.[1] Reading of the presentation report by the secretary;[2] then an intervention by Cardinal Liénart[3] (some incidental remarks and the comment that the schema speaks only of the Eastern Churches), then by Cardinals Ruffini,[4] Browne[5] and Bacci.[6] (Ruffini and Browne: one cannot speak of *unitas ecclesiae instauranda* [the unity of the Church needing to be restored]. It is true, and I would not have written that. *Unitas inter christianos* [Unity among Christians], yes, *uni-*

1. *AS* I/III, 527.
2. After an introductory speech by Cardinal Cicognani, President of the Conciliar Commission on the Eastern Churches (*AS* I/III, 546–547), the secretary of that Commission, Athanasius G Welykyj, a Basilian monk of St Josaphat, presented the schema, *AS* I/III, 548–553.
3. *AS* I/III, 554–555.
4. *AS* I/III, 555–557.
5. *AS* I/III, 559–560.
6. *AS* I/III, 558–559.

tas eorum qui nomine christiano insigniuntur [unity among those who bear the name of Christians].)

At 3 pm, meeting of the working group of French bishops at the Biblicum. Study of the schema *De Virgine Maria*. Very good presentation by Laurentin.

At 4.40 pm, I was taken to Canadian TV. The Father who interviewed me told me that Cardinal Léger had had a half-hour audience with the Pope the day before yesterday. The Holy Father had said to him: 'They have not understood me'. They have not understood what I wanted in summoning this Council (to bring the Church up to date). And, the next day, yesterday, he sent Cardinal Léger a hand-written letter and a pectoral cross.

At 6.00 pm, I was at the Belgian College where I could participate in only the last half-hour of the discussion of the reworking of *De Ecclesia* by Mgr Philips. Rahner, Daniélou and ? were on their way out. That left Ratzinger, Onclin,[1] Lécuyer. Mgr Philips is quite hopeful that his text will be accepted.

At 6.30 pm, lecture to the students at the Belgian College (on the laity) followed by dinner.

Tuesday 27 November 1962

At St Peter's. Felici:[2] a number of bishops have asked that the Second Session should begin not in May but on 8 September 1963.

There will be a vote for general approval of the Constitution on the Means of Communication, so that a commission can shorten it and produce a practical directory.

This vote:

No of voters	*placet*	*non placet*	void
2,160	2,138	15	7

Statement from the Eastern Commission:

1) the title could be changed to indicate that it concerns only the Easterners;

2) the doctrinal sections are meant only to make plain the conditions arising from the separation in the East, and to provide a basis for the practical applications of the second part;

3) the decree is addressed to Catholics in order to give them the means of working for union with the Orthodox.

---

1. Willy Onclin, priest of the diocese of Liège, Professor of Canon Law at the University of Louvain; a Council expert, he was very involved in the Commission on Bishops and the Government of Dioceses; in November 1965 he was appointed assistant secretary of the Commission on the Revision of the Code of Canon Law.

2. *AS* I/III, 613–615.

Cardinal de Barros Câmara[1] (Rio de Janeiro, Brazil): agreed with what was said yesterday. There will be no reunion without a clear declaration of Catholic doctrine. Add to it psychological means: that the Orthodox see unity amongst ourselves. And take into account the special problems of the Easterners.

Maximos IV:[2] Generally speaking, it provides a good basis. However, four comments:

1) Concerning its spirit: Nos. 5 to 12, especially, are expressed too partially and peremptorily. The prominent role is given too exclusively to Rome. Rome counts for nothing in Eastern Christianity, which is descended from the Apostles and the Fathers. In the East, it is necessary to speak first of all of the pastoral collegiality of the Church: then of the Papacy as a basis and centre of this collegiality.

2) There are three schemas on the same subject. 'When there are too many cooks in the kitchen, the food gets burnt' (Arabian proverb). A joint commission should create a single text out of the three.

3) After some general remarks, the schema in fact speaks only of ways of achieving union with the East. In fact, after these common general principles, a special section on the Orthodox is essential. Union is of vital importance for Eastern Catholics: they form a single family with the Orthodox.

Text then read in Latin by Mgr Hakim[3] (who had practised it with me before the session).

Mgr Principi[4] (Italy): (*dilecti observatores*: [my dear Observers]): he recalled the situation at the time of Leo XIII and Solovyov.[5] Do not begin making the same mistakes again. Therefore, postpone discussion of this schema until after that *De Ecclesia*.

Pawłowski[6] (Poland): Prudence! Safety! Sobriety!

He quoted *Humani Generis* on irenicism.

The Latin Church is too often blamed for being responsible for the separation . . . Mary will bring the union about.

Mgr Nabaa[7] (Lebanon) (*observatores carissimi*): *placet tantum iuxta modum* [(most dear observers): I approve it, but only subject to modification]. Not everything in it is well said. Its importance is such that it must be improved considerably.

---

1. *AS* I/III, 615–616.
2. *AS* I/III, 616–618.
3. *AS* I/III, 618–620.
4. Primo Principi, titular archbishop from the Curia, *AS* I/III, 621–622.
5. Vladimir Solovyov, a Russian Orthodox thinker; in his drawing near to Catholicism, he was a forerunner of the ecumenical movement.
6. Antoni Pawłowski, Bishop of Włocławek, *AS* I/III, 622–624.
7. *AS* I/III, 624–627.

1) it speaks only of the East, but that involves special conditions;
2) he suggested ways . . .

Mgr Guano came to look for me in my tribune and took me away. In the bar, I saw Mgr Sauvage,[1] Elchinger, then Roberts and a Czech bishop, Mgr Tomášek,[2] who want something on peace, war and the bomb. The latter told me that the Polish and Czech governments to some extent issued their passports on condition that the Council does something for peace.

I made the acquaintance of Mgr Guano, Bishop of Livorno, to whom I had sent a note about his intervention a few days ago. He is very open. He is chaplain general to the intellectuals.

In addition I met Fr Villain who has also succeeded in getting in. When I returned to my tribune, Cardinal Bea was speaking.[3] I heard only the end of his intervention. I have been told that Mgr Nabaa[4] ended his intervention, which was becoming very interesting, by saying: We should begin by giving to ourselves and to our synods real powers. Then we can be an example and a means of attraction for the Orthodox.

Vuccino:[5] we could have avoided a great many of the imperfections and the waste of time if we had worked together instead of preparing three separate schemas. His personal experience in the Balkans. The schema was based on our own teaching which, far from attracting the Orthodox, repels them: it is too juridical. We need to lay stress on ideas: the Good Shepherd → *diaconia*, SERVICE, not rights and domination.

Mgr Fernández,[6] Spanish: There is only one Church! We cannot speak of *ecclesiae* [churches].

Edelby[7] (very well given, and listened to): he spoke only about the General Introduction, especially Nos. 1–11. Although the body of the schema contains a lot of good things, this General Introduction is very incomplete and not always accurate. There are points arising from the schema *De Ecclesia* in which the consequences for reunion are not taken into account.

---

1. Jean Sauvage, Bishop of Annecy (France).
2. František Tomášek, titular bishop and future Cardinal Archbishop of Prague.
3. This must be a mistake as, according to the Acta, Cardinal Bea did not speak during this general Congregation. It was the Ukrainian bishop of Philadelphia, Ambrozij Senyshyn, who spoke before the intervention of Antonio G Vuccino.
4. *AS* I/III, 624–627.
5. Antonio G Vuccino, Auxiliary Bishop of Paris for Catholics of Eastern rite, *AS* I/III, 633–635.
6. Doroteo Fernández y Fernández, Coadjutor Bishop of Badajoz, *AS* I/III, 636–638.
7. *AS* I/III, 638–640.

1) The spirit is far from the ecumenical spirit which is *spiritus veritatis in caritate et claritate* [the spirit of truth in charity and clarity]. There is some animosity towards the Easterners (for example accusing them of submission to the civil authority).

2) From the historical point of view, the manner of presenting the separation: that the Catholic Church always did everything it could in favour of unity. Whereas the faults are on both sides.

3) The doctrine-theology is not always either felicitous or profound. For example No. 6, where the unity of the Church is based solely on the primacy of the pope and the submission of the faithful to the hierarchy. This is very incomplete.

The popes themselves have referred to the Orthodox as 'Churches'. In No. 9, there is nothing about the relationship of other Christians to Christ. The schema should begin at No. 12, and constitute a special chapter of a schema to be prepared in conjunction with the Secretariat.

Mgr Zoghby[1] (in French): Christian unity from the Eastern and Orthodox point of view.

The Eastern Church has never been part of the Latin Church and does not owe its development to it. It is the SOURCE Church, descending directly from the Apostles.

Two spirits, two different Christian inspirations, Eastern and Western. The same Christian mysteries and the same feasts are understood and lived differently here and there: Trinity, Christology (the divinisation of human nature by Christ). Two Churches which can be united but not fused into each other. Unity but not uniformity, in the image of the Holy Trinity.

(I thought I recognised Chenu).

The collegial power of the Apostles, whereas the Catholic Church evolves towards centralisation.

The overwhelming majority of the Catholic Church is Latin. HERE AT THE COUNCIL there are 130 Eastern bishops, who are lost among 2,500 Fathers, and the patriarchs of the East are obscured and made invisible behind the sacred purple of the 100 Cardinals who today adorn the Catholic Church but who did not exist in the first centuries. One cannot impose this Western development on the East. When the West has rediscovered its liturgical languages, its national synods and its national rites, then a first step will have been made.

Méndez[2] (Mexico): 1) regretted the lack of coordination.

2) there is reference only to the Orthodox and at times it is not clear whether the reference is to the Orthodox or to Uniate Eastern

1.   *AS* I/III, 640–643.

2.   Sergio Méndez Arceo, Bishop of Cuernavaca, *AS* I/III, 643–646.

Catholics. And there is no definition of what the Eastern Church is; etc (other defects);

3) legalism. A monologue and not a dialogue as defined by Bishop De Smedt.[1] At times, it seems that what is envisaged is individual conversions rather than a union of the Churches.

In favour of a new version produced by the three commissions concerned.

A better explanation of the relationship between the primacy and the episcopate. Avoid inserting into a conciliar document quotations from the ordinary magisterium, but quote only from Scripture and the Fathers.

It will be necessary, before 8 September next year, to summon to Rome one in 10 of the bishops, elected by the others, in order to review all of this in the space of one or two months: a *coetus* [gathering] of about two hundred bishops.

Romero[2] (Spanish, but very strong and disagreeable Italian accent).

Athanasius Hage[3] (Superior of the Basilians): *omnino placet* [altogether in favour]: generally speaking it is well balanced. But in detail, and if it is compared with the schema on the Church, there is not complete agreement. And it needs to be shortened. Criticised some harsh expressions. It should be inserted into Chapter XI of the *De Ecclesia*.

A number of telephone calls. Long and good visit from Fr Chenu.

At 8.30 pm, after their supper (I went without mine), a conversation with the priests of the French Seminary. I rediscovered the French priest: good heads, at times ungracious, at times pleasant; good eyes that look straight and questioningly at you; interested in people and in the world; inclined towards freedom and to take hold of the pleasant side of things.

Wednesday 28 November 1962

While looking for some bishops before the Mass in St Peter's, I encountered Cardinal Ottaviani. So I introduced myself. He immediately attacked me (in Italian then, as I replied in Latin, in French). He reproached me for having made an entirely negative and un-constructive critique. I asked him WHICH critique, and of what, so he attributed to me a share in the composition of the schema signed by the Presidents. He added that their approval of this text did not redound to their credit. There will be a critique and a reply to this schema, and the reputation of

---

1. {Cf his intervention on Monday 19 November}.
2. Felix Romero Menjibar, Bishop of Jaén, *AS* I/III, 646–648.
3. The archimandrite Athanasius Hage, Superior General of the Melkite Basilians of St John the Baptist, *AS* I/III, 648–650.

those who have approved it as well as those who prepared it will not be enhanced: their theological weakness will be apparent.

This brief conversation was interrupted four or five times because, one after the other, Cardinal Pizzardo and several stout bishops wanted to say a few words to Cardinal Ottaviani, and each time I stood back.

I told him that K Rahner was my friend, but that I was in no way involved in the preparation of the text he was referring to.

The photographer from *Match,* using flash, took a picture of us at the moment when, deeply shocked by this new assault and this suspicion from which I know I will never be free until I die, I must have had a very unsmiling look on my face.

Cardinal Ottaviani told me that I ought to go to see him, collaborate, see the assessor of the Holy Office.[1] Yes, I will go to see Cardinal Ottaviani. Parente is another matter!

Mgr Collin[2] (Digne) OFM, former Bishop of Suez, buttonholed me; he told me that the Italians were very put out by Maximos IV's proposal, which they interpret as meaning that there would be two churches. It seems that Cardinal Ottaviani has reaffirmed: one single church! Mgr Collin said to me that it ought to be EXPLAINED to them. Yes, but how! The time it would take, and I do not speak Italian.

Ethiopian Mass, lasting a full hour. Strange bawling. It gave me an uneasy feeling. But I liked the enthroning of the Gospel with drumbeat and applause. Evidently, black people must be perfectly at ease with it all.

A sheet containing *emendationes* to Chapter 1 of the text on the Liturgy was distributed. There is to be a vote on nine *emendationes.*

The President, Cardinal Tappouni,[3] explained that the aim of the schema is not to expound dogmatic principles but the attitude of the Catholic Church in approaching the question of union with the Easterners. *Schema mihi placet* [I approve of the schema] (he stressed this). (His pronunciation was Italian, but he pronounced '*-us*' as –US (not as –OUS).)

> Cardinal Spellman:[4] a single Church founded on Peter, but allowing for a variety of rites. Prayer: trust in Mary. *Caveant ne falso irenismo ducti* [They should take care not to be led astray by a false irenicism] . . . etc. He spoke of schismatic Churches, of REDIRE [returning]: they professed Catholic doctrine in the seven ecumenical Councils. *Placet.* (No REAL contact with the REAL problems.)

---

1. Pietro Parente.
2. Bernardin Collin, Bishop of Digne (France).
3. A native of Mossul, Ignace G Tappouni was Patriarch of Antioch of the Syrians, *AS* I/III, 654–655.
4. *AS* I/III, 655-656.

Cardinal Ottaviani:[1] *placet* with some corrections.

> In favour of a SINGLE schema (and not a separate one for the Easterners).
>
> The schema *De Ecclesia*, which is eighty pages long, is too important for it to be dealt with so quickly. He proposed that it should not be tackled immediately and instead, after the schema on unity, to move on to *de Beata Virgine Maria*. Thus one will end by giving a display of the unity of children in the praise of their mother. One will thus offer consolation to the Pope who, on the feast of the Immaculate Conception, will formally approve this schema.
>
> He uttered a SENTIMENTAL appeal to all the holy virgins of the world, and to the [Marian] piety of all the priests.
>
> Applause.
>
> His Beatitude the Chaldean Patriarch of Babylon[2] (*observatores* . . .): He liked the schema and he likes it still. He wishes the Fathers to compose in the name of the Council a prayer for unity: this would be a sign of its concern for this cause.

Mgr Tawil[3] (Damascus): it is necessary to remove the obstacles in the way. He suggested some detailed corrections.

> The term *coetus* [assembly]. It would be better to say: ORTHODOXI [the Orthodox].
>
> The accusation of subservience to the civil authority
>
> No. 26: suspicion of bad morality
>
> No. 52: very inadequate. Because the Catholic Churches of the East will not have their full Catholic status as long as the Orthodox are not in union. At the moment, they have only a provisional status, neither completely Eastern, nor Latin, which can be justified only by their ecumenical vocation.

J Velasco[4] (China): *placet*. However, criticism of the *modus aggrediendi* [the way of approaching] the problem. The schema is too indulgent towards irenicism, the Catholic positions (the monarchical constitution of the Church) are referred to only in passing and diplomatically. Our one aim is to attract to ourselves our separated brethren. And our method = the force and unity of doctrine. And don't let it be thought that Rome bears some responsibility for the separations.

Archbishop of Valencia[5] (Spain) suggested some corrections.

---

1. *AS* I/III, 657-658.
2. Paul II Cheikho, *AS* I/III, 658–659.
3. The Melkite Archbishop Joseph Tawil, of the Patriarchate of Antioch, Patriarchal Vicar of the Melkites in Damascus, *AS* I/III, 660–661.
4. JB Velasco, OP, Bishop of Xiamen, *AS* I/III, 661–663.
5. Marcelino Olaechea Loizaga, member of the Commission on Seminaries, Studies, and Catholic Education, *AS* I/III, 667–668.

Khoury[1] (Lebanon) (*observatores* . . .): In the name of several bishops. The schema calls for several clarifications. There ought to be only one schema. On the other hand, there are several Churches in the East, which appear to have been overlooked (as compared with a privileged concern for the Greeks, for Byzantium).

Against the exaggerations expressed HERE concerning the East and the West (anti-Melkite reaction).

Cathedra unica Petri [the single chair of Peter] (praise for).

What one desires for the East is: the service of the WHOLE Church (less centralised structure, etc.) Maronite thesis; a single Church but a certain provincial freedom.

A single schema should be prepared by a joint Theology/Secretariat Commission. Applause (spoken in a resonant voice and resolutely).

Darmancier[2] (New Caledonia): humility and a spirit of penance are needed. The Roman Church has shown too little of either: he cited Hadrian VI (difficult to hear; the conversations in the side aisles almost drowned his voice which was that of a professor). HE DID NOT GET ACROSS. Rome has sometimes been at fault. He also referred to recent incidents showing a lack of real respect for Eastern traditions. Chapter XI of the schema *De Ecclesia*, namely *De œcumenismo*, does not have the good spirit of the present text. The Secretariat should prepare a new text!

Bishop from Vietnam[3] (*observatores* . . .) this schema and Chapter XI *De œcumenismo* should be combined.

Dom Butler:[4] did he withdraw? Having been announced, he did not speak.

A Spaniard:[5] *placet.*

I went downstairs. I am very oppressed by some of the interventions this morning. I am crushed by them. 'There is no end to the wretchedness', said Van Gogh before he shot himself in the head. As for me, I have hope and prayer. But I am crushed. How can one carry this weight? The number of those who have not understood is enormous. Will one never get out of it all?

The trouble is that when one has gone down to the bar or into the side aisles, one is buttonholed interminably. I missed nearly all of the rest of the debate, ex-

---

1. *AS* I/III, 668–671.
2. Michel Darmancier, Vicar Apostolic of Wallis and Futuna, *AS* I/III, 671–672.
3. The Vietnamese Dominique Hoàng-văn-Doàn, OP, titular bishop living in Hong Kong. In 1963, he was to become Bishop of Qui Nhon (Vietnam), *AS* I/III, 673–674.
4. That Basil C Butler was to speak had been announced at the beginning of the Congregation, *AS* I/III, 653.
5. Vicente Enrique y Tarancón, Bishop of Solsona (Spain), member of the Commission on the Discipline of the Clergy and of the Christian People, future Cardinal Archbishop of Madrid, *AS* I/III, 674–676.

cept for Mgr Ancel,[1] who spoke with real conviction on the spirit of humility and penance that is needed. The first person I spoke to was Fr Lanne, who told me that the renewed vigour of the debate on the schema this morning was the result of a meeting held at the Eastern Commission yesterday; but I have forgotten the details of what he told me. I chatted briefly with Cullmann, who told me that he is preparing something on the Virgin Mary. In his deep desire not to enhance the differences, to seek the maximum agreement, Cullmann is touching. But he does not have much of a THEOLOGICAL approach; he does not clarify matters by means of broad positions of principle.

The Nuncio, Mgr Bertoli, who had said that he wanted to see me and whom I had managed to see for a moment, came looking for me, and took me briefly aside. He began by asking me what I thought of the Council and the way it was going. I replied that I regretted the lack of cohesion in its preparation, the lack of a sense of direction. I referred to my letter to the Pope, which the Nuncio had transmitted, and about which I did not know to what degree it found its mark. Everything will have to be done again!

Mgr Bertoli then told me he was afraid that, between the two Sessions, a number of speeches, books, articles, lectures, would make public the disagreements that have come to light, and would do so without explaining the atmosphere of understanding and respect within which everything has taken place. He also said to me: what one writes is taken by others without nuances; you yourself know where you are going and in what conditions what you say is of value. But others do not make this distinction and draw inferences . . .

I asked him if he was referring to anything specific? No, it is all general.

He said that it would be necessary to meet with the men representing the other school of thought. He is endeavouring to defend the 'integrists' to the liberals and the liberals to the 'integrists'. I should make the effort . . . I asked him if he knew Cardinal Ottaviani well. Yes, he said. Without actually expressing the idea, I made it clear that perhaps he could organise a meeting. He said: Go and see him, he will certainly receive you, and at once.

What a strange coincidence. Too much of a coincidence for it not to have been planned.

That will not make the preparation of my chronicle in *ICI* any easier.

While the Nuncio was talking to me, the Bishop of Leeds[2] was speaking.

I collected the roneoed texts of my *De Traditione et Scriptura* [On Tradition and Scripture] from the bishops' secretariat. I was in the process of correcting them when Ratzinger telephoned me at 2 pm: Cardinal Frings has heard about them and wants to have copies of these texts before the meeting of the sub-commission[3] which is to be held this afternoon.

---

1. *AS* I/III, 682–683.
2. George P Dwyer, *AS* I/III, 685–687.
3. The reference is to sub-commission I, which dealt with the relationship between Scrip-

This sub-commission of the new joint commission consists of: Cardinals Frings and Browne, Mgr Jaeger, Holland,[1] Schöffer and Parente; as experts: van den Eynde, Balić, Maccarrone,[2] and?[3]

I finished my corrections quickly and went at 3 pm to Cardinal Frings under a deluge of rain which had begun at about 10 am.

From there to Saint-Louis. From 3.30 pm until 4.30 pm, a small meeting of the archbishops and bishops representing the different groups.

We were told that the *praesidium* [Council of Presidents] had rejected Mgr Ottaviani's proposal. This proposal had seriously upset Cardinal Liénart for the following two reasons: 1) This retraction would discredit the Council of Presidents; 2) Cardinal Ottaviani's move went against the regulations. He was speaking of something other than the topic for which he had been granted leave to speak, and was putting forward a proposition without having first consulted the other Presidents . . . Cardinal Tisserant was hesitant. Ruffini had suggested that a vote of the assembly be called for. But Cardinal Liénart had said: as we are in agreement, with perhaps one exception, and as this is within the warrant of the Council of Presidents, we should agree to reject this proposal. That was adopted.

We then spoke about the interval between the two Sessions; it would be good to have in Rome a delegation of bishops who would supervise the work of the Commissions and ensure the continuation of the spirit of the Council, such as it has evolved. The best ways of achieving this were sought.

Mgr Veuillot called this a continuation committee.[4] He also mentioned a proposal for the Second Session from the Africans: that those bishops who were not present be allowed to vote by proxy, one bishop not being allowed to act as proxy for more than one other.

We drew up the agenda for the general meeting due to take place immediately afterwards; I was asked to organise working parties.

At this meeting, Fr Gagnebet, when called upon to do so by Cardinal Feltin, presented the history of the writing of the *De Ecclesia*, and the aims sought in each and all of its eleven chapters. He did this objectively, clearly and in such a way as, without a doubt, to prepare the bishops well for a positive approach to the schema. Then it was my turn to speak. It seems to me that, for a discussion which must cover the whole of the schema as such, there are three main points which

---

    ture and Tradition.

1. Thomas Holland, Coadjutor Bishop of Portsmouth (England).
2. Michele Maccarrone, priest of the diocese of Forlì, Professor of Church History at the Lateran Faculty of Theology; he was a Council expert and a member of the Secretariat for Unity.
3. The missing names are Feiner and Eduard Stakemeier; the latter, a priest of the diocese of Paderborn, was Director of the Johann Adam Möhler Institute in Paderborn and a consultor to the Secretariat for Unity.
4. This idea was implemented with the appointment, at the end of the Session, of a Co-ordinating Committee.

will be entrusted to as many working parties: 1) the general nature of the schema; its style. The question of a more synthetic and organic order. Finally, the insertion into it of the *De Beata Maria Virgine* (Daniélou, Laurentin). 2) The concepts used to define the Church, namely the People of God and the Body of Christ. The exegetical question of the σῶμα χριστοῦ [body of Christ] (Fr Lyonnet, Congar). 3) The question of a better text *De episcopis*, regrouping all the elements referring to them and developing those aspects which have hardly been mentioned, above all the question of collegiality (Lécuyer, Thils). Insert something on THE COUNCILS, the conciliar life of the Church.

After that, there would be plenty of detailed objections to be examined, to be studied critically. But that could only be done when the schema is being discussed chapter by chapter. Church and State. Conceived here in their medieval framework in terms of authority; whereas there is the current aspect of the Church being present to the world by bearing witness (the Church, evangelical conscience of the world) and by service. *De Magisterio*: prolix, too detailed concerning the pope and the Congregations. Ecumenism.

On my return after having seen Fr Lyonnet, I found at my door *Sacerdoce et Laïcat devant leurs tâches d'évangélisation et de civilisation.*[1] Another sword. Nice. I would be astonished if it did not turn out to be just as painful.

It was being said today that the Holy Father is very ill: prostate, with diabetes and something else as well. In fact, he has stopped giving audiences.

God preserve him for us, or give us Elisha after Elijah!

Thursday 29 November 1962

Rain without stopping for 24 hours. Storm.

Work of a disagreeable kind on a few pages for *Vérité et Vie*.[2] Everybody is asking me for a few pages! And, with Fr Lécuyer, editing an intervention for Mgr Blanchet.

Lunch at the Embassy to the Holy See. Cardinals Léger and Marella were there, also Mgr the Archbishop of Auch,[3] the Archbishop of Tananarive,[4] his European predecessor,[5] several other bishops and Mgr Mercier. I was seated between him and Robert Bresson,[6] who is here to present his *Jeanne d'Arc* and whom I introduced to Cardinal Marella so that he could be present at the Mass in St Peter's tomorrow.

---

1. Yves M-J Congar, *Sacerdoce et laïcat devant leurs tâches d'évangélisation et de civilisation* (Paris: Cerf, 1962).
2. Yves M-J Congar, 'Quelques aspects de l'Église remis en lumière par le Concile', in *Fiches de Pédagogie Religieuse 'Vérité et Vie'*, 57, No. 437, 1 January 1963: 4–11.
3. Henri Audrain.
4. Jérôme Rakotomalala.
5. Congar added to the typescript 'Mgr Sartre'.
6. Robert Bresson was a film producer: *Le procès de Jeanne d'Arc* appeared in 1962.

Cardinal Léger asked me what I thought about the *De Ecclesia*. He told me that the Pope has a tumour but it is not known whether or not it is of the prostate. It may be cancerous. He told me the gist of what John XXIII had said to him: 'They have not understood me.' He meant by that: in my speech on 11 October[1] I made it clear that we did not need to repeat Trent and Vatican I. That is what they are wanting to do now.

Cardinal Léger claimed responsibility for the chapter *De laicis*. It is quite a claim. I know what a decisive part Mgr Philips played. Perhaps Cardinal Léger improved on it at the Central Commission.

In the evening, telephone call from Mgr Hurley, Archbishop of Durban, asking me to prepare something that would make specific the 'pastorality' of a text, in the way that Mgr De Smedt had made specific his 'ecumenicity'. I will try to do it. But who will make twenty-four hours into forty-eight?

Friday 30 November 1962

Together with Cardinal Marella, I was supposed to bring Robert Besson in for the Mass. But the cardinal had arranged to occupy his seat in St Peter's before I arrived. He certainly vouched for us to the sacristan, but the guard at the entrance absolutely refused to let Bresson in. My approach to Mgr Felici, the Secretary General, made no difference. I was really saddened by this set-back.

I saw a number of new *periti*: Küng, Martelet, Baum.

The voting for the nine *emendationes* to Chapter 1 of *De Liturgia* was explained and Mgr Martin,[2] of Nicolet, explained the reasons and the significance.

Discussion of the schema *De unitate* then continued.

Cardinal Wyszyński:[3] importance of the question; insistence on the solidarity of all believers in confessing Christ in the difficulties of the atheistic world. Need to avoid giving offence. Praise for the East and its Fathers. *Schema placet tanquam osculum amoris et pacis* [I approve the schema as a kiss of love and peace].

Spellman presiding: one does not understand a word he says.

Cardinal Bea:[4] The schema was not written to be separated from the general considerations on unity, but in order to express a particular appreciation for the Easterners, whose problems are particular. One could combine whatever in this schema is contained also in the text provided by the Secretariat. The Eastern Commission has special schemas on *communicatio in sacris* [sharing in the sacraments], on the patriarchs. One could bring them all together. Some detailed remarks:

---

1. His opening speech at the First Session.
2. Joseph-Albert Martin, *AS* I/III, 702–707.
3. *AS* I/III, 707–709.
4. *AS* I/III, 709–711.

the Secretariat has prepared a special schema on prayer for unity, which it has submitted to the Central Commission. Etc. He mentioned the committee that Leo XIII had set up and which had disappeared with his death. This committee had been brought back to life by John XXIII in the Secretariat, which also has an Eastern section.

Bishop *Eboracensis in Lusitania.*[1]

I did not really listen to him. He bored me.

Mgr Hermaniuk:[2] The Council ought to produce a constitution in which the question of the unity of ALL those separated from us is treated in depth. Produce a single constitution out of the three; lay stress on the COLLEGE OF BISHOPS: a dual commission of disparate theologies should be set up: Catholics and Orthodox, Catholics and Protestants, under the direction of the Secretariat.

Addition to be made to No. 49: a good treatment of the question in the catechisms, because the Latin Church is too much equated with the Latin rite.

Youakim,[3] Melkite (but he seemed Italian or Italianised): detailed comments in a good spirit.

Franić:[4] we need to look at the problem *non ex libris sed ex experientia* [not from books but from experience] and without romanticism. There are also Catholics who were brought over to the Orthodox Church, sometimes by violence. Also, he feared an ecumenism which extenuates the differences between Catholics and Orthodox. The present schema is fairly well balanced. So, *placet.* However, some remarks:

No. 31, he is against the idea of equal responsibility. Against the idea of a single faith in two churches (*sic*: Strossmayer[5]). Criticism of the Catholic ecumenists who love their far-away brothers but not those near to them.

A Portuguese:[6] the schema deals more with external, social, unity than internal unity (he was reading very badly). Promote above all charity as a way to unity! He suggested the text of a prayer.

P Sépinski[7] (Superior General OFM). it is well balanced; well corrected by the Central Commission. Keep articles 1–11, which faithfully give

---

1. M Trindade Salgueiro, Archbishop of Évora (Portugal), *AS* I/III, 713.
2. *AS* I/III, 715–717.
3. Eftimios Youakim was the Melkite Bishop of Zahleh and Furzol (Lebanon), *AS* I/III, 717–718.
4. *AS* I/III 719–721.
5. The Croatian Bishop Josip-Juraj Strossmayer (1815–1905), an active member of the minority at Vatican I, fought for a closer relationship between Rome and the Christian East and in particular with Russia.
6. Abílio A Vaz das Neves, Bishop of Bragança and Miranda, *AS* I/III, 721–723.
7. *AS* I/III, 723–724.

the Catholic doctrine and which were composed by experts including several from the East. He proposed some corrections.

Denys Hayek[1] (Aleppo): (*Observatores . . .*) *Placet* in spite of imperfections. He listed some *desiderata*.

Heenan:[2] he spoke at length to say little. HE SPOKE IN TERMS OF A RETURN. Expressed regret at the absence of Observers from Constantinople and Athens. Sentimentality and apologetic. Praise for the Pope.

Philippines:[3] *Placet iuxta modum*. He suggested some alterations, including turning quotations from Scripture into footnotes!!!

Archbishop of Segovia:[4] suggested a few corrections in the interests of greater theological precision (rigour) or of expressing things more positively.

(a Dutchman?):[5] The schema would do more harm than good. Text a monologue that ignores the World Council of Churches.

In favour of an admission of our fault with a spirit of compunction. The style of the schema is self-laudatory. And not to couch this confession in psychological terms, because that gives the impression of something accidental.

What is said about apostolicity (a. 5 end) does not hold together because the pope is never alone but always *caput collegii (episcopalis)* [head of the (episcopal) college].

Bishop of the Ruthenians [6] USA: (very resonant tenor voice): *placet*.

Coadjutor of the Archbishop of Belgrade.[7]

I left the session, because I had an appointment with Cardinal Ottaviani at the 'Holy Office' at 12.15 pm. I arrived hobbling. After a few words of praise, he said to me: in *La Tradition et les traditions*, there are some errors of interpretation of conciliar texts, of the Magisterium and even of the Fathers. I did not dare to ask him which, but I saw at once that he was echoing Parente. Also, he said, in *Vraie et fausse Réforme*, there was a perfectly correct page alongside one that spoke falsely

1. Denys A Hayek, Syrian Archbishop of Aleppo (Syria), member of the Commission on Bishops and the Government of Dioceses from the First Session onwards, *AS* I/III, 724–726.
2. *AS* I/III, 726–728.
3. Alejandro Olalia, Bishop of Lipa, *AS* I/III, 728–730.
4. The reference should be to the intervention of José Pont y Gol, who was in fact the Bishop of Segorbe-Castellón de la Plana (Spain), *AS* I/III, 731–732. The names for Segovia and Segorbe are very similar in Latin: *Segobiensis* and *Segobricensis*.
5. The Dutchman Rudolf J Staverman, OFM, was Vicar Apostolic in {Jayapura, Indonesia}, *AS* I/III, 733.
6. Nicholas Elko, Bishop of the Ruthenians in Pittsburg, *AS* I/III, 734–735.
7. Gabriel Bukatko, who was to become Archbishop of Belgrade in March 1964, member of the Commission on the Eastern Churches, *AS* I/III, 737.

on the same subject. He also reproached me for a purely negative assessment of the schemas, for example in the lectures (in fact, the French bishops had commented that what I had to say about Tradition had been entirely positive and that only at the end, on the basis of this positive assessment, had I made three specific criticisms of the schema). I also perceived (I, Yves Congar) that negative assessments which are not mine are being attributed to me, and I expressly mentioned Parente with his *'alicuius Galli'* [of a certain Frenchman]. These criticisms are not mine; I do not have to reveal whose they are. The Cardinal said: as you are being watched and are under suspicion to such an extent, you ought to be so much more careful and align yourself with the authentic Magisterium.

He went on: Your own experience at the Theological Commission tells you that you were able to speak freely and that, when you asked to speak, I allowed you to. I replied: theoretically, yes, in practice, almost not. The Cardinal said: if you have criticisms to make of the schemas, address them TO US.

I said that no-one has taken much notice of me and that at the Council itself, I have not once been called upon. At the request of the bishops—because I am at the service of the bishops and I do nothing unless they ask me to: the Cardinal approved that and said that the bishops were free to call upon us—I had written a chapter *De Traditione et Scriptura* [on Scripture and Tradition], which I gave to the cardinal because there is nothing secret or hidden. I added that I had sent it to Cardinal Frings for him to circulate to the members of the sub-commission. The cardinal seemed astonished that I have never been called upon, but such is the case. I also pointed out to him that at the Preparatory Theological Commission I had never been asked to prepare a text.

I perceive that I am once and for all and for ever under suspicion. That will not prevent me from working. My work displeases them because they realise very well that its whole aim is to bring back into circulation certain ideas, certain things that they have been endeavouring to shut out for four hundred years, and above all for the past hundred years. But that is my vocation and my service in the name of the Gospel and of the Tradition.

I can hardly write as my whole right side is so tired.

In the afternoon, at 4 pm, meeting at the Belgian College of the group of bishops interested in the theme of the Church of the Poor.[1] Quite a large gathering of bishops from several countries (Brazil, Mexico, Vietnam, Africa, India and various Europeans countries). The primary initiative came from Fr Gauthier,[2] of

---

1. Congar gave a lecture there: cf 'Titre et honneurs dans l'Église. Brève étude historique', in *Pour une Église servante et pauvre* (Paris: Cerf, 1963).
2. Paul Gauthier, disciple of Jean Mouroux, had been a professor at the seminary in Dijon; in his endeavour to share the life of the working class, he had left in order to found in Nazareth the Companions of Jesus the Carpenter, recognised by the local Melkite bishop, Mgr Hakim; he was in Rome during the Council, where his witness and his experience came into contact with numerous bishops who sought a Church that was both closer to the poor and poorer itself.

Nazareth. It was taken to heart above all by Mgr Himmer (Tournai), Mgr Hakim, MGR MERCIER, Cardinal Gerlier (who was to have an audience with the Pope, but the Pope is sick), Mgr Câmara (Brazil), etc. I am always interested in the anthropology revealed by a given group. This one is lovely. The heads of determined men, several of which reflect a true freedom. These men embody the holiest of causes and perhaps the most important. It is unlikely that the Council will be reduced to Byzantine disputations when these men are expecting from it something about peace, hunger, human dignity. But Mgr Mercier told me that even this group deleted from the letter that it sent to the Pope everything that was a bit pointed as well as concrete, for example, the references to 'gold or silver I have none', the suggestion to have pectoral crosses and rings in base metal, or the use of ordinary cars instead of luxury ones.

However, I believe that the resolve that is being created here will produce results. I would like to serve it in some way.

I was so tired I had great difficulty in returning here.

1 December 1962

In the coach that takes us to St Peter's, Mgr Desmazières read me a letter from Cardinal Richaud, whose Auxiliary he is, and which: 1) speaks highly of myself; 2) speaks of Cardinal Ottaviani's allegation concerning the Central Commission's being in agreement and the correction made by Cardinal Döpfner. To say that, wrote Cardinal Richaud, is a 'moral fraud', because there was a great deal of opposition and criticism, but they took account of this only as they wanted to . . .

Fr Gagnebet said that, even after the schema had been passed to the Central Commission, the Commission on Amendments[1] had suppressed or introduced certain things, at times important things. There are notable differences between the text as the Central Commission had corrected it and the printed version we were presented with. The historians of the Council will have a difficult task in writing the history of the eight, ten or twelve successive versions produced by the Commission, then of their being put through the mill, first by the central Commission, then by the Commission for Amendments. Without counting the changes undergone at the Council. And that is not the end of it!!!

I think they have wanted to take on much too much.

At St Peter's. Mgr Felici[2] proposed, with regard to the schema *De unitate,* a vote on this: *Expleta disceptatione* [as the discussion has been completed] the Fathers approve this document in general. However, bearing in mind the comments made, the decree will be sent for revision by the Secretariat and the Theological Commission.

He then gave the results of the votes on the amendments to the first numbers of the schema *De liturgia.*

1. The Sub-Commission on Amendments (cf above, page 146, note 1).
2. *AS* I/IV, 9–11.

Cardinal Ottaviani[1] introduced the schema *De Ecclesia*. He adopted his cajoling voice, but mixed in with it, under a certain humour, a sharp edge of petulance and aggressiveness. The schema, he said, has a concern that is pastoral, biblical, accessible to people and not scholastic. But *'res iam praeiudicata est'* [the matter has already been prejudged]. There are some who are ready to substitute another text for it, one that had been already prepared even before the present text had been distributed. It is a predestination *ante praevisa merita* [in advance of foreseen merits] . . .

Ottaviani is a good comedian but he was speaking ironically and with an element of contempt. He was undoubtedly in the wrong.

The document presenting the schema was read by Mgr Franić.[2] He gave in Latin practically what Fr Gagnebet had given to the French bishops last Wednesday.

> Cardinal Liénart:[3] asked that the relationship between the Roman Church and the Mystical Body not be expressed in such a way as to suggest that the WHOLE of the mystical Body was contained in the Roman Church. The Mystical Body embraces more than the Roman Church militant: it includes the suffering Church and the Church in heaven. And those separated? I would not venture to say that *nullo modo Corpori mystico adhaereant* [in no way are they attached to the Mystical Body]. I would not venture to say *quod Ecclesia, eo ipso quod corpus est oculis cernitur* [that the Church, by the very fact of its being body, can be seen with the eyes]. *Enixe peto* [I strenuously ask] that article 7 of Chapter I be deleted and that the schema be written less juridically. He said this not in a spirit of criticism, but out of love for the truth. *Amicus Plato, magis amica veritas* [Plato is a friend, but the truth is more a friend].

> Cardinal Ruffini:[4] *Placet.* A few comments: that Chapters 5, 6 and 11 be omitted as they repeat what has been said in other prepared texts: that the idea of the necessity of the Church (Chapter II) be joined to Chapter I, the nature of the Church. Then one would have seven chapters: 1) *De Ecclesiae natura* ET FINE [on the nature of the Church and ITS GOAL]; 2) *De membris* [on its membership]; 3) *De potestate ordinis* [on the power of order] with a development concerning the priesthood; 4) *De potestate iurisdictionis* [on the power of jurisdiction], with something on the episcopal conferences and the patriarchal regimes; 5) *Ecclesiae magisterium* [magisterium of the Church]; 6)

---

1.   He was speaking as President of the Doctrinal Commission, *AS* I/IV, 121–122.
2.   *AS* I/IV, 122–125.
3.   *AS* I/IV, 126–127.
4.   *AS* I/IV, 127–129.

Obedience to government and to Magisterium; 7) The relationship between Church and State.

Cardinal Archbishop of Seville:[1] (boring).

Cardinal König:[2] 1) Make it shorter. The Theological Commission should identify the disputed sections or those that have been be dealt with elsewhere. 2) Don't *extollere iura* [extol rights], (Chapter II) but rather mission. 3) Chapter I makes no mention of *indoles eschatologica* [the eschatological nature] and *ministerium verbi* [the ministry of the Word]. 4) Do not present the necessity of the Church solely from the point of view of the individual, but mention the primary basis for membership in one's participation in human nature. 5) Base the episcopate on the idea of the People of God and, for the magisterium, note the participation of the faithful in the indefectibility of the Church.

Cardinal Alfrink:[3] pointed out some duplication: bishops, the laity, ecumenism. The Church is well defined as *Corpus Christi* [the Body of Christ], but there is too much emphasis on the external sense of the comparison. In the same way, the relationship of others to the mystical Body is minimised. 'Residential' bishops? One third of this assembly is, in fact, made up of titular bishops. What is said about the College of Bishops is expressed in a rather negative way. There is the ORDINARY magisterium of the bishops. He quoted Kleutgen at Vatican I. Church and State: there is too much emphasis on RIGHTS.

The schema *De Beata Virgine* should be organically attached to that on the Church.

'*Renovatur a nova Commissione mixta*' [It should be done again by a new joint Commission], established by the Pope.

Cardinal Ritter[4] (St Louis): '*multa desunt*' [There are many things missing]. The faults are connected with the method used. One cannot deduce the Church from its powers. Examples: way of speaking of holiness (whereas we have Eph 5), it is not the magisterium alone that protects the deposit, there are also the faithful (I have the impression that he has read *Lay People in the Church*,[5] either he or the theologian who prepared his text for him). In Chapter IX on Church and State, mention freedom of conscience and of religion.

---

1. José M Bueno y Monreal, *AS* I/IV, 130–132.
2. *AS* I/IV, 132–133.
3. *AS* I/IV, 134–136.
4. *AS* I/IV, 136–138.
5. Y Congar, *Lay People in the Church, A Study for a Theology of Laity*, (London 1967); English translation of *Jalons pour une théologie du laïcat*, 'Unam Sanctam' 23 (Paris: Cerf, 1953).

Bernacki,[1] Auxiliary of Gniezno. He spoke for more than a quarter of an hour in order to say that an essential chapter on the pope was missing.

The results were then given of the vote[2] concerning the schema on unity:

Number of voters	Placet	Non placet	Void
2,112	2,068	36	8

Mgr De Smedt:[3] he began by praising the schema, which had benefited from the progress made in recent years. However, he criticised the underlying concept on three points:

– Triumphalist spirit: in the style of *L'Osservatore Romano* and the documents emanating from Rome, in which the life of the Church is presented as a series of triumphs, whereas Our Lord spoke of *pusillus grex* [little flock, Luke 12: 32].

– Clericalism: the traditional image: the pope, bishops, priests, with their powers: the Christian people is presented as being receptive only, and occupying a secondary role in the Church. Whereas the hierarchy is in fact only a MINISTRY which is derived from the *status viae* [pilgrim status] of the Church, the People of God remains forever; in it we are first and foremost Christians, all enjoying the same dignity and the same goods.

– Legalism: whereas the Motherhood of the Church had been the centre of the primitive ecclesiology (Delahaye[4]), here it is viewed too juridically (above all pages 15-16).

In short, he expressed the wish *'ut a concilio statuatur; remittendum ad Commissionem ut emendetur'* [that it be decided by the Council that it be sent back to the Commission for correction].

Mgr de Smedt was applauded. However, I found his paper less good than the previous one. His criticisms of the Roman ecclesiology in general are very much to the point, but they seem to me excessive when applied to THIS particular text.

Mgr Lefebvre,[5] CCSp: How to produce a text which is both pastoral and rigorous? It is quite simple: produce two texts, one theological and the

---

1. Lucjan Bernacki, *AS* I/IV, 138–141.
2. *AS* I/IV, 141.
3. *AS* I/IV, 142-144.
4. Cf Karl Delahaye, *Erneuerung der Seelsorgsformem aus der Sicht der frühen Patristik* (Fribourg: Herder 1958); Congar was to publish this in French, with a preface contributed by himself: Karl Delahaye, *Ecclesia Mater chez les Pères des trois premiers siècles. Pour un renouvellement de la Pastorale d'aujourd'hui,* 'Unam Sanctam', 46 (Paris: Cerf, 1964).
5. Marcel Lefebvre, *AS* I/IV, 144–146.

other pastoral . . . (not much listened to: his words drop in front of him
without getting across so as to reach and strike the hearer).

Mgr Elchinger[1] spoke much more clearly (*Observatores* . . .): asked a question
concerning the general spirit of this schema. To whom is this text
addressed? To bishops and theologians only, or also to the faithful, who
are waiting for an exposition? The pastoral element is not something
added on from outside. Formerly, the Church was presented as an
institution. Today: as a community. Yesterday: the pope: today: the
bishops (I am a titular bishop).

Yesterday, *episcopus singularis* [the bishop on his own]. Today, the
college of bishops.

Yesterday, the hierarchy. Today the Christian people as well.

Yesterday, with respect to non-Catholics, above all, that which divides.
Today that which unites.

Yesterday, the Church bringing salvation *ad intra* [to those within].

An Italian, bishop *Camerinensis*:[2] there is nothing about the interior life of
the Church.

Pawłowski:[3] *Ex sese* [of themselves] does not mean *sine Ecclesia* [without the
Church]. Better to state this, which would be in accordance with the
nota conciliaritatis [note of conciliarity] of the Orthodox.

Van Cauwelaert:[4] (*Observatores* . . .): A wish from Africa: that the Church
display a pure face to the world, that she present herself as the unity
which human beings need.

The bishops of the Congo are disappointed in this schema: it is too juridical
and does not have the attractiveness of Good News; it is static and does
not show the Church reaching toward eschatology.

Mgr Carli,[5] Italian: he spoke at length. Strongly supported by the Italians.

In the afternoon, working groups at the Biblicum at 5.30 pm. One with Lécuyer
and Colson on the episcopate and collegiality; the other with myself and Fr Lyonnet on the encyclical *Mystici Corporis*[6] and the idea of σῶμα χριστοῦ [the Body of
Christ]. But we did not really manage to produce a precise intervention. However,
Mgr Boillon will put his name down.

1. *AS* I/IV, 147–148.
2. Giuseppe D'Avack, Archbishop of Camerino, *AS* I/IV, 148–150.
3. *AS* I/IV, 151–153.
4. *AS* I/IV, 156–158.
5. *AS* I/IV, 158–161.
6. Encyclical of 29 June 1943.

Sunday 2 December 1962

In the morning, wrote and typed out my *ICI* Chronicle. At noon, Cardinal Lefebvre and some French bishops to lunch. At 2.15 pm, Vogel came to visit. He spoke to me of the article in *L'Espresso*[1] on the defeat of Cardinal Ottaviani, written by a former priest,[2] and of three articles in the *Corriere d'Italia*[3] (middle-class liberal in philosophy and conservative in economics and politics), which insinuated that the Pope was a Modernist: he is a disciple of Buonaiuti[4] who had assisted him at his first Mass; he is from Bergamo, where Modernism had its supporters. What is at the root of Modernism if not the adaptation of the Church to modern culture (allusion, in the actual wording, to the *'aggiornamento'* of the Church, given to the Council as a programme)? The last article attacked in particular Cardinal Bea and Cardinal Alfrink. The latter is anti-Roman. Evidence: at the pontifical Mass he crossed his legs . . . !!! Vogel also told me that Fr Rahner was to give a lecture at the Capranica, but this lecture was forbidden by the Vicariate. I recalled what I was told by the secretary to the Student Association at the Gregorianum . . .

Visit from Mgr Sergio Méndez Arceo, Bishop of Cuernavaca (Mexico). It is he who has Dom Lemercier,[5] author of the report on psychoanalysis[6] as his theologian. He asked me to give a lecture to the South American bishops, and for my advice on the intervention he wants to make at the Council which is pro-episcopal, against the encroachments of the Curia.

From 6 pm to 7.15 pm, I answered the written questions of the English-speaking students at the Angelicum. This will be my only session here . . .

Monday 3 December 1962

I saw some bishops; then Fr Daniélou in order to discuss the organisation of the bishops' working groups during the interval between the two Sessions.

New invasion of experts and assistants: C Moeller,[7] Dom O Rousseau, etc; secretariat people.

---

1. Issue of *L'Espresso* dated 30 November.
2. Carlo Falconi, historian of Catholicism.
3. The reference is to three articles by Indro Montanelli published in the *Corriere d'Italia* on 24, 25 and 26 November.
4. Ernesto Buonaiuti (1881–1946), priest and theologian, he was accused of Modernism and was excommunicated in 1926.
5. Of Belgian origin and formed at Mont-César Abbey in Louvain, Dom Grégoire Lemercier had founded the Benedictine monastery of the Resurrection not far from Cuernavaca, of which he was the Prior; having himself undergone psychoanalysis, he had urged the monks and postulants to do the same.
6. This report was being circulated during the First Session.
7. Charles Moeller, priest of the diocese of Malines-Brussels, specialist in the relationship between modern literature and Christian thought, Professor of Theology at Louvain; present at the Council as personal expert of Cardinal Léger, he was to be appointed a Council expert at the end of the First Session. In 1966, he became sub-secretary of

Daniélou gave me some news from the sub-commissions of the joint Commission. In the one he is on, things are going well (New Testament), as is Mgr Garrone's one (*proemium De revelatione* [foreword on Revelation]); but things are not going well on the sub-commission on the sources. The Secretariat people are weak, he said, and things are close to returning to the idea of the two sources.

Daniélou also told me he had received his nomination as a *peritus* on the Commission on the laity.

First of all, a report[1] on two *emendationes De Liturgia,* on which there is to be a vote.

Cardinal Spellman:[2] comments on Chapter VI *De laicis:* nothing stands out, except that too little space is devoted to Catholic Action.

Cardinal Siri:[3] *Bonum quamvis perfectibile* [Good, though could be improved]. Two comments: 1) Present clearly the VISIBLE Church. He would like a better explanation of the relationship between the Mystical Body and the juridical Church.
2) [ ]

Cardinal McIntyre:[4] No. 9 *membra ecclesiae sensu proprio* [members of the Church in the proper sense].
I do not quite see what he is trying to say . . .

Cardinal Gracias:[5] we are in the last week . . . (. . .)

Chapter X: one-sided presentation without regard for those countries where Catholics are few in number and are ACCEPTED IN a non-Christian country. AS IT STANDS IT WOULD BE CATASTROPHIC FOR THE MISSIONS. There are some provocative expressions. One should not think solely of the separated Orthodox or Protestant brethren but also of the millions of non-Christians. Take into account the methods of presentation that have proved their worth: use their writings.

Cardinal Léger:[6] this scheme will be the *cardo* [hinge] of the Council. The chapter *De episcopatu* especially. There is no time to discuss it adequately. His wishes: 1) that the spirit of renewal be protected by a committee that will AUTHORITATIVELY protect the spirit of the Council in the period between the two Sessions.

---

the Congregation for the Doctrine of the Faith: later he was to be Rector of the Tantur Ecumenical Institute and Secretary to the Secretariat for Unity.

1. The report was presented by Francis J Grimshaw, Archbishop of Birmingham, and a member of the Conciliar Commission on the Liturgy, *AS* I/IV, 170–172.
2. *AS* I/IV, 172–173.
3. *AS* I/IV, 174.
4. *AS* I/IV, 175.
5. *AS* I/IV, 175–178.
6. *AS* I/IV, 182–183.

2). that the remaining time be devoted mainly to VOTING on the *De liturgia*, at least on the first two chapters.

Cardinal Döpfner:[1] the schema has some general defects.

1) It devotes too much space to exterior things: juxtaposition of separate chapters. No treatment of the PEOPLE OF GOD, which should be the basis of the text *De episcopis* [on the bishops].

2) No use of Scripture that is sufficiently DEEP. Church ≠ *Regnum Dei* [Kingdom of God].

3) Too juridical. For example, the way of discussing the membership.

4) No clarifications about theological notes.

Particular points:

The college of bishops is not clearly presented as successor to the Apostolic college.

The question of the conferring of of jurisdiction by the pope ought not to be settled in favour of the opinion currently in possession: the appointment of a person who thus becomes a participant in the power of the college of bishops.

The Church-State question had already been improved by the Central Commission. *Nova reelaboratione indiget schema* [The schema needs to be reworked again].

A new schema should be prepared. The discussion should continue, and then there should be a vote *placet-non placet* on the schema. And other Commissions should collaborate in rewriting those chapters that concern them.

Mgr Kominek[2] (Polish): *placet*. However, there is not enough reference to the Cross of Christ and the Passion. In favour of the idea of the SUFFERING Church (*VERY* long!).

Mgr Marty[3] (his tone a bit sad and affected): two comments:

1) The Church is essentially a mystery; here it is presented too much as an institution. Now the institution is nothing but the manifestation of the mystery. The bishop forms an essential part of the mystery. The faithful ought to be shown as co-workers rather than as subjects.

2) The Church is SENT. The schema should be organised on the basis of the two ideas: mystery and mission (applied to both the bishops and the laity).

Gargitter[4] (Italy: but with a German accent): lay people are not priests merely metaphorically, nor are they simply the subjects of the hierarchy. There

---

1. *AS* I/IV, 183–186.
2. Bolesław Kominek, titular bishop residing in Wrocław, member of the Conciliar Commission on the Apostolate of the Laity, *AS* I/IV, 189–191.
3. *AS* I/IV, 191–193.
4. *AS* I/IV, 193–195.

should be a better presentation of the *iura et officia* [rights and duties] of the bishops and the laity.

Mgr Huyghe,[1] Arras: people's attitudes to the Church. That depends a great deal on the way in which we present it. People will take notice of what the Church says of herself at this Council.

The schema does not sufficiently present the Church as filled with a wide open and truly Catholic spirit, filled with a missionary, evangelical spirit, with a spirit of service, which is different from jurisdiction and domination. The schema should be revised by a joint Commission.

(Listened to attentively in spite of the fact that many of the bishops were missing, having gone to the bar.)

Mgr Hurley:[2] will again be the devil's advocate . . .

Fault common to the entire preparation of the Council: lack of unity and coordination. This should be addressed between the First and the Second Session under the authority of a TRULY CENTRAL commission.

He wishes to propose some refinements on the notion of PASTORALITY (my paper).

Barbetta[3] (Italy): praise of the schema.

Auxiliary Bishop of Barcelona:[4] raised the question of the theological note of the schema.

Take care not to settle questions that are disputed by theologians, or if this is to be done, say so formally. Now there are such points:

The question of the jurisdiction of the bishops coming from the pope, whereas elsewhere it is linked to their consecration.

The question of a single subject.

The bishops are said here not to be judges in the faith and yet infallible. That does not tally.

Mgr Rupp:[5] What one must do is to ask, in relation to each chapter of the schema, what bearing it has on the remote goal of the Council: Christian unity; and on the proximate goal: *aggiornamento.*

He made a heap of allusions, quotations: in search of success. When he spoke of the Magisterium, he assimilated that of individual bishops to this [ ]

He stressed the importance of residential bishops to the point of not even mentioning the titular ones. He caused laughter. He is a comedian! He achieves his success and relaxes.

---

1. Gérard Huyghe, Bishop of Arras, member of the Commission on Religious, *AS* I/IV, 195–197.
2. *AS* I/IV, 197–199.
3. *AS* I/IV, 199–201.
4. *AS* I/IV, N Jubany Arnau, *AS* I/IV, 201–203.
5. *AS* I/IV, 204–205.

Musto[1] (Italian): he spoke for so long that in the end Cardinal Ruffini
   stopped him. A booming voice and great emphasis like my bishop of
   Benevento.[2] He is in favour of the schema as a whole and described as
   almost heretics the bishops who had suggested a new version.

Bishop from Northern Rhodesia:[3] the schema does not correspond to the
   purpose of the Council: the style is too complicated. It is not sufficiently
   christological. Not sufficiently eschatological.

   The Virgin Mary and the COMMUNION OF THE SAINTS should
   be put at the end. He ended with a hymn to the *LEX caritatis* [LAW of
   charity] (not just a counsel). Put above everything the eternal love of
   God. Put the whole of morality under the sign of charity.

Tuesday 4 December 1962

I have the joy of finding Bresson in St Peter's. I stayed with him until the enthroning of the Gospel. He asked to see me in Paris, as he has agreed to make a film on
Genesis.

Cardinal Frings:[4] the schema gives only part of the Catholic tradition: that of
   the last hundred years. But nothing of the Eastern tradition and little
   of the ancient Latin tradition. This is clear from the references and the
   sources, which give quotations from the past hundred years. Is this
   good? Is it universal, catholic, scientific, ecumenical? This fault affects
   the doctrine itself, *qui coarctatur* [which is constrained].

   Example: the notion of the mystical Body, very sociological; there is
   no trace of the Greek doctrine of the Eucharist, of the communion of
   Churches.

   Why separate the section *De Magisterio* from that *De Episcopis*? And,
   in this chapter, one finds nothing about the Word of God.

   Or, third example, the chapter *De praedicatione Evangelii* [on the
   preaching of the Gospel]: there is nothing about the mission proceeding
   from the Father.

   In short, there is a lack of catholicity. Therefore, the schema needs to be
   redone between the two Sessions.

Cardinal Godfrey:[5] *generatim placet* [on the whole I approve]. Look at the
   schema from the point of view of ecumenism. In England, the situation
   is very complex. The mistake of a certain optimism concerning the
   Anglicans, or of allowing the Anglicans to hope for doctrinal and

---

1. Biagio Musto, Bishop of Aquino, Sora and Pontecorvo, *AS* I/IV, 206–208.
2. Cf above, page 202, note 1.
3. Archbishop Adam Kozłowiecki, SJ, *AS* I/IV, 208–211.
4. *AS* I/IV, 218–220.
5. *AS* I/IV, 221–222.

moral concessions (statement of what the English hierarchy has said since 1895).

In the perspective simply of a return and of conversion.

Cardinal Suenens:[1] Reflect on the PURPOSE of the Council in order to CENTRE the work of the Second Session and allow the Commissions to work as parts of a body. Vatican I was the Council of the primacy; Vatican II, according to John XXIII = *Ecclesia Christi lumen gentium* [the Church of Christ, light of the nations]. All should agree on a single overall plan.

The Council should be a Council of the *Ecclesia*.

1) *ad intra* [looking inward]: the Church, her missionary activity (the end of Matthew 28, giving the plan of the whole);

2) *ad extra* [looking outward] in dialogue with the world and showing interest in the human person, in demography, in social justice (ownership, etc), the third world and hunger; the preaching of the Gospel to the poor; peace and war.

In dialogue with the faithful.

In dialogue with our brothers *nondum visibiliter unitis* [who are not yet visibly united with us].

All that is in the Pope's address on 11 September.[2]

He asked that the programme for the remainder of the Council be determined by the Council itself.

The schemas should be revised by the Commissions in accord with the spirit and the aim of the Council.

A secretariat should be set up to deal with the problems of the world of today, which might do work as worthwhile as that done by the Secretariat for Unity (I say that as successor of Cardinal Mercier).[3]

Applause.

Cardinal Bea:[4] A historic moment for the schema. Ecclesiology was born in the sixteenth century. The Council of Trent did not deal with it. Vatican I was unable to complete its proceedings. The question is of interest to Protestants as a new discovery. Therefore the schema is of central importance. He praised the work of preparation. However:

1) it lacks some essential elements. It only deals with the Church MILITANT. After the exposition of the nature of the Church, one would have expected something on ITS PURPOSE.

---

1. *AS* I/IV, 222–225.
2. 'Ecclesia Christi, lumen gentium', John XXIII's Message to the whole world one month before the opening of the Council (11 September 1962). Cf *La Documentation Catholique*, 1962, col 1217–1222.
3. His predecessor, Désiré-J Mercier, had organised the 'Malines Conversations' from 1921 to 1926, with a view to a closer relationship between Anglicans and Catholics.
4. *AS* I/IV, 227–230.

On the other hand, there are some things which are of little use or which are not appropriate in a dogmatic schema. There is discussion of matters which are not yet mature (membership of the Church);

2) the order in which the teaching is expounded: pope, *singuli episcopi* [individual bishops], *collegium episcoporum* [the college of bishops]. The natural and biblical order would call for one to begin with the college of bishops, then Peter as *caput collegii* [head of the college].

The Pope has declared the aim of the Council to be the renewal of the Christian life from the sources of Scripture and Tradition. Now here . . .

The biblical metaphors of the Church are used, but they are not explained and one moves immediately to the SOLE image of the Mystical Body.

There are exhortations (especially in the chapter *De laicis*) which are not appropriate in a dogmatic constitution.

If one seeks the root of everything that is wrong with it, it is that the schema does not match the aim set before the Council by the Pope and which we ourselves declared in our message to humankind.

Cardinal Bacci:[1] 1) the others are brothers *a nobis seiuncti non separati* [cut off from us, not separated from us]. He apologised if our discussions have upset them. But we are never in disagreement about doctrine. *De modo, non de ipse doctrina agitur* [it is a question of manner, not of the doctrine itself];

2) and if our disagreement is only concerning the *modus* [manner], why do people want a new refashioning of the schema? Moreover, those who are pleased with the schema could say *non placet* to the new schema: And then where do we go?

The Theological Commission should reshape and improve THIS schema.

Cardinal Browne:[2] *schema in sua substantia mihi placet* [I approve the schema in its substance]; it can be improved by discussion of each chapter. It speaks of belonging to the Mystical Body.

People complain of the juridical nature of the schema. But *sine iure non vivitur* [one cannot live without law]. Others complain that it speaks too much of the hierarchy. But it speaks of the faithful too.

Mgr Blanchet:[3] (listened to attentively): The schema lacks unity: one detects the work of different authors, and subjects are dealt with in it in more than one place: this also applies to *De episcopatu,* concerning which we still await a complete teaching in order to complete Vatican I. A treatise *De episcopatu* is needed.

---

1. *AS* I/IV, 230–232.
2. *AS* I/IV, 232–233.
3. *AS* I/IV, 233–235.

The doctrine of the episcopate we have is too juridical and not sufficiently Apostolic. There are more than one thousand titular bishops in the world, and they are not mentioned. But the bishop is not defined only by his territory, but also by his *munus* [function]. Pastoral power is being confused with jurisdiction, and it is attributed not to what a bishop is, as such, but is turned into a sort of delegation from the pope.

What is needed is a theology of the episcopate which corresponds with sacred Scripture, with the tradition of the Fathers, with the REALITY OF THINGS.

Rabban[1] (Chaldean): *generaliter placet* [on the whole I approve]. But . . .

Guerry[2] (rather grandiloquent; too long: sentimental): the fatherhood of the bishops.

A Spaniard[3] the text should be revised by ONE PERSON ONLY, in order to have unity, plan . . .

I saw Mgr Flusin in the corridor. He told me that Cardinal Montini is the rising star (behind the scenes!!!). He writes a letter from the Council every week in *L'Italia*.[4] In last Sunday's he struck quite a blow. The Council is accumulating a great deal of paper, of which nothing will remain. It ought to limit itself to ONE question only, namely a treatise on the Church, in itself and in relation to the world. What is needed, between now and the Second Session, is for a small commission to prepare such a treatise and in three months' time for the Second Session to adopt it.

Cardinal Montini is the Pope's guest. He lives in the Vatican. He has a growing influence in the Secretariat of State: it is he who, through Dell'Acqua, makes the nominations. He certainly did not write that unless the Pope agreed with it.

Mgr Suenens and Liénart would agree.

Maccari[5] (Italian): on the laity and Catholic Action.

T Holland[6] (auxiliary, England): disappointed by the section on the episcopate. The separated brethren are hoping, with us, for Vatican I to be completed on this point.

Praise for Tromp (without naming him) on the theology of the Mystical Body. What will the future of our Council be? What will the future of

---

1. *AS* I/IV, 236–237.
2. *AS* I/IV, 240-241.
3. Rafael González Moralejo, Auxiliary Bishop of Vanencia, *AS* I/IV, 242–244.
4. These are his *Lettere dal Concilio*, published in the Catholic daily of Milan, *L'Italia*.
5. Carlo Maccari, titular bishop, *AS* I/IV, 244–246.
6. *AS* I/IV, 247–249.

this schema be? It is not clear what it is aiming at . . . There seems to be a dualism between a kerygmatic text and a dogmatic constitution.

Mgr Devoto[1] (Argentinian): people were expecting things that the SCHEMA DOES NOT DELIVER: the People of God; episcopal collegiality; the preaching of the Gospel to the poor.

Italian:[2] *placet.*

I heard only the end of an intervention by a German:[3] the chapters which discuss the same matters in different schemas prepared by different Commissions should be harmonised.

Doumith[4] (Maronite): what is needed is a constitution *De episcopis* to complete Vatican I. Instead of that, we have a schema *De Ecclesia in genere* [On the Church in general] which contains only one chapter on the bishops. Recommendations for prudence are being multiplied, like a mother who has given a toy to a child and who is afraid it will be misused. There is almost nothing about the bishop *relative ad presbyterium et ad Ecclesiam suam* [in his relationship to the body of priests and to his Church]. The proposed doctrine consecrates the present order of things, itself questionable. The ancient discipline was: consecration FOR A CHURCH. In this way, mission was not separated from order, which is made for it. One does not deny the right of higher authority *'ad moderandum usum potestatis'* [to govern the use of power], but it is necessary to link power with consecration. Today, the two powers are separated, thereby uncoupling what should be united. In my opinion, this intervention (which was listened to VERY attentively), was, theologically, one of the strongest and most important of the entire session.

A bishop from Turkey[5] also said some extremely important things. But he spoke too slowly and he coughed into the microphone which caused laughter.

He echoed all that he had heard from the Orthodox: the Roman primacy is the result of political events . . . But above all: if the pope is infallible, the infallibility of the Church is useless. And if the Church is infallible, what need is there for the infallibility of the pope? That touches the root of the question. It is necessary to explain things. There is a good basis for that in our schema, page 46.

Page 47, No. 30: the relationship between the infallibility of the pope

---

1. *AS* I/IV, 250–251.
2. Giuseppe Vairo, Bishop of Gravina and Irsina, *AS* I/IV, 251–253.
3. Franz Hengsbach, Bishop of Essen (Germany), member of the Commission on the Apostolate of the Laity, *AS* I/IV, 254–255.
4. Michel Doumith, Maronite Bishop of Sarba (Lebanon), appointed member of the Doctrinal Commission, *AS* I/IV, 255–257.
5. J Descuffi, *AS* I/IV, 257–259.

and that of the whole teaching Church should be stated more clearly. The pope must consult the bishops in order to be able to make a definition in the name of the Church. The *ex sese* ought to be replaced, or explained by *'ex ipsius sententia personali'* [by his own personal decision].

In the interval, I saw Fr Daniélou in order to plan the work with the bishops during the interval between Sessions. Daniélou is really extraordinary. He moves quickly, too quickly, but he has an exceptional gift of presence and of getting to the heart of things.

He told me that, from the Roman side, there is a barrier against episcopal conferences. I had already heard that CELAM is obstructed by the Curia. Daniélou interprets in this sense the fact that Mgr de Provenchères, whose name had been down for A VERY LONG TIME to speak on episcopal conferences, has not been called upon to speak. He said he had it from Mgr Zoa (Cameroons) that the latter had yesterday seen Cardinal Agagianian, Prefect of Propaganda, who had said to him: 'Stop speaking as you do about the episcopal conference of Africa, otherwise you will lose your allowance . . . ' Mgr Zoa and the African bishops are very worried by this.

In the coach, on the way back, glancing at the *emendationes* to *De liturgia* which have just been distributed to us, I noticed that the reference to episcopal conferences has been removed. This is undoubtedly not solely on account of the fact that a dogmatic schema must not declare anything other than immutable things!!!

Clarifications that I learned the following day:

1) Mgr de Provenchères: it was an oversight or, rather, he had been put down to speak about THE BISHOPS at the time of the discussion of that chapter and not in order to speak about the schema in general. He has been put down again to speak on Thursday.

2) Mgr Zoa told me that a complaint had been made to him about the unduly violent intervention of Mgr van Cauwelaert as representing the thought of all the African bishops. But, according to Mgr Zoa, in all the episcopal groups, there is one or another individual who does not always represent the ideas of the whole group.

3) In the *emendationes* to the schema *De Liturgia*, the reference to the episcopal conferences has been replaced by another more general formula. Precisely in order not to bind the exercise of the authority of the bishops to a particular form and a particular name in such a way that if, one day, the term 'episcopal conferences' were no longer to be used, one would not be able to eliminate the exercise of the authority of the bishops by arguing from the fact it was now called something else. Thus, what I wrote yesterday was not (or may not be) correct.

Wednesday 5 December 1962

Mgr Garrone, Frs Hamer and Daniélou spoke to me about the work of the joint Commission. Things are going fairly well, with the exception of the sub-commission *De Scriptura et Traditione* [on Scripture and Tradition], where Parente blocks things. Fr Hamer gave me a page of seven points which, according to Parente, constitute the basic principles on which he will rewrite the chapter. I gave him a brief critique of them.

Fr Lanne told me that at the Commission on the Discipline of the Clergy and of the Christian People, Cardinal Ciriaci[1] had said that the Holy Father had decided that, if three bishops requested it, one could bring in an expert from outside. I pointed that out in a letter to Mgr McGrath.[2]

Thurian has heard a rumour that, on Friday, there is to be a vote by acclamation on Mary's mediation. That would surprise me because one can only introduce a vote on a SPECIFIC text that has been previously discussed, or else on something very vague.

Cardinal Ruffini:[3] supported Bacci concerning profound unity. In favour of two schemas: one theological and the other pastoral.

Cardinal Montini:[4] 1) agreed with what Cardinal Suenens had said yesterday: concentrate on the mystery of the Church and its *munus* [function] in relation to the world. He expressed the wish that the Virgin be honoured, but above all that Jesus Christ should be exalted in this schema. Therefore, enlarge on the relationship between Church and Christ, from whom the Church derives everything.

2) As for the teaching on the episcopate, the two chapters which have been presented to us do not correspond with what we were expecting! They are too juridical. It is necessary to present the will of Jesus Christ with respect to bishops.

De institutione collegii apostolici [on the institution of the Apostolic college];

De successione [on the succession] of the college of bishops to the apostolic college;

De muneribus episcoporum [on the functions of bishops] and their basis in episcopal consecration.

3) [ ]

The schema should be revised by the competent Commissions and the Secretariat.

---

1. Pietro Ciriaci was Prefect of the Congregation for the Council and President of the Commission on the Discipline of the Clergy and of the Christian people.
2. Member of the joint Commission on Revelation.
3. *AS* I/IV, 290–291.
4. *AS* I/IV, 291–294.

Maximos IV:[1] This schema is the most important doctrinal text of the entire Council. It is a question of completing Vatican I, so that the primacy and the infallibility of the pope are presented within the framework of the universal shepherding and infallibility of the Church. Chapter I does not contain any errors but it is INCOMPLETE. Against the image of the Church as an army drawn up in battle array.

No. 5 reduces the diversity of the members to the relationship between command and obedience. There is too much insistence on jurisdiction, which results in the failure to mention titular bishops. Unhealthy insistence on the pope; he is thus isolated from the rest of the Church. The positive things that are said are true, but it is not the whole truth. Ecumenism is not a diminution of the truth, but on the contrary a presentation of the FULLNESS of the truth; this is something that a certain Theological School does not do, in accusing ecumenists of diminishing the truth . . .

Against 'popolatry' of which he cites several examples (in Italian). Papacy—mission of love and of service. It is charity that should preside.

Mgr Florit[2] (Florence): *'Immutabilia sunt Constitutio Ecclesiae . . .* [Unchangeable are the constitution of the Church . . .]' etc. One moves into a different spiritual world from that of Maximos. *'ii qui Ecclesiae insidiantur* [those who plot against the Church] . . . '

He approved the schema. Some comments: a few quotations from the Greek Fathers should be included (for him these are purely ornamental). And references to eschatology, the motherhood of the Church, the co-redemptive aspect should also be included. Also corrections of detail.

Mgr Plaza[3] (Argentina). *Placet.* 1) clear doctrine of the Mystical Body; 2) excludes errors, etc.

I went out briefly and was caught by one, then another, from whom I could not escape, and in a way that was very tiring.

Mgr [ ][4] For the sake of our unity, this discussion should take place outside of this hall, in a fraternal manner.

The Secretary[5] gave the result of the votes on the first four amendments put forward this morning.

---

1. *AS* I/IV, 295–297.
2. *AS* I/IV, 298–300.
3. Antonio J Plaza, Archbishop of La Plata, *AS* I/IV, 303–305.
4. This is probably the intervention of the Belgian Bernard Mels who was Archbishop of Luluabourg and Apostolic Administrator of the diocese of Luebo (Congo), *AS* I/IV, 312–314.
5. *AS* I/IV, 315–316.

At midday, the Pope appeared at his balcony, recited the *Angelus* with the Fathers and the crowd, and gave his blessing twice. He said a few cordial words. I greeted Cardinal Montini, with a great crowd around him, and who always has a great spiritual presence.

Afternoon: 1) Visit from a priest of the Society of the Holy Cross, a Canadian, about a thesis on the laity in the Fathers: I suggested to him the idea of the motherhood of the *Ecclesia* in Saint Augustine;

2) Visit from a student at the Angelicum who did his philosophy at Le Saulchoir. Looking for advice about his work. Very baffled and disappointed: in theology at the Angelicum, they are given a highly systematic and scholastic St Thomas. Those who attended Le Saulchoir have been put on the shelf. They have all been put back for solemn profession. The student brothers had all without exception requested that I be asked to give them a lecture, but nobody has asked me for anything!!!

3) At 4.30 pm, lecture to the Latin American bishops on the seigneurial aspects in the Catholic hierarchy.[1] But they were packing their cases. There were seven or eight of them present.

4) Afterwards, at 5.55 pm, I went to Saint-Louis, where the weekly meeting of the French bishops was coming to an end; or rather, it was over, I saw the last of them on their way out.

When I returned from Saint-Louis, at 6.30 pm, I found a priest from Amiens waiting for me. That is what is most tiring about this life; one returns home exhausted only to find someone waiting, or some mail, a telegram, an express letter, telephone calls made during one's absence to which one needs to reply. There is no time to breathe.

5) At 7.00 pm, they came to pick me up for a lecture at the American College (seventy-five USA priests). On ecumenism. Plenty of questions.

Thursday 6 December 1962 Saint Nicholas!
Telephone call from *L'Osservatore Romano*. He[2] wanted a kind of interview on *Chrétiens désunis*. I arranged to meet him in St Peter's, I waited for nearly half an hour and when we finally met, a gendarme put the journalist out!!!

I saw Fr Balić for a moment and Mgr Garofalo, to whom I gave my text on Tradition of which he told me he did not have a copy (though he did know about it).

Mgr Felici[3] presented a kind of balance sheet of the work done: more than 500 Fathers have spoken and a further 300 have also submitted their comments in writing.

---

1. Cf 'Titres et honneurs dans l'Église. Brève étude historique', in *Pour une Église servante et pauvre* (Paris: Cerf, 1963).
2. The journalist who contacted him was PG Colombi.
3. *AS* I/IV, 319–321.

He gave the result of the voting yesterday; an explanation was given of the *emendationes De liturgia*[1] due to be voted on today.

Cardinal Lercaro[2] spoke in support of Suenens and Montini; what is needed is a doctrine *De Ecclesia* which goes beyond the juridical level which is so prevalent in the schema.

Like all the Italians, he spoke appreciatively of the prevailing fraternal unity. Stress the aspect of MYSTERY of the Church, the mystery of Christ. But today there is above all the mystery of Christ in the poor. None of the schemas so far presented deals with this aspect, whereas it was expressed by the prophets (*pauperes evangelizantur* [the poor have the gospel preached to them])[3], it completes the Incarnation of Christ and the Gospel, and it is the subject of one of the Beatitudes.

This point of view must be established as the basis of the work of the Council. The times demand this.

It is not a question of ADDING A SCHEMA on this question, but of incorporating this theme in ALL the matters discussed by the Council ... He suggested:

1) present before all else the doctrine of the poverty of Christ.

2) Give priority to the evangelical doctrine of the eminent dignity of the poor;

3) In all the schemas, the connection between the presence of Christ in the poor and his presence in the Eucharist, in the hierarchy, should be highlighted.

4) In the schemas concerning ecclesial renewal and adaptation to the preaching of the Gospel to the world, the exigencies of the evangelisation of the poor should be highlighted in all settings.

a) limitation of the use made of material means;

b) limitation of episcopal pomp;

c) fidelity to poverty even at community level;

d) *novus ordo de re economica* [new economic order];

If one has these concerns in one's spirit, one will easily find the right way to express even dogmatic formulations (applause).

Mgr Felici[4] read the *ordo* to be observed between the two Sessions. The Pope has decided:

1) *Curandum erit ut schemata* [it is to be seen to that the schemas] are revised, bearing in mind the wishes expressed by the conciliar Commissions.

2) *Finis concilii proprius* [The proper goal of the Council] expressed by

---

1. For the text, cf *AS* I/IV, 322–326.
2. *AS* I/IV, 327–330.
3. Luke 4:18, which quotes Isaiah 61:1.
4. *AS* I/IV, 330.

the Pope must govern everything. Reference to *'neque opus nostrum'* [it is not our task . . .][1] (Address on 11 October).

There is no need to repeat what has already been established and everyone knows. But formulation of doctrine that is ADAPTED TO OUR OWN DAY, and an attitude of kindness and mercy towards the world.

3) Choose, from the existing schemas, the points that are most important and UNIVERSAL.

Matters concerning the revision of canon law will be submitted to a special commission.

4) *Interea* [in the meantime], a commission will be set up to co-ordinate the work; it will consist of cardinals and some bishops. Its *munus* [task] will be to follow and co-ordinate the work of the Commissions and to ensure that the texts produced are in accordance with the purpose of the Council.

Utiliter consultari poterunt alii qui experientia praestant [others who are distinguished by their experience may be usefully consulted], especially in external matters *(LAY PEOPLE?)*.

5) Once the schemas have been revised and approved *in genere* [in general] by the Pope, they will be sent to the bishops for them to study.

6) The conciliar Commissions will then proceed to make the necessary corrections in the light of the bishops' comments.

Mgr Compagnone[2] (Italy): made a critique of what had been done and said at the Council. The President, Cardinal Tisserant,[3] interrupted him by saying: You have said nothing about the question of the Church, you have made the Council's examination of conscience. Thank you!

A Spaniard[4] praise for the schema (spoke very quickly).

Avoid giving the impression of any going back on the existing position regarding the magisterium, and find suitable forms of expression (always *Doctrina*, cut and dried, and some pleasant external touches).

Méndez[5] (Mexico) (the paper of which he had shown me the first draft, but much changed): praised the awareness that had come about through the fact of the Council.

---

1. The beginning of a phrase from the opening speech on 11 October when the Pope declared that it was not a question, in this Council, of repeating more fully what had already been determined by the Fathers of the Church and theologians concerning certain fundamental chapters of doctrine; cf *AS* I/I, 171.
2. *AS* I/IV, 331–332.
3. *AS* I/IV, 333.
4. J Hervás y Benet, *AS* I/IV, 334–337.
5. *AS* I/IV, 338–341.

Chapter III on the sacramental aspect of the episcopate is isolated; in Chapter I the bishops are not even mentioned, it speaks of nothing but Peter.

In *De Magisterio*, the magisterium of the bishops is defined only as derived from that of the pope.

The relationship between the pope and the bishops: in favour of the principle of subsidiarity and for a better balance, more in accordance with the Gospel. He presented two questions: the Jews, the acrimony aroused these past two centuries by certain measures; the question of F∴ M∴ [Freemasonry] (he said a lot of things!!).

Philbin[1] (English pronunciation): he suggested three principles for judging:

1) Our primary aim, from the doctrinal point of view, is to define the truths that are being attacked today. For example, the rights of the Church, the distinction between the two priesthoods.

2) Where there is no danger, do not dwell on the theology.

3) Never give the impression of going back on doctrines that have been established, and do not stay silent about them.

Mgr Renard:[2] something needs to be said in the schema about PRIESTS. The obedience promised by the priest is bound up with the Sacrament itself.

Fares[3] (?) (Italian pronunciation).

I went out and met several bishops: Méndez, bishop from Chile. I heard only a few passages of the very fine intervention by the Superior of the Marists.[4] We must not start from authority, he said, but from the free person and from conscience (Oh, Newman!)

Mgr Stella:[5] replied to the accusations made by De Smedt concerning legalism, etc. In favour of the Hierarchy, Monarchy in the Church, etc. (Italian pronunciation).

Mgr Hakim[6] (in French) returned to the idea of the Church of the poor. Cf population, hunger. That is why we would like to find in the schema *De Ecclesia* not what one finds in the manuals but what human beings are in need of.

The episcopate: the function of the pope and the bishops as a service of love. From the Eastern point of view: no account has been taken of this. Too many juridical categories.

Of the three hundred notes, only five mentions of the Greek Fathers.

---

1. William Philbin, Bishop of Down and Connor (Ireland), *AS* I/IV, 341–344.
2. Alexandre Renard, Bishop of Versailles, member of the conciliar Commission on the Discipline of the Sacraments, future Cardinal-Archbishop of Lyons, *AS* I/IV, 344-346.
3. A Fares, *AS* I/IV, 346–349
4. Joseph Buckley, *AS* I/IV, 353–355.
5. Costantino Stella, Archbishop of L'Aquila, *AS* I/IV, 356–357.
6. *AS* I/IV, 358–360.

> Two examples of legalism stifling the mystical realism of the Eastern Fathers.
> The power of the body of bishops is derived directly from Christ and is defined by the pope for a particular territory.
> The schema should be be sent back to a commission that includes experts in Eastern theology.
> (FINE TEXT, well delivered) (listened to attentively).

The results were given of the votes cast this morning on the *emendationes*. The Council of Presidents asked if it would be possible to proceed tomorrow to a vote on the whole of the amended text of the *Proemium* and of Chapter 1 of *De Liturgia*. Vote by standing or remaining seated.

Returned here at 1 pm. The cardinal[1] and bishops from the Philippines were expected for lunch. I ate only a salad and a slice of ham, as the festivities go on for a long time and I have to prepare a brief summary of my comments on the *De Ecclesia*. Fr General had in fact paid me the compliment of asking me what I thought because, he said, I was competent. I went to Santa Sabina with my text and we spoke briefly. Fr General did not like the Marist General's intervention this morning . . .

I referred to Parente, to the fact that he had attributed the substitute text to me. Fr General knew that it was Rahner who had produced this text: he was very critical of it, and said that there were many things that needed to be corrected or that were missing, that it was more than anything a text of the edifying kind. He added that a number of the bishops had voted FOR the schema *de duobus fontibus* [on the two sources] IN ORDER TO vote against the substitute text. He said he was surprised, indeed somewhat shocked, that episcopates were adopting the attitude of homogeneous groups: the Germans, the Dutch, the Africans and even the French. He said the others were shocked by this and he was against the idea of making ONE person speak in the name of an entire group: that would be to promote a nationalistic spirit and opposition between ethnic groups. He spoke highly of the holy, individualistic anarchy of the Spaniards.

At 3.45 pm, they came to collect me to give a lecture at the Helvetia Romana. Alas, I have so little time and I shall be spending nearly three hours there! The Swiss, as usual, recreate something of Switzerland everywhere: tables with napkins, flowers, singing, snacks. I returned here only at 6.45 pm.

I prepared the reply to the interview that *L'Osservatore Romano* asked me for.[2]

Fr Stirnimann[3] told me that yesterday a 610 page book against the Jews was distributed gratis to the Fathers of the Council. Who pays for such idiotic things?

---

1. RI Santos, the only cardinal in the Philippines.
2. A questionnaire on the unity of the Church, a theme to which a special edition of *L'Osservatore della Domenica* was to be devoted.
3. Heinrich Stirnimann, OP, of the Province of Switzerland, Professor of Fundamental

(perhaps the Arabs?) That ought to evoke a strong reaction from the Fathers of the Council! . . .

(=Maurice Pinay, *Complotto contra la Chiesa*).[1]

Friday 7 December 1962

I have seen the anti-semitic book distributed to the Fathers. I arranged with Mgr Ancel for him to register a protest about it during his intervention this morning. He agreed, but then said that Cardinal Lefebvre, who was due to speak this morning about charity, could do it with greater effect. I saw Cardinal Lefebvre, who passed it on to Cardinal Liénart. The latter thought that it was not a good idea to set off on the path of alluding, AT THE COUNCIL, to things that have been published and distributed. There would be no end to it. A way must be found of reacting, but not in the Council itself. So the idea was dropped.

I said my goodbyes to the Observers.

A sung Mass in Gregorian chant was announced for tomorrow, so that the Fathers could sing with the faithful (applause).

There are seventy-four more down to speak! There is no time to listen to them; the Fathers can submit their papers on the chapters *De Ecclesia* to the secretariat; by 28 February at the latest.

Today, voting on the *proemium* and Chapter I of *De sacra Liturgia*.

I saw Mgr Florit, of Florence, and introduced myself to him, with a view to my January lecture. I did well, as it happens only too often that La Pira takes initiatives without informing him about them.[2]

> De Bazelaire:[3] what has been said about the authority of the Church is too harsh. Many people would listen to the Church if it spoke more maternally.
> In favour of the exercise of authority as service.
> Mgr Ghattas [4] (Thebes, Egypt): three comments:
> 1) Reduction of the Mystical Body first to the Church militant, then to those submissive to the hierarchy, then to the Roman Church. The saints are part of the Mystical Body. It is all built on a false problematic.

Theology at the University of Fribourg; he was later to become Rector of the same University and Co-President of the Swiss Commission for Evangelical/Roman Catholic Dialogue.

1. Maurice Pinay, *Complotto contra la Chiesa* (Rome, 1962); in his copy, Congar left a hand-written note: 'dreadful anti-semitic pamphlet distributed widely to the Fathers of the Council (where they resided) during the First Session of the Council.'
2. Giorgio La Pira, Christian Democrat Mayor of Florence until 1964; in contact with a number of Catholic theologians and intellectuals, he was working for the cultural extension of Christianity.
3. *AS* I/IV, 374–376.
4. *AS* I/IV, 376–377.

2) The schema seems to forget that for many centuries the expression 'Mystical Body' designated the Eucharist. The Copts, in Egypt, have baptism and the Eucharist. How can one look upon them as being outside the Mystical Body?

The notion of membership is ANALOGOUS.

3) Chapter 1 expresses a retrogressive point of view. The Tradition has always spoken of Churches. That includes the idea of collegiality. What needs to be said is: the Church is made up of all the Churches in communion with the Church of Rome.

The schema's formula is INNOVATORY, not traditional.

The schema should be reworked in a more traditional spirit.

Mgr Ancel[1] (listened to attentively by THOSE WHO WERE PRESENT): there is no contradiction between the juridical aspect and love, authority and service, collegiality and primacy. These aspects are brought into unity when one has recourse to the Gospel.

Christ a true king, founding a true kingdom BUT A SPIRITUAL ONE. The juridical organisation is itself subordinate to the spiritual life. The evangelical principles are valid even for the ecclesiastical organisation.

I left the Hall at 10.00 am. At the last minute, I managed to say a quick goodbye to a great many friends. In fact, I had an appointment to meet Mgr Doumith, the Maronite. He wanted my opinion about a document which was distributed to them this morning and which will be discussed this evening at the general assembly of the joint *De Fontibus* Commission, to which he belongs. It was a letter from Cardinal Ottaviani, endorsed by about twenty cardinals, many of them Italians (Bacci, Siri, Ruffini, etc.) and from some other countries (Godfrey, Wyszyński, etc.)[2] and asking the Pope that the revised schema *De Fontibus* condemn the errors manifested, in Biblical matters, in a certain number of publications, including: AM Dubarle's article in the *Revue Biblique* on original sin in Genesis,[3] the Biblical Atlas,[4] a Belgian text with the imprimatur of Namur,[5] which linked the infancy narratives in St Luke with the type of apocalyptic of which Daniel (written under Antiochus Epiphanes !!!) is the prime example. Etc. In short, an eruption of the Spadafora-Romano[6] offensive, although the Biblical Institute was not actually mentioned. On the contrary, there is a quotation from a text by Cardinal

---

1. *AS* I/IV, 379–381.
2. This petition, signed by nineteen cardinals, was dated 24 November.
3. 'Le péché originel dans la Genèse', in *Revue Biblique,* 1957: 5–34.
4. J De Fraine, *Nouvel Atlas historique et culturel de la Bible* (Paris, Elsevier, 1961); J De Fraine, SJ, was an exegete and taught at the Jesuit scholasticate near Louvain.
5. F Neyrinck, *L'Évangile de Noël selon saint Luc* (Brussels: Pensée Catholique, 1960); the author taught at the major seminary in Bruges.
6. Gerrit C Berkouwer, *The Second Vatican Council and the New Catholicism* (Grand Rapids, 1965).

Bea in the lecture he gave at the Italian Biblical Week, expressing concern about serious biblical errors. Cardinal Bea can explain himself to the joint Commission. But Mgr Doumith told me that at this Commission he says very little. After all, Bea the biblical scholar was somewhat conservative!

(For the names of the cardinals who signed this letter, see P Wenger, *Vatican II. Première session* (Centurion, 1963), page 116 note 12. To be corrected by Rouquette, *Études*, June 1963: page 419 note 1)[1]. According to Rouquette, Cardinals Marella, Browne and even Pizzardo, were not among the signatories. He gives the names of eighteen (not nineteen) cardinal signatories. According to *ICI*, 15 March 1963, page 4, five cardinals who had at first signed this letter later withdrew their signatures (which? I think Wyszyński, the Patriarch of Venice[2]???).[3]

I also spoke to Mgr Doumith,[4] about his fine intervention the other day on the episcopate, the text of which he gave me. I also said something to him about the idea of Tradition.

The meeting (the last!) of the joint Commission when it takes place this evening at 5 pm. That will undoubtedly warm up a bit. The others have struck their blow at the last minute, doubtless in the hope that it would go through more easily. Besides, I think that there are some real dangers. Is the Council the place and appropriate means for avoiding them?

I am told that I missed a visit from the Pope who came at noon to recite the *Angelus* with the Fathers and address a few words to them.

Sunday 9 December 1962

I have just returned from a trip to Naples where I wanted to go in order to respond to the invitation of the Fathers who are there making a very interesting attempt at Dominican work aimed at promoting good preaching among the clergy. I wanted to help them. In my opinion everything that is done with a view to converting Italy to the Gospel from political, ecclesiological or devotional ultramontanism, is that much gained for the universal Church as well. That is why, in the coming months, I am going to accept a number of engagements with this end in view.

The Fathers were marvellously kind to me. They received me as if I were a king. On Friday evening, 7 December, at the *studium* in Barra,[5] a session with several of the Fathers and the student brothers. The Province was re-established only in 1937. It is young, it feels it lacks the support of a tradition. But their line of work is authentic.

On the morning of Saturday, 8 December, (a public holiday in Italy), Fr Mongillo collected me at 9 am to take me on a tour by car. By way of Pompeii to the

---

1. Congar wrote in the margin of this paragraph: 'added later'.
2. G Urbani.
3. The text of the letter and its signatories, such as they appear in the archives of Cardinal Ruffini, were published: cf *Cristianesimo nella Storia,* February, 1990: 124–126.
4. Who had spoken on 4 December 1962; see above, page 297.
5. The house of studies for the Province of Naples was at Barra-Napoli.

gates of Salerno. Instead of going into the city, we took the coastal road. A sky with a purity and luminosity that even the Holy Land does not have. Every shade of Mediterranean green: the olive trees, the orange trees, the cedars, the cacti. The sea, at our feet, calm and boundless. A silence which was sweeter and more of a tonic for me than everything else.

We climbed up to Ravello, dominated by towers perched at the top of rugged peaks. We visited the remains of a villa or a Moorish-style castle: a kind of Arabian villa, the various buildings of which follow one another, separated from one another, in the midst of beautiful gardens. That dated from the eleventh to twelfth century. It interested me enormously from the point of view of St Thomas. The land of the Aquino family and Thomas's mother were not so very far from here. I know, of course, that at that time all these roads did not exist. St Thomas cannot have come HERE. It is however impossible that he did not, in this region, brush up against or encounter an Arabian civilisation still at the peak of its power and youth. What I saw explained to me how it was that St Thomas paid so much attention to the Arabs, to the *Gentiles*. I perceived St Thomas FILLED WITH AN EXTREMELY OPEN AND ACTIVE ATTENTION to the world which surrounded him. He experienced there a perceptible revelation of a whole world of great culture.

Amalfi: a little port, the town tightly squeezed into the gorge which goes down to the sea. Cathedral (façade, tower) and cloister in full Arabic style. How these men followed their inspiration and were so little dominated by the fixed rules of the academy!

We returned to the priory in Naples at 1.40 pm. Lunch.

Lecture at 5 pm. Good night. It is curious: since exactly Sunday 2 December, I have been much better. I wonder whether perhaps I am on the way to a cure. I still have difficulty in climbing stairs, and I am dragging my legs a bit, but that is much better than in November when, in the midst of continuing storms and strong winds, things were going far from well.

This Sunday morning, I visited the National Picture Gallery in the royal summer palace. What riches! Italy had local kings, lords and patrons of the arts who assembled splendid collections of paintings.

I returned to Rome in the afternoon; I typed an article which I wrote in Naples, for *Témoignage Chrétien*. I saw Fr Camelot who told me: 1) that the ceremony in St Peter's yesterday was lovely. The Mass, sung by all the bishops, then the Pope came at the end and spoke for a quarter of an hour.[1]

2) The meeting of the joint Commission on Friday evening was a stormy one. At the end, Cardinal Suenens protested very strongly about the letter signed by the twenty cardinals concerning biblical dangers.[2]

---

1. Pope John XXIII's speech for the closing of the First Session of the Council, *AS* I/IV, 643–649; *La Documentation Catholique*, 1963, col 7–12.
2. It was actually De Smedt who protested against the petition of the nineteen cardinals,

Finally, before packing this notebook in my case, I record a few thoughts that came to my mind in the train.

Ottaviani reproaches me for saying sometimes good things, sometimes bad things in my *Vraie et fausse Réforme*. He wouldn't want anything of complementarity, he never either speaks or thinks of the Church dialectically. Everything is praiseworthy, everything must be praised. They know only ONE line: the one that is homogeneous and favourable to the assertion of their authority.

Their way of taking a few lines from a whole page or even from a whole book, is consonant with this. They do not want to assess these few lines in the balance of a whole way of thinking. For them it is the part that does not conform, that is not homogeneous, that must be excluded and reproved.

I was struck, when talking both to Fr General and to Mgr Doumith, by the interest they displayed in the name of Geiselmann, whom neither of them actually knows but about whom they questioned me indirectly. I find myself wondering whether perhaps Parente is seeking to have the Geiselmann thesis condemned by the Council, and whether perhaps he has excluded me not only on account of his personal jealousy but in order, somehow or other, to include me in this without my being able to defend the open thesis forcefully.

If they keep on talking about the two sources and the *partim-partim*,[1] this is because their concept of Revelation is of a series of particular propositions. The declaration that everything is contained, in some way, in Scripture comes from the idea that Revelation is A WHOLE. For me, it is the revelation of a TRUE RELIGIOUS RELATIONSHIP. This point is the principle of the soundness of all the rest.

Why is it THE SECRETARIAT that has been called upon to act as a counterweight to the 'Holy Office'? In a sense, it is not entirely a happy solution. It cannot do everything and it does not always have the most qualified men . . . But it is because it is the (only) instrument of dialogue with the world; hence it represents the need to reply to the questions people are asking, going beyond what is merely accepted.

Tuesday 11 December 1962
Paris. At noon, lunch at the *Études*. Before and afterwards, work with Fr Daniélou and Colson. Daniélou told me about the meeting of the joint Commission on 7 December. Agreement was reached on all the chapters. The only remaining sticking point is the question of Scripture-Tradition. The German bishops (Frings, Volk, Schröffer) brought Fr K Rahner with them, who stood up emphatically to Tromp and in a magnificent Latin. The text proposed, and which Cardinal Bea accepted, said that tradition *'latius patet'* [is wider than] Scripture, *praesertim* [especially] as regards inspiration and the canonicity of Scripture. Fr Rahner, sensing

---

as Daniélou was to inform Congar on 11 December (cf below, page 250).
1. Cf Note on page 228.

that this *'praesertim'* concealed the intention to extend considerably the range of truths of faith not contained in the Scriptures, asked if that was all, if one would limit oneself to these cases, *an non* [or not]? Tromp did not reply.

According to Daniélou, Cardinal Bea was very weak. He was in favour of a compromise formula. The Secretariat followed him. Feiner (a specialist in the matter, or a self-styled one, at the Secretariat), did not say a word. Baum intervened feebly. Thils was not there. Archbishop Heenan declared that his only reason for voting in favour of the text was the fact that Cardinal Bea was in favour of it. Daniélou managed to make a sign to Mgr Garrone and to Mgr McGrath not to vote IN FAVOUR. In the end, there was a narrow majority in favour of the proposed formula. Ottaviani wanted to regard it as agreed upon, but Cardinal Frings objected, arguing for the need of a two-thirds majority.

The meeting ended (after two hours of very tense discussion), and the *Hail Mary* had been recited when Mgr De Smedt got up to protest against the letter signed by the twenty cardinals which, as it was not a document *sub secreto*, had been passed around that morning. This letter overrides permissions to print that had been given by two of the Council Fathers . . . Embarrassed reply by Ottaviani, who claimed the right to intervene in this way for the sake of orthodoxy in Biblical matters.

Wednesday morning 12 December 1962

I went to the Déjerine Ward at the Salpêtrière for a series of tests (x-ray, blood, lipiodol imaging, stomach probe, electro-encephalogram . . .) until the afternoon of Friday 14.

Productive experience of a hospital ward.

On my return to Strasbourg, I found an immense backlog of work, coinciding with a lot of proofs to be corrected. There were also problems due to the fact that my case did not follow me, having been left behind by Secours Catholique. I did not recover it until the evening of 16 January 1963, after many telegrams, letters, visits to the customs and to the station, as well as sleepless nights . . . ! That was for me, for my work, for the manuscripts that I was due to deliver to Fayard,[1] a real catastrophe.

Preached the retreat in Lille. This gave me the opportunity, *ON 4 JANUARY 1963*, to see Cardinal Liénart. I found him astonishingly young and 'involved'. To begin with, he gave me the distribution of the work among the seven cardinals of the Co-ordinating Commission. This was as follows:

| Cardinal Cicognani: | *De Ecclesiis orientalibus* [on the Eastern Churches] |
| | *De Missionibus* [on the Missions] |

---

1. For two works due to appear: *La Tradition et les traditions. Essai théologique* (Paris: Fayard, 1963) and *La Tradition et la vie de l'Église* (Paris: Fayard, 1963).

	De unione fovenda inter christianos [on Promoting Union between Christians]
Cardinal Liénart:	*De Revelatione* [on Revelation]
	De Deposito pure custodiendo [on Keeping the Deposit of Faith Pure]
Cardinal Spellman:	*De Liturgia* [on Liturgy]
	De Castitate et Matrimonio [on Chastity and Marriage]
Cardinal Urbani: (Venice)	*De clericis;* [on Clerics]; *De laicis* [on the Laity]
	De mediis communicationis inter homines [on the Means of Social Communication]
	De matrimonii sacramento [on the Sacrament of Marriage]
Cardinal Confalonieri:	*De Seminariis* [on Seminaries], *De Studiis et Scholis* [on Studies and Schools]
Cardinal Döpfner:	*De Episcopis et regimine diocesium* [on Bishops and the Government of Dioceses]
	De Cura animarum [on Pastoral Care]
	De Religiosis [on Religious]
Cardinal Suenens:	*De Ecclesia* [on the Church]
	De Beata Maria Virgine [on the Blessed Virgin Mary]
	De ordine sociali [on the Social Order].

He, too, told me about the meeting on 7 December. He said it had been 'dramatic'. Since then, he had written to Cardinal Ottaviani in order to say: 'Truth demands' that one does not settle a point about which the Commission itself could not reach agreement. There was not and there would not be the required 2/3 majority for any of the theses in question.

Cardinal Liénart is very determined to force the Commission to work in the spirit and along the lines of the Council. He told me that the other cardinals were of the same mind and that the Romans (Ottaviani) realise that that they will have to give in. He is fairly optimistic about the Pope regaining his health and very optimistic that everything will have been brought to a close by December 1963. Having been made responsible for supervising and directing the work, not only *De Revelatione,* but also *De Deposito fidei pure custodiendo,* his idea is to make of this latter schema a Christian anthropology: man in the thought of God, man the sinner, man restored by Christ the Redeemer and saved.

This could, in fact, be very good. In this way one would bring together, in the light of a single idea, the miscellaneous material in the schema, and do so in a positive, pastoral and kerygmatic way.

On 6 January, I met up again with Fr Daniélou who has given himself, or has arranged for himself to be given, a central role in all the French theological work between the two Sessions. He himself, by drawing things from right and from left, is writing a chapter on episcopal collegiality. Colson, who is there, is nonetheless more competent! Daniélou read me some letters from Mgr Garrone and Mgr Guerry putting him in charge of a kind of theological secretariat. We exchanged a lot of ideas about different points of *De Ecclesia*.

Canon Thils had invited me to Louvain. Knowing, as I did, the task that had been entrusted to Cardinal Suenens, and perceiving clearly that it would come, in the end, to working for him, I felt I ought to accept this invitation. So I went to Louvain for THE EVENING OF 12 JANUARY AND THE WHOLE OF 13 JANUARY, In fact, it was a question of: 1) deciding, with Mgr De Smedt, upon the ecclesiological line (the plan) to be defended by the Secretariat, which will be called upon, sooner or later, and one way or another, to intervene in the *De Ecclesia*;

2) to decide upon a plan which Cardinal Suenens will defend;

3) to point out to Mgr Philips a certain number of desirable improvements in his revised *De Ecclesia*.

Cardinal Suenens was very insistently of the view that *De Beata Virgine* should be put back into *De Ecclesia*. I said that l'abbé Laurentin was, if not the only one capable, at least the one most capable, of indicating how to proceed, the rocks to be avoided, the content and order of the chapter *De Beata*.

We settled for the idea of a *De Ecclesia* in four chapters:

1. *De Mysterio Ecclesiae* [On the Mystery of the Church]: in which one would take up the MISSION of the Church and the essential points *De membris* [on its membership], (but without using this term and presenting the motherhood of the Church in a POSITIVE manner).

2. *De Episcopis.* Developing the concept of collegiality.

3. *De laicis.*

4. *De Beata Maria Virgine.*

A tiring journey, but a fruitful one. After that, I saw Laurentin (21.1.63) at Le Saulchoir. I wrote to Philips. The work continues.

In the meantime, a fairly mediocre Week for Christian Unity.[1] I had refused all commitments and had only those that came up at the last minute.

Florence, Saturday 19 and Sunday 20.[2] Had a long session with La Pira. Also saw the young people associated with him and the review *Testimonianze*.[3] In this way he is preparing a generation of lay people who will transform Italian Catholicism.

---

1. Week of prayer for Christian Unity, organised each year from 18 to 25 January; Congar's custom was to give a number of lectures and homilies during this time.
2. Congar gave a lecture there in the context of Christian Unity week. His theme was: the sense of history and the unity of the Church.
3. *Testimonianze. Quaderni mensili di spiritualità* (Florence).

Monday and Tuesday at Le Saulchoir. Lecture.
Tuesday evening, Lecture to NATO with Roger Schutz.[1]
Wednesday 23, lecture in Strasbourg.[2]

24 January 1963

Spent the day at Mont Saint-Odile with Mgr Elchinger, Flusin, Boillon, Huyghe. Fr Féret was there. Canon Chavasse and Fr Bouyer had come there a few days earlier. We worked on *De Ecclesia*. I feel ill at ease with certain great schemes for a total reworking and with the whole of *De Ecclesia*; very interesting personal syntheses, but that is not what it is about. We must bear in mind:

1) what we are dealing with;
2) for whom we are working.

However, I may well be too timid, too passive, even pusillanimous? I am also very tired. My right leg and my right arm are not working at all. I sleep very little and badly. I am having problems: to do with *'Nec nominetur'* [let it not be named], in which they are convinced I have conducted a publicity campaign on the subject of the Council.[3] I have flu and a little bit of angina.

Friday 25 January 1963

Left for Mainz at 5.10 pm. Stupidly, I had not re-read the letter from Mgr Volk and so I went direct to the bishop's house which is a long way out (by the No. 21 tram). Mgr Volk was not there but his sister invited me to stay the night but, after telephoning, I joined the meeting at Ketteler-Haus.

Saturday 26 January 1963

Working session at 9 am. In addition to Mgr Volk, those present at the meeting were: Mgr Philips, Frs Schillebeeckx and Mulders,[4] Ratzinger, K Rahner,

---

1. Lecture arranged by Noel H Salter (see above, page 204).
2. Congar added to the typescript 'I also prepared, with Mgr Weber, the comments he was to make on the schema *De Ecclesia*, especially on chapter 1'.
3. Cf Eph 5:3 {Congar means he had mentioned things that should not have been mentioned}. Congar was obliged to respond to an article by Carlo Falconi which appeared in *L'Espresso* on 6 January, according to which he was held to have made a number of revelations concerning the preparatory schemas; the Master General of the Order having called for explanations from his Provincial, Fr Kopf, Congar declared to the latter, in a letter dated 25 January, that he had always sought to be discreet with journalists and that he had been moderate in his comments on the preparatory schemas (Congar Archives).
4. Gerard Philips' journal of the Council states rather that it was Piet Smulders, SJ, who was present, a professor of theology at the Canisianum, the Jesuit scholasticate in Maastricht; from being the personal expert for one of his former students, he became a Council expert from the Second Session onwards. Congar must have confused his name with that of another Dutchman, Alfons J Mulders, a missiologist teaching at

Grillmeier, Semmelroth, Schnackenburg,[1] myself, and then, in the afternoon, Fr Hirschmann.[2]

(Shortly before Christmas, the German theologians had held a first meeting in Mainz, specifically to study the official schema. Then, shortly after Christmas, a meeting in Munich with some of the bishops, in order to begin the project of drafting a new text.)

We read and discussed the schema prepared by Grillmeier, with the help of Schnackenburg and Semmelroth. The Germans have thus produced a complete schema: or rather, a TREATISE! I criticised the idea of producing a treatise. The Germans' idea is to perfect a text (that will be done at the meeting of German-speaking bishops in Munich on 5 February), to try to secure for this text the highest possible number of votes in favour, indeed even the votes of the greatest possible number of episcopates, and to present it to the Theological Commission as the expression of what is looked for by a great number of bishops (episcopates). Thus, without being adopted as such, the text would be used more or less extensively for the preparation of the revised schema.

The text has been drawn up very much in relation to Protestants; an effort has been made to support each statement by biblical references.

I myself find the text too long,
  - too scholarly (not scholastic!), being expressed more as a course in theology than a Council document;
  - it includes some points that are not essential to the Catholic faith as such, and represent an option (eg concerning the membership of the Church and the status of non-Catholics).

Mgr Volk receives people with a simplicity and refinement of heart that are extraordinary. He is friendly, engaged, affectionate.

During the conversation, I realised more clearly how the criticisms made of the texts produced by the Preparatory Theological Commission, the speeches made and the votes cast during the First Session, were, and were intended to be, a condemnation of the Holy Office and a rejection of Fr Tromp's theology. It is AGAINST THAT, once again, that the Second Session is preparing itself.

But there is a certain confusion and vagueness about our proposals. I felt again the atmosphere that reigned at certain meetings in Rome: one seeks endlessly and in a vague way for WHAT IS TO BE DONE?

Fr Hirschmann had just returned from Rome where he attended a meeting of the Laity Commission. He is a remarkable man, realistic, precise. He must be very effective, this little fellow with the appearance of a *homo alpinus* [man of

---

Nijmegen and a Council expert.
1. Rudolph Schnackenburg, a priest of the diocese of Würzburg, and Professor of New Testament Exegesis at the University of Würzburg, consultor to the Pontifical Biblical Commission.
2. Johann Hirschmann, SJ, Professor of Moral and Pastoral Theology at the Sankt Georgen Jesuit scholasticate in Frankfurt, Council expert.

the Alps]. According to him: 1) there is an idea to include some lay people, at least on the Laity Commission. 2) Tromp, who has the greatest of contempt for the bishops, is afraid of the Commission comprising the seven cardinals. 3) It is being whispered that Cardinal Ottaviani will withdraw from the 'Holy Office'. The rumour is based on the fact that he has several times got Cardinal Browne to stand in for him. God preserve us from Browne! I much prefer Ottaviani . . . 4) The idea of setting up a sort of Standing Central Commission (meeting once or twice a year), a sort of σύνοδος ἐνδημοῦσα around the pope, is gaining ground in Rome. It is being widely seen as possible. 5) Even now, in fact, Commissions which include bishops and other members from all over the world exist within, or alongside, a number of the Congregations, duplicating them to some extent, and enlarging them.

In this way, there is being sketched out what may well be John XXIII's idea, namely to make the Church move into a largely collegial and episcopal way of operating. The 'transitional Pope' would thus in fact become 'the Pope of transition'. It really seems that the internal result of the Council will be this: to put in place WORLD-WIDE organisms and no longer simply Romano-Catholic ones.

I returned at 3 am by a night train which was delayed so that I had a two hour wait at Karlsruhe.

Letter from Alberigo,[1] asking me a number of questions on behalf of Cardinal Lercaro. But serious questions, which would take me days to answer properly.[2] And also more energy than I have. I replied today—31 January. But I can barely type and my right leg can do no more than drag. Things are not too good and I am VERY tired.

6–7 February 1963

In Angers for the meeting of the bishops of the IIIrd Apostolic Region:[3] fifteen bishops and, on Thursday 7, Cardinal Roques, as negligible as in Rome.

The only bishops who are a little active theologically are Mgr Guyot and Mgr Cazaux[4] (but he speaks at great length, without making things clear). On the Wednesday evening, great presentation on the priesthood by Canon Derouet,[5] superior of the Laval major seminary. Some discussion on priestly holiness, also on the schema for the decree *De laicis*.

---

1. Giuseppe Alberigo, jurist and historian, was Director of the Documentation Centre of the Institute for Religious Studies, founded by Giuseppe Dossetti in Bologna; this Institute, whose principal aim is to work on the history of the ecumenical councils, provided Cardinal Lercaro with some experts during the Council, in particular Dossetti and Alberigo himself.
2. They had to do especially with the improvement of the *De Ecclesia* and the question of the evangelisation of the poor.
3. The Western Apostolic Region.
4. Antoine M Cazaux, Bishop of Luçon.
5. Pierre Derouet.

In the morning of Thursday 7 February, myself on *De Ecclesia*; in the afternoon, discussion, Laurentin on *De Beata Maria Virgine* and conclusions. (Laurentin seems to me to be increasing his tendency to worm his way in, to adapt himself, to have his plan . . .)

Mgr Mazerat received, there and then, documents coming from the Commission on the Clergy of which he is a member. He told us that everything, at the moment, is in a shambles: that is to say, that everything has been demolished, everything is in question; material is filtered, eliminated, reclassified and redistributed . . . The Commission of seven cardinals seems to have decided: there will be no mention of this; that will be re-allocated elsewhere: on another matter the Council will do no more than express its opinion and then appoint a commission which will draft a directory, etc. That just staggers me. I have the impression of a complete mess, an unbelievable improvisation. Everything is to be redone or to be done. And they pretend that it will be ready for September and that the Council will finish at Christmas?

In Angers, I met Mgr Derouineau[1] (at least I think that is his name. He is the missionary bishop who was expelled from China). It is he whom the Pope appointed to to try to win over the Petite Église, which represents just on nine hundred families in all (eight thousand people) in Deux-Sèvres, Lyons and the Cluny region. Mgr Derouineau has contacted everyone. Monsieur Hy,[2] who represents the Deux Sèvres group, would be well disposed, but everything comes to grief on account of the obstinacy of some people called Rolland in Lyons (Sainte-Foy), who are motivated by a sectarian and Jansenist spirit. They come back to the attack every time Mgr Derouineau has settled a point, and take everything back to square one.

A certain Tugdual the First has tried to get hold of the Petite Église. He calls himself Patriarch of the Celtic Church. He has got himself consecrated bishop and, it seems, not only has he administered Confirmation but he has also consecrated other bishops. Evidently, the wretched Kovalevski[3] is mixed up in it and has given his support. I think Tugdual lives in Saint-Dolé(?).

Saturday 9 February 1963

In the afternoon, visit from l'abbé Zimmermann,[4] Mgr Elchinger's secretary. He brought me: 1) the current version of the German schema *De Ecclesia*; 2) some texts which he gave me just to read, namely:

a) the currently planned redistribution of the schemas, under two main headings: the Church in herself, the Church with respect to her presence to the world.

---

1. Cf above, page 76, note 5
2. Jean Hy.
3. The reference is to Pierre Kovalevski or to his brother Eugraph who, within the Orthodox Catholic church, were endeavouring to promote a western Orthodoxy on the basis of Gallican traditions of the first millennium.
4. Jean-Paul Zimmermann.

It really is a major shake-up. Everything has been first pulverised and then redistributed . . . !!!

b) A letter from Mgr Villot saying what had been decided at the meeting of the seven cardinals:

- the dismemberment of *De deposito fidei pure custodiendo*, resulting in its suppression;
- the inclusion of certain elements of *De Magisterio* in a *De Ecclesiae principiis et actione ad bonum societatis promovendum* [on the principles and action of the Church in promoting the good of society].
- the transformation of *De ordine morali* into a *De persona humana in societate* [on the human person in society], which will be incorporated into the above-mentioned schema;
- the dismemberment of *De castitate*, of which only the chapter on marriage and the family will remain.

It is the death knell of curialist theology, of the spirit of Pius XII and *Humani Generis,* of the 'Holy Office'.

That evening, a long telephone call from Mgr Elchinger. He is delighted with the meeting in Munich: more than fifty bishops were there, about ten religious superiors, conciliar Fathers, and a score or so of theologians, including Schauf. The Mainz text had been completed and amended considerably. Mgr Elchinger thought it good, as it now stands: such that one ought to get behind it to give it its best chance. Mgr Philips has already got behind it. Moreover, the Philips text for *De membris* will be taken up. The Germans (Cardinal Döpfner) will send it to Ottaviani, not as a substitute text, but as an expression of what a great number of the bishops desire.

The Pope, it seems, is quite well. He is counting on closing the Council at Christmas and is planning projects for after the Council. The German bishops think that one OUGHT NOT to end by Christmas: it would mean having to rush everything.

The German bishops have worked out a policy for those who will have to adopt a position: 1) state clearly that it is not a question of a dogmatic formulation, but of a wide-ranging presentation of what the Church thinks; 2) reject absolutely Tromp's *De membris*; 3) insist on collegiality, without giving up anything of Vatican I; 4) as regards mariology, propose an expression of what the Church holds while at the same time avoiding whatever might offend non-Catholics and excluding the question of co-redemption and that of mediation.

Mgr Elchinger told me that a meeting of the Theological Commission has been called for 20 February (whereas the bishops have until 25 February to submit their comments): it will have to have completed its work on *De Ecclesia, De fontibus* or *De Revelatione* and *De Beata Maria Virgine* before 10 March!

It is absolutely impossible!

It would seem that the Pope has refused to accept the text for which there was a narrow majority at the meeting of the joint Commission on 7 December. He has said that a two thirds majority is required (this is Liénart's and Frings' position). If agreement cannot be reached, they will simply take up again the text of Trent and of Vatican I.

It would seem that Cardinal Ottaviani appears to be fairly relaxed and makes Fr Tromp responsible for whatever goes wrong.

Mgr Elchinger was very impressed by the atmosphere at the Munich meeting and by the cooperation between bishops and theologians. Here we have anarchy, dispersion. The bishops are not very interested in theology so they do not expect much from the theologians and do not ask them to undertake any serious work. Mgr Elchinger told me he had written along these lines to Cardinal Liénart. He is to see Fr Daniélou in Paris next week.

In fact, I find that the French bishops have expected almost nothing from us. But only very few of them are fit to take a CLOSE interest in theological matters and to WORK seriously with the theologians.

Thursday 14 February 1963

Lecture by Mgr Constantinidis[1] on unity from the Orthodox point of view. He presented a doctrine that seemed to me, on the whole, to be a kind of modernising opening up which has very little basis in Orthodox theology. Either this does not amount to very much, or it is the beginning of quite a new adventure.

He drew a distinction between the absolute unity or unicity of the Church, which exists, and what is being sought, which does not yet exist: in the latter he distinguished between UNION and UNITY. In his view, union is the re-attachment of one Church to another: there is one part that absorbs and another part that is absorbed.

Unity = 'perichoresis of the constituent parts'. It is not the same thing as simple coexistence; nor is it the same as a *modus vivendi*. It is fairly close to what I believe ECUMENICAL DIALOGUE to be in its full dimension. But the basis of this 'unity' is the fact of taking others for what they are and of bringing about between them a mutual penetration.

All that seems to me to be rather improvised and very vague. What minimum common basis would be required? Would Orthodox theology, which in principle (*de iure*) does not recognise the sacraments of other Churches, have the beginnings at least of a theology of the *vestigia Ecclesiae* [traces of the Church][2]? Would mutual penetration go as far as sharing in the Eucharist?

---

1. Chrysostomos Constantinidis, Metropolitan of Myra and Professor of Theology at the School of Theology at Chalki, near Istanbul. Having done his studies in the West, principally in Rome and Strasbourg, during which time he first encountered an ecumenical environment, he was called upon by Patriarch Athenagoras as emissary and counsellor in ecumenical relationships.
2. This expression was used at that time by ecclesiologists to designate those ecclesial elements that persist in Christian communities that do not belong to the one true Church.

My impression is that we are here dealing with a JUXTAPOSITION of a rigid orthodox ecclesiology, that of unicity, that of St Cyprian[1] and of Firmilian,[2] and a theological pseudo-formulation of the ecumenical FACT. I am somewhat disappointed, intellectually. On the other hand, the man himself is extremely pleasant and attractive.

On my way back, dragging my leg, and even dragging myself along, I was approached by someone who offered me a hand. I believe it was l'abbé Heitz.[3] I did not dare to ask him his name. He accompanied me all the way to the Priory, and seemed to know me very well, almost as if he had seen me only yesterday. On the way he said to me: Mgr Constantinidis has just come from Rome and is going to visit Germany. He will be meeting Cardinals Frings, Döpfner, and König, and Mgr Volk. The underlying purpose of his journey or of his mission would be that, in a Church that is becoming, or that is, reunited, the Patriarch of Constantinople[4] does not want to lose his place, which is that of second in the Church. The Secretariat for Unity is apparently seeking to reach an agreement with Visser't Hooft on the one hand, and with the Russians on the other. Constantinople would like to recover an initiative as Premier See, to be looked upon as Premier See.

It is possible. That does not interest me very much. The real problem is quite different. And if John XXIII is making overtures to Russia, it is for the sake of Peace in the world! I said this to him (? Heitz).

Friday 15 February 1963

A visit from Mgr Constantinidis. When all is said and done, he did not tell me anything much. The sending of Observers was impossible, because nine orthodox Churches had stated they were against the idea. I said that there could be some Orthodox there as personal guests of the Secretariat. Mgr Constantinidis agreed, found it a good idea, but seems not to have thought of the idea earlier, which seems to me unlikely.

I spoke about how Constantinople might be kept informed about the Council. I said that Mgr Cassien[5] could produce a report. It is impossible, because he went to the Council in spite of the fact that the Holy Synod of Constantinople was against the idea. As a result, once again it will be through the envoys from Moscow that Constantinople will receive most of its information . . .

---

1. Cyprian of Carthage, third century Father of the Church.
2. Firmilian, bishop of Caesarea in Cappadocia; whose support Cyprian sought and secured against Rome for his rigid position that baptism administered by schismatics was not valid.
3. Alphonse Heitz, having been a parish priest in the diocese of Strasbourg, then attached to the Istina Centre, had joined the Orthodox, and been conditionally re-ordained.
4. Athenagoras: born in 1886, he had been elected in 1948.
5. Cassien Bezobrazov, Rector of the Saint-Sergius Institute of Orthodox Theology under the Patriarch of Constantinople, and titular bishop, guest of the Secretariat for Unity for the first three Sessions, he was to die in February 1965.

Mgr Constantinidis did mention the extremely good relationship between Visser't Hooft and the Secretariat, and the great love that had been displayed at the time of the continuation committee of the World Council of Churches in Paris last August.[1] He was very scathing about the pragmatism and confusion there had been at the New Delhi Conference.[2] It was sheer Babel, he said. On the whole, a very cordial visit. I spoke more than he did. I referred to the extremely positive attitude of the great majority of the Council in ecumenical matters, and the intense desire of the faithful.

Saturday 23 February 1963

Telephone call from Mgr Elchinger, who takes Council matters very much to heart and who is anxious to be effective. He told me:

1) he had received a letter from Fr de Lubac, who had just returned from Rome. Lubac was pessimistic, saying that the Theological Commission would not accept and would not contemplate doing anything other than beginning with the existing schema, and making some improvements to it.

That enraged Mgr Weber, who at once wrote a letter to Mgr Garrone telling him that, if that was how things were, the bishops would demolish the proposed text and would send it back to be redone.

2) the Theological Commission is supposed to have finished ALL its work by 10 March. And, if I understood correctly, not only the Theological Commission but the others also.

3) he had received a letter from Cardinal Suenens telling him this, and asking him to produce something on the problems of conjugal morality.

4) Mgr Elchinger had written a very tough letter to Mgr Garrone complaining about the scandal of the fact that the FRENCH bishops were making almost no use of their theologians.

– He also told me that he had spent two hours with Fr Daniélou but that they had been constantly interrupted by telephone calls. Daniélou, he said, works like a journalist. Many people complain about him. Moreover, he arranges texts as he chooses: there were two complaints about this to the Secretariat of the Episcopate, one from Canon Thils[3].

In fact he re-arranged and cut my own texts: he published one under my name (with that of Holstein) which I had never sent him;[4] he had shortened Fr Lécuyer's text as he chose. Laurentin was very incensed about this too.

---

1. The reference is to the meeting of the World Council of Churches which was held in Paris from 7 to 16 August, 1962.
2. The reference is to the Third General Assembly of the World Council of Churches which was held from 19 November to 5 December 1961.
3. Congar wrote on the second typescript: 'and from Laurentin, I think'.
4. From 15 January 1963 onwards, the Secretariat for the French Episcopate began publishing, under Daniélou's editorship, the first issues of *Études et documents* on the matters discussed at the Council.

Friday 1 March, 1963

This morning at 8.10 I received an EXPRESS letter: just a quick card from Fr Daniélou asking me to come to Rome. I found that a bit casual. I have commitments for Lent, lectures. I could have been given more warning. I hesitated for a moment. Would the journey be worthwhile? I am afraid of once again finding myself working to no purpose. But it might also be important. So I decided to go. Within half an hour I had obtained information about planes. Air France no longer has a flight from Strasbourg to Rome *via* Nice: One has to go through Paris and the plane had already left. In the end, the following itinerary was worked out: Offenburg, Basle, Zurich, then Zurich-Rome by plane.

I telephoned the Cathedral and worked out with Fr Maillard a list of the things for which he will have to find a substitute for me. Fr Maillard was marvellous: he drove me to Offenburg. I packed my things in less than a quarter of an hour, and have surely forgotten something.

The whole of Switzerland was covered with snow: the lakes were frozen, everything was white, except for the woods which were dark patches in the otherwise unbroken white background. It was an Irish plane. In Rome, the all too familiar interminable journey from the airport to the city. I went to the French Seminary, where they made a telephone call to the Angelicum: there are no rooms free.

There I met up with Cardinal Lefebvre, Mgr Garrone, Mgr Martin, Mgr Cazaux and Canon Streiff.[1] Mgr Garrone told me that they had brawled all the week over Scripture and Tradition. THIS EVENING agreement had been reached with a majority of thirty against four or five. The Romans (Parente) wanted absolutely to declare that Tradition had a much larger content than Scripture. They also wanted to condemn a thesis. They were outvoted.

The official schema *De Ecclesia* has been set aside. Officially, another should be produced. Several versions were proposed. There was the one prepared by the Germans, but also one from Chile which is very interesting, it seems, and one from Mgr Parente . . . A sub-commission comprising seven members has been appointed to produce a new text. Each bishop on this commission has chosen a *peritus*: Cardinal Browne chose Fr Gagnebet, Mgr Parente Fr Balić, Cardinal König Rahner, Mgr Schröffer Thils, Mgr Garrone Fr Daniélou, Mgr Charue Philips. Cardinal Léger has two priests: Naud[2] and Lafortune.[3]

In addition there are Mgr Philips, Canon Thils and K Rahner as *periti*. Practically speaking, the work is being done at the Belgian College, centred on Philips

---

1. Jean Streiff, of the diocese of Nancy, Secretary General of French Catholic Action; expert at the Council from the Second Session onwards; he was later to become Bishop of Nevers.
2. André Naud, PSS, of the diocese of Montréal; having taught philosophy in Japan from 1954 to 1962, he was to teach theology at the University of Montréal; he was a Council expert from the Second Session onwards.
3. Pierre Lafortune was a theologian and canonist by training; he was the personal expert of Cardinal Léger, and was appointed a Council expert during the First Session.

and Thils. So it would be better for me to be at the Angelicum . . . But, when all is said and done, I am a supernumerary here and Mgr Garrone said that he will telephone Fr Daniélou tomorrow to find out how and in what capacity to get me in.

Curious, this being everywhere and doing everything of Fr Daniélou . . . In any case, no one knows at all how long the work will take. And I ask myself what I will do.

I am very cold. When I arrived, the airport was a real Siberia.

Saturday 2 March 1963

Things have become a little bit clearer. I saw Mgr Garrone and then, at 9 am, Fr Daniélou. Mgr Garrone showed me the text on Scripture and Tradition which had been agreed upon at the joint Commission yesterday evening. They had had some dramatic sessions, he told me, in particular on Monday last, when Parente read a letter from Cardinal Ottaviani, which created a general brouhaha. Cardinal Ottaviani was actually present, but his text was READ for him on account of his poor eyesight. In it he took Cardinal Bea personally to task. That led to such a discussion that the meeting had to be suspended, Cardinal Bea bringing the Secretariat together in his support. During this time, that is, while Cardinal Bea was out of the room, Cardinal Ruffini read a text of Fr Bea's dating from about twenty years ago with the aim of placing Cardinal Bea in a difficult position. That was looked upon as a shabby procedure by several of those present, and contributed to creating a very tense atmosphere.

In the end, agreement was reached, with some corrections, on a text which I do not find very good. They brawled over a phrase in which the Holy Office people wanted to reintroduce the equivalent of *'latius patet'* [is wider than]. I am amazed that they fought so much over that; for it is true that Tradition is wider than Scripture, but I am told that everyone agreed, but the objection was to the INTENTION, to what lay BENEATH. Because the Romans intended this as a condemnation of Geiselmann. The debate and people's attention were centred on this. Unfortunately, in my opinion. Because in this way they failed to look closely at other points which I consider to be more serious. In particular, No. 5 of the draft seems bad to me: at this point the tradition is presented as being entrusted to the MAGISTERIUM, not to the Church. And the magisterium is there presented as *'regula fidei proxima'* [the proximate rule of faith]—the *depositum* being the *regula remota* [remote rule]—without stating that it is a *regula regulata* [a rule that is itself subject to rule]. That will almost certainly no longer fit in with the *De Ecclesia* schema . . .

This question of substituting the Magisterium for the *ecclesia* occurs again in No. 6, where the three inseparable elements Scripture, Tradition, Church are replaced by Scripture, Tradition, Magisterium!

There are however other points which seemed to me unsatisfactory.

No. 3: Christ conveyed the Tradition to the Apostles *'oretenus'* [orally]; always this fiction of a secret transmission of WORDS and this exclusion of what, in Tradition, is concretely the most important, namely the private and lived realities;

No. 4: the *pari pietatis affectu* [with an equal sentiment of piety][1] is not sufficiently well related to TO THE ORIGIN, as was the case at the Council of Trent.

Fr Daniélou arrived at 9 am. He really has an extraordinary presence. He belongs to three commissions: theological (*De Ecclesia*), on the laity; and also the joint commission which is preparing schema XVII, that is to say the one destined to contain the left-overs from *De deposito* and the chapters on morality, in a kind of anthropology. This joint commission of six bishops is good, with McGrath, Guano, Gromius,[2] etc. But Mgr Glorieux[3] has allowed himself to impose Fr Lio, who is well known, and who wants to bring together all the texts from the official schemas; in the same way as Parente wanted to re-impose a pre-fabricated text on the *De Ecclesia* sub-commission. The people from the 'Holy Office' seem to have done their utmost to make their point of view prevail. They had succeeded in the case of the Preparatory Commission. Now they are defeated. Each time a vote is called for, they have a *SMALL* minority. Hence, Fr Lio is there in order to re-introduce the essence of his ideas. He has just been appointed Consultor (qualificator) of the Holy Office. It was to be expected. A fierce brawl will have to be fought. Fr Daniélou will undertake it. For this reason, he would like to withdraw from the *De Ecclesia* sub-commission and for me to take his place. It is a possibility. Cardinal Léger has two experts and is replacing Naud by Lafortune from today where, in the *De Ecclesia,* they are moving on from Chapter I (On the mystery of the Church: revised) to Chapter II (collegiality). In fact, Mgr Garrone telephoned Cardinal Browne, who is the Vice-President of the Theological Commission, and he had no difficulty about my taking Daniélou's place as Mgr Garrone's expert on the *De Ecclesia* sub-commission. Moreover, Cardinal Ottaviani has twice declared that any expert approved by the Holy Father could attend either the joint Bea-Ottaviani commission or the meetings of the Theological Commission.

It seems that the work will go on beyond 10 March. Moreover, it is very important that a French expert be present and active. So the expectation is that I should remain until 14 March and that Fr Daniélou will take over again from me at that point.

Towards the end of the morning, I went to see Mgr Philips—who was not there!—and to the Angelicum where I met, in five minutes, a whole lot of very

---

1. The expression comes from the Council of Trent and refers to Scripture and Tradition.
2. The name Gromius is not found in the *Annuario Pontificio*. The reference is in fact to the Dutchman, Joseph Blomjous, Bishop of Mwanza (Tanzania), cardinal in February 1965, who was a member of the Commission on the Apostolate of the Laity.
3. Achille Glorieux from the diocese of Lille, ecclesiastical assistant to COPECIAL (Comité permanent des congrès internationaux pour l'apostolat des laïcs), was secretary of the Preparatory Commission and then of the Conciliar Commission on the Apostolate of the Laity; he was later to become Pro-Nuncio in Syria, then in Egypt.

friendly friars, but where there is no room available. So I returned to the French Seminary.

My legs are working quite well. But, on my way back, I was beginning to drag my foot.

At 3.25 pm, visit from Mgr Charue.

At 4.05 or 4.10, I was with Fr Daniélou, who gave me various documents, including the Chile schema.

At 4.30 pm, at St Martha's in the Vatican, sub-commission of experts. Those present included Fr Gagnebet, Rahner, Balić, myself, Mgr Philips, Thils, l'abbé Lafortune and a secretary (Molari,[1] with whom I had had contact previously). Cordial atmosphere. Balić moved from amusing good humour to protestation, frowning and banging his fist on the table, in defence of the authority of the pope. He felt that too much authority was being given to the bishops. I said to him: we will see in September! What he wants above all is for the authority of the ordinary Magisterium (encyclicals) of the pope to be advocated because, according to him, it is being undermined. Example: the Pope had spoken on the question of the members of the Church and now there was silence about what he had said, which is a way of saying the opposite . . . I pointed out to him that, in the matter of the temporal power, for example, the ordinary power of the pope had said many things, from the thirteenth to the sixteenth century, which are passed over in silence nowadays.

The work is being carried out briskly, almost too rapidly for my taste. The draft of a fresh schema is accepted straight off; discussion begins straight off from Philips' text; straight off there is discussion of episcopal collegiality. What a change since the time of the Preparatory Commission, completely dominated by Fr Tromp.

Fr Daniélou, who seems to be well informed, told me that there have been complaints from people in very prominent positions against Fr Tromp, accusing him of making the work of revision very difficult. This could be the real reason, and not the alleged fatigue or illness, why he will not be putting in an appearance. Daniélou even thinks that there are some who are pushing for Mgr Philips to take his place as secretary of the Theological Commission.

It is collegiality that is the occasion of the most serious squabbles, both Balić and Gagnebet wanting to restrict it.

I was given the Parente texts, etc = 1 kg of paper!

The meeting ended at about 7.25 pm.

Sunday 3 March 1963

This has been a day of rest. Cardinal Lefebvre, Mgr Martin and Mgr Garrone invited me to join them on a trip by car as far as Cassino. The abbey dominates

---

1. Carlo Molari, of the diocese of Forlì, taught theology at the Lateran and the Urbanianum; he was attached to the Holy Office, which made use of his services for the Doctrinal Commission.

the scene from a height of 540 metres: immense building, all white, completely rebuilt since the war. Buildings, stairways, courtyards, cloisters, churches! It is immense. Nothing was left of it except a pile of rubble. Not content with mere reconstruction, all the decoration has been renewed in marble, stucco and gilt. It must have cost thousands, if not thousands and thousands of millions. It houses twenty-seven choir monks, very few of whom are young. It is true that there is also the unique treasure of the bones of St Benedict and St Scholastica, and that of the surviving walls of St Benedict's original oratory, right up against an immense pile of pagan and cyclopean stones and a pagan temple. It was from HERE that began the monasticism that created the West. But the fathers of today are spending their time building an immensely luxurious display case for the relics of poverty. Is it legitimate? Is it permissible to do such things ???

The cardinal's red zucchetto opened all doors. For the space of two hours a father conducted us round the church, the crypt, the library (36,000 documents!), the great corridor of cells (176 x 6 metres), pagan remains and stones from St Benedict's oratory ('the window from which he saw St Scholastica's soul flying away in the form of a dove') . . . We had lunch in the refectory. One table, in the centre, for the little oblates of the monastic school. I thought of St Thomas and I looked for a good chubby black-haired fellow such as the young Neapolitan . . . Then, coffee in the Abbot's apartment:[1] an ante-chamber with gilded armchairs, a kind of throne room . . . NOTHING monastic. A charming man, who showed us photographs of the ruins and above all an album showing, moment by moment, the re-discovery of the relics of St Benedict and St Scholastica: a veritable film of the operations.

Return via Gaeta (Pius IX!!! – Rock split in two . . . at the death of Jesus . . . !!!! . . . .), Velletri, the Pontine Marches, Lake Nemi. A marvellously relaxing day, in an extraordinarily beautiful light.

Monday 4 March 1963. In the morning, from 10 am to 1 pm, worked at the Belgian College with Mgr Philips, Moeller, Rahner, then Lafortune, in order to prepare the corrections and often even a new version of Chapter II of *De Ecclesia*. The work went well. Mgr Philips is the man who can get things done, and who is given things to get done. Undoubtedly, our little group is homogeneous; there is no problem at this level. The President of the Belgian College[2] was also working. He typed the texts. In effect, it is THERE that the work is being done. So it was decided that I should move there. A room will be kept for me. That will be for

---

1. Ildefonso Rea, Abbot of Monte Cassino: he had only recently been elected bishop and was to be ordained on the following 12 March.
2. Albert Prignon, from the diocese of Liège, Rector of the Belgian College; he was an expert at the Council from the Second Session onwards.

tomorrow morning. At lunch with Mgr De Smedt—because I lunched there—I learnt a lot of things.

1) Moeller told me how it came about that I am here. It was he who had said, on Tuesday 26, the day on which they started work on *De Ecclesia*: 'what a shame that Congar is not here'. Mgr De Smedt at once picked up his telephone and spoke to Mgr Garrone. It was following that that Daniélou wrote to me. (It seems that Cardinal Léger had also insisted that I should be asked to come).

2) Above all, the worst has been avoided at the joint Commission on Tradition. There is no longer any question of sources (in the sense in which 'they' would like to speak of them); there is no longer any question of the material being distributed between Scripture and Tradition, as though they were two drawers, in one of which could be found what could not be found in the other. Personally, I find the current text bad; flat, superficial. I am told, however, that I ought to see what they started with, and what they have avoided!!! That had been tough going, and it took eight days.

3) At a certain moment, a text was brought to the Commission from Cardinal Cicognani which everyone believed had come from the Holy Father, and hence was not open to discussion. There was consternation. It was then that, in a tense and heavy silence, Cardinal Lefebvre spoke up; one cannot, he said, impose a text that has been completely fashioned in advance. The bishops have said what they think; their own wishes and their own proposals must be taken into consideration. That served to re-launch and reopen the discussion.

I went to the Angelicum to collect my mail. I prepared an intervention that I want to make at the joint Commission.

This Commission met at 4.30 pm in the 'Hall of the Congregations'. At the table in the centre, eight cardinals and twenty-five to thirty bishops. A great many experts along the walls. I found all the big names there. I believe that all these people have been present and have participated in everything, whereas I was there for the first time. Fr General was there, with his experts, Sauras[1] and Ramirez. And Schauf, Fenton, Garofalo, Dhanis, Kerrigan, etc. Only Tromp was missing. No further consideration of No. 5, which was deemed settled, but which I consider very bad and concerning which I had prepared an intervention. Only the last words of the last sentence were looked at, where, extremely timidly and as it were shame-facedly, there is a reference to the CONSENSUS of the laity. Cardinal Ruffini went hammer and tongs for this poor wraith: he can speak only in favour of the Magisterium! I spoke up in favour of a certain active contribution of the faithful. I ended with the idea of '*conspiratio pastorum et fidelium*' [a coalition of pastors and the faithful][2] and quoted the principle '*in ore duorum vel trium*

---

1. Emilio Sauras, OP, of the Province of Aragon, was Professor of Theology at the University of Salamanca and at the *studium* in Valencia (Spain), where he was the Regent of Studies. He was a Council expert.
2. In his comments on the schema, Congar was to write: 'We should add that the most formal documents of the Magisterium attribute a role and a value to the witness borne

testium stat omne verbum' [Only on the evidence of two or three witness shall a charge be sustained].[1] But Ottaviani said that that was not *ad rem*, and he called on Garofalo to support him, which Garofalo duly did, in effect, saying: 'it is not *ad rem*; the reference there is to a juridical procedure. But that is false. The New Testament makes of it a type of action for giving honour.

Garofalo, who was sitting beside me, is a very self-satisfied, mediocre person. Every time a speaker pronounced a word that could be the beginning of a scriptural quotation, he completed the text in Latin. Eg *'Eamus'* [John 11:16]. He went on: *'et nos et moriamur cum illo'* [Let us also go, that we may die with him]. *'Expectamus'* [Titus 2.13]. He continued *'beatam spem . . . '* [Let us await the blessed hope] etc.

Franić intervened several times. Once in order to criticise the prologue, which he found 'paraenetic and poetic', in other words 'existential'. A second, and a third time, pathetically, in order to protest against the journals or newspapers which, in the West, have spoken about the opposition between conservative spirits and open spirits. That did him harm, he said: it was interpreted politically in his country and he was being accused of being a conservative. The Archbishop of Zagreb[2] laughed and signalled his disagreement. After the meeting, I saw Franić and asked him if he was referring to me. He said he was. That, on the basis of a letter from a religious sister living in Belgium . . . Now: 1) I never mentioned a proper name; 2) I spoke in the most general terms and remained *MUCH* more restrained than what was written in the newspapers!!! Moreover, Parente, to whom I had spoken about these things, acknowledged that one ought not to believe anything that one reads in the newspapers as they make up what they do not know.

The presidents of the various sub-commissions reported on the work of their sub-commissions. It is very disappointing. The work has barely started, or is far from finished. A lot of things are being passed on to sub-commissions of the sub-commissions and . . . in May. IT IS NOT ORGANISED! The bishops will never have received the texts before August!! . . .

Tuesday 5 March 1963

At 9 am I moved to the Belgian College. I believe I had to do that. The future will tell whether I was right or wrong to do so.

---

by the faithful to the Tradition: The Bull *Ineffabilis Deus* of Pius XI and the Constitution *Munificentissimus Deus* of Pius XII speak in this sense of the "conspiratio Pastorum et fidelium", an expression borrowed indirectly from Newman (. . .). One could take up this formula'. Cf the schema 'De Revelatione', *Études et documents*, No. 14, 11 July 1963, page 6).

1. Deuteronomy 19:15; which is quoted again in Matthew 18:16 and in 2 Corinthians 13:1.
2. Franjo Šeper was an elected member of the Doctrinal Commission; he was to be created cardinal in February 1965 and was later to become Prefect of the Congregation for the Doctrine of the faith.

In the morning, at St Martha's (Vatican), the experts working on chapter II. Schauf stood in for Balić. He is logically minded, exacting, precise. His questions often force one to clarify details which are not without interest. Good atmosphere. We worked well.

At 3.15 pm, I met l'abbé Alting von Geusau,[1] a Dutchman, at the No. 64 terminus. He is busy publishing (anonymously) documents for the bishops and the serious Press on the principal questions being discussed at the Council. He would like me to collaborate. Poor me!!!

At 4.30 pm, Vatican, Hall of the Congregations, a meeting of the *ENTIRE* Theological Commission to make a start on examining *De Ecclesia*.

Fr Tromp, *redivivus* [back from the dead], proposed that, for the work to be done seriously, SMALL groups would be needed, that the Fathers of the Commission should submit their comments in writing, and that these should then be submitted to the scrutiny of the *periti* and of the Fathers of the sub-commission, who would express their opinion on the suggestions made and give their reasons for either accepting or rejecting them. After that, all the members and the *periti* would be given the comments of the Fathers and the opinion expressed by the Commission.

In addition, Fr Tromp objected to the notice which had been placed at the head of the proposed new schema, stating that the dogmatic constitution would not require that it be accepted as irreformable. For him, that would be liberalism, if not libertinism. A dogmatic constitution must be irreformable.

Cardinal Ottaviani felt that it would be difficult to adopt the working method that Fr Tromp had suggested. But he shared Fr Tromp's opinion concerning the irreformable nature of a constitution.

Cardinal Browne agreed. But Mgr Charue read a passage from the official schema *De Beata Maria Virgine*, page 100, which distinguished between a dogma of the faith and sound doctrine.

Parente insisted on the fact—highly questionable in my own eyes—that *ALL* the texts from the extraordinary Magisterium reflect some degree of infallibility. For him extraordinary Magisterium and infallibility are essentially linked.

Mgr McGrath, Rahner and Gagnebet spoke. I asked insistently to be allowed to speak, but I was not given the nod.

A vote was taken: an enormous majority, almost unanimous, in favour of rejecting the mention of the theological note.

Ottaviani asked what the Fathers thought of Tromp's proposed method of working. Franić supported Tromp, adding that it would make it possible to know the comments that had been submitted by the bishops in writing.

---

1. Leo Alting von Geusau was the Director of the Dutch Centre of Council Documentation, known as DO-C; the purpose of this Centre, which had been created for the Council by a number of Dutch Catholic organisations, and subsequently financed by the episcopate of the Netherlands, was to organise lectures in Rome and to make available theological and historical documentation.

Clearly, 'they' want to revert to the official schema and put off for as long as possible the examination of a new schema.

Cardinal Browne traced the history of the question—very honestly—of the way in which the sub-commission had worked and how the Philips schema had come to be adopted as the working text (it had been adopted by five votes to two).

Ottaviani: the sub-commission overstepped the limits of its competence, it ought to have referred the matter to the general Commission.

Browne: the general Commission left the decision to us.

Mgr Charue (really very courageous): the general Commission left it to the sub-commission to choose the schema: everyone here bears witness to that.

Cardinal Léger: the sub-commission was given the mandate to:

1) prepare a new schema; 2) take the Philips text as a working basis; 3) see what was good in the Parente schema and include it; 4) and also in the others; 5) to point out the items over which there was disagreement.

Ottaviani: we cannot judge whether or not the schema meets with the requests that have been proposed unless we have the WHOLE of the schema in our hands.

Browne: but the two last sections of the schema are in the hands of the joint commissions which are still at work . . . Now *tempus premit* [time presses].

Léger: we were established for the schema *De Ecclesia*. We have already been here for ten days and we have nothing for *De Ecclesia*. We must begin to examine it. We already have two chapters . . . So we would need to remain in Rome for two months . . . !!!

Charue: I do not understand; although the mandate has been given to the sub-commission, we are back discussing the matter again TODAY.

Ottaviani: But what we have before us now is not one of the schemas available to choose from, but a NEW SCHEMA . . .

Charue: No, it is the Philips schema which has simply been improved.

Ottaviani: *Procedatur ad examen* [Let us begin to examine it].

He was beaten. His attempt at postponement was *gescheitert* [defeated] .

Philips explained the work that had been done in accordance with the mandate received. He speaks perfect Latin and is fully in control of what he wants to say.

Tromp: We must have the whole of the work in front of us. Cardinal Ottaviani has said that the sub-commission must take into account the observations made by the bishops. But that would take a lot of time (a month at least) and will produce two kilograms of work . . .

Philips suggested that the work actually being done be completed as a provisional text against which one could match the bishops' comments, taking into consideration at least the most important of these. Cardinal Ottaviani approved this idea and suggested that the bishops' comments BE DISTRIBUTED to the *periti*, each of whom would present his report.

These *vota* are all at St Martha's and available to all members of the Commission.

Garrone expressed the wish that the bishops of the world be informed of the new distribution of the schemas, so that they will not be working in vain.

König: Many of the bishops will be leaving at the end of the week . . . Let us get as much of the work done as possible. For the rest, the text can be sent to the members AT THEIR RESIDENCES.

Ottaviani: Let us begin our study of the text without going into all the details. The style is too oratorical. And there are too many citations from Scripture, not all of which are *ad rem*. A *peritus in Sancta Scriptura* [an expert in Sacred Scripture] would need to revise it.

A letter had just been received from Cardinal Ruffini (in Latin). Ottaviani had it read. The letter said: 1) what has been said about the theological note; 2) the Council is supposed to be pastoral. In order to be so, the text must be clear and simple, WHICH IT IS NOT. There followed further comments on details which will be read in their place.

Long discussion about the use of the word *sacramentum* of the Church. Ottaviani wanted it removed.

After a break, with Cardinal Browne presiding, there was a vote on the amendment proposed by Parente taking up various propositions: '*signum et instrumentum seu quasi sacramentum*' [sign and instrument or quasi-sacrament].

This was accepted almost unanimously, (except for the cardinal from the Philippines [1]).

No. 1 ff: Parente: the text speaks of the relationship of the Church with the Three Persons as though these were related severally, whereas they are related in common.

Franić was against the expression: '*Ecclesiae* MYSTERIUM' [The MYSTERY of the Church]. He wants '*natura*' [nature].

Fr Sauras spoke at length in order to insist on the PERSONAL character of salvation and holiness—and not so much on the social character.

It was announced that Mgr Parente is to be replaced by Mgr Spanedda[2] as a member of the *De Ecclesia* sub-commission comprising seven bishops. (Parente is withdrawing and no longer wants to belong to it).

Wednesday 6 March 1963

At 9 am, paid a visit to Cardinal Léger. He has got thin. He still has his great deep eyes, his ravaged and tragic face. In fact, his sensibility is such that he has a real need of someone sympathetic close to him, to be in contact with people (in prison, he would die!). Thanks to his sensibility he easily sees himself as the centre, and the centre of a drama. He so much likes to open his heart. He told me a number of things.

---

1. Rufino I Santos.
2. Francesco Spanedda, Bishop of Bosa (Sardinia). The Pope had appointed him a member of the Doctrinal Commission.

In the middle of November, he said, I was in an agony. I was asking myself whether I still belonged to the Catholic Church or whether my ideas were putting me out of it. On 20 November, I had addressed the Holy Father on the occasion of the reception of the Canadian bishops. What I said impressed the Pope. He kept me back for a long time afterwards. I said to him: Do you want the Council or do you not? And I spoke to him of the need to set up a commission in order to preserve the spirit of the Council during the nine months intervening between the two Sessions. There and then the Pope summoned Felici (who had gone to bed) and Cicognani and spoke to them about setting up this commission. Then, on the following day, he sent me a handwritten letter and a pectoral cross.

Then there was the *Tempo* affair. I had given a lecture to 1,500 members of Catholic Action. Afterwards, I was asked questions, but the journalists present totally misrepresented my replies and reported me as saying that the work needed to be entirely redone, that the Pope had an incurable illness, etc. The *Tempo* printed an article which provoked demands for explanations from the Curia. But the *Tempo* poisons everything: only yesterday, it printed an article on the presence in Rome of Khrushchev's son-in-law,[1] maintaining that it had been wangled by the Secretariat: in order to discredit it . . .

The cardinal went on to say: It has been my custom, for the past twenty years, to note down every day what I do. Now, in my notebook between Christmas and 6 January there is a blank. I noticed that did I not say Mass on 6 January. I was extremely tired, with the threat of cardiac problems. I ought to rest for three months, but . . .

There have been some tragic days. When, for example, Ottaviani wanted to force the members of the Commission to swear that they believed in Tradition.

I stood up and asked: Are we here in a Commission or on trial before an inquisitorial tribunal?

When I arrived at the Council on 9 October 1962, a very influential cardinal, and one who is steadily more and more influential, said to me: there is a plot against the Council; 'they' want everything to be voted on without discussion before 8 December.

The further we go, the clearer it becomes that the real battle is between the Curia and above all the 'Holy Office' and the *Ecclesia*. That was clear yesterday as well.

I also learnt that Küng and two others (Fr Weigel and a liturgist) were prevented from speaking at the University of Washington. By whom? By the University? By the Apostolic Delegate,[2] who is as narrow-minded as could be?

10.30 am at St Martha's in the Vatican, the seven experts at work: quite a long discussion about the episcopal college. But the same friendly atmosphere.

---

1. Alexeï Adjoubeï, editor of *Izvestia*, son-in-law of Nikita Khrushchev, the First Secretary of the Central Committee of the Communist Party of the USSR.
2. Egidio Vagnozzi.

At 4.30 pm, the Theological Commission, Cardinal Browne presiding. Discussion of various details.

Tromp: at the Theological Commission, only those things had been said which were called for by the times. Now, people want to propose a complete ecclesiological synthesis. Necessarily incomplete, unless one were to produce a whole volume. Hence the dissatisfaction on one side and the other.

I noted down on my copy the numerous corrections that had been suggested. The text evokes many comments. How to proceed? One would need to rewrite whole paragraphs yet again. Then there would be further comments, and so on indefinitely.

Mgr Philips defended himself, gave way, promised to take things into account, and finally succeeded in getting people to continue their reading and study of the text, so that at least the whole of the text of the first chapter was read—but discussion of the very difficult question of the 'membership' was postponed.

Mgr De Smedt left us that evening. He was returning to Belgium by the long way round, over the Dolomites.

Spent the evening in Philips' room, with Thils and Moeller.

Thursday 7 March 1963

Saint Thomas. In the morning, from 8.30 am to 10 am, work with Moeller preparing the corrections to be made to Chapter I of *De Ecclesia*. At 10.30 am at St Martha's, the seven experts' sub-commission. Fr Tromp was there. One senses in him a certain bitterness on account of the official schema having been abandoned but he does not sulk in his tent, although he is not as good at this as Gagnebet and Schauf, whose 'fair play' I admire . . . I find that the authors of the first schema play their game well and have displayed a laudably disinterested spirit.

Except for Cardinal Ottaviani, who makes many obstructions and tries to recover control of what has definitively escaped him.

I lunched at the Angelicum. Feast for St Thomas. Cardinal Ruffini, Mgr Griffiths and Mgr McGrath were there. I worked for a while in the library. The Pope is expected. The time had been originally set for 3.30 pm, but in the end he arrived at 4.30 or 4.35 pm. He has the face of a man who is exhausted. Several more cardinals and bishops arrived, and the lecture hall was packed. I was beside Fr Dingemans[1] (?), a young Belgian sociologist who seemed to me a fine person: balanced, intelligent, with a good feeling for human relationships.

Speech by Fr General. Speech by a black friar speaking on behalf of all the students (that cheered up the Pope for a while, seeing and hearing this black man so close to him). Quite a long speech by the Pope who said he had not prepared anything. I was very far from understanding all that he said. I have the impression that he was telling stories, recounting memories of his childhood. He spoke of the

---

1. Louis Dingemans, OP, of the Province of South Belgium, taught sociology of religion at the Angelicum.

'Wisdom of the heart'.[1] He ended by speaking at length of the *Tabula aurea* by his compatriot Pietro of Bergamo.[2] The atmosphere was that of a meeting of students, who interrupted him repeatedly by laughing and clapping. But the Pope, who seemed extremely tired, is no orator.

In the evening, worked on the corrections with Moeller and Philips.

Friday 8 March 1963

The newspapers are reporting Khrushchev's son-in-law's audience with the Pope. It was this that La Pira had given me to understand in January, except that he was thinking in terms of Khrushchev himself.

By car to St Martha's with Cardinal Léger, who needs to laugh, to feel at ease and to relax his over-stretched nerves.

At 1 pm, lunch at Santa Sabina: Fr Delos' fiftieth anniversary of profession.

At 4.30 pm, at the Vatican, meeting of the Theological Commission. Long discussions, principally about forms of expression.

Speaking of the knowledge of God among some primitive peoples, Fr General told how he had visited some Amazon countries where both men and women are naked. He made everyone laugh by adding that he had some photographs . . .

I am both walking and writing badly (my hand has almost no strength).

After a few minutes' break, reading of a text by Mgr Charue on the importance of metaphors other than that of the body, in particular that of *grex* [flock]. Discussion.

Mgr Prignon, Rector of the Belgian College, described how *De Beata Maria Virgine* had come to be separated from *De Ecclesia*. It was at the request of Cardinal Döpfner. He was afraid that if it was part of *De Ecclesia*, Protestants would have the impression that we had spoken of the Church ONLY IN ORDER TO insert into it the chapter on the Blessed Virgin.

Saturday 9 March 1963

In the morning, work (slow!) at the Belgian College in order to take account of the comments made and re-do a chapter *De corpore Christi mystico* [on the Mystical Body of Christ].

4.30 pm: Vatican. Theological Commission. Relatively easy, albeit slow, discussion of the end of Chapter I. But when we came to the prologue to Chapter II, great conflict over '*in fundamento Petri et Apostolorum*' [on the foundation of Peter and the Apostles]. The Romans wanted absolutely to distinguish express- ly between the way in which Peter (the pope) is the foundation and the way in

---

1. Cf Aimé Forest, 'La Sagesse du coeur', in *Saint Bernard homme d'Église*, 'Cahiers de la Pierre-qui-vire' (Paris: Desclée de Brouwer, 1953), 202–213.
2. Professed in the Dominican priory in Bologna in the fifteenth century; theologian, he composed an analytical table—by words—of the works of St Thomas Aquinas, known as the *Tabula aurea* [Golden Table].

which the other Apostles are. The Romans: 1) reduce the Apostles of Ephesians 2:20 to the same status as the prophets: the reference is only to preaching. So not to the juridical function. So not very important. 2) they rule out Apocalypse 21 by saying that it is metaphorical and refers to the heavenly Jerusalem, hence not to the visible Church on earth. 'They' think of only *ONE* thing: putting the pope in everywhere, putting him above everything, seeing only him, making the entire Church consist only in him!

We were back in the 'Holy Office' atmosphere that dominated the Preparatory Commission: *'Oportet caute loqui'* [One must speak carefully].

'Est res maximi momenti' [It is a matter of the greatest importance] = the pope. Nothing else. And in the end one is caught in the net.

In Rome, in diplomatic circles (but not elsewhere, where no-one mentions it), there is much comment on the audience given to Khrushchev's son-in-law. It is being said that the Democratic Republics would release Cardinal Mindszenty[1] and Mgr Beran[2] and that these would come to Rome. Thus, released from the handicap of the Church of the past and of the presence of 'martyrs', things could start again on a new level. Basically, something like what Pius VII had done in calling for the resignation of all the former French bishops. When all is said and done, up to now the Vatican has acted as if the Communist regimes were not going to last. They are lasting. A way out has to be found.

Sunday 10 March 1963

I thought of all my commitments in Strasbourg that I cannot fulfil . . .

In the morning, work. Mgr Philips accepted my version of the chapter on the Mystical Body and on the images of the Church.

Brief visit to the National Gallery and the Joseph Foret exhibition.[3]

Yesterday evening, Mgr Prignon had telephoned Mgr Cerfaux, of Louvain, to ask him for a competent opinion on the question of the Apostles as a foundation. He had a reply by telephone this morning. Moreover, Mgr Prignon has all the time kept Cardinal Suenens informed of what was happening, spending up to twenty minutes at a time on the telephone.

At supper and afterwards, I told Mgr Philips and Moeller that we needed to be prepared for an offensive along the lines of what, in actual fact, Mgr Parente said to me the following day.

---

1. Jósef Mindszenty, Archbishop of Esztergom and Primate of Hungary, had been living in the Embassy of the United States in Budapest since he had sought refuge there in 1956; he did not leave it until 1971.
2. Josef Beran, Archbishop of Prague since 1946, was forced to live in a monastery in Moravia; he was released in October 1963 and created cardinal in 1965.
3. Art editor, he had in particular conceived and put together an enormous book weighing 210 kg and containing the Biblical text of the Apocalypse of St John, illustrated by means of great paintings and with commentaries written by famous authors.

Monday 11 March 1963

I went to the 'Holy Office' at 9 am to see Mgr Parente. I waited for twenty-five minutes but in the end saw him for about an hour and a half. Two more or less equal parties to the conversation, during which he spoke more than I did. 1) On the subject of what is currently being discussed in the Theological Commission. The Pope has a relationship of head as much to the whole of the Mystical Body as to the college of bishops. But he receives the fullness of power BEFORE the college, and independently of it: so that his supreme power is *LINKED* to the college, of which he is the head, but is not *DEPENDENT* on this POSITION of his being *caput collegii* [head of the college].

There are at present schools of thought that derive all their weight from history (Gallicanism): even Bolgeni and Hamer have exaggerated collegiality. What is said in the Philips schema is true, but is liable to be made use of by the above-mentioned schools of thought. Therefore, one must speak only very prudently and must in no way diminish pontifical authority.

Parente also holds a) that collegiality is biblical and traditional; b) that the bishops receive their power of jurisdiction in and through their consecration; not from the pope. All the pope does is to designate what is subjected to their power. Moreover, he had read my study in *AHDLMA*.[1] He thinks that a great deal of harm was done by the jurists who, being involved in battles between the temporal power and the priesthood, came to conceive of jurisdiction along the lines of political power. It was this juridical point of view that prevailed after the Reformation, in order to oppose Luther. But it was unfortunate. Parente is AGAINST the idea that a lay person, if elected pope, would *illico et ipso facto* [there and then and by the very fact of having been elected] possess universal jurisdiction. The proper subject of jurisdiction is priestly consecration. We need to move away from a juridical conception of the Church to a sacramental one which Parente sees along the lines of the theandric character of the Church.

In passing, Mgr Parente told me that it became obvious at the Council that the bishops are not theologians, but are novices in these matters; they are concerned about other needs and no longer have the time to study theology. For this reason, they rely on experts . . .

I am not an integrist, as people in France say that I am. I have spent my whole life studying and serving theology. All these matters are difficult ones. That is why I consider that the Council is too hasty. I have said so to the Pope. We ought to take much more time. We cannot be finished by Wednesday . . .

2) I have read ET PERLEGI [and STUDIED] *La Tradition et les traditions* in both French and Italian.[2] Great praise for the erudition and intelligence of Fr

---

1. Yves M-J Congar, 'Aspects ecclésiologiques de la querelle entre mendiants et séculiers dans la seconde moitié du XIIIième siècle et le début du XIVième siècle', in *Archives d'histoire doctrinale et littéraire du Moyen Âge*, vol XXVIII, 1961: 35–151.
2. Yves M-J Congar, *La Tradition et les traditions. Essai historique* (Paris: Fayard, 1960);

Congar. But Fr Congar bends the texts of the Fathers, of the Councils, and of the Magisterium to mean what he wants them to mean. This meaning, which is the aim of the book, is the sufficiency of Scripture. Now this is false. There are truths that the Church has defined, that it is necessary to believe, and that are not formally contained in Scripture, even implicitly, but only virtually: the number of the seven sacraments, or the Assumption, for instance, or the Immaculate Conception. They are contained only in the Tradition. In vain I explained that: 1) for me, that is not the principal question, which is much more to define the PROPER MODE of Tradition as compared with Scripture; 2) one cannot accept the fiction of an unwritten doctrine which is communicated VERBALLY from mouth to ear. . . . etc. Mgr Parente is ready to explode against all such views as those of Dreher[1] or Geiselmann, which he criticised severely: moreover, in his Preface to the last volume of the works of Duns Scotus,[2] Balić had crushed Geiselmann, whose good faith can be doubted. At the Council's joint Commission . . . etc. (I stressed two or three times that I had not been invited to attend that joint Commission.)

When all is said and done, Mgr Parente showed me that he was speaking to me as a friend, as friend to friend. Moreover, he is not the integrist he is said to be. Several years ago, he had proposed a procedure which he hopes to see realised, according to which, before people are condemned, they should be listened to and asked to explain themselves freely. He has himself spoken to prevent Teilhard de Chardin[3] being placed on the Index[4] . . .

At 10.50 or 10.55 am, I went to St Martha's. Experts working on (my) new version of the paragraphs on the Mystical Body and the images of the Church. After an attack by Schauf (who maintained that the essential teaching of *Mystici Corporis* was missing), to which Mgr Philips replied forcefully and even indignantly that this was one school of thought sitting in judgement on another, and that he rejected the accusation outright, the discussion went quite well; not much was changed.

It must be acknowledged that, although the teaching of *Mystici Corporis* has in fact been taken up, this has been to a minimal degree, in a totally different equilibrium, where the anthropological-sociological and Pauline idea of the σῶμα χριστοῦ is to the forefront. I hope that things will be left like that. It is my

---

the work had been published in Italian in 1961.
1. Bruno Dreher, theologian teaching at Würzburg.
2. Balić was responsible for editing the complete Works of the Franciscan theologian Duns Scotus. The sixth volume of the *Opera omnia* was published in 1963; in his preface, dated 8 December 1962, Balić made use of Duns Scotus in order to defend the idea of truths transmitted orally and not through Scripture.
3. Pierre Teilhard de Chardin, SJ.
4. Teilhard was never placed on the Index. The Holy Office *monitum*, which was published on 30 June 1962, warned against the ambiguities and grave errors which abound in his books.

contribution. If that is left in, a great victory will have been won for the theology of the years to come.

At 1 pm, Cardinal Léger and his two theologians, Mgr Charue, Mgr McGrath and Mgr Schröffer lunched at the Belgian College (the invitation was issued very nicely, at my suggestion, by Mgr Prignon). Very useful theological conversation about all the problems being discussed at this moment. I told them the gist of what Mgr Parente had said as contained in my No. 1) above and, with Moeller, we prepared for Mgr Philips a little text designed to help him in the discussion.

At 4.30 pm, at the Vatican for the Theological Commission. To begin with, a report on the state of the work being done by the other sub-commissions.

The Spanedda proposal, strongly supported by Ottaviani: FIRST agree on the PRINCIPLES that one wishes to establish, both as regards the episcopal college and as regards the relationship between the college and the pope. THEN, the text can be assessed in the light of the agreement reached about principles. However, after an intervention by Cardinal Browne and an exposé by Philips, it was decided to follow the text and to discuss the fundamental questions as and when they arise out of the text.

Attack by Browne against '*ut collegium* . . .' [as a college].

Franić: *collegialitas nimis extollitur* [collegiality is being extolled exceedingly] and the texts of Ephesian 2:20 and Apocalypse 21:14 have been too much inflated to convey a meaning that they do not have.

Mgr Charue read a paper on these texts, justifying the title of foundation for the Apostles.

Mgr Parente acknowledged that, but spoke of the danger concealed under the theory of the college, which includes, under the same *ratio* [understanding] of college, Peter and the other Apostles, the pope and the other bishops.

Lattanzi, to whom Ottaviani appealed, said: all the difficulties will disappear if one begins by declaring the MONARCHY of Peter.

Good intervention by Fr Gagnebet, who described what one had wanted to do and how one had done it; the secure basis on which all are agreed. He pointed out that the word COLLEGIUM was to be found in the schema produced by the Preparatory Commission and no-one had objected to it. He refuted Lattanzi who, on Saturday, had wanted to liken our position to that of Maret.[1]

Mgr Florit approved Mgr Charue's exegesis.

Gagnebet's intervention produced a good effect. The question was settled with only ONE change: '*ad instar cuiusdam collegii*' [after the fashion of a college of some kind].

D'Ercole:[2] the college is like a *grex* [flock] of which Peter is *THE* Shepherd . . . (he told me afterwards that Ottaviani has asked him to come).

---

1. Henri Maret (1805–1884), Dean of the Faculty of Theology at the Sorbonne; active in the minority at Vatican I, he accepted the decisions of that Council.
2. Giuseppe D'Ercole, of the diocese of Rome, Professor of the History of Canon law at

Tromp: the bishops are successors of the Apostles *ratione iurisdictionis et magisterii* [by reason of their jurisdiction and magisterium], which only applies to residential bishops, at least in a manner that is CERTAIN.

Nevertheless, progress is being made without too many obstacles.

On the whole, a good day. The session began badly, but turned out well. Mgr Philips was marvellously lucid, imposing and focused, prompt to explain and to assuage. The most tiresome ones were, at a deep level, Cardinal Browne, though he is always very humble and very honest—and, at a superficial level, Dhanis and Lattanzi.

Poor Fr Tromp hardly counts at all, now. He had intervened to say that we were discussing the most fundamental and most important question, but when Mgr Parente said that in his view there was no real problem (it was a question of residential bishops and titular bishops), we moved on without further discussion. What a change as compared with the Preparatory Commission, in which he had dominated and decided everything!!! Provided this lasts!

Hand and leg have little strength. I find it difficult to hold my pen.

Tuesday, 12 March 1963

In the morning, reactions to a chapter of schema XVII on culture: very superficial text, with no human, cosmological, christological or theological depth at all. Well-meant, indeed fairly open, but devoid of vitality, vigour, 'vision'.

At 8.30 am, visit from Alberigo, Cardinal Lercaro's adviser. The cardinal has, effectively, no seminary and no professors. In his diocese there is only a general seminary, which is run by the Congregation and not by him. So his advisers are the researchers at the historical Centre.[1]

Alberigo told me that the Italian bishops are very much at a loss and uneasy. This is because, at the Council, they have seen positions questioned which to them were classic and sacred. Hence their reaction is one of DEFENCE. Moreover, they are grouped in their conference under Cardinal Siri, all of whose reactions are negative: AGAINST this, AGAINST that. When I shared with Alberigo my own feeling that the renewal will come from the laity, he shared with me his pessimism on this score: there are no centres or organs (journals) of research; there are no activities or organisms (congresses, journals . . .) in which and through which lay people and clergy come together, talk about things and collaborate.

Cardinal Lercaro feels himself somewhat isolated. Alberigo urged me to pay a visit to Bologna.

At lunch, with Mgr Charue, Mgr Bonet,[2] who is an auditor of the Rota, a very communicative and likeable Barcelonan, whom I used often to see at the Gen-

---

the Lateran, and a Council expert.

1. Documentation Centre of the Institute for Religious Studies; cf above, page 322, note 1.
2. Manuel Bonet y Muixi, of the diocese of Barcelona, a Council expert.

eral Congregations during the First Session. We spoke about the Rota, his work, mixed marriages. But Mgr Bonet clings to his insistence on this: the Theological Commission is preparing a schema containing the general dogmatic principles. Their application remains to be achieved. It is useless to have introduced the principle of collegiality if it is not actually put into practice. In short, the whole question of the canonical forms in which collegiality will or will not be applied remains open. At the Rota, the auditors, above all the Italians, say: let them get on with it and discuss their schema. Afterwards, it is WE who will be writing the articles of the Code! In short, Mgr Bonet suggests that, right from now, projects and applications should be being prepared such as they will later be turned into Law and institutions. And thus to take care that the idea of the Council does not get lost when turned into Law and institutions! . . .

At 4.30 pm, the Vatican.

The question of deacons. Cardinal Ottaviani would like to see the passage leading to the possibility of a diaconate, even a married diaconate, sealed off; but Mgr Šeper (Jugoslav) said: the commission on the sacraments had prepared a whole chapter on this topic, but it has been deleted from the list of schemas as it stands today. So there are grounds for keeping the text as it is. Very fine intervention, given calmly and serenely.

Schauf spoke against including this passage.

Franić too.

Rahner replied to them. Schröffer said that when Cardinal König was leaving, he had given him a note saying that he wished this passage to remain.

Decision: to retain the text for the present, with a note.

A fresh attack against, by Lio.

But Tromp: judging by what their superiors say, the Missions will not be able to survive unless there are married deacons.

Ottaviani in conclusion: *expungenda paragraphus* [the paragraph must be deleted].

In the end, after interventions by Mgr Charue and McGrath, it was suggested that the decision be postponed until the May session, the existing text remaining untouched until then.

Great discussion on the college and the pope: Browne, Gagnebet, Rahner, Tromp, D'Ercole, Dhanis, etc. Dhanis truly horrid. In order to identify them as dangerous errors against which it was necessary to take clear positions, he read two texts by Fr Dejaifve,[1] and one from the secretariat of an episcopal conference—which Cardinal Ottaviani told Cardinal Léger had come from the letter from the Dutch bishops.

Very tough discussion. The papalists want to make everything depend on the pope. What Browne, Parente *et alii* do not want is for the bishops to have the

---

1. Georges Dejaifve, SJ, Professor of Fundamental Theology and Ecclesiology at the Jesuit Faculty of Theology at Eegenhoven-Louvain.

initative of themselves, and not from the pope, in the exercise of their collegial power. According to them, such an exercise would only be possible if the pope not only did not object to it [*non renuente*] but entirely determined it with respect to its origin, its range, and its mode.

For them, the CONVOCATION of the ecumenical Council and the determination of its agenda by the pope have a DOGMATIC value and are a DOGMATIC requirement, because it is a question of the exercise of collegiality '*modo extraordinario*' [in an extraordinary manner]. The fact that the pope did not convoke the first seven ecumenical councils nor determine their agenda does not bother them. They say quite simply that these were particular councils which became ecumenical by having been accepted by the pope. That I would agree with, but that seems to me to imply that *ONLY* THE RECEPTION, or the approval, is dogmatically necessary.

It would seem that the Romans want above all to cut, at its root, any attempt to establish, in whatever form, a permanent council around the pope. Because that would be the end of their reign and the destruction of what they have built up with such dogged patience over the past fifteen centuries.

Cardinal Ottaviani postponed to a meeting, tomorrow at 10 am, of those who wish to take part in the question, the preparation of a text that will satisfy expectations.

A meeting which I found painful, although nothing was lost. But I feel myself totally powerless in the face of their purely ideological-verbal logic, which takes no account either of the realities of history or of the movement by which the Church opens itself to the future, or, indeed, of the legitimate requests of the Easterners.

Wednesday 13 March 1963
Neither of the two references given yesterday concerning the texts read by Dhanis was entirely true. Dhanis told me today that the two texts read in French came from an article written by Fr de Bovis in the journal *Vie Chrétienne*;[1] the other text, which Dhanis had translated into Latin, originated from an episcopal conference's SECRETARIAT and, I believe, from the French text on collegiality (15.1.1963) in which Fr Daniélou had written a very careless phrase which I had subsequently observed was false.[2]

---

1. André de Bovis, SJ, who taught at the Chantilly scholasticate and wrote regularly for *Vie chrétienne*; the reference could be to the following article: 'Église: monarchie ou collège?', *Vie chrétienne*, December 1961: 3–7.
2. The reference is to the first issue in the series *Études et documents* of 15 January 1963, on the subject of 'La collégialité de l'épiscopat', and in which Congar had underlined on page 5 a phrase of Daniélou's that he was doubtful about: 'La prérogative du Souverain Pontife est d'être chef du collège apostolique et il n'est donc ce qu'il est que de par l'existence de ce collège.'

At 10 am, at St Martha's. The meeting was expected to be a difficult one. However, after Philips, then Gagnebet, then D'Ercole (who had produced a new and totally juridical, wordy and dull version of the ENTIRE chapter), Schauf read a text which I then supported and which everybody supported. A few details will be re-written, but agreement has been achieved.

At 11.50 am, at Santa Sabina, where Fr General had asked me to come and see him. It was in order to say some nice things to me: the first time in my life that a superior has summoned me for such a purpose. The trivial affair of *L'Espresso* has been settled.[1] I deserve encouragement; if I run into difficulty, I should have recourse to Fr General who is fully prepared to defend me (but I am still the kind of person who needs to be defended!!!).

Fairly boring lunch at Santa Sabina. Afterwards, I had a long talk with Fr Delos. I asked him about the situation in France. He is very critical of de Gaulle. He thinks we are in an arbitrary moment and that 'the Right' is not respected. He had nothing but banalities to say to me about the visit of Adjoubeï, Khrushchev's son-in-law: we will see how things turn out . . . He asked me about the French bishops, whether Mgr Marty would be suitable for the see of Paris, about Cardinal Confalonieri as a possible candidate in succession to John XXIII. We spoke about the Order, about the so regrettable absence of a living Thomism, above all in philosophy, about our responsibility in this state of things (Fr Delors is strongly critical of Fr Chenu and his sociology which, he says, is not worth much).

I then spent nearly an hour and a half with Fr Thomas Philippe. Poor waif, more or less abandoned by his fellows. A mixture, unfortunately, of very acute intellectual (philosophical) and spiritual perceptions, containing an extraordinary richness, and a poor grasp of reality. He constructs a whole systematised interpretation which, while in many ways being very perspicacious and valid, at times reminds one a little of some of the intuitions of a Joachim.[2] He has suffered terribly. He continues to suffer. But what can one do? Where could one put him, where could he be useful for the Gospel? As chaplain to a reformatory for juvenile delinquents? His memories of the one in Anel(?)[3] are those which are still the most moving and the most precious for him.

What a hash of splendid gifts, in a life which, humanly speaking, has been a failure!

4.30 pm (a little late: I waited for Fr General in the cold of a storm), session at the Vatican. Our formula of this morning did not meet with any difficulties apart from Franić, perfect fruit of the most ultra-Roman seed.

---

1. See above, page 319.
2. Joachim of Fiore, a twelfth century monk and theologian, had developed a theological vision of history and had in particular announced the advent of a new age, marked by the kingdom of the Spirit.
3. He had been chaplain to the Hameau École de l'Île-de-France, at Longueil-Anel, Oise, which afterwards became the IRPR (Institut regional de psychothérapie et rééducation).

The difficulties raised by the Romans all amount exclusively to a SINGLE absolutely unique point (they are quite obsessed): to give as little as possible, and even to give nothing at all either to the bishops or to the Church!!! There is only the pope, one principle or one source: the pope.

An intervention by Mgr Charue restored the reference to the *fides Ecclesiae* [the faith of the Church] which had for a moment been deleted. Moreover, a certain number of expressions to which we attached importance because of their ecclesiological or ecumenical connotations have been either retained or restored. In some cases that are still badly phrased, Mgr Philips got himself entrusted, confidently, with the task of rewriting the text. It is clear that Mgr Philips has gained the CONFIDENCE of Cardinal Ottaviani. And that is very important.

We quite quickly completed the work on Chapter II of *De Ecclesia*. Cardinal Ottaviani finished briskly with thanksgiving to God with thanks everybody, to the *periti*, to Mgr Philips. The meeting broke up, we bade farewell to one another, in an atmosphere of cordiality. I said to Fr Tromp that he too deserved a thank-you. He answered me with a weary gesture accompanied by something that sounded like a sob. In fact, he has in a sense been set aside. Throughout these days, Cardinal Ottaviani himself took little account of his interventions. The sceptre has passed to other hands.

Return by car, as on the other days, with Cardinal Léger and his two theologians, Naud and Lafortune. The Cardinal is relaxed. He told us that the reception of Adjoubeï has aroused very lively opposition in curial circles (or some of them?). It is not clear what effect this new situation will have on the Italian elections. He also told us that he had yesterday met the new French ambassador to the Quirinal,[1] who had just been received by the Pope. John XXIII is not very fond of either de Gaulle or Bidault,[2] of whom he seems to have not very happy memories. John XXIII said to the ambassador: 'I want to shake off the imperial dust that has accumulated on the throne of St Peter since the time of Constantine.' A remark of immense significance, and one which throws a very clear light on some of the Pope's actions.

Cardinal Léger, who is anxiety itself, is now worrying about Cardinal Ottaviani's claim that the texts re-edited in joint sub-commission by the Theological Commission and the Commissions on the Laity, on Religious, and above all by *THE* Secretariat (*De Œcumenismo*) must be fine-tuned and judged by the Theological Commission ALONE.

We bade farewell to our Canadian friends. Yes, a true friendship has been established between us during these days.

---

1. Armand Bérard.
2. Georges Bidault, who was several times Minister for Foreign Affairs between 1944 and 1954, and was so when Roncalli himself arrived in Paris as Apostolic Nuncio. Bidault had sought to secure the deposition of one third of the French bishops.

That evening, champagne in honour of the happy ending of *De Ecclesia.* I, too, have formed or deepened friendships with Mgr Philips, C Moeller and Mgr Prignon.

Thursday 14 March 1963
I slept hardly at all and, not being able to close my eyes (rain, Rome's humid weather, with no freshness at night), I got up at 3.30 am and wrote letters, took some notes, tried again to find some formula for the points still needing to be settled.

Saturday 16 March, 1963
Lecture to the Israelite community in Strasbourg on the Council and the Jews. They are determined in their demand that the Council speak of them. The first Council to be held after Auschwitz cannot say nothing about these things. I told them that they ought to approach Cardinal Bea as the Jewish Community in Strasbourg.

Monday 18 March, 1963
Lecture in Belfort to the priests, Religious and general public on the Council. A very pleasant atmosphere.

Tuesday 19 March 1963
L'abbé Gressor[1] drove me by car to Bossey. The appalling state of the roads in some places and the large number of heavy lorries on the roads in Switzerland resulted in our arriving only at 11 am, an hour late. But the session between Catholics and the *Faith and Order* people[2] was just beginning.

The session continued until Saturday 23 March. Work excessively long drawn out. Discussions not very interesting.

I learnt the following details:

Mgr Galbiati,[3] from Milan, was to come to this session. But he had recently given a lecture in Milan on Scripture and Tradition following the Geiselmann

---

1. Pierre Gressot of the diocese of Besançon, where he was responsible for ecumenical affairs.
2. This was a consultation organised by the Bossey Ecumenical Institute (an Institute founded and run by the World Council of Churches), from 18 to 23 March, 1963, between the Faith and Order section of the World Council of Churches and the Catholic Conference for Ecumenical Matters, to deal with the reports prepared for the Faith and Order Conference due to be held in July 1963. Congar there put forward his comments on the reports of the Theological Commission 'Tradition and traditions'.
3. The reference is probably to Enfiro Galbiati, an exegete, and professor at the Pontifical Faculty of Theology in Milan.

thesis. Parente had written to Mgr Montini and the authorisation for Galbiati to come here had been withdrawn.

More precisely: Galbiati had given a lecture in which he had spoken of the opposition that had surfaced at the Council over the Scripture-Tradition question. The Curia does not want the clergy and the laity in Italy to know that this opposition had existed and was so marked. Italy must preserve the fiction of a gloriously united Church, free of tensions and problems: there must be no sowing of any seed of 'problems' . . . !!!

Cardinal Bea is authorised to sign *tesserae* [tickets] authorising the holders to attend the general Congregations of the Council.

The appointment of three cardinals alongside Cardinal Bea for the Secretariat is a step intended to prepare the statute which will allow the Secretariat to remain in existence after the end of the Council. This is a positive step. But Fr Dumont fears that the Secretariat's best days are already over.

Fr Dumont told me the whole story of the Orthodox Observers, those from Moscow, and Mgr Cassien. From beginning to end, there had been misunderstandings, delays in the sending or reception of telegrams and letters: in short, a whole concatenation of mishaps, gaps, lost opportunities. I asked Fr Dumont to write a little memorandum summarising all this.

Visser't Hooft gave me to understand that there could soon be a more or less permanent delegate from the Holy See at the World Council of Churches.

With reference to the Orthodox Observers, I intoned my refrain to Mgr Willebrands about personal invitations, and I also intoned for him my refrain: 1) in favour of a text concerning the Jews. He told me that a certain Jewish indiscretion in nominating Dr Wardi[1] had damaged the cause they wished to serve. 2) In favour of the preparation of a new formula for the profession of faith, in the spirit and style of the Council.

But it is a very tricky question, he told me. If the person invited belonged to a Church which had refused to send observers, he would be in an awkward position and would put us in a delicate situation with regard to that Church . . .

Fr Bertetti[2] told me that Fr Ciappi had been authorised to supervise all ecumenical matters in Italy. I know Ciappi: ultra-prudent, ultra-curial, super-papalist. This would be frightful. In fact, Bertetti told me the following: the text of a lecture was submitted to Ciappi in which the statement was made that Protestant orthodoxy had created a scholasticism. Ciappi sent back twenty pages of com-

---

1. On 12 June 1962, the World Jewish Congress had caught the Vatican on the hop and provoked hostile reactions in Arab countries by appointing Chaïm Wardi, counsellor for Christian affairs in the Israeli Ministry of Foreign Affairs, as the representative of the Jewish world at the Council. The Secretariat of State had then decided to withdraw the *Decretum de Iudaeis* [Decree on the Jews] from the Council debates.
2. The reference must be to Alberto Bellini, of the diocese of Bergamo, professor at the seminary in that city, who was a consultor to the Secretariat for Unity.

ment on the whole lecture. On this particular point, he noted that it was an attack on Scholasticism . . . !!!

Visser't Hooft told me that at the moment the World Council of Churches is working with l'abbé Chavaz,[1] Fr de Riedmatten,[2] who is much appreciated, and Fr Bréchet, also much appreciated and through whom they are in contact with Fr Tucci of *Civiltà Cattolica*.

Our four days of study were not *VERY* interesting. I have known better. The speakers did not include any of those directly responsible for the relationships that we were studying and the discussion was inclined to wander all over the place.

30 March 1963

I saw Mgr Weber and Mgr Elchinger. The latter said to me: 1) that at the episcopal meeting in Munich, the Germans and Cardinal Döpfner had not adopted a firm position with regard to *De Beata*. Their one clear idea was that, if one were to be produced, in the interests of ecumenism, it should stick to indicating what the Church considers essential in this matter and why. Above all, to avoid reference, in word or in thought, to mediation and co-redemption . . . 2) He showed me a letter from Mgr Gouet in reply to his own suggestion of seeing Frs Martelet and Liégé appointed as Council experts. Mgr Gouet felt that the French bishops would support the appointment of the first of these. He was less sure about the second . . . I had already commented several times, at the Council, that the French bishops did not give Fr Liégé the credit that was his due.

13 May 1963

So I have firmly decided to go to Rome. I will see, when there, whether I am useful or not.

These past few days I have been hearing rumours of the schemas that are going to be discussed and that it seems everybody has received. I myself have received nothing: neither texts, nor an invitation to come. What does that mean? Do people want to keep me away? Laurentin has been invited and is asking me about the usefulness or otherwise of his going; others, too, in Germany and Belgium. Myself: NOTHING!

I left during the night of 13/14 May at 12.27 am. A good night. However, as always after a night-time journey with a sleeping pill, and because it is stormy, I cannot put one foot in front of the other.

---

1. Edmond Chavaz, of the diocese of Fribourg, was parish priest of Grand-Saconnex; he had long been involved in the ecumenical movement.
2. Henri de Riedmatten, OP, of the Province of Switzerland, patrologist by training, ecclesiastical counsellor for the Centre des informations OIC (International Catholic Organisations), in Geneva: Council expert from the Second Session onwards.

Tuesday 14 May 1963

Arrived in Bologna at 11.25 am. Alberigo there to meet me. Visit to the library at his Institute for Religious Studies Documentation Centre. Fine library of religious studies, primarily historical: they buy from four to five thousand volumes per year. Conversation concerning the Council and the texts, which they have not only read, but studied critically. Don Dossetti[1] arrived: a spiritual and cultured man, founder of a cenobitic and somewhat eremitic group completely incorporated into the diocesan structures.

Lunch at an Institute for students. During lunch and afterwards at 2 pm, conversation with Don Dossetti. He finds the new *De Ecclesia* schema bad on two points: the question of the MEMBERSHIP of the Church (baptised non-Catholics have been excluded) and the question of the universal jurisdiction of the bishops, which the schema would deny. These are two points which the schema is able not to formulate, but WHICH IT OUGHT NOT RULE OUT. But it would rule them out. In the street, while making our way (with me dragging my useless right leg) to the archbishop's palace, Don Dossetti went on talking. According to him, the thesis of a universal JURISDICTION, received at consecration, had been the common opinion, particularly of the curialists and the ultramontanists, up to AND INCLUDING Vatican I. It is the thesis of the great ultramontanists of the eighteenth and the beginning of the nineteenth century: Ballerini,[2] Zaccaria,[3] Andreucci,[4] (Muzzarelli[5] ???), Gregory XVI: in short the great anti-Gallicans and anti-Jansenists. It is the thesis of the Vatican Council. Fr Gagnebet has simply made use of Bouix[6] and Palmieri,[7] but, when his references are checked, it is clear that he has taken one or two phrases and inserted them into his context, which is not that of the authors he cites.

We agreed with Don Dossetti's view that, since Vatican I, we have been living under the magisterium of ultra-papalist treatises and that studies that would make it possible to recover a truer and better tradition do not yet exist. We must take steps to promote such studies.

At 5 pm, visit to Cardinal Lercaro. He was in choir dress, getting ready for a ceremony. A little man. He repeated what Dossetti had said to me at greater length about the outcome of the Liturgical Commission. He is convinced that the Council cannot be finished by Christmas. In his view, the Italian episcopate has

---

1. Giuseppe Dossetti, of whom Congar gives a profile on the following page, was the personal expert of Cardinal Lercaro; he was to be the Secretary of the Moderators for a short time during the Second Session, but withdrew of his own accord because of his conflicts with Felici: he was a Council expert during the last two Sessions.
2. Piero Ballerini (1698–1769).
3. Francesco A Zaccaria, SJ, (1714–1795).
4. Andrea G Andreucci, SJ, (1684–1771).
5. Alfonso Muzzarelli, SJ, (1749–1813).
6. Domenico Bouix (1808–1870).
7. Domenico Palmieri, SJ, (1829–1909).

changed hardly at all. He receives NO information in the context of the episcopal conference. In conclusion, he agreed to allow me to dedicate to him my forthcoming little book on *L'Église au service des hommes*.[1] He wants to re-introduce his idea of a Church of the poor at the Second Session, but will await his opportunity. He does not seem to think that much will be achieved. He is sorry that the Council did not have the reform of the Church expressly as part of its programme.

From there, to the tomb of St Dominic where, slumped on a bench and exhausted, I nevertheless prayed as if I were not so exhausted. There was a Mass at 6 pm: attentive congregation. Several fathers or brothers passed by. Suggestive of a monk emerging from his separated and protected silence in order do the rounds of the people visiting their shrine. Anthropologically, not a good impression.

At 7.30 pm, I was collected to go to dine with Alberigo and his wife (two children: Anna and Stefano).

CONVERSATION WITH DON GIUSEPPE DOSSETTI: quite an extraordinary man: during the war, in the resistance and underground; member of parliament; urged on by the cardinal to stand as Mayor of Bologna, but defeated by the Communists. Professor of Law. Priest. Founder of the Religious Studies Documentation Centre. Then, and now, founder of a monastic group under the jurisdiction of the bishop. A man who is greater than the different situations in which he finds himself.

The pope's illness is very serious. A complete morphology of cancer revealed by X-ray. He can now not take anything by mouth except liquids.

Very critical of Cardinal Marella.

He told me that Cardinal Ottaviani's candidate as successor to John XXIII is Cardinal Antoniutti,[2] formerly Nuncio in Madrid, responsible for negotiating the Concordat and a supporter of the Catholic State. Dossetti himself would prefer a non-Italian bishop from a small country.

At this moment in Rome, there is a wave of opposition against those responsible for the new policy of an opening to the left and in favour of peace with Communism, against Dell'Acqua, Capovilla[3] (the Pope's secretary), Toniolo Ferrari,[4] Pavan: the authors of *Pacem in terris*.[5] The results of the Italian elections are not welcome and the slide to the left is blamed on the said opening to the left.

---

1. The reference must be to *Pour une Église servante et pauvre* (Paris: Cerf, 1963).
2. Ildebrando Antoniutti: after the death of Cardinal Valeri in July 1963, he was to succeed him as Prefect of the Congregation for Religious, and President of the Commission on Religious.
3. Loris Capovilla was John XXIII's personal secretary: he was to be appointed a Council expert in 1964.
4. Agostino Ferrari Toniolo, from the diocese of Venice, involved in the Italian 'Semaines sociales'; Council expert.
5. The encyclical published on 11 April 1963.

The work of the Liturgical Commission: the principles have been retained but, as regards their application, things have gone only half-way. However, the door has not been closed to further applications.

The Office: Prime has been suppressed. Compline retained. Lauds and Vespers are the two principal moments. A pastoral duty can take the place of the Little Hours. Matins: fewer psalms and longer readings.

Communion under both kinds allowed for ordinations and religious professions. So, opportunities for 'Church' people. Not for couples at their nuptial Mass (voting: 5 in favour, 21 against). Lay people continue to be the poor relations: it is not allowed for them except in the case of a newly baptised adult.

Concelebration allowed on Holy Thursday. For meetings and conferences of bishops, the diocesan synod, meetings of bishops and priests. THE QUESTION OF RELIGIOUS AND THE POSSIBILITY OF A CONVENTUAL CELEBRATION WAS NOT CONSIDERED.

As regards the breviary in the vernacular: it is allowed that bishops may grant a dispensation from the Latin in certain (rare) cases.

Use of the mother tongue: for prayers in common, readings; with the authorisation of the episcopal conference for the parts of the Mass sung by the people; with the authorisation of the Holy See in some other things. There is a whole scale of permissions.

Don Dossetti was very critical of the first two chapters of *De Ecclesia*.

1) It lacks life, movement. (I agree!)

2) It takes a hard and closed line on two principal points:

a) Membership of the Church: by the words *reapse et simpliciter* [by the very fact and quite simply] it excludes baptised non-Catholics being considered as members, whereas Canon Law (and even more so, he told me, the new Eastern Canon Law) is categorical and so is theology: two things are being confused that should be kept separate: being a member is not the same as being in the communion of the Church and participating in the benefits of communion. But Dossetti rejects the distinction between members and 'subjects' which is a late development borrowed from absolutist ideologies.

b) There is a tendency to subordinate the consideration of episcopal consecration to the consideration of collegiality. There is no mention of the universal jurisdiction that the bishops receive at their consecration. But this is the traditional thesis. At the Council of Trent, the curialists stated: jurisdiction over the whole Church is *a Deo* [comes from God] but jurisdiction over a PARTICULAR territory comes from the pope. It was also the thesis of the great Ultramontanists of the end of the eighteenth century: not only Bolgeni, but also Ballerini, Zaccaria, Andreucci, Cappellari (Gregory XVI). According to them, titular bishops were members of the ecumenical council *iure divino* [by divine right] and that was twice the reply given to Pius IX by the preparatory commission for Vatican I.

According to Dossetti, not only is it essential not to exclude this thesis, as he accuses the schema of doing, but it should be proposed positively as the traditional thesis. In his view, Fr Gagnebet was not straightforward in the way he cited the relevant authors.

Wednesday 15 May 1963
A night of recovery. Even so, I can still only just put one foot in front of the other. Mass at the altar of the tomb of St Dominic. Fast train and first class at 10.46 am. Arrived in Rome at about 3.15 pm. Went straight to the Belgian College.

Meeting of the Theological Commission at the Vatican at 4.30 pm. We greeted one another. We are beginning to know one another.

Introductory speech by Cardinal Ottaviani. Then a report by Fr Tromp (text attached). We were given the detail of the work that had been done WITH THE LAY PEOPLE. It is a sensational moment in the life of the Church: lay people have participated in the WORK OF THE COUNCIL along with clerics. The author of *Jalons* has every right to rejoice.

After that, a *VERY* confused meeting. Fr Tromp and Cardinal Ottaviani proposed that *relatores* [rapporteurs] should be chosen from within the Commission who would study five chapters and would be deputed in this way to carry forward the work of our Commission. Difficult to designate which. In the end, the results were as follows: for the *proemium, De vocatione supernaturali hominis* [on humankind's supernatural vocation], Cardinal Browne, Mgr Garrone; Chapters 2 and 5: *De persona humana in societate, De œconomia, et iustitia sociali* [on the human person in society; on the economy, and social justice], Mgr Roy,[1] Mgr Wright;[2] Marriage and the family: the following were designated to deal with mixed marriages in conjunction with members of the Secretariat: van Dodewaard,[3] Dearden,[4] Franić, Fernandez,[5] Pelletier;[6] Culture and progress: Cardinal Léger, Mgr Charue; Peace, international order: König, Schröffer.

Interminable discussion in order to discover whether *De laicis* and *De Religiosis* should be discussed in a joint commission (and then delegating only some members) or in the full Theological Commission alone. Favouring this point of view was the fact that these two chapters are, after all, chapters of *De Ecclesia*, for which the Theological Commission has the mandate and the responsibility; favouring the alternative solution would be the juridical fact that these texts were

---

1. Maurice Roy, Archbishop of Québec, member of the Doctrinal Commission. He was to be created cardinal in February 1965.
2. John J Wright, Bishop of Pittsburg (United States), member of the Doctrinal Commission.
3. Jan van Dodewaard, Bishop of Haarlem (Netherlands), member of the Doctrinal Commission.
4. John F Dearden, Archbishop of Detroit (United States), member of the Doctrinal Commission.
5. Aniceto Fernandez, OP.
6. Georges L Pelletier, Bishop of Trois-Rivières (Canada), member of the Doctrinal Commission appointed by the Pope.

entrusted, for their final preparation, to JOINT commissions. The law is in favour of this solution. So the final decision was that Cardinal Ottaviani would ask the Cardinal Secretary of State to point the law in favour of discussion by the Theological Commission alone.

In the evening, with Mgr Philips and Moeller, we shared out to some extent the interventions to be made concerning the chapter on the laity.

Thursday 16 May 1963

Before leaving for the Vatican, I read through the texts of schema XVII. I found them bad: very scholastic in the bad sense of the word: all abstract and philosophical, not speaking 'in a Christian way' and not addressed to men and women. But what to do about it? Here we are on 16 May, only three and a half months away from the opening of the next session of the Council. One cannot re-do *ab integro* [from scratch] chapters which, however, really need to be re-written differently from beginning to end.

Vatican at 10.00 am. Once again, difficulty in getting the discussion going.

Cardinal Léger: Avoid the threefold division: hierarchy, laity and Religious. Stick to: hierarchy and the faithful, and include a chapter on Christians. That brings back into question the very order of the material.

We began with doubt, vagueness, a feeling of lassitude.

Tromp said that the Co-ordinating Commission had imposed nothing. There was only a wish expressed by Cardinal Döpfner that there should be a chapter on holiness in the Church, which would include a section on the vows. But nothing had been imposed.

Discussion on different expressions in paragraph 1. One could sense a kind of lassitude at having to recommence, yet again, something that had already been done and concluded.

To St Martha's at 4.30 pm (hence leaving at 3.50 pm): meeting with the bishops of the Commission for the Apostolate of the Laity: but there were only six, as they had been summoned only for next Monday. I have never seen anything so muddled, so discouraging. Everything is still being questioned, being worked on. It is still not known whether or not there will be a chapter on this or on that. And the Council will start again in three and half months' time. The meeting lasted half an hour. Mgr Glorieux, for the apostolate of the laity, spoke in French, which I find very discourteous towards those bishops who do not speak French. In the end, we broke up: we will be summoned again if needed.

I am heartily inclined—and have not been hiding the fact—to return to Strasbourg. I have more useful things to do! We returned here at 5.45 pm, having wasted two hours right in the middle of the afternoon.

I told Daniélou, as I had already told Rahner, Häring and ten others that I find the texts prepared for schema XVII to be frankly bad: all philosophical, abstract, not very Christian. But Daniélou does not want them to be touched. There was nothing left to do but to improve them!

Fr Gagnebet, too, complains of the lack of THEOLOGY and a positive Christian tone in these texts. In this connection, he expressed (and I too!) the same criticism about the encyclical *Pacem in terris*. He told me that he had wanted to insert a paragraph on the contribution that the CHURCH as such makes to peace, but Mgr Pavan rejected it. Mgr Pavan is the SOLE editor of the encyclical, he told me: all the corrections suggested, even by Ferrari, Pavan's friend, were rejected. It is Pavan who inserted this pure consideration of the natural right of the human person.

Friday 17 May 1963
Mgr Garrone telephoned me: I am to be his expert for Chapter 1 of Schema XVII for which he is responsible. So, a meeting with him (French Seminary) at 9.30 am with Mgr Larraín, Fr Daniélou, Mgr McGrath (who arrived very late). We settled on the improvements to be made to the *Proemium*, and to the beginning of Chapter 1. I insisted strongly on the need to combine anthropology with theology, on the need, beginning from Revelation and from faith, to make positive statements that are biblical and Christian—and not only about natural law!—really about the whole theology of the image and likeness applied to a human nature viewed also in its social and historical dimensions. I prepared a text intended to replace § 1 of the *Proemium*.

Lunch: Mgr Charue, Mgr De Smedt, Thils, Delhaye.

At St Martha's at 4.30 pm, meeting of our little sub-commission: the same as this morning, plus Cardinal Browne, Mgr Medina[1] (Chile) and Fr Gagnebet. The fact that Cardinal Browne was presiding made the work very pleasant, because he is calm and objective, but it was difficult to hear as the sub-commission on marriage was meeting in the same room, with Frs Lio, Häring, Tromp and Hirschmann . . .

Saturday 18 May 1963
At 9.30 am, sub-commission working on the chapter *De vocatione hominis* [on the vocation of human beings] at the French Seminary. At 3.40 pm, with Mgr Charrière, to whom I spoke about the question of mixed marriages. He showed me the text which will form the basis of their discussion.[2] I was a bit disappointed in it. It does not give bishops the power to dispense from the *forma Ecclesiae*;[3] this text would be destined simply to REPLACE the current legislation. Now: 1)

---

1. Jorge A Medina Estévez, Professor of Theology at the Faculty of Theology in Santiago de Chile of which he became Dean in 1965; Council expert: he was later to become bishop in Chile and then cardinal and Prefect of the Congregation for Divine Worship and the Discipline of the Sacraments.
2. The matter was discussed by a joint commission composed of members of the Doctrinal Commission and of the Commission on the Discipline of the Sacraments.
3. Church form (that is, the form envisaged by canon law).

there is no reference to guarantees given IN WRITING ; 2) it is not stated that a second ceremony would be ruled out; 3) the marriage would be conducted in the Church, even with Mass (the [Nuptial] Mass *'De sponsis'* being ruled out).

I can hardly move my right leg. It is very heavy.

At St Martha's at 4.30 pm. I would have liked to have gone to the sub-commission on mixed marriages, but my duty is to attend the one on Chapter I of schema XVII. We made very slow progress. Fr Daniélou used some phrases from the text of the Profession of Faith that I had written in October 1962.[1]

Sunday 19 May 1963

To love God with all one's strength. I must be doing so, as I have no strength at all. Except the strength that he grants me each day.

A joyless Sunday. Fairly boring work in the morning, afternoon and evening, for this Chapter I. Fr Daniélou does not examine things too closely. I have seen him drafting *currente calamo* [straight off] in front of me some paragraphs of the dogmatic constitution. He is extraordinary. Whether you turn him upside down or or any other way, he always falls on his feet.

Fairly tedious lunch at the Angelicum. Feeling of lassitude and emptiness. It seems that the news about the Pope is very bad: two or three transfusions every week; he is now able to take liquids only. He is not likely to last beyond the end of June.

Already it is being said that it will be a difficult conclave.

For our work, I am not the only one who is saying that our principal difficulties all converge on the same point: how to get away from a situation dominated by the Holy Office. We have already been working at that for nine months. It is more obvious in the Theological Commission because it was formerly under the thumb of the Holy Office and its men. We are bearing the weight of the original mistake which was to place the Commissions, whatever one said, within the framework of the Congregations. I remember being so struck by this at the time that I wrote an article about it in *Témoignage Chrétien*, in which I drew up QUESTIONS and answers, the questions representing my own thinking more than the replies. All the toil of the Council and of the period between Sessions comes down to getting rid of the primary handicap of the Holy Office and of the Romans so that the *Ecclesia* can really and truly express itself. I know that the same is true of the other groups (marriage, culture, etc).

Monday 20 May 1963

Did my homework, which I took to St Martha's at 10.30 am, (but it took me an hour to get there!!!). Work again at 3 pm; at last our text was ready for the plenary

---

1. On 4 November, Daniélou had already suggested that this *proemium* by Congar be taken up and turned into a dogmatic constitution on humankind in the image of God (cf above, page 181).

session (5 pm). Very quickly, we got a full reading of our text: *Proemium* and Chapter I of schema XVII. After some explanations by Mgr Garrone, the criticisms began: from Parente, Šeper, Castellano,[1] Franić, K Rahner . . . In the end, the sub-commission was asked to look at these criticisms and the others which will be submitted to it in writing tomorrow morning.

Tuesday 21 May 1963

At St Martha's at 9.30 am for this work of revision. Difficult meeting: floundering in a rarefied atmosphere. We needed two and a half hours merely to read the comments submitted to us in writing.

Brief meeting of the sub-commission before the plenary session of the joint Commission. This began with a declaration by Mgr[2] . . . = an appeal for an evangelical spirit in the discussion and against Byzantine hair-splitting in matters which are still evolving. Mgr Garrone gave an account of the criticisms which we had received and said how we would attempt to respond to what was relevant in them: but tomorrow!

A large majority voted in favour of adopting the first heading for schema XVII which was recommended by the sub-commission. We then voted on the *proemium* section by section. Again, discussions leading nowhere: all that does is deprive me of the little strength I have left. Oh! To be able to breathe! To find once more work that is free and true!!!

The interventions of Mgr Ménager,[3] backed up by Mgr Charue, make it clear that the content of schema XVII, as it is planned, is very unsatisfactory with respect to what the Council is expecting from this chapter.

At 6.20 pm we moved on to Chapter II: *De persona humana in societate* [on the human person in society]. Introductory exposition by Mgr Pavan. Mgr Parente criticised inaccuracies concerning the very notion of person: this is not surprising, Franić remarked, as lay people have collaborated in its preparation.

Charles Moeller informed me that Cardinal Ottaviani has gone back on his veto against sending members of various religious orders for the centenary of Mount Athos.[4] Evidently, it is a positive move in the complex interplay which may result in the presence of Greek Observers at the Council.

---

1. Ismaele M Castellano, OP, Archbishop of Siena (Italy), member of the Commission on the Apostolate of the Laity.
2. Tromp's *Relatio* indicates that this was Kominek.
3. Jacques E Ménager, Bishop of Meaux, member of the Commission on the Apostolate of the Laity.
4. The celebrations to mark the millennium of Mount Athos were to take place in June: in the end, Benedictines, Franciscans and Dominicans were represented.

Wednesday 22 May 1963

Bad news concerning the Pope's health. Rumours of criticisms being made of his policy of politeness towards the Communist regimes. It is being said that the Pope is naive to believe that he will achieve anything by this means. In the meantime, it has given a million extra votes to the Communists in Italy.

But I think that there is in the Pope's intentions, on the one hand, a more broad-minded view of the need to contribute to relaxation of tension and to seeking an atmosphere of mutual respect, and on the other hand, the desire to create the psychological conditions needed for an agreement between the Church and some of the Democratic Republics. That implies taking a risk. One cannot change attitudes without losing something. It is also being said that Cardinal König, in his missions to Budapest, would not have sought to arrange for Cardinal Mindszenty to come to Rome,[1] but for a *modus vivendi* on the supposition that he would remain in Hungary.

In the morning, work on the revision of our Chapter I at St Martha's.

That same evening, reading and very rapid discussion of Chapter V on the economic order. Once again, a (very idealistic) taking up of the programme of the Social Weeks. No evangelical motivation!

This criticism has been made. I myself have stated it two or three times.

Cardinal Browne, Mgr Garrone, and Mgr Barbado[2] are basically in agreement about asking for a distinction to be made between the fundamental principles which the Council will discuss, and applications, or reasoned deductions from these principles. But the text would need to be completely re-written. Yet we are going at full speed. Schema XVII must be finished by Saturday. The work is being botched. It is not serious. That will not work at the Council!

Thursday 23 May 1963

The Ascension. No holiday for us. Work in the morning at the French Seminary for the revision of our Chapter I.

At 1 pm, lunch at the Belgian college with Fr de Riedmatten. His own personal point of view is very different from that of Cardinal Browne or Mgr Garrone. There will be an immense feeling of disappointment in the world if, in relation to the subject matter of schema XVII, the Council does no more than enunciate principles or generalities: it is ESSENTIAL for the Council—since, in fact, it is the Council that is today the voice of the Church—to come to grips with concrete

---

1. On 10 April 1963, Cardinal König, as personal envoy of Pope John XXIII, paid a visit to Cardinal Mindszenty in Budapest. Concerning the policy of the Holy See vis-à-vis Eastern Europe, cf G Alberigo (editor), *History of Vatican II (1959–1965), Volume II, The Formation of the Council's Identity. First Period and Intersession* (Orbis/Peeters, 1998), pp 561–564.
2. Francisco Barbado y Viejo, OP, Bishop of Salamanca, member of the Doctrinal Commission nominated by the Pope.

solutions and proclaim a word that is cogent in practical terms. In order for this to happen, Riedmatten would envisage the following: that very soon, at the beginning of the Second Session, the Council should ask questions and reach agreement on the general outline (the prepared texts could play their part here); that it should then appoint one or more small commissions made up of people who really have something to offer, together with some very competent lay people, and that this or these commissions should then prepare PRACTICAL texts.

The argument based on the Conciliar tradition is not valid: it is not true that the Councils have only ever spoken of doctrine and the eternal. Moreover, one could very well accommodate a two-fold plan: texts containing principles, and practical decisions.

I added for my own part that what had been needed during the First Session or will be needed during the Second is to distribute to the Fathers a very precise documentation, according to regions and concerning the major problems, with numbered references, giving a REAL picture of the problems and of the state of things.

At the Vatican at 4.30 pm, discussion on *De Matrimonio et Familia* [On Marriage and the Family]. Neither Lio, nor Häring nor Peruzzo were there. It was Franić, backed up when necessary by Cardinal Ottaviani, who maintained the good doctrine (that of the 'Holy Office'): above all concerning the *finis primarius* [primary purpose] as the proper and specific purpose of matrimony and the setting to one side of love, which is not the purpose of marriage. Every time that the word or the idea of personality is mentioned, either Franić, Castellano or Parente argue against it.

It is clear that the general balance of the chapter represents an improvement on the wholly juridical and brutal notion of the multiplication of children. If the text is approved, this will be an opening towards a renewed chapter on the theology of marriage.

Fine interventions by Mgr Šeper (Zagreb) and Tomášek (Poland: the materialists make of marriage merely a means of procreation), and also by Mgr Charue in the name of Sacred Scripture. The power of the Word of God, too much ignored but always fresh when one gives it a chance to express itself. God has always given conjugal love and fidelity as an expression of the love which he wishes to have with his people. But Cardinal Ottaviani wants absolutely that love be seen only as an accompaniment to marriage, for the purpose of making its exercise easier.

On the whole, things did not go too badly. Very remarkable interventions by Cardinal Léger, Fr de Riedmatten (listened to very attentively, very fine Latin, lovely precision of thought).

After the session at the Vatican, at 7.30 pm, our sub-commission went to the Jesuit Generalate in order to complete the work of revision: the third working session on this day of rest. We finished at 11 pm.

Fr Medina told us what he had heard at the Secretariat of State: the Council represents a revolt by the bishops who ought to be brought back to obedience . . .!

Friday 24 May 1963

First free half-day since I arrived in Rome. So I went to the library at the Gregorianum, then to that at the Angelicum. I also saw l'abbé Ganoczy about his work on the ministry according to Calvin.

At 1 pm, lunch with Don Dossetti. Unfortunately, he could not come on Wednesday, although we had got some people together to listen to him and, today, Mgr Philips was not there . . . Extremely interesting conversation. We spoke about the *ordo concilii* [Regulations for the Council]. He thinks that there is no need to change the STRUCTURE of the existing *ordo*: that would be very risky: there would be a danger of drifting into a kind of strait-jacketing and a limitation of freedom. Dossetti says, quite rightly, that time has to be wasted in the general assemblies. Delays are necessary to allow for things to develop, for example the Italian episcopate, which has still barely begun.

Don Dossetti says he himself is absolutely certain that the Curia (for example, Cardinal Tardini) wanted to make the Council harmless by tying it up in too broad a programme. The same goes for the Roman Synod: there are more canons than the actual Code. So it cannot be applied, no part of it has been realised. In the same way, the Curia wanted a Council *De omnibus* [covering everything], incapable of managing its own programme.

At the First Vatican Council, there was on the agenda a small enough number of items. Four commissions had been set up, each of which was established to deal with ONE specific QUESTION. This time, in order to deal with a universal programme, the Commissions were spread out within the framework of the Roman Congregations. This has been very unfortunate, and has weighed on things since the beginning of the Council. It is true. I remember, at the time, having written an article in *Témoignage Chrétien* in which I myself prepared a list of questions. They were the most important questions at the time. In the article I criticised this kind of confusion between the Conciliar Commissions and the Roman Congregations. That has been catastrophic, above all in the case of the Theological Commission. The idea of the people in the Curia was—quite deliberately, according to Don Dossetti—to make the Council ratify texts prepared within the Roman Congregations and which reproduced the *effata* [utterances] of the ordinary magisterium of the popes. So the way in which the Council has turned into something else is for them a danger and a scandal.

Dossetti also told us that the bishops have received a certain number of schemata with 1) a covering letter from Cardinal Cicognani but also with 2) a note stating that these texts have been approved by the Holy Father. Now they have not been so approved either *in forma generica* [in general] or *in forma specifica* [specifically]. According to Dossetti, Pius IX had made it clear that the texts being presented had not received any formal approval from the Pope and were being presented for untrammelled discussion.

We then spoke of two points concerning the first two chapters of *De Ecclesia*:

1) *De membris Ecclesiae*: all those who have been baptised are members of the Church by the fact of their baptism, and they remain so. But if they are not in communion they do not enjoy a share in the goods of the Catholic Communion.

2) The traditional position, proposed by the papal party at the Council of Trent and maintained by the anti-Gallicans of the eighteenth century is as follows: there is a universal JURISDICTION given to the bishops at their consecration, and a particular jurisdiction over a particular Church, given by each one's mission. Now Philips' text would deny that. Philips, who returned at 3.35 pm defended himself; the matter will be taken up again tomorrow, when we will try to ensure that Lécuyer and Hamer are present.

At 4.30 pm at the Vatican, discussion of the chapter on culture. Over-intellectualist, 'humanistic' and even bookish notion of culture. Nothing about culture through traditions and festivals, through manual labour, through the exercise of responsibilities in society, etc.

In the evening, supper with Laurentin at his place. I walked a little this morning; this evening, not only can I not lift my foot, but I can only just keep my balance when standing.

Saturday 25 May 1963

In the Vatican at 9.30 am, chapter on peace. I was told that Mgr Géraud,[1] a Sulpician, seems to be playing a questionable role here in Rome. Apparently, during the First Session, he reported to the Holy Office on what was being said at the Procure Saint-Sulpice, where Cardinal Liénart in particular was staying. Obviously, I note this subject to confirmation, as something that is being said in Rome.

As was to be expected, a rather tense discussion about over-population. Cardinal Léger, Mgr McGrath and others insisted on the need for the MORAL maturity of young people wanting to get married. Mgr Géraud said some edifying but vague things. Fr Tromp wants nothing said about birth control. But in that case, neither should there be the imposition of obligations which result in total deadlock. Fr de Riedmatten intervened very impressively, saying that the matter is urgent. The note of honesty, IN ITSELF, has great value. But the question remains undecided. There followed a discussion about mentioning the legitimacy of defensive warfare.

At lunch, Don Dossetti, Frs Hamer, Lécuyer. Resumption of the subjects discussed yesterday.

At 4.30 pm, the *De laicis* chapter. The weather is very stormy (I feel it!). The meeting was heavy, with no freshness. But the chapter is good and everything went well.

---

1. Joseph Géraud, PSS, Procurator of the Society of Saint Sulpice in Rome, Council expert.

Sunday 26 May 1963

In the morning, work on Chapter IV, *De religiosis*. It is curious that Fr Tromp has absolutely refused to let the chapter be examined by a joint Theology/Religious Commission: he stated three times yesterday evening that it would be examined by the Theological Commission ALONE. But my own view is that this chapter ought to be rewritten, at least the first two sections. So, will the question of a joint commission have to be brought up again?

At 11.30 am, visit from Mgr Arrighi. He spoke to me about two things:

1) The chapter on religious freedom. The Secretariat had prepared a chapter which discussed both the question of religious freedom and the relationship between the Church and the civil power, in place of the two chapters on these subjects which had been prepared by the Theological Commission and rejected or set aside by the Central Commission. But Fr Tromp had resolutely objected to these two schemas (chapters) being presented to the Council Fathers. However, in July 1962, the Pope let it be known that he wanted the question of religious freedom to be discussed. The Secretariat had then removed from the text the section on the relations between Church and State, but the text had still not been submitted. It had been further shortened and revised in the middle of May 1963 and Arrighi gave it to me as it stands today. The Secretariat could itself present it, but there is uncertainty as to where to place it. In my opinion, there is no doubt: its place is in schema XVII. But everything is still in the air. In any case, I have not yet read it.

2) On the matter of sending representatives of the principal religious orders to the celebrations for the Mount Athos millennium. An invitation has come from Greece: the Secretariat of State passed it on to the Secretariat [for Unity] and, twice, stated explicitly that it was passing the matter over to them. So the Secretariat appointed representatives: for the Benedictines, the Abbot Primate Benno Gut, who is on the Theological Commission; for the Dominicans, Fr Bosco,[1] *socius* for Italy. But when Dom Gut asked Cardinal Ottaviani to excuse him for his absence from the meetings of the Theological Commission (because the celebrations were to have been in May but has been postponed to June because the king of Greece was ill), the Cardinal told him that he was against sending representatives to the celebrations. Mgr Willebrands had been summoned to the 'Holy Office' where he was hauled over the coals and came back totally disheartened: the 'Holy Office' was against the idea of important representatives, and from ROME, going to Mount Athos. That Chevetogne and Istina, having been invited, should send someone was unimportant; but representatives of the major religious orders coming from Rome, No! In the end, the 'Holy Office' had to give way in the face of the formal wish of the Secretary of State, who had entrusted the matter to the Secretariat [for Unity].[2]

---

1. Giacinto Bosco, OP, of the Province of Piedmont.
2. See above, page 293, note 4.

Cardinal Bea is working to institutionalise the fact that the Secretariat should be made definitively responsible for all this type of authorisation even after the Council.

It is one more defeat for the 'Holy Office', which has had to suffer quite a few similar ones in the past two or three years.

At lunch, Arrighi was telling little stories about Rome for more than two hours. He is captivating and can go on for ever. At times he is a bit like Fernandel. To be honest, this kind of thing amuses me, as it amuses everyone else, but it does not really interest me. However, there are some of his stories which imply underlying attitudes in serious matters and arouse in me a deep-seated sense of scandal and vehement indignation. That an imbecile, a sub-human like Pizzardo should be in charge of the department for universities and seminaries is scandalous and extremely serious. When one is acquainted with certain universities, certain deans, certain rectors, and sees how seriously and competently they take to heart a sector which is steadily expanding, when one compares all this with this wretched freak, this sub-mediocrity with no culture, no horizon, no humanity, one feels a wave of anger and revulsion rising within one. This Pizzardo, who has red pyjamas and underpants, who lives with his eighty-four year old and eighty-two year old sisters, who haggles over the purchase of a newspaper, who spends his afternoons counting his pennies for the seminaries of Italy that are his main preoccupation, who gave l'abbé Oraison[1] the famous idiotic reply; who, a few years ago, organised a disastrously stupid meeting of rectors of Catholic universities: this man, in charge of the curial department for Studies and Research! What a frightful comedy!

At 3.30 pm, we left by car with Mgr Prignon, Mgr Philips and C Moeller for an outing. It was the first moment of relaxation since the beginning of this stay in Rome. On the road to Florence, passing through Sutri (at high speed!), stopping in Viterbo: the Palace of the Popes. I thought above all of St Thomas, of the periods he spent at the Curia . . . Then La Quercia. The joy of praying in this cloister which so charmed Lacordaire[2] and his early companions of a romantic age. I understood what PLACES with a monastic tradition, what a true cloister, paintings from the past, gave to their souls, interior invigoration as much as joy and gladness in finding themselves in a place that met with their desires. Outside, there was a market, a country fair, stalls, people milling around enjoying their Sunday rest. In the entrance way, children were playing. But in the cloister, there was calm and silence. At that moment, I felt myself closely united with Fr Lacordaire.

---

1. Marc Oraison, one of whose works on sexual morality had been put on the Index in 1953, recorded in his memoirs what Cardinal Pizzardo had said to him that same year: 'For purity: terror, spaghetti and haricot beans'; cf *Ce qu'un homme a cru voir. Mémoires posthumes* (Paris: R Laffont, 1980), 288.
2. Henri Lacordaire, who restored the Dominican Order in France in the nineteenth century.

Then, Tuscany: in the evening light, the silhouette of the two churches and of the towers which occupy the site of the Etruscan acropolis had something which was both very calm and poignant. Two very fine Romanesque churches with, in the larger one (dedicated to St Peter) a crypt where the setting sun was gilding the pillars. Very fine countryside too, rather like the Argonne. We returned at 9.30 pm.

Monday 27 May 1963

Very bad news of the Pope's health: he has had another haemorrhage. He will not live until the end of June! According to Arrighi, many of the attitudes being adopted at this time are due to the fact that this is known to be the case. The fact that several members of the Holy Office (Ottaviani, Parente, Lio) have not taken part in our discussions in recent days is perhaps linked with these attitudes?

This morning, work: I tried to catch up . . . At Santa Sabina at 12.15 pm: saw Fr Hamer. He was emerging from a meeting of the Studies Commission.[1] He was extremely irritated and upset. He told me that there is no perspective, no movement, that it is all a question of trivial administration. In these conditions, he had nothing interesting to do. He is thinking of asking Fr General to be relieved of his post and allowed to go back to studies, which is what he is made for. I believe, in fact, that his position is a very thankless one and that there is little to be said for working alongside Fr General, who really has no 'vision', but simply administers day-to-day matters. Fr Hamer also told me that the General speaks only about safety and precautions to be taken, and lives under the burden of what is being said at the 'Holy Office': always the same cancer devouring the evangelical heart of the Church!

At lunch, at midday, I saw Frs de Vaux,[2] and Duval,[3] who had come for the Studies Commission: they are being made to revise the *ratio*[4] chapter by chapter. What should be done is first to tackle the question of the overall view!

Fr General announced that at the Holy Office that morning it was being said that the Pope had died, but it was not certain that this was so, he added.

Fr General told me, at St Martha's, that there must have been a mix-up. On the one hand, people had seen the Eucharist being taken to the Pope and it was thought that it was Extreme Unction or the Viaticum. On the other hand, the Roman cardinals would have been notified that the Pope was entering the last phase of his illness . . .

---

1. Commission set up in the Dominican Order following the General Chapter in Bologna in 1961.
2. Roland de Vaux, OP, of the Province of France, exegete and archaeologist, Director of the École Biblique et Archéologique Française in Jerusalem.
3. André Duval, OP, of the Province of France, Rector of the Dominican Faculties at Le Saulchoir, where he was Professor of the History of the Church.
4. The *ratio studiorum*, that is, the programme of studies.

After lunch, I saw Fr Bosco, *socius* for Italy, and president of the *De sacro min-isterio* Commission,[1] to which I also belong. He seemed to me fairly disappointed. Of the twelve members to whom he had written, five had never replied. This Commission had been set up at the General Chapter in Toulouse[2] at the request of a single father, when there was no real and widespread desire for it. That makes no difference '*in vertice*' [at the top], he told me. As regards Fr General, he told me not to be optimistic; he sees to the everyday things, but he has no overall plan or programme. As for this Commission, all that is expected of us is reports on THE QUESTIONS THAT THE GENERAL chooses to put to us, in the event that he does so. We can, however, make suggestions to him as individuals. It was he, Bosco, who secured my nomination, with the idea that ecumenical matters ought to be included, because from now on they have a place in our ministry.

I saw Fr Hamer again for a short while. I left at 4.05 pm for St Martha's, where the meeting on Chapter IV on the states of perfection was being held. It began with a declaration from Fr Tromp, read with his characteristic tone of authority, but less energetically than before.

Fr Tromp, on behalf of Cardinal Ottaviani, began by reading a long report directed AGAINST the idea of producing a more wide-ranging exposition of ho-liness in the Church, and even of placing this chapter on Religious under the heading of the call to holiness, which goes without saying; it must be placed un-der the heading of the Church, an organised body with '*ordines*' [orders], under the heading of organisation, and also under the heading of the services which Religious render to the Church.

Fr Tromp's declaration started a confused discussion. Cardinal Browne, who was presiding, suggested that we should study the chapter as it had been present-ed to us, make amendments, and send it back to the Co-ordinating Commission.

Only eleven members of the Theological Commission were present. Most of the Fathers, who spoke in turn, were of the opinion:

1) that the content of the proposed chapter should be placed in the wider con-text of the call to holiness in the Church, in which there would be express men-tion of priests; 2) to begin at once an examination of the text, which could help to improve it, and then to submit the whole to the Co-ordinating Commission. In all of that, Cardinal Browne was absolutely fair. Had Ottaviani been presiding, the discussion would have been poisoned.

Fairly tense and confused discussion which made it clear that the text would encounter great opposition at the Council.

---

1. The creation of this Commission 'for the Sacred Ministry' had also been called for at the General Chapter in Bologna.
2. Elective General Chapter which had been held during the summer of 1962.

Tuesday 28 May 1963

Work with Mgr Philips and Canon Moeller on the report which Cardinal Suenens is to give on schema XVII.[1]

At 11.25 am, visit from Fr de la Brosse. We spoke about his thesis, and also
about the Angelicum. He told me 1) that the crisis at the Angelicum, far from
being over, has blown up again. The Theology Faculty has elected a new Dean,
in opposition to the Rector, Fr Sigmond: not Fr von Gunten,[2] the candidate of
the people who were open, but Fr Gillon (who gained ten votes as against seven).
So, seeing that there is no wish for renewal of any kind, some Institutes have announced that they propose to withdraw their students: the Oblates have already
done so (forty students), the Blessed Sacrament Fathers are speaking of doing so.
2) Several facts arouse the fear of a hardening and narrowing on the part of the
government of the Order: two Italians who were to go to to Canada for studies
will not now be going. There are five or six cases of this kind. Is it the beginning
of a general rule? That would be an ATTACK on the cultural life of the Order.

So, faced with this situation, and feeling himself powerless, the rector, Fr Sigmond, may be thinking of resigning. Fr Perreault likewise. Fr Duval has said that
if things go on as they are, he would no longer send anyone to the Angelicum. The
Angelicum would become a Spanish house in Rome.

At 12.30 pm Fr Duprey came. He spoke to me about a problem internal to the
White Fathers, and then of the general situation: about the Orthodox Observers
(a matter internal to the Orthodox), about speculations concerning the expected
death of the Holy Father. It appears that the Vatican Administration has not reserved rooms in the hotels for 8 September. So it is thought that the Council will
be postponed . . . ?

I packed my bags, and said my goodbyes.

At St Martha's at 4.30 pm, Mgr Charue began with a harsh criticism of our
text. Fr Tromp wished to reply, but Cardinal Browne did not call on him to speak
until much later.

Discussion of the text resumed. Fr Rahner monopolised the discussion once
again. He is magnificent, he is brave, he is clear-sighted and deep, but, in the end,
he is indiscreet. That was the end of the possibility of speaking: the opportunity,
and even the taste for it, has been lost.

During this time, a heavy storm somewhat lightened this frightfully heavy
atmosphere.

In the end, Cardinal Browne said that the text would be revised, in the sense
of the comments made, by a small commission of three bishops, each of whom

---

1. In the Co-ordinating Commission, it was Cardinal Suenens who was responsible for
    supervising this schema.
2. François von Gunten, OP, of the Province of Switzerland, professor in the Faculty of
    Theology at the University of St Thomas (the Angelicum), editorial secretary of the
    journal *Angelicum.*

could choose a *peritus*. The three Fathers will be Mgr Charue, Mgr McGrath and Fr Fernandez. Somebody signalled to me to be perhaps one of the *periti* but nobody actually asked me; I had to go. In fact, I left at 6.55 pm. Mgr Prignon, wonderfully amicable, drove me to the airport which we reached at 7.45 pm. It was there that I wrote these last lines.

Everything has gone well. The texts have been or will be considerably improved. Cardinal Browne was extremely welcoming, fair and a peace-maker. It is largely due to him that things have gone so well. Moreover, he made us laugh by saying, twice, that Abraham had preserved chastity in intention more than many virgins, although he had had six wives.

Arrived in Paris a little late. Domi was at Orly to meet me, with Anne.[1]

Wednesday 29 May 1963 [2]
Anne acted as my chauffeur. What a lovely girl she is, having an interior life that gives her a deep calm, which adds to her charm.

At Cerf with Fr Bro,[3] then Fr Peuchmaurd,[4] after which I saw two spinster ladies. In the afternoon, recording for Canadian TV, where I followed Fr de Lubac. Brief visit to *Témoignage Chrétien*. Train.

Thursday 30 May 1963 [5]
Mgr Marty was so kind as to drive me to Rheims and back in order to visit Tere.[6] He said in front of her, and told me in more detail afterwards, that he had seen the Pope a month ago, the day before the Balzan Prize.[7] The Pope had said to him: the French bishops are working very well; their theologians also, especially Fr Congar. Mgr Marty said that he was very proud, then, to tell the Pope that I came from his diocese.

Mgr Marty had gone to Rome, having been summoned there by Cardinal Ciriaci, in view of the plans for setting up a commission on the ministry and the apostolate for the period after the Council. He had also seen Mgr Dell'Acqua, who had shown him a list of names for a commission to revise the Code of Canon Law: his own name was on the list, and mine too!!! My God, what would I do in a commission on the revision of the Code?

---

1. Dominique and Anne Congar, nephew and niece of Congar.
2. Congar added to the typescript 'Paris'.
3. Bernard Bro, OP, of the Province of France, was literary editor of Éditions du Cerf and was to become its General Editor in 1964.
4. Michel Peuchmaurd, OP, of the Province of France, worked at Éditions du Cerf.
5. Congar added to the typescript 'Strasbourg'.
6. Tere (pronounced 'Teureu'): nickname given by the Congar children to their mother. This name then came to be used by all the family. Mme Congar, born Lucie Desoye, was a Dominican tertiary.
7. The Pope had received the prize awarded by the Eugenio Balzan Foundation in recognition of his activity in favour of fraternity and peace.

The Pope, who had received Mgr Marty for forty minutes, told him that he had got bored during the first month of the Council: he felt that no progress was being made and that the discussions of the liturgy were without interest. The Pope wants people to move on, to be open! It is necessary, he said, always to see first the good there is in others. He also said that Mgr Pavan had prepared too abstract a text for *Pacem in terris*. During the night of 6 to 7 January, after he had read this text, the Pope had had the inspiration to address himself to all people of good will and not only to Christians: he had also seen the four pillars: truth, justice, love, freedom. I record that for history!

10 July 1963

Since I wrote these last things, great events have taken place, but I have not written anything here about them. There was the last suffering and the death of John XXIII. In this, the Church and even the world have been through an extraordinary experience. All at once, one became aware of the immense impact this humble and good man has had. It has become clear that he has profoundly altered the religious map and even the human map of the world, simply by being what he was. He did not operate by great expositions of ideas, but by gestures and a certain personal style. He did not speak in the name of the system, of its legitimacy, of its authority, but simply in the name of the intuitions and the movement of a heart which, on the one hand, was obedient to God and on the other loved all people, or rather he did both these things in a single action, and in such a way that, once again, the divine law has proved true: God alone is great; true greatness consists in being docile in the service of God in himself and in his loving plan. God raises up the humble. Blessed are the meek for they shall possess the land. Blessed are the peacemakers, they shall be called children of God. Everyone had the feeling that, in John XXIII, they had lost a father, a personal friend, someone who was thinking of and loving each one of them.

Even the incredible Roman ceremonial, those endless shows, were unable to wipe out the deep impression, the sorrow and the intimate heartfelt affection. However, what a contradiction between the courtly pomp and that utterly simple man whose funeral was the occasion of it! The working people followed his last suffering and death as though he were the father of their own family. 'For once we had a good one. . . ' A sort of extraordinary unanimity had come about.

Et nunc, reges, erudimini! [And now, kings, be instructed. Ps 2:10]. It is fairly clear, however, that there is a path to success because it is the path of truth: that the important thing, as Lacordaire said, is not so much to leave behind something achieved, but to have a life. It is not a matter of claiming and loudly asserting that one is the Vicar of Christ, but of truly BEING it. What is really important is not so much ideas, but the heart. And yet, ideas are needed. St Thomas served human beings as much, even if he was less affectionate towards them. I reflect on my own destiny. God has led me to serve him and to serve human beings, from him and for him, above all through the medium of ideas. I have been led to a solitary life, very dedicated to the word and to paper. It is my share in the plan of love. But I want to involve myself with my heart and my life also, and that this service to ideas should itself be a service TO HUMAN BEINGS.

It seemed to me at once that Cardinal Martini was the only one with a chance of winning two thirds of the votes. The non-Italian cardinals who represent nearly two thirds of the College would vote in great numbers for him. So it would be sufficient for a few Italian cardinals also to vote for him, in order to obtain the two-thirds majority. None of the conservative cardinals would ever rally to him.

I have heard it said—but what value has this kind of gossip, or what impact does it have beyond that of being plausible—that, at the very first scrutiny, Montini received forty or forty-two votes and Siri about twenty. At the umpteenth scrutiny, that is on the Friday morning, Cardinal Siri is said to have announced that he would be voting for Montini and to have urged those who had voted for him to do the same . . . (!)

Cardinal Montini[1] is an extremely intelligent and well-informed person. He creates a deep impression of holiness. He will take up John XXIII's programme, but obviously not in the same way as John XXIII and perhaps not altogether in his spirit. He will be much more Roman, more in the style of Pius XII; like Pius XII he will want to decide things on the basis of ideas, and not simply let things evolve by themselves from openings created by a movement of the heart. He will love the world as much, but more by way of solicitude.

I have just returned from spending a few hours at the Caen Social Week.[2] The letter to the Week (from Cardinal Cicognani) rather floored me. It reminded me too much of Pius XII. It is a kind of little encyclical, in which the ideas, which are well balanced, cancel one another out. It is a complete exposition, though very abstract, saying everything that it is necessary to think, to foresee, to avoid . . . Of course, this is rather the style of such texts. It is a style that is difficult to swallow. It carries within it a whiff of paternalism. John XXIII had confidence in human beings, had confidence in the Church, which he allowed to express itself freely. That was the secret of the opening up that he achieved.

In Caen, I lunched beside Mgr Ferrari-Toniolo. He spoke only to me because he had Bouladoux[3] on his right: they talked a lot about trade unions and their Christian label. Ferrari spoke a little to me about Mgr Montini. When he was in the Curia, he had aroused the opposition (if I understood correctly) of those who were opposed to John XXIII and to the Council. 'They' did not want him to be made a cardinal. When Pius XII declared that the collaborators who were closest to him, and the most faithful, Tardini and Montini, had asked not to be elevated

---

1. It was on Friday 21 June, the second day of the Conclave, that Giovanni Battista Montini was elected Pope.
2. The 50th 'Semaine sociale de France' which was held from 9 to 14 July on the theme: 'A Democratic Society'.
3. Maurice Bouladoux was President of the International Confederation of Christian Trade Unions.

to the purple in order to remain close to him,[1] this was only half true. It was the opposition that had secured that. Then, when Montini was appointed to Milan, Pius XII did not make him a cardinal. That was providential. Had he been a cardinal, Montini would have been elected pope after Pius XII and we would not have had the extraordinary opening up achieved by John XXIII. At that time, a non-cardinal could not have been elected. Cardinal Roncalli said as much to Mgr Ferrari: the time has not yet come, he said, when one could elect someone who was not a cardinal.

I asked Mgr Ferrari about the reasons for Montini's departure from the Vatican. He told me: 'they' had persuaded Pius XII that Montini was a source of division in the Curia. For Montini held an important position: in between the temporal or the political on the one hand, and the religious on the other; in effect, a position that was anti-Gedda[2] and pro-'*Humanisme intégral* '.[3] But, according to Ferrari, history repeats itself. It is more or less what happened in the case of Benedict XV. The integrist clan had accused him of Modernist sympathies and had got him moved to Bologna. But he returned. When he was elected, he found three dossiers of accusations against cardinals: the first against the cardinal of Pisa, the second (I forget) and the third against Cardinal della Chiesa . . . [4]

Mgr Ferrari thinks that there will be at least a Third and perhaps even a Fourth Session of the Council. Like Fr de Riedmatten, he thinks that Commissions will have to function as Commissions of the Council and speak in its name without being the Council itself. He urged me to come frequently to Rome.

But how to know whether or not it is opportune to do so? Unless I were to settle there . . .

Beginning of August 1963

During my stay in Voirons[5] with Fr Féret, we spoke a lot together about the Council. Fr Féret is writing up his comments on the schemas. He has a keen, strong perception of things, linked with his reflection and his personal synthesis; but often TOO closely linked with HIS OWN construction. It is this that both gives his remarks their force and makes them not very usable. One cannot rebuild everything from scratch. When it is a question of a work of THE CHURCH in which

---

1. In his consistorial speech on 12 January 1953, Pius XII had announced that Mgr Tardini, Secretary for Extraordinary Ecclesiastical Affairs, and Mgr Martini, who was responsible for Ordinary Ecclesiastical Affairs, had both refused the honour of the cardinalatial purple. Cf 'L'allocution consistoriale du pape Pie XII "ex quo Sacrum Collegium"', *La Documentation Catholique*, 1953, col 78.
2. At that time, Luigi Gedda was president of Catholic Action in Italy.
3. Jacques Maritain, *Humanisme intégral*, 1936.
4. The future Benedict XV.
5. Congar was to stay several times during the summer with his friend Fr Féret at the Priory of Notre Dame de Voirons in Haute-Savoie, where the Little Sisters of Bethlehem were later to settle.

one must co-operate with a GREAT NUMBER of theologians of different schools of thought and work for the episcopate of all countries, one cannot introduce one's own personal synthesis, however well-founded and interesting it may be ...

Fr Féret has been told by Mgr Flusin that the next Session will begin with *De Revelatione*. I foresee a fierce brawl over this. Because, on the one hand, the integrist offensive (the Lateran) against the Biblical scholars has not disarmed.

On the other hand, those who support the thesis of the Two Sources[1] have done their homework and are now producing their arguments. The book for which Fr Balić had asked me for a contribution has now appeared.[2] I have read the conclusion-summary written by Fr Balić himself. I fear that this book will make a huge impression on many of the bishops. It makes it quite clear that the Two Sources have been taught in the Catholic Church, and that this is a majority view, if not quite universal. In my opinion, THIS is not the issue.

The question today is precisely to GET AWAY FROM THIS PROBLEMATIC, which has been conditioned either, in the Middle Ages, by ignorance of the problem of THE Tradition, or, since the Reformation, by a treatment of the question that is dominated by the bad position it has because of the Protestant denials. If only I had the time to show this, to put forward a useful *status quaestionis*. But I have the time for nothing!

The few weeks which separate me from the Council, already so burdened with work to be completed, are getting more and more overloaded day by day. Two new heavy burdens have just recently been laid on me:

1) I have been asked to sit an *Ad gradus*[3] and Fr Provincial has suggested 13 to 16 September, when Fr General will be at L'Arbresle with the French Provincials. Where will I find the weeks necessary for a minimum of preparation, or even the possibility of devoting three or four days to this journey?

2) More importantly. While in Voirons, I received an invitation from Cardinal Suenens to work with a small team, a) on a slight revision of *De Ecclesia*; b) on a major reworking of schema XVII along the lines I had myself suggested in May. See SPECIAL DOSSIER ON THIS QUESTION. It is a major and important matter. But the time!!!

I have been very worried just recently. I was being besieged with requests by the Dutch Centre of Documentation on the Council,[4] so in the end I sent them

---

1. Those who regard Scripture and Tradition as two separate sources of Revelation; they were against Geiselmann's position, according to which all Revelation is already contained in Scripture.
2. *De Scriptura et Traditione,* Pontificia Academia Mariana Internationalis, Rome, 1963.
3. The 'ad gradus' examination is a necessary preliminary to the nomination of a person as Master of Theology in the Dominican Order: owing to the Second World War, Congar had not been able to take this examination which had been scheduled for 1940; the most recent Provincial Chapter had expressed the wish that Congar sit this examination and the Master General had agreed.
4. Cf above, page 268, note 1.

the two critical texts which I wrote on *De Revelatione* and *De Ecclesia* without even taking the time to enclose a covering letter.[1] Now, a word from Mgr Gouet, received on 12 August, made me realise something that I had completely forgotten (and in all good faith), namely, that the Dutch DO-C is more of a press service that is widely reported and disseminated. I realise that I have committed a serious error and a serious fault. My text, which examines secret documents and is addressed only to the bishops, has come into the hands of journalists, seminary professors, Protestants. The press will disseminate all that abroad. I shall be the cause of an enormous indiscretion, of publicity that there will be no way of stopping. What to do? Try to limit the damage. I wrote immediately to Amersfoort along these lines, and also to Fr General and to Fr Tromp, to explain the thing (CF LETTERS ATTACHED). I am getting ready to receive a well-deserved rebuke, which may even take the form of losing my position as an *expert*.

But at the same time, I am at peace on a religious level. On the one hand, I tell myself that this serious *culpa* may well prove, providentially, to be a good thing. Perhaps, once alerted on the question of Tradition, public opinion will serve as a felicitous counter-weight against the reaction of supporters of the Two Source thesis. We shall see. But above all, as in the very difficult situation of three years ago, at about the same time, I entrust myself to the GRACE OF GOD: yes, to so gracious a mercy that, punished for our sins, we are not destroyed thanks to the Mercy of God. To live SOLELY BY **GRACE**, without any reassuring human support, that is the rule that I rely on. God does not deceive us, although his grace is often puzzling.

19 August 1963

Getting round to going through my mail and opening the packets and parcels that had arrived during my absence. The DO-C letter sent with the copies reassured me: it seems that my texts were sent ONLY TO THE BISHOPS, and were also marked 'confidential'. I wrote at once to Fr General and to Fr Tromp to tell them this. That takes a weight off my conscience!!!

21 August 1963

I have just returned from seeing Mgr Weber. Nothing outstanding. He gave me the text of his comments on the schemas, which has already been sent to Rome. He also showed me a printed paper which all the bishops have received: seven pages in Latin, signed '*conciliares quidam Periti qui Romae degunt*' [certain Council experts residing in Rome] and dated St Gregory VII 1963. It is a list of the points on which dreadful danger to the faith is foreseen, because theses inspired by the 'new theology' are being spread abroad. For this theology, the main refer-

---

1. Texts prepared for the series of *Études et documents* published by the General Secretariat for the French episcopate: they were both dated July 1963.

ence is to a work I had not heard of, by a German[1] confrère, Fr AH Maltha, *Die neue Theologie*.[2]

There are theses concerning philosophy (knowledge of God), ecclesiology, classical theology (nothing on ecumenism . . .), but above all on the interpretation of the Scriptures, the historicity of the gospels. So it is a continuation of the Lateran offensive, but undoubtedly with considerable support from Roman circles.

25 August 1963

I had quite a long talk with Mgr Elchinger. To begin with, he spoke of Cullmann's reactions, with whom he had conversed at length at Chamonix. From the exegetical point of view, Cullmann is mainly concerned to thwart Bultmann.[3] It is against Bultmann that he is preparing a new book: salvation is a history.[4]

On *De Œcumenismo*, he maintains that the basic reason for the Reformation was an affirmation of the transcendence of God, without the mediation of the Church; it was, in the name of Scripture, a refusal of the 'plus' the Catholic Church presents. He insists that there should be a reference to mixed marriages.

He enumerates the great points which, according to him, establish an opposition between the Reformation and the Catholic Church: Scripture and Tradition, the authority of a magisterium claiming to be infallible.

Mgr Elchinger was struck by the fact that, on many important points, Cullmann has a very simplistic idea of Catholic positions. He had discovered some very elementary things for the first time.

Cullmann was very touched to have received a long hand-written letter from Cardinal Montini at the end of last January, and one from Paul VI in reply to his own letter of congratulations and good wishes.

Mgr Elchinger is leaving tomorrow for Fulda where he will represent the French bishops at the meeting of the German-speaking bishops. The Germans have asked a specific Conciliar Father to produce a report on one of each of the twelve schemas, which they hope to discuss at this meeting. Each member has received in advance the rapporteur's text, so that they can work fairly quickly. We have nothing like this in France. Our bishops have only held local and partial meetings. There is no overall organisation and any help they ask for from the theologians remains disorganised and haphazard.

I read in particular the critiques of *De Beata Maria Virgine, Matre Ecclesiae*. There is one by ?, perhaps Rahner, not entirely negative, but articulating specific criticisms on 'mediation', etc; another by Mgr Volk, very negative. The German bishops would like to reject the existing schema *De Beata*, and turn the material

---

1. Congar wrote in the margin of the second typescript: 'Dutch?'.
2. Andreas Heinrich Maltha, OP, *Die neue Theologie* (Munich, 1960; this is a German translation of *De nieuwe theologie. Informatie en orientatie* (Bruges, 1958).
3. Rudolf Bultmann, famous exegete and German Protestant theologian.
4. See above, page 159, note 3.

it contains into a chapter or epilogue of *De Ecclesia*, seen from a christological and ecclesiological angle, and entitled

De Maria Matre Christifidelium
                       fidei

[On Mary, Mother of Christ's faithful; Mother of the faith].

In the evening, visit from Fr Vanhengel[1] who is travelling around in order to establish the review *Concilium*: a frightful task. The editor, Brand,[2] who pays well, keeps after him as if for a commercial venture.

31 August 1963

I saw Mgr Elchinger who had just returned, rather disappointed, from the meeting in Fulda. To the degree that the preparations for the meeting had seemed to him fine, to the same degree the meeting itself turned out to be empty. They worked on only three schemas, whereas there had been eleven or twelve on the agenda:

- *De Revelatione*: the German bishops seemed hesitant about my idea that one should speak of the living Tradition. Cardinal Alfrink, who was present, would like to REJECT this schema: it says nothing, it contributed nothing, it is a useless text.

- *De Ecclesia*: the bishops will content themselves with particular comments.

- *De Beata Maria Virgine*: The bishops were agreed, *nemine contradicente* [unanimously], in wishing to see this text shortened and inserted into *De Ecclesia* in the form of an epilogue. But, in my opinion, this would be to assume that the schema would be REWRITTEN from a different perspective and in a different spirit. Mgr Elchinger agreed to my writing to Laurentin about this, so that he could prepare a text. Cardinal Döpfner expressed his *mea culpa*, because IT WAS HE who, a year ago, had prevented the *De Beata* from being envisaged as a chapter of *De Ecclesia*. He said that at the Co-ordinating Commission (which is meeting today) he would seek to have the text so inserted; Mgr Philips, who was present (the only one not a conciliar Father, apart from Karl Rahner), said that Cardinal Suenens would not be displeased if this point were reopened. The German bishops are of the view (unanimously, except for six dissenting votes) that there should be no mention of co-redemption, and, if there is to be a mention of mediation, they would like it to be explained that this is with and in the Church, at the head of the Church, not between the Church and Christ.

Mgr Elchinger told me (this must be in the newspapers) that Paul VI has appointed three new Presidents. So now there will be thirteen, and there will not be a legate, as I was afraid there might be. They are Cardinals Siri, Wyszyński, Meyer (Chicago). I wonder whether perhaps the nomination of Siri is connected with

---

1. Marcel Vanhengel, OP, of the Province of Flanders, was to be the first Secretary General of the journal *Concilium*.
2. Paul Brand.

the fact that there were quite a few votes for him at the Conclave and that, after the third or fourth scrutiny, he had (?) asked those who were voting for him to vote instead for Montini?

Cardinal Döpfner told Mgr Elchinger that Paul VI would have liked to postpone the Council to 1964 with a modified agenda. He had been told that such a move would be very badly interpreted by the world at large.

The German bishops are of the opinion that one ought not to begin with *De Revelatione*. They feel that this schema will provoke difficult questions and that it would be better for the Council to be 'run in' once again: one could begin with *De Ecclesia*. Cardinal Alfrink's response to this was: it will raise as many questions . . .

I shall know the outcome in Malines.

Thursday 5 September 1963

Train to Geneva. Received—indeed welcomed—by the Jesuit Fathers of *Choisir* (Fr Nicod,[1] then, when he returned from Montréal and the USA, Fr Bréchet).

In the evening, my lecture for the Rencontres internationales[2] in the Hall of the Reformation: a sad room, and not many people present. But WHO was there? I don't know. One would need to know in order to assess the appeal of these gatherings and of my presence or participation in them.

Friday 6 September 1963

In the morning, a little lecture with Frs Taymans[3] and Nicod, then with Pastor Widmer[4] and Rist,[5] (thesis on monastic theology).

---

1. Jean Nicod, SJ, on the editorial team of *Choisir,* a journal produced by the Swiss Jesuits.
2. Congar took part in the eighteenth Rencontres Internationales de Genève: cf *Dialogue ou Violence? Textes des conférences et des entretiens organisés par les Rencontres internationales de Genève* (Neuchâtel: Éditions de la Baconnière, 1963): cf in particular Congar's lecture, 'Le dialogue, loi du travail œcuménique, structure de l'intelligence humaine', pages 37–54; it was reprinted in Yves M-J Congar, *Chrétiens en dialogue. Contributions catholiques à l'Oecuménisme,* 'Unam Sanctam', 50 (Paris: Cerf, 1964), 1–17.
3. Georges Taymans.
4. Pastor Gabriel-Philippe Widmer was Professor of Theology at the Protestant Faculty of Theology at the University of Geneva, and contributed to the *Revue de théologie et de philosophie.*
5. Gilbert Rist was preparing a licenciate thesis at the Protestant Faculty of Theology under the direction of Gabriel-Philippe Widmer, the title of which was to be 'Objet et méthode de la théologie d'après saint Anselme, Abélard, saint Bernard, saint Thomas, Calvin et Karl Barth'; he had consulted Congar about the subject of his thesis a year earlier.

Lunch with M Martin,[1] president of Rencontres, with their founder, M Babel[2] (a predestined name!), the secretary M Moeller,[3] Pastors Marchal,[4] and [ ]

At 2.30 pm, a little lecture with a group of pastors who had come for this purpose from Lausanne (Bonnard,[5] Morel,[6] Paquier,[7] and two or three others, plus Bavaud,[8] and [ ]).

At 4.30 pm, preparation for the exchange that was due to follow. I got an idea of the kind of men that one MEETS here. There are some chatterboxes (G Gurvitch[9]), but some interesting people. For some, it provides the opportunity to express the genuine questions that bother them. For others it serves simply as a platform: they take the opportunity of expressing their own ideas, at times on questions which have no connection with the theme under discussion. Several interventions take the form of protests arising from very remote horizons and, for example, from an anti-dogmatic starting point.

All that came out during the dialogue session (5 pm—7 pm) at which about one hundred and forty people were present. I got the opportunity to clarify only a single point.

Supper with the Jesuit fathers, with Frs Cottier and J De la Croix Kaelin[10]: two fine examples of Friars Preachers, cultured, open, intelligent.

In the evening, lecture by President Thorp.[11]

Saturday 7 September 1963

Plane at 5.55 am: a Boeing, much larger and more powerful than the Caravelle: fifty-five minutes to arrive at Brussels, above a sea of fleecy clouds covering Nancy, Metz and Luxembourg. I was to have been met at the airport. There was no-one there. In the end I telephoned the archbishop's house at Malines. There had been a misunderstanding. They had come to meet me yesterday evening and had waited well into the night! . . .

---

1. Victor Martin, honorary professor at the University of Geneva, was Vice-President of the *Rencontres*.
2. Antony Babel, Professor of Sociology at the University of Geneva.
3. Fernand-Lucien Mueller.
4. Georges Marchal, professor at the Protestant Faculty of Theology in Paris.
5. The exegete Pierre Bonnard.
6. B Morel.
7. Richard Paquier, founder of the 'Église et Liturgie' movement which brought together pastors open to an ecumenical contact with Catholics, especially through liturgical research.
8. Canon Georges Bavaud taught dogmatics at the Seminary in Fribourg; he took part in the ecumenical movement and Congar had already had an opportunity to meet him.
9. The sociologist Georges Gurvitch taught at the Sorbonne.
10. Jean de la Croix Kaelin, OP, of the Province of Switzerland, chaplain to the students in Geneva.
11. The lawyer René-William Thorp was the former president of the Paris bar.

In the end, I had to spend more time waiting for a car to come from Malines than to travel from Geneva to Brussels.

Malines: at the major seminary.

Meeting at the archbishop's house at 10 am: perhaps the room in which the 'Conversations'[1] had taken place.

The following were at this meeting: Mgr Cerfaux, Philips, Prignon, Mgr Ceuppens,[2] (vicar general representing the cardinal and there to receive us), Canon Thils, Dondeyne,[3] P Delhaye, Moeller, Fr Tucci, Rahner, B Rigaux,[4] and myself. We were very relaxed and could work well.

I learnt a few things about the Council. That there are three new members of the Co-ordinating Commission: Cardinals Roberti, Lercaro, Agagianian. Fr Tucci said about the text (prepared by the Secretariat) on religious freedom, which I again urged should be inserted into schema XVII, that some of the cardinals, in particular Cardinal Cicognani, the Secretary of State, are against its been inserted and even against its being presented to the Council; because, they say, it would divide the Council. So it seems one will have to be content with saying something along these lines, without presenting a specific text.

In the morning, from 10 am to 1 pm, we completed the work that had been begun yesterday: the comments on *De Ecclesia* and on the constitution of the new chapter *De populo Dei* [On the People of God]. After a more than adequate meal, from 3 pm to 6 pm, we discussed the text of the new chapter requested for Schema XVII: each one said what he thought this chapter ought to contain. In the end, Mgr Philips thought of condensing all the suggestions into four chapters: 1) the Church's Mission; 2) the World: a) in itself; b) the modern world; c) the presence of the Church in the world: general principles; 4) the presence of the Church in the world: applications. After various suggestions as to the best way of following the work through, it was decided that from now until 3 pm to-morrow, each one should prepare, in Latin, suggestions and proposals on what he thought ought to be said in these four chapters.

After supper, each one withdrew. We tried to work as a group, Fr Tucci, C Moeller and myself, in my room at the major seminary, but that did not work. To begin with, we were tired. Then, several people trying to prepare a text together did not work. Each one relied on the others, we wasted time, we floundered. In the end, each one wrote his own section, we began, we tried.

Finally, on **Sunday 8 September 1963,** at 3 pm—or rather 4 pm, because Mgr Philips had been delayed—each one brought the fruit of his *cogitationes* [reflec-

---

1. Cf above, page 233, note 3.
2. René Ceuppens.
3. Albert Dondeyne, priest of the diocese of Bruges, taught at the Institut Supérieur de Philosophie in Louvain and worked on the relationship between contemporary thought and the Christian faith.
4. Beda Rigaux, OFM, exegete, taught at the Institut des Sciences Religieuses at the University of Louvain; he was a Council expert from the Second Session onwards.

tions]. Each one read or summarised what he had written. I had not quite finished a draft covering the whole area. I feel that some of the others, in particular Canon Dondeyne, did not quite see that we are dealing with a dogmatic constitution, and put forward interesting views of the modern world, but which would be rather the material for an article or a lecture.

I maintain that the Chapters 3 and 4 envisaged by Mgr Philips need to be combined into a single chapter (it would seem that every one thinks the same) and that it is impossible to combine in a single new chapter both the question of the presence of the Church in the world *and* the substance of the former Chapter I of schema XVII: that chapter, in my view somewhat lightened, ought to be kept separate, as Christian anthropology.

Finally, Mgr Philips, having received clean copies of all the papers, will try to produce a text taking everything into consideration, and will present it to us at a meeting to be held on Tuesday 17 in Malines. Cardinal Suenens will doubtless be there.

15 September 1963
Evening. I have just returned from l'Arbresle where I passed my *gradus*[1] yesterday. Fr General, no doubt at the instigation of Fr Provincial and Fr Hamer—wanted to do me a kindness. The way in which things were done even gave them the appearance of a public and solemn witness. Fr General made a speech in French which was an unreserved eulogy of my work and of my person. He did not say, he did not even say to me, what he said to Fr Kopf and which for me is of both interest and value, namely that Fr General had recently seen Paul VI who had said to him spontaneously that he held me in great esteem and that he had read my books and knew me.

When Fr General, taking advantage of this conversation, asked the Pope what he thought of Fr Chenu, Paul VI replied: 'I do not know him so well'.

This 18 September 1963
Here in Strasbourg, I copied out the notes I took yesterday in Malines.

We held there the meeting to discuss the Latin text prepared by Mgr Philips for schema XVII in the light of the indications from our meeting of 7 to 8 September. Two journeys at night: I can hardly put one foot in front of the other, or hold a pen.

Those at the meeting: Mgr Philips, Prignon, Cerfaux, C Moeller, Delhaye, Frs Rigaux, Tucci and Congar.

To start with, Cardinal Suenens gave us some news. He was wearing a dark grey clerical suit, without the least sign of office, no red collar, not even a ring. We chatted a little bit at first. I spoke to him about R Laurentin's book, *La question*

---

1. Cf page 307, note 3.

mariale.[1] I told him what I thought: there was discussion on all the theological points regarding which the mariological *zelanti* [zealots] would like 'to add new flowers' to Mary's crown. This maximising theology is not healthy. IT WOULD BE MUCH BETTER TO DO NOTHING.

The cardinal told us that John XXIII had, at first, the idea of a small *Brains Trust* which would direct the Council. He had been seeking the appropriate formula for it, and the establishment, to begin with, of an Extraordinary Affairs Commission, and then of the Co-ordinating Commission had been steps in this direction. However, John XXIII had preferred to leave the Council free to take its chance. John XXIII had asked Cardinal Suenens for a plan for the *ordo tractandorum* [order of things to be dealt with] and, at first, a *NEGATIVE* plan: what was to be excluded. He had said that he entirely agreed with Cardinal Suenens' suggestions which were briefly as follows: make an examination of conscience on the Word of the Lord: *Euntes* [Go out into all the world (Matt 28:19)] (the sending of the Church into the world), etc term by term . . . The Pope had himself taken up these ideas in a speech. John XXIII had pointed out to Cardinal Suenens the names of certain cardinals with whom he wanted him to make contact; these included Cardinal Montini. That explains how Suenens and Montini had intervened at the end of the First Session, after reaching agreement between themselves and showing their text to the Pope. The latter had approved both their interventions and had added, to Cardinal Suenens' text, a passage in praise of Pius XII.

Now, Cardinal Suenens, together with Cardinals Döpfner, Lercaro and Agagianian, has been appointed a member of a group of four cardinals who, within the Council of Presidents, are to direct the work of the Council from the point of view of its INTERNAL content and order. The cardinal has not yet received the text of the Pope's letter appointing them, but he read us the one from Cardinal Cicognani stating what was to happen: this letter uses the word *moderatores* [moderators] which, in Latin, has a strong and wholly positive meaning. The letter speaks, without further details, of 'directing THE ASSEMBLIES of the Council, with an executive mandate'. So it amounts almost to the power of a legate, but without there being a legate, that is to say the Pope's hand everywhere, and the imposition of his authority. It is much more flexible, MORE CONCILIAR.

The cardinal told us that the Council will begin with *De Ecclesia*. The text of schema XVII that we are preparing is a first draft which will be sent on to the joint commission (theology and laity).

He asked us to send on to him, before or during the Session, all the comments, corrections or suggestions that we wish. He told us that Paul VI has told him that he intended to bring into the Council not only lay people, but women. I insisted a lot on the great importance of this step.

As for our work, which we completed at 7 pm, it is quite good. Mgr Philips has an astonishing art of integrating everything in a text. This text is very dense: often,

---

1. René Laurentin, *La Question mariale* (Paris: Seuil, 1963).

an important idea is inserted merely by the addition of *ONE WORD*: for example, the idea of the Lordship of Christ by the addition of the word *Dominus*. Unfortunately, that also gives a fairly pallid text, in which the key and truly decisive ideas are somewhat swamped and covered in grey. But no one other than Mgr Philips would have been able or would be able to do the work . . .

In the evening, five or six of us dined with the cardinal. We spoke in particular about the chapter on religious freedom, of the arguments for and against its insertion into either *De œcumenismo,* or schema XVII.

In favour of schema XVII: this would be the normal place: the presence of Christians in a divided world. Against it: it would not have the whole authority of the Council, as it would be the work only of Commissions of the Council. This fact, however, would perhaps have the advantage of pacifying the very lively discussion that this text cannot fail to provoke.

In favour of *De œcumenismo*: this would be a conciliar text: the Secretariat could undoubtedly present it without first submitting it to the Theological Commission (??). Against it: this would link this more general question with the particular matter of ecumenism, which would mean not presenting it in an adequate light; it would risk seeming to place other religions (Buddhism, Islam, Judaism) on the same plane as the Christian communities: it was this that Bishop Newbigin[1] had warned Canon Moeller against in Montréal.

I am firmly in favour of it being inserted into schema XVII.

In the meantime, stress was laid on the need to state briefly, wherever it is appropriate to do so, the principle of religious freedom. In this way, even if there is no special chapter, or if it is rejected or too much weakened, the essential will always be there.

Cardinal Suenens is very open to the suggestions that are made to him. He is a positive man, well organised, present to those who address him. He spoke again about women at the Council and about women Religious, who need to be SET FREE. He mentioned a case in his episcopal town: a community where, when a man enters the cloister, a plumber for instance, he is preceded by a Sister ringing a hand-bell, as one did for lepers in the Middle Ages!

My leg and my hand are very bad; it has taken me more than an hour to write, with great difficulty, these two and half pages. What to do? There is no diagnosis, and I am not taking any specific remedy.

I am sending additional comments to Mgr Philips.

Rome 29 September 1963

6 pm. Am I going to have the strength to write this journal? I am dead, I can barely move my leg and (slowly) move my hand.

---

1. Leslie Newbigin, theologian, missiologist and ecumenist of British origin, was Bishop of the United Church of South India, after having played a part in its creation. He had worked within the World Council of Churches since it was founded.

Left Strasbourg on Thursday 26 September at 4.20 pm, driven with my trunk by Fr Courbaud.[1] We slept at his mother's house in Vitrey (Jura), which we reached at 9.15 pm. The next day, we arrived at the Priory in Dijon at 7.50 am: problem of fitting the heavy luggage of four theologians into the Opel lent to Fr Féret.

We left at 8.15 am. In Ain and the surrounding areas we were diverted several times by the police: General de Gaulle was visiting the area and would be travelling by these roads. That resulted in our being delayed for more than an hour and having to drive via Aix-les-Bains.

Mount Cenis, after lunch in Montmélian. Great difficulty in finding our way in Turin and getting out of this great city by roads congested with heavy lorries: these forced us to reduce considerably our average hourly speed.

We slept at Asti. Throughout the night, heavy lorries going by on the nearby road. Throughout the journey and at meal times, we talked with Fr Féret and Frs Guillou and Dupuy about the Council and the schemas.

Saturday 28 September 1963

We left at 6.50 am, on a road still congested with lorries and, above all, a mist so thick that visibility was down to about 30 metres, making us hesitate to overtake the lorries as our luggage weighed down our vehicle considerably. After Piacenza, not only had the mist disappeared but we found the Autostrada del Sole. It is an extraordinary work. Between Bologna and Florence, we crossed the Apennines, but there were, so to say, neither mountains nor valley: we crossed from one side to the other of the valley by means of viaducts, from one slope to the other of the hills through tunnels, in the midst of unspoiled countryside.

Lunch in one of the numerous restaurants established along the route, not far from Florence.

Afterwards, Florence-Sea Autostrada, then Livorno. Route often very tortuous, and, again, very congested with heavy lorries.

We arrived in Rome by the Via Aurelia at about 8.30 pm, it took us about three quarters of an hour to find the Via Ulisse Seni, where Frs Le Guillou and Dupuy are staying, then again a further full three quarters of an hour to find the Via Romania, where Fr Féret is to stay. I refused to let him drive me to the Angelicum: I will sleep at the Istituto S Tommaso di Villanova where Fr Féret will be staying with Mgrs Flusin, Boillon, Schmitt and Elchinger. It was just on 11 pm. Fr Féret, who had been driving since early morning and then meandering around Rome for two hours, was exhausted.

Sunday 29 September 1963

Mass at 6 am. We left at 8 am or a little before for St Peter's. We got there at 8.15 am. I found the basilica once again arranged as it had been last year, marvellously

---

1. François Courbaud, OP, of the Province of France.

adapted to its role as a conciliar *aula*. I also saw again many well-known faces, but also some new ones, such as Fr Courtney.[1]

Long tiring wait of nearly two hours, under the floodlights, which hurt our eyes. The bishops came in one by one, in cope and mitre, and took their places. Only as it was coming up to 10 am did we hear, at first from a distance but coming nearer, the singing of the Sistine choir. The Pope was about to enter. First, in front of him, came his court: Swiss guards with their halberds, cardinals in priestly (or diaconal) vestments, wearing very tall mitres, prelates in purple and red, chamberlains in sixteenth century costumes, the insignia bearers (the papal tiara and the mitre), and finally the Pope, flanked by a deacon and a sub-deacon, with the *flabella*-bearers.[2] The Pope was wearing the *pretiosa* mitre; he came in on foot; as he proceeded down the nave, the rows between which he was passing clapped, which shocked me considerably. Fairly faint applause from the rows of young bishops, much louder from the rows of archbishops.

I cannot but interpret the actual structure of the ceremony ecclesiologically. Between two rows of bishops who were silent spectators, the pontifical court passed by, dressed in sixteenth century costume, preceding a Pope who thus appears to be, at one and the same time, a temporal sovereign and a hierarch ABOVE, quite simply above.

The Sistine choir warbled on; the Fathers picked up one or two verses of the *Ave Maris Stella*. Will the Church retain THIS appearance? THIS form of visibility? Will it go on and on giving THIS sign? It seemed to me at that moment that the Gospel IS present in it, but as a captive.

Paul VI intoned the *Veni Creator*. The Church found its voice once more, a voice of great waters, to implore. When the Pope then alternated the verses with the choir of bishops, it was Peter who was praying with the Twelve. It was no longer the sixteenth century temporal prince.

The bishops had asked to sing the Ordinary of the Mass. The Sistine choir warbled a *Kyrie* and would later warble an *Agnus Dei,* not without making use of splendid voices, but the bishops sang the *Gloria*, the *Creed* and the *Sanctus*. One sang with them with all one's heart, at least to the extent to which one had the energy. In this way, in the singing as throughout the ceremony, there was an alternation between the truth of the *Ecclesia* and the ways of the *Renaissance*.

Cardinal Tisserant celebrated the Mass: badly and without fervour.

After the Mass, the Pope made his profession of faith: the *Credo* and the Profession of Faith from the Council of Trent. Once again, it was Peter who appeared and acknowledged Christ. After him, each order, in the person of one of its rep-

---

1.   Congar added to the second typescript: 'Murray'. John Courtney Murray, SJ, was Professor of Theology at Woodstock College (Maryland) and editor-in-chief of *Theological Studies*; he had been silenced by Rome in 1955 on account of his position on religious freedom; Cardinal Spellman's private expert, he was appointed a Council expert in 1963.

2.   Great fans carried around the Pope on solemn occasions.

resentatives; then Mgr Felici read slowly the same texts for all those who had not yet made their profession of faith.

Then the Pope, seated on his throne between a deacon (Cardinal Ottaviani) and a subdeacon, wearing the mitre, read his speech.[1] The bishops were also wearing their mitres. A very long speech, very structured, read, at times, with keen and eloquent emotion. The Pope clearly stressed the role of the bishops, whom he called *'fratres in episcopatu'* [brothers in the episcopate] and who he said were the heirs of the Apostolic College. He said he wanted to pray, study, discuss WITH THEM, during the Council. He will only produce an encyclical later on: the speech he was now making would outline his programme.

He referred to John XXIII's speech on 8 October of last year. For quite a long time, he was speaking directly to John XXIII, thus making him present. He stressed the usefulness of Councils, about which some had recently been in doubt, as if the papal power were sufficient! He emphasised also the PASTORAL character of the present Council. It is not a question only of PRESERVING things . . .

What route to take? Where to leave from? Where to go?

To these essential questions there is only one answer: Jesus Christ. It is Christ who is our origin, our way and our goal. The Pope stated this and developed the idea with very great force and intense emotion. Christ the origin of all. The Pope referred to the mosaic in St Paul outside the Walls in which Honorius III had himself depicted as very small, humbly prostrate before Christ . . .

Christ is our goal. That must clarify the purpose of the Council which is:

1) To define the notion of the Church: what does she say of herself?

The Pope, who enlarged on each of these four points at considerable length and with much emphasis, here laid great stress on the mystical body and on society.

2) The renewal of the Church, in which regard Paul VI spoke of the necessity of the relationship that the Church has with Christ: a historical and human reality, she has never been perfectly what Christ wishes her to be.

3) The restoration of unity among all Christians. Paul VI spoke here at once forcefully, with precision and with emotion. His expressions were carefully chosen. Several times he used the expression: 'the venerable Christian communities' in referring to the Others . . . He recognised that the Others have sometimes developed auspiciously what they had received from Christianity. If there is a fault on our side, he asked forgiveness, while we, for our part, forgive.

4) Dialogue with the world. Paul VI referred to the Message to the World in which he saw a manifestation of the prophetic nature of the Church . . .

He placed the relationship of the Church with the world, with those who are close and with those who are far off, under the sign of the UNIVERSAL love *OF CHRIST.*

---

1. Cf *AS* II/I, 183–200.

It was in this paragraph that he made a comment on the martyrs in the countries where persecution is rife.

A very vigorous, very structured speech which gives precise directives for the work of the Council.

It ended at 1 pm.

Lunch at S Tommaso di Villanova with the four French bishops who are staying there (also there are the Yugoslav bishops: Mgr Franić and some US bishops).

I learnt that, at the meeting of the French bishops yesterday, it had been decided:

1) Who could take part in the weekly meeting on Wednesdays. NOT the theologians, unless they have been specifically invited as lecturers.

2) To set up a commission which would organise and supervise the work of the bishops.[1] It comprises Mgrs Marty, Gouyon,[2] Ancel, Guyot, Maziers, de Provenchères, Elchinger, Le Cordier.

3) To designate a bishop for relations with the other episcopates.

4) Before the Council, a meeting had been held in Florence between some French bishops (Cardinal Lefebvre, Mgr Garrone, Marty[3] . . .) and five Italian bishops (in fact only four[4]) MANDATED BY THE ITALIAN BISHOPS' CONFERENCE. They all agreed in asking for *De Revelatione* to be incorporated into *De Ecclesia*. They sent a communication in this sense to the Council of Presidents of the Council. On the other hand, according to l'abbé Haubtmann,[5] the French bishops are largely in favour of asking that the *De beata Virgine Maria* should also be incorporated into *De Ecclesia* as well as *De Revelatione*.

It was not until 4.30 pm that Fr Féret drove me to the Angelicum, with my luggage. I am only just able to stand.

Fr Gagnebet told me that the Pope had decided that *De Revelatione* would not be dealt with during this Session. The programme has been fixed: five schemas will be examined: *De Ecclesia, De Beata Virgine Maria, De œcumenismo, De Apostolatu laicorum, De regimine Dioecesium*.

---

1. This was the Comité des Réunions des Évêques Français (CREF) of which Marty was elected President.
2. Paul Gouyon, Coadjutor of Rennes, then Archbishop of Rennes in September 1964.
3. As well as Ancel and Veuillot.
4. Florit, Baldassari, Archbishop of Ravenna, Calabria and Carli.
5. Pierre Haubtmann, from the diocese of Grenoble: specialist in social questions and former national chaplain to the ACO (Action Catholique Ouvrière [Workers' Catholic Action]), he taught at the Social Studies Institute of the Institut Catholique in Paris, and was also national Director of the Secretariat for Public Opinion as well as Assistant Director of the General Secretariat of the French episcopate: from the Second Session onwards, he was asked by the French bishops to give a press conference each day in French on the working of the Conciliar assembly; having been appointed a Council expert from this Second Session onwards, he was to become one of the kingpins of the Constitution *Gaudium et Spes*; he was to become Rector of the Institut Catholique in Paris in 1966.

Monday 30 September 1963

(Written in St Peter's). After transport difficulties (buses extremely crowded!), I was very tired when I reached St Peter's. I at once found myself back in the atmosphere of the General Congregations and met a lot of people I knew. I went to greet the Observers, greeting all of them individually. There are many more of them than during the First Session: most of them in suits with, it seemed to me, a much larger proportion than in the Council *aula* itself of men from Asia and Anglo-Saxon America. Like last year, there were tears in my eyes. What a happening! How God has been at work in the world!

Things did not begin until 9.20 am as the bishops' places had been changed on account of the deaths of some and the appointment of others, and the bishops had to find their places.

Mass in the Ambrosian rite celebrated by Mgr Colombo,[1] the new Archbishop of Milan. It is all very well to ask the Fathers to make the responses slowly, with a pause between phrases: the celebrant forces his own rhythm on everyone. It was even worse with Cardinal Tisserant when he recited the *Adsumus* at great speed: it is lamentable.

Mgr Felici[2] began by explaining the changes that had been made in the regulations.

These changes promote DISCUSSION in the true sense, the clash and expression of opinions. Some of the changes are important: we shall see how things work out. There is a certain contradiction between promoting dialogue on the one hand and requiring that the text, or a summary of it, be submitted three days before it is delivered!!!

No more conciliar experts are to be appointed.[3]

A series of announcements was repeated in various languages. During this time, I went to the bar, where I met Mgr Prignon who told me:

1) Some people, of whom Cardinal Antoniutti is one, are critical of Chapter 4, *De religiosis*, and are suggesting that only the part concerning Religious be retained, and that the section on the call to all to holiness be inserted into Chapter II, *De Populo Dei*.

2) Cardinal Browne, as *relator* [rapporteur], will present the schema as it is, but he is sticking to his idea about collegiality: to speak of a COLLEGE is to speak of members who are equal (cf Petit Larousse). This is not possible.

He holds the curial thesis according to which any authority of the bishops that extends beyond the limits of their own diocese, is only a participation in the universal power of the pope, WHICH ALONE IS UNIVERSAL.

---

1. Giovanni Colombo, formerly Auxiliary Bishop of Milan. He was a member of the Commission on Seminaries, Studies and Catholic Education. He was to be created cardinal in February 1965.
2. *AS* II/I, 205–209.
3. This was not to be the case.

As regards the Holy Father's speech on the reform of the Curia, Cardinal Browne maintains that it is of ecclesiastical law that bishops cannot be called upon to participate in the government of the universal Church, except as a pure FAVOUR on the part of the pope.

Introduction to the discussion of the schema by Cardinal Ottaviani[1] and Cardinal Browne[2] (printed text).

The following then spoke:

Cardinal Frings:[3] in the name of sixty-six Fathers from Germany and the Scandinavian countries. The schema is acceptable in general, and he explained why.

More stress could be laid on the Church as *Ursakrament* [primordial sacrament],[4] state more clearly the link with the People of the Old Testament, make clearer the mission of the Church as proceeding from the very nature of the Church.

Something could be said about the [Church's] faults (from the ecumenical standpoint).

It might be thought that the text does not specify WHO is a member of the Mystical Body, but one cannot derive a clear teaching on this subject from the texts of St Paul, because Paul speaks of members from the point of view of the diversity of vocations.

As regards the *munus docendi* [teaching function], more is said about that of the pope than that of the bishops.

Insert the chapter *De Beata*: the Church in heaven belongs to the Mystical Body.

The schema is a good starting point, but needs to be improved.

Cardinal Siri:[5] *idem* (= the schema is a good starting point). However, it needs to be amended and completed: ambiguous points need to be clarified.

Aliqua desunt: progressus non esset si aliqua dicerentur minus praecise quam ante [Some things are missing: it would not be progress if some things were to be said less clearly than previously].

We can move on to discussion of the individual chapters.

Patriarch of the Armenians:[6]

1) 'following the teaching of earlier Councils' is well said.

2) One could be more precise about the Mystical Body (cf Pius XII).

---

1. *AS* II/I, 337.
2. *AS* II/I, 339–342.
3. *AS* II/I 343–345.
4. O Semmelroth had first highlighted this expression in order to describe the Church.
5. *AS* II/I, 347.
6. Ignatius Peter XVI Batanian, Armenian Patriarch of Cilicia (Lebanon), *AS* II/I, 348–349.

3) A good account is given of Catholic ecclesiology from which non-Catholics can come to know it.

4) *Clarior expectatur* [greater clarity is needed] on the relationship between non-Catholics and the Church.

5) Not enough is said about the INEQUALITY OF THE MEMBERS, for example on the obligation to the apostolate.

6) Go back to the Council of Trent on the hierarchical priesthood.

7) What is said about the apostolate of the laity might lead them to lack respect for their pastors.

8) Insist on the need for an inner spiritual life.

This is the head of a Uniate Church speaking!!! Where does he live? He does not say a word about the Eastern Tradition!

Morcillo[1] (Saragossa): it needs to be completed.

It is obscure about non-Christians.

Asked for a great many things, several of which are in other texts!

Nothing is said about the Patriarchs . . . (GOOD THINGS).

[?] Leone[2] (Italian, titular archbishop):

I can barely write!

If Mary really is *Mater Ecclesiae,* why not speak of her in the schema *De Ecclesia.*

Let the two *schemata* be combined! (Cardinal Agagianian, the President, said it was being considered).

The speaker enlarged on all the places where there was no mention of Mary or where one could and should mention her . . . EVERYWHERE!

Florit[3] (Florence): praise for the schema in general.

Pointed out that it is the first time that a document of the extraordinary Magisterium has mentioned certain points: the laity, etc.

However, there are some defects:

The title: *De Ecclesia CHRISTI* [on the Church of CHRIST] – psychologically speaking, is it a good idea to begin with the idea of the Church as MYSTERY? One would need to add to the other images that of the Kingdom of God.

Declaration of the sacramentality of the episcopate: no reference to the theological note.

As regards collegiality: there are more statements than proofs and foundations. And one would need to speak first of the ecumenical council, which is the highest form of collegiality. It would be necessary to repeat, even *ad verbum* [word for word], the teaching of Vatican I.

In favour of incorporating the chapter on Revelation in *De Ecclesia.*

1. *AS* II/I, 350–352.
2. Carlo A Ferrero di Cavallerleone, *AS* II/I 353–354.
3. *AS* II/I 354–357.

Mgr Thuc[1] (Vietnam): the brother of the President [of Vietnam]?

On the Church since the first human being.

He was called to order: that will be looked at when the individual chapters are being discussed . . .

He then said: I salute the non-Catholic Christian Observers but where are the observers from the other non-Christian religions? I have complained to the Co-ordinating Commission, but to no effect.

Mgr Gargitter[2] (Brixen):

1) The document should be written in a more organic fashion in the light of the *IDEA OF THE PEOPLE OF GOD;* the hierarchy itself owes its primary dignity to the fact that it belongs to it.

2) The Church would be better described as the Church of the Cross: it came forth from Christ's side; through baptism . . .

3) When one speaks of bishops . . . (?)

4) Establish a better dogmatic basis for the apostolate of the laity (the remote principle is the solidarity of all human beings which is taken up and made more urgent in the Mystical Body, in which all are made responsible for the salvation of all).

In the evening, at 5.15 pm, visit from Fr Dournes[3] with Mgr Seitz and Mgr Jacq, from Vitenam. They are very isolated (along with the bishops of their country who, they told me, are not living the Council . . .). They are trying to find out what to do in order to live it, to be useful in it . . . In the middle of our conversation, Laurentin arrived; he had produced a draft text for *De beata,* and had brought it for me and asked what I thought of it.

At about 7.30 pm, I brought my three friends from Vitenam to S Tommaso di Villanova, in order: 1) to see Fr Féret, introduce them to him and collect from him a text of his comments; 2) to see Mgr Elchinger, who, as a member of the commission that is organising the work of the French bishops, could perhaps suggest to us a way of proceeding.

In fact, our visit was very fruitful. We saw not only Féret and Mgr Elchinger, but also Fr Liégé. We plunged into work at once. In effect, this little group devised a *De Ecclesia* putting everything together according to the actual progress of the economy or the history of salvation. Though I am in agreement about the ideas, I am less certain that that is what it is about, or even that that is concretely possible. On the other hand, I fully agree with Mgr Elchinger, who wants to speak tomorrow and read us the text of his proposed intervention, designed to emphasise the

---

1. Pierre M Ngô-dình-Thuc, Archbishop of Hué, member of the Commission on the Missions since the First Session, *AS* II/I 358–359.
2. *AS* II/I 359-361.
3. Jacques Dournes, of the Paris Foreign Missions, was a missionary in Vietnam: he was the secretary and personal expert of Mgr Seitz, Bishop of Kon Tum, at the Council.

difficulties that confront the taking of a vote now on the whole of the schema, in order to begin at once the discussion of the *Proemium* and Chapter I. In effect, from one point of view, there are too many unresolved questions concerning the content of *De Ecclesia*. Several people are talking of inserting *De Revelatione*, or *De Beata,* or a chapter on the eschatological Church, or a *De Missione . . .* That presents the problem of the overall concept and plan of the document about which there is no clarity.

The schema reflects its origins. It was never conceived as a *De Ecclesia*; it was never even 'conceived' at all as a single whole. As a result, people are suggesting the addition of one chapter or another rather in the way carriages are added to a train that is being assembled. It needs to be 'conceived' AS A WHOLE, and in accordance with a certain order which would have, in itself, a doctrinal value.

Otherwise, one will keep on adding bits, but it will never become a whole!

Tuesday 1 October 1963

I left at 7.30 am in order to call in at the French Seminary to see the bishops, especially Cardinal Lefebvre and Mgr Garrone.

I also saw Fr Gy, who had arrived yesterday and who told me that he is going from door to door . . . In St Peter's, I saw Rahner, Küng, Liégé, Daniélou, Mgr Philips, Balić, and also a number of the bishops: Charue, Huyghe, and above all Mgr Veuillot, to whom I spoke about the question of a text on Israel. We will have another talk about it

Also Mgr Colombo and Colson. We exchanged addresses.

> Cardinal Silva,[1] Chile, in the name of forty-four bishops from his country:
> A good basis. Approves the idea of a chapter on the People of God: it should speak of the prophetic, royal, and priestly People.
> It lacks the aspect of the Church as a communion of individual Churches (*koinônia*): refer to the text produced by the Chileans.
> There should be a chapter on the Church perfect in her saints: in South America, the cult of the Virgin is often separated from the mystery of Christ: it is important to speak of the Virgin in the CONTEXT of the Christian mystery.
> The exposition of the Trinitarian reference of the Church should not be separated from the exposition of the images of the Church. He submitted a text to the secretariat.
> (The Chilean bishops had shown the connection between the images of the Church and the Three Persons of the Trinity.)
> Cardinal Rugambwa[2] (a black cardinal): *placet* for the breadth of vision of God's design. However, three comments:

---

1.   *AS* II/I, 366–367.
2.   *AS* II/I, 368–370.

1) The mission is not sufficiently stressed: EVANGELISATION.

The formulae are too static: the Church, here below, is in *fieri* [in the process of becoming].

2) Show this missionary function as co-extensive with the *WHOLE* Church.

3) The nature and the vocation of the PEOPLE OF GOD are not made clear enough: the mystery of the Covenant.

Mgr Hermaniuk:[1] *placet propter indolem scripturisticam* [approves its scriptural style] and its reference to the Eastern Fathers; in favour of the insistence on the collegial nature of the Catholic episcopate.

However, there are some defects: 1) Nothing is said about the collegial *regimen* [government] of the bishops over the universal Church to be exercised in two ways:

the pope as *caput* [head];

the college as such.

This power must be exercised in both ways in the WHOLE life of the Church and not merely at the time of a Council.

In favour of a *synodos endêmousa* [permanent synod].[2]

2) The formulae are too abstract;

3) Expressions such as *'collegium episcoporum simul cum Papa'* [episcopal college together with the pope] as if they were two distinct things.

4) Too much of *'Romanus Pontifex'*; it is too 'Roman'.

Mgr Garrone:[3] it needs improvement (in the name of several French bishops).

1) The text on the Virgin should be inserted into *De Ecclesia*.

2) For the definition of the Church, the idea of the Kingdom of God should be put at the beginning. This would provide an eschatological dimension bringing with it a dynamic missionary view of evangelisation (the Church: instrument of the Kingdom).

3) There should be a declaration on Tradition: that would make it easier to make a good beginning on the question of Revelation.

4) There should be more about collegiality.

Mgr Gasbarri[4] (?), auxiliary *Veliternus* (Italy): the schema is more organic and more pastoral than the previous one. It takes up the doctrine of the previous one.

Take care that that does not become obscure!

---

1.   *AS* II/I, 370–372.
2.   See above, page 94, note 3.
3.   *AS* II/I, 374–375.
4.   Primo Gasbarri, Auxiliary Bishop of Velletri, *AS* II/I, 376–378.

The reference to the relationships between Church and State has been removed. This SHOULD be spoken of, either here or in another schema.

Mgr Elchinger:[1] some comments have been made on the order in which the topics are dealt with. The organic unity is important from a pastoral point of view. The ORGANIC unity needs more attention: 1) A *proemium* speaking of the Word of God as founding and convoking the Church. 2) In connection with the chapter on the People of God, something should be inserted about the living tradition. For the Church has an active role with respect to the Word of God which governs it. 3) After the chapter *De vocatione ad sanctitatem* [on the call to holiness], show the eschatological movement of the Church and its positive contribution to the hope of the world. 4) As regards the chapter *De Beata*: this should not be treated in a separate chapter.

Has the vote that we are going to be asked for been clarified sufficiently? (But have people understood this conclusion? I do not think so.)

Mgr Fares[2] (Italy)

Great rush for the bar.

Archbishop from Indonesia[3] speaking in the name of thirty-one bishops from Indonesia: (someone was speaking to me and I lost the thread). Spoke in favour of the idea of the People of God.

Criticism: the Church should speak of herself as obliged and humbly bound by Revelation.

The eschatological aspect is not sufficiently emphasised.

The aim of glorifying the Father is not sufficiently emphasised.

The missionary function of the Church is not sufficiently emphasised.

Mgr Felici,[4] the Secretary General, recalled all the bishops to their seats as the vote was due to take place in a quarter of an hour.

Mgr Joseph[5] ?, titular bishop from Asia? (French pronunciation). He spoke of the workers who are now going about their business. He was called to order and he stopped speaking.

Grotti:[6] there are repetitions: one does not see the connection and the order of the parts . . . ??

Sergio Méndez Arceo[7] (Cuernavaca): supported the request by Cardinal Frings and Cardinal Silva: the Virgin and the saints should be

---

1. *AS* II/I, 378–380.
2. *AS* II/I, 380–381.
3. Adrian Djajasepoetra, Archbishop of Jakarta, *AS* II/I, 381–383.
4. *AS* II/I, 383.
5. The Belgian, Joseph Guffens, SJ, *AS* II/I, 383–384.
6. Giocondo M Grotti, prelate *nullius* of Acre and Purús (Brazil), *AS* II/I, 384–385.
7. *AS* II/I, 385.

mentioned in order to give the foundation, and also the LIMITS of
devotion. In his region, there is such a cult of the saints that the unicity
of the mediation of Christ . . .

Cardinal Browne,[1] *relator* [rapporteur]: the Commission will look into all
that as soon as possible.

Felici:[2] the question to be voted on is *An schema generatim sumptum placeat*
[whether this schema taken as a whole should be approved] so that
we can pass on to an examination of the different sections. This vote
concerns the approval of four chapters, the possibility of inserting new
paragraphs remaining open.

A long break. I spoke to several bishops at the bar; Mgr Rastouil[3] kept me for a
long time with his idea about the sacramental characters (a CONFIRMED lay
person in a state of mortal sin can be active in Catholic Action just as a priest can
consecrate !!!) and about the priesthood.

I spoke to Skydsgaard and Schlink.

Results of the vote:

Present: 2,301

Votes in favour: 2,231

Votes against: 43

Spoilt votes: 24, and 3 *iuxta modum,* that is, null.

At 11.50 am discussion began on the prologue and on Chapter I, but I could
not take it all down: I shall be meeting it all again at the Theological Commission.

Cardinal Ruffini:[4] attacked the idea that all the Apostles constitute the
foundation.

Attacked the use of the expression *sacramentum* for the Church (it was
used by Tyrrell![5])

Criticised several applications of Biblical texts, several ways of
expressing things.

Criticised the relative distinction drawn between the Church and the
Mystical Body: in the name of *Mystici Corporis* and *Humani Generis.*
(All that in a nervous and rather acrimonious tone of voice.)

Mgr Aramburu[6] (Argentina): referring to No. 5, the life of social communion
of Christians should be given expression, on the basis of the Eucharist,

---

1. *AS* II/I, 387.
2. *AS* II/I, 387–388.
3. Louis Rastouil, Bishop of Limoges.
4. *AS* II/I, 391–394.
5. George Tyrrell (1861–1909), English Jesuit who was expelled from the Society of Jesus
    and forbidden to teach at the time of the Modernist crisis.
6. *AS* II/I, 394–395.

of which the *res* [the reality the sacrament points to] is the unity of the Mystical Body.

3.15 pm: I received a telephone call from a White Father,[1] speaking on behalf of the secretariat of the African bishops: asking for a text on Mission to be inserted into the *De Ecclesia*. I arranged to meet him at 7 pm at the Columbus, as I am going there for a meeting of the Observers.

At 3.30 pm, telephone call from Fr Greco,[2] secretary of the French-speaking African bishops, asking for a lecture to these bishops on the *De Ecclesia*. But I do not know to what extent the Theological Commission will occupy my time!!

At 4.30 pm, meeting of the Observers at the Columbus. The Observers were asked to comment on the Holy Father's sermon: he will be told what they said.

Exposition of the *De Ecclesia* by Thils: substantial enough, but *'sachlich'* [factual] and pedagogical. I admire the attention of the Observers, who are really WORKING.

> Cullmann approved of the division, with the introduction of the new Chapter
>   II, the People of God (the aspect of the history of salvation,
>   in the past
>   eschatologically: intermediate time (already and not yet));
>   This notion of the People of God completes the idea of the Body of
>   Christ by expressing the idea of mutuality.
> Schmemann:[3] No. 4 on the Holy Spirit, which is the content of the life of the
>   Church, would be a good place into which to insert what Cullmann
>   has said about the eschatological aspect. This paragraph could be
>   developed in the sense of the new creation. Because there is too much
>   said from the point of view of the individual (gifts of the Holy Spirit
>   in each one).
> Professor Outler:[4] the prophetic dimension of the Church is missing.
>   As is the Church in judgement.

---

1. It will become clear later that this was the Belgian Xavier Seumois, WF: he worked at the secretariat of the Episcopal Conference of Rwanda and Burundi, and in catechetical formation in Africa and at the 'Lumen Vitae' Centre in Brussels; he was a Council expert from the Second Session onwards.
2. Joseph Greco, SJ: he was to be a Council expert from the Third Session onwards.
3. Alexander Schmemann, born in Estonia, educated at the Sorbonne and at the Institut de Théologie Orthodoxe Saint-Serge in Paris; he was Dean of St Vladimir's Theological Seminary (New York), where he taught Church history and the theology of the liturgy; he had collaborated with the WCC since its foundation and was the guest of the Secretariat for Unity.
4. Albert Outler, Professor of Theology at the Southern Methodist University in Dallas; Observer representing the World Council of Methodists.

As is the Church in the process of reforming itself (the relationship between the Church as spotless and the Church as stained).

Nissiotis:[1] the Eucharist as a basis for the structure of the local Church: real participation in the Body of Christ unceasingly recreates the Church.

Professor Berkouwer:[2] everything will depend on what is put into the chapter on the People of God. Is the change that is envisaged purely formal and technical or is it rather a new opening (in the sense of the economy), a deepening of Nos. 8, 9 and 10?

Dr Horton:[3] at the end of No. 3 where it speaks of the Church as a sacrament: he very much liked this idea of the Church-as-sacrament, which expresses the idea of the action of God in humanity.

Pastor Roux: the idea of the Church as the People of God should not be separated from the notion of the Church as a body: this idea belongs quite as much to the MYSTERY of the Church.

Oberman:[4] this schema *De Ecclesia* will be even more important for the future of our relationships than the schema *De Œcumenismo*.

Comments about p 13, l. 13 ff.

Comments about p 8, l. 34.

(The quotation from Scripture is understood as the opposite of what it says.)

There is a certain ambiguity concerning what is attributed to Christians who do not belong to the Roman Church.

Nissiotis: there is no mention of the relationship between the universal Church and the local Churches.

Prof Lindbeck:[5]

1) Nothing is said about forgiveness for sin (for example where the Church is spoken of as a broker of union).

The existence of sin in the Church is not taken seriously enough.

2) Not enough is said about the ministry of the Word when speaking of the bishop.

---

1. The lay theologian Nikos A Nissiotis, of the Greek Orthodox Church, was Assistant Director, and then Director, of the WCC Ecumenical Institute in Bossey (Switzerland): he was an Observer appointed by the WCC from the Second Session onwards.

2. Gerrit C Berkouwer, professor at the Université Protestante Libre d'Amsterdam, guest of the Secretariat for Unity.

3. Douglas Horton, former Moderator of the International Council of Congregationalists, whom he represented as an Observer.

4. Heiko A Oberman, Professor of Church History at the Divinity School of the University of Harvard; Observer representing the International Council of Congregationalists.

5. George Lindbeck, Professor of the History of Theology at Yale University, New Haven; official Observer representing the World Lutheran Federation.

3) The eschatological note is missing (theme: Church of the Cross, the Church is always normally under persecution).

4) Finally, asks in what sense the Church is spoken of as sacrament.

Schlink: believes that Nos. 7 to 9 will increase the difficulties for ecumenical dialogue.

No. 9: there is a reference to non-Catholic Christians but the non-Catholic *CHURCHES* as such are not taken seriously.

Catholic theology today goes further.

Asks what is the theological note of a constitution.

Page 11, No. 7: it would seem that there is a dogmatic definition from line 13 onwards.

Schmemann: concerning No. 9: he fully understands Schlink's question. The historical reality of the separated Churches ought to be taken into consideration.

GOD is at work in HISTORY.

Also No. 10: the Church is not sent only to human beings, but to the world.

Dr Van Holk:[1] Free Church, Holland:

Could room not be found for the idea of the invisible Church?

The concept of the People of God ought to be interpreted in a more general way. There are groups which are not explicitly either Catholic or Protestant . . .

Emphasise the mysterious and ineffable aspect of God's plan.

Canon Pawley: page 12, line 35: the meaning of the word *etiam*.

It is not *even* but *also*.

On the whole, the quality of this meeting was exceptional. It is fantastic: one discusses dogmatic texts with the Others, and in such a way that they feel that these texts concern them, and that we feel that they have something to tell us!

I saw Fr Schmemann for a moment, whom I had not met since he left Paris in 1951. He is EXTREMELY severe about the Greeks: what are they afraid of? They are wasting a unique historical moment. In Montréal too, they had been equally full of complexes and negative.

I saw Mgr Willebrands. To begin with, he told me that Cardinal Bea had just been appointed to the 'Holy Office'. I spoke to him about the question of Israel. He told me that the text of a page, prepared by the Secretariat, was being printed and would be available in a week's time. He added that Paul VI had asked that the question of Israel remain the responsibility of the Secretariat for Christian Unity and not be passed over to the Secretariat for non-Christian religions. I insisted that, in Bea's Secretariat, Israel constitute, by name, a particular section.

---

1. LJ van Holk, professor at the University of Leiden; official Observer for the International Association of Liberal Christianity.

On the way out, at 7 pm, I saw Fr Seumois, of the White Fathers, the brother of the missiologist. He told me the questions and *desiderata* from the Conference of Bishops of Africa; I shall have to give my opinion on some points.

I can barely drag my right leg, which is quite without movement, and I cannot raise it to take a step. However, when I returned, M. De Ridder, a Dutch Protestant, was waiting for me. We arranged to meet tomorrow at 3.30 pm.

In the evening, Fr Gagnebet told me some things about Pius XII during the war. After the particularly cruel execution of three hundred Italians in the Ardeatine Caves, Pius XII asked himself some anguished questions. He ought to have made a public speech of vehement protest. But all the convents, all the religious houses in Rome, were full of refugees: communists, Jews, democrats and anti-Fascists, former generals and so on. Pius XII had LIFTED THE ENCLOSURE. If he had protested publicly and solemnly, all those houses would have been searched and that would have been catastrophic. So Pius XII settled for protesting through diplomatic channels . . .

But Pius XII had great faith in diplomacy. With Pius XI, the whole thing would have been done differently.

Hitler had given orders for Pius XII to be arrested. Kesselring[1] had refused to carry out this order. He may even have warned the Pope of what was being plotted. In any case, Pius XII had certainly been warned. He managed to send a message to Cardinal Lavitrano,[2] Archbishop of Palermo (which was occupied by the Allies), to the effect that if he were to leave the Vatican, it would be by force, he would no longer be pope: the Archbishop of Palermo received the powers in his stead.

Did this amount to the nomination of a successor? History has known such things.

Pius XII had summoned the German Ambassador and had told him: you can take away Mgr Pacelli, but not the pope!

It seems that these things, which Fr Gagnebet knew when they actually happened, are now in the public domain.

Wednesday 2 October 1963
Coach for the bishops from Saint-Sulpice and Saint-Louis des Français. There were some new bishops.

At St Peter's, I met Mgr Griffiths (who wants mention of MEMBERS because there is no body without members), Mgr the Nuncio,[3] Mgr de Provenchères and Mgr Veuillot. I told him what Willebrands had said to me about the chapter concerning Israel. He thought, quite rightly, that, in spite of everything, it would be

---

1.   Albert Kesselring, German Marshal.
2.   Luigi Lavitrano, Archbishop of Palermo.
3.   Paolo Bertoli.

IMPORTANT for the theme to be introduced, in a few lines, in the DOGMATIC schema *De Ecclesia*. Saw Mgr Ancel.

During the Mass, I saw Mgr Onclin on the question of members. We are in agreement. He will arrange for an American bishop to speak about it.

> Cardinal Câmara,[1] Brazil, in the name of [ ] bishops:
> The Council should not define anything as a dogma of faith, and he suggested that this should be clearly stated.
> There should be a word about the poor.
> We share not only in the life of the risen Christ (page 9) but also in the crucified Christ.
> Page 10, line 9, the *Regnum* [Kingdom] should be included among the other images.
> Concerning the members of the Church, do not use the words *reapse* [really] and *simpliciter loquendo* [simply speaking], or the word *votum* [wish].
> Page 12 . . .
> Page 13, line 20: instead of *locupletantur* [they are enriched], say: *pro dolor* [unfortunately] . . . !
> (I shall not copy it all out: it will all be found written down for the Commission. I shall only note down the general remarks.)
> Cardinal Gracias:[2] Does not like the Introduction; the first sentence is too general . . . It would be better to have the history of salvation as an introduction and a statement that Christ is the redeemer of all human beings. The true face of the Church should be shown; it should not appear as wanting to dominate. But in Chapter I, the Church appears as the TERM of Redemption,[3] and as not open to all human beings, and a simple means and service. The Church exists in herself, but not for herself: it is a minority in the service of the majority (he quoted Newman and Paul VI). The missionary nature of the Church must be affirmed, not so that the Church can increase her power, but so that the Church can serve the world; he suggested that No. 6 be completed in this sense.
> Cardinal Alfrink:[4] drew attention to the expression: '*Petrus et apostoli*' [Peter and the Apostles], which is unusual. It would be better to say: *Petrus coeterique apostoli* [Peter and the other Apostles]. He replied to Cardinal Ruffini on the question of the Apostles as foundations. He repeated what had been said (by Mgr Charue) to the Theological

---

1. *AS* II/I, 422–423.
2. *AS* II/I, 425–427.
3. The manuscript has 'Réd'. The typescript has 'Révélation'.
4. *AS* II/I, 428–430.

Commission in March. He added a reference to the liturgy for the consecration of a church.

Mgr Abasolo[1] (India): Spanish pronunciation.

Criticised the first words which seemed to restrict mission to the GENTES [non-Christians] only. It would be better to use expressions from John . . .

Van Dodewaard,[2] of Haarlem, in the name of the conference of Dutch bishops: No. 7: the visible and invisible elements are not well placed.

Nos. 8-10: ought to be under a single heading.

He suggested some changes . . .

De Provenchères:[3] For many people the Church is more an obstacle than a help; they do not see the mystery in it. One could go further in the expression of the mystery: grace—holiness.

He spoke in favour of the ontology of grace, beyond the aspect of the Church as an instrument of salvation.

Mgr Granados,[4] Auxiliary of Toledo.

Mgr Compagnone[5] (Anagni): very much along the lines of Ruffini.

Mgr Franić.[6] Rather against the use of IMAGES: that is all right for the areas where the Church is quite free. For other regions, it gives a glorifying impression, things need to be expressed differently. Insist essentially on the Body of Christ and the Kingdom of God: this would be more encouraging for those who are living in difficult circumstances.

Speak of the Church militant; do not speak only about peace and love, but of a spirit of resistance to the evil world and to atheism. He suggested that a commission on modern atheism be established in the Curia.

I missed the interventions of Mgrs Romero,[7] Carli,[8] and Brasseur:[9] I was told that they were all along the lines of Ruffini. Mgr Carli made an impression. He wanted to show that the application to the Apostles of the idea of foundation, which is

---

1. Of Spanish origin, John A Abasolo y Lecue, OCD, was Bishop of Vijaypuram (India), *AS* II/I, 430–433.
2. *AS* II/I, 433–435.
3. *AS* II/I, 435–436.
4. Anastasio Granados García, who was to become a member of the Doctrinal Commission in 1964, *AS* II/I, 436–438.
5. *AS* II/I, 438–441.
6. *AS* II/I, 442–444.
7. F Romero Menjibar, *AS* II/I, 445–446.
8. *AS* II/I, 447–449.
9. The Belgian William Brasseur, Vicar Apostolic of Montagnosa (Philippines), *AS* II/I, 449–451.

valid in the case of Peter, would be ambiguous. In any case, the idea had been discussed at Vatican I and had been rejected. So the matter has been settled.

I spoke to several bishops at the bar, including Mgr de Provenchères.

Mgr Ancel:[1] in favour of inserting a reference to the *KINGDOM OF GOD;* he quoted several passages from the New Testament.

Mgr Guano,[2] Livorno: show more clearly the link between the Church and the Word made flesh.

Explain the (felicitous) expression Church-sacrament.

Mention the aspect of the Church offering herself in sacrifice.

Retraced a whole plan of the *De Ecclesia!*

Mgr Enciso[3] (Spain): on No. 5, the Mystical Body: it lacks order: he suggested an order. And the content is not perfect: there is no reference to charity and too little mention of the Eucharist.

There is too much concentration on the image of the body, and not enough on that of Bride which complements it.

Mgr Primeau,[4] bishop of Manchester in the USA: he intoned Mgr Onclin's refrain: no distinction between society and community—which would have made it possible to find the right place for page 7, *congregatio iustorum* [assembly of the just].

Page 12 on the members of the Church: proposed a text.

A statement on relations between Church and State is needed.

Butler,[5] Abbot of Downside, suggested additions about non-Catholic Christians in No. 9 in order to state that they are united in communions, groupings which are not simply natural but religious.

He said a few words about the Church and the Kingdom of God according to the New Testament: there is a certain distinction between the Kingdom of GOD and the Kingdom *OF CHRIST* (**_VERY_** interesting).

Mgr Felici[6] speaking for the Council of Presidents: would the Fathers please remain as far as possible in their places! Some of the Fathers and experts are walking about and talking too loudly!

In the coach on the return journey, which was held up for long periods by the police on account of the President of Somalia, conversed with the bishops: Mgrs Ménager, Renard, Blanchet, Weber. We spoke above all about the meaning of

---

1. *AS* II/I, 452–454.
2. *AS* II/I, 455-457.
3. Jesus Enciso Viana, Bishop of Majorca, *AS* II/I, 458–459.
4. Ernest J Primeau: he was to be a member of the Secretariat for Unity from the Second Session of the Council onwards, *AS* II/I, 459–461.
5. *AS* II/I, 462.
6. *AS* II/I, 463.

Ephesians 2:20 and Apocalypse 21:14. The bishops were impressed by Mgr Carli. So, instead of taking a siesta, I put together my documentation on these points.

I spoke to Cardinal Liénart and Mgr Villot about the possibility of Fr Féret being admitted as a conciliar expert. Nothing can be done. During the First Session and afterwards, too many bishops asked for this on behalf of their own private secretaries. In spite of Mgr Villot, they managed to get them all appointed. There had been about a hundred such favours granted. But now, there are too many experts. Requests are still pouring in, so that it had been decided to refuse them all. It is a pity, because a number of nonentities have been admitted and first-class men such as Féret, Liégé and Martelet are left out.

Cardinal Liénart again told me that the Pope had spoken highly of me as a theologian.

At 5 pm at the Vatican, in the stuffy Hall of the Congregations, meeting of the Theological Commission. I arrived a little late. To begin with, I had been busy until 4.30 p.m. with the Dutch protestant, M de Pitter, who wants to write a thesis on present currents in Catholic theology (he is slow and deaf!); then I had to cope with transport difficulties.

Cardinal Ottaviani suggested that five Fathers be entrusted with the task of studying and classifying the changes that have been suggested or proposed.

Cardinal Browne suggested a sub-commission of three members. Mgr Garrone, supported by Mgr Florit, suggested SEVERAL sub-commissions, because there is an immense amount of work to be done. It is more the work of the *periti,* said Mgr van Dodewaard.

The members will be selected from among those who have been most involved in the preparation of the texts. Cardinal Ottaviani suggested as members: Cardinal Browne, Mgr Garrone, Parente, Florit and Franić. After some discussion (Tromp raised some PRACTICAL difficulties), Mgr Charue returned to van Dodewaard's idea: it is a matter for the *periti.* And he asked that all should be given mimeographed copies of the full text of at least the principal interventions.

Cardinal Ottaviani agreed to the idea of the work of classification being done by *periti,* under the direction of three bishops. *Placet.*

He suggested: Brown with Garrone and Parente. The latter said that he had the work of the Congregations every day. Brown suggested Spanedda. Tromp would like the Theological Commission as a whole to deal only with the *maiora* [most important things] . . . Cardinal Browne asked for ALL the comments to be submitted to him . . . The three were increased to five: Browne, Garrone, Florit, Spanedda, Charue.

McGrath insisted that the members should have ALL of all the documents, in their entirety. It is a matter of conscience, he said.

Mgr Griffiths asked that the work should begin DURING the Session, while the whole Commission is in Rome.

A question from Mgr Garrone (is it only the interventions in the *aula* that are to be made available or is it to be also the bishops' earlier written comments . . . ?)

provoked a discussion. Tromp and Ottaviani would only take into consideration what had been said or communicated in writing IN THE COUNCIL . . .

We moved on to the question of the new division of the schema proposed or called for by the Co-ordinating Commission.

All the members, and even the *periti*, should FIRST give their comments IN WRITING, Fr Tromp said.

But, Ottaviani said, it will soon be time for the Commission to declare its position before the Council . . . It seems that Fr Tromp and even Cardinal Ottaviani want to take a long time and perhaps smother the project.

Cardinal Léger read a paper in favour of the new chapter on the People of God. But he raised a difficulty: this would amount to removing from the chapter on the laity much of its supernatural content . . . In conclusion, he advocated a division into three chapters only:

1) The Mystery of the Church;
2) The People of God;
3) The Hierarchy.

When asked what he thought, Mgr Philips explained what he had done. That was so long drawn-out that it was impossible to judge the thing. All the more so since, in this airless room, one feels stifled and sweats terribly.

What to do? The discussion went on, but Parente raised the preliminary question: have we the right to discuss the new arrangement or have we legitimately been required to do so by the Coordinating Commission? Are we under an obligation?

Arising out of this, Mgr Griffiths raised the question of the constitution *De Beata Maria Virgine* which many are asking to be inserted in the *De Ecclesia*. That was shelved in order to revert to the question of the division into four or five chapters.

Ottaviani said that the Pope would be asked whether or not we are obliged to follow the instruction of the Co-ordinating Commission . . . But if the majority of our Theological Commission is IN FAVOUR of the division into five chapters, the question of juridical principle is of little importance. So take a vote on it, said Mgr Charue and Mgr Schröffer.

Fr Fernandez objected to the idea of a special chapter *De Populo Dei* [on the People of God]: what needs to be said should be said in Chapter I (material cause of the Church; members); there would be a danger of inclining towards an exaggerated democratism . . . (!)

Confused and tired discussion. But there have been many requests for the idea of the Kingdom of God to be inserted, Tromp said. It will be necessary to find a place for it too!!! Further confusion.

Conclusion: each one should submit to the secretary of the Commission his opinion in writing for or against.

Thursday 3 October 1963

In the coach, I saw Mgr Weber. We talked about an intervention that he is planning to make about the collegiality of the Twelve.

In St Peter's, I saw Cardinal Léger. He is very unhappy about what he considers to have been, on the part of Cardinal Suenens, an attempt to direct the Council and impose his ideas on it (new Chapter II of *De Ecclesia;* schema XVII). He
is very gloomy and pessimistic. He introduced me to Cardinal Gracias. I also saw
Cardinal Marella who told me that at the request of Canon Boulard he would take
Liégé as his expert in the Commission on the Government of Dioceses.

I saw Cardinal Richaud again. He showered me with praise. He repeated to me
that the Ambassador had seen the Pope for an hour and a half and that Paul VI
had spoken very highly to him of the French theologians, mentioning myself with
Fr de Lubac. Cardinal Richaud added his own compliments to that. I thought it a
favourable moment to speak of Fr Féret. He put on a very serious look and said: I
am much less keen on Fr Féret . . . That's torn it!

The following spoke:

> Cardinal Lercaro:[1] 1) One should look closely at the use being made of the
> words *Ecclesia, Corpus Christi,* etc:
> a) The Church and the Mystical Body are the same thing, but seen from
> two different aspects on the concrete and historical plane; agreeds
> what was said in the name of the Dutch Conference of Bishops; b)
> Concerning No. 8 (*reapse* [really] . . .) put: *'plene et perfecte'* [fully and
> perfectly], because by baptism the heretics are members (Dosseti's
> thesis!); heresy . . . does no more than DIMINISH THE RIGHTS OF
> members . . . ; c) say something about the relationship between the
> Church and the Eucharist, the Eucharist being taken as an action and
> a COMMUNITARIAN action; this is how the Church becomes the
> Body of Christ.
> 2) The biblical images: add the Family of God and the Kingdom
> of God. Their importance: their dynamic value. He insisted on
> *novum genus, nova creatio* [new people, new creation]. It is the link
> between the Kingdom of God and human history. There is a real
> transfiguration, a new birth, by the Cross and the kenosis. The Church
> is the seed of the bringing to birth of the new creation. The presence of
> the Church by witness, by martyrdom, by service, by *diakonia* [service]
> above all of the poor, by mission.
> 3) The Theological Commission *ad altiora vocatur* [is called to higher
> things]. It ought to revise the whole chapter. To do this, it should call
> for the assistance of those Fathers who have spoken so well about the

---

1. *AS* II/II, 9–13.

Church these past few days. This is envisaged in our new Regulations: in particular Silva, Rugambwa, Gracias, Ancel, Guano, etc.

Cardinal Arriba y Castro[1] (Tarragona) on the Virgin Mary: in the name of more than sixty Fathers.

Should there be a Marian schema? Yes. If it is inserted into the *De Ecclesia*, where should it be put?

Mary is the MOTHER of the Church: therefore put it after Chapter I and as a chapter on its own, with the necessary breadth and depth.

Cardinal Confalonieri:[2] Do not forget the sending of the Holy Spirit (quite grandiloquent).

Cardinal Richaud:[3] (careful but very mediocre pronunciation):

1) Ephesians 1 should be quoted.

2) the aspect of the Church as *orans* [praying] is not sufficiently evident.

Cardinal Ritter[4] (St Louis): On the Church as sacrament of union with God; and also as community of human beings united to God. The first point of view is not explained sufficiently.

In No. 7, there ought to be mention of the Word of God, the idea of a Church which proclaims the Word of God: a chapter which is left too much in the shade by our theology!

He cited the text prepared by the Secretariat. There ought to be mention of the Word of God at the BEGINNING of the schema: *Verbo et opere, Verbum et opus* [by Word and by deed, Word and deed]!

Cardinal Bea:[5] Do the chapters that we are scrutinising meet the aim of renewing the Christian life on the basis of Scripture and Tradition? Are the texts being used rigorously? Not always. He gave an example.

Mgr Šeper:[6] (Zagreb): On the images of the Church: what is missing in this exposition.

I went out for a moment and was stopped inopportunely by several people. I returned while Mgr del Campo[7] (Spain) was speaking and asking for more precision in the concepts of Church, Mystical Body . . .

Mgr Hoa[8] (Vietnam): He spoke in favour of the idea of FAMILY (*FATHER* and *BROTHERS*), the relationship of BROTHERS; non-'members'.

This must have come from Fr Dournes. But people were not paying attention. However, he developed his idea well.

---

1. *AS* II/II, 14–16.
2. *AS* II/II, 16–17.
3. *AS* II/II, 17–18.
4. *AS* II/II, 18–19.
5. *AS* II/II, 20–22.
6. *AS* II/II, 32–34.
7. Abilio del Campo y de la Bárcena, Bishop of Calahorra et La Calzada, *AS* II/II, 39–41.
8. S Hoa Nguyen-van Hien, *AS* II/II, 42–44.

Mgr Argaya,[1] down to speak, but did not do so!

Mgr Volk[2] (Mainz) in the name of German-speaking bishops and others. That Chapter I should speak of the Word of God and of the Eucharist (in the celebration of which the Word of God is proclaimed); he suggested a text to be inserted.

Where there is a reference to the pilgrim Church, something should be inserted about the relationship between the visible Church and the Kingdom of God; the two cannot be identified with one another, but there are close relationships between them.

Mgr A Pildáin[3] (Canary Islands): There is no reference to the return to the Church of those who, having belonged to us, are now living separated from the Church; he suggested an addition borrowed from the Bishops of Africa.

Jelmini,[4] Administrator of Lugano, in the name of the bishops of Switzerland: No. 5, pages 9 and 10. There needs to be a reference to the presence of Christ in the Church above all in the Eucharist, and also in his Vicar . . .

Mgr Heenan[5] (Westminster) in the name of the bishops of England and Wales: No. 9 is a matter of the reconciliation of non-Catholic Christians with the Church; No. 10 is a matter of the conversion of non-Christians.

Hence the obligation of the apostolate for all Christians: EVEN IN RELATION TO NON-CATHOLIC CHRISTIANS. He proposed a correction to No. 9.

He spoke in terms of a return to the maternal home.

Mgr Scalais[6] (Léopoldville) in the name of all the bishops of the former Belgian Congo: Concerning the images, which lend themselves to expressing the historical and eschatological aspects of the Church, above all: People of God, Mystical Body, Kingdom of God (but People and Kingdom are not figures!!!). He suggested:

No. 5: *De Ecclesia ut populo Dei* [On the Church as the People of God];

No. 6: *De Ecclesia ut Mystico Corpore Christi* [On the Church as the Mystical Body of Christ];

No. 7: *De Ecclesia ut progrediente ad Regnum Dei* [On the Church as on the way to the Kingdom of God].

Mgr van Velsen[7] (South Africa): There are some things which are not in accordance with concrete reality.

---

1.   J Argaya Goicoechea.
2.   *AS* II/II, 45–46.
3.   Antonio Pildáin y Zapiáin, Bishop of the Canary Islands, *AS* II/II, 47–49.
4.   Angelo G Jelmini, titular bishop, Apostolic Administrator of Lugano, *AS* II/II, 50–51.
5.   *AS* II/II, 52–53.
6.   The Belgian Félix Scalais, archbishop of Léopoldville (Congo), *AS* II/II, 53–54.
7.   Gerard M F van Velsen, OP, was Bishop of Kroonstad, *AS* II/II, 57–58.

No. 9: *reapse* [really] . . . there are disputes about the exact meaning of these words.

Give expression to what is real from the pastoral point of view.

Page 12, lines 15–17: delete *voto* [by desire] on the subject of catechumens.

Page 12, in lines 18–22: the end of No. 8 does not distinguish between Christians and pagans(?)

No. 9 is incomplete: a) If the reference is to Protestants, one cannot be silent about the Bible and the Word of God; b) If the reference is to the Easterners, one cannot be silent about their priesthood and episcopacy, which are constitutive elements of the local Church.

No. 10: The situation of those in a state of grace should be expressed in BIBLICAL terms (cf Rom 2).

Van der Burgt[1] (Indonesia) in the name of thirty-one bishops of Indonesia:

1) *Populus Dei* [The People of God] is the first name of the Church, and its relationship to the Mystical Body should be made clear. He suggested an addition in agreement with the schema *De Liturgia*.

2) Nos. 5 and 7: Church and Kingdom of God: show more clearly the eschatological aspect, with what it implies about our weaknesses.

3) No. 6 on the images of the Church.

4) Page 11, No. 8: express better the necessity of the Church, which is *necessitas medii* [a necessity of the means].

5) Page 12, No. 8: need for corrections (poor Fr Tromp !!!): he suggested *FULL* INCORPORATION for Catholics.

6) Page 13, No. 10: state more clearly that mission is an essential function of the Church.

Mgr Martin[2] (Archbishop of Rouen): There are a number of differences between the way the Church is spoken of in the schema on the Liturgy and in the *De Ecclesia*: concerning the Trinitarian relationship of the Church, the schema *De Liturgia* speaks of the Church being called together by Christ in the Holy Spirit in order to give WORSHIP . . . above all in the celebration of the Eucharist.

At 2.35 pm, at the French Seminary: meeting with Fr Greco, secretary of the African episcopate. He asked me for the principal elements for an intervention that Cardinal Rugambwa wants to make on episcopal collegiality.

At 3 pm, meeting with Mgrs Ancel, Garrone, Maziers, then Elchinger, and with Daniélou, Denis, Lécuyer, Martimort, Colson, Labourdette and myself in order to envisage to some extent the points to be made by the bishops in their interventions and the work they are to do for that with the *periti*. This year the

---

1. Herculanus J Van der Burgt, OFM Cap, Archbishop of Pontianak, *AS* II/II, 59–61.
2. Joseph-M Martin, *AS* II/II, 61–62.

bishops have themselves organised their work. Instead of being led to some extent by the experts, they are organising themselves into small groups and calling on the experts to assist them. They seem to be more in their element and more active than last year. They are living the Council seriously.

With Mgr Ancel, we went through the list of subjects on which the bishops are working and will intervene: while doing so, suggestions were made, information given, comments made. Interesting meeting. Several times, Fr Gy half-opened the door and made a mysterious sign to Mgr Martimort.

It was thought that, in order to explain things to the Italian bishops, for whom the idea of collegiality remains strange, and in order to defuse hostile grenades or objections, it would be good for a bishop to give an exposition of the elementary categories of the question.

At 4.35/4.40 pm I went to Saint-Louis des Français to see Mgr Veuillot and to work on the question of an intervention on Israel. He asked me to prepare one. I was limping dreadfully on the way back.

Friday 4 October 1963

Saint Francis. Yesterday there was a meeting of the Commission on the Apostolate of the Laity. The lay 'auditors' were present and it was agreed that other lay people could be invited.

> Cardinal Gerlier[1] (FRIGHTFULLY French pronunciation):
>> Today the mystery of Christ in the Church is above all to be found in the poor: there has not been enough reference to them. He suggested an addition at the end of the introduction.
>
> Mgr [ ][2] (Burundi, in the name of forty-five bishops): there should be mention of the catholicity of the Church: in accordance with the text prepared by the African bishops. And at No. 10, there should mention of the missionary function of the Church.
>
> Baudoux[3] (Canada): 1) in the section on dissenters there is no mention of Christian communions as such; 2) in the new Chapter II, *De populo Dei* [On the People of God] state the faults in (or of) this people.
>
> Jenny:[4] (text very well given—very pastoral style of preaching);
>> Quite a number of things are somewhat at odds in the schema. He indicated three points.
>> 1) the person of Christ;
>> 2) the Paschal mystery;
>> 3) the people of God as *HUMANITY* renewed in Christ.

---

1. *AS* II/II, 68.
2. Antoine Grauls, Archbishop of Kitega (Burundi), *AS* II/II, 69–70.
3. Maurice Baudoux, Archbishop of Saint-Boniface, *AS* II/II, 70–71.
4. *AS* II/II, 72–74.

And in this way the Church will not appear as alien to people.

Marling[1] (USA): on No. 9: it is insufficient and not well arranged. He suggested a very strong text from the ecumenical point of view, but a bit diffuse.

Baldassari[2] (Ravenna): on the same subject: state more clearly that it is by Baptism that one enters the Church. He suggested a number of additions, veneration for Scripture and the Tradition of the Holy Fathers.

D'Avack[3] (Camerino): the schema says nothing about the foundation of . . . ? CHRIST AS HEAD, priest (sacrifice). It is a regression as compared with *Mystici Corporis*.

His text, read in the Italian way, with great emphases, reviewed all the categories, all the scholastic distinctions, and created an impression of unreality after the four preceding interventions. It is not taken seriously.

Himmer,[4] Tournai, on the Church and the poor.

The Church should show itself to be at the service of the poor. It too will be judged on that (Mt 25). The mission the Church has to evangelise and to help the poor should be given expression; as should the mystery of Christ as identified with the poor.

Cardinal Browne[5] concluded the discussion of Chapter I. Then he said a word about the use of the word *sacramentum* as applied to the Church.

Discussion of Chapter II:

Cardinal Spellman:[6] On No. 15 page 25: the diaconate. A dogmatic constitution is not the place for this. He is against a permanent diaconate. He understands nothing. For him, this would be the kind of archaeologising condemned by Pius XII.

Cardinal Ruffini[7] (a machine gun!): he discussed certain words, the use of certain texts (and once again Eph 2:20), the expression 'college of bishops'. He denied that Christ had instituted a college of Apostles to which a college of bishops would have succeeded.

He rejected the idea (page 26) that the episcopates could decide whether or not deacons would be celibate.

No. 19, pages 29–35: he called for a distinction to be made between the ordinary and the extraordinary magisterium.

Page 30, lines 12-23.

---

1. Joseph Marling, bishop of Jefferson City, *AS* II/II, 75.
2. Salvatore Baldassari, Archbishop of Ravenna, *AS* II/II, 76.
3. *AS* II/II, 77–79.
4. *AS* II/II, 79–80.
5. *AS* II/II, 81.
6. *AS* II/II, 82–83.
7. *AS* II/II, 84–87.

Cardinal Bacci:[1] on page 26: deacons. What is said there is very dangerous! Antiquity is not necessarily better.

Guerry,[2] in the name of the bishops of France on the declaration that the episcopate is a sacrament. It is necessary for the importance and consequences of this point to be more clearly stated.

1) For the formation of the clergy and the theology of the priesthood.

2) By consecration, the newly chosen bishop is incorporated into the order of bishops and, as such, charged with the universal mission. A communion of bishops on a sacramental basis and not a purely juridical one.

Votum: *ut clare et expressius Patres vellent declarare doctrinam de sacramentalitate episcopatus* [Proposal to be voted on: that the Fathers wish to declare clearly and more expressly the doctrine of the sacramentality of the episcopate].

De Castro[3] (Granada): on the episcopate as superior to the priesthood from the sacramental point of view: the opposite was held (unanimously, he said) in t ˙ Middle Ages. The idea is still controversial. And there are the concessions given in the law that allow priests to ordain. He asked that No. 14 be suppressed . . . (I could not follow him).

(I will see his text).

Veuillot[4] (he read his text slowly but coldly. It did not capture one's attention). Page 24: the Apostolic succession of bishops. The biblical texts that prove this have not been cited.

On the foundation of episcopal collegiality: state more emphatically that it is the Apostolic succession itself.

Mgr Vuccino[5] in the name of seven Fathers: he recalled that Cardinal Montini had said during the First Session that it was better not to go into the question of Revelation.

García[6] (Spain) on THE OBJECT of infallibility.

Saboia[7] (Palmas) No. 9. Heretics have been anathematised by all the Councils. Why do things differently this time?

No. 19: he offered an explanation of *ex sese*.

He offered at great speed a heap of things that seemed fairly confused. (= an OFM)

---

1. *AS* II/II, 87–89.
2. *AS* II/II, 89–90.
3. *AS* II/II, Rafael García y García de Castro, Archbishop of Grenada, *AS* II/II, 91–92.
4. *AS* II/II, 92–94.
5. *AS* II/II, 95–96.
6. F García Martinez, *AS* II/II, 101–103.
7. CE Saboia Bandeira de Méllo, *AS* II/II, 114–116.

Pocci,[1] titular bishop of Jericho, in the name of Cardinal Micara, Vicar of Rome. There are some errors which are creeping in . . . about original sin, the Mystical Body, and the necessity of belonging to the Church. This schema does not condemn them: it would seem to be leaving the field wide open to error.

After St Peter's, I was to lunch with Mgr Elchinger at Laurentin's place. But we had difficulty in finding a taxi and Laurentin—who I believe is reporting for *Le Figaro*[2]—kept us waiting for nearly three-quarters of an hour. We made little progress on the question of the *De Beata*. The present text prepared by Laurentin does not satisfy me and does not do what it should do.

Mgr Elchinger told me that the Germans are very reticent about inserting *De Revelatione*, or even a chapter *De Traditione*, in the *De Ecclesia*. They say that they would first like to see a proposed text. Only on this basis could they assess the need for such a step.

He also told me that the secretariat had refused to allow Mgr Blanchet to speak: he wanted to speak about the theological note of our constitutions; the question is (has been) referred to the Pope and, when a question is referred to the Pope, it may no longer be discussed. The same refusal had been given, and for the same reason, to Mgr Volk, but he had persisted in demanding the right to speak as he had something else to say as well. Patriarch Maximos,[3] too, was refused permission to speak, because he wished to speak in French: Latin is compulsory. That must have been very painful for him.

The question [[of the insertion]] of the *De Beata* in the *De Ecclesia* had been put to the Pope. He is personally in favour but HE DOES NOT WANT TO INTERVENE in the Council; it is for the Council itself to reach its decision by discussion and a vote. There will be a vote on this. The Moderators have made a decision about it. But I said to Mgr Elchinger, who will convey it to the Germans and to Cardinal Döpfner, that, in my opinion, one could not ask the Council for a vote unless one has explained the [[full]] import of such a decision. In order to do this, it would be necessary for options 2-3-4 concerning the *De Beata* to be succinctly presented to the Fathers: that one should first give them an idea of what the chapter would be like in each of these hypotheses. That would be difficult to do, but it seemed to me necessary for the honesty of the vote.

On the subject of the *De Beata*, Fr Tillard[4] (Canadian OP), who has just arrived, at the request of Mgr Roy, told me that, with very few exceptions, the Ca-

---

1. Clemente Micara, born in 1879, was the pope's Vicar General for the diocese of Rome. Filippo Pocci was the cardinal's auxiliary, *AS* II/II, 123–124.
2. During the First Session, the correspondent for *Le Figaro* listened only to representatives of Curia circles; for this reason, Laurentin was asked to take over, which he did from June 1963.
3. Maximos IV Saigh.
4. Jean-Marie R Tillard, OP, of the Province of Canada, Professor of Theology at the The-

nadian bishops are deeply Marian. For them, the maximising positions are self-evident, and they have not the slightest suspicion that anyone could ask questions on this subject. Fr Tillard is alarmed at what he has ascertained on this subject.

Lecture on the schema *De Ecclesia* to the French-speaking bishops of Africa at Via Traspontina, at 4.30 pm. There were relatively few black bishops. I spoke to Fr Chenu.

At 6 pm, lecture to the representatives of the religious press. I arrived a little late, in a crowded room, into which three hundred people were crammed, many of them standing, and some listening from outside through the air vents. I spoke again about the *De Ecclesia*, but in a very different way. I thought I would be addressing only lay people; about half of those present were priests, and there were even some bishops.

The question of press coverage at the Council has changed completely as compared with the First Session. Each language group is arranged with a bishop in charge. Thanks to l'abbé Haubtmann, the French have a press coverage with which all the journalists say they are delighted and which attracts a large number of reporters from other countries. From this point of view, it seemed to be a complete success.

I realised this because after my lecture in the Hall of the Augustinians (followed by numerous questions most of which were quite striking), I went to a reception organised for journalists at the Embassy. There I saw a great many people, in particular Pastor Rilliet and Pastor Molard.[1] The ambassador, M. de la Tournelle[2] drew me aside and told me that he had seen Paul VI last Tuesday. The Pope had spoken highly of the French theologians, and of myself in particular, saying that what I write is clear, well-grounded, balanced, etc.

Returned here at 9.30 pm.

Saturday 5 October 1963

At last a quiet morning and not a tiring one as the others have been. Visit from a Polish bishop, wanting my opinion on the question of the diaconate. In Poland, the bishops would be in favour, in principle, but have a great fear that such deacons would be made use of by the Communists, who would set them up against the priests, in the way they set the priests up against the bishops. The further I go, the more I see that the question of deacons is viewed differently from one country to another.

I wrote a memorandum for the French bishops (insistently requested by Mgr Gouet and Fr Daniélou) on the chapters *De Populo Dei* and *De laicis*.

---

ology Faculty in the Dominican College in Ottawa; Council expert during the last two Sessions; very involved in ecumenical dialogue, he was later to become Vice-President of the WCC Faith and Order section.

1.   Richard-Molard (cf above, page 156, note 3).
2.   Guy Le Roy de la Tournelle, French Ambassador to the Holy See.

Sunday 6 October 1963

Telephone call from Mgr Garrone: the work of collating the amendments has got off to a good start. He asked me to prepare one or two paragraphs on Tradition, to be inserted into the *De Ecclesia*. He is reasonably hopeful that this insertion will be taken into consideration. But I am far from being in a state to do any kind of work. Mgr Garrone was very impressed by my two books on Tradition and he thinks it impossible to omit from the *De Ecclesia* this aspect of the reality that the living Tradition is.

In the afternoon, outing with Féret and Liégé, Cullman and H Roux, to Rocca di Papa. At the last minute, Mgr Philips, who happened to be passing, joined us. When conversing with the Observers, one reaches immediately a level of problems beyond the system, whereas amongst ourselves we easily remain at the level of improvements within the system. Basically, without ecumenical dialogue, there can be no complete renewal through a recovery of the sources.

Monday 7 October 1963

Cardinal Siri:[1] on episcopal collegiality. He granted that it existed. However 1) the concept of a college is a juridical concept: it implies solidarity; 2) the basis of collegiality is to be found in the schema: Peter is the principle of unity, and so the bishops have no authority except with and under the Roman pontiff. The college is such because it is *cum Petro* [with Peter]: Peter does not receive from the college but the college receives from Peter (teaching of Vatican I). The crucial point is in the relationship between the college and Peter's successor. One cannot deduce from collegiality anything that would diminish the primacy.

Cardinal Léger.[2] Importance of Chapter II. He expressed the wish that there would be a clear statement of how one is aggregated to the episcopal college: the *munus* [function] of bishops in relation to the universal Church (*ex officio*) should be better expressed, in the sense of *Fidei donum*.[3]

The chapter on the bishops should retain the riches of Chapter I: Christ present and acting in the Church through the bishops.

The idea of service, which is well expressed, should also find expression in titles. Titles, insignia etc. should be reviewed in this sense: they are obstacles to the Gospel.

---

1. *AS* II/II, 222–223.
2. *AS* II/II, 223–225.
3. The encyclical on the Missions promulgated by Pius XII on 12 April 1957.

Cardinal König:[1] the schema says nothing about how collegiality is exercised outside of an ecumenical council. The schema says nothing new, nothing other than what is traditional.

The formula: Church on the foundation of Peter and the Apostles is in no way dangerous.

Cardinal Döpfner:[2] On the question of the diaconate. The text should be left as it is. It is to some extent a backward step from the Council of Trent . . . The text imposes nothing; it simply keeps open a possibility which may be important in some regions, where there is a shortage of priests. Does the text pose a threat to celibacy? Clearly, care would need to be taken that this does not become a solution for men called to the priestly ministry but unable to remain celibate, but it should be available to men who have a vocation to diaconal work.

Cardinal Meyer[3] (Chicago): on the collegiality of the Apostles. All that is needed is to show more clearly that its function is to last until the end of the world (Matt 28).

Cardinal Alfrink:[4] on Eph 2:20: Ruffini is partly right, it would be better not to use this text.

Cardinal Lefebvre:[5] some seem not to see how collegiality is in accordance with the primacy and the infallibility of the pope. They are *AFRAID*, which is a bad state to be in when approaching the question. He explained that this collegiality does not diminish Vatican I in any way. Any more than Matthew 18 takes anything away from Matthew 16, or Matthew 28 . . . A psychological intervention designed to liberate some spirits and provide a better basis for unanimity on this question.

Cardinal Rugambwa:[6] something should be added about solicitude for all the Churches being given by the very consecration of bishops: he cited the pre-twelfth century rite.

The missionary idea is not sufficiently present THROUGHOUT the text; he proposed quite a number of specific corrections or additions in this sense.

Maximos IV[7] (it is not true that he was obliged to speak in Latin; Cardinal Tisserant merely asked him to provide a translation into Latin at the end of his intervention in French).

---

1. *AS* II/II, 225–227.
2. *AS* II/II, 227–230.
3. *AS* II/II, 230–232.
4. *AS* II/II, 232–233.
5. *AS* II/II, 233–235.
6. *AS* II/II, 235–238.
7. Intervention given in French, *AS* II/II, 238–240. It is followed in the *Acta*, by its translation into Latin, *AS* II/II, 240–242.

Complete Vatican I. Several passages need to be further improved.

The only head of the Church is Christ: the Roman Pontiff is the head of the episcopal college as Peter was head of the Apostolic college.

Do not transfer to the universal plane and to the doctrinal plane what was a fact of history in the West: the nomination of bishops by the pope.

I was away for a while (two bishops).

Mgr Florit:[1] on the sacramentality of the episcopate.

On collegiality: its relationship to primacy has not been sufficiently shown .

De Smedt:[2] pastoral action requires a clearer awareness of collegiality, a wider exercise of collegiality, so that Peter can more effectively confirm his brethren, so that the supreme union in the priesthood of Christ can be better realised. This corresponds to the present situation which, for the first time since Pentecost, permits the unity of the Apostolic body to be made actual.

If a wider collegiality calls for a certain internationalisation of the Curia, that is in no sense due to anti-Roman and anti-Italian feeling: a ballad of devotion to Rome.

Zazinović[3] (Yugoslavia) appealed to early Christianity: Chalcedon. The letter to Flavian[4] did not prevent the Fathers of that Council from examining it in the light of the norms of the faith . . . Our text should contain something along the lines of these facts.

He proposed that a Council be held regularly and have authority over the Curia.

Beck:[5] there is no exposition of the New Testament priesthood for priests. This is a lacuna. He suggested a new introduction to No. 15 with these ideas:

unicus sacerdos [the only priest]: Jesus Christ (Hebrews).

The basis of his priesthood is the hypostatic union. No other priesthood, no other sacrifice. However, Christ left a sacrament of his sacrifice and of his priesthood (Council of Trent).

Christ wished this sacrifice and this priesthood to remain among human beings.

Van Dodewaard[6] (Haarlem) in the name of the Dutch conference of bishops: on collegiality. He showed that it is OF DIVINE RIGHT and that its

---

1. *AS* II/II, 259–261.
2. *AS* II/II, 263–265.
3. *AS* II/II, 266–268.
4. Pope Leo I's *Tome to Flavian*.
5. George A Beck, Bishop of Salford (England), member of the Conciliar Commission on Religious; he was to become Archbishop of Liverpool in 1964, *AS* II/II, 268–270.
6. *AS* II/II, 270–272.

power is not DELEGATED by the pope (drawing support from Canon 227).

Accordingly he proposed some corrections.

There were a further twenty fathers down to speak!!!

In the coach on the return journey, Mgr Renard: he is to speak about the priesthood. It was agreed that I should let him have a text on the subject.

It takes longer to get from St Peter's to the Angelicum than to go by plane from Rome to Zurich!

Visit from Mgr Garrone at 3 pm about the question of a paragraph on Tradition to be inserted into the *De Ecclesia*.

Visit from Fr Colombier[1] (international JAC).

Recording for Irish Radio. I prepared texts on the particular Churches, on the priesthood (for Mgr Renard), on the question of *ex sese*.

Tuesday 8 October 1963

Syriac Mass. Tappouni. Rather heavy going, and too long.

Report on Chapter II of the Liturgy, and voting. In the interval, the interventions on Chapter II began.

> A Spanish cardinal:[2] Cardinal Gracias[3] (many things; people were speaking to me . . . The cardinal asked in particular that the essentially missionary nature of the Church be given expression).

Mgr Philips told me that yesterday evening there was a meeting of the sub-commission for the classification of amendments. It had been heavy going: we are once again up against the same mentality and the same obstruction from those on the other side: Tromp dominated and when he arrived he was referring to the stupidities heard in the *Aula*. This will be my siege of Saragossa: line by line and word by word!

> The cardinal from Peru[4] in the name of the Peruvian Conference of Bishops and of some other South American bishops. IN FAVOUR of the diaconate; he stated the reasons IN FAVOUR, and replied to the objections made. With respect to celibacy, leave the text as it is; make it clear that the decision rests with the episcopal conferences.

---

1. Pierre Colombier, OP, of the Province of France, Chaplain General to MIJARC (Mouvement international de la jeunesse agricole et rurale catholique [International movement of young Catholic rural and farm workers).
2. B de Arriba y Castro, *AS* II/II, 308–309.
3. *AS* II/II, 310–313.
4. Landázuri Ricketts, *AS* II/II, 314–316.

Cardinal Suenens:[1] in favour of the permanent diaconate. He cited the New Testament, early tradition and the liturgy. THE CHURCH HAS A SACRAMENTAL STRUCTURE. He refuted the objection based on the fact that one could entrust to lay people the functions envisaged for deacons. Its implementation to be adapted to varying regions and circumstances. He listed the cases in which a diaconate would be indicated.

Very strong text, but too long. He suggested that the issue be referred to the episcopal conferences.

I missed Staffa's intervention:[2] there is only one head in the Church; collegiality would be against the primacy.

Mgr Gori,[3] Latin 'patriarch' of Jerusalem had spoken in the same sense a little earlier.

Mgr Rupp:[4] there is no indication who the members of the college are. ALL the bishops, even titular ones. He made a very strong positive argument.

Mgr Heuschen,[5] Auxiliary in Liège: the patristic tradition on the Apostles as foundation, as FOUNDERS. The idea of the Apostolic sees.

(great attention paid by the audience).

Vote on *emendatio 5* [a] of Chapter II of the schema *De Liturgia*. Results were given for votes already taken. I did not write them down.

Mgr Klostermann[6] told me that there was a meeting yesterday of the *De regimine Diocesium* [on the Government of Dioceses][7] Commission. He was not happy about it. Mgr Carli, who is against collegiality, had been elected rapporteur of this commission. So it will be difficult to harmonise the text with that of Chapter II of *De Ecclesia*.

Mgr Charue:[8] the Scriptural arguments for Christ's will to institute an Apostolic college, and for it to be the foundation of the Church.

Text given with great emphasis and clarity, and listened to with great

---

1. *AS* II/II, 317–319.
2. D Staffa, *AS* II/II, 323–324.
3. Alberto Gori, OFM, Italian, Latin Patriarch of Jerusalem, member of the Commission on the Eastern Churches appointed by the Pope, *AS* II/II, 320–322.
4. *AS* II/II, 329–331.
5. Joseph Heuschen, elected a member of the Doctrinal Commission at the end of the Second Session, *AS* II/II, 331–333.
6. Ferdinand Klostermann, of the diocese of Linz, was Professor of Pastoral Theology at the Catholic Theology Faculty at the University of Vienna.
7. More precisely, the reference is to the Commission on Bishops and on the Government of Dioceses.
8. *AS* II/II, 335–338.

attention in spite of how late it was. He ended by quoting words of Paul VI.

Mgr Guyot asked to speak to me for a moment. He would like priests to be the subject of a chapter following on the *De Episcopis*. He asked me to think about it.

Mgr Martin would be prepared to make the intervention that I would like made about *ex sese,* but he is afraid that it will be too late to put his name down. I am pursuing this important question.

I have been told that the Germans would like to remove the word *potestas* [power] from Chapter II and replace it with the word *munus* [function].

At 4.30 pm, at the Secretariat (for unity). Report by Mgr Philips on Chapter II of the *De Ecclesia*.

Lukas Vischer: on No. 14. In antiquity, the link between the episcopacy and the celebration of the Eucharist was very close. It would seem that today simple priests are closer than bishops to the bishops of the early days.

Greater emphasis on the Eucharist would pave the way for a better theology of the local Church. There is too little said about the action of the Holy Spirit on the ministers.

Canon Pawley: in the Catholic Church there is a certain hesitancy about the episcopacy. The pope can intervene in dioceses, the cardinals who for many years were not bishops; prelatures; episcopacy bestowed merely as a mark of honour for its recipient; prelatures *nullius*; the presbyterian system that one finds in the religious Orders.

Schmemann: there is a certain pluralism in the structure of the Church, which is not reflected here at all: there are other primacies . . . and about *ex sese*.

The document seems to be continually discussing the episcopacy as a concession and every absolute statement is still FOR the pope. Each statement on the episcopacy is related to the pope and his power.

Cullmann's reaction was similar to Schmemann's.

Some preliminary questions, which remained unresolved for Protestants, are here deemed to have been resolved.

Of what ORDER is the primacy of Peter in the New Testament? Was it the primacy of Peter among the other apostles while Jesus was still alive? After Christ's resurrection? After Peter had left Jerusalem?

The succession: the bishops succeed to the Apostles, but in a totally different order. An Apostle is an eye-witness of the Resurrection.

Nissiotis attacked the analogy. I do not quite see how he applied his criticism to the problem under discussion. It is about the succession of Peter and the image of the stone, the rock.

Mgr Philips replied to each question or group of questions.

Mgr Borovoj: the Council is a local council of the Roman Church. It is very delicate for us Observers to say what we approve of or disapprove of: one would think that there was nothing else.

Generalities: we have to make the Roman Catholic point of view comprehensible to our Church, and vice versa. He approved of the insertion of a chapter *De populo Dei*, and the one on the hierarchy after it. That would be to follow a historical order and an order from the bottom to the top.

On the question of collegiality, his Church will ask him: where are the patriarchs in all that . . . Now there is no question of this. The bishops of Antioch, Alexandria and Jerusalem are successors of the Apostles and even of Peter: they are very close to the bishop of Rome . . .

He spoke at length with eloquence and gesticulations.

A representative of the Church of Mar Thoma[1] saw a contradiction between a pope who can do everything on his own and collegiality.

On the way back, it took thirty-five minutes to cross Piazza Venezia!

The weather is hideous, rainy and stormy. I cannot walk well and finish every half-day 'exhausted'.[2]

Wednesday 9 October 1963

(44th General Congregation). I handed to Mgr Martin a text on *ex sese*. He has put his name down for this question.

Cardinal Liénart[3] in the name of more than sixty French bishops: one felt a kind of antinomy between the primacy and the episcopal college. All one needs to do is to seek out what Jesus wanted to do and what the Acts show us of the early Church. Peter has the primacy but he is always IN the college. '*Nec collegium apostolicum a potestate coregendi cum Petro destitutum est*' [The Apostolic college is not bereft of the power of governing in union with Peter]. The Eleven exercised their power collegially with Peter. If one were to look at the authorities from a juridical point of view, there would be competition, but not if what is in question are service and responsibilities.

Cardinal Richaud:[4] *De diaconatu* [On the diaconate]: he endorsed what Cardinal Suenens had said. He believes that the restoration of the diaconate would be likely to promote priestly vocations (he quoted lots of examples and banalities, but it may have been useful).

---

1. CP Mathew, Professor at the Union Christian College, Alwaye, Kerala (South India).
2. {In English in the original.}
3. *AS* II/II, 342–344.
4. *AS* II/II, 346–347.

Mgr Felici[1] said that some of the Fathers had added a question to the vote they had given concerning article 42 of *De S Liturgia* (communion under both kinds). They would have preferred to distinguish or separate a first vote on the actual principle of the restoration of this practice. But the Council of Presidents replied.

Mgr Añoveros[2] in the name of several of the Fathers on No. 15, with reference to priests. It would be better to say more about them. Arguments from Scripture and tradition are called for. The priesthood should be related to the priesthood of Christ and not merely to the fullness of the bishop.

Mgr Blanchet:[3] asked about the weight of the texts and the theological note (he could have said what he said—which he said very well—in three minutes!).

Mgr Conway[4] (Armagh): *cap. II in genere mihi placet* [In general, I approve of Chapter II]. But there is a serious omission on the question of priests and of the presbyterate. His speech made a great impression. But why do the speakers feel they must fill in their ten minutes when two or three would suffice?

Mgr Martínez[5] (Zamora, Spain): Do not give room to errors that have already been condemned. Keep the full truth of the hierarchy (long exposition).

Šeper:[6] The Commission on the Sacraments had prepared a schema which mentioned the DIACONATE. There were so many petitions!

Mgr Weber[7] on the Apostolic college in the New Testament (people were not really listening as they have already heard all that).

Mgr Hurley:[8] the bishop possesses pastoral leadership. This should be mentioned. Unfortunately, renewals have not come to any great extent from the bishops . . .

Mgr Sigaud[9] (Brazil) proposed a theology of the bishop and of collegiality. He distinguished between collegial acts (councils) and collective actions (episcopal conferences). Against the idea of a sort of permanent

---

1. *AS* II/II, 347–348.
2. Antonio Añoveros Ataún, Coadjutor Bishop of Cadiz and Ceuta (Spain), *AS* II/II, 348–350.
3. *AS* II/II, 352–353.
4. William Conway, new Archbishop of Armagh (Ireland), President of the Conference of Irish Bishops: he was to be elected member of the Commission on the Discipline of the Clergy and of the Christian People at the end of the Second Session, and created cardinal on 22 February, 1965, *AS* II/II, 354–355.
5. E Martínez Gonzáles, *AS* II/II, 355–358.
6. *AS* II/II, 358–360.
7. *AS* II/II, 361–363.
8. *AS* II/II, 364–366.
9. *AS* II/II, 366–369.

synod of bishops appointed by the other bishops who would direct the Church collegially with the pope. Equally against a permanent national council. He suggested corrections to pages 24 and 25.

D'Agostino[1] (Italy): The origin of the hierarchy should have been shown more clearly. He proposed a number of corrections, including the deletion of the citation of Ephesians 2:20. On the diaconate, he allied himself with Bacci and insisted on the obligation to celibacy. There is no reference to the duty of priests to obey their bishop. In favour of the primacy of Peter: no college without a head.

Michael Browne[2] (Ireland): nothing is said about DIOCESES.

Mgr Doumith:[3] By his consecration, a bishop receives pastoral power which includes the powers of government, teaching and celebrating. That comes from the tradition and from the liturgy: he cited texts. Consecration includes mission. Consecration is made *ad Ecclesiam* [for Church] and formerly always for a specific church. The canonical mission is *tantum ad moderamen potestatis, sed potestatem ipsam non confert nec aufert* [only for the management of power, but it neither confers nor withdraws power].

Mgr Franić:[4] on the diaconate: Sixteen out of the 21 Latin-rite bishops in Yugoslavia deem it inopportune: how would they be kept under discipline? The proposed text should be deleted. He said that there had been no vote on this point at the Theological Commission and that the text had been inserted without a vote.

On the relationship between episcopate and the primacy: the schema contains a good *via media*, but there are some expressions that obscure the rights of the primacy.

No distinction has been made between the foundation of the Church *ratione doctrinae* [by reason of doctrine] and its foundation *ratione iurisdictionis* [by reason of jurisdiction].

The text of Ephesians 2:20 is doubtful and one ought to delete mention of the Apostles as foundation (he was listened to attentively, in spite of the lateness of the hour).

Vote on correction 9 to the liturgy schema: *non placet*		67
— — — — — — 10	— —	46
— — — — — — 11	— —	96
(= on Communion under both kinds)		
— — — — — — 12	— —	14

---

1. *AS* II/II, 370–372.
2. Michael Browne, Bishop of Galway and Kilmacduagh (Ireland), *AS* II/II, 373–374.
3. *AS* II/II, 376–377.
4. *AS* II/II, 378–380.

After the Congregation in St Peter's, I went to lunch at S Tommaso di Villanova. I had a dreadful headache. The meal was quite a pain for me. Afterwards, at coffee, Mgr Gračanin,[1] whom I had not seen since our time at les Carmes in 1924!

After conversation with Féret and Liégé, we left. I was hoping to spend two hours working at the Angelicum in order to complete my comments on the *De Populo Dei*; but it took us more than an hour to get nowhere; it was impossible to get to Piazza Venezia via the Corso. We turned back and went to see Fr Chenu. Too little time, alas. He was in quite good form, having some journalistic work to do. Féret then drove me to the Vatican for the Theological Commission at 5.30 pm. We all met up once again. Very few experts and (nearly) all friends.

Cardinal Ottaviani said: the question has been asked whether the Co-ordinating Commission has the power to impose a new order on the schema.[2] They have replied that the bishops are FREE to accept it or not.

Mgr Parente gave the reasons for rejecting it. He insisted above all on the fact that it contains a parallelism between the Church and the Jewish people, which implies something both particularistic and nationalistic: and hence not very ecumenical.

Mgr Schröffer defended the plan for a special chapter *De Populo Dei*.

Mgr Florit proposed as a title: *De membrorum in Ecclesia Christi aequalitate et inaqualitate* [on the equality and inequality of the members of Christ's Church]; following that, the chapter *De S. Hierarchia* [on the Sacred Hierarchy], then the chapter *De statibus perfectionis* [on the States of Perfection] (with the text that has just been prepared by the joint Commission of Theological and Religious Life); finally the text *De Laicis* as Chapter 5.

Mgr Charue: the expression *Populus Dei* is in I Peter 2:10. Mgr Philips might be asked to explain it.

Which he did. He insisted on the usefulness of grouping together everything relating to the intermediate and pilgrim state of the Church. He also explained the reasoning behind the drafting of the chapter on the call to holiness: it was in order to avoid speaking of Religious separately. He gave reasons justifying the plan for five chapters such as he had conceived it.

I asked to be allowed to speak but was not given leave to do so: instead Fr Tromp was called upon; he wanted a division into *clerici, continentes, matrimonio iuncti* [clerics, those who live in continence, and those who are married]. – Cardinal Ottaviani hurried things along and wanted a vote on the proposition: *Utrum standum sit primitivae divisioni* [Should the original division be retained]?

Franić was in favour of a chapter *De populo Dei*, but with *De Christifidelibus* [Christ's faithful] as its heading.

A vote was taken on:

---

1. Duro (Georges) Gračanin, former pupil at the Séminaire des Carmes (Seminary of the Institut Catholique in Paris), was a professor at the Faculty of Theology in Zagreb.
2. The reference is to the inclusion of a chapter *De populo Dei*.

1) Is a new chapter required?
Result: yes = 20, no = 4.
2) What heading to give it? *Populus Dei, Christifideles.*
Schauf spoke in favour of *'Christifideles'.*
I spoke in favour of *'populus Dei'.*
Mgr Charue did likewise.
Cardinal Ottaviano would prefer *'De Christifidelibus'.*
Häring: *De populo Dei,* a social term, not an individual one.
The vote was taken:
De populo Dei: 15.
De Christifidelibus: 7.
De aequalitate et inaqualitate membrorum Christifid. = 1.[1]
The issue was settled.

Cardinal Ottaviani said that people had asked whether the *De Beata* should be kept separate, or whether it should be incorporated into the *De Ecclesia*. Cardinal Ottaviani had replied that the Co-ordinating Commission had asked for a separate schema and that Mary well deserved a schema to herself. But he had added that he would put the question to the Theological Commission.

The cardinal said that two of the Fathers and two of the *periti* should be heard. Franić RUSHED to be asked to speak in favour of a separate schema.

Ottaviani added: the schema has already been distributed!!!

Mgr McGrath spoke in favour of it being incorporated into the schema *De Ecclesia*. Several bishops had asked for this; the COUNCIL'S Theological Commission had never either discussed or approved the schema, which had come from the Preparatory Commission.

Spanedda: There should be a separate schema. Mariology belongs more to christology than to ecclesiology. Moreover, in the schema *De Ecclesia*, it is mainly the pilgrim Church and the Church militant that is under discussion.

Fr Tromp: many bishops want a link between the schema *De BVM* and the *De Ecclesia*, but they differ about how it should be conceived and where it should be placed.

Fr Balić, who had only just arrived, was invited to speak, but Mgr Doumith asked WHOSE IDEA IT WAS to produce a schema *De BVM*; if the schema says nothing new, then why a schema? Who had called for it?

That's a good question, Mgr Garrone said.

Ottaviani asked Doumith: Would the Easterners not welcome a text on the Blessed Virgin?

No, Mgr Doumith replied. They have a great devotion to the Holy Virgin, but they are quite content to venerate the *Theotokos* and would not be pleased with

---

1. Congar added to the typescript '= Franić'.

dogmatic texts: we have not yet recovered from the difficulties created by the Assumption!!!

Fr Gagnebet said: a text was produced because a great many of the bishops had asked for one!!!

When Fr Balić was called upon to speak, he READ a text: a clever SALES PATTER, but a sales patter just the same. The separated brethren and above all the Protestants are asking for a clear and doctrinal statement.

At the end, he improvised with eloquence and somewhat ridiculously. He talked and talked without being asked to stop.

Mgr Philips intervened with a few wise and conciliatory remarks; he concluded along the lines of our conversation on Sunday: after the five chapters of *De Ecclesia,* a sixth chapter entitled *De loco et munere Deiparae in Ecclesia* [On the place and function of the Mother of God in the Church] (christological basis—*Deiparae*—and designed to set forth what the faithful owe to the Virgin Mother of God, and her presence in the Church).

Mgr Garrone, speaking very calmly: in the Council, the Church is the CENTRE of interest. For love of the Virgin, it would be good that she should be set forth in connection with the Church, the centre of our work.

One would achieve the same effect, Cardinal Browne said, by placing the schema *De Beata* immediately after that the *De Ecclesia,* thus expressing the link between them. If the ecumenical movement is to achieve its aim: we must place our trust in the Virgin Mary.

Cardinal Ottaviani: that would amount to going back on the progress so far. That would cause astonishment.

Mgr Griffiths supported the Philips proposal. He recalled that there had been a request, in the *aula,* for a clarification of the devotion of the faithful to Mary and the saints.

McGrath: we are only the delegates of the Fathers of the Council; they have not expressed their opinion.

Ottaviani contradicted him fiercely. The normal course is for the Commission to propose a text and for the Fathers to comment on it. There should be a vote on the following:

1) *Schema de BVM maneat ut est* (the schema on the Blessed Virgin Mary should remain as it is)

2) *Schema de BVM fiat caput finale 'De Ecclesia'* [the schema on the Blessed Virgin Mary should become the last chapter of the schema 'On the Church'] (Philips)

3) *Quae dicuntur in schemate inserantur in Schemate de Ecclesia* [what is said in the schema should be incorporated into the schema on the Church].

That could be boiled down to two questions, said Mgr Pelletier:

Ut schema fiat intra schema de Ecclesia

– – – – – – *extra* – – – – – – – –

[The schema should be included within the schema on the Church, or should be separate from it].

Schröffer: Can one vote without having seen the *vota* of the Fathers on the matter? They ought to be seen first.

Ottaviani: the four Moderators have asked the Theological Commission for its opinion. So (after discussion), we will have a double vote:

1) *tractetur extra schema de Ecclesia*   :   9

   ----------*intra*----------------------   :   12

                                       with 2 abstentions

2) if *intra,* where?

By a show of hands, the almost unanimous decision was: as a final chapter.

The decision for a SEPARATE chapter was unanimous.

In the lift, Cardinal Ottaviani said: If Fr General (Fernandez) had remained to the end and had voted, we would have one more vote in favour of '*extra schema*'. I said: 'Was it[1] Providence, or was it the devil?'

It was a great and important meeting from the point of view of the future orientation of things. What has been played out this evening was, partly, the opening towards human beings (*De populo Dei*) and the soundness of a mariology cured of its maximalist canker.

I returned here at 8 pm, exactly twelve hours since I had left my room, absolutely at the end of my tether.

Thursday 10 October 1963

Before the congregation began, I saw Mgr Huyghe about the chapter on Religious. He told me how that had been dealt with at the Commission on Religious and how he had succeeded in bringing together eleven members who are against the current and who hope to prevent certain rather undesirable things.

I also saw Cardinal Liénart and told him privately how the speed with which Cardinal Tisserant intones the *Adsumus* is catastrophic. He must have told him because today Cardinal Tisserant tried to slow down, which only emphasised the cacophony!

Cardinal Câmara[2] (Brazil): in the name of one hundred and thirty bishops
    of Brazil:
    There are too many repetitions about the primacy of the pope. In
    favour of collegiality being by divine right on the basis of consecration.
Cardinal Cento,[3] on the diaconate. Desirable in certain countries. But the
    sacred law of celibacy should always be retained.

---

1. Congar added to the typescript: 'his departure'.
2. *AS* II/II, 388–389.
3. Cardinal Fernando Cento, Grand Penitentiary and President of the Conciliar Com-

Mgr Slipyj[1] (there was applause before he spoke): he will not speak this morning, but tomorrow.

Galea, from Malta:[2] it needs to be completed: there is a distinction between hierarchy of jurisdiction and hierarchy of order.

The order needs to be improved: No. 14 and No. 15 should be switched around. More precision required in No. 13: the power of the Apostles and of the bishops.

Mgr Schick[3] in the name of the German—and Scandinavian—speaking Fathers of the Council:

The concept of the presbyterate should be better expressed, and the concept of local churches: the parish, not in the administrative sense, but the theological one = the frequent meaning of ἐκκλησία. True representation of the universal Church.

Mgr Jaeger[4] (Paderborn): some remarks about collegiality.

1. The prerogatives of the Apostles were different from those of the bishops as their successors.

2. The biblical foundations of collegiality: *Joh. ut maneat vobiscum in aeternum* [to be with you for ever (John 14:16)].

3. On the relationship between the supreme power of the pope and that of the college. It is an original form of power for which there is no analogy in human societies.

Mgr Descuffi[5] (Izmir): in No. 19, the doctrine of the office of teaching in its relationship with the power of the pope. Very important from the ecumenical point of view: he suggested that a paragraph deal exhaustively with the Mystery of the Church and that the *ex sese* be explained, as the formula lends itself to undesirable interpretations.

The pope has infallibility FROM THE CHURCH; hence *sensus Ecclesiae cognosci debet* [the understanding of the Church ought to be recognised].

The word CONSENSUS is ambiguous; it would be better to use the word ASSENSUS [assent]. *Consensus* IS REQUIRED. He suggested a text.

---

mission on the Apostolate of the Laity, *AS* II/II, 393.

1. Josyf Slipyj, Ukrainian Archbishop and Metropolitan of Lvov (USSR), member of the Conciliar Commission on the Eastern Churches, *AS* II/II, 393. From the time of his arrest in 1945 until his release from prison in January 1963, he had known only prison and forced labour in Siberia. He was to be created cardinal in January 1965.

2. Emanuele Galea, auxiliary bishop in Malta, *AS* II/II, 394–395.

3. Eduard Schick, Auxiliary Bishop of Fulda (Germany), member of the Commission on Bishops and the Government of Dioceses, *AS* II/II, 396–397.

4. *AS* II/II, 399–400.

5. *AS* II/II, 402–404.

Mgr Yago (Abidjan)[1] on the permanent diaconate, from the pastoral point of view.

I went to the bar. I saw a Polish bishop[2] from the Commission on the Laity, and Mgr Ménager, who told me how Fr Gagnebet had developed on the question of the episcopate . . .

Maurer, bishop from Bolivia.[3] In favour of the diaconate and for a good theological training of lay people in the faculties of theology.

Shehan (Baltimore):[4] 1) about *ex sese* (page 30), source of difficulties: needs to be better explained. He cited the text of Paul VI on a better presentation of the dogma of the Church; refer back to note 52 and to Gasser's text,[5] an affirmation of which should be inserted in the text. He proposed an addition.

2) Similarly on page 30, line 32 ff, he suggested that the word VEL [or] be replaced by ET [and] (line 14).

Mgr Ghattas,[6] of Thebes: the Council ought to set forth what can unite Christians; create a Church that is more 'catholic' in its forms of government; assert episcopal collegiality more clearly. In furtherance of this, he spoke about: a) the patriarchates; b) the creation of a kind of σύνοδος ἐνδημοῦσα (allusion to Paul VI's discourse).

This ecclesiology is entirely Latin!

VERY strong text. He demanded that the Eastern Churches be taken seriously.

Mgr Renard,[7] on priests: the concept of priesthood.

The idea of the *presbyterium* (St Ignatius, etc); link with the bishop who is the father and also the *perfector*.[8] This needed to be said.

---

1. Bernard Yago, Archbishop of Abidjan, member of the Commission on the Missions appointed during the First Session, *AS* II/II, 405–407.
2. The reference is probably to Mgr Herbert Bednorz, Coadjutor Bishop of Katowice. The other Polish bishop on this Commission, Mgr Boleslaw Kominek, was not present at the Second Session of the Council because, like twenty-four other bishops, he was not issued a passport by the Polish government.
3. José C Maurer, a German Redemptorist, Archbishop of Sucre (Bolivia), member of the Commission on Seminaries, Studies and Catholic Education, *AS* II/II, 410–412.
4. Lawrence J Shehan, Archbishop of Baltimore (United States), created cardinal in February 1965, *AS* II/II, 414–416.
5. Vincenz Gasser, Bishop of Brixen. A theologian, he played an important role at Vatican I, principally on account of the clarifications provided by his *Relatio* on Chapter IV of the Constitution *Pastor aeternus*; the note 52 mentioned here as well as the adjacent notes, are taken from this *Relatio*.
6. *AS* II/II, 416–418.
7. *AS* II/II, 418–420.
8. The one who perfects. For this expression, Renard referred to Denis the Aeropagite and St Thomas Aquinas.

Mgr Morcillo[1] (Saragossa): Only probable arguments, not clinching ones, have been adduced for episcopal collegiality. But he did nothing more than to repeat, in conceptual categories, what has already been said. He drew attention to the distinction between all of the bishops taken collectively, and the college properly so called. In his view, the existence of the college in the strict sense has not been demonstrated.

Fr Fernandez, OP:[2] 1) There are two subjects of infallibility, two subjects of the supreme power.

2) The second subject (the body of bishops) is subject to the first. It is not necessary that the college, as such, be active all the time, but only at an ecumenical council and in certain other circumstances.

3) One cannot say that, by the mere fact of their consecration, bishops possess a jurisdiction, even one subject to limitations, that extends beyond their diocese.

4) If one could institute a sort of central commission representing the bishops, it can only do what the pope asks it to do and gives it to do.

On the diaconate.

Mgr Urtasun[3] (Avignon) in favour of episcopal sacramentality: he replied to the criticisms that had been made (good text, well delivered).

Mgr Yü Pin:[4] On the permanent diaconate: reasons in FAVOUR. And possibly also married deacons.

Van den Hurk[5] in the name of thirty bishops of Indonesia:

No. 13: bishops as successors of the Apostles. But can one say that the Apostles themselves consecrated bishops as their successors? Criticised the reference to Clement's letter to the Corinthians.

No. 14: the sacramentality of the episcopate. Fine, but it should be stated that by means of it a bishop becomes a member of the college. Place the section on priests at the end.

Agreed about the diaconate. There is not unanimity among the bishops of Indonesia about celibacy.

No. 19: on the magisterium of the bishops: this is a certain doctrine. Some people say that the pope would communicate to the Council the power to judge infallibly. But

1) the pope does not COMMUNICATE his infallibility which is personal to him;

2) a power that is communicated humanly could not be infallible.

---

1. *AS* II/II, 420–422.
2. *AS* II/II, 422–424.
3. Joseph Urtasun, Archbishop of Avignon, member of the Commission on Religious, *AS* II/II, 429–430.
4. Paul Yü Pin, *AS* II/II, 430–432.
5. The Dutchman Antoine H van den Hurk, OFM Cap, Archbishop of Medan, *AS* II/II, 432–434.

On the assent owed to the magisterium: disagree, because
a) only the pope is mentioned, not the bishops;
b) the fallible magisterium is too much assimilated to the infallible magisterium;
Some further comments on details, including on the question of *potestas* = better to say *auctoritas* [authority], *munus* [function].
There is too much reference to the pope (more than 30 times!).

At the end of the General Congregation, the results of the voting on amendments 13 to 19 to Chapter II of *De S. Liturgia*. There were 315 *Non placet* for the concelebration of conventual Masses!!! I noted down the results on my copy.

At 5 pm, with His Beatitude Maximos IV and the Melkite bishops. The Patriarch drew me aside for a moment in order to say that it was absolutely essential for me not to mention Israel, as I wanted to do, in the *De populo Dei*. According to him, that would set off a massacre of Christians in the Arab countries surrounding the State of Israel. I objected that, even so, there were other very strong considerations. The Patriarch repeated three times what he had said to me. Mgr Hakim, a little later, said to to me: there will be a chapter on the Jews in the schema *De œcumenismo*; so the intervention that I wished to make in *De populo Dei* could be omitted . . .

I gave them a presentation on collegiality. I linked up different questions, including that of the final formula for the proclamation of the decrees. '*N* . . . , *sacro approbante concilio* [I, . . . , with the approval of the holy Council]. I encountered the same atmosphere as a year ago. They asked me very acute questions, but based less on scholastic categories and technique than on a real sense of the realities: the very meaning of Tradition!

We discussed the question of whether it would be possible to insert a mention of the Patriarchs in the schema *De Ecclesia*.

On the way there, the priest who had come to fetch me said that something very important is going to happen next Monday: the six patriarchs will take their places on a platform opposite the cardinals. This is the result of an approach made by the Melkites to Cardinal Bea and Cardinal Suenens, and, though them, right up to the Pope. In their report, they had based their argument on the precedent of the Council of Florence where the cardinals had been placed on the left when one enters the Church (the place of honour in the Latin Church) and the patriarchs opposite them on the right (the place of honour in the Eastern Church).

The Secretariat, when called upon to seek a solution to the problem, had suggested covering the patriarchs' current places in red instead of green; but the Melkites replied that that would not in any way be a positive response to their request and that green or red made no difference to them.

So, on Monday, they will be opposite the cardinals, close to the statue of St Peter.

After my return, from 7.30 pm to 9.30 pm, except for the time to eat supper, I worked with Frs Féret and Liégé with a view to preparing a section for *De Traditione in vita Ecclesiae* [On tradition in the life of the Church]. Fr Féret had just come from a meeting of the French bishops that had dealt with the chapter on Religious: he found Fr Daniélou extremely muddle-headed and saying all sorts of things, including such enormities as 'There are no counsels in the Gospel'.

Friday 11 October 1963

Today, at the Mass which opened the 46th General Congregation, COMMUNION of the lay *'auditores'* [auditors]. So there was COMMUNION at this Mass. We must get to the point of reading a passage from the Gospel after its enthronement!

The Moderators said that they did not want to interrupt the discussion of Chapter II, but that the Fathers can begin registering to speak on Chapter III.

> Cardinal Quiroga[1] (Compostella): on the expressions: *episcoporum coetus* [meeting of the bishops], *collegium*, etc.
>
> Mgr Slipyj [2] (applauded before he spoke): he recalled the representation of the Ukrainian Church in the Ecumenical Councils. After a long section recalling his own feelings, he gave a very Latin lesson on the pope and the bishops. The same infallibility is in the pope and in the bishops.
> He spoke of the diaconate; he went on and on, wearing everybody out. He asked for Kiev to be raised to the rank of patriarchate.
>
> Mgr Costantini[3] (Italy). On the diaconate: Begin by promoting some lay brothers in the religious orders and some members of secular institutes. On collegiality.
> Infallibility: that of the Councils is not derived from that of the pope.
>
> Mgr Talamás[4] (Mexico): in favour of the diaconate.
>
> Mgr Wittler[5] (Osnabrück): the schema does not state sufficiently the link between the power of sanctification and the power of jurisdiction.
> Episcopal consecration confers THE episcopal power which is a unity comprising several faculties (in the sense spoken of by Mgr Doumith). Half of the Fathers at Trent thought that jurisdiction was conferred together with consecration.
> He proposed a substitute text in this sense for No. 14.
>
> Mgr Cirarda[6] also on No. 14 (in the name of sixteen Spanish bishops): arguments for the sacramentality of the episcopate, but three corrections needed to be made:

---

1. Fernando Quiroga y Palacios, *AS* II/II, 441–442.
2. *AS* II/II, 442–446.
3. *AS* II/II, 447–449.
4. Manuel Talamás Camandari, Bishop of Ciudad Juárez, *AS* II/II, 450–452.
5. Helmut H Wittler, Bishop of Osnabrück (Germany), *AS* II/II, 453–455.
6. José M Cirarda Lachiondo, Auxiliary Bishop of Seville, *AS* II/II, 457–458.

I Peter should not be cited in this sense.

Agreed with what Wittler said about the unity of powers.

One should not speak of CHARACTER in relation to the episcopate.

Mgr Nicodemo[1] (Bari): is everything sufficiently certain for the Constitution *De Ecclesia* to be adopted? Collegiality as it has been presented? Theological notions and juridical ones are being mixed together. It has more than one form: the ecumenical council, etc.

The word covers a number of things.

Mgr Gouyon:[2] on the tradition of the second and third centuries. In relation to no . . .

(=Colson[3]) (very studied but very unnatural pronunciation). The relationships between bishops and Churches (letters) which indicate an awareness of responsibility for the other churches.

Local councils.

The collegial character of episcopal consecrations.

Mgr Flores:[4] (Barbastro): hardly anyone is listening!

De Vito:[5] distinction between the diaconate as a permanent office in the Church, which would require a whole lot of conditions regarding ecclesiastical dignity, and diaconal offices which could be entrusted, by way of exception, to anyone.

He suggested a whole lot of considerations from a narrow and entirely clerical point of view.

Mgr Lefebvre:[6] superior of the Holy Ghost Fathers: the dangers of collegiality (episcopal conferences), including for the authority of bishops, each one in his diocese.

Canon Moeller came to chat with me. He asked me in particular my opinion on the Pope's designation of a new member of the Theological Commission, in place of Mgr Peruzzo, the Infant of Agrigento. Cardinal Suenens had asked him for names. I said that it MUST be either an Easterner (and I mentioned the following: 1) Edelby; 2) Zoghby; 3) Hermaniuk) or a black African: but which of them has sufficient theological training or disposition?

---

1. *AS* II/II, 459–461.
2. *AS* II/II, 461–463.
3. Colson was a specialist in the ecclesiology of the early centuries and Congar had just written a preface for and published one of his works in the 'Unam Sanctam' collection: *L'Épiscopat catholique. Collégialité et primauté dans les trois premiers siècles de l'Église,* 'Unam Sanctam', 43 (Paris: Cerf, 1963).
4. Jaime Flores Martin, Bishop of Barbastro (Spain), *AS* II/II, 464–466.
5. *AS* II/II, 469–471.
6. *AS* II/II, 471–472.

I asked Moeller to say to Cardinal Suenens that thought needs to be given to the form of the conclusion, in order to replace the bad '*N . . . , sacro approbante concilio. . . .*'

> Mgr Boillon[1] on the priesthood of the bishop: it should be linked with that *OF CHRIST.*
>
> Mgr Paul Rusch[2] on behalf of the bishops of Germany and Austria on collegiality: it is traditional.
>> It includes a moral element and a juridical element.
>
> Mgr Pont y Gol:[3] 1) on the word and the idea of *potestas* [power] in this chapter. He gave statistics of its usage; there is far too much of *potestas* at the expense of the idea of service and responsibility.
>> 2) The ecumenical aspect should not be forgotten, even in Chapter II. The true bishops of the separated Churches, above all the Orthodox, should not be forgotten. The share that they have in the power of Christ must be explained.
>
> Auxiliary of Bologna[4] (Bettazzi): the idea that consecration confers all the powers and that it brings the bishop into the episcopal body (Dossetti's ideas) should be better expressed.
>> *Licet iunior in episcopatu et italicus* [Although young in the episcopate and an Italian . . .] he wished to cite some testimonies: he referred to the testimony of Turrecremata,[5] and those of the Council of Trent (the very defenders of the Papacy!) and in particular the future Innocent IX.
>> Trent recognised that at his consecration the bishop receives his episcopal powers.
>> The whole Dossetti-Alberigo dossier[6] given at great speed and with fire.

I had lunch at the Ethiopian College at 1 pm, having been invited by my friend from Cambridge days, Kidane Mariam.[7] In the delightful situation of the Vatican

---

1. *AS* II/II, 476–477.
2. *AS* II/II, 477–478.
3. *AS* II/II, 479–481.
4. Luigi Bettazzi, *AS* II/II, 484–487.
5. The reference is to Cardinal Juan de Torquemada (*circa* 1388–1468) OP, theologian and canonist, and not his brother Tomas who was the Inquisitor General of Spain.
6. A memorandum had in fact been prepared by Dossetti and Alberigo, initially with a view to a spoken intervention by Cardinal Lercaro; cf Marie-Dominique Chenu, *Notes quotidiennes au Concile* (Paris: Cerf, 1995), 142, note 1.
7. Kidane Mariam Ghebray, diocesan priest of the Eparchy of Adigrat in Ethiopia, whom Congar had met at the Dominican house in Cambridge. He was at this time in Rome as secretary to his bishop at the Second Session of the Council.

gardens, and on rising ground, it is a little island of peace and silence. After lunch, lecture in Latin to the students and to three bishops on ecumenism: this does not exist at all in Abyssinia. I tried to instil the beginnings of it in the heart of the younger generation.

At 3.30 pm at the Redemptorists (31 Via Merulana), weekly meeting to coordinate the interventions, or 'conciliar strategy', according to Mgr Elchinger who leads these meetings. Present were: Mgr Volk and his auxiliary,[1] Mgr Musty, Mgr Guano, Mgr Garrone, Dom Butler, Philips, Frs Rahner, Féret, Liégé, Grillmeier, Martelet, Smulders, Martimort, Laurentin, Ratzinger, Häring, Semmelroth, Daniélou and two or three more. We discussed the following:

1) The co-ordination of the interventions on Chapters II and III. We assessed the remaining difficulties which are holding some people back, namely the concept of collegiality and above all that of the relationship between the papal primacy and the college of bishops.

2) The question of the overall vote on Chapter II of *De S Liturgia*. On the formal and pressing advice of Martimort, endorsed by Philips, it was decided that what was needed was, first of all, to do everything to secure approval of the chapter at once and not to throw votes away by voting '*iuxta modum*'. Such votes have to be justified by a concrete proposal for a change and have no chance of securing a change in the text (which one could not be sure would be a better one), unless there are many such proposals in the same sense and at the risk of getting the vote on the text postponed indefinitely.

3) The question of the *De Beata*. The English had prepared a text which Dom Butler handed round and which has already been widely distributed. It seems essential to get it signed as soon as possible. However, there is also a Chilean text. A small team was appointed to look into this.

During the meeting, I realised that I had forgotten my glasses: probably in St Peter's. I went back there. But the roads were sealed off because the Pope was due to come to St Mary Major: hence one of those Roman traffic jams in which one advances 20 cm at a time. At St Peter's I was sent from one place to another; you have to walk kilometres! I could manage no more. In the end, accompanied by a truly helpful and obliging gendarme, I found my glasses at the gendarmes' station in the Cortile di san Damaso. I returned here in a state of complete exhaustion to receive the visit of Fr Cottier, of a Brazilian priest (he told me that the bishops of Brazil do not want to hear talk either of co-redemption or of mediation by Mary) and of a Polish bishop (Vicar Capitular of Cracow[2]): the latter gave me some texts which he had prepared and which are fairly confused, full of imprecisions, not to say of errors or defects. But I am pleased to enter into contact with the Polish episcopate. The Polish bishops, of whom there are twenty-four at the Council (out of the forty-five who ought to have come) received the texts only in September.

---

1. Joseph Reuss.
2. Karol Wojtyła.

They were unable to bring a single theologian with them and are pretty well at a loss, very little or very poorly in touch with what is going on. That is why none of them has yet spoken at the Council.

Saturday 12 October 1963

I read the English text proposed for the *De Beata*. It is a fine text! I hope it will be approved, and WITHOUT DISCUSSION!

I prepared and typed two little memoranda on Collegiality and on the Primacy and the power of the bishops (to be communicated to Philips, Rahner and Garrone).

Visit from Jimenez-Urresti with another Spanish theologian. We went through all the questions. They told me that some of the Spanish theologians accept that there was a college of Apostles, but not a college of bishops. In that case, where is the permanence and the *eadem forma* [same form] that are essential to apostolicity?

I took my memorandum round to the Belgian College, but it was too much for me and I returned unable to move my right leg at all: I had to push it with my hand in order to make it take a little step. I saw Rahner, who was typing the text they had produced this morning in order to print 2,000 copies before Sunday evening.[1] He told me that the Moderators will call for separate votes on:

> episcopal collegiality;
> the sacramentality of episcopal consecration;
> the diaconate.

Mgr Prignon told me again that it was at the Pope's instigation that I had been made Master of Sacred Theology; that as from 4 November, there will be simultaneous translation into five languages, for eight hundred Fathers to begin with. Finally, without going into details, which perhaps he himself did not know, he told me something about the audience which the four Moderators had with the Pope last Thursday. The Pope is extraordinarily well-informed about everything and open to everything. He does not want to intervene in the Council and wants everything to come from the Council itself. He has a plan. He is preparing some sensational steps, of a kind, Cardinal Suenens said, that the press will report with banner headlines: the other cardinals spoke of a 'historic day'. They were all very optimistic.

I spoke again to Mgr Prignon about the final formula of proclamation: this ought to be an act of the College with the Pope at its head.

Afternoon, working for a while with Féret and Liégé in order to prepare a section on the priesthood.

---

1. This was a text prepared with Martelet and Ratzinger: *De primatu et collegio Episcoporum in regimine totius Ecclesiae.*

Evening, supper with Küng and Feiner. Küng, full of intelligence, health, youth and insistent demands. He is extremely critical.

1) About the *De S Liturgia* and the way Martimort has acted. He ought to have begun with proposal that the Canon of the Mass BE PROCLAIMED out loud: '*Mortem Domini annuntiabitis*' [You shall proclaim the death of the Lord (I Cor 11:26)] . . . But Martimort adopted a tactic of effectiveness with a view to secondary practical results, instead of concentrating on the essential, which would have brought all the rest in its train.

2) Above all about the *De Ecclesia* and Philips. In Küng's view, it is full of naiveties and banalities which are absolutely not up to scratch with respect to what intellectual honesty before the facts and the texts, and the necessary dialogue, or simply the inevitable contact with the Others, demands. 'What am I going to say to my Protestant colleagues in Tubingen?'

Küng charges at things, he goes straight ahead like an arrow. He is the exact opposite of Martimort. The latter devotes himself to the 'possible', to the tactical: he is a reformist, he seeks to secure what is possible; Küng demands insistently, like a revolutionary. I believe that I myself am between the two. I am sensitive to what has ALREADY been done, and that it is fantastic. We have to see WHERE we have come from, the road already travelled. In a year, Philips has taken Tromp's place, Häring and Hirschmann that of Lio, Butler that of Balić, etc, etc. Everywhere, the *Ecclesia* is in the process of putting the Curia back in its place. So one should see what had been possible and what is possible. The Catholic Church includes ALSO Ottaviani and Parente, Tromp and the archbishop of Benevento.[1] Küng does not take into consideration anything other than the exigency of the facts, of the texts, of what they impose as questions and as conclusions. He said: 'Ottaviani is in no way a theologian, he knows nothing about the problems presented by the texts and present-day studies, he ought to be replaced.' Maybe so but, in fact, he was there! And replaced BY WHOM? Küng told me that this question of replacing Ottaviani as President of the Theological Commission had been raised with the Pope at the same time as the new regulations were proposed. In Küng's opinion, a great many of the 'experts', who are strangers to the theological science or rather disciplines of today, ought also to be eliminated. But in the meantime, they were there and they are still there.

Faced with Küng, I once again realise the fairly horrifying degree to which I myself have been too timid, especially during the preparatory period, but even after that. I content myself with expressing my opinion, but I do not defend it, I do not stay with it. There is, on my part, a health problem: I no longer have the strength. Have I ever had it? In spite of appearances, I have always been at the end of my VERY LIMITED resources. There is also a question of mystique. I believe profoundly in: 'Each one has what has been given to him. The servant is quite content to be there, outside in the hallway, and to hear the wedding songs'. There

---

1. Reggio Calabria. Cf Above 22 November 1962 and 3 December 1962.

is also the question of destiny: SINCE 1938, I have been UNCEASINGLY under suspicion, pursued, reprimanded, limited, crushed. Finally, there is a question of the extremely keen awareness I have that that some time-lags are necessary and that an active patience has strength. Küng is to some extent an impatient man. He has to be. It is a dangerous position. He worries me a bit, all the more so in that he is so sensitive to Protestant reactions, that he is successful and that he is surrounded by the prestige of success, and lastly that he has not the support of a community of religious and regular life. As for me, I believe profoundly in time-lags, in the necessary stages. I have SEEN that my conviction is TRUE. I have also seen so much progress made in thirty years! I have such a strong feeling that a huge body, such as the Church is needs to move in a measured rhythm . . .

Of course, I am also aware of WHAT IS MISSING in the schema and in the work of the Council. For years I have realised that at no time has the Word of God been encountered in an entirely new and fresh way. There has not been a REAL return to the sources. There have been good elements of Scripture and Tradition, providing the people of today with more than one intention and one method: but these elements have done no more than improve in some points and in certain details on existing expositions based, essentially, on the classical system alone. Exegetes have played almost no part in the work: those from Jerusalem and the Biblical Institute have been set aside. Nothing will redeem this fault, except per-haps the future. For myself, for a long time, all renewal has seemed to me to be linked with a high-level theological teaching which is truly animated by and im-bued with RESEARCH. In Rome, there is no research, except in some peripheral sectors, limited, and purely technical: Byzantine sigillography and *alia huiusmodi* [other things of the kind]. It is by the reform of clerical education that the reform of the Church will really begin. Once that has been achieved, everything will have been gained within one or two generations. But it remains true that we could never give to theology the status that the Protestants give it: it can never be PURE research, without conditions, nor purely personal research, without communion or norms . . .

Sunday 13 October 1963
In the afternoon, an outing as far as the Lido d'Ostia with the four Brothers of Taizé, Chenu, Féret and Liégé. Brother Roger Schutz told me about his audiences with the last three popes. Painful impression of Pius XII who, only towards the end, seemed somewhat open. Brother Schutz seems to me not yet to have realised quite how open Paul VI is. He far preferred John XXIII: a man of God, pure and simple. However, from the ecumenical point of view, John XXIII seems not to have had very structured ideas. He had begun with the idea that Taizé was a min-iature Oxford movement. At the last audience with the Brothers from Taizé, in February 1963 I think, he had said that he understood that there was no question of conversion for Taizé, and he understood this path, which was that of ecumen-

ism. He was severe about the Holy Office people and said of Cardinal Ottaviani: 'He is a child'.

The people from the Holy Office seem to the Taizé Brothers to have still understood NOTHING, even today. A few days ago, Ottaviani said to them: Look at the splendour of the Catholic Church!!!!

The Brothers of Taizé are fairly severe about the immobility of the Orthodox, which does not at all get involved in a positive way.

Monday 14 October 1963

(47th General Congregation). I saw Mgr Maury (Dakar) and Duval (Algiers), our French cardinals. I offered Cardinal Lercaro the first copy I received of my *Église servante et pauvre*.[1] I greeted the patriarchs in their new position in front of the statue of St Peter; I saw Roux and Nissiotis. They are very disappointed in the *De Ecclesia*. I explained to them that one can just as well take things from a critical point of view as from a positive one. One can see all that is missing: there has been no radical re-thinking. One can see the immense progress that has been made, which will cause to shine forth theses which up to now have been kept closed.

There is to be a vote on Chapter II of the *De Liturgia*.

This gave the following result:

No of voters:	2,242
Placet	1,417
Non placet	36
Placet iuxta modum	781

The required majority was not secured.

De Ecclesia, Chapter II:

Cardinal Frings:[2] countered the objections. The case of collegiality is similar to that of the primacy. Collegiality as a function of preserving unity and truth. Historical presentation on ancient governance through communion. I felt that he had not clarified things to any great extent.

Cardinal Ritter:[3] the questions are here approached only from the dogmatic point of view.

Mgr Parente[4] contributed some clarifications: Peter *rupes* [rock]; episcopal sacramentality and the link between jurisdiction and the power of order: there is only one power, one with respect to origin (Christ) and with respect to the goal, so one must not separate the two as has been done. The two are given directly by Christ, *iure divino, sed non extra*

---

1. Yves Congar, *Pour une Église servante et pauvre* (Paris: Cerf, 1963).
2. *AS* II/II, 493–494.
3. *AS* II/II, 495–496.
4. *AS* II/II, 496–499.

Petrum [by divine right, but not without Peter]. The pope does not create the jurisdiction of bishops, but simply stipulates the matter to which it is applied . . . Collegiality: he stated on what conditions it is in harmony with the primacy. The power of the bishop and that of the pope.

The schema is correct on all these points.

Mgr Alvim[1] in the name of thirty-eight Portuguese bishops, on the diaconate. Celibacy should be kept.

Mgr Jacono:[2] not much listened to. People are tired.

Collegiality is traditional.

One should be careful not to impugn the primacy. Some exaggerated things have been said on this score.

He repeated things that had already been said twenty times!

Coutinho[3] (India): there is no episcopal college without the pope. He cited Zinelli.[4]

Mgr Vion[5] (Poitiers): one should say *potestas pascendi* [pastoral power] instead of *regendi* [governing power].

I missed some interventions. Mgr Philips told me that Cardinal Ottaviani had appealed to the Pope not to allow the sequence *De populo Dei – De hierarchia* [On the People of God – On the Hierarchy], but the reverse. It is a whole ecclesiological option! The four Moderators are of the opposite opinion. I am wondering whether or not the conflict will have to go on right to the end, to the point at which Cardinal Ottaviani will be forced to resign as President of the Theological Commission.

Mgr García,[6] Italian: 1) He stated that he agreed with what Staffa and Parente had said. But these two had not agreed at all in what they said, so basically he was simply supporting the Curia as such; 2) He reverted to the question of the primacy, there is nothing but that!

---

1. *AS* II/II, 500–501.
2. *AS* II/II, 502–503.
3. Fortunato Da Veiga Coutinho, Coadjutor Bishop of Belgaum (India), *AS* II/II, 504–506.
4. Federico Zinelli (1805–1879), Bishop of Treviso, who played an important role at Vatican I by the clarifications which he gave, in the name of the Deputation Concerning the Faith, on the papal primacy.
5. Henri Vion, *AS* II/II, 506–508
6. In fact, the speaker was a Spaniard, Segundo García de Sierra y Méndez, Coadjutor Bishop of Oviedo (Spain), a native of the same diocese; he was to be appointed Archbishop of Burgos in February 1964, *AS* II/II, 514–517.

A Yugoslav bishop[1] whose text was read by Franić: all-out attack on the diaconate and above all on the married diaconate.

He told a number of stories showing that there are many inconveniences in being married . . . (widows would be wanting pensions, etc). People were laughing at times.

An Italian bishop[2] speaking about priests: criticised the *De suae paternae plenitudinis* [From his paternal fullness]

PASTORAL [[character]] of the hierarchical priesthood. One is a Christian for one's own sake, and a priest for the sake of others.

Höffner,[3] Münster. At times there is mention of a *triplex potestas* [triple power]. This should be revised. Strictly speaking, there are only two powers, but three *munera* [functions]. The following should be corrected in this sense:

Page 24, line 2;

Page 23, lines 9-10;

Page 25, line 39: *constat 'ratione ordinis'* [allow 'by reason of order' to stand].

The clause referring to the exercise of collegiality outside of a Council: do not speak of the pope as being OUTSIDE: this on page 27, lines 35–40.

Carraro[4] (Verona) on the diaconate. *IN FAVOUR* of celibacy (he cited witnesses from the Tradition).

His speech will make an impression.

However, everything he said is based on abstractions; he made NO reference to the actual life and needs of the Church.

Fares[5] (Italy) on the diaconate: prudence, prudence!!!

Collegiality: great attention should be paid to the exact meaning of the terms used: the word *collegium* is taken in the general, common sense, not in the juridical sense of Roman Law.

Primacy, primacy, primacy!!!

Mgr Kémérer,[6] Argentina, in the name of twenty bishops: in favour of the diaconate, possibly married. Celibacy is a charism, and presupposes psychological and biological conditions which not everyone possesses.

And our shortage of priests: 1 for every 6,000 inhabitants!! And sometimes JUST ONE priest for 20,000 or 30,000 inhabitants.

---

1. Petar Čule, Bishop of Mostar, *AS* II/II, 517–519.
2. The reference is, in fact, to the intervention of Marijan Oblak, Auxiliary Bishop of Zadar (Yugoslavia), *AS* II/II, 520–521.
3. Joseph Höffner, Bishop of Münster, future Cardinal Archbishop of Cologne (Germany), *AS* II/II, 522–523.
4. *AS* II/II, 524–527.
5. *AS* II/II, 530–533.
6. Jorge Kémérer, Bishop of Posadas, *AS* II/II, 534–535.

Mgr Zoungrana[1] (Upper Volta): the diaconate is necessary. But the freedom to permit marriage would be harmful. That would create divisions of categories. And the witness of chastity.

Carli:[2] against the expression *collegium* [college] and in favour of *corpus* [body] or *communio* [communion]. Delete *'statuente Domino'* [as the Lord establishes them].

He tried to reverse the effect of the intervention by the Auxiliary of Bologna.[3] Does not want a college except *ad nutum Romani Pontifici* [at the pleasure of the Roman Pontiff] *(CURIAL THESIS)*.

It is not enough to say ... everything must be left to the discretion of the pope.

The infallibility of the pope has not been well stated, as it was at Vatican I, that is to say, as coming from the primacy of jurisdiction.

There really is a rift in the Church between the curialists and the rest! The whole weight of Vatican I bears down upon us still!!!

On the way out of St Peter's, to the degree that I can stand and that even to speak does not tire me unduly, I said to several of the *periti* and bishops: there cannot be a vote on collegiality if the person who wrote the text does not explain the exact sense and extent before the vote. (I gave a paper in this sense to Mgr Prignon, who will speak to Cardinal Suenens about this.)

I can only just stand on my feet and hold a pencil or a fork.

At 4 pm, lecture at Saint-Louis des Français on the priesthood. Two hundred and fifteen people counted as present. After the lecture, we finalised the setting up, already envisaged with Frs Le Guillou and Dupuy, of a workshop on the question of the priesthood, with a view to presenting a text to the Theological Commission. Those present were Mgr Fauvel, Renard, Guyot, Desmazières and [ ]; we decided to invite also the bishops who had spoken about priests at the Council, and also Fr Lécuyer.

Fr Gauthier told me that Paul VI had been informed of the dossier on the Church of the Poor and had asked Cardinal Lercaro to follow it up, to organise it and bring it to fruition. I arranged to meet Fr Gauthier tomorrow so that we can see how to distribute the work: doctrinal, institutional, pastoral aspects.

Tuesday 15 October 1963

I worked until 9.30 am (such a treat!) and arrived later in St Peter's (delay = slight bus accident). I arrived as the reading of the report on Chapter III on the liturgy was being concluded.

---

1. Paul Zoungrana, Archbishop of Ouagadougou, created cardinal in February 1965, *AS* II/II, 537–538.
2. *AS* II/II, 539–541
3. Luigi Bettazzi. Cf General Congregation for 11 October, 1963, page 366.

Cardinal Siri.[1] Reservations about collegiality.

Cardinal Wyszyński:[2] repeated the beginning of the schema and gave a whole
theology of the People of God—body of Christ—society: in countries
like his own, there is hardly anything left to the Church except her
churches and her deep nature as the body of Christ, united to the
Trinity.

The link with the Hierarchy amounts to that of spiritual fathers. One
should not press the comparison between (the notion of) the Church
as a perfect SOCIETY and civil society, and the Church militant.
Rather, one should stress the Church as sanctifying and vivifying.

His Beatitude Meouchi[3] (Maronite) in the name of the Maronite bishops put
forward quite a good overall theology of the college of bishops and of
the power of the pope (in fourteen points):

'*Collegium tum in concilio tum extra concilium supremam habet
potestatem et magisterium infallibile*' [The college, both in Council
and also when not in Council, possesses supreme power and infallible
magisterium].

'*Summus Pontifex exercet suam potestatem in collegio et pro collegio*'
[The Supreme Pontiff exercises his power within the college and for
the college].

With a brief explanation of *ex sese*.

Jubany (Auxiliary of Barcelona) in the name of twelve Spanish bishops.
On the diaconate: called for more theology and more specifics. On
collegiality: we have heard about that *ad nauseam!*

Mgr Cooray (Ceylon)[4] repeated his paragraph on collegiality, infallibility.

I missed several interventions as I wandered round, in spite of my legs, and met
quite a few people. At 11.45 am, Cardinal Suenens[5] called for a vote by standing
up or remaining seated on whether or not to conclude discussion of Chapter II,
it being understood that those who have not yet been able to speak may submit
their texts in writing. However, those who will ask to speak in the name of more
than five Fathers may still do so. The Assembly rose as one man. After that, the
only intervention was that of Cardinal Browne[6] who cleared the text on collegiality by explaining that the text in no way impugns the prerogatives of the pope
which he strongly reaffirmed, in accordance with HIS ecclesiology.

---

1. *AS* II/II, 572–573.
2. *AS* II/II, 574–576.
3. Paul P Meouchi, Maronite Patriarch of Antioch, member of the Commission on Eastern Churches, created cardinal in February 1965, *AS* II/II, 577–579.
4. *AS* II/II 586–588.
5. He was the Moderator presiding at this General Congregation.
6. *AS* II/II, 600–601.

It was announced that tomorrow there will be several votes on Chapter II; and the results of several votes on Chapter III of *De S Liturgia* were given.

I went to have lunch at La Retraite du Sacré Coeur with Mgr Mercier and Frs Le Guillou and Dupuy. Also there were Fr Gauthier, Mgr Duval (Algiers), Perrin (Carthage), Lallier,[1] Fauvel, etc. Before the meal, (1.15 pm), we had thirty-five minutes in which to work, and again two hours after the meal: very good work on the THEOLOGICAL aspects of the great question of poverty. Mgr Mercier spoke and spoke . . . but even so we managed to clear the ground. I took notes separately. I promised to do some thinking and to collaborate in the preparation and introduction of a text.

At 4.30 pm, in the Vatican for a meeting of the Theological Commission. A great many experts were present.

Fr Tromp gave a report on the work done and to be done in order to classify the amendments.

Cardinal Ottaviani reported on his approach to Cardinal Agagianian and the Moderators, informing them of the results of our previous discussion: *utrum caput de Populo Dei sit inserendum in Constitutione? –Responsum: Largissimum!* [whether the chapter on the people of God was to be inserted into the Constitution? The reply: Most certainly. And on the heading of the chapter: same reply. – Finally the question of the *De Beata.*

We were read the reply (in Italian) from Cardinal Agagianian. He found the vote on the existence of a separate chapter *De populo Dei* , and on the heading for it, sufficiently well supported by a good majority of the Theological Commission, but, as the majority in favour of the other points was weak, there would need to be a vote of the whole assembly. As regards the *de BMV*, it would be necessary for the two propositions to be presented *in aula*: which is what I had said to Mgr Philips.

The Moderators are also asking the Theological Commission to suggest a formula on the question of the theological note of the texts. Accordingly, Cardinal Ottaviani said that it would be necessary:

1) To choose two members for the schema *De Beata:*
- as a separate text (Cardinal Santos, Philippines),
- as an incorporated text (Cardinal König);

2) To appoint three members, each one of whom will choose his own expert, in order to propose a formula on the theological note. Parente, Schröffer and Fr Fernandez were nominated.

Cardinal Ottaviani had reported to the Pope the results of the voting at our last meeting. The Pope had said the same as the four Moderators. He approved the *De Populo Dei*, but added that he would prefer *De Hierarchia* to be put FIRST, followed by *De Populo Dei.*

---

1. Marc A Lalier, Archbishop of Marseilles, member of the Commission on the Discipline of the Sacraments.

I intervened to draw attention to the technical aspect of the content of *De Populo Dei,* which speaks of what is common to the hierarchy and to the ordinary faithful. This provoked a great discussion on this point.

After an intervention by Mgr Philips, Ottaviani suggested that Mgr Philips should produce an exposition of the reasons for the order he had proposed, which Ottaviani would forward to the Pope.

We then began the reading, and discussion, of the new text on the *De Populo Dei.* I saw the possibility and the hope of an account of the People of God from the point of view of the history of salvation disappearing. That was not considered, even as a hypothesis, for a single moment. I cannot intervene all the time.

Discussion on the role of the Church in the forgiveness of sins or rather in the sacrament of penance.

Wednesday 16 October 1963

Coptic Mass: a full hour.

During the Mass, Cardinal Cicognani, Secretary of State, came to look for Cardinal Agagianian and drew him aside in order to speak to him. Before long, the other Moderators joined them. They seemed very preoccupied. The whole thing was repeated THREE TIMES, the Cardinal Secretary of State going away and then returning some time later[1]. Those who saw all that close up and told me about it thought that it was all connected with the disagreement that arose over the question of the three (four) votes that the Moderators wish to submit to the Council:

1) the sacramentality of the episcopate;

2) collegiality;

3) the diaconate: re-establish it with no stipulation about celibacy
                      possibly a married diaconate.

This morning those bishops representing a number of others are due to speak on Chapter II.

> Joachim Amman[2] (Germany) attacked the existence of diplomatic representation of the Holy See, which likens the Church to temporal states. He questioned their episcopal character. He also questioned the greater confidence placed in their reports than in the bishops.
>
> Mgr Jelmini declined to speak.
>
> Carretto[3] (Thailand) in favour of the diaconate as NECESSARY; possibly, ordain men who are married and economically independent.

---

1. On this incident, see below, page 382.
2. Joachim Amman, former missionary bishop, *AS* II/II, 606–607.
3. Peter Carretto, Vicar Apostolic of Rajaburi, *AS* II/II, 608–609.

Henríquez Jimenez[1] (Venezuela), in the name of the episcopal conference of Venezuela: it should be be more formally declared that the bishops hold their power from Christ through the sacrament (the sacramental, not juridical, structure of the Church).

He referred to the correction of the French bishops of the West.

Difficulties have been raised concerning collegiality because people were starting from a JURIDICAL point of view and an administrative conception of episcopacy.

Very good position on the priesthood and the diaconate.

Mgr Zoghby[2] (UAR). The voice of the East has not been heard sufficiently. Asked for a paragraph on particular Churches. He gave a text to the Secretariat.

The doctrine of the primacy has evolved to such an extent in a unilateral sense that the Easterners do not recognise what they have known and accepted up to now. In the schema, the primacy is expressed in an even more unilateral way, unacceptable to the Orthodox. There is too much reference to the pope and so the impression is given that his power RESTRICTS that of the bishops.

There is too little reference to Christ the priest.

It is not stated that the authority of the pope is not absolute, but always linked with that of the college. He was amazed that anyone would question collegiality, which is traditional and is alive in (synodal) governance of the Patriarchates.

In between the speeches, various alterations to *De S Liturgia* were put to the assembly.

Mgr Jacquier[3] in the name of the bishops of North Africa: collegiality has an exterior aspect and an interior one (communion of faith and love).

Theology and mystique of communion (I recognised the hands of Frs Le Guillou and Dupuy).

Pastoral aspect: mutual help.

(All that is very true and correct, but we have been hearing that for the past ten days and very few of those present were listening: many left their places.)

Mgr Holland[4] (England) in the name of the bishops of England and Wales: collegiality must be made concrete and made manifest by making the bishops co-operate in the government of the universal Church, by

---

1. *AS* II/II, 610–613.
2. *AS* II/II, 615–617.
3. Gaston Jacquier, Auxiliary Bishop of Algiers, *AS* II/II, 619–620.
4. *AS* II/II, 621–622.

setting up a means by which the spirit of the Council, and even, in some way, its reality, will be continued.

Echeverria[1] (Ecuador): praise for collegiality from the pastoral and practical point of view (equal sharing out of priests . . .).

Another bishop from Ecuador:[2] in favour of the diaconate.

A Polish bishop[3] in the name of the Polish bishops, about the diaconate: some aspects are positive and others negative (for the Polish situation). They would prefer secular institutes . . . It should be adapted with the consent of the pope.

Discussion of Chapter III of *De Ecclesia* commenced at this point.

Cardinal Ruffini[4] proposed some alterations to be made:

The word *mitti, missi* [5] and everything that seems to place lay people and the hierarchy on the same footing.

This is obsessive! He spoke for twenty minutes (twenty-two minutes), at least, or rather he shouted.

Cardinal Cento,[6] President of the Commission on the Laity: pleased with this theological basis; he spoke with emphasis without saying very much.

Cardinal Bueno y Monreal[7] (Spain): lay people in the Church: a true epiphany! Praised the work done to get away from the idea of an entirely clerical Church.

However, some comments: the expression 'People of God' is new; better to speak of the mystical Body. It can be understood in several ways . . .

Cardinal Bacci[8] on the priesthood of Christians, which is called universal; criticised this expression and some others, and even that of PRIESTHOOD when used of the laity, except in the generic and opposite sense.

The results of the voting on the eight *emendationes De S Liturgia* [amendments to the document on the Sacred Liturgy] were given. I did not write down the figures.

At 6 pm, at the Spanish College in Via Apollinari, a meeting requested by the Spaniards. Those present: Mgr Morcillo (Saragossa), Mgr Guerry, Frs Rahner, Dupuy, Salaverri, Féret, myself, Dournes, Urresti and six other Spaniards including a certain López Gallego,[9] who talked a lot, was deaf, and was shut up in his

---

1. *AS* II/II, 622–623.
2. CA Mosquera Corral, *AS* II/II, 623–624.
3. Josef Drzazga, Auxiliary Bishop of Gniezno, *AS* II/II, 624–626.
4. *AS* II/II, 627–632.
5. Forms of the Latin verb *mittere* (to send, to delegate).
6. *AS* II/II, 633.
7. *AS* II/II, 634–636.
8. *AS* II/II, 637–638.
9. Canon Ramiro López Gallego, in charge of the dogmatic section of the 'Francisco

entirely conceptual definitions as in a suit of armour from the time of Henri II. After some hesitation, we spoke of *De Populo Dei*; the deaf man wanted to see everything within the framework of a definition of rational sociology; the same for the concept of royal priesthood. Rahner, as always, monopolised the dialogue. He is marvellous, but he does not realise that where he is there is no room left for anything else. A desire emerged for a development of the history of salvation. A text needs to be produced. As Fr Dournes had just given me one that he had written, I suggested—without having looked at it!—that copies of his text should be produced and distributed to those present to serve as a first basis for our discussion. The Spaniards would have liked us to produce a text that could be endorsed by several episcopates: they want to emerge from their isolation, build bridges, and that is why, in spite of having an incredible amount of work to do, I wanted to respond to their appeal. But Rahner pointed out, quite rightly, that we are already engaged in a work for our respective bishops and that we should not create a new moral person. In our respective groups, we will report on these meetings, without their giving rise to a separate activity with respect to the the Council.

Thursday 17 October 1963

I saw Cardinal Lefebvre, Mgr Garrone. They told me that there is a French bishops' workshop on the question of the laity-People of God. I am on the outside with respect to all these workshop questions.[1] Immediately afterwards, I also saw Mgr Maziers and said to him, as I had already said to the other two:

1) We MUST seize the opportunity to present a synthetic picture of the Church IN THE HISTORY OF SALVATION. 2) With this in mind, it is necessary to invite Frs Féret, Dournes and myself to attend this workshop.

> Mgr Rastouil[2] on No. 24: dependence with regard to the priesthood of Christ; on the character: a favourite hobby horse!! With the custom the French bishops have of giving the whole of their synthesis, like novices when preaching their first sermon. The Church is entirely priestly (in the end he was told to stop).
>
> Lokuang[3] (China) in the name of fifteen bishops from China: it would not be necessary to prepare a separate chapter on the laity because there is a decree on *De apostolatu laicorum* [the apostolate of the laity]!!! and, in chapter IV, what concerns Religious should be separated from what concerns everybody, to be put into *De populo Dei*.
>
> Universal priesthood: easily understood in China because, in the Confucian tradition, that is all there is.

Suárez' Institute in Madrid.

1. Congar added in the margin of the typescript: 'I was living at the Angelicum, far from all the groups of bishops'.
2. *AS* II/III, 10–13.
3. *AS* II/III, 15–17.

Hengsbach[1] (Essen) on No. 25: against the division of the apostolate into three domains: the division is too abstract and not a good introduction to what is said theologically in *De apostolatu laicorum*. To sum up, the style is not conciliar and not clear.

One should distinguish simply between the spiritual domain and the temporal one. The relationship of the laity with the hierarchy is not the same in the two domains.

The amendments to Chapter III *De S Liturgia* were read and voted on.

Mgr J Wright[2] (Pittsburgh): expressed approval. This was the kind of text one hoped for! He made much of the historic moment of this solemn declaration.

Fiordelli[3] (Prato): *caput laude dignum* [the chapter is worthy of praise].

page 7, l. 30 ff. On married couples, but there is no reference to FAMILIES. He proposed a text.

Dubois,[4] with some emphasis and meticulousness: text and diction very studied. The idea that the People of God includes all Christians, and even all human beings.

GOOD things, but once again a synthesis!! The same as he expounded to me at Besançon two or three years ago. Yet another hobby horse.

Padin[5] (Brazil): approved the idea of a *De Populo Dei* coming BEFORE *De Hierarchia* and, from this point of view, criticised a formula suggesting Hierarchy ≠ people.

He suggested a few interesting corrections inspired by a real awareness of what lay people are. I was witnessing, overcome, the maturing of a theology of the laity in the Church . . . And really of a THEOLOGY and not merely something tactical or pragmatic.

He spoke of the dialogue necessary between hierarchy and laity: the condition upon which bishops would be truly shepherds!

Mgr Gopu[6] (Hyderabad, India); English pronunciation.

The role of lay people in mission countries, where, often, the laity assist the bishop hardly at all, should be better expressed.

It should be affirmed that the Church is always in a state of mission.

Elchinger:[7] Nos. 24–25 which are rather too individualistic. In his usual fashion, he asked questions, and asked them well. He deplored the lack of awareness of belonging to a body and living in it in solidarity. People of today are people without roots. Christian communities are too big

---

1. *AS* II/III, 17–19.
2. *AS* II/III, 19–20.
3. *AS* II/III, 21–23.
4. *AS* II/III, 24–26.
5. Candido Padin, Auxiliary Bishop of Rio de Janeiro, *AS* II/III, 27–29.
6. Joseph M Gopu, Archbishop of Hyderabad (Pakistan), *AS* II/III, 29–30.
7. *AS* II/III, 30–33.

and in them one cannot have AN EXPERIENCE of community that is genuine and personal: the Sects, on the other hand, do make this possible.

Individualism should be condemned as a pastoral heresy.

Hannan[1] (USA) suggested additions to No. 25.

Civardi,[2] on No. 25: the theological and moral motifs of the apostolate of the laity should be still better explained: baptism and above all confirmation, faith and charity.

Castellano[3] (Siena): approved the creation of a chapter II, but pointed out some inadequacies and asked for a more POSITIVE, more BIBLICAL definition of the laity.

Louis Mathias[4] (India): he spoke of the laity as catechists and expressed a wish for the establishment of a Roman office which could be called: *Officium S Pauli ad gentes* [St Paul's Office for the Nations].

I left the tribune. Conversations with Moeller, Daniélou and Laurentin. They told me this: the four Moderators had announced for yesterday a vote on four points. But nothing has in fact been proposed, either yesterday or today. Yesterday, the four Moderators were discussing something throughout the Mass. Cardinal Ottaviani had objected to their initiative for the planned vote, saying it was against the regulations and that the Moderators were overstepping their power. That would explain why nothing had been put to the Assembly.

The Moderators are to see Paul VI this evening: the debate is likely to be cancelled. (The Pope is also due to receive the Observers, who are also due to be received tomorrow by Cardinal Bea.)

Daniélou added that it is considered in various quarters that Ottaviani can no longer preside over the Theological Commission; that the Commission ought to ELECT its own President, and even that the Council ought to ELECT some new conciliar Commissions. Because, on the one hand, the men of worth have been identified and marked out, on the other hand, the Council has revealed its spirit to itself; mentalities have changed: it is only now that the Council is in a position to provide itself with instruments that are suited to the direction of its work.

While this conversation was going on, I saw Fr Balić who, these past few days, has been doing his mariological rounds in the side-aisles. He has had a report printed of which he gave me a copy.

I had lunch with Fr Schmemann and Nissiotis. They invited me to a restaurant in Piazza di S Maria in Trastevere. Both feel intensely the charm and soul of Rome

---

1. Philip M Hannan, Auxiliary Bishop of Washington; he was to become Bishop of New Orleans in September 1965; *AS* II/III, 33–34.
2. *AS* II/III, 35–36.
3. *AS* II/III, 36–38.
4. Louis Mathias was Archbishop of Madras and Mylapore and a member of the Commission on Bishops and the Government of Dioceses, *AS* II/III, 38–40.

as a city that has kept all its past. We had an interesting chat: about ecclesiology. I told them my way of seeing the ecclesiology of the Fathers and of the liturgy, as including anthropology, and we agreed that the best ecclesiology would be, in *De Populo Dei*, a development on the Christian human being. We spoke about the *De œcumenismo*. They told me: these texts ON ecumenism are not very important: an anthropology and a pneumatology in the *De Ecclesia* would be the most positive ECUMENICAL step . . . We also spoke of the *De Beata*. In their view, a *De Beata* is a fairly doubtful step. In the East, Mary is A DIMENSION of everything: of christology, of the history of salvation (continuity with Israel), ecclesiology, of prayer. That is why the Orthodox mix her up with everything without ever producing a treatise *De Beata*.

They also spoke to me about the situation in the USA: Schmemann told me that it was absolutely necessary to go there. In a month, I would make things take a gigantic leap forward. Küng had great success there, but my two orthodox interlocutors were fairly critical of Küng and also of Baum, whom they found overrated. They asked me about Rahner, whom they were inclined to mistrust. I could not quite see why.

We also spoke about the Brothers from Taizé, whom they felt 'exaggerated': on the one hand by an excessively clerical aspect (their cowl in St Peter's), on the other by a systematic policy of making contact with as many bishops as possible. They saw in that a touch of indiscretion or of professionalism. But I stressed the fact that, within its very human limits, Taizé remains a real miracle, a work of God: it is quite out of the ordinary!

In the evening, at the Hotel Botticelli, where the Vietnamese bishops, and also some Melkite and Maronite bishops (Mgr Doumith) are staying.

After dinner, lecture on the *De Laicis* and *De populo Dei*. Then questions and dialogue. I realised that these bishops (thirty to thirty-five of them) are rather ill at ease with the texts and the discussions on the *De Ecclesia*. They even told me so quite forcefully. They do not see themselves in it. They have a tradition of thought, of categories, of lines of interest which are quite other than those.

It is quite disturbing.

I realised once again to what an extent the Catholic Church is Latin, to what extent she deceives herself, in good faith, by believing herself to be 'Catholic'. She is nothing of the sort. Romanism, Italianism, Latinism, scholasticism, the analytical spirit, have swallowed up everything and have almost established themselves as a dogma. What a job!!

Friday 18 October 1963

I was so far behind with important work that I did not go to St Peter's. I began by sorting through and card-indexing the proposed amendments. It is a burdensome task. In half an hour, I had done two cards, and there are SEVERAL hundred to be done!!

In St Peter's it seems that there was a discussion of the definition of a lay person ... !

At 3.30 pm, at the Belgian College for the commission set up to promote studies and steps relating to the Church in the service of the poor. Those present: Cardinal Gerlier, Mgr Himmer, Ancel, Moralejo[1] (very good!), Mercier, Coderre, Hakim, a bishop from Vietnam, one or two others, Dossetti, abbé Denis. Mgr Helder Câmara[2] gave a prophetic and magnificent exposition, a bit theatrical and emotive. He loves the spectacular. He suggested that the Pope should invite some working class and poor people to the closing meeting as guests of honour. Unlike most of those present, I found this suggestion very ambiguous and ultimately bad. That would be a very artificial gesture of condescension; on the whole, rather paternalistic, by which one would ease one's conscience rather too easily.

Much more interesting was the intervention of Mgr Moralejo, which reflected the report of the lay Auditors (which I had already seen) on the *De Ecclesia*. So that it can be understood by the people of today, the lay Auditors would like the Council not to begin by presenting the reality of the Church as a 'mystery' and with the Trinity as its starting point, but starting with what is human, what is visible, and from there moving on to the mystery of Christ and of the Blessed Trinity. I supported the idea of a kind of catechetical formula (the Council of Trent's *Catechismus ad Parochos)*,[3] which would follow, not an analytical order, but a synthetic and concrete order.

It is to be followed up.

At 4.30 pm, work in Commissions until 6.00 pm. Theological Commission.[4] Biblical lecture by Fr Mollat[5] and theological one by myself, along the lines of, and following on from the work we did last Wednesday.[6]

At 7.30 pm, at the Polish college in Piazza Remuria: a magnificent building; supper, lecture on ecumenism (in Latin): fifteen bishops and some students. I got the impression that the Poles have remained rather remote from current ideas, and yet would be open to them. I had a chat with l'abbé Lipinski,[7] of the Polish Institute, on the question of mariology: I will put him in touch with Laurentin.

In the vestibule of the Polish College there is a (very bad: very poor from every 'artistic' point of view) statue of David with, at his feet, the head of Goliath. I thought of the USSR–Goliath!!!

---

1. R González Moralejo.
2. H Pessôa Câmara.
3. Catechism for parish priests (first edition in 1566).
4. Congar wrote in the margin of the typescript: 'of this same group of the Church of the poor'.
5. Donatien Mollat, SJ, exegete, professor at the Gregorianum.
6. Congar's lecture was to be published in Yves Congar, *Jésus Christ, notre Médiateur et notre Seigneur* (Paris: Cerf, 1965), 68–90.
7. Edward Lipinski, exegete, Old Testament specialist.

Saturday 19 October 1963

At 11 am, I went to the the the meeting of the committee for the journal *Concilium* at the Hotel Olympic. In addition to Brand, the editor, Frs Vanhengel, Schillebeeckx, Rahner, Lyonnet, abbés Küng and Jimenez-Urresti, were there, as well as the DO-C secretary.[1] We spoke first of all about the cost price and selling price. I said that a subscription of from 120 to 130 NF would give ten to twenty subscribers in France. Rahner wants us to show from the beginning that we do not adhere to any party; the criterion is to produce something CONSTRUCTIVE. I learnt that Fr Daniélou is resolutely and actively AGAINST *Concilium*. For my own part, I presented two points:

1) Not to do something along the lines of '*Scientia*': that would not arouse any interest. What is of interest are things which, without saying EVERYTHING, rest on a concrete basis, on a tradition from which one can draw out something vital: which does not amount to a 'school' in the strict sense of the word.

2) To move beyond Latinism: work so that Catholic thought does not, in fact, have Latin scholasticism as its NORM.

At 12.40 pm at Santa Sabina: lunch given by Fr General for the Dominican experts. Opportunity to see a great many of the brethren, but only for a few seconds and superficially.

Fr Féret said to me afterwards: Balić is conducting a frantic propaganda: at St Peter's he spends his time doing the rounds of the tribunes and lobbies. He has just given a lecture to the Yugoslav bishops during which he said: 'Fr Congar, who has the greatest influence at the Council, is a minimalist; he has written that the Virgin sins like the rest of us.' Féret is going to protest, through the French bishops at S Tommaso di Villanova and through Fr Hamer, and ask Balić for his reference.

I read the speech the Holy Father made to the Observers last Thursday.[2] It is an admirable document. No one, not even John XXIII, has ever gone that far.

Sunday 20 October 1963

In the morning, worked on writing a section for *De Presbyteris* [on priests]. I wrote to Mgr Garrone and, through him, to Mgr Ancel and Cardinal Lefebvre. I should like, on the one hand, to take advantage of Paul VI's speech to the Observers in order to re-launch, while there is still time, the idea of a chapter on the 'history of salvation' for *De populo Dei*, and, on the other, to see how to achieve a *De Ecclesia* of the catechetical and concrete kind that the laity are asking for.

I also sent the following letter to Fr Balić:

Carissime Pater,

Si causa tua bona est, nullatenus eges me implicandi in re sicut nuper fecisti adloquendo ad Episcopos Croatos. Eo magis quod relata de mente mea circa sanc-

---

1. According to the minutes of this meeting (Congar Archives), it was in fact Alting von Geusau, the Director of DO-C.
2. *La Documentation Catholique*, 1963, col 1421–1423.

titatem Matris Dei erronea sint, si tamen de tuis dictis me recte certiorem fecerunt.
  Tuus in servitio Evangelii addictissimus
  [Dear Father,
  If your cause is a good one, you have no need to involve me in the matter, as you have recently done when speaking to the Croatian bishops. All the more since what was said about my view of the holiness of the Mother of God was false, at least if I have been correctly informed about what you said.
  Yours most devotedly in the service of the Gospel.]
  Outing with Féret, Chenu, Camelot, Hamer, Gunnes:[1] we left at 10.15 for Tarquinia. The Etruscan world: the people who, 2,800 years ago, painted these tombs. The abiding realities of life, of sexuality, of the body, of conflict . . .
  I learnt from Fr Hamer that, when he received Fr General in the month of August, Paul VI spoke very critically of *ICI*, which he accused of being a secret and hidden enemy of the Church. On account of an article on Poland.[2] Very odd.
  In the evening, with the Brazilian bishops at Domus Mariae; but some bishops from Uganda and Ruanda, from Hungary (five), Ecuador, etc. Lecture on ecumenism. Among the questions put to me, that of the *De Beata*. I believe I sensed much hesitation but, all the same, an inclination to make a separate schema of it. In any case, Mary is '*Mater Ecclesiae*': this new title, launched by Balić, has already produced its effect!!
  I said that, from both the internal Catholic point of view and the ecumenical one, the *De BMV* ought to be placed at the end of the *De Ecclesia*: that is the healthy thing to do!! Moreover, the majority of the members of the Theological Commission are of this opinion.
  I was told that Cardinal Ruffini lives there and that he had said: Now, the Protestants are being brought in; shall WE have to leave some day?

Monday 21 October 1963
I left earlier in order to call in at the French Seminary and try to see Mgr Garrone, Ancel and Cardinal Lefebvre about *De Populo Dei* —the history of salvation.
  In St Peter's, a number of often fruitless attempts to contact this one or that one. I telephoned Fr Féret about preparing a *votum* to give to Cardinal Lefebvre on *Populus Dei*.
  I also saw Laurentin who gave me the text that Cardinal König is to read in favour of incorporating *De BMV* into *De Ecclesia*, and a paper written by Lauren-

---

1. Erik-Dom Gunnes, OP, of the Province of France.
2. The Polish bishops had not appreciated some articles in *ICI* about Poland that were suspected of being sympathetic toward the Pax movement, which was animated by some Christians collaborating with the Communist government. In June 1963, the Secretariat of State had sent to the French bishops and major religious superiors a memorandum from Cardinal Wyszyński about the Pax movement which implicated the *ICI*. (Cf *La Documentation Catholique,* 5 July 1964, col 843-853).

tin, Moeller and Martelet . . . giving nine reasons in favour of this and replying to objections. I suggested some further considerations.

Romanian Byzantine Mass which lasted a good hour. This was followed by the reading of the report on Chapter IV of *De Liturgia*. It is very long! I began work at 11 am, already exhausted . . . !!!

> Cardinal Meyer,[1] Chicago: on us sinners, our weaknesses. *Dimitte nobis debita nostra* [Forgive us our trespasses]. And there is the devil *quaerens quem devoret* [seeking whom he may devour (I Peter 5:8)]. In the New Testament, there are always two aspects to the Church: a heavenly one and an earthly one; and also in the liturgy and the witness of the saints. He suggested a concrete emendation.
>
> Cardinal Ottaviani:[2] protested about the fact that three *periti* had distributed leaflets urging the episcopates to vote for a married diaconate. It would be possible to make some married laymen acolytes (in this connection he used the word 'concession').
>
> Mgr Tchidimbo[3] (Guinea): praised the schema which contains a number of good things. He said that colonisation had not yet ended completely from the point of view of the apostolate.
>
> Cooray[4] (Ceylon) on no. 24 (priesthood of the laity). He suggested that one should speak of the sacramental priesthood (hierarchy) and spiritual priesthood.
>
> I sent him some critical comments.
>
> Mgr C Wojtyła, Vicar Capitular of Cracow:[5] in favour of a *De Populo Dei* in Chapter II before *De S Hierarchia* (gave reasons); that would require another revision of Chapter I (partly the text he had given to me, but corrected).
>
> Hurley:[6] not enough attention is paid to the temporal life of the laity, which is to be sanctified.
>
> One of the most frightfully empty and boring sessions.

Mgr Willebrands asked me to speak about the laity to the Observers tomorrow, but I am already booked up, and he has never been in a hurry to invite me!

At 5.30 pm, working at Saint-Louis des Français with the group of bishops (plus Dupuy, Le Guillou) on a *De presbyteris*.

---

1. *AS* II/III, 146–148.
2. *AS* II/III, 148–149.
3. The Holy Ghost Father, Raymond-Marie Tchidimbo, Archbishop of Conakry, *AS* II/III, 150–152.
4. *AS* II/III, 152–154.
5. *AS* II/III, 154–156.
6. *AS* II/III, 157–159.

I sent to Mgr Ancel, for Cardinal Lefebvre, a very good text on *De Populo Dei* by Féret; I also gave a copy to Cardinal Liénart, and I even went to the Procure Saint-Sulpice to explain it to him in a few words, because Cardinal Lefebvre is hesitant: it is a field of ideas with which he is not familiar. Cardinal Liénart welcomed my approach but told me that he prefers to say LITTLE *in aula*.

Tuesday 22 October 1963

I stayed home, not so much in order to work, but to clear to some extent the enormous backlog of post and papers that had accumulated.

I was told that there were some interesting interventions:

> Cardinal Suenens[1] on the charisms (which Ruffini had declared had ceased with the Apostolic age).
> Mgr Ménager[2] [ ]
> A Maronite[3] who spoke in favour of a theology of the Spirit [pneumatology] and said: The true location of the Church is Jerusalem, she is in exile in Rome, which is Babylon, and where she can only await the new Jerusalem.

I am very tired of the sessions in St Peter's. There is no DISCUSSION of a QUESTION, no question is even asked: there is a succession of speeches about a fairly wide-ranging reality. Each one speaks from his own idea, from his own synthesis, riding his own hobby horse, calling for the insertion of an idea which is dear to him. A great many experts push for things, draft texts, fabricate, as it were, a dogmatic constitution, without bothering about what has already been discussed or about the reasons for this or that formula or this or that omission. The debates—which are not even debates but a series of speeches—are not organised in any way. The speaker neither explains BEFOREHAND what he wants to say and why he wants to say it in this way, nor does he intervene afterwards in order to reply, to explain something, to refer to another text.

There is thus a sort of gigantism to the enterprise which risks causing it to collapse, or at least to be exhausted under the weight of its own mass.

Finally, there is no effective organic link between the Observers and the Council, with the result that the many interesting and important things that they say do not flow into the work of the Council or, if they do, they do so only indirectly, in driblets and very partially.

---

1. *AS* II/III, 175–177.
2. *AS* II/III, 208–210.
3. Ignace Ziadé, Maronite Archbishop of Beirut, member of the Commission on the Eastern Churches, *AS* II/III, 211–213.

Wednesday 23 October 1963

Once again I stayed home in order to work. It takes a lot of time to do the least thing and, FOR THIS EVENING, I have to finish
- a text on the priesthood;
- a text on the dogmatic basis of the high value of poverty.

In the tram I took in order to go to the Vatican for the Theological Commission, I met up with Medina (then with Mgr Garrone). Medina told me (having heard it from McGrath) that the Congregation for Religious had sent to the Superiors General a list of dangerous experts . . . (in this connection, the three experts nailed by Cardinal Ottaviani the other day were said to be Rahner, Ratzinger and Martelet: the reference was to the paper they had produced on collegiality, at the end of which there were three lines on the diaconate, WITHOUT ANY REFERENCE TO CELIBACY. Hence, Cardinal Ottaviani's protest was both unfounded and false).

Medina also told me that the Curia was trying to weaken the Moderators and to prevent them from acting. That would be what is behind the crisis that arose about the four questions that were to be put to the vote. There was to be a meeting today between the Moderators and the Presidents of the Council.

He told me that his Cardinal Silva, a fine and courageous man, is having difficulties with the Curia. For instance, he has not yet been given the auxiliary that he has been asking for for several years. On the other hand, only three weeks ago, the Pope had said to him: ask me for an audience, I will give you one the very next day . . . He asked for one straightaway, but he is still waiting . . .

When I got to the Hall of the Congregations, I saw Mgr Griffiths. He told me that today Cardinal Spellman was presenting a petition to the Pope, signed by two hundred and forty bishops, asking for a text on religious freedom to be put before the Council. He would prefer it to be combined with the one on ecumenism because in this way 1) it will come during THIS Session whereas, if it is relegated to schema XVII, which would be the normal place for it, that will not happen until 1965 . . . !!

2) It would be presented by the Secretariat; otherwise the Theological Commission would have to discuss it. What state would it be in when it emerged from that, and when?

At the Commission this evening, all the Italians were absent . . . (?).

Mgr Volk has been appointed a member of the Commission in place of old Peruzzo:[1] it was he who had gained the highest number of votes in the conciliar elections.

> Cardinal König: the Council Fathers are getting worried at how slow the work is going: it would be good for the President of the Commission to report *in aula* on how the work is progressing.

---

1. Cardinal Peruzzo had died in July 1963.

Fr Tromp, in the name of Cardinal Ottaviani: apology for his absence (he had mistaken the day).

We spoke about the four questions that, in the end, had not been put to the Council. This was due to the fact that a matter of such importance must first be discussed in a joint commission of the four Moderators and the Cardinals of the Co-ordinating Commission.

Several sub-commissions are to be established to work on the amendments . . . there will be a central commission and several sub-commissions.

There are also a great many questions relating to topics to be inserted into the schema at the request of the Fathers. That will be a task for the central sub-commission.

Mgr Philips reported on the work: see duplicated sheets dated 22/X/63.

Cardinal König: the Commission ought to give some criteria to help in assessing the proposed *emendationes*. McGrath returned to this idea later.

Tromp: only one Father (Micara)[1] called for modern errors to be condemned. But Cardinal Cicognani had let it be known that the Holy Father had underlined and approved this point in his own hand.

(On the way out, Mgr Prignon told me the true state of affairs: Cardinal Micara had sent his text to the Holy Father. The latter had simply written: *Attente considerandum* [to be considered carefully]. When Cardinal Suenens asked the Pope the meaning and the implication of the annotation, Paul VI had replied (in substance): a polite indication that I had seen the thing.)

Garrone and Charue: take account of the *mens concilii* [intention of the Council].

Mgr Philips went through each of the points in his report and these were discussed.

For the Church of the poor, Mgr Garrone suggested, very appositely, that one should hear one of the bishops, or Cardinal Lercaro, who have insisted on this point. I asked for a special sub-commission to be appointed for that.

After a fairly impassioned debate on what had and had not been accepted by a vote of the Commission on the diaconate, I intervened to insist on the importance of a *De presbyteris*; I asked that one of the bishops who had spoken on this point be invited to address the sub-commission.

With respect to introducing the question of Tradition, McGrath asked if it was known what would happen to the schema *De Revelatione*. Nobody replied. Mgr Garrone explained his thinking on the usefulness of inserting a section on Tradition into the *De Ecclesia*.

---

1. Cardinal C Micara.

Discussion on the composition of the twelve sub-commissions to be set up and on how to proceed. But in the end, members of these sub-commissions were not appointed. It is true that all the Italians were absent.

At 7.35 pm, in Via Ulisse Seni, the group working on the Church and the poor. Fr Chenu was there, having been brought in by Mgr Mercier. The discussion got nowhere.

Fr Le Guillou told me that the Commission on the Missions had rejected the schema *De missionibus*, and that a new one will have to be produced: he is going to do it. He redoes, or does, more or less everything, but much more seriously than Fr Daniélou was doing last year.

Thursday 24 October 1963

It appears that the meeting of the Moderators with the Co-ordinating Commission and the Council of Presidents did not result in a good understanding between them. There were differences of opinion about the wording of the four questions. It seems there were nine votes in favour of the diaconate and seven against. So, not a very clear majority . . . (I have that from Mgr Marty).

Vote on the whole of Chapter IV of *De Liturgia* and reading of the report on Chapter V of the same constitution.

> Cardinal Siri:[1] the definition of the laity should include their submission to the hierarchy.
>
> Against a SPECIAL chapter *De Populo Dei*.
>
> Concerning the universal priesthood: agreed with Ruffini. There is too much of a desire to say things that will please the laity.
>
> On the charisms: need to be very prudent! And even if it is a question of the Holy Spirit, everything must be submitted *regimini* [to the rule] of the hierarchy.
>
> *De sensu fidei* [on the sense of the faith] (mentioned eleven times by the Council of Trent), everything depends on the teaching Church.

He, too, is bent on, and obsessed with, the hierarchy! What wretched outlooks: exactly those pulverised by Möhler[2] (*'Gott schuf die Hierarchie'* [God created the hierarchy][3]...).

---

1. *AS* II/III, 278–279.
2. Johann Adam Möhler (1796–1838) had renewed ecclesiology in the nineteenth century by giving it a theological and supernatural character instead of a merely juridical one. Congar was strongly impressed by his thought, and his most famous work was among the very first titles published in the 'Unam Sanctam' collection: JA Moeller, *L'Unité dans l'Église ou le principe du catholicisme d'après l'esprit des Pères des trois premiers siècles de l'Église*, 'Unam Sanctam', 2 (Paris: Cerf, 1938).
3. The beginning of a sentence from Möhler in *Theologische Quartalschrift*, 1823, page 497: 'God created the hierarchy, and so he has provided more than abundantly for

Fr Fernandez, OP:[1] he gave A DISSERTATION concerning the abuse of temporal goods. He always gives dissertations; whenever he speaks, people offer me their condolences.

I left the tribune: it is all too boring; everybody is fed up with it. I saw Dom Rousseau and Mgr Nabaa. The latter took part in the meeting yesterday evening as sub-secretary. He said that it was a real case of sabotage: the Italians (eleven of them!) with men like Spellman and even Tisserant. The Italians are absolutely AGAINST collegiality and even the WORD has been deleted in the second question. Only Cardinal Liénart had been courageous.

They have been procrastinating for two weeks. Whereas the battle had been well nigh won ten or twelve days ago, the prolongation of tiresome discussions has benefited the reaction. Arrighi, whom I also met, told me: it was done deliberately, they had set out to wreck it.

Mgr Nabaa thinks that it will not even be possible to reach sufficient agreement for the promulgation of a dogmatic constitution. He believes that the *De Ecclesia* will be put off until later. I think he over-estimates the size of the Reaction: he thinks it is nearly half the assembly.

I learnt that Cardinal Suenens has asked Dhanis for a text *de BMV*, a text which has already been written, but he has asked others for one as well.

I saw Guitton: he asked me what I thought. He is to see Paul VI soon and could perhaps give him an indication of my thinking. I told him that the Commission concerned ought to take part in the debate with the Moderators and help to organise it and focus it better.

At 11.22 am, discussion on the chapter *De Laicis* was brought to an end. Applause.

Cardinal Browne[2] added a few concluding words on the chapter and spoke of the holiness of the righteous laity, united to Christ *per fidem et caritatem, non autem per caracterem sacerdotalem* [by faith and charity, but not by the priestly character]—(St Thomas, Tertia Pars[3]); and then on the lay character of human society on earth.

> Döpfner:[4] it has been suggested that the *de BMV* be inserted in the *De Ecclesia*.
>
> Accordingly, two speakers will explain the two theses: Cardinal Santos and Cardinal König, whose text will be distributed tomorrow. The vote on this question will be taken next week.

---

everything until the end of the world.'
1. *AS* II/III, 280–282.
2. *AS* II/III, 297–298.
3. Cf Thomas Aquinas, *Summa Theologiae* IIIa q. 82, a. 1 ad 2.
4. He was presiding at this General Congregation.

Santos[1] read his text (*VERY* long)

> *Maria stat inter Christum et Ecclesiam* [Mary stands between Christ and the Church].
>
> The redemption of Mary does not differs only in *gradus* [by degree] from the redemption of other human beings (hence, *essentia* [it is essentially different]?).

König:[2] much more applause than for Santos, especially from the benches of young bishops.

At 3.30 pm, visit from Fr Gauthier with Marie-Thérèse[3] and two others. Always impressive, they nevertheless run the risk of going round in circles, as they wish, absolutely, that the poor person, *qua talis* [as such], because of his or her being trodden down, is a member of the People of God. They are prisoners of a situational perspective of the masses and do not see clearly enough that in order to belong or not to belong to the people of God, each one must have revealed where his or her heart is.

A little, very little, work with Frs Dupuy and Le Guillou. Then, at 6 pm at the Spaniards' place. The same people were there as last time, except for Salaverri and Mgr Guerry: plus Mgr the Bishop of Münster[4] and another bishop, and Frs Sauras and Iamera[5] (spelling?). Rahner, once again, monopolised the discussion. At one point, there was a scholastic duel between Iamera and Urresti, and then between Iamera and Rahner. This Iamera is a pure scholastic: he could distinguish and counter-distinguish, refute and prove for thirty days and thirty nights on end. It belongs to the world of sport: something like the six day cycle race or the twenty-four hour race at Le Mans.

(The next day, without saying anything about my own impressions, I asked a Spanish Father WHO is this Fr Iamera. He replied: an extremist activist for mariology . . . that does not surprise me: maximising mariology lives only on endless deductions and reasonings derived from words or concepts.)

Apart from an interesting suggestion about the idea of holiness at the beginning, none of that was of any interest; in the end Féret and I left . . . All the same, I would have liked to stay on for a moment, because Mgr Morcillo raised the question of inserting the *De BMV* into the *De Ecclesia*, but Fr Féret had already left the room and I followed him.

I was sorry about that because this point is very important. I have spoken to a great many bishops from different countries (Poles, Melkites, Frenchmen, etc).

---

1. *AS* II/III, 338–342.
2. *AS* II/III, 342–345.
3. Marie-Thérèse Lacaze, of the Companions of Jesus the Carpenter (cf above, page 222, note 2).
4. Joseph Höffner.
5. Congar wrote in the margin of the typescript: 'Iamera'. Marceliano Iamera, OP, of the Province of Aragon, professor at the Dominican *studium* in Valencia.

THEY ARE HESITANT. They do not see any decisive reason *IN FAVOUR* of inserting it. They would not be against it, but are not persuaded by a truly compelling reason. When all is said and done, there is only one: it is THE way to avoid
the making of greater claims. It is the way to get rid of the existing schema. It is a
unique opportunity to produce an ecumenical text. But who FEELS these things?
One either feels them or one does not. It is a question of sensitivity. The outcome
of the vote that has been announced seems to me very doubtful. I think there will
be a majority for the insertion, but whether it will be a preponderant or slender
majority will depend on encounters and conversations to be had in the three days
that separate us from the vote.

Friday 25 October 1963
Moeller gave me the state of the questions discussed on Wednesday and on
Thursday afternoon, as things stood yesterday evening (that could change!). Here
are the four questions which will be put to the vote:

1) The sacramental character of episcopal consecration;

2) That by this consecration the person enters into the *corpus* [body] of bishops;

3) The *collegium* or *corpus* a) *suprema pollet potestate in Ecclesia* [exercises
supreme power in the Church] b) *hoc jure divino* [by divine right];

4) The PRINCIPLE of a permanent diaconate, without raising the question
of celibacy.

Moeller added that 1) Cardinal Suenens had suggested to Cardinal Siri that,
if these wordings did not suit him, he could propose others. By yesterday evening, he had sent nothing, so those of Thursday afternoon were being sent to the
printer; 2) Cardinal Tisserant had been good: he had RULED OUT the question
of right with respect to whether or not the moderators have the right to put such
questions; 3) Liénart had the word *collegium* put back into the third question.

56th General Congregation.

Reading of the text concerning the schema *De BMV Matre Ecclesiae* [on the
Blessed Virgin Mary Mother of the Church] (Felici stressed this title, which was
repeated three or four times).[1]

Further interventions on the chapter *De laicis* and on *De populo Dei* (by bishops speaking in the name of at least five others).

> Mgr Boillon[2] on the poor, along the lines of Fr Gauthier (with a very artificial
> effort at pronunciation).
> (Several bishops from different countries, including Ancel and
> Himmer, told me that this speech irritated and upset the hearers; they
> deemed it unfortunate.)

---

1. *AS* II/III, 349–351.
2. *AS* II/III, 350–351.

Mgr Méndez,[1] Mexico, in the name of more than sixty bishops from Central America. On No. 25, lines 7 ff, on page 18. It is very inadequate for such an important question. People are waiting for a response to this question. How to harmonise the Church's claim to authority with human freedom.

The reference to 'separation' is too simplistic and univocal.

People are waiting for the text *De libertate religiosa* [on religious freedom] prepared by the Secretariat.

Mgr Baraniak,[2] Poznań, Poland, in the name of all the Polish bishops: on Nos. 25 and 27. This cannot speak to the faithful who work in difficult conditions in a country like his own. Something should be added for them and state that their martyrdom is an apostolate.

Applause.

Tomášek[3] (Czechoslovakia, in the name of the Czechoslovakian bishops present): suggested an alteration in favour of the duty of parents to inculcate the faith in their children, and for a catechetical institute for the laity.

During the interval, the *emendationes De Liturgia* were read.

Darmancier[4] (Oceania: Marist—in the name of six bishops of Oceania): there are only three lines about the royal function of Christians. God has given to humankind *dominium* [dominion] over the world and over itself: it is the basis for human activity in and over the world, which ought to reach its consummation in *consecratio mundi* [the consecration of the world] . . . He then went on to speak of toleration (spiritual kingship is in no sense dominating).

Raffaele Calabria,[5] my friend the Archbishop of Benevento. On Nos. 22 and 23, above all with regard to the drafting. No. 24 on the *sensus fidei*: external preaching is the principal and formal element . . . ; he distinguished different aspects or moments with regard to charisms, supported Ruffini and Florit (they are limited to the origins).

Mgr Coutinho[6] (India) in favour of extending the allocation of sacred functions in the Church.

Evangelisti[7] (India) in the name of several bishops from India, Pakistan, Indonesia, China, on the heading of '*populus Dei*' which Christians understand in a biblical sense, but which non-Christians understand

1. *AS* II/III, 352–354.
2. Antoni Baraniak, Archbishop of Poznań, member of the Commission on Eastern Churches, *AS* II/III, 354–356.
3. *AS* II/III, 357–358.
4. *AS* II/III, 358–359.
5. *AS* II/III, 362–364.
6. *AS* II/III 365–366.
7. Joseph B Evangelisti, OFM Cap, Archbishop of Meerut (India), *AS* II/III, 366–367.

in an exclusive sense, which excludes them from it, and makes them the people of the devil. And in pagan countries, there have been too many 'Christians' from the West who were anything but *gens electum, regale sacerdotium* [a chosen race, a royal priesthood] etc. (It would be easy to remove the ambiguity.)

On should speak simply *de populo christiano* [of the Christian People].

Beginning of discussion of Chapter IV: *De vocatione ad sanctitatem* [On the call to holiness].

Unfortunately, my advice, which I had repeated ten times, that, before the discussion, one should explain the meaning, the composition of the chapter, was not followed. Without that, I fear that the discussion will wander from the point more than once.

Cardinal Richaud[1] on holiness, on the aspect of expiation, on the suffering of invalids, on consecration, the basis of all religious life.

Cardinal Silva[2] in the name of fifty bishops from Latin America.

Placet (giving reasons). However, there are some omissions.

Schoemaker[3] (Indonesia) in the name of the Bishops' Conference of Indonesia, more than thirty bishops.

Holiness is seen too much from the ascetic point of view, at the level of activities, whereas, biblically, it is first of all a gift of God to his people, who are sinners.

Thus No. 28 and the beginning of No. 29 need to be rewritten. Criticisms concerning the religious state (the concept of obedience), and self-denial: stress the paschal aspect.

Gonzalez[4] (Astorga): there is no further mention of bishops . . . *Redolet ascetismum* [It is redolent of asceticism]. Include a reference to the relationship to the bishop.

Mgr Charue:[5] the chapter should be retained in both its structure and what it says.

Mgr Urtasun:[6] (high-pitched, thin voice, rather sing-song and 'episcopal'): against transferring the section on the vocation to holiness to *De populo Dei*, as this would mean that this chapter spoke only of Religious.

---

1. *AS* II/III, 368–369.
2. R Silva Henríquez, *AS* II/III, 369–371.
3. *AS* II/III, 372–374.
4. Marcello Gonzalez Martin, Bishop of Astorga (Spain), *AS* II/III, 377–379.
5. *AS* II/III, 382–384.
6. *AS* II/III, 384–386.

Mgr Arrighi told me that the Secretariat's text *De libertate religiosa* had been passed on to the Theological Commission. He was alerting several bishops who were efficacious on this subject: McGrath, Charue . . .

> A Yugoslav bishop[1] showed at great length that diocesan priests, too, are in the state of perfection . . .

Lunch at the Greek College. Mgr Edelby had also been invited. During coffee, he explained how, at the Commission on the Eastern Churches, there had been a total impasse in relation to everything that comes from the Eastern Congregation.

These people are very pleasant when it is a question of generalities but, when it comes to texts, steps to be taken, translating INTO PRACTICE something really worthwhile, there is obstruction, postponement, the force of inertia, the negative vote. Fr Dumont and Fr Lanne say that things are exactly the same at the Eastern sub-commission of the Secretariat for Unity. To say nothing of the fact that at the Council Commission last May the Eastern bishops had not even been invited!

Clearly, that will have to change before one can hope to have a worthwhile dialogue with the Orthodox.

On this subject, Fr Dumont told me that the Secretariat had asked him for a report to submit to the Pope on ways of approaching the Orthodox. Fr Dumont thinks, as I myself do, that it would be necessary to implement to the maximum, IN FACT, the deep community of the Churches, and that reunion will come about in life before it is declared.

At 3.50 pm at the Belgian college for the Committee working on the Church as servant and poor. I presented draft. I was asked to try and reduce the essence into a SHORT SECTION.

At 5.15 pm appointment with a doctor, professor of neurology: Bruno Callieri. He examined me for an hour, very carefully. Difficult case, he said: several things are possible. He adopted the hypothesis of myelasthenia, and gave me some strong medication.[2]

Saturday 26 October 1963

Except for some visitors (a Spanish priest, Fr Féret, two German students, a Canadian Jesuit, the Spanish Dominican Fr Leon . . .) spent the whole day working on the card index for the Commission. Fr Hamer had asked me to go to Santa Sabina for a meeting of experts on the chapter on Religious together with the Fr General, but I thought that Fr Féret was much more competent than I am.

---

1. Stjepan Bäuerlein, Bishop of Djakovo and Srijem (Bosnia), Apostolic Administrator of the diocese of Pécs (Hungary) for the parishes situated in Yugoslav territory, *AS* II/III, 387–389.
2. Congar added to the typescript: 'which had no effect!'

This work on the cards takes a long time, but it allows one to see things close up and to learn something.

Fr Lumbreras[1] asked me, on behalf of the S Penitentiary (Cardinal Confalonieri[2]) about Jean Goss who had left there an appeal for the condemnation of the atomic bomb and mentioning me.

Sunday 27 October 1963

Work: card index for the Commission; brief draft on the Church of the poor.

Lunch: Cardinal Liénart, Mgr Philippe, Guerry, Renard, Marty, Huyghe. During the meal, I listened to the complaints of Fr de Vos.[3] He told me how the Angelicum is collapsing, in his opinion irremediably. They do not want to open up to the needs or demands of the moment. He told me that, in November 1952, he had produced a project for an Institute for 'the historical and critical study of St Thomas'. Fr Gillon, the rector, was in agreement. It all came to nothing. He wonders whether perhaps Fr Garrigou intervened against the project. That would be quite possible. For him, as for Fr Browne,[4] 'historical and critical' were the equivalent of dogmatic relativism and the negation of the principles of metaphysics!

I had another go at Cardinal Liénart in favour of a *De Populo Dei* of an historical kind; what is needed is for the Theological Commission to be pushed by a text coming from a bishop . . .

Mgr Guerry told me that Siri and the Italian bishops want to publish a letter on Marxism. They have in mind the opening to the left and the Italian elections. For them, everything is dominated by preoccupations about political influence. When, at the Council, they call for insistence on the submission of the laity to the hierarchy, and even that this notion be included in the definition of the laity, what they are really envisaging is this: the bishops' dealings with *la Democrazia cristiana*. I have realised for years that many things in the Church can be explained by the Italian situation, and that the Italian situation is itself seen from the political angle.

Mgr Guerry spoke of Cardinal Siri, of his letter (published by *Verbe*[5]), in which several passages clearly refer to the French episcopate; so much so that the bishops, in the person of Cardinal Liénart, protested to the Pope. All he did was to raise and lower his arms, as much as to say: it is discouraging, but what can I do?

---

1. Pedro Lumbreras, OP, of the Province of the Philippines was *sigillatore* at the Sacred Penitentiary.
2. It is difficult to establish a link between Cardinal Confalonieri and the Sacred Penitentiary. The reference is more likely to be to Cardinal Cento, the Grand Penitentiary.
3. Athanase de Vos, OP, of the Province of Flanders, Professor in the Faculty of Philosophy at the Angelicum.
4. Cardinal Michael Browne.
5. The journal *Verbe,* the organ of Cité Catholique (cf page 158, note 1) had published two items by Cardinal Siri in November 1962 (No. 135).

In the afternoon, a very long conversation with Canon Delaruelle.[1] He confirmed to me that Mgr de Solages[2] is dying: a man who will not have had the opportunity to establish himself completely through an outstanding work.[3]

Monday 28 October 1963

This morning, at St Peter's there is only a ceremony commemorating the election of John XXIII: the Pope is to celebrate at the ALTAR OF THE COUNCIL, and Cardinal Suenens will read an address. I did not go. I wrote letters and more letters, and yet more long overdue letters!! It is the cross of my life.

I also replied to an enquiry from the Sacred Penitentiary (Cardinal Confalonieri) about Jean Goss-Mayr, who had introduced himself and mentioned my name. I gave a good reference and added what I myself thought about the bomb.

At 4.30 pm, the Theological Commission. In the Cortile di san Damaso I met up with Cardinal Léger and Mgr Garrone, who were devastated. They had received copies of the questions in which they perceived a manoeuvre aimed at undermining the Moderators' questions.

Cardinal Ottaviani opened the meeting:

Mgr Parente had had an audience of the Pope on 26 October. The Pope had given him, even in writing, instructions on the following points:

    – to speed up the discussion on the *De libertate religiosa*;

    – to speed up the work of the Theological Commission.

The Council needs to have dealt with the *De libertate religiosa* before the end of the Session. The Commission must work *intensior et celerior* [more intensely and more speedily], even if this means meeting every day.

It will be necessary, Parente said, taking account of what the Pope was thinking 'seligere puncta et rogare Patres ut de his suffragium faciant' [Choose points and ask the Fathers to vote on them], 'haec enim sessio non claudetur nisi postquam aliquid magni momenti deliberatum fuerit' [this Session is not to close without some matter of prime importance having been dealt with]. For this reason, the schema *De libertate religiosa* has been distributed this morning and we are to say *si aliquid contra habeamus* [whether we have any objections to it].

Will it be necessary to meet every day? Even on Saturday? But then how will the sub-commissions be able to work so as to prepare the amendments?

Ottaviani had read out a letter from Mgr Felici in which, on behalf of the Holy Father, he asked the Commission's opinion on two questions that had been raised by someone of very high standing: 1) on the purpose of marriage; 2) on the

---

1. Étienne Delaruelle, specialist in medieval religious history, Professor of Ecclesiastical History at the Institut Catholique in Toulouse.
2. Bruno de Solages, theologian and exegete, had been Rector of the Institut Catholique in Toulouse since 1931. He was to resign as Rector in 1964, but he recovered his health and died in 1983.
3. However, his retirement would enable him to complete and publish several works on the gospels and their redaction.

borderline between what is superfluous and what is owed (see sheets of paper). Ottaviani proposed to set up a sub-commission to deal with this.

Mgr Garrone and Mgr van Dodewaard pointed out that this was related to schema XVII.

Mgr Charue: the Moderators have announced that they would be putting specific questions to the Council.

Ottaviani: but the questions that we are raising here are specific! The Moderators cannot take the place of the Theological Commission. Moreover, he suggested it was doubtful that it had been announced that there would be questions . . . We cannot interrupt our work when the Pope himself asks us to get on with it! If the Moderators' questions coincide, there will be no difficulty; if not, we will see how to reconcile them. It is WE whom the Council has appointed to deal with matters of doctrine; the Moderators' task is only to oversee the progress of the work.

Charue: but if the Pope has approved the actual TEXT of their questions?

Ottaviani: then, we will have to suspend our work . . . Do you wish us to suspend our work?

Several: let us select the members of the eleven sub-commissions.

Ottaviani: *'subcommissiones de quanam re'* [sub-commissions for what]?

Mgr Parente saved the situation by recalling that on 15 October we had been mandated to reply to the question concerning the theological note of our texts. The sub-commission (Parente, Schröffer, Fernandez) had composed a text which we began to discuss (*VERY* long exposition by Fr Salaverri), very long exposition by Colombo, along the lines of the pastoral purpose of the Council, very long discussion which was brought to an end at 6.05 pm by sending it back to the sub-commission which will hear all those who have suggestions to make. We then moved on to the appointment of the members of the sub-commissions for the Theological Commission. (Mgr Philips said that for the first two chapters there are 1,500 cards, without counting all the other comments which have not yet been card-indexed, that is, the comments sent in writing before the opening of the Council.) The work can begin at once or very soon. The members of the Commission should write their wishes on a sheet of paper: these will be sorted and the Fathers will be allocated. The results will be announced tomorrow and matters finally settled.

At 6.30 pm, the central sub-commission met to sort out the sheets of paper and set up the sub-commissions; while this was going on, a number of the experts,[1] with Mgr Parente, discussed the formula of the theological note. We improved on the one the sub-commission had proposed.

Strange meeting!! The Holy Office people had staged a manoeuvre designed to torpedo or even eliminate the votes prepared by the Moderators and, through

---

1. Congar added to the margin of the first typescript 'including me', and of the second typescript, 'I was one'.

these votes, the authority of the Moderators themselves. The stage had been set but, at the first sign of opposition, everything came tumbling down; there was no further reference to the questions prepared (*dixit* [according to] Ottaviani) by Parente. Mgr Garrone said to me: it's like a snail. It boldly puts out its horns, but you only have to touch them with your little finger for it to withdraw them . . .

I had supper at the French Seminary. At the end of the meal, Cardinal Lefebvre said that some Spanish theologians had supplied a packet containing papers in favour of a *Non placet* vote with regard to the inclusion of the *De BMV* in the *De Ecclesia*. There were some simple sheets of summary (I took one) and a long duplicated explanatory pamphlet (I left them for the bishops to take, and there were none left). Cardinal Lefebvre smilingly drew attention to the indiscretion of the procedure: we are not in a parliament, subject to propaganda . . . ! '

At 9 pm, lecture on ecumenism at the Jesuit Scholasticate at the Gesú.

Tuesday 29 October 1963

Went to St Peter's. At the door, a leaflet was being distributed signed by Eastern bishops and which is a swindle: they base their argument on the devotion to the Mother of God of the Easterners, whether in union or not, in order to support their demand for a separate schema. Marian devotees of every shade are conducting a massive offensive. I was also told of a paper by Roschini,[1] compared with whom Balić is a moderate. What will be the outcome of the vote? Many bishops are hesitant . . . I would give 52 to 55% in favour of its being inserted. . . . (I had first written 51% . . .).

I met Cardinal Döpfner who asked me how things went yesterday evening at the Theological Commission. I, in my turn, asked him whether or not the four questions were going to be asked. He said: they must have been printed but one cannot tell either if they will be distributed today, or what will come of it, because Cardinal Cicognani or Mgr Felici or Ottaviani are constantly interfering . . .

As I returned to my seat, I encountered Mgr Parente and Mgr Florit in deep conversation, looking very preoccupied . . .

Ukrainian Mass. I dearly love the Easterners, but it is a bit much to keep giving us Masses which last for more than an hour when there is so much work to be done. The time available for work is reduced to very little. And it is very tiring. Many people have been up since 5 am, have said their own Mass, then served another . . . It is absurd. But in Rome, no-one knows what work is.

If I could walk better and was less dependent on means of transport, I would not come here until about 10.30 am.

The meeting began at 10.15 am!!!

---

1. Gabriele Roschini, OSM, Procurator General of the Servites of Mary and President of the Marianum Pontifical Theological Faculty which he had founded and where he taught theology: Council expert.

Felici[1] announced the vote on the *De BMV* and on the amendments to Chapter V of *De Sacra Liturgia*.

De mandato Moderatorum [at the command of the Moderators] (he repeated this several times, and with emphasis), the text of the votes on the various points will be distributed, of which there are now five (so at least they have left the printers!).

Felici read the text. Close attention; intense silence.

Reading of the liturgical report.[2]

The Moderators explained clearly the meaning of the vote *De BMV* :

1) It is not a question of a vote on a minimalist text, but simply of the PLACE where the text is to be put.

2) Whatever the outcome, it will be for the Theological Commission to present the text.

Interventions on the chapter *De vocatione ad sanctitatem*:

Cardinal Cerejeira (Lisbon)[3] [ ]

Cardinal de Barros Câmara[4] in the name of one hundred and twenty-one bishops of Brazil.

Cardinal Gilroy,[5] praised the chapter, approved of the *emendatio* presented by the Germans concerning the bishops' effort at holiness. (I just cannot see that any purpose is served by these speeches.)

Ruffini:[6] (he was visibly either endeavouring to remain calm, or he was out of breath) = same comment: (it would be better to submit a written text).

Quiroga:[7] same comment (all that is VERY tiresome).

Döpfner,[8] in the name of eighty-one German-speaking bishops and bishops from the Scandinavian countries: he praised the fact that holiness was presented and proposed as being for everyone (against the false idea of Max Weber and Ernst Troeltsch), that the counsels are not shown solely from the ascetic point of view, but also ontologically and eschatologically.

He suggested some principles for the correction of the chapter (one sees that the German bishops are listening to and following the advice of the theologians and that the latter are truly in the current of the return to the sources and of the broadening of ideas . . . Our own bishops mix

1. *AS* II/III, 573–583.
2. *AS* II/III, 583–590.
3. M Gonçalves Cerejeira, *AS* II/III, 590–592.
4. *AS* II/III, 592–593.
5. *AS* II/III, 595–596.
6. *AS* II/III, 596–599.
7. Fernando Quiroga y Palacios, *AS* II/III, 600–602.
8. *AS* II/III, 603–605.

their options and, with the exception of one or two, remain syncretists, in a climate of pietistic edification.

Mgr Vuccino:[1] in favour of a more biblical treatment! The life of the just person flowing from FAITH!

What path has God chosen in order to reveal holiness to us. Above all Sacred History . . . (but though this was interesting and valuable, people were no longer listening! It was midday; people were on their way out). I DEDUCE THAT IT IS HE WHO WAS ASKED TO GIVE THE LESSON ON POVERTY . . . FAITH-HUMILITY-POVERTY . . . HE MAKES A JOB LOT OF IT ALL: SPLENDID THEMES BUT *EXTRA OPPORTUNITATEM* [out of place].

Mgr Felici[2] gave the result of the votes:
On Chapter V of the schema on the Liturgy:

present	2,193
placet	2,154
non placet	21

On the question asked about *De Beata MV*:

Present	2,193
placet	1,114
non placet	1 074
iuxta modum	2 (= null)
null	3

It is a very small majority: uneasiness will remain . . . But it has been decided.

Then the various liturgical *emendationes* (which I did not follow).

At 3 pm, left for the recording of two transmission for Swiss TV.

At 4.30 pm, Vatican, Theological Commission.

To begin with, approval of the formula for the Theological note: the vote was 17 IN FAVOUR, out of 24.

Mgr Philips proposed the distribution of the sub-commissions and also general rules for the work of the sub-commissions.

Fr Tromp insisted on the primary task of *periti*: to report exactly the reasons *for* and *against*.

Philips suggested that on the day on which the sub-commissions are to meet to work there not be a meeting of the Commission. This is the recommendation of Cardinal Browne. Truth to tell, Philips plays, IN FACT, the role of secretary of the Commission. He knows where he is going and has the ability to get things through . . . He does not let go of his idea until it has been implemented.

---

1. *AS* II/III, 617–619.
2. *AS* II/III, 627–628.

Philips then took up the idea of informing the Fathers of the work of the Theological Commission and of its sub-commissions.

Rahner raised the question of what will be done with the indications that will be given by the votes on the five points proposed this morning.

On the return journey (during the rush hour!!) in Cardinal Léger's car, he told me that several people resent very badly what they consider to be their defeat this morning regarding the *De Beata*. The Italian episcopate had received instructions which had even been reported on the TV . . . So approaches to the Holy Father are being prepared so that he will intervene and 1) say that as this vote reveals that the assembly is virtually evenly divided, there will be no further mention or discussion of the *De Beata* ; 2) he will himself give a *laudatio Beatae Virginis* [praise of the Blessed Virgin] at the end of the Session.

The way in which the cardinal spoke made me suspect that this could well be the case for several of the Canadian bishops . . .

For my part, I told him, I would regard that as quite a good solution. On the one hand, in effect, it would be very difficult to produce a text. On the other hand, the discussion *in aula* would risk being very difficult. The Virgin Mary, who ought to unite us, would become a subject of division. Now, nothing obliges us to speak of her. On the contrary, one would succeed in eliminating a last vestige of the work of the Preparatory Commission, and that would bring us back into the general movement of the Council.

In any case, this morning's vote marks a first *'parting of the ways'* [1] for the Fathers; tomorrow's votes will be another one, even more decisive.

On my return here, this evening, drafting of a brief text on the mission of the Church, showing how the activity of lay people fits into it, that Mgr Ménager had asked me for. But I can hardly hold my pen!!!

Wednesday 30 October 1963

(58th General Congregation). While chatting with several bishops, including some French ones, I was astonished to see how little they realised what is involved in the five votes that they are to be asked to cast today. They have only vague and fairly pragmatic notions about it all. They do not see clearly what is at stake doctrinally, the foundations . . . Strange business . . . !

Was it like this at Nicaea or at Chalcedon?

This morning, voting on the five points put forward yesterday.

> Cardinal Léger[2] on the holiness of lay people: against the monopolising primacy of a kind of MONASTIC holiness.
>
> On the theology of the consecrated life in a very evangelical sense.

---

1.   {Congar used the English phrase.}
2.   *AS* II/III, 632–634.

Cardinal Urbani:[1] the Church in glory and the communion of saints should be mentioned.

Cardinal Cento:[2] (cited Daniel-Rops[3] but spoke in order to say nothing). Praise for pious associations. He also cited Fulton Sheen.[4]

Cardinal Bea:[5] good but not realistic enough. Care should be taken with the use of the words *perfectio*, etc. when speaking of the pilgrim Church. Nothing on the use of biblical texts in relation to holiness.

I note that, so far, Cardinal Bea has not intervened at the Council except as a BIBLICAL SCHOLAR. I know that it is understood that nobody should speak in the name of the Secretariat, and I note that the most prominent members of the Secretariat (Mgr De Smedt) do not often intervene. Everything happens as if the Secretariat wished to remain very discreet at this Session, or as if it is waiting for the moment when it will itself be presenting its texts on ecumenism and on religious freedom.

Mgr Huyghe[6] (Arras) on No. 31 and No. 32: Féret's comments and theses. (It is curious: many complain of the text restricting the counsels to the vows of religion, whereas the formal intention of the sub-commission, I am a witness to it, was precisely the opposite. But the difficulty, or the ambiguity, comes from the fact that, in re-using the terms of the previous text, one spoke of the counsels (which were intended to be for all) IN TERMS which are proper to their application TO THE RELIGIOUS LIFE.

Mgr Fourrey,[7] bishop of Belley (oratorical tone): that something be added at the request of some lay people.

Mgr Prignon, whom I met at the bar, told me that again yesterday evening Cardinal Ottaviani had tried to get the vote on the five points postponed until later (after the holidays for All Saints); in vain. Thus, right to the end, 'they' have tried to put off what will effectively announce the end of their reign . . .

---

1. *AS* II/III, 635–636.
2. *AS* II/III, 636–638.
3. Henri Petiot, known as Daniel-Rops, French writer and historian, author of works on religious history; he died in July 1965.
4. Fulton J Sheen, Auxiliary Bishop of New York, elected member of the Commission on the Missions during the First Session, was a famous lecturer and preacher in the United States.
5. *AS* II/III, 638–641.
6. *AS* II/III, 646–648.
7. René Fourrey, *AS* II/III, 649–651.

Russell[1] (USA) in the name of several bishops: how is the Church herself holy
while her members are sinners?

Angelo Fernandes, Auxiliary Bishop of Delhi[2] (good English pronunciation):
a certain lack of balance in the chapter between the two parts (the
general call to holiness and Religious). [[Basically, the bishops are
more interested in the notion of holiness than in the theology of the
religious life.]]

One should speak of the holiness PROPER to the hierarchy and to
priests, in dependence on MEANS THAT ARE PROPER to the
PASTORAL life.

Franić[3] on the holiness of bishops (*perfectores* [those who make perfect] even
Religious).[4] On the holiness of diocesan priests.

There should be a SPECIAL chapter on Religious.

There should be a paragraph on poverty as foundation of all holiness
– with commitment to it for major orders so that diocesan priests will
be established in a state of perfection that is being acquired.

Sébastien Soares[5] (Mozambique) *[ ]*

Mgr Hoàng-văn-Doàn[6] (Vitenam): great solemn introduction.

Danger of speaking of an identical vocation to holiness for all.

Dom Reetz[7] (Abbot of Beuron): listened to *VERY* intently: his text was precise,
and well delivered. One should no longer speak *'de statibus perfectionis'*
salva reverentia erga Aquinatem dicetur simpliciter 'status religiosus':
['concerning states of perfection', with due respect to Aquinas, one
should say simply 'the religious state'] this has been a technical term
since the fourth century and St Thomas justifies its use. As regards
exemption: without it the religious orders would never have been so
fruitful. In the Council itself, one third of the bishops are members
of religious orders; the missions and the theological sciences included
a GREAT number of Religious. He compared bishops and Religious
with the columns of St Peter's: the statues of the founders of orders are
placed in niches in the spaces between the columns (= the Apostles).

---

1. John J Russell, Bishop of Richmond, *AS* II/III, 653–656.
2. More precisely, Coadjutor of Delhi, *AS* II/III, 656–658.
3. *AS* II/III, 658–660.
4. Cf above, page 361.
5. Sebastião Soares de Resende, Bishop of Beira, *AS* II/III, 661–663.
6. D Hoàng-văn-Doàn, OP, Bishop of Quy Nhon, *AS* II/III, 664–665.
7. Benedict Reetz, Superior General of the Congregation of the Benedictines of Beuron
    (Germany), member of the Commission on Religious, *AS* II/III, 666–669.

Cardinal Lercaro,[1] Moderator, asked whether discussion of Chapter IV could be suspended, in accordance with regulation No. 57, § 6. A GREAT majority rose to their feet . . .

After the schema *De Ecclesia*, schema *De Episcopis* [on Bishops] and *De dioecesium regimine* [on the Government of Dioceses] will be discussed. The bishops should put down their names if they wish to speak on the schema in general.

Felici gave the result of this morning's votes: on the five points (the five propositions!!):

On No. 1:		On No. 2:	
those present	2,157	those present	2,154
yes	2,123	yes	2,049
no	34	no	104

On No. 3:		On No. 4:	
those present	2,148	those present	2,138
yes	1,808	yes	1,717
no	335	no	408
		null	12

On No. 5:	
those present	2,120
yes	1,588
no	525

So it is the question of the diaconate that aroused the greatest opposition.

There followed the votes on the liturgical *emendationes*.

I learned from Mgr Person, bishop in Ethiopia,[2] that the *internuncio* came to the Ethiopian College yesterday to say to the bishops, on the part of a 'higher authority', that they were to vote 'yes' to the first question and 'no' to the other four. The bishop replied that he would do what he considered best.

I saw l'abbé Naud, in order to speak to him about the *De Populo Dei* (history of salvation) and about the priesthood of priests.

At St Martha's, Vatican, 4.30 pm, sub-commission on the *De Populo Dei*: there were present, together with the bishops of the sub-commission, the following experts: Sauras, Witte, Congar, then Fr Reuter[3] (Oblate) and Naud. Maccarrone has moved to another sub-commission; Schmaus is away until 25.XI.63. On the other hand, Kerrigan is to join us and perhaps Lubac, who has just arrived. Mgr

---

1. *AS* II/III, 669–670.
2. The Frenchman, Urbain M Person, OFM Cap, was Vicar Apostolic of Harar and Apostolic Administrator of the province of Hosanna and Neghelli.
3. Armand Reuter, OMI, Director General of Studies in his Congregation, Council expert.

Philips spent an hour with us, in order to get the work started. It is he who is the real animator.

Fr Tromp, who was in an office nearby, merely put in an appearance, like a shadow. He no longer plays any role. Moreover, he is not particularly gifted for the organising functions of a secretary.

Fr Reuter, who is an expert for the Commission on the Missions, told us what had happened at this Commission. My impression is that it is something of a hornet's nest and that there is no understanding between the President, the members and the *periti*. At the moment they have three texts on the theological basis of the missions, but it will be up to us, in agreement with them (if possible), to introduce a text on this subject in our No. 10 (former numbering). Cardinal Santos, who is supposed to be the President, said: *procedamus in pace* [let us go forth in peace]. . . people chat, waste time, like children who do not know what game to play . . .

The former No. 8 was allocated to Witte and Reuter; No. 9 to Sauras and whoever he chooses; No. 10 to Congar and Naud.

We stayed on to work after the end of this disappointing meeting.

I saw Mgr Colombo, who was pleased about the vote this morning and said to me: It is important above all for the Pope, as it gives him a basis.

Indeed, I know that Paul VI wants to bring residential bishops into the work of the Congregations. If, in order to do so, he bases himself on collegiality, that will be a very firm theological basis.

At 7.45 pm, supper at the Germanicum and lecture on ecumenism.

Thursday 31 October 1963

I did not go to St Peter's: I have too much urgent work to do: index cards for the Commission and preparation for our work on the former No. 10.

Fr Gagnebet informed me of the assurance from Cardinal Antoniutti (through Cardinal Browne) that there was no truth in the report in yesterday's *Le Monde* (H Fesquet) to the effect that the Congregation for Religious had given to the Religious Superiors a list of experts who were not to be trusted, in which my own name figured.[1] I had heard talk of this. Fr Gagnebet added that what may have given rise to this false rumour was the fact that, eight or ten days ago, three experts (Rahner, Thils and Moeller) had wanted to re-do a chapter *De Religiosis* at the Congregation of Religious: Cardinal Antoniutti had said that he did not want that.

At 3.30 pm I saw a new doctor (a consultation arranged on his part by my dear and so good Fr Mongillo): Professor Lamberto Longhi. He examined me fairly briefly. He believes that it is definitely something to do with my circulation. He suggested a medication but, when I asked him if it was compatible with

---

1. *Le Monde* gave the names of twelve Council experts including Congar, Rahner, Küng and Ratzinger.

what I was already taking (without naming Professor Callieri), he told me that the medication he was recommending was sufficient. So I am very perplexed. I find myself faced with three medications, the one recommended by Dr Thiébaut,[1] the one recommended by Callieri (which is neurological and is compatible with the previous one) and the one suggested by Longhi. I cannot take them all at the same time. So I decided, TO BEGIN WITH, to continue with the Callieri medication together with the very mild one prescribed by Thiébaut.

1 November 1963

All Saints. In fact, All Saints' weather: rain.

Profession of Lucie Scherrer at the Charterhouse in Voiron.[2]

I wrote my chronicle for *ICI.* Quite long this time!

From 4 pm to 6.15 pm, meeting with the Goss Mayers, Frs Häring, Rahner and a Spanish Father from the Gregorianum,[3] in order to finish a text on conscientious objection to be proposed to those who are drafting schema XVII, and also to begin preparing a text on the evangelical exigencies with respect to peace. Fr Häring is truly marvellous.

He told me that yesterday Paul VI went to the Lateran for the inauguration of the Academic Year. He finished his speech by saying that the Lateran ought to work POSITIVELY, not in a negatively critical manner, and that negative criticism ought always to be ruled out. The students received these words with a thunder of applause. It was understood that this indicated a disavowal of the spirit of Mgr Piolanti and an end to the attacks on the Biblicum.

Moreover, I bought the *Quotidiano* so as to have a copy of the Italian bishops' letter on atheistic communism: the Pope's little speech was also printed: the passage outlined in red is the one that was applauded by the students.[4]

I also read in it that Fr Dhanis has been appointed a consultor at the 'Holy Office': I had foreseen that since 1960, when I saw him at the Preparatory Theological Commission.

The Italian bishops' text is supposed to be pastoral; it states that it does not wish to judge people, but condemns the atheistic character of communism.

In the same issue, another article by Mgr Staffa: he had written one, eight days ago, in support of the papal monarchy and against collegiality. This time, seeing

---

1. François Thiébaut, neurologist in Strasbourg.
2. The reference is to the Chartreuse de Beauregard in Coublevie par Voiron (Isère).
3. José M Diez-Alegria, SJ, who taught the social doctrine of the Church and the theory of law at the Gregorianum.
4. The passage read as follows: '*della sincera riconoscenza, della fraterna collaborazione, della leale emulazione, della mutua reveranza e dell'amica concordia, non mai d'una gelosa concorrenza o d'una fastidiosa polemica; non mai!*' [sincere acknowledgement, fraternal collaboration, fair emulation, mutual respect and friendly agreement, never a jealous rivalry or a hyper-critical polemic! Never again! (Article inserted into the journal.)

that collegiality is on the point of being approved of, he accepts it, but reduces it to the papal monarchy. He too is obsessed.

All Saints' day very much spent in meditation on the Beatitudes as the charter of Christian ontology or of the Christian human being. THAT is what is still too much missing from our schemas!

Saturday 2 November 1963

The weather has changed. From relatively fresh it has become humid and warm: it is raining. I heard it as soon as I woke up. I have NO strength.

Apart from that, I feel fed up and even crushed by everything. The world is too vast, there is too much that is new, one would need to do and gain mastery of too many things. I feel that I am old, emptied out; I have a headache: my body is heavy and my spiritual resources very uncertain.

Humanly speaking, I am, if not conquered, at least betrayed by life. Humanly speaking, it would be better to disappear now: I would be disappearing in relative beauty. But I know too well that one does not choose and that these feelings are stupid. They are not blasphemous because they remain on the surface of a soul that has been given and takes nothing back. *Sed tu, Domine, usquequo?* [But you, O Lord, how long? (Ps 6:4)].

This morning, I typed my chronicle for *ICI*; in the afternoon painful birth of the beginning of the lecture I am to give at the Week for Catholic Intellectuals on 11 November.

Sunday 3 November 1963

Where am I going? My head feels numb, physically I am half asleep. At times I sit for a long time in front of my sheet of paper, with my eyes open but seeing nothing, with no creativity, in a kind of waking or semi-waking stupor because it easily slides into sleep. Is it the beginning of an incurable senility? I well understand David's need of Abishag: not for her fleshly presence, but for her presence itself. Here I am isolated, I see no-one; the life of the Angelicum is as tedious as the cooking. I am longing to be back in contact with men and women, with friends. The worst thing about old age has to be the isolation.

Monday 4 November 1963

National holiday in Italy.[1] At 10 am, meeting of the working party 'For a Church that is servant and poor', at the Spanish Church of Montserrat. Unfortunately, it is a national holiday; there must be a great parade somewhere. The whole area between the Quirinal-National Museum and Piazza Venezia (and beyond) is closed to buses and cars. I was obliged to go on foot: even the approaches to Piazza Venezia were closed to pedestrians, so that one had to make a detour as far as the Gregorianum; that worked. Afterwards, it went from bad to worse: I covered the

---

1. Anniversary of the First World War Armistice.

last five hundred metres fifteen centimetres at a time, and absolutely at the end of my tether. Moreover, these days nothing goes well for me any more: I have pain in my stomach, in my kidneys, in my back. I am done.

A meeting without ANY interest, absolutely useless. For the sixth time, Fr Gauthier returned to the same topics: we re-read the texts; everyone said: 'we ought to'. Nothing came of it. It is getting nowhere . . . A waste of time.

Visit from a priest from Bologna (for *Il Regno*), de Vogel (*ICI*), from the Rector of the Collegio San Pietro[1] (one hundred and forty priests FROM EVERY-WHERE for the 'missions').

Tuesday 5 November 1963.

The work of the General Congregation recommenced. We are four weeks from the end.

Health: *VERY* bad. During the Mass, unable to make all the gestures; unable to walk. NO strength.

I went to St Peter's mainly because I had arranged to meet Mgr Moralejo.[2] He has redone the texts on the POOR that are to be inserted.

Reading of the reports on the *De episcopis* . . .

Cardinal Liénart[3] (the services that the pope can receive from the bishops should be stipulated (basing himself on the Pope's speech of 29.IX.63[4]).
Cardinal McIntyre[5] (I was absent)
Cardinal Gracias[6]   "
Cardinal Richaud[7] (voice of an old man, and coughing) stressed the lack of agreement with the Council's wish for collegiality: refinements about the competence of the episcopal conferences, that room should be made for bishops who are neither coadjutors nor auxiliaries. He also criticised the plan, the order of the chapters. He gave a complete constructive critique.
Mgr Gargitter:[8] SUBSTANTIAL corrections are called for.
The more detailed questions should be deleted, and one should stick to principles.
Rupp:[9] amused everybody. What has been granted is soon taken back and the important points are glided over as quickly as possible.

---

1. Matthias Schneider, SVD.
2. R González Moralejo.
3. *AS* II/IV, 445–446.
4. The speech at the opening of the Second Session.
5. *AS* II/IV, 446–447.
6. *AS* II/IV, 447–449.
7. *AS* II/IV, 450–452.
8. *AS* II/IV, 453–455.
9. *AS* II/IV, 455–456.

Jubany,[1] auxiliary in Barcelona. *[ ]*

De Bazelaire:[2] the schema is more juridical than pastoral.

Correa[3] (Cucuta, Colombia) in the name of fifty or sixty bishops. Powers should not be not be presented as concessions but as rights.

Garrone:[4] *de ordine* [on order] to be revised in the light of the schema *De Ecclesia* and of collegiality; Appendix II, which ought not only exhort, but determine, should be integrated within the text. The schema is too general and theoretical. It does not take sufficient account of the CURRENT state of the world (socialisation).

He was listened to very attentively, even though it was almost noon.

Marty[5] (precious tone, slow, not catching attention): the collegial aspect should be included; indicate some rules for the relationship between collegial assemblies of bishops and the pope.

Baudoux:[6] along the same lines.

One can say, then, that the basic criticism has been made. Tomorrow there will be a vote on the schema as a whole. It could be rejected. However, it would be good for its various chapters to be discussed: that would give an opportunity for a certain number of things to be said. Also, many of the bishops think, as I do, that it would be better to vote *placet iuxta modum* and proceed to the discussion.

This 5 November is THE worst day I have had over the past three years that I have been ill. I can no longer walk and have absolutely no strength. I am dragging myself along with the gait of a cripple. If I do not improve substantially between now and then, I shall not be able to come back for the Third Session. Of course, the sirocco is responsible to some extent.

However, I went to the Theological Commission. A discussion of *De libertate religiosa* was scheduled.

I did not take this notebook with me to St Peter's: it is too heavy in the brief-case I have to carry! I took notes on a sheet of paper and copied them out as they were.

We were given copies of the *De libertate religiosa* (which the bishops on the Commission had already received).

> Cardinal Ottaviani: a sub-commission should be set up that will submit a report to the Commission.
>
> Charue: What exactly is expected of us?

---

1. *AS* II/IV, 456–458.
2. Louis MF Bazelaire de Ruppierre, *AS* II/IV, 460–462.
3. Pablo Correa León, Bishop of Cucuta, member of the Commission on Bishops and the Governance of Dioceses, *AS* II/IV, 462–464.
4. *AS* II/IV, 465–466.
5. *AS* II/IV, 467–468.
6. *AS* II/IV, 469–471.

Ottaviani: our comments: *utrum conveniat necne* [is it appropriate or not]? Then we will have a joint meeting with the Secretariat.

Charue: is it a *nihil obstat* or a positive recommendation?

Schröffer: Ought we to improve the text or simply say: *transeat* [let it pass]. Have the *periti* had the text? It is important, we are dealing with something important.

Ottaviani: reverted to his idea of a sub-commission which could call on whichever *periti* it chose.

Philips suggested that the members of sub-commission 6 and 7 be chosen as they have no work this week.

This was agreed to. So it will be Wright, Spanedda, McGrath, Šeper, Gut, Fernandez with Cardinal Léger and the *periti* that they select.

Ottaviani: retained the names underlined here.

Philips explained his report on the work of the Commission, to be submitted to the Fathers of the Council. This was approved (but without a vote or a clear conclusion).

Ottaviani: there is:

a) The question of the text *De BMV*: the basis will be the schema that had been proposed. The vote referred only to its insertion, not to the text as such; all we need to know now is whether it will become a Chapter VI of *De Ecclesia* or an appendix: he was in favour of an appendix (which would leave the text as it is).

b) The five points voted on: EVERYTHING has already been stated in the schema. How should we implement the vote? Is it opportune to include the restoration of the diaconate in a dogmatic constitution?

Cardinal König: the Commission should select some members who would consult the bishops' conferences in order to have a text that would avoid the need for a long discussion *in aula*.

Ottaviani: that could not be done either quickly or easily.

Parente: to begin with, WE should reach an understanding about a text: afterwards, contact the episcopal conferences.

Of his own accord, Ottaviani had already twice invited Franić to speak, though he had not asked to speak, as he was not there. But he never stops calling on his own men or pushing them forward: Franić, Spanedda, Fernandez.

Charue (truly persistent and courageous: a real foot-soldier who sticks to his ground!): with regard to the *De Beata*, there is a great deal of sensitivity. The question should be put to some of the Fathers, if need be, not belonging to our Commission. He suggested a sub-commission comprising two cardinals, Santos and König, an Eastern bishop and Mgr Théas.

Garrone: keep something of König's proposal: these four should ask the episcopal conferences to propose a text if they have one.

Barbado: the bishops have studied the question: they should be heard. If in this way one secures widespread agreement, a discussion *in aula* can be avoided.

I asked desperately to be allowed to speak. I wanted to remind them that that text (Butler's) had obtained more than fifty signatures and so, according to the regulations, it ought to be taken into consideration. But, having said that the *periti* would be asked for their opinion, Ottaviani did not call on me to speak; the idea of the sub-commission of four (Santos, König, Doumith and Théas) was settled on; it will propose something.

Ottaviani moved on to the five points: sacramentality had been dealt with sufficiently.

Schauf intervened in order to demolish the five proposals by showing that they were very vague, if not inadmissible, and that they would put beyond question points that were highly controversial.

Cardinal Browne: these intentions have been proposed to us, but we are free to judge.

Gagnebet: if the Moderators want to put questions, they should consult the competent Commission. Had we been consulted, we would have produced a text which would have secured unanimity.

Charue: if the Pope has approved the Moderators' way of doing things, they can create another way of proceeding . . .

Ottaviani drew distinctions: if the Pope indicates something *motu proprio*, then that is settled, but if he merely agrees to something suggested by others . . .

Scherer:[1] if we say anything different from what the Council has voted on, it will be refused! . . .

The meeting ended at 6.05 pm. No progress had been made. It was a waste of time. Always sub-commissions which are to submit a report, then one will see . . . Ottaviani: 1) is trying all the time to gain time, to prolong delays so that nothing is decided; 2) is constantly questioning a decision that he dislikes. Everyone has an impression of underhandedness and, on the way out, harsh comments were made along these lines.

I am to speak this evening at the Collegio Bellarmino: one hundred and twenty Jesuits from all countries who are doing their doctorates and will be professors.

As the programme was changed *in extremis* [at the last minute], and instead of the sub-commission at St Martha's, there was the Commission at the Vatican, I telephoned the Collegio Bellarmino and asked them

---

1. Alfredo V Schlerer, Archbishop of Porto Alegre (Brazil), member of the Doctrinal Commission.

to pick me up in the Cortile di san Damaso. The porter had oddly misunderstood and sent someone to fetch me from San Lorenzo in Damaso. As a result, in spite of four further telephone calls, I had to wait until 8.10 pm. I, who was already so exhausted . . .

However, I gave my lecture at the time arranged.

Wednesday 6 November 1963
I did not go to St Peter's: I am too exhausted.

According to what people have told me, I missed an interesting session.

Ruffini,[1] on the one hand, expressing the Curialist thesis; on the other, Alfrink[2] (primacy of PASTORAL LEADERS over administration); Bea[3] and Maximos IV:[4] the latter strongly criticised the prepotency of the cardinals, who are Roman clergy and represent only the Roman Church, whereas the bishops, and above all the patriarchs, represent the universal Church.

We are observing a confrontation between two ecclesiologies. The after-effects of the pontificate of Pius XII are being challenged. And, beyond them, the regime that has prevailed since the Gregorian Reform, on the basis of the identification of the Roman Church with the universal Catholic Church. The Churches are alive, they are there, represented and gathered together in Council, they are asking for an ecclesiology of Church and Churches, and not just of the papal monarchy with the juridical system with which it has provided itself in order to serve its own purposes.

In the afternoon, visit from Fr Féret, then Cullmann (about a lecture). At St Martha's, sub-commission *De Populo Dei*; not much progress made. At this rate, we will not have looked at the whole chapter before the end of the Session!!

In the evening, lecture at the Collegio San Pietro, for priests of the so-called mission Churches. Supper with Cardinal Rugambwa, in whom I was a little disappointed. His English was not easy to understand, and I cannot say that we 'met' each other.

Very fine audience of one hundred and forty priests, black, yellow, white (Australia): the future cadres of these Christianities . . .

Thursday 7 November, 1963
I did not go to St Peter's. At 11.45 am, brother Clément de Bourmont came to take me to St Peter's Square then—after the bishops had left (they all said that the morning had been deadly boring: pro-curialist reaction. In particular, there was Mgr Batanian,[5] Patriarch of the Armenians, who is more Italian that the Italians, more Roman than the Romans. Every time Maximos expressed himself some-

---

1. *AS* II/IV, 476– 478.
2. *AS* II/IV, 479–481.
3. *AS* II/IV, 481–484.
4. Intervention given in French, *AS* II/IV, 516–519; Latin translation: *AS* II/IV, 519–521.
5. *AS* II/IV, 558–559.

what forcibly (as he had done yesterday), another Italianised 'Easterner' contradicted him . . .)—to the Cistercian abbey of Tre Fontane. Lenten lunch.

Everywhere, lassitude if not actually disgust. Several of the bishops have said to me that they will either leave altogether, or that they will no longer attend *in aula*, or that they are no longer listening. They also find everything too long drawn-out, and the daily Mass too long. They find that time is wasted and they ask themselves if anything will be achieved.

At 3 pm at the French Seminary for a workshop on the schema *De œcumenismo*, with Mgr Gouyon, Lebrun,[1] Martin, Ferrand,[2] Rougé, Desmazières, Elchinger, and Frs Le Guillou and Dupuy, and then, towards the end, Fr Villain, who had asked if he might come and then appeared as if by chance. Excellent critique of the schema by Fr Dupuy. We considered what needed to be said. Some things could be inserted into Mgr Martin's introductory report. Fr Le Guillou left us at 4 pm, he had another meeting. He has gained admission everywhere and does everything. The bishops certainly have a high enough regard for him. The meeting ended at 5.05 pm. I saw Mgr Ancel to raise again the idea of a text of a catechetical-kerygmatic kind.

At 6 pm at the Spanish meeting. There I met up again with Fr Le Guillou who had also got himself invited. We spoke about the *De œcumenismo*. This time, it was quite interesting. Several of the Spaniards would like the schema to begin with a fairly complete dogmatic statement on the unity and unicity of the Church. What has been said does not satisfy them. But there are always very varied positions among them. As against an Alonso, who makes these suggestions, there is a Fr Bredi, who says quite the opposite, in particular in favour of the Easterners.

(Together with Mgr Morcillo) took up the question of making the Observers' comments available to some extent.

Küng, who was there, then took us to dine at his hotel with Moeller and Fr Dournes. The latter is returning to Vietnam with some of the bishops—owing to the threats represented by a political situation that is undoubtedly transitory. He was encouraged to speak a lot about Vitenam. Küng is less pessimistic than he was two weeks ago.

Friday 8 November 1963

By not going to St Peter's, it can happen that that one misses a great moment. And also some boring hours. This morning, some notable interventions that I have been told about:

---

1.   Lucien Lebrun, Bishop of Autun.
2.   Louis Ferrand, Archbishop of Tours.

Cardinal Frings[1] on the Curia. Among other things, there was a passage on the Holy Office, in which he urged that authors who were being investigated should be heard. It is scandalous that they are not.

Both Cardinal Lercaro[2] and Cardinal Rugambwa[3] said that there should be a commission to study calmly the necessary reform. Formerly, there used to be a consistory almost daily, that is to say, a pope's Council: something of this kind needs to be re-established.

Cardinal Ottaviani,[4] who was down to speak, got into a great temper. *Ego altissime protestor* [I protest most strongly] against Cardinal Frings. What had been said could only have been said through *'nescientia'* [ignorance], not to call it something else . . . The Holy Office, it is the Pope himself, he said . . .

Cardinal Ottaviani was applauded quite loudly, I was told, but only by a minority; in the minds of a great many more, his anger caused him to be considered a man whose ideas are fixed, who does not listen even to calm criticism. In the minds of many he is quite discredited.

Today, Saturday, 9/XI/63, I was told that Ottaviani had attacked the Moderators, while claiming to respect them. He said that the questions which they had put to the vote were illegitimate and *nullius valoris* [of no weight]. Why had they not consulted the Theological Commission beforehand? They would have avoided several of the ambiguities contained in the questions.

– People are waiting for the Moderators to sort that out on Monday, as they, ALSO, represent the Pope (they had seen him *THREE* times before proposing the five questions).

Apparently, Cardinal Browne[5] repeated, *in aula*, what he had said at the Commission: the vote on the five points is not binding on the Commission.

Mgr Lefebvre,[6] ex-Dakar, ex-Tulle, Superior of the Holy Ghost Fathers, said that they were witnessing the making of accusations against the papacy. It was as if the pope had assumed the powers belonging to others and they were now being taken back from him while saying to him: *Redde quod debes* [Pay what you owe]!

Now THAT IS TRUE. I have studied and I know this history: it is that of the schemes, pursued by every means throughout the centuries, by which the papacy HAS USURPED the place of the *Ecclesia* and of the bishops.

Moving on to the schema *De Beata*, Mgr Lefebvre was called to order and asked to stop by Cardinal Agagianian, the Moderator.

---

1. *AS* II/IV, 616–617.
2. *AS* II/IV, 618–621.
3. *AS* II/IV, 621–623.
4. *AS* II/IV, 624–635.
5. *AS* II/IV, 626–627.
6. *AS* II/IV, 643–644.

On Saturday 9 I bought the *Tempo* in order to see what the Italian press had to say about the Frings-Ottaviani incident. It did not even mention it; it did not report the name of Cardinal Frings! On the other hand, it gave extracts from Cardinal Lercaro's speech and was right to do so. That speech is held to be very important. Not only must it have been given with Paul VI's agreement, but it suggested things that are POSSIBLE and which are nevertheless far-reaching.

At 4.30 p.m., sub-commission at St Martha's. Fr Naud and Fr de Lubac told me a bit about the work on *De libertate religiosa* that was done yesterday, Thursday, at Cardinal Léger's. Fr Fernandez had criticised the proposed text in the name of texts from the *Syllabus*, Pius IX and Leo XIII: are we always to be tied to the past and to a past as 'dated' as much as that one? Mgr Spanedda did not express any SPECIFIC criticism, but formulated an overall disagreement in the name of the danger of indifferentism.

The three other members of the sub-commission accepted the Secretariat's text, while pointing out some inaccuracies. The experts present were Ramirez (who spoke *LITTLE* but disagreeably, Fr de Lubac told me), Lubac, Naud and Lafortune, Medina.

At 7.15 pm, supper at the residence of Mgr Emanuele Clarizio, Nuncio in Santo Domingo, with Küng (through whom the invitation came), Lubac and Moeller. Also present was a monsignor from the Nunciature in Italy and Mgr Lambruschini,[1] until recently at the 'Holy Office', today professor [[of moral theology]] at the Lateran: an original and interesting man. These curial men are and want to be open. Mgr Clarizio had been in Paris under Cardinal Marella, then in Australia and Pakistan.[2] He explained to us and to some extent justified the role of the nuncios, the incredible difficulty of their task (to take into consideration the most widely varied and contradictory pressures), the procedure for the choice of bishops . . . But we spoke most of all about the 'Holy Office', about denunciations, etc. I do not remember a great deal about all that, which does not interest me much. For these men, Lubac and I are, as it were, miniature versions of the Galileo case. We did not get down to the level of the problems, which is the only important level.

We also spoke a little about John XXIII and Paul VI.

Saturday 9 November 1963

Long and interesting visit from Fr de Riedmatten. With him, one does not talk to say nothing. I have noted down some of the points we touched on.

The CURIA: will there be men, will there be men PREPARED for internationalisation? At the moment, the Curia is pretty well at a standstill: the absence

---

1. Ferdinando Lambruschini, of the diocese of Rome, Council expert.
2. After several years in Oceania, he had been counsellor at the nunciature in Paris from 1954 to 1958, then Internuncio in Pakistan (1958–1961).

of bishops from their dioceses and from their country means for them a kind of paralysis, including at the financial level: the money is no longer coming in . . .

The QUESTION OF RELIGIOUS FREEDOM: Everything should not be based on the individual right of the person. One is led to that because attention is focussed on the case of Spain, of Colombia and, to some degree, of Italy. But Colombia is a special case, entirely dominated by politics. Spain and Italy are opening up and evolving fairly quickly: so much so that by putting all the emphasis on the individual person, one risks linking the question of religious freedom with a problem that is now virtually past history. Riedmatten himself approaches it from a different angle: that of the originality of religion as such. The religions represent an original reality, of which Catholic Christianity is the true and perfect form; but to the degree that a religion really is a religion, it has a specificity. This establishes its independence with respect to the State and to political power, and requires freedom.

We also spoke about schema XVII. It needs to be 'conceived', and first of all a LIST should be made of the chapters that it MUST contain.

On the subject of birth control, Riedmatten told me that if it has been possible to make some progress, this was due to Ottaviani and Parente and that these two had acquired their information from serious reports.

(Journey to Paris (Evangelical group: CCIF) and to Sedan.)

Tuesday 12 November 1963

Saturday afternoon, 9 November, sub-commission at St Martha's. I left from there at 7 pm, in Fr Féret's car, for the airport.

Arrived at Orly at 10.30 pm. My nephew, Dominique, Jean and Françoise[1] were there to meet me. We chatted for a while, even though it was so late and I was so tired. I saw this evening, and would go on seeing throughout my short stay in France, that what was going on at the Council was being followed with attention and in detail. People are very up to date about the deeds, the gestures and comments of Cardinal Ottaviani, who personifies reaction, immobilism, mismanagement.

On Sunday, 10 November, evangelical group:[2] biblical lecture; homily, lecture on the Council from 2 pm to 4 pm.

A few minutes with my nephew Dominique.

Train at 4.48 pm for Sedan, from where I set off again on Monday 11, at 15.47 pm. Each time I tell myself that I may be embracing Tere[3] for the last time.

Monday 11, lecture at the Week for Catholic Intellectuals[4]: hall full (1,900 people). There, too, great sensitivity toward openness.

---

1. Dominique Congar, Jean and Françoise Agar (Françoise was Dominique's sister).
2. Cf above, page 55, note 3.
3. His mother: see page 303, note 6.
4. Cf Yves M-J Congar, 'L'Avenir de l'Église', in *L'Avenir, Semaine des intellectuels catholiques (6 au 12 Novembre 1963)* (Paris: Fayard, 1964).

Tuesday: Orly at 8.55 am. I met Fr Martelet on the plane. Arrived at the Angelicum at 12.15 pm. But I cannot put one foot in front of the other. I no longer have any strength at all. I am beginning to ask myself whether, in a year's time, I shall still be alive: because life is leaving me.

However, after resting for three quarters of an hour, I began to pick up: at the French seminary at 3 pm for the workshop on ecumenism. Frs Dupuy and Le Guillou have done a lot of work. They are constantly in direct touch with the bishops and are very much appreciated. Am I deceiving myself? I have the feeling that the bishops are obsequiously keeping their distance from me, either because my state of exhaustion, which is fairly obvious, prevents them from approaching me, or because the suspicions and problems I have had in the past mean that I am still marked in some way that calls for circumspection (Féret, who is experiencing something of the same attitude, believes that this has a part to play . . .); or else, finally, because I inspire awe . . . The fact remains that the bishops turn much more readily to Martelet, Le Guillou and Dupuy than to Féret or myself. These near-youngsters, moreover, have no doubts about anything, not even about themselves. They have a quite extraordinary self-assurance. This year, they are very definitely taking over from the older men.

On the other hand, I was very impressed by the seriousness and the authenticity of the ecumenical urgency and commitment of some of the bishops who were at that meeting. It was very pure and very good.

At 4.30 pm at St Martha's for the sub-commission.

By questioning various people, I learnt something of how the meeting of the Theological Commission went yesterday, which was given over to examination of the Secretariat's text on religious freedom. I very much regret that I missed it. EVERYBODY, this time, spoke, with the exception of Mgr Šeper and Mgr Florit: those of the experts who spoke were Gagnebet, K Rahner, Häring, Murray and Lio. But Lio, who spoke last, was not able to say very much even though he had prepared a long intervention. Cardinal Browne, Ottaviani and, at the beginning, Parente, attacked the text very violently. But in the end, when Mgr Garrone asked for a vote to discover whether or not the Commission approved the sub-commission's report (attached, in my file, to the duplicated text of *De libertate religiosa*), the vote gave a majority of 18 in favour, with 5 against and one abstention.

Cardinal Léger believes that the blank ballot may well have come from Cardinal Ottaviani himself who, not seeing too well, might have written '*Non placet*' BESIDE the ballot paper, on the blotting pad.

Cardinal Browne urged the great difficulty of the question: he would have liked to break it down into several votes, but things went against him.

It is a fact: every time there is a vote, the result is favourable!

Wednesday 13 November 1963
St Peter's. Slav Mass: over an hour long!
Queue of interventions on Chapter II.

Angelus Fernandes[1] (India): English accent, in the name of several bishops
from Asia, on the resignation of bishops, against empty titles and
dignities: 'rattles for adults';
and two others.
Then discussion of Chapter III: episcopal conferences.
Spellman[2] [ ]
Frings:[3] remarks in favour of the freedom of the bishops (applause).
Olaechea[4] (Valencia) [ ]
McDevitt[5] (Auxiliary of Philadelphia): place of titular bishops.
The votes of 30 October require more than is envisaged in the text.
Applause from the young bishops.
Carli[6] in the name of thirty bishops from various countries. Episcopal
conferences should not be based on the principle of collegiality by
divine right. The vote of 30 October cannot be invoked: it is very
questionable from the legal point of view. And even if this doctrine
were to be proclaimed, the episcopal conferences lack three things
required to satisfy collegiality:
– participation of the head;
– participation of ALL the bishops;
– a question of interest for the ENTIRE Church.
The episcopal conferences have a basis of moral solidarity, of
communion, not of right based on collegiality.
Ancel[7] (pious tone to begin with): *nexus* [link] between responsibility or
mission and jurisdiction. The collegiality of the apostles concerns
primarily MISSION and responsibility, not jurisdiction (the question
really always is to know whether the Church has a primarily juridical
structure, or whether its law is secondary in comparison with mission).
I saw Mgr Baudoux, from Canada, for a quite long time. A marvellous man.
But even a conversation of this kind tires me. I am completely devoid
of strength. I am killing myself here. What can I do?

1. Angelo Fernandes, *AS* II/V, 58–60.
2. *AS* II/V, 65–66.
3. *AS* II/V, 66–67.
4. Marcelino Olaechea Loizaga, *AS* II/V, 69–70.
5. Gerald V McDevitt, member of the Commission on Missions, *AS* II/V, 70-72.
6. *AS* II/V, 72-75.
7. *AS* II/V, 75-77.

Mgr Muñoyerro[1] (?–Spain): against episcopal conferences; only occasional
    meetings on a programme approved and supervised by the pope.
Riobé[2] (Orléans): the necessity of episcopal conferences for the necessary
    cooperation between regions and countries. Example of the World
    Council of Churches.
    Once again, generalities. Our bishops propose syntheses . . .
Bianchi[3] (China) in the name of several bishops: against any authority given
    to the conferences that would limit the freedom of the bishops. There
    should be nothing between each bishop and the pope, who is the vicar
    of Christ!
    In favour of the monarchical structure of the Church.

At 4.30 pm at St Martha's, 'central' sub-commission: a completely useless organism which makes us waste half a day for nothing. In effect, whatever texts have
been prepared in the various sub-commissions that have been set up are submitted to it before being submitted to the Commission in general congregation. It
is pointless, because it will be done in the general congregation. Moreover, one
risks, each time, a flaring up of the debates that have already been fought ten
times: that was how we began to discuss again *'super Petrum rupem et super fun-
damenta Duodecim Apostolorum'* [on Peter the rock and on the foundation of the
twelve Apostles] . . .

Afterwards, I spent an hour with Fr Dournes, who is returning to Vietnam
tomorrow, because the situation is confused and the communists are taking advantage of it to infiltrate precisely into the region to which he is posted. A gifted
man, charismatic, with the spiritual temperament of a missionary hermit, vowed
to living alone . . . In my state of exhaustion, it was really good for me to hear
him saying, as he was leaving: Thank you for having listened to me; without you I
would have remained alone . . .

Thursday 14 November 1963

I did not go to St Peter's as I had work to do for the sub-commission and also I
have had a bit of flu since last Sunday. In the morning, went to see Fr Duncker,[4]
and various telephone calls about the question of the Cullmann lecture. I am going to write down here the facts about this matter, in order to preserve a record of
the stupidity of a state of things that has still not been eliminated.

Cullmann came to see me on ? (eight or ten days ago). He is to give a lecture
on the History of Salvation in the Gospels in the light of ecumenical dialogue. As

1. Luis Alonso Muñoyerro, bishop to the armed forces (Spain), *AS* II/V, 87–90.
2. Guy-M Riobé, Bishop of Orléans since May 1963; member of the Commission on the
    Missions since the First Session of the Council, *AS* II/V, 90–92.
3. Lorenzo Bianchi, Italian, Bishop of Hong Kong, *AS* II/V, 92–93.
4. Pieter Geert Duncker, OP, of the Province of the Netherlands, Professor of Old Testa-
    ment Exegesis at the Angelicum and consultor to the Pontifical Biblical Commission.

the Waldensian hall is small (seating for 100) and very few Catholics would believe themselves free to go there (Cullmann told me that Peterson himself never used to come to HIS LECTURES at the Waldensians. He used to come and see him there *AFTER* the lectures!! . . .)[1]

Cullmann wanted to give his lecture in a larger, Catholic hall. The rector of the Biblical Institute, Fr Mackenzie,[2] had invited him, but then said that the lecture hall at the Biblicum was itself too small, and that it would be better to go to the Gregorianum. That had been agreed when the Gregorianum said that it would have to renege, as the only large hall they had was the covered central court and this could not be closed and isolated . . . A little later, Cullmann was told that THAT was not the real reason. The real reason was that the Gregorianum did not want to compromise itself with the Biblical Institute. Such being the situation, the Director of the Biblical Institute wanted to ask Fr Sigmond for the large hall at the Angelicum for a lecture to be given by Cullmann at the invitation, and under the patronage of the Biblicum. Cullmann had come to ask me to support this request to the Rector of the Angelicum.

The next day, I spoke to Fr Sigmond. He told me that he had received no request from the Biblicum and knew nothing about it. (When I reported back to Cullmann, he told me that the Director of the Biblicum had telephoned the Angelicum twice, but had in fact been unable to contact Fr Sigmond.) Fr Sigmond then added: FOR MY PART, there would be no objection, but I would have to have authorisation from Fr General and he in turn would have to cover himself with respect to the 'Holy Office', without which the arrangement would immediately evoke the kind of remonstrances that one would much prefer not to incur.

I let matters take their course. When I returned from Paris on Tuesday, I inquired of Fr Sigmond how things were. I saw Fr Hamer yesterday in St Peter's. This is the situation: the Biblicum did indeed make the approach, but IS ITSELF NO LONGER INVITING CULLMANN. Cardinal Bea intervened with the Biblicum to say: I am in the process of sorting out the difficulties between the Biblicum and the Curia; just at the moment, the Biblicum must not lay itself open to the least new criticism. On the other hand, Cardinal Bea and Mgr Willebrands do not wish, in the name of the Secretariat, to invite Cullmann, or any other Observer, to speak. At the utmost, if Cullmann were to be invited by someone else, Willebrands would agree to present him.

Well, thank you! In that case he would no longer be needed!

It is the 'Holy Office' that everybody is afraid of and that, here in Rome, blocks the taking of the least initiative. Fr Hamer also told me that a telephone call from the 'Holy Office' last year asked the Angelicum that I not be allowed to speak to

---

1. Erik Peterson, patrologist and historian of religions, came to the Catholic Church from Protestantism. He had taught at Rome since 1937, and died in 1960.
2. The Canadian Roderick Mackenzie, SJ, was Rector from 1963.

the students. In fact, they had asked that I speak to them, and they were refused: I had been told THAT a year ago.

This Thursday morning, I went to see Fr Duncker in order to see if the invitation could not be issued by the Angelicum, as there is no one else as things stand. He told me that he had discussed this with the Rector, Fr Sigmond. When the latter met Mgr Romeo yesterday at some meeting or other, Romeo said to him: it would be very good if Cullmann were to speak, he is the only one who opposes Bultmann!!! So the green light will come from the integrist side, from the very adversaries of the Biblicum, and that, in turn, will perhaps switch on the other green light, that of the 'Holy Office'.

I immediately telephoned Mgr Elchinger, who had spoken to me about the whole affair yesterday, in order to ask him to say to Cullmann simply that the whole matter is not yet settled negatively on the part of the Angelicum (and nothing more). Mgr Elchinger told me that, yesterday evening, he had arranged with the Ambassador and Fr Darsy[1] that, if nothing else was possible, Cullmann would be invited to give his lecture at Saint-Louis des Français.

Immediately afterwards I telephoned Fr Hamer. He was already aware of Romeo's *effatum* [pronouncement]. On the other hand, he had very fairly kept Cullmann informed of the way things were going. He is hoping to speak to Fr General in order to prepare him to react favourably when Fr Sigmond comes to speak to him about it. I gave Fr Hamer a few extra pieces of information in the most favourable direction. Thus, in this frightful and wretched curial Rome, a lecture by one of the most competent and most decent of men that there are depends on a chance *dictum* [remark] of a mediocre Monsignor, and, to top it all, on a telephone call from '*Nec nominetur in vobis*' [one who must not even be named among you] (Eph 5:3)] who is never seen and who controls everything . . .

Pouah!!!

In the afternoon, a visit and telephone calls.

At 4.30 pm, sub-commission meeting for *De Populo Dei* at St Martha's.

Rumours (from Mgr Philips and C Moeller):

1) The idea of re-electing the commissions is gaining ground. The aim is to have commissions and ABOVE ALL A THEOLOGICAL COMMISSION which are more in accordance with the spirit AND WITH THE NEEDS of the Council: the bishops are better known now, and elections among them could now be conducted on the basis of better knowledge than during the first week. It is now currently being thought that the Theological Commission will achieve nothing with the President and Secretary that it has.

2) There is talk of establishing (electing???) a commission charged with making proposals to the Pope for a re-organisation of the Curia and the creation of a

---

1. Félix Darsy, OP, of the Province of France, was the Ecclesiastical and Cultural Attaché at the French Embassy to the Holy See and Director of the Saint-Louis des Français Study Centre, which was run by the Embassy.

central commission attached to the Pope, along the lines suggested by Cardinal Lercaro's speech.

3) Mgr Piolanti is thought to be spreading the rumour that the Council is to be adjourned *sine die*. According to Moeller, either he mistakes his own wishes for reality, or he is trying to make people believe in something well-founded by spreading the rumour to all and sundry. That does not seem to me to be very likely.

It must be acknowledged that, since the beginning, throughout the whole preparatory period, and since the opening of the Council, there has been an ongoing conflict between the *Ecclesia* and the Curia. The further I go, the more it appears to me that the purely Italian structure of the Roman organisms and of the Roman ideology is the tumour that needs to be cut away. Ultramontanism as an ideology certainly exists. And it is very close to being a heresy!

The Curia people (Ottaviani, Browne, Staffa, Carli . . .) are doing EVERY-THING to prevent the episcopate from recovering the rights which have been stolen from it.

Friday 15 November 1963

I went to St Peter's only rather late, having first corrected and typed a text *De Missione Ecclesiae* [On the Mission of the Church]. I can only just stand. However, I saw various people.

Lunch with *Bishof* Silén,[1] Observer for the World Lutheran Federation. We spoke, in German, about many things. Inevitably, the question arose: for you, am I just a layman?

As soon as I returned here (2.30 pm) telephone call from Fr Gauthier; visit from two Polish journalists, then M. Romeu,[2] from Salamanca (he was asking for collaboration in an anthology and for lectures on ecumenism): I see the great usefulness and immense interest of this *REAL* Spanish openness to ecumenism. But who will give me the strength and the time? I cannot do any more, and I already see the table that I shall find when I return to Strasbourg . . .

Sub-commission at St Martha's at 4.30 pm.

In two Roman newspapers there are reports denying what Fesquet said, in *Le Monde*, about an improbable audience of the Pope by Frings, Ottaviani and Siri.[3] These *Le Monde* indiscretions and fantasies are upsetting.

---

1. Sven Silén, Bishop of Västerås (Sweden).
2. Luis V Romeu was secretary of the Ecumenical Centre of the University of Salamanca; the text that Congar was to send him appeared in Luis V Romeu (editor), *Dialogos de la cristiandad* (Salamanca, 1964).
3. According to *Le Monde* of 14 November, on the evening of Friday 8 November, Cardinal Frings had an audience of the Pope, which was followed by an audience for Cardinals Ottaviani, Siri and Antoniutti, during which the Pope reproached Ottaviani for having attacked Frings.

It appears that the Moderators are to have an audience of the Pope THIS EVE-NING.

I saw Mgr Glorieux. He told me that the new text of schema XVII[1] (Chapter I) has only very recently been submitted to the Co-ordinating Commission, which had asked Cardinal Suenens to submit a draft. Cardinal Suenens had sent the text to a number of cardinals, but NOT to the Coordinating Commission, *ut sic* [as such] which had asked him for it.

This text would undoubtedly be looked at by the joint commission on 26 November.

This evening I asked for news about the Cullmann lecture. Reply: the question is going to be put to the Pope's secretariat. That being so, if the reply is favourable . . . One could not select a more highly placed umbrella!!!

Saturday 16 November 1963

Lunch at Saint Jerome, with Mgr Suhr, Dom Butler, Mgr P Glorieux. It is, together with Saint-Louis des Français, the place in Rome that had WELCOMED me at the time of my difficulties with *Nec nominetur* [let it not be named].

Dom J Leclercq, always astonishingly alive, intelligent and friendly, told me that Cardinal Lercaro has submitted to the Pope a memorandum with a view to new elections and a new composition of the Commissions. He also told me, having heard it from Alberigo, that Paul VI is constantly besieged by petitions and pressures of all kinds; he is at the centre of a closely fought battle for influence. On the conservative side, attempts are being made to instil fear into him: this stratagem had succeeded with Pius XII. Possible or threatening dangers are pointed out to him and, for example, in the case of collegiality, the spectre of the synod of Pistoia.[2]

Dominus custodiat eum et vivificet eum [May the Lord protect him and give him life (Ps 40:3)].

At 5 pm, they came to pick me up for the lecture (on ecumenism) to the Cistercians at the abbey of Tre Fontane. From there, supper at the Canadian college and lecture to the student priests (the current ecclesiological movement). Cardinal Léger did not say much and is always fairly sombre. He wants to intervene as little as possible, just like Cardinal Liénart. The latter had been asked to speak on ecumenism: according to Mgr P Glorieux, he will do so only IF ecumenism is attacked. I feel that there is, on the part of several cardinals, a kind of withdrawal, due to the fact that the role of authority they exercised last year to a greater or lesser extent, has passed to the four Moderators who are, to all intents and purposes, legates . . .

---

1. Congar added in the margin of the typescript: 'the one prepared in Malines.'
2. Summoned by the Bishop of Pistoia in 1786, this synod wished to implement the ecclesiological programme of the Jansenists which, far removed from ultramontanism, sought to return to the traditional conception of local Churches and the episcopate.

Sunday 17 November 1963

I prepared a chronicle for *ICI* which I had begun yesterday.

Afternoon, visits from:

1) Fr Chenu.

2) Boudouresques,[1] with two young laymen from Scientific Research ([ ]) about their intervention against the atomic bomb. I gave them the chapter on peace from schema XVII.

Monday 18 November 1963

(Feast of the Dedication of St Peter's Basilica!). A historic day. Discussion of the *De Œcumenismo* begins. I feel very strongly the moment of grace, but, as always, of grace lived in the Church MILITANT.

Before the Mass, in a spirit of intense communion, I greeted the bishops who, in my view, are more particularly involved: Cardinal Liénart (who spoke to me of a section on Islam to be added to the chapter *De Iudaeis* [on the Jews]), Mgr Martin, Cardinal Bea, His Beatitude Maximos IV. I went to assist at the Mass with the Observers, in order to be united in prayer with them. They clearly felt it. We shook hands warmly, and also with Mgr Willebrands, Arrighi, Davis, Frs Duprey, Weigel, Bévenot,[2] Dumont, Lanne, and even Fr Boyer, etc. It was a very great moment for me. We were there above the tomb of St Peter and I begged all the saints to help so that God will lead those who are not yet there, to find their foundation on the apostolicity of Peter, in the way that this ought to happen.

Lercaro[3] read the *relatio* on how the Liturgical Commission had dealt with the *modi* that had been called for.

A bishop[4] of the Malabar rite, speaking in the name of his colleagues, reverted to the question of personal jurisdictions, according to the rite, which is pastorally necessary in India.

Reading of the report on the schema *De Œcumenismo*. Part 1 by Cardinal Cicognani[5] himself. It is a fairly mediocre text, in the style of encyclicals, that is to say, claiming that the Church has always done what it needed to do: which is false. There is no ecumenical soul in this text. On the

1. Bernard Boudouresques, Mission de France priest, polytechnician, research engineer with the CEA (Commissariat à l'Énergie Atomique); he had come seeking a condemnation from the Council of the manufacture and use of atomic weapons.
2. Maurice Bévenot, SJ, taught ecclesiology at Heythrop College, the training centre for English Jesuits, at that time located near Oxford: he was consultor to the Secretariat for Unity.
3. *AS* II/V, 406–409.
4. Sebastian Valloppilly, Bishop of Tellicherry, member of the Commission on the Apostolate of the Laity, spoke in the name of the Syro-Malabar and Syro-Malankar bishops, *AS* II/V, 409–411.
5. *AS* II/V, 468–472.

other hand, the fact that the Secretary of State himself read this text may disarm some of the opponents, or at least calm them down.

This text was not submitted to the Secretariat.

(Fr Hamer told me that Cullmann's lecture will take place at the Angelicum on 30 November.)

Mgr Martin then read the general *relatio* [report] with feeling and a certain tone of interiority. The tone of the text is completely different: there is a Christian pathos!

(very strong French accent: stress on the last syllable of words).

The *relatio* was fairly generally applauded. Certainly, many were moved.

After an interval for voting on the liturgical corrections, the discussion on ecumenism began at 11.12 am.

Cardinal Tappouni[1] (pronounced Latin '-us' not as OUS but as US): The Easterners ought to have been dealt with separately. He was against the insertion of a chapter on the Jews and on religious freedom.

To speak of the Jews is absolutely inopportune and dangerous (Arab countries).

His somewhat tearful tone and his pronunciation in '-US' was odd.

Ruffini:[2] After a gracious word, moved on to criticise:

1) The word 'ecumenism': the Council is ecumenical, but its concern is with the particular. And Protestants, who coined the term, understand it in a sense that cannot be ours.

(People were listening closely: you could have heard a fly buzz although there were 3,000 people present.)

2) He proposed the 'return' thesis, praised the Easterners highly and had some harsh words (with harsh intonations) about the Protestants and their divisions.

One could still hear a fly buzz.

3) Chapter II could be joined to Chapter I, which could be shortened by removing what is already contained in the *De Ecclesia*.

4) If there is to be mention of the Jews, why not also of the adherents of the other religions which are often no more removed from us than the Jews.

5) And the Catholics who have gone over to Communism!

6) Norms are needed on what is to be preserved so that dialogue can be prudent and effective.

---

1.   *AS* II/V, 527–528.
2.   *AS* II/V, 528–530.

Cardinal de Arriba y Castro:[1] on dialogue (contrary to the law of the index) and prayer in common.

It would dangerous for THE COUNCIL to speak of this, above all for those of the faithful who are not well prepared. In fact, proselytism is increasing. A paragraph should be inserted asking our separated brethren to refrain from that.

A catechism of the differences should be prepared.

A serious culture should be promoted.

The Magisterium should not be forgotten.

May prayer and charity towards our separated brethren increase amongst us!

Non placet. Melius esset illud omittere [Against. Would it not be better to omit this]?

Cardinal Bueno y Monreal:[2] *Placet iuxta modum.*

He proposed some corrections.

On the word 'ecumenism' (in the same sense as Ruffini). Discuss both Christians and non-Christians, in other words all those who are outside the Church, in the same pastoral schema.

As regards the internal order of the schema: the first sections should be transferred to the *De Ecclesia*, and remove from that schema the sections on non-Catholics in order to insert them here, or in the schema on the missions. Those who are separated enjoy the gifts of God only *per accidens* [accidentally] and not *in se* [of themselves].

Cardinal Ritter[3] in the name of several bishops of the USA:

The schema *placet in genere* [is acceptable on the whole]: it meets the purpose of *aggiornamento*. There are some gaps. Happily, the one concerning religious freedom is being filled in. It is a necessary pre-requisite. Place this chapter BEFORE that on the practice of ecumenism.

There is something missing in the explanation of the principles of ecumenism: on the Eucharist and the liturgical movement.

If possible, all references that are offensive to the separated brethren should be removed. The title of CHURCH should not be denied them.

A directory should be issued.

Still the same attention and the same silence.

Cardinal Quintero[4] (Venezuela): importance of this schema.

Confess without pharisaism our responsibilities in the separations (allusion to the speech of 29 September).

---

1. *AS* II/V, 530–531.
2. *AS* II/V, 532–534.
3. *AS* II/V, 536–537.
4. José Humberto Quintero, Archbishop of Caracas, *AS* II/V, 538–539.

Suggested that a declaration be added in which the Council does that and asks forgiveness in the same terms as the Pope had done.

Cardinal Doi[1] (Japan) in the name of the bishops of Japan (breathless): *in genere placet.* Comments:

The ecumenical problem should be considered from the missionary point of view also.

Accordingly, the schema should be divided into two sections:

1) ecumenism properly so called,

2) the relationship with Jews and non-Christians.

His Beatitude Stephanos I Sidarouss, patriarch of Alexandria.[2]

Beware of false irenicism! The text lacks precision and is inadequate. The notion of Catholic unity . . .

Do not mention the Jews. That would create great difficulties in certain countries.

Fr Hamer told me that this speech had been inspired by Ottaviani, whose 'liegeman' the patriarch is.

Maximos IV:[3] This is the first schema submitted to the conciliar Fathers that combines doctrinal precision with a pastoral approach.

At last we have emerged from polemics!

It is the sign that we have decided to leave behind the impasses of proselytism and embark instead on the path of spiritual emulation.

Above all, joy in seeing at last the first appearance of a true theology of the Church as a mystery of communion.

However, there are some deficiencies:

Rather too descriptive: lack of sound criticism.

A little too dependent on the causes of division IN FORMER TIMES.

There are not only the cracks which affect the structures; there are also sins which destroy charity.

Finally, he was in favour of removing the chapter on the Jews. If one wants to keep it, it would be better somewhere else: *De Ecclesia* (History of Salvation), Presence of the Church to the World.

If the chapter is to be kept, there should also be mention of Muslims.

It would be sufficient to condemn anti-Semitism and racism.

The Orthodox should be given a privileged place.

The wish expressed at Rhodes[4] should be supported: permanent dialogue with the Orthodox.

---

1. *AS* II/V, 539–540.
2. Stephanos I Sidarouss, Coptic Patriarch of Alexandria, member of the Commission on the Eastern Churches, created cardinal in 1965, *AS* II/V, 541–542.
3. *AS* II/V, 542–544.
4. The second pan-Orthodox conference of Rhodes had been held in September.

Lunch with Mme M Auclair[1] and a Mlle Jeanne.[2] They want to prepare an enquiry in *Marie-Claire*[3] on what women would say to the Council if they were allowed to speak. I gave them some addresses.

Meeting of the Theological Commission at 4.30 pm at the Vatican. Cardinal Browne presided, and began by reading a letter from Cardinal Ottaviani, stating that he had been received by the Pope and that the Pope had said that he wished to see Chapter I, at least, of *De Ecclesia* and the chapter *De Beata* completed by the end of the Session.

As a matter of fact, in the coach, I had asked Mgr Philips how things stood. He told me that they had, that morning, been working in the *De Beata* sub-commission. Having listened to it, and having heard Fr Balić, they had been asked to reach agreement on a text that Philips would produce. Philips has the impression that, deep down, Balić has given up on his own text. He continues to defend it as if it still held sway, but more in order to give himself and receive from others the assurance that he had defended the text. Philips thinks that if HE wished to prevent this or that expression, he would do it. But, he added, he will have to take account of those on the right in order to reach an agreement . . .

After Mgr Charue's report on the work of sub-commission No. 1, Fr Rigaux proposed the text on the *Regnum Dei* [Kingdom of God]. It was discussed. A long and complicated and not very clear intervention by Volk: he laid stress on the obedience of Christ. Then a much improved section on images of the Church.

Poverty. Fairly extended discussion: the text proposed to us is not (very) good; it is too vainglorious, stating that the Church seeks only poverty. Mgr Scherer, Florit and Šeper said it was a lie . . . One should never speak in terms of VOCA-TION to . . . Others (Schauf, Gagnebet) want to hold on to the idea of poverty IN SPIRIT. That would not be enough . . . I intervened. Nothing very clear came of it.

In the end, it was sent to the sub-commission. McGrath insisted that we ought to listen to one of the bishops who had spoken [[about this]] *in aula*.

On the way out, Mgr Prignon gave me some news of the meeting of the Moderators, the Council of Presidents and, I believe, the Co-ordinating Commission, that had been held on Friday evening. Nothing very much. He told me that the question of the renewal of the Commissions had not been tackled, but that the Pope would not be much in favour of such a step. They spoke of the future: one more Session, or two? Most are in favour of ONE, but two would perhaps be needed in order to be able to facilitate some interesting and imperative developments in the matter of the studies and the formation of clerics, by a severe critique of the very weak schemas that have dealt with these subjects. The next session would be from 8 September to 22 November.

---

1. Marcelle Auclair, woman of letters and journalist, who wrote editorials for *Marie-Claire*.
2. Jeanne Dodeman, an assistant of Marcelle Auclair.
3. Cf Nos. 119, 121, 122, 123 and 127 of *Marie-Claire* in 1964 and 1965.

I put together my impressions on this morning's session. It is clear that two mentalities have been displayed, or better, two worlds: what an abyss there is between the evangelism of Mgr Martin's *Relatio* and those who, like Ruffini and the two Spanish cardinals, are simply attached to a past . . . that has been passed by!!!

Tuesday 19 November 1963

I got a lot of odds and ends done, and a little text for Cardinal Liénart (on Islam) and for Mgr Jacq (on the novelty of the word 'ecumenism').

In the coach, conversation with two Armenian bishops. They combine the narrowness of a Latin scholasticism with the particularism so common among the Easterners. They see nothing in the light of critically assessed general principles but in a kind of concrete particularism. For example, they told me, on the one hand, that Muslims are much more Christian than Jews. The Muslims, according to them, acknowledge the divinity of Christ, because they call him 'Spirit of God' (!!!). But, on the other hand, they deny to Islam any mystical value: they say it has only the mystique of sensuality.

They also said that in *La Documentation catholique* (*sic* = the *ICI*), I, Fr Congar, take no account of dogma: I accommodate the dogma and tone it down in order to please the non-Catholics!!!

Where did they get that from? From Patriarch Batanian?

It is painful to see men so little open, so badly informed, having so little of what is needed in order to confront the real, modern world!

Frs Gagnebet and Labourdette spoke to me about Fr Hermand,[1] with whom *Candide* has published an interview. It is very painful, but it was bound to happen. He will be USED by all that there is of 'the flesh'; he will be drawn to an impure context. He is going to drift inevitably into a mediocre world, and what he sought to say will inevitably become an ATTACK on celibacy, indeed on chastity. Instead of helping to improve matters, he will add his voice to a work causing trouble and destruction.

Perhaps I was not firm enough when I wrote to him.

God help us!!!

They spoke to me about it again in the coach on the way back. They told me, which I did not know, that Fr Hermand is himself caught up with a woman. It seems there were two Fathers with the same woman, and that, during the divorce proceedings, the husband produced letters from the two Fathers.

It is dreadfully sad.

The reports on Chapters III ff of *De œcumenismo* were read. The introduction to the chapter on the Jews was read by Cardinal Bea.[2] It is too long, with repeti-

---

1. Pierre Hermand, OP, of the Province of Toulouse: Congar was corresponding with him on account of a book he was writing that appeared during the Second Session: *Condition du prêtre, mariage ou célibat?* (Paris: Calmann-Lévy, 1963); Hermand was to leave the Dominican Order the following year.
2. *AS* II/V, 481–485.

tions, but it is very strong and very fine. And it is good that these things are being said in front of the episcopate of the entire world. This, too, is a great moment, a decisive one, in the life of the Church.

Mgr De Smedt read his long report on religious freedom.[1] He did so with force and with fire, but, nonetheless a little theatrically, in the manner of someone who knows that his success is assured and is doing everything to make sure that it is so. IT IS A GREAT TEXT, although it does have some weaknesses. It, too, is a DECISIVE moment in the life of the Church AND OF THE WORLD.

What a contribution to the centenary of the *Syllabus*[2]—which is, it must be said, referred to and placed in its historical context . . .

The interventions on ecumenism in general did not begin until 11.07 am!

Cardinal Léger:[3] called to mind John XXIII and the prophetic moment experienced by the Council with respect to the cause of unity. The schema is good and necessary.

However he had two criticisms to make: a lack of homogeneity; chapters IV and V ought not to be there. It would be better to leave them as separate schemas.

Concerning the second part of chapter III: one ought not to put forward a description of other Christian communities in a conciliar decree. It is too complicated and too delicate. Place all that in an appendix, thereby avoiding discussion *in aula*.

Cardinal König:[4] everything that is most opportune, most in accordance with the purpose of the Council. Before union, and in preparation for it, there is need of a process of becoming neighbours to one another.

Some comments:

On the word 'ecumenism', which has had, and continues to have, different meanings.

It should be stressed that what is presented is CATHOLIC ecumenism, in dependence on Catholic ecclesiology—and at the same time that this ecumenism is neither closed nor imperfectible. Dialogue makes us understand things, and ecumenism itself, more deeply.

Catholic doctrine certainly requires a distinction between the Eastern 'Churches' and the Protestant 'communities'; but this word 'communities' is inadequate for describing the ecclesial elements that they contain. One should speak of 'ecclesial communities'.

---

1. *AS* II/V, 485–495.
2. Cf page 110, note 3.
3. *AS* II/V, 550–552.
4. *AS* II/V, 552–554.

Cardinal Rugambwa:[1] *Nobis placet* [We approve]. However
1) speak humbly of the gifts received from God: these are to be found amongst all human beings. Do not impose human traditions on others;
2) on the ecumenical activity that is so necessary from the missionary point of view. Seek the greatest possible co-operation in mission countries.

His Beatitude Gori[2] (Jerusalem): *Satis mihi placet quoad tria prima capita* [I am satisfied with the first three chapters]. But do not forget the distinction between Orthodox and Reformed; solicitude for all religions (while avoiding the mention of one in particular).

His Beatitude Batanian:[3] Ecumenism is timely, and hence so is the schema.
However '*veritatem facientes in caritate*' [speaking the truth in love (Eph 4: 15)]. Here and there, Catholic doctrine is not sufficiently clearly stated (in the Roman sense).
Do not conceal the fact that the aim is union in the Catholic Church.
The content of Chapter IV should be dealt with ELSEWHERE.

Mgr Garrone:[4] two comments: 1) *De locis œcumenicis* [on the sources of ecumenism]. Ecumenism is founded on faith and hope: it is quite other than a wish not to wound, or a benevolent sentimentalism. There is in Revelation such a declaration of unity = creation, incarnation, redemption, eschatological kingdom: everything is a mystery of unity and of reconciliation.
2) Ecumenical charity that purifies and enlightens faith, that dissolves the malformations that attach to our faith, the residues of polemical times, through which we diminish our own treasure.
It purifies us of all possessive spirit in the faith.
The providential nature of ecumenism.
Very fine text, given in a very interior and religious spirit, though in a rather maudlin tone.

Elchinger:[5] This text is a grace of God for our times, the crowning of the difficult efforts of our predecessors.
The condition for the success of ecumenism is a profound reformation of OUR attitudes with regard to the revealed truth.
Situations upon which ecumenism is able to bear:
1) The refusal to confess our historical faults and the historical truth, harsh as it may have been.
What the reformers WANTED, was not to destroy unity, but to re-state authentic truths.

---

1. *AS* II/V, 555–557.
2. *AS* II/V, 557.
3. *AS* II/V, 558–560.
4. *AS* II/V, 561–562.
5. *AS* II/V, 562–565.

The initiators of ecumenism came from among the Protestants, while those from amongst ourselves who first engaged in it encountered difficulties more than anything else (Mercier). Exegetes have experienced a warmer welcome among Protestants than among us (Fr Lagrange).

2) In the age of polemic, we often rejected ALL their doctrines, whereas there were some very fine partial truths.

3) It is time to give up a passive attitude and to adopt an attitude of SEEKING.

4) Up until now, unity has been confused with uniformity. The time has come to get away from that. We have had the beneficial experience of diversity in unity. The separated brethren deserve our praise and our acknowledgement of their legitimate differences.

McQuaid[1] (Ireland: Dublin): *Schema in genere placet.* [I approve of the schema as a whole]. However, *teste experientia* [as we learn by experience], at times we confuse doctrine with somewhat vague expressions.

De Provenchères:[2] *In genere valde placet* [I very much approve the schema as a whole]: for its ecclesiology of communion, for the POSITIVE way in which it states the problems (recognise the positive and start from there); in favour of the distinction that is drawn between Easterners and Protestants.

He then proposed different levels of ecumenism, from simple politeness to deep conversion, pretty much along the lines of what I have said and written.

An English (Irish) Mgr whose name I do not remember, told me anxiously that it seemed to him that the Pope was beginning to be affected by the assaults to which he was being subjected on the part of the conservatives, who seemed to have managed to alarm him.

I do not know what there is to this.

In the afternoon: sub-commission at St Martha's. I had just time, in the interval, to READ a PART of my mail, and not to reply to any of it.

Mgr Garrone told me that Fr G de Broglie[3] had produced a terrible critique of the chapter on religious freedom for the bishops of North Africa. In it, he said, the rights of an erroneous conscience are limited only by the common good. But what is to be put under 'Common Good'? Either it is a question of the TRUE common good, and then one has reverted to the *Syllabus*, or it is a question of a common good defined by human reason alone, and then one is moving towards

---

1. *AS* II/V, 566–567.
2. *AS* II/V, 567–569.
3. Guy de Broglie-Revel, SJ, who taught fundamental theology at the Gregorianum, had taught this subject for a long time at the Institut Catholique in Paris.

liberalism, or even to state totalitarianism, because the State will declare sovereignly what the common good requires.

Fr Witte, with whom I returned in the bus, spoke of Fr Tromp. He was recalling Fr Tromp from the preparatory period: his absolute dictatorship. He spoke of a meeting at Domus Mariae at which Fr Tromp, without having said anything beforehand, so that one was not able either to prepare a reply or to discuss the matter, had pulled out a text of Pius XII from the letter to the Chinese, and said: it is absolutely forbidden to say that non-Catholics are members of the Church. He was shouting with his imperious voice and banging on the table. That epoch is gone. Fr Tromp has virtually been replaced by Mgr Philips. This man has been providential. It is true that he does not possess ALL the gifts: his texts are a little pale and do not have much energy. But one has to see WHERE we have come from. A year ago, the schema produced by the Preparatory Commission held sway. Without creating problems, and imperceptibly, Philips has taken over everything. HE ALONE COULD HAVE DONE THAT . . . As for Fr Tromp, he is tired, a little embittered, but he has not given up the battle. He fights above all through his confidant, Schauf. He wants at least, in this way, to avoid the worst, he says.

Wednesday 20 November 1963

(71ˢᵗ General Congregation). Bus strike this morning. Had to wait half an hour in the noise of car horns and the stench of petrol. I could only just stand and my brain was in a kind of void, not at all painful, but disturbing. I told myself that, unless there is a VERY noticeable change in my health, I shall not be able to come back for the Third Session.

Yet more explanations of the *modi* and votes on Chapter II on the Liturgy. We are fed up with it! If they retain the same procedure of *modi* and votes, we will *NEVER* get to the end when it comes to the *De Ecclesia*, and a minority of four hundred Fathers could block the text. That would present us with an unbearable Third Session.

> Cardinal Meyer:[1] *in genere placet tamquam basis ulterioris disceptationis* [I approve on the whole, as a basis for further discussion]. And Chapters 4 and 5 should be retained, and in the schema *De œcumenismo*.
> Cardinal Bacci:[2] two comments:
> 1) does not like the title *De œcumenismo*:
> a) the word is understood in the non-Catholic sense, and lends itself to being understood in the sense of inter-confessionalism;

---

1. *AS* II/V, 597.
2. *AS* II/V, 598–599.

b) Chapters 4 and 5 have no business to be here. Or else it would be necessary to change the heading: he suggested one, covering all religions.

2) *Verbosum* [verbose], and at times ambiguous: for example, on page 7 'Petrum' [Peter] . . . and page 23 *'officium Romanae Sedis* [duty of the Roman See] . . .

(really, they never think of anything except JURISDICTION! . . .)

He said that he had asked to speak BEFORE the vote on the five articles on October 30, and that he had not been allowed to do so. He had protested about this to the Pope.

This revelation evoked a murmur from the assembly.

Jelmini[1] (Apostolic Administrator of Lugano) in the name of the Swiss bishops:

Christ is the A and the Ω of the ecumenical spirit.

Show clearly what already belongs to the Church everywhere.

There is need for a deep *aggiornamento* in the life of the Church.

It is good to make a distinction between Eastern and Protestant churches. There are also the Old Catholics.

Do not speak of the Jews only, but of the Muslims and of all those who believe in God.

Do not speak of the freedom of the human person only, but of that of communities and religions. That is related to ecumenism as its condition *sine qua non.*

The question of the Jews also comes back to that of ecumenism: the first schism was with the synagogue.

Sapelak,[2] visiting Bishop of the Ukrainians in Argentina:

1) Create two separate chapters for the Easterners and Protestants.

2) Lacks clarity.

3) Seems to ignore the centuries of efforts for union with regard to the East; there is no reference to the Uniates, who have often paid for their Catholic fidelity with their blood. Importance of the Uniates, whose status could be improved (he gave the idea of what would be the status of the Orthodox after their reunion).

He thinks only in terms of reunion.

Most of the former schema on the Eastern Churches should be brought back. If Chapter 5 *De libertate* is to be retained, the Council should first raise her voice solemnly against persecution in Communist countries.

---

1. *AS* II/V, 600–602.
2. Andrea Sapelak was a member of the Conciliar Commission on the Eastern Churches, *AS* II/V, 602–605.

Morcillo:[1] fairly complex: I could not really follow it as Fr Hamer was talking
to me. It was a report of the meetings with the Spaniards.

Fr Hamer told me that the question of the Cullmann lecture, which yesterday
was very problematic, today seems again to have been resolved. The Secretariat of
State was in favour, but a favourable indication is required from the Holy Office.
PARENTE IS IN FAVOUR, but he said: if it were only a question of a Catholic hall
in the city, there would be no problem, but it is a question of a hall in a pontifical
university: that would create a precedent. So a vote from the Congregation of the
cardinals of the Holy Office would be needed. They will be meeting this evening.
Nothing can be settled before 10 pm. Hamer added that Fr Sigmond had been
marvellous and active throughout this whole affair.

Baudoux:[2] emphasised the profound and supernatural aspects of ecumenism.
He emphasised what already unites us:
'We must walk together' (John XXIII to the Taizé Brothers).
Christ is our starting point, our way—renewal of the Church.
Heenan,[3] in the name of the whole hierarchy of England and Wales.
Welcomed the schema with joy because it gives an authentic direction
(coming from on high) for our action.
It has been said that the English hierarchy was OPPOSED TO the
meddling of Catholics of other countries in Anglican questions. The
dialogue must be conducted in the conditions proper to each country
and under the control of the hierarchy of that country.
I find that declaration SENSATIONAL. It is an official declaration of
conversion to ecumenism and to dialogue on the part of the English
hierarchy.
I did not dare to expect that.
He pointed out a lacuna in the schema: the nature of ecumenical action
is not clear and neither is its purpose. Assert, as well as dialogue, the
need to set forth the whole truth.
(But one cannot express in a dialectical kind of clarity something
which is emerging from the movement of history, from a process that
is gradually coming into being.)
In the name of the whole English and Welsh hierarchy, he declared an
absolute readiness for dialogue.

---

1. *AS* II/V, 606–608.
2. *AS* II/V, 608–610.
3. *AS* II/V, 610–612.

Weber,[1] Strasbourg: asked that what was said about *communicatio in sacris* [sharing in the sacraments] in Chapter XI of the schema *De Ecclesia* last year be inserted here.

Catholics should be able to receive the Sacraments of the Orthodox, and vice versa.

Mgr Méndez[2] (Cuernavaca): he began by quoting the words of St Paul: *Benedictus Deus* [Blessed be God] . . . who has blessed you (Eph 1:3).

Ecumenism, God's blessing, of which we have had an experience at the Council.

Speak of Churches or of ecclesial communities; one ought also to consider the Pentecostals.

Mention the immense ecumenical importance of the biblical and liturgical movements (he cited Dom Beauduin in this connection).

In speaking of the Jews, there is no reference to the fact that they are still the chosen People. They must not be excluded from this schema. He suggested that one should BEGIN with religious freedom, then move on progressively from non-Christians to Christians, mentioning Muslims and Jews on the way. Then it would be necessary to draft new chapters (even the F∴M∴ [Freemasons]).

Mgr Chopard-Lallier:[3] two things to note, from the missionary point of view:

1) The dogmatic principles would be better in the *De Ecclesia*.

There is too little reference to the Holy Spirit.

2) A point missing: unity in the promotion of family life in certain circumstances. It would be possible to say together prayers other than those approved by the Church.

He recommended that in certain circumstances THE UNITY OF THE CHRISTIAN PEOPLE should be manifested to non-Christians; he replied to the objection of the danger of indifference.

It is also necessary to recognise those cases where unanimity in evangelisation already exists (he cited the Taizé Brothers in Abidjan).

At 11.45 am, a vote was called for on Chapter II and on the whole of the *De S Liturgia*. The result was:

Present:	2,152
Yes	2,112
No	40
Null	[ ]

---

1. *AS* II/V, 613–615.
2. *AS* II/V, 615–618.
3. Robert Chopard-Lallier, Prefect Apostolic of Parakou (Dahomey), *AS* II/V, 618–620.

In the name of the Moderators, Cardinal Agagianian[1] explained the incident spoken of by Cardinal Bacci: he had wanted to point out a mistake in the Latin and say *ius primatus* [right/law of primacy] instead of *ius primatiale* [primatial right/law]. So the Moderators had decided that there was no place for further insistence.

Applause.

> Mgr Jacq[2] (read his text very badly, at the head of which he had put my paper).
> Showed the importance of ecumenism in a very authentic way.
> Showed the timeliness of ecumenism.
> Ferreira[3] (Bishop of Porto): in favour of introducing scholasticism into the schema (and into everything): distinguish the essence of the Church and its concrete situations or historical conditions (he was called to order).
> De Uriarte,[4] (Capuchin from Peru, whom Fr Tascon told me he had known there: he is eighty-five years of age). He made everyone laugh—it is a shame to laugh at an old man—because, with enthusiasm and volubility, he developed the idea that everything is ecumenical:
>> God is ecumenical
>> The Blessed Virgin, Saint Joseph are ecumenical
>> The bishops, parish priests, are ecumenical . . .
>
> The President called him to order, asking him to speak of the ecumenism OF WHICH the schema speaks. But he went on, imperturbably. In the end he was applauded as a way of easing the strain.

On the way out, the Superior of the Congregation of the Holy Cross[5] told me that this morning, in the tribune of the general superiors of the Orders, an unsigned two-page document was being circulated and signed. This paper was asking (the Pope) for the question of collegiality to be postponed until the next Session. Because it is not yet ripe, it is ambiguous, it is full of dangers . . . Apparently, about seventy out of eighty superiors had signed, beginning with Fr Fernandez.

Mgr Charue, to whom I spoke immediately afterwards about this, told me that he got wind of it two days ago and thought that it had come from the Spaniards.

In the afternoon, visit to Dr Callieri. He gave me a paper for Garcin[6] and Thiébaut, giving his opinion about my case.

---

1. *AS* II/V, 622.
2. *AS* II/V, 622–625.
3. António Ferreira Gomes (Portugal), *AS* II/V, 625–627.
4. Bonaventura León de Uriarte Bengoa, OFM, born in 1891, Vicar Apostolic in San Ramón, *AS* II/V, 629–631.
5. Germain Lalande.
6. Raymond Garcin, neurologist, was the Clinical Director of La Salpêtrière in Paris.

Callieri has reached no conclusion. It could be either a slow degeneration—which would end in paralysis—or a compression of the marrow at the joint of the occiput and the first cervical, which could be improved by neuro-surgery—or an inflammation of the marrow.

Callieri gave me a letter for Garcin and Thiébaut.

Sub-commission at St Martha's. In the evening, lecture on collegiality at the White Fathers.

Thursday 21 November 1963

(72nd General Congregation.) Before the Mass, I saw Cardinal Silva, the Apostolic Nuncio, Mgr Bertoli, whom I had tried several times to see, in vain, and finally Mgr Heenan. I was determined to express to the latter my deep gratitude for his lovely, moving and important declaration yesterday: an HISTORIC act.

Mgr Marty told me that today the election of six new members for the Commissions would be proposed, four to be elected, and two to be chosen by the Pope. The purpose of the operation: to modify the make-up of the Commissions in line with the spirit of the Council. But that will also have the effect of weighing them down!!!

Mass in Croatian: it is the Roman Mass but in a Slav language. During this Mass, singing in unison by strong male voices, accompanied by the organ. These chants have a serious and somewhat nostalgic style. They are in the style of German choral singing, and it seems to me that the synthesis between Slavism and Romanism is matched by a synthesis between that itself and the Germanic sense of choral singing. It is at the same time very Balkan and very Central European. How deep and interesting the human being is everywhere!! How one, and yet how different. It wants to be itself, quite simply, to be what it conceives itself to be.

Felici[1] announced that, in order to speed up the work of the Commissions, the Pope, in response to numerous requests, had raised the number of members of the Commissions to thirty. Thus, five new members will be needed, except for the Eastern congregation, which will have only three new members and the Secretariat twelve.

The Council will elect four members and the Pope will appoint one, except for the Liturgical Commission, which has finished its work.

The presidents of the episcopal conferences are to convene their conferences and indicate three names for each Commission (six for the Secretariat), who can be voted for in the General Congregation. To be submitted to the secretariat before Monday. These lists will be distributed to the Fathers on Wednesday and the election will take place on Thursday.

After these elections, the Pope will grant the Commissions the right to ELECT a new vice-president and a new secretary in addition to the existing ones.

---

1. *AS* II/V, 635–637.

A list was then read of the thirty-one names of those who have asked to speak, and have yet to be heard, on ecumenism in general. It will be impossible for them all to be heard!!!

Then yet another *relatio* [report] on the *modi* called for in the liturgy. What a bore! However, it is a question of things that are important: mother tongue in the sacraments and in the liturgy. I have not been much interested in the liturgical question at the Council, but one cannot do everything: I have not even got the time to READ all the post every day, and even less time in which to reply to it.

Laurentin gave me to read a report which he has produced (for whom?) on the work of the Commission that is dealing with the Marian question. What he says is very distressing and even horrifying. Balić's people, in fact TWO Sicilian bishops, have infiltrated and led the work and are pushing it in a maximising direction, at times using some very dubious dirty tricks. That does not surprise me: mariology has been living only on that for a long time. AT LEAST THAT KIND OF MARIOLOGY THAT ALWAYS WANTS TO ADD SOMETHING. It is a real cancer in the tissue of the Church.

The discussion of ecumenism resumed.

> Flores[1] (Barbastro) spoke very positively. In favour of dialogue (though he did not see all that that implies).
> *VERY* long speech: he could have said that in three minutes, but the Spaniards always go back over the whole question. They produce encyclicals.
> Florit[2] offered some comments designed to improve the schema.
> Once again the reference to Eph 2, 20 that we have had so many times in the Theological Commission: page 8 on the elements of the Church that are present among those who are separated from us.
> Page 16 on common prayers: Florit said that they are common only externally, but that each has a different intention.
> The fact is that he has not personally reached the level of a true prayer for unity.
> Etc.
> I missed Mgr Aramburu,[3] from Tucumán (Argentina): in the bar I saw Laurentin: who added to his dossier that he had heard it said that yesterday evening Balić had made some concessions. That remains to be seen.
> Mgr Höffner:[4] those who are CHRISTIANS in another communion are not the only separated brethren, there are also the brethren who are separated because lapsed, those who are far from the Church.

---

1. J Flores Martin, *AS* II/V, 661–663.
2. *AS* II/V, 665–667.
3. *AS* II/V, 668–670.
4. *AS* II/V, 670–671.

Hervás,[1] Dora, Spain: proposed another distribution of the material, excluding from the schema Chapters 4 and 5. The question of religious freedom is not in the right place, but should be in the chapter in schema XVII which speaks of the rights of the person. Placed in the schema on ecumenism, the chapter on freedom, as it is, would encourage a Rousseauan idea (subjective norms only) and proselytism. The first part of the encyclical *Pacem in Terris,* which is concerned with the rights of the person, deals with this topic.
I THINK THAT IS FAIR.

Ziadé[2] (Maronite): very warm general approval of the principles outlined in the schema: in third place respect for freedom and differences (example of the First Council of Jerusalem).
A few comments and *desiderata.*
The time has come to live from a Catholic fullness by taking up everything that has evolved everywhere and amongst all.

Hamvas[3] (Hungary). Hungary has always promoted peace between East and West: Saint Stephen . . . He recounted the history of the fate of the Calvinists in Hungary. He went well over his allotted time but he was allowed to continue (because he is Hungarian): Cardinal Lercaro interrupted him, but he went on.

Cardinal Lercaro,[4] on behalf of the Moderators, asked the Fathers to signify whether or not they agreed to terminating the discussion of the schema *in genere* [in general]. It was 11.15 am.

The vote was by standing up or remaining seated.

It was agreed to end the discussion; those who were to speak in the name of at least five Fathers may still do so.

The Moderators asked for a *placet* for the first three Chapters, after which the same question would be put separately for Chapters 4 and 5. The wording of the vote was: *An placeat tria prima capita globatim sumpta ita approbari ut assumentur sicut fundamentum basis ulterioris disceptationis* [whether the first three chapters, taken as a whole, are approved such that they can be taken as a basis for further discussion]?

That gave the following result:

Number of voters	2,052
Yes	1,967
No	87

1. J Hervás y Benet, *AS* II/V, 671–674.
2. I Ziadé, AS II/V, 675–676.
3. *AS* II/V, 677–679.
4. *AS* II/V, 681–682.

Mgr Martin,[1] *relator* [rapporteur] for the first three chapters, then spoke: the Secretariat has already examined the written comments; if the first three chapters are approved in principle, it will take everything thoroughly into account.

Discussion of Chapter 1 began (it was 11.25 am).

Mgr Nicodemo[2] (Bari, Italy): importance of this first chapter.

The whole of Catholic doctrine in unity has not been given (yet another reference to Eph 2: 20).

It is not mentioned that Christ built the Church on Peter (really and truly, ultramontanism does exist !!!).

No 2, lines 17 ff: there is attributed to the heretics a certain communion with us whereas, although there are some links, there is not the least degree of communion.

One should describe at least WHAT ecumenism IS, and what are its theological principles. In this, the greatest clarity is needed, without ambiguity.

Mgr Volk:[3] the word ECUMENISM has two meanings:
- universal: ecumenical council;
- the activities connected with Christian unity.

Ecumenism must also be applied in the Church with respect to universality or catholicity. The historical character of the Church means that everything that is POSSIBLE for the Church is not all at once REAL.

One cannot be aware of being only PARTIAL, unless one knows the whole and recognises oneself in the whole. The Catholic Church, then, must develop and show its full catholicity (he had to be reminded that he had overrun his time).

Talamás[4] (Mexico): suggested that the text of the schema *De œcumenismo* be altered on page 10, lines 29 . . . in the sense of not entering into dialogue unless well prepared.

Carli:[5] make the heading more precise: *De œcumenismo catholico*, because it does not have the same meaning! There should be a *proemium* in which division is deplored, and the maternal solicitude of the Church towards those who are separated is stated; the unicity of the Church, its unity and what union must consist in should be well defined.

And in Chapter I, principles should be set out, principles which he expounded in the most rigidly dogmatic manner. And he quoted once again Eph 2: 20 and the college!! He triggered some murmuring: the

---

1. Joseph-M Martin, *AS* II/V, 682–683.
2. *AS* II/V, 683–686.
3. *AS* II/V, 687–689.
4. M Talamás Camandari, *AS* II/V, 681–690.
5. *AS* II/V, 691–694.

other Apostles, he said, were given to Peter as CO-OPERATORS!!!
Peter must be declared the foundation of the entire Church and head and foundation of the apostles.

I SEE THAT THERE IS A PROFOUND AMBIGUITY UNDERLYING THE SAME WORD 'ECUMENISM', BETWEEN THOSE WHO SEE ONLY **RE-UNION** WITH THE **CHURCH** (FAVOURED BY CHARITY) AND THOSE WHO SEE SOMETHING QUITE NEW AHEAD OF ALL OF US, THAT CALLS FOR A PROFOUND REFORM.

Mgr Elchinger came to tell me that Hamer had telephoned him yesterday evening at 10.30 pm to say that the hall at the Angelicum could not be used for the Cullmann lecture, by order of higher authority. He thought that this authority was Staffa. I said to him: higher than that. He wants to let the Pope know what has happened.

So Cullmann's lecture will be at Saint-Louis des Français under the chairmanship of the French ambassador to the Holy See.

And that happens at the very moment when ecumenism is being discussed *in aula*.

Mgr A Abed[1] (Maronite, Tripoli): pronounced Latin '-us' as 'US' (not 'OUS'). There are more useful things than the primacy of Peter to let our separated brethren hear about: Christian faith and the hope of the resurrection.
They are Christian brethren who do not need to be CONVERTED but embraced.
He proposed some corrections in this spirit.

The results were given of the votes on Chapter III of the liturgy:

Number of voters	2,143
Yes	2,107
No	35
Void	1

In the coach on the way back, the bishops were talking about the elections to be held for the Commissions.

At St Martha's at 4.30 pm, for the sub-commission.

Mgr Philips confirmed to me that Fr Balić HAD TOLD HIM explicitly that he was creating a smoke screen in order to conceal the fact that he was giving up on the Marian question. But Fr Balić is full of curious, successive and at times contradictory reactions. He can, in succession, go quietly, bang his fist angrily on the table, circumvent and play dirty tricks . . . And all that with an incredible ability to bounce back.

---

1. Antoine Abed, Maronite Archbishop of Tripoli (Lebanon), *AS* II/V, 694–696.

Friday 22 November 1963

Conversation with various bishops (Schmitt, Boillon, de Provenchères) about the *De libertate religiosa*. Then with Liégé and Mgr Méndez about priestly celibacy.

More reports on the *modi* to the liturgy!! What a bore! After that, a rush to the bar . . .

Queue for the discussion on ecumenism in general.

> Mgr Da Veiga Coutinho:[1] went back over chapter 4 which he would like to see removed.
>
> Mgr Pont y Gol:[2] chapter 4 should be sent on to the Secretariat for non-Christian Religions.
>
> There are differing opinions concerning chapter 5; he thought time should be set aside to study the question.
>
> He spoke in favour of an expression of mutual forgiveness requested and given.
>
> Makarakiza[3] (Burundi): on renewal in the Church by means of a less conceptualist and more total-existential notion of Faith.
>
> To be possessed by Christ. Example of John XXIII.
>
> (Nobody was listening; it did not get across.)
>
> Discussion of Chapter I was resumed.
>
> Mgr Mazur:[4] (Lublin) in the name of the bishops of Poland:
>
> This chapter lacks order: he suggested one, not very interesting and with little real feeling for ecumenism.
>
> Huyghe:[5] pointed out that what was under discussion was the *aditus* [approach] not the *reditus* [return] of those separated from us.
>
> Today one can see all that needs to be done on our side. The conversion of ALL Christians. COMMON action . . . both in prayer and in the raising of funds (a Cullmann idea[6]), as well as in theological reflection on such matters as poverty; lastly, in a certain pastoral activity in common.
>
> Romero[7] (dreadfully boring tone): on the necessity of belonging to the Church.
>
> Jaeger[8] (Paderborn): with reference to his own experience.

---

1. *AS* II/V, 744–745.
2. *AS* II/V, 746–747.
3. Andreas Makarakiza, Bishop of Ngozi, *AS* II/V, 749–751.
4. Jan Mazur, Auxiliary Bishop of Lublin *AS* II/V, 751–753.
5. *AS* II/V, 753–755.
6. Cf Oscar Cullmann, *Catholiques et Protestants. Un projet de solidarité chrétienne* (Neuchâtel-Paris: Delachaux & Niestlé, 1958).
7. F Romero Menjibar, *AS* II/V, 757–759.
8. *AS* II/V, 759–761.

Flusin:[1] suggested some corrections and additions to Chapter I in which I recognised Fr Féret with his biblical references.

Mgr Chang(?):[2] dreadful Germanic diction: enough to shatter the amplifiers. In favour of the ecumenism of Confucius; in favour of ecumenism— *simpliciter dictus . . . fuit homo missus a Deo* [simply put . . . there was a man sent from God (cf John 1:6)] (John XXIII).

The human being is enlightened for its salvation.

Fairly dismal session which ended with the proclamation of the results of the vote on the schema *De S Liturgia* as a whole.

Those present	2,178
Yes	2,158
No	19

On the way out of St Peter's, I saw Mgr Oesterreicher. He seemed to me to be full of enthusiasm and rather self-satisfied. Clearly it is to do with Chapter IV on the Jews.

Lunch with Skydsgaard and his assistant.[3]

At 3 pm, workshop on the chapter *De libertate religiosa* at the French Seminary. I had arranged for Fr de Riedmatten to be invited, as he is by far the most interesting of the experts that have been heard at this session. But the bishops seemed to have specially invited Frs Daniélou, Martelet and Cottier to speak. Dupuy and Le Guillou were also there. It emerged from the colloquium that it would be necessary:

1) to make it clear that the problem of religious freedom is not being discussed IN ITS ENTIRETY;

2) to make it clear that the text concentrates mainly on *libertas a coactione physica et morali* [freedom from physical or moral constraint];

3) not to link this freedom solely to the dignity of the human person, but to formulate OBJECTIVE foundations in the transcendence of faith with respect to temporal structures and in the NATURE of the religious fact and of religion.

At 5 pm, lecture by l'abbé Houtart at the Angelicum. Afterwards, at the Angelicum, meeting of the 'Church poor and servant' group. Painful meeting. Fr Gauthier, who has this ONE idea and who sees NOTHING else, went round in circles.

It is extremely disappointing. The more worthwhile a man is on the charismatic level, the more the group he is supposed to be animating is left feeling lost, caught up in a battle of words, lacking initiative. WE ARE NO MORE AHEAD THAN WE WERE A YEAR AGO. Mgr Himmer did not add an ounce of struc-

---

1. *AS* II/V, 762–764.
2. V Chang Tso-Huan, *AS* II/V, 765–767.
3. The Danish Lutheran Pastor Gerhard Pedersen.

ture, precision, or effectiveness. Mgr Mercier read the text (too long) of an address to the Pope, the most positive aspect of which was an urgent request that
the next Session should BEGIN with schema XVII. I added my own idea that
it should begin with a realistic assessment of the world, accompanied by some
direct testimonies.

After that, we went with Chenu to another meeting with Frs Cottier, Labourdette and Voillaume.[1] The purpose was the same, but the idea was to succeed in
producing, for this question of poverty, a book that would serve a purpose similar
to that played by *L'Épiscopat et l'Église universelle* for the question of the episcopate (this book had been decisive).

We began to plan the main outline. This all happened in a small restaurant. I
encountered there a Fr Voillaume quite different from the one whom I had come
to know through his books or his *Lettres aux Fraternités*:[2] a much more realistic
man, in touch with the real world, modern, progressive.

We heard there, only an hour after it had happened, of the assassination of
President Kennedy. Everyone was deeply moved. One felt that an opportunity for
peace had been taken from the world in the person of a brave and upright man,
who loved and served humanity.

Saturday 23 November 1963

Very indifferent day. Telephone calls. Work interrupted by visits: in the morning,
a Polish priest, in the afternoon Mlle Thouzellier.[3]

At 11 am: Television: a recording for the Sunday Catholic programme and
one for 'Cinq colonnes à la Une'. But the *speaker* for this transmission arrived
very late, and altered the arrangement; Italian radio had brought spools that only
lasted two and a half minutes, so they had to keep changing them. In short, two
and half hours in the middle of the day for very little. Moreover, the interviewer
himself simply did not tell me (nor want to tell me) what he proposed to ask me
about, so that he took me by surprise with questions on collegiality and the Holy
Office or the conservative current. How can one speak to twenty million viewers
who have not the least idea about all that?

At 4.30 pm, sub-commission meeting at St Martha's. Mgr Garrone told me
that Cardinal Suenens had said yesterday that the Pope will come *in aula* on 3 and
4 December: that he will consult the Fathers on the date of the next Session; and
finally—this, in my view, is very important and concerns a matter to which I have
several times drawn attention—that he is looking for a formula for proclaiming
the decree on the liturgy that ASSOCIATES THE BISHOPS with the Pope. Some-

---

1. René Voillaume, in the footsteps of Charles de Foucauld, had founded the Little Brothers of Jesus, of which he was at that time Prior General, as well as the Little Brothers
   and Little Sisters of the Gospel.
2. René Voillaume, *Lettres aux Fraternités,* vols I and II (Paris: Cerf, 1960).
3. Christine Thouzellier, specialist in the sects and heresies of the medieval West, was
   responsible for research at the CNRS [Centre national de la recherche scientifique].

thing other than *'Paulus, sacro approbante concilio'* [Paul, with the approval of the sacred Council] . . . !

Mgr Garrone also told me that there was a split within the Secretariat for unity. A goodly number would like to detach Chapter 4 (on the Jews) and Chapter 5 (Freedom) from the schema on ecumenism. It would be stubborn of Cardinal Bea to defend the unity of the five chapters.

Sunday 24 November 1963

Work for the sub-commission, in so far as I was able. In the morning, visit-interview for the newspaper *La Rocca* (Assisi);[1] at 12.30 pm Fr Féret came to fetch me, with Fr Liégé and Mgr Schmitt, for a pleasant outing: Via Appia, lunch in front of the Catacomb of St Sebastian; then, further along the Via Appia. Rome has kept everything. In the midst of cosmopolitan-style suburbs, this narrow road remains intact, bordered by moss-covered walls and gardens, tombs and ruins, cypresses and stone pines. Everything here is as it was two thousand years ago. A poetry without sadness emanates from these remains of an antiquity that was grandiose, and, in spite of everything, also very human. Everything here speaks, nothing is mass-produced; the past is present. We trod the same paving blocks as those on which St Paul walked . . . On the way back, we stopped at St John at the Latin Gate, which I did not know: charming little basilica, bare, humble and peaceful.

In the evening, visit from l'abbé J I Tellechea Idígoras,[2] who brought me a book on the ideal bishop at the time of the Reformation.[3] An intelligent and open-minded man, dedicated to the truth and the historical method: one of those who will form a Spanish Catholicism synchronous with the world of today and tomorrow.

Fr Liégé and Fr Féret told me that: 1) on the occasion of their reception by the Pope last Monday, the French bishops had been quite disappointed: I knew this. I did not know that the Pope had reminded them that they were required to watch over all that was being published. That concerned especially *ICI*. The Pope had been very scandalised by an article on Poland[4] and said that the *ICI* people were enemies of the Church in disguise; 2) Fr General, in consequence of what the Pope had said to him on this subject, had written to the French Provincials asking them not to allow any OP to be involved with this journal or its running, but also saying that it would be a good thing if some reliable theologians were to write in it in order to give a reliable account of things. I knew nothing about this letter which Fr Kopf, it seems, has not passed on in order not to damage *ICI*.

---

1. 'Incontri all'ora del Concilio. Yves Congar', *La Rocca*, 15 February, 1964: 22–28.
2. José Ignacio Tellechea Idígoras, professor of the history of the Church.
3. *El obispo ideal en el siglo de la Reforma* (Rome, 1963).
4. Cf above, page 386, note 2.

Monday 25 November 1963

In the coach, some news about the election of additional members for the Commissions. It seems that a list was compiled, signed by fifty-six episcopal conferences. If that is true, it is a sign that the episcopates have got themselves organised since a year ago.

There was also a meeting of the episcopates of the European Union. It is also being said (Haubtmann, Moeller) that the Pope is being put under a lot of pressure to have Chapters 4 and 5 removed. The votes that have been announced for these might not even be held. The Spaniards and the Italians in particular are against Chapter 5, *De libertate*. The Italians claim that that would contribute to the opening to the left, which would bring with it a flight of capital. Or else the chapter *De libertate* could be transferred to schema XVII. That has always been my own position, and it is what I have been saying every day now, adding however, that it would be necessary for the text to be discussed during this Session in order to provide guidance for those who will correct and improve it. In the confidence of friendship, I told Moeller how, while working these past two days on the chapter *De Populo Dei*, I had had in my hands the corrections suggested by Mgr Philips. He is without the slightest doubt a providential man: he alone could do what he has done, that is to say replace the official text by a new one, without struggle or crisis. He has an astonishing gift of welcome, that gift of peacefully disarming every adversary. It is marvellous and one can never overstate what he has done. But his thinking is limp, and his texts are flat!

Everything is there, but without vigour, sunk in a facility without depth.

On the way into the Basilica this morning, a paper bearing a great many signatures was being distributed, calling for the suppression of the schema on the means of communication, deemed to be puerile and inadequate. It is not the only paper with this intent. Mgr Schmitt, Bishop of Metz, at the instigation of Fr Féret, organised something similar. It was he who said: it is a text for Coeurs Vaillants.[1]

Also being distributed was a little book by M Guarducci[2] on the excavations of St Peter's and the tradition of St Peter in the Vatican.[3]

De mandato S Pontificis [At the behest of the Supreme Pontiff], on Wednesday 4 December at 9 am there will be held the public session of the Council at which the decrees already approved will be examined and voted on. On 3 December, again at 9 am, the Pope will come *in aula* and there will be a commemoration of the fourth centenary of the Council of Trent with an address by Cardinal Urbani.

---

1. The 'Coeurs Vaillants' (Valiant Hearts) was a Catholic Action movement for children.
2. Margherita Guarducci, Professor of Epigraphy at the University of Rome.
3. On 18 November, Felici had announced the forthcoming distribution of this book (*La Tradizione di Pietro in Vaticano alla luce della storia e dell'archeologia* (Rome: 1963)), made available in translation into various languages: the French version was entitled: *La Tradition de Pierre au Vatican, à la lumière de l'histoire et de l'archéologie*.

Discussion of chapter I of *De œcumenismo.*

Cardinal Léger:[1] in favour of a more precise presentation of the mark of unity, which seems too monolithic and uniform; the schema should state better how to overcome the DOGMATIC difficulties.

Veritas non tantum in caritate, sed etiam in humilitate [Truth not only in charity, but also in humility] (intellectual humility). This, in the name of the transcendence of dogmatic [[spirits]], struggles against intellectual immobilism.

Cardinal Ritter:[2] in favour of a better expression of the doctrinal bases of ecumenism (christological basis).

Cardinal Bea:[3] on the title. *De christianorum unitate fovenda* [On promoting the unity of Christians] had been suggested. The Secretariat will study it. There has been reference to the possible dangers. It is for the local ordinaries to supervise ecumenical activity. The episcopal conferences should establish a local secretariat. Doctrinal dialogue should be conducted only by well-prepared and sound theologians: this is something that the local ordinaries can appreciate better than the Roman dicasteries.

It has been said that the schema praises highly the good that is found among non-Catholics and does not sufficiently set forth Catholic doctrine. But the schema is addressed TO CATHOLICS.

There has been an objection to the advisability of prayer in common on the grounds that each person will bring to it his or her own concept of unity.

Cardinal Tisserant:[4] on the way in, a leaflet was being distributed calling on the Fathers to vote against the schema on communications. The Council of Presidents and the Moderators deplore this procedure, which is unworthy of the Council.

(Why did nobody protest when leaflets about the text on the *De Beata* were likewise distributed?)

Mgr Stourm[5] read the *relatio* [report] of the *modi* that had been inserted into the schema in question. I went out for a while during this time; I saw Jedin. I spoke to him about the question of how the Pope would promulgate the Decree on the liturgy. They had had a meeting at which Mgr Colombo and Dossetti were also present. They had suggested: the

---

1. *AS* II/VI, 10–12.
2. *AS* II/VI, 12–14.
3. *AS* II/VI, 14–17.
4. *AS* II/VI, 17.
5. René Louis M Stourm, Archbishop of Sens, member of the Commission on the Apostolate of the Laity, appointed by the Pope at the beginning of the First Session, *AS* II/VI, 19–20.

Pope, having received the agreement of the Council, *assentitur* [gives his assent] and promulgates the decree passed by the Council. It is not known what the Pope will do with this suggestion, but the matter has been raised and this suggestion has been passed on to him.

Mgr Guano[1] distinguished three progressive moments in the ecumenical approach:

a) collaboration in Christian social action;

b) dialogue;

c) a deeper communion, based on prayer and paving the way for eucharistic communion.

Mgr Tawil[2] (Syria): The title: *De catholicis principiis œcumenismi* [on the Catholic principles of ecumenism].

In the schema there is no theology of discord, whereas there is one in Sacred Scripture. He enlarged on it admirably. He spoke of the different traditions and explained their existence in the East, not without saying a word about Latinisation. The Uniates have no ecumenical sense except in relation to Orthodoxy which they represent in the Catholic Church.

Fr Fernandez, OP[3] (many departures for the bar):

The title: *principia catholica de œcumenismo* [the Catholic principles of ecumenism], or the title suggested by Cardinal Bea.

The most important result of the Council will be the opening to the others and to the world. However, some comments:

1) Individual conversions, which ecumenism does not harm.

2) On the doctrinal preaching of the faith: 'witness' is not sufficient.

Mgr Gahamanyi,[4] in the name of the episcopal conference of Rwanda and Burundi: tone and content very tiring: mostly warnings.

Mgr Pangrazio[5] (India): in favour of a more dynamic, more historical presentation of the Church.

Canestri:[6] Auxiliary of the Cardinal Vicar of Rome: detailed comments for a more precise formulation.

page 8, line 20: l. 27 etc.

In favour of '*clarae distinctiones*' [clear distinctions].

'*unum Christi ovile sub uno pastore Petro*' [A single flock of Christ under the one shepherd who is Peter].

---

1. *AS* II/VI, 20–23.
2. *AS* II/VI, 23–25.
3. *AS* II/VI, 26–28.
4. Jean Gahamanyi, Bishop of Butare (Rwanda), *AS* II/VI, 30–32.
5. In fact, Andrea Pangrazio was Archbishop of Gorizia and Gradisca (Italy), *AS* II/VI, 32–34.
6. Giovanni Canestri, Auxiliary Bishop to Cardinal C Micara, Vicar General of the Pope for the diocese of Rome, *AS* II/VI, 35–36.

Felici:[1] results of the votes on the *modi* to the schema on the means of
communication:

Number of those voting	2,032
Yes	1,788
No	331

This evening, at 5 pm, at the Lateran, Requiem Mass for President Kennedy.

Mgr Granados,[2] on No. 1: the description of the unity of the Church is vague.
The hierarchy as principle of unity.

The Moderators suggested that discussion of Chapter I of *De Œcumenismo*
should now be ended. Voting by standing up or remaining seated. It
was agreed. It is always possible to speak further about it in accordance
with the regulations.

With Cardinal Döpfner as Moderator, discussion of Chapter II on the practice
of ecumenism began immediately.

Cardinal Bueno y Monreal:[3]

Comments on details, some of which concerned notable points. Good
things on the harm that divisions do to the cause of the Gospel.

Against proselytism, in measured and quite appropriate terms.

Mgr Darmancier[4] on No. 7 concerning prayer for unity. Specify its spirit
and its purpose if one wants it to be possible for it to be common.
Only the prayer of Christ is adequate to the mystery. It is a matter of
our associating ourselves with it or rather of making the Holy Spirit
associate itself with it in us.

The unity that Christ wants by the means that he wants.

Margiotta:[5] (Italy: Brindisi): that, even though the Index be retained,
excommunication of those who possess or read books by separated
brethren should be be suppressed.

Mgr Desmazières:[6] on the ecumenical objective, the ecumenical moment of
all pastoral action.

Emotional evocation of John XXIII.

Pious and sentimental tone, exhortatory and somewhat oratorical,
though also virile. He said some good things.

Fr Martin[7] (New Caledonia): in favour of a real dialogue in which one really
faces the problem of one's own reformation.

---

1. *AS* II/VI, 36–37.
2. *AS* II/VI, 37–39.
3. *AS* II/VI, 40–42.
4. *AS* II/VI, 42–43.
5. Nicola Margiotta, Archbishop of Brindisi, *AS* II/VI, 43–44.
6. *AS* II/VI, 44–46.
7. *AS* II/VI, 46–48.

The result of the vote on the means of communication was then given:

No of voters	2,212
Yes	1,598
No	503
Void	11

So the schema has been adopted. Without glory. Moreover, it brings no further glory to the Council. From what I see, many place their confidence in those who have drafted a text. They say: they are competent people . . .

At the Vatican at 4.30 pm. Prior to that, a visit from Mlle Frassati, Pier Giorgio Frassati's sister.[1] She spoke to me about her brother. It was very interesting. Frassati was a deep soul, very humble and very hidden. His family never had the least idea of his holiness. It was a worldly family (his father was ambassador in Berlin), and spiritual questions were never discussed. His sister herself had no idea that her brother was a saint. It was only after his death that this was realised. They then received hundreds of testimonies of his charity. When his sister undertook to study his life, she herself did not really believe it all. But then it became apparent that this tough young man (he died of poliomyelitis) had a life of constant union with God. He loved and visited the poor; he saved his money for them, at the cost of his own fatigue. He studied in the mineralogy section of an engineering school in order to work with the miners. His father, who died only a couple of years ago, never understood his son; indeed he was inclined to regard him as a half-wit (because of his humility); he never wanted to get involved in this whole affair. The whole story interested me greatly.

On the ride to the Vatican, Mgr Philips told me how things were as regards the *De Beata*. Balić has produced two new texts. Basically, now, with the support of Ciappi, Llamera, Garcia Garcés, Bélanger,[2] etc, he would like Philips to be responsible, as 'editor', for a text that is even more Marian than the official schema. He seems to have the idea that, as regards the content, a maximising text would be accepted by two thirds of the Fathers if Philips takes it over and becomes its editor. They had held a long meeting this morning at St Martha's during the General Congregation: each expert said what he thought. Finally, they had not got any further than they had been two weeks ago, except that the trend is to keep on adding to it . . .

At the Commission, I was beside Fr de Lubac. He is very pessimistic. He thinks that, although nothing of this is as yet perceived *in aula*, or in the thinking of the Council, the conservatives are in fact in the process of winning points

---

1. Pier Giorgio Frassati [1901–1925]. His sister had collected the testimonies concerning her brother: Cf Luciana Frassati, *Mio fratello Pier Giorgio, vita e imagini,* Geneva, 1959; he was later to be beatified by Pope John Paul II, who named him a patron of young people.
2. Marcel Bélanger, OMI, of the Faculty of Theology at the University of Ottawa, was a Council expert.

and that they are manoeuvring in order to secure the defeat of things that are advantageous. Fr de Lubac believes that the Spaniards and the Italians HAVE SECURED from the Pope the transfer of chapter 5 of the *De libertate religiosa* to schema XVII, that is to say, in his view, to the graveyard. He sees manoeuvring everywhere. Perhaps I don't see enough. He says: they are gangsters.

Great discussion on *'ab Abel iusto'* [from the just man Abel]; a vote gave fifteen in favour of the text proposed by the sub-commission, which said *'inde ab Adam'* [from Adam onwards], *'ab Abel iusto . . .'* Then, one moved on, from one skirmish to another, from one phrase to the next.

Tuesday 26 November 1963
I am keeping this little journal as a witness. I do not mix in the expression of my personal feelings. That is why I simply record here my departure for Sedan at midday to-day. Yesterday evening, I telephoned Sedan at 8.20 pm. My mother was still alive, but would certainly not last the night. At 10.40 pm, I had a telephone call from Sedan: 'She is with the good Lord'. If it were a question of the mystical history of the Council, my mother would have an important place in it. During years of suffering, she has never ceased to pray for the Council, for my own work. The Council has been borne along by many prayers and suffering offered for it. But who knows, who could write this history?

Dom Rousseau had a very serious operation on the very day on which discussion on the schema on ecumenism began . . . My own health problems, the total exhaustion that I have been experiencing these two months, is not this also something in the invisible and mystical history of the Council? I believe so strongly in the Gospel's 'the one who loses, gains'. I believe so strongly in *'Cum infirmor, tunc potens sum'* ['When I am weak, then I am strong', (II Cor 12:10)] . . .

Saturday 30 November 1963
I returned from Sedan yesterday evening: reaching the Angelicum at 10.15 pm. Once again, I leave out of this journal everything touching my family and my mother. I merely note here what concerns the Council. I have little news of the past few days. While driving me back from the airport, Fr Féret told me that few French bishops had been elected to the Commissions: Mgr Ancel was, for the Theology Commission; Mgr de Provenchères for the Eastern.

The bishops have received the text of a message to priests, to be voted on on Monday. According to Fr Féret, the document is not entirely satisfactory. It is somewhat paternalistic. Whose initiative was it? And who wrote it?

Fr Labourdette told me a bit about the meeting of the joint commission on schema XVII yesterday evening. Almost the entire session was devoted to a very confused discussion on the origin and value of the new chapter I, on the mandate that Cardinal Suenens had had. By what right had he produced a text outside of the normal Council channels?

Mgr Prignon intervened to say that on the way out from the Co-ordinating Commission meeting, Cardinal Suenens was of the opinion that this was what he had been asked to do. Cardinal König concluded, quite rightly, that Cardinal Suenens himself should be asked about it . . .

It is true that to some extent Cardinal Suenens is directing the Council and that the little Belgian group is practically running things . . .

Finally, a joint sub-commission was appointed to co-ordinate the work on schema XVII:

From the Theological Commission: Ancel, Schröffer, McGrath.

From the Commission on the Laity: Hengsbach, Guano, Ménager.

The principle of two levels was accepted: a conciliar text, to be discussed *in aula*, and conciliar decrees prepared by sub-commissions that have been designated or confirmed for this.

Fr de Riedmatten completed this picture. He told me that many people were greatly disturbed: McGrath, Daniélou in particular, but also Hirschmann. They were saying: what is this new text? For what reason has the Chapter I that had been discussed in the Commission in May been suppressed? What has Cardinal Suenens been up to?

Fr de Riedmatten made them come to the meeting at the Belgian College on Thursday (to which I was supposed to go!); that calmed them down somewhat and inclined them more towards co-operation than opposition. However although, in the end, they have begun to collaborate once more, yesterday evening, at the joint commission meeting, Fr Tromp launched a fierce attack. There was a real feeling of discontent about the role that Cardinal Suenens has assumed, and it has not been entirely dissipated. Things need to be done *conciliariter* [in a conciliar manner] and they have not been . . .

At lunch, Cardinal Wyszyński. I spoke with him for some time. He spoke to me about the article by J De Broucker[1] in *ICI*.[2] This article had been felt in Poland as a stab in the back. The Cardinal thought that de Broucker was a pure intellectual, who was deluding himself in believing that one could come to terms with communism and who, not finding this same attitude among the Polish bishops, had accused them of negativism and a lack of openness. He has no sense of the humble reality of the Church, of the simple forms of a widespread fidelity among the people. However, the Cardinal regards intellectual formation as extremely important.

During this conversation and throughout the long toast at lunch (a real lecture of information), he showed himself very optimistic on the religious fidelity of the Poles. It seems, (according to de Riedmatten) that there is actually a serious crisis and that Cardinal Wyszyński is very much aware of it . . .

---

1. José de Broucker was the editor-in-chief of *ICI*.
2. Cf above, page 386, note 2.

I also encountered once more in him the fiercest and most monolithic Polish nationalist foundation: to be among Poles . . . Whatever is Polish is marvellous . . .

At 5.30 pm at Saint-Louis, lecture by Cullmann:[1] the lecture which he could not give at the Angelicum. Four cardinals, the ambassador, a lot of bishops, a huge crowd, above all of clerics (but not exclusively). VERY FINE lecture, which called for reflection.

Unfortunately, I was obliged to leave before the end (which must have sketched out an application to the present situation and to ecumenism) because there was an audience of experts with Paul VI. We waited for an hour. I protected myself as best as I could from my neighbour, a Korean priest, who was trying to breathe his flu into my face, and persisted in talking to me. In the end, I was _VERY_ disappointed in this audience: an address by Mgr Colombo, in Latin, in the name of the experts, the Pope read a text in Latin, prepared by a scribe. There was not the shadow of an idea in either the one or the other speech. I was not expecting either revelations or confidences. I was expecting a word on theology, on its place in the present situation. But there was nothing. Two hours wasted. What a frightful thing Rome is, reducing everything to ceremonies.

Medina told me that things are going very well at the sub-commission on the diaconate: they have even gone further than the text of the schema (married deacons). On the other hand, at the sub-commission on collegiality, they are faced with two opposing theses, which will result in two different reports between which the Commission will have to decide.

Afterwards, Delhaye and the Canadians (Naud and Lafortune) took me to dinner at the Columbus. I again received evidence of the attitude of the Canadians to 'Malines'. Cardinal Suenens, the new schema XVII, and even Mgr Philips, with the monotony of his lifeless statements, have clearly wearied the Canadians. They said that there would be no vote on Chapters IV and V of De œcumenismo, but that the Moderators would declare that these texts would be taken up later on . . .

Sunday 1 December 1963

I finished preparing my lecture for this evening. And I also got some correspondence out of the way. Chores.

But I was thinking back over the past week. Eight days ago, Tere was still alive. Now, it is all over. One will never now say what has not been said. One will never do the kindnesses that have not already been done. I feel this emptiness very painfully today. I was loved by someone and I loved. I tell myself that if priests wait, in some way, for the death of their mother in order to leave the priesthood and at times also the Church, it is not only because they have, up to that point, been held by a fidelity, nor because they have wanted to spare their mother this pain. It is also because, suddenly, they no longer feel themselves loved and they

---

1. 'The History of Salvation in the New Testament'.

themselves no longer have anyone on whom to bestow their affection . . . At Sedan, I experienced and understood better what a home is: a place where people love one another, where stable bonds of affection exist. I feel very strongly the sweetness of these bonds, which are tied not only at the level of a single generation, but from one generation to the next. One sees this extraordinary treasure of mutual confidence, of mutual giving and devotion, of the communicative contact of hearts which are committed: in short, there is a strength and a truth in affective bonds.

What will become of me? I have no strength left. I feel I have half-ruined my life. I have only half-succeeded in it. Will I have the courage always to have before my eyes the ineluctable end, so as to fill the days which may still be given to me with what I shall be happy to have done on that day without a tomorrow when it will be too late to do what I have not yet done? To love, to give, to be useful, to leave behind only the memory of having been loved . . .

Will I be willing to live the rest of my life, the decline of which is already being announced in my unspeakable exhaustion, in loving and in giving?

In the afternoon at 5 pm, lecture at the Biblicum on Scripture and Tradition. There were too many people, we moved to the large lecture hall at the Gregorianum (eight hundred seats). By applauding me, the students drew attention to some ideas or things which they took as criticisms, the evocation of Fr Teilhard . . . However, I felt inadequate. I was dragging myself along on the way back, and have a very bad headache. I am done for! Mgr Fulton Sheen came to see me before and after my lecture: he told me he had read all my books, some of them twice or three times . . . Flowers cast onto a shadow which is disappearing! I can hardly stand.

Mgr Baudoux (one of the Canadian bishops who was at lunch at noon) was saying that a concelebration of twenty bishops with the Pope had been planned for Wednesday: the first implementation of the Constitution on the Liturgy which is due to be promulgated that same day. A ritual had been worked out. But it all fell through. For what reasons, or because of what interventions?

Monday 2 December 1963

(79th General Congregation.) I have had a nosebleed since yesterday evening. It is a great nuisance.

Mgr Felici[1] spoke briefly about the faculties granted to bishops by the Pope (*Munus Pastorale*[2]) and about the work of the Commissions during the intersession.

The Fathers could send in their comments until 31 January 1964 on the schemas that have been discussed and those that have not.

---

1. *AS* II/VI, 337–339.
2. The reference is to the *motu proprio 'Pastorale Munus'* which was due to be read in *aula* the following day.

He spoke of the message to priests which had been distributed last Friday. As there had been a number of comments and emendations (more than sixty), the Moderators were postponing this message until later (some applause from the young bishops).

On Chapter III of the *De œcumenismo*:

Cardinal Ruffini[1] wished to recall several points:

The infallible Church founded on Peter (the pope).

One cannot impute any fault to the Roman Church as such (they live in a fictional world)—but only to some sons of the Roman Church; and there are the faults of those who '*Ecclesiam Romanam misere dereliquerunt*' [those who, lamentably, have left the Roman Church].

With all its heart, the Roman Church waits for those who stray. Prayer for this through the intercession of the Virgin (some faint applause).

Mgr Green:[2] (South Africa): on the question of Anglican ordinations. Need for dialogue between the Catholic Church as such and the Anglican Church as such. The case of Anglican pastors.

Mgr Muldoon:[3] (Australia): drew attention to the seriousness of the section analysing the meaning of the sixteenth century Reformation. That does not apply to Anglicanism. He spoke of his experience with Protestants who look for nothing but what they can turn against the Church. They will find there a new cause for complaint. If one wants peace, this section needs to be deleted.

Against those who advocate the making of a solemn act asking for forgiveness: let them go and find their confessor, but let them not plague us (in my tribune, some contented chortling from some of the religious superiors); some applause, showing that certain emotional declarations are upsetting ...

Thangalathil[4] (India) against the idea that the Orthodox had kept the whole patrimony: they could only have done so in union with the Apostolic See.

(What a lot of work remains to be done!!)

Costantini[5] (Italy): on No. 12, lines 7–10. Do not speak as if the faults are all on the side of the Catholic Church (very boring).

Hermaniuk[6] great praise for Chapter III.

The Council is calling for ecumenism, but it should itself give good

1. *AS* II/VI, 339–340.
2. Ernest A Green, Bishop of Port Elizabeth, *AS* II/VI, 341–342.
3. *AS* II/VI, 343–344.
4. Gregorios B Varghese Thangalathil, Archbishop of Trivandrum of the Syro-Malankars, member of the Commission on the Eastern Churches, *AS* II/VI, 344–346.
5. *AS* II/VI, 347–350.
6. *AS* II/VI, 350–353.

example and DO something: declare that the Church did not wish to impose anything more than what was necessary.

I missed Tomášek [1] (Czechoslovakia) and only heard the end of Mgr Srebnič's intervention.[2] He said: things are moving and ripening very quickly today! What has not been done for several centuries is now being done in a few years. May the time come when there will be a Council in common with the Orthodox!

Layek[3] (Aleppo, Armenians) drew attention to things missing in the schema: deplored the new canon law on mixed marriages and the laws on *communicatio in sacris*.

(About half the seats in the *aula* were empty; the bishops were chatting in the side-aisles.)

Dom Butler[4] on pages 23 and 25: on Anglicanism and its claim to have kept continuity with the ancient church; in his view, one should not say '*exortus*' [departed] in the sixteenth century, but 'separated'.

He replied to Muldoon regarding his rejection of a public confession of our sins: even though this point is the first article of spiritual striving. Perhaps the noise of it has not yet reached Australia, but historians have shown the faults that we have committed. The Council ought to associate itself with the Pope for this confession. He proposed a text for page 25.

Ziadé,[5] Archbishop in Lebanon: he praised the first section of Chapter III; suggested three amendments in order to improve it.

There are not only the Byzantines! Plurality in unity (not only the East-West duality). He spoke, remarkably well, of the Syriac Church (= the Easterners really have an INTERIOR feeling for things).

Mgr D'Mello[6] (India): proposed a practical conclusion: that the Fathers should recite the priestly prayer and the Lord's Prayer *WITH* the Observers and the Auditors, here, in St Peter's.

(Normally, there would have been general applause, but half of the Fathers were chatting in the side-aisles. It fell flat.)

Roborecki:[7] (Ukrainian): the principal difficulty is not the primacy itself, but the way it is exercised, centralisation . . . and also the fear of Latinisation (too many real facts feed this fear).

---

1. *AS* II/VI, 354–355.
2. In fact, this was said by F Tomášek, *AS* II/VI, 355. Congar must have mixed him up with the Yugoslav Bishop of Maribor, Maksimilijan Držečnik who, according to the *Acta,* was to have spoken after Mgr Tomášek, but did not do so.
3. Georges Layek, Armenian Archbishop of Aleppo, (Syria), *AS* II/VI, 356–358.
4. *AS* II/VI, 358–360.
5. *AS* II/VI, 360–361.
6. Leo D'Mello, Bishop of Ajmer and Jaipur, *AS* II/VI, 362–363.
7. Andrew Roborecki, Ukrainian bishop of Saskatoon (Canada), *AS* II/VI, 363–364.

It was 11.25 am: there were no further speakers listed for chapter III of *De Œcumenismo*. Cardinal Bea[1] brought things to a close. He expressed thanks for all the comments, all would be examined. There remained two chapters that had not been discussed due to lack of time, and for no other reason (he repeated these words twice). There could have been a vote on these chapters as a BASIS for discussion, but that would have been precipitous. It should be the subject of tranquil meditation, and preparation for a fruitful discussion at the Third Session. Any comments, whether on the content, or on the best place for inclusion, should be sent to the General Secretariat for the Council by 31 January.

Mgr Hengsbach[2] was going to give a brief report on the schema *De apostolatu laicorum*: genesis of the schema, content . . .

Mgr Felici,[3] General Secretary: instructions about what to wear tomorrow and the day after.

Lunch with Küng and Fr Daniel J O'Hanlon, SJ,[4] (the journal *America*), in order to plan the publication of the best forty speeches that had been made. We looked at the possibilities; a lot of work has already been done by Küng and O'Hanlon, who have employed a secretary. But I was being asked to seek the agreement of some ten of the bishops, and collect their texts (seven copies of each). That is why, not having returned to the Angelicum except to see an American priest for three minutes (thesis on the parish), I saw this very afternoon Cardinal Léger, Mgr Doumith, Mgr Jacq, Mgr Henríquez Jimenez and Mgr Charue.

Küng and O'Hanlon told me that they had been told by Mgr Helder Câmara that, during the last days of the life of John XXIII, Cardinal Ottaviani had come to see him and had shown him that he had done a lot of good, but that, after his death, there were some people who might misinterpret and misuse some of the things he had said. For this reason, the cardinal had asked him to sign a document, which he presented to him. The Pope had made a sign of refusal. Shortly afterwards, he had it said that he loved ALL the cardinals and thanked them for their kind collaboration.

Küng and O'Hanlon think that Paul VI is very good while he is hesitant, which is his first reaction: but then, in the end, he decides in a conservative direction. He is now being subjected to intense pressure, which is always of a somewhat PO-LITICAL kind, and is connected with the Italian situation. It is now being put to him that the various openings (ecumenism, collegiality, religious freedom) would promote the slide to the left and even, with the flight of capital, an economic crisis

---

1. *AS* II/VI, 364–367.
2. *AS* II/VI, 367–370.
3. *AS* II/VI, 370–371.
4. Daniel J O'Hanlon, SJ, specialist in ecumenical matters, was Professor of Theology at the Jesuit College in Los Gatos, California; he was the personal expert of a bishop from Jamaica.

in Italy. Hence, on the part of the Pope, attitudes that will disappoint the hopes that had been raised by the way he had begun.

I record this as it was told to me . . .

On the way out of the restaurant, Küng introduced me to Paul Blanshard,[1] who was dining at a nearby table. I told him that I had read his books ('and in spite of that you remain in the Catholic Church?') and that I am a son, not of *American Freedom,* but of *Christian Freedom*[2] . . .

I left for the Vatican with my Belgian friends. Mgr Prignon said that, on Wednesday, the Pope will announce something sensational concerning himself. What?? Mgr Philips told me that Balić is wilder than ever and that in eight days he had sent three different texts for *De Beata.* The Pope is concerned about the work and had told Mgr Théas and Mgr Charue so last Saturday.

Can one vote to elect a vice-president, even though the Pope has not yet made known the name of the member whom he wishes to nominate. Discussion.

Mgr Philips reported on the work of the sub-commissions, cf sheet attached *hic,* (in a remarkable way).

That ended in the practical conclusion that a meeting of the Theological Commission be held immediately after Easter. Great discussion on the possibility of settling on a date that coincides with that of the Commission *De apostolatu laicorum.*

After a break for an exchange of views, the question of whether or not one could proceed to elect a vice-president and a second secretary was asked. Since no-one objected, the election took place.

After two ballots, Mgr Charue was elected Vice-President (12 out of 21 votes). Mgr Philips was elected as second secretary on the first ballot (six people voted for Fr Gagnebet). So, two Belgians.

The meeting ended at 6 pm. Afterwards, I went to ask for copies of their speeches for the volume that is planned from Mgr Henríquez Jimenez, Mgr Huyghe and Mgr Gouyon. It is quite a task getting all these texts together, and in seven copies (often the bishop has ONLY ONE copy): it must all be done by tomorrow evening because, immediately afterwards, everybody will be leaving . . .

Tuesday 3 December 1963
I did not go to St Peter's: it would be nothing but ceremony. I worked on getting the texts together, then for the *De Populo Dei* sub-commission.

Visit, as expected, from Fr Dumont.

---

1. This American official had criticised the authoritarian functioning of the Catholic Church in his publications, comparing it to the Soviet system.
2. The reference is to the title of a book by Paul Blanshard, *American Freedom and Catholic Power* (Boston, 1950).

In the afternoon, visit from the Dean of the Theological Faculty of Notre Dame University,[1] who invited me to give a course of lectures. I refuse all offers from America . . .

I took the texts to Küng and O'Hanlon, who were working hard, seeking to be finished by tomorrow morning.

De Populo Dei sub-commission. As we worked on the text in detail, it became painfully clear how much both the *De Ecclesia*, and this chapter *De Populo Dei* in particular, have suffered from never having been THOUGHT THROUGH. Bits have been taken from here and there: a friend of Philips, who had the ear of Cardinal Suenens, had inserted here and there the idea which appealed to him (likewise with the no *De populo uno et universali* [on the one and universal people], inserted by Thils, regarding which one can see neither what it is doing, nor what it is doing there): that does not produce A TEXT! Philips satisfied all requests *currente calamo* [with hesitation], with a disconcerting facility, adding 'something' on the Eucharist here, 'something' on the mission there, 'something' on the diversity of cultures somewhere else. I have his index cards, written directly and almost without crossings-out. But it is without vigour, without unity of thought. What is lacking is ONE idea that controls and arranges the whole.

Afterwards, meeting with Alberigo and supper with him and Dossetti at the home of three old, or middle aged, spinsters dedicated to Christian Democracy and to social works, in a house built by St Philip Neri near the church that bears his name.

Dossetti and Alberigo are fairly pessimistic about the present situation as regards the Council and the Pope. Throughout the month of October, Dossetti had been the secretary of the Moderators, but he was pushed out after 30 October, thanks to the influence of Felici. I was not at all surprised that 30 October had provoked such a turning point. That was a decisive *'parting of the ways'.*[2] The Pope himself began to change, partly due to the assaults to which he was being subjected, and partly *motu proprio* [of his own accord]. He was very struck by a speech in which Carli had evoked the spectre of the Synod of Pistoia. Felici is one of those, or even the one, leading the charge against the 30 October vote. Unfortunately, he is active and influential. I am wondering what has happened about the form in which, tomorrow, the Pope will proclaim the Liturgical Constitution and the Decree on Communications. Dossetti and Alberigo took part, with Jedin and Mörsdorf[3] (not a single Frenchman at all these key moments!!) in drafting a proposal in which the Pope would: 1) express his own VOTE (*assentimur*); 2) make the proclamation. Five weeks ago, the Pope had himself asked for suggestions to be made to him about this. But today, the formula suggested by Jedin

---

1. This was Robert S Pelton, CSC, President of the Theology Department of Notre Dame University.
2. {The phrase is in English in the original.}
3. Klaus Mörsdorf, priest of the diocese of Munich, was an eminent specialist in canon law, which he taught at the University of Munich; he was a Council expert.

and Dossetti has been set aside. The Pope has referred the matter to Felici who wants a formula: '*Paulus . . . approbante concilio*' [Paul . . . with the approval of the Council]. Mgr Colombo tried to discuss the matter with Felici, but one might just as well discuss it with a wall. For this reason, Dossetti and Alberigo feel that, although it is bad, it would still be better to use the formula envisaged in the regulations, which has the advantage of having been drawn up two years ago, before all the discussion on collegiality, and so of not prejudicing anything.

IT IS VERY SERIOUS.

It seems that Paul VI, after having been informed, and having moved from one idea to another, has a tendency to leave the final decision to the departments. That is to say to the Curia . . .

Dossetti and Alberigo told me that they had reached the same conclusion when I said to them: what is most important, what is most decisive, is the work done at the base. Things have gone well where such work was done: the liturgy, for example. So it is necessary to keep on working. Work has not been done on this question of the episcopate. So I made an overture to Alberigo for the publication of his book,[1] in Italian or in French, in *Unam Sanctam*.

30 October was decisive. It seems (Dossetti saw this from close quarters and continues to do so, with Cardinals Lercaro and Suenens) that in the month of October, Cardinal Agagianian was collaborating well with the other Moderators. After 30 October, he broke off this good co-operation with the three others, which, in its turn, has had the effect of bringing the other three closer together and uniting them.

Alberigo and Dossetti are very harsh about the half-measure taken by the Pope in response to the VERY insistent and numerous requests (for example from the episcopate of Africa) for new Commissions that respond to the spirit of the Council.

The Council is also bearing the weight of the original sin committed by John XXIII in conceiving the Commissions of the Council as corresponding to the Roman Congregations. Not only did he appoint the Presidents of these Congregations as Presidents of the Commissions (first the Preparatory ones, then the Conciliar ones), but he conceived the Commissions of the Council after the pattern of the Congregations, like permanent offices dealing with one section of things. It is not at all clear why the Theological Commission: 1) is competent for ALL doctrine, in all fields, as well in marriage as in episcopal collegiality or in original sin; 2) must remain in place from one end to the other. At Trent, a commission was appointed for each [[major]] problem, according to the matter being dealt with: for example, *De Iustificatione* [On Justification]. As they were few in number, there was a direct understanding between the presidency and the assembly, for the setting up of this commission of competent individuals.

---

1. Giuseppe Albergio, *Lo sviluppo della dottrina sui poteri nella chiesa universale* (Herder: Rome-Fribourg-Basle-Barcelona-Vienna:), 1964).

I had seen even when, immediately after the Preparatory Commissions had been established by John XXIII, I had asked myself some questions to which I replied in *Témoignage Chrétien*, that the important thing is not so much the answer as the question. This original sin continues to weigh things down. The Pope has not been able to remedy it. He has not solved the real question that is posed by the presidency of a Marella (who has gone ahead without calling a meeting of his Commission), of a Pizzardo (imbecile), of an Ottaviani (partisan and too cunning without at the same time being at all skilled).

I have written all this down this evening, although it is late, so that it is all fresh.

Alberigo was telling me (gossip?) that a libel against the German cardinals and theologians has just appeared, signed 'catholicus'.

This morning, not only was there a speech by Cardinal Urbani, but one by Guitton (in French) and one by Veronese.[1] I have received a great many laudatory reactions to Guitton's speech. But one Holy Cross Father (an American) said to me: his aim for a long time had been to speak at the Council. Alberigo and Dossetti told me that he spoke like a Father of the Council, not like a layperson.

All the same, I find his speech quite good, although too academic, too optimistic, and even too smug about ecumenism. It is not very real. But I am happy that a lay person has spoken at the Council and that he has spoken about ecumenism. After all, it is the first time, and it is very significant.

But I am more and more struck by the fact that all that is very much amongst ourselves. And that it has little or no contact with the real world. These are disputes between clerics, as in the fifteenth century. There ought to be contact with real men and women, with a real world! We produce paper, make speeches, and then what?

In the end, a list was read this morning of the faculties that the Pope grants to bishops: 'concedimus' [we grant], 'impertimur' [we impart]. Whereas, in reality, all he is doing is to give back—and not graciously!—a part of what had been stolen from them over the centuries!!!

Ah! How much we need a visit from the Holy Spirit and the help of all the saints! Tere, who prayed so much for the Council!!

Wednesday 4 December 1963

I did not sleep. I have too many things to think about and to do before I leave. And this situation of the Council worries me greatly.

At St Peter's by 8.30 am; lots of very friendly goodbyes, above all Maximos IV. How many bishops have said to me that they are praying for Tere, that they have said or are going to say their Mass for her . . .

---

1. Vittorino Veronese, former President of Italian Catholic Action and former Director of UNESCO, was a Director of the Banco di Roma; he was a lay Auditor at the Council, then a Consultor to the Secretariat for Non-Christians.

At 9.20 am the singing was heard to begin. The same procession as for the opening: the entire pontifical court in Renaissance costumes or in the royal pomp of the epoch of the Congress of Vienna. After the long cohort of cardinals, bowed down under their high mitres and their chasubles (preceded by the Patriarchs; but Maximos was not there. This admirable and upright man sticks to his position: he does not belong to the Roman clergy), the Pope, like an idol, seated on a throne carried on the *sedia*; he was surrounded by the *flabella*, like Darius. I protested in my tribune at the applause. I felt a deep discomfort. THAT must come to an end one day!

The dialogue of the Mass (with Cardinal Tisserant) was cacophonous as, alas, it has never ceased to be, with, however, an effort to control the body of participants.

At 10.30 am, reading of the Constitution *De sacra Liturgia* began (only the chapter headings). This was preceded by:

Paulus episcopus servus servorum Dei, una cum Patribus Sancti Concilii ad perpetuam rei memoriam [Paul, bishop, servant of the servants of God, together with the Fathers of the Council, in perpetual memory of the fact].

Phew! The formula was correct . . . But we await the promulgation . . . Only the beginning of each chapter was read. The Fathers were invited to vote by *placet* or *non placet*.

The intervening time was filled with the *Ave Maria, Magnificat, Salve Regina* = babies dummies to keep them quiet.

At 11.05, the result of the vote on the Liturgy was announced:

Yes: 2,147
No: 4

Applause. The pope then promulgated the text in these terms:

'In nomine Sanctissimae et Individuae Trinitatis, Patris et Filii et Spiritus Sancti. Decreta quae in hac sacrosancta et universali synodo Vaticana Secunda legitime congregata modo lecta sunt, placuerunt Patribus.

Et Nos Apostolica a Christo Nobis tradita potestate, illa, una cum venerabilibus Patribus, in Spiritu Sancto approbamus, decernimus ac statuimus, et quae ita synodaliter stabilita sunt ad Dei gloriam promulgari iubemus.

[In the name of the Most Holy and undivided Trinity, of the Father and the Son and the Holy Spirit. The Fathers have expressed their agreement with the decrees just read out in the presence of this legitimately assembled Sacred and Ecumenical Second Vatican Council.

And We, in virtue of the Apostolic authority passed on to Us from Christ, and in union with the reverend Fathers, approve, establish, and ordain them in the Holy Spirit, and We order that what the Council has so ordained be published for the glory of God.]

I breathed a sigh of relief. The formula is good [[((I have written it down as best I could . . .)]] It will come into force on 17 February 1964.

There is a deep objective and doctrinal coherence between 'in the name of the Three' (who concelebrate in unity) and *'una cum venerabilibus Patribus'* [in union with the reverend Fathers]: the Council is in the image of the Three in unity!

Schema on the Means of Communication:

Yes:	1,960
No:	174

The Pope began to speak at 11.40 am. In the interval, I went down; I saw Mgr Boillon. He has known the Pope's secretary[1] for fifteen years, and saw him recently. Mgr Boillon conveyed to him the general impression that the Pope had moved backwards in comparison with the beginning of the Session. The secretary denied this absolutely. Nevertheless it is the impression of many. The speech that the Pope read while I have been writing was far from the one he gave on 29 September. It is academic and tired. Why speak in this way about the schema on Revelation, about the schema on *De Beata Maria 'Matre Ecclesiae'*? A very long speech. How can they create ceremonies that last for four hours?

It is 12.16 pm. He added something that was not found in the printed text. HE HAS DECIDED TO GO AS A PILGRIM TO THE HOLY LAND (a response to Fr Gauthier's invitation?), to return to the place from which Peter departed, where the Church came from. There he will pray earnestly for the unity of Christians, for peace. He asks all to support him with their prayers.

Loud applause.

The Holy Land. That will be a centring on the Word of God and on Christ; it will be the source; it will be the grace of God in the poverty of men. Undoubtedly, the Pope will have much to endure by going as a pilgrim. He will be beset by the arches of triumph, the speeches and the banquets. But he will meet Abraham, David, John the Baptist, Mary, Jesus . . . The Church, in the person of its head, is going to refresh itself at the sources! The Pope ought to leave there his *sedia* and his *flabella*!

On the way out, Mgr Mercier told me that he had passed on to Cardinal Gracias my suggestion that the Eucharistic Congress in Bombay ought to be a congress of Christian charity in the midst of a poor people, and that all religious triumphalism ought to be avoided: he had given him my text from *ICI* suggesting that the Third Session SHOULD BEGIN with schema XVII and with an assessment of the world. The cardinal had welcomed these ideas and inserted them into his intervention on [ ]; they may well have reached the Pope himself.

Afternoon, packing (exhausting); in the evening, at the French Seminary, dialogue with the seminarians and priests. Among the bishops living there, an air of leaving for the holidays, with luggage of all kinds heaped in the entrance. I myself feel a certain nostalgia. After all, a kind of fraternity had been established amongst us. Once again, one needed to say goodbye and set off on one's own, each

---

1. Pasquale Macchi, priest of the Diocese of Milan.

following his own route and his own affairs. I react with sadness to separations and departures . . .

Thursday 5 December 1963

I finished my chronicle for *ICI*, the last one.

Belgian Radio-TV (on religious freedom).

At 3.15 p.m., visit from five Argentinian priests, three of whom are writing a thesis on the laity.

Then, correcting the proofs for *Chrétiens en dialogue,*[1] which I began in Sedan, near Tere's body.

Visit from an American priest who, like one of the Argentinians who came earlier, wants to write a thesis on the *consecratio mundi* [consecration of the world].

Friday 6 December 1963

Fr Prior[2] arranged for me to be driven direct to Fiumicino. I am overcome by the extent to which people have been and continue to be kind to me.

At the airport, I met a Scottish bishop,[3] (Scanlan), who recognised me, then Rahner (with a German novelist[4]) and the abbot of Beuron[5] with whom I am to travel. The route from Rome to Fiumicino was filled with lovely autumn colours, beneath an extremely beautiful, pale and golden light. It was light and so delicate!

Blue sky, then above the clouds. In the distance, the Alps completely white. Stopover in Zurich: shrouded in mist with a temperature of one degree.

Then Geneva.

From Geneva to Grenoble by car, via Annecy and Aix. Visited the Chartreuse of Beauregard (Lucie Scherrer). In the evening, in Grenoble, lecture[6] before a hall packed to the rafters. Supper with the Jesuits (Fr Chailler[7] was Superior), who had invited the Dominicans.

---

1. Yves M.-J Congar, *Chrétiens en dialogue. Contributions catholiques à l'Oecumenisme,* 'Unam Sanctam', 50 (Paris: Cerf, 1964), 1–17.
2. Sigmond.
3. James D Scanlan, Bishop of Motherwell.
4. This was probably Luise Rinser.
5. B Reetz.
6. The theme was 'the Laity in the People of God'.
7. During the Second World War, Pierre Chaillet had taken part in the Resistance and in the foundation, in 1941, of the *Cahiers de Témoignage chrétien;* after that he had worked for *Études* until 1963.

Saturday 7 December 1963 [[Paris]].
In the afternoon, ENT examination by Professor Aubry[1] (65, avenue Georges-Mandel) and neurological examination at Professor Garcin's (19, rue de Bourgogne). He thinks in terms of a diffuse disease of the nervous system, the first symptoms of which may well go back to December 1935, and the kind of collapse that I experienced then. According to him, at my age, that should not develop further to any great extent; I ought not to become paralysed . . .

I slept at Le Saulchoir.

Sunday 8 December 1963
A celebration in my honour at Le Saulchoir. Programme: 10 am Mass, at which I preached (profession of brother de Monléon[2]); 11.30 am Fr Chenu spoke of me and interpreted what, even so, I do not dare to call my work. It is too ridiculous. However, I must confess that everything he said was true . . .

Lunch. At 3 pm, a lecture by me on the present ecclesiological moment. In the evening, lecture in the Pleyel hall, as part of the 'Connaissance de l'Église'[3] series.

The Brethren were marvellous. Those from Le Saulchoir had set up a kind of biographical exhibition about me. I wonder where they can have got all those photographs. There were some that I had never seen. It was done with great taste, precision and affection. There too, ridiculous as it seems, it was all true.

It seems to me that the whole of this day was very homogeneous, or all of a piece. What was so lovely was that the younger brothers were able to have a concrete experience of the authentic tradition of Le Saulchoir, thanks to the evocation of our work, in which my one regret was that Fr Féret is no longer there. Chenu showed well what a theology committed to the service of the church was and could be, in accordance with the needs of the time, situated in the teaching of St Thomas. The aims have radiated from living people in a climate of fraternity. That is not so bad from the point of view of a 'Friar Preacher'.

How did I RECEIVE all that?

Monday 9 December 1963
My table! 40 cm of letters, printed matter and parcels spread over more than a square metre. More than 200 letters: many about Tere, that do not require an answer, but many others also, and proofs to correct!!

---

1. Maurice Aubry, ear, nose and throat specialist at the Paris hospitals and professor at the Paris Faculty of Medicine.
2. This was the solemn profession of Albert-M De Monléon, OP, of the Province of France: he was later to become Bishop of Pamiers and then of Meaux.
3. Lecture on the Council.

22 January 1964

I have heard virtually nothing about the Council since 5 December 1963.

On 17 and 18 January 1964, together with Frs Voillaume, Cottier, Loew,[1] Régamey,[2] Hayen,[3] (+ Le Guillou and Henry,[4]) we set up a project for a book on the Church and poverty.[5] The bishops want it. They have in mind the volume *L'Épiscopat et l'Église universelle*, and the significant part it played in giving them a concrete idea of collegiality. They wanted something analogous done for the question of poverty. We worked well. But I have collected a good deal more work to be done: sections to be drafted or organised.

Today, at Marienthal, with the bishops of the eastern apostolic region, to talk about the *De Apostolatu laicorum* [on the apostolate of the laity]. I did not learn much. It seems that the Pope wants the Third Session to be the last. So the Co-ordinating Commission is making some dismal cuts, some draconian abridgements. A schema such as this will have to be cut down to three pages. Many things will be excluded from the Council's programme. (That came from the Co-ordinating Commission of 28 December, not from the one that is in progress at the moment . . .)

I, too, wish that the Third Session would be the last, or that the Council would be adjourned for several years. But it seems to me that this is technically impossible.

---

1. Jacques Loew, OP, of the Province of Toulouse, founder of the Workers' Mission of Saints Peter and Paul, which was to be erected as an Apostolic Institute in 1965; together with R Voillaume, he was later to establish the School of Faith in Fribourg, Switzerland, for the doctrinal formation of lay people.

2. Pie-Raymond Régamey, OP, of the Province of France; specialist in Christian art, former collaborator with Marie-Alain Couturier, OP, on the journal *L'Art sacré,* he also worked in spiritual theology, on questions of poverty, and pursued themes of warfare and non-violence.

3. André Hayen, SJ, taught philosophy at the Jesuit Scholasticate at Eegenhoven-Louvain.

4. Antonin-Marcel Henry, OP, of the Province of France, had, for a long time, worked at *Éditions du Cerf* where, amongst other things, he was principally responsible for the celebrated *Initiation théologique*, published from 1952 to 1954. He was one of the founders of the journal *Parole et Mission,* which had as it goal the renewal of matters concerning mission in the Church.

5. Cf *Église et pauvreté*, 'Unam Sanctam', 57 (Paris: Cerf, 1965).

For the *De apostolatu laicorum*, the Co-ordinating Commission wants a few pages of texts and then a *Nuntium* [message] to lay people and a Directory. . .

The bishops are talking among themselves about the application of the Constitution on the Liturgy.

Negotiations about my *Unterbringung* [lodgings] during the sub-commission on *De Populo Dei*, in Rome, 30 January 1964; in addition to this there will be a spell of work with the Secretariat for Unity.

I shall leave various letters concerning this here, but take a fresh notebook to Rome.

Rome, 30 January 1964
I left Strasbourg at 7.17 this morning. I took a train to Mulhouse; visited the Hermanns.[1] Mme Manolesco[2] drove me to the airport at Basle-Mulhouse. I had begun reading when Cullmann arrived, on his way to the USA. We chatted, and since he was also going to Zurich to catch his plane, we spent nearly two hours together.

I can see just how interested he is in the Council. He told me that Barth[3] would willingly have come to the First Session, but now he feels tired. He is not able to write and will not complete his *Dogmatik*. However, he might, perhaps, be able to come for a fortnight. I will speak about this in Rome.

Cullmann regrets that the WCC had deliberately not sent their top-ranking people. This was dictated by politics, he said. He was against 'politics', including the type, he said, engaged in by Mehl[4] at the Protestant Theology Faculty in Strasbourg, and by Casalis[5] in the Paris faculty. What he believed in he believed in profoundly: in ecumenism, in the criticism and the rejection of Bultmann that had to be made. Cullmann deplores the fact that young Catholic theologians or exegetes are allowing themselves be seduced. He gave me some examples. We spoke of Malet[6] . . .

I reached Rome at 2.15 pm, and was met at the airport. I found it all as if I had left only yesterday. I made this journey again with the nostalgic memory of having traversed it with Fr Féret coming back from my mother's funeral. The weather is fine and even hot here.

---

1. Michel and Renée Hermann, an interchurch family; Congar had officiated at their wedding.
2. Marthe Manolesco, member of the Lay Dominican Fraternity.
3. The Protestant theologian, Karl Barth, who had taught in Germany and then in Basle, had a profound influence on the evolution of Protestant theology. At the time, he was working on his monumental *Church Dogmatics,* which would run to 28 volumes.
4. Pastor Roger Mehl, of the French Reformed Church, taught ethics in the Protestant Faculty of Theology in Strasbourg.
5. Pastor Georges Casalis, of the French Reformed Church, was Professor of Practical Theology in the Protestant Faculty of Theology in Paris.
6. André Malet, a Protestant philosopher and theologian, was a specialist on Bultmann.

At the Belgian College Mgr Philips—who has had a heart attack, and speaks like a man careful of his strength—brought me up to date somewhat.

The *De collegialitate* [on collegiality] has been going well. With regard to the text of Ephesians 2:20, it has been agreed to use a quotation from the Gregorian Sacramentary: *in apostolis condidit et super Petri fundamentum aedificavit* [he established it on the Apostles, and built it on the foundation of Peter]. This is to abandon the notion of the Apostles as foundation.

The *De sanctitate* [on holiness] has gone well too. The religious would really prefer A SEPARATE chapter. There were seven who voted for this in the joint sub-commission, against four bishops who wanted a single chapter in two sections: a) the universal call to holiness; b) the religious life. Among the *vota* of the Council Fathers there were 600 for keeping the section on the vocation to holiness in Chapter IV (henceforth Chapter V) against 500 for including it in the *De populo Dei*. But as Philips said to me, on a closer look, it was apparent that among the 600 there were many bishops who were religious, who had followed the advice of their religious superiors. (Is that true? I don't know.)

It seems that a rather long development has been introduced into the chapter *De laicis*, somewhat by way of parenthesis, about the sharing of the laity in Christ's royal, priestly and prophetic power; and, in applying this to the activity of Christians, without distinguishing the specifically religious sphere from the temporal: a distinction that was described as specifically 'French'. This text would have been revised by Fr Häring, at the request of Mgr De Smedt, who had collected a fair number of signatures.

It seems that there is currently in Zurich a meeting of the people dealing with schema XIII: Moeller is taking part. This would be the third proposed version for this schema. Both Pavan's drift and the drift of our text of May and September would come in for criticism: the former considered to be too much that of 'natural law', and the latter considered to be too theological.

I spoke to Mgr Philips about an insertion—that I would like—of a chapter on the Jews in the *De populo Dei*. He told me that it had been decided to leave that to the *De Oecumenismo*, as an appendix.

At 4.30 pm at St Martha's. I went by car with Mgr Onclin: he is entirely re-working the *De regimine diocesium* [on the Government of Dioceses]; Mgr Charue went with Thils in the other car. I found myself again in the climate of 'the Council of Louvain held in Rome', of which Dossetti had spoken to me in December 1963. It is clear that the Belgians are, to a great extent, the 'drivers'. But what have OUR Faculties of Theology done?

The only members of the sub-commission there were Mgr Garrone, Fr Reuter, Witte, Kerrigan and myself . . . My text on universality and catholicity was considered. We took up again as though we had left off two days before. We went back to Latin. We found ourselves very much at home.

Fr Tromp, alone in the secretarial offices of the Commission, seemed like an elderly, rather broken-down chatelaine, who had gone on living in a stately home that was too big and empty. What can he do?

This evening, I learned from Mgr Philips that he is drafting a report on the comments made by the bishops on the subject of the (new) *De Revelatione*. For there really is talk of taking up this text again. Mgr Medina, who dined this evening at the Belgian College, even said that a group (?) had drafted a new text. (Mgr Medina had stayed in Rome after the end of the Second Session to keep Cardinal Silva informed, who has on side probably half of the Latin American episcopate. He came this evening to draw the attention of Cardinal Suenens, through Mgr Prignon, to the subject of the *Motu proprio*[1] . . .) In any case, according to Philips, the prospect of the *De Revelatione* being taken up again has caused the removal from the *De Ecclesia* of the chapter on the living Tradition that Mgr Garrone had proposed, and for which he had asked me to draft a text.

The letter from Cicognani-Ottaviani requiring silence, or at least great discretion, from the experts, was discussed.[2] Mgr C Colombo gave a commentary on these letters: experts might publish scientific studies, but should not create currents of opinion by using interviews or behind-the-scenes manoeuvres . . . I am not conscious of ever having done this. But I have certainly sought to influence opinion.

The Pope's *Motu proprio* on the liturgy was discussed. This document virtually takes away from the Council what the Council had decided. It lays down that texts for use in the vernacular must first be submitted to the Holy See, and approved by it. This is the very negation of the worth of the Council, and it seems to me that if it does not react, that will be the result: it will abdicate. The Curia wants to take back what the Council has decided. This is the first instance of this. There must be a reaction TO THIS, or else one might as well give up in advance gaining anything over the existing Roman system! Mgr Medina detects the hand of Mgr Dante in the *motu proprio*.

The *De BVM* was discussed. Mgr Philips described his encounters with Balić, who in 1963 had drafted FOUR texts one after another. Various formulas were discussed. It would appear that Paul VI is not in favour of the mediation of Mary.

The meeting of curial cardinals that is to take place tomorrow was also touched on briefly. It seems that the Pope wants to bring them up to date about his pilgrimage to the Holy Land, on the prospects opened up, and to sound out the opinion of the Curia on this subject.

---

1. *Sacram liturgiam*, dated 25 January 1964: it required Roman approval for translations of liturgical texts into living languages.
2. Ottaviani passed on this request to the experts of the Council in a letter dated 9 January. He had himself received it from Cicognani, in a letter dated 3 January.

Friday 31 January 1964
This morning, sub-commission on *De populo Dei* at the Belgian College, with Mgr Philips.

Mgr Philips told us that there are more than 4,000 amendments for the *De Ecclesia*. If it was desired to vote on each amendment, 100 votes would be needed just for Chapter I. But it is only possible to take five votes in each sitting . . . ! Clearly the process must be simplified, and voting must be section by section, which would reduce the votes for Chapter I to 8 or 10. But it will also be necessary to find a reasonable solution for the *modi* . For example, if there are fifty DIFFER-ENT *modi* for a single section, that would entail a new drafting, which would require MONTHS of work.

Cardinal Cicognani made it known (on behalf of the Commission), that there would not be a fresh discussion on the *De Ecclesia*, but only a brief discussion on sacramentality and collegiality.

Evening, at St Martha's, work in the sub-commission.

Saturday 1 February 1964
Morning and evening, sub-commission work on *De populo Dei* at the Belgian College. We finished it. In the evening Mgr Philips got me to read the present text of *De Beata*. This is a text drafted by him in the first place, revised three times by Balić, then by Philips, then by Balić. Not bad. However it seemed to me that, given that it is to become Chapter VI or VII of the *De Ecclesia*, its ecclesiological aspect is diffuse and rather weak. The battle rages over two points in particular: 1) Mediation: Fr Balić wanted a mediation that went well beyond intercession. But Philips produced references from three different sources showing that Paul VI wanted no talk of mediation. 2) Balić wanted it said that all this was without prejudice to what is taught in Catholic schools, or by the ordinary Magisterium.

For myself, I compare the mariological developments made by popes in the past century with the situation for three or four centuries when the popes assert-ed their power over the temporal authority, and their right to depose kings. They did this under the pressure of an opinion that was itself formed with the help of the abundant use of a method of reasoning that was vague and inconclusive, with narrow or questionable foundations. Nowadays mention is no longer made of such solemn pronouncements. I think that, when the return to the sources, the christological and paschal recentring, ecumenical dialogue and real concern for the world will have at last reached the hearts of the bishops and of the Pope, these mariological developments will experience a reversal, and that health and sobri-ety will again be found in these areas, too.

There was some brief discussion of schema XVII, which is at present being discussed in Zurich, and of some forecasts of what might happen at the Third Session. The Co-ordinating Commission dealt with this question from after Christ-mas until mid-January. The Pope does indeed want the Third Session to be the last, but HE WILL NOT IMPOSE THIS. Doubtless he realises that this is technically impossible. Cardinal Döpfner had a plan, a procedure, even a carefully timed schedule, for getting everything finished at the Third Session. (Cardinal Liénart, speaking first among the cardinals of the Co-ordinating Commission, criticised and even virtually demolished Döpfner's proposal.) This would have led to some brutal measures, and, in the end, to a total loss of any conciliar sense. It allotted THREE sittings for voting on the whole of the *De Ecclesia*: but it is not possible to get more than five or six votes into a sitting! How can he think like this, given the importance of this text, of which it must not be said afterwards that it was imposed without the minority being able to make its reasons heard? How can Cardinal Döpfner not see that the main point of the Council is not to vote on some texts, but to establish a spirit and a new awareness, and THAT THIS REQUIRES TIME? Can't he see the profound anthropological reality of a council, that has its own weight, and its own demands?

I want more than anything else that the Third Session should be the last: because it is not possible to go on working further, and there would be the risk of loosing momentum, of seeing lassitude spreading. But I remind myself that it is technically impossible. What is needed is that it should be known beforehand that the Fourth Session will definitely be the last, and that it will be devoted to the CONCLUSION of whatever will have been discussed in the Third Session, under clearly defined conditions.

But what can I do about it?

Sunday 2 February 1964

I typed a large part of the Chapter *De populo Dei*, so that Mgr Philips could take away a complete text. —Preached a little fervorino for the Sisters. In the afternoon I typed some texts for Cullmann, with regard to his chapter on Scripture at the Council.[1] (Cf letter attached here.)

At midday, Mgr Philips told me that he had spent two hours with Balić this morning. There was a fair number of points on which they could not agree.

1) Mediation. But Balić knows that the Pope does not want this spoken of. That is good. It is a considerable support; but I am uneasy with the thought that such an important point should hang on the opinion or the position of ONE person. If it had been Pius XII or Pius IX, many things would have looked different! Pressure could have been applied in a maximising mariological direction! The Pope has only to follow the inclination of a good Italian Catholic, and the Church would be dragged along in this direction. That is not right!

2) Balić would like to introduce '*alma socia Redemptoris*' [gracious associate of the Redeemer]. He would put something else into the same sentence that would counterbalance the idea, but the idea would be there, and it would gain ground by its own force of words. Basically, his idea is that Mary and Christ form a single

---

1. Cf Oscar Cullmann, 'Bible et second Concile du Vatican', in *Le dialogue est ouvert. Le Concile vu par les observateurs luthériens* (Neuchâtel-Paris, 1965), 133-146.

principle of redemption. Mgr Philips categorically rejects this. But, for me, this idea is ABSOLUTELY alien to Revelation, to the Gospels and to St Paul. It has no place in the Apostolic faith. What sort of religion do people like Balić have, then? A Mariano-christianity. They will have to end up with the idea that Mary is the *Caput (secundarium!) Corporis mystici!* [(secondary!) head of the mystical Body!].

3) Balić does not want us to quote the phrase *'Beata quae credidisti'* [Blessed are you who believed (Lk 1:45)]. The reason: certain theologians hold that Mary did not have faith, because she had the beatific vision. It is incredible! For the sake of a crack-brained notion of theologasters Scripture must be wrong, and must keep quiet!!!

Nor does Balić like the words of St Augustine any better: *'cooperata est caritate ut membra Christi nascerentur'* [She co-operated by charity, so that the members of Christ could be born][1] (I am quoting from memory).

For him, Mary is not really in the Church, even in an eminent place in it, but above it! So, outside it.

Philips, on the other hand, did not quote the expression *'Mater Ecclesiae'* and alluded to it—very implicitly—only in the moral sense: according to which Mary has a maternal care for the Church.

4) Balić did not want the phrase *'propter nostram salutem'* [for our salvation] applied to Mary in any way whatsoever. Deep down, he was following a Scotist idea, pushed so far as to say: the Word of God became incarnate SO THAT he could be the son of Mary. It is incredible!!!

Neither Scripture nor Tradition admits any such thing!

Balić ended up by saying: the Council will decide. To which Philips replied: but for you a majority vote of 1,900 out of 2,100 (the vote of 30 October) does not count!!! Finally, Philips said: I do not concede your point. I will not change anything in my text. There is nothing more to say, except that we disagree on such and such points. Let the Commission decide . . .

(I cannot go on writing. I have done too much typing.)

In the afternoon, after taking Mgr Philips to Fiumicino, I typed some texts for Cullmann: in order to give him documentation on the Bible at the Council, for a symposium which the Observers want to put together.

Conversation with Mgr Prignon, who told me several things: (I thus learnt that Mgr Charue saw Ottaviani who had confirmed for him that *De Revelatione* would come up for discussion. The text would first be revised to respond to the wishes of the bishops. But Ottaviani thinks that it would be reviewed ONLY by the Theological Commission, without the Secretariat. Mgr Prignon and Mgr Charue urged Arrighi to keep a prudent eye on this . . .)

1) On the background of the five propositions (30 October):

---

1. St Augustine, *De Sancta Virginitate*, 6.

The idea and a first draft came from Dossetti. He acted as secretary for the Moderators. But Felici had wanted that position, and conceived an animosity for Dossetti.

So there was this text. At 7 o'clock in the morning on the day when it was to have been put to the vote, there was a telephone call from the Secretary of State[1] to Cardinal Agagianian, to halt the matter. That was the day when the Secretary of State had been in discussion with the Moderators throughout the whole of Mass. Felici had intervened. It was he who had led the opposition to the initiative of the Moderators. Two days later there was the weekly reception of the Moderators by the Pope. Although the Secretary of State had claimed the authority of the Pope against the questions, the Pope himself declared that he had never seen them. He read them without making any fundamental reservation. But he said to the Moderators: you should have made yourselves understood by the Co-ordinating Commission and kept Felici informed . . .

On the Friday there was a meeting of the Moderators with the Co-ordinating Commission. Döpfner was supposed to see Felici. Felici telephoned during the day to say that this wouldn't do, and put it off to the Wednesday of the following week. Cardinal Suenens then went to see the Secretary of State, who told him: Felici does not want it. He went to see Felici, who told him: Cicognani does not want it! It was decided that there would be a meeting on the Saturday (or on the Monday at the latest), with the Secretary of State. But half-an-hour later the Secretary of State said: that won't do. The Council of Presidents must ALSO take part in this meeting.

The meeting took place. The Moderators explained their business (the questions). Cardinal Tisserant said immediately: that's not our business. It's your job as Moderators.

The Moderators went back to see the Pope, who helped them to reach a solution.

A meeting of twenty-one or twenty-two people: the Co-ordinating Commission (so Felici and the Secretaries), the Presidents and the Moderators. Cardinal Roberti, prodded by Felici, posed the preliminary question of the rights of the Moderators. But Tisserant broke in: don't let us waste our time discussing that. Let's discuss the basics. A vote was taken on each of the questions. The first two got through. There was no agreement on the third. Siri was opposed to Suenens. The latter then proposed that Siri should draw up a text, and that both these texts should be presented to the Council to be voted on. The final question, on the diaconate, comprised three subsidiary questions. At first the vote was negative on the whole thing. Half-an-hour later Tisserant put the question again. Alfrink advised Suenens not to insist on questions *b* and *c* (concerning marriage). In fact, question *a* had nine votes in favour and eight against, but questions *b* and *c* had

---

1. A Cicognani.

eight in favour and nine against. Curious: there were twenty-one or twenty-two people present, but only seventeen votes were cast.

When everything had been thus legitimately agreed, Cardinal Siri had Calabria produce a text (Calabria had no doubt drafted it. He was my bellowing Censor from 1962 at the Capranica . . . !) Siri wanted his text only to be put to the vote.

Suenens saw the Pope on the Monday and told him about all this manoeuvring. He said that he himself had got stirred up; he put to the Pope the question of the authority of the Moderators (who in this crisis had offered their resignations). Suenens said: if the Pope gave way on this, the newspapers would soon carry banner headlines: Paul VI has betrayed John XXIII . . .

It was decided to take no notice of the text of Calabria-Siri. It was then that the definitive text was drawn up by Dossetti, Philips, Rahner and Prignon (in all of this, the French were bypassed).

On Thursday the Moderators were received by the Pope. With his agreement they re-introduced the words suppressed by Siri: *'vel saltem libre recipiat'* .[1]

On the Sunday after the vote, the Moderators dined with the Pope, who offered them a chalice and said: you have made your way of the cross. I congratulate you. I have supported you, but be more prudent.

In going to the Holy Land, the Pope wanted to beg for light especially on this question. Dossetti's impression that a change had come about in him after 30 October could be due to the somewhat gloomy pessimism displayed by Dossetti concerning the end of the Session.

2) The question of the renewal of the Commissions. Cardinal Suenens has spoken to the Pope about this. The Pope had said: I cannot dismiss the Presidents already in place. They have not committed a public crime: Ottaviani is not a malefactor . . . It would be seen as my taking sides. It would be said: the Pope is on the left . . .

3) Concerning the text for promulgation: there were drafts by Rahner, Dossetti, Thils, Colombo, Philips. Colombo wrote the definitive version.

4) The appointment of Moderators. The creation of this function had been decided in July. The original intention was rather to have a brains-trust that would consider the progress of the Council. Ottaviani was against Lercaro, and advocated Siri or Ruffini. In the end, instead of the three that were planned at first, there were four of them: the Pope added Agagianian as a curial man.

---

1. 'Or at least may freely accept'. (The formula had to do with the role of the pope in the episcopal college).

The Pope has put the various Moderators in charge of different questions: he asked Lercaro to attend to the question of poverty; Suenens that of conjugal morality. On this point the Pope himself is very conservative. He believes that it is his duty to speak out, but Cardinal Suenens restrained him by pointing out to him that the Council has taken up the matter.

5) Reform projects.

The speech Cardinal Lercaro made about the Curia was a tactical one. There was indeed a Siri project, and Lercaro did not want it to be the only one. He spoke in order to declare his interest and to enter the arena.

Regarding the committee of bishops, the Pope is following the question. There are five suggestions, but the Pope wants to let the question mature.

It was the Pope himself who had asked Cardinal Suenens to talk to the Council about women, being unable to do so himself.

6) The duration of the Council, Third Session.

The Pope wants the Third Session to be the final one. Döpfner made a draconian proposal to this end. Suenens showed that it is impossible.

As to the order of the day, Suenens recommended that it should start with the vote on *De Ecclesia* and put the discussion of *De Revelatione* AT THE END. Because the latter will be on the agenda. Tromp is presently working on a report on the bishops' comments, and a text will be put forward taking account of these comments. Mgr Charue saw Ottaviani yesterday, and Ottaviani told him this . . .

7) The visit of Athenagoras. The Pope wants to receive him in Rome, and doubtless himself wants to go to Constantinople. But he says he is not so sure that the people in the Curia are disposed to welcome Athenagoras. They would be thinking, in order to dilute things a bit, of a visit of the Patriarch to Rome coming AFTER a visit to Ramsey[1] (Canterbury) . . .

Dinner in the evening with Mgr Arrighi. I picked up some bits of information.

Paul VI had received Mgr Willebrands and said to him: Tell me frankly what you have to say to me. Willebrands said: There must be no talk of a 'return'. Paul VI replied: Yes, in Bethlehem, at the moment when I spoke about a single fold, I felt that it was not quite the right note.

(Mgr Willebrands told me of the incident himself. He had told the Pope frankly that there must be no talk of a 'return'; it is contrary to what he had himself said on 17 October. Against maintaining the status quo, the Pope said: I understand what you are saying. Willebrands also said that the Secretariat had corrected the phrase about the Fold: Mgr Dell'Acqua had accepted this correction. Unfortunately the corrected text was not the one that had been sent back to the Pope and read out by him. —After a reception for Protestants whom Willebrands had accompanied, the Pope had called Willebrands back and asked him: tell me FRANKLY, without flattery: was THAT it . . .)

---

1. Arthur M Ramsey had been Archbishop of Canterbury since 1961; he was one of the Presidents of the World Council of Churches.

This morning the Pope said he would send Candlemas candles[1] to the Patriarchs and Catholic bishops who had received him in the East, to the Orthodox and to the heads of Christian communities. So the World Presbyterian Alliance is going to receive a candle. It has been given notice of this, insisting, as the Pope had done this morning (at the request of the Secretariat) on *'lumen ad revelationem gentium'* [a light for revelation to the Gentiles (Lk 2: 32)].

Mgr Capovilla, while talking to Arrighi, observed that John XXIII never dared to use the word 'dialogue'. Paul VI had done so during his enthronement address, and, of course, on 29 September 1963.

The chapter on the Jews will form an appendix to *De oecumenismo* (I said that, in my opinion it should be put back into the *De populo Dei*); there will also be a text on the Muslims, and perhaps on non-Christian religions.

At 9.00 pm, I fastened my suitcase and was driven to the place where the experts of the Secretariat were to meet: Bethany of the Holy Spirit, 14 Via Achille Mauri, Monte Mario. It was a long way away.

It is a sort of pilgrims' hostel run by the Dominican of Bethany, a branch of the foundation of Fr Lataste[2] adapted to Dutch realism. It is where Mgr Willebrands lives. A gleaming house, neat and tidy, very resonant, in a district where every square metre not already built on is being filled in with concrete structures.

Monday 3 February 1964

Some news at breakfast (with Willebrands and Thijssen[31]). I myself spoke of inviting Barth. He had been sounded out (by Küng) for the First Session, but he had declined, though noting with appreciation the fact that people had thought of inviting an old 'savage' *(Wildmann)* like himself. Another attempt could be made, said Willebrands, who told me that Boegner had just written asking to be invited.[4] This will be done.

We talked about the Pope's journey to the Holy Land, about how things were working out in connection with Athenagoras, at the last moment (nothing had been known before 28 December), of the reactions of the World Council of Churches and of Visser't Hooft. Rome is anxious not to isolate Athenagoras.

---

1. On 2 February, the feast of the Purification, the traditional offering to the pope of candles for Candlemas takes place; according to custom he sends them to the four corners of the earth, in particular to the Vatican Diplomatic Corps.
2. The Third Order Dominican Sisters of Bethany of Venlo (Netherlands).
3. Frans Thijssen, a priest from Utrecht and friend of Willebrands, was his assistant in the setting up and running of the Catholic Conference for Ecumenical Questions. He was a consultor to the Secretariat for Unity.
4. Marc Boegner, pastor of the French Reformed Church, was President of the Protestant Federation of France and one of the founders of the World Council of Churches, of which he was one of the first presidents; he was to be one of the guests of the Secretariat for Unity during the two final Sessions.

It would seem that the meeting of cardinals on 31 January went well from the point of view of the Secretariat. Mgr Willebrands and the people of the Secretariat, who know that they are still barely tolerated in certain Roman circles (Arrighi reported to me the remark of a highly placed prelate after the death of John XXIII: Now the Secretariat is going to pay up!), seem to me to see things very much FROM THE POINT OF VIEW OF THE SECRETARIAT and of the general attitude towards it. The Pope did not come to this meeting, which was presided over by Cardinal Tisserant—who now seems to be back in favour. There is talk of his returning to the Eastern Congregation, from which Testa[1] would resign. Maximos IV will have asked for this return . . . The cardinals were brought up to date about the Pope's pilgrimage, about what had happened, about the possible consequences.

Mgr Willebrands said that we must go very gently here. Besides, when he saw the Pope and told him of his wish to have the FUTURE of the Secretariat more firmly established, the Pope replied: Pay your dues, and that will come.

What would be envisaged would be an exchange of letters with the East at Christmas and Easter, some exchange visits, in short a becoming re-accustomed to living together, and the progressive establishment of a situation in fact bordering on communion. Dogmatic questions would not be discussed to start with, but rather pastoral ones.

On the part of the Secretariat the idea is to create a sort of Catholic Bossey.[2] I spoke of the plan mentioned to me by Mgr Elchinger, of an open college, attached to a Jesuit University in California, at Strasbourg. Mgr Willebrands thinks that Strasbourg will become important from the ecumenical point of view, but for this Catholic Bossey, he thinks rather of Gazzada. That is tenable.

This morning (since no one had yet arrived), I did a bit of work on the proposed *emendationes* to *De Oecumenismo*, a packet of which Mgr Willebrands had sent me.

I made a note, too, on the subject of a Secretariat for Non-Christian Religions, the creation of which has been officially announced.[3] It seems that there is not a clear view of WHAT TO DO. Will there perhaps be a DIALOGUE between Catholicism and Buddhism, or Confucianism? There does not seem to have been progress towards anything specific. And, Mgr Willebrands said, where will we get suitable MEN?

I spent the whole day reading the dossier of the bishops' *Animadversiones* [comments] on *De Oecumenismo*. I did not quite get to the end.

---

1. Cardinal Gustavo Testa, who had been Secretary to the future John XXIII when he was in Istanbul, was at the time Secretary of the Congregation for the Eastern Church.
2. The Ecumenical Institute at Bossey had been founded by the World Council of Churches.
3. Paul VI announced its creation on 10 September 1963.

In the evening—when Frs Dumont, Tavard,[1] Lanne, Baum, Stransky . . . arrived—we shared out the work. Then we talked. Very interesting. I learned that the WCC under Lukas Vischer, had made some attempt to direct the Observers. For example, there had been a directive not to go to the celebration commemorating the Council of Trent. The Russians (Borovoj) and the Anglicans reacted by asserting their freedom: they were answerable only to their own churches.

From this question we went on to the current reactions of the WCC, which is fearful that Rome might pursue direct conversations, either with the Orthodox, or with the Anglicans. That would weaken the WCC and would prejudice the action it is able to take in certain conversations between the churches. Among ourselves, some insisted on the freedom the churches enjoyed, according to the statute of the WCC itself, to seek unions, and also on the fact that we have not waited for the WCC to search for unity! Others (G Baum) underlined the gravity of our responsibility if we were to weaken the WCC and leave it to deal with just the Protestants. This was a matter of emphasis, for we are all agreed that neither the Orthodox nor the Anglicans should be cut off from the WCC. We must proceed with great prudence and do nothing behind Geneva's back.

Tuesday 4 February 1964

I read the article by Fr L Ciappi, 'Unico Pastore e uncio Fundamento della Chiesa universale' [A Single Shepherd and a single Foundation of the Universal Church], *L'Osservatore Romano* 29.1.1964. It is the ultramontane thesis according to which 1) all ecclesiology is reduced to the pope or is deduced from his powers; 2) Only the pope has power over the UNIVERSAL Church: the college of bishops is not mentioned, but it is excluded.

Thus they seek to influence opinion. The prohibition of doing this, expressed in Cicognani's letter, applies only to those who are not of the right persuasion—theirs!

In the morning, work in the sub-commission on Chapter I.

At table, Mgr Willebrands recounted that there had been pressing requests at the Council for the enthronement of a statue of the Blessed Virgin after that of the Gospel. (I asked Mgr Willebrands: BY WHOM? It is Ottaviani . . . ! Extraordinary!!! In the face of objections from the Secretariat, Cardinal Cicognani had come up with this solution: that the enthronement should not take place every day, but that on one side of the Gospel there should be placed a statue of the Blessed Virgin which would stay there, and, on the other side, a statue of St Joseph. Fortunately the Secretariat had [[made]] a WRITTEN note of this, and John XXIII, having read it, said NO. Otherwise, Mgr Willebrands said to me,

---

1. George Tavard, an Assumptionist priest of French origin who worked in the USA, was a Council expert and was a consultor to the Secretariat of Unity.

Cicognani would have been perfectly capable of not passing anything on. For one cannot trust him. —And to think that Cicognani was Prefect of the Eastern Congregation!!!). —One of the reasons invoked was that this would please the Orthodox!!!!! This came from above, and it went a long way. It was because this reason was invoked that the matter was submitted to the Secretariat. Fr Hamer told how, as *socius*, he had passed on to Cardinal Browne a request from an American Jesuit seeking to have a liturgical honour rendered to the *Summa* of St Thomas after the book of the Gospels.

By contrast, I took up again my idea of reading a few verses after the rite of the enthronement of the Gospel.

I also learned this: that a few years back there was question of re-establishing relations between the Vatican and Israel. Cardinal Tardini said to Cardinal Tisserant, who repeated it to Mgr Willebrands: How could we establish diplomatic relations with a people that killed Jesus? (sic).

There are in Rome some relics of the head of St Andrew, which the town of Patras sent to Rome at the time of the Turkish invasion. Cardinal Bessarion[1] received them in the presence of the pope and said: *Pollicemur* [We promise] . . . We promise to return them when . . . Recently the municipality of Patras asked for this famous (and, no doubt, inauthentic) relic. The Secretariat is making efforts to have it sent back. I foresee the Pope going to Constantinople to pay his visit to Athenagoras and taking this relic with him.

Obviously, other requests will follow, for the crusaders brought back a good many relics to the West. Timothy and Titus, John Chrysostom etc would have to be returned!!! Why not?

Paul VI had planned to give each of the orthodox Patriarchs that he would meet in Jerusalem a piece of the head of St Andrew. But this manner of breaking up a relic and dividing up its ownership would have been worse than anything. The Pope was dissuaded, which safeguarded the possibility of the gesture that, I hope, he will make one day make. Meanwhile, the Orthodox have been asked not to raise the question in the newspapers, in order not to compromise the possibility of a happy outcome.

We worked until 9.30 pm on the *Animadversiones* concerning Chapter I. There are a lot of them, sometimes mutually contradictory. A good number of them called for the presentation of the dogma of the papacy in all its brutal precision, and an ecclesiology seen (only) in this light. But the point is precisely to get beyond such an ecclesiology. For many, ecumenism is just a gentle, easy tactic to lead people to the pope. Franić said so explicitly.

---

1. John Bessarion (1395–1472): Metropolitan of Nicaea, he played an active role in favour of the reunion of the churches at the Council of Florence; created cardinal, he settled in Rome.

Wednesday 5 February 1964

Worked on the bishops' comments. I counted the number of those for whom ecumenism is just a pleasant way of leading the others to submission to the pope! Wretched ultramontane ecclesiology . . .

Mgr Willebrands told me about his reception by Mgr Meouchi, Patriarch of the Maronites. His Beatitude was in bed, dressed in an incredible, somewhat feminine fashion. It would appear that he often receives people in bed like this. After the Pope's pilgrimage to the Holy Land, he got King Hussein of Jordan to give him the magnificent car the Pope had used during his pilgrimage . . .

When the English bishops, and in particular Dom Butler, were accused by *Il Tempo* of advocating a text *De Beata* in which the dogmas of the Immaculate Conception and the Assumption were played down, even passed over, Dom Butler went to *Il Tempo* to protest. The director who received him categorically refused to print a clarification and said: for us, the Council is a purely political affair, and we treat it only from that angle.

Thursday 6 February 1964

Work. On the subject of *De libertate religiosa*: Cicognani said, in a purely personal conversation with Welykyj: it can no longer be avoided. Nevertheless, by 15-20 January, hardly any but critical *Animadversiones* had reached the Secretariat. Many Spanish bishops had written against the present text, invoking thesis and hypothesis. So Fr Ahern (American Passionist and biblical scholar, who had played a major role in fostering 'good ideas' among some bishops of the USA: already at the time of the First Session on the matter of Scripture and the historicity of the gospels; at the Second Session on the question of *De Beata* . . . The Secretariat had taken him on as a biblical expert) had alerted Cardinal Meyer, for whom he had drafted various papers during the Second Session, and Cardinal Meyer had written personally to various American bishops in such a way that, within a few days, about thirty letters were received praising *De libertate religiosa*, and expressing the ardent wish that it be taken up again.

It is certain that its proper place would have been in schema XVII, just as the proper place for the *De iudaico populo* [on the Jewish People] would have been in the chapter *De populo Dei*: Willebrands would willingly surrender the text to schema XVII, but on the condition that it remain substantially as it is. But, in schema XVII it would run the risk either of being reduced to ten lines, or of not being a Conciliar text, but simply a text of the Commission. It might be an idea, in order to give it still greater weight, and to take it out of the context of ecumenism, which is too narrow, to present the schema *De libertate religiosa* as an INDEPENDENT schema, and have it put forward by both the Secretariat and the Theological Commission. But besides the fact that the Co-ordinating Commission would have difficulty in accepting that another schema should be added to the NUMBER of those it already has, one wonders what would become of the text if it were submitted to the Theological Commission. That is why the Secretariat, even while recognising that the framework of ecumenism is too narrow and specific for this question, will keep this chapter as Chapter IV of ecumenism, though it will improve its text. Mgr Willebrands expects to do this work during April, inviting the help of experts like Mgr Pavan, Fr de Riedmatten, Fr Courtney Murray (but he is ill: heart trouble. However the most recent news is good). I insisted that it should be clearly stated in a *proemium* that the PARTICULAR link between ecumenism and the question of religious freedom extends far beyond this context.

However Mgr Willebrands would be happy if it could be arranged that this text be presented jointly by the Secretariat and the Theological Commission. That would assure it of a much wider agreement. The historic role of the Secretariat has been to introduce the question, to open the breach. Without it, the question would not have been tackled in this way.

Friday 7 February 1964

I should have left this morning, in order to be in time for my course this evening in Strasbourg.[1] But I would not have been able to finish my work, or rather my part of the work, on Chapter I and the *Proemium*. So, although this is rather inconvenient, and although it will seriously disrupt things on my return, I shall stay on until Sunday.

Recently, Paul VI's speeches during public audiences have returned constantly to the absolute divine mission of the papacy. I read in *L'Osservatore Romano* as recently as 6 February a speech in Italian to some pilgrims. There the Pope developed the idea that Peter received a name that the Old Testament gives to God and the New Testament attributes to Christ, that of Rock. He quoted St Leo on the subject: *id quod Ipse erat voluit (Petrum) nominari* [He willed that (Peter) be called what he himself was] (*Ep* X, 1 = Patrologia Latina 54, col 629). All this makes me think, and fear, that the Pope, disturbed by the development of the idea of collegiality, and having hoped for some light on these questions from his pilgrimage to the Holy Land, has brought back from there a reinforced awareness that he is THE foundation of the Church, THE Vicar of Christ . . .

In *L'Osservatore Romano* for 7 February 1964, there is an article by Balić on 'Maria Madre e tipo della Chiesa' [Mary Mother and symbol of the Church]. I compared it with the article by Ciappi, cited *supra* on page 483, and I note that the people of the Curia are making a tremendous effort to ensure that the ultramontane theses prevail.

Saturday 8 February

A day of all of us working together. Under discussion were my *proemium*, which was demolished, and Chapter I. I found the same method of working as in the Theological Commission: questions were again discussed which had been discussed ten times already, words which had been taken out were put back in, ones

---

1. Part of a course on religious culture organised by the Catholic parishes of Strasbourg.

which had been added were removed, and so on, two or three times over. I must say it is rather boring work. And the Secretariat has not yet come to the end!

This morning an article in *Il Tempo* (a conservative paper, often informed by the Holy Office) reporting a papal audience for Ottaviani and Carli. It interpreted this audience as a riposte to Cardinal Döpfner (Döpfner has been vilified for saying that only the Truth itself is an absolute and that dogmatic formulations are approximations that bear the mark of history) and to the French bishops who have promulgated the Constitution *De Sacra Liturgia* with the employment of French translations not approved by the Holy See. This is bluster from the Holy Office, of which the Pope is the head: the head not of a mere Council, which will pass, but of the Church, which will remain.

Lunch at 1.00 pm with Fr Lécuyer. He is working on collegiality. It seemed to me that he was glad to be able to speak somewhat freely about matters close to his heart. His General (Mgr Marcel Lefebvre), for whom he is Procurator, has taken as his theological adviser l'abbé Berto,[1] of *Pensée catholique*. During the whole session, Lécuyer was opposite him at the table, with the consequence that he was not able to say anything.

In the evening Mgr Willebrands recounted various memories and anecdotes of the Pope's pilgrimage to the Holy Land.

Sunday 9 February 1964
Departure at 10.05 am. I found Thils at Zurich. We had travelled together without realising it . . . In Rome there had been an unsurpassed purity and beauty of light. Above the Po the fog started. At Zurich, where the temperature was 1 degree, clouds. In Alsace these clouds became a continuous layer between the sky and the earth. At Strasbourg I again found the frosted glass, the endless sheet of blackish cloud that hangs over us for ten months of the year.

In the evening, preached at the priory.

Milan, 29 February 1964 (Saturday)
My last week in Strasbourg was terrible: such numbness and weakness that I could scarcely walk. In my room, with feet I could not lift, I bumped into everything.

As I have often found, a journey, even a tiring one, rather does me good. I left Strasbourg at 12.30 am (having given my lecture yesterday evening). In the same couchette compartment was a gentleman who walked with two sticks. In the morning we chatted, and he recognised me. It was Mgr Elchinger's brother, who has multiple sclerosis (paraplegia). We have remarkably similar symptoms, and experience the same inconveniences and benefits: difficulty in lifting a foot (I noticed that in order to put his shoes on he picked up his right leg with his hand just as I do), difficulty in getting into a car, difficulty in going up and down

---

1. Victor-Alain Berto, priest of the diocese of Vannes, had participated in the creation of *La Pensée catholique*.

stairs; the benefit of high altitude, total collapse in low atmospheric pressure and stormy weather . . . He told me of some conclusions from his own experience and of various pieces of advice he had been given by doctors: to avoid numbness keep moving; on the other hand, when tired, stop and rest; don't carry parcels; live in a human climate that is joyful and optimistic, with people who appeal to you; avoid excess at table. The inconveniences increase with boredom and misfortune. In the light of this I told myself that it is useless to expect any improvement as long as I have so much correspondence every day, so many requests, difficult letters which take several hours to answer . . .

At Milan I was met by M. Falchi.[1] We spent what there was of the morning making a summary of my lecture in Italian. (I am staying at San Fedele with the Jesuit Fathers.) At 11.30 am, I was taken by car to Venegono, a seminary for philosophy and theology. There are three other 'seminaries', two 'junior' ones, and one for pastoral work. Altogether 4,400 students. There are 700 here. The theologians applauded me beyond all measure. Lunch with the professors (80 in all). A lecture at 2.45 pm presented by Carlo Colombo. Excessive applause.

Colombo told me various details about the Holy Father, whom he continues to see regularly.

The Pope had formed his plan for a pilgrimage as early as July: a simple pilgrimage, for him, and for the Church, which, in his person, would confess Christ. The meeting with Athenagoras was grafted on only afterwards. The Pope showed great stamina of nerve. On the plane coming back, he spent an hour discussing a particular matter with Mgr Dell'Acqua and Mgr Colombo.

His prayer had been:
   at [   ], the *Pater* [Our Father]
   at the church of the Primacy (*'Pasce oves'* [Feed my sheep (John 21:17)] . . .),
      the *Veni Creator*
   at Capernaum, the *Pange Lingua*
   at the Beatitudes, the reading of the text of St Matthew
   at Tabor he had wanted to read the account from the Gospel, but a New Testament could not be found . . .

The Pope works until midnight or 1 am. He gets up at 6.30 am. He continues to read a great deal. During the Council, he has frequently read *ICI*. It was he who pointed out to Mgr Colombo the passage where I relayed to the Observers his words about a theology that was historical and concrete . . .

On this matter, it was, for the Pope, something much more than a nice remark spoken by chance in response to Skydsgaard. He really thought about it. He would envisage a complete faculty of theology where all the teaching was done from the angle of the history of salvation. One could well see what might come

---

1.   Franco Falchi, a layman much involved in ecumenism, was the Secretary of the Committee for the diocese of Milan of Fr Boyer's international association 'Unitas'.

of that . . . But the Pope does not have a settled view, and Colombo told me that any suggestion that he passed on might have a chance of having an effect on him.

The Council: 1) The number of votes should be increased. They are favourable every time, observed Colombo, as we have often remarked. THIS Session would be envisaged as more a session of votes and proclamations. On the subject of collegiality, the Pope would not be opposed, or even reticent; but his wish is that on such an important matter serious work should result in sure and precise conclusions.

On the subject of the Secretariat for Non-Christian Religions: it would not be a matter of an organism for action, but simply for information and contact. In the long run, what is good in these religions would be brought into relief.

We returned to Milan at 5.30 pm. At the women's college of the Catholic University, a room full of young women and men awaited me, and welcomed me warmly. For the space of an hour, the most wide-ranging questions. I replied as best I could in French (the questions had been put to me in Italian.)

Return to San Fedele at 7.00 pm. Dinner at 8.00 pm.

My lecture on the requirements of ecumenism: a packed auditorium, very attentive. Some good questions. Bed at 11.30 pm.

Sunday 1 March 1964

Train at 7.40 am for Turin. Don Rolando[1] came from Turin to welcome me at the railway station in Milan and travelled with me. I am quite overcome by the status attributed to me and the kindness shown me. I meet people ten times more worthy than myself who show me a hundred kindnesses.

Mass on arrival in Turin. A lecture[2] in the—very modern—hall of the Museum of Modern Art. A very good audience; people standing in the aisles and at the back. I felt that I had given a mediocre lecture, difficult to follow. Nevertheless, I was listened to with great attention. Many young people, many university people . . . Lunch at the seminary at Rivoli. It too is a grand building of the imposing and imperial style of Pius XI, but the view over the mountains is magnificent. One feels the Alps very close. This is indeed Piedmont.

Don Rolando spoke to me about Fossati,[3] the old Cardinal of Turin. At the Council—and everywhere else as well—he goes to sleep. He is nearly 90 years old, of the same generation as Pizzardo,[4] and has close ties with him. Pizzardo, originally from Savona, was sidelined (accused of anti-fascism) when he came to Genoa, where Fossati was secretary (to the bishop?). Fossati sent Pizzardo to Rome. There Pizzardo had had the opportunity to be involved with the Lateran Treaty. This led to an improbable career for this man who, Don Rolando told me,

---

1. Giovanni M Rolando, professor at the major seminary of Turin.
2. A lecture on the laity.
3. Maurilio Fossati, Archbishop of Turin, was born in 1876.
4. Born in 1877.

is an imbecile. Pizzardo, being a cardinal, was one of the opponents of Montini, one of those who brought about his departure from Rome.[1]

Dinner in the evening with Count Dal Verme,[2] whose two unmarried daughters are involved, respectively, in the San Fedele Centre and AC [Catholic Action]. The elderly Count, who had been a soldier, is ninety-one years old. He spoke with indignation about Combes and also about Luther: how could Protestantism be true, given that it was founded by an un-frocked monk? One of his daughters had been connected with Countess Ciano,[3] and I was told various details about the death of Ciano, about Mussolini, about their surviving relations and descendants. There was also a journalist present, very intelligent, cultivated and well-informed. We talked about the Council, the Curia, and the Pope. They told me they prefer to have Montini as Pope than as archbishop. He was often hesitant. John XXIII once called him the Italian Hamlet. Knowing that he would not remain in Milan, but that he would one day return to Rome, he never really gave himself fully . . .

What a strange milieu is this milieu of ancient nobility (the family has been known in Milan since the twelfth century) that still has something of a fortune: others no longer have anything, and live in two or three rooms, strangers to the modern world. These are VERY cultivated people, but I was conscious of how artificial, empty and unreal was the set-up of drawing rooms hung with old paintings, of domestic servants in white gloves etc. It is a bit like the set-up of the Vatican . . .

Before leaving Strasbourg I read the Acton-Döllinger correspondence.[4] It is the set-up Lord Acton knew: a leisured aristocracy pursuing a life of high culture in travels and visits to Count X or Countess Y, but juxtaposed to [[or superimposed upon]] the real life of the people of its time . . .

Monday 2 March 1964

Mass, lunch with some of the Fathers, with whom I felt a close affinity, because they know what's going on.

The Countess Dal Verme drove me to the airport.

Rome. An indifferent journey: no flight information at Milan, a strike of some service or other, dissatisfied people. Nobody to meet me at Rome, though I had telephoned, and there should have been someone. I got no reply on the telephone. After waiting for an hour I took the ordinary bus and a taxi. (Mgr Prignon apologised: he had a great many things to worry about, and was not able either to come to collect me or to let me know this in advance . . .) I reached the Belgian Col-

---

1. Montini was at the time *sostituto* of the Secretariat of State; he was appointed Archbishop of Milan in 1954.
2. Guiseppe Dal Verme.
3. Edda, daughter of Mussolini, had married Count Galeazzo Ciano, who became her father's Minister of Foreign Affairs.
4. John Acton (1834–1902), a pupil of Döllinger, historian and journalist.

lege at the end of the meal: Mgr Charue, Mgr Heuschen, Philips, Moeller. I was brought up to date on what was waiting for us in the Theological Commission this afternoon. And also on what had happened about the Pope's *Motu proprio* regarding the liturgy. Paul VI had not realised that his text contradicted the conciliar decree; that seems to me hardly credible!!! He gives in, a little, to everyone. On one hand to the French bishops: the text of the *Motu proprio* was modified.[1] *Il Tempo* commented: this was in order to give in to the French bishops, who once again, were quicker than the music. But, on the other hand, translations must all be submitted to Rome. The Pope received Mgr Martin, who said to him: if the restriction comes from the Pope personally we will all submit to it; but we want to know if it comes from the Pope or the Curia. Paul VI replied, telling him to disseminate this response widely: it comes from me personally. My reasons for requiring the submission of translations to Rome are: 1) to establish from now on a uniformity within linguistic regions (there is a great variety, and later on it will be too late to bring them back into unity); 2) to avoid translations that are paraphrases. Finally, even translations already approved by Rome must be submitted, in order not to make distinctions between countries. I do not find these reasons cogent: the national episcopates are perfectly capable of responding to these requirements. It is even their proper function.

At 4.30 pm a meeting of the Theological Commission at the Vatican. We gathered and exchanged news among ourselves.

The meeting began with a *De Profundis* for Mgr Griffiths, who had recently died. He had been a member of the Preparatory Commission and was a member of our sub-commission *De populo Dei*: a man of independent judgement, mischievous, somewhat abrupt, and not much given to compromise . . . It passes quickly, does life . . . !

Fr Tromp read Cicognani's letter about the discretion imposed on the *periti* (on this subject I was later told that this warning would have been aimed either at people like Küng and Laurentin, or else at certain *periti degentes Romae* [experts living in Rome], who had campaigned against others (the Lateran) . . .), then a letter on the speeding up of the work concerning the Third Session; to shorten the schemas. But as our schema was already approved *in genere*, this hardly concerned us.

Then a letter from Cicognani was read on the subject of the discussion to be had on the *De Revelatione* and on the revised text on collegiality (text HERE).

General report by the Secretary (Fr Tromp) on the work done, and on the unfolding of the work to be done. We learnt that Cardinal Larraona has a schema prepared on the relationship between the Church and the Church Triumphant, a text that would be inserted before the chapter *De Beata*. The Pope has forwarded this text to the Theological Commission (Ottaviani proposed that a sub-commis-

---

1. The official text appeared in *Acta Apostolicae Sedis* of 15 February 1964; less restrictive than in its first version, it allowed a certain ambiguity to remain concerning the Holy See's control of vernacular translations.

sion be set up to examine this text and its insertion in the *De Ecclesia*. Mgr Cha-rue said that a paragraph in the *De Beata* would doubtless be sufficient). There had also been handed over to us an enormous *Relatio* on the bishops' comments on the *De Revelatione*, which will have to be presented to the Fathers at the Third Session . . . We have also been sent the bishops' comments on *De oecumenismo*. I thought I understood that our Commission would have to discuss certain pas-sages in *De oecumenismo* (religious freedom).

Discussion then went on to the question of the formula for the theological note of the conciliar texts. I was not aware that, during my absence, Mgr Felici had read out, *in aula*, the text dealing with the theological note, while introduc-ing into it some short phrases which our sub-commission had not put in.[1] How strange. Who had fiddled with the text in this way? A sub-commission was set up = the three previous members (Fernandez, Parente, Schröffer) plus Ancel and Dodewaard, to look into this affair.

During this session, we looked at the first two Numbers of *De populo Dei*. That went well enough.

In the evening, at the Belgian College, two or three small changes were fi-nalised. For my Belgian friends, the 'Cerfaux *dixit* [said]' ranks a little above the Gospel . . . !!!

Tuesday 3 March 1964
This morning, I read some of the papers they sent us yesterday: the documenta-tion on the discussion concerning collegiality and a text by Fr Tromp about (and against) the same subject. Fr Tromp is still completely stuck in a Bellarminian perspective of juridical presuppositions and pontifical monarchy.

At 4.30 pm, a meeting of the Theological Commission at the Vatican. First of all, a long explanation by Parente of the formula assigning the theological note to the texts of the Council.

The discussion lasted an hour and ten minutes.

Mgr Henríquez proposed the setting up of a sub-commission (of bishops and) of experts to study the comments made on the *De Revelatione*. But Fr Tromp had done the work and said—in vain—that pages would be distributed in which all this would be explained.

A very tedious meeting. In two days we have done only three Numbers.

Wednesday 4 March 1964
Worked on texts during the morning. Lunch at the French Seminary: Mgr Guer-ry, Garrone, Ancel, Cazaux, Urtasun, Ménager, Streiff, Gouet.

At 4.30 pm, at the Vatican, Joint Commission with that of the Apostolate of the Laity, on the new schema XVII. Some lay people helped or participated.

---

1. On 29 November, at the beginning of the session, when Congar was away in Sedan for his mother's funeral.

A *Relatio* by Mgr Guano on the manner in which the work is being done, the content and the plan of the schema.

Lectio textus [reading of the text]: we got no further than Chapter I, because the rest was not yet ready in Latin!!!

Ordo laborandi [the order of the work to be done]. The setting-up of sub-commissions:

1) *Centralis*

[central sub-commission]: already constituted

2) *De persona humana in societate*

[on the human person in society]:

President: Mgr Roy + Garrone, Wright. . . László

3) *De matrimonio et familia*

[on marriage and the family]

4) *De culturae progressu rite promovendo*

[on the correct promotion of cultural progress]

5) *De ordine oeconomico et de iustitia sociali*

[on the economic order and on social justice]

6)*De communitate gentium et pace*

[on the community of nations and on peace]

Ottaviani suggested that two or three lay people should be added to sub-commission 3, not as experts, but as MEMBERS.

A wholly muddled and disappointing meeting.

A TOTAL WASTE OF TIME. Endless preliminary or elementary questions were raised. At 6.30 pm we still did not know if the properly conciliar schema should set out the general principles of each of the chapters, which will make as many annexed documents . . .!!!

But what authority will such documents have? Some time was given to discussing the question.

At 6.40 pm the distribution of the LATIN text of the schema began.

A truly pitiful meeting. Ottaviani was completely bucked up: he can present his Commission as a model of orderly work . . . With regard to the proposed text of schema XVII, a very quick reading of it amid this noise and disorder, led me to think that it was very paraenetic. It is half-way between a theological text and a MESSAGE—with some very good things, but a somewhat sermonising tone and a liberal use of grandiose words . . .

In the evening, at 9.30 pm, Mgr Daem, bishop of Anvers,[1] asked me to produce, for tomorrow morning . . . A PLAN of the text on Christian schools—universities . . . !

---

1. Jules V Daem, member of the Commission for Seminaries, Studies, and Catholic Eucation since the First Session.

Thursday 5 March 1964

Session at the Vatican at 9.30 am. Mgr Philips started by showing mathematically that timing demanded that at least three Numbers should be done at each session, and that the Chapter *De populo Dei* should be finished today.

That went well enough.

At 4.30 pm, a second session. First, Cardinal König and Mgr Garrone reported the conclusions of the sub-commission set up to deal with holiness in the Church Triumphant. Fr Fernandez raised the question of a special chapter for Religious: Fr Gut was in favour of this.[1]

Work continued on the chapter *De populo Dei*: No. 15. There was debate over the first or second formula for non-catholic Christians (the second formula takes account of people who say they are Christians, but are not baptised). There were twelve or thirteen votes for the first formula and seven for the second.

In the evening, after dinner at the Belgian College, with Fr Lécuyer and Mgr Onclin, there was discussion of the draft corrected by Mgr Heuschen of the section on apostolic succession. A USEFUL discussion.

Friday 6 March 1964

At 9 am, a short meeting with Mgr Parente on the question of the theological note that is to be indicated.

9.35 am, session. The chapter on the episcopate was started. Much debate about the repetition of *'vicarius Christi'* [vicar of Christ] and the pope's titles. Fr Butler said that too much repetition will give the impression that there is some doubt about it. He began his intervention by recalling an English poem in which someone asserts the existence of a monster. By virtue of its being stated, a thing must be true: 'When I have repeated something three times, it is true.'[2] Many would like to suppress *'Christi vicario'* (the bishops are vicars of Christ), indeed, the whole of the last sentence of the prologue. But Tromp, Parente and Schauf intervened. A vote resulted in fourteen in favour of retaining the petrine formulas, when there were twenty-seven Fathers there. So that remains established.

Medina had worked out that there were still twenty-one formulas of this sort in the chapter (instead of the twenty-six there were previously). He confidentially submitted a paper containing his comments.

The discussion of Christ as foundation, and the Apostles or Peter as foundations, threatened to resurface . . . It was broken off.

At 11.15 am No. 21 was begun, No. 20 being postponed until later, so that the text of sub-commission 3, and that of Mgr Heuschen could be better harmonised and presented.

---

1. Bruno Gut, OSB, Abbot Primate of the Benedictine Federation, member of the Doctrinal Commission since the First Session of the Council.
2. {Lewis Carroll, *The Hunting of the Snark*.}

Thus the very important question of whether or not pastoral powers are given to bishops at their consecration was broached. Doumith and Parente intervened: *Episcopus, vi consecrationis, fit aptus ad participandum, habet participationem potestatis etiam iurisdictionis substantialiter; iurisdictio non creatur a missione canonica'* [the bishop, by virtue of his consecration, becomes capable of participating, he has an essential participation even in the power of jurisdiction; jurisdiction does not come into being with the canonical mission].

(Parente's intervention was sensational. He gave it a certain character of solemnity. He set out his way of looking at it (he had already done so a year before) in a very complete manner, in great silence. Tromp, who had been about to intervene, stared and listened, unhappy, and as though stunned.)

Mgr Parente and Mgr Doumith were asked to collaborate in preparing a formula to be voted on.

It was a pity that the vote was not taken on the spot. The case would have been won!

In the afternoon, at 4.30, at the Vatican.

First, approbation of the formula, corrected this morning, *De nota theologica* [on the theological note] of the Council's teaching: unanimous except for three. Florit wanted the sacramental character of the episcopate to be treated first, and then the grace. There were twenty votes in favour of Florit's line. It was made clear that the mention of the character in no way settled the dispute about whether episcopal character is a new character, or simply an extension of that received at priestly ordination. I thought of Fr Bouëssé.[1]

Reading of No. 22. Ottaviani again started to deny that the Apostles had formed a college.

It is starting all over again!!! A feeling of oppression.

After a few exchanges, Charue and Henríquez demanded a vote. A very charged atmosphere. König also demanded a vote.

Interventions by Charue, Henríquez, Volk, Doumith, Browne. Volk and Doumith emphasised that there is in collegiality a valuable Christian reality.

D'Ercole, Lécuyer, Rahner, Gagnebet, Butler again intervened in favour of the college.

At 5.52 pm (and after Charue, Ancel and Henríquez had insisted that a vote be taken . . .): Who approves the text as it is? EVERYONE! Even Ottaviani!!! This had gone on for over an hour.

---

1. Humbert Bouëssé, OP, of the Province of Lyons, specialist on the sacrament of orders and at that time opposed to the existence of an episcopal character, had just made a *retractatio* in a postscript to a colloquium he published: cf: 'Postface. Le caractère épiscopal', in H Bouëssé and A Mandouze (editors) *L'Évêque dans l'Église du Christ. Travaux du symposium de l'Arbresle 1960* (Bruges: Desclée De Brouwer, 1963); Bouëssé hoped, nevertheless, that the Council would not pronounce on this episcopal character, which required further research (page 368).

Discussion of the next bit. Cardinal Browne proposed a new formula which expressed the curialist thesis that a universal collegial power could be exercised only at the invitation and by the concession of the Pope.

Discussion. Voting: A LARGE majority in favour of retaining the text suggested by the sub-commission, and a second vote in favour of re-inserting *una cum capite* [together with the head] instead of *sub capite* [under the head]. This was achieved at 6.30 pm. An interval.

After the interval, and when the text of the chapter had been VOTED, Cardinal Ottaviani proposed that a vote should be taken on Monday or Tuesday on Browne's text, which would be distributed (in fact it already was).

Garrone protested: it has been voted, accepted and approved . . .

Ottaviani said: but we are all agreed . . . Browne's formula is merely an explanation which says the same thing . . .

Charue and Henríquez: no! It is a different text. What has been voted has been voted. It can't be gone back on.

Ottaviani: Very well! Browne's text will be distributed merely '*ut prae oculis habeatur*' [so that we may have it in front of us].

We moved on to discuss the end of the section. Philips, supported by Schröffer and Heuschen, pressed for a return to the original text: '*saltem libere recipiat*' [at least may freely accept]. Butler did the same . . . Doumith questioned what was said about the convocation of councils, and Henríquez even what was said about the RECEPTION of Ecumenical Councils!

At 7.04, we went on to No. 23. It would have been possible to finish this and clear the last few lines in the momentum of this end of meeting. Sadly it was put off until tomorrow.

Saturday 7 March 1964 St Thomas.
At 9.30 am, at the Vatican. Ottaviani (at the request of Philips), asked that a sub-commission be set up to study the question of the *De Revelatione*. The following were named: Florit, Charue, Pelletier, Dodewaard, Heuschen, Barbado, Butler (Garrone and Poma[1] declined). The question of collegiality had been virtually settled by yesterday's discussion. Even Fr Tromp did not intervene. He had drafted, duplicated and distributed copies of a rather long paper against collegiality, vigorous and dull, juridical and thoroughly Bellarminian,[2] wholly conceived along the lines of the pontifical monarchy. Nothing at all was said about this, no one made the slightest allusion to it.

We returned to the final lines of No. 23 where we stopped yesterday. These were speedily dealt with. An intervention by Doumith to the effect that the differences between the churches should not be given too much importance. It should

---

1. Antonio Poma, bishop of Mantua (Italy), appointed a member of the Doctrinal Commission at the time of the Second Session of the Council.
2. In the spirit of Robert Bellarmine (cf above, page 77).

simply be stated that they enjoyed their own customs and usages. I suggested that fine text from St Cyprian on *'salvo iure communionis'* [while retaining the right of communion].[1] This fell flat. There was a lot of hair-splitting, time was wasted the discussion of No. 25 *De munere episcoporum docendi* [On the teaching office of bishops]. Many felt that it had too much to say about the pope (half of the text).

After a short interval, there was discussion of the formula proposed by Parente and Doumith for the link between the powers of the episcopate and episcopal consecration (No. 21). A long discussion.

Tromp wanted to teach his doctrine in his trenchant and definitive tone. He raised a storm of opposition.

Philips' proposition, which he dictated and on which he asked for a vote, at least as regards the idea. The experts spoke. Finally SECRET votes were taken (at the request of Doumith):

1) Lines 19–21 with the words *sollemniter* [solemnly] from the duplicated text: UNANIMOUS, by a show of hands. The question was raised whether this would be a dogmatic definition. Dom Butler was against that. Cardinal Browne said it was solemn teaching, not a definition.

It was suggested that *sollemniter* be removed, or better, that the Moderators should suggest two formulas.

Sollemniter was suppressed.

2) The second part of the text: *Consecratio autem episcopalis confert cum potestate sanctificandi munera quoque, saltem radicitus, docendi et regendi: quae tamen nonnisi in communione cum Collegii capite et membris exerceri possunt* [However, episcopal consecration confers, together with the power of sanctifying, the offices of teaching and ruling, at least radically. These however cannot be exercised except in communion with the head and members of the college]—without *'radicitus saltem'* [at least radically]. A secret vote. Twenty-seven (including Ottaviani): 19 *placet*, 8 *non placet*.

Lunch at the Angelicum: with four cardinals. Saw Frs Philippe[2] and Hamer briefly. A somewhat formal feeding ceremony in a freezing and noisy refectory. Nevertheless, a wonderful young Dominican student body.

From 4.00 pm to 7.00 pm worked with Mgr Philips and Moeller to make a fair copy of the corrections that had been accepted.

In the evening, Mgr De Smedt at dinner, having returned from the meeting of the Secretariat. He was delighted with the revision of the *De libertate religiosa*. He

---

1. Congar had cited this statement previously in, amongst other places, *Jalons pour une théologie du laïcat*, 'Unam Sanctam', 23 (Paris: Cerf, 1953), 482. The complete sentence is: *'Salvo iure communionis, diversum sentire'* [while retaining the right of communion, to hold a different opinion]. {This is, in fact, Augustine's extrapolation from what Cyprian had said; cf Augustine, *On Baptism, Against the Donatists* III.3.5 and Cyprian, at the beginning of *Sententiae Episcoporum numero LXXXVII de Haereticis Baptizandis*.}

2. Paul Philippe.

explained its principal points, especially its extension to religious societies. It is all based on the vocation and the dignity of the human person.

At dinner, Mgr Heuschen and Mgr Charue described the joint meeting of sub-commission III and the biblical sub-commission, on the subject of the section on apostolic succession: 'Mgr Cerfaux will be pleased' they concluded . . .

Sunday 8 March 1964
From 5 am, and especially from 6 am, I had a sort of lumbago, or gout? I had VERY bad pain in the sacrum, and in the right hip and leg. This morning it took me half an hour to tie my shoes because I could not find a position which made it possible. It was painful to walk and I could not bend down. It is really terrible. What shall I do? I must carry on as usual and put a good face on it, but it is VERY hard!

Work.

Midday, at lunch, Mgr van Cauwelaert. He spoke first, and at length, about the Congo. The Belgians had failed to prepare the transition to independence so that, when this came suddenly, there were no indigenous structures in place. Now there is really no public order, everyone lines his own pockets and looks after himself. It seems as though there is a plan to create the greatest possible disorder, and at the same time prepare for a Chinese intervention. There seem to be no forces presently in existence capable of controlling the disorder and bringing order to the country . . .

He then spoke, at my request, about what the Commission on the Sacraments, of which he is a member, is preparing with regard to mixed marriages. The conciliar text itself, drawn up in twelve or fifteen propositions, asks only that these articles be reviewed in the light of ecumenism. But the recommendations made by the Commission introduce the following: 1) the undertaking to bring children up as Catholics should be required only of the Catholic partner; and even, if this proves impossible, it should not to be insisted upon; 2) the possibility of the bishop dispensing from *forma Ecclesiae* [canonical form] BEFOREHAND, so that a marriage celebrated in a non-catholic church would be valid; 3) the suggestion that there be an understanding between priests and non-Catholic ministers.

In the afternoon, work to finalise the corrections accepted. A meeting with Medina and Mgr Henríquez. In effect, they objected to the section explaining the phrase *ex sese*. When they explained their concern, the sequencing was revised. We agreed on a text which I will explain after supper to Mgr Garrone and Mgr Ancel. Medina is extraordinary. He lives the Council intensely (from the angle of Cardinal Silva) on the level both of ideas and of tactics, if not, indeed, of scheming. He sniffs around a bit everywhere, often with perspicacity. He knows everything that is going on, he goes from one to another carrying his bits of information, his comments, his instructions. He is one of the creators of the Council at this level of alliances and coalitions.

But, this afternoon there was something to excite him. Fr Dhanis, rector of the Gregorianum, said that yesterday's vote on the episcopate as a sacrament, and the conferral of the three *munera* [offices] by episcopal consecration, is a scandal: the bishops, he said, do not have the right to do this. They should allow freedom for theological options, and not take it away . . . With the result that the rumour is going about that yesterday's vote will be challenged. Mgr Charue telephoned this evening to say that, if the vote was challenged, he would immediately take the floor to say that it is inadmissible to challenge what has been settled, and that immediately afterwards he would walk out of the room, inviting the bishops to follow him.

But perhaps Medina had turned Charue's head. We shall see tomorrow.

Mgr Carlo Colombo has been named a titular bishop. No doubt he will get a post in the Curia . . .

Monday 9 March 1964

9.30 am, at the Vatican. A date for the May session was considered.

Discussion of the exclusive character of the right a bishop has to ordain priests and even other bishops. A solution was accepted that will perhaps be regretted one day: it was affirmed that only bishops can consecrate bishops. And yet the Commission was clearly warned!!! (myself, Lécuyer, Moeller). A discussion followed on the infallibility of bishops when they all agree in teaching a PARTICULAR doctrine.

- The text drawn up yesterday passed without question.

Cardinal Browne raised a question about the text that says that THE POPE makes use of the services of *periti*. Parente also, and others. Idolatry? The mention of experts was suppressed!

Butler returned to the question of the ordination of the bishops of Alexandria and proposed the formula '*Episcoporum est* . . . ' [it pertains to bishops].[1] Mgr Philips said, very rightly, that there could not be a new vote unless *EVERYONE* agreed on this. Only a few were prepared to allow another vote. Consequently this was not done, and the matter remains in an unsatisfactory state. At least the Holy Spirit did not make use of this ignorance or even thoughtlessness to lead the Church to affirm that ONLY bishops are able to consecrate other bishops . . .

Lunch at Santa Sabina. I went by car with Fr General, Mgr Barbado and Fr Ramirez (always very silent). Fr General told me about a lecture in a church in Paris[2] by G Hourdin,[3] which the public prevented him from giving, shouting out, 'You have been in Poland at a congress with the Communists . . . '

---

1. The formula indicates that it pertains to bishops to ordain newly chosen members of their body.
2. Lecture in the church of Notre-Dame-de-Grâce, 26 February.
3. George Hourdin, great patron of the Catholic press, he had founded *La Vie catholique illustrée* and also *Actualité religieuse dans le monde*, which subsequently became *Infor-*

Fr General and Fr Barbado made a great deal of a letter from the Pope to an American group set up to finance the Leonine edition of St Thomas. For them this letter was a document of the utmost importance, a victory. It stated two things: 1) St Thomas is the teacher always adapted to the spirit and needs of OUR TIMES; 2) St Thomas is FOR ALL COUNTRIES . . .

Thus I find myself, with these few men with whom Fr General always comes to the Vatican, and leaves it—who are his conciliar milieu—in a Hispanic climate of anti-communism and of the triumph of Thomism.

After lunch I saw Fr General for a moment, to bring him up to date about the plan for the volume *Discours au Concile*.[1] This scared him a bit. He doubts that one has the right to publish these texts. He himself, when he had been asked in Spain to publish his own interventions, did not believe he was able to do so. But, after all, he was not sure that it was forbidden. I suggested to him without mentioning my own plan (rather more than a plan!), that he should enquire, as though in his own name, whether it is permissible to publish his text.

At 2.30 pm Fr Hamer gave me the corrected text *De libertate religiosa* to read. It is a very homogeneous and coherent text. It bases everything on the rights of the human person, and gives living together [*convivere*] in society, or the common good understood in this sense, as the only criterion limiting liberty. This will certainly disconcert more than one Father . . . No appeal is made to objective considerations outside the human person.

4.30 pm. Joint commission for the doctrinal chapter of schema XVII.

General discussion: not enough scripture (Florit); exhortatory tone, not sufficiently dogmatic (Civardi); language sometimes remote from the use that people of today make of words or concepts, for example, 'technical', which has a much more precise meaning for people of today than for clerics. We, for our part, say 'there are spiritual things and technical things'. . . For lay people this is much more *PRECISE*, concrete. There is the technical sphere but also the sphere of politics, of trade unions, of the family: THINGS that are precise, concrete. . . ; condemn atheistic communism explicitly (Franić); recover the style of John XXIII (Helder Câmara), which is not just a style but also a content (Poma): the question of humanism, of the relationship to humankind.

At the interval, Fr Häring took me aside to tell me, under secrecy, that Parente had written to Don Giovanni,[2] editor of *La Rocca*, to protest against the interview with me they had published, in which they praised my person and my work. I should not, said Parente, be commended in this way.

---

mations catholiques internationales, of which he was then the editor.
1. Yves Congar, Hans Küng & Daniel O'Hanlon (editors) *Discours au Concile Vatican II* (Paris: Cerf, 1964).
2. Giovanni Rossi, the founder, at Assisi, of the association *Pro Civitate Christiana* [For the Christian City], that formed young lay people for the apostolate; a friend of John XXIII, to whom, on 9 January 1959, he had confided his intention to call a council.

Fr Häring told me that he was going to send a photocopy of this letter to the Pope.

When the meeting resumed, an intervention by Veronese. He insisted on the primacy of the importance of the CONTENT.

Long, VERY long response from Mgr Guano.

A great critique from Rahner: the schema over-simplifies questions to which we do not have the answer.

Ferrari Toniolo: it would be good to have the *a quo* [starting point] and the *ad quid* [goal] of the temporal and natural connection to the integral Christian human being (the connection must then be supernatural). Start with a clear distinction between the Church and the World; show their relationships in everyday life. This is in three stages:

- the situation of our times,
- the doctrine
- the pastoral applications.

Basically: see, judge, act . . .

A dreadful meeting, which made me think of some Catholic Action meeting where one spends one's time discussing

what one will do,

what one can do,

the method and procedure to be employed . . .

If only they would do it!!!

This evening, at dinner, Cardinal Suenens. He mainly asked questions, in order to bring himself up to date about things, about the work, about what was being said about the likelihood of a Fourth Session, etc. All this with a certain seriousness of a man who is realistic and precise.

Tuesday 10 March 1964

I typed out four copies of the French *votum* for *De presbyteris* [on priests].

9.30 am, at the Vatican (taxi). Almost the whole meeting was devoted to *De presbyteris*. Very good interventions by Mgr Heuschen, McGrath and Garrone. I also intervened, in favour of a priesthood that is evangelical and apostolic. This article absolutely must be revised and improved. It will be a big job.

At 11.54 am the section was accepted as approved, subject to the corrections and additions to be made. A start was made on the section on deacons.

At lunch, with Cardinal Suenens, there was discussion of the changes envisaged for the regulations, particularly with regard to THE VOTE on the schema *De Ecclesia*. The inclination is to allow a vote, section by section, or by important points, as determined by the Council of Presidents and the secretariat of the Theological Commission, which would be already indicated on the printed text: it would still be possible for bishops to ask for a particular vote, on the condition that they gather fifty signatures.

Again I noticed the realistic and concrete attitude of the Belgians, which makes them so EFFECTIVE.

[[I received the proofs of *Discours au Concile . . .* !!!

At 3.15 pm, work on the *De presbyteris* with Philips, Mgr Heuschen and Moeller.

At 3.30 pm, sub-commission. Discussion of *De Diaconis*.]]

Ottaviani would be favourable to the restoration of the diaconate, quite apart from the shortage of priests. Parente said that the Pope is thinking of the restoration of the permanent diaconate, to last for several years, to test the chastity of young people. But that is quite a different idea.

Henríquez commented on it. There are two separate things:

- the restoration of the PERMANENT diaconate;
- the restoration of the diaconate *ad experimentum* [as an experiment] for a longer or shorter period: this is a matter of the intervals between the reception of different orders: a question of canon law that is not being addressed here.

The real question that we should be dealing with, Doumith said, is to specify what are the purpose and the effect of the sacrament given to the deacon.

There should be two sections:

- a dogmatic one on the sacrament and the office;
- a pastoral and canonical one on the restoration and its conditions.

Franić read a long paper against the restoration of the married diaconate. He proposed that the two opposed positions should be set out at the Council (his own by Cardinal Wyszyński), and that a vote should be taken on this point.

Ottaviani returned to his idea of acolytes. A long discussion: interventions by Henríquez, McGrath, Doumith (listened to with great attention). A long discussion in which the problems came and went with varying results.

Šeper said that the question had been discussed by the Commission on the Sacraments AT THE POPE'S REQUEST. A splendid intervention, calm, full of realism and humour. The text leaves room for freedom, and allows that if a deacon is not wanted there does not have to be one. It is good. It should be left alone.

Mgr Šeper said: If lay people perform the functions of a deacon they should be given the order—which Christ instituted precisely FOR the fulfilment of that service. One should not invent an order of acolyte or some other artificial structure when the diaconate exists!

A formula needs to be prepared for the Fathers to vote on (Charue, Schröffer and eventually even Franić)

A vote on the words *'praesertim in absentia sacerdotis'* [especially in the absence of a priest]: three in favour of retaining it.

- on the first lines of the second, disciplinary or pastoral, part (= the possibility of instituting a permanent diaconate)

either: *resitituti poterit* [it will be able to be restored]: 22 *placet*

or: *viris maturis:* {*exerceri poterit:* 11 *placet*

                       {*conferri*

[it shall be able to be exercised by mature males]

[it shall be conferred upon mature males]

- on the ending: decisions about WHETHER OR NOT IT IS OPPORTUNE should be left to the bishops' conferences with the approval of the pope: 15 *placet* out of 27;

- on WHETHER OR NOT IT IS OPPORTUNE TO RAISE *IN AULA* THE QUESTION of the possibility of ordaining married men (with double formula).

After an interval of a quarter of an hour, or even more, discussion began on the Chapter *De laicis*. During the interval, Fr Balić came to moan near me: a minimalist text *De Beata* has been drawn up (it does not speak of Mary as *Mater gratiae, Mediatrix gratiarum* [Mother of grace, Mediatrix of graces]). Philips would not concede anything: he wanted his text and that of Balić put side by side in two columns. But the Pope wanted there to be unanimity on this text. But the Spaniards will never accept that text. Fr Llamara had sent a long report to Fr Fernandez. He had also sent it to Fr Balić, but the latter did not want to duplicate and distribute the text. We will see . . .

Mgr Garrone told me that Mgr Villot, coming out of a papal audience, had reported to him that the Pope was considering a procedure to speed up the debates: discussion would take place in a limited assembly made up of representatives of groups. Only the voting would require the plenary assembly.

But is this fair?

In the evening, we finished tidying up the article *De Presbyteris*.

Wednesday 11 March 1964

9.30 am, at the Vatican. First, No. 20, on apostolic succession.

After an interval of five minutes, which became a quarter of an hour, the chapter on the Laity was taken up again at 11.15 am.

At 3.30 pm, a little meeting to prepare for the meeting at 4.30 pm on the *De Revelatione*: to see how the work will be organised, and the people assigned.

The meeting at St Martha's went well. Fr Tromp spoke first about a text sent by Cardinal Silva Henríquez; he went on to point out that the Joint Commission set up by John XXIII no longer existed as such, because it had finished its work. But Cardinal Bea will judge whether the corrections introduced are such that the text should be submitted to the Secretariat: Mgr Florit suggested dividing us up into three sub-commissions, *De Revelatione, De Scriptura, De Traditione*. Mgr Philips and Charue preferred two sub-commissions, with each again having two sub-commissions:

1 {*De Revelatione*
  {*De Traditione*
2 {*De Inspiratione*
  {*De V et NT* [On the Old and New Testaments]

This was adopted, and the members of our sub-commission were assigned:

Prima sub-commissione: Florit, Pelletier, Heuschen, Butler

a) *De Revelatione: Periti:* Smulders, Moeller, Prignon and Colombo;

b) *De Traditione: Periti:* Congar, Betti, Rahner, Schauf;

Secunda sub-commissione: Charue, Barbado, van Dodewaard:

a) *De Inspiratione:* Gagnebet, Grillmeier, Semmelroth, Garofalo;

b) *De V et N Testamenti:* Turrado[1] (of Salamanca), Rigaux, Castellino,[2] Kerrigan.

[[It was agreed that we should reconvene on 20–25 April, to establish the definitive text. The text of the *relatio* and of the propositions should be sent to Fr Betti, secretary of our sub-commission, for 10–15 April.]]

Rahner was of the opinion that we should not touch *De Traditione*, the subject of such difficult negotiations. But Betti, Schauf and I said: YES! Tradition must be treated in a POSITIVE way, without touching on the agreement reached, with such difficulty, on the delicate points.

We went over again, with Mgr Florit, what would need to be done. This boiled down to:

1) Establishing the *nexus* between Revelation and Tradition.

2) The nature of Tradition (and its existence); its importance in the life of the Church.

3) Tradition and Scripture.

4) Tradition and Magisterium or Church.

I was made responsible for preparing the *relatio* on 2 and 4; Rahner and Schauf will prepare the *relatio* on 3. But it was agreed that, with the *relatio*, each one will propose either a plan of the text, or some propositions concerning his part of it, and even the whole of the chapter, which will need to run to two or three pages.

Went home with Rahner and Colombo, and then by taxi with Rahner.

In the evening, Cardinal Suenens familiarised himself with the different points concerning schema XVII. (I explained my idea of a day at least on the 'world situation'). He spoke of the discussions that were going on with a view to the speeding up, and a good scheduling, of the work. The Session will last only forty days: eighty hours of discussion. It is very little! It will start with the *De Apostolatu laicorum* or with the *De libertate religiosa*. The Moderators are trying to organise the debates. In my view, they should focus on certain questions decided by the competent Commission and perhaps introduced by a *Relator*.

This evening, revision of the corrections to be made to the texts.

---

1. Lorenzo Turrado, priest of the diocese of Salamanca, Professor of Holy Scripture at the University of that city, Council expert.
2. Giorgio Castellino, SDB, Orientalist, professor at the University of Rome, he was a consultor to the Pontifical Biblical Commission, and a Council expert.

Thursday 12 March 1964.

At 9 am at the Vatican, continuation of the chapter *De laicis*. Mgr Philips presented it and defended it with less commitment than the rest: it does not come from him but from Mgr De Smedt, from Cardinal Silva, together with more than three hundred South American bishops, and from Fr Häring. It is rather wordy and often not very precise.

For myself, I got sinusitis on Monday evening (there was a draught at the Joint Commission). This, together with the lingering lumbago, or the painful ankylosis of the sacrum, tired me very much.

Since my arrival in Rome the weather has been very poor.

The interventions of Browne, Parente and sometimes Florit are unfailingly in favour of suppressing everything that could extol, in however small a way, marriage, freedom, and of amplifying everything that affirms the EXCLUSIVE rights of the hierarchy, of the clergy!

It was a real race against the clock to FINISH the chapter *De laicis* this morning.

At 12 noon there was a ceremony in St Peter's for the inauguration of the funerary monument of Pius XII.

In the afternoon: work (corrections to the proofs of *Discours au Concile*): I did not go to the Joint Commission on schema XVII: the two previous meetings were too disappointing. And above all, I did not have the time to work on the proposed text in such a way as to be able to intervene usefully. I will have to do it. . .

At supper, the talk was about schema XVII. In the opinion of the Belgians, schema XVII will not be ready if it is desired to go sufficiently deeply into the questions with which it ought to deal. It would be better, they think, not to hurry things, but to allow time for certain questions to mature, such as those concerning peace, and especially birth control. My Belgian friends have spoken a lot in the past few days about an article by Canon Janssens, in *ETL*.[1] Cardinal Suenens wants to encourage the development of a new way of judging these things.

The Belgians say: If schema XVII does not present something new and forceful on the questions that interest human beings, there will be terrible disappointment everywhere. So time should be taken to develop something good. But, there is no such time available between now and the summer; besides we are all more than fully occupied. So the Belgians suggest that schema XVII should be quite simply postponed for two or even five years, with the Council suspended for the whole of that time.

There was agreement, too, on the idea that there should be a more THEO-LOGICAL Latin text, accompanied by OFFICIAL translations that EXPLAINED things further in accessible terms in the major world languages.

---

1. L Janssens, 'Morale conjugale et progestogènes', in *Ephemerides Theologicae Lovanienses*, 1963: 787–826.

Friday 13 March 1964

Slept badly. I am worried about the publication of *Discours au Concile*.

At 9.30 am, Vatican. Beginning of discussion on the chapter *De Sanctitate* [On Holiness].

At the interval, I saw Fr General. I showed him the proofs of *Discours au Concile*, and gave him an account of the question. He told me he had asked Mgr Parente and Mgr Felici. The reply was: No. The texts should not be published. He said he will ask Cardinal Browne, and will, if need be, go to the Secretary of State. I pointed out that *THESE MEN COULD* give only a tutiorist and constrained reply . . .

He suggested that I should wait until the end of the Third Session to publish the book. I pointed out that the other editions which are now appearing, or have appeared, carry my name. Yes, he replied, but they involve me less. . . That is true, and I think I am coming round to the idea of publishing the book only towards 10 or 15 October . . .

At 4.30 pm, Vatican. We continued with the *De sanctitate*. One sensed an overall feeling of lassitude. For myself, I felt flat. The weather was stormy and oppressive. There was no longer any freshness of spirit.

I asked to speak several times but was not called.

At the interval I again saw Fr General on the question of *Discours au Concile*. I insisted on two points: 1) the number and quality of those who had given me their texts with permission to publish them; 2) those with whom Fr General had discussed the question (Parente, Felici . . .) could only give the most tutiorist and most constrained advice . . . Fr General would allow publication during the Third Session, but he added that he did not 'give permission' for it . . .

Discussion began on the chapter *De Religiosis*. Fr Gut read a paper with emotion (his hands were trembling) and in heavy silence. He had recourse to more than 700 bishops in order, in some way, to impugn the text. Mgr Philips made a very lively response: How could these Fathers judge a text they had not read? The whole thing should be read first, and then it could be seen whether or not the text deserved this wholesale criticism that was being thrown at it. A little later Fr Fernandez intervened in a rather disagreeable tone in which decided opposition was apparent and little disposition of welcome. This left a painful impression. Cardinal Ottaviani, for his part, decided to move on quickly and just about declared that the whole chapter had been voted, when it had not.

Once again, for the fourth time, I asked, in vain, to speak. Thils and Moeller were called to speak without difficulty.

In the evening, a visit from Michel Le Guillou[1] and Fr de la Potterie. Nevertheless, Laurentin was at dinner. We had to speak about the *De Beata*. This went badly. Philips rather dug in his heels. He is tired: that is only to be expected. But I also

---

1. Younger brother of the Dominican Marie-Joseph, he was training to be a hospital doctor.

noticed in him the same attitude as when I introduced Dossetti last May. There are some people before whom Philips digs in his heels, and from whom, from his first impulse, he will accept nothing. He called on Laurentin to say whether he approved or disapproved of his text *De Beata*, and as Laurentin did not say yes or no, he left the dining room. Discussion of the question continued after he left. This is proving to be ***INSOLUBLE.*** The group of maximalists, stirred up by Balić, who alerted and is alerting the Spanish bishops, considers that the Virgin is being betrayed. But one absolutely must not give in, and the others do not want to give in, to this formal demand for maximalism. On the other hand the Pope has said that he does not want DISCUSSION *in aula* of the *De Beata*. He asks that the Theological Commission come to a unanimous agreement, on a text which the Assembly would be able to pass at one stroke.

But THAT would appear to be impossible. It has reached a point where the demands for maximalism are so enormous, so absurd, that one cannot keep up with them. THEY SHOULD, MUCH RATHER, BE CONDEMNED. So, it is insoluble.

Mgr Prignon said to me: Cardinal Suenens is IN FAVOUR of mediation. I spent two hours persuading him not to intervene along these lines. Finally he said: I won't do so, but don't ask anything more of me. If the question is put, I shall vote IN FAVOUR.

This evening, late, a little correspondence and then packing.

I am writing this on 14 March at 9.00 am, in the Boeing which is taking me to Geneva. I regret that I shall not be taking part in the discussion from today about the last part of the *De Religiosis*, and about the *De Beata*. How will these things turn out? Will there be last-minute scheming? Balić will certainly intervene. He will quote the encyclicals, Bittremieux[1] etc.

This maximalist Mariology is a canker.

JESUS CHRIST *ALONE* IS THE HEAD OF THE CHURCH.

I left Rome on Saturday morning, 14 March. By air from Rome to Geneva; by train from Geneva to Lyons.

A celebration in honour of Fr De Lubac.[2] He was presented with the three volumes of essays: *L'homme devant Dieu.*[3] Not much ceremony, really. Almost no outside guests (except the theological faculty of Lyons). No festivity. Just a lecture,[4] after which Fr Guillet[5] presented him with the essays and made a very good little speech.

---

1. The mariologist Joseph Bittremieux, who died in 1950, had taught dogmatic theology at Louvain until 1945.
2. The celebration was for his fifty years of religious life as a Jesuit.
3. Cf particularly Congar's contribution to Volume I, 'Le thème de *Dieu-créateur* et les explications de l'Hexaméron dans la tradition chrétienne', in *L'homme devant Dieu, Mélanges offerts au Père Henri de Lubac (I)* (Paris: Aubier, 1964), 189–222.
4. Congar gave a conference on the theme: 'The present ecclesiological moment'.
5. Jacques Guillet, SJ, was Professor of Fundamental Theology and Sacred Scripture at the

I spent the evening with my confrères at Place Gailleton. An atmosphere like that of Éditions du Cerf, though less anarchist.

Night train to Strasbourg. I thought about the meetings in which I am unable to take part, on such important subjects: *De religiosis, De Beata*! How are these things going in Rome? I wish I had some news . . .

I would like, at the end of this notebook, to express my opinion on one point. I write, in fact, if not for the sake of history!!! at least so that my testimony will be set down.

This Council has been called: *Primum Concilium Lovaniense, Romae habitum* [The first Council of Louvain, held in Rome]. That is true enough, at least as regards theology. Since I had many contacts with my Belgian friends and (willingly) stayed frequently at the Belgian College, I want to say here what I think.

And, first of all, I do not want to say anything discourteous of my Belgian friends, or that would appear as a criticism. Facts are facts. I want only to say how I know them and see them.

1)THE STRUCTURES

(I am copying out again in Strasbourg notes taken in Rome.)

The Belgians are not numerous: five or six of them, but they are EVERY-WHERE. Not only do they put their own into all the interesting posts, not only have they had named as conciliar experts those who would work effectively (Moeller, Prignon), but they spread themselves around. While I was told that I could not be on the Secretariat because I was on the Theological Commission, Thils, who is on the Secretariat, is on the Theological Commission, and Moeller is everywhere: Theological Commission, Commission for Religious, schema XVII, the Secretariat, etc! He was present at all the decisive moments and places.

They all come from Louvain or take their bearings from there. They know one another, often having been students together, and they are on familiar terms with one another. They cohere, and have the same points of reference. THEY TRUST THE COMPETENCE OF THEIR OWN; what comes from Louvain is sacred. This goes even so far as *Magister dixit* [The Master said]. I have several times reacted openly, and more often still internally. Whatever the subject, there are only THEIR references, although so many others, all just as competent, have dealt with the question. As soon as one of their own, and especially someone from Louvain, has said something, everyone takes it seriously and makes it a point of reference. What Cerfaux has said is a bit above the word of the Gospel . . .

Jesuit Theology Faculty of Lyon-Fourvière; he was later to become the Dean.

It is not as though they are completely homogeneous: for instance, Philips is a little irritated by Thils. However he tries to satisfy him. When a question is about to be raised, a new focus of work opened up, they alert one another, they get themselves involved, or have themselves called in, they share amongst themselves opinions on the sensitive issues. And what one of them passes on to another, or prepares for another, is made use of. They organise themselves, meet each other again and again. The result is that, where one of them is, they all are . . .

This is a very effective system. They rejoice in their effectiveness. At meals in the Belgian College they congratulate each other, boast of having said this, or got that accepted. With some of them (Moeller) it is partly egocentric, but the reality is there: they are very effective.

It is well known. It is known that the centre of work is there. That is why people come to them to try to get this or that matter passed. Before and after meetings, during the intervals, Philips and Moeller are bombarded. During the Second Session, the Belgian College was the place where Tucci, Dossetti, Medina, Rahner came . . .

There are some personal centres of this effectiveness. Mgr Prignon provides the link and informs the cardinal, who follows matters very closely. Thanks to this agent that he has in place, Cardinal Suenens is up to date with everything, and acts effectively. It was said to me: 'his stocks are falling in Rome'. They were very high during the Second Session.

- The theological centre is Mgr Philips. He combines an extraordinary gift with average qualities. No one else could have done what he did and have succeeded as he has. He owes this:

– First to great intellectual sturdiness. He knows his business very well. He sees clearly. He has present to his mind the elements and the documentation of the matter. He is very good at putting problems in context.

– Then there is his character: peaceable, pleasant, conciliating. He is welcoming to everyone and everything. He then does what he wants, but everyone has been welcomed, everyone's trust has been won. He combines this with a great fairness. He does not appear to anyone as a party man. In fact, he acts straightforwardly, along the lines of openness, along the lines of what D Beauduin used to call 'good ideas'. But he is not passionate. He has the reputation of never having promoted a personal preference on any question. He is truly fair, and never plays tricks, although he knows how to be deft. That is why he enjoys everyone's trust. He completely won over the trust of Cardinal Ottaviani, of Tromp himself (they talk Dutch together: that makes things a lot easier). IN PRACTICE, PHILIPS DOES AS HE PLEASES. Whatever he says (and he has the art of saying it), is accepted immediately.

– This applies also to the qualities OF STYLE. First, his Latin is easy and clear. But there are also his extraordinary qualities as a *debater*. He knows how to propose a question in a such a way that, disarming preconceptions, neutralising objections in advance, he points the others towards the solution he wants WITH-

OUT THEIR REALISING IT. With a consummate skill, innocently intended and fully conscious, he draws attention to some inoffensive point of detail, and gets the big question passed without its even being noticed. He never gives others the impression that he wants to 'have' them, but, really, he does have them. He scatters his *'si Patres velint'* [if the Fathers wish], that give the impression that a decision has been made freely, but, really, he leads the Fathers where he wants. He has always got an answer ready. When the discussion has been exhausted with no outcome, he innocently suggests his solution without in any way imposing it. It is nearly always adopted.

Without any doubt, Mgr Philips is the architect No. 1 of the theological work of the council.

The Belgians hold all the stakes in the 'biblical sub-commission': Cerfaux, Heuschen, Charue, Rigaux. Under the guise of the monitoring of biblical quotations, this sub-commission actually exercises a final monitoring of the texts. In its defence, one can still modify these texts after the work of the relevant sub-commission: it is possible to reintroduce something. In any case, there is a monitoring of all the work. Sometimes this monitoring is not even done in Rome, but in Louvain. It is a final means by which the Belgians, closely linked in solidarity, influence the content of the texts.

2) THE SPIRIT and action which make these structures possible.

The Belgians have a militant, pro-active attitude. They are not content, as are the French, timidly to propose corrections of detail while accepting the text as it is; THEY ALTER THE TEXT. They have set themselves certain objectives, they want to get certain things through. They act, they intervene, they mobilise their friends until they have got what they want. There are none who stick together as much, apart from the Chileans, with Medina, and to some extent the Germans.

The Belgians DARE. They have not been scolded, they do not feel they are under surveillance, as we do. I am convinced that this plays a great part. Personally I have never, I have still not, escaped from the apprehensions of one who is under suspicion, punished, judged, discriminated against.

The Belgians have remarkable qualities for the work that they do. They are CONCRETE, they have an instinct for effective action. At the Council, our bishops always set forth a grand synthesis full of pastoral charity and piety. Even their interventions on points of detail betray these preoccupations. Our bishops have no technique. They do not work with the experts. Among the Belgians, the bishops and the experts work *ex aequo* [on an equal footing], on the level of ex-students of Louvain. Moreover, with us, most of the experts are religious. But, in spite of everything, there is a slight barrier between the bishops and the religious. The Belgian experts are diocesan priests (except for Rigaux, and his being an ex-student of Louvain makes up for the defect of being a religious) . . .

All this means that the Belgians, directing their efforts to CONCRETE objectives, even in the matter of ideas, are effective. We are not.

I thought of the view of Lord Acton and of Newman, that is so right, about the part played, in the nineteenth century, by the suppression of universities outside Rome, and their replacement by the Roman Colleges. At the moment we have a sort of reversal of this situation. The whole movement of the Council, in its Theological Commission, has been to pass from the Roman Colleges to theological centres outside Rome. But, among such universities, Louvain is the only one that has been effective. What have the theological faculties of our Catholic Institutes done? Practically nothing. Not one of our bishops coming from these has contributed anything.

A very sad observation!!!

15 March 1964

The climate of the Theological Commission has changed. For the better. I believe this is due to: 1) The fact that members know each other better. Instead of their looking at one another with a certain distrust, there is now confidence and collaboration. There have been many more sessions of working TOGETHER, in which, to a certain extent, the atmosphere of the sub-commissions is prolonged; 2) Mgr Philips, who enjoys everyone's confidence, and who fosters an atmosphere in which people are not prejudiced; 3) the new members. They are all very good, they have entered into the work. Their presence balances the Commission in a favourable way.

I do not know whether Fr Tromp and Cardinal Ottaviani have 'understood', if they have accepted. Perhaps, to a certain extent. In any case the former no longer dominates everything; he scarcely comes out of his burrow to intervene; when he does so, he is hardly listened to. Many of the bishops don't like this man's tone, who always has the air of teaching them their lessons, nor his kind of intellect, which they find to be without openness, without truly THEOLOGICAL reference points. As for Cardinal Ottaviani, it seems that he has resigned himself to certain matters. Perhaps someone in high places has read him his lesson too. Perhaps he objectively trusts Mgr Philips, and sees that what is being sought is not a victory for a particular school as such . . .

18 March 1964

Mgr Elchinger (whom I brought up to date on *Discours au Concile:* this morning I received the first copy of the German edition: *Konzilsreden*[1] . . .) told me: the Nuncio recently said to Mgr Weber: your coadjutor gets too worked up, he rushes ahead. Too much. What drives him or inspires him? What is his connection with Mgr Huyghe, who also rushes ahead (too much)?

It is certain that the Council has released a breath of freedom and a wave of hope. From different sides I hear echoes of disappointment among the laity AND

---

1. Yves Congar, Hans Küng and Daniel O`Hanlon (editors), *Konzilsreden* (Einsiedeln-Cologne, 1964).

AMONG PRIESTS. The reform of the liturgy is insufficient ('Is that all?'). The story of the *Motu proprio* has caused disturbance and disquiet. Some are driven to despondency and to lose interest: 'There is nothing to be done' . . . ! Others are inclined to take things into their own hands: 'Since that is how it is! . . . '

I can understand that Rome is a bit worried. The sense of a great putting into question, where there is no longer a totally assured discipline, must play a part in the Pope's desire to close the Council without delay. The conciliar situation allows too many uncertainties. In Rome, the Belgian bishops are finding this too . . .

Sunday 19 April 1964

Departure after the sermon at the cathedral. Lunch at Ayroles,[1] with Fr Catão.[2] Two students who were his friends drove me to Zurich in his car. It took twice as long to drive the ninety kilometres from Basle to Zurich airport as from Kehl to Basle. Appalling Swiss roads, cluttered with dawdlers at forty kilometres per hour. But it was even worse going from Fiumicino to Rome. It was a Sunday evening and people were coming back from the coast. It took us more than an hour and a quarter. I was met, and taken by car by M. Darry de Bavier, the ex-ambassador, a friend of Fr Maillard, accompanied by a young girl, Narguès.

At the Belgian College I found Mgr the Bishop of Liège,[3] Mgr Heuschen, Mgr Philips and C Moeller. We talked a little about the work of the Liturgy Commission, which is going well. I learned that the Arab states have threatened to break off diplomatic relations with the Vatican (and so cause very grave inconvenience to all Catholic works) if the text on the Jews remains in the schema *De oecumenismo*. The Cardinal Secretary of State is asking that it be removed. There is some thought of burying it to some extent in an extended text that will discuss either racism or other religions.

I am dead from fatigue and headache.

Monday 20 April 1964

I saw Mgr Prignon who told me quite a lot of things, especially to do with the Co-ordinating Commission, which has been meeting in Rome these past few days.

1) About collegiality. It was Cardinal Agagianian, who, very briefly, presented the *De Ecclesia*. (Cardinal Suenens, who should have done it, thought he would be involved in a lecture tour in America, and had asked Cardinal Agagianian to do it. But, as it turned out, Cardinal Suenens was in Rome.)

Cicognani intervened: this text must not be sent to the bishops because it was heretical. Collegiality was the negation of primacy. It was then argued from the fact that the vote in the Theological Commission was UNANIMOUS, and from

---

1.   Roger Ayroles, Congar's comrade in captivity in Lübeck (Oflag XC).
2.   Bernardo Catão, OP, of the Province of Brazil, who was preparing his doctoral thesis in theology at Strasbourg, under the direction of Chavasse.
3.   Guillaume M van Zuylen.

the fact that this would be a scandal . . . Cardinal Cicognani denied the unanimity of the Theological Commission, saying that Browne had not voted and that Cardinal Ottaviani had written to the Pope to withdraw his vote.

Mgr Felici said to Cardinal Suenens: in reality it was Browne who had written to the Pope; Ottaviani had not written, but had told the Pope *viva voce* that he regretted his vote: 'I allowed myself to be carried along by the atmosphere of the Commission'.

Someone said to Cicognani: You are one member among the others, nothing more than that here. We should vote. The vote was unanimous against Cicognani (including Agagianian).

Döpfner suggested that when the vote on this point was to be taken *in aula* there should be two rapporteurs, one for and one against. This was accepted.

2) The text on the government of dioceses. Mgr Onclin, knowing about the vote in the Theological Commission, had rather hastily drafted a text on 'collegiality'. Carli, rapporteur for the Commission, protested and asked that his critical comments be added to the text that would be sent to the bishops. The Co-ordinating Commission judged that here Carli had only the status of a member, and that his comments could not be added to the text as though coming from the Commission *De Episcopis*,[1] but only as amendments coming from a member.

3) *De oecumenismo*. Cardinal Cicognani was the rapporteur, but it seemed that he was no longer much good at it. He confused and mixed things up. In any case he re-echoed the protests from the Arab countries against the text on the Jews. The Co-ordinating Commission does not want to sacrifice this text. It was agreed that this text would be introduced in a wider context. So Cicognani proposed that the *De libertate religiosa* should be introduced into the *De Ecclesia*. (Was this so that it would come before the Theological Commission?) It was decided that the *De libertate religiosa* and the ENLARGED text on the Jews would be added to the three chapters of *De oecumenismo* AS TWO DECLARATIONS, that on the Jews introduced into a declaration against racism.

4) *De Missionibus*. In addition to the official schema of the Commission, there was presented (Agagianian) a schema put forward by the superiors of the missionary Congregations. It was decided that the *textus receptus* [received text] should be retained, but that the text of the missionary superiors would be added to it as an amendment [[especially]] recommended to the attention of the Fathers.

5) Seminaries and universities.

a) the Pope had suggested to Pizzardo that he should offer his resignation. Pizzardo refused.

b) The schema has been reduced to twelve propositions which are to be voted on without discussion. Cardinal Suenens said that, in view of the importance of the matter, two days should be devoted to hearing the comments of the Fathers.

---

1. This refers to the Commission on Bishops and the Government of Dioceses.

There was objection to the length of the Session and to the desire that it be the last. Cardinal Suenens suggested waiting for the meeting on 15 June, or, better, the beginning of the Third Session, to decide whether there should be a Fourth Session, and the precise schedule of the Third (it is obvious that it cannot all be finished in one go!).

6) The schema on the Eastern Churches. Cicognani, who had become confused and lost his grip (so Suenens told the Pope) raised some difficulties.

After an intervention—Mgr Prignon did not know more precisely whose it was: Liénart or Confalonieri—it was agreed that the text should be sent back to a special commission of EASTERN bishops, leaving them to decide, and telling them that their decision would be accepted in advance.

(At last, and for the first time, the Easterners have been treated as Christians with full rights, and not as minors for whom others make decisions.)

7) There would be a schema on priests, made up from bits from the Message to Priests (so bad) presented at the end of the Second Session, and the earlier *De cura animarum* [on the care of souls].

There was a sentence exhorting them to abandon purely honorific titles. Cardinal Suenens remarked, CAN WE, WE cardinals, address that exhortation to them, without first setting the example ourselves? Someone replied: try convincing Cardinal Tisserant and Mgr Dante first!!! At his next audience Suenens will suggest to the Pope that he should make a gesture. To move the question forward, an example needs to come from above!

8) *Discours au Concile.* This was not raised at the Co-ordinating Commission. But Cardinal Suenens had received the English and German editions and was very pleased with them. He asked: when is the French edition coming out?

9) On the subject of the rumour, spread by certain newspapers, about the appointment of Mgr Guano as secretary of the Italian Conference of Bishops.

Cardinal Siri is ill. According to Cardinal Lercaro, it is not just physical illness, but he sees his 'ideas' as good as rejected, even by the Pope, and he is completely at a loss. He did not come to the meeting of the Italian Bishops, of which he is President. This is what gave rise to the rumour that he and Mgr Castellani[1] would be replaced by Cardinal Urbani and Mgr Guano. But that did not happen. Instead of and in place of Siri, it was Ruffini who drafted a text for the final message. But this text was so negative, so 'anti', and especially anti-communist, that it was not accepted. The Conference set up a little commission (which included Guano) to draft another.

Thus the reactionaries are being progressively sidelined. We are slowly coming out of the tunnel.

---

1. This is probably Alberto Castelli, titular archbishop, Permanent Secretary of the Italian Bishops' Conference.

As for the Pope's speech to the Italian bishops,[1] it was truly interesting and open: Cardinal Suenens, at his audience, had commenced by congratulating the Holy Father. The Pope replied that he was not at all conscious of having made a keynote speech, and that he had simply said, entirely spontaneously, what was in his mind.

It would appear that Felici's influence, which has been preponderant for two or three months, is diminishing. A certain reaction against it is becoming apparent, which might originate from Mgr Dell'Acqua. The latter never stops suggesting to people who are open that they should see the Pope, who otherwise risks hearing only the other side of the story.

10) On the subject of the *Motu proprio* on the Liturgy. A text had been drawn up by people like Martimort. But it came out a fortnight later transformed (Felici, Mariani[2] and others).

The corrected text was reworked by Martimort, and introduced by Mgr Martin and Mgr Gouet . . .

This is how it came about that the Commission *De liturgia* was rather suddenly announced.[3] Nothing was happening. But then the Congregation of Rites produced a text in which it represented itself as being in charge of the application of the Constitution. Cardinal Lercaro reacted, speaking directly to the Pope, which resulted in the post-conciliar Commission, of which HE (and not Larraona) was appointed President.[4] Martimort's plan envisaged the participation of only RESIDENTIAL bishops (except perhaps for one or two auxiliaries, like Jenny). This would eliminate people like Dante, who, in fact, is not a member. But Dante is busy on all sides trying to get himself nominated. It seems inevitable that he will get in. In any case, it is really an organ of the *ecclesia* and not of the Curia.

11) This comes from Mgr Capovilla. John XXIII did not originally want the Preparatory Commissions to be presided over by the Presidents (Prefects) of the corresponding Congregations. But there was a veritable siege of the Pope, conducted by the personnel of the Curia, who delegated to the besiegers the intonation of their refrain:

- Cardinal Giobbe[5] (friend of John XXIII);
- Cardinal Testa (friend of John XXIII);
- Cardinal Jullien,[6] a pious man.

---

1. Speech of 14 April; cf: *Documentation catholique*, 1966: col 545–552.
2. This could be Bonaventura Mariani, OFM, Professor of Sacred Scripture at the Lateran and Assessor at the Holy Office.
3. The Council [Consilium] for the Implementation of the Constitution on the Liturgy, members of which were appointed in March.
4. Cardinal Lercaro, Archbishop of Bologna, was appointed President of the Council for the Implementation of the Constitution on the Liturgy. Cardinal Larraona, Prefect of the Congregation of Rites, and President of the former Commission for Liturgy, was among the members of this Council.
5. Paolo Giobbe, papal datary, was created cardinal by John XXIII in December 1958.
6. The Frenchman André Jullien, Dean of the Rota.

Their argument was: residential cardinals would not be sufficiently in touch with affairs; they could not be constantly leaving their dioceses to come to Rome to conduct business . . .

John XXIII had, in the end, let himself be persuaded, and given way.

At the end of the morning I went to the Secretariat for Unity. I was able to see Willebrands for only a moment: he was leaving immediately, with Fr Duprey, for Istanbul. Fr Duprey said to me: 'God is great! The deadlocks are being broken in a sensational way.' His Holiness Athenagoras is to have an operation for prostate in Switzerland (a neutral country). The situation with regard to Turkey is very difficult. It is not impossible that the Patriarch will be expelled. And basically, he has little support. America is not interested and will leave him to his fate.

I saw Arrighi for a moment. He spoke to me about the Little Church[7] and the steps taken towards reunion. Willibrands and Arrighi have taken over this task, which always moves me profoundly, and even to tears, from Mgr Derouineau. They went to Poitou. They saw several of the families. These are aware of the fact that their secession no longer makes any sense, because the villages are no longer isolated but are involved with the life of the towns. The young ones are losing all religion, and that is all. But Arrighi noticed that in some old declarations the faithful of the Little Church used to say: 'as long as the wrongs committed against us have not been put right'. The idea came to him to make use of the passage in the speech of Paul VI where he asks pardon. The Pope agreed that these words could be used in that way. So a letter was composed in the name of Cardinal Bea and of the bishops who are members of the Secretariat, and sent personally to 1,200 families. A good number were affected by it. A significant minority, Arrighi said, is ready for reunion. The idea would be that they should come to Rome to make a pilgrimage in a church, and that a bishop would come and explain the situation. But Arrighi thinks that not all will be reached. He was called away and left me just at the point when he was starting to talk about the group in Lyons: the one that, until now, has foiled . . .

We came back with Fr Betti. From him I learned:

1) That Fr Lio had made a speech against collegiality to the assembled Italian bishops. But according to Fr Betti, there are no more than seven or eight Italian bishops opposed to collegiality. Some implacable ones. The Pope's speech to them on Holy Thursday made an impression on several of them.

2) That Fr Balić is in Spain, and must be assembling his forces to defend his threatened Marian doctrine.

At 4.30 pm, at St Martha's. The whole sub-commission *De Revelatione*: There were too many people! First there was a long discussion on the manner of proceeding, about what can or cannot be changed in the *textus receptus*. Fr Tromp said, incidentally, that the Pope wanted a vote without discussion on the *De Ecclesia* and the *De Revelatione*, except for a brief discussion on collegiality.

---

7. Cf above, page 62, note 2.

At 5.45 pm we divided into two sub-sub-commissions. It would appear that in the second one, *De Scriptura,* this went quite well. Ours (*De Revelatione, De Traditione*), was rather muddled. Smulders explained how the work had been conducted. Betti introduced a discussion on the possible weight of a *Proemium* (at Vatican I, Mgr Simor[1] declared, in the name of the Deputation of the Faith, that the *proemium* had no doctrinal weight!!!) Should the *De Revelatione* have a *proemium*, or a *caput* [chapter] 1?

This evening, the idea of respect for the *textus receptus* was dominant. It must be departed from as little as possible. I think my *De Traditione* totally contradicts this principle. I drew up a text that has almost nothing in common with the *textus receptus*. This seemed necessary to me in order to pursue an interesting idea. The *textus receptus* says NOTHING!!!

Tuesday 21 April 1964

In the morning, work on the report I have to make on the Tradition text, and reading the *proemium* for *De Revelatione*.

At 4.00 pm (not 4.30 pm!), at St Martha's, sub-commission, discussion of the *Proemium* to *De Revelatione*. A long discussion of two points especially: 1) the relationship between *gesta* [deeds] and *verba* [words] in Revelation: Fr Tromp is stuck in the idea of an absolute priority of *verba*, because the faith is *auditus* [heard], and all the texts of Scripture or of Tradition talk about the WORD of God; 2) Primitive revelation, through knowledge of which people were able to be saved. Rahner maintained this point of view with obstinacy, on the grounds of the link between salvation and faith, faith and revelation. For him the revelation that stands over against this saving faith is THE social and public Revelation.

For the first time since I have been a member of the Theological Commission, I heard the voice of Fr Ramirez. Usually, he is there like a sphinx, without a word, without any indication on his impassible countenance of any reaction whatever. He intervened about the usage of the word *persona* [person] used about Christ in an everyday sense, which is not the strictly dogmatic sense.

The meeting lasted until 7.30 pm.

Wednesday 22 April 1964

At 8.30 am with Fr Smulders, a little council of war, to find a formula on the point discussed at such length yesterday: the place of *gesta* in Revelation. I suggested a text (attached).

Since yesterday, I have been wholly in the atmosphere of the Belgian group. I again encountered their TACTICAL point of view: to be in agreement in advance, to know very precisely what one wishes to avoid and what one wishes to

---

1. János Simor, at the time Archbishop of Esztergom (Hungary), was one of the minority at Vatican I.

get through; to prepare a line to fall back to; to win some people to one's own point of view and to neutralise the others.

It is effective.

In fact, this morning the discussion again took up the question of revelation first of all by DEEDS, and then by words. Dom Butler gave a long exposition of the priority of deeds. But the Smulders-Phillips text, prepared this morning, received the vote of Fr Tromp.

Next it was decided to make the previous *Proemium* into a *CHAPTER*, the Chapter I of the *De Revelatione* = *De ipsa Revelatione* [Of Revelation in itself]. The first lines, somewhat amplified, will be a brief *Proemium* (the proposition of Florit and Betti).

After a (long) interval I read my *relatio* on the chapter *De Traditione*, which I proposed to call: *De transmissione Revelationis praesertim in S Traditione* [On the transmission of Revelation especially in Sacred Tradition].

On the way home, and at the table, my Belgian friends congratulated themselves on their interventions and the results obtained. Mgr Charue was satisfied with the work of the sub-commission *De S Scriptura*: 'Mgr Cerfaux is pleased.' He said a lot in favour of the Spanish exegete, Turrado.

At table, Mgr Prignon reported news received from Canada. Cardinal Léger is not coming to the May-June meeting of the Commission. He is disappointed with the way things are turning out. He feels he has been excluded from a role in the direction of the Council (he confided something of this to me during the Second Session, with a certain animosity towards Cardinal Suenens). He thinks that the Council is deviating from the pastoral intention of John XXIII, and is getting bogged down in byzantine disputations about theology.

In the afternoon, at St Martha's. Mgr Florit proposed—as expected—that Betti's text should be chosen (Betti's text was already a synthesis with some extensive borrowings from my 1962 text). It will probably be completed with elements taken from other texts. Then discussion started. Unanimous agreement in favour of an improvement of the text. Rahner and I insisted on the actual Tradition.

Tromp announced to us that Cardinal Ottaviani wished Fr van den Eynde to be added to our sub-commission. According to my Belgian friends, the one who once wrote *Normes de l'enseignement*,[1] had become very integrist since he had been living in Rome.

In the evening, after dinner, together with Mgr Heuschen and Moeller, we made a start on a text about Tradition itself, intended to replace the—pretty awful—one of Betti.

---

1.   Cf Damien Van Den Eynde, *Les Normes d'enseignement chrétien dans la littérature patristique des premiers siècles* (Gembloux-Paris: Duculot, 1933).

Thursday 23 April 1964

In the morning: before leaving, we looked at a few points of the text that we wanted to include. The Belgians always do this. They study each paragraph BEFORE the discussion, carefully preparing the points on which they wish to intervene, agreeing about this among themselves and with Mgr Philips, planning, if need be, a manner of procedure and a line to fall back on. This is indeed (so far as concerns theology), 'the first Council of Louvain, held in Rome'. They are very conscious of it. I heard Mgr Philips say to Mgr Heuschen: 'The best text is still the one that was drawn up at Louvain' (it was about the *De Traditione*). And, at midday, the other Belgians indicated to Mgr Charue, who will be presiding, the points to which attention should be paid.

At 9.30 am, at St Martha's. Mgr Charue said he knew that Cardinal Ottaviani would have wanted a vote on the two opposing positions: but everyone is agreed not to go back over controverted points, and to arrive unanimously at a text which will not settle these.

With truly remarkable skill, playing the innocent or the fool, proceeding calmly, and in a frank and peaceable tone, Philips read out our replacement text as though it were the text proposed to the sub-commission. This got by at first, but Betti spotted that another text had been substituted for his. He jibbed at this and, vehemently supported by Mgr Florit, he protested, dug his heels in, and refused to budge. He was told that there was no intention of replacing his text, but merely of inserting some additions. That is how it was taken, and eventually accepted. At least, after a confused discussion, Philips and Betti were given the task of coming up with a draft.

I want to note down here what concerns the HISTORY of the question. Florit and Betti (*idem sunt* [they are both the same]) had, from beginning to end, an OBSESSION, yes an obsession about the respective CONTENT of Scripture and Tradition. They never ceased to suspect, beneath whatever criticism of words, or proposal to substitute one adjective for another, a cunning plan to canonise Geiselmann's position. Even this morning when, in all innocence, I suggested qualifying the scriptural witness as *eximium* [eminent], I was suspected by Betti, and then immediately afterwards by Florit, of wanting to say that Scripture is SUFFICIENT. The second time I got hopping mad, even using 'le mot de Cambronne',[1] and saying that this obsession was entirely alien to me, that I was entirely untouched by it and free of it. That is true. But those who have not made any original, fresh reflection of their own on the question of Tradition, think of nothing else. Perhaps they used to have a mandate for that. In any case, it was expressly understood by everyone at the beginning of our work that we would not go back again over this debate and that we would formulate matters in such a way that neither of the two positions would be canonised, or condemned and excluded. It must be said that Betti and Florit have very faithfully observed this

---

1. {'Merde'. Widely, but falsely, thought to have been what General Cambronne said on the occasion of the surrender of the Old Guard at Waterloo.}

agreement. But the dread of it has stayed with them. Ottaviani was so much of the same position that he asked that the 'majority' and 'minority' should each draw up a text. But a tolerable text that was accepted UNANIMOUSLY was arrived at easily enough.

At the very end of the meeting (we had finished the *De Traditione*) Mgr Glorieux appeared and, on behalf of Fr Häring, invited me to join the discussion of the revised schema XVII, next Tuesday and Wednesday. This puts paid to my return to Strasbourg on Saturday and my preaching in the cathedral on SUNDAY. My sermon was ready!

On the way home, Moeller remarked: 'My intervention succeeded all the same'. 'I said . . . you did well to insist etc.'

In the afternoon, I chatted with Dom Butler and Fr Hamer for a moment. With Hamer I talked about *Discours au Concile*. I stuck to my position: to publish at the beginning of October; we mentioned Fr General (no 'vision'). He told me that Mgr Parente is not exactly fond of me. I knew that.

In the evening, revision of the text with Philips, Heuschen, Cerfaux, Moeller, so as to be in agreement for tomorrow. This method of the Belgians is effective!

Friday 24 April 1964

At St Martha's, at 9.30 am. As the WHOLE sub-commission was assembled, we reviewed the texts revised by the two sub-sub-commissions. This morning the first two chapters. It is extraordinary, one would not believe it, but it is so, and I have experienced it twenty times: in a text read ten times over, discussed word by word, something is always found, to be changed and improved, sometimes mistakes or ambiguities to be corrected. It is because one does not see the faults of a text until one has FINISHED WITH that text.

Several more points were corrected, some of real importance.

In the afternoon, a fairly intense discussion of Chapter III, bearing on the interpretation of the Sacred Scriptures. The sub-commission worked in a kind of euphoria, but it was not able to justify its text very well. After an hour and a half, this chapter was finished, but the rest of the text was not quite ready and had not been duplicated. The session closed before the usual time.

On the trip home, the usual remarks: 'I was right to say that'; 'Mgr Cefaux . . . Mgr Cerfaux . . . '

Saturday 25 April 1964

At 9 am, at St Martha's. The *De Revelatione* was finished. Not much discussion. However, on the subject of the use of Scripture, Fr Tromp wanted to multiply the warnings. It should not be given to everyone in all its parts. The story of Susanna is very dangerous, and a priest who spoke about the Song of Songs to a penitent in confession would be suspected of the crime of solicitation . . . Scripture was not given to the faithful, but to the teaching Church as such . . . Poor Fr Tromp did not have much success.

For Fr Tromp the speeches of Job's 'seven' *(sic)* friends have no importance. Such things are not inspired as to their contents, it is only inspired and infallibly true that these things were said. On the other hand, *'verbum Dei scriptum et Traditio'* [The written word of God and Tradition]:

Tradition is the word of God IN THE SAME WAY as Scripture. *Sic* Fr Tromp . . .

Mgr Heuschen, Cerfaux, Rigaux and Philips leave this afternoon.

At 4.00 pm, at the Secretariat for Unity with C Moeller: we were invited by Mgr Willebrands to work on the drafting of an ENLARGED text in which the Declaration on the Jews would be included. Mgr Willebrands told us about his journey to Constantinople, from which he had just returned. The situation of the Christians, and especially of the Greeks, is difficult and very distressing. They are subjected to all sorts of annoyances and pressures (in retaliation for Cyprus). It has come to the point where many are thinking of leaving, as all opportunities for a future are closed to them. The situation, Mgr Willebrands said, is more distressing than in Moscow. In Moscow everything is controlled, a police state is in command. In Constantinople an illiterate and unreasoning people can, at any moment, sack a shop or set fire to a church. The Pope has already intervened with the Turkish government, and will do so again. The visit of his envoys (Mgr Martin, Willebrands, Fr Duprey) was some comfort for the Christian community.

After this he told us what he wanted of us: to prepare a text in accordance with the indications of the Co-ordinating Commission, or at least those of Cardinal Cicognani: a *Declaratio de Hebraeis et de gentibus non christianis* [declaration on the Jews and on non-Christian peoples] (I find this title odd and unsatisfactory), according to the following criteria:

- to emphasise the link between the Jewish People and the Catholic Church;
- to avoid all reference to 'deicide';[1]
- to speak of other non-Christian peoples as children of God, and to affirm the principle of brotherhood in condemning any slur on a race or on human beings for racial reasons.

According to Mgr Willebrands, there should not be any specific reference to Muslims. All the experts and the missionary bishops say that an attitude like that of Massignon[2] is, in practical terms, contrary to the realities. We are at peace with the others everywhere else, except the Muslims, who fight against us.

---

1. The previous schema had explicitly rejected the antisemitic description of the Jewish People as 'deicide', that is, as having killed God.
2. Louis Massignon (1883–1962), orientalist and sociologist, ordained priest in the Melkite Church; influenced by his encounters with Charles de Foucauld, he had developed a very positive approach to Islam, especially to its mystical strains.

The text envisaged should have about forty lines and will be sent to the bishops together with the rest of the schema *De oecumenismo,* without being either discussed again at the Secretariat or submitted to the Co-ordinating Commission.

I proposed starting from the following ideas (I had brought a written plan with me): God the Father of all; all human beings are brothers and sisters to one another. Further, all those who worship God have a further link between them; we believe that no human being is a stranger to Christ.

God has always linked the true relationship to himself to the true relationship with other human beings:

dimitte nobis . . . [forgive us (Matt 6:12)],

the second commandment is like to the first,

vade prius reconciliari fratri tuo [go and be reconciled with your brother first (Matt 5:24)].

Every denial of human brotherhood is a denial of God, or leads to it.

Racism . . . in addition, destroys the charity which is at the heart of Christianity.

Returned at 6.00 pm. I got down to it at once as best I could. Neither my leg nor my hand was working well! Year by year I lose a little more. I would not have been able, this year, to go from the Belgian College to the Angelicum. I will write today to ask for a room in the French Seminary for the Third Session. . .

I come back to this question of the Jews. Really, it is quite scandalous and unacceptable that the Church, in order to please some Arab governments that obey no other reason than just an instinct that is simplistic and all-inclusive, should have to refrain from saying what should be said on a question which comes within its province, and on which it has a duty to speak. I believe that the WHOLE of the Secretariat's text should be retained, while removing only the WORD 'deicide', and expressing the idea in some other way.

Sunday 26 April 1964

I was supposed to be preaching in Strasbourg. The Council is endlessly useful. The course it has enabled me to run is fantastic. Oh, but I wish it would end!!! I am unable to do anything more. I have scarcely time in the intervals between my periods in Rome to deal with day to day correspondence and minor commitments. Besides, a crowd of people are engaged, at great expense, people who already have more than enough to do are further weighed down, for an outcome that is rather mediocre. Our texts, in the end, are pretty banal. So much effort, so much time spent, to achieve middling declarations . . .

However, 1) What if they are frankly limited and unsatisfactory? The opening up of dialogue, the gaining of liberty, are of an incomparable value . . . ; 2) In certain countries things that seem commonplace to us will be taken very seriously, and will allow some substantial advances; 3) I have just reread the whole of the *De Ecclesia,* with a view to a paper for the French bishops. There is, after all,

MUCH that is very good; sometimes a great density of dogmatic thought, and, throughout, openings, seeds.

I believe in seeds. As I always say: between 100 grams of living wheat and ten tons of dead wood, I don't hesitate . . .

In the morning, work: comparison of the *tentamina* [rough drafts] by Moeller and myself for the text for Willebrands. Study of the new text of schema XVII, distinctly improved. At least, so it seems to me. Perhaps because I am reading it in a different frame of mind from before. Self-criticism is difficult.

After lunch, conversation with Mgr Prignon and Moeller. Since I am recording here what I know of the minor history with respect to the greater, I want to record an appreciation of Mgr Prignon. The Council, in its theological aspect, was to a large degree put together in the Belgian College. What was done in the Commission was done largely thanks to Mgr Philips, to the combination of qualities (exceptional enough in itself) that he possesses. But the Belgian College and the small group of Belgians (five or six people in all) could not have played the part they did without the personality of Mgr Prignon. He too, in his own way, holds together a collection of qualities that are themselves rare enough. He has, at once, a theological sense, a practical sense and a sense of tactics. He followed everything, in conjunction with Cardinal Suenens and on his account, but also in conjunction with Charue, Philips, Moeller, Cerfaux. He is very well-informed. He is alert to all the details, without losing track of larger lines of interest. But all of this paid off to the full, because of Mgr Prignon's talent for making people welcome, and this flows directly from his human sensitivity, certainly, but chiefly from the religious and Christian quality of his soul. Mgr Prignon is very much a man of the gospel, entirely DEDICATED, very oblivious of self, who has made the service of others a sort of ABSOLUTE rule for his own conduct. Without all of this, the Belgian College and the Belgian group would neither have been what they have been, nor played the part that they have played.

Mgr Onclin arrived at 2.30 pm for the Commission *De Episcopis*. Not that there was a meeting of the Commission, but simply of a small group purely for redactional tidying up. He told how Carli's position is of the pontifical monarchy, pure and simple. He always looks upon the episcopate or the Council as REALLY distinct from the Pope, and contrasts them as two concurrent realities. But there is no Council without the Pope.

Carli wanted to have added to THE TEXT SENT TO THE BISHOPS a report of his own AGAINST that text. But in virtue of what?

On the other hand, Onclin holds that the Pope enjoys the *plenitudo potestatis* [plenitude of power] only in as much as he is *caput collegii* [head of the college]. I think he is wrong.

Monday 27 April 1964
In the morning, work. At 1.00 pm (2.00 pm) lunch with Fr Maillard's friend, M. Darry de Bavier. He lives at the top of a villa which overlooks a fairly large garden

and a whole ring of woodland with pines and cypresses. On the near horizon are the Baths of Caracalla. An apartment full of beautiful things. But a life in which futility is combined with family cares bordering on the dramatic. My God, how like a soap bubble is the futility of the rich, all gilded by the sun, but empty! How one wishes that such lives were filled with things that weighed more in the scheme of eternity!

At 6.00 pm, at the Secretariat. A great deal of time was spent on things that should have taken half an hour. The rhythm of Willebrands and Moeller is not mine. They repeat three or four times what they have already said once. Three times, Moeller sang the praises of the text (quotation) from Malachi 2: 10: 'I did well putting that in'; 'The text I discovered', etc. In the end, the inclination was to make no specific reference to the Muslims, and to retain intact (except for the WORD 'deicide'), the Secretariat's text on the Jews. Our text was accepted by Willebrands.

Willebrands showed us a report submitted by the internuncio in Cairo[1] after the last meeting of the Arab League. One of the points discussed by this meeting was 'the efforts of international Zionism to obtain from the Council that the Jews should be acquitted of the crime' of having had Jesus crucified.

Dinner with Mgr Willebrands in a small restaurant nearby. He spoke to us about:

a) Princess Irene.[2] She really has been rebaptised. The Holy Office told Cardinal Alfrink that the investigation about her baptism had been made. The Cardinal was no longer worried about it. But no investigation seems to have been made. The princess had on three occasions had an hour of catechism. It is true that she had close ties with a Catholic family and was already acquainted with Catholicism. But all of this, the fact that the Dutch people have not been honestly kept up to date, and that things seem to have been kept from them (they learnt of the conversion, the baptism, the engagement, only through the foreign press) . . . finally this marriage, which will be celebrated on Wednesday, and which it seems the Bourbon-Parma family have promoted without much delicacy: all this seems less than pleasant . . .

b) About Constantinople. The restitution of the skull of St Andrew to Patras has been approved by the Pope. Patriarch Athenagoras is pleased about it, even though he says: it doesn't matter much whether it is in Rome or in Patras. We are a single Church. Rome's relics are ours and Constantinople's are yours . . . The Patriarch will send Observers to the Third Session; that is decided;

c) Concerning the Little Church. Willebrands recounted to us in detail his visits to the principal families of Bressuire and of Vendée. It was very moving. He is

---

1. Mario Brini.
2. Younger daughter of Queen Juliana of the Netherlands, was to marry Prince Carlos-Hugo of Bourbon-Parma on 29 April. On 25 April Alfrink announced that he had conditionally re-baptised the Princess, since he was not sure about the validity of her Protestant baptism.

certain that a fairly good number of the families will be reconciled. A Council Father will be sent to them for this. Mgr Willebrands has to go to Lyons soon (after *Corpus Christi*) to make similar arrangements. The faithful of the Little Church had written to the first Vatican Council; they got no reply. Vatican II is replying, ninety years later . . .

Tuesday 28 April 1964

At St Martha's, at 9 am, for schema XVII. Present were: Mgr Hengsbach, Schröffer, Ménager, Ancel (who had just come from the train), Glorieux, Moeller, Sigmond, Hirschmann, Häring, Congar, and Messieurs Veronese, Habicht,[1] Vanistendael[2] (International Trades Unions). It was not a matter of REWRITING the text, even partially, but of improving the current draft. On the whole, this won approval, particularly from the laity (a letter from Folliet was read out[3]). So I saw that the plan for a new, more theological, draft of Chapter I had no chance, and that it did not square with what was asked of us.

Interventions, in particular from Mgr Hengsbach and from Vanistendael who, in the light of his experience of Asian countries, would like there to be reference to a feeling, that he had often encountered, of a lack of spirituality.

Fr Häring read out the text and commented on it extensively and enthusiastically.

At 4.00 pm, at St Martha's again, until 7.30 pm. During the meeting, there was a telephone call from a Mgr Gillon.[4] I do not know what that is about. I cannot at the last minute change my arrangements, which had been difficult enough to set up in the first place. So, in the evening, at 8.15 pm, I telephoned Paris, Carnot 44 74. I was told that no one knew anything about this, that Mgr Gillon was at a meeting and would not be back until late. I said that I could not make any further changes to my arrangements.

(Mgr Gillon, Rector of the Lovanium, had wanted me to come to Paris for a meeting about the Institute for the History of Salvation in Jerusalem.[5])

In the evening, at 8.15 pm, a lecture to the students of the Belgian College.

---

1. Mieczyslaw de Habicht, a Polish naturalised Swiss, was the Permanent Secretary to the Conference of OIC (Catholic International Organisations) and lay Auditor at the Council.
2. The Belgian, Auguste Vanistendael, President of the International Confederation of Christian Trades Unions, was a lay Auditor at the Council.
3. Joseph Folliet, an outstanding figure in Social Catholicism in Lyons; Professor of Sociology at the Catholic faculties in Lyons, he was editor of *Chronique sociale de France* and Vice-President of *Semaines sociales*.
4. Luc Gillon, of the diocese of Malines-Brussels, Rector of the Lovanium University at Leopoldville (subsequently to become Kinshasa) in the Congo.
5. The Ecumenical Institute for Theological Research that was to be founded at Tantur, between Jerusalem and Bethlehem.

Wednesday 29 April 1964

At St Martha's, from 9 am until 12.10 pm. Departure for the airport with M. de Bavier. The unpleasant airport of Fiumicino: hundreds of metres on foot, extremely tiring noise, discomfort. Delay and waiting. That gave me the opportunity to meet l'abbé Baier,[1] a former student of L'Eau Vive,[2] who is now Assistant to Professor Haag[3] for Old Testament at Tübingen.

Zurich. Fr Eichenberger[4] met me at the airport and drove me to the house of the Fathers, Augustinerhof. There are three Fathers there with premises for high school and junior students. Three other Fathers live elsewhere: the beginning of a new Dominican foundation 730 years after the first one (by a Father from Strasbourg in 1229). Across the road from them, the presbytery and parish offices of the Old Catholics, with a very fine Augustinian church from the middle ages, devoid of believers, and which would make a very good Dominican church. . .

Indifferent train journey. I didn't get to the Priory until 10.00 pm, seven hours after my arrival in Zurich, a distance of 250 kilometres!

Sunday 3 May 1964

Telephone-call from Mgr Elchinger. We have been trying, in vain, to meet these past few days. Hence the telephone call.

In the conventional terms (that he always uses on the telephone) he told me of the audience he had had with the Pope. He spoke first of his project for a chair of Ecumenism in Strasbourg, and of conferring it on me. Because he had been told that, to overcome various objections, it would be necessary to go to the top. The Pope took note. At the allusion to the difficulties that would be encountered (from Pizzardo and Staffa, if I understood correctly) the Pope said: it will be necessary to wait a little longer. That will work out. It would seem that he was thinking of a change in the personnel of the Congregation.

The Pope is thinking of founding a Faculty of Theology in Jerusalem, in response to the wish of Skydsgaard, the wish for dialogue and for 'a historical and concrete theology'. He said: everyone must be able to speak frankly and to feel at ease. The Easterners do not feel like that amongst their own in Rome. So a place for dialogue must be sought outside Rome.

(This will be sponsored by a union or association of Catholic Universities. Is this what Mgr Gillon (of the Lovanium) wanted to talk to me about the other day?)

The Pope expressed himself in an astonishingly bold and forthright manner about the need to overcome a fossilised tradition; everything must be started again, as though we were in the first centuries of the Church.

---

1. Werner Baier of the diocese of Basle.
2. Cf above, page 33, note 1.
3. Herbert Haag taught Old Testament at Tübingen.
4. Ambrose Eichenberger, OP, of the Province of Switzerland, former pupil of Congar at Le Saulchoir.

Mgr Elchinger spoke of the drawing up of a new profession of faith. The Pope who seemed not to have thought of this, was very interested and highlighted it twice in the margin.

Cardinal Bea told Mgr Elchinger that the Pope had said to Cardinal Ottaviani: You must not go on like this. If you go on like this you will do harm to yourself, you will do harm to the 'Holy Office', you will do harm to the Church. But is Ottaviani ABLE to change?

I saw Mgr Elchinger on 6 May. He told me all this even more fully, even reading me passages from the notes he had submitted to the Pope, and those he had made immediately after the audience.

It was Cardinal Bea who told Mgr Elchinger what Cardinal Ottaviani had confided in him about the rebuke he had received from the Pope. But Ottaviani said to Bea, What do you expect? I am almost blind, I cannot read now. And then I am impulsive, I explode.

For the project of an ecumenical institution in Jerusalem: the Pope wants to do this in memory of his pilgrimage, and also in response to Skydsgaard. The Pope envisages a modest beginning: a simple faculty of theology, but destined to become a place of encounter where all spokespersons from other Christian communions would be able to set out their positions freely. The Pope realises that this cannot be done in Rome, where the Others will not come! Cardinal Cicognani suggested that this should be entrusted to the Franciscans, and established within the framework of the operations of the Custodianship. That is, either he undersands nothing of the new venture and its demands, or he knows nothing of the weight of defensive conservatism that the Custodianship carries. Cardinal Bea himself thinks that the institution is called to become a university and to extend its scope.

The Pope said to Mgr Elchinger: EVERYTHING MUST BE RETHOUGHT. There must be a new start, as though we had returned to the first centuries.

With regard to the ecumenical chair in the Theology Faculty at Strasbourg, Mgr Elchinger told me that he was aware of the reactions of the Faculty. For them, it is not scientific (basically nothing is scientific except the study of the past!). They would want merely to invite me to give some courses, and that *ratione personae* [in a personal capacity]. To which Cardinal Bea replied: it is as just as scientific as archaeology, which does have a chair!

Mgr Elchinger went to the Congregation for Seminaries and Universities, and saw Mgr Romeo. His reaction to the project: Why not? So, fairly favourable. However, when Mgr Elchinger asked him if he could say (to the Pope and to others) that the Congregation was in favour, Romeo said: one can say that the Congregation looks on it favourably, not that it approves. Mgr Elchinger said that he thought of entrusting the chair to me. Romeo's reaction: Certainly Fr Congar is well regarded, but, all the same, at the Congregation . . . — It was when Mgr Elchinger made allusion to this in the presence of the Pope that Paul VI replied: Patience!

Things will get better little by little.

As for Cardinal Bea, he said: For Fr Congar to be engaged simply to give some courses does not require the approval of the Congregation, nor need it be submitted to the Congregation.

I returned (on 20 May) from the symposium on collegiality at Constance.[1]

I note down here a number of points I learnt on that occasion.

1) From Dom O Rousseau. He explained to me (as I had suspected) that the telephone call received in Rome from Mgr Gillon on 28 April did refer to the Jerusalem Institute project.[2] That was what the Pope had spoken about to the cardinals at the mysterious meeting on 31 January last. But under the seal of absolute secrecy. Now, Mgr Esburgh (I am not sure of the spelling),[3] Rector of the University of Notre Dame, came to Rome, on 15 February I believe. He was received by the Pope, who even had him stay to lunch. He had made some changes of personnel that had not been approved by the Congregation, because it thought these men were too new. The Pope confirmed them. But, above all, the Pope spoke to him, under conditions of secrecy, about his Jerusalem project. He entrusted it to the Union of Catholic Universities. That was the reason for the meeting in Paris on 28 April. Present there were: the Rector of the University of Laval,[4] Gillon for Africa, a Jesuit from Lima, the Rector of Lille (Mgr Lefebvre[5], also l'abbé Lepoutre[6]), Dom Rousseau, Fr Daniélou, and myself, if I had gone.

It will probably be a matter of building on a piece of land given by the Knights of Malta, between Jerusalem and Bethlehem: thus in Arab territory. I noted immediately that Jordan is very much cut off from the world: there are no intellectual contacts. The École Biblique suffers very much from this. There they notice the change as soon as they cross from the Jewish side.

There was some thought of entrusting it to the Benedictines (six Fathers) because of their reputation for combining prayer, work and hospitality . . . At first it would be a kind of hostel, with a group of permanent scholars.

2) Fr Lécuyer told me that Pizzardo, having been at the Gregorianum a few days earlier for the feast of St Robert Bellarmine, had there repeated all the most stupid accusations of Romeo against the Biblical Institute.

---

1. A colloquium organised by Stanislas Dockx, OP, of the Province of Flanders; thereafter, he was to organise each year a colloquium of theologians, under the aegis of the International Academy of Religious Sciences, officially created in 1966, and of which he was to be the first secretary; certain of the works of this colloquium were to be published by Congar. Cf *La Collégialité épiscopale*, 'Unam Sanctam' (Paris: Cerf, 1965).
2. Cf above, page 525, note 5.
3. Congar added to the typescript: 'Hesburgh'. Theodore M Hesburgh, CSC, President of the University of Notre Dame and also of the International Federation of Catholic Universities.
4. Albert Vachon, priest of the diocese of Gravelbourg.
5. In fact, it was Mgr Georges Leclercq, a priest of the diocese of Lille.
6. Gérard Lepoutre, of the diocese of Lille, was the Vice-Rector.

The Congregation for Studies, with the imbecile Pizzardo, Staffa and Romeo, is the archetypal concentration of cretins.

3) Sunday 17 May 1964 (Pentecost): Conversation with Fr Vanhengel, secretary of *Concilium*. He described to me the difficulties the proposed journal has met with from the Roman side.

If I understood rightly, at the beginning of the year, the editorial committee composed a letter signed by four members and the editor, Brand, to put the Pope in the picture. It would seem that one cannot launch a journal, intended for bishops, and bringing together 200 theologians as collaborators, without Rome being kept informed. The reply came from Mgr Colombo, not in the name of the Pope, in February 1964, I think. Mgr Colombo laid down the following conditions: 1) that Küng be struck off the editorial committee (Rahner and the others refused: he was, in fact, the one who had initiated it in the first place); 2) that there should be a committee or a group of bishops drawn from different countries to exercise control over its theology and its suitability. Colombo suggested, for example, Mgr Wright for the USA, Scherer for Brazil; 3) that there should be among the collaborators, and even on the editorial committee, some representatives of Roman theology. Fr Gagnebet or Mgr Garofalo were suggested for the editorial committee (Fr Balić had been nominated first, Concilium had categorically refused, and Mgr Colombo had not insisted). Finally, they wanted the title to be changed. If these conditions were not complied with, not only would Rome not approve of the enterprise, but it would create a concurrent international review of Catholic theology which would respond to their theology.

I have forgotten the exact order of the discussions which Fr Vanhengel recounted to me. They were conducted on Rome's side by Mgr Colombo. He never once quoted the Pope, but he claimed to have spoken to the Pope, and it was obvious that these conditions did represent the Pope's thought. As a matter of fact, the announcement of the *Concilium* project did stir up great anxiety in the world of the Curia, and especially in the Holy Office. In fact, I put myself in the Romans' shoes. They already know that these are the theologians—and not their own!: others . . . —who have made the Council. They had seen a plan to continue the regime of indoctrinating the bishops, after the Council, in the direction of an open theology, that is to say, in a direction which would mean the end of their reign. They were particularly fearful of exegesis. This is their main preoccupation at the present time. (And yet, it does seem to me that this should be the most prudent area of *Concilium*, as the bishops are not ready for anything very critical, or for anything technical.) That is why Rome insists that the Roman member of the editorial committee should be Garofalo. I know him a little; I have had dealings with him since the Preparatory Commission over the question of Tradition. He is the confidant and the instrument of Cardinal Ottaviani. For myself, I would prefer to deal with Fr Gagnebet.

I said to Vanhengel that it seemed to me necessary, either to give up the project, or to give a guarantee. With Rome having this suspicion, and laying down these conditions, one cannot not do anything to satisfy them, without giving up the project. But how to give a guarantee, and hold on to liberty, or avoid being entangled in the logic of the system?

Vanhengel told me that he is certain that Fr Daniélou (who was opposed to the project from the start) is, in his opinion, the instigator of these difficulties. I asked him what indications he had of such activity. He cited four or five that were actually telling.

4) Fr Hajjar,[1] a Melchite, spoke to me about his work, which he had already discussed with me, ten years ago in Jerusalem. In particular, he told me of the influence this work had had on Maximos IV. Since the end of the last century, when he was twelve or thirteen years old, this man had been destined by the White Fathers to be Patriarch one day. He was Rome's man. But the historical work of Fr Hajjar, and the documents placed before his eyes, had opened those eyes round about 1954–1955. Maximos saw and understood that Rome and the Latins had sought only to tame the East, and to lead it towards Latinism. Then Maximos opened his ears to what Fr Kéramé was saying, though, beforehand, he had been harsh toward him.

He became the man who, at the Council, was the champion of the East, and, in a certain manner, the voice of Orthodoxy.

5) Moeller gave me further details about Mgr Willebrands' recourse to us on the Declaration about the Jews. I learned in this way that there was a CONTEXT to this . . . The bishops of the Secretariat had taken a special vote on 'deicide', and had decided, unanimously, except for one vote (Mgr Rhamani[2]), to retain this word. So Mgr Willebrands had to some degree taken advantage of us by not telling us this. It was due to his being caught between the Secretariat [for Unity] and the Secretariat of State: Cicognani was shaken by the report from the Nuncio in Cairo.[3] Mgr Willebrands should not now use our names (Moeller's and mine) to justify, against the Secretariat, the suppression of the word 'deicide'. At least, I had introduced the mention of the pardon of Christ on the cross, and both of us, Moeller and I, had insisted (against Cicognani) that, except for this WORD, the WHOLE of the text on the Jews should be kept, and that we should not be content with a few vague words. On this subject, the evocation of Hochhut's accusations in 'The Deputy'[4] is very unsettling.

But, on this very subject, I note here an interesting fact. It has to do with the very threatened situation of the Patriarchate of Constantinople, and the kind of

---

1. Joseph Hajjar, a Melchite priest of the diocese of Damascus, dedicated himself to the history of Christianity in the Middle East.
2. The name Rhamani does not appear in the *Annuario Pontificio;* the reference must be to Raphael Rabban, Chaldean Archbishop of Kerkuk, and a member of the Secretariat for Unity appointed by the Pope.
3. Mgr Brini.
4. Rolf Hochhut, *Der Stellvertreter,* Hamburg 1963; French translation : *Le Vicaire* (Paris: Seuil, 1963).

suffocation of the Patriarchate that the Turks are pursuing. Two bishops of the Synod, two who could one day provide for the replacement of the old patriarch, have been expelled by the Turks, even though they are Turkish subjects. When they arrived in Paris they said: there should be DIPLOMATIC action to help the Patriarch, but official protestations will do us more harm than good and risk aggravating the persecution.

The Hungarian bishops said something analogous during the First Session of the Council. These convergences are not without interest.

26 May 1964

I saw Mgr Elchinger, who has returned from the meeting of German-speaking bishops at Innsbruck. These German bishops have eight or nine schemas, while the French bishops have not yet received any (however Cardinal Feltin told me yesterday evening, at Le Cerf, that he had received these eight or nine schemas). The German-speaking bishops have reached agreement on the changes they want to secure. However, Cardinal König was not there. On the other hand, the German-speaking bishops from behind the Iron Curtain did come. These had intervened very little during the Second Session: Mgr Elchinger thought that this was deliberate.

The German bishops would like the chapter on the saints, presently planned as the conclusion of the *De Ecclesia*, suppressed, and replaced by a brief epilogue on the end and eschatological consummation of the Church (but it was pointed out to them afterwards that it was THEY [Frings] who had asked for it. Not in Larraona's form, certainly . . .). They are unanimous on this point, except for three.

On mixed marriages they are very divided, and rather cautious.

The schema on Schools and Universities: they consider that it says NOTHING and that it should be suppressed. Mgr Elchinger intervened in order to criticise the sort of exclusivism or absolute character of the rights of parents.

The schema on priests. They consider it inadequate.

On the government of dioceses: the German bishops are not much in favour of auxiliary bishops. For them, a vicar general is preferable.

Mgr Elchinger thinks, again this time, that the German bishops' meeting was very well prepared and organised, but that the meeting itself, as such, was not very interesting. It was rather monarchical and authoritarian.

Monday 1 June 1964

Got up at 4.00 am. Three solid hours of work before leaving at 8.20 am. A very difficult journey: not only was the weather everywhere dreadfully oppressive and stormy, but the agency had given me the wrong timetable (the train timetables changed this morning) so that at Basle I had to run to catch a plane for Zurich at the airport (by train I would have missed my plane). The plane was full, but they gave me a seat all the same. I cannot lift my right leg even a centimetre! It's terrible.

I was met at the airport in Rome. Arrived at the Belgian College at 3.45 pm. Left again for the Vatican at 4.00 pm.

There I found not only all my Belgian friends but also the members of the Commission. Absent were: Cardinals König, Léger (ill), Santos, Mgr Van Dodewaard, Doumith, Scherer, Florit. Various papers were distributed, in particular a letter from Mgr Felici who, on behalf of the Pope, asked for thirteen *emendationes* in the Chapter *De Episcopis*.[1] On this subject, Mgr Parente said to several people (Philips, Charue) that the Pope is at present the object of intrigues and of an all-out siege. They are trying to make him afraid. But Mgr Prignon has it from Mgr Charue (the chair of the Commission) that the Pope is not IMPOSING these *emendationes*. He is merely taking precautions.

Mgr Granados García, Auxiliary Bishop of Toledo, replaces Mgr Barbado, who has died. No one knows what he will be like.

Fr Tromp announced the order of the day for this session:
- discussion of *De Beata*;
- collegiality. The Pope has submitted two questions of exegesis to the Biblical Commission; we shall have its response;
- schema XVII (Tromp always calls it: *'famosum illud schema'* [that famous schema]), which has now become XIII (a lucky number in Italy!). We will have three days of Joint Commission for this;
- *De Revelatione*: Cardinal Bea announced the Secretariat's *placet in genere* [generally in favour] and did not ask for a joint meeting.

He added that the Pope wants the texts of *De Revelatione* and *De Ecclesia* to be sent to the Council Fathers *quam primum* [as soon as possible]. The latter will be sent chapter by chapter: chapters I and II at first, chapter III needs to be further discussed by us . . .

We began to look at *De Beata*. There were corrections of detail proposed by Mgr Philips (Philips, seconded by Moeller, got quite a lot of Laurentin's corrections accepted: Laurentin himself did not say a word).

Balić wanted to re-introduce *'mater Ecclesiae'*. There was good resistance from Philips, on the grounds of Tradition, also good interventions by Dom Butler, from Mgr Henríquez, Garrone, Semmelroth, Rahner and Moeller (in contrast, Franić and Ottaviani insisted on saying that it was the Pope's wish: Butler challenged the relevance or cogency of this). The text was accepted by twenty-three votes to twenty. The introduction of a new and very doubtful title was avoided.

Fr Baraúna, a Brazilian OFM,[2] suggested that a biblical commission should be created to check the biblical quotations, as had been done for some other chapters of the *De Ecclesia*. But, Mgr Philips said, such a sub-commission already exists . . . It will be consulted.

---

1. For this letter and the proposed amendments, cf *AS* V/II, 507–509.
2. Guilherme Baraúna, OFM, consultor for the Brazilian episcopate, Council expert.

Regarding the section on the Virgin and the Infant Jesus, Rahner said: one must be fair and ALSO quote the verses where the Virgin is seen to suffer some difficulty in the episode about Jesus in the Temple. He spoke vehemently and movingly. Balić, questioned by Ottaviani, was even more vehement: either the texts Rahner wanted should not be included, or they should be accompanied by the explanations of the Fathers and of the Magisterium. But Philips said that this episode NEEDED to be evoked. He got himself appointed to write a draft on the matter.

Ancel attacked the word *offerens* [offering] in regard to the role of the Virgin at the crucifixion.

On the whole, it did not go too badly. Fr Balić continued to lose points. He fought a rear-guard action, arguing from the encyclicals. But Dom Butler made an important intervention. We have not been given the task of echoing all the words of the Pope: *'habet curiam suam'* [he has got his own curia]. We are a Commission of the Council!

Tuesday 2 June 1964

This morning I read the thirteen corrections proposed by Felici on behalf of the Pope. As to their origin, Mgr Parente—who said that the Pope is subjected to very strong pressures: that is why bishops who have other views should also go to see him. Mgr Charue asked for an audience—Parente said to Mgr Philips that this came from Cardinal Browne (doubtlessly together with Fr Gagnebet). The intent of these corrections is perfectly coherent. They mean to locate the pope, not within the Church, but above the Church (*super Ecclesiam* [over the Church], in place of *in Ecclesia* [in the Church]; *uni Deo vinctus* [bound to God only] . . .). For this reason, they also replace, as far as possible, the *capitalitas* [headship] of the pope over the college of bishops (and thereby his *capitalitas* over the Church) by his *capitalitas* over the Church alone, in virtue of his being *vicarius Christi* [the Vicar of Christ].

This is the sort of ecclesiology which renders union with the Orthodox completely impossible.

9.30 am, at the Vatican. Mgr Prignon had just seen Fr Dhanis. The latter had got wind of the thirteen corrections. He thought they had come from a fear that had been sustained by certain exaggerations. The Pope must have been presented with a little florilegium of texts by Daniélou, Küng etc, which tend to subject the Pope to the Church to some degree (I had, at one time, drawn attention to a very faulty text by Daniélou, in the notes on the episcopate, but Daniélou had suppressed that passage in my text). Tromp had this to say regarding the question decided yesterday about Mary's 'offering'. Rahner was wrong in wanting to DISCUSS the question when Mgr Henríquez very rightly observed that it had been voted on, and we should not go back over it. In this one gets a sense of the degree to which mariology lives only on theological subtleties that are scarcely tenable.

Much debate about whether the Immaculate Conception should be mentioned: where? In what terms? (those of the Dogmatic Constitutions of Pius IX and Pius XII, or in patristic terms).

Balić wanted the Constitutions to be taken on board. Interventions by Poma, Butler, who spoke in favour of a mode of expression accessible to Protestants: an idea which totally escaped Franić.

Parente intervened very solemnly to ask that mediation (with or without the word itself) be dealt with differently from the way it has been. It seems that, in the text, all of Mary's mediation is reduced to her intercession. That is what all the other saints also do. He said: I, who have committed myself and am ready to commit myself in favour of collegiality, cannot be suspected of not being open. It should be stated, clearly and frankly, that the Virgin is associated with her Son in his role as the Redeemer,

-    she co-operates,
-    she is *omnipotentia supplex* [suppliant omnipotence],
-    she participates in the unique mediation of Christ, which remains unique, but into which the Virgin enters. The concept of instrument should be used here, which will salvage everything.

Ottaviani: 1) Let us deal with the concept of mediation,
        2) Parente should draw up a text that will be discussed (Browne said the same).

Henríquez: GENUINUS conceptus Mediationis [the AUTHENTIC concept of mediation] means: accepted by all Catholics.

Fernandez.[1]

Garrone: FIRST, Mary should be shown AS THE HEAD of intercessions, IN the Church; then, on the mediation that is PROPER to Mary (the mediation of cooperation) the question is not so clear among theologians that one could affirm it without difficulty.

Heuschen: A VOTE should be taken to see whether or not the present text should be kept as the basis for discussion.

Ottaviani invited Ciappi to speak, but it was pointed out to him that he was no longer there. So, it had been agreed IN ADVANCE that Ciappi should intervene!!!

Various interventions: Balić, etc.

Ancel: I am one of those who asked for the defining of mediation, because I have come to recognise this doctrine as true; but I have listened to the difficulties of others, and our discussion itself shows that the question is not fully ripe, and that we should not go beyond the text.

---

1.   Aniceto Fernandez, OP.

Philips: summed up what all are agreed on, and pointed out what there is in
   the text that justifies this.

Ottaviani: a sub-commission of three Fathers and three experts should
   examine this text and suggest corrections or additions: Parente, Ancel,
   Fernandez, with Philips, Balić, Rahner . . .

McGrath criticised the composition of this sub-commission, and suggested
   that it should be put under the presidency of Mgr Charue. The latter
   objected, and suggested a smaller group: Parente, Balić and Philips.

After the interval, Garrone and Henríquez were added to the sub-commission.
Each member will choose one or two *periti*.

After this great moment of discussion, things went quickly enough and three
Numbers were done in half an hour, when two-and-a-half hours had been spent
on a single section. It was finished at almost 12.20 pm. Rahner, with my support,
asked that the section on Mary and unity be taken out. At the suggestion of Mgr
Garrone, it was decided to consult Cardinal Bea about this.

As Mgr Charue had said that several of the Fathers were planning to leave on
6 June and for this reason had asked that the *De Collegialitate*[1] and the *De Revelatione* be looked at before they left—even if it meant dropping schema XVII for the
time being, Cardinal Ottaviani decided to start the *De Revelatione* this evening.

I found myself back in the atmosphere of militant cooperation and effective
tactics of my Belgian friends. At table, no one talked about anything except this.
At 3.00 pm a number of Fathers (not experts) met, to study together the thirteen
corrections made by Paul VI-Felici. Truly, they conduct the work of the Council
as they would a battle. Mgr Prignon had also, yesterday evening, alerted Cardinal
Suenens by telephone, and the Cardinal is going to write to the Pope . . .

I saw Fr Duprey very briefly. He came to express to me his fear about the place
in the *De Ecclesia* where it is said that the mystical body of Christ exists in the
Catholic Church, which is governed by the pope and the bishops in communion
with him. He fears that this text will have a negative and destructive impact on
the hard work currently being done with the East. For this hard work is based
on the following idea, formally accepted by Athenagoras, and, basically, by Paul
VI—that is to say: the Orthodox Church and the Catholic Church are the same
Church; the Orthodox Church is the Church in the East. It is simply that it is not
in communion with the See of Rome . . .

Fr Duprey communicated to me, under the seal of discretion:

1) The Pope sent an Easter greeting not only to Athenagoras but also to the
other Orthodox patriarchs. In his letter to Patriarch Alexis,[2] he added in his own

---

1. On collegiality; but the word *collegialitas* is not found in the Council texts; Congar
   here intended to refer again to No. 22, *De Collegio Episcoporum eiusque Capite* [on the
   college of bishops and its head].
2. Orthodox Patriarch of Moscow.

hand a phrase on 'the portion of Christ's flock which you govern'. These letters will not be published and circulated by ourselves until the Eastern patriarchs have published them. Some extraordinary responses have been received at the Vatican.

2) Patriarch Athenagoras wants to convene an Orthodox Prosynod this year, doubtless in Belgrade. His idea is to come to Rome himself, with several other patriarchs, towards the end of the Session, WITHIN THE FRAMEWORK OF THE COUNCIL (this would remove from his visit to the Pope the appearance of a visit just to the Pope as such). *THAT WOULD BE TREMENDOUS*!!!

3) The matter of the restitution of the head of St Andrew to Patras has gone forward. Fr Duprey has just returned from Athens and was, happily, able to keep the secret throughout. The matter is accepted. The Russians have declared that this gesture would have repercussions far beyond Greece.

I told him that, on the matter of the text of the *De Ecclesia*, we can now proceed only by way of *modi*. It would be necessary for the bishops of the Secretariat unanimously to sign such a *modus*. And the signatures of other episcopates could be obtained.

Before going into session at the Vatican, I saw Laurentin for a moment. I asked him why he does not speak and does not want to speak. He told me: every time, I have been reported to the Holy Office. This time I am accused of: 1) having inspired Fesquet for his article in *Le Monde* on birth control;[1] 2) having given out information about the work of the Theological Commission, as has Fr Congar.

Even though everyone in France criticises me for my absolute silence!!!

The *De Beata* was finished.

We came back to the section on Mary as mother of unity. Interventions by Rahner, Schröffer, Volk, Butler, Balić (selling mats or braces! A fairground tumbler!!!)

Finally it was agreed to accept Philips' proposition to combine the two last sections, adding only a sentence saying that Catholics pray to Mary for unity.

At 5.05 pm we began the *De Revelatione*. Mgr Charue gave a brief account of the work done so far.

I had been told that Fr Tromp would announce that experts were requested not to intervene. He did not do so.

Smulders gave the commentary. It was VERY long, and one's attention tired terribly.

At the interval, I found myself all alone with Ottaviani. I paid my respects to him: He said: have you got something to say to me? I replied: nothing, but do YOU, perhaps, have something to say to me?—He said: you are suspected of having sometimes communicated information to the press . . . I said to him: NOTHING, *EVER*.—He seemed to believe me, and, more relaxed, he added that my interventions are very satisfactory (they are rather discreet and rare . . .).

---

1. {Congar used the English term.}

Byzantine discussion. I was struggling. There was no fresh air in that room with all the windows sealed. Nothing more could be done and this discussion was boring. How did people still have the energy to go on discussing? I, myself, no longer have ANY. I am dead.

Wednesday 3 June 1964

No meeting of the Theological Commission this morning: Mass for the anniversary of the death of John XXIII. On the other hand, we do have a meeting of the sub-commission on the mediation of Mary. Mgr Garrone and Ancel asked me to come to it. It took place in the meeting room of the Holy Office, all redecorated, red hangings, hermetically sealed.

Present were Mgr Charue, Garrone, Ancel, Parente, Henríquez, Frs Tromp, Philips, Balić, Gagnebet, Rahner, Salaverri, Laurentin, Moeller, Rigaux. Arriving late (as always) Fr Fernandez, accompanied by Fr Philipon.[1]

> Parente read out a text he had prepared: awful, putting *in nuce* [in a nut shell] the whole theology of the mariologists. But Mgr Henríquez had also prepared a text: much better, very christological. Opinions were invited.
>
> Ancel: two difficulties with Parente's text: 1) the idea of *particeps mediationis Christi* [participant in the mediation of Christ]; 2) one cannot put forward in a conciliar text a doctrine that is not accepted by ALL. Nothing should be said about mediation, either for or against.
>
> Garrone: the same ideas. It is not yet mature. One should speak of the Virgin, of her intercession, in general terms; it should be suggested that, later on, it might, perhaps, be possible to go further.
>
> Fernandez: a better text should be made, out of the two proposed. There is more than just intercession in the mediation of Mary. (He did not say WHAT!)
>
> Parente: we should make a formal response to this question: is there something more than intercession?
>
> Philips explained at length what he had put into the text and what his thought was. Say that *'singulari modo cooperata est'* [she cooperated in a singular manner]. *Consentire DE RE* [agree ABOUT THE REALITY] while letting the words go.
>
> Rahner spoke with the kind of forcefulness and candour that demands to be heard.
>
> Myself: mediation: we have shown (earlier) how the Virgin was associated with the work of salvation on earth; with regard to her mediation in heaven, I learnt that she does not intervene in the communication

---

1. Michel Philipon, OP, of the Province of Toulouse, who taught theology at the Dominican *studium* of Saint-Maximin, then of Toulouse, was a Council expert.

of *SACRAMENTAL* graces. I have also heard it said that the Pope is AGAINST 'mediation'. Finally, I again insist that we should speak
a) about the unique mediation of Christ;
b) ABOUT A CO-OPERATION OF THE WHOLE MYSTICAL BODY;
c) about a singular and eminent co-operation of the Virgin Mary.

Fernandez [   ].

Henríquez: had often heard or read real heresies about mediation and co-redemption. We must not encourage such things!

Tromp: make a synthesis of the two texts: that of Henríquez demonstrates better the dependence on Christ, that of Parente explains better Mary's positive co-operation by her consent *TO THE SAVIOUR* to come. The WORD 'mediation' is correct, but it can be omitted. Mgr Ancel's difficulty about PARTICIPATION is not real: we participate in the divine life. . . The degree and nature of Mary's intercession are different from those of other members of the mystical body (this was aimed at me).

Charue: Henríquez' text has the advantage of deriving from the *textus receptus*. He proposed that Philips should make a single text out of the three. Which one should be taken as the basis? He suggested that of Henríquez.

Parente: the *textus receptus* should be the basis. He has already prepared a text which would do no more than simply add some expressions to the received text. (But he neither read out, nor distributed this text.)

Gagnebet: he set out what is held by all: that includes mediation (but, for Mary in heaven, it is confined to intercession).

Balić gave us a wonderful circus number. He began with a sorrowful account of his own role in this affair. UNITY WILL NEVER BE ACHIEVED: THE BISHOPS WILL TALK! If we do not want to talk about Mary's mediation we must also refrain from talking about the mediation of Jesus. Because to talk about the latter, while remaining silent about the former, would amount to denying the former. He cited the *votum* addressed to John XXIII by the Faculty of Theology of TOULOUSE; he cited Canisius[1]. . . What a clown!!! He added, for my benefit: the Pope has been mentioned, but the bishops are quite happy to speak for themselves about what they want. There was no more unanimity about the sacramentality of the episcopate, or about collegiality!

Henríquez [   ]

Parente: Philips should be given the task of drafting the text; he should improve the formulation of how Mary's co-operation goes *praeter intercessionem* [beyond intercession]. The titles *mediatrix* or *mediatio*

---

1. St Peter Canisius (1521–1597).

should be avoided, but it should also refrain from mentioning the mediation OF CHRIST.

Philips insisted that the three last lines of the paragraph be kept (bottom of page 53); he came back to this.

There was further discussion on the text of St Paul, I Timothy 2: 5–6.

Gagnebet: one should not avoid mentioning the mediation of Christ, even if the words *mediatrix, mediatio* were not used about the Virgin.

Fernandez: in the case of Mary, one should speak only of co-operation.

Charue proposed that it should say: '*Si B Virgo Maria titulo Mediatricis decorari consueverit, S Synodus declarat hoc intelligi non posse in sensu quo uni Christo Mediatori officit*' [if it has been the custom to honour the Blessed Virgin Mary with the title of mediatrix, the Holy Synod declares that this cannot be understood in a sense that obscures the fact that Christ is the one mediator]. (I suggested *quoad sensum* [with respect to the meaning] for the end of this sentence.)

Balić's face lit up. He and Parente declared themselves in favour of this solution, which would bring peace.

But Garrone objected to it, as did Philips. 'They want the WORD', he said.

Ancel supported Philips. Don't use this TITLE. There would be peace only in appearance. As Philips asked, keep the last three lines of the section.

Tromp took up Charue's idea in a more indirect manner: 'If the Virgin is invoked as 'Mediatrix' BY THE FAITHFUL...'

Laurentin intervened in a somewhat confused manner. If one did not just say 'mediatrix', but EXPLAINED the two titles *Mediatrix* and *Mater Gratiae* [Mother of Grace] side by side, one would have a better balance. But, when Parente interrupted to criticise this, Laurentin got the huff and said: if I am not allowed to speak I will shut up!

(Laurentin was, at that moment terribly nervous, anxious, suspicious. He looked from one to the other, from Ottaviani to Parente, as though he had to justify himself and wanted to be restored to grace...)

Moeller: the history of the councils has taught me that it is better not to employ new expressions unless it is absolutely necessary. Avoid the title '*Mediatrix*'. Our separated brethren are waiting for us here...

Tromp: the Protestants will say that, if we avoid the word, we are not sincere: we avoid the word, but we hold on to the reality.

Henríquez (rather nervous): yesterday it was voted to keep Philips' text as the basis. Introduce into it some precisions taken from Parente, while avoiding things that are the subject of dispute among ourselves. And put the unique mediation of Christ in first place.

Ancel: we should agree to vote first on whether to use, or avoid, the word '*Mediatrix*'. Then, if the vote is in favour of using the word, we should adopt Charue's formulation.

Charue: we should vote first, *HERE*, in the sub-commission. Only Fernandez
and Parente are in favour of the word '*Mediatrix*' . . .

It was agreed:

1) to take Philips' text as the basis;

2) to speak FIRST of the mediation of Christ;

3) to speak positively about Mary's co-operation, without the word '*Mediatrix*';

4) to keep the three last lines of the existing section;

5) that Mgr Philips will propose a text.

On my arrival at the Belgian College, I met Fr Duprey who had come to see me. He wanted to draw my attention to some other passages in the *De Ecclesia* that would create difficulties for the Orthodox. It is evident that we are at a point with them which offers an extraordinary historic opportunity. The Patriarch of Moscow said: we want dialogue, but we are waiting for the end of the Council before engaging in it, so as only to take it up when there is some chance of success. Because failure would be worse than anything.

I had Duprey stay for lunch so that he would have the opportunity to speak of his difficulties in the presence of such effective people as Charue, Heuschen, Philips, Moeller and Prignon. In fact, after the rather disappointing first part of the meal, during which my Belgian friends thought only of recalling the events of this morning, this happened. Duprey repeated almost the whole of what he had said to me yesterday. It made a great impression. It was agreed that the Secretariat should keep in contact with the Theological Commission and with the episcopates. Efforts will be made to see to this in an effective manner.

Duprey chatted briefly with me about the Jerusalem project. We are in agreement about the objections to be made. He told me that Fr Bouyer is in Rome and has seen the Pope. I will try to meet Bouyer. For my part, I passed on to Duprey the papers on the thirteen points (concerning Chapter III) for him to show to Cardinal Bea: Bea should see the Pope tomorrow, or on Friday at the latest. It will then be seen how much of this comes from the Pope. (Mgr Charue and Philips will have a meeting with Bea as early as this evening.)

On this subject, Mgr Charue reported the following details to us: not only was Parente not aware of the thirteen corrections before they were distributed, but Ottaviani seems not to have been aware of them. On the other hand, Cardinal Browne was not satisfied with the proposed text. It seems he wished for SOMETHING MORE. That would give one to understand that the text of the thirteen corrections is a compromise, or the remainder of some more lively propositions. Extracts from some articles were sent to the Pope in order to worry him. Mgr Charue said that Ottaviani had his audience on Friday, and that he probably asked the Pope to what extent is one bound by the text of the thirteen corrections.

In the car that took us to the Vatican, Mgr Philips said that yesterday evening Mgr Colombo had REPEATED to him that the Pope does not want the words '*Mediatrix, Mediatio*'.

On reaching the Vatican, Mgr McGrath told me that a letter from the Holy Office yesterday evening had restored to Frs Lyonnet and Zerwick,[1] the right to teach.

At the beginning of the meeting Cardinal Ottaviani said that, to speed the work up, the experts will speak only if they are asked a question.

At my side, Rahner was champing at the bit, and said to me 'what are we doing here . . . ?'

There was much confused discussion about a proposed text of Parente's about primitive revelation.

Discussion on the chapter *De Traditione* began at 5.05 pm. But the ban on experts speaking greatly diminished my attention. However, the meeting became impassioned when Franić asked a question of Schauf (who had passed a note to him) to know if it must be said that there are TRUTHS that the Church knows with certainty only through Tradition.

Rahner got himself invited to speak by Cardinal König, who had just arrived. After this, Charue protested against the reopening of a question on which the sub-commission had decided to observe, and had in fact unanimously observed, discretion. Schauf then intervened (Ottaviani gave him leave to speak without his having asked for it, or having got himself asked a question by one of the Fathers); he set out his position and concluded: if what the ordinary Magisterium has been teaching for four centuries is not Catholic doctrine, then neither has the teaching of the Council any value: and I will say so!

Butler intervened along the same lines as Charue. And when the testimony of Florit, who was absent, was invoked here, Ottaviani said that Mgr Florit had declared at the time of the conference of the Italian bishops that it was his opinion that there are, in Tradition, truths that are not contained in Scripture.

Ottaviani told Mgr Heuschen that Florit had said to him, in reference to the work of the sub-commission: 'my hand was forced'. —That is a bit strong!!! Florit is not candid.

After this (it was 6.00 pm) Ottaviani said there would be a break. Both sides set about rebuilding their support, each along its own lines.

After the break, Ottaviani said: Since no agreement can be reached, and we are doing this in conjunction with the Secretariat for Unity, there will have to be two *relationes in aula*, one for the majority and one for the minority, as the regulations provide.

---

1. Maximilian Zerwick, SJ, was an exegete, and a specialist in Biblical Greek. Lyonnet and Zerwick had been forced to give up teaching at the end of the academic year 1961–1962, at the request of the Holy Office.

Charue: the Pope ought to be asked!

Ancel asked for two (secret) votes:

1) are there some truths that are not found in Scripture?

2) ought the Council make a declaration about this, or keep silent about it?

Henríquez: there should be a vote on the text! *Placet* or *non placet*.

Butler: there should be a vote, a secret vote, *utrum legatur an non* [should it be read, or not]?

Šeper: if neither we ourselves, nor the Joint Commission, have been able to reach agreement, it will cause scandal if it is discussed in the *aula*.

Therefore, take two votes: the one that we are expecting, and another on the point: should there, or should there not, be two *relationes in aula*?

It was pointed out to him that, if this second vote were negative, this would result in choking off the minority.

A vote was taken: is the text as it stands acceptable on the point under debate? Result: 17 *placet*, 7 *non placet*.

The meeting ended with brief questions on the rest of the Chapter *De Traditione*; this ending of the discussion was hurried through for the sake of getting the Chapter finished.

After the meeting, Mgr Charue, Heuschen and Philips went to see Cardinal Bea. They will be able to speak to him not only about the thirteen *emendationes*, but also on this question of Tradition. For the Secretariat has a stake in it. It has given its approval to and expressed confidence IN THE TEXT OF THE SUB-COMMISSION. But if this text is called into question precisely on the point to which the Secretariat became party in the Joint Commission, the Secretariat obviously has the right (and the duty) to want to become party to it again.

Franić and Schauf reopened a discussion without result!!!

Mgr Heuschen and Philips came back from Cardinal Bea rather disappointed. He refused to try to find out from the Pope if the thirteen corrections did indeed come from him, and are virtually imposed. He thinks that the terms of Felici's letter move along these lines. With regard to the debate reopened on the subject of Tradition and Scripture, he said that, since the COMMISSION ITSELF has not altered its text, the agreement with it is not broken. Therefore he is not going to intervene further.

At 10.00 pm Mgr Heuschen was called to his mother's bedside. We examined together the thirteen corrections, comparing our reactions with those of Medina.

Thursday 4 June 1964

It is only today that I have recovered a LITTLE from the exhaustion into which I was thrown last Monday.

Mgr Philips reported to me that Ottaviani said to him yesterday, with reference to the discussion of Tradition: all the trouble comes from the plot by which, at the time of the setting up of the Commissions, a group of Belgians, French, Germans and Dutch was brought into the Theological Commission . . . A strange thing to say, and rather revealing. It is obvious that the Curia (and the Holy Office) had their own plan, and counted on imposing on the Council their own personnel and their own texts, with only simple corrections of detail. The freedom to elect to the Commissions was a decisive victory. It allowed the Council to be, laboriously, a slow but progressive victory of the *Ecclesia* over the Curia.

A Joint Commission (Theology and Laity) for schema XVII—which has now become XIII. Fr De Lubac, who was beside me, thought that it was lacking a certain sense of Christian self-respect: all the same, the Church knows, in Jesus Christ, what is the truth of humankind.

I saw a crowd of faces not normally encountered: Frs Lebret,[1] Thomas, SJ,[2] Mgr Larraín, Câmara, etc.

Garrone proposed, in order for the Theological Commission to be able to continue its work, that joint meetings should be held only in THE MORNING, and that a certain priority in speaking should be given there to the members of the Theological Commission—this would also allow the Commission on the Laity to have a daily meeting on its own, that is, with a smaller number of people present, which would speed up the work.

This suggestion was accepted.

A discussion that was not without interest. These criticisms especially were made of the beginning of the schema:

1) it is too optimistic;

2) it does not distinguish sufficiently between the supernatural order of salvation, which is the subject of the Church's work, and the natural order of the construction of the terrestrial city, which falls to the faithful as a task to be accomplished in the spirit of Christ;

3) the ambiguity of the 'world' is not sufficiently emphasised.

4) it uses biblical texts outside of their own meaning, and in particular it applies to the TERRESTRIAL history or task many texts whose meaning is eschatological;

---

1. Louis-Joseph Lebret, OP, of the Province of Lyons; his work on socio-economic structures had led him to found the Economy and Humanism Centre during the war; thereafter, interested mainly in questions of development in the Third World, he founded IRFED, the Institute for Research and Formation, and exercised an international influence; he was Director of Research at CNRS, and the Holy See called on him to represent it at various international conferences; he was appointed a Council expert at the beginning of 1964.

2. Joseph Thomas, SJ, Chaplain General of the Social Union of Catholic Engineers (USIC) and of the Movement of Engineers and Leaders of Industry of Catholic Action (MICIAC), which decided to unite to become, in 1965, the Movement of Christian Executives, Engineers and Directors (MCC).

5) (Rahner) it deals with things too much on a moral, even moralistic, plane, without indicating that moral questions arise from an OBJECTIVE or real situation that is technically very difficult. For example, the problem of hunger.

I left the room at 11.25 am, to go, as I had been invited, to see Mgr Poupard at the Secretariat of State. He questioned me and showed me round the areas accessible to outsiders. I insisted on saying that the Pope's gestures to create a new ecumenical situation do not have the requisite ecclesiological foundation. An ecclesiology of the Church as a communion of churches is needed. Yet even the liturgical movement is boxed in, whereas we are working with a very medieval and counter-reformation ecclesiology, which is absolutely inadequate.

I added: if the Pope receives me, this is one of the things I would like to be able to say to him.

Lunch at the French Seminary, with Mgr Garrone, Ancel, Ménager, Rodhain[1] and Haubtmann. A very different atmosphere from that of the Belgian College. There conciliar tactics are put into action, and that is all that is done. Here the talk is about the most general pastoral problems . . . At coffee, Mgr Lefebvre, Superior General of the Holy Spirit Fathers. I found it amusing to talk to him, knowing who he was, and that, in his report to the Pope preceding the Council, he had asked for the condemnation of my errors . . .

At 3.45 pm Fr Bouyer arrived with Fr Duprey. I saw him only rather briefly (the time it took to go by car from the French Seminary to the Belgian College, where I needed to look out my papers on Tradition and Scripture, for I supposed that the whole day would be devoted to schema XVII) and then to the Vatican. Fr Bouyer saw the Pope yesterday. He found him just as open, just as eager for contact and direct information as he had been in Milan. Astonishingly open to the ecumenical point of view.

On arriving in the room, I saw Rahner for a moment about schema XVII. He was extremely disappointed and dissatisfied. He found it verbose and moralising. We were agreed in thinking that Fr Häring is in some degree prejudicial to the cause. For it is from him that this kind of thing comes.

Since the meeting started ten minutes late, Fr Fernandez was on time.

Cardinal Browne's *Animadversiones* were distributed.

Chapter III was discussed. Stubborn, repeated and boring intervention by Fr Fernandez to assert, right from the beginning, that THE FIRST THING that an EXEGETE has to do is to be submissive to the Magisterium.

Fr Fernandez is really tiresome.

Betti was asked to give an account of his visit to Mgr Florit. He confirmed the two contradictory statements attributed to Florit by Charue and by Ottaviani: he

---

1. Jean Rodhain, a priest originally from the diocese of Saint-Dié, Secretary General of French Catholic Aid which he had founded in 1946; he was a Council expert.

was in agreement on the text of the sub-commission, but he had also given to the Italian bishops the text of the remarks he had made on the schema the previous year. His own view is that Tradition *latius patet quam Scriptura* [is wider than Scripture].

He himself declines to set out his personal view in the conciliar text and will fall in with yesterday's majority.

Friday 5 June 1964

Moeller and I finished a general note about the thirteen points to be corrected (and also in reply to a paper from Cardinal Browne).

Joint Commission on schema XVII. We were given an account of the corrections made yesterday by the Commission for the Apostolate of the Laity.

I said to Fr de Riedmatten that Cardinal Suenens will doubtless reject Chapter I at the Co-ordinating Commission. He answered: no. I saw him last Sunday; Cardinal Suenens said: there are still two official levels at which the text can be corrected and improved: that of the bishops' comments, and that of the discussion *in aula*. So it can be corrected. But, on the other hand, if one were to reject it now, even partially, one would run the risk of there being no schema XVII (XIII) at all. Because certain people do not want there to be one, and it is possible that the Pope himself will be satisfied with a declaration or a message.

The text that we reviewed was open to the same criticisms as yesterday; confusion, lack of distinction between the order of creation and the order of supernatural salvation.

4.30 pm. Vatican. Theological Commission.

I checked back with Cardinal Browne who explained to me what part he had played in the questions again addressed to us about the college of bishops and the pope. Browne has been to see the Pope and put to him his difficulty concerning a passage in the former No. 16 (new No. 22, page 21, lines 11–15): he would prefer it to say: the college of bishops CAN be the subject of the supreme power, if and when the pope summons it to be such. It has within itself something that disposes it to be such, but it is such only if the pope summons it to be such.

The discussion of the *De Revelatione* was completed.

Mgr Charue reopened the whole question of Scripture-Tradition, wishing absolutely and with a curious stubbornness to deny that Tradition has a claim to belong to the SOUL of theology, in order to reserve this role to Scripture alone.

Afterwards, a vote to choose between the texts composed by Parente or Smulders in response to the difficulties raised by primitive revelation (No. 3).

This resulted in eleven votes for Parente's text and eleven for Smulders'.

People said: my, how well they have agreed with each other!!!

At 5.45 pm we began reading and examining the thirteen corrections. Then there was an interval, during which I said to five or six people that the text voted on the historicity OF THE GOSPELS COULD NOT GO THROUGH: *sic* to Garofalo, Garrone, Daniélou, Rigaux, Grillmeier, Kerrigan, Cardinal König. (When we returned, Mgr Philips told me that Garofalo had given him a text somewhat different from the one which had been voted on, and which corresponded with what I wanted. That is good, but one can see immediately that the Romans do not have much scruple about changing a text already voted on . . . !!!)

The question was asked whether the thirteen corrections are, or are not, imposed by the Pope. Ottaviani had asked him: the points are left to our free discussion. It seems that our responses will be submitted to him before being sent to all the bishops.

Parente intervened because he was implicated, since these questions touched on a text approved almost unanimously by the sub-commission UNDER HIS PRESIDENCY. But rumours had immediately been spread calling into question the orthodoxy of the text. It was insinuated that collegiality put in question the primacy of the pope. The Pope had questioned Parente on this point. Parente had replied that the text was orthodox, and did not call papal primacy into question.

The corrections proposed did not substantially change the text. Even if they were adopted, the doctrine of the text would remain substantially the same.

Mention of the primacy of the pope was made at least sixteen times in the text.

He reviewed the points and criticised them, showing that they were unnecessary. What they are seeking is already to be found there. He took them one by one and demolished the correction that had been requested. The authors of these observations seemed to think that the existence of the college would limit or place conditions on the primacy. That was what inspired them.

He moved on to Cardinal Browne's observations: the schema speaks of a SINGLE subject of *potestas* [power]. But even if it spoke of two subjects (which it does not) it would not follow that it is asserting two *potestates* [powers].

Finally, what is being suggested is in no way necessary and not very important. But since this is all that is being asked of us, this confirms the orthodoxy of the text.

Mgr Ancel wanted to add some general remarks. Since the POPE had suggested these corrections to us we could examine them and improve them, eliminating what would make the text worse. The Pope should be thanked for leaving us free to discuss these points. Our President should express this to the Pope. — The votes should be secret. —Our Council does not want to speak about the primacy and infallibility of the pope, but of the bishops. Therefore, the additions that would needlessly reiterate the power of the pope SHOULD NOT BE RETAINED.

(Mgr Ancel said all this in a whining tone which was embarrassing. I think he is lacking in Christian simplicity and self-respect.)

Cardinal Browne: did not want to get involved in a controversy. He had made no difficulty (and had expressed none) except on ONE point. It should be proved from Scripture (the Biblical Commission had said: *non constat* [it is not certain]) and from Tradition that the college is the subject of the supreme power together with the pope. Mgr Staffa's objections should be answered.

We moved on to the discussion of the points. I noted the results in red pencil on my copy.

I made the most of the fact that one passage in the thirteen points brought into question again one of the places to which Fr Duprey had drawn my attention as being capable of disqualifying the Orthodox with respect to Ministries and Church. Short discussion. Schauf intervened: the schismatics have no power of magisterium or of jurisdiction. It is simply a matter of *Ecclesia supplet* [the Church makes good].[1] What horizon of thought is this? What a miserably mechanistic approach!!! For him the Orthodox Churches do not have the true quality of Church. And he pronounces this with assurance, with smugness!!! Mgr Philips replied to him: all the same, the fact that the Orthodox faithful believe in Christ and in the Holy Trinity on the word of their pastors, and that they do it in the way they do, that is not nothing!!! He said to me later: this Schauf has no sensitivity in his guts!—I replied: no: those sausage casings are empty!

A strange meeting. Mgr Parente was very firm. He had been appalled that a text established by his sub-commission, and for which he had been responsible, had been criticised without his knowledge.

In the evening Fr Bazille[2] (who by mistake, had been kept waiting in vain for an hour) brought me my ticket for the audience at midday tomorrow. He had telephoned Mgr Poupard THIS MORNING: Poupard asked about it. Nothing had been done. The request for an audience had been made only this morning . . .

Saturday 6 June 1964

Before leaving I prepared some arguments and texts (Zinelli) which could be useful in the discussion. At the beginning, those who will make the *relationes* were named:

De Ecclesia:

Chapter I:	Charue
Chapter II:	Garrone
Chapter III:	Sacramentality, König
	Collegiality: Parente
	Priests and Deacons: Henríquez
Chapter IV:	(laity) Wright
Chapter V:	(religious) Gut
Chapter VI:	(Mary) Roy

De Revelatione:

Chapters I & II: Florit, with Franić for the minority
Chapters IV-VI: Van Dodewaard.

---

1. A canonical saying, indicating that Church makes good what is lacking.
2. Marie-Joseph Bazille, OP, of the Province of France, was the French language secretary of the General Curia of the Order.

Maccarrone, claiming to speak at the request of Cardinal Browne (who returned to his doubt arising from the *non constat* of the Biblical Commission), suggested introducing the following passage into No. 22 (*De collegio episcoporum* [on the college of bishops]).

'*Ordo autem episcoporum qui collegio apostolico in magisterio et regimine pastorali succedit, imo in quo corpus apostolicum continuo perseverat, una cum capite suo Romano Pontifice et nunquam sine hoc capite, cum collegialiter agit suprema hac plena potestate in universam ecclesiam pollet, iuxta capitis ordinationem exercenda.*' [But the order of bishops, which succeeds to the Apostolic College in teaching and pastoral rule, or rather, in which the apostolic body continues without interruption, together with its head, the Roman Pontiff, and never without this head, when it acts collegially, is possessed of this full and supreme power over the universal church, to be exercised according to the regulation of the head.]

He explained the text at great length.

> Charue: raised the question of principle. There is no need to repeat the fundamental question in order to reply to the Pope's thirteen points.
> The Biblical Commission's response IN NO WAY contradicts our text. It should not be used to put this text under question again.
> Parente: the only real change is the introduction of the phrase '*quando collegialiter agit*' [when it acts collegially]. Nevertheless, the received text has been changed (which was not required of us, and is contrary to its having been accepted by vote).
> Henríquez: it goes a long way beyond the points made by the Pope. There should be a vote on the principle of reopening the discussion!!!
> Poma: it should not talk about the *actus collegialis* [collegial action], but de *ipsa potestate, de subiecto potestatis* [about the power itself, about the subject of power]!
> Ciappi: having been called on by Ottaviani to speak, he read out a text: *Mirum est* [it is astonishing] that the schema had been approved almost unanimously by the Theological Commission, when neither Scripture nor Tradition proves that the college is the subject of supreme power (he developed this idea with a very brief documentation). Besides, Fr Ramirez, a theologian of renown, is against it. The bishops, in Commission, are only theologians, and their conclusions are only as valid as their reasons. Here these are insufficient.
> (All this was said in an aggressive tone of superiority and smugness!)
> Ancel: (who before the meeting had confided to me that he had said to Cardinal Browne: if Patriarch Athenagoras were to hear that we are calling collegiality into question he would back-pedal!): we must scrupulously keep this secret. If the Orthodox learn that we are again casting doubt on the doctrine of collegiality, unanimously approved in the Commission . . .

There was scarcely time to respond to the Pope's questions . . .
We must prepare these responses. If we could get back to that!!!

Betti: it is the SUBJECT that should be spoken of, not the exercise. The Biblical Commission's replies could be clarified . . . Pius XII spoke about *suprema potestas* [supreme power] (Speech to the Rota, 2 October 1945). And the Vatican cited the text of Zinelli (*Mansi* 52, 1109) which I had been ready to cite from Torrell, page 153[1] . . .

König: in proposing these comments, the Pope had, in a sense, approved the text of the Commission. We should continue the examination of the points proposed!

This examination was taken up again.

Philips on *'praesertim concilia oecumenica'* [especially ecumenical councils].
Point 5 [ ]

Point 6: 'They' want to re-introduce Vatican I and not go a step beyond it. And yet, the whole future of ecclesiology, and that of ecumenism, is bound up with going beyond (without negating) Vatican I.

Philips: appealed to a biblical mode of speaking: refer to the pope as *pastor* rather than *caput* [head]. He spoke with emotion: 'I have never sought anything except concord'.

Ottaviani sided with him.

Butler: in the proposed additions, there is continual repetition of Vatican I. This is NOT what should be done. It will give the impression to our separated brethren that we are not sincere in what we say about collegiality.

Parente: if the chapter is read as A WHOLE these additions appear pointless. They have been proposed only because a few sentences have been read as cut off from the others, and from the whole.

Volk supported Butler in a somewhat confused manner. He spoke against such an emphasising of only the juridical aspects, even in the primacy.

Ottaviani: appealed to Colombo.[2] Colombo: Vatican II must try to combine and harmonise primacy and collegiality. What is suggested in the thirteen points is intended to facilitate this. There have been certain expressions at the Council which call for some adjustments.

(But, myself, I find that the proposed corrections do nothing except repeat the doctrine of primacy without casting ANY light on the harmonisation of the two.)

---

1. Cf Jean-Pierre Torrell, *La Théologie de l'épiscopat au premier Concile du Vatican*, 'Unam Sanctam', 37 (Paris: Cerf, 1961)
2. Carlo Colombo, after becoming a bishop, continued to share in the work of the Doctrinal Commission and thus ensure an official link with the Pope.

Point 7: Philips spoke along the lines of Medina's remarks. The formula
should be supplemented in such a way as not to exclude a directive
made BY THE COUNCIL at the invitation and with the approval of
the pope.

D'Ercole began a course of history of the constitution of the Church: the
communal government of the early church. He was stopped after the
False Decretals.[1]

Fernandez came to the aid of Browne.

Colombo recalled the terms of the explanation which had accompanied the
vote on 30 October: *'regitur ab ordinationibus Romani Pontificis haec
potestas collegii.' —Est enim potestas intrinsece subordinata voluntati
capitis* [this power of the college is controlled by the ordinations of the
Roman Pontiff. For it is a power intrinsically subordinated to the will
of the head].

Philips: yes, the expressions of 30 October should be taken up again.

Browne: the Biblical Commission considered *non constat* [it is not certain]
that the power of the college is *potestas suprema* [the supreme power].

Lécuyer explained the reply of the Biblical Commission, and cited the text
of the schema *De Ecclesia* of Vatican I, prepared by Kleutgen, on the
identity of the supreme power of Peter and of the other Apostles.

Salaverri, (appealed to by Franić) commented on Kleutgen's intention in the
sense *'cum episcopi a S Pontifice in partem sollicitudinis vocati'* [when
the bishops are called by the supreme pontiff to share his care (for the
Church)]. Thus, they SHARE in the *plenitudo potestatis S Pontificis*
[fullness of power of the supreme pontiff].

Betti repeated Zinelli's text.

A vote was taken to choose between Parente's proposition: *'quae quidem potestas
independenter a Romano Pontifice exerceri nequit'* [this power cannot be exercised
independently of the Roman Pontiff], and that of Colombo, *'cuius actuale exerci-
tium regi debet secundum ordinationes a Romano Pontifice approbatas'* [its actual
exercise must be governed by regulations approved by the Roman Pontiff].

The result was: thirteen votes for Parente, seven for Colombo, with two abstentions (including that of Browne who had declared that he wished to abstain).

Point 9: *remanet* SUIS [remains TO HIS] (I intervened on this subject.)
Point 10: on *CAPUT* [HEAD]: Tromp quoted the bull *Unam Sanctam*.[2] Our
constitution is not sufficiently christological . . .

---

1. An apocryphal canonical collection dating from the ninth century, long attributed to
   Isidore of Seville.
2. In this bull, dating from 1302, Pope Boniface VIII affirmed that the pope, the Vicar of
   Christ on earth, was the sole head of the Church, and that all human creatures should
   be subject to him.

Papa uni Domino devinctus [the pope is subject to the Lord only].

Henríquez: proposed *'cuius auctoritas a nulla alia ecclesiastica auctoritate pendet'* [whose authority depends on no other ecclesiastical authority].

Rahner: If one wanted to prevent any application to Protestants one could not have put it better!

Charue: this will be a new *ex sese* [of himself].

Point 12: I intervened, as did Moeller, for the retention of *caput collegii* [head of the college]. This was done.

Examination of the thirteen points was completed.

At 12.30 pm, Parente broached the subject of the text proposed by Philips on 'mediation'. He said he did not agree with the way things had been done. There must be a formal mention of mediation.

Charue: is the Pope not against it? Have recourse to him.

Franić and Ottaviani: there should be two texts and two *relationes*.

It was suggested that we should meet at 4.00 pm[1] and discuss the question. But there would not be time and people's arrangements would be disturbed.

Ottaviani: who wants the text to contain the WORD or the title *Mediatrix*?

The result of this was 13/22 (including Ottaviani).

This end of session was hurried through between 12.30 pm and 12.42 pm.

I should have had my audience at 12 o'clock, but at 9.45 am I had a telephone call here to say that the audience had been deferred. I said: very well, but I am leaving on Tuesday morning.

We will see. But if I do not get my audience this time, I shall not ask for it a second time.

Fr de Lubac is invited to lunch. But I could have believed that I was at the Priory in Strasbourg: it is ludicrous how little people know about welcoming a guest and showing interest in him. Each one belches out what is of interest to himself, and takes no notice of the other.

We all noted how much the atmosphere of the Theology Commission has deteriorated. In March there was an atmosphere of co-operation and trust. In April, also in the sub-commission. Today we are back to the old days of distrust and strife. This has arisen from the offensive mounted against collegiality.

Mgr Charue thinks that the thirteen points were drawn up in the entourage of Felici, the secretary of the Council. The name of a certain Mgr Carbone[2] was mentioned.

Parente said to someone who repeated it to me: I hear now that the Holy Office must hear authors before condemning them.

---

1. Congar added to the typescript: 'that is to say, half an hour before the meeting of the Commission for schema XIII'.

2. Vincenzo Carbone of the diocese of Monte Vergine (Italy) worked at the General Secretariat and at the Administrative Tribunal of the Council; he was a Council expert; he would later become responsible for the Archives of the Second Vatican Council.

4.30 pm, VATICAN, JOINT COMMISSION ON SCHEMA XIII (XVII)

Guano: some propositions.

> Details of grammar should not be discussed. The members of the Theological Commission should be called to speak first. The discussion should go on until 8.30 pm. Thanks to Semmelroth and Rahner for being willing to collaborate. They are open to criticisms.

The examination began again at No. 22, *Dignitas matrimonii et familiae* [the dignity of marriage and the family].

Franić opposed Häring, who seemed to want to have the Council canonise his position, according to which love is the essential element of marriage: a point of view which he defended against Fr Hürth. Furthermore, there was too much talk about natural love and not about conjugal CHARITY. The style of the whole schema was 'Häringian' . . . It should be a more Catholic work.

> (This attack of Franić's was violent and crude. It did him a good deal of harm, and rather rallied sympathy for Häring.)

Ottaviani got Fr Lio to make an intervention: love is necessary for marriage in the moral order, but not in the constitutive order.

McGrath: all the Fathers of the sub-commission and almost all the *periti* are agreed that the style should be changed to one of positive exposition of the values concretely bound up in the conjugal life. Fr Häring cannot be considered the only person responsible for the work of the whole sub-commission.

Poma: all the same, a distinction should be made between method and substance. The substance is good and the *modus* [method] excellent.

Hirschmann justified at length the doctrine, and the way the exposition unfolded.

Ottaviani had Tromp read out some replies of the Holy Office approved by Pius XII. THIS IS THE GREAT CONCERTED OFFENSIVE: Franić, Lio, Tromp . . . , in short, the Holy Office.

I asked to be allowed to speak.

The text was read out. After it was read, Ottaviani gave a reminder that the *periti* could not speak unless invited to do so by one of the Fathers (this was not the only time he had cut me out).

Šeper: we are pastors. Do we want to put doctrine in a sort of inaccessible ghetto, or do we want to engage with humankind? That is the question of THIS SCHEMA. I am not denying anything the Holy Office said twenty years ago. But today's problem is to speak to people whose lives, at the present time, are lived and unfold outside the Church.

Ancel: supported Šeper. It is a matter of applying what John XXIII said, not of repeating things that are already accepted, but of speaking to the people of today.

Browne proposed that just a few words be added; after that he would have no objection.

Häring accepted this.

Tromp read out a letter from a Dutch layman on the relation between copulation and love-play.

Garrone: these questions need to be distinguished: Is there anything in this text contrary to doctrine? - No.

Is the text appropriate for the purpose we have in mind? - Yes.

St Paul speaks about men and women, never about children.

Ottaviani: with the addition proposed by Browne, can we pass on to the next Number?

Franić spoke against a line which said: marriage is not merely an instrument of fecundity. Häring explained the abuses against which these words had been introduced. Philips continued the explanation.

At 5.43 pm No. 23, on culture, was read out.

Garrone gave expression to the criticism that I had already made: the culture envisaged was of a humanist kind; technical culture had been overlooked.

Philips added further to Garrone's comments.

At the interval, when I congratulated quite a lot of people on the Victory of Love, Mgr Charue said to me: this motto should be printed at the head of every page of every document: PRIMACY, MEDIATION, BEGETTING OF CHILDREN . . . !!

Lubac told me yesterday that he had seen a personal letter from Ottaviani to the Bishop of Assisi, dating from five or six days ago. The periodical *ROCCA* had printed a page of praise for Fr de Lubac. Ottaviani said that one could not speak in that way about an author who had elicited express reservations (it was not said which). And, for this reason, he was appointing an ecclesiastical censor for the journal.

It is the same journal that got a letter from Parente on the subject of the interview it published with me.

At 6.15 pm No. 24, on economic life, was begun.

At 6.30 pm No. 26, on peace, was begun (skipping No. 25). A new draft of the text was distributed.

Butler raised the question of a politics of peace by force of nuclear dissuasion. The question had been discussed at the sub-commission. Nuclear war had been condemned, while at the same time avoiding any formal statement on this point, which is so much debated, and on which opinions differ so much.

Butler: in other words, every time a problem is raised which is truly urgent for humankind, we acknowledge that we have nothing to say about it. So it is with marital practice, over-population, the politics of dissuasion and of peace . . . That is what is wrong with this schema, which will be a great disappointment.

Häring: this text will provoke discussion and new developments. Other responses from Philips, Riedmatten.

Ancel: could something be said about the disproportion between military expenditure and aid to poor nations?

It does not deal with the causes of war: imperialisms (including economic imperialism.)

At 7.01 pm, we went back to No. 25. Much discussion about what can and SHOULD be said about the rights of the state in the matter of family planning. In Venezuela, in certain clinics, women are sterilised after the fourth child . . .

It was decided to be more explicit about this in the accompanying appendix.

The schema was approved as a whole at 7.25 pm. Mgr Guano announced that it would be reviewed for accuracy of theological detail by a small commission: Gagnebet, Rahner, Thils, Congar, Moeller, Daniélou.

Sunday 7 June 1964

Reviewed the responses to the thirteen points with Mgr Philips, so that he could prepared a report on them. —Visit from Frs Lyonnet and de La Potterie, about the projected volume; 'La vie selon L'esprit, condition du chrétien'.[1]

They told me that Mgr Willebrands has been named a bishop as well as Dom Salmon.[2] This would have been required by his visits to the East: the Patriarchs expect the messengers sent to them to be bishops. I am very pleased with this nomination, a step, I hope, towards the cardinalate and succession to Bea.

The fathers think that the postponement of my audience is intentional. They have known of numerous similar cases: when it is known that a person is about to depart, his audience is postponed. Thus it is not refused, but nevertheless it does not take place . . . I cannot take part in this sort of machination. 'Let your word be: yes, yes!'

---

1. I de La Potterie & S Lyonnet, *La Vie selon L'Esprit, condition de chrétien*, 'Unam Sanctam', 55 (Paris: Cerf, 1965).
2. Dom Pierre Salmon was the abbot of St Jerome, the pontifical abbey charged with the revision of the Vulgate; he had just been named a bishop on 4 June.

I spoke too soon, and foolishly: at 1.00 pm, I received my ticket for a PRIVATE audience at 12.15 pm tomorrow.

After we had together corrected the report prepared by Mgr Philips on the Commission's replies to the Pope's thirteen points, we went, again together, to a meeting organised by Fr Balić, to prepare for the mariological congress which is to be held in Santo Domingo next March, on 'Mary in the Bible'.[1] Ten or twelve people were there (Balić, Rahner, Lyonnet, Fenton, Ciappi, Castellino, Garofalo, Baraúna, myself, Philips, and finally Mgr Roche[2] (= Opus Coenaculi), to whom Fr Balić spoke as if he were able to extract a nail from his eye. . .). It is a matter of studying Mary in the Scriptures SERIOUSLY. The nuncio in Santo Domingo[3] had already invited two Brothers from Taizé, and the question has been raised of whether other Protestants should be invited, and WHICH? I suggested consulting the Faith and Order Commission of the WCC.

Rahner, myself, Philips and some others, spoke about the serious character, and the freedom of this work.

Fr Balić asked what subjects we would be working on. Alas, I have neither the time nor the strength: I can scarcely stand up, I am exhausted, and the weeks and months pass without advancing by a single step the work I owe to editors!!! If one could be sure of being able, by the sacrifice of time and strength, to help to direct the international mariological academy and the currently pretty stupid mariology that makes its home there to become true again, that, perhaps, would be worth the effort.

That might also contribute to narrowing the gap that separates true biblicists from theologians, or even those theologians who are exacting, and who attend to the sources, from those who do not. For the situation is rather troubling. That would also work towards the PEACE which the discussions of the past week have shown to be so precarious, if not profoundly lacking. But how are a few, already overburdened, to struggle against the enormous mass of fanatical mariologues?

Will a change of direction perhaps come about, nevertheless? I would be sorry to miss out on it, even at the moment when I must record that I have neither the time nor the strength for that, or for anything else.

Monday 8 June 1964 *(St Médard!)*

This morning examination, of the Chapter on the Church triumphant, at Cardinal Browne's (a very enviable apartment, a haven of calm). Present were the Cardinal, Mgr Philips, Moeller, Frs Molinari, SJ,[4] (principal redactor), Rahner, Tromp, Salaverri, Gagnebet and myself. It went well.

---

1. The Fourth International Mariological Conference was to be held in Santo Domingo in March 1965, on the theme: 'Mary in the New Testament'.
2. Georges Roche, a close collaborator of Cardinal Tisserant, and founder of the Opus Cenaculi, a diocesan Secular Institute.
3. E Clarizio.
4. Paolo Molinari, SJ, Postulator General of the Society of Jesus, was a Council expert.

I left at midday for my audience. A series of antechambers and salons, with *tronetto* [throne] or without. Cardinal König emerged from his audience. The Czech bishop from the Commission on the Laity, Mgr Tom,[1] was waiting and went in before me. About 12.40 pm I entered the Pope's private library. While I was waiting I chatted with a colonel of the Swiss Guard, and with the chamberlain, Mgr Del Gallo.[2] He told me about the habits of the popes. Pope John XXIII sometimes had a little snooze between audiences. He put his head down on his arms and went to sleep. Sometimes he snored. The doors were carefully shut. He used to work until 2.00 am.—He will not hold out.—It is forty years now since that was said, etc. (*De minoribus* [of minor matters]). We spoke briefly about *ICI* and Hourdin. I said frankly what I thought.

The Holy Father was seated at a table with little on it. First I offered him my books: *Sainte Église*[3] and *Chrétiens en dialogue; Tradition* I & II; *Foi et Théologie;*[4] my two chronicles of the Council,[5] and *Église servante et pauvre.*[6]

The Pope congratulated me and thanked me for my fidelity and my service, especially at this time of the Council, when things had to be explained in a new way.

I said to him that the ecumenical openness and the gestures he had made towards the Patriarchs call for (just as the renewal of the liturgy calls for) an ecclesiology that has not yet been worked out, an ecclesiology of Communion, in which the Church would be seen as a Communion of Churches. The Holy Father said he did not see quite what I meant. I explained a little further. But the Pope said: there is only one church. Our Lord wanted only one. Certainly it admits of a variety of rites, usages and customs. But it must be ONE single church.

> Myself: Yes, but not monolithic. It is not a question of a federation. But neither of a monolithic organisation.
> He: The others (he seemed to be thinking of the Orthodox) will have to come round to this idea.

---

1. On the typescript, Congar completed the name as 'Tomko'. Is he referring to the Czech F Tomášek, or to the Slovak Josef Tomko, the future curial cardinal? (Eduard Nécsey, Apostolic Administrator of Nitra, was the only Czech bishop on the Commission for the Apostolate of the Laity.)
2. Luigi Del Gallo Roccagiovine, of the diocese of Rome.
3. Yves M-J Congar, *Sainte Église. Études et approches ecclésiologiques,* 'Unam Sanctam' 41 (Paris: Cerf, 1963).
4. Yves M-J Congar, *La Foi et la Théologie,* 'Le mystère chrétien' (Tournai: Desclée, 1962).
5. Yves M-J Congar, *Le Concile au jour le jour* (Paris: Cerf, 1963), and *Le Concile au jour le jour. Deuxième session* (Paris: Cerf, 1964).
6. More precisely, *Pour une Église servante et pauvre* (Paris: Cerf, 1963).

Myself: Yes, Most Holy Father. But it will be necessary, without denying the concept of a communion of churches, to widen their outlook to accept an idea that they have never well recognised.

From there, I went on to the disgraceful article in *L'Osservatore Romano*.[1] The Holy Father told me that he disapproved of it and had already made this known. This gave me the opportunity to give the Holy Father the text of Nicetas of Nicomedia, which I had copied out for him,[2] and which explained the difficulty of the Easterners. He took the text and said he would read it. But (he pointed to the library), he added, I have the Patrology here . . .

I spoke about my wish that the Council would draw up a new profession of faith, as Lateran IV or Trent had done, but in a more biblical and kerygmatic style, adapted to our own times. The Holy Father agreed with me, and said: draw up a text, I am asking you as a private request. I replied: I will try. I will send you my attempt through Mgr Colombo.

- You know him?

- Yes, very well.

- He is a great asset to the Council, as a Council Father.

Then I spoke about the journal *Concilium*. The Holy Father told me that there should be two or three Roman theologians on the committee, not to supervise or impede, but to establish contact with the Roman milieux. He asked me if I had any names to suggest? I mentioned Fr Gagnebet. The Pope, replied (after repeating the name, which meant nothing to him): I do not know this religious. Tell him to come and see me (but I am going to write to *Concilium* first) . . . But, he added, there ought to be a diocesan priest as well. The Pope also asked me if the journal was about to come out . . .

He spoke to me, I no longer know on account of what, about Guitton, saying that he has spoken of me. He thinks Guitton is capable of making the voice of the Church heard among the laity, which he represents well.—I was cowardly. I did not dare tell him that that was only half true. I said nothing.

I said a word about the project of the Ecumenical Institute in Jerusalem which could, the Pope said, study theology according to an historical method (I completed the sentence—historical and concrete theology). I made my critical remarks about Jerusalem as the place for it. The Holy Father replied: No, it is THERE that all must return.

Then I said that this should be linked with some other ecumenical institute, established for example at Gazzada.

---

1. Cf, Bernardino Bilogeric, 'Pensieri sulla collegialità episcopale' in the edition of 7 June 1964; the article opposed ecumenical currents, and relied particularly on the proposal of Anselm of Havelberg in his discussion with Nicetas of Nicomedia.

2. The theologian Nicetas of Nicomedia, Byzantine metropolitan of the thirteenth century, had been a defender of the collegial and conciliar structure of the Church; he considered that papal primacy had come about for only historical reasons.

The Pope did not prolong the conversation. I sensed that this was the end. I asked him to sign the photo of himself with Patriarch Athenagoras. He did so. He gave me a medal of the Council. He blessed me, and my intentions and my family (while repeating his pleasure at my fidelity and service to the Church). I asked for a special blessing for my sick sister-in-law. He went back to his desk and took from it a rosary for Annette.[1]

I wanted to say something about Galileo, but I was not able to. A clock struck as I came down into the cortile di san Damaso. After me there were the mayor and town council of Bergamo, and then other visitors.

I do not now know at what point or in what connection the Holy Father said to me: things will change little by little. There are some journals in Holland and Belgium that are 'too energetic'. I wondered for a moment whether, with regard to Belgium, he was thinking of Janssens' article for *Ephemerides Theologicae Lovanienses* about the pill.[2] I asked a question to get greater precision. The Pope was referring to an article in *Église vivante*, where *L'Osservatore Romano* was criticised for something like yesterday's article, and where Rome was criticised. I took the opportunity to say how well and how hard the Belgians had worked in the Council, on the Theological Commission (which had just finished the work of drawing up a response to the Holy Father's thirteen questions. He did not take this up.) And I referred to Mgr Philips, saying that he was the one who had done most. The Pope replied: I do not know him, but I am waiting for him to ask to come and see me. For the moment I want to leave him completely free.

Perhaps I have not noted down this interchange very well. I got the impression that the Holy Father is a man under strain, intensely attentive, knowing how to affirm what he has seen needs to be retained. It seemed to me that, on the ECCLESIOLOGICAL plane, he does not have the theological vision that his openness calls for. He is very bound to a Roman point of view.

In the evening, Mgr Philips told us that he could do nothing with Parente. It was absolutely necessary to introduce *mediatrix* into the *De Beata*, and even (this had neither been asked for, nor voted on by the Commission), *prae coeteris socia Christi Redemptoris* [more than others the associate of Christ the Redeemer].

So, the division among Catholics about the *De Beata* remains profound.

Likewise, Parente had demanded of Smulders that HIS text on the *Protoparentes* [first parents] should be inserted in No. 3 of the *De Revelatione*. Fr Smulders refused.

Dinner, to which Mgr Prignon invited us (Philips, Moeller, Thils) at a restaurant in the Piazza Navona, in the open air. We saw normal people again, to whom our byzantine intrigues would have absolutely NOTHING to say!

---

1. The wife of Robert Congar, Yves Congar's brother.
2. Cf above, page 505, note 1.

Tuesday 9 June 1964
Took the plane home.

31 July 1964
Since Les Voirons, a visit to Cullmann at Chamonix (with Fr De Ménil[1] and Fr Peuchmaurd, whom we visited at Sallanches). Cullmann has a very fine villa and yet he has had built a little house (in the Savoyard 'treasury' style), where he sleeps and works, with his assistant below him. I discovered an unknown Cullmann; in one aspect, he is somewhat bourgeois, if not the confirmed bachelor. He cultivates his plants, calling each species by its Latin name; he collects rare stones; he goes for walks in his forest. He told me that creation plays a major role in his history of salvation. He also has an odd timetable. He gets up at 3.00 am and works until 6.00 am. Then he sleeps again from 6.00 until 9.00 am. In the afternoon, he tends his plants, walks, goes swimming (at the beach) . . . He was very pleased to see me and immediately started to talk to me about the Council. He had just received the schemas (even those that I do not have), in particular, the *De Ecclesia* and the *De Revelatione*, printed in two volumes, as well as the *De oecumenismo*, which included the *De Iudeis*.

He talked at length with me on this subject. The text of the *De Iudeis* has stirred up an extremely violent storm in America (USA). The Jews maintain that the word 'deicide' had been suppressed in order to continue to accuse them of this crime. There were some very violent articles in the newspapers saying that the Council was a spiritual pogrom. They accused Paul VI of being totally under the thumb of Ottaviani, who, according to them, is the one responsible for the suppression of the word 'deicide', and so for the accusation of deicide that this suppression conceals. A certain Heschel,[2] of their major Hebrew seminary, even maintains that there is a complicated conspiracy, that the microphone was cut off when Cardinal Bea spoke at the Council. However much Cullmann told him that this is not true, that he had been THERE and had heard the discourse over the public address system, Heschel believed none of it, and accused Cullmann of naivety. This Heschel had just sent a long telegram to Cullmann, and another to Barth, asking them to write to the Pope to protest. Happily, Cullmann was able to dissuade Barth from writing. He had copied out the new text for him, in which the WORD 'deicide' does not appear, but where the same thing as was said previously is to be found . . . Truly, one cannot allude, even distantly, to the Jews without a violent reaction of offended protest on their part! Even to speak well of them evokes a violent reaction of offended and accusatory protest on their part.

But, Cullmann told me, the Protestants of the USA have voiced their agreement with the Jews: they are saying that, since John XXIII, nothing is going forward any more, and that the Council either is getting nowhere, or is a reactionary

---

1. Raphaël Menu de Ménil, OP, of the Province of France.
2. The Rabbi Abraham J Heschel taught at the Jewish Theological Seminary in New York.

device. It seems that the American Observers have not given objective reports, much less sympathetic ones. Negative criticism is rife in the Protestant world.

We spoke about the next Session, and about the Observers. Several will be changed. It is a very questionable principle, but many churches are changing them. If Roux returns it will be simply as a guest of the Secretariat (but at his own expense . . .). Boegner will come for at least a fortnight. Barth does not want to come, although Cullmann invited him, in agreement with Willebrands: he has recently had a haemorrhage of the bladder. His son Markus,[1] who does not exactly sparkle with equilibrium of spirit, is one of those on the Protestant side who are leading the campaign against Paul VI and the Council. He has taken up, on his own account, the ridiculous phrase 'spiritual pogrom'. . . !!!

6 August 1964

Fr Dupuy came to join us (Féret and myself) at Les Voirons, in order: 1) to work on the schemas, and prepare the *modi*, or to anticipate some interventions; 2) to make remote preparations for the book of commentary on the Constitution *De Ecclesia* (and also, possibly, on *De Revelatione* and *De oecumenismo*) which I am planning to publish. Since Fr Féret had only got part of the schemas (Mgr Flusin's copy), and Cullmann had suggested lending us the later ones, we went to Chamonix this afternoon to get from Cullmann the whole of *De Ecclesia, De Revelatione, De munere episcoporum. . . De oecumenismo II* (= Declaration on the Jews and *Relatio*). An interesting conversation, excellent tea with Cullmann, his assistant and his sister, in the marvellous setting of the Villa Alsatia.

During the following days, alternation between private reading or study of the texts, and working together: we put our comments together and perhaps drafted a *modus*, or anticipated some interventions to be made. We also tried to decided WHOM we might usefully interest in it.

For this reason, in order to approach Mgr Provenchères in particular, we sent a message to Fr Cottier, who was coming to see us on 12 August. A nice brother, an intelligent and pleasant collaborator. He told us, among other things, that M. Jauch,[2] a physicist professor at Harvard, will be in Rome in September. There is to be a scientific conference on the subject of Galileo. A lecture by Jauch, who is to be received by the Pope. The Pope will be asked for a review of the trial of Galileo. Not just a speech, BUT A REVIEW OF THE TRIAL. It would appear that one of the documents was a forgery . . . That would be marvellous, much more effective than a speech!!!

---

1. Markus Barth was an exegete, a specialist in the New Testament, and taught in the United States.
2. Josef M Jauch was professor at the University of Geneva.

13 August 1964

I wrote to Mgr Ancel to suggest an intervention (because according to new regulations, in order to speak on the last two Chapters of the *De Ecclesia*, a summary of the intervention must reach Rome before 19 September) on the Chapter ON THE ESCHATOLOGICAL CHARACTER OF OUR VOCATION . . . the text is too limited to the personal-spiritual aspect, it lacks the cosmic and historical dimensions;

and to Mgr Weber, to suggest to him an intervention on the *De Beata*: to propose some corrections (*'Virgo filia Sion'* [Virgin daughter of Sion]), and especially to make a *laus capitis* [praise of the chapter] against those, the maximalists, who will attack it. It should be said that this text is capable of reconciling the two parties . . .

14 to 17 August 1964

Perhaps the worst days of the last three years. To take a step is a real problem, requiring a real effort. It is beyond my strength. What shall I do at the Council?

18 August 1964

Lunch at the bishop's residence. Conversation before and afterwards with Mgr Weber about his intervention *De Beata*.

I then saw Mgr Elchinger on his own. He is very disappointed with the encyclical *Ecclesiam Suam*.[1] He finds it paternalistic, hollow, speaking in a superficial and empty manner about atheism, claiming for itself an ecumenical initiative that does not correspond with reality, reaffirming Roman rights in a disturbing manner.

He told me he would be calmer at the Council.

I asked him how things were going with regard to the chair on ecumenism. He told me he had had a visit from Nédoncelle who is very discontented. Nédoncelle had received a notice from the ministry, pursuing it, if I understood him rightly. He asked Mgr Elchinger: why have you approached the ministry?

Elchinger: It was Mgr Weber who did so first: ask him. But look here: when I spoke to you about this chair, you told me that all the posts were occupied, that their number was limited, that you yourself could do nothing, as the matter depended on the ministry. So I addressed myself to them.

Nédoncelle then articulated four comments which were in fact criticisms in regard to the creation of this chair (and indirectly of its being given to me):

1) The number of hours of the course: even though Elchinger himself had complained that the seminarians were over-burdened.

Reply: this course would not be obligatory . . . But Elchinger admitted that he had not considered this aspect of the question.

2) The Protestants are not doing it.

Reply: They will follow. —And I pointed out that they have, nevertheless, a Lutheran Ecumenical Institute which has *de facto* connections with the Faculty.

---

1. The encyclical had been published on the preceding 6 August.

3) There is already teaching on these matters, that of M. Chirat.[1]

Elchinger: that is not the same thing.

Myself: (*in petto* [to myself]) I do not rate myself highly, but everyone, unanimously, rates Chirat's teaching very low.

4) In practice, this chair would be created for Fr Congar. But we do not want to take on religious.

Elchinger: There had been Fr Renaudin.[2]

Myself: I could not be sure of staying in Strasbourg. Fr Daniélou has several times offered me two chairs in Paris.

Mgr Elchinger told me what I already knew, that the most lively opposition came from Giet.[3]

30 August 1964

Telephone call from Fr Benoit,[4] from Paris. He had met Fr Rigaux who had said to him: there will be a meeting of the Theological Commission at St Martha's, on 10 September. Come to it. Be at St Martha's by 9.30 am. Fr Benoit has not much idea of how, or where, to get himself in. He asked for my advice. He is counting on Fr General. I told him that Fr General is not very efficient or interested. As far as I know, the biblical work for the *De Ecclesia* is almost finished, except for the Chapter *De Beata*. It is for schema XIII that Fr Benoit could be useful. For the rest, I know nothing about a meeting of the THEOLOGICAL Commission on 10 September. He should come to St Martha's and get involved in the work on schema XIII . . .

1 September 1964

As I had received no reply from Mgr Ancel about his signing up to speak about eschatology, I was anxious, and went to see Mgr Elchinger and asked him to sign up. I explained to him what it was about.

2 September 1964

At his request, I prepared a summary of the intervention, a copy of which I sent to Fr Féret.

---

1. Henri Chirat taught the History of Religions in the Catholic Faculty of Theology.
2. There had been no teacher of theology of this name; Congar probably confused Fr Paul Renaudin, a Benedictine of the abbey of Clervaux, who had published some works of historical theology, with Fr Paul Séjourné, a Benedictine of the abbey of Oosterhout, a historian and theologian, who taught dogmatic theology at Strasbourg from 1946 to 1952.
3. Stanislas Giet taught ecclesiastical history at the Catholic Faculty of Theology.
4. The exegete, Fr Benoit, OP, of the Province of France, was a specialist in the New Testament: he taught at the French Biblical and Archaeological School In Jerusalem, of which he became Director in 1966, and edited the *Revue Biblique*; he was a Council expert for the last two Sessions.

Thursday 10 September 1964

From 3 September to the evening of 9 September, a week of theology with students of L'École normale supérieure. Departure on 10 September at 3.30 am from Schauinsland (after a sleepless night). By car to Zurich. Plane: departure at 7.00 am. Stopover at Geneva. Arrival in Rome at 9.30 am. Mgr Declerck,[1] Vice-Rector of the Belgian College, was waiting for me. But it took half-an-hour to travel 500 metres in Rome, and I arrived at St Martha's just as everyone else was leaving. It had been nothing more than a quick first contact. I saw Mgr Glorieux. He gave me the comments made up to the present on schema XIII. He explained that the Pope wanted simply an emphasis on the world of work, of culture, of science; there would be a special appeal to youth. It is not yet known whether we are to compose a text which would be given to the Fathers before the discussion, or whether our corrections would simply be put to them in a *Relatio*. In my view, this is something that cannot yet be known or stated. It remains to be seen.

I was as exhausted as I have hardly even been before. I can scarcely hold a pencil and keep my balance. (I am copying out my notes again a little later on.)

At the French Seminary, a room overlooking the street... At lunch, Mgr Garrone, Devreesse.[1] Conversation about the witticisms of bishops, of cardinals, of John XXIII. I saw that Mgr Garrone and l'abbé Haubtmann had got my *modi* on the *De Ecclesia*. So Mgr Gouet must have passed them on.

In the afternoon, at 3.30 pm, at St Martha's, with McGrath, Mgr Roy, Schröffer, Garrone, Hengsbach, Daniélou, Philips, to agree, in a small group of like-minded people, about our attitude and action. (I communicated my *modi* to McGrath, Roy, Schröffer.) What should be inserted into the text? Six points were retained:

- Make the aim of the text clearer: it is not dealing with the mission of evangelisation for its own sake, but with the mission of the Church with regard to the World.
- Be clearer on the notion of the world (nature and grace).
- Broaden the *signa temporum* [the signs of the times] so that these are not seen solely in the western context (Europe and North America), but also that of Africa, Asia and South America.
- Make it clear that in Chapter II it deals with the People of God as a whole, and in Chapter III more especially with Pastors.
- Find a better way to introduce a note of historical TRUTH. Is it true, as Cardinal Siri says, that it would be necessary to affirm the Church's right to certain privileges?
- Nature and grace. Some theological principles concerning earthly realities. Demonstrate better the ONTOLOGICAL connection of THINGS to eschatology.

---

1. Leo Declerck, priest of the diocese of Bruges.

It seems to us that if all this is better expressed, many of the objections will be satisfied beforehand and will fall away.

At 4.30 pm general meeting (list attached). Mgr Guano summarised the principal criticisms, in French (in this smaller Commission French is used as much as Latin). HOW EFFICACIOUS WAS THE WORK DONE AT LES VOIRONS!

Mgr Garrone explained our six points very well and with great force. Philips completed and proposed the text he had prepared (taking up the one from Malines): once again the Belgians had used their little biblical commission to improve the text. I advised Fr Benoit to insert himself into this group, and he is beginning to do so effectively. He made an impression straightaway by his competence, his seriousness and his balanced approach.

McGrath and Lebret intervened on the Signs of the Times. Lebret emphasised: 1) the aspiration of the modern human being to be a human being, due to the impact of the West and of science; 2) humanity is no longer in the same situation with regard to God: everywhere it manifests a quest for self-transcendence, and ultimately for divinisation. The longing for a happy immortality is inscribed IN ITS NATURE.

Hirschmann, relayed by Rahner, wanted a gnoseological definition of the notions of World and of dialogue.

Häring agreed that a small sub-commission should make a revision of the whole text from the point of view of the distinction, and the relations, between Church and World.

Cardinal Cento: In the light of the encyclical (to be quoted!).

(Mgr Ferrari Toniolo told me that, for *Mater et Magistra*, on which he had worked, he met with opposition from the Holy Office and the Secretariat of State. For *Pacem in Terris* he collaborated DIRECTLY with John XXIII.)

A theological sub-commission, a sub-commission on the Signs of the Times, and further precision about the exact purpose of the schema (Garrone and Ferrari) were agreed to.

Moeller intervened against all disincarnate spirituality ('a Platonism for the people'), and in favour of an anthropology. He was insistent.

Benoit spoke of the (multiple) biblical concept of 'World'.

The general comments were read out.

Friday 11 September 1964

I slept in spite of the noise: I had a night to catch up on! But neither my right arm nor my right leg is working!

Mgr Rodhain took us by car. He is always full of plans, particularly for a City of St Abraham to be built in Jerusalem on the Mount of Offence.

Moeller told me that the Moderators would decide today about the procedure for voting on *De Ecclesia*. Mgr Felici has suggested that there should be:

- ONE vote on Chapter I;
- ONE vote on Chapter II;
- THIRTY-NINE votes on Chapter III!

'They' want to reopen the discussion on collegiality: Ruffini has asked for it. If it is reopened, Ottaviani will speak. That presumes that there will be a vote in the Assembly on the reopening of the discussion. And, as Moeller said, it will be sufficient for it to be known that it is wanted by Ruffini in order for a large majority to pronounce AGAINST the reopening of a debate. But Moeller thinks, as I do, that the anti-collegialists will keep on right to the end, and that it will not be surprising if the Pope does not change or add a few words at the very moment of the promulgation of the text.

Delahaye told me that Mgr Roy not only has, as his theologians, Fr Lambert[1] and a layman (De Koninck[2]), but he has brought with him a report drawn up by the latter in favour of the contraceptive pill . . .

Mgr Guano concluded as follows yesterday's discussion with respect to the *ordo laboris perficiendi* [programme of work needing to be completed]:

1) Garrone and Ferrari Toniolo on WORLD and the direction of the schema;
2) Nature-grace: this returns to the competence of the Theological Commission;
3) Theological Commission: Garrone, Rahner, Congar, Rigaux, Benoit, Moeller, Philips, Ferrari;
4) Commission *De signis temporum*: McGrath, Lebret, D'Souza, Tucci, Ganebet, Daniélou, Delhaye, Habicht, plus some persons from Asia, Africa, Latin America, to be consulted. This Commission should also consider the appendices;
5) Historical realism: Congar;
6) On progress: Lebret, Congar;
7) Rahner will propose IN WRITING how he sees *caput* [chapter] I;
8) Delahaye, Moeller, Daniélou (Congar), and possibly all the others, will prepare the documentation: something that several of the Fathers have asked for.

Guano and Häring: were against the inversion of Chapters II and III, but wanted these chapters, and especially Chapter II, revised in such a way that it is more apparent that Chapter II is speaking about the whole Church, the whole People of God, and Chapter III specifically about the particular office of pastors.

Ferrari and Hirschmann spoke of a presentation concerning the relations of Church and State.

---

1. Bernard Lambert, OP, of the Province of Canada, an ecclesiologist active in the ecumenical movement, was a Council expert.
2. The neo-Thomist Charles de Koninck taught philosophy at Laval University in Québec.

Plan of work for today: in the morning, comments on each chapter. In the afternoon, at 4.00 pm, sub-commissions; at 6.00 pm, meeting of the whole Commission together.

Everyone should write down which chapter he wants to work on: except for Chapter IV, which is already assigned to the commissions preparing the appendices.

The bishops have only until 1 October to present their observations. Guano thinks they will not change much, but that the essential comments have already been made.

In order to avoid discussions and useless criticism, it is thought to be a good idea to tell the Council Fathers the criteria and principles of revision adopted by our Commission.

As for the wishes of the Pope communicated by Felici, Guano said that in the audience he had had on 8 September, the Pope had been more specific: apart from schema XIII, a message should be composed addressed to workers, people involved in science, people involved in culture, and especially the young.

At 10.36 am Garrone put forwards the comments that had been asked of him, on the direction of the schema, and the concept of world.

Lunch at the Belgian College with Fr Benoit, whom I was glad to see integrated into this effective team. Philips saw Felici and his secretaries this morning. In effect, they want ONE vote on Chapter I, they had envisaged one also on Chapter III, but three have been introduced, because certain parts are new; these chapters did not interest them much. But they want thirty-nine on Chapter III: THAT does interest them.

For fifteen years I have known that their ecclesiology is summed up in the assertion of THEIR POWER. That is all.

Interesting conversation about the text *De Iudaeis* and Israel in the history of salvation.

At 3.30 pm departure for St Martha's. Meeting of the theological sub-commission at 4.00 pm. Mgr Garrone said that we must: 1) somewhere clearly define the aim of the schema, and the status of world with respect to Church; 2) revise the whole text from the same point of view.

Rahner: Our role is to put into the first of these what ought to be found there from the point of view of theology. But the idea of the total vocation of humankind is not enough.

Extensive exchange of views and reflection in common about the principles and distinctions that should be proposed at the beginning as a basis for the whole. This is very important.

At 6.00 pm we moved on to the third stage. Meeting of the WHOLE Commission. Hesburg and D'Souza were present.

In the evening, at 8.30 pm, dinner at the priory of the Angelicum with the participants (at least those who were there this evening) in the study days of Dominicans engaged in the apostolate in Muslim countries.

Saturday 12 September *1964*

Got up early and was exhausted by 8.00 am!!! Several bishops have arrived. Telephone call from Fr Hamer. Fr General wants to see me. I had counted on doing a little work . . . Fr General had to speak to me about my autobiographical preface in *ICI*.[1] The Holy Office is attacked in it . . . I asked him if he had been ordered to tell me this. He replied that he was not able to say anything, but that he was OBLIGED to speak to me. He (they) reproached me: 1) in the first place and in the highest degree for what I had said about Fr Chenu (but I would be prepared to give my life for that!); 2) for having spoken about the Holy Office, about Fr Suarez,[2] about personal matters that should have remained secret, even though this was pointless. Fr General added: 1) people whose esteem I had regained would hereafter take a very dim view of me; 2) if the Holy Office were also to be indiscreet, and put forward an account seen from its side, I would not perhaps come out of it so gloriously. Fr General said I would have to write another article paising the Holy Office and the services it has rendered to the Church.

I found all this wretched. I thought Fr General appallingly small-minded and lacking in vision.

I spoke to him about the continuation of my collaboration with *ICI*. Fr General told me he did not approve of it (but he did not forbid it). He told me that it is a journal that attacks the Church, that saps confidence in the hierarchy, that insists on criticising. It is said that they often come to Rome, to collect their information in Rome . . . I said very plainly that the accusation alleged is false.

After this, I spoke to Fr General about *De munere episcoporum*, and of the necessity of intervening on the paragraph concerning exemption—but I had not the courage to mention either the request for collaboration I had received from *Le Monde*, or the publication, these last few days, of *Discours au Concile*. Dear God! How petty this all is, with no bearing on the immensity of the Apostolic tasks and the demands of the world!

At 10.00 am, at the Belgian College, to work with Mgr Philips and Moeller. I am glad that, yesterday evening, I asked for and obtained (from Mgr McGrath) the appointment of Fr Chenu to the sub-commission on *De signis temporum* . . . I believe he was glad of it too.

I stayed at the Belgian College for lunch with Cardinal Suenens and the Auxiliary Bishop of Bruges.[3] Cardinal Suenens did not tell us anything of much importance: some details. The bar will not be open until 11.00 am (there will be such a crush!) and the Fathers will be invited at least to leave their places. There will, perhaps, be some meetings this afternoon. The minority will be given leave to

---

1. 'Chrétiens en dialogue, souvenirs oecuméniques', *Informations catholiques internationales*, 1 June 1964: 17–32, reproduced and completed in the preface of *Chrétiens en dialogue. Contributions catholiques à l'oecuménisme*, 'Unam Sanctam', 50 (Paris: Cerf, 1964), X-LVII.
2. Emmanuel Suarez was Master General of the Order from 1946 to 1954.
3. Maurits De Keyzer.

speak against collegiality. The Moderators proposed that Cardinal Browne should speak for the minority (he would not have been much understood, listened to even less . . .) but this was not kept to . . . 'They' know very well what that would have meant. There has been consideration of ways of better maintaining secrecy when sensitive topics need to be discussed. Some were proposing that in such a case there be a meeting of cardinals by themselves, but that was rejected for the sake of conciliar truth.

I spoke to the Cardinal about the matter of Fr Féret. He told me I should approach Mgr Felici, when a favourable moment occurred . . .

Fr Rigaux said he had it from two Italian OFM bishops that there had been a meeting of the Italian bishops yesterday, and that a pronouncement had been made there in favour of purely and simply rejecting schema XIII. But I made inquiries: 1) of Mgr Ferrari Toniolo. It is not true. On 12 August the bishops of Lombardy and Triveneto had a meeting, at which they decided to accept the schema as a basis for discussion. But, he added, Mgr Vallainc,[1] head of the Press Office, had been spreading it around IN PRIVATE, that this Session will be the last, which would be a way of burying schema XIII. 2) Mgr Guano purely and simply repudiated Rigaux's information. There are only some individuals who are opposed. (Ferrari also told me that Cardinal Siri is pretty ill with a nervous condition.)

Meeting of our sub-commission at 4.00 pm. We went over again with the whole group what had been done this morning at the Belgian College. But this was not without value: agreement and some very valuable refinements were progressively achieved in this way. Work like this is very burdensome and tiring. It takes days of meetings to reach a result, but that is the nature of the case. It seems that the *THEOLOGY* that was to have been included in it fifteen or eighteen months ago, and that the Zurich meeting excluded from it (under the influence of Habicht), is now about to be put back in schema XIII.

General meeting at 5.30 pm. I am terribly exhausted. Dear God! Help me if you want me to serve you . . . I am summoned to live only on the manna of a grace for which I haven't even a quarter of an hour's reserve.

First, Mgr Hengsbach proposed his additions and corrections.

Then Garrone proposed his draft reworking of the *Proemium*. He was rather strongly against the present text. It is strange how the lay people, Daniélou, Lebret, do not react critically to the tone of *captatio* [rhetorical seduction] at the beginning of it . . .

Mgr Philips proposed (and got accepted) our sub-commission's draft revision of Chapter I. What an effective man!

Mgr McGrath gave an account of the work of the sub-commission on the *signa temporum*, which wants further to extend its work (Chenu was there, wide-eyed, very alert and young). Finally, Mgr Guano gave an account of what it is

---

1. The Italian Fausto Vallainc was Director of the Council Press Office.

intended to say to the Fathers about the rules, according to which the work of improving the text is carried out. Their comments were asked for by 1 October.

At 7.30 pm a Cadillac took us, Mgr Garrone and myself, to the Hotel Flora where, after a very sumptuous dinner, we took part with Alain Galichon[1] in a direct broadcast for Radio-Luxembourg, with a link-up to Paris. Until midnight. Got back at 12.30 am . . .

Sunday 13 September 1964

The French bishops arrived yesterday evening. Lunch with Cardinals Lefebvre and Richaud. I saw Fr Gy, who was there for the approval of the translations of the missal.

Fr Daniélou called to pick me up at 10.45 am; we went to see Fr Lebret at the *convitto* of the Angelicum, to hear his ideas on the theme of Progress—because he is leaving tomorrow for Rwanda, and we three have been charged with suggesting something on that theme. Fr Lebret was interesting: he has a concrete and profoundly well considered view of the situation and movement of the whole world.

In the evening, a visit from Frs Féret and Dupuy.

Mgr Gouet is going to have our *modi* roneoed.

Monday 14 September 1964

I had an unexpected bit of luck. As Mgr Pailler and Martin took me by car, we entered by the door for ambassadors and cardinals. A great crowd of men dripping with decorations, ribbons etc, with elegant women, some beautiful, some mainly stout. My 'Council Father' *tessera* [ticket] admitted me as far as the Confession. There I found, on either side, in front of the tribunes, all the Observers: Cullmann, Schlink, Boegner, L Vischer, Nissiotis, Borovoj, Skydsgaard, etc, and the people from the Secretariat. Fr Duprey told me: 1) that he had distributed 300 copies of my *modi*; 2) that the Patriarch of Constantinople was sending two personal Observers; 3) that Fr Scrima[2] has been appointed a parish priest in Rome, where he will also be a delegate for the Orthodox. —I went to greet Maximos. He too had drawn up some *modi*, very similar to mine, and had distributed 400 copies of them. Fr Duprey found me a place with the Observers and the Secretariat, in the best position in front of the Confession. The altar above it is surrounded by a large platform for concelebration. All around us, everywhere, in the tribunes, on the benches, on the chairs, were delegations and guests. Great deployment of chamberlains in ruffs, the Noble Guards, the Swiss Guards, etc under the arc lights.

---

1. Secretary General of Independent Catholic Action (ACI).
2. Andreas Scrima, monk of Romanian origin, devoted himself to ecumenism, and had stayed at the Istina Centre near Paris; he became an archimandrite of the Patriarchate of Constantinople and was appointed Observer for the Patriarchate of Constantinople and representative of Patriarch Athenagoras at the Council during the last two Sessions.

At the moment when the procession entered St Peter's, I caught sight of Cardinal Léger in his seat. We made signs to one another, I went to greet him, gave him my *modi*. He looked well enough, better than I had been led to expect. I also greeted Guitton and the lay Auditors, who named me an honorary layman and invited me to sit with them.

The papal procession entered: more simple than the previous year: no *flabella*, the tiara was not carried in procession. From his *sedia* the Holy Father made his great gesture with his arms. Mass started straightaway.

What progress! And how clearly the road taken by the Council is inscribed in the three celebrations:

- 1962: the Sistine.
- 1963: a combination: the Holy Father assisting from the throne.
- 1964: concelebration by twenty-four Council Fathers—truly a dialogue Mass, sung with the congregation; the Holy Father himself gave communion to a dozen of the lay Auditors.

The communion of the concelebrants took a very long time, but one had the feeling of a common banquet. So there was a concelebrated dialogue and sung Mass. Just as the consecration was about to begin, Cullmann fell down. He was made to lie flat, cared for, and taken out on a stretcher. Between the two consecrations, Cardinal McIntyre collapsed. It is true that it was very hot and oppressive.

After Mass, the Pope gave an address.[1] Fortunately, I had a French text, without which I would not have understood well. The Pope FEELS things in a very profound and dramatic way, he has some fine images and moments of emotion. But he is not an orator, he is lacklustre and sad, and he is badly served by a rather unattractive voice. He did not come out of himself: only towards the end were there a few restrained gestures. Fr Martelet, who came to sit beside me, said: Paul outside the walls and Peter in chains, all at the same time. The Pope goes out to people in his heart, but he himself remains tightened up. He IS very present, but he HAS no 'presence'.

With regard to content, his speech was an invitation to construct a theology of the episcopate. But he started from the top down, he did not start with the People of God, his categories are not those of an ecclesiology fully informed by the sources. The laity exist very really for him, but rather as a particular *ordo* of the Church rather than as the People of believers in which are to be found structures of service and presidence.

I gave my *modi* to Fr Martelet (for the African bishops), to Mgr van Dodewaard (for the Dutch bishops); to Cardinal Léger, that's done; Maximos IV has them; two Lebanese priests also told me that they had them and were ready to duplicate and distribute them. So that is already a good distribution.

---

1. Cf, *AS* III/I, 140–151; cf also: 'Discours prononcé par SS Paul VI lors de l'ouverture de la III*e* session du Concile', *La Documentation catholique*, 1964, col 1217–1228.

I saw Mgr Ancel and telephoned Mgr Elchinger to get them to intervene in favour of a more historical and cosmic-collective eschatology. I started work on a text concerning Progress. But,

I received visits from: Le Guillou, Hua,[1] de Surgy;[2]

a visit from Falchi, whom I later presented to Mgr Ancel.

Martimort (with Etchegaray[3]) is worried about the possibility that the anti-collegial minority might succeed in achieving a third plus one of the votes. I do not believe it, but this eventuality cannot be excluded. Moeller and Heuschen have prepared a note in order to respond to hesitations or difficulties. They want to have it signed by a bishop and we went together to see Mgr Ancel for this reason. But it would be better if it were someone who is not on the Theological Commission. Mgr Ancel suggested Cardinal Lefebvre, and will see him about it this evening. This would be much better, in fact, as the cardinal is known as a man of peace, a stranger to particular schools of thought or currents of opinion.

Then a visit from the good Fr Camelot, then from Fr Lécuyer, who wanted to involve me in some work on the *De Presbyteris* tomorrow. The French bishops are unhappy with the text and want to propose some *modi*. I agreed.

Falchi himself wanted two meetings. So the circus begins . . . One is going to be pulled in all directions.

Tuesday 15 September 1964

At St Peter's, at 9.00 am. We started late. People met and chatted, looking for their places etc. For many of them all this was already familiar. Mgr Villot asked, in vain, that we should respond at Mass '*choraliter*', that is to say, *una voce, lente, graviter* [as one voice, slowly, with gravity]. But for this request to be effective one would need 1) a celebrant who was consistent; 2) a master of ceremonies. But there was neither. The result was painful. My God!

A short discourse by Cardinal Tisserant[4]: thanks, welcome. A call to prayer and penitence. The PASTORAL goal of the Council. The general desire that this Session be the last. So, keep to the regulations for work. Reminder of the law of secrecy with regard to discussions.

---

1. Maxime Hua, priest of the Paris Mission, of which he was superior.
2. Paul de Surgy, priest of the diocese of Quimper, was an exegete and taught at the Catholic University of the West, at Angers; he was the personal expert of Mgr Fauvel, Bishop of Quimper.
3. Roger Etchegaray was the director of the Pastoral Secretariat of the French episco-pate; he was in charge of the secretariat for the conference of delegates from episcopal conferences, called the 'Conference of Twenty-two' (cf above, page 172, note 6) he was later to become Archbishop of Marseilles; created cardinal, he was afterwards to become President of the Pontifical Council for Justice and Peace, and of the Pontifical Council 'Cor Unum'.
4. The Dean of the Council of Presidents, *AS* III/I, 27–30.

80th General Congregation, presided over by Agagianian.[12] A short inaugural discourse.

Felici:[2] new rules approved by the Pope and already known (speeches to be deposited five days ahead etc). Very insistent reminder of the law of secrecy for the *periti*. If they break it they will lose their places as *periti*. The bar will remain closed until 11.00 am.

Cardinal Browne[3] read the *relatio* on the chapter which they persist in calling 'the seventh': our eschatological vocation. He indicated its structure, then its dogmatic (ecclesiological) and even ecumenical interest.

Ruffini:[4] comments on biblical texts or allusions. Repetitions and gaps. *Caput iterum retractetur* [the chapter should be gone over afresh].

Cardinal Urbani:[5] *caput placet.*

Cardinal Santos:[6] *idem*: profound and well-balanced from the dogmatic, pastoral and ecumenical point of view.

Cardinal Rugambwa:[7] repeated what had already been said three times. Everyone was bored!

Mgr Gori:[8] What a bore!

Nicodemo[9]

Mariani:[10] (?) Indonesia: it speaks only of INDIVIDUAL eschatology; rather critical.

Ziadé:[11] no reference to the mission of the Holy Spirit. Without that there is no epiclesis! Eschatological = pneumatological. The eschatological times are those inaugurated by the Resurrection of Christ who acts through his Spirit. Already, but not yet . . . He developed a very good theology of the Holy Spirit and its activity. The west is purely christological . . .

Hermaniuk:[12] *placet secundum modum.* Too individualistic. The sacramental and collective aspect is lacking.

{individual and ascetic

---

1. *AS* III/I, 155–156.
2. *AS* III/I, 156–157.
3. *AS* III/I, 375–377.
4. *AS* III/I, 377–379.
5. *AS* III/I, 379–381.
6. *AS* III/I, 381–382.
7. *AS* III/I, 382–383.
8. *AS* III/I, 383–385.
9. *AS* III/I, 385–386.
10. This in fact refers to the intervention by Justin Darmajuwana, Archbishop of Semarang (Indonesia), *AS* III/I, 386-388.
11. AS III/1, 389–91.
12. *AS* III/I, 391–394.

Eschatology → keeping vigil → fasting   {communitarian and sacramental
{ (eucharistic fast)

Felici:[1] invited people to put themselves down to speak on the schema *De munere episcoporum*; the part on *De cura animarum*. He asked whether the mode of voting proposed for *De Ecclesia* was accepted. He explained it.

Pont[2] (Spain): it takes note only of the transcendent aspect, the immanent aspect is missing.

Elchinger:[3] my text, somewhat enriched (the idea of *pars pro toto* [part for whole], and of recapitulation) and comparisons between modern ideas and the biblical manner of presenting eschatology. —A text well presented, and listened to attentively.

Dom Butler:[4] proposed to amend the text. He criticised the use of the term *Corpus Christi mysticum* [Mystical Body of Christ] for the Church on earth, the Church suffering and the Church glorious.

García de Sierra[5] (Burgos): criticisms. He went on too long: he was stopped.

An Indian:[6] it is very good. It should be keep as it is.

I saw Mgr Willebrands and Fr Hamer.

At 3.15 pm, work on *De Presbyteris* with Lécuyer and Denis. *Modi* had been drawn from 500 submissions (these were ultimately reduced to 200).

In the evening, Cardinal Lefebvre read us the peace-seeking text he had prepared on the subject of collegiality.—Mgr Guerry brought me copies of the letters in which a certain abbé 'George de Nantes'[7] attacked me. This does not interest me, but Mgr Guerry thought that a response SHOULD be made: ten thousand copies have already been distributed, and it has its patrons to support it.

Mgr Ancel told me that Parente read his *relatio* to the Theological Commission today: apparently, it was very forceful, showing how it came about that the ancient tradition of collegiality was forgotten. Parente asked Franić to read the text in which he was to set out the difficulties felt by some of the Fathers. It would have been good if Philips had been able to reply to Franić simply from the point

---

1. *AS* III/I, 395.
2. J Pont y Gol, *AS* III/I, 417–418.
3. *AS* III/I, 419–420.
4. *AS* III/I, 420–421.
5. *AS* III/I, 422–424.
6. Louis Mathias, *AS* III/I, 424–426.
7. Georges de Nantes, from the diocese of Grenoble, settled in the diocese of Troyes, where he founded a religious community; from 1962 onwards, in his 'Letters to My Friends', he attacked the Council, which he accused of betraying the Catholic faith, and came into conflict with the Bishop of Troyes; he was suspended *a divinis* [from priestly functions] in 1966.

of view of the printed text. The Theological Commission (members only, no experts) is to meet again on Friday, to finalise these questions of procedure.

Wednesday 16 September 1964

At the Mass, communion for seminarians AND FOR WOMEN. Those who want to speak on religious liberty and the Jews need to put their names down from today.

They are still talking about the Church in heaven:

> Suenens:[1] in favour of the canonisation of members of the faithful from all walks of life and from all countries.
>
> 85% of those canonised are male or female religious.
>
> 90% represent three countries in Europe.
>
> So, the method of canonisation should be changed: it is too long, too expensive, the process is too centralised.
>
> He proposed that beatifications should be entrusted to episcopal conferences, with canonisations reserved to the pope for those whose reputation for holiness extends beyond the frontiers of one country.
>
> Ancel:[2] against any escapist mystique. The eschatological dimension of our vocation and activity on earth.
>
> D'Agostino:[3] not enough is said about Purgatory, and eternal damnation.
>
> Mgr Roy:[4] read out the *relatio de Beata Maria Virgine*. Good.
>
> Vote on the manner proposed for voting on the *De Ecclesia*. Felici[5] explained it again.
>
> Result:
>
> yes: 2,204;
>
> no: 32;
>
> void: 2.
>
> Discussion on the *De BMV*:
>
> Ruffini:[6] found the text insufficient on several points. Cited Leo XIII and St Pius X.
>
> Wyszyński:[7] (in the name of seventy Polish bishops): they had sent the Pope a text requesting the declaration of Mary as Mother of the Church and of Mary's spiritual maternity, that a consecration of the whole of humanity to the Immaculate heart of Mary be renewed at the Council in

---

1. *AS* III/I, 430–432.
2. *AS* III/I, 432–433.
3. *AS* III/I, 434–435.
4. *AS* III/I, 435–835.
5. *AS* III/I, 438.
6. *AS* III/I, 438–441.
7. *AS* III/I, 441–444.

collegial manner, that the chapter *De BMV* be put in Chapter II of the schema, BETWEEN GOD AND THE PEOPLE OF GOD.

Cardinal Léger:[1] in favour of a theological and pastoral renewal. With regard to style, avoid amplifications:

- concerning the relationship between the Church and Mary, and especially the title 'mediatrix'. This title is difficult to interpret; it is of late date; it seems to go against the biblical affirmation of '*unicus Mediator*' [a single mediator (1 Tim 2:5)]. It can only be properly understood in a certain context, whereas it is being used here without giving that context;

- concerning the cult of the Virgin Mary. The text is inadequate, it speaks as though Marian devotion will, *ex sese* [of itself], lead to Christ. That is not true.

Döpfner:[2] in the name of ninety Fathers from Germany and Scandinavia: *in genere placet*. He explained a good number of corrections needing to be made with great *PRECISION*.

Silva Henríquez:[3] in the name of Cardinal Quintero and forty-three Fathers from Latin America: he praised the balance of the text. The biblical quotations should be revised by a sub-commission of biblicists. There are dangers with 'mediatrix'.

Bea:[4] does the schema respond to the present needs of the Church and the purpose of the Council? Is the topic of mediation ripe? He indicated several points at which theological agreement has not been sufficiently attained: 'Protoevangelium', John XIX . . .

Djajasepoetra[5] (Indonesia) [   ]

Plus some eloquent speeches. I went out. I saw a GREAT number of bishops.

At 11.50 am Mgr Charue[6] read out the *relatio* on Chapter I. Asked for a *placet*.

Rusch (Innsbruck):[7] he was called to speak, he wasn't there!

An Italian:[8] *placet*, but he wants the consecration to the Immaculate Heart of Mary.

Cambiaghi:[9] he will give his text to the Secretariat.

---

1. AS III/I, 445-447.
2. *AS* III/I, 449–450.
3. AS III/I, 452–454.
4. *AS* III/I, 454–457.
5. *AS* III/I, 459–460.
6. *AS* III/I, 466–467.
7. *AS* III/I, 467.
8. G Ruotolo, *AS* III/I, 468–469.
9. *AS* III/I, 469.

Hervás:[1] *'Mater Ecclesiae'* [Mother of the Church] should be taken up again, from the title onwards.

Abasolo[2] (India): a Spaniard: on the marriage between Joseph and Mary. Give honour to St Joseph. What vision, what theology do they have?

A Czechoslovak bishop:[3] see the Council and its primary and secondary ends in the light of the Marian cult.

A vote was taken on Chapter I, but the results were not given immediately. I think it is very hurried to take a vote immediately after the *relatio*. It always used to be left for at least a day. This is going to neutralise many of the *modi*. I will have to hurry up and distribute my papers.

At 3.10 pm, Fr Féret came to find me for this procedure. We tried to plan the journey a bit. But some addresses were missing and some that I had been given were no longer correct. We spent four hours going to eight or nine addresses, through crazy streets, constantly coming up against one-way streets. . . I could not stand any longer. Had I done the right thing? In any case I had done what I could.

In the evening, a visit from a Brazilian couple, Fábio Konder Comparato;[4] a short meeting with Moeller, Martimort, Mgr Ancel at Cardinal Lefebvre's, for his little text. Moeller told me that Cardinal Suenens wanted to speed up the discussion on the *De Beata*, in order to avoid possible upsets, or tiresome speeches.

Thursday 17 September 1964

I forgot my notebook. I made notes on this sheet of paper. I saw a lot of people, distributed some *modi*, and noticed that those distributed five days ago have had their effect. It is attracting close attention.

Felici:[5] The vote on Chapter I:

Placet	2,114;
Non placet	11;
Placet iuxta modum	63.

Thus the chapter is *APPROVED*. Forecast of votes. Chapters I & II will be dealt with very quickly, but the votes for Chapter III will be wrapped round with all possible care. That is all that interests 'them'.

- The last day for asking to speak on the schema *De Revelatione*: 25 September.

- The last day for asking to speak on the schema *De Apostolatu Laicorum*: 28 September.

---

1. *AS* III/I, 472–473.
2. *AS* III/I, 473–475.
3. E Nécsey, *AS* III/I, 475–476.
4. Fábio Konder Comparato and his wife Monique, who was French; he was a barrister and Professor of Law at the University of São Paulo and campaigned against poverty and in support of development in Latin America.
5. *AS* III/I, 497–500.

- The last day for submitting [[written]] comments on *De Praesentia Ecclesiae* [on the presence of the Church] ... and the other schemas: 1 October.

A sheet of paper was distributed today in which the relevant Commission set out the criteria in accordance with which it proposed to revise schema XIII.

Reading of the *Relatio* on Chapter II: Good. We passed immediately on to the vote on Nos 9–12. The result was: *Placet [ ]; non placet [ ]*.

Suenens:[1] Mary is too much in evidence as having exercised her role in the past, and not sufficiently as doing so in the present.

Rendeiro:[2] praised the chapter, but wanted three corrections that would express the truth more POSITIVELY. In the name of eighty-two bishops, he asked for the retention of mediation.

Sapelak:[3] (Argentina): there is no mention of Mary's Patronage and Help.

The results of the vote on the (new) No. 13 of *De populo Dei* were announced. They were:

Placet	2,173
Non placet	30
iuxta modum	3 (these were null).

Van Lierde:[4] in favour of the title: *De Maria Ecclesiae Matre* [on Mary Mother of the Church].

Results of the vote on Nos 14–16:

Placet	2,186
Non placet	12
iuxta modum	2

Jaeger:[5] on the relations between Mary and the Holy Spirit, and various remarks.

Ancel:[6] we should look for unanimity in the vote on this text. The text had been drafted to allow this. He said again in public what he had said about Mediation in the Commission: he has changed his mind and thinks that the Council cannot canonise this doctrine.

Kempf:[7] [ ]

Fr Betti told me that *simul* [together] instead of *semel* [once] in the quotation from Jude 3, in the *De Revelatione* was not a typographical error, but was requested by Fr Tromp[8] !!!

1. *AS* III/I, 504–506.
2. Francisco Rendeiro, OP, Bishop of Faro (Portugal), *AS* III/I, 506–507.
3. *AS* III/I, 509–510.
4. *AS* III/I, 511–513.
5. *AS* III/I, 517–519.
6. *AS* III/I, 519–520.
7. *AS* III/I, 521–522.
8. According to Betti, this had to do with supporting, by this means, a much greater in-

De Uriate:[1] a real belly-aching to say that the chapter should be entitled *De Maria Matre Jesu* [on Mary the Mother of Jesus].

Reading of the fourth text of the *De Populo Dei* for voting (No. 17):

Placet	2,038
Non placet	38
Placet iuxta modum	1, and 2 null.

Fr Fernandez:[2] the chapter should remain substantially as it is; he proposed some corrections.

Gasbarri:[3] against the 'minimalism' of the ecumenists. Mary has always favoured ecumenism. It will be favoured if Mary is proclaimed Mediatrix of all graces.

Monta,[4] Superior of the Servites.

Garcia[5] [   ]

Mgr Prignon told me:

- that the Belgians (bishops and experts) were furious at Cardinal Suenens' speech;
- that the Pope is still receiving papers against collegiality every day; the Moderators will see him morrow, and will respond;
- that Mgr Palazzini,[6] the Secretary of the Congregation of the Council, has addressed a request to the Moderators that collegiality be withdrawn from the text as being not yet ripe.

Le Couëdic:[7] praised the fact that certain ambiguous titles had been avoided, like Mediatrix, Co-Redemptrix. In favour of seeing a model for Catholic Action in the Visitation. Suggested an addition in this sense.

Méndez Arceo:[8] in the name of more than forty bishops from South America. Praised the *via media* adopted by the Commission. On '*Mater Ecclesiae*' (along the lines and with the documentation of Laurentin, almost to the point of indiscretion).

I am campaigning, AS MUCH AS I CAN, against a consecration of the World to the Immaculate Heart of Mary, because I can see the danger that a move in this direction would constitute.

---

dependence of Tradition with respect to Scripture; cf, Umberto Betti, *La dottrina del Concilio Vaticano II sulla trasmissione della rivelazione. Il capitolo II della Costituzione dommatica* Dei Verbum (Rome: 1985), 125, note 59.

1. *AS* III/I, 523–524.
2. *AS* III/I, 525–527.
3. *AS* III/I, 528–530.
4. Alfonso M Montà, Prior General of the Order of the Servants of Mary, *AS* III/I, 530–532.
5. R García y García de Castro, *AS* III/I, 536–538.
6. Pietro Palazzini, titular bishop.
7. Julien Le Couëdic, Bishop of Troyes, *AS* III/I, 539–540.
8. *AS* II/I, 5415–43.

Lunch at the Columbus with Mgr Delacroix,[1] who also invited Arrighi, Philips, Fr de Lubac and Laurentin. (During the conversation Laurentin once again took out his notebook and made notes. He does not realise just how tiresome he is in this.) Anecdotes from Arrighi. He confirmed that Palazzini, the secretary of the Congregation of the Council, is one of those who are fighting against collegiality. He is perhaps prompted, certainly supported, by Cardinal Ciriaci, who, with Ottaviani, is one of the main (or intelligent) opponents.

I returned at exactly 3.10 pm for the meeting with Denis and Lécuyer about the priesthood. But Lécuyer had to leave us very soon: he was going to a meeting arranged by Moeller: the Pope, who continues to receive the onslaughts of the anti-collegialists, was, it appears, very impressed by two reports along these lines. A report must be prepared that might thwart these two. I told Lécuyer to try to join up with Dupuy, who has been working for a week on a refutation of Staffa.

I myself spent the evening working on the *modi* for No. 28 of *De Presbyteris*. Because of this I missed the reception at the embassy, interesting because one meets a lot of people there.

I have been especially struck these last two days by the quite appalling MEDIOCRITY of the discussion *De Beata*. The basic questions have barely come to the surface. The East remained silent.

Friday 18 September 1964

At the beginning of Mass, l'abbé Denis and I looked at the text I had prepared yesterday evening on priesthood.

There was a meeting yesterday of the Italian Episcopate. Ruffini and Carli made a thoroughgoing assault on the schema (that is to say, on Chapter III, because the rest does not interest them). But Colombo defended it very strongly and was listened to with attention.

They went back over the *De BMV*, in the name of seventy bishops:

Frings:[2] appealed for consent to a *via media* and so for unanimity.

Alfrink:[3] recalled the true purpose of the chapter: to enunciate the teaching THE CHURCH must give. That is why maximalist and minimalist touches have no place here. It is a matter of a document of the highest teaching authority (≠ any pontifical document).

He spoke of the question of 'mediatrix'. This title expresses badly the teaching that is intended by it. IN ITSELF it assimilates Mary too closely to Christ, the *UNIQUE* Mediator. This title should be avoided.

---

1. Simon Delacroix, priest of the diocese of Cambrai, Professor of Ancient History at the Catholic Institute in Paris, was Director General of the Apostolic Union of the Clergy, as well as of its journal, *Prêtres diocésains;* he was a Council expert.
2. *AS* III/II, 10–11.
3. *AS* III/II, 12–14.

Castán (Spain):[1] in favour of '*Mater Ecclesiae*' because the Church is a family (of God) [in that case, Mary is the wife of God].

Actually, he said Mary is *Sponsa spiritus Sancti* [the spouse of the Holy Spirit].

Mother of human beings, if she were not, she would be Mother of a monster, that is, of a head without a body. . .

IDIOCIES: a combination of verbalism, abstract dialectic and sentimentalism.

He replied to Méndez (Laurentin).

Vote on the whole of Chapter II of *De Ecclesia*. Result:

Placet:	1,615
Iuxta modum:	553 = the Muslims!!!
Non placet:	19.

Reading of an introduction by Marella[2] on *De Munere episcoporum*, and of the *Relatio* by Veuillot[3] (not striking).

Discussion started straightaway.

Cardinal Richaud:[4] indicated some omissions: on the *amotio et translatio parochorum* [removal and transfer of parish priests].

I went out with Fr Grillmeier, who wanted to see me about *De Presbyteris*, but I was mainly buttonholed by l'abbé Dulac,[5] with whom I spent a good hour. I realised that he was finding in the terms of the schema theses that were not there, and that were not intended to be there. I explained what it was intended to say, and what it did say. Since he did not really believe me, I referred him to Mgr Philips, D'Ercole, Maccarrone. That seemed to pacify him. I concluded, in agreement with him, that it was necessary that an IRENIC explanation be given on Monday morning by Mgr Philips. That would greatly clarify, and calm things down. Rather like the way Zinelli had clarified, with explanations, the vote on infallibility at Vatican I. It was decided—and Philips agreed; Otttaviani would too, he said—to try to obtain this from Cardinal Ottaviani, who would be able to explain it to the Theological Commission this evening. I pushed for what seemed to me would be conducive to peace and truth. We tried to see Ottaviani after this morning's meeting, without success. We at least saw Cardinal Browne, but he, as usual, saw mainly, or only, the difficulties in the matter. On my return, I spoke about this to Mgr Garrone, who promised to introduce the idea at the meeting of the Theological Commission this evening (a meeting of members ONLY, without the experts.)

---

1. Laureano Castán Lacoma, Bishop of Sigüenza-Guadalajara, *AS* III/II, 15–18.
2. *AS* III/II, 58–59.
3. *AS* III/II, 60–66.
4. *AS* III/II, 69–71.
5. Raymond Dulac, priest of the diocese of Versailles, collaborator in *La Pensée catholique*.

During this time I missed all the interventions, particularly Carli,[1] who seems to have made an impression. The results were also given of the vote on Chapter II as a whole.

I saw a good many people. Especially Mgr Zoghby, who asked me for the elements of an intervention to be made on the *De Ecclesiis Orientalibus* [on the Eastern Churches]. Also Fr de Lubac, always very pessimistic. He thinks the Holy Spirit has been forgotten everywhere, and that there is no breath of the Spirit at the Council. For myself, I am optimistic, perhaps too much so, sometimes.

At 3.00 pm a visit from M. Menz, an English Canadian convert from Lutheranism (partly under the influence of my books) who is wondering about his vocation: Friar Preacher? Oratorian? Benedictine? Holy Cross?

At 4.00 pm, at Saint-Louis: workshop for the bishops on priesthood (from the pastoral point of view and for the pastoral decrees). I don't know how I got back, as I was hardly able to take a step. The weather was very sultry.

Visit from l'abbé Dulac. Obsessed, gnawed at by anxiety. To settle him I went to see Mgr Garrone, who had just come back from the Theological Commission. He told me: 1) that Parente had raised a vehement protest, relayed by Tromp, who was even more vehement. There are a lot of manoeuvres around Chapter III, manoeuvres to which the Secretary General is lending his support. He vituperated in particular against three Italian experts, who had inundated certain episcopates, for example those of South America, with sheets of paper pointing out to them the course to be followed in the voting, Number by Number. 2) As for Philips' intervention, it was very vague. Cardinal Browne, timid and sheepish, pronounced himself against. It had been thought that Parente's text was so clear that it answered the objections by itself.

Short visit from Fr Dupuy. Moeller and Martimort had indeed made appeal to him. He told me that the Pope is very impressed by two reports to which a response must be made, even though they have not been seen . . . Fr Dupuy had been commissioned to draft this response, to which Lécuyer has added some notes. At this very moment (7.30 pm) Cardinal Suenens is being received by the Pope: he is taking to him the text of Cardinal Lefebvre and that of Fr Dupuy, and will comment on them to him. —At least on first reading, I do not find Fr Dupuy's text very good: neither strong nor convincing. But I will not speak of it to anyone.

Dupuy told me that Cardinal Cushing would like to reopen the debate; he has collected seventy signatures, and nothing, it seems, will prevent the reopening of a debate declared closed last year. It is indeed possible. But it is endless. Dulac said to me that Cardinal Browne had told him of his own wish that Chapter III should be deferred to a Fourth Session. Scarcely any progress would have been made.

Saturday 19 September 1964

I have just read the *relationes* prepared for Chapter III. In my view, Parente's is no match for Franić's, from the psychological point of view. Franić will perhaps

---

1. AS III/II, 72–74.

succeed in having the text sent back for recasting. It will make an impression on many bishops formed in the ideas of the time of Pius XII.

At 5.00 pm, a meeting of about thirty bishops or experts, representing about fifteen episcopates, to agree upon the *modi:* not only on content or text but also on the procedure to be followed. After some excellent explanations by Philips and Martimort, it was concluded that:

- it will be necessary to vote *placet*, Number by Number, in order to assure that the text has the status of being in possession;
- it will be necessary to vote *placet* for the final vote on the chapter in its totality, because if there were to be a large number of votes *iuxta modum*, the chapter would be *'in aere'* ['up in the air'] (*dixit* [said] Felici) and, psychologically, the assembly would have a sense of having been disqualified.

One individual could propose several dozens of *modi*. When it is a matter of disciplinary questions, the NUMBER of Fathers asking for a *modus* comes into consideration; when it is a matter of doctrinal questions, it is the weight of the text and of the reasons supporting it that counts. So: vote *placet;* arrange to have all the *modi* that are desired proposed by a small number of men of weight, indicating, if necessary, that others are in agreement with them.

The Commission will take great account of *modi* presented in this way.

Mgr Etchegaray gave me some more precise details on the text of the Italian experts. It had been distributed yesterday in ST PETER'S SQUARE [so Felici should be in thunderous form on Monday!!!]. It was anonymous, but was drawn up by three Italians, of whom Lio was one. It gave this instruction: Vote *non placet* to all the Numbers and *placet iuxta modum* at the end.

Etchegaray added [he was informed by Gargitter about what had been done and said at the meetings of the Italian episcopate], that at the meeting of that episcopate last Thursday, Carli had given the same advice, with very great violence.

Let's hope things will become clearer. What should happen is that, on Monday, the Secretary—or better, the Secretary of the Theological Commission, should declare CLEARLY and in the five modern languages: 1) the exact meaning of the strange procedure for the *modi;* strange because, as Mgr Edelby says, in order to get them through we are asked to vote *'iuxta modum'* as little as possible; 2) the exact meaning of certain terms in the proposed text.

Etchegaray told me that at a meeting of representatives of about twenty episcopal conferences which took place yesterday (every Friday[1]) everyone signed a petition to the Council of Presidents, asking for a written response concerning this procedure for the *modi*.

Sunday 20 September 1964

I finished writing my chronicles for *ICI* and a text for Mgr Zoghby. I finished typing my chronicle with one finger, because my right hand can do no more. After

---

1. This refers to the 'Conference of Twenty-two', of which Etchegaray was the secretary (cf, above, page 172, note 6).

that, I had to prepare a plan of work on the *De Revelatione*, and my two lectures for tomorrow. A visit from Laurentin, and from André Cruiziat.[1]

Monday 21 September 1964

At St Peter's, a somewhat nervous atmosphere. It seems that yesterday fifteen cardinals went to see the Pope to ask him that Chapter III be deferred until later. 'They' had pulled out all the stops . . . I saw Mgr Guano, who told me that he was thinking of associating Fr Häring with Mgr Philips as redactor of schema XIII and as Secretary of the Commission. I wholly agreed and had thought for ten days that this was happening *via facti* [in fact].

I intoned two refrains to as many as I could: 1) to vote *placet* on the sections and on the chapter and to have the *modi* presented by a small number of authoritative men, who will vote *iuxta modum* at the end. 2) There will be no peace for Chapter III, unless Philips explains the meaning of the terms and of the principal propositions. That is becoming more and more obvious to me. Because the opponents read into the text a meaning that is not there.

It was announced that Mgr Gawlina[2] (who had spoken in the Council on Friday) died last night; that on 23 September the Pope will bring to the Basilica the head of St Andrew, which will be exposed for veneration by the Fathers.

Reading of *relationes*: Franić.[3]

Cardinal Tisserant protested, but in a rather academic fashion, against the experts who meet together to create currrents of opinion.

König's[4] *Relatio*, then Parente's,[5] WHICH WAS APPLAUDED, then Henríquez's.[6]

I went out briefly during this *relatio*, and saw Mgr Prignon for a moment. He told me that at 9.00 pm yesterday evening Cardinal Cushing had refused to sign the request for a reopening of the debate. The Moderators, he told me, have decided, if the request for reopening is presented, to allow another to be proposed in the contrary sense, and to argue from the opposition of the two in favour of disallowing the reopening. In any case they will not reopen the debate without having asked for a vote of the assembly.

At 11.45 am the first vote was announced.

---

1. André Cruiziat was a layman engaged in the liturgical renewal, in the Catholic Scouts' Movement of France, and in La Vie Nouvelle (on this Christian movement see J Lestavel, *La Vie Nouvelle, histoire d'un mouvement inclassable* (Paris: Cerf, 1994).
2. The Pole Joseph Gawlina, curial titular archbishop, member of the Commission for Bishops and for the Government of Seminaries. In fact, he had intervened *in aula* the previous Thursday.
3. *AS* III/II, 193–201.
4. *AS* III/II, 201–204.
5. *AS* III/II, 205–210.
6. *AS* III/II, 211–217.

At 11.50 am Cardinal Léger[1] spoke to propose that the role of the bishop should be spoken of in a less atemporal manner, and one more adapted to the MODERN world, some characteristics of which he described. He spoke in favour of a more pastoral understanding. He was applauded by the young bishops.

> Cardinal Confalonieri:[2] on the pastoral care of displaced persons.
> Mgr Compagnone[3]
> Angelus Rossi[4] (Brazil) in the name of 108 bishops of Brazil.
> Staverman[5] (Indonesia): the bishop is too much spoken of in the manner of the past; today co-operators want to be taken seriously. There is talk of an attitude of mercy, but this needs to be translated into actual practice.

I spoke to Mgr Villot about my idea of getting Mgr Philips to speak *in aula*. He was interested. He said it would be necessary to get in touch with the Moderators. In fact, at the end of the meeting, I spoke to Cardinal Döpfner. He said to me: Yes, but isn't there a risk that the Others will also want to speak? I replied: it is provided for in the regulations . . . Cardinal Döpfner said he will raise this at the meeting of the Moderators.

Visit from Fr Hussar,[6] who stayed for lunch.

At 4.30 pm, a lecture to the French-speaking bishops of Africa about collegiality. Then a lecture to the lay Auditors on the *De Revelatione*. That was interesting for me and I enjoyed being in their group and seeing them responding. Their response to my lecture was good; they are concerned about the pastoral impact of what is said about exegesis, about literary genres, about the historicity of the gospels and the concrete consequences all this will have in the Church.

Tuesday 22 September 1964

I did not go to St Peter's this morning. I had too much correspondence and work that had got behind. Work on a text about progress. When the bishops came back they said there had been eight votes, that the highest number of *non placet* had been 391, and that discussion of religious freedom would begin tomorrow.

---

1. *AS* III/II, 219–221.
2. *AS* III/II, 222–223.
3. *AS* III/II, 224–227.
4. Agnelo Rossi, Archbishop of Ribeirão Preto, member of the Commission for the Discipline of the Clergy and of the Christian People; he was to become Archbishop of São Paulo in November 1964, and cardinal in 1965; *AS* III/II, 227–228.
5. *AS* III/II, 229–231.
6. André (in religion Marie-Bruno) Hussar, OP, of the Province of France, was in charge of the Maison Saint-Isaïe which he had founded in Jerusalem: a centre for Dominican studies of Judaism. He was sent to Rome during the Third Session to follow the question of the schema on the Jews there.

At 4.00 pm, at the *Foyer Unitas* for the meeting of the Observers. My tiredness prevented me from seeing each one as I would have liked. For this short walk is my limit, even with a stick.

Exposition by Fr Benoit, wholly biblical (with, nonetheless, some excess of piety in regard to John 19) on the mystery of Mary, seen in the perspective of the *Virgo Filia Sion* [*the Virgin Daughter of Sion*], [I had made a formal request for this to the Commission; I had asked Mgr Weber to intervene about it. But his text never arrived in Rome . . .]

There followed interventions by:

Blakemore[1] (Disciples of Christ)

Cullmann: Mary is an instrument in the history of salvation exactly like Abraham or the Apostles; there has not been constructed an abrahamology or a paulology . . . The gospels speak of some weaknesses of Mary in faith: Mark 3: 21–25, for Cullmann believes that this is all one and the same pericope [Cf 6: 3–4]: John 2: 4 ff. In John 19 it is apparent that it is the cross of Christ that creates the true family of believers.

From the point of view of the use of texts, on page 207, 2 Peter 3:10 and Hebrews 13 and 14 are quoted just for the sake of THE WORDS, not for their precise context.

Fr Scrima made an intervention of very fine quality. He was looking for the implicit gnoseological presuppositions of a Mariology: they are of the order of a liturgical understanding. The connection should be demonstrated between Mary and christology, pneumatology, anthropology.

Schlink: 1) in the same sense as Cullmann. Mary was tempted and wavered. But she was confirmed in her faith by grace. It is much rather in that way that she is the type of the Church;

2) criticism of MEDIATRIX: the title mediator is reserved to Christ alone as Saviour and Lord. It cannot be applied to Mary except by way of an analogical transposition which theologians know about, but of which the faithful are unaware;

3) the text that is now INSERTED as the last Chapter of the *De Ecclesia* is, in effect, the previous text, scarcely changed. But the previous text was independent. One would have expected a new draft text on Mary AS A MEMBER OF THE CHURCH. [[But Mary is presented over against the Church, distinct from the Church.]] This will have serious ECCLESIOLOGICAL consequences. The Church will emerge as hypostatised, triumphant.

---

1. William Barnett Blakemore, Dean of the Disciples' Divinity House at the University of Chicago, and Observer delegated by the World Alliance of the Churches of Christ (Disciples of Christ).

Nissotis: spoke at length in English, in a rather obscure manner. Once again he poured out all his complexes, demonstrating that he is not, TO ANY DEGREE, a man of dialogue. In addition, he was also irritating, negative and excessive. For Scrima, sitting beside me, it was a source of suffering to listen to him. He criticised the absence of the Holy Spirit, and the attribution to Mary of what belongs to the Holy Spirit: the Comforter, the source of the Church . . . Mariology suppresses pneumatology. The schema puts Mary between authority and the people, when in fact she prays with the Christian people. The interpretation given by Fr Benoit of John 19 attributes to Mary the role of giving birth to the Church, a role which belongs to the Holy Spirit at Pentecost. Etc.

In the evening, after my return, a visit from Mgr Sauvage, for the question of the *modi*, especially to *De Presbyteris*. Moeller said to me: The Pope refuses to intervene on Chapter III. On the other hand, he is reserving to himself what concerns marriage in schema XIII.

The opponents want to introduce into No 16 of the *De Ecclesia* (p 64, lines 4ff) a *modus* scaling down the *plena et suprema potestas* QUANDO COLLEGI-UM AGIT COLLEGIALITER [full and supreme power WHEN THE COLLEGE ACTS COLLEGIALLY]: that is to say, in practice, to the ecumenical council. Their idea is always: outside the council—which is convoked, presided over and approved by the pope, and thus entirely dependent on him, and, according to them, receiving its authority from him—there is in the body of bishops only a passive capacity to be, together with the pope, the subject of the *suprema potetstas* [supreme power].

Wednesday 23 September 1964

At St Peter's, I saw Mgr Colombo for a moment. He intoned the refrain: there needs to be the greatest unanimity for this Chapter III. To achieve this some points need to be better explained (and then it was I who intoned my refrain: Philips should be got to speak *in aula*). And also, added Colombo, add a few words here and there.

It was also apparent from this conversation that there is a great deal of obscurity on the question of how the *modi* are to be VOTED ON. Colombo said: a FEW *modi*, but supported by a great number of people. This is the opposite of the conclusions of the meeting last Saturday.

Thus, as Fr de Lubac, who was beside me, noted with somewhat pointed criticism, the very small minority will achieve its aims, at least in part. In the end, their cries will be given in to, just as parents end up giving in to their recalcitrant children, for the sake of peace . . .

At 9.00 am the Sistine choir began to be heard in the distance. The Pope drew near, carrying the head of St Andrew. Mass by Cardinal Marella, archpriest of St

Peter's, in the presence of the Holy Father. After Mass a fairly brief address by Cardinal König.[1] The Pope left the basilica amid applause, while the Sistine choir briskly chanted a complicated motet.

This morning's newspaper gave the names of the members of the delegation who will go to Patras with the relic: Cardinal Bea, Willebrands, Duprey, Raes, Mgr Jacques Martin,[2] etc.

It is a blessed moment for ecumenism.

86th General Congregation. End of the discussion on the pastoral *Munus* [function] of bishops.

Mgr Greco,[3] USA: as President of the Confraternity of Christian Doctrine (a lay association): asked for it to be mentioned in the schema.

Mgr González Moralejo:[4] on the recently added No. 18 *(ter)*, on the freedom of episcopal elections. Asked for some POSITIVE criteria and the involvement of the episcopal conference.

The presbyterium of the diocese concerned, and even the laity, should be heard.

Mgr De Smedt[5] read out his new *Relatio* on religious freedom: very good. Although the voting was for the *suffragationes* [propositions] 13 and following of Chapter III, we were listening to interventions on religious freedom.

Ruffini:[6] associated freedom and truth. And here below, tolerance. In favour of making room for the Catholic state. Be careful! This is serious. The old warrior Ruffini has lost none of his punch.

Cardinal Quiroga:[7] put forward *doctrinam integram, non imminutam* [the whole teaching, undiluted]. The text is responding to the spirit of so-called Protestant regions, not that of Catholic countries. According to him, one moves from the private and subjective order to an objective rule.

Cardinal Léger:[8] in the name of several Canadian bishops: Praise for the schema. Asked for a better description of religious freedom (it only speaks for people who do have a religion), a better formulation of

---

1. *AS* III/II, 285–287.
2. The Frenchman Jacques Martin was a titular bishop and worked in the Secretariat of State.
3. Charles P Greco, Bishop of Alexandria (Louisiana, United States), member of the Commission for the Discipline of the Clergy and of the Christian People, appointed by the Pope at the time of the First Session of the Council, *AS* III/II, 289–290.
4. *AS* III/II, 294–295.
5. *AS* III/II, 348–353.
6. *AS* II/II, 354–356.
7. *AS* II/II, 357–359.
8. *AS* II/II, 359–360.

the FOUNDATION, in such a way that everyone could agree with it, namely: respect for that which is held to be most precious.

Cardinal Cushing[1] in the name, almost unanimously, of the American bishops (very solemn pronunciation, at the same time very American, which caused undisguised amusement). *Declaratio debet manere intacta quoad suum sensum essentiale* [the declaration should remain intact in its essential meaning] . . . Allusion to John XXIII. Applause.

Cardinal Bueno[2] (Seville): not against the text, suggested some improvements.

Cardinal Meyer:[3] in the name of almost all the American bishops on the OPPORTUNENESS of this text (Lacordaire and Montelambert would be thrilled!) Suggested some modifications.

Cardinal Ritter:[4] on the notion of freedom and on its foundation. Suggested that a simple DECLARATION should be made, without argument or the giving of reasons: greater unanimity would thereby be obtained. The Moderators should separate the two things in proposing the vote. (It seems that an expert had given him this paper at the last minute, but this text did not express his own thought, but was even rather the opposite. Ritter was very unhappy. But why did he read it?)

Cardinal Silva Henríquez:[5] in the name of forty-eight Fathers from Latin America: approved the declaration. Its importance as a foundation for evangelisation in Latin America. It is a condition for that. One will be led to a more authentic pastoral action (≠ proselytism).

Cardinal Ottaviani:[6] the Church has always professed the principle: *Nemo cogatur* [no one should be constrained]. But certain exaggerations in the text should be eliminated. The schema lacks a declaration in favour of the liberty of those who profess the true faith. Some remarks along the same lines as Ruffini. Against affirming the freedom of propaganda. The text could be harmful to the unity of certain Catholic nations.

Parente:[7] asked to speak TOMORROW. Granted.

X[8] . . . (Yugoslavia): a rather long intervention, which was applauded, but which I could scarcely hear, because I was chatting to Guitton. The Pope, he told me, is tired and strained (I learned elsewhere that Guitton had been consulted by the Pope for *Ecclesiam Suam* = the section on ecumenism).

---

1. *AS* II/II, 361–362.
2. *AS* II/II, 363–365.
3. *AS* II/II, 366–368.
4. *AS* II/II, 368–369.
5. *AS* III/II, 369–372.
6. *AS* III/II, 375-376.
7. *AS* III/II, 378.
8. Smiljan F Cekada, Bishop of Skoplje, *AS* III/II, 378–381.

Mgr Prignon told me that Ruffini had made an approach to Cardinal Suenens, claiming to have been put up to it by the Pope, and saying: it is necessary to converse, it is necessary to come to an understanding.

This ties up with what Mgr C Colombo said to me about the same time. The minority would like to bring about a rallying to their cause, at the cost of some concessions. But which concessions? I cannot believe that any could be accepted that would touch on THE DOCTRINE of Chapter III.

On going out I saw Cardinal Wyszyński, who advised me against ANY collaboration with *Za i Przeciw*,[1]—then His Beatitude Maximos IV, who was delighted with the votes achieved. Indeed, they are remarkably favourable. The most disputed sections still garnered more than 85% of the votes.

In all, a very interesting morning: 1) St Andrew and the *rapprochement* with the East; 2) the votes; 3) the quality and positive character of the debate on religious freedom. Lacordaire prevails a hundred years after his death.

Mgr Henríquez and Mgr Ancel told me that the object of this evening's meeting of the Commission (without the experts) is to decide on the title for the chapter *De Beata*. *Mater Ecclesiae, Mater fidelium* [Mother of the Church, Mother of the Faithful]? Mgr Henríquez is against the first title, but would willingly accept the second. I spoke to the contrary. In the end (I learned from Mgr Garrone), it was a question of whether this title could be added to the Litany of Loreto. Mgr Garrone had raised a prior question: should ANY title be added at all? The question was dismissed.

Mgr Etchegaray told me that he had seen a Canadian bishop who had been invited, by mistake, to the meeting held every Tuesday, by the anti-collegial group:[2] about thirty of them, including Ruffini, Staffa, Carli, Dom Prou,[3] Mgr M Lefebvre. It seems that quite incredible expressions of extremism and negativity are voiced there.

[Here are some more precise particulars: this Canadian bishop was Mgr Hacault,[4] auxiliary of Mgr Baudoux. The participants in this meeting were very disappointed, for they were counting on 700, and even 800 in the important votes . . . One of them said: when the leaders betray the cause, the troops take the initiative . . .]

Nevertheless, I believe we are on the way to rebalancing Vatican I.

The French bishops had their meeting at Saint-Louis. There they adopted the *modi* (a selection of those prepared at Les Voirons, plus those that I had prepared

---

1. The journal *Za i Przeciw* had been created by a dissident group of the Pax Movement; they had published at Easter an article that Congar had sent them.
2. The *Coetus Internationalis Patrum*; on this group, see Luc Perrin, 'Il "Coetus Internationalis Patrum" et la minoranza conciliare' in: *L'evento e le decisioni. Studi sulle dinamiche del concilio Vaticano II* (Bologna,1997), 173–187.
3. Dom Jean Prou, OSB, Abbot of Solesmes and Superior General of the Benedictine Congregation of Solesmes.
4. Antoine Hacault, Auxiliary of Saint-Boniface.

for *De presbyteris*) and designated Cardinal Lefebvre to present them, while voting *iuxta modum*; the other bishops voting *Placet*. It seems that other episcopates are making similar agreements, perhaps with more or less the same *modi*. It is sorting itself out. What is achieved in St Peter's first takes shape in very small units. The Council now has its own self-awareness and its incipient structures. All the bishops are aware that, with the votes taken yesterday and today, the turning point has been won, Vatican I has received its necessary complement.

Thursday 24 September 1964

Mass, DURING WHICH a choir sang chants in honour of the Blessed Sacrament. Why the blazes can't we just have a Mass that is a Mass! The Constitution on the Liturgy is already a dead letter for many! And they have been determined this year, for the enthronement of the Gospel, to replace the *Christus vincit*, a strong chant, easy to sing, with the Palm Sunday hymn, *Pueri hebraeorum*, which is sung too high, and not well known by the Fathers.

Felici[1] announced the closing dates for signing up to speak on the *De Revelatione*. The discussion on religious freedom was taken up again.

> König:[2] we cannot remain silent about the fact that there are whole countries where religious freedom does not exist. This is contrary to the declaration of the United Nations, contrary to common knowledge, to social progress and to human dignity.
> Applause.
> Cardinal Browne:[3] the text cannot be approved as it is, and it is not necessary for ensuring peace. He believed and said that in the text religious freedom is grounded on the rights of conscience. *THAT IS NOT TRUE.*
> Parente:[4] some account has been taken of his difficulties, but not enough on all points. Called for greater rigour and force in the affirmation of certain very delicate points.
> The schema might have dubious effects in many international circles (an allusion, I think, to Fr Riedmatten). Take the route proposed by Ritter to avoid contentious statements. He suggested a plan for a statement of principles and an all-embracing declaration by way of conclusion.
> Cantero[5] (Saragossa): *in genere placet.* But some comments: either on the internal order . . . (Impossible to summarise, a text to READ carefully).

---

1. *AS* III/II, 467–478.
2. *AS* III/II, 468–470.
3. *AS* III/II, 470–471.
4. *AS* III/II, 471–473.
5. Pedro Cantero Cuadrado, Archbishop of Saragossa, member of the Secretariat for Unity, elected during the Second Session of the Council, *AS* III/II, 472–477.

Abasolo[1] (India): a Spanish dissertation.

Nicodemo[2] (Bari): in favour of a declaration which included in a better manner the statement of principles, which he recalled clearly along the classical line.

I went out for a moment. Conversation with Fr Scrima. He spoke to me about: 1) a plan for meetings *HERE* with the Observers of the Ecumenical Patriarch, to help them to get involved and to become accustomed to ecumenical dialogue with us. One of them calls the Catholic Church 'the papist Church'; 2) a plan to have Catholic observers present as PARTICIPANTS at a conference on Orthodox theology to be held in Romania in 1965. Fr Scrima asked me what I would think about a visit by the Patriarch to Rome.

I returned to my place to hear an attack against the text by Mgr Marcel Lefebvre.[3] He criticised, in terms of *fas et nefas* [right and wrong], practically the whole of it, from the point of view of a man with a wholly negative attitude, seeking to oppose what the text said, without reflection.

Buckley[4] [   ]

Primeau[5] also gave a very elaborate dissertation. No one much listened. Half the assembly was chatting pretty well everywhere.

Nierman[6] in the name of the episcopal conference of Holland and of some bishops from Indonesia. Approval of the declaration. The legislation on mixed marriages will need to be reviewed in the light of this declaration. He will propose some emendations in writing.

Temiño? Spain:[7] the text should be brought into agreement with that of Vatican I on the sufficiency of the evidence for the Catholic Church. Always the affirmation of the *en-soi* [self-evident].

Klepacz[8] in the name of the bishops of Poland: he, too, gave another dissertation. It is very wearisome!

Dubois[9] (Besançon): too philosophical and juridical. It should be based more on RELIGIOUS principles. . . The text is presented in a pedantic fashion, and with considerations that are too much *ex communibus* [from commonplaces].

---

1. *AS* III/II, 477–480.
2. *AS* III/II, 481–482.
3. *AS* III/II, 490–492.
4. *AS* III/II, 493–494.
5. *AS* III/II, 495–497.
6. Pieter A Nierman, Bishop of Groningen (Netherlands), *AS* III/II, 498–499.
7. A Temiño Saiz, *AS* III/II, 499–501.
8. *AS* III/II, 503–505.
9. *AS* III/2, 505–507.

Granados:[1] *Ius pro Ecclesia, pro errore, tolerantia secundum quod exigit Bonum commune* [rights for the Church: for error, tolerance to the degree required by the common good]. The text should be reviewed by the Theological Commission.

As we were going out I remarked to Cardinal Liénart how exhausted I was, going out after having to listen to fifteen disssertations; he said to me: we have a copy of the summary sent to the Secretariat; it makes it easier to follow. One can also sometimes see that the speaker has changed something. Mgr Parente and Marcel Lefebvre have toned down their texts. The latter said at first that the adoption of the Declaration would be a veritable revolution in doctrine.

I spent the afternoon (except for a visit from Féret and Urresti) studying the *De libertate religiosa* and the reactions it has aroused. I remain uneasy. This text is, in the end, premature.

It sweeps the place entirely clean of what had been there, that is, of the manner in which this matter has been spoken of hitherto, and replaces all that with something else. This can perhaps be done, but it should be done only after mature reflection. But there has not been time for sufficient reflection. There is some truth in the objections raised against the text, in the criticisms of Fr de Broglie. What is required is addition, *augere vetera novis* [to augment the old by means of the new], not substitution pure and simple. But, on the other hand, in the former position, there is something of the 'theologico-political treatise', closely connected to the times, to Christendom and its after-effects, that must also be subjected to criticism and from which we need to be set free.

I went to see Mgr Garrone, to suggest that he might say something along these lines tomorrow (he is due to speak), and to ask for a period of reflection, perhaps a revision of the text in a Joint Commission with the Theological Commission. But the text must retain a tone that is accessible to people, and open to the kerygmatic and missionary spirit. That is what Fr de Broglie has not done.

Friday 25 September 1964

Mgr Elchinger, who had just seen Cardinal Döpfner, told me that the Pope is at last reassured. He had been on the point of intervening in a way that would have thrown everything into question, but he has personally studied the text and the question of collegiality. He is now settled and reassured. —Mgr Philips confirmed this to me.

Mgr Etchegaray recounted how the Pope had said to Mgr Capovilla that last Monday and Tuesday were the best days of his life.

I saw Mgr Huyghe about the question of the *modi* to the chapter on holiness, and on religious life. He had prepared the *modi* for the French episcopate, along with those of Féret and myself, of Dom Dupont and G Lafont.[2]

---

1. *AS* III/2, 508–509.
2. Ghislain Lafont, OSB, of the abbey of Sainte-Marie de la Pierre-qui-Vire (Yonne),

For the first time a female Auditor, Mlle Monnet,[1] and, among the Auditors, a Black in the full costume of his country (from Togo).[2]

Felici[3] announced the closing dates for the submission of the text of one's intervention: *De apostolatu laicorum*: 2 October; schema XIII: 5 October!!! What a rush!!! Afterwards there will be voting on certain schemas without discussion. However, the Moderators do allow a brief discussion. It will be possible to introduce some *modi* in the voting for these texts. The text of *modi* must be submitted by these dates:

> *De Ecclesiis Orientalibus:* 10 October.
> *De Missionibus:* 11 October.
> *De sacerdotibus* [on priests]: 12 October.
> *De religiosis:* 13 October.
> *De Matrimonio:*[4] 14 October.
> *De institutione sacerdotali* [on priestly formation]: 15 October.
> *De Scholis* [on schools]:16 October.

(Felici had wanted these small schemas to be simply put to the vote, without discussion. On the order of the Moderators he announced that, nevertheless, there will be discussion. The bishops strongly insist on this!!!)

Resumption of the discussion on religious freedom:

Cardinal Roberti:[5] freedom of conscience is not the same as freedom of consciences.

Hurley:[6] the setting up of a society in and through which the human being renders to God the SOCIAL duty which is owed to him SOCIALLY, exempts (and excludes) civil society from having to render this social cult. The old thesis of the union of church and state must be dropped. Freedom, even to make mistakes, is a concrete condition for arriving at the truth.

Cibrián[7] (Bolivia): the objective right of God, of truth alone.

---

taught theology.

1. Marie-Louise Monnet was the founding President of the International Movement for the Apostolate of Independent Social Milieux (MIAMSI) and, in France, of Catholic Action of Independent Milieux (ACI).
2. Eusèbe Adjakpley was the African Regional Secretary of the International Federation of Catholic Youth.
3. *AS* II/II, 513–515.
4. The *votum* on the sacrament of marriage.
5. *AS* III/II, 515.
6. *AS* III/II, 515–518.
7. Ubaldo E Cibrián Fernández, titular bishop, prelate *nullius* of Corocoro, *AS* III/II, 518–519.

Melendro[1] (China): criticised the text on behalf of the rights of truth, and even of ecumenism, because people would not be urged to seek the truth.

Wojtyła[2] (Crackow): the schema includes two aspects which should be distinguished: the ecumenical and the socio-political. UNITE truth and freedom.

Garrone:[3] in favour of a declaration of the historic evolution that the Church has known in this matter. On exactly the same lines as what I requested in connection with schema XIII. There is no contradiction because one is not talking exactly *de eodem et sub eodem adspectu* [about the same thing and from the same point of view].

Hoa Nguyen-van Hien[4] Vietnam [   ]

Alter[5] (USA, Cincinnati) [   ]

Fernandez, OP:[6] praise of the schema, but several serious things in it are inadequate. Is it not too bound to CURRENT, relative, ideas and structures? Aim for a shorter declaration, on which everyone would be agreed. It speaks too much of holy things in a non-religious manner. It deals too much with the relations of human beings among themselves and not of human beings with God.

Rectae norma conscientiae (John XXIII) ≠ *recta conscientia* [the measure of a right conscience is not the same as a right conscience][7] (text) [Mgr Pavan, who drafted both texts, expressly denies this . . .]

Lucey[8] (Cork, Ireland) [   ]

Colombo Carlo:[9] on the composition of the declaration. On the doctrinal principles, none of which should be passed over in silence. The Catholic doctrine on religious freedom:

1) —the natural right to seek and to know the truth; from which flows the freedom of research, and that of communication, of dialogue;

---

1. *AS* III/II, 522–524.
2. *AS* III/II, 530–532.
3. *AS* III/II, 533–535.
4. *AS* III/II, 535–536.
5. Karl J Alter, Archbishop of Cincinnati, member of the Commission for Bishops and the Government of Dioceses, elected during the First Session, *AS* III/II, 537–539.
6. *AS* III/II, 539–542.
7. A reference to the encyclical *Pacem in Terris* of John XXIII, on a point of which the interpretation was disputed.
8. Cornelius Lucey, Bishop of Cork and Ross, *AS* III/II, 552–553.
9. *AS* III/II, 554–557.

2) – the right to follow one's certain conscience, even in religious matters;

3) – the revealed principle: the freedom and supernatural character of faith, of the act of faith. This step is never subject to the civil powers.

These principles are bound up with the nature of things, and so are always valid, for everyone.

Add these two things:

– the obligation to seek the truth, especially in religious matters;

– the value of revealed truth as an element of the common good in any society.

At 11.55 am, Cardinal Suenens[1] proposed that the discussion of *De libertate religiosa* be terminated. —*YES*.

Cardinal Bea[2] read out the *relatio De Iudaeis* . . .

I met Mgr Lambruschini. He asked me: what's this about this letter you wrote to a bishop in which you call collegiality into question? Mgr Piolanti has circulated it in photocopy among the Italian bishops and others. It took me a moment to understand what this could be about. It could only be about my letter to Dulac where: 1) I acknowledged receipt of his offprints from *La Pensée catholique;* 2) I reproached him for being purely negative, and for combating a caricature of collegiality; 3) I said that there was a need for some historical, canonical, and theological studies about it; ; 4) I invited him to do some positive and constructive work.

(L'abbé David[3] (Luçon) told me this evening that he had known about this for four or five days and wanted to speak to me about it.)

I have to rely on memory to restore the contents of my letter, but I am sure about the sense. So 'they' have gone so far as to publicise a private letter, and make use of it far beyond its meaning. If not even contrary to it. It is true there is a lack of studies, that is why I was so keen on making them, stimulating them, publishing them. But what is affirmed in the schema is, as such, sufficiently established. And yet my idea was simple, and I printed it last year: for a thousand years everything among us has been seen and constructed from the papal angle, not from that of the episcopate and its collegiality. Now THIS history, THIS theology, THIS canon law needs to be done. That's all.

The general feeling: We are ahead of schedule. The Council could well be finished this year, and even, after a short interval, the bishops could be recalled to vote on the texts. Thus those from more distant parts would not have to go back.

---

1. He presided at this General Congregation, *AS* III/II, 558.
2. *AS* III/II, 558–564.
3. Jacques David, of the diocese of Luçon, was secretary to his bishop, Mgr Cazaux; he was later to be Bishop of La Rochelle, and then of Évreux.

Balić, it seems, is advocating that the *De Beata* should be accepted purely and simply.

Afternoon, work on drafting a section on eschatology, cosmic and historical, for the chapter *De indole eschatologica* [the eschatological character].[1] I was asked to do it.

Saturday 26 September 1964

In the morning, a *LITTLE* work on *De indole eschatologica*. A visit from Fr de Lubac. Féret, with Liégé, were supposed to collect me at 12.00 pm for a fraternal 'symposium'. They arrived at 12.25 pm. We spent two hours looking for Dupuy and Chenu and in getting out of Rome. We did not get to Monte Cavo until 2.45 pm!!! A good encounter. Returned at nearly 7.00 pm; conversation with Liégé.

In the evening, I saw Mgr Leclercq, Rector of the Catho of Lille. He spoke to me, among other things, about the plan for the foundation in Jerusalem. I remember and note the following: 1) he maintained that it could not be done ALONE, that it would have to be done together WITH THE OTHERS, that is to say, with the Protestants and the Orthodox; they would have to be included in the running of it. He went to see Schutz at Taizé, and Schutz had said to him: it is necessary not only to SEARCH and WORK together, but also to PRAY together. This idea of 'doing together' must be elevated to the level of a rule of life, of prayer and of the hospitality of the House. 2) The financial resources for starting the project have been secured by an American donation equal to 150,000,000 old francs. 3) Mgr Gillon suggests the following administrative or juridical formula: that the Union of Catholic Universities should be the owner, and should rent the premises to the Foundation (for a nominal sum). In the event of a hitch or difficulties, this would allow for the tenancy to be terminated, with appropriate notice, and for one's freedom to be regained. 4) The meeting of the Rectors of Catholic Universities had a half-hour audience of the Holy Father last Thursday. Mgr Leclercq spoke on behalf of the others. He explained his idea for an institution for three parties. The Pope reacted negatively at first. Then after a quarter of an hour, he accepted the idea. He even remarked: not only for three, room must be made for the Anglicans . . . The Pope said nothing must be done in haste: 'speeding is forbidden' . . . 5) Since then, there was a meeting in which Fr Duprey took part. He revealed, under the seal of discretion, that the Faith and Order Commission, at its recent meeting at Aarhus, had decided to found an ecumenical institute in Jerusalem[2]. . .

Mgr Leclercq considers this to be providential: the two projects should meet and combine. . .

---

1. This refers to the future Chapter VII of *Lumen Gentium*.
2. From 15 to 27 August a plenary meeting had been held at Aarhus (Denmark) of the Faith and Order Commission of the WCC; in his opening speech L Vischer, Secretary of this Commission, had suggested that an Institute for Ecumenical Research should be founded by the WCC.

I then told Mgr Leclercq what Visser't Hooft had said about an organic participation of the Catholic Church in the work of the World Council of Churches: not joining the World Council, not even joining the Faith-and-Order Commission, which would be juridically possible without joining the Council. But to create a permanent Joint Commission made up of members of the Faith and Order Commission and some Catholic theologians. —This could also be taken into consideration . . .

Sunday 27 September 1964
In the morning, I completed and typed out my text on cosmic eschatology and took it to the Belgian College for Mgr Philips.

In the afternoon, I tried to catch up a bit with the necessary or useful reading which accumulates on my table. —I had little strength.

Monday 28 September 1964
Raining, damp weather.
The speeches on religious freedom commenced again.

> Heenan[1] praised the schema unreservedly with a view to the English situation, which is excellent. Applause.
> A bishop from Uganda:[2] praise for the schema.
> Wright[3] (USA) developed the consideration of the common good under its spiritual aspect. Quoted J Maritain. He got very worked up . . . (Experts have been excluded from a large part of the tribune to make room for the Auditors. There is nothing to lean on and I can hardly write. I am wondering whether, in these conditions, I will come to St Peter's again . . .)
> Zoa[4] [ ]

I collected my thoughts. At 10.45 am discussion on the Jews resumed.

> Cardinal Liénart:[5] despite the difficulties raised by the Arabs, the text is necessary from an ecumenical and pastoral point of view (against the notion of a reproached People).
> Text not at all striking; given without force. I was expecting better. It is true that I am so tired that I have hardly the strength to pay attention.

---

1. *AS* III/II, 569–571.
2. H Ddungu, *AS* III/II, 572–573.
3. *AS* III/II, 573–575.
4. *AS* III/II, 576–578.
5. *AS* III/II, 579–581.

Tappouni[1] in the name of the Eastern Patriarchs. They have nothing against the Jewish religion or against any nation. But this text would cause grave difficulties for their apostolate. This declaration is inopportune. Some applause, ISOLATED and thin.

Frings:[2] some comments.

Felici:[3] gave the results of the votes, said that the Theological Commission had asked that this Chapter III be divided into two for the final vote, that is, Nos 19–23 and 24–29. The reason: there really are two parts and the division would make the Commission's work easier.

Ruffini:[4] supported what Bea had said: one cannot call the Jews 'deicides'. But it would be a good thing to invite the Jews to recognise that Christ had been unjustly condemned, and to respect, to esteem, not to molest or attack Christians.

Lercaro:[5] emphasised that the Declaration on the Jews comes from the depths of the consciousness the Church has taken of its own mystery. Also noted the connection with the liturgy and the Constitution *De sacra liturgia*.

Cardinal Léger[6] [   ]

Cardinal Cushing[7] [   ]

I understood almost nothing. Afterwards, I went out for a pee. But I was stopped by an Argentine bishop (at their recent meeting one of them had said that I had written that collegiality was not sufficiently mature to be proposed as doctrine. He wanted to be clear in his own mind about this. Always that letter to Dulac!!!), then by Dulac, desperate and protesting that he did not have liberty to speak or to vote—that was a bit strong!—then Mgr Guano, then one of the five Hungarians who have been nominated as bishops and are participating in the Council: he had read all my books, he is a disciple . . . then Fr Benoit—who considered that the New Testament truth about the rejection of the gospel by the Jews is not being told . . .

Lunch at the Greek College, where Dumont, Rousseau, Lanne are. E Beauduin.[8] Then a session at the dentist's, because I have some problems with my teeth. I cannot walk two steps and it is painful to stand up: one of my worst days.

---

1. *AS* III/II, 582.
2. *AS* III/II, 582–583.
3. *AS* III/II, 584–585.
4. *AS* III/II, 585–587.
5. *AS* III/II, 587–589.
6. *AS* III/II, 590–591.
7. *AS* III/II, 593–594.
8. Édouard Beauduin, nephew of Lambert Beauduin, edited *L'Oeuvre d'Orient,* in Brussels.

The reception of the relics of St Andrew at Patras was, it seems, sensational. It is gestures like this that will, actually, change the atmosphere.

I have been told that, each year, the Council costs 1,400,000,000 lire.

Visit from Fr Dupuy, from Alberigo. He told me that, according to Dossetti (and, it seems, Cardinal Lercaro) Paul VI is tending more and more to distinguish himself from John XXIII. How? By an accentuation of the government of the Curia. From the liturgical point of view, Lercaro is in despair; his Commission works very well, but comes up against the Congregation of Rites. Every time the Pope finds in favour of the Congregation.

I note down these impressions just as they were given to me.

Visit from a young Spanish priest, of the *Sons of Charity* (St John of God)[1] about a subject for a thesis!

The bishops have each received, in a sealed envelope, a statement claiming that Cardinal Bea is of Jewish descent . . . !

Anti-semitism is not dead!

Tuesday 29 September 1964

I did not go to St Peter's. I was too exhausted by this damp, humid and pre-stormy weather. I was told yesterday evening that there were still forty-two or forty-four down to speak on the *De Iudaeis*. But the Moderators will doubtless want to finish it this morning.

On their return, the bishops told me that, in fact, they had heard once again grand general declarations in favour of the Jews, and the debate had been declared closed. What is more serious is that Felici had said, twice over, on the subject of tomorrow's vote on Chapter III as a whole, that if it resulted in two thirds of the *modi* being accepted, the text would be up in the air. But that is not true. The text has already been accepted by more than two thirds: IT IS IN POSSESSION. This morning, the diaconate was accepted, and the possibility that it might be conferred on married men.

Felici also said that those who have *modi* should vote *iuxta modum*: a *iuxta modum* allows the presentation of *modi* for only ONE person. That is true. But it is a tactical move. One is obliged to take it into account: the others have theirs, which Felici seconds . . .

I dragged myself to the *Foyer Unitas* for the weekly meeting of the Observers. It had been transferred to Friday—I was not aware of this—as the Observers are being received at the Vatican. But if I could have spared myself the journey! I am worn out and do not feel well. Can I hold out? As St Albert used to say: *Numquid durabo* [will I last]?

I saw Frs Hamer then, quickly, Dupuy and Le Guillou: brothers!

---

1. Probably the Hospitaller Order of St John of God, whose members are often called 'Brothers of Charity' in France.

Wednesday 30 September 1964

I was told that Felici had protested yesterday (without naming him) against Mgr Henríquez, who had drawn up a paper and signed it, asking that a single person might propose the *modi* of many. Obviously, that would mean only ONE person requesting the *modi*. But this was agreed to in order to prevent Felici and the anti-collegialists proclaiming everywhere that a text voted with so many *iuxta modum* votes 'stat in aere, non est probatus' [remains in the air, is not approved].

Felici had this announcement made: first, the advice of the Assembly is sought on the division of the vote on Chapter III into two votes. It was agreed to by standing or remaining seated.

He repeated that anyone who had any *modi* should submit them himself by voting *iuxta modum*.

He announced a vote to be taken on Nos 18–23: The results of this turned out to be:

Present:	2,242
Placet:	1,724
Non Placet:	42
Placet iuxta modum:	572
Null:	4

Reading of the *relatio* on Chapter IV
The second vote, Nos 24–29:

Present:	2,240
Placet:	1,704
Non Placet:	53
Placet iuxta modum:	481
Null:	2

Relatio on Chapter V a and b or V–VI
Vote on Chapter IV:

Present:	2,235
Placet:	2,152
Non Placet:	8
Placet iuxta modum:	76
Null:	0

Reading of the *relationes* on Chapters I & II of *De Revelatione*. Franić[1] first—the reading was interrupted by votes—then Florit,[2] whose explanation was much too long!!! Three times longer than the text itself . . . (and yet he was applauded).

---

1. *AS* III/III, 124–129.
2. *AS* III/III, 131–139.

Utrum instituendum sit caput speciale de Religiosis [whether there should be a special Chapter on Religious] (a simple majority vote):

Present:	2,210
Placet:	1,505
Non Placet:	798
Null *(iuxta modum)*:	4
Null:	3

Vote on Chapter V:

Present:	2,177
Placet:	1,856
Non Placet:	17
Placet iuxta modum:	302
Null:	2

Vote on Chapter III *De religiosis*

Present:	2,189
Placet:	1,736
Non Placet:	12
Placet iuxta modum:	438
Null:	3

We heard Mgr Gahamany[1] (Rwanda) in the name of seventy Fathers on the Declaration *De Iudaeis*. Praise for pagan religions.

At midday discussion commenced on the *De Revelatione*.

Ruffini[2] [   ]

Döpfner:[3] praise of the schema. The facts recalled by Franić are not denied by anyone, but are differently interpreted by some good theologians.

Some corrections that could truly improve the text in a biblical sense.

Cardinal Meyer[4] on No. 8 (*De ipsa Traditione* [on Tradition itself]): indicate the obscurations of the Tradition. He suggested a text.

I saw Fr Duprey for a moment. He told me that Patras was tremendously impressive. The Pope signed the Greek text of his letter IN GREEK, which thus authenticated it. But yesterday's meeting of the Observers at the Vatican did not have the

---

1.   *AS* III/III, 141–142.
2.   *AS* III/III, 142–145.
3.   *AS* III/III, 145–147.
4.   *AS* III/III, 150–151.

same warmth as last year's: especially the speeches of the Observers. It was good, but with less warmth.

Lunch at Saint-Sulpice. Conversation with Weber and Bannwarth.[1] At coffee, Cardinal Liénart came and sat beside me. He is pleased. We talked about collegiality. He told me that, after having heard Ottaviani say, *in aula*, that there had never been any collegial action by the Apostles, he had written to him to call his attention to Acts 6, the institution and ordination of the deacons, which are presented as an act of the Twelve. Ottaviani had replied to him IN WRITING: the text says: the Twelve, but it means: PETER, and Peter is what it wanted to say.

Unbelievable!!!

When I told the cardinal what I had heard said about Cardinal Lercaro's disappointment with respect to the *De sacra Liturgia* Council,[2] and the authority retained by the Congregation of Rites, he said to me: the Pope is leaving it be SO LONG AS THERE IS A CONGREGATION OF RITES . . . I took the matter up: are there plans to replace the Congregations with something else?' The cardinal indicated yes.

So the reform of the Curia would be a stage on the way to the expression of collegiality?

The cardinal insisted on explaining: the Church, which up until now has been predominantly European, must become worldwide in its structures.

Visit from Mgr Poupard. He said to me: the titles of several of your books could be put into *Ecclesiam Suam* as sub-titles.

At 5.00 pm I gave a lecture on Scripture and Tradition at the Dutch Documentation Centre. It went all right. There were questions afterwards. But I collected five or six engagements!!!

Thursday 1 October 1964 (92nd General Congregation)

Felici[3] said: it has been asked what is the status of the appendices to schema
  XIII = private documents but prepared by the Commission to explain
  the understanding it had put into the schema itself.

Cardinal Léger:[4] in favour of a stronger affirmation of the transcendence of
  revelation.

Cardinal Landázuri[5] [ ]

Cardinal Browne:[6] it was definite!!! He spoke against 'experientia' [experience]
  with allusions to *Pascendi*.[7]

---

1. Alphonse G Bannwarth, Bishop of Soissons.
2. The Council for the application of the Constitution on the Liturgy, the members of which were named in March, and of which Lercaro was the President (cf above, page 515, note 5).
3. *AS* III/II, 181–182.
4. *AS* III/II, 182–184.
5. *AS* III/II, 185–187.
6. *AS* III/II, 187–188.
7. Encyclical of Pope Pius X against Modernism, published in September 1907.

His Beatitude Batanian:[1] exegetes should work in submission to Tradition and the Magisterium.

Kowalski[2] [ ]

I was caught by Fr Baraúna about his plan (enormous, but very interesting) for a volume on the *De Ecclesia*. I therefore missed a lot of speeches: Constantini,[3] Jaeger,[4] Romero,[5] and part of Shehan.[6] But I will get all that in writing.

Vuccino:[7] Eastern sense of Tradition as embracing everything, and from the angle of the Trinity and the Spirit.

Reuss:[8] on the proposed description of the act of faith.

Compagnone[9] {Great weariness among the Fathers, who strolled around
Ferro[10]   {and chatted.

Guano:[11] Revelation as the communication of friendship; harmonise what is said of faith with this. And explain better the mutual interiority of Scripture and Tradition.

At 11.00 am Felici, on behalf of the Moderators, gave a clarification: this is not a purely private text, because it has been composed by a Joint Commission (Theological Commission and Commission for the Apostolate of the Laity). We will come back to the question.

In the car, Cardinal Suenens gave me this clarification of the matter: an integrist bishop had sent a letter expressing indignation at the distribution of such a text (the Appendices) which reverses the whole of the Church's teaching(!!!). Felici had made the declaration *proprio marte* [on his own initiative], which he then corrected, on the intervention of the Moderators (*'de mandato EE Moderatorum'*.)

Wyszyński:[12] useless words!!!

Zoungrana,[13] in the name of numerous bishops of Africa: Revelation is Christ himself.

---

1. Ignatius Peter Batanian, *AS* III/III, 188–190.
2. Kazimierz J Kowalski, Bishop of Chełmno (Poland), *AS* III/III, 190–192.
3. *AS* III/III, 193–194.
4. *AS* III/III, 195–196.
5. F Romero Menjibar, *AS* III/III, 197–199.
6. *AS* III/III, 199–200.
7. *AS* III/III, 201–203.
8. *AS* III/III, 203.
9. *AS* III/III, 203–205.
10. *AS* III/III, 206–208.
11. *AS* III/III, 208–210.
12. This in fact refers to Tomasz Wilczyński, titular bishop (Poland), *AS* III/III, 210–211.
13. *AS* III/III, 212–214.

Arattukulam[1] (India): pure dialectic of the Spanish kind. And, as with Spanish
dissertations, rapid and interminable. Along the lines of Franić.

Fares:[2] in favour of a development of the act of faith as a PERSONAL act.

Attipetty[3] (India): against maintaining silence on the question of constitutive
Tradition, a point, he said, that was defined by the Council of Trent(!!!)

Rougé:[4] (the twenty-first speaker) [   ]

Before going to lunch at the Belgian College, in order to work there afterwards,
I looked in vain for Mgr Heuschen's car, which should have taken me. Cardinal
Suenens took me in his car which gave me a chance to talk to him. First, about
how things are going. There are only seventeen people down to speak for the rest
of the *De Revelatione*, which means that it will certainly be finished on Monday.
After that will come the *De apostolatu laicorum*, for which there are lots of people
down to speak. It will be possible to allot two weeks to it.

Felici had got the Pope to agree, somewhat by surprise, that schemas reduced
to a few propositions would be simply VOTED ON, without discussion. The
Moderators got discussion restored, which Felici announced by speaking of a
'*brevis disceptatio*' [brief debate]. But the Moderators are disposed to allow ALL
THE TIME that is necessary: these are very important matters which touch directly on the *aggiornamento*.

There will remain schema XIII. Cardinal Suenens thinks it should be discussed in depth and reworked in the interval between Sessions so that it can be
voted on in the Fourth Session. This is necessary. First because of the subject
matter, and also because otherwise it will be said in public: the bishops spent
two years talking about the Church *in se* [in itself] and about themselves, but
dispatched the question of the world in a fortnight . . .

I took the opportunity to remind Cardinal Suenens of my idea, taken up again
recently by the bishops of Fr Gauthier's group: to begin the discussion of schema
XIII with some expositions of the situation of the world, given by lay people. I
added, even by a woman. The Cardinal said: yes, I would be in favour of that,
and I shall speak to the Pope about it this evening. I can very well see Mrs Ward,[5]
American specialist on under-development, giving an exposition in English at
the Council. For my part, I added: very good, but a voice should be heard coming
from real people, people at the bottom . . . I also said: there should be a COUPLE,
as a couple, among the Auditors. The Cardinal said that that was his idea too, and
that he would talk about it, too, to the Pope. He went straight on to the question

---

1. Michael Arattukulam, Bishop of Alleppey, *AS* III/III, 214–217.
2. *AS* III/III, 217–219.
3. Joseph Attipetty, Archbishop of Verapoly, *AS* III/III, 219–221.
4. *AS* III/III, 222–223.
5. Barbara Ward.

of *'birth control'*,[1] which he has very much at heart. He asked me what I thought of it, and what I thought of the chapter on marriage in schema XIII.

At table, allusion was made to Cardinal Suenens' discourse on the canonisations. He said that he concluded his paper by conjuring the thought that John XXIII be canonised by acclamation. He thinks that such a canonisation would find a very great echo in the world. But in fifty years' time it will be too late.

At 3.15 pm, work with Mgr Heuschen and Fr Rigaux to shorten my text on collective eschatology. We broke off at 4.30 pm to go with Mgr Philips to Balić's meeting of the International Marian Academy: it is a matter of organising the Congress in Santo Domingo, in March 1965, on Mary in the New Testament from the exegetical point of view. Balić is more of a fairground tumbler than ever. He always lands on his feet, but he also knows what he wants. His great argument is: the Pope wants it, all we have to do is to carry it out.

We returned to the Belgian College at 7.00 pm, to continue our work, which was interrupted by dinner, and which was finished (?) at 9.00 pm.

I got back unable to stand up, obliged constantly to prop myself up on something, and only able to move forward like some poor cripple, at the cost of efforts which completely exhaust me. Where am I headed?

I have also taken note today: of a conversation with Mgr Leclercq and Honoré,[2] rectors of Lille and Angers: Mgr Romeo said to one of them, on receiving him at the Congregation [[for Studies]]: 'it is above all necessary to fight against pantheistic monism' . . . !!! Where are their brains? With Pizzardo, stupid and emptyheaded, this Congregation is, in Rome, my (single) scandal. It is shameful! In a world where schools and universities are such serious things, to have at the head of the schools and universities of the Church such imbeciles as Pizzardo.

Mgr Himmer told me, on the subject of the Church of the Poor, that a letter is going to be sent to the Pope. It will be suggested that honorific titles be given up, and also that bishops should be able to dress in the same way as all other priests; as for liturgical vestments, aim for simplicity.

Friday 2 October 1964

I did not go to St Peter's this morning in order to be able to 'work' (?) a little. Basically, there is little point in going to St Peter's . . .

Yesterday I asked Mgr Philips if we (experts) were going to be invited to the Theological Commission. From what I can see, recourse to experts is being greatly limited. Is this in order to avoid new discussions, and so loss of time? In practice, examination of the *modi* is done by a small group: Philips, Tromp, Charue, the bishop of the relevant section (the one who presided at the sub-commission for drafting or revision), one or two others perhaps . . . Obviously this does save

---

1. {The phrase is in English in the original.}
2. Jean Honoré, of the diocese of Rennes, he was later to be Bishop of Évreux, then Archbishop of Tours, and was to be created cardinal in 2001.

time. But I shudder for this or that text that I care about . . . As for meetings of the Theological Commission, if experts are invited it is a matter of a very limited chosen few . . .

The bishops, on their return, told me that discussion had continued on Chapters I & II of *De Revelatione*. Mgr Calabria[1]—the same with whom I had a run-in two years ago at the Capranica—quoted me, saying: Fr Congar himself admits that there are in Tradition some truths that are not found in Scripture . . . The *relatio* of Chapter III–VI was read out and discussion of them was started.

I meant to go to the meeting of the Observers, but I realised that I would have difficulty in going there and back to the Piazza Navona on foot. Especially as I shall be speaking to the bishops of Brazil this evening. I am obliged, now, to look after myself. I have difficulty in writing, in keeping my balance. I find this very trying.

Dinner with the Brazilian bishops and a lecture on Scripture and Tradition. Fr Antõnio Guglielmi,[2] who came to collect me, told me that he has a lot of business to deal with in the Roman Congregations. On all sides he hears bitter complaints about 'this cursed Council' which is 'ruining the Church'; not a financial ruin, but an ecclesiological one, I venture to say. What Church? What ecclesiology? They say: if only it was over, and these bishops went back home!!! But is 'back home' not the Church? The Romans have a strange conception of things. For them, there are bishops and dioceses: these are *materia circa quam* [the matter about which], and there is 'the Church': that is, themselves, their authority, their administration, their legalism. This 'Church' is bound up with forces and with forms of conservatism, including political and social conservatism. At bottom they are 'Maurrassians'.[3]

A long wait in an incredible racket: the small staff of Italian women of this Domus Mariae recreates in this beautiful house the intolerably noisy atmosphere of Fiumicino airport, with horrible, squawking calls on the loud-speakers.

I saw one of the Hungarians who had come to the Council. He was also nourishing himself on Congar . . . That went well, he said.

A mediocre lecture, as far as I am concerned.

I saw the bishops of Rwanda and also Mgr Selis,[4] Auxiliary Bishop of Iglesias (Sardinia), who had invited me to speak at his AC [Catholic Action] Congress: VERY good. All these last days, besides, I have been accosted by many young

---

1. *AS* III/III, 262–264.
2. Antõnio Guglielmi, Professor of Sacred Scripture in Brazil, was the organiser of the lectures given at the *Domus Mariae*, under the aegis of the Brazilian bishops; he was a Council expert.
3. {Follower of Charles Maurras, French political thinker of the late nineteenth and early twentieth centuries.}
4. Enea Selis.

Italian bishops (of Crema,[1] of . . .) who congratulated me, being wholly of the conciliar point of view and my point of view. There are some, then. But Fr Guglielmi, driving me back, recounted how the secretary of Cardinal Siri,[2] a fool, he told me, had attempted to prevent K Rahner from talking to the Brazilian bishops on collegiality by interrupting repeatedly, until he was given notice either to shut up, or to leave the room. . .

Saturday 3 October 1964

Worked on my paper for the *ICI*. Dentist. Very sultry weather, hot and clammy. A sauna.

This evening, dinner beside Mgr Veuillot. He saw Cardinal Suenens after the audience for Moderators last Thursday evening, 1 October. It seems that this audience was very difficult. The Pope is once again hesitant about Chapter III of the *De Ecclesia*. He is made the object of daily assaults and pressures by the anticollegialists, and this has ended up making some impression on him. The position of the minority, to which it hopes to win over the Pope, is: accept (some of) the *modi*, water down the doctrine.

Since reading *Ecclesiam Suam*, I have thought that the passage in which the Holy Father says he hopes to be able to add his agreement presages some last minute changes in the text that has been voted on by the Assembly . . .

How fortunate that the Belgians are so determined.

Sunday 4 October 1964

I finished, and typed my chronicle for *ICI*. Visit from Fr Iglesias,[3] from Chile, who came to put some questions to me about the *De Revelatione*.

Monday 5 October 1964

On arriving at St Peter's I saw Mgr Carlo Colombo. I asked him if he knew anything about the plan for a Profession of Faith that I had sent to the Holy Father: yes. The Pope had read my text attentively and had brought to him Fr Tromp's text [not accepted for the Council]. He had given my text to some theologians to study. He likes its biblical tone, but thinks that, for a profession of faith, one needs to put things in a more formal manner.

Colombo then told me that the Holy Father's desire is that the greatest possible unanimity for Chapter III (collegiality) should be arrived at. For this, I said, the terms need to be better explained (my idea from the beginning). Agreed, said Colombo. A meeting should be arranged, for example, between the Theological Commission and some representatives of the minority. He asked me who I knew. He ruled out Dulac, who, he said, did not represent anything or anybody. I had to

---

1. Carlo Manziana.
2. Giacomo Barabino.
3. Daniel Iglesias, of the diocese of Santiago, was a professor in the Faculty of Theology of the Catholic University of Chile; he was a Council expert.

admit that I had seen scarcely any of the others. I named some Italian bishops. He told me that Ruffini has drawn much closer.

I will go to see him with my Belgian friends and Mgr Garrone.

Relatio on Chapter I of *De oecumenismo*, read by Mgr Martin,[1] who made an effort at correct pronunciation (without wholly succeeding).—Applause.

Votes on Ecumenism, Chapter I. I noted down the results on my copy. Discussion of the *De Revelatione*, Chapter III–VI, was resumed.

> Cardinal Meyer:[2] on the concept of inspiration reduced to its intellectual aspect, and thus to inerrancy. But the Word (of God) has other functions: personal communication and efficaciousness.
> Bea:[3] praise for the schema. Somewhat professorial critical comments.
> Mgr Weber:[4] [ ]
> Mgr Simons:[5] in favour of a broadening of the notion of biblical inerrancy.

I went out for moment, but it was impossible to avoid a great number of encounters and conversations:

- Fr Gilliardi:[6] about the volume on atheism.[7]
- a Brazilian on the relationship of the Assumption with Tradition.
- Mgr Charue to whom I spoke about what Colombo intends to do.

But I went out, walked around and stayed standing far less than I had done in the preceding sessions, in order to conserve my limited strength. This *GREATLY* restricts my contacts.

A Brazilian bishop who had heard me on Friday, said to me: what a transformation! Some years ago I had to give a talk in Rio de Janeiro, a report on the laity. I drew my inspiration from your *Jalons*, and I even quoted you. But Mgr Samorè and Cardinal Piazza[8] said to me: your report was excellent, but you must suppress the quotations from or allusions to Fr Congar, because he is an author suspected of not being wholly orthodox.

---

1. *AS* III/III, 280–282.
2. *AS* III/III, 283–284.
3. *AS* III/III, 284–287.
4. *AS* III/III, 290–292.
5. *AS* III/III, 293–295.
6. Congar wrote on the typescript: 'Girardi'. Giulio Girardi, SDB, taught philosophy at the Pontifical Salesian University; he was to be appointed a consultor to the Secretariat for Non-Believers in 1966.
7. *Des chrétiens interrogent l'athéisme* (Desclée, 1967-1970).
8. Adeodato G Piazza, OCD, who died in 1957, became President of CELAM (Episcopal Conference of the Bishops of Latin America) in 1955.

Edelby:[1] gave the Eastern point of view, based on the duality of the mission
of Christ AND OF THE HOLY SPIRIT. Scripture is a liturgical and
prophetic reality. Get away from points of view arising from the
controversy with Protestants. Tradition is as it were the epiclesis of the
history of salvation.
Mgr Schick[2] . . . etc.

Almost no one was listening. After 11.00 am, or even 10.50 am, the Fathers leave
en masse, and stroll around until about midday. There is a general buzz of conversations.

Medina, who is like a radar detecting rumours and intrigues, said to me: you
know that Mgr Philips has not yet received the *modi* for Chapter III. I am sure the
Pope has had them sent to him and is studying them. I will not rest easy until the
Constitution is promulgated.

Lunch with the Trappist Fathers at 'Tre Fontane' with my comrades from
Oflag IV D.[3]

At 4.30 pm, Theological Commission.

Tromp read a letter from the General Secretariat to Cardinal Ottaviani (absent). For the first part of Chapter III there have been submitted 4,055 *modi*, and
for the second part 1,551 *modi* (if I have correctly understood Tromp's Italian). It
would take at least ten days even just to sort them.

Discussion about the TITLE of Chapter VII, which Molinari once again reduced to the CHURCH, totally failing to see that it must include HUMAN BE-
INGS and THEIR vocation. Alas, few of the bishops understand this.

Molinari's text, in my view very unsatisfactory, was discussed. He said to me
as I arrived: I have retained almost the whole of your text, but there was a text
from the Germans and I was obliged to take account of both of them. —As far as
I can see, the Germans think above all about the eschatological aspect *OF THE
CHURCH*, not about our vocation as human beings. I am very discouraged by
this IMPOSSIBILITY of getting something so essential through. And then, in
spite of everything, the experts are scarcely able to speak. I raised the question of
the title, but was not able to speak again.

The 'Platonism for the people' continued . . . No pneumatology, no anthropology, no cosmology. Fr Molinari's corrections and additions very much belong to
a Counter Reformation outlook.

A great storm (how I felt it coming and longed for it!). McGrath brought us
back by car, but going first by way of Monte Mario! We got back at 8.30 pm. Away
from my room for exactly twelve hours. I found the morning's post at 9.00 pm!
Mgr McGrath spoke to us about South America, and especially about the role of

---

1. *AS* III/III, 306–309.
2. *AS* III/III, 309–311.
3. Cf above, page 200, note 3.

the nuncios there. With rare exceptions (he named two of them), in South America the nuncios have a role that we have no idea of in the west. They constantly intervene in diocesan affairs in the smallest details (whether or not to hold a procession), in conferences and meetings, in teaching, in political affairs. They do so in the most clerical manner, the most ultramontane, the most narrow and, in a word, the most *STUPID* way possible. They are one of the factors which maintain in those countries cretinous structures and reactions, preventing an open and happy evolution. A whole history of Catholicism in South America could be written from the point of view of the activity of the nuncios. Along with this (the two go together) an authoritarianism bordering on that of the little village dictator. They are backed up in Rome by Mgr Samorè and they nominate bishops who will be at their service. It is very sad!

How differently things should be done!

Tuesday 6 October 1964

In the morning, I stayed at home to do a little 'work'. Work = recopying, letter by letter, my article for the Mélanges for Chenu.[1]

After lunch, a visit from Dr Maurice Marois,[2] founder of the Institute of Life. I was able to get him an interview with Cardinal Suenens and to present him to Mgr Willebrands. —At 4.30 pm, at the *Foyer Unitas* for the meeting of the Observers. The first part of the meeting was about the *De Iudaeis*:

> Lukas Vischer: 1) is Israel still the chosen people of God? God has a particular plan with respect to it. Israel is a sign of GOD'S PLAN. The Declaration looks too much to the past, to the origin of the Church, to the *patrimonium* [patrimony] we have received. But Israel and the Church have a relationship—a mysterious one—in the plan of God. 2) The people of Israel is of great importance for the understanding of the Church itself: it is though it that one understands that the Church exists by grace. The text does not give sufficient expression to this. It presents the Church too plainly as the continuation of Israel. 3) Line 23, the word *adunatio* [reunion]. Paul says: The whole of Israel will be saved. This does not mean that Israel will come into the Church, will submit itself to the Church. Israel will reach its fulfilment as completely TRULY JEWISH. The text reflects the notion of concentric circles, of which the Catholic Church is the centre and core.

---

1. Yves M-J Congar, 'Le moment "économique" et le moment "ontologique" dans la *Sacra Doctrina* (Révélation, Théologie, Somme théologique)', in *Mélanges offerts à M-D Chenu maître en théologie* (Paris: Vrin, 1967), 135–187.
2. Maurice Marois, Professor of Histology at the Faculty of Medicine in Paris, founded the Institute for Life, a non-confessional organisation, with the aim of putting science at the service of human life.

Cullmann: accepts *'adunatio'* in the sense of Romans 11: 4, re-insertion into their genuine olive tree. The problem is to discern what is the role of unconverted Israel, at the present time. It is to be a witness to the history of salvation seen in two essential traits: the fidelity of God, of Christ; God writes straight with crooked lines.

Schmidt:[1] the Declaration poses questions that it does not answer. Gratitude to the Council for daring to pronounce these words, and so to offer a sign of peace. We German Protestants are conscious that it does so also ON OUR BEHALF.

One Easterner, and then another, again took up the protestation of the Easterners, emphasising that the OTHER Christian Churches are involved, for all practical purposes, since the Arabs make no distinction.

Thurian: there has been anti-semitism. Let us not be too pro-semitic. Don't forget that the Jewish people profess a religion that statutorily excludes the rejection of Christ (in the sense of Fr Benoit). We moved on to the schema *De Revelatione*, which the Observers praised a lot.

Thomas[2] (Reformed, USA): the *De libertate* is based on reason as a theological *locus*. The place of reason, if it really is a theological *locus*, should be indicated in the *De Revelatione*.

Aldenhoven[3] ('a young "Old Catholic" . . . ' he really was rather young): on Chapter II: 1) The absence of the Holy Spirit. The proclamation of the gospel by the Apostles is not referred to the Holy Spirit, although, according to the New Testament, it is a *Geistgewirktes Geschehen* [something that happened by the working of the Spirit]; likewise the preservation of the Gospel intact, which is spoken of only in terms of *assistentia* [assistance]; 2) The growth of Tradition: if *intelligentia* [intelligence] is taken as an ablative, it would be saying that it is Tradition itself that grows . . . ; 3) The relationship between the Magisterium and the Church: the Magisterium is too isolated from the Church. Attempts have been made to remedy this isolation but it has stopped half-way: at the beginning of the chapter preservation seems to be attributed solely to the successors of the Apostles; 4) The boundary between Tradition and the things that go on in the Church, but that are not Tradition: the distinction is claimed to be made by the

---

1. Pastor Wilhelm Schmidt, Vice-Rector of the Evangelische Michaelsbrudershaft, was one of the guests of the Secretariat for Unity.
2. John Newton Thomas, of the United Presbyterian Church, Professor of Systematic Theology at Union Theological Seminary, Richmond (United States), Observer representing the Presbyterian World Alliance.
3. Herwig Aldenhoven, parish priest at Walbach (Switzerland), Observer representing the Old Catholic Church.

Magisterium. Very well! But not only, like the reforms that are prepared by those on the periphery, at moments when the Magisterium is silent!

Wednesday 7 October 1964

I didn't go to St Peter's. I notice that I have less interest this year. I am less involved in the work; more tired; going around less, I meet fewer people. Many of the meetings are boring and I come away empty. Nevertheless my semi-indifference worries me. Am I less a man of desires, less the servant of the Design of God? Am I failing in my duty?

Five minutes on Irish Radio, on Tradition.

Thursday 8 October 1964

Yesterday evening there was a meeting of the Co-ordinating Commission, but nothing is known about it. Moeller told me only that it lasted two-and-a-half hours and that Cardinal Suenens came back with a long face. But it seems that nothing was decided either for or against a Fourth Session. Cardinal Suenens said: 'If there were to be no schema XIII it would be a scandal for the world'! So THAT is in question at the moment. It seems that there is an enormous amount of activity in the way of movements, negotiations, initiatives . . .

Discussion was resumed on *De Apostolatu laicorum*:

D'Souza:[1] against clericalism and paternalism. Applause.
De Smedt:[2] the laity should respect *TOTALLY* the freedom of persons in the apostolate.

I no longer make summaries of (boring !!!) speeches: they will appear in the press.

I went out at 11.00 am and saw a lot of people. Among them, Mgr Prignon. He told me: there are some who want to bury schema XIII. Either because they are AGAINST it, or because they see in this a means of closing the Session very quickly and impeding or postponing the vote on the *De Ecclesia*. For it is ridiculous that, for three weeks, the minority have contrived to avoid chapter III of *De Ecclesia* being brought to its conclusion. If I told you everything, Mgr Prignon said, it would take me more than an hour. So Mgr Prignon had asked Martimort, and he was asking me, to spread the word that schema XIII was being called in question and was in danger. He said that even Fesquet should be approached, because the Pope reads *Le Monde* everyday. (The idea would be: to replace schema XIII by an encyclical!!!)

I set to work immediately to speak to this one and that about schema XIII being put in question, WHICH WOULD BE A CATASTROPHE—but I will not do anything with regard to Fesquet.

---

1. *AS* III/IV, 58–60.
2. *AS* III/IV, 58–63.

Mgr Ancel reported the same things to me, and added: there has been a major offensive in the Co-ordinating Commission; some people were asking also that there should be no more than two General Congregations a week, and that the Commissions should work in such a way that everything can be finished this time.

Lunch with the Taizé Brothers, wearing albs or something like them. Schutz a little bit starry-eyed, and sentimental, but, even more, luminous and a man of God. It is so obvious that the grace of God is with them! There is a Taizé 'man', a Taizé anthropology, very spiritual.

At table I spoke in particular with Fr Courtois,[1] of the Sons of Charity. He knows everybody. He filled out what Mgr McGrath was saying about the nuncios, especially in South America, but also in the Far East: he works at Propaganda and has contact there with Mgr Jacqueline,[2] who is responsible for the Far East. Now, Mgr Jacqueline said, out of seven nuncios, only two are any good.

The rest are narrow-minded schemers. Courtois said: it is a plague. They are careerists. They are archbishops at forty, they interfere everywhere and play politics. Finally, sooner or later, they occupy important posts in the Curia, where they continue this petty Roman political and juridical imperialism. Only a third of them have a truly pastoral vision.

Courtois also spoke to me about Pizzardo, Staffa and the Congregation for Studies: They know nothing about anything, and pretend to control it all. In his youth Pizzardo was rejected by the Society of Jesus, as being intellectually inadequate . . .

In the afternoon, a visit from a journalist from *La Rocca* who had interviewed me last year.[3] He told me the story of Parente's letter following the publication of the interview, and that of Ottaviani following a similar article on Fr de Lubac. His bishop, a good Benedictine, eighty-seven years old,[4] had refused to issue a reprimand, he objected to the intervention of the Holy Office. But this journalist has had to keep quiet and not be published since then. What, he asked me, would have happened if he had published an article on Fr Chenu!!! He told me that, if I had already had my audience with the Pope, Parente would not have written his letter.

Rome is a court, where favour from on high is decisive.

At 5.00 pm I took part in a workshop studying schema XIII. It was a report of the work done by the under-workshops. VERY INTERESTING. These work-

---

1. Gaston Courtois, Procurator General of the Sons of Charity, was Chaplain General for the International Catholic Child Bureau (BICE), and the international secretary of the Pontifical Missionary Union of Clergy.
2. Bernard Jacqueline, of the diocese of Coutances, was *minutante* at the Congregation of Propaganda and chaplain of the Chateaubriand School in Rome; he was later to become a bishop and Pro-Nuncio in Burundi, and then Morocco.
3. Vincenzo D'Agostino.
4. Giuseppe Nicolini.

shops have done some very good work which should be incorporated into the schema. Fr Daniélou is working for this.

Friday 9 October 1964

I did not go to St Peter's. Very early in the morning, I finished typing two texts written yesterday evening: one for an intervention on the idea of THE mission, that Mgr Geeraerts,[1] of the White Fathers, will give, and the other on the comments of the Lay Auditors on the *De Revelatione*.

I studied the *modi* accepted by the small sub-commission for Chapter II, *De Populo Dei*. Mgr Philips sent them to me. I asked him to have a look at the *modi* for Chapter II of *De Ecclesia* and Chapter II of *De Revelatione*, of which I had been to a large extent the redactor (and also at the text on cosmic eschatology). The changes accepted are insignificant and almost entirely of a stylistic character. The text remains virtually what it was. This is due to the criteria adopted by the Commission for assessing the *modi*, criteria which I copy out here because they are very interesting:

1) *Textus a duobus e tribus partibus in aula probatus, gaudet possessione: ideoque nullus Modus accipi potest qui textui probato contradicet* [A text approved in the Council Hall by a vote of two thirds enjoys possession: therefore no amendment can be accepted which contradicts the approved text].

2) *Eadem de causa non possunt admitti notabiles expunctiones vel mutationes ordinis* [For the same reason, no notable deletions, or changes of order, can be accepted].

3) *Item admitti nequeunt longiores additiones, etiam si in se sint pulchrae. Nam nullus numerus est qui non augeri possit pulchris citationibus vel ampliationibus* [Similarly, longer additions cannot be accepted, even if, in themselves, they are fine. For there is no Number that could not be extended with fine quotations or amplifications].

4) *E contra admitti possunt breves additiones, transpositiones, mutationes, quibus clarius et melius apparet sensus textus, vel etiam expunctio superflui* [On the other hand, brief additions, transpositions or changes by means of which the meaning of the text is better and more clearly seen, or even the deletion of what is superfluous, can be admitted].

5) *Non tangi debent ea quae scripta sunt post serias discussiones in commissione. Textus enim probatus a Commissione debet manere in decisis, nisi ab altiore auctoritate nova discussio imponatur* [What has been written after serious discussions in commission should not be touched. For a text approved by a Commission should stand in matters that have been decided, unless a new discussion is imposed by higher authority].

6) *Fieri potest, maxime in rebus ordinis positivi, ut irrepserint unus alterve error. Quod si ille clare iudicatur, error erit corrigendus, ut clarius apparebit in ulteriore relatione. V. gr. Filii Ismael habet sensum controversum; non omnes pagani*

---

1. The Belgian Xavier Geeraerts, WF, had been Vicar Apostolic for Bukavu (Congo).

colunt idola; non OMNES *baptizati gaudent iis qualificationibus de quibus in textu*
[It is can happen, especially when dealing with facts, that one or another error
will creep in. If this is judged to be clearly the case, the error is to be corrected,
so that this will be seen more clearly in the later report: for example, 'the sons of
Ishmael' has a controverted meaning: not all pagans worship idols; not ALL the
baptised enjoy the qualifications spoken of in the text].

These criteria allow the text to be retained almost unchanged, and the work to
make rapid progress. But they are draconian in excluding several important *modi*
that we have suggested for Chapter III, IV and V . . . !

I spent my morning putting on index cards some interventions on the *De
Revelatione*, since in the Theological Commission this work comes back to the
experts, and is not be done by the secretaries, as is the case in the Secretariat for
Unity . . .

I had to lunch M. Vajta, a Lutheran Observer.[1]

At 4.30 pm, at the Belgian College, a meeting of the Church of the Poor group.
I met some friends. Fr Häring told me that he had heard it said in a group of bish-
ops that Fr Congar had written to the Secretariat of State, to retract on collegiality
. . . Look what has become of my letter to Dulac: an insane fabrication!!!

This very morning, *in aula*, Fr Gagnebet told me that he had seen photocopies
of my letter, widely distributed: he said: For myself, I don't reply to the dispatches
of *La Pensée catholique*, because I know them . . .

Fr Häring has also heard it said that Fr Congar and Fr Rahner are against
schema XIII, which they consider to be bad.—Fr Häring did not bother to reply
that I had worked on it!!! Certainly I have voiced my criticisms, but quite openly,
and the Commission made roneoed copies of them . . .

Fr Häring gave us (in French) a very fine exposition, very rich, ELOQUENT
and impressive, on the place of poverty in schema XIII. Not only does the idea
appear at many points; but it is there as the central and inspiring idea, not as an
added flourish. It is at the heart of what the presence of the Church to the world
calls for most deeply, and of the dialogue which is the means and the expression
of this. Häring rightly points out that it is not only MORAL but ONTOLOGI-
CAL. It is part of the ontology of the Christian, of priesthood, of the bishop, of
mission. In short, what I recently demonstrated in connection with service applies equally to poverty, which is intimately connected with it.

Mgr Rougé and Mgr Riobé have received invitations to a meeting on Tuesday
of a group under the patronage of Cardinals Ruffini, Siri, Browne, Larraona and
Santos.[2] The point of the meeting is to ask the Pope that the schema *De Revela-*

---

1. Vilmos Vajta was originally from Hungary, where he was ordained pastor in the Lutheran Church. He was Director of the new Institute for Ecumenical Research in Strasbourg, created by the World Lutheran Federation officially and inaugurated at the beginning of 1965. He was an Observer representing the World Lutheran Federation.
2. The Coetus Internationalis Patrum (cf above, page 589, No. 2).

tione should be purely and simply withdrawn . . . This must be the same group to which the Auxiliary of Mgr Baudoux[1] was invited [[and where he heard some frightful things. And Mgr Rougé must have been invited to it]] because his (favourable) intervention on Tradition was presented by *Il Tempo*, an abominable newspaper, reactionary and liberal, as an appeal to the Magisterium of the Pope, superior to all else! *Il Tempo* never stops presenting Council affairs, contrary to their most certain meaning, in the light of the exaltation of the Pope and of the Curia. It recently ran the headline: 'The Chimera of Ecumenism . . . ' etc. Here, once again, one sees verified the mainly POLITICAL character of these integrist exaltations of authority.

Saturday 10 October 1964

A plenary session of the French episcopate all day: the third since the beginning of the Council.[2] The French episcopate is organising itself, taking some concerted measures from the pastoral point of view, is studying the texts of the translations of the liturgy . . .

Work (indifferent: storm, sirocco). A visit from Fr Guglielmi, who wanted to have copies made here by roneo of the observations of the Biblical Institute on the use of scriptural texts in the chapter *De Beata* of the *De Ecclesia*.

At midday, some bishops passed on a rumour that is going about (source: Mgr Blanchet, Elchinger) according to which Felici has made an approach to the Pope—poor Pope!!!—asking that: 1) the Declaration on the Jews be reduced to a few lines; 2) the Declaration on Religious Freedom be revised by a commission to include Cardinal Browne, Mgr Marcel Lefebvre. I do not attach much importance to this rumour.

At 7.25 pm, Fr Hamer telephoned and told me this, which totally contradicted the impression I had got at midday:

Two documents were sent to Cardinal Bea during the General Congregation yesterday morning. Cardinal Bea communicated them to the meeting of the Secretariat at 5.00 pm yesterday:

1) a letter concerning the schema on the Jews: there should not be an independent schema, but it should be mentioned in the *De Populo Dei* of the *De Ecclesia* [this would, in itself, be the normal place]. For this there will be a Joint Commission of the Theological Commission and the Secretariat;

2) concerning the *De libertate*, a letter from Felici making three points:
    a.   the Holy Father wants the text revised;
    b.   Cardinal Cicognani says: for this there will be a Joint

---

1. A Hacault.
2. The first plenary assembly took place on the eve of the Second Session; the second in May 1964, at which it was decided to create a French episcopal conference; the third plenary assembly, charged with finalising the statutes of the French Episcopal Conference, took place on several days during the course of the Third Session: 26 September, 10 October and 8 November.

Commission composed of the Secretariat and the Theological Commission;

c.   Cardinal Browne, Mgr Marcel Lefebvre, Fr Fernandez, Mgr Colombo will be members of this commission.

Fr Hamer clarified: it is not known from WHOM the third point comes; Fr Ramirez had sent Fr Fernandez an extremely violent document of eleven pages; Cardinal Suenens, Mgr De Smedt and the Belgians are in Belgium where there is an election tomorrow. Suenens has been informed by telephone.

Fr Hamer is VERY worried: 'One does not know what to do.'

I spoke to Mgr Garrone, who had been put in the picture by Mgr Martin. He thinks that there should be some reaction, and Cardinal Liénart is going to intervene, perhaps first through Mgr Dell'Acqua. On the other hand, Cardinal Döpfner saw the Pope on Thursday evening: it was very relaxed (according to Mgr Elchinger).

There was some talk at table this evening about letters to the Secretariat. Mgr Ancel, charitable by the standards of the charitable, had some extremely hard words for Felici—and not *per transennam* [glancingly], but, he insisted, by making reference to facts that he said he knew. He believed that Felici will not back away from anything, and has, more than once, used means that are objectively dishonest.

I want on this occasion to note here the atmosphere at table among the French bishops, different in the extreme from that of the Belgian bishops and at the Belgian College. At the Belgian College the meal would be spent discussing the small details of the day in a manner resolutely distrustful of and hostile toward the anti-collegial party and toward the personnel of the Curia in general.

The French bishops are much more calm, peaceable, kindly, much less passionate; much less actively and efficaciously engaged in conciliar strategy. They are good and charitable men, but not very energetic, and absolutely not waging a battle for certain theses, certain formulas, etc. In fact, they have scarcely played an active role in the Council. Mgr Garrone and Mgr Ancel (Theological Commission) have their positions, they are firm, but much less active, much less tacticians than the likes of Heuschen or Charue. The French bishops have little (too little) of the 'irascible' . . .

Sunday 11 October 1964

Work. Poor work. I had already spent almost the whole of yesterday preparing my lecture for tomorrow, on 'Church and World'. When I proposed it and it was accepted, I did not realise that it would take me so long!

Mgr Pailler met Mgr Edelby and reported that: before the presentation of the schema *De Ecclesiis Orientalibus*, Cardinal Cicognani would take the floor to say that three points in this schema should be removed from it: what is said about an Easterner remaining in his own rite upon entering the Catholic Church; what is said about the possibility of Catholics receiving the sacraments of the Orthodox; and what is said about mixed marriages.—And yet, these points were voted on in the Commission, with seventeen in favour and three against. If Cicognani does that, Edelby said, I will take the floor in order to resign from the Commission.

These events, these past days are contributing to the maintenance of a kind of distrust with respect to the people of the Curia, who are felt to be trying to sabotage the Council.

Monday 12 October 1964

Cardinal Lefebvre told me that there was a meeting yesterday at Cardinal Frings' place. Present were Cardinals Frings, Léger, Lefebvre, Meyer, Ritter, Silva, Döpfner, Alfrink. They decided not to intervene on the question of the Jews, in which there must be political influences at play, but to make an approach to the Pope, through Cardinal Frings, in order that responsibility for the revision of the text of *De libertate* will be left to the Secretariat.

I am not going to St Peter's. It seems that I have not missed much. Fr Lebret was at lunch; realism, or rather, REALITIES.

At 4.00 pm, a lecture at Saint-Louis on 'Church and World'. On the subject of schema XIII. A very good audience.

Visit from M. J Zabłocki,[1] a Pole, the editor of *Wiez:* he was looking for collaboration in the survey of the journal, and for some lectures in Poland.

— Fr Dupuy.

It seems that the Pope has stated that he did not take the initiative in connection with Felici's letter on religious freedom.

Tuesday 13 October 1964 = 100ᵗʰ General Congregation

A (token) presence of some PARISH PRIESTS.

Three speakers in the name of more than seventy,[2] on the Apostolate of the Laity: Guerry[3] and Santos Quadri[4] spoke of the autonomy of the temporal order and its harmonisation with the supernatural order; Zoghby[5] spoke on the commission of lay people attached to the patriarch in the Eastern Churches, a good model for the Latins . . .

A Lay Auditor, Keegan,[6] spoke on behalf of the Auditors. Applause. He emphasised what he was himself a sign of: the complete insertion of lay people,

---

1. Janusz Zabłocki was vice editor-in-chief of *Wiez* a journal promoted by Polish Catholic intellectuals.
2. Congar added to the typescript: 'Fathers'.
3. *AS* III/IV, 210–212.
4. Santo B Quadri, Auxiliary Bishop of Pienerolo (Italy), *AS* III/IV, 213–216.
5. *AS* III/IV, 217–219.
6. Patrick Keegan, President of the World Movement of Christian Workers, member of the directing council of COPECIAL (Permanent Committee of the International Congresses for the Apostolate of the Laity).

definitively consecrated, into the life and activity of the Church. He discreetly underlined the fact that the schema is a step on the way. He did not praise the schema as such, but the discussion: an important nuance.

Mgr Hengsbach[1] concluded the debate on the Apostolate of the Laity. The text could be improved in the following ways:

- a better adaptation to the schema *De Ecclesia;*
- an exposition of the relations between nature and grace;
- the spirituality of lay people;
- the relationship between the apostolate of the laity and leadership in the temporal order;
- a better connection between the different forms of the apostolate.

One heard in the *aula* debates that had already been abundantly discussed in the Commission, on the concept of the apostolate, on Catholic Action etc. A certain generality was deliberately maintained in order to respect the freedom of bishops and of laity in the Church. The greatest freedom, the greatest flexibility should be aimed for . . . etc. There must be a text that is suitable for the whole world. To complete the text it will also be necessary to know a little more closely the final text of schema XIII (Possibly, this implies a Fourth Session. He did not say this, but it was understood. Applause).

Mgr Marty[2] read his *relatio* on priesthood (as always his diction was too careful and artificial).

Cardinal Meyer[3] was pretty severe about the schema. There was need for A SERIOUS DISCUSSION of it. It is highly inadequate. *APPLAUSE.*

I saw for a moment Veronese, Sugranyes,[4] Habicht. Veronese told me that the minority opposition might well be using the tactic of STIRRING UP the majority, in order to make them take on an attitude of fanaticism, which would enable them to say: Look! They are hot-heads.

I declared that I could not enter into such considerations . . .

I told them all that I would like to be involved in the work if there was to be work on the spirituality of the laity.

I also intoned my refrain to these layfolk and to Don Dossetti (who promised me he would speak of it to his Cardinal[5] this evening): that the sessions for discussion of schema XIII should begin with some expositions of the world situation.

1. *AS* III/IV, 222–224.
2. *AS* III/IV, 241–243
3. *AS* III/IV, 244–245.
4. Ramon Sugranyes de Franch, outgoing president of Pax Romana (International Movement of Catholic Intellectuals), and of the Conference of OIC (International Catholic Organisations) was a Lay Auditor at the Council.
5. Congar added to the typescript: Lercaro.

Dossetti finds the text of *De Ecclesiis Orientalibus* unsatisfactory, very backward in comparison with the *De oecumenismo*. For myself, I have been aware above all of the many good things to be found in it.

Habicht and Sugranyes think that certain criticisms from theologians, like Rahner and Schillebeeckx, could harm schema XIII. In wanting something better, they could do harm to what is good. The chances of schema XIII should not be put at risk.

Mgr Theas[1] gave a great fervorino on priesthood, in which I confess I could not see the relevance. What use was it??? However it was tending towards the same conclusion as Cardinal Meyer.

I left the tribune and was caught up in a whole lot of encounters . . .

- Peter Meinhold,[2] from Kiel,

- Cardinal Meyer, whom I thanked for his speech; I say almost everywhere how indifferent I find this *De Sacerdotibus* to be,

- a Mexican expert who asked me what truth there was in the question of the ICI,

- Mgr Philippe[3] (a word about the affairs of the Congregation of Ribeauvillé),

- Fr Hamer, with whom I discussed the *De libertate,*

- Mgr Guano, to whom I intoned my refrain about concrete examples concerning the world situation,

- Mgr Del Gallo, the papal chamberlain; *idem.* He told us:

1) Felici's two letters to the Secretariat are as though they had never been written. It was Mgr Dell'Acqua who served as intermediary to the Pope;

2) the day before the opening of the Third Session the Pope had received a letter signed by several cardinals (Ottaviani, Ruffini, etc) saying to him: Beware! You are leading the Church to ruin. So the Pope did not sleep, and on the day of the inauguration, 14 September, he was appallingly tired.

So, the affair of the two letters about the Jews and Freedom[4], should be settled. However, it is not clear that that is the end of it. At 3.35 pm this afternoon Mgr Garrone said to me: This morning I received a letter from Cardinal Ottaviani saying to me: We are charged with drafting a section on the Jews for the *De Populo Dei*. I am asking you to join the small sub-commission that I am appointing for this purpose, and that consists of Cardinal Browne, Cardinal Santos, Mgr Franić and the Superior of the Carmelites.[5] Mgr Garrone has composed a reply which he is going to send straightaway to Cardinal Ottaviani, saying: I cannot agree to

---

1. *AS* III/IV, 246–8.
2. Lutheran and specialist on Luther, he was Professor of Church History and Dogma at the University of Kiel.
3. Paul Philippe.
4. Congar added to the typescript: 'religious'.
5. Anastasio (Ballestrero) del SS Rosario, superior of the Discalced Carmelites, member of the Doctrinal Commission. He replaced Mgr Griffiths who died on 24 February 1964. Later he was to become Cardinal Archbishop of Turin.

join a sub-commission that has not been appointed by the Theological Commission.

Mgr Willebrands telephoned me: the question of freedom has been sorted out; the question of the Jews is well on the way.

At 4.30 pm, Joint Commission of Theology and Laity. Mgr Guano read his *Relatio* for schema XIII. (I finished distributing the Biblical Institute's comments on the mariological texts in the schema *De Ecclesia*, which I had roneoed.)

> Mgr Petit[1] (England): this schema should not be presented for discussion *in aula*. It takes up a position on the two questions of the pill and the bomb. But the bishops are not well placed to judge these properly, as they lack the necessary studies. And yet these are questions of such great popular interest that the press will seize on everything that is said ... It is for the papal magisterium to decide on these ...
>
> Guano and Ottaviani: that is not the point. We are assembled to see if this report can be presented in the name of the Commission. That's all.
>
> Browne: it should be said clearly that these problems are being considered from the point of view OF THE CHURCH, the point of view PROPER to the Church.
>
> Castellano: *relatio placet*, however he made some rather subtle and precise comments. He was of the opinion, rather like Petit, that the Fathers should be warned not to enter into questions which are not yet mature. [But these are the questions which interest people and on which they explicitly question the Church.]
>
> Petit: *haec disceptatio est academica, idealistica, non realistica* [this debate is academic, idealistic, not realistic]. No one replied to him. Guano's *reltio* was approved almost unanimously. 'Verba, verba' [words, words], said Petit.
>
> Spanedda came back to Petit's idea.
>
> Guano: (who defended himself very well today) said: 1) those who are not in agreement should speak *in aula*; 2) the Moderators should take care that dangerous questions or words are avoided.
>
> At 5.50 pm discussion moved to the question of the appendices.
>
> König: the appendices should be put forward under the authority of the Joint Commission [not of the Council].
>
> Butler: that would require a long discussion in the Joint Commission. But say simply that the Joint Commission HAS TAKEN NOTE of the texts.

---

1. John E Petit Bishop of Menevia (Wales), member of the Commission for the Apostolate of the Laity.

The Council itself would be able to do and say that. He cited the example of the Anglicans in this regard.

Fr Anastasio: along the same lines as Butler, but the text should be revised because it often says: 'the holy synod teaches . . . ' etc.

Doumith: recalled what had already been accepted: texts drafted at the request of the Commission and to be presented at the same time as the text for discussion.

Guano: (very much in form this evening): responded.

Parente: the text of the schema is sufficient in itself; if the appendices are brought up in the discussion this could do harm to the text itself. The appendices should remain as *'acta commissionum'* [acts of the commissions] but without having any authority: unless they are debated in depth. The Commission gave the mandate to draft these appendices, but did not give them any authority.

Ancel: there should not be a discussion of their authority, but there should be simply an explanation of WHAT HAS BEEN DONE.

Pelletier: agreed, but the question of authority cannot be avoided.

Ottaviani agreed.

Guano: they are texts drawn up by sub-commissions under the mandate of the Commission, but they were not discussed and approved as such by THE Joint Commission as a whole.

König: practically the same opinion as Guano.

Browne: at the meeting of the Moderators . . . (he spluttered).

Poma: their weight should be stated clearly, otherwise the bishops will mix up texts and appendices in their discussion. Present clearly the HISTORY of the appendices, that will explain what kind of text they are. He suggested that they be presented as POST-CONCILIAR texts.

Henríquez: they are documents like NOTES explaining the text, which alone should be discussed and approved.

Mgr Nécsey (Czech): one should say nothing more than the note which appears at the head of the printed text.

Hengsbach: 'the Joint Commission has considered these texts and accepts them as ACTS according to which the text of the schema can be interpreted and taken further.'

Ménager: agreed with Hengsbach; the appendices cannot be too much seprated from the text because they talk about things not mentioned in the text, about which people are expecting some statement.

Fernandez (nothing precise or constructive).

Garrone: referred to a passage (approved by the Joint Commission) of Mgr Guano's *Relatio*.

Castellano: the history should be explained; these are some of the Commission's working documents, from which the text was composed, but they have a historical value. Do not present them as a commentary, because then the Fathers would have the right to discuss them.

Guano: yes, but they are working documents, coming not from individuals but from sub-commissions and in that sense from an official work.

László and Quadri: something to this effect should be changed in the PRINTED text of the appendices, page 2.

Yes, agreed Guano.

Tromp: there were some lay people on the sub-commissions: this has to be said!!!

YES.

Spanneda: but are these documents going to be published? Because the newspapers are going to publish them and that will make them appear to be texts of the Council.

Ménager: the Joint Commission SHOULD discuss some appendices, because it is there that there are some elements of a response to the problems of humanity. WE SHOULD NOT SHIRK OUR RESPONSIBILITIES.

Ottaviani appealed to Philips as the sage from whom enlightenment might be expected. If the appendices are brought up for discussion *in aula*, that will do harm to the text of the schema itself.

Could the Joint Commission discuss it? YES but later on: it would be impossible this month. The Theological Commission will have to work non-stop. Simply state *in aula* the situation as it is.

This produced agreement.

Wednesday 14 October 1964

Felici:[1] tomorrow there will be votes on the *De Sacerdotibus*.

1) *proemium* and No. 1;

2) on No. 2;

3) on No. 3;

4) on No. 4;

5) on Nos 5 and 6;

6) on Nos 7 and 8;

---

1. *AS* III/IV, 401–403.

7) on Nos 9 and 10;
8) on Nos 11 and 12,
by *placet, non placet, placet iuxta modum.*
There will also be a Message to Priests that needs to be corrected. After that there will be the discussion on the Eastern Churches: then schema XIII.

Barros Câmara[1] supported what had been said by Meyer and Théas, and thus the criticisms of the insufficiency of the text.

When I met Mgr Edelby, he gave met the point of view of the Melchites on the *De Ecclesiis Orientalibus*. It seems that Cicognani has changed his view because, on the three delicate points, his *Relatio* supports the text of the schema. Edelby also told me that, after all, the Declaration on the Jews would not cause so many difficulties in the Arab countries. The bishops stole a march by saying to the governments: it is not with US that you should take it up, but with the oil companies . . .

I went out and got caught in fifteen or twenty encounters. One was particularly interesting: Cardinal Suenens came up to me and asked what I thought: should the Moderators propose a vote by *placet* and *non placet* for the schema *in genere* [in general]. That could have the effect of having it rejected and sent back to be done all over again.—I am myself of this view, and say everywhere that this text should be rejected, because it is weak, moralising, paternalistic, without any vision, inspiration or prophetic spirit. It does not contain any deep re-examination, any biblical re-grounding, it does not address the real, burning questions of priests themselves . . . —But Cardinal Suenens said to me: we are afraid that if this schema is rejected this may become an example that will be followed: the other small schemas will be also. That would commit us to a fifth session . . . —Later, having thought about it, I shall tell the cardinal that this would be no bad thing . . . —a fifth session, because they would need to be recast in order to be submitted to discussion during the Fourth Session: they could be VOTED ON only in a fifth session . . .

But the text is bad.

In any case, Mgr Fernando Gomes[2] (Brazil), in the name of more than 120 bishops, said this very strongly. He was applauded twice. So the idea of rejecting it is making headway. But if the text comes back to the Commission, the same people will do the same things, just as an apple tree produces apples . . . There is need for a new inspiration, for new men.

I waited for Cardinal Suenens at the end of the General Congregation to give him my complete view, after reflection: that the vote should be *De retinendo vel non retinendo* [whether it should be kept or not kept]. If the other small schemas were, in the same way, sent back to be recast, that would be so much the better!

---

1. *AS* III/IV, 403–404.
2. Fernando Gomes dos Santos, Archbishop of Goiânia, *AS* III/IV, 420–421.

Cardinal Suenens said to me: it is in order to take a step in that direction that the Moderators have just postponed the vote until later.

Lunch in Via Ulisse Seni with the bishops, Frs Dupuy and Le Guillou, and the small group of worker priests around Fr Depierre.[1] After lunch, conversation with them. One was immediately in the midst of the serious and the real. Am I mistaken? I had the feeling that my concept of priesthood and what I call the consequent monotheism could provide an answer to many of the questions raised, or at least, open up promising possibilities for them.

While waiting for 4.30pm (I was early), I chatted with Fr Philipon: we were much more thoroughly in agreement than I had expected on the schema *De Sacerdotibus*, collegiality etc.

At 4.30 pm, Theological Commission. Discussion on the text concerning collective eschatology.

Spanedda found the whole thing useless. Henríquez and Daniélou the same.

At 5.00 pm we went on to the *De Beata*. Philips gave a very conciliatory *relatio*. Also very deft.

Cardinal Santos insisted on the TITLE of the Chapter: *'De Maria Matre Ecclesiae'* [on Mary the Mother of the Church]. But that did not encounter much support. Almost everyone wanted no further discussion of the title (a unanimous vote except for Santos).

Discussion of *Maria Mater Ecclesiae* under another form: *'Ecclesia . . . matrem suam . . .'* [the Church . . . her Mother]. Spanedda and Parente were IN FAVOUR. Parente brought forward the witness of Paul VI. But he came over to Philips' proposal simply to quote the words of Benedict XIV, *'tanquam matrem amantissimam'* [as a most beloved Mother] (page 198, line 9).

Some biblical questions on Genesis 3:15 and Isaiah 7:14.

Philips won, without striking a blow, the suppression of *'Quoniam Beatissima Virgo haud minor poterat esse quam Dei Matrem decebat'* [For the most blessed Virgin could hardly be less that what befitted the Mother of God] (page 199, lines 22 ff). It was fantastic! It was one of the bad arguments of the professional mariologues. He simply argued from the fact that the text of St Ambrose had been taken in an extended sense that did not belong to it.

Fr Balić spoke ONLY ONCE to support a correction proposed by Cardinal Bea. No notice was taken of it.—What a transformation! Might we have escaped from the runaway, maximalist mariology?

Ancel, supported by Butler, tried to have inserted in the text: *'Summe Deo grata seu gratia plena'* [most highly pleasing to God or full of grace]. Benoit, Hen-

---

1. André Depierre, originally from Jura and incardinated in Paris, was a worker-priest and in charge of the Mission of Paris; at the beginning of the Second Session he was delegated to the Council by his fellow French worker-priests whose turn for this had just come round.

ríquez came to the rescue; Parente was against it . . . As Moeller said to me, the Fathers take an interest in some trifling matters of theological technique, but for a question of such importance as this they have no sensitivity: 14 out of 26 were in favour of the text AS IT IS, without '*Summe Deo grata*'.

At the interval, Parente said to me: 'My friend Jean Guitton—a Frenchman!— said to me: for us layfolk the schema *De beata* is poor. One could have gone much further.' But, Parente added, *transeat* [let it pass]! . . .

It went on, often dealing with small details. We stopped just before broaching the question of mediation. Parente called a halt. That is for tomorrow, but I shall not be able to be there.

In the evening, at dinner, there were some bits of information from the meeting that the French bishops hold every Wednesday. They had talked about *De Sacerdotibus*. The feeling was confused. Some wanted to reject it; it seems that the Brazilian bishops have so decided. Others were hesitant, either because they found some good things in it, or because they were fearful of the very adverse effect it would have on priests if, once again, there was a failure to speak either to them or about them. (Mgr Guyot, in charge of the studies about priests, was not at the meeting, but he had sent a message asking for a vote *non placet*.) They also feared that this might set off a series of rejections of the little schemas. On this subject, Mgr Lallier and Mgr Bézac[1] said how disappointing the schema on marriage seemed to them, and what a cruel disillusionment it will be for lay people.[2] It is silent about the most delicate questions that they raise.

This Council has not been thought though. Each group has worked in ignorance of the others, as though it were the only one . . .

I have been given to read the CURRENT text of the schema *De libertate*. Hardly anything is left of the previous text. In these circumstances a new discussion is needed. I find that there is a certain superficiality in this approach. The redactors (especially Pavan and Murray) have no idea of the difficulties that their text will raise. The BIBLICAL part is mediocre. De Broglie's objections have not been taken up. In short, I don't find it REALLY satisfactory . . .

Thursday 15 October 1964.

At St Peter's, I saw Mgr Marty about the *De Sacerdotibus*; I offered to help him. He said he was very touched at this.

> Mgr Prignon: There is going to be need for vigilance about schema XIII. Cardinal Frings came back rather uneasy from a meeting with the Pope. It is feared that the discussion will not touch much on the

---

1. Robert Bézac, Bishop of Aire et Dax (France).
2. This refers to the *votum* on the sacrament of marriage finalised by the Commission for the Discipline of the Sacraments, which was to be voted on and communicated to the Pope at the end of this Session with a view to the reform of the Code of Canon Law on mixed marriages.

question of 'the pill'. The French bishops need to be alerted to the danger that exists.

Felici[1] asked that requests for attendance at Mass and at the General Congregations be limited.

There are still numerous requests for interventions on the *De Sacerdotibus*, this morning's session will deal with them. What a bore!!!

Alfrink:[2] the image of the priest and of priesthood in the world of today is inadequate. The questions that engage priests today are not dealt with or are dealt with superficially.

It needs to be looked at again.

Applause.

Köstner (Austrian)[3] [ ]

Jenny:[4] look at the priesthood within the whole mystery of Christ and of the Church: priests are like the bishop's council, like the apostles of Christ (reference to Dom Gréa[5]). The unity of the priesthood with the bishop and amongst priests. He took up the three functions and set out the function of the priest. ONCE AGAIN A SYNTHESIS in its entirety.

Defer the schema, not indefinitely, but to later THIS Session.

Modrego:[6] boring!

Gugić:[7] (Yugoslav) [ ]

Sartre[8] retired Archbishop of Teneriffe. Emphasised the connection with Christ, the Church, the world. Nothing on the Holy Spirit, etc. The text should be revised and redone as a substantial schema. He suggested a plan in several points:

Begin with the mission of the whole Church, which is essentially apostolic. The priest as sent to the World.

The mission comes from the Father, through the Son, in the Holy Spirit. Christ as head is represented by the hierarchy. The mission is hierarchical.

Cooperation in this mission is essentially sacramental, not simply spiritual.

1. *AS* III/IV, 453–454.
2. *AS* III/IV, 454–456.
3. Joseph Kostner, Bishop of Gurk, *AS* III/IV, 457–458.
4. *AS* III/IV, 458–460.
5. Dom Marie-Étienne-Adrien Gréa (1828–1917) priest and founder of a congregation of male religious; his researches prepared for the renewal of ecclesiology in the twentieth century.
6. G Modrego y Casáus, *AS* III/IV, 461–463.
7. J Gugić, Auxiliary Bishop of Dubrovnik, *AS* III/IV, 469–471.
8. *AS* III/IV, 471–473.

This sacramental initiation does not reduce the mission of the priest to the sacramental and cultic order. The priest is always sent to all human beings, even unbelievers.

The mission of the priest, flowing from Christ, can never be separated from the spiritual life: it is a matter of being united with Christ as head. One does not function except through Christ.

Nourishment by Eucharist, the Scriptures, Prayer.

Flores[1] (Barbastro) [   ]

The Moderators asked (this was before 11.00 am, the moment when seats are vacated) if it was desired to halt the discussion on *De Sacerdotibus*. The great majority stood up, but it was not clear.

Cardinal Lefebvre spoke in the name of seventy Fathers:[2] the priest consecrates HUMANITY ITSELF.

Mgr Marty[3] read a *relatio conclusiva* [final report] (his diction still broken up into short bursts, like a little girl timidly reciting a lesson).

Reading of the *relationes* on the Eastern Churches. I went out for a moment: Don Dossetti told me that Cardinal Lercaro immediately accepted my suggestion regarding concrete reports at the time of the discussion on schema XIII: he will speak to the Pope about it during the Moderators' audience this evening.

Mgr Conway, Archbishop of Armagh, came to see me about the question of mixed marriages. I offered to meet him one day about this question.

Discussion of *De Ecclesiis Orientalibus* began exactly at midday.

Cardinal König:[4] the schema is not sufficiently ecumenical, not consistent, in this regard, with *De oecumenismo*. The Eastern Churches appear too much as exceptions. He made a number of remarks along these lines. Revise the text in a truly ecumenical way.

(A very remarkable intervention).

SB Sidarouss,[5] Patriarch of Alexandria: recommended approval of the schema.

Maximos IV:[6] there was a religious attention. Absolute silence. Almost all the Observers and many of the Fathers stood up. This was partly because Maximos spoke in French, and many turned an ear to him and sharpened their attention. A strong, virile, candid, somewhat abrupt

---

1. *AS* III/IV, 473–475.
2. *AS* III/IV, 479–481.
3. *AS* III/IV, 482–484.
4. *AS* III/IV, 528–430.
5. Stephanos I Sidarouss, *AS* III/IV, 530–532.
6. *AS* III/IV, 532–535.

speech, from this admirable old man who was giving an historic address.

It was a grand and moving moment. The assembly felt this. Maximos explained the patriarchal system and the theology of communion.

An allusion to the meeting in Jerusalem.

He was applauded.

At midday I brought Fr de Lubac back for lunch. I am astonished and saddened that the bishops no longer approach him and take so little interest in what a man of this quality could tell them.

At 4.30 pm, with the Observers. I gave an introductory exposition on Scripture and Tradition (which caused me to miss the Theological Commission).

Questions:

Cullmann took up his position (the difference between the Tradition of the Apostles and post-apostolic tradition: the sense of the fixing of the canon: I criticised this in my response. . . etc).

Cullmann, who repeated himself at length—recognised that the gap has been narrowed; his chief criticism is the absence of *'Gegenüber'* [reciprocity] on the Catholic side.

Nissiotis found it lacking in dynamism, and the way the Magisterium is presented as equivalent to a 'christomonism': Apostolic Succession does not have any relationship, for us, with Pentecost.

The Russian Observer hardly did anything more than to repeat in Russian some positive affirmations of the schema, which thus seemed to satisfy him.

Müller:[1] who will guard the guardian? The Scriptures.

Fr Scrima underlined the coherence of the Council's work.

I asked Willebrands to get Fr Féret to speak, to bring it to a close.

At 7.00 pm, at the American College. A very warm, simple welcome. I feel very much at ease with these simple men who, encountered in their American setting, are authentic. Three hundred seminarians from 105 dioceses. My lecture (the one from the Dutch centre translated into English) went well.

I missed the Theological Commission. I was told (by Ancel and Philips) that there was a serious set-to on *'mediatrix'*, but that it was a *via media* formula that was passed. On the other hand, a proposition of Ancel was rejected that said one should not give to Mary titles that belong ONLY TO Christ. As a whole, the chapter is certainly not along the lines of the runaway, maximalist mariology. It is a *via media* text. *'Mediatrix'* could not be avoided. The manner in which it is spoken of is still the most discreet. I really do believe that the rampant movement

---

1. There was no Observer of this name, but it could be a reference to Walter Muelder, Observer appointed by the World Methodist Council.

that Pius XII had favoured, perhaps PARTLY in spite of himself, has been reined in, if not brought to a halt.

Mgr Philips told me that, to avoid the indiscretions of the press with regard to the discussion of schema XIII, it will no doubt be requested that the two most burning questions, the pill and the bomb, be addressed only in WRITTEN communications.

Friday 16 October 1964

Khrushchev has resigned.

This morning, Melchite liturgy celebrated by Mgr Hakim, with Maximos presiding. It lasted one hour and a quarter, but this is part of the current discussion, it is an object lesson. The East speaks through liturgical action.

DISTRIBUTION of the *motu proprio* (approved by the Pope *speciali modo*[1]) on the application of the *De Sancta Liturgia*, — the *relatio* on schema XIII, — the amended text of chapter VII of *De Ecclesia*.

The question was asked: are the Fathers agreeable that the schema-propositions be sent to the relevant commissions after a brief discussion, or, if the text can be voted on by articles, straightaway. That was the decision of the Co-ordinating Commission. THE TEXT OF THIS NOTIFICATION WILL BE GIVEN IN WRITING.

Discussion was resumed of *De Ecclesiis Orientalibus.*

Cardinal Barros Câmara[2] (Brazil): in favour of its application to Easterners dispersed among the Latins.

Gori,[3] Jerusalem: in favour of converts having freedom to choose a rite.

Batanian:[4] on No. 18 (mixed marriages): in FAVOUR of the new legislation concerning mixed marriages, but his speech did not really have an ecumenical tone.

Slipyj:[5] in the name of all Ukrainians and of others. In favour of ensuring the LIFE of the Eastern Churches. They matter to CATHOLICITY.

Ghattas:[6] there is a lot of good in the schema, but why a SPECIAL schema on the Eastern Churches? From the outset there has been a sense of distinguishing them from the Catholic Church . . . He enumerated what is there, or what is lacking but would have its place in the other schemas.

---

1. 'in a special manner' (a canonical term).
2. *AS* III/V, 11–12.
3. *AS* III/V, 13–15.
4. *AS* III/V, 15–18.
5. *AS* III/V, 19–21.
6. *AS* III/V, 21–23.

De Provenchères:[1] (appallingly French pronunciation). Interventions by the French bishops are nearly always grand personal syntheses, or particular remarks marked by a certain dose of sentiment. However they do express some good things from the ecumenical point of view.

Zoghby:[2] in favour of a true notion of catholicity. Against a confusion between this, and the *de facto* universality of the Latin Church.

Doumith:[3] this schema is ENTIRELY DISAPPOINTING. Prejudices have not been eliminated. Etc. He also spoke about unity of jurisdiction in places where there is plurality of rites. He held to the Maronite thesis: Unity of the Church, unity of discipline, except for the recognition of particularities.

I was absent for a moment. At the end of the sitting, an allusion by Mgr Stangl[4] to a Fourth Session was applauded.

Mgr Elchinger said, when I encountered him: I have just seen Cardinal Frings and said to him: have you asked the Pope for a replacement for Felici as Secretary General? Frings let it be understood that something of the kind might well be being staked out, and that, in such a case, Mgr Dell'Acqua would be under consideration; because it would have to be someone from the Curia.

Saturday 17 October 1964
Worked on my *ICI* chronicle.

In the evening, dinner with Mlle Stevens,[5] together with Nicolas Zernov[6] and his wife.[7] Theological conversation. This gave me the opportunity to see, albeit in artificial light, the EUR quarter—a reasonably successful concept of Mussolini's: wholly modern homogeneous architecture, of a certain grandeur.

Sunday 18 October 1964
I did not go to the ceremony for the canonisation of the martyrs of Uganda. I am against such ceremonies, full of ostentation and of HUMAN glory, and I have always declined tickets or opportunities that have been offered to me. I finished my *ICI* chronicle and the text Mgr Ménager asked for, on the theological basis of the participation of the laity in the mission of the Church.

---

1. *AS* III/V, 29–31.
2. *AS* III/V, 32–34.
3. *AS* III/V, 36–38.
4. Josef Stangl, Bishop of Würzburg, member of the Secretariat for Unity, appointed in March 1964, *AS* III/V, 42–43.
5. Hélène Stevens, whom Congar knew from his ecumenical rounds, worked for the FAO.
6. Nicolas Zernov, a Russian émigré in Great Britain, was Professor of Eastern Orthodox Culture at the University of Oxford; his ecumenical involvement had led him to found the Fraternity of Saint Alban and Saint Sergius which linked Anglicans and Orthodox.
7. Militza Lavrov.

In the afternoon, I worked on the *De Sacerdotibus* for Mgr Marty.

L'abbé Haubtmann told me this, which he must have directly from the Cardinal concerned (doubtless Liénart). In the meeting of the Co-ordinating Commission which preceded the votes on 30 October 1963, there was question as to whether the Moderators had the right to put to the assembly the famous five questions. Felici had announced the result of the vote in a manner which gave the negative a majority by one vote. This cardinal, having noted the fact, had contested the accuracy of the result announced. There was a recount which gave a majority in favour by one vote.

Haubtmann concluded, as did others: in an industrial enterprise, Felici would receive thanks. . .

This evening, prayer and dinner with the Brothers of Taizé. I experienced once again the miracle of this creation. Taizé seems to me to give a striking example of a Gospel response, and I would say, a priestly response to the expectation of human beings. They communicate God, they live God, and that is all. And that is enough. One comes to them because there one finds oneself in the presence of God. But Schutz combines a mystical gift with a rather extraordinary sense of the concrete and an ability to translate the mystical expectation into concrete realisation. He immediately seeks to engage with the CALL and find for it a concrete response. Very many young people come to them: they convey to them, first of all, entry into the presence of God and his demands, and then, not theories, but the suggestion of simple, immediate, concrete undertakings.

Many priests, monks, religious come to them. Schutz told me that in this way people have made him the confidant of their great distress. Not only many young Catholics, young married couples questioning ecclesiastical structures in a VERY radical way—, it is not only among the young that one finds a total absence of reference to a tradition, of an even elementary knowledge of history, of what should be THEIR history, but there is a profound questioning among priests and monks about their vocation. I have been aware of it.

Schutz and Thurian went eight days ago to the village which was the birthplace of John XXIII, whom they venerate. They saw his brothers, his nephews and nieces: a very poor background. 'Because you have been faithful in small things I will place you over great things.' They also visited Brescia, the Oratory, with its school where the Montini were educated. The old teacher of Paul VI, Bevilacqua[1] is still there. They told me: this place was a school of courage, an education in courage. And a place of resistance to totalitarianism.

---

1.   The Oratorian, Giulio Bevilacqua, friend and confessor of the Pope: created cardinal by him in February 1965, he died in the following May.

Monday 19 October 1964

I did not go to St Peter's.[1] Correspondence. Worked on *De Sacerdotio*.[2] At 1.15 pm, lunch with Nissiotis, who had invited me. He is VERY pleased with Cardinal König's intervention,[3] and this morning's session on the Eastern Churches. This morning it was Cardinal Lercaro[4] and a German abbot[5] who were excellent. He did not tell me what I learnt later, that there was a painful intervention by a Chaldean bishop[6] against Maximos, or rather against the theology of patriarchates. These are a purely ecclesiastical institution and the patriarchs are named by the pope, on whom they depend. The western bishops find these conflicts amongst the Easterners very tiresome. It makes them hesitant: if only they would agree amongst themselves!!

Nissiotis said to me: write a paper on the points that need to be broached in a theological dialogue between the Orthodox and Rome, and on the order to be followed (which ones to put FIRST). He promised me that he would present it in Rhodes, at the Pro-synod,[7] and, he said, coming from me, it will be accepted. For I am well known and it is known that I have always served the truth, without any spirit of connivance or of controversy.

In the afternoon, I worked on the definitive redaction of the text on Mission that Mgr Geeraerts had asked me for. However, I had visits from Fr Dingemans and from Fr Guy Leger[8] for: 1) the volume of essays in honour of Fr Chenu;[9] 2) the serious difficulties of CIREC[10] in relation to Istina and the Eastern Commission.[11]

In the evening, supper and a lecture at the Canadian college (Church and World).

Tuesday 20 October 1964

I have received some news of the Theological Commission meeting that was held yesterday evening, and to which I could not go. The *modi* for Chapter II were

---

1. Congar here added to the typescript: 'Return to the Commission of the text on priests'.
2. This refers to the schema on priests.
3. This refers to Cardinal König's intervention *in aula* on the preceding 15 October.
4. *AS* III/V, 64–47.
5. Johann D Hoeck, OSB, Abbot Primate of the Benedictine Congregation of Bavaria, member of the Commission for the Eastern Churches, *AS* III/V, 72–75.
6. Raphaël Bidawid, originally from Mosul, Chaldean Bishop of Amadiyah (Iraq) later Patriarch of Babylon of the Chaldeans, *AS* III/V, 100–102.
7. The third Pan-Orthodox Conference of Rhodes was to be held from the first to the fifteenth of the following November.
8. Guy Leger, OP, of the Province of Paris.
9. Cf *L'Hommage différé au Père Chenu* (Paris: Cerf, 1990), 239–245.
10. The International Centre for Research and Cultural Exchange, set up in Paris by the Dominicans.
11. The reference should rather be to the Congregation for the Eastern Church, on which the Istina Centre was dependent; a plan envisaged the transfer of the Centre to the CIREC premises in Paris.

discussed. The text concerning Non-Catholic Christians has been somewhat further spoilt, by making it less ecumenical. More especially there was a discussion which lasted half an hour. A letter was read from Mgr Dell'Acqua, asking that Mgr Franić and Granados be added to the small sub-commission which is examining and evaluating the *modi*. It is obvious: we have got to the *modi* for Chapter III, which is the ONLY chapter that is of interest to THEM. It's collegiality!—Confused discussion. Mgr Ancel proposed, and this was accepted in the end, that Fr Tromp be delegated to go to Mgr Dell'Acqua to explain to him the manner of working in the small sub-commission, and that he should bring back the cardinal's final decision.[1]

I asked Mgr Philips (the evening of 20 October) for news of this affair. He told me that Fr Tromp did not want to take this step, which would imply distrust of the small working commission. But Mgr Philips thinks, more realistically, that it would be tactically better to take Franić into the small group, given that he will be at the Commission in any case. This would disarm him a bit.

This morning I was summoned to the sacristy[2] at 9.00 am to preview the work to be done on the text of the *De Iudaeis,* with Cardinal König, Moeller, Frs Pfister[3] and Neuner.[4] It seems that the text will have to be added to the chapter *De Populo Dei,* as a *consectarium* [corollary] or *Appendix.* (This was decided by the Co-ordinating Commission, the Council of Presidents, and the Moderators. The Pope agreed. But it should be voted on by the Assembly. . .) This would be a good solution: it would give the text a purely religious colouring, indeed a dogmatic one, and also, by that very fact, great dignity. But how shall I do the necessary work, given that at the same time the *De Sacerdotibus* needs to be done, I have to go to Naples, take part in the Board of *Concilium*, etc!!!, and prepare and complete the volumes on collegiality and on poverty.

At the General Congregation, the completion of *De Ecclesiis Orientalibus*: those who spoke in the name of more than seventy Fathers:

Mgr Hakim:[5] who recommended a positive vote for the schema *in genere*.
Mgr Baudoux:[6] *idem*, and he replied to the Chaldean bishop of yesterday.

---

1. A Dell'Acqua was not yet a cardinal, cf above, page 136, note 1.
2. Congar added to the typescript: 'St Peter's'.
3. Paul Pfister, SJ, of German origin, had been a long time in Japan. He taught in the Faculty of Theology of Sophia University, run by the Jesuits in Tokyo; he was a Council expert.
4. Joseph Neuner, SJ, of Austrian origin, was Professor of Theology at the Pontifical Athenaeum of Poona (India); he was a Council expert.
5. *AS* III/V,106–107.
6. *AS* III/V, 107–110.

Mgr Athaide[1] (India): in favour of unity of jurisdiction in the same area.
He ended with the request that Patriarchs should be cardinals!

The conclusion of the schema *De Ecclesiis Orientalibus*, by its rapporteur, Bukatko;[2] he presented the schema as a child of John XXIII . . .

After this the vote was proposed: *an placet Patribus ut transeatur ad votationem per placet et non placet* [are the Fathers willing to move on to a vote for or against]?

The two *relationes* on the Church in the world were read: Cardinal Cento,[3] Mgr Guano[4] (he made some cuts).

There will first be a discussion on the general principles of schema XIII; after which the Moderators will ask if it is desired to move on to the discussion of each of the points: *proemium* and Chapter I; Chapter II and III together; Chapter IV by sections, after a brief *relatio* on each point listed by Felici.

The result was given of the vote on Chapter VII as a whole:

Present:	2,184
Placet:	1,921
Non placet:	29
Placet iuxta modum:	233
Null:	1

Mgr del Portillo[5] asked me to be at the chapel of the baptistry at 11.00 am tomorrow for the *De Sacerdotibus*. He has prepared a text for a message to priests which he will bring me tomorrow.

I would like to do my utmost for these texts about priests. I offer myself to God for this in accordance with the apostolic prayer that is mine without ceasing.

I note that Mgr Willebrands saw the Pope yesterday evening . . .

I saw Fr Duprey for a moment, who said to me: pray for me. I am leaving this evening. He said no more, but I understood that he was going to prepare for Patriarch Athenagoras' arrival at the Council. Certainly, that too, is in the apostolic prayer!

General vote on the *De Ecclesiis Orientalibus*:

Present:	2,180
Placet:	1,911
Non placet:	265
Placet iuxta modum:	1
Null votes:	3

---

1. Dominic RB Athaide, OFM Cap, Archbishop of Agra, *AS* III/V, 110–112.
2. *AS* III/V, 112–114.
3. *AS* III/V, 201–203.
4. *AS* III/V, 203–213.
5. Alvaro del Portillo, Secretary General of *Opus Dei*, was secretary of the Commission for the Discipline of the Clergy and of the Christian People and a Council expert; he was later to be named titular bishop and Prelate of *Opus Dei*, which had, in the meantime, become a personal prelature.

Tomorrow the vote will be section by section: Felici[1] indicated the distribution of votes (7 in all).

At 11:10 am: discussion began on *De Ecclesia in Mundo.*[2]

Carinal Liénart:[3] the tone is not good; too exhortatory and homiletic; the natural and supernatural orders should be better distinguished (a large synthesis). Not a very strong text.

Spellman[4] who had just arrived at the session; very boring.

Ruffini:[5] criticisms of detail and too many repetitions; a preaching tone; some inaccuracies and imprecisions. How simplistic, this Ernest! He is perfectly consistent with himself and with his attitude of rejecting real openings. *Ut schema funditus reficatur* [the schema should be fundamentally remade] in line with the encyclicals of recent popes.

Lercaro:[6] in favour of a thoroughgoing discussion of the schema. He recalled the PURPOSE of the Council, and even the Message to the World.

There should be a fourth Session, perhaps, even, not in 1965, but later. Applause.

Cardinal Léger:[7] a good foundation. It should be discussed, including the family, and peace . . .

Each specific subject in chapter IV should be preceded by an exposition of the question given by an expert, male or female.

Döpfner:[8] in the name of eighty-three German or Scandinavian-speaking Fathers: A good basis for discussion. There should be a wide-ranging discussion. On the most delicate points (responsibility of spouses, peace) the discretion of the Fathers should be trusted.

He agreed with Lercaro on the question of necessary extensions of time.

Meyer:[9] in favour of thoroughgoing discussion. The relationship between daily human toil and the kingdom of God is not sufficiently brought out. THE WORLD is a beneficiary of redemption. The *munus cosmicum Christi* [cosmic function of Christ].

Silva Henríquez:[10] like many others this morning, having prepared his text when schema XIII was under challenge, he spoke in an apologetic manner. He added that the God of the Bible reveals humankind to itself—V[ery] G[ood].

---

1. *AS* III/V, 214.
2. This refers to the future Constitution, *Gaudium et Spes.*
3. *AS* III/V, 215–217.
4. *AS* III/V, 217–219.
5. *AS* III/V, 220–223.
6. *AS* III/V, 223–226.
7. *AS* III/V, 226–228.
8. *AS* III/V, 228–230.
9. *AS* III/V, 232–234.
10. *AS* III/V, 235–237.

The French bishops have received, in personally addressed envelopes, a report from medical doctors which seems to have been written at the instigation of Louvain.[1] However there are many American, Dutch and French names. The report is a calling into question of the norms that official documents give for the human practice of conjugal relations. I have NEVER been completely in accord with these norms . . .

At 4.30 pm, sub-commission on *De Revelatione*. Schmaus, Schauf and Fr Trapè have been added to our sub-commission, but Rahner was not there.

Betti gave the report on the comments concerning Chapter II: he did it very well. It was discussed at GREAT LENGTH. Mgr Florit did not guide the work.

Wednesday 21 October 1964

A difficult morning. L'abbé Ernoult,[2] national chaplain to the men's ACG wanted to see me; he did not arrive until 8.45 am. I left for St Peter's at 9.15 am, with Mgr Gouyon. Mass had not finished because it was a very long Romanian mass. But I had a conflict of obligations. There was the sub-commission on *De Revelatione*, with the delicate question of constitutive Tradition,[3] at St Martha's at 10.30 am; and there was a meeting with Mgr Marty and Fr del Portillo on the *De Sacerdotibus* at 11.00 am at St Peter's. I had originally decided to go there (in order to get a foothold in this working group), but after having seen del Portillo, Lécuyer, Mgr Marty, I changed my mind and went to St Martha's. Since the Mass finished at 10.10 am, I missed the whole Congregation and several interesting speeches.

At St Martha's, the work made only slow progress, so that, by 12.20 pm, we had still not got to the '*vexata quaestio*' [vexed question]. Fr Tromp intervened several times. So did I, especially to safeguard mention of realities (*rerum*) as the object of Christian experience: Philips, referring to Cerfaux, wanted to speak only of gifts of the Spirit, which everyone would have understood as the 'gifts of the Holy Spirit', entirely interior—and also so as to avoid it being said that Tradition IS also (together with Scripture) '*verbum Dei*' [the Word of God]. No. It CONTAINS the Word of God, and transmits it, together with various other things, but it IS not the Word of God.

Moeller, returning after an absence, came immediately to the rescue. Dom Butler, one of those who were asking for this, thanked him as he was leaving, hav-

---

1. This refers to the *Address to the Vatican Council about the Problems of the Family*. Among those who had taken the initiative in this were Herman and Lena Buelens-Gijsen and also Jan Grootaers; they were later to publish the text in *Mariage catholique et contraception* (Paris: Épi,1968), 275–281.
2. Eugène Ernoult, of the diocese of Rennes, was the National Chaplain of the Men's General Catholic Action; he was later to become Auxiliary Bishop of Nantes, and then Archbishop of Sens.
3. The idea of an oral tradition coming from Christ and containing truths not found in the Gospels.

ing at last seen what was at stake in the matter from the ecumenical point of view (but there was also a question of truth).

I brought Mgr Jacq back to lunch.

At 4.30 pm, I could not, alas, go to the sub-commission on *De Revelatione*, where the *'vexata quaestio'* was undoubtedly going to come up at last. There was a meeting at the Secretariat for Unity about the declaration on non-Christian religions. The Secretariat had had two good paragraphs prepared on the Jews and on the Muslims.

Stransky, Neuner (India), Pfister (Japan), Moeller and I were there. Neuner and Pfister have a rather difficult English. We spoke especially about THE ORDER to be followed and the contents of the paragraph on non-Christian religions other than Jews and Muslims.

After discussion, the following was arrived at;
- a brief introduction,
- the unity of the human race, to which would be attached something about the great religions inasmuch as they offer a response to the great questions of humanind.
- and the desire for dialogue,
- the former No. 33, minus the last two lines,
- the Muslims,
- the Jews.

I insisted that there should be a sentence, short but pithy, stating that the answer that human beings are seeking is found in its fullness in Christ, but avoiding any missionary allusion.

We also discussed where it should be placed. The presence of the section on the missions at the end of Chapter II of *De Ecclesia* is a very serious difficulty in the way of placing the Declaration as an appendix to this Chapter II. Perhaps it could remain as an independent text after all.

Since our meeting ended at 6.05 pm, we went with Moeller to St Martha's, for the *De Revelatione*. They had finished the chapter on Tradition and had just started the one on Revelation. Schauf, Trapè and Salaverri looked to be very relaxed, even jovial. Seeing this I was fearful that they had got their way on the question of constitutive Tradition. Someone told me later: they put the question with vehemence, but without success. The Fathers on the sub-commission did not want to follow them. Tromp noted that, in his (inaugural?) address the Pope seemed to have alluded to a constitutive tradition. It was decided to put the question at the *plenaria* [plenary meeting] as to whether to ask the Pope to make known his intention. It seems that that calmed down Schauf and Trapè.

I have heard it said on one side (De Lubac) that there would be a new Joint Commission on religious freedom, and on another side (Mgr Heuschen) that there would be a Joint Commission for the *De Iudaeis*. If that is the case, should we continue our work?

This evening, at the French Seminary, there were five Italian bishops at dinner: (Florit, Baldassarri, Carli, the Bishop of Cremona[1] and ... ?). And also the people from *La Croix:* Wenger,[2] N Copin,[3] and the editor of *La Croix.*[4] Wenger told me that Mgr Méndez and Fr Lemercier who accompanied him, would be the two who kept Fesquet (*Le Monde*) informed.

Thursday 22 October 1964

As there was a sub-commission on *De Revelatione* at 10.00 am, I took advantage of this to: 1) see Fr Féret for a moment about the *De Presbyteris* (he had redone a complete text which the sisters were going to roneo) and about the Message to Priests, on which he had asked my advice; 2) go to the Vatican to claim my expenses for four journeys to Rome for the Commission. So I managed only a brief moment *in aula*. I caught the end of an intervention by Mgr Heenan;[5] extremely violent. For him schema XIII would be the disgrace of the Council. What is said about the family cannot go through. The evil comes from experts who pick and choose among pontifical teachings. But they are not infallible [implying: for all that they seem to believe that they are!].

Heenan would have had in mind particularly Küng and Häring who had intervened in the English situation. Häring had spoken about birth control. There had also been the intervention of Mgr Roberts. In short, the English bishops do not want to hear mention at the Council of either the pill or the bomb.

Heenan was strongly applauded. By some perhaps, because of the humour of his speech; by many, especially at the top of the assembly, because they saw in his speech a savage attack on schema XIII, which they do not want. From the experts' tribune, one saw that it was Felici who, if he did not actually start the applause, at least encouraged it as soon as it started. There was applause also from the table of the Council of Presidents.

Yesterday, Mgr Petit (always very much for the *sed contra* [on the other hand]) had already criticised the schema along the same lines. Conversely, someone told me, only this morning, that Mgr Beck,[6] Heenan's successor in Liverpool, had spo-

---

1. Danio Bolognini.
2. Fr Antoine Wenger, Assumptionist; after having taught Eastern theology at the Catholic Faculties in Lyons, he was from 1962, editor-in-chief of *La Croix*, and covered the Council in Rome during the Four Sessions; this led him to publish, at Éditions du Centurion, four volumes of chronicles: *Vatican II. Première session*, 1963; *Vatican II. Chronique de la deuxième session*, 1964; *Vatican II. Chronique de la troisième session*, 1965; *Vatican II. Chronique de la quartrième session*, 1966.
3. Noël Copin, editor at *La Croix,* covered the Council in Rome from the Second Session; he was later to become editor-in-chief of that daily newspaper.
4. Jean Gélamur, President and Director General of *La Croix*, and also of the firm of Maison de la Bonne Presse (which later became Bayard-Presse).
5. *AS* III/V, 318–321.
6. *AS* III/V, 360–361.

ken like almost everyone else: the schema needs a lot of improvement, but it is a good basis for discussion. Mgr Glorieux told me that Guano will respond after the discussion of the schema *in genere*: Moeller told me that Cardinal Suenens would respond from tomorrow.

At 10.30 am, at St Martha's, for the sub-commission on *De Revelatione*. We finished the work on Chapter I. Smulders and Betti have done some very good work.

I saw Fr Lebret at lunch: 'schema XIII must be saved. Three or four of us must set to work at once to draft a new text. Only the French can do this, because they have a lead in experiencing what it is to be confronted by a world.'

At 4.30 pm, Theological Commission, at the Vatican. Since it was dealing with Chapter III, on this occasion we saw Lattanzi, Ciappi, Ramirez, D'Ercole turn up [Moeller said to me: the whole of the front line of Waterloo is here].

The end of the *modi* for Chapter II.

Mgr Roy got approval for the text of the *Relatio* on the revision of Chapter VIII, *De BMV* (a text which is Philipon's from beginning to end!).

Colombo's wish is that we do not speak of a *via media*, and several shrink from the frank admission that there are differences among us. A misleading cloak of Noah [cf Genesis 9:23]!!!

Philips announced that the small working group that was looking at the *modi* for Chapter III asked Franić to join it. What a tactician! (I learned on 25 October that THE POPE had asked that a bishop from the majority party and a bishop from the minority (without mentioning Franić by name) should be added to the small working group.)

Smulders clarified the precise meaning of the vote on the possible ordination of young people to the diaconate.

Granados presented an entirely new text for No. 18, where the idea of a hierarchy as SERVICE seemed to him to smack of democracy. But it was pointed out to him that: 1) we could only deal with the *modi* proposed *in aula*; 2) the text said nothing along the lines of democracy.

Spanedda raised, with warmth and force, the question of the theological note of the text. For him there is no middle ground between UNCERTAIN and infallible teaching. '*Doctrina certa*' [certain teaching] is only certain if it can, and should, be called infallible. I believe that this point is decisive in the Italian mentality.

A sub-commission was appointed which worked up a text. This conclusion was accepted by the Commission, but had never been made public *in aula*. It would be possible, Fernandez said, to introduce it in to the *Relatio*.

A great discourse by Salaverri, who really does have the dogmatic tone.

Tromp—who seemed to have, *motu proprio,* suppressed the word '*dogmaticae*' in the title, '*schema Constitutionis dogmaticae de Ecclesia*' [schema of the Dogmatic Constitution on the Church]—intervened several times. He retired into his shell, somewhat abashed, because the Commission reacted in a rather lively fashion when the question was asked: who removed the word, and on what authority?

Charue asked for the restoration of the word, and that a vote be taken on the point. Garrone came back to it, with emphasis, and Charue once again.

Henríquez insisted: WHO changed the title, and by what authority?

Tromp did not say a word. Nobody knew. . .

What would the work of the Theological Commission have been like if Tromp (a few years younger) had been all-powerful there, as he had been at the beginning, and if Philips had not been there? He brings peace and clarity to everything.

Colombo said that the Commission could speak its mind, but that the Pope will have to reserve to himself the right to specify, in the way that he will choose, what is to be the note of these texts.

Schauf: it is not known on what understanding of the theological note the Fathers voted *Placet*. Nothing is known about that . . . What was it they wanted to do and to approve?

Various speakers discussed the point: the Council is PASTORAL: and yet it is DOGMATIC . . .

Friday 23 October 1964

This time I really would have liked to have gone to St Peter's to hear the end of the debate on schema XIII *in genere*, and the beginning of the discussion on Chapter I. But I must leave for Naples at 1.00 pm, and I have some visitors and many things to do.

A visit from Mlles Grandjean and Lebaindre, for the background of what was, at least according to their version, a new '*Eaux Vives*' affair,[1] on a larger scale: Fr Tempels, OFM, and his Congolese group, JAMA.[2] Once again, a mariological gnosis.[3]

I went to see M. Brand for a moment, about *Concilium*. He told me that Fr Vanhengel had seen Colombo again, who had pointed out to him, as Roman theologians, Garofalo and two others who, according to the *Annuario Pontificio*, are members of the Index . . . I will see, tomorrow, what came of this, if, that is, my activities in Naples will permit me to attend the meeting of the Board of *Concilium*.

I worked on my lecture for Naples, and on a short report for Nissiotis, and, through him, for the Orthodox conference in Rhodes.

---

1. An allusion to events that had disturbed the life of the Dominican Centre of l'Eau Vive, (cf abov, page 33, note 1) and led to its closure.
2. The Belgian Franciscan, Placide Tempels, for long a missionary in the Belgian Congo, where he had studied Bantu philosophy in particular, and where he had founded a spiritual work, the 'Jamaa' (the 'family'), widely known in missionary circles.
3. Congar was to reply a little later to these two consecrated virgins that their fears had little foundation; he was to concede to them only some reservations about Fr Tempels' theological formulations (Congar Archives).

Mgr Gouet, returning from St Peter's at around 11.00 am, told me: 1) Felici had expressed praise for the experts (to balance Heenan; 2) that the Council will finish on Saturday 21 November.

Along the same lines as Felici, a very funny intervention by Dom Reetz[1] (Beuron), who took Heenan up, point by point.

It seems that the schema on Religious Freedom will have to be (not given to a Joint Commission, but) revised by Browne, Parente, Franić, Granados, Colombo and Fr Anastasio[2] . . . On the other hand, those on the Jews and the Muslims remain TEXTS OF THE SECRETARIAT: the Theological Commission is being asked only IF this text can be inserted into Chapter II of the *De Ecclesia*. The reply will no doubt be negative: the text will then come back to the Secretariat as a Declaration. But, it seems, the other non-Christian religions would need to be considered by the Secretariat of the same name.

Saturday 24 October 1964

Yesterday evening, a lecture in Naples,[3] in the theatre of the royal palace. Departure by car at 1.30 pm with Mgr Primeau and Fr Hamer. An incredibly fraternal welcome from the fathers in Naples. The students regard me as a star. Dear God, is it possible? This royal palace: everything for show, processional parades between two ranks of grenadiers! So also this theatre, with its sumptuous royal box. A good audience. It went well. Returned at night on the motorway.

This morning, from 9.00 am to 1.20 pm, the *Concilium* meeting, then lunch at the Hotel Raphaël. A gigantic enterprise, even one suffering from gigantism, but which, after this morning's meeting, does not look to be achievable. Only the Dutch or the Germans could be successful in this sort of thing.

Mgr Colombo told me that the Pope has asked me, through him, to get him a copy of Moehler's *Unité*.[4]

A long visit from Fr Dupuy. He spoke, we spoke, about Istina, about the schema on the Eastern Churches. He is of the same mind as myself: publication should be deferred until the Orthodox have become acquainted with it and given their views. But what can be done now, to recapture a favourable vote? If my legs would let me, I would spend a whole day going to see the dozen or so men on whom an adjournment of the schema could depend: Maximos, Cardinal Bea, the Moderators . . . It seems that Fr Lanne campaigned for the rejection of the schema. He never said anything to me and I was entirely ignorant of the paper in which he explained himself. It seems that the Orthodox Observers were expecting the rejection and are very disappointed with what has happened. But they

---

1. *AS* III/V 374–377.
2. Anastasio del SS Rosario.
3. On the subject: 'The ecumenical problem and the Second Vatican Council'.
4. J-A Moehler, '*L'Unité dans l'Église ou le principe du catholicisme d'après l'esprit des Pères des trois premiers siècles de l'Église*', 'Unam Sanctam' 2 (Paris: Cerf, 1938).

hardly spoke along these lines. Neither Nissiotis nor Fr Scrima told me anything of this . . .

We also discussed the schema on religious freedom, which is pretty poor, it seems, in its current draft. I am not acquainted with it. I notice that, when all is said and done, I am somewhat outside the current of affairs. It is true that Fr Dupuy is involved in them in an extraordinary manner.

In the evening, a chat with the priests of the French Seminary (plus some seminarians).

Sunday 25 October 1964

I worked all morning and until 4.00 pm on a text on non-Christian religions. It was a waste of time, because, at our working meeting at 4.30 pm, with Mgr Willebrands, Moeller, Neuner and Pfister, my text was of no use. A combination was made out of those of Neuner and Pfister, that did compel recognition, it must be said. Willebrands said there was no truth in the rumour about a Joint Commission for *De Iudaeis*.

In the evening, a lecture to a small international group from Vie Nouvelle.

Monday 26 October 1964

A little work on the *De institutione sacerdotali* [on priestly formation]. I left at 9.15 am, with Mgr Gouyon. Arrighi told me that there are, on the part of the Secretariat, fairly major difficulties of a doctrinal order (see following page).[1]

Felici[2] announced that, on Wednesday, the occasion of the anniversary of the election of John XXIII, there will be a Mass concelebrated with twelve parish priests.

Discussion of the *proemium* and of Chapter I of *De Ecclesia in mundo* [the Church in the world].

> Cardinal Léger[3] [ ]
> Dom Prou:[4] Against a synthesis (Teilhard? Schillebeeckx) that would attribute to STRUCTURES that are in themselves natural, a supernatural, ontological consecration from the time of the Incarnation, or even from the beginning, in view of the Incarnation.
> Guerra,[5] Auxiliary Bishop of Madrid: he summarised the Marxist position in an interesting way.
> A Pole:[6] On apostasy from God . . . It is evident that the bishops have a more dramatic and more profound perception of the situation than does the schema itself.

---

1. For what Arrighi said to him, cf below, page 645.
2. *AS* III/V, 515–516.
3. *AS* III/V, 516–518.
4. *AS* III/V, 519–520.
5. José Guerra Campos, *AS* III/V, 520–523.
6. This in fact refers to a Yugoslav, Josip Pogačnik, Archbishop of Ljubljana (Yugoslavia), *AS* III/V, 525–527.

Tenhumberg:[1] we speak of the signs of the times, but those who have discerned
them have been criticised and persecuted. In future, provision must be
made for finding means by which this function can be honoured in the
Church: a more biblical theology, an esteem for charisms, a new style
of exercising authority in the Church, a more trusting one . . .

I thought of Lamennais,[2] who had seen all this from 1808!

De Roo,[3] with a fine Canadian accent: in favour of the union of natural and
supernatural values, and against all contempt for earthly realities.

All this morning's interventions contained good doctrinal density.

All this has little interest for the Fathers; theology is too strange to them
and tires them out.

Santo Quadri:[4] praise of WORK.

Chapter II and III together:

Ziadé:[5] one must not forget the eschatological and christological sense of the
signs of the times. It is only the sacrificed Lamb that opens the seals of
history. Everything should be seen in the light of Christ who is risen
and who is to come again.

Relate everything to the history of salvation. Show the vocation of the
human being in relation to the history of salvation.

- Speak about the prophetic character of the people of God.

Ancel:[6] demonstrate better the union between the care of earthly realities
and the heavenly life. Without this there can be no reply to those who
say: heaven is no longer of interest to anyone, the Church turns its
attention to earthly affairs . . . Show the integral mission of the Church,
which includes earthly affairs.

I am going to stop making short summaries.

Towards the end of the sitting I walked about a bit. I went to see the Observers.
I met a lot of people:

Häring: Mgr Heenan has done us a service. He has focussed the attention of
the Fathers on the question of birth control. . .

The secretary of Maximos IV:[7] I told him of my idea (which I had

---

1. Heinrich Tenhumberg, Auxiliary Bishop of Münster (Germany), *AS* III/V, 528–529.
2. After having been one of the chief promoters of Catholic renewal after the French
   Revolution, l'abbé Félicité de Lamennais (1782–1854) saw his politico-religious positions condemned by Rome, and he gradually withdrew from the Church.
3. Rémi J De Roo, Bishop of Victoria (Canada), *AS* III/V, 529–531.
4. *AS* III/V, 532–534.
5. *AS* III/V, 534–536.
6. *AS* III/V, 536–538.
7. The Archimandrite Adrien Chacour, a Basilian.

discussed in recent days with Cardinal Lefebvre, Mgr Willebrands, Gouyon and Martin): that *De Ecclesiis Orientalibus* should not be promulgated before dialogue has been entered into with the Orthodox. He told me that the Patriarch would certainly accede to this suggestion, and asked me to compose a letter to the Pope which Maximos would sign, copies of which would be communicated to the Moderators.

Arrighi: it is on the subject of the Little Church, of which I had spoken to him a little earlier, that there are some doctrinal difficulties. For the people of the Little Church are in favour of the superiority of a council over the pope. . . Mgr Willebrands explained to them that the *De Ecclesia* of Vatican II balanced Vatican I: THEY TRUSTED HIM. For the first time since the Restoration they assisted at a Mass, celebrated by Mgr Willebrands in a forest. They did not received communion, saying that they were unworthy, but it was agreed that on 6 December Willebrands and Arrighi will go to hear their confessions, and that they will have a Mass with communion on 8 December. Willebrands and Arrighi saw their prayer-books: they are those of Paris before the Revolution. These good folk asked for Benediction of the Blessed Sacrament after the Mass. The women were weeping. Willebrands said that he had not himself felt emotion like this since his first Mass.

I saw Cullmann. He was received by the Pope the day before yesterday. They talked chiefly about the project of the foundation in Jerusalem, and about the excavations at St Peter's (the Pope has read Cullmann's book[1]). The Pope gave Cullmann an incunabulum: the first printed Italian translation of the Bible.

None of this was possible ten years ago, it was scarcely conceivable.

At 3.15 pm, a visit from Fr Dingemans, very excited. Fr Sigmond is to participate tomorrow in a small meeting where the question of the revised and transformed plan of the *De Sacerdotibus* is to be dealt with. And yet Sigmond (who is there on behalf of the Hungarians) is conscious of knowing nothing about it; he asked Fr Dingemans, who doesn't know any more about it, for his suggestions. Dingemans' reaction: 'It is like it was with schema XIII: they are floundering, they have reached an impasse; anyone who at this point provides a possible plan will seem like a saviour; his text will be accepted. As I, Dingemans, know only the pastoral-sociological side of it, I have come to find you for the rest.' Dingemans thinks that he was, behind the scenes, the real father of schema XIII (which Häring, he said, had subsequently ruined); he could, with the help of others, behind the scenes, rescue *De Sacerdotibus* . . . I said that Fr Féret had made a plan and a revision, I passed the text of it on to Fr Dingemans. We tried in vain to telephone Fr Féret and arranged to meet after dinner this evening. But I was shocked

---

1. Oscar Cullmann, *Saint Pierre, Disciple, apôtre, martyr. Histoire et théologie* (Neuchâtel-Paris: Delachaux et Niestlé, 1952).

to see such important matters left in the hands of men so little competent, even in their own opinion . . .

At 4.30 pm, Theological Commission. First the question of the *relationes* on each of the sections of Chapter IV of schema XIII. No one was ready. It was suggested that the discussion of schema XIII be interrupted for a while, to allow for the composition of these *relationes* . . .

Examination of the *modi* for No. 22 of Chapter III of *De Ecclesia* was resumed: there are fifteen big pages of *modi* for this single Number.

Discussion of the situation of a layman or a simple priest, elected pope.

One sees how heavily centuries of drawing distinctions between one thing and another, and of legalism, weigh down upon us. In an obscure way, the Council wants to retrieve the unity between mission and consecration. But how difficult it is!!!

Philips wants to go quickly. We move on, without having the time that is necessary for consulting the text and reflecting a little. What should be done? The Fathers accept anything whatever, without having had or having the least possibility of calmly and seriously looking at the text, the *modus* and its arguments, and finally, the response (it is true the Fathers had the text of the *modi* YESTERDAY). We function only because we have faith in Philips and because he follows the work through with an extraordinary 'presence'.

I was sad to see that the *modi* that we prepared and had proposed did not get through at all. I was upset and discouraged by this.

It is true that the pressure from the anti-collegialists and the pro-papalists (maximalists for papal power) was so strong that it was against it that Philips chiefly directed his efforts.

At the Commission, Colombo insisted VERY MUCH (one sensed the Pope behind him) that the formula '*quae potestas [collegialis] independenter a Romano Pontifice exerceri nequit*' [which {collegial} power cannot be exercised independently of the Roman Pontiff] should be altered. He wanted it mentioned that there can be no collegial act except *ad nutum pontificis* [at the will of the pontiff] and governed by the pope.

An intervention by Fr Ciappi, who wanted to give a particular meaning to the expression '*TOTA plenitudo potestatis*' [ALL the fullness of power], was refuted by Thils and Betti who showed, from the history of Vatican I, that the expression does not have THIS sense.

In the evening, from 8.45 to 10.00 pm, with Fr Dingemans and Fr Féret on the question of a plan for a *De presbyteris*[1] = Féret's plan with, in addition, a chapter of biblical theology on the ontology of Christian priesthood.

---

1. Up to this point, the expression *de presbyteris* was used to indicate what was to become section 28 of *Lumen Gentium*, on priests; from now on it will indicate instead the schema on priests, which was to become the decree *Presbyterorum ordinis.*

Tuesday 27 October 1964
Before leaving for St Peter's, I drafted a letter to the Holy Father for Maximos IV, on the subject of the adjournment of the vote or of the promulgation of *De Ecclesiis orientalibus*.

On Chapter II–III of *De Ecclesia in hoc mundo*:

Frings:[1] against a certain Platonism: (St Augustine: God and my soul); in favour of a theology of earthly realities in the light of the incarnation and of eschatology. That is the basis of the distinction between Church and world and of the freedom of the Christian in the very midst of their engagements.

Caggiano:[2] speak about (social) justice.

Silva Henríquez:[3] on poverty as a mode of Christian life. With a proposition for the creation of a secretariat to co-ordinate the efforts made in favour of the poorest. He set out its structural characteristics (an allusion to Cullmann's idea of fund-raising[4]).

Maximos IV:[5] in favour of the education of Christians for maturity and freedom. In favour of a revision of the teaching of morals, against legalism and in favour of a christocentric ethic, in a climate of personal life and freedom, of responsibility. For example, the way the commandments of the Church are set out in the catechisms.

[This old man is much younger than many of the young ones. But Pius IX must have been uneasy in his grave!!!]

He quoted John XXIII: 'We have not yet discovered the demands of charity'. He proposed the creation of a commission of theologians to study the presentation of morality in this sense. Some applause.

Gand:[6] on No. 18 (dialogue): in favour of the study of the world and its problems; in favour of a knowledge by means of the heart. The dispositions for dialogue. Its locations and its modes or degrees.

Once again, a grand, ardent synthesis, after the manner of the French bishops.

(Yesterday Mgr Fourrey[7] fell very flat because of his appalling diction and his emotional, sentimental and oratorical tone.)

Zoghby:[8] this Chapter II lacks warmth. Simplify titles (*'feliciter regnans'* [happily reigning); he quoted the words of John XXIII: 'I have loved all those I have met during my life.'

---

1. *AS* III/V, 562–563.
2. *AS* III/V, 563–565.
3. *AS* III/V, 565–567.
4. Cf above, page 446, note 5.
5. *AS* III/V, 567–569.
6. Adrien Gand, Coadjutor of Lille, *AS* III/V, 570–572.
7. R Fourrey, *AS* III/V, 555–557.
8. *AS* III/V, 572–574.

Himmer:[1] on poverty. A text delivered with much warmth and vehemence. The essential value of CHRISTIAN poverty. Poverty a SIGN.

Afterwards, I asked some bishops what significance, what welcome this discourse had had: it didn't get across, they told me: it was not well understood, and this manner of treating us as novices, of wanting to influence us and get us on side, incites us to shrink back . . .

I went out for a moment. Lots of people about everywhere, in chapels, the side-aisles, the bars. THIS DISCUSSION IS NOT FINDING INTEREST . . .

I saw Dr Marois again, and introduced him to Mgr McGrath, Cardinal Alfrink, Mgr Guano. I left before the end, because Mgr Pailler wanted to return to some urgent correspondence.

A visit from a young Pradosian:[2] Very good (they usually are very good) on the question of poverty, which he wants to work on.

At 4.30 pm, meeting at my place with Frs Lécuyer, Denis, Daly (Irish), Herranz[3] (Spanish), Martelet, on the question of the Message to Priests. We agreed at once on this: that the schema *De Presbyteriis* should have priority. If this is what it should be there will be no need for a Message, except for a VERY BRIEF and purely amicable message, without theoretical pretensions. After that, we spoke about the *De Sacerdotibus (Presbyteris)*. The text of the comments by bishops will be available on Thursday morning. We shall suggest a plan to the Commission. We were agreed on the proposal to take Féret's plan as a basis, while adding to it a theology of priesthood.

At 8.00 pm, dinner arranged by Éditions L'Orante (M. Lafarge[4]) in honour of the publication of the volume by R Aubert[5] on Vatican I.[6] Other guests besides these two were Fr Dumeige,[7] Monachino,[8] another Jesuit, Daniélou, Hamer, Laurentin, Maccarrone. We sat down to table at 9.00 pm! and got back at 11.30 pm. Aubert is always the same, welcoming, open, intelligent. Maccarrone: candid???

---

1. *AS* III/V, 574–576.
2. Member of the Institut du Prado, founded in Lyons by Blessed Antoine Chevrier.
3. The canonist Julián Herranz, of Opus Dei, was *minutante* at the Commission for the Discipline of the Clergy and of the Christian People. A titular archbishop, he was later to become President of the Pontifical Council for Legislative Texts and the Disciplinary Commission of the Roman Curia.
4. Jacques Lafarge, literary editor of Éditions de l'Orante.
5. Roger Aubert, priest of the diocese of Malines-Brussels, Professor of Ecclesiastical History at Louvain, edited the *Revue d'histoire ecclésiastique* and the *Dictionnaire d'histoire et de géographie ecclésiastiques*.
6. *Vatican I*, coll 'Histoire des conciles oecuméniques', 12 (Éditions de l'Orante, 1964).
7. Gervais Dumeige, SJ, Church historian, President of the Institute of Spirituality at the Gregorianum, edited the collection 'Histoire des conciles oecuméniques'.
8. Vincenzo Monachino, SJ, Professor of Church History, was the Dean of the Faculty of Ecclesiastical History at the Gregorianum.

Wednesday 28 October 1964

Terrible weather. We have been having stormy weather for a month, and even worse for the past six days. I have difficulty standing. I am also disheartened by the way in which the little group Philips-Tromp-Charue have dealt with the *modi*. We have spent eight days full of 'holidays' preparing them. The number of approaches made to get them adopted by the episcopates, having them roneoed, distributing them . . . Our acceptance of having them presented by only one person so that all the others would vote *Placet* . . . And, in the end, NOT A SINGLE ONE of our *modi* has got through up until now. Those that seemed to us advisable, even necessary, in order to keep the text open to the Orthodox did not get through any more than the others. Philips has not enough sensitivity for this. He contented himself with saying that the text did not envisage these cases. Yes, but in actual fact they implicitly destroyed them! I understand that Philips wants to go quickly. I understand that he was chiefly concerned with fending off the attack of the anti-collegialists. I realise that, for this reason, he is making use of the *Normae generales* [general norms] in virtue of a text once voted on cannot be altered. But the result of this is that, in practice, a text is not MODI-fied, is not improved, indeed is unable to be improved. I have seen three, four, five final opportunities lost, one after the other. Many of our *modi* are of real interest.

This disturbed me very much and discouraged me, unable as I was to do anything, from witnessing this check. Because one can no longer intervene. It is moving too fast. And, in fact, if the Constitution is to be voted on in this Session, it does have to move fast. But it is a defeat.

This morning I did not go to St Peter's. Work on *De Sacerdotibus (Presbyteris)*.

(There was a concelebration at St Peter's this morning, by Mgr Felici with twelve PARISH PRIESTS).

I invited to lunch Nissiotis, who is leaving tomorrow for Athens and Rhodes. Thanks to the cordiality and intelligence of Mgr Martin[1] who presided at table, it was a very successful occasion and I think Nissiotis left well pleased.

Mgr Ancel said to me: the Pope has asked, through Cardinal Lercaro as intermediary, that a text on poverty be prepared for him. A small group of bishops has been set up for this, which has already met twice, and of which Mgr Ancel is part: he asked me to be his *peritus* for this purpose, together with Fr D Mollat. There will be a meeting on 3 November, at Mgr McGrath's. Of course I accepted, as an undeserved favour.

In the evening, a lecture to the seminarians (Church and World).

Thursday 29 October 1964

This morning, I wrote and began to type my contribution to a volume of essays in honour of Fr Chenu (I finished typing between 2 and 3.15 pm).

---

1. Congar added to the typescript: 'Rouen'.

It would appear that this morning's sitting was a great one: after Ruffini,[1] always negative and mean, Cardinals Léger,[2] Suenens,[3] and Maximos IV[4] spoke about marriage along the lines of the re-examinations that are currently being undertaken. Cardinal Suenens even asked that the commission set up by the Pope to study the problems connected with birth control should become public and work with the corresponding organisms of the Council.[5] This is important. It was courageous on his part since the Pope keeps control of it as HIS commission, and as working in secret. But can such duality be maintained at a time when the Council is studying these things?

Cardinal Léger told me that he was still in a sweat (it is true: his hands were clammy). He told me that a Canadian bishop had said this morning: I have never heard so many heresies . . .

At 4.30 pm, Theological Commission. It was concerned with the *modi* to No. 28 (*De Presbyteris*). It was noticeable that neither Ciappi, nor D'Ercole, nor Maccarrone, nor Lattanzi were there. It is no longer dealing with collegiality, so it no longer interests them . . . I continue to go. THIS TIME, Philips welcomed a fair number of *modi* I had prepared, which the French bishops had adopted and Cardinal Lefebvre had presented. I was pleased because these few changes do nevertheless somewhat transform the physionomy that is presented of the presbyteral priesthood, and in a way that is dear to myself and to the French.

I tremble each time a point is discussed.

Colombo raised some questions about the exact sense (the exact content) of the vote on the authority that re-establishes the diaconate.

At 6.40 pm, examination of the *modi* of Chapter III was completed: there were more than 5,500 *modi* for this Chapter. A start was made on the *modi* for Chapter IV, but attention was flagging a bit, and the Fathers were saying 'yes', without really making an effort.

In the evening, until 8.15 pm, a visit from l'abbé R Izard,[6] who is involved with the journal *Vocations*.[7] I had already decided in advance to agree to what he asked of me, as far as possible, because I consider the problem of priestly vocations to be a problem of the first order, and I would like to do as much as I possibly can for him.

During this afternoon's sitting Moeller drew my attention to how Cardinal Browne, good and decent as he is, has a truly dreadful cast of mind. He has re-

---

1.　*AS* III/VI, 52–54.
2.　*AS* III/VI, 54–56.
3.　*AS* III/VI, 57–59.
4.　*AS* III/VI, 59–62.
5.　This refers to the Commission for the study of problems of population, the family and birthrate set up by John XIII towards the end of his pontificate.
6.　Raymond Izard, of the diocese of Montpellier, was director of the National Centre for Vocations.
7.　The journal *Vocations sacerdotales et religieuses* was to be called *Vocations* from October 1964 onwards.

mained, without budging an inch, what he was when I knew him as 'Master of the Sacred Palace' and General. Renewal through the return to the sources has not dented him by so much as a micron. For him, today, just as twenty years ago, the pope is *episcopus universalis*' [universal bishop]: that is the whole of his ecclesiology; 'the encyclicals have corrected St Paul'; everything that affirms submission is good, everything that speaks of freedom is to be restrained and, if possible, excluded. He NEVER MISSES *A SINGLE* OCCASION to speak along the lines of these miserable 'principles'. With Moeller, one sees it coming, one tells oneself in advance what is going to be Browne's reaction that THE WORDS alone are enough to trigger: and it never fails. One can be certain that if the words 'love', 'experience' occur, there will be a difficulty; and that if it is asserted for the twenty-ninth time, that everything must happen *'sub Petro'* [in subjection to Peter], and that it is necessary *'reverenter oboedire'* [repectfully to obey], that will be very good. This afternoon, he persisted in rejecting the following order for the acts of priesthood: word, community, sanctification. Priesthood absolutely had to be DEFINED by the power to say Mass. I quoted Romans 15:16, but he replied: theology has explained that. There was no way of appeasing the obtuse spirit of this gentle giant, except by saying that this was following an ascending order of dignity. He then fell in with it. But this is obviously not true: it follows the logical and real order that Revelation shouts aloud by so many voices!

Friday 30 October 1964
Very tired. A little correspondence. At 9.30 am, at St Peter's. Discussion on the family continued.

> Alfrink:[1] don't hasten to formulate solutions. In favour of a permanent commission for the study of human problems in liaison with psychologists, doctors, sociologists etc.
>
> Ottaviani:[2] against the invitation given to spouses to learn about the spacing of children; in favour of a birthrate with confidence in Providence. Don't alter anything that has been held up until now. (Ottaviani appealed to the emotions: 'I, the son of a workman, the eleventh child in a family of twelve . . . ')
>
> Browne:[3] repeated the 'doctrine' *'finis primarius-secundarius'* [primary-secondary goal], and on a sort of concurrence between *amor amicitiae* [love arising from friendship] and *amor concupiscientiae* [love arising from desire] . . . With him, distinctions become separations and abstractions. He admitted, nonetheless, that these questions might be

---

1. *AS* III/VI, 83–85.
2. *AS* III/VI, 83–86.
3. *AS* III/VI, 86–88.

studied in the context, in short, of an improvement of Ogino.[1] In a restricted Commission.

Reuss:[2] supported Suenens, Léger, Alfrink. Presented a precise text in ten points, and concluded also in favour of a study commission.

Urtasun:[3] a synthesis that could scarcely be heard, given in an oratorical tone with French pronunciation. It was very boring.

I went out for a moment. I saw various people. Fr Duprey told me that the Pope had sent a letter to Rhodes, in French, Greek, Russian and Arabic.[4] That is something!

The discussion on the family was halted. Perhaps at the Pope's instigation? The discussion on culture was commenced.

I saw Dossetti to ask him to intervene with Cardinal Lercaro in order to arrange that at the resumption on Wednesday a prayer should be said for Rhodes.

At table Mgr Jenny reported that, in June 1962, he had been received with a group of six bishops by John XXIII. The Pope said to them: Pius IX convoked the Vatican Council to deal with the question of the temporal power, according to the history I studied, and not much was done in preparation for it. It will be quite different this time, and the Council has been well prepared. —I note this down just as I heard it. What is it worth?

From 4.00 pm until 7.00 pm, I worked with Lécuyer, Martelet, Daly, Herranz, on the *De Presbyteris*. The Commission formally accepted that the Message to Priests be postponed *sine die* and that a proper schema *De presbyteris* be prepared.

Dinner with my friends from Cambridge, Jacques and Jacqueline de Groote.

Saturday 31 October 1964

I worked on the part of the *De Presbyteris* assigned to me, that is, the *munera* [functions]. As a matter of fact, I must play a very tight game during these days of 'vacation', that is to say, of more intense work. I have established an order of urgency, because I have to write the chapter on the *munera* of priests for Sunday evening: for midday Tuesday, something on poverty; for Tuesday evening my article for *ICI*. My text on the ontology of priesthood will perhaps not be of much use. Yesterday evening it was considered that THAT manner of proceeding would confuse the bishops and would exceed their comprehension, and that it would be better to start, as Fr Martelet suggested, from the mission to establish a People of God, and from the episcopate as the fullness of priesthood.

Etchegaray spoke to me (at breakfast) about the *De pastorali episcoporum munere in Ecclesia* [on the pastoral function of the bishops in the Church], the revised

1. A method of natural birth control, named after its inventor, a Japanese doctor.
2. *AS* III/VI, 88–90.
3. *AS* III/VI, 105–107.
4. The message was to be read out in all four languages.

text of which was distributed yesterday. Some people (Kéramé, etc) pounced on No. 4, from which the word *plena* [full] had disappeared, because the Commission had reproduced, word for word, a passage from the *De Ecclesia*. They saw a ploy in this, and immediately spread a current of suspicion and some proposals of protest. The same people said that the text had been deliberately distributed yesterday, on the eve of a fairly general departure for the holidays, while asking for the vote to be taken next Wednesday so that, in view of the departures, the episcopates would not be able to consult together.

I note this as evidence of the suspicion that is widely held regarding Carli,[1] the secretary of the Commission: the bishops do not have confidence in the anti-collegialists. But for my part, I find this stirring up of suspicion and almost of passion much exaggerated. I looked very quickly at the new text of *De pastorali munere* and found that it did not justify these suspicions. Some people were already talking about a massive vote to reject certain sections. However, I would vote *non placet* on No. 35[2] (the former 33) which does not satisfy me. I have alerted Fr General on this subject: I don't know what he will do. He did not intervene *in aula*.

Almost all the bishops have gone away for the three days of leave, some on retreat. There are ten or eleven now instead of forty.

Sunday 1 November 1964
Work on *De Presbyteriis (de muneribus)*.

An enjoyable visit from Fr Chenu. I reproach myself for never seeing him. Very much in form. How bursting with life he is!

From 5.00 pm until 7.30 pm, work with Lécuyer, Martelet, Herranz, Daly, del Portillo, on the *De presbyteriis*.

At 8.00 pm, dinner at the Embassy. The Ambassador, M. R Brouillet,[3] was alone. He got me to talk about the Council, about the different groups of bishops. He made an interesting remark to me. He has served the state at the Élysée and in various posts. There, one scarcely saw anybody except when they were ASKING for or INSISTING on something. In the case of the Church, one sees people who are not asking for anything but who offer their generosity and whose plans are only for giving and advancing.

He thinks his post is rather meaningless. The principal disagreement between the Church and the French State has been overcome. On the other hand, the papacy no longer has, as it still did under Pius XII, the merit of a diplomatic outlook

---

1. Luigi Carli was, in fact, the rapporteur for the Commission for Bishops and the Government of Dioceses. Cf above, page 351, and above, page 513.
2. This No. 35 (*Principia de apostolatu Religiosorum in diocesibus* [principles concerning the apostolate of religious in dioceses]) dealt with the question of the exemption of religious.
3. René Brouillet, Ambassador of France to the Holy See.

on the world. Pius XII and Tardini still made wide surveys of the political horizon, which were, as such, of interest. Since then, the Church has been occupied with purely religious affairs; in this way a situation has been established where there are neither clashes nor competition. The difficulties and minor differences of opinion occasioned by decolonisation have been sorted out. There are no major matters left.

M. Brouillet gave me the impression that he finds his post pretty uninteresting. I understand that!!!

Monday 2 November 1964

Work, this time, on poverty for Mgr Ancel and the small group of bishops that the Pope has consulted.

At midday, Etchegaray told me that this morning he went to Cardinal Frings' place; Ratzinger had been invited there. A move is looming to secure more than a third of votes *iuxta modum* for the *De pastorali munere episcoporum*, so as to OBLIGE the Commission to take seriously the requests for amendments by means of which the authority of bishops would be given greater emphasis and close dependence with respect to the pope less. (Four *modi* (the most important concerns No. 4: where a theology of the ecumenical council is at issue) have been prepared AT THE BELGIAN COLLEGE.)

In the afternoon I began, painfully, to write my chronicle for *ICI*. I have got a touch of flu.

Tuesday 3 November 1964

Mild flu. I finished my *ICI* chronicle in the morning.

At 11.00 am, the sister had not arrived; I returned to my text on poverty, which I had given her to type, and typed it myself, which I managed with one finger, and by holding my right hand in my left, since it would not work by itself.

Lunch at the Hotel Cesaraugusto, beyond the Milvian Bridge, with Mgr Ziadé and Mgr Doumith, who had asked me to come and see them about the *modi* for the *De episcoporum munere*. I brought them (also for distribution) the ones that had been prepared with the Belgians and the Germans. It was agreed to vote *placet* for No. 4, even though they want to modify it, because if there were more than a third of *Non placet* votes, the first text would automatically be reverted to; but there would have to be more than a third of votes *iuxta modum* on the whole of Chapter I in order to oblige the Commission, and its secretary Carli, to take account of the *modi* that were presented, or risk seeing its text rejected.

Mgr Doumith explained to me the *modi* that he had thought of on his own account.

But there are the *modi* of the anti-collegialists. I insert here those distributed by the group that meets on Tuesdays and of which Ruffini, Siri, Browne, etc are the sponsors. It is truly a hatred of all 'democratic' spirit, and an expression of integrism, just as I described it in *Vrai et fausse Réforme*.

At 4.00 pm, a meeting at Fr McGrath's (Fathers of the Holy Cross, Via Aurelia Antica 391) for the text on poverty to be prepared for Cardinal Lercaro, and through him, for the Pope. Mgr Ancel, Coderre, McGrath, Puech[1] were there. Likewise the Superior General of the Holy Cross,[2] Fr Mollat, Urresti and, a bit later, Tillard. Work until 9.45 pm, with a break for prayer and dinner. In the end, the drafting of the first part (analysis, or phenomenology of the situation) was entrusted to Mgr McGrath, and of the second part (theology) to me. I don't know how I will manage it. And it is urgent . . .

Wednesday 4 November 1964

Tidying up of the *ICI* text. Revision of my text on the *munera* [functions] of the presbyterate. I did not go *in aula* until 10.25 am (by taxi). They were getting to the end of the reading of the *relatio* for *De episcoporum pastorali munere* [on the pastoral function of bishops], so I did not miss anything. In any case, I stayed only twenty minutes. A speech by Lercaro on culture.[3] Outdated forms of clerical culture should be dropped: this will be the best way to demonstrate that one is taking culture seriously. Lercaro even wished that bishops would again become teachers, not in the scholastic sense, but along the lines of the Fathers of the Church.

It was very good, but very idealistic!

I saw Fr Scrima for a moment, who had just come from Rhodes, and was going back there. He was quite radiant and very happy. The Pope's message, so precise in its theological terminology, had made a great impression. Dialogue seems to be decided on! But His Holiness Athenagoras will not be coming. He had intended to, not in a personal capacity, nor as Ecumenical Patriarch, but at the head of a delegation from Rhodes. As Rhodes is due to finish on 12 November, and the Session on 21 November, this will be too short an interval . . .

At 11.00 am at St Martha's, for our text *De Presbyteris*, which is taking shape. There will be something to present to the Commission tomorrow.

When I got back, I heard some news of this morning's sitting *in aula*. Chapter I of *De episcoporum munere* had gathered more than 800 votes *iuxta modum*. So the work done by the tactical teams (Belgian College, Etchegaray, Martimort, Medina. . .) has been effective. There is a well established voting discipline. The Commission will be obliged to revise its text . . .

Mgr Elchinger[4] presented an exoneration for Galileo.

In the afternoon, I began to think about the new chapter entrusted to me: the evangelical form of priestly life. Headache and flu. Brief telephone-call from Fr Hussar. 'The text' [on the Jews] is not making progress all by itself.

---

1. Pierre M Puech, Bishop of Carcassonne (France).
2. Germain Lalande.
3. *AS* III/VI, 249–252.
4. *AS* III/IV, 266–69.

Thursday 5 November 1964

In the morning, work. I finished the drafting of the section on the *forma evangelica* [evangelical form] of the life of priests (a rather long text . . . ! Too long?).

I was told that, this morning, a layman, M. Jacques Norris[1] (FAO), spoke about poverty in the world. He spoke IN LATIN. This was the realisation, to a very small degree, and in a timid fashion, of what I had asked for and suggested last year, and for which I have expressed the desire several times this year. I was not there to experience in my own heart of flesh the satisfaction I think I would have felt.

I was told that the Pope will come *in aula* tomorrow to open the discussion on the schema *De Missionibus*. The discussion of schema XIII will be interrupted for this. The Pope will sit, not on his throne above the Confession, in front of the altar, but at the table of the Council of Presidents. It seems that there was some hesitation, although the Holy Father had expressed the desire to come FOR THE DEBATE ON THE MISSIONS, because this will be rather bitter, and because there is a risk that the schema will be rejected . . .

On 13 November (St John Chrysostom) there will be a celebration by Maximos IV, with some bishops from different patriarchates, under the presidency of the Pope.

Lunch at Arrighi's place, with the Anglican Bishop of Ripon, Canon Pawley, Observers, Mgr Marty, Le Cordier, the Auxiliary Bishop of Ajaccio.[2]

As we were leaving, Arrighi told me that again this morning there were some objections to the *De libertate religiosa* and the *De religionibus non christianis* on the part of the Secretary of State.[3] Moreover, Cardinal Ottaviani claims that *De libertate* should be revised by the plenary Theological Commission: that will amount to, if not its being buried altogether, at least to the vote of the Assembly being adjourned for a long time!!!

According to Arrighi (a reliable source) there is a chance the Fourth Session will have to finish by 29 June 1965: it will be very hot!!!

I was supposed to have attended the meeting of the Commission *De disciplina Cleri*,[4] for the reworking of the *De Presbyteris*. Fr Lécuyer was supposed to pick me up; I did not know even WHERE the meeting was taking place, I waited at the door from 4.00 pm until 4.35 pm. I tried in vain to telephone. The long and the short of it was, Fr Lécuyer had forgotten me, and no one let me know. This disappoints me, and even hurts me, because I put my whole heart into this work, and I see that no one cares about my presence, that I will not be there to explain and, if necessary, to defend a text that is dear to me. Yes, disappointment and real pain.

---

1. James Norris, President of the International Catholic Commission for Migration.
2. André Collini.
3. A Cicognani.
4. The reference is to the Commission for the Discipline of the Clergy and of the Christian People.

Friday 6 November 1964

At St Peter's. Arrived at 9.30 am. Ethiopian Mass: interminable. On the one hand I was touched to see that Christ is proclaimed in a language and by a people of Africa, and that the poor of that region have been evangelised. But on the other hand I found their chant terribly painful. It put me in mind of the ravings of drunkards.

At the end, tom-toms for the enthronement of the Gospel. Just before this, the Pope had come in quickly and without ceremony. He took his place on a throne in the middle of the Council of Presidents.

He introduced the discussion on the *De Missionibus* with a short speech.[1] He hopes that the schema will be approved, with a view to its being perfected. (Even though, as I know, the superiors of missionary congregations have sent a letter asking that this schema be rejected and replaced by another that they are proposing.)

Before his making his *relatio*, Agagianian[2] gave a great fervorino to the Pope in the conventional and flattering style. The *relatio* itself is very triumphalist: everything is glorious. And the history of the missions is presented as a history of pontifical acts and encyclicals.

After this the Pope blessed everyone present, and the pious objects they had with them, and then left. There was applause, and that was it.

Voting continued on the *De Episcoporum munere pastorali*. Our tribune, which had been full (especially of Italians) to the point where people had to sit on the steps, emptied: it had been a real invasion of frogs. The spectacle over, they slipped away.

As for work, it is something other than that! Why, as soon as the Pope appears, does everything turn into ceremony and triumphalism?

This sitting left me with a very unpleasant impression.

There was the LONG and deadly boring reading of two *relationes*. Discussion began at 11.45 am!

Lunch at the Albergo Sant'Angelo with Fr Scrima, M. Moustakis[3] and various theologians or friends of the Secretariat. The purpose was to have a little gathering around this last (M. Moustakis) who has created, in Athens, the *Orthodox Religious Encyclopedia*[4] and a journal, *Orthodox Presence*.[5] He directs this effort in a spirit that is ecumenical and open, very interesting, and with a great future. This effort is EXACTLY what is needed today.

But I had a very bad head and could not move a step.

Nevertheless, at 4.30 pm, at the Vatican. I did not know that the General Congregation was at 4.00 pm. I was late. Some additions to the *Relatio generalis* on

---

1. *AS* III/VI, 324–325.
2. *AS* III/VI, 326 and 336–339.
3. Vasileios Moustakis.
4. The *Encyclopédie religieuse et morale*, in twelve volumes.
5. *Orthodoxos Parousia*, a quarterly journal concerned with theological education.

Chapter III, proposed by Mgr Philips to appease the opponents, were discussed.[1] A discussion stirred up by Parente on *consentiente* [consenting].

A start was made on the *modi* for the *De Beata*.

Discussion and votes on '*gratia plena seu summe Deo grata*' [full of grace or most highly pleasing to God], which was adopted by eleven votes out of twenty.

After an interval at 6.00 pm, discussion was resumed. Philips: at this rate it will be finished by the end of NEXT week. Another vote was taken on the retention of the text AS IT WAS. This resulted in eleven out of twenty.

People were very tired, attention was flagging. The Fathers accepted what Philips proposed, almost without examination. They followed the text closely, but there was no longer much of the 'irascible', of 'attack'.

Very tired. My eyes hurting so much I could hardly keep them open.

In the evening from 9 o'clock until 11, I was with a group of young Italians (male and female) from Catholic Action, on ecumenism. But I hate being tape-recorded. They asked me some very delicate questions. I replied honestly. They promised me that they would not use the tape in any way.

An extremely critical reaction from Fr Féret to the *tentamen* [attempt] on *De Presbyteris* which Onclin had to pass on to him. This reaction, excessively harsh and negative, was hurtful to me. Fr Féret seems to believe that his way of seeing things is the only one possible. That is not true. Certainly, there are always acute perceptions in what he says or writes. But dialogue is practically impossible because, if one does not say things exactly as he sees them and formulates them, one has not said anything worthwhile.

(Written on 7 November). Today, I twice had the opportunity to say (to Dossetti for Lercaro; to Colombo for Paul VI directly): the next time the Pope comes to a General Congregation *in aula*, he should come in carrying the Gospel! I still have a painful impression of this Friday morning's sitting. Would it not be possible for the Pope to come to participate in a working sitting, in the normal way, as A MEMBER OF THE COUNCIL? Does his being HEAD isolate him in such a way, and elevate him to such a degree that he has to stay outside? In fact, the Pope has not TAKEN PART in the assembly. He has made a 'gesture' (he has made many, and some good ones, but while retaining another ideology, and one not so good). He has not fitted in, and it seems that he is not able to. From the time he appeared, and throughout his brief presence, he was like a marshal

---

1. See below, page 676. This refers to what was to become the *Nota explicativa praevia* [preliminary explanatory note] which was to be placed at the beginning of the *Relatio* on the *modi* to Chapter III; it was requested by the Pope as a norm for the interpretation of this chapter, and to appease the minority; the text he was to propose was to be modified by the Doctrinal Commission. On the history of this note, cf Jan Grootaers, *Primauté et collégialité. Le dossier de Gérard Philips sur la Nota Explicativa Praevia (Lumen Gentium, chap III)* (Leuven, 1986).

visiting his troops and taking a spoonful of soup at the field kitchen. The papal theology, worked out SOLELY as *'potestas supra'* [power over], throws a deadly shadow over conciliar theology, the theology of communion. It has no insertion into it. But conciliar theology has come to life again, the theology of communion is indefeasible. So the theology of papal *potestas* will have to adapt itself.

Ecclesiologically, the Pope's visit to the conciliar assembly struck a note that, to my ears, was disharmonious, and painful to hear.

Saturday 7 November 1964

The Father Superior[1] passed on to me the issue of *Le Monde* for 4 November, in which Fesquet gives the text of a letter from Cardinal Antoniutti, forbidding students in religious houses of formation to attend lectures by experts. This prohibition is, in fact, extended to seminarians: the Father Superior received a telephone call from the Congregation for Seminaries and Universities (presided over by that imbecile Pizzardo), asking him if some seminarians were attending the lectures given at the Domus Mariae (organised by Fr Guglielmi, for the bishops residing there, especially the Brazilians) which are very interesting and oriented towards openness: nothing more. When the Superior asked: is this prohibition to be communicated to the seminarians?, the answer he got was no, because this is always the way with the Romans: not to take a measure frankly and openly.

Truly, this stupidity could be a sin. Because it is contrary to the dignity of the RATIONAL creature. Deplorable cretinism! If they want to censure an erroneous statement they should say what it is!

Would that have something in common with the Pope's address, published in *L'Osservatore Romano* for yesterday, 6 November, speaking of Protestant and Modernist currents that undermine authority and mistrust it? In any case authority is not here adopting a good means of consolidating itself in people's minds.

I know from Boegner that Cullmann has written to the Pope to protest. It would appear that the word 'Protestant' figured only in the ITALIAN text of the address, which was also made available in other languages, without it. If that is true, this refinement does not amount to much.

I did not go to St Peter's. I continued with my work on poverty.

Propter verbum labiorum tuorum	}	
Propter Testimonium Agni	}	*ego custodivi*
Propter amorem Veritatis, Dominae meae	}	*vias duras!*
Propter homines, fratres meos,	}	
quibus servire intendo	}	

[For the sake of the word of your lips	}	
For the sake of the testimony of the Lamb	}	I have kept to

---

1. Roland Barq, a Spiritan, was the superior of the French Seminary in Rome.

For the sake of truth, my mistress	}	difficult paths!]][1]
For the sake of human beings, my brothers,	}	
whom I intend to serve	}	

At 1.30 pm, lunch at the Spanish Embassy to the Holy See. I have often admired this palace from the outside. Inside it is absolutely regal. Sumptuous reception rooms, but restrained, even a little austere; domestic staff like that of a great house, footmen everywhere. Numerous guests, several *periti* (Urresti, Häring. . .), only two Spanish bishops, Mgr Morcillo and the Auxiliary of Seville.[2] A faultless meal. A little speech from the ambassador, in French. Afterwards, over coffee, some conversation with the Auxiliary of Seville, very 'collegial' and very open. We also talked about religious freedom.

I had noticed in Spain how everything about reception rooms, drawing rooms of public buildings, is always very sumptuous and very grand. It is the same tradition here, on a grand scale.

It was not until afterwards that I noticed this: there was not A SINGLE woman at this luncheon for thirty or thirty-five people. Is the ambassador married? I don't know. He told me he did not have a SON. In any case, it was entirely ecclesiastical and masculine (there were some attachés of the Embassy, and M. Ruiz-Giménez,[3] an Auditor at the Council, and editor of the journal, *Dialogue*[4]).

(He is a widower!)

Mgr Morcillo seems to be in favour of the Fourth Session being adjourned until later and, at the same time, of the finishing of this 'constitutive' period of the Council, which is getting in the way of work and the applications.

I gathered some bits of information about this morning's sitting at St Peter's. Cardinal Suenens, I was told, protested against the interpretation that the press gave of his speech about birth control. Anxious as I know he is to 'open a breach' (*mihi dixit* [he told me this]), he should not be upset by these interpretations. But he takes his precautions, and had he, perhaps, been asked to do so?

The missionary bishops have made a thoroughgoing critique of the schema *De Missionibus*. They recommended a *Non placet*, and were applauded each time. So there was in this case a demonstration of conciliar freedom, made by this morning's speakers with a certain petulance, according to what I was told. That's good.

The missionary bishops are very much against Agagianian and the Propaganda. When the Pope heard the complaints of Cardinal Agagianian he came to give him his support.

---

1. Cf Psalm 16:4 for the beginning and the end.
2. JM Cirarda Lachiondo.
3. Joaquín Ruiz-Giménez, former President of Pax Romana and a former minister to Franco, advocated a liberal evolution of the Franco regime.
4. *Cuadernos para el diálogo*.

Cardinal Richaud (who will vote *non placet*) told me that the heart of it is opposition to Cardinal Agagianian and a desire to escape from the tutelage of Propaganda. The young churches want to be churches like the others. Cardinal Richaud also told me that it was on a higher command that the Co-ordinating Commission had the schemas reduced to simple propositions: which is now shown to be catastrophic.

Each time, the Council wanted to go back to a rather fuller, theologically based, exposition.

This sort of protest by the missionary bishops, contrary to the desire expressed yesterday by the Pope himself, raises a question about this intervention of the Holy Father, and, in a more general way, about the relations between the Pope and the Council (or rather, the conciliar assembly). The Pope, who should have the last word, on this occasion has given himself the first. And it was not followed. The more I think about it, the more painful yesterday morning appears to me.

In the evening, from 4.00 until 5.00, work with the usual small group, on the *De Presbyteris*. It was finished. But our text is too long, especially this second part. It is full of repetitions and it often veers towards exhortation. It will be presented, as it is, to the Commission on Monday, but with the question: should not the spiritual applications be reduced and (at least in large measure) be woven into the objective, 'doctrinal' part?

Today's *L'Osservatore Romano* gives the text of the reply to the Pope from the Rhodes Conference. The TONE is RELIGIOUS and cordial, analogous to that of the Pope's own letter. I note with joy that the letter mentions the UNANIMITY of the Orthodox Churches in replying in this way. Including the Church of Greece, then.

The return of the head of St Andrew has borne fruit!

Mgr Ancel told me that the Theological Commission should examine the *De libertate religiosa* on Monday. This will set back the examination of the *De Revelatione*, but it was the Pope who has asked that priority be given to *De libertate*.

Sunday 8 November 1964

Worked on the correction of my text on the evangelical form of the life of the priest, and then on the continuation of the text on poverty. Today the bishops had the final meeting for the constitution of their collegial organisation at the level of the French Episcopal Conference.[1]

Lunch at *Salvator Mundi* with His Beatitude Maximos IV, Mgr Nabaa, Edelby. Maximos: Galileo must be rehabilitated. Far from harming the Church, this would enhance it in the eyes of people generally. —I said: if YOU were to say it. — Yes, if I can find the opportunity.

---

1. Cf above, page 616, note 2.

According to Mgr Nabaa, sub-secretary of the Council, the reduction of schemas to propositions comes from Cardinal Döpfner, whose officiousness I have recently taken note of. So he might take to heart the criticisms made of the schema on the Missions, as a bloodless schema, reduced to a skeleton. The Moderators were wanting to save the schema in order to save their proposal to reduce some texts to propositions. (On this subject, Fr Féret told me that, according to Galli,[1] who is well informed, Cardinal Döpfner disclaimed having pushed for the reduction to propositions.)

These Eastern bishops give me the impression of being a bit isolated, of not knowing much about the workings of the Council. For them many of the ecclesiological realities which we have difficulty in conceptualising, are evident and near to hand. A lot of things will need to be recovered that have been lost from the Catholic Tradition!

At 3.30 pm, lecture to the Ursuline Sisters at Via Nomentana 236. Then back to work. I did my best, which was pretty mediocre!

Monday 9 November 1964

A storm has been going on since 3.00 pm yesterday! Oh, this Roman autumn! That makes a good month of constant storms, rain without any freshness.

Finished poverty. At St Peter's at 9.30 am, with Mgr Gouyon. I came in at the moment of communion; *Ubi caritas* was being sung (well). An atmosphere of great recollection, while outside cataracts were being discharged from the heavens.

Fr Wenger, back from Rhodes, told me that many of the Eastern bishops are saying: we cannot follow Patriarch Athenagoras, we will go little by little, always in the same direction, but little by little. —The Orthodox have interpreted the schema *De Ecclesiis orientalibus* very unfavourably, they are saying that it impedes dialogue. They take offence at the expression 'separated brethren', saying that they are the Church . . . They find that the Third Session has not fulfilled the promises of the first two. In brief, they are hesitant. The Russians, for their part, are waiting, uncertain about the new political conditions in their country.

There will be need of great patience!

It has barely begun.

Resumption of discussion on the Missions. I shall not make a summary of all of it. Most of the Fathers speak in the name of a great number of Fathers.

I heard my text very well presented by Mgr Geeraerts.[2]

Intervention by Fulton Sheen,[3] (the first) with a remarkable speaking technique at the microphone: a confident tone, posing questions and leaving an in-

---

1. Mario von Galli, SJ, covered the Council for the journal *Orientierung*, of Zurich, of which he was editor-in-chief.
2. *AS* III/VI, 431–433.
3. *AS* III/VI, 443–445.

terval of suspense in which they could be pondered. Expansion of the notion of mission by that of dialogue. In favour of the unity of the mission, the dimension of the whole Church. In favour of poverty . . . He commanded attention, despite a somewhat theatrical and artificial manner. He was applauded (not by me).

At 10.55 am, the Moderators asked whether it was desired that discussion be brought to an end on the *De missionali* . . . The result was: yes.

A brief closing report from the rapporteur of the Commission.[1] He concluded: it is appropriate that the schema be redone by the Commission. For this purpose, the Fathers should submit their comments before leaving Rome.

Applause.

Felici:[2] applause has no juridical value. So there will be a vote on this: *Utrum placeat schema propositum De activitate missionali Ecclesiae iterum refici a Commissione competenti* . . . [should the proposed schema on the missionary activity of the Church be redone by the relevant commission]?

Those in favour of revision should vote: *placet*.

The interrupted discussion of schema XIII was resumed; Chapter IV, Nos 24 and 25.

I went out for a moment. A large number of encounters. Medina and Dossetti were very worked up about the four Numbers added by Philips to the *relatio* on Chapter III of *De Ecclesia*. They thought that this emptied collegiality of its content. I don't think so. But a distinction has to be made between the collegial ACT in the strict sense, and collegiality in the wider sense, or communion, an act accomplished in communion . . .

At 11.45 am, a start was made on No. 25, on peace.

Alfrink:[3] the Council should not say less on these questions than *Pacem in Terris*. And yet the text retreats from the encyclical. A very remarkable text, listened to with religious attention.

Ancel:[4] was also heard with GREAT attention. Universal disarmament by the permanent renunciation of war. With international organisation and support.

That is my position.

Applause (not very strong).

Mgr Guilhem,[5] bishop of Laval, who said in a kind and weak tone (with a terrible accent): *non possumus non loqui* [we cannot not speak] (against the bomb).

---

1. Lokuang, *AS* III/VI, 446–447.
2. *AS* III/VI, 447.
3. *AS* III/VI, 459–461.
4. *AS* III/VI, 462–463.
5. Jacques Guilhem, Bishop of Laval (France), *AS* III/VI, 466–467.

Vote on the schema-propositions *De Missionibus*:

Voters present:	1,941
Placet [= rejection of the schema]:	1, 601
Non placet:	311
Null:	1+1

At 3.00 pm, visit from seven students from the Capranica (one American, two Swiss, four Italians) who came to ask me questions about priesthood, how to find their way, the usefulness and the arrangement of their studies.

At 4.30 pm, at the Commission *De disciplina cleri* for the *De presbyteris*. I had to choose between this and the Theological Commission, where the *De libertate* was to be discussed, and perhaps a start made on the *De Revelatione*. This would have interested me much more, but I was told that it would be more useful to go to the *De presbyteris*.

A big room, a big long table around which the *periti* were interspersed with the bishops. No microphone, so that sometimes, around that long table, three or four separate conversations were going on. No one chaired it. The 'debates' were not directed. Or they were a little by the secretaries, del Portillo and Lécuyer. The latter was something of a king and made Philips his child. The bishops did not say anything of note, or only some comments on details. It could not be said that any work was being done. Soon, tea or fruit juice was served to us where we sat. This had nothing in common with the Theological Commission, which, nevertheless, does have another way of conducting itself, and which does work. I realised that the somewhat strained atmosphere created in the Theological Commission by Cardinal Ottaviani, by Franić and by those who are opposed, has played a beneficial role in stimulating work. There was no one here of the stature of Rahner or even Parente.

Lécuyer, del Portillo, Herranz did more less what they liked. They rearranged and somewhat shortened the texts; I found that they had ruined mine, on the evangelical form of life, deleting some vigorous statements and adding words of piety. With fairly extensive collaboration, this will be to some degree Lécuyer's schema, in the sense that the *De Ecclesia* is the schema of Philips or the Belgians. I am afraid that it will be more pious and verbose, not sufficiently theological or ontological.

Nevertheless, for the first time, l'abbé Gay (Lyon)[1] and l'abbé Maxime Hua, whom I saw this morning, were satisfied.

In the evening [after waiting an hour for his car!!], dinner at Mgr Höfer's,[2] with the German Ambassador to the Holy See,[3] M. and Mme Brouillet. Mgr Hengs-

---

1. Canon Jean Gay, parish priest of the Primatial Church of St John in Lyons, was one of four French parish priests invited to follow the conciliar debates on the ministry of priests.
2. Josef Höfer, of the diocese of Paderborn, was a counsellor to the German Embassy to the Holy See; he had been involved for a long time in the ecumenical movement and was a member of the Secretariat for Unity.
3. Hilger van Scherpenberg.

bach, Ratzinger, Cullmann and Alessandrini,[1] deputy editor of *L'Osservatore Romana*. A pleasant, but rather insignificant dinner.

Tuesday 10 November 1964

Work on some corrections for the De *presbyteris* (which the Commission should approve on Thursday and pass on to Felici on Friday). I was intending to go to St Peter's, for the end of schema XIII, and the beginning of *De religiosis*, but this tiresome work of revision and patching-up took me beyond the time, and I stayed at home.

3.00 pm. It would appear that I did not miss much.

Telephone-call from Mgr McGrath. He asked me for my impression of yesterday's meeting of the Theological Commission. I had not been there . . . He told me: it was very confused. It was not known exactly what was being asked of us. The Theological Commission has been, for some time, more or less paralysed. Neither Fathers nor experts any longer express themselves really freely there. This is obviously to a large extent due to the fact that time has not allowed us to discuss the *modi* prepared by the small group Charue-Philips-Tromp. But there is a risk of losing interest in discussing matters freely. There are also small irregularities that amount to the diminution of full freedom and of the seriousness of the work of the Commission. Also, it is said that there are some *modi* by the Pope to the *De Ecclesia* which the College of Presidents is to discuss at 4.00 pm this afternoon. There was also, unknown to the plenary Commission, a small sub-commission to talk with religious. Mgr McGrath said there is need for vigilance, and for the restoration of the habit of full discussion, as we have known it.

At 4.30 pm, at the Vatican. Theological Commission: examination of the corrected text of *De Revelatione*. Philips explained the various alterations or deletions.

> Parente wanted to introduce into No. 5 a mention of the external signs of credibility. 'They' are not at ease except with the external aspect. Intelligent resistance from Dom Butler. Philips cajoled the combatants, pacifying them and imputing the matter to himself. It was agreed to speak again about signs and miracles in *No. 4.*

> There was not much reaction from the Fathers. Moeller said to me: 'They are fed up'!

> Granados again raised the question of constitutive tradition. Browne supported him, but feebly, by asking simply that the words of Vatican I should be repeated, here, or somewhere else. A Denzinger was sought, in vain.

> Henríquez: there should be a vote on whether the question should be put again. If the answer is 'yes', it would be necessary to consult the Secretariat again.

---

1. Federico Alessandrini.

Franić said: two texts should be proposed to be chosen between by vote *in aula*. There should be a vote.

Florit: don't upset a balance that has been achieved with difficulty. But if they are set on it, the vote should be: should the *via media* proposed here be retained, or not?

Charue: if the question is to be taken up again, the Secretariat will have to be consulted again.

It is fortunate that Florit is responsible for the text: that reassures Cardinal Ottaviani.

Browne returned to his idea of quoting Vatican I.

Betti: I myself proposed this addition, but it will not be sufficient to pacify those who are uneasy. Trent and Vatican I spoke not of the *Tradition* but of *traditions*.

Butler confirmed Betti: this was discussed in the sub-commission and the discussion came up against this plural. And we have, in the *proemium*, declared our fidelity to Vatican I.

Tromp: there is another text in Vatican I: '*verbo Dei scripto vel tradito*' [The word God, written, or handed on].

Betti: this formula was taken up in No. 10.

Florit: a note could be inserted here, referring to Vatican I.

Parente supported this solution.

Would Browne be satisfied? Ottaviani asked.

Browne: '*esset aliquid*' [it would be something].

That was agreed. It was left like that.

But in No. 9, in the description of Tradition, the fullness of the original text has been lost; now it speaks only of *verba* [words], not of examples and of the *instituta* [things instituted] by Christ. I intervened in vain. Browne is evidently in favour of '*verbum*' on its own.

Mgr Ancel told me that the meeting with Cardinal Lercaro on poverty was excellent. Only the texts prepared by McGrath (excellent), myself and Wright (practical applications) were read. These texts will be given to the Pope on Thursday. The Pope wants to make a declaration on poverty.

I acquired a little information about yesterday's meeting of the Commission, on religious freedom. It was a very confused meeting. Discussion went on for an hour and a half about what, exactly, had to be done, about what the intervention of the Commission bore upon, and on what grounds? It was concluded that the Commission was being asked simply for a *Nihil obstat*.

Then there was a vote ON THIS. The result of the vote was:

- 15 = nihil obstat,
- 7 = aliq uid obstat [there is something in the way]
- 6 = abstentions.

(There were twenty-eight present, a figure seldom achieved.)

Then, as this had not settled the question, since, in a doctrinal matter the rule of a two thirds majority is observed, there had been a second vote, on the intervention of Mgr Wright:

Placet: there were   12
Non placet: 6
Placet iuxta modum: 9

There was also one abstention.

Those who voted '*placet iuxta modum*' were invited to submit their *modus* today: it being understood that this *modus* was proposed in a personal capacity, not in the name of the Commission.

This evening, Arrighi was waiting to take these *modi* to the Secretariat.

Wednesday 11 November 1964

Mgr Desmazières (Auxiliary of Bordeaux) told me that Cardinal Richaud has a photocopy of a letter from Franić to the Pope putting him on guard against the immense peril of collegiality. I asked Cardinal Richaud if he would be able to show me this letter. He took it rather badly: it is a text that concerns me personally. Mgr Desmazières should not have spoken to you about it . . . I said: this will not go beyond me!

During these days several experts (Dossetti, Medina, Lubac) have been very worked up about the four additions Philips made to his *Relatio* on Chapter III.[1] They think that some of the words are excessive and that there is the risk of emptying collegiality of its content. I find this impression very exaggerated. It is true that the four additions have been made in order to appease the minority. They play a part at this Council analogous to that of Zinelli's great discourse before the final vote at Vatican I.

(In *Études* for January 1965, page 104, Fr Rouquette recounts the facts and the history of the *Nota Praevia*. He had in hand the report of Fr Bertrams[2] that accompanied the letter of the Pope (10 November) asking or ordering the Theological Commission to draft a note. —Roquette has an interesting note on the NB,[3] concerning the jurisdiction of the Easterners. It is along the (optimistic) lines of Fr Duprey.)

At St Peter's at 9.30 am.

Vote on Chapter II of *De oecumenismo*.

---

1. This refers to the *Nota explicativa praevia*, cf above, page 658, note 1.
2. Wilhelm Bertrams, SJ, was Professor of Canon Law and of the Philosophy of Law at the Gregorianum; he was a Council expert.
3. The *Nota Bene* that concluded the *Nota explicativa praevia* makes clear that the Doctrinal Commission did not want to settle the question of the validity of ordinations in the Orthodox Church.

Discussion on the *De religiosis*:

Cardinal de Barros Câmara,[1] in the name of 300 bishops from Brazil.
Ruffini,[2] against novelties, and a vehement appeal for an authentic religious
    life. Quite strongly applauded.

After this vigour, the cracked and tired voice of Cardinal Richaud[3] made little
impression. With dreadful mistakes of accent: '*schemátis, contemplátivo, stúpore,
canoníco . . .* ' Criticisms of the title and of the extension of the concept; on cloister; on the lack of mention of the Holy Spirit . . .

Döpfner:[4] the schema gives no indication about the adaptation of religious
    life TO THE CONDITIONS OF OUR AGE. This had been the case
    with the fuller, previous drafts. He developed some points WITH
    GREAT FORCE. None of our bishops spoke like this!!! Our bishops,
    with the exception of two or three younger ones (Huyghe, Elchinger
    . . .) have NO DESIRE, nothing of the 'irascible', no coherent will for
    REFORM . . . It is a little like 'Gamelin'[5] confronted with 'Guderian'[6]. . .
    There was applause.
Cardinal Landázuri:[7] made an impression by his calm tone after this fine
    Germanic storm. He was also applauded.
Suenens:[8] *schema non placet* because it contains nothing about a renewal of
    religious life. Especially female religious: in favour of a much greater
    development concerning their human worth and their apostolic
    activity. In short, Cardinal Suenens gave his book,[9] in a very self-
    assured and somewhat domineering tone.

I left the *aula* at 10.55 am (unfortunately missing the rest of a very interesting
debate in which the bishops were also interested) for a meeting at St Martha's of
the group on *De Presbyteris*. The text on celibacy was revised: Lécuyer, who is
somewhat intrusive in this schema, has redone the beginning in an interesting
way, starting from the idea of a ministry of heavenly espousals and of the new
human being. We also looked at the suppressions that Lécuyer and Herranz want
made in the Number on pastoral ministry. They, who were ready to extend the

---

1. *AS* III/VII, 422–423.
2. *AS* III/VII, 426–429.
3. *AS* III/VII, 429–431.
4. *AS* III/VII, 431–434.
5. Maurice Gamelin, French General, Commander-in-Chief of National Defence in
   1938.
6. Heinz Guderian: German General, organiser of the German armoured divisions
   (1935–9).
7. *AS* III/VII, 436–439.
8. *AS* III/VII, 439–442.
9. Cf above, page 124, note 2.

spiritual considerations and to stretch out the whole moralising part, had made ruthless cuts here without taking account of what they were suppressing. I look like I am defending MY text. No, but some important ideas, which it is timely to formulate!!!

I was given the task of producing a CONCLUSION for the schema by tomorrow.

At lunch, the Observers from Constantinople and Alexandria, with Mgr Arrighi, Fr Duprey, Mgr Willebrands. Arrighi said to me: I had to ask for an admission for the wife of a Dutch Observer. I was asked if she was of mature age . . . Because some cardinals have complained that one sees, in St Peter's, quite young women walking around with priests (it has happened, in fact). Without commentary.

As the Observers that had been invited were due to visit the excavations under St Peter's with a good guide, I joined them. Indeed, today the weather was sunny and fresh, I felt rather well. So I made this visit. I came back dead with fatigue, but gratified. I *SAW* the originals: that pillar of the tomb, from the time of Marcus Aurelius, still embedded in the Constantinian wall. The archaeological proof is very strong. It consists in the continuity and the fact that nothing has ever been created or invented. It was persuasive enough, and for this reason, enormous efforts have been made TO PROTECT WHAT WAS THERE BEFORE. Constantine was the first to do this. He who had the power, and no doubt the wish, to erect a grand funeral monument, had left everything as it was, a little like the Franciscans at the *Portiuncula*, in building above and around. I was very moved. Once more, in Rome, one TOUCHED the thing itself, without any intermediary. Once more, in Rome, the centuries respect, and protect what is most significant from the past . . .

We saw, from the side, one of the columns of the famous little monument, embedded in the wall by Constantine, but we did not go into the chamber of this monument itself, or in front of it. When I expressed surprise at this, our guide replied, in a brisk and detached tone: there is some work going on at present. There was now no longer the time, but there could have been.

I understood, when some days later, I gathered from a suggestion of Cullmann (bound to secrecy) that the excavations are continuing. Perhaps they have found the body, or the bones of Peter himself . . . This is surely why we did not walk in front of the *edicula* itself.

Since I was on the spot, and since Mgr Hanrion[1] (OFM, Gabon) drove me in his Citroën 2 CV, and I had missed the Theological Commission, I went to the exposition of Ecumenical Councils from 1215–1870, from the Vatican Archives. I did not regret this either, in spite of the fatigue. What treasures! The ORIGINALS of so many things (see the catalogue). *THIS IS ALSO PART OF THE COUNCIL AND OF ITS GRACE*, to be in touch in this way with the previous councils. THE

---

1. Barthélemy P Hanrion, OFM, was, in fact, the Apostolic Prefect of Dapango (Togo).

ORIGINAL of Massarelli's diary[1] and the verbatim records of Trent! One of the three originals of the bull of union of Florence[2] (I felt like falling on my knees)! The original subscription of a decree of Trent, etc, etc!!!

I met Fr Smulders there who asked me, on behalf of the members of the Commission on Missions, if I would be willing to draft the theological chapter of the future revised schema *De Missionibus*. How could I refuse? I said yes.

On my return I received a visit from the Director of *Éditions S. Paul*,[3] Don Valentino Gambi.[4] He came to see me about questions regarding translations. He told me that already in 1958-1959 the 'Holy Office' had prohibited him from translating my *Jalons*, and, in general, any book signed Congar. The same for K Rahner. Now, the 'Holy Office' no longer says anything . . .

Shortly afterwards, a visit from a Mgr (Drago[5]) of the Secretariat of State. I wondered what he wanted, I waited right up to his departure to find out. I still don't know. Perhaps he just wanted to see a Father whom he considered famous, *'Doctor totius Ecclesiae'* [Doctor of the whole Church], etc, etc.

Telephone call from Canadian TV for tomorrow: I can't, I am already engaged.

Thursday 12 November 1964

Yesterday evening and this morning, before going to St Peter's, I drafted the conclusion of the *De Presbyteris*.

121st General Congregation. It was announced that there would be a *capella papale* tomorrow, with a concelebrated Byzantine Mass, for the (Byzantine) feast of St John Chrysostom. Fr Duprey told me that this was arranged in order to avoid a celebration of St Josaphat, asked for by the Ukrainians, which would have taken on a political dimension . . .

The discussion of the *De Religiosis* was completed.

> Huyghe,[6] speaking first, gave an excellent text, one that was at last on the same level as the better ones given by the Germans, the Dutch and the Belgians. He criticised the schema for not viewing and presenting religious IN THE CONTEXT OF THE CHURCH, and in harmony with the ecclesiology of the Council (and thus with the missionary mind of a Church fully 'present to the world'). *'Novum schema conficiatur quia*

---

1. Angelo Massarelli was the Secretary of the Council of Trent, during which he kept a precious diary.
2. The union with the Greeks at the Council of Florence in 1439.
3. More precisely, the *Edizioni San Paolo* of Milan, not to be confused with the *Éditions Saint-Paul* of Fribourg in Switzerland.
4. Priest of the Society of St Paul, who was the director of the *Edizioni San Paolo*.
5. Giacomo Drago, of the diocese of Bergamo, attaché at the Secretariat of State.
6. *AS* III/VII, 472–475.

vetus insanabile est' [a new schema should be prepared because the old one is beyond repair]. The Superiors General of WOMEN religious should be consulted. Applause.

Hoffer,[1] a Marianist, in favour of teaching brothers, with insistence on fidelity to God AND TO THE WORLD.

Lalande,[2] (Holy Cross), with a fine Canadian accent, in the name of more than 140 Fathers of whom 43 were Superiors General. The adaptations suggested cannot be justified merely internally. They must also be presented in relation to the renewal of the whole Church and to the needs of the world.

He put a lot of heart into this (he has a lot of it, and of evangelical spirit).

The schema should be sent back to the Commission, to which some experts, men and women, should be added, especially ones who know about the dispositions of young people.

Mgr James Carroll,[3] in a nasal tone, slow, a bit soporific. *Placet*, but he wanted some additions.

I was prevented from hearing Baraniak[4] by a Pole who wanted to write a thesis about my ecclesiology (and that of K Rahner)!!! He wants to come to Strasbourg to hear me!!! Dear God!!! I have not constructed an ecclesiology . . .

Van Kerckhoven,[5] Missionary of the Sacred Heart: 'the apostolic life is not a sheer danger to religious life' . . . Obviously!!! Announced banalities as though they were new discoveries.

Fiordelli:[6] we are forgetting the Secular Institutes.

I went out for a moment. Mgr Riobé asked me again to work on the theological part of the *De Missionibus*. —Mgr Larraín said to me: this is going very badly. Staffa has spent an hour this morning in the *aula*, gathering signatures to a paper . . . It seems that Chapter III is in danger and that the Pope is asking for *modi* that

---

1. Paul J Hoffer, Superior General of the Society of Mary (Marianists), member of the Commission for Seminaries, Studies and Catholic Education appointed by the Pope during the Second Session of the Council, *AS* III/VII, 474–477.
2. *AS* III/VII, 478–480.
3. James Carroll, Auxiliary Bishop of Sydney, member of the Commission for Bishops and the Government of Dioceses, elected during the Second Session, *AS* III/VII, 481–482.
4. *AS* III/VII, 483–485.
5. Joseph van Kerckhoven, Superior General of the Missionaries of the Sacred Heart, *AS* III/VII, 486–488.
6. *AS* III/VII, 488–490.

really would be an attack on collegiality. I knew that the Fathers [not the experts] of the Theological Commission were to meet at 11.00 am this morning. This must be for that. We agreed with Mgr Larraín that prayer is needed, because it is a spiritual battle.

It should be noted that as long as Chapter III of *De Ecclesia* has not been voted on, there cannot be a vote on *De pastorali Episcoporum munere* [on the pastoral function of bishops], which refers to it . . .

A little after 11.00 am the Moderators asked if it was desired that the discussion on *De Religiosis* be brought to an end. The answer was 'yes'. So the *relator* brought it to a conclusion. The results of the vote were given:

Voters present:	2,042
In favour of accepting the schema as a basis:	1,155
In favour of rejecting the schema:	882

There were s3 votes *iuxta modum*, and 2 null.

Felici announced the arrangements for the nine votes to be taken on the *De religiosis*, starting on Saturday. Because it has been accepted as a basis by an absolute majority. Therefore it will be necessary, from this Saturday, to prepare the *modi* for those who want to vote *iuxta modum*.

And, at 11.25 am, the *relator* (Carraro), read his *relatio* on *De institutione sacerdotali* [on priestly training].

Discussion began at 11.46 am.

Cardinal Beuno y Monreal[1] spoke (somewhat poorly) about the vocation to the priesthood.

Meyer:[2] good points, but '*magis elaborandum*' [in need of further development].

Drzazga[3] in the name of the bishops of Poland.

I left the tribune a little before the end of the sitting. I saw a number of experts, often already chatting in twos and threes. An atmosphere of great disquiet was apparent everywhere. Collegiality is under threat. I said: first wait and see WHAT it is about. Perhaps it is very serious, perhaps it is something quite small. I refuse to stir up a climate of distress, as some people do, before knowing what the matter is.

However, I learnt that the signatures Staffa had collected this morning are for the purpose of asking the Pope that Chapter III of *De Ecclesia* be withdrawn. Staffa was even then, at that very moment, in earnest conversation with Schauf, Lattanzi . . . It is clear that the anti-collegialists are mounting a major offensive.

---

1. *AS* III/VII, 552–54.
2. *AS* III/VII, 556–59.
3. *AS* III/VII, 559–61.

And they will still be doing so, if they have not got their way, five minutes before the proclamation of the text.

I met Daniélou, who was delighted that the schema *De Religiosis* has been accepted as a basis: without that, he said, we would have been given over to Huyghe and Charue (Huyghe had given him the slip last year, in the workshop on this question . . .). Daniélou was furious, on the other hand, about the text from the Secretariat for Non-Christian Religions, which, he said, made Christianity one religion among others. (I had myself insisted, in my *tentamen* [essay], on the affirmation of the absolute truth of the Gospel, and the duty to proclaim the Gospel.)

At the 1.00 pm meal, Mgr Garrone and Mgr Ancel said to me: it is not over yet, it will be continued at the beginning of this afternoon's meeting, but it is not very serious. There is no need to be disquieted.

At 4.30 pm, first at the Commission *De disciplina cleri* for the *De Presbyteris*. We looked at the changes made to the text (additions and suppressions, changes of detail). But I left at 5.30 pm for the Theological Commission. The meeting did not start for the *periti* for a long time (because the Fathers first continued their work from the morning). Besides, there were only eight *periti*, because Cardinal Léger had told them there would not be room for them to stay . . . (Daniélou left with almost all the *periti*. I wanted to give him his opportunity and alerted Mgr Colombo, who telephoned to call him back. But he did not come.) The *Declaratio de habitudine Ecclesiae ad religiones non chrsitianas* [declaration on the relation of the Church towards non-Christian religions] was examined. The Commission was not in favour of accepting this as an appendix to the *De Ecclesia*. Because one does not want to adopt a child one has not produced. ('Let us leave the child of Hagar to be washed and "perpoliendum" [brushed up] by its own father') (Henríquez). But, if this is made an appendix to the *De Ecclesia*, the public will attribute this text to the Theological Commission. That must be avoided.

Various discussions. In particular about the Jews, 'deicide' etc. Doumith intervened with fervour. Wright defended the text well; Šeper said that it certainly must be admitted that there has existed, and does still exist, a Christian anti-Semitism based on the idea that the Jews killed Christ. On the other hand, Franić wanted to exclude the word 'deicide'. Šeper's intervention made a profound impression.

> Ottaviani wanted a vote on the retention of the text. McGrath opposed this: we are to decide only *de fide et moribus* [on matters of faith and morals], so we are not to vote about whether or not it is opportune.
>
> Poma: mention Christ's harsh judgments, do not silence the texts which condemn the Jews. One could bring in one or another of them without doing harm.
>
> Ottaviani: WE have to say only whether there is anything here contrary to faith and morals.

> Charue: one cannot draw from the New Testament the idea that Christ condemned his people. Scripture has more and more distinguished between the people taken collectively, and individuals.
>
> Ottaviani: the Fathers who have *modi* to formulate should draft them and hand them in signed.
>
> Doumith, very passionately: this should be an exhortatory text, not a doctrinal one!

A vote was taken: those who think there is nothing here contrary to faith or morals, raise their hands. It was almost unanimous (Doumith remained with arms down, and discontented).

Since the Theological Commission finished at 7.00 pm, and the window of the Commission *De Disciplina Cleri* was still illuminated, I went across there for a moment. They had just finished with the *modus procedendi* [the manner of proceeding]. The text was approved by the Commission.

Mgr Kervéadou[1] told me that *Ouest-France*—and other newspapers of the province that are dependent on it, carried the text of a petition to the Pope asking that: 1) he proclaim Mary 'Mother of the Church', and 2) he put a stop to the doctrine of collegiality. There was this sentence: 'We, Christians, want the universal motherhood of Mary over the Church, and the universal fatherhood of the Pope over the Church' (quoted *ad sensum* [according to the meaning]). This comes from l'abbé Berto (*Pensée catholique).* I don't think the minority at Vatican I moved heaven and earth like that. In any case this shows: 1) there is a connection, at least temperamentally, between the OVER-exaltation of Mary, and that of the Pope; 2) that the basis is political. At Vatican I also, the papal question was bound up with politics. For me, the end of the eleventh century and what followed sheds light on this!

Friday 13 November 1964

Etchegaray told me that, yesterday, they worked until midnight on the *modi* for the *De Religiosis*, which have to be given in tomorrow, and to be roneoed in the meantime. Once more, everything is being done at the Belgian College, with Moeller and Prignon. Indeed, Moeller was accepted as an expert in the Commission for Religious. The Belgians are only three or four in number, but they have got one of themselves in everywhere. As soon as one of them is there, the small group is there, and takes over the work. 'Union makes strength'. The Commission for Religious has been very closed in, and has admitted experts only lately, and sparingly. I realised once again how broad and open to work the Theological Commission has been in comparison with some others. I suggested calling in Fr Féret. It is too late for the *modi*: they are done [but how competently?]. But for later on, for the work of rewriting. I wrote to Mgr Huyghe along these lines. But

---

1. François L M Kervéadou, Bishop of Saint-Brieuc (France).

Féret is not a conciliar expert, and I am afraid that will prevent his entry into this ghetto-group.

On the other hand Fr Martelet (who certainly has something to say and has just finished *Sainteté de l'Église et vie religieuse*[1]) is in on it. Yesterday the presbyterate no longer interested him, but THIS question did.

I did not go to St Peter's this morning: there was a Byzantine mass celebrated with *capella papale*. For the first time for a long time I was able to do a little work for myself: in fact, I finished recopying the text (not the notes!) of my article for the collection of essays offered to Chenu.

I was given some information about this morning's ceremonies. The Pope brought his tiara and offered it for the poor. If this is the discarding of the tiara, if there is not another one after it, that is good. Otherwise, it would be a spectacular gesture without consequence. In short, he should have put on the altar, not A tiara, but *THE* tiara. It would appear that, at the moment of entering the basilica, the Pope was already seated on the throne of the *sedia*; they were getting ready to lift up the whole thing. He signalled to them to leave it on the ground, got down from the throne and entered on foot.

The same thing. Is this the beginning of an overhauling of the seigneurial? And how far will it go?

Lunch with Cullmann, who has invited Liégé, Féret and me. There was very much a feeling of communion of spirit and of service. Cullmann told us of some reactions of the Observers. A very great mistrust with regard to Fr Boyer. At first they gave to the *Foyer Unitas* [centre for unity] the name *Duplicitas* [duplicity]. Now they are very much at ease with this Centre, to a large degree because of the Bethany Sisters who are wonderful, but they have not changed their opinion of Fr Boyer.

Fr Scrima came in for a good deal of comment. They find him too pro-Catholic. Subilia[2] with whom the World Alliance of Reformed Churches has replaced H Roux, is VERY anti-Catholic. This is causing tension, at the Waldesian faculty, with another current (Vinay[3]) who is less anti.

Cullmann, whom I questioned about his visit to the Pope, and about a point touched on in the course of the visit, that is, the excavations under St Peter's, said he was bound to secrecy on this point. Nevertheless, from what he did say on the subject, I thought I was able to deduce that the excavations would be continued, and that they might well have found the body, or some bones of St Peter.

At 4.30 pm, at the Belgian College for the group dealing with 'the Church of the Poor'. A lecture by Fr Chenu, a Chenu 200% better: intelligence, vitality,

---

1. Gustave Martelet, *Sainteté de l'Église et vie religieuse* (Toulouse: Éd. Prière et Vie, 1964).
2. Vittorio Subilia, Professor of Systematic Theology at the Waldensian Faculty of Theology in Rome, was an Observer delegated by the World Presbyterian Alliance at the two final Sessions.
3. Valdo Vinay was also Professor of Theology at the Waldensian Faculty of Theology.

propheticism, presence. An analysis characterised by both a propheticism and an intellectual rigour that were sensational.

Fr Paul Gauthier insisted that I go to have dinner at his place, with his small group and some bishops who come on Fridays. 'It is quite close by.' He does not take account of what 300 metres means for me . . . and a whole evening. In the end I agreed to go. There were present, besides Marie-Thérèse and a new (Belgian) girl, Ghislaine, two lads (Brazilians) doing their theological studies, Mgr da Mota from Vitória[1] (Brazil), Mgr Távora[2] from Aracajú (Brazil) and, arriving very late, Mgr Gand (Lille). But we clashed, Marie-Thérèse and I. I resisted what seemed to me to be simplistic views. She persisted with a feminine passion and a refusal to see anything other than the needs of the poor. In short, it was a VERY trying evening for me. Physically, as well: I had been under lights or lamps for twelve hours, and my eyes were burning.

I acknowledge that I would see things differently if I lived among the poor. I reject impassioned simplistic views.

Saturday 14 November 1964
In another week I will say: Phew!

Rodhain has transferred the *Caritas Internationalis* Study Day on the Diaconate to today. I am sorry to be missing a sitting of the Council which interests me, but I promised to go to the Diaconate at the *Domus Mariae*. In fact, there were nine of us (plus a tenth): twenty had been expected. It was wholly Franco-German. The old man Hornef[3] was there: he is the grandfather of the restored diaconate. But a young German forester, H Kramer,[4] is the still more effective father. This lad had, in the forests, a true and compelling vocation to the diaconate, at a time when no one talked about it. IT WAS HE who organised the *Diakonat-Kreise* [diaconate circles] in Germany that later inspired similar efforts in France. It was he who prepared the Rahner-Vorgrimler volume *Diaconia in Christo*[5] . . . These men now see their efforts coming to fruition, more quickly and more extensively than they imagined it . . . René Schaller,[6] of Lyons, was also there, awfully well, in the more mystical style of the French.

We spent the morning exchanging ideas about a programme, proposed by Rodhain, concerning the study days to be held in 1965 on the now restored diaconate. But our discussion lacked vigour. The most interesting aspect of the ques-

---

1. J-B da Mota e Albuquerque, Archbishop of Vitória.
2. José V Távora, Archbishop of Aracaju.
3. Josef Hornef, a retired magistrate.
4. Hannes Kramer, a social worker, founded the first diaconate circle at Freiburg-im-Breisgau.
5. Karl Rahner and Herbert Vorgrimler, (editors) *Diaconia in Christo: Über die Erneuerung des Diakonates* (Freiburg-Basle-Vienna, 1962).
6. René Schaller, father of a family and social worker, was the founder of the Community of the Diaconate of France; he was later to be ordained a permanent deacon.

tion is not so much the diaconate in itself, but rather the connections between the restored function and the general evolution of ecclesiological ideas: ministry, evangelical concept of priesthood, the presbyterium, collegial pastoral work, communion, the criticism of legalism, and the vitality of the obligations arising from MISSION and COMMUNION; etc.

The meeting in the afternoon was not much heavier. Mgr Guyot arrived at 3.30 pm, Mgr Motta[1] at 4.00 pm . . . At the end we briefly previewed the 1965 session, its style . . . I was nabbed to give an exposition, obviously!!!

Before returning, I visited the exhibition of pastoral work in the Church in Spain. Certainly, these pictures and graphics lend themselves to showing especially the ORGANISATIONAL aspect. But that aspect is very much emphasised here. Everywhere photos of new buildings, impressive numbers of convents and seminarians. A country where the ideal of life and the great surges of underlying life coincide largely enough with the Catholic Church, with the encyclicals, and even coincided rather well with Pius XII . . .

I gathered some bits of information on this morning's sitting, which had greatly interested the bishops (and in the course of which the *modi* for Chapters III-VIII of the *De Ecclesia* were distributed. Relief among the Fathers! At last the deadlock is broken . . . It appears that when Felici announced the distribution of the *modi* for the *De Ecclesia* there was great applause. There had been fairly widespread anxiety (stirred up by some men who were importunate and too 'irascible'): this anxiety was now put to rest), and also some rumours about what has been going on these past few days. It was said that at one point the Pope had thought of sending a message to the assembly about primacy and collegiality. I was told (by Etchegaray) that the meeting of the Theological Commission without experts was for the purpose of hearing and examining the comments of Fr Bertrams (one wonders what role he plays) and of Mgr Colombo: the Pope being, PERHAPS, behind the pair of them??? However it is VERY probable that there was also question of some modifications that Don Dossetti wanted to have introduced into the few general explanatory notes placed at the head of the booklet of *modi* for Chapter III. In fact, the printed text is not exactly the same as the roneoed one we had been given on 6 November, and in the discussion of which I had hardly taken part, as I arrived late. Dossetti had told me about his anxieties, his dissatisfaction with certain terms. For my part, I had explained that, in the fourth paragraph, it was a question of collegial acts in the STRICT sense. And I saw from the printed text that some small corrections had been made on precisely the points about which Dossetti was annoyed, and along lines that would give him some satisfaction. There does not seem to be any question that the Theological Commission had to approve the small modifications, which Philips had, dutifully, submitted to it. On the other hand, the *relationes* have often been dealt with by the Commission WITHOUT the *periti*.

---

1. This must refer to J-B da Mota e Albuquerque.

This morning's votes on the schema *De Religiosis* resulted in a very large number of *modi*. They went a long way beyond a THIRD, and so the Commission CANNOT allow a text to pass without taking account of them.

This evening, I telephoned Mgr Colombo to tell him that I had received the Möhler asked for by the Pope. He told me to have the book brought to him tomorrow MORNING. Doubtless this is because he is going to see the Pope in the afternoon ... (I also sent Colombo Fr Dupuy's text.) He asked my views about the text of Chapter III: 'it has not been changed, has it?' He told me spontaneously that the East was not wholly satisfied. I told him my view: WE had presented three or four *modi* to preserve the ecclesiological opportunities of the Orthodox in the *De Ecclesia,* especially in Chapter III, but also in other places. I have gone to a lot of trouble to distribute these *modi* everywhere; Fr Dupuy drew up some explanations which I signed and had roneoed. However, Mgr Charue and Philips have not taken account of them. Now, an NB has been added at the beginning of Chapter III saying that the Council does not invalidate the de facto situation of the Orthodox: the task of looking for explanations is left to theologians ... (where does this NB come from? From the Pope? From Colombo? It was he who first spoke to me about it). This note has hurt me very much. Thus the Council leaves it to the theologians: it is not a matter that is of interest to IT!! Mgr Colombo said to me: it was all that could be done NOW. [Is that certain?] – It will be for a latter council ... !!!

That did not satisfy me.

I am afraid that our *De Ecclesia* will create a new obstacle on the path to rapprochement.

Sunday 15 November 1964

Correspondence, and a hundred little things I was late with. I wrote to Mgr Colombo and to Fr Duprey. There must be something for the Orthodox, for example, from the Pope in his final discourse.

I began to look at what I will put into my final chronicle for *ICI*; I wrote my piece. Pretty feeble, like everything else I do.

Telephone-call from Fr Schillebeeckx: the Dutch bishops are wondering if the *modi* that have been accepted do not bury collegiality.

Monday 16 November 1964

Correspondence.

At St Peter's at 9.30 am, for Mass, Malabar rite. Dreadfully sad music. The mass was too long. I am glad that Christ is proclaimed and sung in all languages. But there are the demands of work: it is daft not to start work until 10.00 am, already tired.

Felici[1] corrected the absence of a *quaesitum* [question].[2]

Certain Fathers had it noted that in the vote on Chapter III, the *ordo concilii* [regulations of the Council] had not been observed.[3] Their objections were examined and the response was: the *ordo* had been followed exactly and all the methods of procedure had been carefully evaluated. The same ones made some criticisms of the doctrine: these were examined by the relevant Commission.

The question of the theological note of the texts was raised. See the reply on page 8 of the booklet of *modi* for Chapter III. He read out the text of it.

By virtue of higher authority the *Nota praevia* to Chapter III was communicated to the Fathers, according to which the doctrine set out in the chapter is to be interpreted. Felici read this note, which thus really played the same part that the speech of Zinelli had played at Vatican I.

This morning's debate was very boring. I went out for a moment, but in the end I stayed out until it finished. Thus:

First I saw Mgr Heuschen. He said, 'Now it is the collegialists who are uneasy. They say, or they fear that the *Relatio praevia* will damage collegiality. But, Mgr Heuschen said, what could be done has been done. The NB does not have the meaning that is attributed to it. It was a way of avoiding a phrase that the Pope wanted put into the Number: *'qua deficiente (communione cum Collegio et capite eius)* [when (communion with the College and its head) is lacking] there is no power of magisterium or of jurisdiction'. (This would have come, perhaps, from Fr Bertrams.) This would have categorically excluded the Orthodox. Mgr Philips and the Commission rejected that. The result was the NB.

I saw once again that the Pope does not have the ecclesiology that goes with his grand ecumenical gestures. I think the note I wrote yesterday to Mgr Colombo, and what I also wrote yesterday for *ICI* is of a completely different spirit.

Almost everywhere I am stopped by experts, bishops, or even groups. I was almost holding a press conference: sitting on the step of a confessional, with several bishops, including Mgr Zoghby, Fr Kéramé, Manteau-Bonamy[4] etc. They were all anxious and worked up. Several of those I met this morning were considering voting *Non placet*. I explained that such a vote would have only one outcome: it would increase the number of anti-collegialists and, at the same stroke, feed the Pope's anxieties. I explained that the preliminary declaration was made in order

---

1. *AS* III/VIII, 9–13.
2. A question that should have been submitted to the Fathers had been omitted from the booklet concerning the *modi* for Chapter III of the *De Ecclesia*.
3. The *Ordo Concilii oecumenici Vaticani II celebrandi, Editio altera recognita,* [Order for the conduct of the Second Vatican Ecumenical Council (second, revised edition, 1963)].
4. Henri-Marie Manteau-Bonamy, OP, of the Province of France, former Professor of Philosophy at Le Saulchoir, summoned to Rome by several bishops during the Third Session, as a mariologist.

to reassure and rally the minority, that it does not damage the doctrine of the text. But I added that I do not like the NB, that I find it pitiable and that I have made this known.

In fact, just before this, Mgr Colombo told me in passing that yesterday he had passed on to the Pope, Möhler, my letter, and Dupuy's paper on the *modi* that are desirable from the Eastern point of view.

Kéramé and Zoghby said that the NB is an insult to the Easterners. They seem to believe that text of the *Nota explicativa praevia* FORMS PART of what they will have to vote on tomorrow. Obviously not. In any case, Mgr Zoghby was going, *illico* [there and then], to find Cardinal Suenens so that it would be expressly declared tomorrow that these two pages do not fall under the vote. But it remains the case that they explain the meaning of the text that will be voted on, exactly as the *relatio* of Zinelli did in 1870. Kéramé wasn't having any of that and said that one will have complete freedom to interpret the text.

Fr Guglielmi told me that the Brazilian bishops, dissatisfied and uneasy, had been to see Cardinal Frings, asking him to approach the Pope and get a discussion opened on the text of the *Nota explicativa praevia*. He would envisage a speaker in the name of the German episcopate, another in the name of the French episcopate, etc. I told him that I was absolutely not in agreement. If the discussion is reopened: 1) the minority will also ask to speak, there will be an exposition by Franić, and people's minds will be even more in the dark; 2) that will reinforce the Pope's anxiety; 3) we will end up with what the minority wants: not having time to complete it and postponing Chapter III to the next Session.

It is regrettable perhaps, but that is how it is; they are now cornered into voting *Placet*, even if not everything is acceptable.

(Felici announced that some bishops had asked how to respond to the Pope's gesture of giving up his tiara, and the reply given to them (by the Secretary of State),[1] was: by a collection of money. —A very dim view was taken of this by the French bishops whom I heard speaking about it.)

For myself, today as seven weeks ago, I would like Mgr Philips to explain *viva voce* the *Nota praevia*. But it does not seem that the Moderators will accept this, for the same reason, not valid in my opinion, as six weeks ago: the fear that if the opportunity to speak is given to one it will have to be given to others.

But it remains the case that I hear tell, through other channels, of the same unease that I have encountered: ill-founded unease. But it exists. I am told that *I* would be able to allay it. As I did this morning. Several have come to the conclusion: once they know that YOU think that this changes nothing about collegiality, people are reassured . . . —But what can I do? Except by conversation as one person to another.

---

1. A Cicognani.

A little correspondence (it never ceases! That is my cross).

At 4.30 pm, Joint Commission on schema XIII.

Fr Tromp read out a letter from the Pope to the members of the Theological Commission. The Pope sent back the documents relative to Chapter III of the *De Ecclesia*. He thanked the Commission for its work.

Guano took stock:

Regarding an enlargement of the joint sub-commission. It has eight members: he suggested that eight more should be nominated from each of the two Commissions, and that a few more should be added who do not belong to these two Commissions, representing different countries. He gave seven names, which were accepted. The election produced these results:

THEOLOGY		LAITY	
Garrone:	14	Laszlo:	11
Šeper:	13	Morris:[1]	10
Poma:	13	Larraín:	9
Butler:	8	Fernández Conde:[2]	9

Regarding the reworking of the schema, there are three points in particular to be noticed:

1) to whom is it addressed and in what manner?

2) should it speak from the beginning about the current world situation?

3) in addition to more temporal problems, should it also speak of the spiritual situation, and in particular about atheism?

The Moderators thought it would be better not to raise these questions *in aula*. Their own opinion is that, on the first point, it is addressing Christians, while also having the others in mind.

On the first point, some were for addressing the world (Butler, Ancel), while others were for addressing Christians (Poma, König, Yü Pin, Henríquez). A vote was taken: a *GREAT* majority in favour of directly addressing CATHOLICS.

The time required to produce an acceptable text was discussed.

It seems that this would presuppose a fourth session in the AUTUMN.

Ottaviani asked Philip's advice. He insisted on the value of good work done by sub-commissions. Tromp added: the work of the sub-commissions should be communicated to ALL. —Philips: and there should be a sub-commission to co-ordinate the work of the sub-commissions.

---

1. Thomas Morris, Archbishop of Cashel and Emly (Ireland), member of the Commission for the Apostolate of the Laity elected at the First Session of the Council.
2. Emanuele Fernández Conde, Bishop of Cordova (Spain). He was elected a member of the Commission for the Apostolate of the Laity at the Second Session of the Council.

Helder-Câmara (in French): have in mind lay experts and non-European experts.

This meeting finished at 6.15 pm. Like almost all the meetings of this Joint Commission this one was empty, without great content. It reminded me of the meetings of Catholic Action before 1939, where one asked oneself interminably what Catholic Action was, what it was going to do, what methods one should use . . .

While I was leaving with the Belgians, I learned that Cardinal Frings has decided against intervening, and has gone over to a *Placet* vote. But the situation is not yet clear and tomorrow's vote remains unpredictable.

Mgr Prignon and Mgr Philips can do no more. They have had some terrible days: everything coming at once! I told Mgr Philips about my dissatisfaction with the NB to page 6. He told me he would explain this to me LATER; meanwhile I should read the *modi* concerning the Easterners. He could not, and did not want to go any further. (Especially Nos 40, 43 and 153.)

I spent the rest of the evening, until quite late, closely examining the *modi* for Chapter III. No! They do not alter the doctrine, any more than the *Nota praevia*.

Tuesday 17 November 1964

Correspondence (always!!!). At St Peter's; some private matters. I again saw several (four or five) excellent *periti* who are still full of disquiet and doubt about the meaning of the vote on Chapter III. They absolutely do not want to include the *Nota praevia* in it. —It certainly does not constitute part of the text as voted, but it gives the meaning of the text that will be voted on. I am afraid that many do not give this text its exact meaning, but something wider, I don't know what. The fact remains that the *Nota praevia* has sown anxiety and dissatisfaction among the 'collegialists'. Although, as far as I can see, it changes nothing.

The text of the *De libertate* was distributed.

Felici read out the *modi* for Chapter III. But there was no declaration specifying that the *Nota praevia* does not fall under the vote.

A brave critique of the Congregation for Studies, by Mgr Garrone.[1]

Mgr Méndez[2] raised the question of celibacy. But the Fathers were preoccupied with their vote so this did not get MUCH attention.

At 10.32 am, Felici gave the result of the vote on Chapter III. It surpassed all my hopes. Here it is:

Voters present:	2,146
Placet:	2,099
Non placet:	46
Placet iuxta modum (null):	1

---

1. *AS* III/VIII, 171–173.
2. *AS* III/VIII, 174–177.

Pretty solid applause. The storm has passed. One can breathe again.

Reuss[1] spoke again about the *De institutione sacerdotali* [priestly formation], in the name of more than seventy, because, in principle, the debate is closed. He too spoke about celibacy, which should not be made a purely juridical condition necessary in order to be ordained . . .

The *relator* brought the debate on *De institutione sacerdotali* to a conclusion. The first, general, vote resulted in:

Present:	2,117
Placet:	2,076
Non placet:	41

At 11.30 am, there followed the detailed vote:

Vote on the *modi* for *De Ecclesia*	Chapter IV;	Chapter V:
Present:	2,144	2,146
Placet:	2,135	2,142
Non placet:	8	4
Null:	1	

Very little applause.

Then the question of schools was taken up. *Relatio* (too long!) by Mgr Daem.[2]

Fr de Lubac told me that yesterday the minority had received a paper saying: vote *Placet*. We have obtained satisfaction . . .

On the other hand, Cardinal Browne was not deceived by it: Philips told me that he had remarked: 'But there is nothing changed in the text . . . '

This morning's *Il Tempo* presented the matter thus: it is a purely administrative question. And it saw in it a victory for the good cause.

So it is perfect. As in *Alice in Wonderland*, everyone has won.

Mgr Prignon said to me: forgive us for yesterday evening. Mgr Philips could not do any more.—Certainly I understand! But, I said, there remains the enormous problem represented by the NB, and various turns of phrase in the *De Ecclesia*: these, if taken literally, will 'unchurch'[3] the Orthodox. And the job of explaining is pathetically handed back to the theologians. But THE COUNCIL ought to have taken on this concern and this task!

Prignon said to me: the experts were excluded. The Commission was faced with a text by Fr Bertrams, annotated in the hand of the Pope, for whom Betrams is the theologian listened to . . . It was a photocopy. The wording of this text, which would, itself, have disqualified the Orthodox, was avoided. Prignon agrees that the Pope absolutely does not have the ecclesiology implied by his gestures. He once asked: how far can we go in the 'concessions' to the Orthodox? . . .

---

1. *AS* III/VIII, 177–178.
2. *AS* III/VIII, 218–222.
3. Congar used the English word.

In such conditions dialogue is, humanly speaking, still-born!

The minority considers today's vote a victory. Stickler,[1] a canonist of the Staffa persuasion, said: 'today the Fathers have voted for the opposite of what was voted for on 30 October last.'

That is false!

Correspondence. Visit from some people from American TV. Visit from Le Guillou.

At 4.15 pm, at St Martha's, for the Commission on schema XIII. We did not start until 4.45 pm or a little later. And there were far too many: forty-five people. It has always been a vice of the Commission for schema XIII to accumulate people and overburden itself.

Häring enumerated, with the pathos of his oratorical temperament, the points to be worked on. One is drowned in abundance, one does not feel engaged in the work.

Häring made a long speech about what should be done.

After him, Guano: it will be necessary to speak of the goal to be sought = directly the evangelisation of the world, of the method to be followed, of the order of the subject matter.

Häring: nothing of value can be done unless the human vocation is considered in its fullness.

Ancel: we should not be thinking directly of converting people, but of speaking in such a way that the mission of the Church, which includes action in the temporal sphere, will be seen with its value as a sign.

Hirschmann: we should FIRST study the comments of the Fathers.

Guano: but we must formulate some working principles this evening.

It came back to asking Philips, who said: there should be a general *relatio* on the *desiderata* of the Fathers, drawn up by a central commission, that, on the basis of this, would distribute the work. Then the work of the sub-commissions would be gathered together, and ONE person, or a very small group, would be entrusted with the task of harmonising, unifying and organising the text.

But what does the schema want to achieve? One wants also to reach out to non-Christians. How to cooperate with them in this TEMPORAL and human work?

Set out first some broad general principles: relation with the world, with humankind; then deal with the principal problems (the matter in Chapter IV).

There are two functions:
    - the *relatio generalis* [general report]
    - the secretary who will keep the work moving.

---

1. Alfons M Stickler, SDB, Professor of Canon Law and the History of Law, was Rector of the Pontifical Salesian Athenaeum; he was a Council expert; he was later to become a cardinal and Prefect of the Vatican Apostolic Library.

Philips seemed to insinuate that he would be able to organise it, but perhaps
   not to draft it in a Latin text that spoke directly to humankind. [THAT
   IS TRUE.]
Do not desire to redo everything anew, starting from scratch: it would never
   be finished; but start from what is already there.
Philips was applauded.

Hengsbach: what would be the steps to be taken most immediately? Examine
   the comments of the Fathers, because we are here only to be at their
   service. So set up a small sub-commission for this. And Philips would
   be the first to be designated.
Philips: I cannot do it all alone. There needs to be people who will put
   everything on index cards. I am able to collate the work of five or six
   aides, or *relatores*, as was done for the *De Revelatione*.
I agreed with all that. But the more important question is the tone to adopt.
   —Philips made another great speech about the style, those to whom it
   would be addressed etc.
McGrath: on the small central commission and the work it will have to do.
   And that a second vice-president should be elected.
Guano: it is necessary to know first what we want in this schema . . .
Hengsbach: first of all, take account of the comments of the Fathers: Philips,
   Hirschmann and Haubtmann would be able to prepare this work.
Philips: YES, and the different sub-commissions should each elect a *relator*.
   And the same applies to the third stage (the trials of the *De Ecclesia*).
González Moralejo took up again (in a difficult Latin) the general goal of the
   schema.
For the small sub-commission that needs to make the index cards there
   were chosen: Lebret, Hirschmann, Medina, Haubtmann. Philips will
   supervise the group.
Guano proposed the following sub-commissions:
1)   a general *conspectus* to be put at the beginning of the schema;
2)   revision of Chapters I, II and III; as required   } Chap I
      sub-divided, with right of superivsion   } Chap II-III
      over the rest
3)   several sub-commissions for each point of Chapter IV, which would
      see to the unity of the whole.

At 7.00 pm, in the midst of noise, the names of the presidents of these sub-commissions were given:
   -

- *De persona humana* [on the human person]: Wright
- *De matrimonio et familia* [on marriage and the family]: Dearden? or Poma?
- *De Cultura* [on culture]: Charue
- *De vita oeconomica* [on economic life]: Hengsbach
- *De communitate gentium et pace* [on the community of nations and peace]: König.

And a vice-president should be elected: Ancel.

Butler: we should find names for the sub-commissions. We have twenty minutes left.

We went round in circles, wasted time. Nothing was ready, nothing was decided. Everyone was very dissatisfied.

I note down here that Mgr Philips said to me: the *Nota praevia* was drawn up in place of another one, rather bad, which was sent back three times,—and what Gagnebet told me. A week previously, he had spoken to Staffa criticising his false image of collegiality. In the end the minority had agreed on this: that they would be content to set forth in the text what was held in common, without canonising a particular theory.

That was to ask for what has always been the rule of the Commission, and what has always been done!!!

This evening, there was a meeting at the Belgian College, to prepare the *modi* for religious freedom.

When I got back, worn out, from St Martha's, finding it difficult to stand, there was the day's correspondence, telephone calls, a visit from a Spanish priest who wanted my views on the difference between Constance and Vatican II . . .

Wednesday 18 November 1964

I did not go to St Peter's. Correspondence. I tried to make some headway with the backlog of work . . . I am in fact behind with a hundred important and urgent items!

Accounts of this morning at St Peter's. Presence of the Pope for the Armenian Mass (50th Anniversary of the Turkish massacres. The Patriarch of the separated Armenian Church asked him for this[1] . . .) Felici announced that some of the Fathers felt that they had not had all the time appropriate to study the new *De libertate* and so tomorrow there will be a preliminary vote to ask if the Fathers want to postpone the vote, or to go ahead with it, all the same. —To a certain extent, I understand the reaction of these Fathers: such an important text does require thorough reflection. But it is certain that there is also some manoeuvring. Mgr

---

1. This must refer to Vasken I, Catholicos of Etchmiazin in Soviet Armenia, who had a primacy of honour in the Armenian Apostolic Church.

Pailler told me that Mgr Marcel Lefebvre (the great adversary of any ideas of free-dom) and Carli conferred for an hour. Passing close to them, he had overheard a proposal regarding 100 signatures that had been obtained. This can only refer to a manoeuvre against the schema *De libertate.*

The definitive text of the *De Ecclesia* was distributed this morning (on which there will be a general vote tomorrow) .

In the afternoon, to the RAI studio for American TV (which will be broadcast on Sunday morning) with Fr Häring, Outler, an announcer, and a USA ecclesi-astic. What a horror TV is! They kept us two hours under the spotlights before starting whatever was going to be done. This disregard for others, disregard for speakers, is rather disgusting. I returned after three-and-a-half hours' absence (when I have got so much to do!) at once disgusted, revolted, worn out and with a very bad headache!

And that doesn't help matters. Mgr Rougé, who had been there, said that at the general audience this evening the Pope announced that on Saturday he is going to proclaim Mary *Mater Ecclesiae* [Mother of the Church]. He asked for prayers for this.

Truly, there was no need for them!

Thursday 19 November 1964

At St Peter's, I saw Mgr Philips. I brought him up to date about the background to *Mater Ecclesiae*. He said to me: that doesn't surprise me. The Pope is authori-tarian, he wants absolutely to affirm his superiority over the Council. He was extremely mortified by the rejection of the schema *De Missionibus.* (Another side of the story: the Pope holds it against Cardinal Agagianian that he tricked him, and, in getting him to present the schema in that way, that he caused him to be disavowed.) He wants to have an opportunity to demonstrate his personal magis-terium. We have resisted as far as we could . . .

It is worse than that. Ecumenism is in question. Since the beginning of the week, there has been a concerted effort around the Pope to stop its being pro-claimed. Yesterday evening, it was even settled. In the end, the Pope is going to make a certain number of modifications to the text. This text was to be printed tonight, for distribution tomorrow morning. We'll see.

But I reacted very strongly: so? the embraces in Jerusalem? Was that just a charade? The Pope makes gestures, and that's all? In no way does he have the theology implied by his gestures, he even has a theology that is contrary to them.

We'll see. I don't want to get carried away by what is, perhaps, something imagined. I also tell myself that I do not pray enough; I do not campaign suf-ficiently in the other direction.

The distribution of the *modi* on the Eastern Churches was announced: they will be voted on tomorrow. Whereas it would have been better if it were not pro-claimed, so as not to impede dialogue with the Orthodox. There is still a huge number of speakers who have signed up for *De Scholis*. But Felici announced the vote on *De Ecclesia* as a whole, in accordance with the *Nota praevia* that was read out on 16 November. And the vote on Saturday too will be conducted under the same conditions. The result of today's vote:

Present & voting:	2,145
Placet:	2134
Non placet:	10 + 1 null vote.

I went to see the Observers, to express my communion of feeling with the people of the Secretariat. Arrighi said to me: Willebrands and I have not slept for three nights. The *De oecumenismo* is being called into question. However, it is being printed with some corrections by the Pope, which, Willebrands thinks, touch only on matters of detail, and do not change it fundamentally. Arrighi thinks that, when he is with the Pope, Colombo plays a role of anxiety and scruples.

I chatted at length with H Roux. He is very critical of what he sees at present: these are behind-the-scenes manoeuvres: this really calls into question the status of the rule of the Holy Spirit in the Church. It lacks candour!

I saw some other people: Thijssen, Mgr Gand, Laurentin, Villain. They were all saying: why is there no more talk about religious freedom?? It should have been voted on this morning. What manoeuvre is going on beneath that?

I also saw Cardinal Meyer and told him this: he should intervene and publicly ask what is going on.

Meanwhile the Moderators have asked if it is desired to put an end to the discussion on schools. This was agreed at 10.45 am. But those who were down to speak in the name of more than seventy were still able to do so. This was the case with Fr Fernandez,[1] who gave an interminable dissertation. Cardinal Döpfner[2] asked him to bring it to an end, and this request was strongly applauded.

Shortly after, about 11.05 am, Cardinal Tisserant[3] took the floor: Certain Fathers had complained that the time was too short to study seriously the new text on religious freedom; a text whose *relatio* itself recognised that the structure was new. In these circumstances, the Council of Presidents thought that this schema could not be put to the vote today. The Fathers are invited to submit their comments before 31 January.

This declaration was welcomed with applause from a rather small number of men who clapped their hands as hard and for as long as possible, to make it seem that they were very numerous.

At 11.20 am, Felici announced[4] that the vote would be taken on *De oecumenismo* tomorrow. But some corrections have been added to the *modi* already

---

1. Aniceto Fernandez, *AS* III/VIII, 408–411.
2. He was the Moderator who presided at this General Congregation.
3. *AS* III/VIII, 415.
4. *AS* III/VIII, 422–423.

approved. This *BY THE SECRETARIAT*, according to suggestions proposed *'auc-toritative'* [authoritatively].[1]

No reaction.

Felici READ OUT these additions or corrections. From what I could hear, and without having been able to compare it with the text, it did not seem to me to be very serious.

At 11.35 am, the preliminary vote on the schema *De educatione christiana* was proposed.

Then De Smedt spoke:[2] he read out (in part) the *relatio* prepared for the *De libertate*, and printed. I wondered a little why he read a *relatio* when it was not going to be followed by a vote. But it was an opportunity of making a point. Because, the end of his delivery was broken into by vigorous and prolonged applause. Three times there was applause like this. All the area around the Confession was full of small groups of bishops and experts, especially experts, who were chatting, with great animation. The atmosphere was that of the lobbies during an important sitting of parliament. It was midday. Many were very agitated. But this applause was the response of a very large majority to a minority who wanted to impose its law on the majority. Because today it is only a matter of a generic vote to accept the text, with the possibility of *modi*. But some people, who do not want the Declaration on freedom, believe that to suspend this vote is to defer it until next summer, and thus to gain several months which will be able to be made use of to do something else. Others hold the view, I think legitimately, that there has not been enough time to study the text. So they must be given an extension to submit their *modi*.

In any case the majority is very worked up. They thought that others wanted to catch them by a ploy. They responded. Immediately five stations were set up where a petition to the Pope could be signed, asking that the vote intended for this morning should take place tomorrow. The Americans telegraphed their newspapers. After the sitting had finished, Cardinals Meyer (what exactly had his role been? Cardinal Tisserant consulted the members of the Council of Presidents. Cardinal Meyer denies having given his assent. But Mgr Delacroix, who followed it all from our tribune, maintains that he was consulted, and after he had been, had signalled to another American cardinal who was some distance away, by a gesture of his arms, that everything was overturned), Ritter and Léger, went to the Pope, carrying a petition covered with more than eight-hundred signatures, asking *instanter, instantissime* [urgently, most urgently][3] that the vote should be taken before the end of this Session, that is to say: tomorrow.

At table (Cullmann, Bishop Moorman and Féret had come to lunch), Cardinal Richaud said that Cardinal Alfrink, who is a member of the Council of

1. This indicated an intervention by the Pope.
2. *AS* III/VIII, 449–456.
3. These words were found at the beginning of the petition.

Presidents, had said to him: the Council of Presidents thought it had been told that there would have been a large number of *non placet* votes (eight hundred, it was said), especially from the Spanish and the Italians, if the vote had been taken today. It was in view of this, and in order to avoid it, that they had taken the decision to cancel the vote that had been announced.

Cullmann (and also Boegner and Thurian, whom I saw for a few seconds on the way out) were also rather affected by the *modi* that came from the Pope in the *De oecumenismo*. Several are entirely anodyne, but there are also three or four that are bad. The last retracts what had been recognised in the Eucharist of Protestants. Another speaks of what they are LOOKING FOR, and no longer of what they FIND in the Scriptures. As Cullmann said, if it had been worded like this from the beginning, it would be passable. But since there have been other, more favourable expressions, these changes had the appearance of a retreat and a hardening. It is more serious. It is no longer said that the Eastern Churches have *'ius et officium se secundum proprias disciplinas regendi'* [the right and duty of governing themselves according to their own disciplines] but only *facultatem* s[the ability]. The Pope (for it comes from him) wants the Eastern Churches to depend on him and not have, of themselves, an internal right of self-government.— The whole thing clearly debases the *De oecumenismo*, and impairs what was rather good about it: its unhesitating, unreserved ecumenical SPIRIT. Now, a little of what is given is taken back in the very moment of giving it: hesitations are introduced in the very movement that is made towards the others.

It is undeniable that this morning was CATASTROPHIC from the point of view of the ecumenical climate. It is obvious that the Pope makes grand, symbolic gestures, but that, behind these, there is neither the theology nor the concrete understanding of the things that these gestures invoke.

A crowd of people asked me what I thought. I said that I still go on hoping; that for religious freedom, everything could be retrieved tomorrow, and that, over all, this shows that the work has scarcely begun! Everything, or almost everything, remains to be done.

A visit from Fr Legrand[1] about his thesis. A subject I gave him eighteen months ago: the relation between ecclesial communion and Eucharistic communion.

At midday I saw Fr Seumois for a moment. He is one of the experts charged with the redoing of the *De Missionibus*. He told me that Cardinal Agagianian had totally failed to understand the meaning of the vote. He remembered nothing

---

1. Hervé-Marie Legrand, OP, of the Province of France; his lectorate thesis was entitled: *Essai sur les rapports entre l'Église et l'eucharistie selon l'Écriture et, principalement, selon les expressions qu'en donnent les rites et les institutions.* He was later to become a professor at the Catholic Institute in Paris (in the Faculties of Theology and Canon Law); a recognised ecclesiologist, he was to share in the work of the International Catholic-Lutheran Commission, and in numerous instances of ecumenical research.

save the ironical comment of one Father that the mountain had gone into labour and brought forth a mouse. He holds obstinately (as also, it appears, do the Germans) to the idea that identifies MISSIONS with a specific territory still coming under Propaganda. In the Commission, which is poor, it seems, they reject the category of 'young Churches'. Furthermore, they do not see the connection of the missions with the temporal sphere, with social changes. Finally, the work is very poorly organised. So I intend to bring up the example of the Theological Commission at tomorrow's meeting. There would need to be a good secretary. Fr Seumois told me he was willing to take that on.

At 4.30 pm, at RAI, for French TV this time, with Haubtmann, Bourdarias.[1] We did not go on air until 6.30 pm. THIS IS THE LAST TIME I SHALL CONSENT TO SPEAK ON RAI. Two afternoons wasted when, at present, every SECOND counts.

The news about the cardinals' approach to the Pope is that the Pope declines to intervene. This morning's decision was taken by the Council of Presidents; it is for them to do what they think ought to be done.

This evening, Mgr Garrone and I recalled the history of the *De Ecclesia*. I called to mind the visit Mgr Philips made to me during the First Session: he tried to put together again a *De Ecclesia* sthat was more organic and better oriented, while making extensive use of the text of the earlier one . . . Ottaviani was very dismissive of it . . . Mgr Garrone told how Philips' *De Ecclesia* had been taken as the working text. That was in February 1963. Only eighteen months ago . . . There were in contention Philips' text, a text from Parente, a Chilean plan, a German plan and some French propositions. Cardinal Ottaviani had appointed, or caused to be appointed, a small sub-commission of seven members to study the matter of which was to be chosen as a working text: Browne, Léger, Garrone, Parente, Charue and two others. They met at the Holy Office. They were ushered into a room where Cardinal Ottaviani was seated at the end of a table. Ottaviani said to them: there is an excellent text, that of Mgr Parente, which meets all the requests voiced *in aula*. I am expecting you to defend it . . . Then he went out. Cardinal Browne took the chair in his place and said: *'Bene. Quid faciemus?'* [Good. What are we going to do?]. In the end, a vote was taken. This resulted in five votes for Philips' text and two for Parente's. At the plenary meeting of the Theological Commission, Ottaviani presented Parente's text as the one adopted. But Browne said: no, there was a vote . . . —Ottaviani protested, saying that the sub-commission had gone beyond its remit, but he had to admit that it had been appointed IN ORDER to choose a working text . . . So Ottaviani said no more, and the history commenced of the *De Ecclesia* that was voted by the assembly this morning. I have noted its stages, so far as I knew them, at the relevant times.

---

1. Jean Bourdarias covered the Council as religious affairs commentator at Radio-Luxembourg.

Friday 20 November 1964

129th General Congregation: the last before the public and final sitting. It appears that when the Pope received the cardinals all together yesterday evening, Cardinal Frings raised the question of the vote on freedom. The Pope maintained his position: that is the business of the Council of Presidents. But the Pope spoke about the reform of the Curia, and asked the cardinals to give him their suggestions.

The *De presbyteris, De Revelatione, De oecumenismo* were distributed. The Fathers were asked for their comments on the *De presbyteris* before 31 January 1965.

The vote on marriage will have this content: to give to the Pope, with the comments of the Fathers, the responsibility for promulgating the law, with the help of the competent departments. I note that this was simply a *votum.* sSo that's the meaning of this term *'votum'.*[1]

Today the vote was taken on the Eastern churches:

Voters present:	2,104
Placet:	1,964
Non placet:	135

On the *De oecumenismo:*

Voters present:	2,129
Placet:	2,054
Non placet:	64 + 5 null

De Ecclesiae habitudine ad religiones non-christianis [on the relation of the Church to non-Christian religions]:

Partial votes

Voters present:	1,987	1,986
Placet:	1,838	1,770
Non placet:	136	185
	+4 and 9	+7 and 7

Total and final vote:

Voters present:	1,996
Placet:	1,651
Non placet:	99
Placet iuxta modum:	242 + 4 null

---

1. Cf, above, page 626, note 2.

De Matrimonii Sacramento:[1]

Voters present:	2,024
Placet (thus in favour of leaving the matter to the Pope):	1,592
Non placet:	427
Placet iuxta modum:	2 +3 null

The discussion of the *De matrimonio* continued.

Before this, Cardinal Tisserant read out a statement:[2] many of the Fathers have asked the Pope that the Session not end without a vote being taken, one way or the another, on the *De libertate*. But the opportunity that exists for the text to be able to be studied seriously does not permit this. It will be discussed at the next Session, even as a matter of priority.

Numerous declarations on mixed marriages:

Döpfner,[3] Ritter,[4] Heenan,[5] Charrière[6] were approving of the new dispositions.

Mgr Riobé asked to see me with Zoa and Fr Seumois. Mgr Sartre could not be found. This is the situation. Yesterday, Cardinal Agagianian made it known that he did not want me called to the Commission as a conciliar expert. Mgr Riobé could consult me as a private expert . . . Now:

1) At the meeting of the Commission *De Missionibus* a few days ago, Agagianian had said that three experts should be chosen. Then he left. In his absence, the Commission unanimously agreed on these three names: Neuner, Ratzinger, Congar. —And now Agagianian dismisses me and wants Reuter in my place, Reuter, who was more or less dismissed from the Commission on Missions and then came to the Theological Commission and even to the sub-commission for *De populo Dei*. He is nothing but a canonist, aligned with the Congregation and with Agagiaian;

2) The Congregation and the Cardinal have this idea: mission is a matter of territory. Missions are those churches that are under Propaganda. For the Church to be in a state of mission means supporting Propaganda;

3) The Commission did not give the Fathers the text of the comments made *in aula*, or submitted in writing, but only some comments connected with the schema, as kinds of *modi*. This was because its idea was not to touch the structure of the schema, but simply to improve it with regard to detail. Agagianian is dismissing me *BECAUSE* he did not want a new schema, that was theological and with a different orientation, he did not want a text with some life in it.

It is a matter of importance: not about me personally, but about the cause of Mission and the chances of a new, worthwhile schema. Fr Seumois, who was prepared to remain in Rome FOR this work, said that if I am expelled he will resign.

---

1. This was the *votum* referred to on page 226, note 2.
2. *AS* III/VIII, 554–555.
3. *AS* III/VIII, 626–627.
4. *AS* III/VIII, 629–631.
5. *AS* III/VIII, 658–659.
6. *AS* III/VIII, 654–656.

Mgr Riobé thinks it better that I should not go to the meeting this evening. It is agreed that Zoa and he, who are isolated there (except that they form a group with Mgr Sartre) will speak strongly RESTING THEIR CASE ON THE REGULATION, WHICH IS CATEGORICAL.

I said: yes, I won't come, but if you win your case about me, telephone me, and I will be there in a quarter of an hour. Because I would immediately take my place and position.

I went for a moment to say goodbye to the Observers.

Arrighi and others from the Secretariat told me: yesterday evening, at 9.30 pm, the Pope still wanted to make some modification to the *De oecumenismo.* And Felici did not want to put on the cover: 'to be voted on in the public Congregation of 21 November 1964'. He said: perhaps there will be 400 *Non placet!* —There were in fact sixty-four . . .

A bit later on, Fr Duprey told me that on Thursday 19 November he saw Mgr Dell'Acqua in the morning, as he had seen him once or twice each day during the Council. Mgr Dell'Acqua said to him: the *De oecumenismo* will be for the next Session; not for this time. There are some changes. These were the forty *modi,* half of which (the most dangerous) the Pope has crossed out, and of which there remain the nineteen that have been made known to us. So it was accepted by the Curia that the *De oecumenismo* would be put off until later . . . stogether with the text on religious freedom. Fr Duprey said that these *modi* were being attributed to Frs Boyer and Ciappi.

Obviously, the Session will end with a sense of half-failure. To members of the Secretariat who asked me what I felt, I said: the decree *De oecumenismo* has, as it were, lost its virginity, or a measure of purity . . .

Mgr Riobé came to see me this evening after the meeting of the Commission on Missions. There had been no experts there. Fr Reuter was there, but he was made to leave. Straightaway, Mgr Riobé had tackled the matter of my designation as an expert by the unanimous decision of the members of the sub-commission— and not a private expert, but a CONCILIAR one. Agagianian did not deny this, but said that his reaction had been justified by the fear that he had had that the new experts would eliminate the old ones. But, he said, why make a change, why bring in others, why Fr Congar?—Because one of the complaints made about the *De Missionibus* was that it should have a theological foundation. But Fr Congar has been on the Theological Commission, on the *De Ecclesia,* and he has the confidence of Cardinal Ottaviani and of the Pope.

In short, I was admitted. A date was fixed for working in Paris, 13 December, with Mgr Riobé and Fr Seumois.

The Commission will meet again, starting on 12 January 1965. Alas! Precisely my week for Unity . . .

What shall I do ?

In the evening, at 9.30 pm, a lecture to the Catholic Laureati [graduates][1] of Rome on the outcomes of the Third Session. —Afterwards, a Mgr Del Giudice,[2]

---

1. The *Laureati* movement brought together Italian Catholic Intellectuals.
2. At that time there were several Monsignori with the name Del Guidice, but none at the

of the Holy Office, asked me unpleasant questions in an unpleasant manner: why, since some errors do exist, is the Council not condemning them? And he cited, insistently, Marxism, existentialism, dogmatic relativism . . .

Saturday 21 November 1964

Cardinal Frings made an approach to the Pope to tell him about his unease over a proclamation of Mary as *Mater Ecclesiae*. The Pope replied to him. It seems that there will simply be a sermon along pious lines this afternoon, at St Mary Major: nothing this morning in the proclamation of the *De Ecclesia*.

So we have, indeed, reached the end. I have packed my bags: more than forty kilos heavier than when I arrived. We have received so much paper!!! So behind with everything, I could well have stayed home to push on a bit further with the writing of my contribution to the volume *Église et Pauvreté* that I have begun. It was for a mystical reason that I decided to go to St Peter's this morning: to participate in the grace and the occasion of the Council at its most decisive moment. This time, there is no dogma. There will be neither the legend nor the mystique of a Pius IX illuminated by a ray of sunshine at the moment when he declared himself infallible. But there will be the two great acts of proclamation of the *De Ecclesia* and the *De oecumenismo*. I wanted to participate in that at the top, just as I had at the bottom—and in the splendour, as I had participated in the sweat and the tears.

Strasbourg, 22 November 1964

I forgot (left behind) in Rome the previous notebook of this journal. So I am copying out on a loose sheet the notes I took during yesterday morning's ceremony. At St Peter's at 8.45 am. I had an excellent place, very close to the Confession, among the Observers. While waiting, I had a conversation with Fr Corbon.[1] A theological conversation. However, a few details in passing. The twenty or so *modi* introduced into the *De oecumenismo* came from Fr Ciappi. I must say this does not surprise me. Fr Ciappi is a poor and petty soul, for whom the papal system, understood in the most literally unyielding and limited manner, is an absolute, which occupies the ENTIRE space. There is nothing else. The psychological and moral elements, so decisive in ecumenism, do not exist. HE IGNORES THEM. It appears, too, that Cardinal Tisserant wanted to postpone the Declaration on Non-Christian Religions, along with that on Religious Freedom. It was Cardinal Lercaro who succeeded in getting it voted on.

Every light they could possibly have there was turned on. Incredible décor of red and gilt. The ambassadors and their wives arrived, led by Noble Guards

---

Holy Office.

1. Jean Corbon, member of the Dominican Third Order, worked in the Near East in the areas of Islamology and Ecumenism; he was an interpreter for the Orthodox Observers at the Council.

in black velvet doublets and French breeches with a kind of Golden Fleece and multiple decorations. The fancy for décor, for theatre, for grand ceremony was triumphant everywhere in that place. The pontifical procession entered, there were heads that Dreyer would have made something of. There was no tiara: not only not on the Pope's head, but not even in the hands of the insignia bearers, but simply a mitre. The Pope was on the *sedia*, but there was singing and no applause. The Sistine choir sang well, but more or less anything at any moment. During the consecration, instead of listening, in the silence of a general recollection, to the words pronounced by the twenty-five concelebrants, there was a blare of (silver?) trumpets that was totally out of place. Apart from that, the celebration was beautiful and solemn. However, with concelebration, the communion, by itself, lasted as long as the rest of the Mass. After Mass, the *Adsumus*, the *Veni Creator,* alternating with the Sistine choir, which turned the verses into beautiful music—the votes. Felici read out the beginning and end of the eight chapters of the *De Ecclesia,* of the three of the *De Ecclesiis orientalibus,* and finally of the *De oecumenismo.* The votes were as follows:

    De Ecclesia: (result announced at 11.32 am):
        Placet: 2,151   *non placet*   5
    De Ecclesiis orientalibus
        Placet: 2,140   *non place*   38
    De oecumenismo
        Placet: 2,137   *non placet*:   11

There followed the Pope's speech:[1] thirty-seven minutes. I did not see in it the inspiration, the vitality, of his previous speeches. He spoke about Chapter III of *De Ecclesia*, emphasising the good balance achieved. He spoke—without warmth— about the *De oecumenismo.* He did not say a word about *De Ecclesiis orientalibus.* On the other hand, for a quarter of an hour he gave a very devout eulogy of the Virgin Mary. Though his text contained little substance, he spoke at length, then he turned to using words like '*declaramus*' [we declare] and announced the title *Mater Ecclesiae*. The seven protonotaries, sitting just near me, stood up: so also the two cardinals assisting the Pope, the other cardinals, almost all the bishops. The enthusiastic applause was very strongly supported by the mob of insignia-bearers and the various members of the papal court. They gave the impression of believing that the Pope had just made a dogmatic definition. But a definition OF WHAT? What is the CONTENT of '*Mater Ecclesiae*' ???

    The Observers have a very bad impression of these last two days and of this final act. They saw, and we saw with them, that no account had been taken of them, that the demands of a true ecumenical sensibility had not been observed. Cullmann said: 'It will take two generations to efface this and cause it to be forgot-

---

1. *AS* III/VIII, 909–918.

ten'. At the airport, on the plane, and at Zurich, Shlink was downcast. He told me he was *'sehr traurig'* [very sad] and that the schema was *'sehr entwertet'* [very impoverished] by the *modi* added. Cardinal Döpfner and the Bishop of Rottenburg[1] were equally very much saddened. The session ended badly. I said: they threw ashes on our flowers and then, afterwards, they throw flowers on the ashes!!! For my part, I stand back a bit, detach myself from the blunt reality of what has happened, from the restiveness and the excitation of these last days. I am getting things back into proportion. I see more clearly that certain circumstances, certain imponderables were in play, had come together to produce this result. But, looking at things coolly, what took place is VERY serious. We have gone back several years. THE SEPARATED BRETHREN HAVE GONE BACK TO HAVING DOUBTS ABOUT US. And one sees that, among ourselves, almost nothing is being done since so few people REALISE this. We will not be able to win back what has been lost except by the path of ABSOLUTE HONESTY. On the other hand, I tell myself, without this sowing of enemy seed among the wheat of our hope, OUR victory would have been too complete. It would indeed have been a victory of one group over the other. The Pope, who is the man for all, wanted to give satisfaction to all. But in doing this he has come to appear like someone who cannot be fully trusted. Once again, he has neither the theology, nor the intellectual backing for his gestures.

I ask myself what is to be done. I know that, whatever I tell myself, there will be only one conclusion for me: the work has to be done. The check we have come up against indicates the limit of what our work has achieved. But overburdened, literally crushed, living constantly way beyond my strength, I ask myself what is it better to do, to what should I bend my efforts by way of priority? I am overloaded with a heap of things. Otherwise, I think that the history of ecclesiology should have first priority. It alone will break the deadlock for certain questions, by showing where this or the other position comes from.

The ceremony in St Peter's ended about 12.45 or 12.50 pm. A hurried lunch; the plane was to leave at 3.10 pm; in fact it left thirty-five minutes late. On the plane to Zurich, via Geneva, were several Germans, including Schlink, Cardinal Döpfner, Cardinal Rugambwa, the Bishop of Rottenburg.

Reached the Priory at 11.00 pm. I have never been more exhausted, with a very bad headache, which I still have today, Sunday.

Once back in Strasbourg I had a crushing amount of work. During the session I had not let up FOR A SECOND. Back home I had to work three times as hard. I would need six months before Christmas to get through what I HAVE to do!

First I must sort out my papers, then, when my trunk has arrived, sort out the contents of that.

Clear the stock of correspondence, of papers that have arrived in my absence.

---

1. Karl J Leiprecht.

Write a chapter for the volume on poverty: the chapter the text of which I took to Fr Henry when I went to Paris on 30 November[1] for the colloquium for *Parole et Mission*.[2] But I have still got two chapters to write for the same volume.

After 15 November,[3] I started on a plan for the schema *De Missionibus*, which I presented to Mgr Riobé and Fr X Seumois in Paris on 13 December. For this I had to make a detailed study of a certain number of documents, conciliar and otherwise.

This work was followed through here in Strasbourg with Fr Seumois, Fr Kaufmann,[4] and Fr Glazik, of Münster, on 19 and 20 December.[5] A plan was agreed (for the theological part = mine) during an exchange of some interesting remarks about the content. Fr Glazik was won over to our ideas.

Mgr Riobé told me that my presence was indispensable at THE BEGINNING of the session of the Commission in Rome (starting on the morning of 12 January, so the evening of 11 January 1965). He himself intervened to ask Fr Le Guillou to replace me in my lectures in Brussels, Liège, Louvain, Fribourg. This has been done. But all this had to be arranged = dozens of letters!!!

I prepared and gave various lectures. The one on sciences and theology for the Latin-American Week[6] required a good deal of tedious work. But I had already written my lecture on Church and World, which I have sent to *Esprit*,[7] to *Aggiornamenti Sociali* of Milan,[8] and to my Polish confrères, whom I try to help a bit.

After that I put the finishing touches to my volume on the Third Session,[9] in which *Church and World* is to be published. I wrote the note on the priesthood of women, a new page on religious freedom, and finally '*Les derniers jours de la session*' [the last days of the Session], which I have also sent to *ICI* and to *De Bazuin*.[10]

I have written some comments on the theological chapter of schema XIII that Mgr Garrone asked me for: I took them to him on 14 December, at the meeting of bishops and pastors, during which I gave a presentation about the Council's *De oecumenismo*.

It was that evening of 14 December [between the above-mentioned meeting, which finished at 4.30 pm, and this lecture, that I recorded my text for the Latin-American Week, then I was at Cerf for dinner and to deal with various questions

---

1. {Although this part of the diary is recorded for 22 November, it is plain that it was written up some time before Christmas 2004}.
2. Missionary journal, cf above, page 471, note 4.
3. Congar added a question mark to the typescript here.
4. The Swiss, Leonhard Kaufmann, of the White Fathers.
5. Joseph Glazik, MSC, missiologist, was Director of the Institute of Missiology at the University of Münster; he was a Council expert.
6. Yves Congar, 'Théologie et sciences humaines', *Esprit*, July–August, 1965: 121–137.
7. Yves Congar, 'Église et Monde', *Esprit*, February, 1965: 337–359.
8. 'Chiesa e mondo', *Aggiornamenti Sociali*, February, 1965.
9. *Le Concile au jour le jour. Troisième session* (Paris: Cerf, 1965).
10. A weekly journal published by the Dutch Dominicans.

with Fr Bro] that I gave that lecture at the *Mutualité*, which an integrist commando tried to interrupt and sabotage.[1]

I wrote the Introduction to the *De oecumenismo* requested by Elchlinger for the Centurion edition.[2]

I revised the translation of the constitution *De Ecclesia* made by Fr Camelot.[3] There were some mistakes and omissions. I also had to prepare the notes of the Latin text for a French translation. I wrote a brief foreword.

I prepared my lecture for Turin (16 January 1965) in order to send the outline requested by the organisers.

I TYPED and put the finishing touches to the notes, masses of them, for my contribution to the collection of essays for Chenu.

I wrote the ten pages requested by Mgr Molari for a commentary on certain paragraphs of *De Ecclesia* (Nos 30–33, and 48). I could not have refused him that!

I wrote nine pages of introduction to the enormous collection prepared by Fr Baraúna,[4] the French version of which I am to publish in 'Unam Sanctam'.

I read the manuscript proposed by Dom De Vooght for 'Unam Sanctam',[5] and wrote a brief introductory note.[6]

I wrote and had typed, and then revised, my chapter on 'Schism and heresy',[7] compiled with a view to *Mysterium Salutis* (Feiner's project), in order to propose this text to Fr Dumont—in the same way as I had sent my introduction to the *De oecumenismo* to the journal *Quatember*.[8]

And then—correspondence, correspondence, correspondence.

Every day—twice a day,

My cross.

On the morning of 24 December, I began the Latin DRAFT of the theological part of the *De Missionibus*, the pastoral part of which Fr Seumois is drafting.

---

1. Lecture organised by the CCIF on the assessment of the Third Session.
2. This refers in fact to Charles Ehlinger, at that time editor at Centurion. Yves M-J Congar, 'Introduction' in *Concile Vatican II: L'Église, L'Oecuménisme, Les Églises orientales* (Centurion, 1965), 165–192.
3. Cf *L'Église de Vatican II: La Constitution dogmatique sur L'Église 'Lumen Gentium'*, 'Unam Sanctam', 51a (Paris: Cerf, 1966).
4. The reference is, in fact, to his conclusion to *A Igreja do Concilio Vaticano Segundo* (Rio de Janeiro, 1965); his original version appeared later: 'En guise de conclusion', in Guilherme Baraúna and Yves M-J Congar (eds), *L'Église de Vatican II. Études autour de la Constitution conciliaire sur l'Église*, 'Unam Sanctam', 51c (Paris: Cerf, 1966), 1365–1373.
5. Cf Paul De Vooght, *Les Pouvoirs du concile et l'autorité du pape au concile de Constance*, 'Unam Sanctam', 56 (Paris: Cerf, 1965).
6. This refers to a foreword signed by 'the editors', without further precision, in which they distance themselves to some degree from the theses of the author.
7. 'Les ruptures de l'unité', *Istina* 1964: 133–178, reprinted in Yves Congar, *L'Église une, sainte, catholique, et apostolique*, 'Mysterium Salutis', 15 (Paris, Cerf, 1970), 65–121.
8. 'Zum Dekret über den Oekumenismus', *Quatember*, Ostern, 1965: 82–85.

I am copying out these notes on Christmas Eve.

God help me! I can't do any more!

There is still nothing known about the date of the Fourth Session. Liégé reported the rumour: Spring 1966. I had already heard that. I don't know what it's worth. Neither the bishops nor Mgr Gouet knew anything on 14 December.

After all this there still remain untouched:

- the preparation of the volume on collegiality (for 'Unam Sanctam'[1]) and if possible, its completion by a preface and by a study on collegiality in the Middle Ages. I have had ALL the manuscripts for a month, except that of Dom Dupont, who has not yet got his baggage from Rome, sent by express;

- the WRITING of the volume of commentary on the *De Ecclesia*!!![2]

25 December 1964

I preached in the cathedral and saw Mgr Elchinger for a moment. He told me:

1) that he was soon going to see Mgr Colombo and Fr Bevilacqua (thus people who are close to the Pope); 2) that he knows NOTHING about the Fourth Session; 3) that Haubtmann has been appointed Secretary for schema XIII, replacing Fr Häring (I said: he should be seconded by Philips!); 4) that Mgr Elchinger had recently seen the minister for National Education, Christian Fouchet, who said to him: 'you are doing a bad job at the Council. You are calling everything into question. What was true yesterday is no longer true today . . . '

In fact, the press (Fesquet), to some degree looking for the sensational and wanting to give a shove to the renewal, has given something of this impression. They too often present as the word OF THE COUNCIL everything that is said there . . .

29 December 1964

This morning, at 10.00 am, I finished typing and revising a plan for *De activitate missionali Ecclesiae I. Pars theologica.* [on the missionary activity of the Church. I. Theological Part].

6 January 1965

I saw Mgr Elchinger briefly, because he came with his secretary to record my comments on the *De presbyteris, De libertate, De religionibus non-christianis*, schema XIII, for the meeting of the bishops of the East at Sainte-Odile, in which I shall not be able to take part, as I shall be in Rome. He told me:

The bishops have just received a Christmas letter from the Pope, all about collegiality. The Pope is convinced, intellectually.

---

1. Cf *La Collégialité épiscopale*, 'Unam Sanctam', 52 (Paris: Cerf, 1965).
2. Cf Guilherme Baraúna and Yves M-J Congar, (eds) *L'Église de Vatican II, Études autour de la Constitution conciliaire sur l'Église*, 'Unam Sanctam', 51 b and c (Paris: Cerf, 1966).

According to Mgr Colombo, whom Mgr Elchinger saw a week ago at Assisi: it was Fr Boyer who was behind the Pope's *modi* on ecumenism. The Pope was very much astonished by the emotion stirred up by these *modi*. He had no idea of the psychological state of the Council. But, Colombo said, it was the fault of the Secretariat: the text of the *De oecumenismo* had not been communicated to the Pope in the way that the text of the *De Ecclesia* had been. So he was late in communicating his reaction.

Fr Bevilacqua (eighty-six years old, a former teacher of the Pope) is VERY cross about Staffa.

The Pope, it appears, is not taken in by the requests and reports with which he is assailed by the integrists. He knows what this represents, and how little.

Mgr Elchinger, in response to his greetings to the Nuncio,[1] received from him a rather dry letter—which he did not show to Mgr Weber. The Nuncio warned him: the others must not be excluded, those who think differently . . . ; one must not cut oneself off from one's predecessors, say the opposite to them . . .

Is this an allusion to an intervention at the Council when Mgr Elchinger asked for the rehabilitation of Galileo? It appears that the Pope might be amenable to such a step. He was impressed by a letter from non-Christian Japanese scholars asking for a gesture along these lines, because, they said, this would have a symbolic value. I passed this information on to Fr Dubarle this very evening.[2]

Yesterday evening it became known that the Fourth and last (phew!!!) Session of the Council will open on 14 September 1965.

11 January 1965

Since my return to Strasbourg on 22 November 1964, I have had a crushing load of work. I have never worked less than thirteen hours a day. And also an enormous amount of correspondence: the past few days as many as twenty-one letters in A SINGLE delivery. Nevertheless, yesterday, 10 January, I sorted a great deal of papers, which tired me terribly. I had to make several attempts to get on to the platform at the railway station with my luggage.

At Mulhouse, a buffet dinner with Brothers Gobert and Lacoste.[3] I found them very isolated and as though rootless.

A lecture (fairly good).

Monday morning, 11 January, a lecture at the Capuchin Fathers at Hirsingue. Also fairly good. They drove me to the airport of Basle-Mulhouse, where we arrived at 10.30 am. But what a business!! The Zurich airport was out of action:

---

1. P Bertoli.
2. Dominique Dubarle, OP, of the Province of France, a physician and a philosopher, taught philosophy at Le Saulchoir and the philosophy of science at the Catholic Institute of Paris; he was appointed a Council expert during the Third Session, and was to work on the chapter on peace during the last Session.
3. Daniel Gobert and Pierre Lacoste, OP, of the Province of France, were worker-priests at Mulhouse.

black ice. All planes were landing here, at Basle. One arrived every ten minutes, from all over the place. The waiting room, already so inferior and so uncomfortable, was full of groups speaking different languages, with women sometimes very badly dressed, with ridiculous hats. The confusion was indescribable. The staff were overwhelmed and knew nothing. The loud-speakers never stopped making announcements or calling people. It was atrociously painful and that completely exhausted me. There were two (Dutch) bishops there who were returning to Indonesia, with an expert. Smoking strong cigars, they took all this quite philosophically. In their part of the world, one has weeks to spare. Nothing arrives, or very little, and with enormous delay. Out there, they still haven't received information about the Third Session. In order to arrive in time they have to set out two months in advance, not knowing when there will be a boat. One of them, on his island, gets post (by boat) only once a month, and not always even then. In order to say his first Mass in his home village, a priest spent three months on the journey, even though it was in the same diocese.

I had no notion of all this! It made me blush at my impatience. But that was consonant with my rhythm of work. I had just come from working like a maniac for six weeks, without wasting a second, and Swissair made me stupidly waste five hours!

We did not leave until 4.00 pm, instead of 11.25 am, but direct for Rome without stopping in Zurich. A rather bumpy flight.

Arrived at Fiumicino at 5.30 pm. The chauffeur of Fr Schütte,[1] General of the Divine Word Fathers, was waiting for me: 'better late than never', he said.

With the Divine Word Fathers, overlooking Lake Nemi. A magnificent house of forty, very comfortable, rooms. An excellent welcome: aperitifs, cigars. How poor and austere we are in comparison with all this. Nearly everyone arrived shortly after me (see attached list). We were introduced. We spoke mainly in French and German. Mgr Zoa, always so magnificently free, intelligent and frank, spoke of his agony about the situation in Africa. The Chinese are everywhere and spread their ultra-simple slogans among the people: 'it is the fault of the Americans, the French, the Westerners, the Catholic Church.' They make use of any and every means to overcome the barriers that still restrain them: now the rulers, whom they soemimes bribe, now the unions, now the nationalist parties. It seems that the Congo will soon collapse into complete chaos, and one absolutely cannot see what might be done to prevent this. It seems that within ten years Africa will be a land of fearful dramas and confrontations.

The atmosphere of our first meeting was good. We will see what it is like tomorrow.

---

1. Johann Schütte, titular bishop, Superior General of the Society of the Divine Word, member of the Commission for Missions, elected during the Second Session of the Council.

Waiting for me on my table were some 'Suggestions for a new schema', by a Fr Legrand,[1] a plan from Fr Neuner, who is here, always very nervous (and talked to us about India, about Bombay), and some *Considerationes* concerning the theological foundation of the Missions, by Ratzinger (in Latin). That will have to be studied.

Tuesday 12 January 1965

First working session, from 9.00 am to 1.00 pm. Fr Schütte briefly presented the present drafts: that of Mgr Lokuang (with Grasso[2]), of Fr Peeters, OFM,[3] of Riobé-Congar-Seumois-Glazik, the plan of Fr Neuner, to which was added the text from the Missionary Religious Superiors. We spoke in Latin, Italian and French. I stuck to Latin. We discussed Mission in both the strict and the broad sense: the missionaries wanted us to stick to the strict sense. I supported Neuner's suggestion: that we should speak successively about the mission of the Church, which is one:
- the missionary situation in the strict sense: in places where people are not yet evangelised;
- the even more precise situation, where the Church does not have in itself all the resources and where the people have not got the resources of the Church at their disposal.

To all intents and purposes, my text was accepted, and we began to discuss some points, without much order, in particular the opposition (insoluble here below) between the salvation of individuals without the formal intervention of the Church, and the Church as the necessary, positive means of salvation [but necessary, *non natura sua, sed ex institutione* [not by its nature, but by institution]].

In the afternoon we waited for Cardinal Agagianian. He arrived about 4.30 pm. Fr Peeters read a report of what had been done this morning. The cardinal made a speech in favour of the STRICT sense of mission. For him, the point of the schema is to stimulate missionary vocations and financial assistance.

We went on to the work to which the evening meeting was to be devoted: discussion of the plan to be followed in the second, pastoral and practical part of the schema. Fr Seumois explained at length the order of ideas in his text. Mgr Lokuang explained his plan.

The cardinal, before he left, a little before 6.00 pm, reverted to his fear that by giving a broad concept of mission, one would turn aside the attention and the efforts of missions directed towards the pagans. We reassured him. The order to be followed in this third part was discussed, but the session closed at 6.50 pm,

---

1. François Legrand, a Belgian Scheutist, former missionary in China, editor of the missionary journal *Le Christ au Monde.*
2. The Neopolitan Jesuit Domenico Grasso, Professor of Pastoral Theology at the Gregorianum, was a Council expert.
3. Hermes Peeters, OFM, Consultor at the Congregation of Propaganda, was a Council expert, and assistant secretary to the Commission for Missions.

without this having been fully clarified. For this, the texts of Seumois, Lokuang and Peeters will need to be read with care.

This evening, overlooking the lake encircled by the lights of the town and the road, I thought of how I should have been in Brussels and, at that very moment, speaking there. Until the Council finishes, I shall miss a lot of opportunities. But we must work where the priority of duty places us.

Apart from this, we have perfect comfort here, and no less perfect service. I am beginning to give in to the satisfaction of all this. The Divine Word Fathers, who are German in origin, and whose members are still 38% German (followed by the USA), have the abundance of plain food and the huge coffees customary in the Nordic countries. Their Superior General, Fr Schütte, is a dynamic man, precise, very pleasant socially, and very attentive to his guests.

Wednesday 13 January 1965

In the morning, work in a small sub-commission with Mgr Lecuona,[1] Mgr Riobé and Frs Neuner and Grasso, on my chapter, while the others were working on the *Proemium*. We saw how to deal satisfactorily with the eight or ten points raised yesterday, and we began to correct the text. I have to draft two new sections—I am going to start on this straightaway.

Afternoon. We looked again at: 1) texts or bits of text already reworked; 2) the theological chapter as a whole. This revision resulted in the need to rework some small pieces again.

Current forecasts:

The schema will be submitted to the Commission, which will meet to discuss it on 22 March: it will be necessary to return to Rome for that. After that it will be sent to the bishops, who should submit their comments by the end of April: comments will be examined in mid-May.

For schema XIII, Mgr Glorieux telephoned me to say that it will be necessary TO HASTEN THE WORK.

The session on 14 September will follow this order: religious freedom; schema XIII (new discussion); *De missionali activitate* (new discussion); *De Presbyteris* (new discussion).

Yesterday evening, I saw Fr Le Bourgeois,[2] Superior General of the Eudists, who is a member of the Commission for Religious. He told me that there are more than 15,000 *modi* for the schema, of which 750 are completely different. He

---

1. José Lecuona Labandibar, titular bishop, Superior General of the Spanish Institute of St Francis Xavier for the Foreign Missions, Vice-President of the Commission for the Missions.
2. Armand FM Le Bourgeois, Superior General of the Congregation of Jesus and Mary (Eudists), was a Council expert, and assistant secretary of the Commission for Religious. He was to become Bishop of Autun in 1966.

had spent a month sorting through and classifying all these. The Commission meets on Monday.

It appears that it was Cardinals Cicognani and Confalonieri who insisted at the Co-ordinating Commission that the schemas should be reduced to propositions. They made a very grave mistake.

Fr Peeters, a member of the OFM General Curia, who has information about the Custody of the Holy Land, told me that ten parishes have gone over to Orthodoxy in reaction to the Declaration on the Jews. The Orthodox Patriarch enticed them, saying: WE are total strangers to this declaration; WE did not even want to send observers to this political and philosemitic Council.

C Moeller, who has now (11 January 1965) returned from Jerusalem said to me: it is false that some Catholic parishes have gone over to Orthodoxy. It is true that the Orthodox are very worked up against the Jews, and that they dissociate themselves entirely from the conciliar declaration.

Thursday 14 January 1965

Work. We finished the *Proemium* and Chapter I. This evening, I got an example of the reactions of Mgr Lokuang. He can be a real mule, not listening to anything, stubborn, not changing from his reaction, even when it is beside the point!!

Friday 15 January 1965

I began to draw up a *relatio* on Chapter I, because I must leave tomorrow morning.

We began the discussion of the second, practical, part. Somewhat confused discussion at first, from which it emerged, however, that the most delicate point is to know where to put the FORMATION of indigenous clergy. On the one hand, they should have the same formation as all the rest of the clergy (Mgr Zoa was insistent on this), and on the other, it should still be missionary in the strict sense and not be without adaptation, despite a formation inevitably influenced by the West. On the other hand, missionaries coming from outside (missionaries in the strict sense) do not come just to act as missionaries *ad pagano* [to pagans], but also to take on, in the young Churches, some normal pastoral tasks of the Church, in keeping with their own formation (seminaries, Catholic Action etc).

In the end, there was agreement on a division into three chapters, which I propose to entitle:

I *De opere missionali et eius exigentiis* [on missionary work and its requirements]

II *De institutionibus et operariis ad opus missionale destinatis* [on institutions and workers destined for missionary work]

III *De cooperatione universali* [on international co-operation]

And our sub-commission was divided into three corresponding sub-commissions:

1) Zoa, Schütte, Seumois, Neuner
2) Lokuang, Lecuona, Glazik
3) Riobé, Grasso, Peeters

I continued and finished my *relatio*, which I typed at the beginning of the afternoon. It was read in the evening. There was agreement on the content of the three chapters, and on the distribution of the material within each.

I finished reading a book lent me by Mgr Riobé. Michael Serafian, *Le Pèlerin. Les secrets du concile.*[1] Certainly, it is a book to read from beginning to end, even though it is long and sometimes tedious. It is in the same vein as Rynne (= Murphy[2]). The author poses as a former diplomat, but he is certainly a cleric. (It appears, actually, that he is an unfrocked American Jesuit, who at one point took up with the wife of Mr Kaiser,[3] an American journalist at the Council.) The book annoys me because it seems to me that, while saying a good number of things that are true, it yet distorts the truth. It politicises everything. It finds in the smallest things ulterior motives, intentions, connections with grand (or petty!) politics. Now, we know that 'the *per accidens* [accidental] is the father of many of our actions', that the Council was never properly conceived and directed. The author gives Cardinal Bea a role which he did not have to that extent. And also to Fr Courtney Murray and to the Americans. (He presents Fr Courtney Murray as coming to defend religious freedom, with eloquence, in the Theological Commission. That is not true. Every time he recounts something of which I have direct personal knowledge, it is not accurate. So it must be the same for the rest . . .). On the other hand, not a word about the Belgians, and I know what role they played.

It all looks as though the author, having entered on index cards all the details he knew (more or less accurately), whether they were in the public domain, or whether he knew them through corridor-gossip, had set his cards side by side on the table, and had reconstructed, or imagined, the facts and motives that allowed a reconstruction of the chain of events. But this must often be pure conjecture. It is true that Paul VI changed after 30 October 1963: I heard that said at the time, and noted it in my journal. But that was in relation to collegiality, to his doubts, rather than to politics. It is true that one of the purposes of his pilgrimage to the Holy Land, or one of his intentions, was to shed light on collegiality, on his doubt. It is true that on his return, at the beginning of 1964, he made a series of papal affirmations, in the purest Pius XII style. But all that certainly did not have as political a context as the author outlines. He also gives the Declaration on the Jews an exaggerated importance. Everything revolves around that. In this regard the

---

1. Michael Serafian, *Le Pèlerin. Les secrets du Concile* (Plon, 1964).
2. The mysterious Xavier Rynne, who provided news of the Council in the *New Yorker*, was, in fact, the Redemptorist, Francis Xavier Murphy, a Council expert.
3. Robert Kaiser, correspondent for *Time* in Rome.

distortion of the truth that this book presents will do harm. Finally, what he says about the Theological Commission, and the role played there by Cardinal Ottaviani is, as he presents it, inaccurate. See, for example, pages 46 and 227. Many things THAT I KNOW ABOUT with certainty, are inaccurately presented. That makes me form a bad estimation of the rest. He seems to think that the members of the Theological Commission are less than children!!

Saturday 16 January 1965

Farewells. Departure at 8.25 am. When I arrived at Fiumicino (at 9.10 am) I encountered once again its detestable, atrociously noisy atmosphere. I arrived at Turin airport at 11.30 am. Fr Rector[1] and Fr Piras[2] were there to meet me. A very warm welcome from the Jesuit Fathers. But how lacking in charm are these lodgings for old bachelors, and how very nearly coarse, in the end, are these heavy meals!

Lecture: neither very good, nor bad. A good public. In the evening dinner in the little eighteenth century palace, located in the garden of the Fathers' college, that comes from the d'Aoste family and serves as the premises for the students' club. Then, after dinner, answers to questions from a group of young people, or of young men and women.

Sunday 17 January 1965

At 10.30 am, the Rector drove me to the Dominican Fathers. Conversation. He said so me: yesterday evening you attributed a great deal to John XXIII. Certainly he had a great goodness, but one can ask if, in the end, he did not do a great deal of harm to the Church. He opened things up. But are we not moving towards sacrificing 'the truth'?—I asked WHAT truths. Truly, some people miss the Catholic ghetto. But the basis is political. For them, John XXIII means peace with the communists, and they don't want that.

And yet, it is certainly true that opening-up should be done with prudence, while keeping closed the foundations of truth and Tradition. The world situation is full of grave dangers. Africa is deeply troubled by the Chinese . . . Nevertheless I believe that an attitude of shuttered orthodoxy and 'holding on' to everything, that is to say, chiefly structures of a social and political conservatism, would be the worst of attitudes.

A very tiring journey: eleven hours by train! Arrived (late) at Toulon, exhausted, at 11.25 pm. Stayed at the bishop's residence with Mgr Sartre.

I note down here the great anxiety of my Italian Dominican confrères: a very serious crisis of recruitment. They have a sense of decline for which there seems to be no remedy. The young ones are good, but very few in number: not even two novices[3] a year for each of their five provinces.

---

1. Pasquale di Girolamo, SJ.
2. Francesco Piras, SJ.
3. The typescript quotes 'monks'.

A terrible journey: eleven hours by train! Towards the end, from Menton to Toulouse (four hours!) soldiers, one of whom, one of the 'new generation', spent the whole time, in full view of the compartment or the corridor, touching up a girl, while singing snatches of songs.

Then followed the week for Unity: Toulon. Religious sisters. A public lecture.[1] Some slight commotion at first, but it died down.

A day for priests at Brignoles, Tuesday 19 January, from 10.00 am to 3.00 pm, and, also at Brignoles, an hour at the camp of the Conscientious Objectors,[2] under canvas.

In the evening, a lecture at Aix, at 6.00 pm. After dinner a meeting with the students at the Protestant Centre.

Wednesday: Marseilles. Lunch with Mgr the Archbishop and the pastors Marchand[3] and Roux. At 2.30 pm, a lecture to priests. At 6.00 pm a public lecture (two canisters of tear-gas). In the evening, dinner and a friendly meeting at the presbytery of Saint-Victor. Prayer in the basilica.

Thursday at Dieulefit. Lunch with Pastor Brémond.[4] In the afternoon, a lecture to the Dominican contemplatives nuns beyond Theu.[5]

In the evening a public lecture. This region, with a population of 3,000, produced an audience of six hundred people, including some who had come from outside, even from the Ardèche.

Friday 22, we went to take Fr Benoit to a little Orthodox hermitage. Spent the day (from 10.00 am to 4.30 pm) at Nyons: priests and pastors, about sixty in all. —By car to Nîmes. A very long journey in a rather slow car.

Saturday morning: a joint meeting of the diocesan secretariat for unity and the Protestant committee. A good atmosphere. Co-operation is making headway. Lunch together.

In the afternoon, a meeting of twenty-five pastors and about sixty priests, with Mgr the bishop,[6] in a Protestant venue. I gave a presentation of the *De oecumenismo*. Questions. A few minutes on the radio, but we had to wait a long time for the journalist who did the interview.

Sunday 24 January 1965

Preached in the cathedral. A very beautiful celebration. I was very moved. Then at 11.15 am, at St Baudile; in the evening at St Perpetua. The norms for celebration are very far from uniform. Here there is no longer any Latin in the fore-mass;

---

1. On the subject of the Third Session.
2. Congar had campaigned for the recognition of conscientious objection and the status of non-military service.
3. Jacques Marchand, of the French Reformed Church, Pastor in Marseilles.
4. Arnold Brémond, Pastor at Dieulefit (Drôme), had long been active on the ecumenical plane.
5. The monastery of Clarté Notre-Dame at Taulignan
6. Fr Rougé.

there, there still is. A certain disorder prevails in all this . . . Lunch at the bishop's residence. Afterwards, Canon Bost[1] drove me to Aigues-Mortes, to the Tower of Constance, which I had wanted to see for a long time.

In the evening, a public lecture.[2] A great commotion of maniacs, of the OAS[3] kind. Fifteen or so, armed with whistles, or who chanted: Congar to Moscow! Unity, yes; Pax,[4] no! etc. It was impossible to give the lecture until they were eject- ed. This was done, partly by the police, partly by the men in the audience, after thirty-five minutes of uproar. Once again I was deeply traumatised and wounded, not by being spoken against, but by the impossibility of uttering a human word. I was humiliated in my humanity. The actions of these people have NOTHING to do with truth, with anything reasonable, with any possibility that there might be of explaining oneself, of dialogue, of using speech for the purpose for which it was made. And I suffer in sensing, here or there, a sort of virtual schism. There are some people who do not accept the Council and the opening it represents. They are capable of causing an outright schism. They are already in a state of virtual schism.

Monday 25 January 1965
By air, Nîmes-Orly-Strasbourg. More than fifty letters on my table, an accumu- lation of books and papers. —In the evening, I added a closing word after the lecture by Hébert Roux.

Tuesday 28 January 1965
I have not yet finished dealing with the papers that had accumulated on my table, even though I have done nothing else for three days.

Sunday 31 January 1965
Left the Priory at 8.20 am. Stopped at Mulhouse, then by air, Basle-Zurich-Rome. Antoine, the son of M. de Bavier, drove me straight to Ariccia. One of those in- numerable retreat-houses of which we have no real equivalent: rooms facing North-West. View over Lake Albano and the town of Castel Gandolfo. Comfort- able house, well designed, practical, but terribly noisy.

After dinner, a meeting. There are nearly seventy of us and not everyone has arrived yet. So, once again, this is going to be the great gathering, the grand ex- hibition? Mgr Guano gave a general presentation: we are to work this week in sub-commissions, then next week, in a smaller group, all together.

---

1. Albert Bost, of the diocese of Nîmes, diocesan director of works and of Catholic Ac- tion.
2. A lecture on Vatican II and Ecumenism.
3. ('Organisation de l'armée secrète': a far-right movement supporting the continuation of French rule in Algeria.)
4. Cf above, page 386, note 2.

After that, l'abbé Haubtmann gave an account of the state of the work: unfortunately in poor Latin and rather bad pronunciation (*'schemâtis problemâta; dogmâte'* . . . ') Almost all the Fathers who had commented asked that the text be addressed to all people, but eventually they settled for what had already been agreed upon: it would be addressed to Christians in the first instance, and also to all people. —It is necessary to proceed *'modo inductivo'* (pronounced *indûctivo*) [by induction]. Content: a Christian cosmology (the human being in the world; a Christian anthropology: the human being in society, the values to be promoted in a socialised world; many wanted atheism to be mentioned, without polemic).

We shall know tomorrow how people are to be divided into sub-commissions.

Mgr Ménager told me that, three days ago, *Il Tempo* reported my lecture at Nîmes, describing me as *'prete rosso . . . Progressista bene noto'* [the red priest . . . the well known progressive],[1] etc. The ambassador, Brouillet, was annoyed by this article, but what can I do? Perhaps I will write a letter to *Il Tempo,* or make my reaction known in some other way.

L'abbé Haubtmann told me that he had received a letter from Franić, asking that Fr Lio be invited. Fr Lio is there, with Franić and Tromp, who was very amicable towards me this evening [but Lio and Franić are not on the sub-commission for marriage, and neither is Fr Häring: they are on the sub-commission *De Re economica* [for economic affairs]].

Monday 1 February 1965

I have read the new text of the *Ia pars* [first part]. It is by Haubtmann, following the IDEAS of the old schema, the comments of the Fathers, the consultation with thirty-five international organisations and comments received from here and there. It was Fr Lauras, SJ,[2] who put it into Latin.

In my view, this text is clearly better than the Zurich-Häring one. IT HAS FOUND THE RIGHT TONE, and that is half the battle. It is a text that the people will be able to read; it brings in doctrine [perhaps not enough, and not sufficiently] WITHIN THE CONTEXT of human realities. It is more theological *in actu exercito* [obliquely] than in *actu signato* [intentionally]. I note as I go along a certain number of *requisita* [things required] that have not been achieved, or not sufficiently so (sheet attached here.)

I have been put on the theological commission that has responsibility for: 1) the drafting of the more general first part, and 2) also the examination from a doctrinal point of view of the applications in the second part. —Meeting from 9.15 am, to 12.35 pm. The first question raised concerned the legitimacy of making an entirely new text, at least as far as concerns its presentation because, Haubtmann

---

insisted on this, the ideas are the same. Tromp considers that we are heading for serious difficulties. However, many of the Fathers (eighteen) have asked for a text addressed TO PEOPLE in general [but, Tromp said, the sixty members of the Joint Commission had approved its being addressed first to Christians, to Catholics, and through them to people in general]. It was acknowledged that this change will need to be given a serious justification in the *relatio*. In my view, if the Fathers see that it succeeds in speaking TO PEOPLE, they will be in agreement. I emphasised this point. There was also a preview of how the work was to proceed. The Co-ordinating Commission was not in agreement with the original idea of sending the new text to the bishops FIRST, so that it could be corrected in accordance with their wishes, and so that the discussion could be confined to a text already revised, which would have allowed for a shorter discussion. The reasoning of the Co-ordinating Commission was that our new text will be the text of a sub-commission. Legally, one cannot send the text of a simple sub-commission that has not been approved by the plenary Joint Commission. That is why the meeting of the Joint Commission has been brought forward and will take place from 29 March to 7 April.

After three-quarters of an hour for reflection on the comments to be made on the text *in genere*—the French-speaking experts met, that is Haubtmann, Daniélou, Girardi, Thils and myself, and assembled their comments, virtually my own, which Fr Daniélou will present—we reconvened. There is a summary of the comments made on the sheet attached here. Each one made his comments in turn. These were noted down. When this general survey had been made, the comments were taken up one by one and discussed.

In the afternoon, Mgr Wojtyła[1] (Cracow), who arrived this morning, said: the Poles had made a plan for schema XIII before the Third Session, and they took it up again afterwards, taking account of the comments of the Fathers. They had conceived and composed it in the light of THEIR situation in a communist society. He read out the beginning of this text, and indicated the structure of what followed. It was conceived and drawn up FROM THE POINT OF VIEW OF THE CHURCH ITSELF which formulates ITS principles, and gives ITS justifications. —It was thought that all this will need to be taken into account, but this text, a private one, cannot take precedence, as the basis for our discussion, over the one drawn up on the mandate of the Joint Commission . . .

The points raised this morning were taken up again. (I had asked that the dimension of interiority, the HEART, be emphasised. That is what Daniélou has done: quite well.) When I explained how a profound anthropology calls for a pneumatology, and said that the Observers, unanimously, reproached us for the

---

1. Karol Wojtyła, who was not a member of any conciliar commission, was nevertheless invited to share in the drafting of schema XIII, at first in the sub-commission on the signs of the times that was created in September 1964, and then in the central sub-commission of the Joint Commission charged with schema XIII, beginning from November 1964.

lack of pneumatology, Tromp intervened: that, he said, is because they do not have a magisterium. For us, it is enough to have it said once and for all: '*Ego vobiscum usque . . .* ' [I am with you until . . . (Matt 28:20)]. THEY insist on the Holy Spirit because they have eliminated the magisterium . . . —I replied that this might be true, but WE should not do the opposite . . . —Tromp responded: Jesus Christ could have acted on human beings without the Church, through his Holy Spirit alone, but he chose to act on them THROUGH THE CHURCH, by putting the Holy Spirit in the Church.

I think we have touched on an important point there!

Once again, and indeed several times over, Tromp commented: Beware! We are tending to suggest our OWN ideas for introduction into a new text, rather than to try to satisfy the requests of the Fathers. —There was some truth in this comment . . .

At 5.10 pm, Fr Schütte, SVD, came to bring me the schema on the Missions. With reference to the theological part, my part: 1) several people found some sentences difficult, or at least obscure; they need to be formulated more clearly; 2) Fr Kaufmann suggested some stylistic corrections; 3) Fr Peeters has drafted some of my sections differently. But I made it clear that Fr Peeters did this *motu proprio* [on his own initiative], while my text has received the approval of the official sub-commission . . . I will have to respond to his comments and propose an amended text for 15 February . . . Fr Schütte told me, on the other hand, that Cardinal Agagianian was happy enough with our text.

The work has arrived, piles of it . . . Dom Mayer[1] asked me for my reactions to the *modi* proposed for *De institutione sacerdotali*, and sent me the whole dossier. The Polish plan for schema XIII, too, will have to be studied *quam primum* [as soon as possible]. Finally I have been sent the first issue of *Concilium*, for which I must write a presentation in *La Croix* . . . [2]

At the end of the evening, the critical revision of Haubtmann's text was begun. There was some hair-splitting and bickering over details in No. 1. There were too many of us (twelve or fourteen) to do any useful work at the level of drafting.

Fr Gagnebet, who arrived this evening, told me that the Pope had asked Maritain for a *votum* on truth, and another on religious freedom. But Maritain had bronchitis and was unable to get these done.

Fr General arrived with Gagnebet. He said a word to me about the article in *Il Tempo* that described me as a 'red priest', and added that Fr Hamer had sent a

---

1. The Germnan Benedictine, Augustin Mayer, Professor of Dogmatic Theology, was Rector of the Pontifical Athenaeum of St Anselm, and of the College of the same name; a Council expert, he was Secretary to the Commission for Seminaries, Studies and Catholic Education.
2. Cf '*Concilium*, Une nouvelle revue théologique sous le signe du Concile' , in *La Croix:* 14–15 February 1965.

letter of protest.[1] I thanked Fr Hamer, but added that there is nothing to be gained while the allegations against the *ICI* have not been officially declared to be no more than lies.[2]

Tuesday 2 February 1965

The sub-commission *De signis temporum* [on the signs of the times] joined us at the beginning of the morning session. Mgr McGrath gave an account of his work, already carried out during the whole of the Third Session and concerned with ensuring for the *conspectus generalis* [overall view] (the phenomenology of the world as it is) a character that is sufficiently complete and sufficiently universal (not a purely western one). They pointed out two deficiencies: 1) humankind emerges as too much determined by technical changes: put in higher relief the value of HUMANKIND, the Church's special point of interest; 2) the explanation is too narrow in scope, applying mainly to developments in Europe since the Renaissance.

Also, the effects of technocracy on the Christian conscience (No. 10) do not have much application in those regions where 70% or 80% of the population are illiterate, and where religion has rather a superstitious form, tied up with subjection to the physical elements. The Church, for its part, ought to put forward a message acceptable to minds formed along scientific lines.

Other comments about details.

Moeller, who had come with the sub-commission on the *signa temporum*, even though he is allotted to the sub-commission *De cultura* [on culture], remained with us. (But he is on the drafting committee and it is good that he takes part in our discussions.) He told me yesterday evening that he would rather have been put on the Theological Commission. That is just like the Belgians: few in number (although their number far surpasses their numerical proportion) they go everywhere and position themselves where they expect to have the most efficacious influence.

We worked individually, then in common. We returned to the *proemium*. After lunch, I familiarised myself with the Polish plan. It is a well constructed text, but one which makes a DOCTRINAL DECLARATION of the principles and justifications of the CHURCH in the face of a society that is officially atheist. The text in no way addresses people in general; it sets out categorically and *in actu signato* [intentionally] what would come over better if expressed *in actu exercito* [obliquely], in a text CAPABLE OF BEING READ BY PEOPLE IN GENERAL. There is much more of Pius XII than of John XXIII [[although Haubtmann's text recovers something of the vigour of John XXIII]]. Even with regard to the ques-

---

1. Hamer had written to the editor of the paper on 30 January (Congar Archives).
2. Certain integrist publications were conducting a campaign against the *ICI*, making use for their purposes of the concerns raised by the Polish episcopate (cf above, page 386, note. 2).

tions this text is intended to answer, that is, those of Marxist atheism, there is certainly a coherent affirmation of Catholic truths opposed to the positions of that atheism. Is there an effective ANSWER to the QUESTIONS of Marxism?

At the afternoon meeting, in discussion of the comments on Chapter II as a whole, Mgr Wojtyła made some remarks of an extreme gravity. He said: we are considering only the questions posed by the new world situation supposedly described in Chapter I; but this modern world also provides ANSWERS to these questions. And we must reply to these answers, for they constitute a putting in question of our own response. And yet, we are not taking into consideration either these answers or the questions posed for us by the fact of their existence. The Marxist answer really exists: it is not truly being considered here, although it is shared by two fifths of humanity . . . There it is not presented simply as an academic mode of THOUGHT, but it penetrates and shapes the whole of life in which humankind is called to live and work.

Wojtyła made a very great impression. His personality is imposing. A power radiates from it, an attraction, a certain prophetic force that is very calm, but incontestable.

It was resolved that there will be included, not a specific answer to Marxism, but some general elements of an answer, especially in the chapter on anthropology that it had already been decided to add. Daniélou seemed to be already selected: he will have to draft something together with Mgr Wojtyła. —But, during the interval, almost all the experts doubted whether Daniélou, quick and superficial, was the right man for this; Girardi in particular complained that Daniélou monopolises the discussion, takes over, speaks in the name of others without really expressing their position . . .

Fr Tromp once again contested the worth and legitimacy of Haubtmann's text, on the grounds that it is a NEW text, and not just the correction of the original text in the light of discussion . . .

After the resumption, Mgr Wojtyła said that in his view there was not enough emphasis on the soteriological or salvific dimension.

Discussions about the detail of the text, conducted in a lacklustre way.

Several people arrived today: Folliet, Prignon, in the evening, Tucci . . .

Wednesday 3 February 1965

Very beautiful light. Yesterday, too.

Mgr Wright floated the idea: what if schema XIII were to take the form of a collective pastoral letter from the whole episcopal college? I find this a very interesting idea; in that way one would determine the literary and theological genre of the text.

In the morning, the end of Chapter II was discussed. A real depth has been achieved in the view of the unity between anthropology and theology (and also cosmology): my great preoccupation!—and in the idea that creation is the basis of the internal autonomy of things: a critique of any sort of 'Platonism for the people'.

The schema drafted in Cracow was then discussed. Mgr Wojtyła first outlined its history: Cardinal Wyszyński had brought it in May 1964. And yet, Mgr Glorieux, Secretary for schema XIII, said that he had not received it before the drafting of Haubtmann's text . . .

Mgr Wojtyła had sent it to the Council Secretariat a second time, together with the text of his intervention in the discussion of schema XIII. And he had communicated it a third time to the sub-commission charged with the revision of the schema.

From the point of view of method, the Cracow experts had revised their text after the Third Session in order to include in it the changes called for by the discussion. They had retained the central idea of Häring's text, that of vocation. But they had looked for a way of tackling the question of atheism, and of finding a platform for dialogue with atheists.

From the point of view of content: in Haubtmann's plan, humankind and its problems are the OBJECT of the Church's REFLECTION, which tries to connect with them. In the Cracow plan it is not so much a matter of reflection as of affirmation of three FACTS that determine the work of the Church in the contemporary world: 1) the work ensues from the will of God; 2) from the grace of Christ; 3) from the human conscience, to whose demands it responds. This approach develops a presentation of the Church as SALVIFIC, of a salvation that is not just supernatural, but that implies achievements in the temporal order, in which the relationship of 'Church-world' comes into effect.

Mgr Wojtyła, who got his passport *in extremis* [at the last minute], believed that Providence had permitted –or rather, willed –that he should be able to come in order to make us think about all this, and, at last, give the Polish point of view its opportunity.

Reactions to his text were expressed. It was thought that it would be necessary to take up several elements from it, in particular in the new chapter on formal anthropology that needs to be drafted.

In the afternoon, Fr Daniélou and Mgr Wojtyła read the plan of the text that they had prepared for a new chapter on anthropology, the text (in French) by Fr Daniélou, was quite good, though a bit literary and written *currente calamo* [just as the ideas came to him]. Mgr Wojtyła read us some long chapters from the Cracow text. There were reactions to it. With a very great and wonderful frankness, Haubtmann said: it is a possible option, but the orientation of this text and that of mine are so different as to be incompatible.

Mgr González Moralejo observed shrewdly that the Polish text envisaged the Polish situation where, in the face of the attraction and influence of Marxism, one could still rely on a strong Catholic majority. But such a presentation would not meet the situation of Marxism in other countries like China or the USSR.

It was agreed that the Cracovian passages would not be taken up as such, but great account would be taken of the ideas that could be assimilated from them.

After this, a plan for a text on atheism by Fr Girardi was discussed. Daniélou reacted with the passion, instinctiveness and subjectivity of a woman. Girardi will revise his text. The general inclination is to place it at the end of the *conspectus generalis*, then to present the human being in its profundity, then the human being in the world, the human being in society—finally it will say that to do all this is the work of the Church, which will be presented in its HIERARCHICAL STRUCTURE as the People of God.

I note down here various pieces of information or minor facts that I learnt this afternoon.

In the building located between the Holy Office and the street, the Pope is having made not only a large audience hall, but also a meeting room for the collegial Advisory Council that he wants to establish.

Progress is being made towards the suppression of the appendices to schema XIII: many of them will be incorporated into the text of the schema itself. That is logical: these appendices were a stage in our work, but it was not possible to find a satisfactory status for them.

Fr Gagnebet told me that if Fr Schillebeeckx is not a conciliar expert this is because of the annoyance he caused the Pope by an article written at the beginning of the Council (and the idea of which Schillebeeckx later took up in a lecture) according to which, when one speaks of the infallibility of the pope EX SESE, 'semper subintelligitur collegium' [IN ITSELF, the college should always be understood]. It is somewhat like Rahner's thesis, but less nuanced.

Fr Lebret said to me: in our sub-commission (on economic affairs) we have a Franciscan father who blocks everything! He is called Lio . . .

As for Fr Tromp, he blocks; he still comes out with his great doctrinal declarations, simplistic and peremptory. But the old lion has grown weak and mellowed; he no longer has claws, and he coughs like an old man. To me, he is charming . . .

Thursday 4 February 1965

This morning, snow! Then sunshine.

Mgr Garrone is trying to see how the different parts look within the context of the whole, and to give them a title. —The general comments on Chapter III, 'the human being in society', were reviewed. They are fairly critical.

Finally, a list was made of the chief points in this first part of the schema that call for further elaboration, or rather a new drafting. This led to the establishment of four small sub-groups:

- on the question of atheism: Garrone, Girardi, Haubtmann,
- the human person in itself, anthropology: Moralejo, Daniélou, Tromp, Miss Goldie[1] and Sr Mary Luke,[2]

---

1. Rosemary Goldie, Executive Secretary of COPECIAL (Permanent Committee of the International Congresses for the Lay Apostolate) was a lay Auditor at the Council.
2. Mary Luke Tobin, Superior General of the Sisters of Notre-Dame-de-Lorette, was a lay

-   the human being in society: Poma, Thils, Gagnebet,
-   the Church (to be put at the end of the chapter): Wojtyła, Grillmeier, Semmelroth and myself.

A draft text will have to be ready by 3.45 pm, tomorrow.

In the afternoon, a little of my own work; at 4.00 pm, meeting with the Commission on the *conspectus generalis*. It explained, and read out its text: it has given a somewhat different arrangement to Haubtmann's text, by bringing into it some new elements and by abridging it. This produced a very dense text, very convoluted, that is to say, too dense. It had lost its warmth and was a bit like a table of contents.

Afterwards, a brief meeting with Wojtyła, Grillmeier and Semmelroth. They agreed with the *ordo dicendorum* [order of things to be said] that I had prepared. I started work on a draft.

Friday 5 February 1965

Worked on the drafting of my small section. I presented a roneoed text to the meeting of our small group at midday.

Mgr Charue brought back from Rome a rumour that an attack is being planned on the *De Revelatione*. Moeller filled me in about this. The group *'Coetus Internationalis'* (Sigaud[1]), had produced two texts at the beginning of January, in the context of the comments asked for by 31 January: a critique of the *De libertate*—which accuses the text of *sapere indifferentismum, liberalismum'* [smacking of indifferentism, liberalism], etc, and reverts to the old positions about tolerance, the thesis and the hypothesis—and a critique of the *De Revelatione*. The Biblical Institute replied to this text by itself producing some *modi*.

It seems that Cardijn[2] has asked for a working-class parish in Rome for his 'titular' church. For him, the question of a simplification of cardinals' robes is raised. It is agreed that silk is given up. Phew!! As for the Eastern Patriarchs, it seems that they have secured it that they will PRECEDE the cardinals, except the cardinal Dean, considered as legate, or representative of the premier patriarch, the bishop of Rome. Further, they will not have the title of ROMAN. This would be the beginning of a significant change not only in a state of affairs, but also in the way in which these are regarded.

This evening we revised:

1) the *proemium* and the *conspectus generalis*,
2) the four chapters of Part I of the schema, except that dealing with humankind in the world.

Auditor at the Council.

1. G de Proença Sigaud.
2. Joseph Cardijn, priest of the diocese of Malines-Brussels, had founded the Young Christian Workers' movement; he has been a Council expert since 1963; he had just been named a cardinal.

At supper I saw Fr Tucci. He passed on to me a photocopy of the comments of the 'Coetus internationalis' on the *De libertate*. He got the document from Fr Greco.

He told me that it was only a fortnight ago that two Jesuit priests (Fr Martini and another[1]) had been entrusted with the task of classifying Pius XII's papers and of possibly getting something from them in order to respond to *The Deputy*.

He also told me that *Le Pèlerin*, published under the name of Serafian, thought to be a diplomat, comes, at least as far as the basic documentation is concerned, from a Fr Martin,[2] a Jesuit, formerly of the Biblical Institute, who suddenly disappeared from there, and had been in Jerusalem and in contact with various Jewish ambassadors. (Arrighi told me that this Fr Martin knew Cardinal Bea very well and that several passages of the novel presuppose information from the Secretariat.)

Finally, he told me that he HAD SEEN a list of *modi* presented to the Pope by a group (who??) which included about forty *modi* for the *De oecumenismo*. The Pope had crossed out (in red or blue) about half of these *modi*, thus excluding them: these, it appears, were the most serious. He had let the other nineteen pass, to which the Secretariat had sometimes given a softer form.

It appears that the reactionary group, in their approach to the Pope, had made use of the publicity given to the steps taken by the cardinals on the subject of religious freedom, causing him to remark: when WE take an initiative, it remains secret . . . But, in the Vatican, secrecy is preferred to publicity.

Tucci concluded: the Pope has been the object of continual approaches and pressures. He has resisted, rightly, nine times out of ten.

In what time I had left this evening, I began to read the comments on the *De libertate*, taking some notes. There are two small booklets, one of twenty-two pages, of *Observationes criticae* [critical observations], and one of fifteen pages, of *Emendationes textus* [emendations of the text]. A new text is suggested for a number of passages.

Fr Tromp, decidedly much softened, congratulated kindly me this evening on the Latin of my short chapter on the *munus* [function] of the Church. Don't mention it!

Saturday 6 February 1965

I did not have time to read PROPERLY the WHOLE text of the two booklets on religious freedom. The photocopy is in very small print and the ink often faint, so that, even with respect to the form of the letters, I was not able to decipher it all. In any case, it was a serious attack, forcefully made. The force is not so much perhaps in the number and weight of the opponents; it is in the argumentation, especially in the manner and the basis of the argumentation. The basis is the 'clas-

---

1. The project was initially entrusted to three Jesuit historians : Pierre Blet, Angelo Martini and Burkhart Schneider.
2. Malachy Martin, SJ, an Irish exegete.

sic' doctrine, the manner is that of a scholasticism of distinctions and syllogisms as in the days of Occam, or the quarrels *De Auxiliis*.[1] The *Animadversiones criticae* [critical observations] conclude that the Secretariat is incapable of proposing a satisfactory text, and that higher authority will have to provide for this by some other means.

The position is that of a distinction between a real right and toleration. No real and full right exists unless it conforms to the eternal law. Without this conformity one has a deficient right: not a real right, but a toleration.

This political Augustinianism is even applied to the concept of human dignity. The metaphysical or ontological quality of the person is distinguished from that person as he or she expresses himself or herself on the level of acts: on that level, the full dignity of the human person exists only if he or she acts *in vero et bono* [in truth and goodness] . . .

I feel sorry for the Secretariat, which will have to face up to this offensive. I would not be surprised if the Pope asks it—without imposing this—freely to co-opt some supplementary experts.

This morning, at 9.15 am, the final meeting: everyone. Each sub-commission gave an account of its work:

Mgr McGrath: *conspectus generalis.*

Mgr Garrone: theological chapter.

Mgr Wright: the person in society.

Schillebeeckx for the sub-commission on the family: A VERY BELGIAN-DUTCH GROUP. He said that the sub-commission had left the pastoral question to the extraordinary pontifical commission.

Mgr Hengsbach and Fr Calvez:[2] economics.

Mgr Charue: culture.

Mgr Schröffer: international life and peace.

After this, a few words from Habicht underlining the fact that, for the first time, there had been collaboration with lay people, men and women, on an equal footing. Really, this is remarkable.

At 10.45 am, common thanksgiving in the chapel.

At 11.00 am, departure for Rome (in a car sent by Fr General). Arrived at the French Seminary at 12.15 pm.

In the afternoon, correspondence. Work on the *De Missionibus*. It is a matter of saying what I accept in two big dossiers of proposed corrections: one from Fr Kaufmann and someone else: stylistic corrections in the main. I accepted most of these. The other, from Fr Peeters, OFM, which suggests the SUPPRESSION of a large number of theologically important IDEAS, of which he does seem to have understood the scope or even the meaning.

---

1. Disputes about the relation between grace and free will at the end of the sixteenth and beginning of the seventeenth centuries.
2. Jean-Yves Calvez, SJ, a specialist on the thought of Karl Marx, was Director of the Institute of Social Studies at the Catholic Institute of Paris, and edited the *Revue de l'Action populaire*.

I borrowed Michel de Saint-Pierre, *Les Nouveaux Prêtres*,[1] and spent the rest of the evening reading it.

Sunday 7 February 1965

Work on the *modi* for *De Institutione sacerdotali*. But I am not very well. A very indifferent day; painful, even.

This evening at dinner, Mgr Del Gallo and Arrighi. I did not learn much that was new. When I happened to mention the remark of a South American nuncio about bishops at the Council having been found in brothels, I got this further detail from Mgr del Gallo. He told me that cases are known, that he knows of two cases: a South American bishop, but 'protected' in the Curia, and a bishop from Mexico, who approaches the papal gendarmes, gives them gifts, and propositions them.

My God!

Arrighi spoke to me about the Little Church. About a hundred of the Poitou families are going to be reconciled on *Laetare* Sunday.[2] These decent folk are asking that their marriages be blessed, because their last priest, over a hundred years ago, had told them that when they got good priests again, they would have to have their marriages blessed. It will not be Arrighi who will receive their confession, because, as a Frenchman, he could be suspect for them. It will be Mgr Willebrands, as representative of the Council, that is, of the College, and of Catholicity.

I cannot hear the Little Church spoken of without tears coming to my eyes.

Arrighi gave us a short history of the last two days. On Thursday evening, 19 November, at 9.00 pm, Felici had given the order that the *De oecumenismo* should not be printed. Because, he said, the bishops will vote against it, because, for the *modi*, there will be 200 or 300 *non placet* votes, and, in these conditions the Pope would not be able to proclaim it. At 9.00 pm, Mgr Willebrands went to Mgr Dell'Acqua; there were telephone-calls. In the end, on the direct order of the Pope, the printing machines were set in motion.

But on the Thursday afternoon, the Pope was still asking for the introduction of two *modi*, which Willebrands refused.

Arrighi also said that the Latin Patriarch of Jerusalem[3] had written, insisting that the Declaration on the Jews be changed. Cardinal Bea was disposed to suppress the reference to 'deicide'. Garrone, Haubtmann and I said forcefully, that this is impossible. It would be catastrophic.

Arrighi, after seeing Fr Hamer at midday, insisted that I should come to the Secretariat at 5.00 or 6.00 pm: because they would be glad to have me, not just concerning non-Christian Religions, but also concerning religious freedom.

---

1. Michel de Saint-Pierre, *Les Nouveaux Prêtres* (La Table Ronde, 1964).
2. The fourth Sunday of Lent, popularly so called from the opening words of the *Introit* at Mass, 'Rejoice', announcing the approach of the feast of Easter.
3. A Gori.

God grant me the strength and the time to complete the services that are being asked of me!

Monday 8 February 1965

This morning there was an article in *Il Messaggero* with information about the current machinations of French integrism, and of the 'Promotion of the Laity' group.[1] The French episcopate is depicted as being vassals of de Gaulle for the purposes of a 'Neo-Gallicanism' and under the influence of Chenu and Congar in a Marxist direction. It's unbelievable!!!

At 9.30 am, at the Vatican, in the Hall of Congregations. Meeting of the whole sub-commission. It was accepted that the Fathers would speak, but not the experts. Philips arrived. He said he had received a letter from Cardinal Döpfner on the subject of the *De Revelatione*. He said that there was no need to change anything in the *De Revelatione*, that it should be presented for the votes just as it is, along with the *modi*.

It is so obvious! It is juridically in order!

The chapter on marriage and the family was looked at this morning. An interesting text in that it does not separate love and marriage. But the text is somewhat dogmatic in tone, and does not take up the question of birth control, because the Pope has reserved that to himself. So the text remains handicapped.

Mgr Ancel was received by the Pope this morning. The Holy Father (who has read the book), asked him what he thought of the impression given in *Les Nouveaux Prêtres*. The Holy Father also thought it an over-simplification, a false image, made up with some accurate fragments.

He had not granted the author, Michel de Saint-Pierre, the audience he had requested.

But (Del Gallo told us) the Holy Father is rather uneasy about the Dutch situation.

At 4.30 pm, at the Vatican. Examination of the chapter *De vita oeconomico-sociali* [on socio-economic life]: the experts were passive, and several of them left.

Monday 9 February 1965

Terrible weather: snow driven by the wind. Impossible to find a taxi! At St Martha's at 9.30 am. Several were missing and not a few were late. Chapter on the dignity of the human person (+ political life).

For us experts it was a waste of time. Several departed. I could have gone back to Strasbourg last Saturday without missing anything here. I could have done a little work. I have got so much to do. I am behind with everything!!!

Lunch at the Embassy with M. Brouillet, his wife and a daughter (Christine). M. Brouillet wanted to see me ALONE (he had invited others on another day). I

---

1. This clandestine group, made up of young people organised in commandos, had disrupted a number of lectures by those in charge of the *ICI*.

admit I did rather wonder why. Certainly, he likes me well enough, and is interested in the way I think. But the way in which Fr Martin[1] passed on the invitation to me led me to think that the Ambassador had some important things to say to me. Fr Martin alluded to some rumours concerning me. M. Brouillet questioned me about the integrist reactions, he talked about various things (about the nomination of new cardinals, about the creation of a collegial advisory council to the Pope . . .) but without seeming to have a very specific point of interest. But perhaps he wanted to express his sympathy to me in regard to the recent incidents and to discover my own reaction to them. He questioned me about Maritain.

The streets of Rome are difficult to negotiate. There are twenty centimetres of snow, turned to frozen mud here and there. If it freezes tonight the flow of traffic will be impossible tomorrow morning. Many trees have come down, or have had their big branches broken off. The garden of the Villa Bonaparte[2] is a real disaster.

Afternoon, at the Vatican, where M. Brouillet's chauffeur drove me at 3.40 pm. The text on culture. Very long. Rather boring, thoroughly stodgy.

Dinner with Arrighi. Two hours of stories about the incredible Roman crowd. Very racy. Of no interest at all for the cause of the gospel in the world. It is even a serious *impedimentum* [obstacle]. And nevertheless, 'our Church is the Church of the saints'.

Wednesday 10 February 1965

At the Vatican. *De communitate gentium et de Pace* [on the community of nations and on peace]. Some vigorous interventions, in particular from Mgr Ancel and others. Riedmatten made a remarkable response. He, like Philips, has the knack of establishing an interior relationship with meetings and commissions.

In the afternoon, a start was made on the *conspectus generalis*. But: 1) there was not complete agreement between Haubtmann and the sub-commission for *De signis temporum* [the signs of the times]. The latter complained that it had been deprived of the right to draw up and present a text itself (McGrath *et alii*, among whom Houtart sees everything in sociological terms, while Martelet systematises all the time . . .); 2) the Latin is appalling and often comprehensible only if one refers to the French text. [[This is the INEVITABLE outcome of a text composed first in French.]] The experience of the text of February 1963 should have been decisive; 3) Haubtmann reads badly and has not got the necessary voice; 4) as to the core of it, after the dense and technical texts of recent days, this one appears rather vague and elementary.

At the interval, it was obvious that everyone was disappointed, that no one was satisfied, and that everyone was asking what should be done? An awkward

---

1. This refers to Marcel Martin, of the Holy Spirit Fathers, who was the Procurator for the French bishops at the Holy See.
2. The seat of the French Embassy to the Holy See.

moment. We seemed to be back at square one. Discussion was resumed. Mgr Guano posed three questions: 1) *quis sit scopus huius conspectus generalis?* [what is the scope of this general overview]; 2) *de modo procedendi, generice* [about the manner of proceeding, in general]; 3) what ideas would one want to see expressed here?

> Philips said: set out the general problematic of humankind today: If God exists, humankind does not stand a chance. He cited Robinson, *Honest to God*,[1] which had such enormous success because it gave expression to the question of humankind.
> Garrone: envisage the situation of humankind in our own age.
> Hengsbach: a short prologue, with three points: 1) what are the questions?; 2) *reductio quaestionum ad fontem suum* [taking the questions back to their source]; 3) the Church wants to give its testimony in the face of these difficulties: love and truth.
> Guano: begin with what everybody feels: questions that really grip people.

I myself, before 7.00 pm, had drawn up a short note for the Secretariat, along much the same lines as Hengsbach.

The final practical solution: a small group composed of Folliet, Rosemary Goldie and Fr Tucci will make a plan of a *Proemium*.

(I gather that during an audience recently given to Mgr Ancel, the Pope spoke about schema XIII. He made it quite clear that he knows that Felici is at the source of many of the difficulties and *impedimenta* [obstacles]. The need for vigilance remains.)

Thursday 11 February 1965

I am very annoyed with the state of affairs. We are once again in a complete shambles. The French team is still, in a way, in the dark. This certainly would not have happened with a Belgian team. One would have had a text by now, not definitive, certainly, but already solid. Now, for example, my short text on the Church was the object of corrections at Ariccia . . . But these corrections have not been inserted into the text we were given today. This should have been done since Saturday. For my part, I was quite ready to work. All that has remained as it was, in the dark.

In contrast, Mgr Garrone and Haubtmann maintain a serenity and optimism which seem to me to share something of those of the cicada.

At the Vatican, at 9.30 am. Fr Häring, who does not want to say anything in public, so as not to seem to be defending his original text, confided his annoyance to me. It seems to him that they have arbitrarily cut loose from and departed from the original text, the density of which has been lost, and that MANY things are missing from the current text: for example, in the chapter on the vocation of

---

1. John AT Robinson, *Honest to God* (London, 1963).

humankind, the response to the Marxist concept, the capacity to love inscribed in the image of God.

Reading of the text by Daniélou, in an affected style, because he was keeping a check on his naturally rapid and jerky flow. Discussion. In the end, the text went well enough. An altercation over atheism. In my opinion, what was said at Ariccia, with Fr Girardi, has not sufficiently borne its fruit. What remains is not adequate.

On the whole, things went well enough.

At 4.00 pm, at St Martha's for questions about the text to be typed. Then at the Vatican (I went up on foot and arrived no longer able to stand upright!!!) Discussion of the chapter on the relationships between humankind and the universe. Haubtmann's text is a little light and would need a lot of clarifications, or of better developments. A long time was spent in discussion of the question whether the christological affirmation of faith should be put first, or the place of humankind in the world should be set out first, so that everyone would conceive of it on the basis of reason. There seemed to be agreement in favour of a simple introduction placing the Christian affirmation in the situation and problems common to all human beings.

Haubtmann's text appeared rather light, rather general, rather journalistic. Haubtmann has a good mind, but I saw once again how far the pastoral point of view and being trained in Catholic Action has led the French clergy towards generalised syntheses that do not make great practical demands.

A slight altercation over the mention of Galileo, which many wanted to suppress. I intervened to ask that the allusion be retained while saying nothing either against the honour of the Church or against the historical truth.

Moeller supported me by referring to Brecht' play.[1]

I was asked to produce a text for tomorrow.—*Libenter* [willingly].

In the evening, dinner at the Belgian College. Philips recounted a little about the drafting of the *Nota Praevia* for Chapter III of the *De Ecclesia*. The Pope had provided a formula saying that the separated Easterners DO NOT HAVE jurisdiction. That was the origin of the *Nota Bene* that so much offended me, but which avoided this unsustainable wording. On the other hand, it was the Pope himself who put the following: the documents (of Pius XII and even John XXIII) that speak of a derivation of all jurisdiction *a Papa* [from the pope] must be interpreted according to the doctrine set out concerning the radical possession of the *munera docendi et pascendi* [teaching and pastoral functions] in virtue of episcopal consecration. Fr Fernandez OP had even then remarked that, nevertheless, such an interpretation would be difficult.

Apart from that, nothing. Moeller is back from Jerusalem, where he had been for the business of the Institute of the History of Salvation. But he obviously did not want to talk about it, asking me to keep quiet about even his journey, and, moreover, he stayed out of the way.

---

1. Bertold Brecht, *Leben des Galilei* (Berlin 1967).

Friday 12 February 1965

9.30 am, at the Vatican. It was I who was in the hot seat this morning, because the chapter on the Church was under discussion. Plenty of criticisms and questions. Mgr Wojtyła defended his text for the first section.

A grand lunch at the Spanish Embassy: we lunched over schema XIII, for which the ambassador hopes to be 'a stumbling block'.

Mgr Garrone has had an audience of the Holy Father. The latter had just read an article by Michel de Saint-Pierre, to which he tended to attribute too much importance, not giving their right proportions to what are bursts of 'reaction', pure and simple, that crop up among us at the moment.

At 6.00 pm, at the Vatican. At 4.30 pm there had been a meeting of the presidents of sub-commissions and the secretaries. Fr Lebret, who was sitting beside me, and who is at present much engaged with the affairs of the Holy See as well as his own, said to me: in the years 1948 to 1952, when the French were under suspicion in 'Rome', Montini always upheld Fr Lebret and his activity. Fr Suarez had told Fr Lebret that, FOR THIS REASON, Montini had, at the time, been denounced to the 'Holy Office'.

Lebret also told me that a secretary was being sought for the Secretariat for Non-Christian Religions. Because this Secretariat does not have much of an idea of what to do. Mgr Dell'Acqua asked Fr Lebret to give him a name . . . and Fr Lebret put the same question to me. I said: Voillaume, Blomjous, a Dutchman (to be found . . .)

Reading and discussion of the new *Proemium*, drawn up by Folliet in French, put into Latin by Tucci. But the Latin is incomprehensible without the French text . . .

We went fairly quickly, and grew tired!

At the end of the session, Mgr Guano summarised the conclusions of the meeting of the presidents of sub-commissions. Insistence on the tone, the style, the reference to the PRESENT situation. On the necessity of taking more account of the previous text, of aiming for greater brevity, on the concern for the unity of the text.

Knowing that Mgr Guano was to have an audience of the Holy Father today, I had asked him to try to find out the Pope's attitude towards the mention of Galileo in schema XIII. He sent me the reply this evening: the Pope thinks that he should not be mentioned in the schema, but he does want to do something himself, and asked Mgr Guano, who passed on the request to me, to suggest something to him. I can imagine that the Holy Father would indeed like to make a GESTURE. But what? It would be easier to take advantage of a scientific congress that he could receive and address. One could prepare a text.

This evening, a telephone call from the White Fathers. It seems they still have some anxiety about the *De Missionibus*. They insist strongly that I should come to Nemi on 22 March. Of course, I will go!

Saturday 13 February 1965

I again encountered the noisy atmosphere of Fiumicino that I so dislike.

Return journey without incident.

I have mixed feelings about the past fortnight, and overall some dissatisfaction. This comes partly from the fact that there was not much work to be done, especially during the second week. I like to have something to do, I don't like being primarily a spectator. However, I realise that, before sharing together in the work, and becoming a team with others, one does have to sit through these long sessions where one IS PRESENT at the work of others. It is required if one is to get an idea of the whole.

However, it is with what we have done that I remain dissatisfied. There has been too great a departure from the earlier text, especially in the first part. There has been too much new work done *ab ovo* [from scratch]. Each team has done its work too much as though the chapter for which it was responsible formed a whole, without really keeping constantly in view the fact that it was dealing with a fragment of a single schema and that this schema is not meant to be some fragment or other, but very precisely SCHEMA XIII: a NOVEL schema, that must speak to people in general. An enormous work of drafting still remains to be done. THE SCHEMA HAS TO BE WRITTEN! It must be thought through as such in its unity and its originality. Is the drafting team capable of doing this?

Haubtmann is a bit disappointing. First, he does not know Latin well, in practical terms, that is a very great handicap. Moreover, he has a sort of calm and transcendent serenity, but what does this really cover? He speaks little, he listens (which is a good point) and, when something is said, he takes it up, giving to his formulation a very general turn, full of nuances that could well be 'emergency exits',[1] as though he were giving expression to the outcome of a profound reflection that was pre-occupying him, and which, at last, he is announcing. In his draft there are some generalities and some slogans. When one reads this for the first time it is rather seductive. When one looks at it more closely it is full of imprecisions, and more than one formula is shown to be incapable of being retained.

But the experience of the *De Ecclesia* shows that the impression of a barely organised shambles can be followed soon enough by that of a work that holds together. Mgr Garrone himself sees this with a serenity, an optimism and an untroubled confidence. He has the gift of taking things 'philosophically' and of doing away with anxiety as, so he thinks, the problems are sorted out and the work done. It is a strength. It enables him to deal with problems in their turn, without anxiety. When he is convinced about something it is, for him, settled, sorted, sure. He calmly moves on to something else, without going back over what has been settled.

I found this evening, as usual, a terribly overloaded table; hundreds of papers all mixed up together. It was like an enormous traffic jam, with cars coming from

---

1. Congar used the English phrase.

all directions to a big junction without traffic lights. It is not easy to get out of this imbroglio! It's killing me. However, I am thinking of the work of drafting, so important, even decisive, for schema XIII. It is on this that will depend whether or not the text can be absorbed, its acceptability, and thus its worth for people in general.

Sunday 14 February 1965
I made the small additions or corrections for the chapter on the Church, in schema XIII, and sent them by express to Haubtmann.

Thursday 18 February 1965
Left the Priory at 8.25 am; by air from Basle to Zurich, then from Zurich to Rome. I studied again the *De libertate*. Fiumicino. I fell and hurt my left knee, the better one. I reached Monte Mario at 3.30 pm. Tea with Stransky, Thijssen, Pavan, Murray. On my table I found the big dossier of comments on the *De libertate*. I settled down to it at 4.00 pm.

Mgr Willebrands is not here. Today he is in Geneva with Cardinal Bea. The World Council of Churches has, indeed, sent a delegation to Rome to announce officially its declaration regarding a Joint Commission of theologians. It appears that the Vatican has done things well: the Pope gave a lengthy reception for the delegation; two days later, *L'Osservatore Romano* made a 'banner headline' out of that. The Cardinal and Willebrands are formally taking the response. I will get the details, either from reading *L'Osservatore*, or from listening to this one or that.

At supper Hamer, just arrived, told me that it was not the GENEVA folk who had been received in Rome, but the Orthodox Metropolitans.

I spent the whole evening reading the comments on the *De libertate*. I was not able to read more than a quarter of the dossier. The battle is a tough one, the critics are determined, proceeding, moreover, nearly always from the same principles. I got the impression, all the same, that the Secretariat has been too optimistic. It lacked the benefit that the presence of opponents—Browne, Franić, Spanneda, etc, who made it necessary to go deeper—brought, in the end, to the Theological Commission. Has not the Secretariat worked too much in the euphoric unanimity of men won over to open ideas? Opposition is coming, in the assembly. It is not negligible. If one accepts the principles of the opponents, everything is ineluctably logical. But this bears no relation to the situation of the Church and of the world on this side of the eschaton.

Friday 19 February 1965
A very poor night. Hard bed: I have a lot of pain in the hollow of my back.

Mgr Willebrands returned at 8.15 am, from Geneva. He told us about it. At 10.00 am the first plenary meeting: Willebrands, Thijssen, Murray, Pavan, Hamer, Feiner, Stransky and me. We made a general survey: what are the criticisms, what are the requests in relation to the text as a whole?

Each one gave his point of view. I suggested that, after a very short *proemium*, the biblical idea of humankind restored by God to its own counsel, should be developed, seen through the history of salvation. After that, a few brief words saying that the Church has lived this in the course of a very varied history, then that it finds itself today confronted by a reality that is widespread, or that tends to be widespread, of the recognition of a juridical structure that, with its idea of *immunitas a coactione* [freedom from constraint], answers to this profound biblical and Christian appeal. THAT is what will be spoken of, from this point onwards, in this declaration.

This was accepted, and I was asked to prepare it in cooperation with the biblical people. This will satisfy those who say, with good reason, that the Council has a duty to pronounce a word that proceeds from the Revelation of which the Church has the deposit, and that it lives and develops in its tradition. In this way we will stay within the framework of what the Council Fathers are asking for.

At the end, it was remarked that it would be a good idea to have the essentials in place before the arrival of Mgr De Smedt. There seemed to be a little apprehension about this arrival, because Mgr De Smedt is a great worker, but rapid and determined, and who does not deal with detail . . .

We were agreed that the current No. 3 (defence of nineteenth century texts) should move to the *Relatio*, and should be wholly rewritten to answer to the historical reality, quite simply, to the truth . . .

In the afternoon, we each worked on our own.

Mgr Willebrands asked me if I could take part in the conversations requested by the World Lutheran Federation in Strasbourg next May: six members from each side.

Of course, I said yes. But I saw even the few poor scraps my time that still remained being carried away by the flood. Fr Bosco asked me to come to Rome in MAY for the Commission on the Apostolate; Fr General[1] insists VERY strongly that I accept some lectures in Burgos in August, which I would certainly have otherwise refused. The very little time I have left is disappearing like water running through my fingers . . .

Willebrands told me that he had met Fr General in Bombay. The General said to him: is Fr Congar a serious theologian, or a risky one? He has been criticised in the past . . . Willebrands replied: those who criticised and suspected him knew nothing about the SUBJECTS in question. They judged in ignorance, and out of their ignorance.

This evening, Willebrands spoke about the alterations made to the *De oecumenismo*. There were three interventions by the Pope. The nineteen alterations concerned the second of these. But the Pope had received (from whom?) a list of forty alterations. When he sent for Mgr Willebrands, he had himself already underlined, in blue-pencil, the most serious of these corrections, those which really affected the text. Mgr Willebrands discussed the others with the Pope. Paul VI

---

1. Aniceto Fernández, OP.

retained the one which, instead of 'Spiritu Sancto movente . . . inveniunt' [moved by the Holy Spirit . . . they find], said 'invocantes Spiritum Sanctum . . . inquirunt' [invoking the Holy Spirit . . . they seek]. The Catholic Church, through the supreme voice of the Council, COULD NOT, he said, proclaim the first wording in general.

As for the third intervention, in the middle of the night of 19–20 February, Mgr Willebrands had purely and simply refused.

It is true, Willebrands told me, that the Pope complained that he had not received the text of the *De oecumenismo* in time. It had been overlooked. Whose fault was it? Paul VI said to Willebrands: that of the bureaucracy.

In contrast, the Pope is asking that our text on religious freedom should be communicated and explained to him even before it is given to the bishops of the Secretariat. He said to Willebrands: you will bring it to me, with two or three of your experts, and, there and then, around a table, I will pose some questions, they will explain to me, and I shall see if it is satisfactory.

But will the Pope have the time? And will we? That would have to take place in eight days . . . [On the other hand, this evening, I received a reply from Fr Dubarle, for Galileo. I am going to copy out certain passages of his letter and I will transmit the documentation to Mgr Guano.]

Saturday 20 February 1965

A dreadful bed. Awful pain in my lower back, which further hinders my ability to walk, already so limited.

Mgr Felici had telephoned Mgr Willebrands: 'I have just seen the Holy Father. I want to see you'. This was in order to repeat to him what the Pope had already said directly to Mgr Willebrands: the Pope wanted to see the text *De libertate*, with some experts, if possible before 7 March, or even before 1 March. But this will be difficult, as the Holy Father's time this week is very much over-loaded with the ceremonies for the twenty-seven new cardinals and their reception.

This afternoon, I went to the Biblical Institute to see Frs Lyonnet and Mc-Cool[1] about the biblical part of the Declaration. I submitted to them my plan for a *proemium* and we went on to talk about No. 12 (*Doctrina evangelica* [gospel teaching]). I did not gain much from this.

I went on from there to the French Seminary. I saw Haubtmann. He is redoing the text IN FRENCH; Philips will put it into Latin. Daniélou's text, and mine, were considered too abstract, too pedestrian. It must, he said, begin from the current situation. In short, Haubtmann is rewriting everything. So, in the main, the time spent at Ariccia and at the Vatican had been largely wasted. It seemed to me (and I told him so), that the drafting team—that is to say, in practice himself—is taking a good deal of liberty with a text that had been discussed and accepted by the sub-commission and the Commission.

Haubtmann has had an audience of the Pope. He had asked him (because it was a point on which many, including Cardinal Cento, had been reticent) if it

---

1. Francis J McCool, SJ, was a professor at the Pontifical Biblical Institute.

should be said that the Church had sometimes been too much the friend of the rich. The Pope replied: it is a delicate matter to express, but it does have to be said. —The Pope asked if atheism was mentioned and said: it must be spoken of in a PASTORAL WAY, that is to say, more about atheists than atheism. —Finally, the Pope insisted that the text be submitted to him BEFOREHAND. He seems to be haunted by the incident of the *De oecumenismo*, and himself said that it must not be repeated. In short, he said about schema XIII what he said about the *De libertate*, or very nearly.

I stayed for supper. Cardinals Richaud, Martin, Mgr Gouyon, Lebrun were there, having come for the new cardinals, with a certain number of priests especially from Rouen. Insignificant conversation.

Bad news in this evening's *L'Osservatore Romano*: the Cardinal Patriarchs will come after the Suburbican Bishops. We had been led to understand something else, and better: that only the Dean of the Sacred College, as the representative of the Pope, Patriarch of the premier See, would precede them. I find that painful!

—This afternoon and this evening, I have largely wasted my time, and 1,500 lire on taxis!!!

Sunday 21 February 1965

Mgr Willebrands, to whom I spoke about this (the matter of the Patriarchs) this morning, told me that the Patriarchs,[1] (and especially Maximos) have received assurances for the future. This is only one stage. It will go further. The Pope always proceeds gradually, without rushing, in progressively bringing future structures into the present ones. He waits for certain posts to fall vacant in order to suppress them *via facti* [by way of deed]. For example, when the major-domo died, he did not appoint a new one. He is proceeding with the reduction of the number of Italian bishoprics by waiting for the death of the holders of the condemned sees. Then, he combines that bishopric with another one. In this way about ten sees have already been combined with others. It is a less spectacular means, but more prudent, and it does not arouse the conflicts and the reaction that an immediate, and directly radical measure would be capable of arousing.

This morning I finished the section asked of me, a kind of *proemium* setting out the gradual education towards freedom in the history of salvation, and concluding by making an introduction to a declaration on freedom as a juridical structure of civil society: the goal of the schema, which, in my view, will have to be strictly adhered to.

Work in common at 4.15 pm. Mgr De Smedt arrived at 6.20 pm. What had been done was explained to him. I got the impression that he was not happy that the *textus emendatus* [emended text] had been changed so much. His silence

---

1. Three Eastern Patriarchs were created cardinals on 22 February: Paul-Peter Meouchi, Maronite Patriarch of Antioch; Stephanos I Sidarouss, Coptic Patriarch of Alexandria; Maximos IV Saigh, Melkite Patriarch of Antioch.

weighed heavily, as though somewhat disapproving. In fact, the group wanted to have already done some work before his arrival because, when he is there, he intervenes . . . He fears that the text is being altered too much. Mgr Willebrands also. This would give a purchase to the criticism already articulated against this text: the Secretariat does not know what it wants, and has not been sufficiently serious about its work.

Fr Murray is less precise than I thought, and has no gift at all for elegant expressions. He is dry and brief. A certain imprecision reigns over our work. In my view, it would have been preferable if a single person had conceived the text as a whole, and we had made that our starting point.

In the evening Fr Hamer—who saw Fr Dumont yesterday and Fr J Bonduelle[1] this evening—brought me up to date about the present situation, truly very complicated and very badly handled, of the negotiations for the transfer of Istina to St Jacques.[2]

Monday 22 February 1965

This morning I had one of the worst half-days of my life. Thank God I had done some work beforehand. But I went with Willebrands and Hamer to the presentation of the *bigletto* [note][3] to the new cardinals. There were three groups: Italian-speakers at the *Domus Mariae*; French-speakers at Propaganda; Anglo-German-Swiss at the American College. We arrived at Propaganda at 9.30 am. The bearers of the note did not arrive until 10.40 am. The reading of the double document to Mgr Cooray, Martin, Villot, Zoungrana, Duval, Cardijn.[4] I had come mainly for the sake of Cardijn, Journet and Duval. Journet was not there. After this double reading six times over, a speech by Cooray, then a speech by Martin (three times too long; some warm, friendly strokes; good seminarian's wit). I greeted the cardinals, especially Cardijn. He embraced everyone, giving pats on the back, a bit like Fr Chenu. He was the most genuine (along with Šeper) of those whom I saw. He said: 'They have given me a voice. I hope to make good use of it.' His consecration yesterday had been, it seems, magnificent with 800 Jocists from Belgium there, singing and praying. To me he said: Help me! Keep on helping me, I will need it. We still need to forge ahead.

After Propaganda I went to the American College. I wanted to greet them all, but one had to wait a long time, in very tiring conditions. At Journet's door, I was turned out fifteen times by some ambassador, or bishop, or photographer, or Mgr Felici. I was furious and refused to sign the register. Journet embraced me and said: Pray for me! This is a very heavy cross!

---

1. Jourdain Bonduelle, OP, of the Province of France, was the *socius* of the Prior Provincial.
2. The Istina Centre was to be set up in Paris, near to the Priory of Saint-Jacques, in 1967.
3. The document sent by the Secretariat of State, announcing their official nomination to the new cardinals.
4. All six were created cardinals.

I saw Jaeger and Roy for a moment; I was not able to see the others. Finished up at the Eastern Congregation. I saw at once Fr Villain, dramatic, and Fr Lanne, furious. The cardinalate for Maximos has been taken very badly by some people. Zoghby sent in his resignation and sent Fr Villain a telegram telling him to make it public everywhere. Fr Lanne told me that at the Eastern Congregation, where he had been present at the presentation of the *bigletto*, he had conspicuously omitted to greet the patriarchs. I do not, myself, have this intransigence. The cardinalate for Maximos astounded me: I do not understand. But I have confidence in Maximos. From any point of view, this must be a painful moment for him; I wanted to demonstrate to him my respectful friendship. I saw Cardinal Meouchi, Maximos, Mgr Beran (a poor little fellow, who seems to know neither French nor German. I had imagined him quite differently). Šeper (wonderfully simple and frank, and who seemed radiant!), Slipyj and Sidarouss (surrounded by his family). Around Maximos, Mgr Edelby seemed preoccupied, crushed: he had the look of someone who throws a careless punch, is surprised at the reaction this brings on, who boxes on but is a little stunned. Maximos wanted to keep me for a moment in order to explain to me. He made me sit down beside him. The Pope had communicated his intention on 17 November; Maximos had at first refused. He had written the Pope a letter of eight pages, setting out all his objections. Despite these, the Pope had insisted that Maximos accept. Maximos considered that he was not able not to accede to this desire of the head of the Church. On the other hand, the Pope accepted almost all his requests and conditions: the patriarchs will remain a distinct group at the Council; Maximos will not walk in front of the *sedia*; they will receive the biretta in their hands, not on their heads. They will not prostrate themselves, they will not kiss the Pope's slipper; they will not be silenced . . .

In spite of all, it is painful. What possessed the Pope to make a gesture that is possibly so full of repercussions for the East? According to Lanne the reaction of the Orthodox Patriarchs is either disapproval, or silence.

We returned at 1.20 pm. Five hours of toing and froing, doing nothing. And not only by us, but by the hundreds of people mobilised by this fourfold ceremony. I emerged morally deflated. It was a void, a mere nothing. While the world was at work, while for us, an hour of work is so valuable, we have here been in the most complete human void: a matter simply of performance, of the ecclesiastical ballet, of the *'bella figura'*. It is fortunate that there were those genuine human beings, such as are, each in his own way, Cardijn, Maximos, Šeper, Journet. I was happy, too, to be able to demonstrate friendship or reverence for Duval, Beran. But what a weight of dead wood there is in the ecclesiology of those who find this wonderful, and see in it the Church at one of its greatest moments!!!

To work!

This evening, from 3.00 pm to 7.30 pm, fairly good work on the *De libertate*.

Frs Neuner, G Baum, Mgr Oesterreicher arrived this evening for the Declaration on Non-Christian Religions.

Tuesday 23 February 1965
A poor night. I woke with very bad pain in the small of my back and my legs.

The Pope continues to read a great deal: books, pamphlets and articles. Willebrands reported to me that he had recently read an article by Küng on the Third Session, which appeared in *Civitas*,[1] a Swiss journal. Küng holds Rome very much accountable for the facts that marked the end of the Third Session, and says that it is for Rome to repair this damage, and that it cannot do this except by reforming itself, by reforming the Curia. At least, that is how I understood the summary that Willebrands gave me. The Pope is somewhat hurt and disappointed. He said: Küng is young. I was hoping he could be a theological leader for the future. But he is without love. He will not be able to be that.

I find this remark profound. Küng is critical. He loves the truth, but has he any mercy for human beings? Has he the warmth and the measure of love?

In the morning, continuation of *De libertate*; at the end of the morning, a bit on *De Iudeis*.

In the afternoon, continued *De libertate*; in the evening at 8.00 pm, a lecture and then dinner at the Spanish College (on Chapter I of *De Ecclesia*). —Moeller arrived this afternoon (but he has barely put in an appearance here.)

Wednesday 24 February 1965
In the office for St Matthias, some wonderful, collegial texts!

De libertate. There arrived, but one after the other, Mgr Primeau, Fr Degrijse[2] (Skeut), Mgr Cantero (Saragossa). Each time, Mgr Willebrands explained what had been done and where we were at. This took up time.

I proposed and defended the order according to which the *Declaration* (No. 3) should be followed immediately not by the rational and anthropological argument, but by the bases of Revelation, including in these (very briefly) the current Number 12 (*Doctrina evangelica* [gospel teaching]) and Number 11 (*libertas actus fidei* [the freedom of the act of faith]). But my idea met with opposition or criticism from Hamer, Murray, Mgr Primeau, and even Willebrands, while at the same time being supported by Feiner and Thijssen. It was decided to come back to the question when the whole thing had been considered paragraph by paragraph, and comment by comment. This is what was done this morning for Nos 10 and 11.

In the afternoon we looked at: 1) a *tentamen* [outline] that I had been asked to make for No. 10; 2) Nos 12–14. I was charged with reworking No. 12, on the basis of the existing text. It was understood that wherever the 'theological part'

---

1. A monthly journal of the Society of Swiss Students.
2. The Belgian, Omer Degrijse, Superior General of the Congregation of the Immaculate Heart of Mary (Missionaries of Scheut), was a member of the Secretariat for Unity, appointed by the Pope.

was to be placed, the order to be followed will be: *Exemplum Christi* [the example of Christ]; *Libertas actus fidei* [the freedom of the act of faith]; *Libertas Ecclesiae* [the freedom of the Church]; *Munus Ecclesiae* [the function of the Church].

Thursday 25 February 1965
Good work on No. 4 of the *textus emendatus* [emended text]. Murray explained the comments made, with great precision. It became apparent soon enough—and there emerged an agreement on this, which I encouraged—that we will need to proceed thus:

- Objective truth the transcendent rule of action.

- The mediation of conscience, which: 1) should be formed according to the truth, and which has for this the duty and the right to listen to other human beings (and to the Church's magisterium itself); 2) has the right not to be constrained to act against itself.

- The right to act ACCORDING to conscience. But here it is a matter of EX-ERCISE, and so there come into play considerations and possibly limitations arising from the public good and the right of other human beings.

It was agreed that, this evening, Murray and Pavan will propose an *ordo dicendorum* [order of things to be said] in accordance with this scheme. They asked me to join them. It was agreed (it was Willebrands who said so) that the drafting should be done by Murray, with advice from Feiner and myself.

But Mgr De Smedt was not happy with this last decision. He said so to Hamer. In general, De Smedt does not like Murray's intervention very much. For him, Murray is the one who transformed the first text (De Smedt) in the *textus emendatus*; he is also, and this is true, a man of a dry and too juridical style; he sees things from a rather individualistic angle. De Smedt, for his part would have wanted to do the drafting, doubtless going back as much as possible to his original text. But in the group there was some fear (especially from Willebrands), of his brisk and rather peremptory manner of intervening.

In the afternoon it was said: Murray and Feiner (for the drafting).

Mgr De Smedt arrived half-an-hour late, Willebrands twenty-five minutes late. People were a bit tired. The *ordo dicendorum* that we had prepared with Pavan and Murray was discussed, without freshness of spirit, and also the revision of No. 12 (the old '*Doctrina Evangelica*) that I prepared. Pavan said to me at the end: how one can waste one's time!

Friday 26 February 1965
Dreadful early hours–kept waking up. My back and lower back were so painful, making any movement so difficult, that I could hardly slide my feet along the floor one after another. I think it is due to the bed, which is too hard. But is it only that?

This morning: 1) revision of No. 6; 2) re-revision of the beginning of the text, already refashioned. In our small group, Mgr Cantero (Saragossa) is a little what

Mgr Wojtyła was for schema XIII: the man who, in his own country, with his colleagues and experts, had drawn up a text on the question, who holds on to it, who brings it back for each chapter, whom one listens to without following, who defends his own position and who ends by committing it to the judgement of all the others, with the disagreeable feeling that it will be found, on his return, that he had not defended well such an excellent, so well-grounded text.

We reread together the beginning of the text. From this it was apparent that it did not emerge sufficiently clearly from the text itself that we begin with a simple recognition of the fact of a generalised attachment to religious freedom today: people believe that at this moment the Council has already begun to declare its own spirit. So we were agreed (and we corrected the text in consequence) to put at the beginning the *proemium* which will consist of two Numbers:

1) *De vocatione ad libertatem in historia salutis* [the vocation to freedom in the history of salvation].

2) *Conceptus modernus libertatis religiosae* [the modern concept of religious freedom].

After this would come the DECLARATION, and then its justifications.

In the afternoon, work on *De libertate* only until 4.00 pm; the three Belgian members left for a papal ceremony connected with the assassination of missionaries in the former Belgian Congo, so the sub-commission suspended its work. I went to the group for *De religionibus non christianis* [on non-Christian religions]. They were obviously dealing particularly with the Number on the Jews and with 'deicide'. Mgr Willebrands explained clearly that the Arabs of the Near East (whose very lively reactions we had to hand) had been very much disturbed by the propaganda put out in Arabic by Israeli Radio: they listen to their broadcasts a lot. But this radio chanted the refrain: the Council has declared the Jews innocent. Our diplomacy has been more skilful and efficacious than that of the Arabs. The Arab agitation comes in large part from this propaganda. Here, this evening we were all in agreement about keeping '*deicida*' [deicide]. Mgr Willebrands found a good solution: while keeping the elements of the text, to reverse the order of two sentences. Thus the caution against accusing the Jews of 'deicide', will be prepared for and explained in advance by what is said about their responsibility in the death of Christ.

Deo gratias! Provided that this text is kept as it is!

De Smedt and Hamer returned at 7.45 pm, from the ceremony at St Paul Outside-the-Walls. The Pope had used some very hard words to stigmatise the barbarity of the rebel Congolese tribes. But above all he baptised twelve black people and confirmed them. The Church goes on !

Saturday 27 February 1965
In the morning, a critical study of No. 4, revised by Murray. The latter certainly has a lovely ability to make welcome the questions of others, which implies an interior humility and an authentic intellectual code of ethics. He also brings to his response a serenity characterised by a composure and a courteous distinction more British, even Oxonian, than American.

In the afternoon, we looked at the end again. I was asked to draft the pastoral addition that I have been promoting. But everyone was very tired. Cantero left, saying that he could not do any more. As for me, I have had flu since yesterday.

Our work as experts is more or less finished. A text will be offered to the Fathers of the Commission. There will still be THEIR discussion, that of the Council, the revision of the text, its being put to the vote, the *modi* . . . Not to mention its being read and assessed by the Pope. He is, it appears, very favourable to the text. But I am sure he will be subjected to terrible pressures. It will be represented to him that, in sanctioning this text, he will contradict the teaching of his predecessors, put the Church at risk, favour indifferentism and individualistic and anarchic relativism. Now, it is true that there is a danger along those lines. But the text should be taken together with the entire work of the Council, which is on the brink of a powerful revitalisation of the Catholic Church and its dynamism.

This does not prevent me questioning myself this evening. Have we done our best, have we done well?

I believe that God does pursue, through human history, a liberation of human beings. But is it THIS liberation that we have served? Yes, I am convinced of it, in so far as it depends on us. But this declaration will be abused to support fraudulent liberations, or to bend true freedom in other directions.

Doubtless we have not prayed enough. We have not sufficiently situated this juridical and civil freedom within the unfolding of the History that is guided by God. We should have proceeded HISTORICALLY, by demonstrating the novelty of the New Testament in relation to the Old. I did do a little of this in my biblical *Proemium*, but too little!

Yesterday's *L'Osservatore Romano* published the appointments of the new cardinals to the Congregations. A good number, and good ones (Cardijn) are appointed to that for Studies and Seminaries. Is this the sign that we are getting away from the regime of Pizzardo and the other cretins? The Pope, I know, believes in culture and is very concerned about it. Only two cardinals have been appointed to the Secretariat for Unity: Shehan and Heenan.[1] —Jaeger and Martin, who currently belong to it, are not appointed to it. Is this an indication that they will remain *durante concilio* [while the Council lasts], in as much as the Secretariat has its conciliar *raison d'être*, that to which it owes its existence, while Shehan and Heenan would be (only through this promotion) intended for the Secretariat under its post-Conciliar and permanent form? Would this even be an indication

---

1. They already belonged to it, as bishops and for the Council.

that the Pope is thinking of giving the Secretariat the structure of a Congregation, characterised by being composed of cardinals? Willebrands is apprehensive that this is so. He thinks, with good reason, that such a structure amounts to giving POWER to incompetent men. Whereas, if the Secretariat has done some good work, this is because it is in the hands of competent and worthwhile men.

Unless it is the case that the Pope wants, from now on, to nominate some cardinals BECAUSE OF their competence in the matters in question?

Sunday 28 February 1965

An almost completely sleepless night. Fever.

I drafted the text on St Thomas for the Studies Commission, a short *relatio* on the new *Proemium*, a presentation on the Declaration *De libertate* for the French episcopate (to be completed when I shall have the definitively decided text).[1]

In the afternoon, Frs del Portillo, Herranz and Lécuyer came to see me. They brought me the bishops' comments on the *De Presbyteris:* 500 bishops had addressed it, which is a very high number. It will be necessary to study these before 22 March, and to prepare some *relationes*. They are optimists. According to them, the work will be interesting.

Departure with Willebrands for Ariccia. He did not tell me much. Only that the Pope had written a letter, not yet published, attaching the Jerusalem Institute to the Secretariat—and also some details about the beginning of the Secretariat:

A request, a project, had come from Paderborn that an organism should be created in the Curia for dealing with ecumenical questions.

When Fr Bea was named cardinal he told the Pope that he would be glad if his cardinalatial dignity gave him more credit for consecrating his final years to the cause of unity. Thus, when John XXIII created the Secretariat in the context of the Council, it was entirely natural that he nominated him to it. Bea has been the absolutely providential person, because he is devoted to ecumenism with faith and competence.

Reached Ariccia at 6.35 pm. Already there were people everywhere, looking for their rooms. Not everyone has yet arrived tonight. I made the acquaintance of new bishops, a good number speaking ENGLISH: friendly and simple men with whom I was at ease straightaway.

But I feel so ill! I cannot lift my right leg more than three centimetres; I slide it along the ground. And I have developed very painful neuralgia in my shoulder and right arm. I have seldom been as low as this.

---

1. Cf Yves Congar, 'La déclaration sur la liberté religieuse', *Études et documents*, No. 15, 14 June 1965.

Monday 1 March 1965

I have atrocious pain in the pelvic bones. I can hardly stand upright. Even vesting for Mass is too much, with all the movements it demands. What have I got? What shall I do?

Opening session. Cardinal Bea gave an overall survey: a list of the chief interventions of the Secretariat since the Third Session, and of its President; attitudes with regard to the Decree on Ecumenism, to the Catholic Church and to the Declaration *De non-christianis* [on non-Christians]. On this point, he noted that the Arab countries had REFUSED to publish any explanation coming from us, either on the radio or IN THE PRESS. He said, too, that care must be taken, before the definitive publication of the declaration, to provide, as far as possible, a psychological preparation. The Arabs make no distinction between politics and religion. They interpret every religious declaration favourable to the Jews as the taking of a stance in favour of the State of Israel.

After a *Relatio generalis* from Fr Hamer (he read his roneoed paper), and a few words of explanation from me, about the *proemium*, there was announced the division of the Fathers and the experts into three sub-commissions, each of which should discuss the text and make a report of its remarks to the general meeting.

Unhappily, the sub-commission to which I was allotted, with Murray, has Cardinal Jaeger for president. He is a much weakened man. He is not there; he falls asleep, he is incapable of putting a precise question at the appropriate moment and directing the discussion, which follows its course whether he is presiding or whether he is absent.

The work of the sub-commission resumed at 3.30 pm, a man in a red zucchetto seated in the middle. A rather painful session. The Fathers were terribly glum, and seemed deflated. It is true that there was a terrible storm raging outside. We discussed interminably, and without finding a solution. Mgr Cantero brought in one or another of the things that he had proposed at Monte Mario, or others. How many times each sentence will have been put through how many mills!!

At 6.00 pm, a meeting of the full Secretariat. Another mill. In a good two hours we did only No. 1 (freedom in the history of salvation), of which more than one passage will need to be revised.

The tiny amount of vitality I used to have, somehow, in my leg is reduced to just as much as is needed to avoid speaking of paralysis. This is certainly my worst day for four years.

Tuesday 2 March 1965

From 7.30 am to 8.15 am, with Mgr De Smedt, to draft the corrections requested.

Continuation of the work on the Numbers for which I am least useless: doctrine in the light of Revelation—because tomorrow I shall no longer be there.

But we pushed on with the work, and, at least in the sub-commission, we did succeed in looking at everything.

After supper, a little work with Pavan to improve the pastoral conclusion.

Mgr Willebrands said to me: this evening's *L'Osservatore Romano* has published on its front page, inset, as though it were an official notice published as such by authority, a statement according to which the *Nota praevia* to Chapter III of the Constitution *De Ecclesia* was an 'authentic source' for the interpretation of the text.[1] But, Fr Duprey has just telephoned Willebrands: the Secretariat has received a telephone call from Mgr Martin of the Secretariat of State, informing him that they are very displeased there with this publication, which does not come from on high, and is in no way official. Willebrands and I had the same reaction, at the same time: if that is so, they should say so in the newspaper itself. It is always the same behaviour, in which a complete honesty is not to be found: 1) 'someone' manages to introduce his preferred idea into the official organs; 2) an unsigned document, with no indication of from where or from whom it comes; 3) it is contradicted quietly, by telephone, not openly, in the public view.

Wednesday 3 March 65 (Strasbourg)

Left Ariccia at 8.00 am, with Fr Hamer. Mgr De Smedt came to see me for a moment before I left. I had the distinct impression that he had really suffered yesterday evening. He is certainly rather sensitive. In fact he had put his heart into this text, especially in certain passages. When one criticises a text 'objectively', one crushes what for its author are the living links, the sensitive connections. I distinctly felt yesterday evening that this had been the case with a criticism made of a section, to which De Smedt was much attached, on prayer as the first act of the *Munus Ecclesiae* [function of the Church]. This morning, Mgr De Smedt said to me: I cannot do any more. I am going to leave this evening. When I told him that I was afraid that, as in the case of Chapter III of the *De Ecclesia*, the Pope might try to rally the minority by some intervention, De Smedt told me to rest very assured on that point. THIS text, and the foundation it provides for religious freedom, are close to his heart. Not only has he several times expressly encouraged Mgr De Smedt in his private audiences, but he has held this position for a long time. Mgr de Smedt has seen the minutes of the meeting of the Central Commission [before the opening of the Council] where the question was debated. There Cardinal Montini had strongly upheld the current point of view against Cardinal Ottaviani and the others.

Thursday 4 March 1965

Visit from Fr Seumois. He came to warn me about certain changes introduced into the *De Missionibus* after his departure, that of Mgr Riobé, and *a fortiori* after my own departure. These changes spoiled the text somewhat and damaged its

---

1. In *L'Osservatore Romano* for 3 March, 'La *Nota explicativa praevia* fonte autentica d'interpretazione della Costituzione dommatica *De Ecclesia*'.

coherence. They are intended to return to the theses dear to Propaganda, and to please the South Americans, to whom it had been said that there was no longer a question of Mission where they were concerned. But this has made a dent in the full notion of Mission, which is co-extensive with the life of the Church. It will be necessary to keep a very attentive watch, and perhaps there will be a confrontation eighteen days from now, at Nemi . . .

Monday 22 March 1965

A Roman again. After some days of unremitting work, very worn out, the usual itinerary: Mulhouse, Basle-Zurich-Rome. Fr Lécuyer met me at the airport. French Seminary. Within a few minutes, I saw Arrighi and the drafting team for schema XIII: Haubtmann, Moeller, Hirschmann. I found myself again in what has become my element and where I feel more at ease than in Strasbourg, where no one is interested in what I do.

Lécuyer told me that the boxed statement in *L'Osservatore Romano* on 2 March, about the *Nota Praevia* to Chapter III of the *De Ecclesia*, would have been prompted by a text of Fr Schillebeeckx that said: if it were not for this Note it would have been possible to interpret the text of the Constitution in the sense that the pope is OBLIGED to consult the bishops in order to promulgate a dogmatic decision. Fr Gagnebet arrived one day brandishing this article and saying: see how necessary the note was.

Fr Gagnebet also told Arrighi that the minority would do their utmost to prevent the *De libertate* from getting through. That was why the Secretariat was considering adding to its side the weight that an agreement with the Theological Commission might have, by submitting the text to it once again. Arrighi insists that I should come to Rome from 3 to 9 May, for the final revision of the *De libertate* (which is currently with the Pope) and for the Ecumenical Directory of the Secretariat.

Arrighi also told me that the Pope has just received the new delegate from Canterbury.[1] He had HIMSELF raised the question of Anglican Orders. He said: I don't believe that one can go back on the judgement of Leo XIII,[2] but it will be necessary to find a way to change things. In my view, it is an appeal to Canterbury that it should refine the propositions already sketched out by Ramsey.[3] This is important and remarkable.

At 4.30 pm, at the Commission *De disciplina Cleri*, at the premises of the Congregation. Present were Frs del Portillo and Herranz, Lécuyer, Sigmond, Mgr Onclin and I. We looked at the comments on the *proemium*, No. 1, and the begin-

---

1. Canon John Findlow was the Observer delegated by the Anglican Communion, and the representative of the Archbishop of Canterbury during the Third and Fourth Sessions.
2. In the bull, *Apostolicae Curae* of 13 September 1896, Leo XIII had declared null the ordinations which had taken place in the Anglican Church since the schism.
3. In an interview given to *The Economist*, he had suggested for the Anglican Church a status analogous to that of the Eastern Catholic Churches.

ning of No. 2. I was completely exhausted and scarcely able to move my right leg. It is awful to have to keep on walking and working when one has no longer *ANY* strength!

In the evening, at dinner, there were three of the drafting team for schema XIII and Mgr Kominek, a Polish bishop from the Commission on the Laity. He talked inexhaustibly about the situation in Poland, with an enormous confidence, with something, even, of that daring confidence in Poland which I often noticed in my Polish comrades in captivity. According to him, communism is changing; there is an evolution, a certain liberation. The Russians are detested in Poland— and they are in China, too. The Russians think a great deal about the Yellow Peril. In Poland no one believes in Marxism. The young? Not even them now. They look at the Church in a rather critical manner, but if a young and sympathetic priest puts himself forward, they follow him. Etc.

Later on he said: at home one cannot have this sort of conversation, or express oneself so FREELY.

Tuesday 23 March 1965

As Fr Lécuyer was occupied this morning, there was no meeting. I worked on the text on the tradition of the Church with regard to its temporal possessions.[1]

Moeller (who doubtless had it from Onclin?) reported on the subject of the *De Episcoporum munere:* the opponents are mounting a terrible offensive to make the Pope alter, or reject, two points: 1) that the Council express the desire to see the Pope create an advisory council for himself. The Council is not able even to formulate such a wish. That would be to limit the *plena potestas* [plenary power] of the primacy; 2) that nuncios should be excluded from episcopal conferences.

On the first point, Moeller said that the Pope was on the point of giving way. But Haubtmann said: this would greatly astonish me because THIS point WAS INTRODUCED INTO THE TEXT AT THE WISH OF THE POPE (audience given to Mgr Veuillot). *Videbimus* [we shall see].

At 4.30 pm, work. Onclin was absent. Sigmond told us—under secrecy—a little about the papal commission on birth control.[2] It consists of about fifty members, half of whom are medics. These have said that the Church will make itself ridiculous if it does not speak about the pill; because it is the pill today, but it will be something else tomorrow. The commission has therefore considered an enormous volume of documentation, but it will have great difficulty in giving truly concrete indications. It will inevitably remain on the level of theological and moral principles. However, the Pope has said: give me some precise conclusions, so that I might be able to say something . . .

For my part, I think that opinion should be got ready to receive a MORAL teaching. Public opinion in this area is very materialistic. It wants a 'thinguma-

---

1. Cf Yves M-J Congar, 'Les biens temporel de l'Église d'après sa tradition théologique et canonique', in *L'Église et pauvreté*, 'Unam Sanctam', 57 (Paris: Cerf, 1965), 233–258.
2. Cf above, page 650, note 5.

bob' which, if it is 'allowed', will dispense people from seeking to act virtuously. It is true that the casuists were the first materialists. They thought they had hold of there a marvellous matter where sin could be weighed and numbered, measured and assigned a price, bound, as it was considered to be, to the material thing as such. So public opinion must be got ready not to accept a material 'thingumabob', or a statement of permission or prohibition about such a material 'thingumabob'.

Wednesday 24 March 1965

Work on *De Presbyteris* in the morning (in the absence of Sigmond), and in the evening. In between, I prepared the corrected text of the paragraphs I had drafted, and a text on mission and presence to the world.

Fr Sigmond absent (→ the Commission on birth-control).

This evening at 7.30 pm, on leaving our afternoon session, I was collected by a Father of the African Missions. Actually, I was invited by the Superiors of the missionary congregations. About ten people but not all were superiors. These (African Missions, Picpus, Capuchins, an Augustinian, Fr Seumois . . .) were mainly Dutch. It is the group that—with some others—drafted the schema *De Missionibus*, called the group of Superiors of Missionary Societies.

A sumptuous and super-abundant dinner (although I ate little I shall sleep badly!); a very congenial atmosphere, straightforward and open.

After dinner, we discussed the schema for an hour and a half. Reactions of the Augustinian Father, a Dutchman, sharp enough, but hyper-critical. Useful. They were pointed in the direction that I believe is true. It appears that an attack is being prepared, for the meeting at Nemi, by the recognised missiologists who are stuck in a territorial and juridical concept of Mission, although a conciliar ecclesiology requires a dynamic conception: not considering the territories and organisations so much as the living goals and the situations and tasks that correspond to them.

Thursday 25 March 1965

Work. Made some progress. But it is so long![1]

Friday 26 March 1965

In the morning, we each worked on our own to refine the Numbers so far looked at as a whole. It is longer than I thought. And to think that the Commission is going to mix up lots of things in what has been so carefully arranged, and that afterwards there will be the discussion *in aula*, the revision of the text, the *modi*, the *expensio modorum*.[2] It is a galley-slave's job!

And this will start over again for schema XIII and the Missions as well!!

---

1. Congar added to the typescript: '*De Presbyteris*'.
2. This term indicates both the analysis of the *modi* that had been proposed and the augmented response made to them; the term indicates both this work and the written report that was submitted to the Council Fathers.

Saturday 27 March 1965

This morning we finished the *De presbyteris*. I did all my Numbers and the *Relatio* for each of them.

At lunch, Mgr Ancel and Garrone, who have come for schema XIII.

Afternoon, work: I started again to draft my paper of the tradition concerning the Church in the temporal sphere.

The same for **Sunday 28 March 1965**

Departure for Nemi at 6.15 pm. We got there at 7.20 pm (Fr Superior and Fr Bouju[1] took me by car). A house built three years ago by the Divine Word Fathers: architecture rather dry and hard, functional; a thoroughly modern installation, and finished to the last detail. I thought of Le Saulchoir, that we have not managed to finish!! We are poor . . .

The Fathers and experts who had already arrived were at supper. Not everyone was there yet, but I got a first impression of the situation.

On everyone's table there is a pile of papers representing the reactions to—inevitably the criticisms of—the schema. There is an extremely violent attack by Fr André Seumois against the whole of the schema and its doctrine; his violence will do him harm! Another totally negative reaction from a Fr Buijk, SJ,[2] Rome(?). I feel myself rather overwhelmed by so many comments, many of which are pertinent. Finally a page in Italian, coming personally from the Pope. He criticised the notion and the definition of MISSION as referring to the people of God, and not to apostolicity, to the mission of the Twelve and of the Hierarchy. Certainly, I was not excluding that. I envisage a structured people of God. Obviously, it will be necessary to make careful refinements in this sense, and establish clearly the Mission of the Twelve.

Monday 29 March 1965

What a house! Everything is complete: marble and panelling, ornaments, everything . . . At breakfast, everyone around me was laughing at the excessive and violent reaction of Fr Seumois OMI: *'detestabilis, insanabilis . . . peccatum originale'* [detestable, incurable . . . original sin] . . .

I finished becoming acquainted with the dossier.

At 10.00 am, the inaugural session. I met Fr A Seumois in the corridor and we went in together . . . Cardinal Agagianian was presiding. Almost all the Fathers were there. There are eleven *periti*.

For five or six days now I have had a VERY great intensification of the buzzing or whistling in my ears, and, when I shut my eyes tightly, I have a sort of vertigo.

---

1. Daniel Bouju, Holy Spirit Father, Director of the French Seminary in Rome.
2. The Dutchman, Lodewijk Buijk, SJ, Professor of Canon Law at the Gregorianum, was a consultor for the Congregation of Propaganda; after having been a consultor for the Preparatory Commission for the Missions, he was a Council expert.

I am breaking up bit by bit. *'Licet is qui foris est noster homo . . .* ' [but though our outward man {perish} (2 Cor 4:16)].

The cardinal quickly came to: 'the purpose of THIS commission' = not the whole evangelisation of the world but missionary activity *'quantum ad aliquid signum minus generalem'* [in a less general sense], that is, with respect to a *'particularis conditio quae verificatur in certis locis'* [particular situation that exists in certain places]. Mission is concerned with (IS) *'illa territoria pro quibus ex ordinatione Sedis Apostolicae'* [those territories for which, at the direction of the Apostolic See], the Congregation *Pro Propaganda fide* pays out subsidies and is the administrative authority. *'Procedamus ab aliquo facto contingenti'* [let us start from a contingent fact]: that one. They begin from it and remain in it!

The cardinal left immediately after having formulated his idea thus (and so naively). He appointed Fr Schütte as Vice-President in his absence. Schütte thus took the chair at 10.35 am. He DIRECTED the debate well, but he did not really PRESIDE. Unceasingly, instead of allowing the Fathers to speak, he immediately expressed his own position or reaction.

Mgr Lecuona read out a *relatio* on the *ordo agendi* [order of procedure]. Its proposals were accepted (in principle!). Then a sub-division into sub-commissions was proposed:
- Chapter I: Lokuang, D'Souza, Yago, Sevrin,[1] Cavallera;[2]
- Chapter II: Zoa, Sison,[3] Sartre, Perrin, Kerketta;[4]
- Chapter III: Lecuona, Pollio,[5] Mabathoana,[6] Deschâtelets;[7]

---

1. The Belgian Jesuit Oscar Sevrin, a titular bishop living in India, was elected a member of the Commission for the Missions during the First Session.
2. Charles M Cavallera, Bishop of Marsabit (Kenya), a member of the Commission for the Missions, appointed after the Second Session.
3. Juan C Sison, Coadjutor of Nueva Segovia (Philippines), a member of the Commission for the Missions, elected during the First Session.
4. Pius Kerketta, SJ, Archbishop of Ranchi (India), a member of the Commission for the Missions, elected during the First Session.
5. Gaetano Pollio, Archbishop of Otrante (Italy), a member of the Commission for the Missions, elected during the First Session.
6. Emmanuel Mabathoana, Bishop of Maseru (Basutoland), a member of the Commission for the Missions, appointed during the First Session.
7. Leo Dechâtelets, Superior General of the Oblates of Mary Immaculate (Canada), a member of the Commission for the Missions, appointed during the First Session.

- Chapter IV: Schütte, Ngô-dình-Thuc,[1] Mahon,[2] Ungarelli;
- Chapter V: Riobé, Escalante,[3] Sheen, Comber,[4] Bolte.[5]

At Zoa's suggestion, the sub-commission on the *Proemium* will be formed LAT-ER, of one member from each of the other sub-commissions.

Schütte read an objective *relatio generalis*. Fr A Seumois, sitting beside me, reacted in a rather lively manner at several points.

F Sheen suggested adding a chapter (a section?) on ecumenism, and changing the title. He would prefer *'De Ecclesia missionali'* [on the missionary Church]. His suggestions did not meet with much support.

We then moved on to the question of the nature and the definition of mission. The bishops gave expression to different points of view. Several bishops from the younger churches (Yago, D'Souza) were in favour of a territorial definition.

I was asked for my view. I said this: 1) If what is wanted is a definition with a THEOLOGICAL foundation, one must necessarily start from a broad notion, of the mission OF THE CHURCH itself; then one can specify a stricter sense. 2) That, or the missions, should be defined by their object or their goal. These are not territories, but PEOPLE: those who do not know Christ, or do not believe in him. Mission has in view groups of people in the situation of unbelief. It can very often be the case that, in *FACT*, these groups are to be found in large numbers in certain *PLACES*, and that, therefore, in FACT, Mission has in view certain PLACES: this might very often be the case, but it is ACCIDENTAL: the cardinal himself used the word 'contingent'. Territory, AS SUCH, is not a formal part of the definition. 3) So one cannot oppose as CONTRADICTORY a geographical definition and a sociological one (I prefer to say anthropological): they are not on the same plane. The one is essential, the other is accidental. In my view, one ought to be able to LOCATE the territorial notion within the definition that has HU-MAN situations in view. It should be possible to agree and to arrive at unanimity.

The next to speak were Fr A Seumois (territorial notion, *'plantatio Ecclesiae'* [planting of the Church][6] UNDERSTOOD IN A TERRITORAL SENSE, Grasso, Glazik, Buijk, FX Seumois). When No. 17 of the *De Ecclesia* was invoked, I said: I

---

1. PM Ngô-dình-Thuc.
2. Gerald Mahon, Superior General of the Mill Hill Society for the Foreign Missions, recently made a member of the Commission for the Missions.
3. Bishop Alonso M Escalante, Superior General of the Institute of Our Lady of Guadaloupe for Foreign Missions (Mexico), a member of the Commission for the Missions, elected during the First Session.
4. Bishop John W Comber, Superior General of the Maryknoll Missionaries (United States) and a member of the Commission for the Missions, elected during the Second Session.
5. Adolf Bolte, bishop of Fulda (Germany), a member of the Commission for the Missions, elected during the Second Session.
6. A technical term used by missiologists.

drafted it. It was not intended to introduce there a juridical-static concept, but to apply there the DYNAMIC concept of the Church which is that of the Constitution. The notion of *plantatio* should be understood in the same manner.

At 11.35 am, the experts were dismissed, while the sub-commissions remained behind to choose the experts they would invite.

At 5.00 pm a plenary meeting. Mgr Lokuang gave a *relatio* (somewhat mediocre, not precise) on Chapter I. But, as I had requested of him, he asked the Commission for a secret vote to give direction on various points, for the work of the sub-commission on Chapter I.

1) On the notion of Mission:
   a. Is a purely territorial definition wanted?
      Yes =1, No =21.
   b. Is the TOTAL EXCLUSION of the territorial idea from the notion of Mission wanted?
      In favour of exclusion =1; Against total exclusion = 20.

2) On the retention of Nos 9 and 10 in Chapter I, or their transfer to Chapter II? Mgr Riobé intervened in favour of retention. The vote favoured this by 19 to 3.

3) Finally the motives for mission, and its necessity, were discussed. Mgr Perrin intervened in favour of insisting on charity [but Fr A Seumois, sitting beside me, said: 'That is external to mission! It is purely moral . . . '].

The sub-commissions met separately. See previous page for the list of their composition. The notion of mission was discussed first. Fr A Seumois several times wanted to bring in his own concerns, and read a (very pedestrian) text he had prepared. But it was not only Ratzinger who criticised his text: Mgr Lokuang told him it was off the point, that our text should be taken as the basis. Mgr Lokuang saw to it that we stuck to the strict line of the text and the mandate received from the Commission, the same stubbornness that had sometimes made our work difficult in January.

It was agreed that the experts will meet tomorrow at 8.15 am, that they will present a text to the five Fathers of the sub-commission before lunch, and that it will be discussed from 4.15 pm, after tea.

Sunset, with an immensely empurpled horizon. I prayed in the spirit of Tere: Tere the missionary, Tere the contemplative. I always work with her, or rather—I hope and believe—SHE works with me.

This evening, after a short recreation, work on what has to be presented tomorrow.

(We had a much too copious fare. Not only no sign of Lent, but a real excess of everything. In the evening, there was a gathering for drinks. It is obviously useful for creating an atmosphere of cordiality, and that is why Fr Schütte does it. But what expense!!)

Tuesday 30 March 1965

At 8.15 am, a meeting of our sub-commission. I proposed that there be sent all round a No. 5, where THE general mission of the Church or apostolate will be defined—and a No. 6 which will go on expressly to the *apostolatus missionalis* [missionary apostolate] in the strict sense. This was accepted well enough, and I was asked to produce a proposal for drafting at midday.

We reached a unanimous agreement . . .

I realised that the Preparatory Commission on Missions had been completely under the influence of Fr Buijk. He teaches canon law and particularly missionary law. He had arranged and drafted everything from the point of view of canon law. In his criticisms of my text which, according to him, should be entirely rejected, he said that the missions have no relationship at all with the Trinitarian Processions!!! In truth, the movement of the Council from one end to the other—and most especially here—will have consisted in moving from the purely juridical towards a supernatural ontology. Frs Seumois (A) and Reuter are of the same bent as Buijk. And, this morning, Mgr Pavente[1] too: for him the 'real' (his expression) begins with the juridical definition. Otherwise it is a matter of spirituality or of poetry.

Our epoch is at last overcoming the divorce introduced between mysticism and theology; the study of the Fathers has been both a cause and a result of this.

At the general meeting this evening, there was discussion of the CENTRAL COUNCIL FOR EVANGELISATION that we want to recommend in the schema. First a vote was taken to decide whether or not to retain the allusion to the senate of bishops spoken of in *De episcoporum munere pastorali* [on the pastoral duty of bishops]. The Commission was unanimous in favour of retention.

With regard to the Central Council for Evangelisation, there were two contrasting conceptions: either make of it, in the context of Propaganda, a motivating instrument that is directive and DECISIVE, made up of true representatives of the episcopate that is engaged in the Missions and of the Superiors of Congregations—in place of the current cardinals who make up the Congregation, who have authority, but neither competence nor dynamism—or make of it an organism apart from Propaganda, and above it. But this second concept turned out to be inconsistent. A vote will be taken tomorrow on the first one.

Work began on the revision of Chapter I in the sub-commissions, but this evening, after the plenary meeting, there was a lack of freshness.

Wednesday 31 March 1965

I slept badly; lay awake for a long time. I ruminated on our affairs and was worried about having been too welcoming of the strict definition of the properly mis-

---

1. Saverio Paventi, of the diocese of Benevento (Italy), was professor of Canon Law of the Missions at the Pontifical Ecclesiastical Academy; a Council expert, he was Secretary for the Commission on Missions.

sionary apostolate by *plantatio Ecclesiae*. However, it is true, and if this *plantatio* is related not to territories but to people or to groups of people, then my idea of a unique mission immediately specified by the conditions in which it is exercised will have been met.

We had to make peace and avoid rousing an opposition which the likes of Fr André Seumois would certainly have stirred up. The majority of the Fathers on the Commission and of the missionaries want to speak not of THE mission of the Church, but of the missions. THAT IS THE SUBJECT OF THE SCHEMA.

A plenary session on Chapter V and the *Proemium*.

Two hours of work in the sub-commission for the revision of the text of Chapter I. Fr A Seumois really is an ass. He has HIS set of ideas, he has HIS answers all prepared. Not for a moment, in any degree, does he try to be open to anything else, to entertain the point of view of someone else. Whatever does not coincide with his idea, his formula, is empty, stupid, useless, to be rejected. It is ABSOLUTELY impossible to have a single minute's DIALOGUE with him. Everything has been judged in advance, arranged in advance. Not even Fr Tromp, at the time when he prospered, was so immovable. In contrast, in our sub-commission: Mgr Yago says nothing and appears to be very bored; Mgr Perrin scarcely follows what is going on and is no help; Mgr Cavallera agrees; Mgr D'Souza says nothing, except occasionally, to set forth in dramatic and prophetic tones, ideas or difficulties from which nothing can make him budge. It is Mgr Lokuang who is still the one most engaged, and the best. Sometimes he shuts A Seumois up, by telling him that we have heard enough of him, or that he is off the point, or that he was not asked to do that. I have confidence in Lokuang. But, for myself, I am one who tries to compromise for the good of peace. Fortunately, Ratzinger is there. He is reasonable, modest, disinterested, a great help. These meetings of the sub-commission, under these conditions, are wearing me out. And since I am exhausted by the dreadful work of these pernickety discussions, and the meticulous revision I have been doing non-stop since 22 March, I would like to send the whole lot packing. I am clinging on. I look for strength in prayer.

Thursday 1 April 1965

Still a LITTLE insomnia. This worries me and even plagues me. Fr A Seumois said to Mgr Riobé: 'I have come here to introduce some of my theses into the schema'. This morning, I am preparing the sub-commission's discussion on the diverse conditions encountered by missionary activity. There will be three propositions:

- Ratzinger, who has made a single text out of this section and the one defining missionary activity (text already approved); that is the solution I would prefer because it reaffirms my idea of the unity of mission, diversified according to the conditions in which it is exercised;
- a revision and conflation,[1] made by me, of the current text;
- a proposition by Seumois (OMI): yet to be seen, and that I am dreading.

---

1. The space for this word was left blank in the typescript, Congar added it in his own hand.

In the end, that went well. Ratzinger's text was accepted, on condition that I complete it. At 3.30 pm I finished the polishing up of the text of Chapter I, and sent it to be typed.

We waited an interminable time for the cardinal, who was supposed to come. After which there were several photos, both outside and in. The session did not start until 5.15 pm. So much time lost! Discussion of Chapter V in the presence of the cardinal, in a somewhat artificially well-behaved atmosphere; in which people laughed at nothing in a climate of equally artificial benevolence. Fr Schütte insisted a lot on unanimity and asked that when the schema came to be voted on by the Commission, a bloc should be formed to support it (*in genere*, while nevertheless retaining liberty in one's estimation of the detail). The reference to twinning was removed from the text. After this, discussion of the revised text of Chapter III commenced immediately. Interminable quibbling. But these two chapters are very little changed and present no difficulties. If Chapter I is dealt with in the same way tomorrow, how will that go?

Friday 2 April 1965

In the morning: discussion of Chapter III was completed, Chapter II was discussed; Mgr Lokuang gave, in a most confused manner, a very incomplete *relatio* on the changes introduced into Chapter I.

During the 'siesta' I composed the *relatio* on Chapter I.

At 4.30 pm, discussion—or rather non-discussion!—on Chapter I: only two or three stylistic comments were made . . . Perhaps the Fathers were tired. They had, however, had leisure to read the text, distributed this morning. It is also true that 'theology' frightens them; they do not feel well at ease in this area. In the end, I had about ten appreciative comments from them, they trust me and give me enormous credit. To such a degree that, very quickly, a UNANIMOUS vote was obtained. This was a great achievement. The unity of Mission is affirmed!!!

After this, a fairly animated discussion of the new text of the *Proemium*, written too quickly, without inspiration, without that certain tone of nobility that seems to me to be appropriate for a *proemium*. I found it bad. It is a great shame!

Then the election of the *Relator in aula* = Fr Schütte, unanimous except for one vote in favour of Zoa—as a joke.

I copied out my *relatio* again.

Saturday 3 April 1965

I finished at exactly 7.30 pm. At supper on Friday evening, I was offered the opportunity of going back to Rome immediately, by car. I accepted. (At dinner Ratzinger told me that the Declaration on the Jews was thought to be again in question. The Pope was thought to be convinced of the collective responsibility of the Jewish people in the death of Christ. And that would cause some fresh difficulties.) Immediately afterwards, I was given a telephone message from Fr Mayer, Secretary of the Commission for Studies and the training of priests; he had asked me to come to the Commission for half a day, and that was planned for this Saturday morning. That was why I was going back to Rome. But he telephoned me to say that it was not worth the effort of coming. Good. All the same I went back to Rome. Our work was finished. This Saturday morning there will be only a eucharistic concelebration (with three experts) presided over by the cardinal, then the final, overall vote on the schema and the reading (approval) of the *Relatio* that they want to add to it to explain the meaning of the sequencing of the chapters and the paragraphs. In Rome I will be able either to work, or to go to schema XIII . . .

Departure on Friday at 8.35 pm. At the French Seminary at 9.30 pm. I met Mgr Garrone. He brought me up to date about the work on schema XIII. They are working every day, morning and evening, except Sundays. They are about half way through (today: the family). The experts are not allowed to speak, unless they are asked a question. It is going well. For the first part, Mgr Garrone told me, they followed fairly closely the Ariccia text, but improved it. It is readable, even though the Latin will need to be revised again.

This Saturday morning I got up early after a poor night. (The buzzing in my ears has got a lot worse in recent days. It is such as to keep me awake. It is like the sound of an unremitting electric motor.) I was wondering whether I would work here, or to go to schema XIII instead, to meet the people and renew contact with the team.

Eventually, I decided on the latter. It is important to renew contact with these people. In fact within a few minutes I saw about a hundred people whom I already know well, and with whom the conciliar work has created close and trusting bonds; and then Cardinal Ottaviani who was friendly, even cordial (he asked me what work I had on the go). This morning, they are to deal with the *De Matrimonio et Familia*: there is the MAXIMUM presence of Fathers and experts. Mgr Dearden told me that Cardinal Mayer is finished.[1] His brain operation has revealed cancer. Since then he has not regained consciousness except for ONE brief moment. What a tragedy! He could have been the guide to the USA hierarchy. I had a real, human and intellectual fellow-feeling for him . . .

Cardinal Florit again raised the question of the ends of marriage, of the balance between contract and love in the proposed text. Doumith and McGrath are insisting on this: to talk about love is all very well, but it could be ambiguous because people of today, Christians and non-Christians, mean very different things by 'love'. The word, and what it designates, are so exalted and so perverted in our erotic age that the text could be dangerous, not sufficiently envisaging the concrete REALITY. (And similarly van Dodewaard). Cardinal Browne also intervened again on *amor concupiscentiae* [love arising from concupiscence] and *amor amicitiae* [love arising from friendship]. Mgr Fernandez, Cardinals Ottaviani, Spanedda (along the lines of Lio), Colombo.

---

1.   He was to die on 7 April 1965.

I found myself among men who: 1) know how to express themselves in Latin with precision and brevity; 2) have a good knowledge of the requirements of doctrine, and attack a subject on the level of a real discussion of IDEAS. After having frequented some other commissions, I became still more aware of what the Theological Commission, whose members chiefly intervened this morning, has represented in terms of value, of strictness, of precision, of attention in the work.

Volk asked that the personalist element should not be diminished. But his intervention, which was laborious, was a bit vague in its profundity. He insisted on the connection between the personal relationship with God and the personal nature of the matrimonial bond (of the nature of *Foedus* [covenant]).

Garrone and Wojtyła: make very clear on what grounds the Council speaks to Christians and speaks to Non-Christians.

Tromp intervened at Ottaviani's request. He recalled what had been prepared by the Preparatory Commission.

Dearden, then Charue: the text itself answers many of the criticisms made. The difficulties fall away if it is read as a whole.

Philips will have to respond to everything. That is a dreadful piece of work to impose on him. But as Fr de Lubac, who was sitting beside me, said: he has the satisfaction of making what he pleases of the Joint Commission.

After the interval, Cardinal Ottaviani announced that Fr Tromp was going to make a declaration. In fact, Fr Tromp, with his imperious voice as of the highest tribunal, said: just as faith without being informed by charity, is truly the assent of faith, in the same way the marriage contract, without being informed by charity, is the essence of marriage.

This unleashed a hilarious reaction.

The continuation was read and it appeared that it did answer many of the objections raised before it was read. But, all the same, many questions were put again. Doumith: it does not bring out that marriage is both a natural and a supernatural institution over which no human will, no decision, either individual or of the civil powers, has the slightest authority. Cardinal Roy: give more affirmation to the absolute value of the bond. Etc.

Fr de Lubac (like Fr Sigmond a while ago) drew my attention the place taken by the Belgians in this work. In his view, there is some indiscretion on their side. Thus, yesterday or the day before, Dom Butler, who is a good exegete, made an exegetical comment. Mgr Charue intervened to say: we will look at that with the exegetes. That meant: with Rigaux and possibly Cerfaux, in short, Louvain. This was one of the most remarkable things—I have mentioned it previously: by this roundabout means of the verification of biblical quotations, the Belgians have accorded themselves a sort of right of revision. Yet there are other exegetes, quite as able. But, on the other hand it is true that: 1) the Belgians have done this work well; 2) they have rendered, and are still rendering, immense service. They have been effective. Philips has been crucial. Without him the work of the Theological Commission would never have been what it has been. Again for schema XIII, he has been extremely valuable. And Moeller has also done excellent work every-where, very effective.

At the French Seminary, an ordination lunch. A very agreeable atmosphere. I managed a little correspondence. Mgr McGrath came to collect me at 4.00 pm, to drive me to the airport, but more particularly, to secure my participation in a Theology Week at Notre Dame in March 1966. Given the way things are turning out, and the great objective interest of the project, I will not be able to refuse. And yet yesterday I received an official invitation to do a lecture tour in Poland. My poor weeks are being whittled away without let-up!!!

Sunday 4 April 1965

This morning, in Paris, for a meeting with the Marxists of the *Nouvelle Critique*. On the Catholic side: Chenu, Jolif,[1] Duquoc[2] and me. On the Marxist side: Mury,[3] Casanova,[4] Milhau,[5] and a fourth.[6] The object, preparation of an issue of the *Nou-velle Critique*[7] on the Council and the Church on the move.

29 April 1965

I saw Mgr Etchegaray for a moment. He has come from Rome. He gave me some bits of information from there:

The journal *Concilium* seems to be under threat. He heard some criticisms of it in various places and congregations where he went. My own impression is clear since the meeting in Rome of those working together on DO-C[8] during the Third Session: 1) the editors will not manage to keep up the rate of ten fascicles per year with translation into several languages; 2) there are going to be difficulties there on the Italian side. But the specifically Italian problems of timeliness reverberate in the Curia in as much as it is a Curia that calls itself universal. The theologi-cal personality of someone like Schillebeeckx is rather *ingrata* [unwelcome], and Rome keeps a careful eye on anything that could threaten its primacy, not just from the dogmatic point of view, but with respect to its claims, in practice, to be in charge of everything.

On the other hand, the minority will threaten the work of the Council during the Fourth Session on three points: 1) in the *De pastorali Episcoprum munere*, the participation of nuncios in episcopal conferences; 2) *ibidem*, the power of

---

1. Jean-Yves Jolif, OP, of the Province of Lyons, taught philosophy at the Dominican *studium* of Éveux and at the Catholic Faculties in Lyons.
2. Christian Duquoc, OP, of the Province of Lyons, taught philosophy at the Catholic Faculties in Lyons and at the Dominican *studium* in Éveux.
3. Gilbert Mury, sociologist, attached to the Centre for Marxist Studies and Research.
4. Antoine Casanova, historian.
5. Jacques Milhau.
6. Jacques Arnault.
7. A Marxist review.
8. (Dutch Centre of Council Documentation).

bishops; 3) *ibidem*, the establishment of an Advisory Council to the pope. The latter, after having himself made an overture in this direction publicly and even solemnly on three or four occasions, has been impressed by the difficulties that have been presented to him. To such a degree that it seems obvious that if the thing is not achieved under pressure from the Council and the atmosphere that the conciliar meeting itself will create one last time, it will not be achieved for a long time!

On the other hand, the Pope is wholly in agreement with the text of *De libertate*. I shall find out next Monday.

Etchegaray told me that there are grounds for fearing that the Co-ordinating Commission, which meets on 11 or 12 May, wants to shorten the *De Missionibus* and, for this purpose, will remove from Chapter I some paragraphs that are considered to double up on Chapter I of the *De Ecclesia.*

Also today, 30 April, I wrote to Cardinals Liénart, Lercaro and Suenens, to give them the reasons that seem to me decisive in favour of keeping the text as it is.

(I received good replies from the first and third of these. It seems that Lercaro never answers letters . . .)

2 May 1965

Departure from Strasbourg for Paris at 8.00 am. Lunch for the twentieth anniversary of the liberation of Lübeck.[1] I met again a number of my comrades, a lot of Jews. In the welcome of almost everyone, I felt a sense of trust. Marx from Lyons, spoke to me about John XXIII, who was for them the man by whom they felt they were loved. Jacob came to tell me that someone, coming back from Rome, said to him that there is still a lively opposition to the Declaration on the Jews; some people wanted it elevated to the theological level . . . The Pope will need to be strengthened in the right direction; now, there are two men he listens to: M. Maritain and Fr Congar.

I pass over the naivety of this last suggestion, but I can see that the information is pretty accurate. I will find out tomorrow.

I was pleased to find myself among so many comrades, Jews in particular. Sadly, I had to leave at 3.45 pm, so I had only a little time to clasp so many hands, and try to recognise so many faces. Jeanjean[2] looked awful. He has been, and still is, pretty ill.

At Orly I felt like death, and had all the difficulty in the world in taking even a few steps, or rather in dragging my poor leg. Even my arm was without strength, and I leaned on my stick by intention and will, but without the least strength. It was the same at Fiumicino, all the more so as Rome is in its worst stormy weather.

---

1. Congar had been liberated on 2 May 1945, at the time he was in Oflag XC, near Lübeck.
2. Paul Jeanjean, from the Ardennes, a priest of the diocese of Rheims, who was a friend of Congar from their time in the junior seminary, had caught up with him again during their captivity in Germany.

I have no longer anything to offer to God except the total absence of strength. If *'virtus in infirmitate perficitur'* [power is made perfect in weakness (2 Cor 12:9)]—the principle on which I have lived my life—I should not have come in vain. For it is a complete nothing that God will be making use of. At Rome, St Dominic received the staff and the book, but it was a pilgrim's staff. I carried there only a staff of weakness.

However, I do have a certain joy in finding myself back here. So many things are familiar to me, or evoke agreeably happy memories! I reached Santa Sabina at 7.45 pm.

I am afraid I may have come for nothing, at least as far as this phantom Commission *De apostolatu* [on the apostolate][1] is concerned. I have received no programme, no documentation. I fear that this commission is only meeting for the sake of form, in order to be able to say to the General Chapter at Bogota[2] that it did meet. That too I will find out tomorrow.

Monday 3 May 1965

Fr Bosco told me: No meeting before tomorrow, Tuesday. And there is not much business, Fr Congar being the only, or almost the only one, to have replied last year. So I went to the Secretariat (for Unity) at 9.00 am. The Secretariat is in its new premises, which Mgr Willebrands showed me round with a good humour. The Vatican has done a good job. There are plenty of offices, anterooms, everything smells of paint and new furniture. It is pleasant to see something expanding. The people we met also had, even outwardly, an openness, a dynamism, a note of joy. A contrast with Santa Sabina, where the impression is one of conservation, of inactivity, although in a charming fraternity.

We waited a good while before starting the meeting. Mrg Willebrands said: there are three subjects:

RELIGIOUS FREEDOM: the text has been submitted to the members of the Theological Commission, who have forwarded their comments. These will have to be studied by a small sub-commission; Murray, Pavan, Feiner, Congar.

The Pope himself approves the text. He asked if (my) *proemium* is really *ad rem* and is not just an hors-d'oeuvre . . . But Pavan wants it kept.

DIRECTORY:[3] Willebrands would like to be able to proceed to a rather wide consultation. To have the authority to do this he had sought the authorisation of the Pope, because the Secretariat is at present only an organisation linked to the Council: one would need to be assured that some other organism would not consider itself to be more suitable. The Secretariat has received many suggestions in response to the short questionnaire circulated to friends; these have been typed up.

---

1. This refers more precisely to the Permanent Commission on 'the Sacred Ministry' (cf above, page 301, note 1).
2. This General Chapter was to take place in July 1965.
3. The Secretariat for Unity was responsible for preparing an Ecumenical Directory (cf above, page 740).

THE DECLARATION ON NON-CHRISTIAN RELIGIONS.

For the paragraph on non-revealed religions; Mgr van Cauwelaert and the Archbishop of Léopoldville[1] have asked that African religions should be spoken of.

The difficult questions concerned the section on the Jews. Mgr Willebrands has made two trips: Lebanon, Jerusalem, Egypt, Addis-Ababa. He made himself aware of the precise situation. In the East, the Christians as well as the Jews and the Arabs, and, on the Christian side, the Orthodox as well as the Catholics, take this Declaration in quite a different sense from its true meaning. Between Arabs and Jews, any statement touching the Jews falls into a situation of war. Even if governments were reassured by the explanations, the ordinary people would not understand either explanation or nuance. The Jews for their part, will exploit the text, as they have done already. Certain ones among them will find in it a justification for their presence in Palestine: because they are the children of the Covenant they have a right to the lands of the Covenant.

Inevitably, too, a conciliar declaration would compromise ALL Christians in the eyes of the Muslims. The latter make no distinctions between Orthodox, Copts and Catholics. And their reactions can be extremely brutal. Already this year, when a muezzin said on a Friday evening, in an Egyptian village: What? You call yourselves Muslims, and tolerate two Christian churches in the village . . . ? Coming out of the mosque, the mindless mob set fire to these two churches . . . There is extreme pressure on the Copts in Egypt; more or less everywhere, Christianity is being picked on in thousands of ways. There is no doubt that a Declaration on the Jews would unleash a persecution with the burning of churches and the murder of Christians. Already the prospect of it has created tension between the Orthodox and ourselves. The Orthodox keep their distance with regard to Catholics and present themselves as the better patriots . . . If the Council proceeds with its declaration, and if this leads to grave difficulties in which the Orthodox or the Copts are caught up with the Catholics, the Orthodox will reproach us bitterly for having proceeded by ourselves, for having sold-out the possibilities for a Christian presence in the Near East, in short, for having acted in a hostile manner in their regard.

And who would accept responsibility for unleashing a persecution against Catholics when it is not a matter of Faith??

When Mgr Willebrands asked us for the strictest secrecy about all this, I told him that the Jews were already aware of a good deal of it; I cited the evidence I had received yesterday in Paris. Then Davis spoke about what had been reported in *The Observer*; Long[2] and Stransky said that the papers were even talking about

---

1. J Malula.
2. The American, John F Long, SJ, was *minutante* at the Secretariat for Unity.

a commission the Pope had appointed (four members, including Cardinal Co-lombo[1]), to inform him about certain points touching this question.

The Pope himself is in favour of the declaration, but is trying to avoid the risks by suppressing the word 'deicide' and the section on anti-Semitism.

In the East, the Christian people, and even the clergy, do not understand the intention of what is being said about the accusation of 'deicide'. They are saying, 'All the same, who did kill Jesus? And wasn't Jesus God?' They are impervious to distinctions and explanations.

So the solution is to suppress 'deicide' and the lines explicitly about anti-Sem-itism: this is the position of the Pope and of Cardinal Bea. The latter has always been personally against the text on deicide, even though he defended it in public out of loyalty to the Secretariat which had voted for it. If I understand rightly, at the time of the last meeting of the Secretariat, there was a vote on this point (after my departure) and the text was retained by 15 votes against 9 (Bea had always voted against).

Against this solution one could also assert a point of law. The text is actually a conciliar text over which the Commission has no rights except in the context of *modi* which do not affect its substance. But wouldn't this be the case if one went ahead with these two suppressions? At least if the decision does not come from the Pope . . .

Another solution—that Mgr Willebrands positively recommended: annul the Declaration purely and simply, with the Council stating that it has come up against difficulties not yet resolved, and asking the two Secretariats (Unity and Non-Christian Religions) to continue working along the lines of the declaration first voted by the Council and which remains a document giving direction to the work to be done.

What persuaded Mgr Willebrands to recommend this solution was his con-viction that, in the context of the certitude that a text would unleash some serious persecutions of the Christians in the Near East, cutting out a few words would do nothing to alter these reactions. People will not examine the CONTENT of the Declaration but, whatever that might be, will become inflamed, simply on the grounds that it is favourable to the Jews. It is even thought that bishops from Arab countries will leave the Council before the vote.

Whatever happens, we are in agreement that the odium of simply not pro-mulgating the text should not be foisted on the Pope; the Council must accept its responsibilities. But several of us insisted that it will have to accept these in the full knowledge of the factors involved, on the basis of a precise documentation and FOR THE REAL REASONS, CLEARLY SET OUT. These reasons will also have to be made known to the public, in complete frankness.

For myself, however, I am in no way in favour of the pure and simple with-drawal of the text. Twenty years after Auschwitz, it is impossible that the Council

---

1. Giovanni Colombo.

should say nothing. World opinion has been so aroused, the Jews are to such a degree on the look-out, that it is impossible to conclude in such a feeble fashion. I would be in favour of putting forward a new text that would propose dialogue in terms both strong and generous, that would condemn all violence motivated by race or religion, with allusion to the massacre of the Armenians as well as the Jews, that finally would set forth, in dignified terms, some of the points that call for elaboration and which, because of their under-developed state, the Council is sending back to the two Secretariats: the relation of non-Christian religions to Christianity, the place of the Jewish people in the history of salvation, etc.

In passing, Fr Lanne told me that *Concilium* has appeared in Italian; but the Italian edition only gives part of the text: it will have only four fascicules per year; the choice of texts retained would make plain the exclusion of certain others; in the bookshops, the Italian edition is not selling well, people prefer to buy the French edition. Whereas the production of an Italian edition would have been intended to discourage the reading of the French edition . . .

Lunch at Santa Sabina: dismal. And afterwards, as 'recreation', we hung around for a quarter of an hour. Again I had the impression of emptiness, of desert.

In the afternoon, after writing up this journal, work. I studied the comments made on the *De libertate*, and with a view to a Directory.

A long visit from Fr Baraúna, as always, about his book on the Constitution *De Ecclesia*. I think he needed to talk a bit and to get some support.

How cold I am! I am frozen to the bone.

Tuesday 4 May 1965
Two good hours of work, 7.30 am to 9.30: I read the dossier put together with a view to the directory. I put on paper a plan for a very brief general declaration that would replace the current Declaration on non-Christian religions. For, in my opinion, neither the solution of Paul VI and Bea, nor that of Willebrands, can be satisfactory (cf, leaf *hic*).

At 9.30 am, meeting of our commission *De Apostolatu*. Present were eight members and the president, Fr Bosco: that is, Frs Sancho Morales,[1] Bonnet,[2] Brachthäuser,[3] Spiazzi,[4] Reed,[5] Reeves,[6] and Hanley (USA).[7] First Fr Bosco gave a long exposition: we are not a study congress. We are not expected to give our opinion on the *postulata de S. Ministerio* [recommendations concerning the Sacred Ministry][8] that might have been submitted by the Provinces in view of the

---

1. Silvestre Sancho Morales, OP, of the Province of the Philippines.
2. René Bonnet, OP, of the Province of Toulouse.
3. Wunibald Brachthäuser, OP, of the Province of Germany.
4. Raimondo Spiazzi, OP, of the Province of Piedmont.
5. Gérard Reed, OP, of the Province of Canada.
6. John Reeves, OP, of the Province of England.
7. Earl Matthew Hanley, OP, of the Province of New York.
8. *De S. Ministerio* was the precise name of this commission.

General Chapter. Fr General[1] did not want to send them to us, as he considered that they had been sent to the preparatory commission OF THE CHAPTER, not to us, or to him with the liberty to share them with us. It is our job to form a judgement, to give an opinion about what should be submitted as a question to the General Chapter on the subject of ministry, especially in its relation to the juridical structure of the Order. Various things must be renewed or adapted, while respecting what is unchangeable. There are already many excellent pointers for this in the General Chapters of Bologna 1961, and Toulouse 1962 (thirty-three articles at Bologna, thirty-eight at Toulouse . . .).

Munus ordinarium nostrae Commissionis: convenire saltem semel in anno [the ordinary role of our commission is to meet at least once a year] to examine the problems submitted from various sources to Fr General. But NO province has ever sent anything to Fr General, and Fr General has never passed any question on to us. He has received only one, very recently, from Spain: a request for the creation of a secretariat for the means of communication. As for Fr Bosco, he has had six replies to twelve letters he sent out, and only three addressing questions to be discussed *De apostolatu*. In any case, many of these questions have already been touched on by the last two General Chapters. Moreover, secretariats or commissions already exist for the Missions, the Rosary, the Sisters, etc. Does our commission want to cover everything?

Munus extraordinarium: Schema parare de rebus ministerii tractandis in Capitulo Generali [the extraordinary role: to prepare a schema about matters concerning ministry that need to be considered at the General Chapter]. And also to assist the preparatory Commission for the General Chapter; to formulate a *votum* on Ministry in relation to the juridical structure of the Order.

However, questions that are not yet mature, or that would be of interest to only some Provinces, must not be put forward for the whole Order. We need to see what is possible, we must be realistic, we must take into consideration the small Provinces that do not have either the men or the resources of the large ones . . .

After this long discourse, we were each invited to state our position and make suggestions. I found myself very close to Fr Brachthäuser. However he had a more particular slant. It seems that, in Germany, the young ones are more radical, that the gap is more dramatic. There are not two Fathers, Brachthäuser said, who have read the Acts of Bologna and Toulouse. What comes from Rome is received with disdain and laughed at by the younger ones. He considers that, at the moment, it is as though there were two Orders, side by side, close to breaking into two.

For my part, I said we should look at the prescriptions of Bologna and Toulouse together, reduce them to their essentials, confront them with the direction of the Council, and complete them (for example, giving real status to a laity that

---

1.   Aniceto Fernandez, OP.

would be something quite different from the Third Order regarded as an extension of the Order itself . . .) then formulating the whole in terms that are neither
juridical nor pompous, but simple, direct, real, by means of affirmations such as:
'A friar preacher is a man who . . . ' etc.

In the afternoon, I remembered that we had a meeting at the Secretariat at
4.00 pm, on religious freedom. I got there at 3.45 pm. There was nobody there,
nobody came. I left, I went to the Columbus where Fr Murray is staying; the
meeting, he told me, was YESTERDAY!!! What a stupid mistake: yesterday, I was
free . . . So I went back to Santa Sabina in a taxi and arrived in time for the second meeting of our commission at 4.30 pm. We read the articles of the General
Chapter of Bologna (they had been photocopied and distributed) while chatting
about the subject of each of them. But it was agreed that we will take as a basis the
general and preliminary report that I had made in response to Fr Bosco's request
on 15 June 1963, and that we will try to draw out some POSITIVE principles
about what is SPECIFIC to the Dominican apostolate, the priority of which over
all the rest should be assured.

What a lot of time spent for very little result!!! Should I take these days as
relaxation and holidays? However, I want to remain attentive to the opportunity
to serve in holiness the holy cause of the vocation and the grace of St Dominic
and St Thomas.

Wednesday 5 May 1965

As on previous mornings, Mass in the room of St Pius V, whose feast it is. But I still
don't like him, and the office for his feast is too pompous. How the Renaissance
left its mark on Rome and the Curia! Oh! How institutions do retain the mark of
their origin! The modern papacy is indeed Tridentine and post-Tridentine . . .

At 9.00 am, at the Secretariat. First, I saw Mgr Willebrands for a moment. He
confirmed for me that the Pope wanted to publish his *motu proprio* on mixed
marriages before Easter. But he wanted to send the text first to certain bishops to
get their reactions. Some difficulties were being raised, especially by the English
hierarchy, so that everything is in suspense and the Pope doesn't quite know what
to say.

Work with Murray, Pavan, Feiner on *De libertate*. We looked especially at the
corrections asked for by Colombo. In the end, the small group had not accepted much from the comments made by the Theological Commission. I insisted,
but without success, that some satisfaction should be given to the comments of
Heuschen and Garrone, amounting to asking for a still stronger affirmation of
the obligation for conscience to be formed according to true rules. In effect our
Declaration—whose doctrine I accept—is going to have some unforeseen consequences over two or three centuries. I am convinced that it will bear some good
fruit: it will dispel some of the accumulated distrust with regard to the Catholic
Church. But we must not delude ourselves: in practice, it will cause to turn faster
the mills of religious indifference and of the conviction, so widespread today, that

ALL rules of morality are a matter of sincerity and subjective intention. We will not be creating this disposition: it already exists. But it is up to us, conscious of our pastoral responsibility, to do all we can to struggle against these erroneous dispositions.

I did not have much success. I realised that my colleagues did not see eye to eye with me on this point. All the same, I was able to save a section on the *Libertas Ecclesiae* [freedom of the Church] as being of positive divine right, irreducible to the common right based on the freedom and dignity native to the human person.

A difficult return journey. At Santa Sabina the door is shut at 12.30 pm and there is no second table. This is certainly not the place to stay if one has to work on conciliar Commissions! It is marvelously calm, but very remote, and distant from everything.

At 4.30 pm, the Dominican Commission. I am really annoyed and embarrassed that this commission, that is of so little interest, prevents me from participating more fully in the activities of the Secretariat. It is extremely regrettable.

My preliminary report of May 1963 was taken as a basis: that was two years ago! Before the Council had taken even one of its decisive steps. Each one expressed his opinion about it. Everyone accepted it and praised it; Brachthäuser and Bonnet wanted to complete it on several points (certainly!); Sancho and Reeves contested in particular what I had said about devotions and the Rosary; I explained and defended myself, explaining with heat the need to bring back the instinctive elements of 'religion' into the 'Faith'. I found myself wholly in agreement with Spiazzi, who seemed to me to have a very authentic vision that was also balanced and realist, but first of all a VISION, and that is not so banal. Spiazzi had put my report into Latin, but his text is too long. I myself had drafted, in Latin, four very general paragraphs: I read them out and they were adopted. They would have adopted pretty well anything because they had nothing to do, and yet they wanted to send something for the Chapter. Each of us is going to look at one point (mine is ecumenism) and will bring a short text on that point tomorrow afternoon . . .

Thursday 6 May 1965
Before 8.30 am, I wrote a page in Latin on ecumenism in Dominican ministry.

At 9.00 am, at the Secretariat for Unity. A brief period of work on the Directory, then when 'the *De libertate* people' arrived, work with them. We continued the examination of the *relatio* drawn up by Fr Murray: the part explaining the theses of the conservatives and replying to their arguments.

On the way out, I saw Mgr Oesterreicher for a moment. He was tense. He thinks that—IF one really must give way before the reasons developed on Monday by Mgr Willebrands—the solution is: to suspend the PUBLICATION of the text, which has already been voted by the Council (except for the *modi*), and would remain as the definite expression of the *mens Concilii* [mind of the Council]—while declaring frankly to the public for WHAT reasons of human politics and of peace the Council wanted to stay its publication.

Yes, everything would depend on the way in which these matters were presented.

At Santa Sabina at 12.30 pm, lunch with the curia, under the presidency of Cardinal Browne, who is celebrating his seventy-eighth birthday today. I spoke to him briefly about religious freedom. In summary:

He: I do not agree with the text, I shall vote against it.

Me: The Pope is in favour.

He: If the Pope is in favour, I have nothing more to say, I suppose.

At 4.30 pm, meeting of our Dominican Commission. First it was decided to ask Fr General that my brief Latin report in four points should be incorporated, in one way or another, into the Acts of the General Chapter. Then there was discussion, in turn, of a text by Brachthäuser on preaching, mine on ecumenism, one by Spiazzi on the social apostolate; finally there was discussion of the conditions for the functioning of our permanent commission, and of various points. We finished at 7.50 pm.

Friday 7 May 1965

I was almost dead when I arrived on Sunday; the following days were not too bad. These last few days and this morning I am WITHOUT ANY STRENGTH AT ALL. What am I going to do?

This morning, at the Secretariat at 9.00 am. I saw Murray first. Yesterday he had received an unexpected visit from Mgr Colombo, who was on the way to catch his plane for Milan but had stopped off to see Murray, on the subject of the Declaration on Religious Freedom. It should be underlined that this is not freedom with respect to God and is very much limited to the level of civil freedom *a coactione* [from coercion], and this should be clearly stated at the beginning. The *proemium* runs the risk of being interpreted as a charter of freedom WITHIN THE CHURCH, with regard to the Church (on this point, Mgr Willebrands, who seems to me to have got it from somewhere else, told me that this fear is not unrelated to the crisis concerning the Young Christian Students movement in France.[1] Since the beginning of this crisis I foresaw and said that this case would have some repercussions on us and even on some steps taken by the Council . . .).

Feiner is very annoyed by interventions of this sort. He feels things the way Protestants will feel them. As long as a text is not published, he says (rightly) one can never be sure, one is (it is) always under threat.

---

1. Following a disagreement between the French Episcopate and the national team of the Young Christian Students, a new team, which accepted the directives of the Episcopate, took up the baton in March–April 1965.

Perhaps it will lead to the abandonment of the *proemium*, which was trying to show how God has educated his people for freedom. It is curious: the Pope, who is in the process of establishing an Institute for the History of Salvation, does not seem to have noticed the significance of this (very elementary) presentation of the cause of freedom in the history of salvation.

I took part in the meeting of the commission preparing the Ecumenical Directory. But my head was completely empty.

And also, since the beginning of this spell in Rome, I have had a large general feeling of emptiness in my life. I am divided between the Secretariat, in the work of which I am not really involved, and this phantom commission, from which no one expects anything, and which even itself does not really know the reason for its existence. I see other people very much involved in their work. For myself, I am a sort of wandering Jew, here today, somewhere else tomorrow. I am like a stranger, cut off from that which has a kind of assurance and peace through the regularity and the usefulness of life. I realise that I shall never be really involved anywhere, but always ready on the instant, without close friends, without confidants. I have never once been integrated, except in the house of studies, but, since then, in nothing. I go hither and thither, I work, without forming part of a team, of a friendship, of an enterprise. . .

I think this feeling of emptiness comes partly from staying at Santa Sabina. Santa Sabina is a VERY regular priory, perhaps the most regular in the whole Order, the one that conforms most closely to the Constitutions. It is also a house where there is some fraternal spirit. But it is a house outside time. It is already protected by its situation. The Aventine, on this side, is a haven of peace; there is no traffic; the square in front of the priory is as quiet as that of a village right in the middle of the day . . . The house is no more affected by the problems than by the noises of the world. Sometimes I ask myself: Where are we? Under Pius IX or Benedict XIV? Who is the General: Fr Cormier?[1] This is charming, but it is terrible. . . The curia seems to share this timelessness, this immunity with regard to the questions of the day which are also the questions of human beings. Perhaps it does harbour real apostolic anxieties under the cover of secrecy and discretion. It remains a house which gives the impression of being outside time.

This Friday afternoon the work of our phantom commission was concluded in scarcely more than an hour, which prevented me from really taking part in the work of the Secretariat.

Saturday 8 May 1965
No strength left. Like this every day, and every day I must go on as if I had some.

At the Secretariat at 9.00 am: Directory. This started well but after 11 am we were flagging.

---

1. Hyacinthe Cormier, who was Master General of the Order from 1904 to 1916.

This afternoon, work on a (careful) text for the Jewish symposium.[1] To avoid problems I have chosen to present, in a fairly bland fashion, the circumstances of the declaration which, after all, even if it is not published in the end, had been accepted in its substance by an enormous majority on 20 November last. The Church, the Council have declared their *mens* [mind].

Monday 10 May 1965

At 9.00 in the morning, at the Secretariat. I wrote on the sheet attached here, during the session itself.

I finished typing my brief and bland article for the Jewish symposium and gave it to Mgr Willebrands for a private and fraternal *nihil obstat*.[2] The bishops of the Secretariat arrived. I find these men to have a candid and open mind.

Cardinal Bea opened the meeting. He related what had passed since the meeting of the Secretariat: the Joint Commission with the WCC,[3] the Catholic members of which had just been named (including Duprey and Hamer); a visit to Athenagoras in Constantinople: they continued the dialogue of charity and spoke of pastoral, social questions, the formation of the clergy, *caritas* [charity]; they decided to form a Joint Commission to prepare, one day, for doctrinal discussion. But many political difficulties . . .

An enthusiastic welcome from the PEOPLE: a real plebiscite . . . the opposite of what had followed Florence . . .

Bea then went to London where practical questions were discussed. In the Episcopal Conference that had taken place under the presidency of Cardinal Heenan, it was decided that there should be an ecumenical committee in each diocese.

Bea returned from the USA: lectures on the unity of the human family under the aegis of ecumenism. In the USA, a decision to create eight commissions, each presided over by a bishop, each of which will be concerned with a specific communion.

Willebrands and Duprey visited both Orthodox and Uniate Patriarchs in the East, to inform them about the Declaration on Non-Christian Religions.

Bea had seen the Pope for an hour-and-a-half on the subject of the two Declarations, but the Pope wants to leave the Secretariat free, yet himself free to intervene later; so Bea did not pass on what he had said . . .

On the Declaration *De habitudine Ecclesiae ad religiones non christianas* [on the relation of the Church to non-Christian religions]: Bea recalled the vote of 20

---

1. Organised by the American Jewish Committee.
2. Willebrands was to show himself hostile towards this publication which could have appeared to be a means of external pressure on the Council; Congar was to record this opinion when he forwarded his text (Congar Archives).
3. In January 1965, the Central Committee of the WCC proposed the formation of a Joint Commission; in February Cardinal Bea went to WCC headquarters to bring Rome's positive response.

November 1964: it is such that the first work to be done is to evaluate the *modi* proposed. But there is a further question, that of its timeliness. Willebrands will speak about this.

On the subject of the Directory, Bea reported what the Apostolic Delegate to the USA[4] (who is an ass) said to him: he had received 'from the Holy See' (but from whom?) a report setting out complaints coming from the USA about abuses committed in the matter of ecumenism. But he was unable to give Bea any specific information about what this might be.

The *Veni Creator* was recited with deep feeling.

Willebrands opened the session on religious freedom (those working on the Directory wanted to go on with their work).

On behalf of the sub-commission, Murray explained the few changes made, for the sake of more clarity, after study by members of the Theological Commission and after fresh reflection on the text.

Introduction: they went back to the printed text, or got closer to it, in order better to indicate that what was under discussion was SOLELY religious freedom IN SOCIETY (and not freedom IN THE CHURCH).

De Smedt: but in this way we are we tending towards the very thing we were criticised for: multiplying REPETITIONS. (De Smedt was not satisfied with the simple fact that something had been changed. This had been done in his absence, in a text which he tended to consider his own.) A very brief introduction had been made in order not to say there what was going to be said later.

And so the text was extended.

Cantero took up the same criticism.

Marti: *idem*; the French bishops had complained about length and about repetitions. Others expressed themselves for (Charrière) or against the current introduction.

We moved on quickly enough to the *proemium*: Mgr Willebrands did not hide the fact that he would prefer to see it suppressed.

I suggested an idea: start straight off with the Declaration, without other introduction, and put into the chapter on Revelation the idea of the human being created free by God, without the other developments of the current *proemium*.

Murray explained with honesty, clarity and force, the reason why the *proemium* had been composed AND PLACED THERE.

De Smedt made a rather grand disquisition in favour of putting the whole theological part AT THE HEAD. I disagreed.

Cardinal Martin (who spoke frequently, and whose authority seemed to have got a recharge) spoke along the same lines as I did.

Then Mgr Primeau, then Cantero, too. And also, briefly, Willebrands.

Bea: Many questions that pose difficulties are raised in the *proemium* (basically, WITHOUT SAYING SO, Willebrands and Bea were echoing the Pope).

---

4. E Vagnozzi.

At 11.10 am, a secret vote was taken on the choice: to begin with the Declaration (after a few lines of introduction) *omisso hoc loco proemio* [with the preface omitted in this place].

The result was unanimously *placet*.

I had thus almost proposed the destruction of my own child. But I realised that: 1) *VERY FEW* understand the link between the content of this *proemium* and the declaration; 2) that runs the risk of leading the mind in a given direction that is not that in which the Declaration and its whole substance later situates itself. It was apparent to me, on reflection, that the whole thing would be much stronger if it were situated straightaway on the ground of JURIDICAL freedom. ONE WOULD THEN HAVE A MUCH WIDER AREA OF AGREEMENT, verging on unanimity.

For the rest, it is almost sure that if it were not done in this way, the Pope would get it done later on.

The content of the introduction that will precede the Declaration was then discussed.

Hermaniuk: set out in the introduction THE FACTS that confront us; then, in the Declaration, give the JUDGEMENT of the Church.

Unanimous accord, except for one *non placet*, for the suppression of lines 4–7 of the text of the Introduction proposed this morning by the sub-commission.

Discussion of an addition made to the end of the text of No. 2, which had actually been made at the request of Colombo. But no one could say what was the real reason for this addition: everyone thought it pointless, and no one knew what was at the bottom of it. Wouldn't it be better to state clearly what it was about?

In the end, Colombo's addition was deleted by unanimous consent.

The miniscule changes of detail were tidied up.

The session ended at 12.35 pm.

On the way out, Cardinal Bea told me he had to smile a bit at the sort of suggestion I had made in the third place for the Declaration on the Jews (a new text, short and general).

But I replied to him that, for my part, after I had reflected better, I thought it would be better to postpone the promulgation of the text which, having been voted, does express in an official manner the spirit of the Council, to say frankly WHY it did not go on to a formal promulgation, and recommend that the two Secretariats should work in the spirit and the direction of the text.

At 4.00 pm, at the Secretariat, to finalise the insertion of the substance of the *proemium* into Chapter IV of the Declaration. Fr Lyonnet was invited by Mgr Willebrands to join us.

Willebrands himself would basically like to suppress this entire text, or to reduce it to practically nothing: but then he should not have invited Lyonnet, who would rather go further in the direction of its themes, Christian freedom etc.

Tuesday 11 May 1965

Sleepless for a long time because of the cramp in my leg and, lasting some hours, the consequent nervous contraction. Brother Ass is a poor specimen.

At 9.00 am, at the Secretariat. Religious Freedom was completed. At 11.00 am a (secret) vote on the text as a whole, as it now stands. Unanimity. After a short interval (during which I saw Cardinal Martin, getting dressed to go to an audience of the Pope. I told him about my efforts for a new Profession of Faith; he was interested and told me he would make a note to speak to the Holy Father about it). Fr Murray presented his general *Relatio* explaining the doctrinal line of the schema, and responding to the difficulties of those who wanted to hold on to civil toleration, while rejecting religious freedom in the sense of the Secretariat.

At 4.30 pm, at the Secretariat: beginning of the examination of the Directory. This provided the opportunity for a very wide and interesting exchange of views. Those who had most to say:
-    De Smedt (who wanted a sort of code, something very definite),
-    Cardinal Heenan (who likes to play the fool a bit),
-    Cardinal Bea, full of nuances and experience, who spoke with self-control and great freedom, all at once. It was apparent that many things concerning ecumenism are currently fluid in Rome. One sensed that his idea is that the Secretariat should be the only final authority in this matter.

Extremely serious work. No verbosity.

When I consider what Catholic ecumenism is today, at the summit, I am astounded. It is fantastic! THE STEP HAS BEEN TAKEN!

I am sad that this is my last meeting. Tomorrow morning they will start on the Declaration on Non-Christian Religions. I would have liked to be there. . .

I wrote a letter to Mgr Willebrands that Fr Hamer will give him tomorrow, telling him my views on: 1) the Declaration (on the Jews): precisely for the solution, *IF* the PROCLAMATION of the text MUST be abandoned, say frankly why, making reference to the text already voted and asking for further studies of it in its own spirit; 2) the second part of Murray's *Relatio*, which does not seem to me to answer, in a totally effective manner, to the position said to be classical. But I do not think it would be possible to answer to it in a totally effective manner.

It is a matter of two positions, one purely theoretical-juridical, the other presupposing knowledge and consideration of history.

Wednesday 12 May 1965

At Fiumicino. Much too early, as always. Nearly an hour's wait. Fiumicino truly detestable, was frankly odious this morning: a level of noise such that one could not even hear the strident announcements of the loud-speakers; a draught such that everything was blown all over the place and that one could scarcely hold open the pages of a book. Horrible airport.

The rest of the journey was rather bad. Swissair has changed its timetables in such a way that I had a two-hour wait at Zurich. I arrived in Strasbourg supporting myself against the walls, and unable to put one foot in front of the other.

July 1965

Fr Courtois (of the Sons of Charity), whom I saw at Lyons on 5 July, told me that in Rome there is much fear that the month of August may see a move to the use of atomic weapons in the conflict between the USA and China over Vietnam. There is a party in the USA that thinks it is time to put China out of the affair. At the moment, China does not have a really effective bomb; Russia supports China only from a distance. In a few years' time it will be too late. . . It is now that the future of the free world is in the balance. The Pope, conscious of the immensity and, he thinks, of the imminence of the danger, would like to go to New York, to the tribunal of the United Nations, to stop that danger. He has formally asked to be invited by the United Nations Organisation. But, on the other hand, he wants to make this gesture only if he has, in advance, some assurance that he will be listened to. If he goes and speaks in New York and a week later the bomb is dropped, what impression will that give?

But it is no use waiting until one can be sure of being heard before speaking! It is this very word that must ACT and stop the evil! If the Pope is convinced that there is a very imminent danger, obviously he must act. He should be haunted by 'The Deputy'!

Sunday 11 July 1965

I saw Mgr Elchinger. Some time ago he told me a story which I did not note down at the time, and of which I do not remember all the details. It concerned the *Motu proprio* on mixed marriages and Cardinal Döpfner, and also the Archbishop of Berlin.[1] It had to do with what I had been told about how, at Rome, certain reactions had been reported to the Pope in an inexact manner. The reaction from Munich had been represented as negative, when in fact it was not. Cardinal Döpfner has since informed the Pope directly.

On the same subject: Mgr Elchinger had got the permanent committee of the French bishops to write to the Pope about ecumenical questions.[2]

He had also written to Cardinal Jaeger of Paderborn, from whom he had just received a reply. The latter had also written to Cardinal Heenan, suggesting that he should make a similar approach to the Pope, telling him that it was urgent; that people will be very disappointed if nothing comes of it; that responsibility for the application of the *Motu proprio* should be given to national episcopates.

Mgr Elchinger had just seen Mgr Reuss, Auxiliary of Mainz. Two anecdotes:

---

1. A Bengsch.
2. More precisely, The Episcopal Committee for the Unity of Christians.

1) It was from the hands of Mgr Reuss that Felici had violently snatched a packet of leaflets against the vote on the Decree on the Means of Communication. Reuss had intended to bring a complaint against Felici before the administrative tribunal of the Council. He was asked to withdraw his complaint, but stuck to his position. In the end, he was given to understand that it would please the Pope if he gave way, because the tribunal would find in his favour and against Felici. He then withdrew his complaint. The Pope had thanked him personally for this.

2) More recently, he had received a letter from Felici, following on an article on birth control, a translation of which had appeared in the supplement to *La Vie Spirituelle*.[1] Felici asked him (in the name of higher authority?), not to publish anything more on this subject. Reuss replied that he had a conscience and that he would write whatever he believed in conscience he ought to write. He then received a letter from Cardinal Cicognani insisting that he refrain from publishing material on these questions. I believe he again refused to obey. But at that point he saw the Pope about the previous affair. He told the Pope that he would like to speak to him about another matter, and, for an hour, he conversed with him about the problems of birth control. The result—all to the honour of the Pope—was that Reuss was invited to sit on the Commission set up by the Pope to study these problems.

I gave Mgr Elchinger some reactions to the schemas to be discussed. From now on, it will be necessary to start anticipating interventions (those on religious freedom are supposed to arrive in Rome for 9 September). I wrote to Cardinal Cardijn.

I had not thought that my letter would have such an effect and such a result!

*At Les Voirons, **13 July 1965—10 August 1965**, except for two days at Bossey[2] (**2–3 August**)*. I had a good rest there, and yet was able to work well enough there:
a) I drafted four, even five articles:
- a lecture on the diaconate with a view to the Congress at Assisi;[3]
- an article on Poverty, for *Concilium*;[4]

---

1. Josef M Reuss, 'Suggestions pour une pastorale des problèmes du mariage et de la fécondité', in *Supplément de la Vie Spirituelle*, No. 72, February 1965: 5–12; translation of : 'Hinweise zur Pastoralen Behandlung der Fragen um Ehe und Elternschaft', in *Theologie der Gegenwart*, 7, 1964: 134–139.

2. Congar gave a course at the Ecumenical Institute at Bossey.

3. Yves M-J Congar, 'Le diaconat dans la théologie des ministères', in Paul Winninger and Yves Congar (editors) *Le Diacre dans l'Église et le monde d'aujourd'hui*, 'Unam Sanctam', 59 (Paris: Cerf, 1966), 121–141.

4. 'Situation de la pauvreté dans la vie chrétienne au sein d'une civilisation du bien-être', in *Concilium* 15, 1966: 45–62; reprinted in Yves Congar, *À mes frères*, 'Foi Vivante', 71 (Paris: Cerf, 1968), 105–132.

- an article for *Le Monde* on Fr Duployé's *Péguy*,[1] which I read;
- an article for *ICI:* perspectives and prospectives for the Fourth Session;[2]
- an article for the German journal for the use of priests in the diaspora.[3]

(b) I worked on schema XIII and read the one on the Lay Apostolate.

We had some useful discussions with Fr Féret, who studied the texts I had brought with me. He made an effort, with some success for the *De libertate religiosa*, which at first he had taken in the wrong way, to understand the perspective of these texts. But he barely manages to place himself within the real line of sight of the Council: he is stuck in that of an ideal council and still doesn't really see the texts except in relation to his synthesis. The latter is grand and strong, very structured; it is organised in accordance with some profound insights. But Fr Féret ends up being unfair towards views which are not precisely those of this synthesis. For example, he does not see the value and the interest of the idea of the image of God for a Christian anthropology; the biblical paragraph of the *De libertate*, for him, says nothing!!! In short, this year we have had a little more DIALOGUE than last year, but still limited.

I wrote to Mgr de Provenchères about the anthropology of schema XIII (the new human being) and its pneumatology,

     to Mgr Elchinger about its eschatology

     to Mgr Garrone about the chapter concerning the Church.

(c) But the great moment, from the point of view of Conciliar work, was the arrival of Cardinal Cardijn. He had written to me, insisting that he wanted to see me. On 1 August I telephoned him in Brussels. He arrived on 4 August at Geneva airport, at 12.40 pm. We spoke at once, then in the car. This was for us an extraordinary feast of St Dominic, two half days of grace. I believe that it was not for nothing that THIS was given to me.

About Rome, the plans of the Pope, the reform of the Curia, the progress of the Council, Cardinal Cardijn said he knew nothing, and indeed I believe he

---

1.   Y Congar, 'La Religion de Péguy. Un Livre du R P Duployé', in *Le Monde,* 17 August 1965.

2.   Cf *Informations catholiques internationales*, No. 248, 15 September 1965: 3–9, reprinted in Yves M-J Congar, *Le Concile au jour le jour. Quatrième session* (Paris: Cerf, 1966), 11–28.

3.   'An meine Brüder im Priestertum, Zeugen des Evangeliums in der Einsamkeit', in *Lebendiges Zeugnis*, October 1966: 52–66; the article was to appear first in French: 'À mes frères prêtres, témoins de l'Évangile dans la solitude', in *La Vie Spirituelle,* November 1956: 501–552; it was to be reprinted in: Yves Congar, *À mes frères,* 'Foi Vivante', 71 (Paris: Cerf, 1968), 199–218.

did know next to nothing. He said he had not received a single paper since his cardinalate, informing him of what was expected of him. As a member of the Congregation for Studies and Seminaries he went to see Pizzardo. He came away alarmed. Pizzardo is a nothing, he said. He spoke to us about his cardinalate, how the Nuncio had announced him, how the Pope had said to him: 'Stay Cardijn!'; how, since his elevation to the purple, everyone in Rome smiles on him, bows and scrapes to him ('it is disgusting', he said, 'it is ignoble. I would never have believed it'). Cardijn is very relaxed, he remains completely himself. What drive, what enthusiasm; what vigour this man of eighty-three years of age has!

We talked about religious freedom, about schema XIII, the Lay Apostolate, Missions, Priests. Cardijn had prepared reflections on these texts; he is counting on me, on us, to test them and put them into the form of conciliar interventions. Basically Cardijn has only one idea, but it is consubstantial with himself, he is as absolutely faithful to it as he is to himself. It lights up everything. His great idea is to start from the real, the concrete. People must be taken as they are. He criticises the new schema on the Lay Apostolate for starting with a distinction between different sorts of apostolate and for suggesting a 'spirituality for the laity'. If I had started like that, he said, I would have done nothing. I have never met anyone to whom these schemas could be applied. You must always start by taking people as they are, without wanting to plaster over them our framework, our ideas, our requirements. It must come from them, it must be authentic for them. When one starts from a system, one easily forms the idea that it has nothing to do with this or that person. And one achieves nothing. Cardijn was teaching in a seminary or a school when Cardinal Mercier appointed him curate of Laeken. He was badly received by his parish priest, the dean, who immediately stuck labels on him: poor health, did not speak Flemish, came from a seminary, and knew nothing! Now there was a district of poor people, which neither the Dean nor any other priest had ever visited: 'There is nothing to be done there!' And, as Cardijn was notifying his intention of going there: 'They won't receive you'. But Cardijn went there the next day. They opened the door to him. He drank coffee. A year later, he had a group of a thousand Catholic women in that district!

He made similar criticisms of schema XIII, of the schema on the Missions. Little by little, we decided on a certain number of interventions to be made on the basis of his notes and our conversation.

After the cardinal's departure, when we took him to his plane at 1.40 pm on 5 August, we shared out the work, Fr Féret and myself. On 10 August I sent him a proposed intervention on Religious Freedom.

See the dossier.

10 August 1965

Departure for Spain, plane at 6.10 pm. After light cloud with some breaks, which hid from me Lyons, St Etienne and Le Puy, France was covered in clouds that lay beneath us like a fluffy blanket. At a certain point this layer was pierced by black reefs; they were the Pyrenees. It was curious how the chain of mountains marked the edge of the layer of cloud: on the French side everything below us was white, on the Spanish side there stretched out an arid and furrowed land. Soon, in the rays of the setting sun, the whole Spanish land appeared to be blazing red.

A car. Reached Burgos[1] at 12.05 am. The seminarians were not yet in bed!

11 August 1965

In the morning I was present for part of the concelebration. The Church was there. *Inveni Ecclesiam tuam cantantem!* [I found your Church in song]. The Catholic vitality of Spain: vocations, resources (seminaries and convents being built everywhere) application to work. Here all the public and social work of the Church is held in honour; life is lived according to its reference points and its norms.

I have here an insane standing. I have given more than a hundred autographs. I am constantly being photographed. People come to see me, they ask my advice about theses, about their work. I am regarded as 'somebody' although I am so stupid, so empty. And so tired! So dead that on each of the two evenings they offered to have supper brought to me in my room.

On 12 August, at 4.00 or 4.30 pm, I left to spend the night in the Dominican Priory (St Peter Martyr) of Las Covendas,[2] at the gate of Madrid. Very good conversation with Fr Martínez,[3] who passes for a 'naturalist' in this conservative and closed milieu. I did not get to sleep until 5.00 am in the morning, so sultry was the weather, and so violent the spasmodic reactions of my leg.

13 August 1965

An afternoon of work for Cerf. I returned to Strasbourg in the evening: more than a hundred parcels of books, booklets, letters, manuscripts etc covered my table!

25–27 August 1965

A meeting with the Lutherans.[4] I shall not make notes here about this meeting as such—the first as official as this since the sixteenth century discussions. I am getting into the matter of Luther, and it seems to me that in doing so I am coming close to him—but two or three details that Willebrands told me.

At the General Congregation preparatory to the Council (which one, exactly?) only two people out of a hundred objected to the presence of Observers at ALL the General Congregations.

---

1. Congar took part in the 18th Spanish Missiology Week and gave two lectures at it, one on the Church as the universal sacrament of salvation, the other on the Church as the seed of unity and hope for the whole human race.
2. A Priory of the Province of the Philippines.
3. Eusebio Martínez Peña, OP, professor of psychology and anthropology.
4. This was one of two consultations that were held in Strasbourg in 1965 and then 1966 and that led to the formation of an International Catholic-Lutheran Commission that was to meet from 1967 onwards.

The Holy Office had said to Willebrands: tell Cardinal Bea that he can no longer speak as Fr Bea. He cannot go on speaking, as he does, about brothers and a common home. —Willebrands replied: Tell that to the Pope! He's the one who speaks like that.

With regard to the *Motu proprio*, still awaited, on mixed marriages: the Pope wanted to promulgate it before Easter this year. But he sent the plan to some bishops and some episcopates. Some difficulties emerged from all sides, but especially from England. The Pope is very put out and does not know what to do. He said to Willebrands: this is the tenth draft; what have you got to say?—Willebrands replied: I am waiting for the eleventh.

On this subject Willebrands said: a council has the means of dissipating opposition, of overcoming the objections of a minority. The Pope does not have those means.

4 September 1965

My trunk is being dispatched by *Secours catholique*. I shall put this notebook in it, and not see it again until I get to Rome, when the Council recommences. A grand affair!!! *Dominus qui incipit, ipse perficiat!* [May the Lord who has begun this work bring it to completion].

Monday 13 September 1965
Beginning of the Fourth Session. ROME.

Departure from Strasbourg at 8.45 am, with Mgr Elchinger. He gave me his reactions to schema XIII: very severe, excessively severe. He finds it lacking in this and that, and what he says is often just. But: 1) I challenged him to put that in a UNITY that holds together, to make a WHOLE of so many things; 2) many of the things he wants said go beyond the average and common tenor that a document of this sort MUST have. I have often noticed that an idea that is a bit strong, a bit sharp, has eluded the average intelligence of the bishops. This has sometimes even been a cause of astonishment for me and a bitter experience. However I agree with Mgr Elchinger about several serious defects in the whole thing: 1) the absence of vigorous direction and movement of the whole. It ought to have been christological and anthropological: to have given the 'human' face of biblical-Christian affirmations; 2) sometimes, there is a little demagogy. It is rather ACO [Catholic Workers' Action]. And certain sections, on the economy for example, list all the *requisita* [requirements] without allowing sufficient latitude for the development of new forms, or sufficiently providing a deep SPIRITUALITY. It remains too much on the level of formulas, of a programme, of dodges. Elchinger is not mistaken when he says that it is too much a casuistry that presupposes a stable situation; it should have indicated some main lines of direction, major needs, and what means are envisaged to begin to address these.

Everything, or almost everything, is said, but often in a rather involved manner. This comes, I think, from its being put together too much by accumulation. That is Mgr Guano's tendency: an over-loaded Joint Commission, numerous sub-commissions, a mass of documents, as well as requests to be dealt with. One person, or a very small group, should have thought the synthesis through.

There was some gigantism in the undertaking of schema XIII.

At Fiumicino, we waited an hour-and-a-half for our cases (Elchinger and I). Amid all the racket we watched the arrival of various groups of bishops: from Nice (Lyons and Provence), from Germany, from Brussels (at least twenty bishops: many of them missionary; Mgr Philips. I saw De Smedt, Daem, Prignon . . .), finally the Caravelle from Paris: in the space of a few minutes we saw about thirty bishops and experts . . . But our cases had stayed in Zurich! We will have them this evening PERHAPS, if they can be found. Mine contains the papers I need immediately, and several working dossiers. A manuscript etc.

Is this the cost of paying so dearly to waste so much time and be unable to get on with one's business?

At supper, contact with the bishops: the same ones as last year plus three new auxiliaries. Cordiality. Everyone is a year older, but this is not very obvious, except for Mgr Guerry, who has been very much changed.

Tuesday 14 September 1965

Departure for St Peter's at 8.15 am. The St Peter's of great occasions: the arrival of ambassadors with their wives, in ceremonial dress, a crowd that began to pile up. I again found a seat among the Observers. This time there were ninety-eight of them. Many figures known already. I greeted Boegner, Cullmann, Roux, the Brothers of Taizé, Evdokimov[1] etc. Newcomers included Mgr Emilianos,[2] whom I had already met yesterday on the plane, and a Romanian metropolitan.[3] It seems that a delegate from the Serbian Church is waiting only for the *placet* of his government.[4]

I saw Fr Duprey for a moment. He told me that the contacts made in Russia had been extraordinary. He spoke to me about the messages that the Pope had sent, and I repeated to him that, for me, the problem was that the Pope should

---

1. Paul Evdokimov, a lay theologian of Russian origin, was a professor at the St Sergius Institute of Orthodox Theology in Paris; he was a guest of the Secretariat for Unity during the Fourth Session.
2. Bishop Emilianos Timiadis, titular metropolitan of the Patriarchate of Constantinople, the representative of the Patriarchate at the WCC, was the Observer delegated by the same Patriarchate during the Fourth Session.
3. There was no Romanian Metropolitan among the official Observers; Congar is perhaps referring to the presence of an archimandrite of the Bulgarian Orthodox Church, which sent an Observer to the Council for the first time.
4. In the end, there were two Observers delegated by the Serbian Orthodox Church.

have the theology of his gestures and his messages. But Duprey responded with something I believe is interesting and true. The Pope and Rome must be left to make gestures and send messages, even if the thinking is not yet at the level of these. Because it will catch up one day. If one were to FORMULATE today the implications of these gestures and messages it is likely that Rome would retreat from such a formulation of ideas. The gestures will create a familiarity and when that has been done, one day, the formulas will be able to be accepted. And that goes not only for Rome. Among the Orthodox, the theologians are behindhand about the real ecumenical situation. Among them also a period of familiarisation, beginning from concrete action, is desirable.

I also saw Mgr Willebrands. He immediately spoke to me about the encyclical on the Eucharist.[1] Plainly, he wanted to create a climate of opinion. All the Italian press is saying that the criticisms are aimed at the Dutch theologians and that a schism in Holland is to be feared. The Dutch bishops are very annoyed about these insinuations, and Cardinal Alfrink has already given a press conference on the subject. Willebrands thinks that the encyclical is not that significant and that in five years' time it will not be spoken of.

Fr Lanne, for his part, thinks the encyclical 'catastrophic': the tone especially, seems to him objectionable. Besides the Pope has published it just two days before the Council, as though to affirm the independence and the superiority of his magisterium . . .

I note here that, at the end of the ceremony, I saw Fr de Lubac with H Roux on the steps going up to St Peter's. He was defending, to Roux, a totally different point of view. The encyclical, he said, has a benevolent tone. It is discreet and explicitly says that research must continue. But it was necessary given what is being said even in France, which is rash, if not even unacceptable.

About 9.10 am, strains of *Tu es Petrus*. The Pope entered ON FOOT, wearing a mitre, and a cross functioning as a crosier in his left hand. (The bishop of Rome has never had a crosier). There was singing and not a single sound of applause. No guards or procession of a princely court. There was, all the same, something new. It was the entry of a bishop, a pastor, the entry of a priest, no longer that of a prince.

And the Mass began straightaway, dialogued and sung, without long delays, concelebrated by the Council of Presidents, the Moderators and the Secretaries of the Council. Alongside this there were some survivals: all the gentlemen in doublet and hose, swords at their sides, ruffs and the golden fleece around their necks. Some had horrifying heads, others heads like Henri II or Henri IV. One could have believed that portraits of that period had left their frames, come down from their canvas and started walking.

1.　*Mysterium Fidei*, dated 3 September 1965.

A speech by the Pope[1] (after he had enthroned the Gospel: a suggestion I had made to Colombo). He spoke about charity as the soul of the Council. He announced the creation of a synod of bishops around the pope, bishops elected for the most part by episcopal conferences.

Féret told me yesterday that Cardijn would ask us to come to lunch after this morning's ceremony. But I knew no details; I didn't know where, or at what point to join Féret and Cardijn.

I looked around. I went out by the Square, at the shuffling pace of that enormous crowd, having scraps of conversation with this and that person.

I saw all the coaches, all the cars leaving one after the other and the Square emptying. I was limping and I waited in broad sunlight. Thank God, Mgr McGrath was one of the last to leave and took me as far as Via Ulisse Seni. Cardijn was not expecting anyone. Fr Féret had been told not to come until 4.00 pm. But, in the end, he was reminded; he arrived after an hour-and-five minutes. Something of a farce as dinner was over and the cardinal, tired out, went to take a siesta.

When he came back, we did a little work while drinking coffee in the garden. He knew nothing, had seen nobody, had not been involved in anything. But his interventions were ready and he was prepared to deliver several good punches. Féret has resumed the spirit of systematisation. He dogmatises against dogmatism and had the single-mindedness of a man inspired. He sees salvation only in his way of looking at things. With all this he was in very good form and wonderfully fraternal.

He brought me my bag which had at last arrived.

This afternoon at 5.00 pm, a penitential procession from Santa Croce in Gerusalemme to the Lateran. The bishops did not get back until 9.00 pm. Everyone said it was beautiful, with a big crowd (a point of contact between the Fathers and the faithful of Rome), but too long, exhausting. Everyone said that the great penance was the sermon by Cardinal Traglia.[2]

Wednesday 15 September 1965

To the Secretariat to collect the schemas.

At St Peter's. Mass of Our Lady of the Seven Sorrows. Too long: singing of the *Stabat* . . . An interesting innovation: the celebrant entered carrying the book of the Gospels during the processional Psalm.

The Pope came to preside. In his presence the *Motu proprio*, instituting a synod of bishops around him, was promulgated.[3] Marella presented the text.[4]

---

1. *AS* IV/I, 125–135; cf, also: 'Discours prononcé par SS Paul VI, lors de l'ouverture de la 4ᵉ session du Concile', in *La Documentation catholique*, 1965, col 1653–1664.
2. Cardinal Luigi Traglia, Vicar General for the City of Rome, Grand Chancellor of the Lateran University.
3. *Apostolica sollicitudo*, *AS* IV/I, 19–24.
4. *AS* IV/I, 140–142.

The situation in our tribune (invaded more than is allowed) was pretty awful because of the experts and the fifty-two Lay Auditors. So I took hardly any notes. The Pope left after the reading of the *Motu proprio.*

An allocution by Cardinal Tisserant:[1] peace.

A few words from Cardinal Agagianian.[2] A telegram was read (in French) from the 'Ecumenical Patriarch Athenagoras', rather vague, almost nondescript, but the fact is important.

At 11.00 am, discussion started on religious freedom. *Relatio* by Mgr De Smedt,[3] who doubled the text that had been distributed by reading the two pages of the *Relatio* attached to the text, so that everything would be clear!!!

There spoke in succession: Cardinal Spellman,[4] Frings,[5] Ruffini[6] and Siri,[7] who began again with religious freedom what the minority had done with collegiality: criticising something other that what the text said.

Arriba y Castro:[8] the Syllabus.

Urbani,[9] in the name of several Italian bishops: *EXCELLENT.*

Cushing[10] and Alfrink[11] (who also spoke rather to the side of the perspective of the text).

As yesterday, I have already met dozens and dozens of people: bishops, experts, lay people. All seem to have an extraordinary good will towards me. It is daft that people are so kind to me, often friendly, even affectionate.

At 5.00 pm, at the Secretariat. Previously, I had read the numerous papers, of real value, that had already been sent to me about religious freedom. Papers are now beginning to arrive EN MASSE: there is hardly time to study them SERIOUSLY.

One had the pleasure of meeting up again. The anthropology, the typical man of the Secretariat, is appealing. As always, Cardinal Bea gave an account of what had been done since the last meeting.

Regarding the Declaration *De Iudaeis* [on the Jews], it should be printed as soon as possible.

The drafting of the Directory must be speeded up, because questions are coming from all sides.

---

1. *AS* IV/I, 24–25.
2. *AS* IV/I, 143–144.
3. *AS* IV/I, 169–199.
4. *AS* IV/I, 200–201.
5. *AS* IV/I, 201–202.
6. *AS* IV/I, 204–207.
7. *AS* IV/I, 207–208.
8. *AS* IV/I, 209–210.
9. *AS* IV/I, 211–213.
10. *AS* IV/I, 215–216.
11. *AS* IV/I, 217–218.

Willebrands: calculates that a corrected text of the *De libertate* could be presented around 8 October, the vote with *modi* could then be taken, and the text could be proposed for the definitive vote round about 15 November.

The state of the work on the Directory, which will have to be submitted to the Council's Theological Commission. It will be submitted to Bishops' Conferences and to the Observers before being definitively promulgated.

This evening was chiefly concerned with the text of the Declaration on Non-Christian Religions. The Pope wanted a delegation from the Secretariat to go and see the Eastern Patriarchs to present and explain the new text to them: these were De Smedt, Willebrands and Duprey.

All were satisfied with the corrections that had been made.

The Pope also wanted the Muslim world to be better informed not only about this text but about the work of the Council in general. An attempt is being made to provide reliable information and explain things on the radio, to bring together various competent and influential people to create a favourable climate of opinion.

However, Maximos has submitted some new *modi*. The Pope, on learning this, remitted the evaluation of them to the Secretariat.

Willebrands explained the three *modi* of Maximos.

De Smedt pointed out that the attitude of the Easterners had been good once they had seen the amended text in May, and it had been explained to them. They had declared then that there would still be grave difficulties, but that they were ready to defend the text, to explain it, and to cooperate so that things would go better.

Willebrands read out the letters sent to the governments of Syria and [ ] by Maximos: it was a complete and honest defence of the Council.

Tappouni: once the text is promulgated the whole Syrian Church will follow the Council.

Cantero and Lamont[1] favoured the acceptance of the first *modus*.

There was long discussion and a vote (secret vote) on each point: cf my page dated 15 September 1965.

It seems that the *De Revelatione* will be voted on (with the possibility of *modi*) on Monday. As last year, for Chapter III of the *De Ecclesia*, it is to be hoped that the 'good' will make as little as possible of it.

I have flu. A slight fever.

Thursday 16 September 1965
The first day went well. I even found I had a little energy, but already by yesterday I was not brilliant. This morning I can hardly stand up. I shall not say Mass: it is too far away and too tiring.

---

1. Daniel R Lamont, Bishop of Umtali (Southern Rhodesia), member of the Secretariat for Unity elected at the Second Session.

Before breakfast I reread the *De Revelatione* to look out for possible *modi*.

Went to St Peter's in spite of everything. The liturgy of the Mass now has a much better format: 1) the celebrant makes his entry bringing in the Gospel-book, from which the Gospel reading for the day is read. Thus the unity between the two ceremonies is affirmed, and Christ is proclaimed as the Master of Truth; 2) everyone present sings the proper of the Mass, with a system of antiphonal psalms, which is a bit overdone and of which one will soon grow tired. Each day, four times over, a sometimes humdrum antiphon is alternated with some rather long psalms; 3) for the epistle, a *lectio continua* [sequential reading] of the Acts of the Apostles has been introduced, and, for the Gospel, of the final chapters of St John.

Thus the book, which used to be only an object of ceremonial, is now speaking!!!

First, Felici gave out the order of the discussions and the votes to be taken.[1]

Then a long, very long, series of discussions, some very long. Very fortunately, Cardinal Jaeger[2] showed how the text itself provides the answers to most of the difficulties raised yesterday. Cardijn did not speak, I don't know why. There were some very lively attacks (Morcillo[3]). It emerged from the discussion that the text is not entirely clear, nor satisfactory, and that many of the bishops are finding difficulties in taking THIS step.

I could not stand any longer and was unable to have all the conversations I should have. I envy those who are able to come and go, walk, be alive to the questions of others with enthusiasm and vigour. I haven't the strength for any of that.

I brought the Lay Auditor from Togo back for lunch.[4]

At 5.00 pm to Via Transpontina, a lecture to the bishops of Africa on religious freedom. It went well enough. A lot of them, from Arab countries, are against any mention of a confessional State: that is not essential; the Muslims will argue from it, without taking any notice of the rest of the declaration, to justify their fanaticism. For them, the person does not exist, being submissive is everything. The day a Muslim sets himself to think and react as a person, he ceases to be a Muslim.

A visit from l'abbé Ganoczy, who has just returned. I could scarcely talk.

Friday 17 September 1965
I missed the coach by a few seconds, so I am staying here. I am drafting a text for Mgr Elchinger.

It appears that the session was interesting: six interventions by cardinals, among whom Heenan,[5] who quoted Newman: 'conscience first, then the pope'.

---

1. *AS* IV/I, 223–225.
2. *AS* IV/I, 239–241.
3. *AS* IV/I, 245–248.
4. Eusèbe Adjakpley.
5. *AS* IV/I, 295–296.

Mgr Elchinger[1] produced out a paper in which I recognised Fr Féret: suppress the biblical section; speak of respect for ALL the values that transcend the domain of the state; mention and identify with the international examples of defence of religious freedom.

At 4.00 pm at the 'conciliar strategy' meeting (Elchinger) at *Regina Mundi*. Present were: Mgr Elchinger, Volk, Garrone, Ancel, Marty, Reuss, Hengsbach, the Auxiliary of Freiburg[2] and a Dutch bishop; as *periti*: Haubtmann, Schillebeeckx, Daniélou, Rahner, Ratzinger, Semmelroth, Moeller, Hirschmann, Philips, the canon from Louvain, Neuner.

I wrote this up only after I got back, so in a summary fashion. Volk opened the meeting, but it was Elchinger who directed it, translating from German to French. The point was to come to an agreement (the German bishops on one side and the French on the other should decide on their common attitude by Monday) in order to work together. Schema XIII should not be rejected or demolished, because that would play into the hands of the conservatives, but it should be improved.

Hirschmann explained the current attitude of the Germans with great precision: on the foundation, on the genre and the style, on the title (several of them do not want a 'Pastoral Constitution' and prefer the form of a letter).

Rahner insisted on the problem of gnoseology: who is speaking, in whose name, with what certitude; where does what is being said come from?

Ratzinger had lots of criticisms. Two in particular: 1) it is situated too much on the natural, ahistorical plane; 2) it is too optimistic, there is no mention of sin until page 20 (this will later be shown to be incorrect).

Volk ... (He made such grand gestures that he lost his ring!)

Ancel and Garrone returned to the concrete conditions in which the text has been drawn up. One had not done what one wanted to do, but what the Fathers wanted.

Daniélou replied to Ratzinger and showed how the first part sought to say only what is necessary in order to give a Christian clarification of the second part.

I said how I had passed through two phases: one euphoric, after what I was told by the Agars[3]—with, however, some criticisms since then (the ones expressed in the letters I wrote at the time to Provenchères, Garrone, Elchinger); and then a more critical one, when I was more aware of the lack of synthesis in the area of anthropology and christology. The major question is the union between anthropology and theology.

Haubtmann: what has been done is what was called for, required by the Fathers. He read out some favourable testimonies.

But there are critical testimonies: Schillebeeckx brought some from the Dutch universities and made some remarks along the lines of Rahner and Ratzinger.

---

1. *AS* IV/I, 313–314.
2. Karl Gnädinger.
3. Jean and Françoise Agar; Françoise was Fr Congar's niece.

Hengsbach then spoke about the chapter *De vita oeconomica* [on economic life] and the reactions of M. de Rosen.[1]

Philips: We must consider what is POSSIBLE. To want to redo the whole schema would result in having nothing at all, which would be a terrible disillusionment. So start with what we have got, and improve it. We should agree on these three points:
- THE CHURCH speaks in the name of its Faith.
- The Church addresses itself to all people.
- We are not claiming to give a definitive and final teaching.

Philips spoke about the setting up of ten commissions (which will be done tomorrow) each of six Fathers and about ten experts; unofficial experts can be invited.

Mgr Hengsbach: this is pressing. The discussion could start on Monday!!! Agree these three points:
1) Don't speak in such a way as to destroy the credit of the schema, but to recognise it as a possible basis.
2) Agree on improving it at the stage both of the discussion and of the *modi*.
3) Recognise that it is an imperfect text, a beginning of dialogue with the world, not an absolute and finished teaching.

He would be in favour of it being presented as a LETTER.

Overall, this meeting was useful and interesting. The Germans will doubtless be less critical than there was risk they would be.

It was agreed to meet again next Friday.

I have another touch of flu and a temperature (due to being out in the sun on 14 September with my bald head.)

Saturday 18 September 1965

This morning there was a meeting of the Joint Commission on schema XIII, to: 1) approve the *Relatio* that will be read on Monday. As Mgr Guano is seriously ill and still in hospital, it was Mgr Garrone who drafted it and will read it out; 2) set up the central commission and the ten commissions, corresponding to the chapters of the text, that will have to rework the text in the light of the discussion.

I did not go to it; I sent a note about my preferences for this or that subcommission.

I wrote my chronicle for *ICI*.

At 5.00 pm, at the College of Propaganda for the meeting of the commission on missions. I waited interminably. I was too tired to join in the groups chatting here and there.

---

1. Léon de Rosen, President of the International Christian Union of Business Leaders, was a lay Auditor at the Council.

After a very friendly and very flowery speech by Cardinal Agagianian we wished him a happy birthday, and he left. Fr Schütte presided: three questions:

1) the approval of his plan for a *Relatio*. But, in this very large room, it was difficult to hear and we were too far away from each other. There was some hair-splitting over details. There was only one important point: what was said about the reorganisation of Propaganda. The commission for the reform of the Curia has already put forward some principles: among others, that only cardinals should be members of Congregations. Schütte offered two solutions for page 22, lines 17–22 of the printed schema;

2) the question of the meeting of sub-commissions: Where? At Propaganda.

I spoke with several French bishops living at the French Seminary about religious freedom. I saw among MANY a hesitation to vote this text through. Many think that it will not get the 2/3 majority. They freely agreed that what the text says is sound, but they find it insufficient on the whole: it does not state, or say enough about, essential points: about objective truth, and the duty to seek it.

Sunday 19 September 1965

I feel crushed by the consciousness of the mediocrity of my life and my work.

I had a word (separately) with Martimort, with Haubtmann, with Mgr Garrone, about my fears for the *De libertate*. I believe that, to ensure a favourable vote, the Commission must explain the exact sense and content of its text, and show that it responds to many of the difficulties that have been raised. Martimort, it seems, is looking after the matter, and also ensuring that there will be a vote, because Cardinal Suenens did not appear to be sure of this.

Mgr Garrone told me that Martimort is attending to the TERMS in which this vote will be presented, in order to allow a significant rallying of those who are hesitant. Martimort can be relied on. If I had strength in my legs I would, all the same, try to join De Smedt or Willebrands . . . Haubtmann told me that De Smedt is very discredited in general estimation. He has successively presented different texts, in a very triumphant tone. This has not left an impression of seriousness. Haubtmann told me that very little attention was paid to his *Relatio*: it was known beforehand that he would defend his own position. This seems very regrettable to me. I note these things down just as I heard them.

I saw Mgr Etchegaray this evening. It is he who arranges the external relations of the Council tactics. He is very uneasy about tomorrow. One knows neither what there is a risk of happening, no what to do. He is recommending two votes: the first on this question: Do you wish that there should be a declaration on religious freedom? The second on: Do you agree that the Secretariat should rework its text in the light of discussions? But, he said, it is not certain, this evening, that there will be a vote. That does not depend only on the Moderators, but also on the Council of Presidents. The Pope, he said, is very shaken by the speeches, which he has followed from beginning to end.

There is a restricted meeting at the Secretariat this afternoon, to approve the *Relatio conclusiva* [final report] of Mgr De Smedt.

I said again that, in my view, much will depend on the terms in which there is explained to the Fathers exactly what it is about and what is not about.

Monday 20 September 1965

At St Peter's. Within five minutes, three invitations to give lectures (Brazil, Argentina, and at Brescia).

Felici[1] read out (in the name of the Cardinal Dean[2]) a letter which it is proposed to send to the Pope, thanking him for the encyclical on the Eucharist, and assuring him of support during his trip to the UN.

Voting on the *De Revelatione* began. I noted down the results on my copy.

> Cardinal Lefebvre:[3] *pro pace* [for the sake of peace] responded to six difficulties.
>
> Wyszyński:[4] countries that are subjected to dialectical materialism have completely different categories of thought.
>
> Beran:[5] the harm done to his country by the absence of freedom of conscience in the past; this is what it is atoning for in the present.
>
> Cardinal Shehan[6] tried to demonstrate that the teaching of Leo XIII and Pius XII was along the same lines as the declaration.
>
> Cardinal Rossi:[7] Brazil, carried the votes of eighty-two Brazilian Fathers.
>
> Cardinal Browne,[8] who seemed to me to have made considerable progress towards the text.
>
> Cardinal Cardijn[9] followed him. This was not in the same style. He was stopped after twelve minutes.
>
> Marcel Lefebvre CSSP[10] followed: the Declaration = eighteenth century philosophy = a thing condemned by the Church since Pius IX.

Such a simplistic attitude grieves me: in my humanity, FOR THE SAKE OF HUMAN BEINGS!

At last, this morning, the text has gained some points. But considerable uncertainty reigns about the vote, about the terms in which it will be put (there should be a vote of ORIENTATION), and even whether it will happen. One Fa-

---

1. *AS* IV/I, 335.
2. This refers to the letter from Cardinal Tisserant, *AS* IV/I, 25–26.
3. J Lefebvre, *AS* IV/I, 384–386.
4. *AS* IV/I, 387–390.
5. *AS* IV/I, 393-394.
6. *AS* IV/I, 396–398.
7. *AS* IV/I, 399–401.
8. *AS* IV/I, 403–405.
9. *AS* IV/I, 406–408.
10. *AS* IV/I, 409–11.

ther this morning suggested that the matter should be remitted to a new commission of theologians and jurists.

At 3.30 pm, Bourdarias, for Radio Luxembourg.

This evening, at 9.00 pm, a telephone call to Willebrands, about something else. He does not know whether there will be a vote tomorrow.

Tuesday 21 September 1965

At St Peter's. Gregorian sung Mass. Discussion did not start until nearly 10.00 am.

The Pope has appointed a delegation, representing the Council, to accompany him to the UN: of cardinals of different nations (and rites, someone said: Agagianian!![1]).

> Cardinal Journet[2] gave an assessment of where there is unanimity among us, and of differences. Journet gave a very clear lesson, but one that added nothing. He concluded that all this is in the Declaration, and therefore he would entirely approve it. THIS WILL CARRY GREAT WEIGHT.
> He had delivered his text very well. It was a complete approbation.
> At 10.40 am, Agagianian[3] said: sixty-two Fathers have spoken, shall we terminate this discussion? It was thought that the majority were in favour of closure... (This form of *quaesitum* [query] always obtains its effect. There is an impetus. A person gets up when he sees the others standing up...)
> De Smedt[4] read a conclusion. He expressed thanks and promised that the Commission would study all the comments. He listed a number of points on which more clarity had been asked for.

His conclusion was GOOD. Always optimistic. The impression made was good.

At 10.53 am the Moderators proposed the vote (secret ballot) on the following question: *Utrum textus reemendatus de libertate religiosa placeat Patribus tamquam basis definitivae Declarationis ulterius perficiendae iuxta doctrinam catholicam de vera religione et emendationes a Patribus in disceptatione propositas et approbandas ad normam ordinis concilii?* [whether the re-amended text on religious freedom is agreeable to the Fathers as the basis of the definitive declaration, still needing to be further perfected in accordance with Catholic doctrine concerning true religion and with the emendations proposed by the Fathers during the discussion that remain to be approved according to the norm of the order of the Council?]

---

1. AS IV/I, 421.
2. AS IV/I, 424–425.
3. AS IV/I, 431.
4. AS IV/I, 432–433.

The result:

Voters:	2,222
Placet:	1,997
Non Placet:	224
Null:	1

So, there was a vote. When I arrived at 9.00 am, someone said to me: there ought not to be a vote, but they are trying to get it through.

Cardinals Tisserant and Agagianian did not arrive until the end of Mass. I was told they had been with the Pope. Doubtless some approach had been made to him and doubtless the text put to the vote was the result of this step.

But the text of the vote was odd. Only those who did not want a Declaration at all could have voted no to it . . .

I went to greet Cardinal Journet and could not pass unnoticed because I missed a step and fell over.

Reading of the *Relatio generalis* on schema XIII by Mgr Garrone.[1]

At 11.37 am, the GENERAL discussion on schema XIII began (it will be followed by a vote to determine whether there will be a discussion of each chapter).

Spellman[2] began the discussion. Other cardinals.

I gather that the Council of Presidents met yesterday afternoon. There was a majority against taking a orienting vote on the *De libertate*. This morning, the vote was proposed in the name of the MODERATORS, not of the Council of Presidents. Basically, the Council of Presidents does not mirror the assembly well, and this is the source of many conflicts. If the Council of Presidents had won this time a deeper doubt would have hung over the project of the Declaration, from the PSYCHOLOGICAL point of view.

Cardinal Agagianian was with the Pope at 10.00 pm.

It was between 10.00 pm and midnight that Willebrands and Arrighi sent the Pope a report which decided him to intervene in favour of a vote. The result was the text just now voted on. This does not say very much, from the point of view of content: one could have voted *placet* for several different reasons, and voted *non placet* equally. But it is important from the point of view of public opinion. It announces to public opinion that THERE WILL BE a Declaration *De libertate religiosa:* that the Council is IN FAVOUR OF religious freedom.

Veronese said to me: this vote is Paul VI's passport for the UN!

At 3.50 pm, a visit from two young students of history at the École normale supérieure, M. Levillain and M. Jeanneret.[3]

---

1. *AS* IV/I, 553–558.
2. *AS* IV/I, 559–560.
3. Philippe Levillain and Jean-Noël Jeanneney, students from the École normale supérieure in rue d'Ulm, were taking a course of studies in Rome and helping René Brouillet, French Ambassador to the Holy See, keeping him informed about the progress of the Council; P Levillain was later to become professor of contemporary history in several universities (cf the publication of his third-cycle doctoral thesis, dedicated to the Am-

At 5.20 pm, meeting of the Secretariat for Non-Believers.

Before going in I met Fr Chenu, who was recovering from lumbago, but apart from that was in good form.

There were present, under the presidency of Cardinal König, with Miano as Secretary:[1] Chenu, Moeller, Rahner, Cottier, Häring, Lubac, Houtart, Girardi, Veronese, La Valle[2] (editor of *L'Avvenire d'Italia*), Sugranyes. I did not make a note everything.

> Rahner: are we concerned with atheism ALONE, or with the atrophy of the religious sense?
> Houtart: make an assessment.
> > Compose a typology of atheism. Houtart finds the Number on atheism in schema XIII very bad.
> Moeller: certain works or films, which seem at first sight to be atheistic, are in fact full of questions about transcendent problems.

I insisted on the profound character of the questions posed by atheism, on the profound sameness of method with that of ecumenism (if we are dealing with atheism as a spiritual world of values and not simply with the fact of abandonment), on the necessity of making the theologians and pastors of the Church sensitive concerning it: the Council could be a unique occasion for this, either during the discussion of schema XIII, or if, after the discussions, some explanatory talks are given to the Fathers (a suggestion Moeller had from Suenens).

From the practical point of view, the creation of local secretariats was suggested.

From the pastoral point of view, Häring drew attention to co-existence, dialogue, and the need to find the appropriate language.

Wednesday 22 September 1965

Was I wrong? Am I going to miss something interesting? I did not go to St Peter's this morning. I was afraid it would be terribly boring. I will get the texts *in integro* [in full] at the Commission, and the lack of strength I suffer from so much

---

bassador and his wife: *La Mécanique politique de Vatican II. La majorité et l'unanimité dans un concile* (Éditions Beauchesne, 1975); J-N Jeanneney, after teaching, was to make a career in radio and television, he was to sit in two governments and later to become President of the Bibliothèque nationale of France.

1. Vincenzo Miano, SDB, Dean of the Faculty of Philosophy at the Pontifical Salesian Athenaeum until 1966, Council expert, he was Secretary for the newly created Secretariat for Non-Believers.
2. Raniero La Valle was editor of *Avvenire d'Italia*, a Catholic daily newspaper in Bologna.

prevents me from seeing people and chatting, as the others do. However, I would very much have liked to speak a little with the Observers.

It seems that there were some interesting interventions, but I did not miss much. Etchegaray passed on to me from Cardinal Suenens that the latter had seen the Pope yesterday. The Pope had on his desk my treatise for the bishops (*Études et Documents*[1]) on religious freedom, with lots of passages underlined. The Pope had praised in particular the way in which I present the events of 19–20 November 1964.

A visit from Lison Millot[2] and her companion, who have come to prepare the meetings of a group of lay people with some bishops.

A visit from l'abbé Caminetti of Bergamo,[3] who would like to come to study protestant theology in Strasbourg—then Dr Marois (Protection of Life). I went to the Gregorianum to check some references: it would have taken me half-an-hour in Strasbourg . . . I was only just back when there was a telephone call and a visit from Fr Müller SVD,[4] on behalf of Fr Schütte, for the commentary on the *De Missionibus*.[5]

At almost every meal the French bishops talk, at some time or other, about integrist currents and activities. They are all annoyed with these. They are all AGAINST: many of them have among their clergy some priest or other who make problems for them about this.

Thursday 23 September 1965

At St Peter's. The ambassadors' cars were seen arriving. It is because Cardinal Cicognani is celebrating his sixty years of priesthood, which cost us a few chants from the Sistine choir and some odious flash-lights for photographs.

The morning was not very interesting: the end of the GENERAL discussion of schema XIII; the beginning of discussion of the preliminary statement. This threatens to be very boring. The whole thing was punctuated by votes on the *De apostolatu laicorum* (after the *Relatio*).

Cardinal Cardijn spoke, a little oratorically.[6] He is well-liked, but that won't help. That has no influence and there was gentle criticism of his style.

I spoke to Mgr Prignon: how are the bishops going to occupy themselves after about 8 October? He told me: the Coordinating Commission once asked that

1. Yves Congar, 'La déclaration sur la liberté religieuse', *Études et documents,* No. 15, 14 June 1965.
2. Lison (Marie-Louise) and her husband Georges Millot belonged to the *Vie Nouvelle* movement which was to send a delegation to Rome the following October to meet with the French bishops there.
3. This probably refers to the theologian Mario Cuminetti, who was very much involved in the ecumenical movement.
4. Karl Müller, SVD, was Secretary of Studies for the Society of the Divine Word.
5. J Schütte (editor) *L'Activité missionnaire de l'Église*, 'Unam Sanctam', 67 (Paris: Cerf, 1967).
6. *AS* IV/II, 394–396.

question. Felici said: with visits to museums and concerts. That had not been taken up and the matter stopped there. The Pope is thinking of holding a meeting of the Presidents of Episcopal Conferences—who will afterwards call meetings of their conferences—to consider together the application of the conciliar decrees, and their consequences for Canon Law . . .

In the afternoon, I was torn between a workshop of the French bishops on the *De Presbyteris*, a meeting of the Secretariat to take stock of the matter of religious freedom, and the Joint Commission on schema XIII. I opted for the first meeting, which seemed to me the one that more pertinently required my presence. Taking part were: Mgr Marty, Atton,[1] Bannwarth, Mazerat, Gand, Gufflet,[2] Alix,[3] Théas, Guyot, Polge,[4] Vilnet,[5] Bazelaire, Brunon[6] and, as experts, Colson, Frisque,[7] Denis, Salaün[8] (Mission de France), Camelot.

Each expressed his *desiderata* and essential criticisms of the text. A list was drawn up of the points on which improvement was desired and sub-groups were set up that will draft something; all this will be looked at again next Thursday.

This meeting was interesting and, I think, very useful. If there are requests from the Fathers backed up by precise propositions, the schema could be greatly improved, and it needs to be. I well recognised that the way in which we have worked has been catastrophic. The synthesis should have been the work of a single mind. But the work was shared out: a different person responsible for each Number, etc. When each one pursued his own work, for myself I did not want to assert myself too much, I wanted each one to have his chance, and for this reason, I let the others do the talking. It was, in fact, impossible to say to the others: my idea is good, my text is excellent, yours is no good!!! I did indeed find this or that Number verbose, even poor, but it was not I who had been made responsible for it.

I think many things can be retrieved by provoking some good interventions and injecting a dose of this or that into the text. This procedure of injection produced some good results for No. 28 of the *De Ecclesia*, which was, in any case, more difficult, since the Commission did not want to retain more than a small number of *modi*. Those that I drafted, that the French bishops asked for, that the Commission accepted, were sufficient to modify profoundly the appearance, the

---

1. Alfred Atton, Bishop of Langres (France).
2. Henri Gufflet, Coadjutor of Limoges.
3. Bernard Alix, Auxiliary Bishop of Le Mans.
4. Eugène Polge, Auxiliary Bishop of Avignon.
5. Jean Vilnet, bishop of Saint-Dié (France).
6. Jean-Baptiste Brunon, Auxiliary Bishop of Toulouse.
7. Jean Frisque, of the Society of the Helpers of the Missions (SAM) founded by Vincent Lebbe, taught ecclesiology at the Seminary of the *Mission de France* at Pontigny (Yonne).
8. René Salaün, priest of the *Mission de France*, where he was in charge of pastoral research.

balance and so the teaching of that No. 28. That was one of my meagre satisfactions.

Friday 24 September 1965

I did not go to St Peter's. It is too boring and exhausting. For us, poor experts, it is even rather dreadful. Yesterday I talked to Fr Gagnebet about this. The prospect of entering on index cards nine hundred pages of Latin, of discussing this over again, of redoing some texts that will provide further occasions for *modi*, to review all this again . . . this prospect, this enormous process is draining and crushing. Nothing more can be done. All the non-conciliar experts used the morning session to chat and meet people. They have the strength for that. And they provoke, or write papers that come raining down on us, adding still more to the weight of paper under which we are suffocating! Oh! If only there was an end to this. I can't do any more.

And then there is the correspondence. EVERY DAY there are people asking to see me, who telephone just when I am most exhausted, just as I have come back in . . .

At 4.00 pm, at *Mater Dei* for the meeting with the Germans, the Dutch and the Belgians. A lot fewer participants. From the outset it was obvious that this would not be up to last Friday's meeting. Some newcomers: Klostermann, Küng, Smulders and another Dutchman, Grillmeier, Mühlen[1] Mgr Martensen.[2] It was obvious that schema XIII leaves the Germans very dissatisfied. They are looking for a dogmatic density that is not there . . . Küng would prefer that instead of telling the world what it should do the Church should say what IT ITSELF DOES! Garrone keeps going back to concrete realities: we began from what the Fathers asked for in the Third Session, BUT IT IS OBVIOUS THAT THE ATTITUDE OF THE COUNCIL HAS CHANGED QUITE A LOT SINCE THEN: Mgr Martensen: How differently the New Testament (Romans, Apocalypse) speaks about the world!!!

There was rather good agreement on several points. Mgr Elchinger would like a certain number of theologians to meet to define the main lines along which, and according to which the text needs to be revised. I insisted, as also did Mgr Garrone, that one could only indicate WHAT HAD BEEN ASKED FOR BY THE FATHERS. I was afraid that this group of theologians would say above all what IT wanted to see emphasised. Mgr Elchinger suspected the commissions of having done as they pleased (at least, ONE of those who did the drafting, in the sub-commissions). But that is not true. All the work of the Commission begins with a study and precise analysis of the interventions made *in aula* or submitted in writing. It is only on this basis that the work planned, that would be very useful in

---

1. Heribert Mühlen taught dogmatic theology in the Catholic Faculty of Theology at Paderborn from 1964 onwards; he was a Council expert during the last Session.
2. Hans Martensen, SJ, Bishop of Copenhagen.

itself, can be done. So, in my view, either this work should be done by the theologians OF THE COMMISSION, or else the theologians of whom Mgr Elchinger is thinking should do the work of detailed analysis and entry on index cards.

Fr Smulders told me that Schauf hopes for a kind of *nota praevia* or for some *modi* from the Pope for the chapter on tradition in the *De Revelatione*. He will have to see Cardinal Florit.

From *Mater Dei* I went on to *Domus Mariae* for a lecture about schema XIII. A pretty large audience. It had been advertised: there were some journalists, some Observers, a few Protestants (I only knew this afterwards).

I saw the Hungarian bishops for a moment and it was agreed that we shall meet again.

Saturday 25 September 1965
I did a little work, wretchedly. Nothing serious. Then correspondence. At the end of the morning, at 1.00 pm, a telephone call from Fr Hamer. There was a meeting this morning at the Secretariat, on religious freedom. They must have forgotten to call me to it. On Tuesday at 4.30 pm there will be a meeting of the particular sub-commissions:

1 = Nos 1–3;
2 = No. [ ];
3 = [ ].

I am on sub-commission 3 with Hermaniuk and Lorscheider.[1] Wednesday, a meeting of the WHOLE sub-commission. Between now and then the observations will need to have been read.

A little work *(De Presbyteris)*. Visits: l'abbé Bardés,[2] Frs Refoulé,[3] Benoit.

Sunday 26 September 1965
Rain. The poor gypsies whom the Pope is supposed to visit this afternoon and who have had to make some festive preparations! A rotten year for weather!

Work on the texts for *De libertate*: there are 105 interventions. Many of them extremely carefully considered. It cannot be said that the question has been treated in a slipshod manner. What are we going to do???

---

1. Aloísio Lorscheider, OFM, Bishop of Santo Ângelo (Brazil), elected member of the Secretariat for Unity during the Second Session of the Council; he was later to become Cardinal Archbishop of Fortaleza, and then of Aparecida.
2. Josep M Bardés i Huguet, of the diocese of Barcelona, had brought Congar to Barcelona for a series of lectures in 1961.
3. François Refoulé, OP, of the Province of France, worked at Éditions du Cerf, where he was in charge, on the Catholic side, of the ecumenical translation of the Bible into French (the future TOB); later he was to become editor of Éditions du Cerf, then director of the École biblique et archéologique française in Jerusalem.

At 5.00 pm, a small French group in my room endeavouring to improve the concept of priesthood itself in the gospel sense in the *De presbyteris*. Present: Mgr Marty, Guyot, Lebrun, Brunon, Frs Salaün, Frisque, Colson. Colson explained his (my—our) concept of the priesthood of the Gospel, starting with Romans 15:16. Mgr Guyot had prepared an intervention on: 1) the place of consecration by the Holy Spirit (supported by some texts from the major seminary at Autun; but Mgr Lebrun did not wish to intervene); 2) on the missionary opportunity with respect to unbelievers (intervention by Salaün, whose drafts were less happy). They will settle on: a WRITTEN intervention of Brunon along the line of Romans 15:16. It will be reported to the meeting on Thursday.

We did not manage to catch up with Lécuyer. He was not there this time.

Fr Gy confirmed for me what I had thought: it was by deliberate choice that Father General did not take part in the discussion on religious freedom. He knew that he would be criticised for not fully representing the Oder. He wanted to make this gesture of goodwill. Equally, he said to Mgr Boudon[1] that the Order will follow whatever the Council decides, not only in a spirit of obedience, but joyfully.

Monday 27 September 1965

At 8.30 am, at St Martha's, for the plan for a volume on the *De Missionibus* (Fr Schütte). Then at St Peter's (I arrived at the Gospel). The votes on the *De apostolatu laicorum* and the discussion of Part I of schema XIII continued side by side. All this in an atmosphere of lassitude and boredom.

Among others who spoke was Maximos[2] (with a criticism of No. 19 on atheism, too negative according to him. But what he said was vague and too facile); König[3] also criticised Nos 18-19 on atheism, which are inadequate; Florit[4] too.

I left the tribune and so missed a good number of interventions. I was given a summary of the one by the Father General of the Jesuits,[5] which was described to me as 'horrible'; he envisaged a great mobilisation against atheism, like an army under the orders of the Pope.

I am overwhelmed on the one hand, by the feeling of my own powerlessness, of my intellectual and spiritual mediocrity, and, on the other hand, by the expression of immense credit and friendly interest of which I am the object. I sat down for a moment on the step of a confessional box. More than forty people came up to make kindly remarks: 'I have read all your books', etc. From the USA, from Ceylon, from Africa, from South America, Australia etc. How ridiculous

---

1. René Boudon, Bishop of Mende (France).
2. *AS* IV/II, 451–453.
3. *AS* IV/II, 454–456.
4. *AS* IV/II, 456–458.
5. The Spaniard, Pedro Arrupe, elected General of the Society of Jesus in May 1965, *AS* IV/II 481–484.

that people are good to me, and the credit or influence attributed to me: 'You are very well known among us' etc.

I am extremely weary. Stormy weather.

At 4.00 pm with the bishops of Chile: a lecture on the priesthood. A friendly atmosphere. But when I came home I could not stand up. I did not even read things that would require that I take some notes. I was unable to write. I am writing these few lines only after supper.

I had a visit from Thils. He told me: it will not be possible to revise schema XIII, submit it to a vote with *modi*, and do the *expensio modorum* with a view to a final vote. Why not close the Council as soon as the vote with *modi* is assured? The text with the *modi* could be SENT to the bishops who would vote *placet* or *non placet* by mail. The Pope could take up these votes in a collegial act and promulgate the text in the spring or at Pentecost of 1966, during the first meeting of the *Synodus episcoporum*[1] ... No one would see in this deferral a means of getting around the schema, since it would have been voted in substance. It would be a way of saving time.

But this evening, Etchegaray [whose weekly meeting (started by him) brings together representatives of practically all the espicopates, and serves as an official organ recognised, and made use of, by the official authorities of the Council] saw Döpfner today. Döpfner was very much in form: he had spent his weekend mountaineering ... He is optimistic about the length of the Session: it could finish by the end of November. And Döpfner, under the seal of discretion, has proposed a hypothesis similar to that of Thils for the vote and declaration of schema XIII: the schema which, moreover, if it were left to him, he would gladly see totally suppressed.

Tuesday 28 September 1965

I stayed at home to work on *De libertate*. I finished reading the 105 texts submitted to the Secretariat (sixty-two of which had been spoken *in aula*). Some are VERY sophisticated. Very great seriousness about this discussion.

I am frequently obliged to revive my courage and my attention, motivating them by the spirit of obedience to God in the service of truth and of my brothers: because this work is very dull and very trying. What fatigue is crushing us all in this Fourth Session!

At the Secretariat at 4.30 pm: the sub-commission which has to deal with Nos 8–14 of the Declaration on Religious Freedom. Present were: Mgr Hermaniuk and Lorscheider, Frs Hamer, Benoit and myself. We were not in very good form. The weather was sultry and stormy. A list was made of the changes asked for: they were not so very great. Fr Benoit outlined a plan of development according to the general sense of Holy Scripture. But it is not certain that it will be able to be followed throughout: we can do only what the Fathers ask for. In the Commissions

---

1. The Synod of Bishops had been instituted by the Pope on the previous 15 September.

there is fidelity to this rule. It is true that the Secretariat has received a GENERAL mandate to correct and complete the text in a sense that would be able to satisfy the whole body the Fathers: this mandate gives us A LITTLE latitude. We succeeded in determining precisely the attitude of our sub-commission on the main points raised by the interventions. They are still coming in. This evening the score was 127.

Wednesday 29 September 1965

At 9.30 am, at the Secretariat: the whole sub-commission for the *De libertate*. The vote that had been taken, Mgr Willebrands said, was due to the Pope personally. Mgr Carlo Colombo will be invited to the sub-commission, through whom there is contact with the Pope, and also Mgr Ancel. Because the Pope has intimated that he had been very impressed by Mgr Ancel's intervention and by the final *relatio* of Mgr De Smedt.

Felici asked for the revised text for 15 October. It will therefore be necessary to put an end to the papers which keep on coming (we were given more of them this morning).

The problems posed by the Declaration and the 'rational' part were discussed. De Smedt, Cantero and Murray had each produced a text. It was agreed soon enough (it was my idea and I pushed in this direction) that there should be a rather ample *proemium* in which there would first be presented the ideal position of the Church, its mandate for evangelisation, the duties that human beings have towards revealed truth—then one would pass on to the situation of the world and to the idea of religious freedom in as much as it applies to all human beings. It was also agreed to put ALL the teaching into the text of the Declaration. There was less agreement on the subject of the arguments from reason. Heylen[1] defended the idea that the Council makes this Declaration ON ITS OWN AUTHORITY, by simply AFFIRMING it, and does not have to offer REASONS, some of which could turn out to be questionable, indeed, invalid. In any case, it was agreed to put forward reasons as indications, as *suasiones* [spurs]. In the end, it was said: as we are preparing an emended draft, it will be seen later, in each instance, where a particular piece should be put, and on what basis it should be presented.

The meeting finished at 12.25 pm. I said my prayers. Afterwards I had great difficulty in finding a way of getting to the embassy. I was assailed by two Italians from Palermo, who came up to me, asked me if I was Fr Congar, wanted an article for their journal *Dialogo*. I saw La Pira for a moment. I arrived a bit late at the reception of M. and Mme Brouillet.

Lunch with Cardinal König, Mgr Marty, Vial, Schmidtt, the Guittons, several members of the two embassies . . .

---

1. Victor Heylen, priest of the diocese of Malines-Brussels, taught moral theology at the University of Louvain.

I tried to see Cardinal Journet at 3.50 pm. I had informed him earlier. He probably did not get the message. He went out.

I took a quarter-of-an-hour to get from the Porta Sant'Anna to the meeting room. I could no longer take two steps.

'I am walking for a missionary' and so that THE CHURCH MAY GO FORWARD![1]

The members of the Theological Commission arrived. But I had to stay sitting down, unable to greet them. I was unable to stand up.

Philips explained the *expensio modorum*.

Tired as I am, I am here again. I realised this evening that, basically, I love the work and the atmosphere of the Theological Commission. But everything (or a lot!) depends on Philips, on his clarity, his presence of mind, his obvious fairness. He has created and continues to create the climate of the Commission.

We did the *modi* for Chapter I, with some moments of hair-splitting… sometimes it is the most minute points that one discusses for the greatest length of time.

In the evening, at dinner, M. Boegner.

Thursday 30 September 1965

At St Peter's. I really need to regain contact. That's the only way I can do my *ICI* chronicle.

Continuation of the votes (after a LONG *Relatio*) on the *De episcoporum pastorali munere* [on the pastoral office of bishops].

Discussion on marriage. Journet[2] replied in an abrupt fashion to Zoghby[3] who had yesterday referred to the Greek Fathers on the indissolubility of marriage. He sees no other solution than heroism for broken and destroyed marriages.

I did not take notes of the discussions, they will appear in the newspapers.

The bishop of Treviso[4] came to see me to ask me to come and talk to his priests …

The text of the Declaration on Non-Christian Religions was distributed this morning.[5] This is an important step. I read the very well prepared *expensio modorum*.

On the way out I saw Chenu. He told me that we were attacked in a filthy conservative rag called *Lo Specchio*. I bought this rag.[6] Chenu (with a photo) and myself (with passages cited from my article in *Esprit*) are presented as the agents of an introduction of Marxism into the Church. The title of this issue is 'I Rebelli

1. Cf above, page 3, note 1.
2. *AS* IV/III, 58–59.
3. *AS* IV/III, 45–47.
4. Antonio Mistrorigo was Bishop of Treviso, Italy.
5. *AS* IV/IV, 690–696.
6. This refers to the issue of 3 October of this weekly paper.

del Concilio' [the Conciliar Rebels]; that of the article is 'La cellula del Concilio' [the Council cell].

This comes back to what I wrote in *ICI* for 15 September, and which Fesquet quoted in *Le Monde*: 'the watchdogs have to be let bark at the moon.'[1] But it is tiring, all the same, to have to listen to their barking . . .

At 3.00 pm a visit from three priests from Chambéry: Manificat, Porcheron, Paravy.[2] They had worked a lot with Taizé and they are planning to set up an ecumenical community for evangelisation. A brother from Taizé is going to join them. On the one hand, from the ecumenical point of view, the moment has come to take actions, to make gestures which open up and prepare the future. On the other, there is a profound link between ecumenism and mission. I was impressed by the truth of what they told me: ecumenism practised and lived brings a momentum, something efficacious, to mission, to evangelisation. It really answers to an expectation. Particularly among the young.

I saw that THIS was missing from the schema on the missions, and I told them to go and find Mgr Darmancier, on my behalf, asking him to intervene along these lines. It seems to me that the case of these three priests—who made a good impression on me of spiritual seriousness—is part of that miraculous character of Taizé. Miraculous because it is part of God's plan of salvation. That is the only source, the only norm. I have the feeling that what these three priests want to start comes from the Holy Spirit. I said to them as they were leaving what I have myself heard everyday for forty years: *Et tu puer propheta Altissimi vocaberis; praeibis* . . . [And you child shall be called a prophet of the Most High; you shall go ahead . . . (Luke 1: 67)].

At 5.00 pm at Saint-Louis des Français, for the workshop on priesthood. The work is becoming clearer.

At 6.15 pm with Frs Benoit and Hamer: examination of what Fr Benoit had prepared for the biblical Numbers of *De libertate*.

When I got back, at 7.35 pm, Pastor Leuba was waiting for me.[3] I had him until 9.45 pm for the preparation of the lecture that we are to give jointly in Strasbourg on 24 January 1966. We chatted about various things. A truly original spirit, lively, sharp.

Friday 1 October 1965

I did not go to St Peter's: work on the *De libertate religiosa*. I have to choose this afternoon between three meetings in which I should be taking part:
    - *De libertate religiosa*.

---

1. Congar wrote there, in reference to attacks on himself, 'Such attacks always remind me of the saying of St Francis de Sales: "The watchdogs have to be let bark at the moon"'.
2. Maurice Manificat, Edmond Porcheron and Gaston Paravy.
3. Jean-Louis Leuba, an eminent Reformed theologian, was a professor at the Faculty of Theology of the University of Neuchâtel.

- the Theological Commission: Chapter II on Tradition: one of my subjects.
-The meeting on the ecumenical Bible.[1]

I shall go to the *De libertate*: that is my most pressing duty. For Chapter II of the *De Revelatione* I wrote a note on a text from St Irenaeus that they want to quote (*'charisma veritatis certum'* [2]) and made forty photocopies of it. I will entrust it to Mgr Garrone.

Yesterday morning, the votes on the *De episcoporum munere* was stopped earlier than expected. It was suspected that something was up. Mgr Guerry told me that the Commission had, indeed, had an extraordinary meeting yesterday evening. It found itself faced with *modi*, supported by Carli, who had some texts all prepared. Two *modi* were dangerous, touching episcopal conferences. They were able to be stopped.

Yesterday Fr Camelot told me that on the previous day (that is, Wednesday) there had been a rather painful session of the Commission for Studies: Staffa wanted to have something about fidelity to St Thomas inserted in the text on SCHOOLS (thus including universities).

This morning I was told that Mgr Pellegrino,[3] just recently appointed archbishop of Turin—and that by the Pope's personal choice and despite some opposition—intervened this morning on the subject of culture. He is well able to: he is himself very cultured. He asked for freedom of research in the Church and spoke of a religious sent into exile not long ago who is now quoted at the Council . . . I was told he was referring to me. It is possible. I met Pellegrino in Strasbourg; I saw him a couple of days ago at the Council and he was very friendly towards me.

At 4.30 pm, at the Secretariat. The sub-commission, plus Mgr Ancel: Mgr De Smedt gave an account of the fifty-minute audience he had had yesterday. The Pope said to him: this is a major document. It establishes the attitude of the Church for several centuries. The world is waiting for it.

The Pope approves the line of the Declaration.

---

1. In the Spring of 1965 an agreement was concluded between Éditions du Cerf and the Universal Biblical Alliance for an ecumenical translation of the Bible into French; François Refoulé OP, and Pastor George Casalis undertook the editing; after the Epistle to the Romans, in 1967, the New Testament was to appear in 1972, and the Old in 1975.

2. 'The sure charism of truth'; Congar wanted to demonstrate that the expression, suggested in a *modus*, did not clearly indicate a ministerial charism for the interpretation of revelation. The reference to Irenaeus was to be deleted from the schema.

3. Pellegrino had declared : 'Only a few years ago I met a religious who was living in involuntary "exile" because he had expressed some opinions that today we rejoice to read in pontifical and conciliar documents. And we all know that his case is not unique'.

When Mgr De Smedt asked: what must be done by way of revision? The Pope said: indicate in a few words that this teaching is the logical continuation of the teaching of my predecessors.

The Pope praised Ancel's speech. The ontological foundation of freedom must be shown, he said.

He gave De Smedt a document signed by about 125 bishops asking that, before the discussion there be a full presentation *in aula* of the position of the Others (Truth and Tolerance); the Secretariat does not represent the thought of the WHOLE Council . . . The Moderators received this text AFTER the vote had been taken, and thus it has only documentary value.

It would be a good thing if the revised text were presented to some members of the opposition but the Pope did not insist absolutely on this.

Willebrands was absent; De Smedt presided and took control of the meeting. Before the opening of the session, Murray came towards me, drew me aside and said: I think the method they are following is very bad. It should be done as it was in February: a small number of experts working on it. Now there are too many. We have moved at once to the level of the WHOLE sub-commission. Murray finds the draft prepared by De Smedt VERY bad. But De Smedt took the whole thing in hand. To some extent he thinks that it is HIS business (Fr Hamer told me yesterday evening that that was also his impression). In fact, Mgr De Smedt had written a plan, which he distributed. At the end of the meeting, he was asked what was the status of this text. He replied: it is only an *'elementum ad cogitandum'* [something to think about].

During this meeting the plan for the drafting of Nos 8–10, prepared by our small group, was examined.

This evening, I asked Mgr Garrone for news of the Theological Commission: 1) about my remarks on the text of St Irenaeus, *'charisma veritatis certum'*, I got the impression that he had not had my forty copies distributed. He had warned Mgr Philips, who had said: there are some difficulties about the meaning of the text in St Irenaeus. Let us take these three words as a nice expression, but without citation or quotation marks. This was accepted; 2) in regard to *modus* 40 D, that is, the addition of *'quo fit ut non omnis doctrina catholica ex Scriptura directe probari queat'* [from which it comes about that not every Catholic teaching can be proved directly from Scripture], I had given my agreement that these words state a FACT, that, as such, is certain, very certain. It was a fine concession that the sub-commission and the Commission made to the minority. But Parente, at this proposal, reopened the whole debate. It was apparent that, under these words, he (they) wanted to re-introduce constitutive Tradition and some more or less unlimited possibilities of development. A vote was taken: Parente and his friends, in wanting too much, lost everything. The *modus* was rejected. The text stayed as it was.

I was told afterwards that Parente had organised his coup. He brought Fr Boyer [who quoted me] in to speak, and had Fr Gagnebet speak.

Does the Holy Spirit make use even of such means?

It is probable that the minority will complain that NONE of their requests have been met. And yet the sub-commission dealing with the *expensio modorum* and the Commission were disposed to give them fairly substantial satisfaction. It was a maladroit and over-ambitious spokesman of that very same minority who compromised its cause.

Mgr Charue told me afterwards that the Pope's letter said: the expression *veritas salutaris* [saving truth] could be used in a bad sense by some people (to limit inspiration and inerrancy). But the Pope hopes THAT IT WILL BE STUDIED AFTERWARDS.

This evening, a visit from an Italian priest wanting an article, two telephone calls for meetings, letters: requests from here and there . . .

Saturday 2 October 1965

At 9.00 am, at the *Foyer Unitas*, for a meeting to discuss and finalise the statutes for the 'Concilium' FOUNDATION. They envisage something rather grand. I said: a kind of Rockerfeller Foundation! We in France are accustomed to achieving things with nothing . . . What they envisage disconcerts us. But why not? Present at the meeting were M. Brand, Rahner, Küng, Schillebeeckx, v den Boogaard,[1] Vanhengel, myself.

Rahner filled out what I had been told about the meeting of the Theological Commission yesterday. According to him: 1) Philips was too diplomatic: he had spoken of indicating in the *Relatio* that the sub-commission for the *expensio modorum* had accepted *modus* 40 D for Chapter II; 2) according to Rahner, this will be useful for those who want a kind of *Nota praevia*. And, in fact—I said so to several people—the minority hopes to get one; 3) Florit has moved from the minority side, or at least is wavering and open to some concessions.

I came back here at noon, as I have some appointments.

First a photographer. I let myself be taken only after grilling him for a long time. Because, as I told him, I have no wish to further the bad work of some newspapers like *Lo Specchio*. The list of people whom he is supposed to photograph consists precisely of those who are being attacked. But he said to me: I could just as easily take you in the street or at the Council. It is for an agency: we have to be able to produce a photograph of everyone who is mentioned.

I let myself be taken, under protest. But what have I got to lose in that? 'They' will always be able to get hold of my photograph!!!

A visit from Etchegaray. He relayed to me the reactions of the meeting of representatives of episcopal conferences that takes place every Friday, about the schema on the Missions: it is not sufficiently discussed in the context of the new churches, and starting from them. It is still too much stuck in the frame of mind

---

1. Anton van den Boogaard, a Dutch businessman was the treasurer and was soon to become the President of the Concilium Foundation.

of Catholics from the old Christendoms; it does not speak sufficiently about the laity; it does not speak of the MISSIONARY VOCATION of lay people; and it should show more clearly that the first missionaries are the indigenous inhabitants (who very often, so I am told, do not have the missionary spirit).

On the schema on priests: two major questions: WHAT IS the priesthood; celibacy.

On the schema on Christian education: many think that this mediocre text should be discussed again; seventy-two per cent of its content is new!!!

At midday, at lunch, the three priests from Chambéry. I have prepared a plan for a projected intervention. They have seen McGrath, Darmancier, others from Brazil etc; these bishops would be disposed to sign the text of an intervention about what is lacking in the schema on the Missions from the ecumenical point of view. At 3.00 pm, the three made me remember a very short paper by Thurian that I used in the drafting, to which I turned immediately. Because the discussion on missions could come up from Tuesday . . . This sort of work, so often undertaken, so often useless, is very burdensome, very tiresome. I feel little inspiration . . .

In the evening, a visit from Jean Bosc.[1]

After supper, someone came looking for my text; Fr Vanhengel and M. v den Boogaard came to invite me to supper tomorrow evening: I declined.

Sunday 3 October 1965
Worked on my *ICI* chronicle. At the end of the evening, when I had finished that work, I returned to work on the *De libertate*. But my hand was tired and I could neither write nor type.

Monday 4 October 1965
The Holy Father left by plane for the UN. I did not go to St Peter's, and continued the adjustments to articles 12–14 of the *De libertate*. This is urgent.

I saw Fr de Lubac briefly, he was very tired, crushed, and down in the dumps: he is not employed in anything, he is not resorted to, he is not given notice of meetings. . . What can be done? I am going to try to get him invited to the workshop on atheism.

At 2.15 pm, the arrival of the Pope in New York was shown live on TV (2.27 pm). Thus we witnessed it at the very moment it was happening. It's fantastic.

At 3.00 pm a visit from M. Pyronnet of the l'Arche community.[2] He explained to me its background, its position, what the community is. The presence of six or

---

1. The Pastor Jean Bosc, of the Reformed Church of France, was Professor of Dogmatic Theology at the Paris Faculty of Protestant Theology; editor of the journal *Foi et Vie*, he was active in the ecumenical field, particularly in the *Groupe des Dombes*.
2. Joseph Pyronnet was a member of the l'Arche Community, an inter-confessional and non-violent community founded by Lanza del Vasto; from l'Arche, he founded an association for non-violent civic action of which he was the national Secretary, with a

seven members in Rome arises from the initiative of forty women who decided to observe a ten-day fast, which they are keeping at the Cenacle.[1] I would certainly fast for one day, but not for ten. I already don't have much strength for that. But I am happy to unite myself spiritually, and humanly, to these witnesses. I have not yet been able to go and see their little exhibition,[2] but I want to.

At 4.30 pm, Theological Commission. I had thought the *modi* to Chapter II were finished. But they are up to No. 42.

At *modus* 65 we again came up against the question that had given trouble the other day with regard to *modus* 40 D. Philips asked that we hear it through to the end before there was any discussion. He pointed out that everyone was agreed on this, that not EVERYTHING is formally expressed in Scripture. Philips suggested a formula; he explained it. Colombo suggested another formula, to be inserted at No. 9 [but that is already completed . . .] We listened to several Fathers, several experts (Rahner, Gagnebet, myself). Philips replied. This lasted nearly an hour. Parente proposed: *Sancta Scriptura et sancta Traditio, quamvis invicem plane distincta, unum tamen depositum constituunt* [Sacred scripture and sacred Tradition, although clearly distinct from each other, nevertheless constitute a single deposit]. I think that very bad.

Throughout this whole discussion Schauf did not open his mouth. Franić was absent.

A vote was taken:

1) SHOULD THERE BE an addition?

> Yes   13
>
> No   11

2) Which?

> – that of Philips?
>
> (*Sacrae Scripturae complexum mysterii christiani referunt,*
>
> *quin omnes veritates revelatae in eis expresse enuntientur*
>
> [the Sacred Scriptures record the whole of the Christian
>
>   mystery without all revealed truths being explicitly enunciated
>
>   in them])
>
> - that of Colombo?
>
> - that of Parente?

Philips got fourteen out of twenty-four votes. It was accepted.

---

view to obtaining status for conscientious objectors.

1. On 8 October, Mgr Boillon, Bishop of Verdun, was to inform the Council Fathers that a group of twenty women were observing in Rome a ten-day period of fasting and prayer for the cause of peace and in union with the Council; this fast took place from 1 to 10 October at the Cenacle Convent.
2. This exhibition, entitled 'Non-violent combat, a sign of the times for Christians' and put on by the l'Arche Community with the co-operation of Non-Violent Civil Action, was held at the *Foyer Unitas*.

This procedure itself stirred up a great discussion: where to put the *modus*, the manner of voting . . .

The text of Philips' that was accepted doesn't amount to anything, it states something so evident (Denzinger is not part of Scripture!) that the minority will be in no way satisfied with it. To the degree that the formula does say something, it rather favours the thesis of the material sufficiency of Scripture: this is certainly traditional. But Cardinal Browne raised a difficulty: where is it to be found that the Scriptures contain the whole of the Christian mystery? I have not seen that anywhere, he said . . . Does he have only a list of theses in his head?

On the subject of *modus* 8 to Chapter III, there was discussion about *veritas salutaris* [saving truth]. After the intervention of Benoit, and despite those of Gagnebet and Garofalo, the phrase *'veritatem SALUTAREM'* remained. I am VERY happy about this. It is a move forward in the direction that I have long advocated. But I asked in vain to be allowed to speak (Ottaviani rarely allows me to do so).

Father General[1] told me that he had seen the issue of *Lo Specchio:* he thought the attack stupid.

I brought Fr de Lubac back with me so that he could make contact with the workshop on schema XIII.

At 8.15 pm, the Pope, LIVE TELECAST, at the UN! Great nobility in his gestures, his attitude, his words.

Tuesday 5 October 1965

A little work on *De libertate* before leaving for St Peter's. The approached to the Basilica were difficult: arrangements for the Pope's return. Inside, we were turned out of our tribune, which was reserved for the Observers (their tribune was reserved for the diplomatic corps) and the Auditors. This Council will have been largely one of theologians who (not all, but a certain number) have contributed an enormous amount of work to it. But they have not been pampered. We have only the right to get on with the job, but not with any help or favour, or any consideration . . .

Very tedious discussion of schema XIII. Cardijn spoke:[2] less oratorically than the first time. Contrary to what I had thought, he attracts little support. I went out for a while. Cardinal Silva told me that he will not speak on the priesthood. But it so happened providence sent me Mgr JA Plourde (Canada),[3] and Mgr Albert Ndongmo,[4] who wanted to intervene on the question. I will draw up a text for

---

1. Aniceto Fernandez, OP.
2. *AS* IV/III, 364–365.
3. Joseph A Plourde, Auxiliary Bishop of Alexandria, Ontario (Canada).
4. Albert Ndongmo, Bishop of Nkongsamba (Cameroon).

them. According to what the latter told me, Fr Martelet stirred up the African bishops on a number of points. That's good. Not only was he within his rights but that sort of work is often beneficial. However there is also something rather awful about it. There are, in Rome, accompanying the bishops, some two-hundred theologians. Each one has HIS idea: he must express THIS idea, see things from THIS angle ... And so he stirs up a bishop, or a group of bishops in consequence. The poor theologian of the Commissions is thus assailed two hundred times. He can do no more.

For myself, today I can't stand up—yes, simply stand up—except with great difficulty. The sessions in St Peter's exhaust me to an incredible extent. There is no movement in my right leg. I have not the least strength. I am always, and every day, without vitality and strength: like a tree struck by lightning, no longer alive, exhausted, except by a centimetre of bark and wood by means of which a minimum of sap still rises. All the same, it produces some apples or some plums.

Oh, but it's hard!!!

I met Fr Tucci who told me that there are a lot of frictions at the Commission for Schools and Universities. Staffa wants absolutely that St Thomas be imposed as the rule. Tucci said to me: If he does not win his case, he will produce a document from the Congregation after the Council! Will St Thomas be for Staffa the last means of holding back a movement which is invading everything on all sides? That would be to use St Thomas against himself!!!

The Holy Father arrived from New York at 12.50 pm. Very abundant applause. An address by Cardinal Liénart (the speech to the UN should be placed in the Acts of the Council. In fact, the Pope wanted to finish his journey AT THE COUNCIL. For him, his arrival at that moment was still part of his undertaking). Speech by the Pope: words must be put into action. This afternoon I read his speech to the UN which I followed with great difficulty yesterday evening because of the Italian translation which a presenter read with great effects of intonation. It was an admirable text, in a language like Kennedy's, very pure, very vigorous, astonishingly human. Has the Church found the language in which to speak to the world?

Lunch at 2.00 pm ...

At 4.30 pm to *Unitas*: I was asked to present the schema on Missions to the Observers. I am very impressed with the quality of the men gathered there. It is a very important achievement.

Willebrands told me (I knew it since yesterday) that Murray is ill. When I said, that is a great pity, because he was necessary to counterbalance Mgr De Smedt, Willebrands replied to me: Murray had been able, EARLIER, to provide a plan of the text and it is that plan that will be taken as a basis.

I was brought home by car. I absolutely could not have walked it.

Wednesday 6 October 1965

This morning, drafting of an intervention on the *De sacerdotio* for Mgr Plourde and Mgr Ndongmo. I communicated it to Mgr Vilnet.

From 2.00 pm until 4.10 pm, correspondence and study of a plan for the *De libertate recognitus* [revised], that Mgr Ancel passed on to me.

At 4.30 pm, at the Secretariat for the *De libertate*. But Medina told us that there will be a major offensive in the Theological Commission and it would be a good thing to go there. I reflected, and concluded that it would be better to go there. Fr Degrijse drove me. I arrived before the prayer. I realised immediately that all the big wigs were there: Ciappi (whom one never sees), Spadfora, Lio, Ramirez . . .! At the outset Ottaviani said: Parente wants to set out a question. Parente has suffered anxieties of conscience. He again raised the question of the relationship between Tradition and Scripture, in the direction of a wider material content for Tradition.

> Ottaviani invited the Fathers to express their thoughts on Parente's question. He was met by absolute silence.
>
> König: leave it where it is. Butler: the same.
>
> Charue: to go back over a point already decided requires the unanimous consent of the Commission.
>
> Ottaviani: but if it touches the Faith numbers make no difference.
>
> Henríquez: for x-number of Fathers who have a doubt of conscience there are x-number who are satisfied with the text as it is.
>
> McGrath: the text leaves the doors open, it resolves nothing. But that was the intention of the assembly and of the Joint Commission. We are not here dealing with doctrine, but with OPPORTUNENESS. But the mind of the Council is against its opportuneness. A *modus* would be required only if there were a two-thirds majority.
>
> Someone said: the *modus* proposed by Philips did not have that!
>
> That's true, McGrath admitted, it should have had two-thirds.
>
> But, Ottaviani said, it was said before the vote that it was in the majority . . .

The text of the *Ordo concilii* [Regulations for the Council][1] was read out: it was clearly for the two-thirds. So, Parente said, it would be better to leave the text as it is. Ottaviani was of the same view.

Thus they will stay with the text as it is: 19/24. So, for a second time, the opposition, by trying to gain more, lost everything.

At 5.02 pm, the *expensio modorum* for Chapter III was resumed at *modus* 12: the offensive was not strong. No expert spoke.

In the end, in leaving the Secretariat and coming to the Theological Commission I had perhaps backed the horse that could not lose.

I drew the attention of Cardinal König to the danger, which did not seem to me to be fanciful, that the minority would try to get satisfaction by way of a

---

1. Cf above, page 679, note 3.

modus from THE POPE. He replied: I must see the Pope soon. I will speak to him about it.

I added: bring Cardinal Florit in, too.

The sheets giving the composition of the sub-commissions for schema XIII were distributed.

The last three-quarters of an hour were passed in torpor and fatigue. The room was very hot and there was no fresh air.

At supper, Mgr Ancel briefly brought me up to date about what had been done at the *De libertate* meeting. He also told me that he had launched the project of a message from the Council to all governments. He had asked for a green light from the Secretariat of State. He got the reply: no problem.

Thursday 7 October 1965

At 9.30 am, at the Secretariat for Unity: religious freedom. Difficult and muddy discussion about where they will place the affirmation that religious freedom leaves intact the Catholic doctrine of the one true religion and the one true church. Put it in the *proemium*, or at the end of the Declaration, or within the very framework of the Declaration???

For my part I would have put it as a sort of *nota praevia* and I would move from that kind of 'thesis' to the consideration of the world situation, which would thereafter be addressed.

But the solution that prevailed was to put it at the end of the Declaration.

But later on (11.20 am) when Mgr Colombo had arrived and Cantero returned, they went back to the idea of putting it in the *Proemium*.

I left the session at midday: Mgr Nabaa came to find me for lunch at *Salvator Mundi* with Patriarch Maximos. This gave me the chance to see Fr Murray. He was lying down, with oxygen tubes in each nostril. His right lung is no longer working . . . But he has all his vitality. He told me that he had a lot of comments to make on Pavan's text, which we are discussing at the moment. They MUST be passed on to the sub-commission, I told him. And, after I left him, I telephoned Mgr Willebrands about this. Willebrands told me that, after I had left, I was allotted the task of drafting a *Proemium* along the lines that I had proposed and that seemed to me to be suitable for the literary and theological status of a 'Declaration'.

Thus Fr Murray was ill, and seriously so, at the moment when a text was being finalised which had been, to such a great extent, his work. He himself told me that he is taking this mystically, in the sense of the cross, and that he is perhaps more useful to the text in bed and powerless, than up and active . . .

I had scarcely returned from Fr Murray when I had a telephone call from Fr Hamer telling me the same thing as Willebrands. He added that Colombo had insisted that it should be put in the prologue (and from there onwards), and that afterwards he had said to De Smedt that this was the Pope's wish.

Maximos IV gave me to read, in order to ask my advice, the text of an intervention he wants to make on celibacy: to show the good of the Eastern discipline that has a celibate clergy and ordained married men side by side, and to suggest that this could be beneficial to the rest of the Church. Personally, I think that is right. Is it opportune that this should be said to the Council? I doubt it. That is why I spoke of it, in a personal capacity, to Mgr Ancel: I asked him to warn Maximos of the reverberation and the consequences of his intervention.

After lunch, the Declaration on the Jews was discussed. Maximos certainly has some anti-Semitic reactions: that was obvious to me. The younger bishops are much more favourable to the Declaration. For Maximos it is unfortunate, for him it would have been better if it had never been born. However, he knows that it will be voted in, and he will defend it.

I was told that this morning FOUR French bishops had put themselves down, one after the other, to speak about peace: Gouyon, Guerry, Ancel, Boillon. But the discussion was cut short after Gouyon . . . The discussion of the *De activitate missionali* [on missionary activity] was commenced.

A visit from Cardinal Journet. Very friendly. We talked about the Council, about different texts. 'This schema XIII has made me suffer: it starts from below, as though Christ came at the end, at the conclusion of a movement.' But the Cardinal liked the *De Ecclesia*. He did not seem to me to have read EVERYTHING truly closely. He repeated to me his formulas on the Church as in process of coming into being, on the two cities of St Augustine, on the grandeurs of holiness, and the grandeurs of hierarchy . . . He seemed to me to be the prisoner of certain schemes from the milieu of Maritain and de Menasce.[1] On Maritain, he told me that he had come a few weeks ago, only in the interval between two flights. The Pope had let him know that he would be glad to receive him. He did not come to Rome. The Pope received him at Castel Gandolfo. They talked, among other things, about the Lay Apostolate.

At RAI, video-taping for the TV, to be broadcast next Sunday, on war and peace.

I received two parcels of proofs from Cerf. That has got to be done TOO! They have to do with volumes for *Unam Sanctam*. I did not go to the reception at the Embassy. One does see a lot of people in a short time there, but I had neither the strength, nor the two hours to spare that it would have cost me.

So I spent the evening reading the proofs. Tomorrow I will get down to the drafting that I have been asked to do for *De libertate*.

Friday 8 October 1965
I wrote a letter to Maximos, asking him to limit himself to speaking about the Eastern practice, and drawing his attention to the repercussion and the conse-

---

1. Jean de Menasce, OP, of the Province of France.

quences that his intervention would have. Mgr Ancel will forward my letter to him, and he has written one too.

At 9.30 am, at the Secretariat: *De libertate*. Work in a somewhat jaded atmosphere, at least, with little freshness and drive.

At 3.45 pm, a visit from Mgr Elchinger. Thurian had been to see him. None of the bishops that had been approached agreed to read out the text I had prepared on the ecumenical aspect in the schema on Missions. No missionary wanted to deliver this speech. Mgr Elchinger certainly would, but he was afraid that it would be thought that he was abusing the right to speak . . . For my part, I did not want to add further to the reputation he has of being the man who makes all the shock speeches . . . On the other hand, it was now too late to sign up to speak, because the debate on the Missions will be terminated on Tuesday. But there are already more than thirty signatures and it is easy to collect another forty. Besides, it would be sufficient to send the text to the Commission without its having been read out *in aula*: but that would be a pity from the point of view of the Observers . . .

The *De libertate* was taken up again at 4.30 pm. Examination of the 'theological' part. I have never lived through a more painful, more dismal, session. An hour and a half was spent on ten lines, without any result.

Fr Benoit suggested an addition to No. 9, on the Pauline theme of freedom from the Law. The Fathers, Colombo in particular, were very impressed, but, they said, will the assembly of the Fathers understand it? Our investigation livened up a little. I have great admiration for Mgr Willebrands, who has a presence, a precision, a respect for ideas and nuances, that are truly extraordinary.

Mgr Willebrands told us that Felici (he had told him so this morning) did not know what was going to be done at the Council when it resumed on 25 October.

Fr Benoit had in his hands quite a booklet in Arabic: It is the commentary on the Declaration on Non-Christian Religions intended for newspapers, offices and departments of the Arabic world. Seven hundred copies have been distributed. Certainly the Vatican and the Secretariat have done everything possible to get this declaration accepted. But the most important effort was the revision of the text in a manner that makes it biblically and theologically more exact. Certainly, emphasis is placed on the favourable aspects, as the very goal of the text desires. But the attitude of the Jews towards the Gospel and towards Jesus is presented in a truer fashion, and the word 'deicide' is suppressed. In spite of this, André Chouraqui[1] expressed his satisfaction (*Le Monde* for 6 October 1965). It seems that the PRACTICAL goal of the Declaration will be achieved.

In the evening, a visit from Jean Stehly and another seminarian from Strasbourg.

---

1. Originally from Algeria, this Jewish writer and thinker was very active in inter-religious dialogue; he was the permanent delegate of the Universal Israelite Alliance and, a little later, was to become joint mayor of Jerusalem.

Saturday 9 October 1965

Etchegaray told me (on the basis of the meeting of representatives of various episcopates that takes place every Friday) that the bishops are asking themselves what
they are going to do. They want to work. And yet, during the 'blank week' of 17
to 24, only ONE question has been submitted to them: about the discipline of
penitence (fasting, abstinence) . . . They have a feeling of EMPTINESS.

I did not go to the Theological Commission this morning (where the examination of the *modi* for the *De Revelatione* was supposed to be completed). I
worked on the *proemium*, for which I had been given the job of proposing a draft.

Approaches for the text on the ecumenical aspect in the *De missionali activitate*. Fr Degrijse, Superior of the Scheutist Fathers, agreed to read it. As I was
unable to meet Mgr Elchinger, who was away for the whole day, I took the papers
to him, duplicated and signed.

At 4.00 pm, at the Secretariat, to look at my plan for the *proemium* with Mgr
De Smedt and Pavan. De Smedt had also prepared a text, and one was also sent
to us from Murray (who is very much overloaded with responsibility for various
matters and who would even like to turn his mind to other themes). So my text
was taken up, examined and, with minor corrections, accepted by our sub-commission. The second part was then addressed. Cantero said he wanted to disclaim
responsibility for the second part, which is weak.

It was nevertheless examined. It was considered (by me, too) that Fr Benoit's
text about the regimes of law abolished by Christ would go beyond the understanding of the Fathers, and thus ought not to be taken up, all the more since it is
a long, entirely new text. A vote was taken on the removal of No. 9 (*in historia
salutis radicatur* [takes root in the history of salvation]), and it was decided to
retain only some elements of it in the Number on the freedom of the act of faith,
which would be put before No. 10 on the *modus agendi Christi* [Christ's manner
of acting].

Sunday 10 October 1965

In the morning, work on a *conflatus* [conflation] of the former Numbers 9 and 11
of the *De libertate* (history of salvation and the freedom of the act of faith), then
various small matters which gave me a bit of a break from conciliar texts; a brief
trip to Santa Sabina. In the evening, an hour with Chenu, and then from 6.00 pm
until 10.00 pm (with a break for supper), the New Life group on the dialogue
between laity and bishops.

Monday 11 October 1965

At 9.00 am, at St Martha's, for the distribution of work on schema XIII. The text
must be ready, *dixit* [said] Felice, by 10 November. But it will take the Joint Commission ten days to look at the text: that will be 20–30 October. So the plenary
Joint Commission should have the text by 19 October. We have only eight days
to do our work.

For Numbers 18 and 19, Daniélou has already made the *relatio* on the basis of the index cards. Cardinal König said he is working directly with Daniélou. I asked if Frs Miano and Girardi could be invited. König said that he was working with them and would bring their point of view to Fr Daniélou.

Daniélou read out, and commented on, his *relatio* in a dreadful, nervous manner.

It was recognised that the exposition of the question will need to be developed (while keeping it in this spot).

There was also the question of the placing of the two Numbers on atheism. Benoit thinks that, at present, they interrupt the line of development running from the creation of humankind in the image of God to sin and to the re-creation by Christ.

Semmelroth gave the *relatio* on the remainder, or the whole of Chapter I of the first part.

Rahner raised the question of the ORDER of the sections, which, according to him, was very questionable. The Fathers would have to come to a decision on this order, before the work is undertaken. Ménager: the opinion of the central sub-commission will be required.

Poma: there is a complaint that the text lacks dynamism.

Ménager: the redactors followed a pedagogical order, from the more known to the less known.

In fact, the criticisms that one could very legitimately make on the basis of a logical and THEOLOGICAL order collide with the intention of the redactors to follow a phenomenological order.

However, Benoit said, one could have a better exposition while keeping the present sequence as a whole.

At 10.42 am, Kloppenburg[1] gave his *relatio* on Chapter II. There was much less criticism of this Chapter.

The Fathers and the experts of the sub-commission were organised into three sub-sub-commissions. I would have liked to be on atheism. Daniélou and de Lubac were the only ones put there. I advised the latter to make sure that he complemented the former, and that Miano and Giradi really were consulted.

Since the meeting ended at 11.15 am, I went to spend the rest of the morning at the Secretariat, where the sub-commission was finishing the examination of the *De libertate*.

At lunch, I picked up some bits of information from this morning's General Congregation. It appears that the discussion on the Missions was well conducted, and that, if it put forward some elements to enrich the schema, it contained few criticisms. Ruffini gave his examination of school homework, which is what a

---

1. Bonaventura Kloppenburg, OFM, Professor of Dogmatic Theology at the Franciscan Scholasticate at Petropolis (Brazil), was a Council expert and consultor for the Brazilian episcopate.

schema is for him . . . A letter was read out from the Pope addressed to Cardinal Tisserant: the Holy Father had learned that the Fathers wished to raise questions about celibacy. He certainly did not wish to restrict the freedom of the Council, but he asked that this subject not be debated publicly: questions and suggestions should be sent to HIM.

Canonically, the Council can only debate what the Pope submits to it; so the Pope can withdraw this or that question from the order of the day.

Correction of proofs and correspondence.

At 4.30 pm, at the Secretariat: A plenary Commission for examination, at this level, of the *De libertate* such as it now is, having been corrected by the sub-commission.

Willebrands gave an account of the work done by the sub-commission. He read the text and De Smedt commented on it. The Fathers were rather tentative and taciturn. However, this roused them and there were some good comments.

The first part was finished this evening, but they may return to it next time.

Tuesday 12 October 1965

At St Martha's at 9.30 am: sub-commission on schema XIII Chapter I.

Discussion of the order to be adopted, starting with that suggested by Fr Benoit. His plan was adopted.

They went on to the text and the evaluation of the proposed corrections. How appalling is the Latin of schema XIII!!! It is not good enough to have proposed THAT to the Council. All the same, one sees that the text often proposes synthetic views in which several points of view are mixed together: that lacks rigour, *'non formaliter loquitur'* [it does not use speak formally] . . . A lot of time was spent looking for more precise, more Latin expressions. Because it certainly won't do as it is. Rahner, whom the text does not please, but irritates, added further to the difficulties raised. He sees approximations and informal expressions everywhere.

As Mgr Parente left at midday the session was interrupted. I went to the Council for half-an-hour, to sample the atmosphere, for I never go there. They were finishing the discussion of the *De Missionali* . . . That on the *De presbyteris* will start tomorrow.

At 3.00 pm, a visit from someone from RAI: He wants a ten minute interview on the text on priests, but in Italian. I can't speak Italian. I put forward the name of Mgr Garrone. I was told: IMPOSSIBLE. We must not have any Council Father speak. And he explained it to me: the situation of RAI from the point of view of religious information is very difficult. As soon as they do anything, within limits that are already narrow, they are reproached, bawled out. . . In short, from the Vatican side, they are closely watched, have very little freedom.

At 4.30 pm, at the *Foyer Unitas*. I have to present the *De Presbyteris* to the Observers, but first to respond to questions remaining concerning the Missions. This took up two hours (all in English).

Afterwards, I put in an appearance, a gesture of friendship, at the Spanish Embassy reception. I know that the Spanish are sensitive to a token of esteem and friendship. As always, a royal etiquette, lots of nobility. Obviously, I was questioned about religious freedom. I greeted Cardinal Tisserant, who once again responded with a contemptuous look. *In petto* [under my breath] I said 'shit' to him.

Thursday 13 October 1965

A very poor night. Correction of proofs.

At 9.00 am, at St Martha's; sub-commission on schema XIII. It started with endless hair-splitting. Doumith, when he really gets down to it, is terrible: he pursues his own idea without listening to anything. After that it went quicker.

Bits of information from the General Congregation: still ELEVEN speakers on the Missions, with the right to speak because speaking in the name of seventy; speech by a layman;[1] reading of Mgr Marty's *Relatio* on priests.[2]

At 3.55 pm, eight minutes of recording on the Missions for Radio Ireland.

At 4.30 pm at the Secretariat. Fr Degrijse told me that he had received congratulations from various bishops for his intervention this morning;[3] he was asked for a translation. He seems delighted to have done it.

Mgr Willebrands said that Cardinal Journet had said to him: not only is the Declaration very good, but it is very worthy of note.

Mgr Willebrands said he had shown the text of the first part to the Latinist. That enabled him to introduce some modifications, softening the expressions in the *Proemium*. I got the impression that he had had recourse to the Latinist to obtain without difficulty some changes that several—including himself—wanted, in an irenic direction.

The first part was voted, then, after its reading and a few remarks, it was approved unanimously. There will remain the enormous work of the *Relatio*, which will fall on Feiner especially. Then the vote, the *modi* . . . It is not finished.

Someone spoke to me about two pamphlets against the Declaration on Non-Christian Religions. (I got hold of them courtesy of Mgr Ramanantoanina. I have also got a photocopy of an incredible pamphlet, of four pages, signed by a whole series of organisations of the extreme right, often more of a limited membership than really substantial.[4] In it the Council is treated as a conciliabulum, and there is even talk of a right of resistance, based on the right of legitimate defence against international Jewry and its subversive plans. The bishops are said to have been bought by Jewish gold! . . . 'If only it were true', Cardinal Martin said to me.

---

1. Eusèbe Adjakpley, *AS* IV/IV, 328–330.
2. *AS* IV/IV, 332–335.
3. *AS* IV/IV, 290–292.
4. This text was signed by, amongst others, *La Cité catholique,* the journal *Itinéraires,* the Traditionalist Catholic Movement (Congar Archives).

These stupid pages, which seek to persuade that the Declaration be rejected, simply demonstrate how much it was, and remains, necessary. Last year, when Mgr Elchinger made an intervention that was very favourable towards the Jews, some neighbours asked him, when he sat down, 'How much have they paid you?' . . . !!)

In any case, I have received the paper of the *'Coetus internationalis'*, signed this time by Sigaud,[1] Marcel Lefebvre and Carli: it advises voting *Non placet* to the whole Declaration. I do not blame these men for having their own opinion, but for being purely NEGATIVE. That is my first criticism with respect to the integrists. They do not look for any dialogue, any collaboration. They are stuck in a narrow system of ready-made formulas, they reject or condemn, without opening themselves up to any problem at all. They provoke a reaction as simplistic as their own. For many people, it is sufficient for these people to take up such and such a position for the contrary position to appear to be the only acceptable one!

At 9.30 pm, a visit from six priests of the diocese of Namur. They brought me a bit of news they had gathered from two or three Brazilian bishops. According to the latter, the Council is sliding into error. 'Judas also was an apostle', they are saying. The new Fathers of the Church are Teilhard, Congar, etc.

What can be done to enlighten these people? They are stuck in a ready-made system, hermetically sealed. But how will they behave when the Holy Father promulgates the two Declarations of the Secretariat?

Some lectures are being held in Rome just now of an organisation called ROC[2] (Roman Encounters). Thibon,[3] Daujat,[4] de Corte,[5] lecture there. Daniélou, who was to have given the final lecture, withdrew when he saw the context and the real purpose. Lubac got up to speak after a lecture on Teilhard,[6] made up of scraps of quotations strung together to establish that, during the Great War, Teilhard was converted to something other than Christianity. Lubac demolished this ridiculous construction. Certainly, the thought and many of the writings of Teilhard give rise to question marks. But they should still be understood in an intelligent manner.

---

1. G de Proença Sigaud.
2. The acronym is from 'ROmana Colloquia'.
3. Gustave Thibon, essayist and self-taught philosopher.
4. Jean Daujat, a philosopher with scientific training, founded and directed, in Paris, the Centre d'études religieuses, neo-thomist in orientation, for the philosophical and theological formation of lay people; he gave a lecture at ROC on the relation between science and faith.
5. Marcel de Corte collaborated on the journal *Itinéraires* and taught philosophy at the University of Liège.
6. A lecture given on 11 October by Henri Rambaud entitled 'La "conversion" du Père Teilhard de Chardin'; Henri Rambaud was a professor of letters and a literary critic.

Thursday 14 October 1965

No commission this morning; I could have gone to the Council. That tempted me, but these sessions so tire me, I am so behind with work—proofs, correspondence, necessary reading—that I stayed at home to try to shift this backlog: not much of a fun chore, in any case. I no longer even have the time to read the papers that concern the work I am supposed to be doing on the schemas. . .

At 4.30 pm, at St Martha's, sub-commission. Rahner told me that he is worried about the *De Revelatione*. It is CERTAIN that the Pope has been influenced by requests for interventions. The Pope has received Florit and Parente, and also Charue (was this at the Holy Father's summons, or did he take the initiative?). It was undoubtedly in connection with this.

Rahner had spoken to Cardinal König to ask him to intervene. I told him that I had already done this, because I had been convinced, from the day of the discussion in the Commission, that there would be pressure put on the Pope to obtain a *modus* or a *nota praevia*.

Revision of the text continued. Daniélou got on my nerves. He is as excitable as a high-spirited racehorse. He does not even wait for someone to finish a sentence before saying, four or five times, *Ita* [that's right], or *Bene* [well said], or *Perfecte* [exactly], or the opposite. Or 'Absolutely! Absolutely!' He makes a law of his own immediate reaction, without bothering himself about what others think.

We finished at 7.20 pm. As I had the opportunity of a car I went to the Belgian College, to acquaint myself with the situation concerning the *De Revelatione*. Supper had started when I arrived. During supper, nothing much was said. Philips said nothing. He seemed to me subdued, less sociable than formerly.

As we went out, I saw Cardinal Suenens for a few minutes. He confirmed that the Pope is preoccupied with the question of Scripture and Tradition: he has spoken to him about it twice. He asked me if I thought there was a crisis of faith. I replied: in France, no. There are, in point of fact, here and there, some presentations that are a bit *ad hoc*, for example about the Eucharist, but I am not aware of any real crisis of faith. That could come about, especially with regard to the biblical question, that of historicity. I developed this a bit further: there should be conversations between exegetes and theologians . . . The cardinal said: it is not actually France that is spoken of in this connection, but Germany, Holland . . . I said that one is not able to avoid the crisis just by putting up barricades, no more in that case than in the case of obedience. A true affirmation must take on board the reasons for doubt or for objection. Lastly, the cardinal asked me for some details about the congress on the diaconate. Only the Pope had spoken to him about it, no one else knows anything about it. The Pope had praised the good spirit and obedience of the organisers, who have moved the Congress with respect both to date and place.

As I was not able to see Mgr Philips, who had gone out for his usual walk, or Mgr Prignon, who was occupied with the return of the students and overwhelmed by a thousand concerns (he seemed VERY tired), I saw:

1) Mgr De Smedt, who told me: the *De libertate* has been submitted to three cardinals: Browne ('I cannot subscribe to this'), Journet (who had repeated and written: 'not only excellent, but admirable'), Urbani (who was in agreement).

2) Mgr Heuschen. He confirmed for me that Mgr Charue has been SUM-MONED by the Pope, who has also received Cardinal Florit. The Pope is personally pre-occupied with two points: the formula *'veritas salutaris'* [saving truth], about which, however, the note from the Biblical Institute[1] is sufficiently conclusive—and the question of Tradition. On the latter, he is not only moved by the people of the minority, but has a personal conviction. He had written a letter to Ottaviani,[2] and it is partly as a result of this letter, and to avoid a later papal intervention, that the small commission for *expensio modorum* had introduced (accepted) *modus* 40.[3] But the people of the minority, Parente, have manoeuvred skillfully: twice—on that occasion and at the time of Philips' proposition[4]—they have managed to leak the propositions of the sub-commission, so as to be able to complain: not a single concession has been made to us! Mgr Heuschen, who saw Mgr Charue after his audience, believes that it is inevitable that the Pope will impose a *modus*: doubtless worded like one by Parente. Mgr Charue called the Pope's attention to a possible reaction from the majority, along the lines of that of 1962: it would be possible that the majority would reject the Chapter!!!

Mgr Charue thinks it would be good for Florit to see the Pope again.

For myself, I wondered whether I shouldn't write to Colombo? I am almost resolved to do so.

Friday 15 October 1965

I wrote the attached letter for Colombo,[5] on the hypothesis, which Mgr Heuschen has presented to me as a certainty, that the Pope will intervene in the direction of constitutive Tradition. At St Peter's, before delivering my letter, with offprints of my note in *RSPT*, 1964, page 645 ff,[6] I saw Moeller. He told me he found my suggestion very dangerous. I was not at the session where *modus* 40 D was discussed

---

1. This must refer to the *modi* proposed by the Pontifical Biblical Institute, dated 25 January 1965.
2. Cf *AS* V/III, 408–410.
3. Cf above, page 796.
4. Cf above, page 799.
5. In it, Congar regrets that *modus* 40 D had been rejected by the Doctrinal Commission. If the Council of Trent certainly had not taught the material insufficiency of Scripture, it had affirmed that Revelation is to be found in Scripture and in unwritten traditions. The Gospel cannot be known solely from Scripture or solely from Tradition, and so the *modus* is right. In conclusion, Congar communicated to Colombo his wish that the Pope would ask the Commission to reconsider this *modus* so that it might be able to accept it.
6. 'Le débat sur la question du rapport entre Écriture et Tradition, au point de vue de leur contenu matériel', *Revue des sciences philosophiques et théologiques*, 1964, 645–657.

(Moeller insisted, almost with a note of reproach. But I was working at the meeting on religious freedom!). If I had been there, I would have seen that the minority was giving this text a meaning that I would be the first to reject. That is where the immense danger is. So Moeller insisted on the rejection of every *modus* and the retention of the text as it is. He himself believed that it was not certain that the Pope had decided to change anything in the text.

That was not what Mgr Heuschen had told me. I wrote my letter according to what Mgr Heuschen told me was certain.

Nevertheless, I added a PS to my letter in the sense that it would be better not to change anything.

Dominus providebit! [the Lord will provide Gen 22:8)].

A Lebanese Mass, the rite rather Latinised.

Resumption of the discussion on priesthood.

About 11 am, I went to circulate a bit: Wyszyński → appointment.

Féret told me about the difficulties encountered by Liégé. This year he had been refused his entry pass because, in lectures, he had spoken critically of the minority. People who speak ill of the Council cannot be admitted to the Council. Liégé explained himself; Mgr Schmitt and the Provincial of Brazil[1] intervened on his behalf with Fr General. That is how things stand.

I saw Cardinal Florit on the question of the *De Revelatione*. He told me that he was in favour of the adoption of *modus* 40 D, which does not affect the balance of doctrine; he does not understand why the Commission rejected it. I said: for fear of what the others (Parente etc), would see beneath it and draw out from it. But Florit thinks—and I think too—that it would be better for the Pope to invite the Commission to revisit this vote. Florit confirmed for me that Parente had been to see the Pope.

At the end of the morning, the result was given of the vote on the Declaration on the Church and Non-Christian Religions as a whole:

Present and voting:	2,023
Placet:	1,763
Non placet:	250 + 10 null

The *non placet* votes are ambiguous. Some voted in that way because they were against the Declaration, or against some part of it. Others because they wanted to go back to the previous text, including in particular the words '*deicidium*' [deicide] and '*[deplorat et] damnat*' [{deplores and} condemns]: *sic* the bishops of the USA. I believe that the bishops of Arabic-speaking countries voted *placet*. Their requirements had been accepted and honoured. The Arab governments had had

---

1. Alexandre L Figueiredo, OP.

things explained to them and were pacified. And these bishops are able, in virtue of the votes *Non placet*, to let their governments understand that they were among the opponents . . .

At 4.15 pm, a visit from the Bishop of Treviso.[1] I agreed in principle to go and talk to his priests, because I have tried for three years to agree to everything that has been asked of me in Italy: if one wins Italy, one wins a lot! We agreed on 24 November, but I accepted this in the dark, not knowing what will be my work at that time, what possibilities I will have.

At 5.00 pm, at Propaganda: meeting of the Commission on Missions. First we had to wait: during this time the presidents of sub-commissions were reaching agreement. I had leisure to take in the surroundings. It was on the first floor. Everything felt run-down. A dismal office had for its name 'Holy Childhood'.[2] Everything was cramped, grey and mediocre. On the other hand, distributed in several rooms, there was an admirable library, built up over centuries; an inexhaustible mine for works and possible theses!! Our sub-commission listened to Mgr Lokuang. The idea is for the group that prepared the text in January, very slightly enlarged (Ratzinger), to work at Nemi on Tuesday, Wednesday and Thursday. Fr André Seumois reacted: he began again making dogmatic affirmations about the definition of Mission in the great missionary encyclicals. Mgr Lokuang cut him off as he had done at Nemi. For my part, this will prevent me from participating as I should in other commissions; I said that I would have to return to Rome on Wednesday morning for the *De Presbyteris*.

In the end this was understood.

I went from there to the Procure Saint-Sulpice to let Mgr Marty know and to reach agreement with him. He insisted that I should come back on Wednesday for the Commission *pro disciplina Cleri* [for the discipline of the clergy].

Dear God! How hard it is to sustain this wandering and activist condition!

I think the French bishops are ineffective. They have no sort of discipline that would permit them to be so. I said this to Mgr Vilnet and Mgr Marty in connection with the *De Presbyteris*. Our bishops had a workshop which worked very well. And yet, what has come out of that workshop, which, in principle, is for preparing interventions? The intervention of Mgr Guyot.[3] That is all. In contrast, Mgr Renard[4] this morning, Cardinal Lefebvre[5] and Mgr Weber[6] tomorrow, bring out their business quite independently of the existing workshop, in which they have taken no part (Cardinal Lefebvre came once, partly at my instigation). Each one wants to bring out his own small business, his hobby-horse, his personal synthesis. The result is ineffectiveness.

---

1. A Mistrorigo.
2. It indicated the Pontifical Missionary Work of the Holy Childhood.
3. Cf his intervention the following day, *AS* IV/IV, 744–746.
4. *AS* IV/IV, 813–814.
5. *AS* IV/V, 12–14.
6. Mgr Weber was not, however, to intervene during this Session of the Council.

The Germans work differently: at least they give that impression, for I am not sure that they really do cooperate so much.

Saturday 16 October 1965

Prolonged insomnia. I was thinking about the question of Tradition. The result = letters to Florit, Colombo, Charue.

At 9.00 am, at St Martha's. But I was not at the Commission yesterday and did not know that the meeting was not until 10.00 am. While waiting I read the text on atheism.

Philips said to me: no doubt there will be two or three suggestions from the Pope for the *De Revelatione*. Perhaps at the Theological Commission on Monday. (This is true. THE BISHOPS have received a summons. Are they going to exclude the experts, as they did for the *nota praevia*? We have been told nothing. In fact it was Tuesday. I shall not be able to take part in it.)

Sub-commission: examination of the two Numbers on atheism. All together, I had not missed much by my absence yesterday.

At 3.40 pm, a visit from an American priest: an ambitious programme for a Faculty of Theology in a university in Colorado. Have you got the men? I asked him. —We will get them. . .

He told me he had seen Fr Schillebeeckx this morning. Schillebeeckx had said yesterday that he was having some problems over *Concilium*: a claim by the Curia and, he told me, by the Theological Commission (???), to control the journal . . .

At St Martha's, at 4.30 pm.

Rahner said to me: Daniélou gets on my nerves in the extreme by his habit of taking up, one minute later, as his own, an idea expressed by someone else, and that he had, at first, dismissed . . . This is certainly true, but it must irritate Rahner more than others because of his particular personality and because he is so intellectually honest.

Chapter II was examined: presentation by Fr Nicolau, SJ.[1] A large part of the time was spent in trying to find formulations that would be LATIN, and Latin formulations that would be comprehensible.

In the evening, from 7.35 to 8.05 pm, a visit from the Millots: frankly, the events of their week . . .

Sunday 17 October 1965

Writing up my *ICI* chronicle. After I finished it and sent it to be typed, a few odd jobs for myself: it relaxed me a little to do some work of feeble value, but different from that of the Council. After supper, a little work for Cardinal Lefebvre. There was a bishop from Peru at supper: a diocese as large as Belgium, with thirty-two parishes and, in all, twenty-three priests . . . The altitude goes up to more than

---

1. Miguel Nicolau, SJ, Professor of Dogmatic Theology at the University of Salamanca, was a Council expert.

5,000 metres; 400,000 inhabitants, of whom 70% are illiterate. The archbishop's place is 200 kilometres away, and has to be reached on horseback... My God! What can be done? What meaning can our schemas have for such men in such situations? I feel so wretched, undisturbed, in the midst of a profusion of resources! The religion of these men, who still speak their native language (seventy-five per cent are Indians) is a religion of fear. They practise in fear of damnation. How to get them out of that? Christ has acknowledged them, loved them, he died for them. Me, I am an imbecile, in the Latin sense of the word. What can I do?

My work, as least badly as possible.

Monday 18 October 1965

As I have to be at Nemi tomorrow, and will not be able to take part in the meeting of the Theological Commission (in any case, I do not know if the experts are invited) I wrote two notes which I sent to Mgr Garrone, Charue, Heuschen, Colombo, Cardinal Florit, Fr Butler and also to Mgr Philips, Rahner, Betti, and Mgr Ancel. I also wrote a note for Mgr Garrone on the discipline of penitence, which the French bishops are supposed to discuss on Wednesday, in order to respond to the consultation which the Pope addressed to the whole episcopate on this question.

Then the reading of the documents with a view to the revision of the *De Missionibus*. An enormous task, and rather trying. But it MUST be done! It is a considerable task: bigger than I had thought.

Tuesday 19 October 1965

Departure at 8.00 am for the house of the Divine Word Fathers, from where a car took us to Nemi: a not very powerful car, or very fast.

This little group for the revision of Chapter I consisted of: Mgr Lokuang, Ratzinger, Congar.

At Nemi, Italian TV was there for our arrival and the beginning of the meeting. We made a survey of the major questions or requests expressed, and discussed some points in order to work out an initial direction. But before starting on this work of revision, the comments had to be read. We were given here the third booklet of these, but the rest still has to be typed...

Fr Greco asked my views on the canonisation of John XXIII, for which Mgr Bettazzi had recently been campaigning. On that occasion he told me that, when he went to see Mgr Roncalli in 1952 (on his return from the Philippines) he found him in the middle of reading *Vrai et fausse Réforme*. The Nuncio said to him: 'Can one speak of the reform of the Church, can the Church, or ought it, reform itself? However, the author of this book is a good theologian and historian...'

I sometimes asked myself if John XXIII knew me: yes, because he spoke of me to Mgr Marty... —if he read me? There is the answer.

This copy, annotated and scribbled on by John XXIII, should still exist. I would be interested to see it. And also to meet Mgr Capovilla one day.

At 3.30 pm, another eighty-two pages of comments were received. And there will be another 180 pages tomorrow morning . . .

Despite the agreeable character of the group, and the cordial hospitality of Fr Schütte, I had a certain sense of loneliness—and also of lassitude. Once again to take one's bag and go . . . Once again to take up texts, read the criticisms, search for formulations, insertions for these formulas . . . It is extremely wearisome.

Wednesday 20 October 1965

Departure at 8.30 this morning to participate in the meeting on the *De Presbyteris*, at the Congregation *De Concilio* [of the Council]. Present were Mgr Marty, Nagae[1] (Japanese), Vilnet, del Portillo, Herranz, Lécuyer, Martelet, Frisque, Onclin, Denis and I. They all spoke French. Fortunately, there were two Germans, Tilmann[2] (an Oratorian) and Wulf[3] (Editor of *Geist und Leben*). There is quite a serious difference between the Germans and ourselves. The French are much more mystical. They are more used to making something out of nothing, or almost nothing. The Germans are better equipped; they have the resources. For them, things exist. They think within the framework of concrete situations.

First, Marty summarised the main requests expressed *in aula*:

1) Two concepts of priesthood: as consecration (personal union with Christ), as having been sent!

Exactly, the Council has rediscovered the unity between consecration and mission!

2) Not responsible JUST for the faithful.

3) Reply to the expectation of priests IN THE PRESENT DAY.

4) A more vigorous, less exhortatory style: there should be fewer subjunctives, more verbs in the present tense: fewer recommendations.

Then Mgr Marty suggested a plan that was a little new. It was discussed. Even a plan from Döpfner and one from Suenens were discussed. Finally Marty's plan was adopted with some modifications.

In the course of these discussions, when speaking of this or that paragraph, the contents were discussed and the principal requests made were recalled. There were interesting exchanges about the double relationship in which the priest is SITUATED: in relation to the *Ordo episcoporum* [order of bishops] and to people, or to the world. On the subject of the counsels, in order to present them less in a

---

1. Lorenzo Satoshi Nagae, Bishop of Urawa, not long since a member of the Commission for the Discipline of the Clergy and of the Christian People.
2. The Oratorian, Klemens Tilmann, who had been in charge of the work on the catechism for German dioceses that had come out in 1955, was a specialist in religious education; he was a Concil expert.
3. Friedrich Wulf, SJ, was the editor-in-chief of the journal *Geist und Leben*.

manner that is too reminiscent of religious life, del Portillo told us about a letter signed by Dell'Acqua. The Pope has received a report from Maximos IV: the Pope asked the Commission to take it into account, that is to say, to better explain and respect the situation of Eastern married priests.

Finally, the work was distributed:

I.   *proemium*, former Numbers 1, 6, 7, 8 and 19: Congar (for a long time I remained the only one). Eventually, I was joined by Martelet.[1]

II. Numbers 2, 3, 4 (*tria munera* [the three offices], drafted by me): Nagae and Martelet.

III. Numbers 11, 12 , 13 and 5: Vilnet, Denis, Tilmann, Frisque.

IV. Numbers 14, 15 and 17: Lécuyer, Wulf.

V.   Numbers 16 and 18: Onclin.

Mgr Marty, who was pushing the members of the Commission, had wanted to have the texts revised by Friday. I said that was quite impossible! The comments received had to be read. I greatly regretted that only an extract had been received this morning. This was totally insufficient for the ones that really proposed novel ideas. For myself, I will not be able to TOUCH this work before Friday afternoon ... The Commission is being hurried because the Fathers want to be able to leave for holidays on 29 October. I think it scandalous that it should be 'holidays' that impose their law on the work, and cause it to be botched. Because it is necessary: 1) seriously to consider comments; 2) to work out a renovated text, sometimes quite deeply renovated; 3) to submit this to the whole Commission of revision; 4) to discuss the whole thing in the plenary Commission; 5) to write a *relatio* ...

And all this (so far as concerns me) at the same time as the *De Missionibus*, the congress on the diaconate, the meeting of the *Concilium* committee, without taking into account appointments and unforeseen events!!! It's impossible.

In the end, a meeting was fixed for Sunday at 4.30 pm, for the Numbers that are ready, and a second for Monday at 4.30 pm.

I will do as much as I can. But I am starting the most heavily burdened days of all my conciliar activity.

I went back to Nemi for 12.25 pm. In the afternoon, reading of the texts we had been given this morning. Another bundle was brought to us at 4.00 pm, and there will be still others tomorrow ... It is impossible to arrive at a corrected text before having taken into account ALL the comments!!!

At 5.00 pm, I tidied up a few Numbers with Mgr Lokuang and Ratzinger. The greatest part (of a very great deal!) remains to be done.

This evening, after dinner, a recording of the psalms and the Mass in the language and music of Cameroon.

---

1. Congar added to the typescript: '(who in fact did nothing)'.

Thursday 21 October 1965

Another 150 pages of texts! Our revision of Chapter I had to be finished off before taking account of this. That is not right.

At midday I heard news indirectly of the Theological Commission, to which the Pope had proposed three *modi*. But I expect to get more precise information from Mgr Garrone and others. I will make a note of them then.

As our work was finished, I returned this evening with quite a large group. Arrival at 9.00 pm. Sorting through correspondence and newspapers.

Friday 22 October 1965

Several bishops at breakfast told me that the Pope had quoted me in his discourse at the general audience last Wednesday, on the subject of the holiness of the Church. There were a good many French pilgrims present, and it was in his speech in French that he did it.[1] Obviously this gave me a little pleasure. Further, I was not surprised that it was my article in *Angelicum*, which appeared a month ago.

A visit from [ ] about the programme for the Social Weeks. She was seeking my support for a session on the theme: Third World (Bandung), human progress and universalism.

At 9.30 am, at Propaganda. A meeting of everyone for each sub-commission to examine the chapter relevant to it as it was prepared at Nemi. The members of the sub-commission thus had before them a PROPOSAL for amendment, not an imposed text. They were able to discuss. Fr André Seumois was not too stubborn this morning. Certainly, he brought up his unyielding, closed concepts, devoid of any openness to points of view other than his own, but he did not argue a lot. In any case, he would soon be stopped by Mgr Lokuang who would say (who has already said) 'Shut up, it is the bishops who decide', or 'this has been discussed for three years without agreement being reached. Now *causa finita est* [the case is closed], nothing more is going to be changed.' Besides, the sub-commission will meet again tomorrow, but I shall not be able to take part: there is the congress on the diaconate and the *Concilium* meeting.

After lunch, Mgr Garrone gave me some news from the meeting of the Theological Commission meeting (last Wednesday) on the *De Revelatione*.

A letter had been read out, indirectly from the Pope, bearing on three points:

1) Scripture and Tradition. On the second scrutiny, a two-thirds majority had been achieved fairly easily for a formula close to the one with which I had declared myself in agreement. I was told that my suggestion had been followed, of putting: '*PER Sanctam Scripturam*' [THROUGH Holy Scripture, not '*EX Sancta Scriptura*' [FROM Holy Scripture], which could have been open to the idea of two sources.

2) '*veritas salutaris*'. The letter recognised the positive value of this formula for exegesis and its future. However, there were grounds for fearing that it might be wrongly understood, and that some people might misuse it to restrict inspi-

---

1. The Pope quoted this phrase from Congar: 'To the degree that it is of God, the Church is absolutely holy', an extract from 'L'Église est sainte', *Angelicum*, July–September 1965, 279.

ration, and thus inerrancy, to religious truths. Mgr Ancel told me that he had it from Mgr Colombo that this fear originated with Cardinal Bea, who had powerfully impressed the Pope with it. Bea had himself come to that session of the Theological Commission, and he had defended with fervour his criticism of the formula. There had been three successive votes on it without the required majority being attained. At the first vote, there were four abstentions 'out of reverence for the Holy Father'; at the second vote, three abstentions with the same motivation. At the third, after Bea intervened to say that reverence for the Holy Father could inspire something other than abstention, one of those who had abstained voted AGAINST the proposition. Mgr Philips then produced a formula that came from a text proposed by seventy-three Fathers, and that saved SOMETHING (not much!) of the idea contained in *'veritas salutaris'*, that is, by attributing to GOD the Revealer the act of revealing for our salvation. That had been accepted.

3) On the question of historicity. The formula proposed by the Pope spoke of *fides historica* [historical faith]. It was not found difficult to observe how unfortunate this was: it would make Bultmann happy . . . This time Philips proposed a solution that, all the same, went back to introducing the word *'historicitas'* [historicity]. That had been accepted.

It seems that the matter rests there. The correction of the proofs of the text, which is unchanged, is under way: in other words, the Pope would not otherwise intervene. The Holy Father's idea is even that the text could be voted on 25, 26 and 27 October, and promulgated on 28 October, after a definitive vote bearing on the whole as such. That would be a great thing, for this text is VERY important.

In the afternoon, reading and study of the comments on the *De Presbyteris*, at least of those comments concerning the parts that have been entrusted to me.

Also correction of proofs (*L'Église de Vatican II*).

I was extremely disappointed by the reading these comments. This was because, in place of giving us the text of the speeches, they have given us only an extract, reduced to specific suggestions for changes. That might do for working on *modi*, but ABSOLUTELY NOT for the work that has been asked of us. It lacked precisely the ideas, the suggestions, the inspirations. NOTHING was left here of several important speeches that had put forward perspectives rather than modifications of detail.

And yet, we have been asked for a fairly profound reworking—that was clear last Wednesday. It is IMPOSSIBLE to do this IN ACCORD WITH THE WISHES OF THE FATHERS on the basis of the documents that have been given to us.

For my part, for example: I am supposed to transform Numbers 6, 7 and 8 into a description of the SITUATION or POSITION of presbyteral priesthood in relation to bishops, laity, other priests. The kinds of *modi* that have been passed on to us have almost no significance for such work. Consequently, I am in a void. In these conditions I am seriously thinking of resigning from THIS work, which I WILL NOT BE ABLE to do properly.

In the afternoon, several telephone calls. Also, at 3.30 pm, a visit from l'abbé Hänggi,[1] Dean of the Faculty of Theology in Fribourg (Switzerland). He told me that it had been decided unanimously to give me a doctorate *honoris causa*; that the Roman authorities were in agreement, and that Fr General, prevented from coming on the proposed day (according to university regulations, this should take place on the first day of the new academic year, that is, 15 November), will come later to perform a ceremony himself. Fr General asked that it should be postponed until his arrival, but the regulations do not permit this.

I replied that I was very sensible of the honour . . . etc, but that I was opposed in principle to exercises of this kind. I do not see St Dominic or St Thomas as doctors *honoris causa* . . . For me it is the office that counts, not the honour (at least in that sense of the word).

And, if I accepted one offer of this kind I would be obliged to accept others (for there will be others). Better not to START on this road, WHICH IS NOT MINE.

But Hänggi insisted: this is very special. It concerns the public recognition of my merits(??!!!) That means something. At Fribourg, they are very keen on it.

I replied that I would think about it and give an answer tomorrow. But whom can I ask for fraternal advice?

In the evening, as Van Hengel insisted that I go and dine with the *Concilium* group, I went there—after ascertaining that it was objectively important, because, these days, I have to save every MINUTE. So, dinner at *Dodici Apostoli* with Küng, Schillebeeckx, Vanhengel and M. Brand. *Concilium* is having difficulties. The Pope told Fr General that there were too many Dominicans in the journal; he criticised two articles on Natural Law. The Pope would like to give *Concilium* a kind of board of governors or higher board of censors made up of bishops. For my part, I do not think this would be a happy arrangement. On the one side, the bishops know almost nothing about the questions that might be being discussed. Hence, they will either let through things that really are doubtful or they will block ones that are in fact inoffensive . . . Fr General, for his part, summoned Fr Duquoc and criticised an article in *Lumière et Vie*, in which Duquoc said that the atheist had a right to his atheism and to the expression of it, without distinguishing between the objective, absolute right and the external and civil right. Fr General repeated his criticism of *ICI*, which had repeated something from an article in *De Bazuin*[2] criticising the encyclical on the Eucharist. In fact, I was aware of that article in *De Bazuin* through *ICI*, and had asked myself whether I shouldn't distance myself from that weekly by ceasing to send it my articles. Schillebeeckx [whom the Pope is going to receive soon in private audience, especially in order to talk to him about *Concilium*] told me that the article in question is fundamen-

---

1. Anton Hänggi, Professor of Liturgy at the University of Fribourg, was the founder and director of the Swiss Liturgical Institute at Fribourg.
2. A religious weekly published by the Dutch Dominicans.

tally sound, but was unacceptable in tone. I am going to write to Fr Hamer on the subject.

Schillebeeckx told me that there is a schism, well and truly, in Holland: latent but nevertheless real. Cardinal Alfrink was optimistic in his press conference. He had to be, in order to cut short the accusations of the Italian press. But this does not stop the situation from being worrying.

At 9.00 pm, at the Hotel Minerva, for a reception in honour of the section editors and co-workers of *Concilium*. There were many people there that it would have been interesting to see, but I had to sit down, and also to leave a little after 10.00 pm.

Saturday 23 October 1965

Not sleeping very well recently.

At 9.30 am, at *Domus Mariae*, a lecture to the Congress on the Diaconate. Presided over by Cardinal Döpfner, Silva Henríquez, Šeper, Rossi. A very good public, not very numerous, but good quality. This caused me to miss the meeting of the sub-commission on Missions, but one can't do everything ... At 11.00 am, I went round to the *Concilium* meeting, until 1.00 pm.

After lunch, I went back to the *De Presbyteris*. May God have mercy on me and supply my deficiency, I am conscious of just how deep it is!

[[I met Fr Bazille for ten minutes and also saw Fr Gy on the question of the Fribourg doctorate. Both of them said: however stupid it may appear to you, it is important for Fr General and still more for Fribourg. It demonstrates the desire to be open and to give a sign of that openness. You will certainly wound them by refusing.]]

Sunday 24 October 1965

Work on *De Presbyteris*. At 10.00 am, Martelet came to work with me. He also brought me the *modi* he had prepared for the *De libertate religiosa*. We discussed these.

Martelet is very curious, he only goes to what interests him and only for as long as it interests him. He came to see me only this once; he was seen two or three times in all at the Commission, and then he did not appear any more; he had gone on to other things. He never finishes anything. This humble and tedious work puts him off.

At noon, at the house of the Holy Cross Fathers: a meeting to prepare the Theology Week for next April at Notre Dame. I gathered from Moeller and de Lubac further details about the meeting of the Theological Commission on the subject of the *De Revelatione*. They were pretty severe (and Willebrands too) about the role played by Cardinal Bea, who had already caused disappointment at the time of the so-called 'two sources' Joint Commission. He had attacked *veritas salutaris* bitterly. He told Tromp that all his life he had fought against what he suspected beneath this expression. There had been a battle to know how the votes would be counted and whether the blank forms should be deducted from the number of votes. Canon Law was invoked on the side of a negative response, the Conciliar Regulation in favour of a positive one ... At the end of the meeting, when everyone was on the point of leaving, Fr Anastasio del SS Rosario very nearly put the whole question back in doubt by saying that his conscience was not at ease with the solution adopted, and that he had put the question before the Administrative Tribunal of the Council. That can't have been done, or if it had been, the Pope carried on regardless, since, I was told, the text is printed (without new changes), it will be distributed tomorrow, put to the vote on Tuesday and Wednesday, and probably promulgated on Thursday ...

Fr Tucci, who was beside me at the table, told me: there is at present a campaign in the press and public opinion in Italy to have the Council condemn communism. On the ecclesiastical plane, Carli, and I believe, almost 180 Fathers have signed a request to the Pope along these lines. The press, especially that section which represents a bourgeoisie for which the Church, an unchanging Church, was the bastion of its privileges and of the 'established order', is conducting a campaign and, in advance, attributing the progress of communism to a Council that avoided condemning it. But it does not seem that there will be such a condemnation. To tell the truth, the Council, and within it schema XIII (against which the same press thunders), is, throughout, a criticism and a rejection of communism. But the Pope and the Council opted for a pastoral attitude directed towards caring for people and trying to heal them. At the UN, the Pope did not conspicuously shake Gromyko's hand,[1] he had a (brief) personal conversation with him, as he did with four other people. Tucci told me that he believed there was agreement in principle about a visit of Gromyko to the Pope when he comes to Rome.

Tucci told me that *Il Borghese* is VERY widely read in the whole of Italy, even in Roman ecclesiastical circles. When it comes out it is delivered in heaps to the newspaper kiosks.

At 4.40 pm, at the sub-commission on *De Presbyteris*.

At 8.45 pm, a visit from l'abbé Winninger:[2] a brief look at the plan for the volume on the diaconate.[3]

Monday 25 October 1965
In the morning, work on *De Presbyteris*. I spent a lot of time typing out my texts. No one had told me that the meeting had been cancelled. So I went in vain to the Congregation: a disrupted afternoon, time wasted, fatigue. Eventually, visits from

---

1. Andreï Gromyko, Foreign Minister of the USSR.
2. Paul Winninger, of the diocese of Strasbourg, who taught philosophy at the philosophical seminary of St Thomas Aquinas in Strasbourg, had been interested for several years in the question of the diaconate.
3. Cf Paul Winninger and Yves Congar (editors), *Le Diacre dans l'Église et le monde d'aujourd'hui*, 'Unam Sanctam', 59 (Paris: Cerf, 1966).

Frs Bro and Bonnet,[1] with whom I considered the questions concerning the edition on which I am engaged.

I saw Lécuyer this evening. The postponement of the meeting (about which he had been asked to tell me, and forgot, just as he forgot to pick me up yesterday), was caused by the need to review and redo the work of Fr Tilmann. The latter does not know what conciliar work is. He has not retained a single word of the former text, so the revision and harmonisation group was obliged to redo the whole thing!!! Lécuyer also brought me a text from Mgr Vilnet who is also not very well acquainted with what a conciliar work is. It was 100% a 'French bishop's' text: the Council knows the difficulties of priests, and gives them all its sympathy. . . Truly, our bishops are good, extraordinarily disinterested, pastoral, devoted to their task. But they easily replace the intellectual framework with piety or spirituality. Mgr Marty, for his part, is too good. He says Amen to everything.

The *Expensio modorum* for the *De Revelatione* was distributed at the Council this morning.

Tuesday 26 October 1965

I became aware of the totally negative reactions of the '*Coetus Internationalis*' on *De libertate*. It is undeniable that this presents a doctrine that is OTHER than that of the *Syllabus*. But WHO would dare to hold, just as it is, that doctrine and that of *Quanta Cura*[2] from which they quote a passage? On the other hand, in its critique, the '*Coetus*' always takes *ius* [right] in an ABSOLUTE, undetermined sense. But the schema speaks only, in a very precise fashion, of the '*ius AD IMMUNITATEM*' [right TO IMMUNITY]. Now, WHO could deny THAT right?

Work on the *De Presbyteris*. There is a sub-commission meeting this evening, Fr Herranz telephoned me. And yet I should be presenting the *De Presbyteris* to the Observers.

Taking advantage of the opportunity of a car (Frisque, who came to see me), I made a dash to St Peter's to come to an agreement with Mgr Willebrands (at St Peter's, I had a conversation with Jimenez-Urresti. He does not allow religious freedom as a right of COMMUNITIES), then to St Martha's to see Mgr Marty. It was agreed: I shall go to the Observers only from 4.30 to 5.30 pm. Mgr Marty was in a dreadful smoke-filled room with the little drafting group. I told them my opinion: our work is not good enough, it is much too hasty. There are too many interventions, speeches and comments from the Fathers of which we have no trace, not even an extract, in the documentation that has been given to us. We have neither an adequate conciliar basis, nor the necessary time to remake the text.

---

1. Henri-Noël Bonnet, OP, of the Province of Lyons, worked for Éditions du Cerf.
2. The encyclical *Quanta Cura*, published by Pope Pius IX in 1864, and accompanied by the Syllabus (of Errors).

At 3.40 pm, recording session for Radio Française, in honour of Rondenay[1] (to be broadcast on 11 November). At 4.30 pm, at the meeting with the Observers. I presented the schema on priests. I could stay only for the beginning of the discussion: a question from Skydsgaard: it sets out the programme for a way of living and for a holiness that are impossible. Who could achieve it, or even tackle it? It should have presented OUR weakness and the victorious holiness of Christ. In short, a reaction somewhat along the lines of '*simul justus et peccator*'.[2] But Skydsgaard was right when he noted that this could turn into LAW, into a legalistic programme of perfectionism. The 'Gospel' was not being proclaimed to priests . . . The Gospel proceeds rather by way of the setting forth of a CONCRETE example and a dynamic involvement in its meaning . . .

Nissiotis made a remarkable intervention. In the East, the problems about which I had spoken (tension between consecration and mission. . .) don't exist. The priest (the presbyteral priesthood) is never separated from the community: the priest cannot celebrate by himself, in the absence of a community of the faithful . . .

I heard Fr Vanese[3] make some comments, but I had to leave at 5.35 pm, to go to the sub-commission on *De Presbyteris*. It is a pity that the bishops present were so feeble. There were only three Frenchmen there: Marty, Mazerat and Vilnet. Good as a group, but Mgr Marty has not ANY position of his own, he says yes to everything. Much as I like him, it hurts me to see him so ineffective.

In the evening, a visit from priests of the 'Better World'.[4] At supper, Fr Scrépel.[5] He going to go home to Lille. The chapter of the worker-priests has reopened.[6] Tomorrow he will celebrate a Mass of thanksgiving in the Catacombs. Little by little, we are escaping from Pius IX and Pius XII (I mention them here only from the point of view of their refusal of the world as it is). Everything is cohering: the

---

1. André Rondenay, whom Congar had known during his imprisonment, escaped twice from prison camps; having become a colonel in the Free French Forces, he was again captured by the Germans; after having withstood torture, he was shot on 15 August 1944; made a Companion of the Liberation, he received a state funeral; cf Yves Congar, *Leur Résistance. Mémorial des officiers évadés anciens de Colditz et de Lübeck morts pour la France. Témoignage d'Yves Congar* (Paris, 1947), 74–85.
2. 'Righteous and a sinner at the same time': Luther's famous formula summing up his theology of justification.
3. This no doubt refers to the Indian, Paul Verghese, a priest of the Syrian Orthodox Church of the East, Assistant Secretary General of the WCC, Observer delegated by the WCC; he was later to become Metropolitan of Delhi, and President of the WCC.
4. The Movement for a Better World had been founded in 1952 by the Italian Jesuit Riccardo Lombardi, with the encouragement of Pius XII.
5. Jacques Scrépel, OP, of the Province of France, was in charge of the team of Dominican worker-priests in Hellemmes, near Lille.
6. On 23 October, the plenary assembly of the French bishops had re-established, with Roman endorsement, the possibility of priests taking on full-time work. There was a commentary on this decision by Mgr Veuillot in *La Croix* of 26 October.

work of the Council, even though it was so little thought through in advance, and has been conducted [from a human point of view] in the way that it has been, is extraordinarily coherent. The page is being turned over on Augustinianism and on the Middle Ages. Pretensions to temporal power are being renounced. New structures of relationship with the world are being put in place, beginning from the Gospel and in the light of Jesus Christ. . .

Mgr Philips has had a heart attack. The doctor said: Stop! You are on the brink of a serious collapse!!!

Wednesday 27 October 1965

A little correspondence: I am VERY much behind with regard to this. At 8.45 am, at St Martha's, drafting work (very long!) with Onclin, Lécuyer, Mgr Marty and Vilnet, M. Denis and the two Spanish secretaries. Felici is asking for our text, immediately if possible (!!!), in any case by Saturday. That is absolutely impossible. There is an ENORMOUS amount of revision and drafting to be done. The text is becoming overloaded with things, though they are excellent IN THEMSELVES . . .

The votes on the *De libertate* were much more favourable than I was expecting. The pure and simple *non placet* votes were fewer than seventy. The *modi* were numerous, but they will: 1) come from opposed intentions, in favour of a harder line, or of a softer one; 2) be repetitive, to a rather large degree.

I was told this morning that the idea of a formal condemnation of communism has been rejected by the Pope. On the other hand, it has been announced that he will go to Poland on 2 May. The Pope has opted for an adjustment of relations, with a view to facilitating, and even favouring, the life of the Church in the place in which it lives, in a communist regime.

After 2.00 pm, a long visit from l'abbé Rétif.[1] We discussed the priesthood. At 3.00 pm, recording session for Radio Luxembourg. Correspondence. At 4.30 pm, at Propaganda College for the plenary commission on the Missions. That went off without incident. Mgr Ungarelli, spokesman for several Brazilian Fathers, raised the question of prelatures *nullius* (there are more than 40) in Brazil. He asked for an expansion of the concept of mission, to include their case. After discussion, there were two successive votes on this subject: 1) to approve a rather long explanation that Fr Schütte wanted to put into his *Relatio*, and that showed how, at many points, the case of these prelatures REALLY is included. This resulted in unanimity except for one vote; 2) to decide whether the concept of mission in the text should be extended by the word 'praesertim' [especially]. This resulted in only five *placet* votes.

---

1. Louis Rétif, of the Sons of Charity, for a long time parish priest of the parish of the Sacred Heart at Colombes, was now working in pastoral formation and conducting courses and retreats.

I suggested (to save my conscience) two fairly long additions that Mgr Mercier wanted to introduce on poverty. In my own opinion, what is already there is sufficient, but Mercier, like Fr Gauthier, wanted it put in everywhere. Several Fathers were sick of it. It was not accepted. Finally, Mgr D'Souza felt that the missionary vocation was being spoken of in a way that would encourage the Missionary Institutes to look out especially for their OWN recruitment.

At 7.45 pm, the meeting still had not finished. I left. In the evening, at dinner, Skydsgaard.

Thursday 28 October 1965

This morning, there was a public session for the promulgation of the texts:
- Declaration on Non-Christian Religions.
- Decree on Religious Life.
- Decree on the Pastoral Office of Bishops.
- Decree on Christian Education.
- Decree on the Training of Priests.

However fine such a ceremony, whatever joy I might have in joining in the prayer of the Church, in listening to the promulgation especially of the first of these texts, in hearing the discourse of the Holy Father, I shall not go. We have a meeting of the drafting (drafting-revision) sub-commission for the *De Presbyteris:* at Mgr Onclin's place in the *Viale Romania*. That was at 9.00 am.

Quite good work. We had, after all, on TV in a nearby room, the Holy Father's speech (nothing very remarkable: the Church IS ALIVE!), and the result of the votes:

	Voting	*Placet*	*Non Placet*	Null
On the Pastoral Government of Bishops:	2,322	2,319	2	1
Religious Life:	2,325	2,321	4*	
Formation of Priests:	2,321	2,318	3	
Christian Education:	2,325	2,290	35	
Non-Christian Religions:	2,309	2,221	88	

(Mgr Bézac was beside a Yugoslav bishop who voted *Non placet*. His reason: as far as I am concerned, religious do (only) as they please. . .)

Back again at 4.30 pm, this time for the plenary meeting of the Commission. There were twenty to twenty-five bishops. They listened attentively. Cardinal Conway presided and did it very well, with authority and precision. Fr Lécuyer read out and explained the text. The Fathers made some detailed comments, sometimes not without interest. The text was improved, but it remains overloaded and heavy. The priesthood and the ministry of priests is one of those subjects on which there are the most comments and suggestions; everyone holds to his own little idea.

When I got back at 7.50 pm, two American Maryknoll priests were waiting to take me out to dinner with two others. The American priests were simple, direct, sane, full of longing and openness. My poor writings are much read among them. They questioned me as though I were a prophet about everything: 'anonymous Christians', hell, Teilhard, how to approach atheists, the theology of tomorrow, original sin, etc, etc!!!

Friday 29 October 1965

At 9.00 am, at St Martha's, small group for the revision of the text of *De Presbyteris*. We finished this work at 12.40 pm, though we have to wait to perfect it further after the vote by the Commission.

During this time, in St Peter's, the assembly had the final vote on the *De Revelatione*. A great moment.

At 3.00 pm a visit from Mühlen. He was a little uneasy about the position he had taken in a recent article about the Holy Spirit and the dissident Churches (in *Theologie und Glaube*[1]): it is a difficult question. Should one consider the dissident Churches only as having some ELEMENTS taken from the true Church, or do they rather have in some degree the Holy Spirit, THE SAME who is the soul of the Church? Is the Spirit THEIR soul? I believe the Spirit is bestowed as soul only on the complete and authentic (legitimate) *sacramentum* that is the Catholic Apostolic Church (of East and West), but it is also at work in the others.

At 4.00 pm (earlier than usual) at the Commission for the *De Presbyteris*. Several absences—there are sixteen bishops in all—particularly among the cardinals! We started with the Number on the nature of presbyteral priesthood. I was dreading difficulties, because the idea of Romans 15:16 had been introduced. But the members of THIS Commission were looking only at the details, not the whole of the teaching. They went over the text with a fine-tooth comb for some expressions, they scarcely followed it at all at a fundamental level. This meant that the text got through without meeting any opposition. It was incredible! It could not have been hoped for.

There was lengthier discussion on some points. Should the word *legitime* [legitimately] be retained to characterise the commands of authorities to which priests ought to be obedient? A vote was taken: a majority was against the use of this word. One must not even APPEAR to limit the authority of the pope. But that authority was not in question, only certain instances of its exercise. Tradition as a whole restricts the duty of obedience to what is commanded legitimately . . . The reply was given that this goes without saying, it is to be understood . . . I suggested saying *iure* [by right], but this had no success.

---

1. Cf 'Der eine Geist Christi und die vielen Kirchen nach den Aussagen des Vaticanum II. Zur Frage nach den dogmatischen Prinzipien einer ökumenischen Ganzheits-Ekklesiologie', *Theologie und Glaube*, 55, 1965: 329–366.

In connection with a formula envisaging the case of worker-priests several difficulties were raised, not unreasonably: (a) this only concerns one or two countries; (b) we would be canonising something that has been conceded only temporarily (three years) by way of experiment; (c) we would be risking that a large number of priests would use the conciliar text as an argument for taking up work without mission or authorisation. The text will be kept, but the formula will be toned down, or made more precise.

Everything was finished when, at the last hour, Mgr Rusch, Bishop of Innsbruck, suggested four additions, in general fairly verbose and exhortatory, which said nothing beyond rather banal generalities. Only the first was accepted, by a weak majority. The others will come back in the form of *modi*, because Mgr Rusch is VERY stubborn and brings back the same things in a hoarse and hollow voice . . .

At 7.55 pm, it was finished! Phew! All that remains is some work on the final drafting revision.

Saturday 30 October 1965

Correction of proofs (Baraúna volume). At 9.00 am, Viale Romania, Mgr Onclin's place, for the drafting revision of the *De Presbyteris*. We were not able to finish it all by 12.45 pm. For my part, I cannot come back either this afternoon or tomorrow, because I have to finish my article for *ICI*.

I got down to this at 2.00 pm.

At 3.00 pm a visit from a Catalan priest about the translation of three of my books into Catalan (which ones is yet to be decided).

At 3.30 pm, a visit from Mgr Willebrands. We started by talking about the votes of recent days. He told me that THE DAY BEFORE the promulgation of the Declaration on Non-Christian Religions, there was yet another approach made to the Pope in order that this promulgation should not take place. They argued from an inaccuracy in the quotation from Romans 11: 28–29, where it has *manent* [remain] instead of *sunt* [are] . . . A few days before, Felici had announced the promulgation of only four texts . . . At that point, Maximos IV had prepared a letter to the Pope asking him that the text of the Declaration be promulgated on 28 October. That is interesting.

We also talked about the *De Revelatione*: this title, Willebrands said, originated with John XXIII, who had used it (instead of *De fontibus Revelationis* [on the sources of revelation]) when he instituted the Joint Commission. Willebrands repeated to me that Cardinal Bea had disappointed him during the meeting of last week. He also said that he was somewhat scandalised by the way in which Cardinal Ottaviani had insisted on a majority of two-thirds of the votes on a text that the Fathers did not want. Cardinal Ottaviani had just given an interview to *Corriere della Sera*, in which he had compared himself to an old, blind policeman who had, all his life, seen to it that certain laws were observed. Now the laws are being changed. He will have to change his norms, that will be difficult for him, but he will give himself to the new rules, and will see to their observance.

There is in this a certain nobility of the faithful old servant.

Willebrands came to see me, in particular, about the report I must give, conjointly with Schlink and Nissiotis, on dialogue, for the next meeting of the Joint Committee of the Catholic Church and the WCC.[1] It seems to me that Schlink is not welcoming of the ideas of others. Faced with the Council, faced with Catholic theology, his reaction is always to find the point of criticism that will allow him to justify his own positions and change nothing in them.

We spoke a little about this reality of dialogue and of the conditions in which it can be undertaken and led.

This evening, only four or five bishops out of forty remained. A good many had returned to France, others are on retreat at Ariccia, lastly, others are touring (Mt Gargan, Sicily . . .). Only the galley slaves remain behind.

Sunday 31 October 1965

Wrote my *ICI* paper; visit from Fr Camelot; correction of proofs (Baraúna volume: a very bad article by Daniélou on the religious life[2]).

Sunday 1 November 1965

All Saints' Day. It is beginning to get cold. I got down to what Willebrands had asked of me for the Joint Committee with the WCC: a paper on dialogue. This necessitated some preliminary reading. (*Dialog unterwegs.*[3])

There were only six of us at table, of whom two were bishops: the Cinderellas of the Council . . . having finished my text on Dialogue fairly quickly (5.00 pm), I went back to the proofs of the Baraúna volume.

Propter verba labiorum tuorum, ego custodivi vias duras [for the sake of the words of your lips, I have kept to difficult paths (cf Ps 16: 4)].

---

1. The first meeting of the Joint Working Group (of the Roman Catholic Church and the WCC) took place at the Ecumenical Institute at Bossey from 22 to 24 May 1965; it was decided there to have an exchange on the nature and the conditions of dialogue, and three theologians were asked to produce a document for this work; those involved were Schlink (the problems of theological dialogue), Nissiotis (the problems of dialogue) and Congar (comments on the nature of dialogue according to the Roman Catholic understanding).
2. Cf Jean Daniélou, 'La place des religieux dans la structure de l'Église', in Guilherme Baraúna and Yves M-J Congar (editors) *L'Église de Vatican II. Études autour de la Constitution conciliaire sur l'Église*, 'Unam Sanctam', 51c (Paris: Cerf, 1966), 1173–1180.
3. George A Lindbeck (editor) *Dialog unterwegs, Eine Evangelische Bestand-saufnahme zum Konzil* (Göttingen, 1965).

Tuesday 2 November 1965

Correction of proofs as long as eye-strain would allow.

I learned that Cardinal Ottaviani had very recently summoned Mgr Garrone to tell him: the Pope wants absolutely that schema XIII should go through, as should religious freedom. It is you who have to direct the business in the absence of Mgr Guano.

Fr Bernard Lambert, who is working with Haubtmann on the drafting-revision of schema XIII (especially on Chapter III of the first part, of which Smulders had done an unsatisfactory draft in an unsatisfactory order), had made the same gloomy observation as myself. We tired ourselves out preparing interventions for the bishops, who agreed to present them. In the end, they didn't; with the result that there was no basis, in the Commission, for introducing such a thought. It can be introduced only if at least one Father asked for it. So, one goes to see a Father, one spends time preparing a text for him . . . and he does nothing with it. Nearly everything that I prepared at Les Voirons has fallen into the void in this way:

- On the Holy Spirit and the new human being (of Provenchères, then Volk).
- On messianic anthropology (Elchinger).
- On priesthood in the NT (Plourde).

It is sometimes discouraging. So much work has come to nothing! I am thinking also of the two texts on the Church in the world: the one drawn up in Rome in 1963, and that compiled in Malines in September of the same year. And so many others! I could have written three volumes in the time I have spent on such works that have fallen into the abyss of nothingness!

A visit from a confrère from the Priory in Pistoia.

I took my text on Dialogue to Mgr Willebrands: via dell'Erba was closed. I went to Monte Mario. Willebrands was absent!

Wednesday 3 November 1965

The weather has changed. I had already noticed that 1 November is a deadly date with regard to the weather in Rome. Until now we have had, in general, very fine weather, bright and fresh all at the same time: physically that suits me. Now it has become overcast, rainy, and damp. I felt it immediately and walk distinctly less well (or more badly).

The papers are talking about the closure of the Council for 8 December. It appears that this date is firmly fixed for the Secretariat of State.

Thursday 4 November 1965

At 10.20 am l'abbé Michalon[1] arrived with the *modi* for Numbers 9–15 of *De libertate*. We got down to them. I never thought this work would be so deadly boring and thankless. But it has to be done.

---

1. The Sulpician, Pierre Michalon, Professor of Sacred Scripture at the University Seminary of Lyons, and Director of the Christian Unity Ecumenical Centre at Lyons which was set up to continue the ecumenical work of l'abbé Paul Couturier, was a consultant of the Secretariat for Unity.

At 12.30 pm at the Gregorianum, where the Fathers had invited the Dominican experts present in Rome. A very warm welcome. A rather indifferent setting, utterly lacking in grace, even in humanity. But it is like that in almost all religious houses. I was beside Fr Alfaro:[1] very open and well informed.

At 2.45 pm, two priests or students from the USA who questioned me about the chapter on the People of God, which they have to work on.

At 3.00 pm, Michalon: *modi* for the *De libertate* until 5.45 pm. Then someone came to collect me for a lecture at the scholasticate of the White Fathers on Chapter II of *Lumen Gentium*. It went well, although I was very tired. After supper, a meeting with the Fr General of the White Fathers,[2] Fr Kaufmann and Fr van der Weijden[3] (Hermits of St Augustine): they brought up certain difficulties about Numbers 5 and 6 of Chapter I on the missions. Also, they thought that the brief few lines on ecumenism (the search for unity) would be better placed, theologically, at the end of No. 5 (*Ecclesia a Christo missa* [the Church as sent by Christ]: this Number should end with the evocation of the two essentials that accompany mission in as much as it is received from Christ: poverty and unity.

This last idea greatly attracted me. It is odd that it had not been thought of when, together with Ratzinger, we were looking for a place for this brief paragraph on ecumenism. It is true that unity is cited as a sign of mission . . . If this text could be transferred to there, it would take on an extraordinary force; work for unity would be seen to be placed at the heart of mission and intimately bound up with it.

I said to the Fathers that it will be possible to allow, under the form of *modi*, changes that, with respect not only to teaching but also to the text, would be an improvement of it. Even transpositions. But I recommended to them: 1) to be very modest (the best is the enemy of the good); 2) to speak about it to Fr Schütte in advance; 3) not to try to collect too many signatures, so as not to multiply the 'iuxta modum'.

If they do this, perhaps the changes they are suggesting will get through as *modi*, for the improvement of the text.

But, when all that is finished, we shall thank God, and say 'Phew'!

Friday 5 November 1965

I slept poorly. For eight days the buzzing and hissing in my ears has come back VERY strongly; I am hypersensitive to noise; I hear others and I hear myself in a hollow and strange manner. And then, I thought about yesterday evening's questions on the *De Missionibus*. I sent a letter (had it taken) to Fr van der Weijden.

---

1. The Spaniard, Juan Alfaro, SJ, taught dogmatic theology at the Gregorianum where he was the Prefect General of Studies.
2. Léon Volker, Superior General of the White Fathers.
3. Athanasius van der Weijden, Procurator General of his Congregation.

At 8.45 am, Michalon, then Feiner, arrived for the *modi* for the *De libertate*. I would never have thought this work could be so tedious and so tiring. It is awful: there is no intellectual object to be pursued, but simply attention to be given successively to a litany of disparate comments. Each time, one has to refer to the text, weigh or assess the reasons; these raise new questions, to which, however, one can give neither satisfaction nor even a following up, because it is not our job to rewrite the text . . .

A break between 1.00 and 3.00 pm. Resumed the chain-gang work from 3.00 pm until 5.50 pm. It was finished . . . until tomorrow!

At 6.30 pm a lecture to the community of seminarians and priests, on the priesthood. After supper, conversation with the priests. All sorts of questions.

Saturday 6 November 1965
I slept very badly. Dreams. Head too full of worries. Woke at 2.00 am, and impossible to get back to sleep. I looked at all I have got to do, all that is behindhand, the meetings and journeys to be fitted in. I am too weighed down by requests that are unceasing, and of every kind.

A visit from E Schlink, who brought me his own writings on dialogue. This will have to be read between now and Monday! It seems that Nissiotis, Schlink and I are going to present three separate papers at the discussion of the Joint Committee with the WCC, and that it will be only afterwards that a single text will be produced.

Visit from a Dutchman, a professor from Amsterdam, who explains Catholic theology to Protestants there. He is deaf, hesitant and stammering in his speech, often changing from French to German in the same sentence. He told me that he was very tired, but he dragged me into his own fatigue!

At 12.25 pm, Mgr Poupard and Joulia,[11] together with Laurentin, came to take me to have lunch with them (and Mgr Riobé) at the Dominican Sisters of the Union of St Dominic, near La Storta. A magnificent building. What a joy to see trees again, and breathe air that didn't stink of petrol!!! The light was beautiful, and the trees, whose leaves were beginning to turn yellow, had autumn tints of such a soft brightness that my old love for them became wholly joyful.

We talked a little about everything. Nothing really noteworthy. Laurentin occasionally asked questions, but most of the time spoke forcefully and in an imperious manner without listening to anyone else. He is fully preoccupied with the small goings-on of the Council or of the Curia. I felt myself out of sympathy with him.

---

1. Henri Joulia, Procurator General of the Missionaries of the Immaculate Conception, attached to the Congregation for Religious; he was, like P Poupard, a chaplain to the Sisters of the Union of St Dominic, where they took him to lunch.

At 4.30 pm, at the Secretariat: a meeting of the three sub-sub-commissions for the *expensio modorum*: Willebrands, De Smedt, C Colombo, Primeau, Degrijse, Hamer, Feiner, Becker,[12] Murray, Pavan, Michalon, myself. Great joy to see Murray again, out of hospital, and, he said, ninety-two per cent cured. But he spoke in a voice that seemed like that of a ghost, and as though it came from the other side of the veil. Interesting work and discussion, but it took up a lot of time. We attempted to give satisfaction to a letter from Cardinal Wyszyński, in the name of the bishops of Poland (not to assert the transcendence of religion in such a way that the Communists could make use of it in order to confine priests to the sacristy), and also to some extent, to a curious letter from Fr Boyer transmitted, it wasn't known why, *via* Cardinal Traglia. Boyer presented two requests or *modi*, saying that if these were met, it would bring on side a quasi-unanimity of the Fathers. He is deluding himself. The 200 opponents know very well that a different doctrine from the one they would like is being maintained!

This evening, the proofs of the second part of schema XIII: the text of it was sent YESTERDAY (before that of the first part, which is still being revised). The Vatican Press knows how to work quickly and well. When I said it would have been possible, two years ago, to save ten days and present *De libertate* in good time, Tucci said to me: the text has been held up all this time by Cardinal Cicognani, Secretary of State, who does not want it.

Sunday 7 November 1965

I spoke to Cardinal Richaud about the question of the economics of the Council: How much is all this costing? He did not know anything, although he is a member of the Economic Commission.[2] This commission has met only twice, at the beginning: once for a little more than an hour, the other time for less than an hour. On this matter of finances, there is a black-out!!! It appears that at first it was envisaged that the Council would be held IN A TENT, set up in the Cortile di san Damaso. That shows that, at the beginning, no one had any idea what it would be like, neither how long it would last, nor what would be the programme of work, nor what would be the technical requirements . . . John XXIII spoke truly when he said, at time of the First Session: in the matter of councils we are all novices.

This morning, work in preparation for this evening's session; a short visit from Fr Le Guillou: he has prepared (together with Fr Mollat and Mgr Mercier) a *modus* on poverty to propose for No. 5 of *De Missionibus*: a text of more than fifteen lines, somewhat obscure and complicated. It was impossible. A conciliar text must be comprehensible on a simple reading; a *modus* must be brief.

Then, correspondence.

---

1. The Oratorian, Werner Becker, of Leipzig, appointed by the bishops of East Germany to follow the ecumenical movement, was a consultor to the Secretariat for Unity.
2. The Council Regulation had provided for a Commission for technical and organisational matters.

At 11.45 am, Fr Féret came to collect me. We went to pick up Chenu from where he lives on the outskirts of the city. Lunch on the terrace of a restaurant on the shore of Lake Bracciano. It is the first time we have met since the beginning of this Session. It is, moreover, also my first outing, my first and only hour of relaxation. We talked about the Council and about AFTER THE COUNCIL, which many are concerned about. How will things go? What structures, what commissions will be in place? How will the spirit of the Council be maintained at the top, and even in the episcopates? The Council has largely been made by the contribution of theologians. The time after the Council will only preserve the spirit of the Council if it takes up the work of the theologians. I said this in my piece for *ICI* on 15 November, but it will be necessary to come back to it.

At 4.00 pm, at the Secretariat. There we finished, in the small sub-commission, the *expensio modorum*, which I presented for Numbers 9-15.

Mgr Garrone came back at 8.10 pm, having seen the Holy Father for a full hour about schema XIII. I asked: is the Holy Father optimistic? Reply: he wants to be, to have good reasons for being so.

I several times offered my services to Haubtmann and Garrone for the literary revision of schema XIII. But they did this between them, with help from Tucci and sometimes from Daniélou(!) In any case, I am fully occupied with other things and would have found it difficult to add this work, or ensure that it was done effectively.

Mgr Philips left by train at 2.00 pm, rather sad to go, but serene. So much is owed to him! Without him, the Theological Commission would never have functioned as it did function, nor would it have produced the fine texts that it did produce. He was not alone in having given these texts to the world, but he was, nevertheless, the father of them. During his illness, as soon as he learnt of it, the Pope sent him a personal, hand-written letter.

Mgr Philips has been considered for the post of Secretary of the *Synodus Episcoporum* [Synod of bishops]. Others mentioned the name of Felici. Since the latter knows how to make use of his facility with words, and of a certain agreeable dynamism of his personality, he has acquired the reputation of being well thought of by the bishops. That favours the likelihood of his chances. But he would perpetuate in the *Synodus* the curial spirit that he gave evidence of at the Council. Philips would certainly be preferable. But either one could well, quite as much, be made a cardinal . . .

Monday 8 November 1965

I feel very tired and sluggish. The weather must have changed . . . In the morning, a little correspondence. But especially the reading of the two articles of Schlink on the conditions for THEOLOGICAL dialogue. And also preparation for my lecture this evening.

Visit from a Spanish bishop from Galicia, Mgr Mondoñedo[1] with two of his priests. He spoke very quickly and enthusiastically. The bishops, he said, are the successors of the Apostles, but Fr Congar is the successor of all the doctors and all the prophets!!! He has all my publications and he has read them all. He wants to establish a sort of archive of the Council, with all the documents, all the *vota*, all the documentation of the Commissions, extracts from the press etc. I could not give him copies, as he asked, because I have not got any. I directed him to the documentation of the Belgian College (Moeller-Louvain), and told him to go and see the secretaries of the various Commissions. At Tromp's place, there are stacks of speeches made about the *De Ecclesia* and the *De Revelatione*.

Finally, after having asked a great many questions and talked a great deal (he is a great friend of Fr Sauras) he left with, all in all, very little . . .

At 1.00 pm, lunch at the German deaconesses, with Schlink, L Vischer, Nissiotis and Kantzenbach.[2] We talked about our three reports on dialogue. They are very different, but will be able to be linked together sufficiently well; after discussion with the Joint Committee, we will get together again to draw up a single document, intended for the Central Committee of the WCC.

At 3.00 pm, a visit from six young Protestant students from Heidelberg, mostly theologians, who are working on ecumenical questions. They have spent the whole period of the Fourth Session in Rome, and are studying the theology underlying schema XIII. They asked me a hundred questions and recorded my replies in bad German. But what a novel thing, and how promising it is to see young Protestant theologians taking an interest in all of this with earnestness, precision, and an authentic spirit of openness . . .

At 4.30 pm, at the Secretariat: a plenary meeting. At the moment of leaving I saw Mgr Ménager. He told me that, while the schema *De apostolatu laicorum* was being printed, they received some *modi* from the Pope. The Commission rejected some of them (this was relayed at second hand); the others will be given out with the schema, but on a separate sheet. These *modi* come, Mgr Ménager told me, from bishops who went to lament to the Pope and complain that notice had not been taken of their comments. And so the poor Pope is beginning again what turned out so badly for him at the end of the Third Session . . . In a less delicate matter.

I left the session at 5.45 pm (Hermaniuk and Cantero had raised some difficulties; at that time they had just looked at No. 1, and, at that rate, they will not finish it). Also, it was agreed that the whole thing would be gone through today, and that the vote would not be held until tomorrow. Murray regretted that the

---

1. This refers to J Argaya Goicoechea, Bishop of Mondoñedo-Ferrol (Spain).
2. Friedrich Kantzenbach, Professor of Church History and Dogmatic Theology at the Augustana-Hochschule at Neuendettelsau in Bavaria, was also research Professor at the Centre for Ecumenical Studies in Strasbourg, which had just been created by the Lutheran World Federation; he was an Observer delegated by the Lutheran World Federation.

general statement of the theme of the dignity of the human person, with its support from *Pacem in Terris*, had been removed from the beginning of No. 1. He had been absent when someone (me!) again redrafted this No. 1. This showed once again that when someone other than the one who drafted it corrects a text, he hardly enters into the perspective and the detailed intentions of the previous drafter at all, and risks making a botch of things that were dear to him. This has happened to me in texts that I had drafted.

That is why I shudder somewhat when I think about the drafting-revision of schema XIII that is presently being done. They worked through the whole night from Monday to Tuesday. That was necessary in order to send the text back to Felici, as promised, on 10 November. It was a small, rather closed group: Haubtmann, Garrone, Tucci, with, to a small degree, Ancel and Hirschmann. Daniélou got himself into it. They did not call for me. I am afraid they take too little account of the work of sub-commissions. Garrone got himself covered by the Pope for the editorial changes that he introduced into a text already approved by the Joint Commission, and the final version of which will not be submitted to this Commission. I recognised that, in the revision by sub-commissions, the text had lost something of its tone of speaking to humanity, in order to turn to a dogmatic tone. A lot of repetitions had been introduced. A more theological, less concrete order had been adopted. The drafting-revision sought to re-establish the character intended for this text.

Lecture to the 'Better World' movement, near Rocca di Papa.[1] I was not really at ease in front of this audience that I did not know, equipped with headphones for simultaneous translation. I had the feeling of not making contact. Nonetheless, afterwards, I received a great number of very warm expressions of satisfaction. At supper, a cheerfully informal atmosphere. The American element is less starchy than is the case among us: they laugh, they clap one another on the shoulder, the religious sisters are more informal . . .

Tuesday 9 November 1965

The bishops have returned: from France, from Sicily, from Paestum etc etc. Full of vigour. They left at 9.30 am. I did not go: it will only be a matter of voting. Correspondence, disposal of the crazy backlog that has accumulated on my table from everything I receive every day!

At 12.30 pm, lunch with François de Seynes and his wife.[2] Old memories, always very vivid.

---

1. Cf above, page 825, note 5.
2. François de Saynes de Larlenque, scion of an old Huguenot family, he had been Assistant Secretary General of CIMADE, a Protestant solidarity movement, and in that capacity had invited Congar to various ecumenical meetings; at the time of his marriage to a Catholic, Marie-Camille de Chamberet, Congar had helped them in their canonical proceedings with the Catholic authorities.

Then odds and ends, correspondence, telephone. Great joy at a visit from Fr Jacques Dournes, who has just come from the High Plains of Vietnam. It is a pity that, from the point of view of the missions, he has arrived after the battle!

I did not go to the Secretariat for the vote of the bishops on the *expensio modorum* for the *De libertate*. I thought that my presence was not necessary, and I had some appointments here. These really must be dealt with too.

Before his departure for this session, I saw Cardinal Martin. He was very shaken by the criticisms he had heard of the first Number of *De Libertate*. If the Pope had started his speech to the UN in that way, people would not have listened to him. But I rejected this comparison: If the Pope had made in New York a DOCTRINAL DECLARATION ON RELIGIOUS FREEDOM he would have said what this No. 1 says. It says only some things that we hold, which figure even in the opening of the *De oecumenismo*. I think that, at the moment, too many of our theologians seem to forget that we are the Church!

Moreover, since the beginning of my collaboration on the *De libertate*, I have told myself that, if I were a bishop, I would be asking myself a good many questions on the subject. Anyone with a sense of pastoral responsibility could not view without anxiety either the threat that comes from the offensive by the sects, or the weakening of absolute convictions among Catholics. The document ought, so far as it is able, to fend off both of these. So some of its formulas could be softened, some have already been softened, but this Number must be kept, and kept at the beginning.

Several visits from bishops concerning *modi* for the *De Missionibus*, Chapter I: Riobé, de Cambourg,[1] Gouyon.

Visits from: a journalist from *La Rocca* (reproduction of part of my article on the diaconate[2]); P Burke[3] (Chicago); a Spanish priest who wants me to answer a dozen questions for the journal *Palabra*,[4] read by 'all the priests' in Spain and in South America.

But just recently I have received three requests of this sort, for Italy, for the USA. I am doing nothing but odd jobs of this kind. It will kill me. My days are torn in shreds: the hours fray away like an old, worn-out garment. Everything works unremittingly to prevent me doing anything serious. And it gets worse. I often think only death will sort things out.

---

1. Jean de Cambourg, Auxiliary Bishop of Bourges (France).
2. Cf above, page 768, note 3.
3. Thomas Patrick Burke, Australian by origin, was director of the John XXIII Research Centre, an inter-confessional theological centre attached to St Xavier's College in Chicago; at his invitation, Congar was to go there the following year for a colloquium; cf T Patrick Burke (editor) *The Word in History: the St Xavier Symposium* (New York, 1966); French translation, *Théologie d'hier et de demain,* Cogitatio Fidei, 23 (Paris: Cerf, 1967).
4. Cf 'La Iglesia tiene ahora necessidad de un momento de calma', *Palabra*, December 1965.

From Cardinal Martin: The Pope would like the *De libertate* to be proclaimed on 8 December, for the closure of the Council, officially announced for that day (letter from the Pope to Cardinal Tisserant, read out this morning *in aula*). This, he said, would be a fine ending. But it was impressed on him that, between now and then, the opponents will be on the move, that they will multiply their approaches to him, and that it would be preferable to hasten the promulgation.

From Mgr Garrone: the Pope said to him, in an audience the day before yesterday, on the subject of the chapter on marriage in schema XIII: it is evident that love is the soul of marriage and determines its real nature. That has always been the tradition of the Church, only it has been expressed differently. At bottom, that is what consensus means.

Wednesday 10 November 1965

I got down to the chore that is the article requested by *CCIF* on the past twenty years from the point of view of theological research.[1] I am not in good spirits. I will only be able to do something very mediocre. This is a real piece of drudgery for me.

From 2.00 pm until 7.30 pm, with P Peuchmaurd to get the commentaries on conciliar texts under way.

These past two days, at the Council, and continuing in the following days, the episcopal conferences are giving an account of their reactions to the proposal for the *aggiornamento* of indulgences.[2] The idea that this should be open to a public debate in the presence of the Observers! That is going to damage the climate of this end of Session. Have they not realised that beneath this there are all the elements of tragedy. It is true that points of profound disagreement should not be concealed. But this is neither the time nor place to bring them up again. In fact, Schlink and Roux are greatly shocked. This occasioned a very good speech *in aula* this morning from Maximos.[3] I also read the reply from the Germans, which will be given tomorrow. It is solid and detailed, too detailed to be listened to, but it does not go to the root of the questions.

Thursday, 11 November 1965

I interrupted my *CCIF* article, scarcely begun, to deal with the writing of the *ICI* article, because tomorrow and the following day I have to go to Nemi for the *expensio modorum* for the Missions. This rhythm of perpetual interruptions of what cannot even be called work, is incredibly trying: it destroys all calm and all possibility of thought. There is more than one way of carrying one's cross!

---

1. Cf 'La recherche théologique', *Recherches et Débats,* No. 54, April 1966: 89–102, reprinted in *Situation et tâches présentes de la théologie* (Paris: Cerf, 1967), 26–40.
2. The Sacred Penitentiary had proposed to the Presidents of Episcopal Conferences a project for the reform of indulgences.
3. *AS* IV/VI, 292–294.

At midday, lunch: I invited Mgr Seitz, Jacq, Fr Dournes (who did not come), Peuchmaurd, with whom I worked a little. He did not waste his time. Mgr Mc-Grath asked me to go to a meeting at the Belgian College: it was about popular devotions, especially in South America. Everything was in English. It was very interesting. The speakers were: McGrath, a Jesuit from Chile, Häring, myself, Fr Pin (a sociologist from the Gregorianum),[1] Houtart, Cardinal Suenens, Mgr De Smedt and several others. I said a little along the lines that 'Religion' ≠ 'Faith' and that 'religions succeed each other in the same place . . .' Despite my incredible pressure of work, and the three hours that this cost me, I am glad I went: I believe I contributed a mite to the cause of the Gospel.

At supper, three bishops and a priest from Hungary. They invited me to visit Hungary where, they told me, I am very well known and appreciated.

At 9.00 pm a visit from Laurentin: he has not read the schema on priests and has to speak about it in *le Figaro*. He asked me what to say, and took notes. I made the effort to reply amicably, but I was embarrassed by this utilitarian spirit, the sort of unabashed confidence that journalism has developed in Laurentin.

By the way, he has written some very good, sometimes courageous articles in *Figaro*.

Friday 12 November 1965

Answers to the questions from the journal *Palabra*.

At 8.50 am, outside the Holy Office to wait for the car that was to take us to Nemi, for the *expensio modorum* for the *De Missionibus*. It rained VERY heavily. In rainy weather, the streets of Rome are even more congested: one has to go step by step.

People arrived late. We went by way of the Divine Word College. We finally reached Nemi at 10.40 am. What a loss of time! For such an *expensio modorum* it would have been better to stay in Rome; that would have allowed us to take note of a good many of the requests that fell outside the main work.

We got down to work straightaway after the distribution of our batch of *modi*: Ratzinger, Lokuang and myself. We started again straight after lunch, because Mgr Lokuang had to leave at 4.00 pm. We moved ahead quickly enough. We identified the packets from the *Coetus internationalis Patrum*, of which it was easy to draw up a list. They are against the new paragraph on ecumenism: it would favour indifferentism.

Saturday 13 November 1965

We finished (with just Ratzinger: Lokuang had left at 4.00 pm yesterday) the *expensio modorum* for Chapter I. It was all finished by 4.00 pm. Ratzinger will re-copy the lot. We accepted a rather large number of improvements, and we gave

---

1. Emile Pin, SJ, taught general sociology and sociology of religion in the Institute for Social Sciences at the Gregorianum.

careful, rather detailed replies: this had to be done since the Fathers had taken the trouble to explain their own reasons in detail.

From 4.13 pm to 7.00 pm, correction of the proofs of the Baraúna volume.

Conversation with Fr Greco. I questioned him about the history of the schema and the work of the Commission. Why was it that, for such a long time, no progress was made? He told me: the ante-preparatory commission had drawn up a wholly juridical schema. It remained (and the Conciliar Commission itself remained for a long time), under the thumb of the Congregation. The Congregation had blocked everything right up to June 1963 (the death of John XXIII). Paul VI had instituted the four Moderators [one of whom was Cardinal Agagianian . . . !]. These, together with some other cardinals like Cardinal Liénart [the Co-ordinating Commission?] then intervened to pressure the Conciliar Commission to respond to the wishes of the Missionaries. The Congregation did nothing. On 17 October 1963, the Moderators asked the Co-ordinating Commission: 'will there be a schema on the Missions?' The reply came on 31 October: there IS a schema and it has been drawn up at top speed. After the meeting of the Co-ordinating Commission in January and especially in May 1964, this schema was reduced to some propositions, because it was not certain, at that point, that there would be a Fourth Session, and the idea was to get everything out of the way in one go.

In the course of the Third Session, it became evident that there would need to be a Fourth Session (necessary because there was a schema XIII). The schema on the Missions, in its reduced form of propositions, was rejected in November 1964. That was when I was brought into the work. I have recorded the rest in this journal, to the extent that I was involved.

A brief interchange with Mgr Höfer (counsellor at the German Embassy): 'You are winning all along the line', he told me.

That has often been said to me, but, as far as I am concerned, it is not like that in any degree or any manner. I know myself to be so unequal to the task to which I have been called, by pure grace. But however badly I have fulfilled it, I am profoundly happy to have been able, among others, to serve two things that are so dear to me: the Missions and priests. In this (and other ways) I feel myself very much in communion with little Thérèse and with Tere[1].

Departure after supper. At the French Seminary at 9.50 pm.

Sunday 14 November 1965

Perusal of the correspondence that had arrived in my absence.

A little work on my *CCIF* article.

Departure for this ridiculous doctorate from Fribourg.

---

1. St Thérèse of Lisieux (and Congar's mother).

Monday 16 November 1965

Physically, this journey was rather difficult for me: departure from the seminary at 2.50 pm: very fine as far as Geneva; I saw Les Voirons from very close by, passing just over Thonon. But afterwards, the Swiss railways, the fast-moving tram-cars! Sixty times the door opened and all the cold air (for it was cold) came into the carriage . . . At the Albertinum.[1] A charming welcome from the Fathers, though many were away. On Monday, a great academic session under very tiresome spotlights. Afterwards on foot through the melting snow—for it snowed quite a bit and some flakes were still falling at intervals—to a speech and the blessing of the foundation stone of some science buildings. An interminable meal; 400 people in the same room . . .

Departure at 3.30 pm, with Riedmatten and l'abbé A Müller.[2] Got to Zurich airport at 7.00 pm. A long wait. Cardinal Journet arrived for the same plane. He had brought two croissants and, wrapped up in an old travelling cloak, he ate them in small bites with the bag open on his knees: he looked like an old monkey eating his peanuts. Or rather, a poor old fellow. The total simplicity of this man, for whom the cardinalate has not touched or changed anything. That morning, when he was presiding, he had made a conclusion of very great spiritual purity, even if it was, to a small degree, the 'wisdom' of *retirement*.[3]

In the end, because one of the engines of our plane was not functioning properly, we left two hours late and (with Féret waiting for me all that time at Fiumicino!) I did not get to the Seminary until twenty minutes past midnight.

I had the experience of a great solemnity in the Fribourg fashion. People exchanged titles. The way public offices are arranged there means a multiplication of offices and titles. There are whole echelons of councillors and of presidents. They love long speeches in which each personality is passed in review, named, praised . . . THE ADMINISTRATION IS VERY MUCH PERSONALISED. On the other hand, people are known, everyone knows everyone, and the maiden names of women etc. It is a product and a form of Swiss democracy, which starts FROM THE BOTTOM, and rests on a common citizenship that is local and concrete. Napoleon did not pass through here; not that the city or the university resembles a barracks, but the Army reflects the local particularism and the personal character of undertakings in the city. But a taste for titles and ceremonial covers it all in a slightly heavy patina of folklore and of fairly stultifying solemnity. I would not live there willingly, or I would get away from there.

On my table there was an accumulation of correspondence, books, proofs, envelopes of *modi* for the *De Presbyteris*.

First I finished the final touches to my *ICI* chronicle –*De Bazuin,* with a reply to *De Bazuin* on the subject of my criticism of the article concerning the encycli-

---

1. The Dominican house of studies in Fribourg.
2. Alois Müller was Professor of Pastoral Theology at Fribourg.
3. Congar used the English word.

cal *Mysterium Fidei*.[1] Then after a visit from Fr Peuchmaurd, I got down to the *modi* for the *De Presbyteris*.

At 6.00 pm, a visit from one of the editors at Fayard,[2] a friend of J-M Paupert,[3] and a [[close]] collaborator of Daniel-Rops. We talked about him, and the gap left by his death. Rops had, in 1934, foreseen his death. In *Mort, où est ta victoire?* (page 283) his spokesman gave the date: 1965, and saw himself being buried, like Rops, in the cemetery of a mountain village on the side of a valley . . . [4]

Wednesday 17 November 1965

I was supposed to be in two places at once: at the *modi* for schema XIII, Part 1, Chapters I and II, and at the *modi* for the *De Presbyteris*. I chose the second, where my participation is active, effective and efficacious—although I have had a lot of disappointments over my successive collaborations each time schema XIII was put through the mill again. Each time, the work provided has been very little taken into consideration. This time, the small drafting group did just as it liked. It took great liberties even with respect to the text which had been accepted by the plenary Joint Commission. Mgr Garrone said to me: if Philips had been there, he would not have allowed it . . .

Peuchmaurd told me that Lubac did not want to collaborate in a volume of commentaries on schema XIII, given the way he feels because Mgr Garrone excluded him from collaboration. I could well feel the same way. It turned into a closed team. Perhaps that was necessary for it to succeed.

In fact, the result is not bad. The anthropology is the weakest part. Furthermore, I have difficulty seeing the Council promulgating the text of the second part as a 'constitution', even if it were 'pastoral'. I campaigned for each of the two parts to be given a different theological note.

The journey was very difficult on the 'C'[5] as far as Viale Romania: rough-going, jolted about . . . I finished the journey on foot. Very tired. '*Deus qui laborem et dolorem consideras*' [Lord, you have seen our trouble and sorrow (Ps 10:14)] . . .

I saw Liégé for a moment.

---

1. In his reply to the journal *De Bazuin*, Congrar wrote, on the subject of the article about the encyclical: 'This is what I think : *one does not speak like that about a document of the ordinary pontifical magisterium* [. . .] The challenging is crude and simplistic.'
2. Robert Toussaint confirms that this refers to him: at the time he was Secretary-General of Fayard.
3. Jean-Marie Paupert, after a philosophical and theological education, during which he had known Congar, became a close collaborator of Daniel-Rops at Fayard, in the religious section, and on the journal *Ecclesia*, as editor-in-chief.
4. Congar added to the typescript: 'Madame Daniel-Rops wrote to me subsequently to say that there was nothing of a premonition there, and that her deceased husband was not a man given to premonition.
5. {*Circolare* tram}.

I was told that the Pope had conveyed his comments on celibacy. Without imposing anything, he would like priestly celibacy to be made a formal vow, which priests would renew each Holy Thursday. He asked the Commission to study this.

This would presuppose a better separation between the commitment to chastity, a PERSONAL undertaking answering to a personal grace, and ordination for MINISTRY.

I learned in a rush, without details, that there have been some difficulties concerning the *De libertate religiosa*. Some of the Fathers of the minority (and Felici among them), had intervened in favour of having the printing and distribution of the text with the *expensio modorum* postponed again. They were hoping to gain more time and, doubtless, to the end that the text would not get through at all. It was on the personal intervention of the Pope that the text was printed. It was distributed to the Fathers this morning.

Roman rumours, tittle-tattle of Rome. Certain libraries have received from the Holy Office and the Congregation of Seminaries and Universities the recommendation to display in their windows the latest book of Michel de Saint-Pierre.[1]

The same integrist group wanted to make a success of a book by l'abbé Prévost,[2] about which I wrote on page XXXIX of *Chrétiens en dialogue*. Prévost was presenting his book, *Pierre ou le chaos,* in a Roman bookshop this evening. Michel de Saint-Pierre and Pierre Debray[3] were there, but a VERY small audience and no one of note. But those people enjoy the support of the Holy Office and those around Pizzardo and Staffa. L'abbé David told me he got from someone that Cardinal Ottaviani had said to this someone: if you want to know the French clergy read *Les Nouveaux Prêtres*.

At lunch, Peuchmaurd, who stayed with me until 4.10 pm. Fr Smulders was supposed to have come, and had agreed to be the editor of a commentary on the *De Revelatione*. He did not come. I bumped into him just as I was going out myself. He told me that he will not be able to do anything!

As a matter of fact, I left at 4.10 pm to go to the Commission on Missions. I was expecting they would start with Chapter I, and that I would be able to leave at 5.30 pm, to go to the *expensio modorum* for the *De Presbyteris*. But Fr Schütte started with the most delicate question of Chapter 5, so that at 5.35 pm I left the session (in the evening, Ratzinger telephoned me to say that everything had gone well and had been finalised). During the hour I was there, there was discussion and voting on:

1) The formula concerning the participation of bishops and missionary
    superiors in the Congregation *de Propaganda Fide* [for the Propagation of
    the Faith]:

---

1. Michel de Saint-Pierre, *Sainte colère,* (La Table Ronde, 1965).
2. Robert Prévost, priest of the diocese of Lille; in conflict with his bishop, he had left his diocese in 1954.
3. This Christian militant and journalist, who came from the progressive milieux of *Témoinage chrétien,* embodied a conservative current that was anxious to maintain dialogue with the French episcopate.

In favour of retaining the text: 12.

Against retaining the text: 10.

2)   Mgr Riobé suggested a formula which was adopted by 17 votes to 5: '*partem actuosam habeant cum voto deliberative*' [they should have active part with a deliberative vote].

3)   On the formula '*auditis conferentiis episcopalibus*' [after having listened to episcopal conferences]. It was also accepted by 17 votes to 5.

I arrived at *Viale Romania* at 5.55 pm; Mgr Marty was there, with Onclin, Lécuyer, del Portillo and Herranz.

In the evening, after 9.00 pm, a visit from Mgr Izard, and several telephone calls. Wretched days, disjointed, mangled, ragged, tiring.

Thursday 18 November 1965

I got up early and set about typing the *modi* and my responses for Numbers 1–3. I worked non-stop until 4.00 pm, except for the interruption of lunch with Chenu and Peuchmaurd. It was a very long and very demanding job, that had to be done with care.

Consequently I did not going (and probably would not have gone anyway) to the public session where there was to be the promulgation of the *De Apostolatu laicorum* and the *De divina Revelatione*: a great text which provides theology with THE MEANS of becoming fully evangelical. The Pope made a speech[1] in which he did not speak about these texts, but spoke, in a fairly developed fashion, about what will come after the Council. He also announced a Jubilee Year, and the opening of the beatification process for Pius XII and John XXIII. This announcement saddened me. Why this glorification of popes by their successors? Are we never, then, to get out of the old Roman habits? At the moment when *aggiornamento* is announced, things are done that do not accord with it.

At 4.30 pm, *Viale Romania*, for the *expensio modorum* for *De Presbyteris*. Onclin was glowing. He was one of the experts called to concelebrate with the Pope (along with Courtney Murray, Lubac, Pavan, Feiner, Medina, Schmaus, who, even so, did not write a single line of a conciliar text! Fr Benoit was designated, but he has already left Rome). Onclin was appointed second secretary of the Commission charged with the revision of the Code: the first TRULY GOOD news for the period after the Council. This will oblige him to spend ten days of each month in Rome, but that is an excellent thing for the general good, and for the preservation of the spirit of the Council. After 8.45 pm, further work on the *modi*.

---

1. *AS* IV/VI, 689–695.

Friday 19 November 1965

I got up early [I always sleep too little these days; I have difficulty in getting to sleep], work on the *modi* until 8.00 am. At 8.00 am, Stransky picked me up to take me to Ariccia, where there is a meeting at present of the Joint Committee of the World Council of Churches and the Roman Catholic Church.[1] The day was to be devoted to 'dialogue'. I was pleased to meet some old friends again: Visser't Hooft, Oliver Tomkins[2] (plus Nissiotis, Borovoj, etc). The morning was somewhat disappointing. Nothing precise. Confused interventions from Nissiotis, Borovoj. This vagueness of the conversation aggravated my headache.

Fr Verghese said to me: two days ago an expert from the Commission on Missions said to me: 'We have put Fr Congar back in his place'.

During our 'work'(?) the Fathers voted on the *De libertate religiosa*. On this subject I was told:

1) There was an intervention with the Pope from the *Coetus internationalis Patrum*, asking that the *De libertate* be crossed off the order of the day. The reason was: the text ignores the magisterium, and so undermines in advance the authority that belongs to it; it derives from conciliarism. The text will raise many and serious difficulties.

2) After the *expensio modorum* by the Secretariat, the Pope proposed some *modi*, one or another of which have got into the text. But the Secretariat rejected those that would have ruined the text, in particular, the one that said: '*[Ecclesia] indulgens moribus modernis*' [{The Church} making allowance for modern customs]. This would in effect lower the text to the level of timeliness, and even of a rather lax indulgence.

The Pope did not insist.

What will he do? I learned at 12.30 pm, by telephone, that the first vote this morning produced 246 *Non placet*. I wondered if some of the Fathers of the minority would not do what had been done by those at Vatican I: leave Rome before the last public session in order not to vote against texts they disliked and which, nevertheless, were going to be passed: *De libertate* and schema XIII.

Meeting of a restricted group at 2.30 pm; and then the whole group at 3.30 pm.

Willebrands has returned to Rome. I realised more clearly this evening what it is he brings to a meeting by means of his calm, his attention, his concrete and precise mind: that kind of gracious welcome and prudence that he has. However, the discussion reminded me of those at the beginning of schema XIII: subtleties

---

1. The second meeting of the Joint Working Group of the Roman Catholic Church and the WCC took place at Ariccia from 17 to 20 November 1965.
2. Anglican Bishop of Bristol, he was President of the Executive Committee of the Faith and Order Commission of the WCC.

and vagueness. Wouldn't that stem from the very nature of work that is to be done by a group that is not homogeneous? Schema XIII made me better understand that it is never easy to determine the relations between the Church and the temporal sphere. Here, one is among Christians, who are nevertheless different, and on ground that is Christian, but points to worlds of a different structure. Nothing is simple, everything is multilateral and must be considered and nuanced very closely.

For the whole of the rest of the evening there was a violent storm. Despite difficulties to do with the car, I got back at 8.10 pm. Work.

I note down here two or three details I learnt in the past few days.

Mgr Garrone said to Mgr Marty: Pay attention to this or that in the *De Presbyteris:* those who drafted it are members of religious orders. . . At bottom, the bishops do not have 100% confidence in us. And yet, without the religious, what experts would there be, and, without the experts, what work would they have done?

That hurt me, just when I am tiring myself out beyond measure on the *De Presbyteris*.

A few days ago, perhaps a week, Felici declared *in aula*, that the lectures given at *Domus Mariae*, under the aegis of the Brazilian bishops, had only a purely private character (which goes without saying), and that everything that was said there was not equally indisputable.[1] A curious declaration. Some Brazilian bishops protested. Felici replied that he had made this declaration under orders. Fr Baraúna told me that this referred in particular to a lecture by Fr Schillebeeckx on marriage, unless it was on the question of transubstantiation.[2] Poor Fr Schillebeeckx does not have a chance: in Rome he is dogged by suspicion and persistent critics.

Baraúna also told me that Fr D van den Eynde, with whom he lives, worked on the drafting of the encyclical *Mysterium fidei*.

Saturday 20 November 1965

I got up early to get down to work on the *modi*, without stopping until 4.00 pm, except for brief visits from Fr Peuchmaurd, and a Polish journalist from *Znak*[3] (he told me: the Polish bishops have distanced themselves from the others in the context of the Council. That is true enough. The Poles are always a people apart, with whom it is difficult to get on: they have their own ideas and do not seek to get on with anyone, except for some individuals), and the president of *la Table ronde*. I would never have believed that this work on the *modi* would be so hard. It is

---

1. Felici intervened on 12 November; cf: *AS* IV/VI, 341.
2. Schillebeeckx had given a lecture on 9 November at the *Domus Mariae* on the encyclical *Mysterium Fidei* under the title: 'Transubstantiation, transignification, transfinalisation'.
3. A journal published in Cracow by the Znak movement, which brought together Polish Catholic intellectuals, and which has friendly links with Wojtyła.

VERY hard. I am working on some Numbers that I did not draft, with the result that, for the least thing, I have to read the whole paragraph very attentively. But I want to do this work very conscientiously. It is important. Sometimes, even, I am almost a little afraid: am I capable of deciding, for the whole Church, and for the holy, catholic priesthood, this or that delicate point? I do my utmost, and even a little more than that. This evening I cannot stand up, and then I find it difficult to speak, because of tiredness.

At 4.30 pm, at Onclin's, for more of this work. And it isn't finished! Onclin is beaming, if not even a little thrilled. This morning there was an audience for the members of the Commission for the revision of the Code. The Pope, it appears, spoke in a remarkable way. He said a few words to each one. To Onclin he said: We have concelebrated. Now we must work together, and really hard. I shall see you again soon, and often.

I am pleased, both that the Pope has chosen Onclin, that he has shown this confidence in him, and that the Pope has linked working together with concelebration. I believe that, in his mind, this comes from a profound conviction.

In all these recent days I have not had time either to recite the whole of my breviary, nor to READ the correspondence that has arrived, and still there is some! I have not stopped for a second.

Sunday 21 November 1965

Last year this was the end. Still another eighteen days!

A certain number of *modi* for the *De Presbyteris* came from the French workshop. They can be recognised at twenty paces. They are missionary, pious, well-intentioned, not always rigorous. The French seem incapable—but they are not the only ones—of getting beyond their own particular horizon—and rising to a truly general view. I do not know why Mgr Vilnet was introduced into the work at one point by Mgr Marty; both of them are rather dependent on Frisque. Mgr Vilnet did not know what conciliar work is. He took very little notice of the previous text, drafting some whole paragraphs anew. These paragraphs are undeniably slanted in a particular direction: sanctification through ministry, with little insistence on personal effort of the ascetic or moral type. Some *modi* make complaints, with a good deal of exaggeration, moreover. The Germans (Fr Wulf) have been, in their own way and on their own lines, just as particularist. Through Döpfner, Fr Wulf had wanted his ideas and, for example, a distinction between holiness, acquired absolutely at baptism through the action of Christ, and perfection, to which a person inclines by his or her own efforts, to be put in all over the place.

In the morning: Correspondence! Correspondence! At least ten letters. I am so much behind!!! At 10.00 am, at Viale Romania, for the *modi* for the *De Presbyteris*, which, decidedly, are taking up much more time and demanding much more effort than I would ever have imagined. If a work really is worth what it costs, this one must be of great value. But, on the whole, the cause is worth this effort.

There were very nearly 9,700 *modi* for the *De Presbyteris*, some of them, undoubtedly, repeating others.

The work is almost finished at the level of our small sub-commission (Onclin, Lécuyer, del Portillo, Herranz, myself). I shall not go either to the very last meeting of this sub-commission, or to the two meetings of the Commission. Thus, for me, at 1.00 pm today, the Council finished . . .

It was apparent to us again this morning how the introduction of Mgr Vilnet into the work has not been altogether happy. He considered that the work had to start again from square one, he has taken practically no account of the *textus prior* [previous text]; he had expressed HIS ideas or those of his friends (Frisque, Denis to some extent), he significantly changed the style and general orientation of the text. It appears that he frequently asked to come to our sub-commission for the *expensio modorum*, and even wanted to be invited to the Commission. Now, I have nothing against him personally, on the contrary, he seems to me to have very great quality, but I have [little] appreciation for his work, so very 'French' in character, and I am astounded that Mgr Marty should have brought him on board in this way.

In yesterday's *L'Osservatore Romano*, the text of the Pope's speech at the audience last Wednesday. In it, he quoted my *Mystère du Temple*.[1]

In the afternoon, more correspondence, and I went back to my article for *CCIF*, three times interrupted, three times taken up again: it will be a wretched text!

I have been told that the Pope is preparing an encyclical on priesthood. Haubtmann told me that among the *modi* for schema XIII, there are 220 requests for the condemnation of communism. (In fact, there are 220 + 110 of them = 330: see the booklets of *modi ad No. 20*, but the second series largely reproduces the first: Mgr Garrrone assured me that the score was 330.) So that represents the real number, lower than the number given by the right-wing press, which is campaigning for the Council to pronounce a solemn and categorical condemnation. Among them, Carli.

This evening, a lecture on the priesthood at the Belgian College. Mgr De Smedt is very optimistic about the religious freedom document. All the people he has met are delighted with it. I saw Moeller and Prignon only briefly. It seems a long time ago that I was a member of the house and was looked upon as such. I spent some good times there.

Monday 22 November 1965

I am not going to any more of the meetings planned for the *modi* for priests. So I have the feeling that, for me, the Council is finished! One never knows. Cardinal

---

1. *Le Mystère du Temple, ou l'Économie de la Présence de Dieu à sa créature de la Genèse à l'Apocalypse*, Lectio Divina (Paris: Cerf 1958).

Browne, it appears, is profoundly dissatisfied that the priest is not being defined by the celebration of the Eucharist and he wants to warn the Pope.

Correspondence; I am carrying on, somehow, with the article for *CCIF.* Telephone-calls, invitations to Padua, to the USA again, etc. But how good it is to have a few hours for work by oneself!

This evening, at 8.00 pm, l'abbé Heidsieck[1] took me to dinner at Sencourt's place: other guests included the permanent representative of Canterbury[2] and his wife (Russian by origin and Orthodox) and a Scottish priest. Nothing of note, except an incredible apartment and draughts. What Rome can be, made of shacks and of old, patched-up palaces!

Tuesday 23 November 1965

Correction of proofs (I have a heap of them!) and preparation for my lectures.

The French bishops are having their plenary meeting at this time. Everything is being arranged. Etchegaray told me yesterday that the work to which he is dedicated is bearing fruit. Every Friday he has brought together delegates from the bishops' conferences to take stock, and to some extent to arrange the positions to be adopted. Now, it was agreed yesterday that cooperation would be organised between the episcopal conferences of Europe, including Poland and the People's Democracies.

The French bishops had their collective pontifical audience yesterday. The Pope gave them the impression of being very relaxed. For him, too, the end is in sight! It is not the first time in recent weeks that people who have got close to the Pope have reported the impression of a relaxed and calm Paul VI. Even the 246 negative votes for the *De libertate* do not seem to disturb him. He congratulated Cardinal Bea on the positive vote last Friday. But he is going to be the object of repeated approaches and pressures . . .

I have agreed to give a lecture to the Salesians. But neither they nor anyone else has the least idea what my life is like and what five minutes means to me. They came to collect me at 12 noon, instead of 12.30; three quarters of an hour was wasted before the meal in very cold draughts; I did not get back until 5.45 pm. Certainly, they were charming, they have a fine and very worthy group of young people, they have built an immense and magnificent university with five faculties (philosophy, theology, law, religious education and advanced Latin): very grand buildings with windows that are too large for a sunny climate. But who finances, who will maintain all that? But they should realise that they have asked too much of me in terms of time. It is the same people who are constantly asking me: 'What are you working on at the moment?', 'When will your commentary on *Lumen Gentium* appear?' who prevent me from working.

---

1. Patrick Heidsieck, of the diocese of Rheims, worked on the Catholic Committee for French Friendships Worldwide.
2. At the time, this was Canon Findlow, but Congar is doubtless referring to Canon Pawley, whose wife Margaret was Orthodox and of Russian origin.

Besides, my current work is: correction of the proofs of the Baraúna volume.

Departure from Rome, Ciampino, 8.10 pm. A view of the city: the streets and avenues picked out by lights: the Earth of human beings!

Brief stop at Forli. Afterwards, we saw on the right the Adriatic coast marked by a continuous, curving line of light. Soon Venice, the quays and lagoons.

Cold. It snowed today in Treviso and in Venice.

The seminary: Formerly the Dominican Priory. Calm, and a more lively atmosphere: what a change from Rome!

A very friendly welcome.

Wednesday 24 November 1965

I celebrated Mass for the seminarians. Except for a very few, they were not in cassocks. Not a very handsome physical type: spotty faces, big noses, sometimes reddish hair, not many faces that reflected an alert and intelligent adolescence. I said a few words after the Gospel. After Communion they sang the *Magnificat* in Italian, to a slightly altered Gelineau tone.[1] But after every second verse there was a refrain celebrating 'Mary, Queen of the world'. What a betrayal of this wonderful text!!!

Since yesterday evening the question has been asked: what shall I talk about, and in what language??? They insist that I speak in French: they do not understand Latin, and I sensed an aversion to it. When I was with the bishop, it was envisaged that my article 'Chiesa e Mundo' [Church and World][2] would be read out. But a READING OUT does not appeal to me, as I believe in speaking directly, and I fear that that article might be too theoretical for priests directly engaged in ministry. I decided *in extremis* [at the last minute] to prepare a synthesis on the priesthood and to speak in Latin.

It went well. Three hundred and eighty priests.

On the return journey, a quick visit to the church of St Nicholas, our former church, begun in 1231: an immense nave, an immense auditorium for preaching: a church of the Dominicans of Colmar, of the same dimensions and the same rose-red bricks as the Jacobins of Toulouse. What inspiration that suggests there was in those first generations of Dominicans!

The priory is almost intact. In the former chapter house, the motif depicted and tirelessly repeated, is that of study and writing. Is it original? There we find the famous St Albert the Great at his desk, wearing a mitre. What life had this priory sheltered? This chapter house? What had been said here? If only these walls had recorded, and could reproduce the images and sounds of the past!!!

---

1. Joseph Gelineau, SJ, musicologist, composer of liturgical chants, and especially of psalm tones for the *Psautier de la Bible de Jérusalem*, which were adapted to several languages.

2. Cf above page 698, note 8.

Lunch with the bishop and the THIRTY-FIVE professors of the major and minor seminaries (for which there is only the one administration). Work: but some sort of muffled motor which apparently feeds the water-storage tank, had an irresistibly soporific effect on me. Never mind, I shall have a rest during these twenty-four hours in Treviso. The atmosphere is good, and here there is neither the stench nor the din of the streets of Rome, dreadful city! Something is going wrong with my hearing. Often I have, all at once, or simultaneously, the sensation of an echoing void (of no longer hearing anything) AND a sensitivity such that sounds irritate me and tire me out, in short, they distress me to an abnormal degree. I have noticed this for a long time, but it has become much more marked since 11 November this year.

After supper a short exposition with questions, for the professors, on ecumenism.

Thursday 25 November 1965
Anniversary of Tere's death.

I celebrated Mass for the seminarians; a short homily. At 9.00 am, a sort of course for theologians and teachers; they asked me all sorts of questions. Even some of the professors, afterwards. They told me that some years ago the bishop [of Treviso][1] had secured a condemnation of them from the Congregation of Seminaries for their French sympathies, naturalism and activism. . . French authors, including Congar, were banned. I said: But then, why has the same bishop invited me to come and handed over to me his clergy and his seminary? —The reply: because now you are on top! This explains for me some words the bishop said yesterday in front of his clergy: he professed to have altered some of his ideas as a result of the Council, to have come to understand a number of things.

Lunch at the College of St Pius X. Questions (on Teilhard, etc). The bishop, with rather exaggerated insistence, alluded to my cardinalate, which will be so well deserved. God preserve me from it! It was during my stay in Rome at the end of January and beginning of February that I was told about this for the first time as a current rumour. Since then, it has been mentioned to me several times. It is something I do not want to think about.

Train to Mestre (at 3.00 pm) for Milan. From Padua to Verona, snow in the fields, the sky—hues of a Breughel. Falchi met me at Milan with Fr Favaro[2] and another: friends. They took me to the Hotel Continental: not super-luxurious, but luxurious for me: a room with *en suite*. I had supper. At the tables were young people, or young couples, or even older men with wives who had a rather dazed appearance, their fingers covered with rings, their nails varnished. What a bunch! A sense of idleness. It is true that the service was impeccable, and everything was designed for relaxation in the Anglo-American style, one really was able to

---

1. A Mistrorigo.
2. Arcangelo Favaro, SJ, Director of the San Fedele Cultural Centre in Milan.

relax. Businessmen have some chance of delaying the onset of their coronaries. But I prefer our bare cells, our floors without carpets, our meals without excess. Tremendous male service. The lift-boy told me he would be there until 2.00 am.

I thought about Tere, whose anniversary it is, of her infinite poverty. That is the way I try to follow in my own fashion, but without that absoluteness of pure interiority and of total gift.

Lecture at 9.15 pm. It did not go too badly in its own way; average nevertheless. Back to the hotel at 11.45 pm.

Friday 26 November 1965

Chenu arrived two days ago to speak at the University; Lubac is to follow me tomorrow at San Fedele. So the turn and the conversion to these 'French' ideas, that some people dread so much, is under way.

Mass at San Fedele. A little—very little!—work in the stifling atmosphere of this hotel with under-floor heating. Writing the article 'Enfances ardennaises'[1] [childhoods in the Ardennes] and correction of the Baraúna proofs.

Lunch at the Dominican priory: fat Dominicans with bulging stomachs coming down the stairs swinging their arms. The Fr Prior,[2] who made an EXCELLENT impression on me, gave a sort of toast in my honour that was very fraternal, and, at bottom, truly in the spirit of a Friar Preacher. But at table the opening speech of Fr Fernandez at the last General Chapter was being read: a wholly abstract and analytical scholasticism, with a clear distinction between natural and supernatural, an invitation to 'supernatural' motives and means . . . Something that was, for me, insupportable, and rather empty. Why not just speak the language of the Gospel and St Paul. It is so much more manly and more true!

I visited the four cloisters of the priory, restored after the war, because everything had suffered greatly from the American bombardments. And especially the church, Our Lady of Graces. I have seldom seen two such different styles of architecture harmonised in this way. The nave is Lombardy Gothic: peaceful and calming, humble and glorious at the same time. From the back, one can see the altar but one does not realise that it is situated beneath Bramante's cupola. As one approaches it one finds oneself in a different space, under a different style of architecture. There one can see clearly how the cupola represented an extraordinary conquest of space. One really has the impression that cosmic space has been taken up and crowned, that from now on it is included within human architecture.

A moment of work. I spoke a little with the Fathers, especially with the Prior and Casati.[3] From what I have been told elsewhere, they are outside the main

---

1. 'Enfances ardennaises', *La Grive*, October–December 1965: 14–16.
2. Giordano Ghini.
3. Innocenzo Casati, OP, of the Province of Lombardy, who defended a thesis on Fénelon at Le Saulchoir in 1940.

current of affairs. They carry out the Church's classical ministry and occasional preaching; they are not involved in the life of this university town (two universities and two big technical colleges of university level). St Dominic had chosen the university towns, above all Paris and Bologna, the two cerebral hemispheres of the Christian world . . . My Milanese brothers are worried about the problems that could arise for simple folk from a presentation of the Council as reform and novelty in an overly simplistic way: before, after . . . I am very well aware of the genuine ground for their anxiety. On the other hand, I do not think my confrères are sufficiently aware of the quite remarkably new or renewed things brought in by the great texts *Lumen gentium, De divina Revelatione,* etc.

At 4.00 pm, I left by car (with Mgr Sarkissian,[1] who had just arrived from London. He told me that the Armenian Catholicos who had died recently[2] had heard me in Aleppo in January 1954:[3] he often recalled it. It had been decisive for his own ecumenical orientation) for the meeting of the Academic Committee of the Jerusalem Foundation dedicated to the history of salvation desired by the Holy Father, with which Fr Hesburgh is involved—as also, very actively, are C Moeller and Fr Duprey. The meeting took place at Bellagio, in the Villa Serbelloni, at the junction of two branches of Lake Como. At this close of an evening in winter the lake could be made out, somewhat obscured by the fog: at the foot of the coast road were the lights that traced the contours of the great sheet of water.

The villa, which now belongs to the Rockerfeller Foundation, is a former palace of the beginning of the seventeenth century, old furniture, tapestries everywhere, carpets, mirrors, and yet, modern comforts. I was a bit ashamed, as a religious vowed to poverty and, indeed, a faithful old companion of it, to find myself in these conditions of luxury. But in this case, IT SERVES A PURPOSE.

I went down for the preprandial drinks at 6.45 pm, in order to meet the others; I found Fr Georges Florovsky,[4] very much aged and shrunken . . . I learnt a number of things which I note down here:

From Medina. The sub-commission for schema XIII on marriage has received (I believe three) *modi* from the Pope, with an almost threatening letter from the Secretariat of State. One of these *modi* excluded all usage of contraceptives. It seems that that came from Mgr Colombo. It seemed that these *modi* could not

---

1. Karekin Sarkissian, superior of the seminary at Antelias (Lebanon), was an Observer delegated by the Catholicosate of Cilicia (Apostolic Armenian Church); he was later to become Catholicos of Etchmiazin, under the name of Karekin I.
2. Zareh I Payaslian, Catholicos of Cilicia, died in 1963.
3. Congar had done a lecture tour in January 1954 in the context of the week of prayer for Christian unity; Zareh Payaslian had been Archbishop of Aleppo, before he was elected Catholicos.
4. Georges Florovsky, Russian Orthodox theologian, had taught at the Orthodox Institute of St Sergius in Paris, then in the United States from 1948; at this time he was professor at Princeton (New Jersey).

even be DISCUSSED. Two cardinals (doubtless Léger and Roy) went immediately to see the Pope, with the Mexican couple who are Auditors.[1] However, it had later been allowed that these *modi* could be discussed. No doubt they have been discussed even today. (Cardinal Léger had prepared a paper, and he read it in a silence in which you could have heard a pin drop. He said: something that had not been discussed at the Council could not be introduced by a simple *modus*.) —Medina told me that, in May, the question had been put to the Pontifical Commission on birth-control: must the teaching of Pius XI and Pius XII on this subject be considered irreformable? Twelve theologians out of eighteen replied: it is reformable.[2]

Medina told me that the tactic settled on by those drafting this part of schema XIII (Heylen) was: to accept the *modi* of the Pope, but to express them in such a way that they said nothing.

Cullmann told me that he greatly regretted that Skydsgaard was not there. He did not want to come (even though he was, in part, father of the idea) because Geneva is reticent with regard to the project, fearing competition . . . Indeed it seems that, as fas as Geneva is concerned, it alone has the initiative in ecumenical matters . . .

Schlink, though, would have come, but he has a touch of flu. Fr Benoit is ill and in hospital in Jerusalem . . .

Cullmann told me that the Pope would have liked to have a service of prayer with the Observers. But several people had raised difficulties, and the idea had has had to be abandoned. There will be only a reception at the end of the Session.

Fr Duprey told me that a document is being finalised that will remove the obstacle caused by what happened in 1054. With regard to the plan for the Jerusalem foundation, they are waiting for King Hussein to give his agreement to a transfer of property.

After the aperitifs, an interminable supper, with the service and the menu of a great hotel: the Rockerfeller Foundation is paying for it.

After supper, coffee and alcohol (the American regime!) in this obviously very agreeable historic and princely setting.

Then the first meeting. Fr Hesburgh (who unfortunately made no effort at pronunciation that would make him intelligible to all) gave an account of the history of the idea, and the different stages accomplished so far. I note down simply what he said about the long audience that the Pope had granted him at the beginning. The Pope had said that he wanted to do something, wanted to do everything (in the order of the possible) for the unity of Christians. He had been very impressed by two things: 1) the Observers, their religious bearing; 2) Jerusalem. Jerusalem is for all, it is there that the place of encounter should be . . . The foundation must on

---

1. Señor and Señora José Alvarez Icaza, founders in Mexico of the Christian Family Movement.
2. The fact is confirmed by Pierre de Locht, *Les couples et l'Église. Chronique d'un témoin* (Centurion, 1979), 153; however, that deals with the session of March 1965.

no account be a foundation of the Curia; the Pope confided it to the Federation of Catholic Universities. It must remain entirely a university responsibility. Its link with the Holy See would not be made by a Roman Congregation (that would have been the Congregation of Pizzardo and Staffa!!!), but through the intermediary of the Secretariat for Unity.

We ran through the list of those present. Alas! Many of the Orthodox were missing. I regret this profoundly. I am afraid that a start made without them will bring about problems afterwards. But what could be done?

Sunday 27 November 1965

A concelebrated mass (nine priests) in the parish church. Unfortunately, the sky is cloudy; mist; nothing could be seen of the countryside, which could just be made out, and which must be extraordinarily beautiful.

Meeting at 9.00 am. After a brief introduction by Hesburgh, each one was invited to express his reactions. I noted down only a few points.

The Americans asked above all practical questions: who will finance it, who will come, what will be the specific character of the new foundation in comparison with institutes and faculties that already exist? They made no allusion to the decisive theme of the history of salvation, which does not seem to enter into their categories. The question was raised (by the Easterners) of union with the concrete life of ecclesial communities; Medina raised that of the style of simplicity and of poverty that is particularly necessary in Jerusalem.

All were agreed about the necessary independence with respect to one Church or another, even in the matter of financial resources. However, Howard[1] strongly expressed his conviction: that reference to the initiative of the HOLY FATHER should be preserved, because this gave the project a major part of its worth and its specific character.

For my part, I insisted, backed up later by Feiner, on the specificity and strength that the proposed objective has of itself: the study of the history of salvation, and of everything else in the light of it. I will hand in a written and more developed note to recall what I said, or wanted to say.

At 3.00 pm, resumption and conclusion of comments. Cullmann spoke of the hesitation of certain Protestants, who see in the project simply a tactic of Catholics; the fact that the money is coming from Catholic universities confirms them in their fear of a kind of stranglehold. There would have to be a permanent joint secretariat in Jerusalem.

Cullmann also found the suggested title too vague and general. He moved on to give, once again, his course on 'the history of salvation'.

Kelly[2] spoke with a conviction and a fervour that were impressive. He got stuck into these Protestant hesitations and criticisms. In two years, he said, the

---

1. Howard E Root, Professor of Theology at Cambridge, where he was the Dean of Emmanuel College, was an Observer delegated by the Anglican Communion.
2. The Anglican patrologist, John ND Kelly, was Principal of St Edmund's Hall, Oxford, and deputy Vice-Chancellor of the University of Oxford.

Roman Catholic Church has moved an immense distance: 'We have done nothing comparable'. The Protestant side knows only how to be suspicious, but would be incapable of doing as much as this!

Mgr Sarkissian, with great precision and delicacy, made two comments: 1) thought must be given to relationships with the local churches: just as one cannot separate a theological activity that would be wholly academic from the life of the Church. It is necessary to take account of the delicate situations and the susceptibilities that are peculiar to this corner of the earth; 2) It is desirable to enter into relations with the Jews on the other side of the armistice line.

Fr Duprey gave some details about the approaches made to the local religious authorities and to the Orthodox. Patriarch Benediktos[1] seemed to view the project with all the more favour, since he hoped that the advent of Orthodox professors would give him some opportunities to offer his clergy some degree of theological formation, the absence of which he deplored.

After tea, there was discussion, especially of questions about the statute: two-and-a-half hours that were very difficult for me. On the one hand, so many trifling details and waste of time. On the other hand, the manner in which Fr Hesburh 'spoke' was extremely trying for me. He does not open either his lips or his teeth, so that one hears a hoarse, inarticulate sound from his throat, on top of a heavy soporific tone. My malady makes my ears more and more sensitive. The noise of an engine or strident sound, or the raised tone of an over-enthusiastic conversation in a place that resonates, really makes me suffer. Thus I have developed an excessive sensibility and jumpiness. I can't stand noise, or certain sounds—while silence or moderated tones are agreeable to me.

Immediately after supper, a meeting until 10.25 pm. The liturgical aspect of the foundation was discussed, amongst other things: the proposed group of monks (from Montserrat),[2] and perhaps some brothers from Taizé. Fr Hesburgh said how the Holy Father had welcomed this idea, saying: We do not at present have a form of prayer in common with the Others. Perhaps the Institute will be the place and the means for creating such forms?

Following on from an intervention by Outler, the question of the future director of the Institute was raised. Moeller's name was proposed. Each one was then asked to say what he thought. Since Moeller was in the room next door with two or three others drafting the communiqué, we discussed him in exactly the same way as we discuss a candidate in the *tractatus* [discussions] that precede our Dominican elections. For an hour I was party there to something extraordinary, even of a moving nobility. An overwhelming unanimity became apparent. Each one eulogised Moeller, it turned out that he had been for all and for each like a personal friend, that he had been deeply immersed in the life of the Council, and

---

1. The Greek Orthodox Patriarch of Jerusalem.
2. The Benedictine Abbey of Montserrat (Spain).

in everything that happened in connection with it from the ecumenical point of view.

I saw then, in an instant, how a destiny is shaped. It seemed to me—it even seemed like a physical impression—that one was the human instrument of Providence, in deciding a person's life according to the realisation of the plan of God. One was conscious of what one would be imposing on Moeller by way of sacrifice: Louvain has been his life. But 'the Master is here and is calling you'. It seemed to me that Dom Lambert Bauduin, of whom Moeller is the spiritual son [he wears his watch and told me: it is always fast!], carries on the work started at Amay and at Chevetogne.

Mgr Leclercq put forward an interesting proposition: it is too early to name now a director for something that does not yet exist. On the other hand it is normal for the future director to oversee the maturation of the project, the development of the programme, the construction of buildings, the appointment of the initial team. Moeller could be given a temporary mission with a view to the definitive formation of the Institute. That is what was accepted.

Sunday 28 November 1965

This morning, the lake and the mountains were visible. The sun rose behind them and reddened the clouds from the East. Peace arose from that sheet of water in which the whole of earthly creation was mirrored.

Concelebration at 8.00 am, with a parish congregation. A mixture of deep faith and piety and unacceptable forms of devotion. The priest gave out the notices in Italian while Moeller read the preface in Latin! At communion a dreadfully sentimental hymn set to insanely vulgar and jejune music! As soon as Mass was finished, exposition of the Blessed Sacrament. But in all this, the deep faith of the people.

Discussion was resumed at 9.30 am.

Some practical questions: two meetings were arranged: 30–31 May and 4–6 September 1966 (in Jerusalem); the communiqué.

Mgr Colombo arrived at 11.00 am. Hesburgh spoke of what had been said yesterday evening about Moeller: the referendum of yesterday evening was repeated in a few minutes. Cullmann said: there are some hesitations on the Protestant side; Moeller is the man whose name alone would be a guarantee for them and would facilitate their acceptance of the idea. —Moeller said he would accept but asked for the help of an executive committee: presuming he will have the agreement of his bishop and of his Rector.

Before dinner, the director's wife took me by car up the hill which forms the park of the Villa Serbelloni, and right to the top. It was an extraordinarily beautiful view of both arms of the lake.

I saw Moeller for a moment.

At dinner, I was seated between Hesburgh and Colombo. The latter told me some interesting details, which I note down here:

1) The *modi* about marriage in schema XIII. Their intention was not doctrinal but pastoral. The Pontifical Commission must be left with all its liberty, without being subjected to pressure. But, TO BE SILENT about methods of birth control was to allow it to be understood that the position adopted by Pius XI and Pius XII was being changed. IT MUST BE SAID THAT NOTHING IS CHANGED. [I must say that this does not please me, nor does it greatly set my mind at rest. . .]

2) On the subject of religious freedom. The Pope is deeply delighted at the results of the votes. He thinks that the majority is more than sufficient to allow one to say that THE CHURCH is truly committed. Colombo seems to espouse the idea of Willebrands and De Smedt: if anything, opposition justifies the text!

3) The Pope reads a great deal, but recently he has made a point of reading those who think differently from himself: in order to make calm and fully informed decisions, having overcome the objections. Last year he read Billot[1] and Siri in this way; this year, some critics of religious freedom. Colombo greatly insists on the need to take decisions, or to inform oneself, in a calm and serene atmosphere, and so with sufficient maturity.

4) Reform of the Curia: this will come; there will be an end to Pizzardo. One thing is certain: the appointments will be temporary.

5) From time to time the Pope sends books to Ottaviani to lead him towards better ideas. The first book he sent him in this way was Mouroux, *Sens chrétien de l'homme*.[2]

Colombo told me that there was much mirth in the Joint Commission when, after someone asked why *'Malignus'* [Malign] was written with a capital letter, Ottaviani replied *'Propter Reverentiam'* [Out of Reverence], while laughing himself.

Departure at 2.20 pm (someone came from Brescia to collect me). The road ran along the side of the lake. We went through Bergamo Basso. I was offered the chance of a detour through Sotto il Monte, the village where John XXIII was born; but I was told that my lecture had been brought forward an hour, and fixed for 5.00 pm. I had not the time and I declined.

Brescia. The Oratory, where Paul VI received his early education. A lecture on schema XIII. Quite a good public, very attentive. It went, I think, quite well. Some open and sympathetic faces.

Afterwards, until supper, correction of proofs.

Supper with the Oratorian Fathers. The graces were said any old how, such that it would have been better if they had not been said at all. Several of them had known Paul VI well, but Bevilacqua (whom they said I resembled in the face) was not there. I would have liked to have met him.

The Fathers present each had their own job and did not seem very interested in what goes on in my poor life.

---

1. Louis Billot, SJ (1846–1931), Professor of Dogmatic Theology at the Gregorianum University; valued by Pius X, who created him cardinal; he resigned after the condemnation of *Action française* by Pius XI.

2. Jean Mouroux, *Sens chrétien de l'homme* (Paris: Aubier, 1945).

Monday 29 November 1965

Got up at 5.50 am. Mass; departure at 7.15 am. The reason is, Milan is often very much covered by fog, and Alitalia requires one to come an hour early, not to the airport, but to Aria Termini (the station), because they do not know in advance which of the three possible airports will be useable and in fact in use.

The dawn rose behind us, gradually invading a very clear and luminous sky; on the right the first mountains, dominated by a line of snow-covered ridges and peaks. As we got closer to Milan the industrial concentration became greater: chimneys belched out reddish or off-white clouds of smoke, spreading over everything a great stench of cement, zinc and chemical products. The inhabitants of the city are expected, indeed obliged, to inhale all this. Tower blocks ten storeys high follow one other, more and more tightly packed, traffic becomes impossible, the people rush about. This is the city!!! The modern city, the lodging machine, the slaves' quarters . . .

We reached Termini at 8.30 am; we did not leave by coach until 9.20 am. . .

At Fiumicino, Mlle Stevens and Mlle Guillou were waiting for me. It seems that the latter will become my secretary.

At the French Seminary at 12.20 pm: the porter told me: Mgr Marty is here waiting for you. In fact this is the day for the lunch previously arranged for the sub-commission for the *De Presbyteris:* Mgr Marty, Mgr Mazerat, Onclin, Lécuyer, del Portillo, Herranz and myself. A pleasant lunch, but they did not know anything and did not tell me anything interesting. Onclin was in very good form. He has, one hundred per cent, that Belgian combination of practical sense and scientific competence, together with perfect health!

I returned to my room at 3.30 pm. An enormous amount of correspondence; and, already, telephone calls, reporters . . . This too, is THE MODERN CITY!!!

Supper: I took a certain pleasure in realising that the bishops had noticed my absence and welcomed my return with friendly interest, and even affection.

Tuesday 30 November 1965

Worked on finalising some articles (with Mlle Guillou); correspondence. I offered my services to Haubtmann for the correction of the proofs of the *expensio modorum* for schema XIII. He accepted. So I got down to this.

I saw the Fr Superior of the Seminary.[1] He told me from a direct source that the seminaries financially and administratively dependent on the Congregation for Seminaries and Universities have been banned from teaching collegiality.

This afternoon, at 2.05 pm, a visit from an editor of *Razón y Fe:*[2] he wanted me to work on a Spanish commentary on *Lumen Gentium:* impossible!

---

1. Roland Barq.
2. A Spanish monthly, edited by the Jesuits.

At 2.15 pm, a visit from Fr Matías García,[1] who spoke to me about his thesis on the unity of the human race according to Staudenmaier,[2] and of a plan for a thesis on the theological foundations of politics.

At 3.00 pm a visit from two Polish journalists from *Znak.*

At 3.40 pm, departure for the meeting organised by Küng, in Viale Romania. Present were: Mgr Elchinger, Mejía, Ochagavía[3] Schillebeeckx, Laurentin, G Baum, Féret, a priest from Bologna, and the one who wrote about Fr Sarpi, Ratzinger, myself and Küng. The purpose: to anticipate theologically, in some way, the period after the Council, and to draw up a little appraisal.

Interesting and congenial. Laurentin presented a very solid picture of the schemas, but he made notes of what the others said and asked questions: one will find all that in his articles and his book . . . Schillebeeckx and Ratzinger made some relevant and subtle comments, as did the priest from Bologna (from the Dossetti group), but Küng is always very radical. He says some true things, but in which the critical research into what is true is not sufficiently tempered by concern for concrete situations. —The discussion was resumed after supper.

Wednesday 1 December 1965

For midday today, an invitation to the Spanish Embassy: impossible, Father General is gathering the experts for a concelebration with him, and for lunch. There is no way I could not go to it. This afternoon and evening, Fr Schütte wants to gather the Commission on Missions at Nemi, to celebrate yesterday's vote on the schema. But I am invited, this evening, to the Taizé Brothers. Lunches everywhere, a life far removed from the peaceful setting of the cell in which one works . . . Even settling all this by telephone takes quite a lot of time!

In the morning: correspondence, correspondence, correspondence!

At 11.30 am, arrival of Fr Bro, with whom, from 4.00 pm until 7.00 pm, we clarified the plans for the publication of conciliar texts, beginning with Peuchmaurd. Frisque arrived just in time to work out with him the principal axes of the volumes on priests and their formation. He is to see H Denis as soon as possible, and together they will work out a more precise plan on this basis.

At 8.00 pm, (with Fr Bro) at the Taizé Brothers' place. I did not feel at ease with Br Roger Schutz because, although he never stops talking about dialogue and listening to others, at the same time he never stops expressing and asserting himself. He is a man of God, but, this evening I found him trying.

Thursday 2 December 1965

Correspondence and correction of proofs. At the end of the morning, a dash by car to the Council Press Office. I gather that some people go there regularly: one

---

1. Matías García Gómez, SJ, private expert of Mgr Cantero.
2. Franz Anton Staudenmaier, German Catholic theologian of the 19th century.
3. Juan Ochagavía, SJ, was Professor of Dogmatic Theology at the Catholic University of Santiago (Chile).

sees a whole crowd of people in the space of a few minutes. Rather too many; I was assailed and had to begin defending myself against the requests for appointments which came raining down. I went there for a photo which *Life* wants of the experts of schema XIII. Those they gathered were not very representative: myself, Häring, Lio, Delhaye, Daniélou . . . That was all! Häring told me that he is pleased with the chapter on marriage, and that the Holy Father has been very understanding and humanly very fair.

But Haubtmann and Garrone told me that right up to this night there had been an alert about several points in schema XIII. Felici wanted to change the terms of Mgr Garrone's *Relatio*. The latter held fast, but we should 'keep an eye out for trouble', and if necessary, fight to the end. Earlier, for the *De Ecclesia*, Philips used to say that one could not be sure until AFTER its solemn promulgation.

Some bishops told me this morning that *ICI* was repeating the Roman rumours about the cardinalate for de Lubac and me. Encountering Vogel at the press office, I scolded him seriously: why repeat these bits of gossip? That puts me in a ridiculous situation. He replied that he had it from *Civiltà*, where this rumour is taken seriously.

I am no longer going to St Peter's, but the votes being taken there these days do concern my humble work: Tuesday, the Missions; this Thursday morning, priests.

I began writing my *ICI* article, but was soon interrupted. In addition, at 5.30 pm, at Saint-Louis, for the presentation of the one hundredth volume of *Sources Chrétiennes*, with a lecture by Mgr Pellegrino on the study of the Fathers and Vatican II. Then a presentation on St Irenaeus by Cardinal Villot. Short speeches by Daniélou, de Lubac and one (of a delightful freshness) by Fr Bro: a group of university quality, not at all 'parochial'.

A fortnight ago I had received four volumes of 'Unam Sanctam' (Lyonnet-Potterie;[1] De Vooght;[2] de la Brosse;[3] *Église et Pauvreté*.[4]

Today I saw Mgr Poupard. Since it is no longer necessary to have books bound in order to offer them to the Pope, I presented these four volumes to the Holy Father, *via* Poupard, with a letter from me.

The bishops told me that, at the recent general congregations, Fr Paul Gauthier was *in aula*, and gathering signatures. This must be about the petition to the Holy Father, prepared four years ago in secret (!), for the abolition of pompous titles. Or rather, resolutions of some kind in thirteen points, the text of which had been put in everyone's pigeon-hole today. (It must rather have been about what has been called (they have called) schema XIV: resolutions of some kind on poverty.) I want to note here—I have perhaps already done so in this journal—that the activity of Fr Gauthier has been both positive and negative. Positive: he intro-

---

1. I de la Potterie and S Lyonnet, *La Vie selon l'Esprit, condition du chrétien*, 'Unam Sanctam', 55 (Paris: Cerf, 1965).
2. Cf above, page, 699, note 5.
3. Cf above, page 69, note 4.
4. *Église et Pauvreté*, 'Unam Sanctam', 57 (Paris: Cerf, 1965).

duced the idea or the concern for poverty to a great number of Fathers, and even imposed it on them. He has succeeded in having the subject introduced into all the conciliar texts, or nearly all of them. But he has also very much antagonised the bishops as a whole, except for a small number of those who have more or less gone along with him. Often, it was enough to refer to these subjects in order to provoke a reaction of nausea. Even the effort made to introduce the mention of the poor and of poverty, *per fas et per nefas*, [by fair means or foul], everywhere, has quite antagonised people. I supported this effort, but without tipping into monoideism or over-simplification.

The volume, *Église et Pauvreté*, which is about to appear in 'Unam Sanctam', sought precisely to tackle the question, without either romanticism or over-simplification. But it lacks, perhaps, the inspiration of Fr Gauthier the mystic, who is, in the end, the most irrepressible force.

Friday 3 December 1965

I slept very badly and far too little: I woke up between 2 and 3.00 am and could not get back to sleep. (The ringing or whistling in my left ear also had something to do with it. At present, it is very loud. It keeps me awake in bed . . .) I have too many things to do, I am too weighed down by multiple worries and obligations. So I got up at 5.00 am, despairing of further sleep, and I corrected some proofs.

I gave a good hour to Fr Dournes, to Fr Bro; verification with him of the translation of the *De Revelatione*; at 2.30 pm, TV for Radio Luxembourg. I got down to my article for *ICI* after 5.15 pm.

The bishops have received a paper from the Americans[1] protesting against the condemnation of the bomb: there are bombs that can be tolerated, with effects that be controlled. One cannot condemn the fact of possessing a stock of atomic weapons. Where would the free world be, where would peace be, if the USA did not have them? Etc. The document asked for a *non placet* to the WHOLE of schema XIII. It was signed by about ten names, among them Spellman, the bishop of New Orleans,[2] Hurley . . .

Mgr Dearden told Mgr Garrone that there are not many American bishops behind Spellman. It is chiefly Mgr Hannan who is leading this campaign. Dearden added: there is nothing in the text except what is true and Christian, and if some people are scandalised by this, that just shows that we needed a text like this!

Saturday 4 December 1965

A crushing load of work to clear away my backlog of correspondence (I finished the letters typing with one finger, because my right hand can't do any more) and correction of proofs. There is no end to them!!!

---

1. In fact, the bishops who signed it were not all Americans: certainly they included Cardinals Spellman (New York) and Shehan (Baltimore), as well as Hannah (New Orleans), but also Hurley (Durban), Miranda (Mexico) and Khoury (Tyre).
2. PM Hannan.

The bishops came back from this morning's Congregation very moved by a letter from the Observers to the Council Fathers [drawn up by Lukas Vischer] a text, it would appear, of great nobility and lofty religious feeling. A bishop told me that an Italian bishop beside him was weeping with emotion. For myself, I would not have been able to restrain myself, for these things move me deeply. The reading of the letter provoked very prolonged applause.

Furthermore, I was invited to go this evening to the ceremony at St Paul-Outside-the-Walls. This is reserved to Council Fathers, but I will get in with Cardinals Richaud and Martin. In fact, not a few others have done as I have.

A lively monastic chant of the entry psalm (Ps 26); lessons from the Old Testament, the Epistle from St Paul, the Gospel (Beatitudes) read by an English-speaking Observer in English (Outler), l'abbé Michalon and a Greek-speaking Observer (the Rector of the Greek Orthodox Church in Rome, from the delegation of the Patriarchate of Constantinople: Maximos[1]. . .). The prayers of intercession: Maan (Old Catholic from Utrecht) and Mgr Davis.

An address by the Pope.[2] I noted down there and then: the change of the form of address from 'Sirs' to 'Brothers'.

'Your departure will create around us a solitude we used not to be aware of before the Council.'

'Your presence: we have been conscious of its influence.'

'The historic significance of the fact of your presence.'

To examine 'the mystery that your presence seems at one and the same time to conceal and to point to'.

Your departure 'will not put an end to a dialogue that has begun'.

All of this, 'many used already to know about it; now the number of those who think like this has grown'.

Then the Pope spoke of the fruits of the Council from the point of view of the approach to unity:

'a heightened awareness of the existence of the problem itself,'

'the hope that the problem will be able to be solved, certainly not today, but tomorrow'

'we have learned to know each other a little better'

'through your persons, we have entered into contact with Christian communities who pray, act in the name of Christ' . . . 'with some treasures of great value'

The Observers have been 'associated' with the work 'right up to the formulation of doctrinal and disciplinary expressions. . . '

'the Christian patrimony that you conserve and develop'

'we have begun again to love one another'.

---

1. The Archimandrite Maximos Aghiorgoussis, Observer delegated by the patriarchate of Constantinople.
2. The Pope spoke in French; cf *AS* IV/VII, 624–627, and *La Documentation catholique*, 19 December 1965, col 2159–2162.

I found this ceremony almost natural. And yet, five years ago, who would have thought it was possible? Here at the highest level, and as the first act of the conclusion of the Council, there unfolded what was almost a concelebration of the Word, in the presence of the Pope, WITH him, who read out the prayers and introduced the *Pater*. On leaving the basilica, shaking hands with people (Fr Villain was there, deeply moved), I stopped for a minute on my knees at the tomb of St Paul: because he was there. I spoke to him. I spoke to him about Luther, who had wanted to re-affirm 'the Gospel' for which Paul had struggled. I asked him, and I implied that it was in the nature of an obligation, and for me, something assured, to intervene in this new phase; to guide the Pope and ALL OF US!

Cardinal Martin, who had seen the Observers, told me that they were very favourably impressed with the monastic lunch they had had at the abbey: the Father Abbot himself served them at table. But H Roux was a bit indignant while listening the Pope's address, admirably given in French (he is a much better orator in French than in Latin!). Roux is fearful of optimism, and that people will believe that it is already achieved. He rehearsed all the demands of a difficult dialogue!

He is not wrong. But I feel sorry for the one who does not sense what new thing the grace of God has brought about!

John XXIII announced the council at St Paul's, at the end of the worldwide week of prayer for Christian unity. The Council is ending in the same place. John XXIII should be pleased.

I received an invitation to lunch tomorrow with all the bishops (who come originally) from the diocese of Rheims—and to supper in the evening with the Superior of the White Fathers. That would have been very agreeable, but I cannot go. Not only are there so few hours left to me before the end of the Council and my departure in which to complete the most urgent of the things I have to do, but by 4.00 pm tomorrow I must finish the paper on Dialogue for the Joint Committee with the World Council of Churches.

Arrighi telephoned me late in the evening to invite me to lunch with the members of the Secretariat on Monday, at the Columbus. He told me, in secret, that the abolition of the reciprocal excommunications of Rome and Constantinople will take place on Tuesday: simultaneously, an Orthodox delegation will come from Constantinople and a Catholic delegation (Cardinal Shehan) will go to Constantinople: the things will take place simultaneously.

Vidimus—et videbimus mirabilia! [We have seen—and we shall see marvels! (Lk 5:26)].

Arrighi clarified that the Pope had written his speech HIMSELF, and the people of the Secretariat only learnt its contents when they heard it.

Sunday 5 December 1965
Worked without stopping until [ ], on the writing of the paper on dialogue for the Joint Committee of the WCC–Catholic Church. In between visitors (Baraúna,

Spanish fathers) and telephone calls. All about invitations, appointments, requests to visit, lectures, ceremonies . . . It could not have been done better if the intention had been to KILL someone. But each one has only the best of intentions, it is the accumulation that is homicidal. No one takes account of the fact that I can do no more, even though each one apologises, knowing—so he says—how much work I have to do. And many have the cheek to ask what I have in preparation!!!

I had was writing almost the last word of my text on dialogue, when Nissiotis came to collect me at 3.50 pm; I spent an hour and a half with him and Schlink in discussion of my text, but it will be necessary for them to have the WRITTEN text in front of them. We made an appointment for this after the ceremony on Tuesday. I am completely DRAINED.

A visit from the Holy Cross Father who founded the Rosary crusade.[1] He would like a chapter from me for a book on the family.

I had the greatest difficulty in the world to make him realise that, since I was already very much beyond what I could do, and beyond my strength, I was not able to accept.

I have done almost nothing of what I was hoping, in spite of everything, to write during these twelve weeks in Rome . . . I am catastrophically behind with everything, and each day I receive SEVERAL requests for something. Again this morning, some Spaniards, formally recommended beforehand by a personal telephone call from Fr General:[2] for me that was decisive.

At 7.30 pm, a telephone call from Fr Peeters. Ruffini wrote to the Pope a week ago, to attack the expression of the *De Activitate Missionali*, Chapter I, No. 2, '*et Spiritus Sanctus per Filium procedit*' [and the Holy Spirit proceeds through the Son]. I had heard something about this yesterday evening, but it was not precise. I had prepared a correction, drawing on the Council of Florence (Denzinger 691; D Sch 1300–01),[3] but this had kept me awake for a while last night.

The Secretariat of State passed on the Pope's desire that account be taken of this request of Ruffini's. I suggested to Fr Peeters that it should read: '*ex quo [Patre . . .] Spiritus sanctus per Filium* UNICA SPIRATIONE *procedit* [from whom [the Father . . .] the Holy Spirit proceeds through the Son BY A SINGLE SPIRATION] with a reference to Florence, or: '*ex quo Filius gignitur et* SIMUL AC EX FILIO UNICA SPIRATIONE SPIRITUS SANCTUS PROCEDIT' [from whom the Son is engendered and THE HOLY SPIRIT PROCEEDS AT THE SAME TIME AS FROM THE SON BY A SINGLE SPIRATION].

Mgr Garrone told me this evening that there were 470 *non placet* votes (Etchegaray told me 497) for the final chapter of schema XIII on peace. That was the result of Spellman's campaign. But, on the other hand, Mgr Dearden, of Detroit,

---

1. Patrick Peyton, CSC.
2. Aniceto Fernandez, OP.
3. The references Congar gives are to the 1960 edition (revised by Karl Rahner), and the 1963 edition (thoroughly reworked by Adolf Schönmetzer) {of H Denzinger, *Enchiridion Symbolorum Definitionum et Declarationum de Rebus Fidei et Morum*}.

discussed it with Spellman, who withdrew his criticism. Cardinal Ottaviani accepts that tomorrow *in aula*, Mgr Garrone will announce this publicly: that will alter the result of the definitive vote.

Cardinal Richaud told me that one of the chamberlains of the Pope said to him: the Pope is very tired, assailed by all these who put difficult cases to him.

Lécuyer told me that Cardinal Ruffini has written to Mgr Marty to congratulate him on *De Presbyterorum ministerio et vita* [on the ministry and life of priests].[1] That's good. But the Commission *De Disciplina cleri et populi Dei*, as such, really had no big part in it. It is a pretty feeble Commission. I have never once seen the President, Cardinal Ciriaci, there, scarcely another of the other five cardinals who are part of it. Lécuyer told me that the *expensio modorum* had been examined and voted on in it by thirteen members (the only ones present, out of thirty). No, really, this Commission is in no way comparable, for seriousness and work, with the Theological Commission. Mgr Marty himself is goodness itself, but he says Amen to everything . . . The work has been done, essentially, by Lécuyer, Onclin and myself.

(I note down these small items as I learn them . . .)

This evening, a performance (Ionesco, *The Rhinoceros*[2]), given by the seminarians for the Council Fathers. Despite my incredible overload of work, I went to it, remembering our own feelings when we were young and our lecturers did, or did not, come to things like this.

Monday 6 December 1965

I did not go to St Peter's for the FINAL General Congregation. At last, I had a few hours for a final tidying up of my manuscript on the four marks of the Church for *Mysterium Salutis*.[3]

At 1.00 pm to the Hotel Columbus (where I gave Nissiotis a typed copy of my text on dialogue[4])for a lunch put on by Cardinal Bea (who was not there) as a token of gratitude to those who had worked at the Secretariat, and as interpreters for the Observers. Unfortunately, I was worn out, and the noise of thirty of us in this small room exhausted me to breaking point. . . I learnt some interesting details.

The ceremony on Saturday evening (at which only forty-one cardinals were present), stirred up some criticisms. Several had expressed these even to the Pope, in particular Mgr Vagnozzi(?) the Apostolic Delegate at Washington, a man of very narrow views, and Cardinals Roberti and Siri.

---

1. The future *Presbyterorum Ordinis*.
2. Eugène Ionesco, *Le Rhinocéros* (Paris: Gallimard, 1959).
3. It was to be further reworked before its publication; cf Yves Congar, *L'Église, une, sainte, catholique et apostolique,* 'Mysterium Salutis' 15 (Paris: Cerf, 1970), 65–121.
4. 'Propositions sur le dialogue', published in *Voix de Sainte Paul,* March, 1966: 6–7.

On the other hand, ecumenical EVENTS continue. Willebrands was late for our lunch because he had been to Fiumicino to welcome Mgr Nicodim[1] who had arrived from Moscow to assist at the closure. It is more than probable that the Russians waited to see what the Council would, or would not, say about communism before deciding to come. The direction taken by schema XIII decided them.

The Catholic delegation left for Constantinople at 1.00 pm (Cardinal Shehan, Fr Dumont, etc); the Greek delegation is about to arrive. Arrighi told me that he had heard some very disagreeable things about this in the Roman offices: 'We are not going to bow down before these people!'

Duprey told me that, right up to 10.30 pm yesterday, there were difficulties and danger concerning the declaration of the abolition of the excommunications of 1054. He said it was Maccarrone who had rescued the situation, and that, already in Constantinople, he had been astonishing, seeming to have understood some things there (I heard another side of the story from Fr Dumont).

Hromádka,[2] invited by Fr Becker, was at the Council this morning.

Fr Lanne told me that the Eastern Congregation does not know about the Decree on the Eastern Churches. The deputy[3] seems even not to know of its existence. He NEVER set foot in the Council. The Cardinal Prefect, Testa, made only very rare appearances there.

The Pope has this morning given every bishop a gilded (or gold???) episcopal ring. The Vatican doesn't worry about expense. How can one still talk about the Church of the Poor?

On Saturday, he gave to each of the Observers a little hand-engraved bell, equally of very high value. Obviously, it is good that he made this gesture, but again, what expense!!!

I got back at 3.15 pm, scarcely able to stand. There was a visitor waiting for me: l'abbé Snoeks,[4] professor at the major seminary at Malines. I had hardly the strength to receive him decently.

At 5.00 pm, in accordance with the invitation I had received, I dragged myself to DO-C, where Fr Dockx wanted to have a meeting of some members of his International Academy.[5]

No one came. I said my prayers. In this way God often has what one cannot use oneself . . . In any case, I had to leave at 6.15 pm, to give a lecture to the African Missions of Verona:[6] in Latin. I did what I could in spite of unimaginable

---

1. Metropolitan of Leningrad, he was the President of the Department of External Relations of the Patriarchate of Moscow.
2. The evangelical pastor Josef L Hromádka was Professor of Systematic Theology in Prague.
3. Amerigo Giovanelli, priest of the diocese of Rome, Council expert.
4. Rémi Snoeks.
5. Cf above, page 528, note 1.
6. A lecture on schema XIII.

fatigue. It was for the Missions. After supper, questions. On my return, I found parcels and correspondence.

Tuesday 7 December 1965

Why is it that one CANNOT rest when one is most tired?

Exhausted as I was yesterday evening, it took me four hours to get to sleep . . .

This morning, I would not have gone to the public session were it not that the ending of the mutual excommunications between Rome and Constantinople was to be declared there. But I wanted to take part in this event, and share in the prayer of the Church. Before leaving, I was able to get the finishing touches done for my text on the four Marks, so that I was able to give it to Feiner.

Congestion such as I have never seen, to get into St Peter's, by the Cardinals' door. The basilica was flooded with light, an excessive light for TV, which hurt my eyes very much, even though I protected myself as best I could. But the ceremony lasted nearly four hours. Everywhere was already packed when I got in; the ambassadors and delegations were arriving. Thanks to God and my friends, I had a seat with the Observers. I greeted on the sacristy-side, in relation to the altar, some Orthodox bishops who had come from London, Vienna, Geneva.

Everything was very beautiful. However, there was still too much of the theatre, with spectacular gestures, strange and sumptuous vestments, elaborate chants. It was bound to be, on the whole, too long! Why sing a polyphonic version of the *Veni Creator*, when we had just said the *Adsumus?*

The communion rite of the concelebrated Mass was also excessively long. But what a day! What a moment!

Felici[1] read out the beginning and the end of the principal parts of the schemas to be voted on. I was waiting for the passage from No. 2 of the *De Missionali Activitate*: it was read out just as it was printed, without addition or correction. I was astounded and happy at this. I had introduced there a little bit of Eastern theology.

After that, Willebrands read out, in French, the text of the abolition of the mutual excommunications between Rome and Constantinople.[2]

It is a fine text. Right at the beginning, the name of Athenagoras was applauded and cheered at length. The document itself was also warmly applauded.

'Nine hundred years later!'[3]

I could feel the historic moment. Not that the difficulties have been resolved into nothing, but they can be the better tackled.

What a reversal of history!

---

1. *AS* IV/VII, 650–651.
2. Cf *AS* IV/VII, 652–653 and *Documentation catholique*, 2 January 1966, col 67-69.
3. Cf Yves M-J Congar, 'Neuf cents ans après. Notes sur le Schisme oriental', in *1054-1954 – L'Église et Les Églises – Neuf siècles de douloureuse séparation entre l'Orient et l'Occident* (Chevetogne, 1954), 3–95.

It was 10.20 am, when this was read out: the date 1054 begins to fade on the screen!

The Pope's speech:[1] very much in the tone of '*Ecclesiam suam*'; a veritable declaration of the complete acceptance of the modern human being and of the primacy of anthropology. (The Holy Father's speech was remarkable: he gave expression to the fundamental intention of schema XIII: to renew contact with humanity, to re-introduce the consideration of humankind into theology. The Pope thus responded to those criticisms according to which the Council was tipping towards humanism.)

After Mass, the results of the final votes were given. I was expecting 120 *non placet* against the *De libertate*. But it was quite otherwise:

	Voting	*Placet*	*Non Placet*	Null
De libertate	2,386	2,308	70	8
Missions	2,399	2,394	5	
Priesthood	2,394	2,390	4	
Pastoral Constitution (schema XIII)	2,391	2,309	75	7

This is a triumph (without triumphalism, I hope).

VERY strong applause.

After this announcement of the results of the voting, and the promulgation of the texts by the Pope (*vacatio legis* [not legally binding] until 29 June 1966), Cardinal Bea read out the pontifical brief about the events of 1054 (in Latin):[2] it was very much the same content as the French text read out by Willebrands. Bea was again greatly applauded. Mgr Meliton of Tyre[3] had gone up near to the altar. After this reading, the Pope embraced him, and two or three of the Pope's close assistants also embraced him. There was thunderous applause, which was redoubled while Meliton returned to his place, walking right the way round the altar. If there had been a popular plebiscite in favour of union at Constantinople, there was also a popular plebiscite in Rome!!

The public session concluded, before the final *Te Deum,* with a liturgy of penance imploring God's forgiveness for the sins committed during the Council, and because of it.

I left slowly and with difficulty, barely able to stand. A great many bishops congratulated me, thanked me. To a good extent, it was my work, they said.

Looking at things objectively, I did a great deal to prepare for the Council, elaborating and diffusing the ideas that the Council consecrated. At the Council itself, I did a great deal of work. I could almost say '*Plus omnibus laboravi*' [I worked harder than any of them (cf 1 Cor 15:10)], but that would, no doubt, not

---

1. *AS* IV/VII, 654–662.
2. *Ambulate in dilectione* [walk in love] (*AS* IV/VII, 861–862).
3. The metropolitan, Melito of Heliopolis and Tyre, was head of the delegation from the Patriarchate of Constantinople.

be true: think of Philips, for example. At the beginning, I was too timid. I was coming out of a long period of suspicion and difficulties. Even my spirituality had acted on me in the direction of a certain timidity. In fact, I have lived all my life in the line and the spirit of John the Baptist, *amicus Sponsi* [the friend of the bridegroom (John 3:29)]. I have always thought that it was not necessary to take hold of whatever it might be, but to be content with WHAT HAS BEEN GIVEN TO US. That is, for each of us, our *'logikè latreia'* [rational worship (Rom 12: 1)], our spiritual sacrifice, our way of sanctification. So I have accepted what has been given me, I have forced myself to do well (?) what was asked of me. I have taken very few—too few, I believe—initiatives. God has overwhelmed me. He has gifted me profusely, infinitely beyond my absolutely non-existant merits. Even at the Council, I was involved in a great deal of work, over and above a general influence of presence and spoken contributions. I contributed:

Lumen Gentium, the first draft of several Numbers of Chapter 1 and Numbers 9, 13, 16, 17 of Chapter II, plus some particular passages.

De Revelatione: I worked on Chapter II, and No. 21 comes from a first draft of mine.

De oecumenismo: I worked on this; the *proemium* and the conclusion are very nearly mine.

Declaration on Non-Christian Religions: I worked on this; the introduction and conclusion are very nearly mine.

Schema XIII: I worked on this: Chapters 1, IV.

De Missionibus: Chapter I is mine from A to Z, with borrowings from Ratzinger for No. 8.

De libertate religiosa: I cooperated on all of it, and particularly on the Numbers of the theological part and on the *proemium*, which is from my hand.

De Presbyteris: three quarters of it is a draft by Lécuyer-Onclin-Congar. I reworked the *proemium*, Numbers 2 and 3; I did the first draft of Numbers 4-6; I did the revision of Numbers 7–9, 12–14, and the revision of the conclusion of which I wrote the second paragraph.

Thus what was read out this morning came, to a very large extent, from me.

Servi inutiles sumus [we are unprofitable servants (Luke 17: 10)].

While waiting for Mgr Gouyon's car, in front of St Martha's, I saw M. Maritain go by, very pale and leaning on Mgr Baron. He had been personally invited by the Holy Father. I told him what joy it gave me to see him here, especially as his residence at Kolbsheim seems difficult of access.

Lunch at the embassy to the Holy See. Everyone was late (St Peter's did not finish much before 12.45 pm). Unimaginable traffic jam. Mgr Le Cordier told me that the secretaries were received by the Pope on Friday evening. He had seemed very relaxed. Although, he told them that he was receiving masses of letters every day recently, asking him to intervene, to prevent this or that. For example, the Pope said, this letter, and he started to read it out, punctuating each sentence with an assessment. It was the letter (he did not say from whom[1]), asking him to correct the wording about the procession of the Holy Spirit, in the *De missionibus*. But, the Pope said, one can understand what is said in a good way. I do not wish to intervene in the Council, and I NEVER have intervened. On only two or three occasions I asked for some clarifications. This text was voted by the Council, I do not wish to change it.

An excellent lunch. The Minister of Foreign Affairs, Couve de Murville,[2] is pleasant, but cold. Cardinal Tisserant, for whom we waited a long time, did not look at me and half-heartedly offered the extreme tips of his fingers. I kissed his ring because he is my hierarchical superior, but I immediately turned my heels and back to him. At table I was next to M. de Beaumarchais[3] (who had married a Cochin[4]), department head at the Quai-d'Orsay: a man of a fine human and Christian culture. We talked about the elections, about Europe, about Russia etc. I had the pleasure of there meeting again Pastor Boegner, Guitton, the French cardinals and several French bishops (Mgr Veuillot was not much more welcoming than Cardinal Tisserant).

And so the Council is over! However, it appears (from Garrone and Gouet) that the Pope is keeping some surprises for his speech tomorrow, and that M. Maritain will speak. However, I am fearful I shall not be able to go to the ceremony: it will be too tiring for me, all the more as I must pack my trunk, which is always far beyond my strength.

At 5.45 pm, I went to *Domus Mariae*, for the presentation of the Italian edition of the Baraúna volume. I went because I was afraid there would not be many people there, everyone is engaged in various receptions (the embassy, the Capitol, etc). I did not manage to find a French bishop who would take an interest in this Baraúna volume . . .

Afterwards I went to the audience given to experts. I saw again a hundred well-known faces, including so many Americans whom I saw in the tribunes but never in the Commissions.

The Holy Father, who was giving audiences that evening, one after another, to diplomatic delegations and I don't know what other groups, to experts, to bishops' secretaries, did not appear to be tired, however. He started by reading a paper in French, then continued off the cuff in French, in a way that was very remarkable not only for the manner but also for the depth.

He spoke about the dialectic of truth, which exists even within the Church. (For what Paul VI said on 8 December 1965 about the 'dialectic of truth', compare *Ecclesiam Suam*, quoted by de Lubac, *Le mystère du surnaturel*, 1965[5], page 217.)

---

1. Ruffini.
2. Maurice Couve de Murville.
3. Jacques Delarue Caron de Beaumarchais, Head of Cabinet of the Ministry of Foreign Affairs.
4. Marie-Alice Le Couteulx de Caumont, related to the founder of the Cochin Hospital in Paris.
5. Henri de Lubac, *Le Mystère du Surnaturel* (Paris: Éditions Montaigne, 1965).

He said, rightly, that the period after the Council would have need of theologians, and that, far from being finished, the work was beginning.

As we went out, we were given a New Testament in Latin, a 'token' the Holy Father rightly said. I found the token a little stingy considering the unbelievable expenditures he outlaid elsewhere, the expenditures we had outlaid, and the work that some, at least, had put in.

Fr Meersseman[1] recounted that, at the last moment, at the request of the Holy Office, ONE word had been changed in the common text concerning 1054. It had been necessary to go to Constantinople to get the agreement of Athenagoras. He had said: So be it! We don't go in for Byzantine hair-splitting here! If that is a true story, it's not bad.

Mgr Glorieux said that tomorrow there will be different messages addressed to different groups of people, by a Council Father accompanied by lay people. Perhaps that is where a role for Maritain has been envisaged.

Medina, whom it is always a pleasure to see, because one senses a true friend and encounters a man incredibly up to date with everything, told me that he had the original and had made a photocopy of the correspondence between Ottaviani and the Pope on the subject of marriage and the family. (Medina has given a photocopy of these documents to the Belgian College. He offered to make one for me, but it is not worth it.) The *modi*, he said, came from Ottaviani, assisted by Frs Lio and Gagnebet. At a given moment Ottaviani said that the text could not go any further BECAUSE THE MAJORITY OF THE COMMISSION DID NOT WISH IT! *(sic).*

Fr Betti told me that, in the DEFINITIVE text of the *De Revelatione*, No. 7, *communicantes* had been changed to *communicans*.[2] I checked this: it is true! That changes the sense: CHRIST is made the subject of the verb to communicate, and not the Apostles, as the Commission had wished. The intention of those who drafted the text was to express, already with reference to the Apostles, the idea of tradition as REAL, and not simply a means to knowledge. The meaning of the text has thus been deeply betrayed, on an essential point. Betti, who suspects it was down to Fr Tromp, complained to Cardinal Ottaviani.

Wednesday 8 December 1965
EVERY DAY these days, I have received several requests for articles, or co-operation for some commentary on the conciliar decrees. They rain down!

This morning I did not go to the final ceremony in St Peter's Square. To pack my trunk and my suitcase is already a very serious test of my spinal column and

---

1. Gilles-Gérard Meersseman, OP, of the Province of Flanders, Professor of Church History at the Theology Faculty in Fribourg (Switzerland) was a member of the Pontifical Committee of Historical Sciences.
2. Cf Umberto Betti, *La dottrina del Concilio Vaticano II sulla trasmissione della rivelazione. Il capitolo II della Costituzione dommatica* (Dei Verbum, Rome, 1985), 229, note 92.

my strength; I could not stand there. And I certainly needed the whole day to clear up and dispose of everything. For I have more than 40 kilos more of papers, schemas, documents and odd books, than when I arrived. But I watched the whole thing on Italian TV. Pretty good reporting, with a well-prepared text, varied and technically excellent pictures. First the long, slow procession of the Fathers from the Bronze Door to the precinct of St Peter's. Unfortunately, in silence. Then the trumpets, the music: the Pope. On the *sedia*, wearing a mitre, carrying a pastoral cross in his left hand (yesterday he entered the Council carrying the book of the Gospels—a suggestion I had made to Carlo Colombo. On leaving, he had shaken hands with Boegner and some Taizé Brothers—a detail I learnt this morning). Paul VI has been remarkable. However, from the ecclesiological and ecumenical point of view, I felt some unease in watching the very beautiful ceremony this morning—and seeing it, thanks to TV, better than if I had been involved. The Pope got all the attention. He sat enthroned as a sovereign; everything had reference to him. He did not appear to be so much IN the Church, as above it.

I understand the intention of today's ceremony by comparison with that of yesterday. The two correspond to the schema: the Church in itself, and the Church in the world and for humankind. Yesterday we had, as it were, the internal closure of the Council. Today, the Church is being sent out into the world, *ad gentes, ad populos. Incipiendo, non a Ierosolyma sed a Roma* [to the nations, to the peoples. Beginning, not from Jerusalem, but from Rome]. The Council is going to shine forth in the world. Today it is achieving its Pentecostal moment, of which John XXIII had spoken.

The Pope's homily[1] was less remarkable than yesterday's, but he announced at the end of it that, after Mass, there would be a series of messages to different categories of people.

In fact seven messages followed one another. They were delivered in such a way as to be, at the same time, from the Council, from the Pope and from the Christian People. Each message was read by a cardinal, flanked by two other cardinals (the Council), and by some lay people (the Christian People): after the reading this group went towards the Pope who welcomed each one (this suggested a sort of prize-giving).

The order was as follows:

Cardinal Liénart, Alfrink, Colombo[2] and some diplomats: message to the governments of peoples.[3]

Cardinal Léger with Maritain (to whom the Pope spoke for a moment) and Guitton: to intellectuals.[4]

Cardinal Suenens: to artists[5] (!!)

---

1. *AS* IV/VII, 868–871.
2. Giovanni Colombo.
3. *AS* IV/VII, 875–876.
4. *AS* IV/VII, 877–878.
5. *AS* IV/VII, 878–879.

Cardinal Duval: to women.[1]

Cardinal Zoungrana: to workers.[2]

Cardinal Meouchi: to the poor and the ill.[3] Some people who were ill went up towards the Holy Father; a blind man with his dog, which received a ribbon for its collar.

Cardinal Agagianian[4] to the young: some young boys, one in short pants, came up to the Pope. But why had no young girls been put with them?

As to the form: all these messages were in French: what an honour for our language, which is thus given the glory of a kind of catholicity! (These texts were written at the Secretariat of State and imposed on those who read them out.) I found the style a bit bombastic, but that was almost inevitable. With respect to the content, I was not entirely comfortable. I recognise the good intention and even the deep significance. How often had we said, Mgr Elchinger and I, that the Council should conclude with a new message to the world. I had, RIGHT FROM THE FIRST SESSION, made some notes along these lines. To tell the truth, schema XIII is a tremendous message to the world. But there remained a place for something more brief, and above all promotional. The meaning of the gesture was evident, and it was good. I am not sure that the right note was always found. There was a whiff of *captatio* [rhetorical seduction] about it: the Church, now that the world is distancing itself from it, cries out to it in every possible way: But I am with you, you have no better friend than me!! I felt that the Church was too much TURNING ITS ATTENTION WITH SOLICITUDE TOWARDS . . . I did not like the Message to workers, where 'the Church' said it was interested in them, as though they were not the Church . . . *Pro quo supponit 'Ecclesia'?* [to whom does the word Church refer?]

But, when all is said and done, the Council concluded with a message to humankind!

Felici[5] read out the brief declaring the Council closed.

There were some 'praises' in the Carolingian style, wishing peace and prosperity to all and for all.

Then the footlights were turned off.

It was over.

After the meal (at 2.15 pm), some of the bishops were departing. We had got used to one another and to this sort of extended seminary life. Many of them were extraordinarily good and kind to me, friendly even. They considered me almost as one of themselves. Several spoke to me about the cardinalate: always the same rumour. I think, like Brother Thomas, that I would be more use to the Church as

1. *AS* IV/VII, 897–880.
2. *AS* IV/VII, 880–882.
3. *AS* IV/VII, 882–883.
4. *AS* IV/ VII, 883–884.
5. *AS* IV/ VII, 885.

a simple Friar Preacher and theologian. However, if this trial should await me, my two successive stays at the French seminary would at least have made the bishops accustomed to my personality, and made me acceptable to them.

For myself, I have never sought anything other than to place myself where God really wanted to ask me to serve him. 'Obedientia et pax' [obedience and peace].[1]

After 3.00 pm, several visits, in particular a Canadian priest who wants to write a thesis on Faith and Order. I directed him towards a study of the work of the last thirty years on Tradition (and Scripture).

After supper, cordial farewells. An atmosphere of general DEPARTURE, but not at all of departure FOR HOLIDAYS . . .

Thursday 9 December 1965

Strasbourg. I got up at 5.30 am. Mass; departure by car with Mgr Weber at 6.40 am. We arrived at Fiumicino almost an hour early. Departure of several Dutch and Netherlands (Polynesia) bishops on the same plane as us as far as Zurich, including Cardinal Alfrink. We reached Zurich at 9.40 am. We were told there was no flight to Basle: it was impeded by fog at the airport of Basle-Mulhouse. In fact, there wasn't any fog: the atmosphere everywhere was clear, a beautiful, luminous sky above a ground covered with hoarfrost. But some planes were diverted to Basle yesterday evening, had not come back to Zurich, and were not going to come back just for us three unfortunate travellers. So, a long wait, then a train to Basle (where I saw Schlink again for a moment). Mgr Weber's secretary was waiting on the station platform; Fr Vachette[2] was waiting for me. Returned to Strasbourg by car with him; I was at the Priory at 3.20 pm.

What a table-full! There are piles of books and journals everywhere: on the table, on the chairs, on the floor! What a job!!!

5 February 1966

The day before yesterday, I learned of the nomination of Mgr Garrone as pro-Prefect of the Congregation of Seminaries and Universities.

This is important. Specifically, for this Congregation that is so important, where some imbeciles are in charge: Pizzardo, Staffa, Romeo . . . I recall that Mgr Garrone had specifically asked for the reform of the Congregation in a speech at the Council. That means the formal notice for him to put his idea into action. . . It also means his being bound, for a second time, to an old cardinal who is finishing up,[3] but this one is less intelligent than the earlier one. I feel sorry for him. It is a

---

1. The motto of Pope John XXIII.
2. Francis Vachette, OP, of the Province of France, from shortly before, the Prior of the priory in Strasbourg.
3. He had been co-adjutor to Cardinal Saliège from 1947 to 1956.

big sacrifice that is being asked of him. Generically, it is the first notable sign of the internationalisation of the Curia. And that in line with the Council. It seems that the Holy Father wants to have the application of the Council done by the people who were active at it.

Three weeks ago, we heard that the CONCILIAR commissions, five of them, at least, including those for Missions and Seminaries, would purely and simply continue on. Some people reacted rather badly because they saw the names of the Presidents, for example those of THESE TWO commissions, and because that disturbed them with respect to openness and dynamism. But I see above all that the Pope wants to continue the work of the Council with the men who carried it out. However, these men would not have done what they did without the experts. Now, some experts will be able to be summoned to these post-conciliar Commissions, but none has been made a statutory member of them.[1] I have long seen that one of the major problems of the post-conciliar situation will be to preserve the organic co-operation—which alone permitted and brought about the Council—between bishops and theologians.

This morning, a visit from Fr Baraúna. He told me about the difficulties encountered by the Italian edition of *L'Église de Vatican II*.[2] Fr Baraúna was supposed to have an audience in order to present the book to the Holy Father. When the audience didn't happen, he became uneasy, he saw Mgr Dell'Acqua. He learnt that there was opposition to this audience. The publication has been accused of being tendentious, of diminishing the force of the *Nota praevia*, which is the Gospel for the curialists.

So the Pope had the book examined by two censors whose evaluations were passed on by Dell'Acqua. The first, who would have been Ciappi, was very critical: a tendentious, dangerous book (which diminishes the force of the *nota praevia*). The second, who would have been Colombo, was favourable with some slight reservations: it is a line of interpretation: Ratzinger does diminish a little the force of the *nota praevia* . . .

In the end, Baraúna had his audience, but the Pope was very diplomatic and behaved as if he were seeing the book for the first time.

5 March 1966

I take up this notebook again on the eve of departing for Rome. Because I have been summoned to a meeting of the post-conciliar Commission for the Missions, for 7 March at 9.30 am. I was supposed to have arrived in Valencia on Sunday 6 March for the meeting of Dominican ecclesiologists. It had all been planned and arranged: to Paris, to Madrid, to Valencia. It has all had to be altered and arranged

---

1. Congar was to be called only to the Commission for the Missions.
2. Guilherme Baraúna (editor) *La Chiesa del Vaticano II. Studi e commenti intorno alla Costituzione dommatica 'Lumen Gentium'* (Florence: Vallecchi Editore, 1965).

otherwise. Moreover, there is no agenda, and we do know how long we will be kept there. I would rather spend only 48 hours in Rome, and take the good plane that I would have on the evening of Tuesday 8 March. We'll see.

I have also received my appointment as expert to the Secretariat for Non-Believers. I have sent in the suggestions I was asked for. Above all, we should be trying to engage with non-believers, to get them involved. We need to work with them, and lead them to work with us.

But the two great events of these past weeks were the appointments of Mgr Garrone to the post of Pro-Prefect of the Congregation of Seminaries and Universities, and of C Moeller to that of Under-Secretary of the Congregation for the Doctrine of the Faith, which replaces the defunct 'Holy Office'. Both nominations are significant, and even rather sensational, especially the second. It was Mgr Garrone who, at the Council, specifically criticised the Congregation and demanded its reform. He wanted to see it transformed into an open organ, an organism for the promotion of studies and ideas. After having been for several years tied to an elderly cardinal who was disabled, he is going to be tied to an elderly cardinal who is an imbecile . . . But he is an independent man, who knows how to discern what is essential among the details, and to hang on to it: he is endowed with a great faculty for work and a placidity that is proof against all irritation. . .

With Moeller, what we have is 100% ecumenism, what we have is openness to humankind, interest in human searchings, in culture, what we have is dialogue. I remember the extraordinary and moving unanimity regarding him that came about at Bellagio. The Pope has assured him that his new post would not prevent his taking up that of rector in Jerusalem. That appears to me to be fanciful. He will have to be replaced in Jerusalem. But what a change! Here is the spiritual son of Dom Beauduin, the man of all the dialogues of Chevetogne, the man of all the schemes at the Council, installed in a house where he will not be spied on . . . It is a marvellous harbinger of the springtime of reform. It will also be a support for the three Secretariats (Unity, Religions, Non-Believers).

I shall try to see Moeller during the few hours that I shall be in Rome.

6 March 1966

Departure from the priory at 8.15 am. We flew over the snow-covered Alps; reached Nice at a few minutes past ten. There I had a four-hour wait. The weather was fine and bright, but there was the noise of the very frequent arrivals and departures of aircraft. A little before arrival in Rome at 3.20 pm there were great storm clouds. It was sultry. I was extremely tired.

French Seminary. At 7.00 pm, I telephoned Fr Peeters to know how it was shaping up. Tomorrow morning, the meeting is at the College of Propaganda, but we shall go to Nemi in the afternoon. I shall try to leave on Tuesday evening.

7 March 1966

St Thomas: I have celebrated the feast in Rome several times. A difficult night. I had a lot of pain in my back, in the sacrum, and I woke up more than a hundred times, getting back to a half-dozing state after changing the position of my legs.

9.30 am, at the College of Propaganda. Twenty or twenty-one members of the Commission and the regular experts (not Ratzinger) arrived and caught up with one another. A speech by Cardinal Agagianian, very laudatory, very grateful to everyone. After which he slipped out and left the conduct of the meeting to Fr Schütte, whom he had appointed Vice-President, as at the time of the Conciliar Commission. Schütte had had an operation and, like me, walks with a stick.

According to the Central Post-Conciliar Commission,[1] our meeting should observe the following norms: simply explain the existing decree. Not create a new one. Prepare the decrees that will come into effect at the end of the *vacatio legis*; don't reject things already decided. If there are some new suggestions, submit them to the Central Commission, which will decide to which commission to forward them: for example, the revision of the Code; liturgical questions.

But how to go about it? Some *periti* from Rome have drawn up an *elenchus* [list] of twenty-seven points to be dealt with. Buijk commented that 'someone' has deleted from their paper what they had put in about the application of the Decree *Ad Gentes* concerning the representation on the Congregation of Propaganda of missionary societies, bishops and *periti*.

I suggested that we meet in smaller groups to study this *elenchus*, and possibly to complete it so as to sort out the points to be studied. But Mgr Yago said that we must first study these things PERSONALLY, and that it will be only TOMORROW that we will be able to get together and commence the work. In consequence, at 10.15 am we broke up and each one went off by himself. So I studied the *elenchus* of twenty-seven points, and decided that I would leave tomorrow evening for Valencia. Because there is no great work for me here. We are going to Nemi this afternoon: leaving at 3.30 pm.

I worked at writing a paper on five points that seemed to me the most important. Fr Che[2] (Chinese) picked me up at 3.20 pm; we went to collect Mgr Lokuang way up to the North (near the catacomb of St Priscilla) and made an immense detour to rejoin Ciampino and the road to the Lakes. We got there at 4.50 pm, for tea. The first meeting was arranged for 6.04 pm! It seemed to me that we had wasted most of the day. If the two sheets that had been distributed to us had been sent out beforehand, we could have started work this morning. Whereas in ordinary life we niggle over five minutes, here we are made to waste several hours!

---

1. This had the responsibility for coordinating the works of the different Post-Conciliar Commissions.
2. Vincent Che-Chen-Tao, of the diocese of Ningbo (Ningxia, in the People's Republic of China), was the ecclesiastical attaché at the Nationalist Chinese Embassy, and taught Canon Law at the Urbanianum; he was a consultor to the Preparatory Commission for the Missions, and a Council expert.

One could even doubt that the arrangement for us to meet at Nemi was, from every point of view, a good idea. Certainly it is comfortable at Nemi and one can work well. The external conditions are excellent. It is, all the same, the house of ONE missionary institute, and one might ask oneself if it is appropriate for the Commission to be associated with it in this way?

At 6.00 pm, a rather poor meeting. We asked ourselves what we should do and how we should proceed. Since we have to prepare some elements for the *motu proprio* and the instruction of the Congregation, the best thing to do is to follow the text of the Decree closely, to which one always has to refer.

That is why the Fathers were divided into three sub-commissions: 1) Chapters 1–4: ZOA, Cavallera, Lecuona, Pollio, Ungarelli (experts: Seumois, Congar, Smulders). We got down to work straight after supper—instead of that recreation with whisky that Fr Schütte so much enjoys.

Tuesday 8 March 1966

A bad night: back pain; woke up more than a hundred times.

Work in the sub-commission from 9.00 am until 12 noon. After lunch, we drafted eight points with Fr X Seumois. A meeting of the sub-commission at 4.00 pm. We finished specifying what was to be proposed to the plenary commission.

I left the group and the work at 5.15 pm, to go to Fiumicino. The two Fathers who drove me there were very interested in theology. They gave me (as did Cardinal Rugambwa) a great eulogy of *Concilium*. We arrived at Fiumicino in good time at 6.15 pm: the plane was to leave at 6.55 pm.

But at about 6.35 pm, it was announced that the plane would leave an hour late. I took steps to confirm my connection to Barcelona, which seemed threatened. I was reassured about this.

But at 7.15 pm, it was announced that the plane would not leave until 8.20 pm, that I would miss my connection, and that a seat would be reserved for me on the plane the following morning.

That's Spain for you! For me it is catastrophic. Where shall I sleep? I can scarcely stand up, and all this involves some very great additional fatigue. Fortunately, at this hour, Fiumicino (where I am writing these lines) is not too noisy.

I note what followed, because there I find Spain, with its total absence of a sense of time and urgency; with its desire to do everything very well, to the point where the best is the enemy of the good. The plane which was to take us arrived at 8.15 pm. We left at 8.45 or 8.50. A group of seven or eight Americans from the USA was kicking up a mighty fuss because they were going to miss their connection for Palma, on Majorca.

We arrived in Barcelona a little after 10.00 pm. The Yanks ranted more and more, demanding to see the 'Manager', saying that they wanted to start again from Switzerland. I tried to send a telegram to Fr Hamer at Torrente, telling him to come and meet me at the airport on Wednesday at 10.40 am. But I was told that it was not certain that there would be a seat on that plane. What a business! The

Iberian Airline will pay for a night at a hotel for us. But we had to get there and this did not happen at once, nor in a single trip. We got there at midnight.

Wednesday 9 March 1966

An acceptable bed, but in a room that smelt of paint, the latrine, and acetylene. From 3.30 am, a hullabaloo of conversations, calls, discussions, hustle and bustle. I was told that we would be collected (there were two of us for Valencia) about 8.00 am. I was there at 8.00 am. We left at 8.50!

When I arrived at the airport I bumped into Fr General,[11] who had just arrived from Torrente, fresh as a daisy.

Arrival at the Valencia airport at 10.45 am. Luggage, reservation for Saturday. But no one was there to meet me. I tried to telephone to Torrente. I was told that it was impossible before 11.30 am!!!!! I would be necessary to wait longer. And I will have to wait until someone came to get me. I could no longer stand up.

At 11.30 am, I was told: in twenty minutes. I finally made my telephone call at 11.58 am. The car arrived to pick me up at 12.40 pm, exactly two hours after my arrival.

We went up the gentle slope to the heights on which the new priory is built, which has given Fr Sauras nervous depression! Groups of white robes in discussion. A thoughtfulness was shown me that my ravaged appearance intensified; I was served lunch in my room. In the course of a few minutes I saw Fathers Ryan,[22] Hamer, Ortuño.[33] The Spaniards had prepared the Congress with meticulous care. Each had in his room a set of explanatory papers, postcards, note paper, etc. That is their grand manner, gracious and thoughtful.

Thursday 10 March 1966

Meeting of the OP ecclesiologists.[4] Not very good. The problems were not sufficiently tackled by SPECIALISTS. Some major questions were raised that there was not time really to deal with. The important thing, as at the Council, is the contact. This is sometimes a confrontation. Again, as at the Council. There are partisans for conceptualism, and those who have a more historical and more existential approach. But even among these latter there are some who received their formation BEFORE Heidegger and the current queries, and there are those who take their bearings from the level of those queries: two generations. I understand the current problem of the younger ones, for whom Tradition does not have a value in itself. Some posed these questions in a genuine and basically serious way,

---

1. Aniceto Fernandez OP.
2. Columba Ryan, OP, of the Province of England, Professor of Dogmatic Theology, was Regent of Studies at the Dominican *studium* in Oxford.
3. Roberto Ortuño, OP, of the Province of Aragon, was Master of Students, and Professor of Dogmatic Theology at the Dominican *studium* of Torrente.
4. The lectures were to be published in *Angelicum*, December 1966: 307–510.

like Fr Dominguez,[1] from Portugal, who seems to me to be a man of the future. Others are more radical (Fr Willemse,[2] from Nijmegen). The tension exists. The great majority admit that we have to be open to some rather profound putting in question, and believe that this is acceptable within the framework of a fidelity to a Thomism conceived in all its depth, and not like the orthodoxy of the manuals. Over and above, or alongside this, questions are raised about the method of teaching and the *ratio studiorum* [programme of studies]. Apologetics has been pretty nearly abandoned by nine out of ten. The greater part question the division between the years of pure philosophy and the years of theology.

At 10.45 am, we set off in a coach on a grand excursion, through Valencia and then some rich orange orchards; we crossed a whole tourist region that is in process of development between Valencia and Alicante. Hotels and great apartment blocks are under construction. But if life gets better in Spain, tourism will decline, and these apartment blocks will remain half-empty . . . After an hour and a half in the coach, lunch at a very fine hotel in Gandia. A more than plentiful meal. This morning's gospel was about the rich man and Lazarus. We are the rich. I would not have dared to enjoy this pleasure and this abundance if the gospel had not said that the rich man '*epulabatur QUOTIDIE splendide*' [feasted splendidly EVERY DAY (Luke 16:19)]. That '*quotidie*' [every day], which does not overlap our '*hodie*' [today], only just rescued our meal today . . . On our return, I had a conversation with Fr Schillebeeckx, in so far as it was fair to make him talk, because he is ill and sleepy. Fr Willems[3] was able to give more detail about what he had told me of the seriously worrying situation in Holland. Willems had submitted his resignation as Regent. He could not take responsibility for the teaching of five or six lecturers who, Schillebeeckx told me, reduced Christianity to a mere humanism, and radically espoused the theses of Bultmann, or those of '*Honest to God*'.[4] I was very disturbed by what he told me.

Conversations with Dupuy, Le Guillou, Nicolas,[5] and others.

The Fathers asked me for a whole heap of things, including lectures. I would have to come back to Valencia, where I have been invited to speak at the university; I would have to visit the Fathers from the Philippines in Madrid, to go and lecture in Avila, in Salamanca. And, at the same time, they all ask me what book I am working on, and say that they are impatiently waiting for my *De Ecclesia*, etc.

---

1. Bento Domingues, OP, of the Province of Portugal, taught at the Dominican *studium* in Fatima.
2. Johannes Willemse, OP, of the Province of the Netherlands, taught theology and exegesis at the Albertinum in Nijmegen.
3. Bonifac Willems, OP, of the Province of the Netherlands, taught dogmatic theology at the Albertinum in Nijmegen.
4. The book by John AT Robinson; cf above page 723, note 1.
5. Jean-Hervé Nicolas, OP, of the Province of Toulouse, Professor of Dogmatic Theology at Fribourg (Switzerland).

The same people who keep me constantly on all the roads of the world and ask me to come, to speak etc, say that they are hungering and thirsting with impatience for my books. No one has any conception of what my life is like, and how I can barely face each day, no longer having the time either to read or to write. They do not realise that I am in demand EVERYWHERE, and that what I give out here and there is in fact multiplied 200 times. I often think: only eschatology will resolve this insoluble problem of my poor life!

Friday 11 March 1966

This morning, it was principally I who held the stage.[1] But Le Guillou raised some serious problems of pneumatology on which we did not have time to linger. Requests continue to pour in: Naples, a theological congress in Rome (which I cannot and ought not refuse), the editor from the Radio wants my text of this evening: Fr Ortuño took notes yesterday evening and will make a translation of them.

Conversation: 1) with the Italians (who want to escape from the stupid elementary scholasticism that the Curia imposes on them); 2) With Frs Hill,[2] Horst[3] and Willemse: more reasonable than I had feared and than I had been led to anticipate.

In the evening, a lecture in Valencia, in the assembly hall of the secondary school run by our Fathers. Fr Ortuño translated paragraph by paragraph. Still more requests: Barcelona, the Summer School at Santander.

Saturday 12 March 1966

Concluding meeting. Still more requests: Fr Ryan: I must come and lecture in Oxford; the ecumenical situation there is interesting. Fr Dominguez: I must come to Portugal; we are so isolated there!

10.30 to 11.45 am, with the students of the *Studium*.[4] They asked me some interesting questions touching the points of contact and of joining between the 'traditional' positions and the queries of today's world. Numerous farewells and departures after lunch.

---

1. Cf Congar's lecture: 'Traditio thomistica in materia ecclesiologica', *Angelicum*, 1966, 405–428.
2. Edmund Hill, OP, of the Province of England, was Professor of Theology and Master of Students at the Dominican *studium* at Hawkesyard (England).
3. Ulrich Horst, OP, of the Province of Germany, taught fundamental theology at the Dominican *studium* of Walberberg near Bonn.
4. The lecture concerned: 'Tradition as the Word of God in the Christian Community'.

March 1966

Trip to the USA:[1] separate notes and dossier. What Willebrands told me about Ramsey's visit to Rome: *idem.*

July 1966

Fr Féret, who had it from Fr J Hoffer, Superior General of the Marianists, told me (at the end of July 1966) these facts which concern the delay in the decrees of application which were supposed to have appeared by 29 June 1966, and still have not appeared. The chief hold-up concerned the decree *Christus Dominus*, on the pastoral office of bishops. The Commission had prepared the elements of a *motu proprio* in fifty articles, half of which concerned Nos. 33–35 of the decree bearing on Religious. These twenty-five articles went into such details as, for example, the duty of bishops to check on the sanitary installations in religious houses, and reflect an attitude of interference by bishops in the lives of Religious. This provoked a spirited reaction from religious superiors, who addressed themselves to the Pope, who was very displeased and ordered the work to be done again.

The appointment of Fr Le Bourgeois, a Eudist, to the bishopric of Autun, is not unconnected with this incident. He was in effect Secretary of the Union of Religious Superiors in Rome.

Friday 23 September 1966

Left Strasbourg by car at 4.30 pm (with Fr Humbrecht,[2] Mlle Guillou). Got to Zurich just in time to get through the boarding gate for the plane. Reached Rome at 10.15 pm (11.15 local time). Spent the night at Hélène Stevens' place at EUR.

Saturday 24 September 1966

At 9.00 am at the Secretariat for Non-Believers. The meeting was held in the familiar room of the Secretariat for Unity. I knew and acknowledged Frs Miano, Girardi, Lubac, Rahner, Voillaume, C Murray, Sigmond, M Veronese, Sugranyes. But there were many experts whom I did not know:

De Rosa,[3] Reid,[4] Wetter,[5] de Toth,[6] Pfeil,[7] Alvarez-Bolado,[8] etc, and two priests from Yugoslavia . . .

---

1. There, amongst other activities, Congar participated in the Theology Week at the University of Notre Dame (see above pages 752 and 822), its acts were published in *Vatican II: An Interfaith Appraisal* (Notre Dame and London, 1966), and in a Symposium in Chicago (see above page 838 note 3). He wrote a little manuscript journal during this trip.
2. Joseph Humbrecht, OP, of the Province of France, of the Strasbourg Priory.
3. Guiseppe de Rosa, SJ.
4. John Patrick Reid, OP, of the Province of New York.
5. Gustav A Wetter, SJ.
6. Giovanni de Toth, priest of the diocese of Rome.
7. Hans Pfeil, priest of the diocese of Meissen.
8. Alfonso Alvarez-Bolado, SJ.

At first, GENERAL comments on the text of the proposed 'Directory'.[1]

I opened the attack: if it is a question of a Directory for the activity of the Secretariat, it should deal with quite different topics, for there is question there only of dialogue as a kind of specific activity, having its own internal consistency.

Rahner: to whom is it addressed? Is it a legal framework for the Secretariat as such, or are these directives for dialogue to be carried on by other people? There would be a good many other things to say: by whom? which? about what? should the episcopal conferences take initiatives.

X: attention is focussed on the Marxists, but there are also the Masons.

A Yugoslav OFM read a paper that he had prepared: dialogue is *novitas* [novelty]; it needs to be better explained as such. Furthermore, it is a bit concerned with pure dialogue *in vacuo, non in concreto* [in a vacuum, not in the concrete]. Together with the explanation of the *novitas*, we need to affirm our sincerity.

Veronese, in excellent Latin! It overlooks the object and the goal of the Church's solicitude, which is human beings, along the lines of the Pope's speech on 7 December 1965. It also lacks mention of literature, the arts, culture. That is a not unimportant sector!

Sugranyes: dialogue is taken in too limited a fashion, it is too institutionalised. It is seen as an object in itself: 'Now, we are dialoguing!' And one sets up an abstract figure of the non-believer, while the non-believer is what the modern world is normally made of.

Alvarez-Bolado, a Jesuit from Barcelona was one of the more caustic. He must have studied in Germany; his Latin was not fluent and he sometimes mixed in a German word. He said: dialogue should not be made into a kind of structure that would be external to ourselves. Insist on its anthropological necessity. On the other hand, it is never a matter of a single individual, it always expresses the attitudes of a community. The Church should frankly recognise that it has to create the CONDITIONS that make dialogue truly POSSIBLE. In my country, these conditions do not exist. If the Church truly believed in it, it would behave differently.

Courtney Murray: in the USA, from the Christian side, dialogue is inconceivable without the participation of Protestants.

Voillaume: why are those who are called non-believers not interested in dialogue with the Church? What would be the subject of dialogue? Why does it not exist? Because no one expects much from Catholics about the problems that the present world raises, and that are those that concern the future of humanity, the building up of humankind.

---

1. This refers to a plan for a Directory *de dialogo cum non-credentibus* [for dialogue with non-believers].

Miano: the activity of the Secretariat is much wider than this directory. The
    object of the latter is: some general norms for dialogue which will take
    place WITHIN THE CHURCH, and not just by the Secretariat.
Rahner [   ]
Myself: I insisted:
    1) On the necessity of PROVING OUR SINCERITY. The example
    of John XXIII. He put human beings before the assertion of his own
    power. What is expected of the Church is that it declare its belief in
    human beings;
    2) On the necessity of working with the others, with the WCC. I said
    a few words about my idea about the Secretariat for development
    and social justice. This poses a particular question in Rome, where
    everything is very compartmentalised. But everything involves
    everything else. In fact,
    3) what we recommend about dialogue involves not only Christian
    unity and the Missions, but the training of the clergy, which ought
    to be done with reference not to the past, to the Middle Ages, but to
    the present. It involves public opinion among Catholics, accustomed
    to regarding unbelief as a falling away, a sin; and so the direction of
    pastors . . .
Lubac was favourable to the inclusion of non-Catholics on the Christian side
    in our dialogue: the Secretariat for Non-Christian Religions want to
    do this. Note that OUR 'faith in humanity' is not the same as that of
    the others . . .
Murray: agreed with me and Lubac: In favour of the introduction to be given
    to the document, following not so much the texts of the magisterium
    (Paul VI and the Council) as the example of *Gaudium et spes:* show
    the Church in the world of today in order to show the sincerity of the
    Church in this dialogue and why we are setting it up.
Alvarez-Bolado: the Church should PROMOTE dialogue.
Miano raised some questions about the second part of the proposed
    document: are the distinctions (action—truth) valid? And it should
    speak about the difficulties the believer will have in dialogue.

There was a short break, which allowed me to get to know two or three whom I
did not know. Discussion of the text was resumed.

De Rosa: adopt the concept of dialogue in *Ecclesiam Suam*, or a wider one?
Giradi made the point that had been raised before the break, in particular an
    introduction to the text, where one would speak about the *novitas*, and
    the ecumenical point of view.
Wetter: proposed a different distribution of the material.

There was discussion about whether the concept of dialogue was the same in *Ecclesiam Suam* and in *Gaudium et Spes*. If not, how does it differ?

Pfeil, who seemed to me to have a rather systematic German mind:

> *Ecclesiam Suam*: the dialogue bears on SUPERNATURAL matters.
>
> *Gaudium et spes*: the dialogue bears on NATURAL, worldly, terrestrial affairs.

Rahner: OPENNESS is part of dialogue. It includes the possibility of transcending ourselves, going beyond ourselves, of going further [thanks to the other], even in what we hold.

Alvarez–Bolado.

Lubac.

Myself (in response to Pfeil):

> 1) The *colloquium salutis* [dialogue of salvation] of *Ecclesiam suam* is that of a doctor with his patient; the Church SUPPLIES, it does not receive. In *Gaudium et Spes* No. 44: the Church receives something from the world;
>
> 2) In opening myself up to dialogue, I am not necessarily seeking as the final goal, to bring the other to my faith. Dialogue has its own internal validity, and its immediate object is that 'going beyond self' that Rahner spoke of. It is quite distinct from preaching for the purpose of conversion.

Rahner: don't load everything on to dialogue. The Church has, and should have, other ways of talking to the non-believer.

Miano raised the question: WHAT IS LACKING IN THE PROPOSED TEXT?

Giradi: an admission of our development, a certain self-criticism. But if we make that admission, will the Congregation for the Doctrine of the Faith agree?

Murray: some words of repentance, as there are in the documents on Religious Freedom, Ecumenism, and *Gaudium et Spes*.

An Italian: the change is not only on the side of the Church but also on the side of the world.

Voillaume: indicate and state that, in the present promotion of humanity, the Church has something to learn and to receive from Non-Christians. That would be sufficient, without the confession of past sins. That would be wholly positive.

Sugranyes took up Veronese's idea: dialogue on the level of the sciences, the arts, culture.

Lubac: if there was a fault, it was rather that of confusion. He spoke along the lines of Voillaume.

> He made some comments about the use of the word 'values': page 14, lines 19–20: V{ery} G{ood}.
>
> Page 11, line 31–2: 'Christian values' is not a happy expression. It is really referring to our faith in God and in Jesus Christ.

Discussion went on to the question of the order, but it was nearly 12 Noon, and people were tired (I was).

> Wetter: it mixes up dialogue with the Communists and every other kind of
> dialogue. Shouldn't there be a special paragraph on the first of these?

This point was discussed. There was general opposition to a special paragraph concerning dialogue with Marxists. Rahner warned against any appearance of an offensive, militant aim. Rahner, when he speaks, has A DEPTH of thought, of HUMANITY of speech, of courage and of fairness. He is truly a gentleman.

From what he said, he and some others, it was agreed: no special paragraph for Marxists; that what one says always follows on from the requirements of dialogue, and that the unbeliever can (should) make his or her own the rules thus enunciated.

Since we were asked to return at 4.30 pm, to discuss the details of the text, I did not go back to EUR, and lunched at a nearby trattoria, Da Roberto. But how Italians do love noise!!!

At 3.30 pm, at Mgr Garrone's, who lives above the former premises of the Secretariat for Unity, at 64 Via dei Corridori, on the third floor. Mgr Garrone is just as I knew him: calm, envisaging the work to be done without bias or deviation. There are some truly intelligent people in his Congregation, but there are Staffa and Pizzardo. The latter arrives at his office at 8.30 am every morning, sits down in his armchair, and stays there, immobile, staring into the void, doing NOTHING. He signs papers without reading a line of them. When he has to chair a meeting, and say something at it, someone else writes his paper. And it is said 'The Congregation for Studies' thinks or says . . .

Mgr Garrone wants to work WITH people: WITH the bishops for the seminaries, which depend on them, WITH the universities.

On arriving at 64 Via dei Corridori, I met Mgr Willebrands. He told me about Barth's visit,[1] he is currently in Rome and is to be received by the Pope on Monday. Barth studied the conciliar texts for a month. He has drawn up some questions on each of them, and he has come to the source, to Rome, to hear the answers. Yesterday, he examined *De oecumenismo* and *De libertate religiosa* in this way. —I fill this out with what I heard from Barth himself. 'I have come to Rome to be clear about what it is that the Council wanted to say.' —The *De libertate* does not please him. It is aligned with the modern and entirely human idea of the dignity of the human person. The best text, in Barth's eyes, is *Ad Gentes*. Today, this morning, Barth spent three hours at the Gregorianum on the *De Revelatione*; just

---

1. On this visit cf Karl Barth, *Ad limina Apostolorum* (Zurich, 1967; French translation in: Karl Barth, *Entretiens à Rome après le Concile*, Cahiers theologiques 58 (Neuchâtel, 1968).

now, at 4.30 pm, he is at the Secretariat, that will be about the *De Sacra Liturgia*. Willebrands invited me, if I wanted to come. And so, at 4.30 pm, instead of continuing at the Secretariat for Non-Believers, I went into Mgr Willebrands' waiting room. Barth arrived with his wife and a young (assistant?). I embraced him. Also there were Fr Jungmann,[1] Dom Raphael Schulte[2] and another OSB,[3] a co-worker with Feiner on *Mysterium Salutis* in German, Willebrands and myself. Rahner arrived after 6.30 pm. Barth and he had never met before. This was the first time. I got the impression that they were profoundly in sympathy straightaway. See here the questions posed by Barth about the *De Liturgia,* and in general. They were taken up one by one. I intervened, reasonably well, in German or in French. Jungmann, who knows the liturgy like no one else, did not seem to me to be much of a theologian. It was touching to see the old prophet trembling a little, but still so attentive, forcing himself to understand from the theological angle, what had happened in Rome.

At the end, Barth insisted strongly that the Catholic Church should not make the same mistake as Protestantism which, since the end of the seventeenth century, had followed all the fashionable philosophies in turn. Let the Catholic Church profit from this lesson of history! Don't let it now put itself in tow to Heidegger and Bultmann!!! Barth fears that a trend in this direction is becoming apparent among us. But he added: I say this TO YOU. I shall not say it to those of the con servative trend that I shall meet!!! They would take advantage of my 'admission' to oppose an open attitude!!!

Barth repeated: Why, and in what way am I '*seiunctus*' [separated]?

Tomorrow this will be taken up again at the Gregorianum; on Monday afternoon at Santa Sabina on the *De Ecclesia*. As I have not been specifically invited, I do not count on going there. Besides, this will be the Theological Week[4] . . .

That finished at 7.15, or 7.20 pm. Return to EUR by taxi.

Return, too, to standard time.

Sunday 25 September 1966
A little work in the calm atmosphere of the apartment of Hélène Stevens. This evening we are going to the *Domus Pacis*. Some difficulty in getting there because of a street that is one-way only in THE EVENING, or even only on Sunday eve-

---

1. The Austrian, Josef A Jungmann, SJ, was one of the major makers of the liturgical movement in the twentieth century; he was Professor of Liturgy and Pastoral Theology at the Faculty of Theology in Innsbruck; after having been a member of the Preparatory Commission on the Liturgy, then a Council expert, he was a consultor for the Committee for the application of the Constitution on the Liturgy.
2. The German Benedictine, Raphael Schulte, of the Abbey of Gerleve, was Professor of Theology and Liturgy at the St Anselm Athenaeum.
3. Magnus Löhrer, of the Abbey of Einsiedeln (Switzerland), was Professor of Theology at the St Anselm Athenaeum.
4. This refers to a theological congress on Vatican II; Cf: A Schönmetzer, SJ, (editor), *Acta Congressus Internationalis de Theologia Concilii Vaticanii II*, (Rome, 1968).

nings. In the end, it was full of pilgrims, it was noisy, it was a real caravanserai. I went back to EUR to sleep. We will see what tomorrow is like!

Monday, 26 September 1966

At the *Domus Pacis* for 9.45 am. Within a few minutes I saw a crowd of friends or acquaintances, Roman and others. Dear Fr Lalande offered me the hospitality of the Holy Cross Fathers, whose house is quite close by, and where Frs de Lubac and Medina are already installed, and where Mgr McGrath will also be. So this problem was settled in an unexpected way.

A few words of introduction from Pizzardo: quite incomprehensible.

Reading of the Pope's letter, interesting, full of fine texts from the Council, and he is in favour of research.

A good introductory lecture by Mgr Garrone: in the same spirit.

Presentation of the origin and organisation of the Week by Fr Dhanis. Lecture by Parente.

A brief interval, during which I saw quite a few people, including Cardinal Ottaviani (I asked for an appointment: he VERY graciously gave me one for 11.00 am tomorrow morning), the attaché to the French ambassador,[11] Max Thurian, Fr General, etc.

Discussion of Parente's lecture. I was the first to intervene: he had identified the Church too closely with Christ. —Cardinal Ruffini thanked me for this intervention: he thought the same. There followed a second, rather long, intervention, then a third by Fr Tromp, on the relationship between the encyclical and *Lumen Gentium* on the question of the mystical body.

This Monday morning, between 11.30 am and midday, I thought about the audience that the Holy Father was giving to Barth, and I prayed to God in the perspective of his design of grace!

As I went out, clusters of young clerics, especially Spaniards, fell on me. Each one put HIS own question or sought direction for some work.

Lunch with the Fathers of the Holy Cross, where I have the room(s) of a Father who is away.

After lunch, a visit from Fr Desjean,[22] who is writing a thesis on me, on my ecumenism. He wants to come and see me in Strasbourg. . .

At 4.15 pm, the afternoon session. Fr Dhanis asked me to intervene in Colombo's lecture. This would definitely give him pleasure, he told me. Among other questions, I asked this one: what is the significance of the Reformation in the plan of God? This had me surrounded and assailed afterwards by dozens of young participants . . .

I sang to whomever I could my refrain about a Secretariat for Development and Justice: that is 1) an autonomous organism; 2) very much open to lay people;

---

1. This must refer to Paul Henry, first counsellor at the Embassy to the Holy See.
2. Georges-Étienne Desjean, CSC.

3) working in union with Geneva. I sang this refrain to Cardinal Roy, who came here for this Secretariat, to Mgr McGrath, who arrived at 2.00 pm; I will sing it to Mgr Colombo.

Tuesday 27 September 1966

An atrocious night. The father whose room I am in sleeps on a wooden board. But, even after I had removed the board, about midnight, I turned over more than a hundred times, with pain in every part of my back. I did not sleep much, and this morning I felt as though I had received one hundred blows with a staff.

Concelebration in French. At 9.15 am, in the Congress hall. I left between the presentation by Fr Braun[1] and that of Fr Balić (who, ALWAYS making the most of tactical opportunities, said to me beforehand: you will have some objections to raise!). I went to the Holy Office, where I had an appointment at 11.00 am with Cardinal Ottaviani. He received me at once, very cordially, and it lasted for ten minutes. It was concerned with the possibility of re-editing *Vrai et fausse réforme*.[2] This was his reply: there were some debatable passages (open to criticism) in the book, which were counterbalanced two or three pages later. The text should be revised in such a way as to be, in itself, beyond the reach of criticisms. I should, in the next few days, write a letter to the Cardinal, saying that I am prepared to revise, by means of discussion (for instance with Gagnebet), the passages that needed to be reworked. The Cardinal himself will present the matter to the next Congregation. I will then be able to have the discussion in question and to republish, taking it into account.

As he showed me out, the Cardinal said to me: one should always follow the Magisterium. If the Magisterium were not there, everything would collapse. One should espouse, explain and defend the thought of the Pope. In certain countries the Pope and the Curia are unjustly attacked. A theologian, who claims to be such, has attacked Paul VI in an ignoble manner. One should follow the Magisterium and the papacy. I am a good Dominican. Now, the Order of St Dominic has always been distinguished by its defence of the Holy See.

During the conversation I recalled what Mgr Montini had said to M. d'Ormesson:[3] Congar should be given the right to re-edit *Vrai et fausse réforme*. But, I added, I do not wish make use of these words.

I am rather crushed by this obsession Rome has with its authority. I know from history that it has only ever thought of that.

On the other hand, Gagnebet told me this morning that I was attacked in today's *Il Tempo* and treated as a 'progressive theologian'. Intellectually, that leaves me totally indifferent, but psychologically it wears me out!

---

1. François-M Braun, OP, of the Province of Belgium.
2. A first, abortive, attempt was made after the war. The book was to be re-edited in 1968, with a new preface and postface ('Unam Sanctam' 72.)
3. Wladimir d'Ormesson had been the French Ambassador to the Holy See from June to October 1940 and from 1948 to 1956.

In the afternoon, a physically very trying meeting, without a break until 7.15 pm. I received FIVE requests for articles or interviews. I refused them all. I can hardly stand up.

After supper, a long session with Fr Desjean. He does not know much. He will have to do a lot of work, and under the conditions demanded by his subject.

I hesitate to go to bed because I still have such pain in my sides as well as my back. I dread this bed!

Wednesday 28 September 1966

I slept in the armchair. It was better. This morning, quite a good session. First Barth came to join us. He was loudly applauded. I am afraid there was some whiff of triumphalism at the source of this applause. The same people had, I was told, yesterday applauded the mariological pirouettes and extravagances of Fr Balić . . . But, all the same, it does show that something has changed. Because this would have been impossible four or five years ago. *Deo Gratias.*

A very full presentation by Rahner,[1] in magnificent Latin and given with total human conviction. After him Fr Masson[2] seemed somewhat pale: it is undernourished, Daniélou said to me. After a discussion of the two reports, four shorter presentations on the Missions. Fr A Seumois commented on *Ad Gentes* in HIS understanding of it, and he was certainly not faithful either to the totality of the text or to its meaning.[3]

At 12.30 pm, with the Fathers of the Holy Cross, so marvelously hospitable, reception for Mgr Colombo, Mgr Nag.[4] Mgr Colombo told me that the Pope wants to see the theologians: not at audiences, but privately, with a relaxed timetable, in order to ask them questions and receive their suggestions. He likes to receive suggestions. Colombo told me that he would try to get me invited like this some time.

In the afternoon, a visit and several further requests for articles on this and that. I refused them all. The way that people have no regard for the work involved is very tiresome.

A very good session, though overloaded. The lecture by Fr Alszeghy,[5] on what theology could or should be, from the point of view of salvation history, caused a great stir. Piolanti threw himself on Cardinal Ruffini. He seemed to be very ex-

---

1. '*De praesentia Domini in communitate cultus: synthesis theologica*' [on the presence of the Lord in the community of worship. A theological synthesis].
2. The Belgian missiologist, Joseph Masson, SJ, gave a presentation on '"Love-as-Source", the mover and form of all mission'.
3. A presentation of which the title was '*Finis proprius activitatis missionalis*' [the proper goal of missionary activity].
4. Probably Lorenzo Satoshi Nagae.
5. Zoltan Alszeghy, SJ, taught theology at the Gregorianum; his lecture was entitled: '*Quid reflexio ad historiam salutis a theologia exigat?*' [What reflection on salvation history is called for by theology?].

cited. However he paid me some compliments: I am a true disciple of St Thomas .
. . It is certain that Alszeghy allowed himself to be carried away by his subject. But
Piolanti (and Ruffini) seemed equally very unhappy with the (admirable) paper
of Fr Benoit and with the intervention of Fr de la Potterie which followed it.[1] La
Potterie wished that the Council had adopted the BIBLICAL concept of truth,
instead of the *Adaequatio rei et intellectus* [equivalence between the intellect and
its object].

In the evening, dinner at EUR at Hélène Stevens' place; Madame Parisot, who
had just arrived from Hungary, was there. I slept there: a stormy night: I had felt
it coming!

Thursday 29 September 1966

Fr de Lubac told me how that the original plan for the Theology Week (proposed
by the Congregation for Studies, that is to say, by Staffa) was very restricted and
rather pointed with respect to the men invited. Tucci had told Lubac this last
April. The Pope had then declared himself dissatisfied with this plan, and asked
that it be expanded. Hence what is now happening. The appointment of Mgr Garrone to the Congregation had even been hastened by this fact.

This morning, some very good papers: Fr Betti[2] dense, solid; Fr Murray[3] a true
gentleman, with a sensational command of Latin! Afterwards, among the interventions, Mgr Colombo reverted to Alszeghy's exposition: this was to give him
the opportunity to explain himself and so to respond to some lively criticisms that
had been addressed to him.

A quarter-of-an-hour's paper by Chenu, for whom Latin is evidently a shackle.
But it got by, all the same! All morning, thunderstorms: the worst sort of weather
for me!

After lunch, an hour with the students to respond (?) to their questions. In the
afternoon, after Mgr Wright, who sweated profusely, it was my turn.[4] I did what
I could, but I could do no more. Assailed by people who questioned me on every
imaginable subject, I had no voice, no strength left.

In the evening, dinner with the Chargé d'affaires[5] (in the absence of the Ambassador, and with myself due to be absent on Saturday): guests included Fr Le

---

1. *'De indole veritatis in Sacra Scriptura'* [On the innate character of truth in Holy Scrip-
ture].
2. *'De Sacra Traditione iuxta Constitutionem dogmaticam, "Dei Verbum"'* [on sacred Tradition according to the dogmatic Constitution 'Dei Verbum'] .
3. *'De argumentis pro iure hominis ad libertatem religiosam* [on the arguments for the
right of humankind to religious freedom].
4. *'De commercio inter ecclesiam et mundum secundum Constitutionem "Gaudium et spes"*
(N. 44)' [on the exchange between Church and World according to the Constitution
'Gaudium et Spes', No. 44].
5. Paul Henry.

Blond, SJ[1] (who is at present at the General Chapter of the Jesuit Fathers: Second session!), Fr Humbertclaude,[2] Secretary to the Secretariat for Non-Christian Religions, Fr Wenger and Max Thurian. Conversation was mainly about China and Vietnam.

Last night a tremendous storm which was still going all the morning of [ ].

Friday 30 September 1966

Presentations by Daniélou and Hamer, under the chairmanship of Cardinal Bea. An objector to Murray, who had been kept away up until this, managed to get himself heard. He was a poor fellow, traumatised by a stupid adventure, but who had within himself all the tenacity of a paranoiac or schizophrenic. (Mgr [ ] had been a long time at the Holy Office, as a right-hand man of Cardinal Ottaviani. One of his objects, Gagnebet told me, was to get Maritain condemned. One day when he was at Fiumicino on his way back, he was more or less kidnapped in a car falsely carrying the badge of the Vatican, and represented as having come to collect him, and taken to a brothel . . . He has remained permanently traumatised by this. He now has a sinecure as a canon of St Peters.)

Departure from Fiumicino at 11.10 am. Zurich. Strasbourg without incident.

---

1. Jean-Marie le Blond, SJ.
2. Pierre Humbertclaude was the Procurator General of the Marianists.

POINTS OF REFERENCE

1959
January
This was when John XXIII, according to his own admission, had the first inspiration for a council.

25 January
The Pope announced to a group of eighteen cardinals, meeting at St Paul-Outside-the-Walls, his intention to convoke a council. The Vatican published a communiqué the same evening: 'The purpose of the Council, in the mind of the Holy Father, is not only the spiritual good of the Christian people, but seeks equally to be an invitation to separated communities to search for unity.'

29 January
The cardinals of the entire world were invited to give their views about the Pope's intention.

27 April
In a speech broadcast on radio, the Pope invited the Catholics of the world to pray for the Council.

27 May (Pentecost)
Inauguration of the 'ante-preparatory phase'. This was to last until 1 May 1960. It was to allow for the gathering of suggestions for the Council from bishops, from universities.

1960
5 June
John XXIII created ten commissions and three Secretariats for the preparation of schemas to be submitted to the Council.

14 November

Solemn opening of the preparatory works. The Pope explained to the members of Secretariats and Commissions the orientation he wished to give to the Council.

1961

The year 1961 was almost entirely occupied with the work of Commissions and Secretariats.

Christmas

Signing by John XXIII of the bull, *Humanae Salutis* which announced the opening of the council for 1962. The precise date would be fixed later. It was to be 11 October.

1962
11 June

Final session of the Central Commission. The Pope had declared on the previous day, the day of Pentecost: 'The Church which is about to go into council, rejects nothing of the riches and beauty of the present world. . . It wants to assist and to love the people of today.'

6 September

A *motu proprio* from the Pope laid down the regulations for the Council.

THE FIRST SESSION

11 October

Opening of the First Session of Vatican II in St Peter's basilica. In the evening, arrival in Rome of two Observers from the Russian Orthodox Church, from Moscow.

12 October

John XXIII received the representatives of diplomatic missions in the Sistine chapel.
John XXIII added fourteen new experts to the 201 already appointed. He received the special diplomatic missions in the Sistine chapel.

13 October

Meeting of the first General Congregation, intended for electing the 160 members of the ten Commissions. It dispersed after half-an-hour: because Cardinal Liénart, supported by Cardinal Frings, proposed deferring the first rounds of voting to Tuesday 16 October, so that the Council Fathers could get to know each other, and consult among themselves about the candidates, a proposition accepted by acclamation.
The French bishops met in the afternoon.

John XXIII received the thirty-nine non-Catholic Observers in the Hall of the Consistory, and journalists in the Sistine Chapel.

14 October
A further meeting of the French bishops. Other national episcopates held similar meetings in the following days. In a press conference, l'abbé Haubtmann, director of the religious information office of the French episcopate, insisted on the fact that the French bishops wished, at all costs, to avoid the formation of blocs.

15 October
John XXIII received the Observer delegated by the Methodists, Bishop Fred Colson.
Mgr Cassien (Bezobrazov), Russian Orthodox bishop, Rector of the St Sergius Institute in Paris, accepted an invitation to be present at the Council. This was the second Orthodox bishop, with Mgr Antoine (Bartasevic) of Geneva.
Cardinal Bea offered a reception to Non-Catholic Observers.
The Pope named four under-secretaries to the Council.
Meeting of the Eastern patriarchs around Mgr Meouchi.

16 October
Second General Congregation: the Fathers had only until 6.00 pm for submitting their lists for the Commissions. The counting of votes (430,000) was to continue until Saturday 29 October, the date for the Third General Congregation
The Pope had a long session with the ten members of the Council of Presidents.
Second meeting of the Non-Catholic Observers at the Secretariat for Unity.

18 October
The Pope named Cardinal Wyszyński, Primate of Poland, as the seventh member of the Secretariat for Extraordinary Questions. He also appointed a fifth under-secretary for the Council.
Meeting of the ten members of the Council of Presidents.

Between 18 and 21 October
Various meetings of national or regional episcopates prepared the discussions on the *schema on the Liturgy*. In particular, the bishops of Africa (indigenous and missionary), who had created a Secretariat for themselves, presided over by Cardinal Rugambwa (Tanganyka), held a meeting with the French bishops, and in the course of another meeting, Canon Martimort (France) gave them the explanatory lecture on the liturgy that he had already given to the bishops of France.

20 October
Third General Congregation, presided over by Cardinal Liénart. John XXIII set aside article thirty-nine of the regulations (which called for an absolute majority)

so that the sixteen candidates who, for each Commission, received the highest number of votes were elected. The names of the members elected for seven of the ten Commissions were published.

From 21 October to 15 November
The schema prepared by the Commission for the Liturgy formed the basis of the Council's work.

22 October
At the fourth General Congregation, presided over by Cardinal Gilroy, Archbishop of Sydney, two presentations were made to the Fathers regarding the *Schema on the Liturgy*, one by Cardinal Larraona, the other by Most Reverend Fr Antonelli. Immediately afterwards, and again the following day, 23 October, numerous interventions were offered on this schema as a whole.

25 October—15 November
The preambles and the eight chapters of the schema were examined by the Fathers, and gave rise to multiple interventions. 14 November: first votes on 'the guiding principles of the *Schema on the Liturgy*, which seek, with prudence and understanding, to render the different parts of the liturgy more alive and more formative, in conformity with current pastoral requirements', and on the sending back of amendments to the Commission (nearly 2,000 of them).
 Results of this vote: In favour: 2,162; against: 46; null: 7.

Other votes, producing rather similar results, were to take place on 17 November. During this same period, there a great deal of peripheral activity on the subject of the *schema on the Liturgy*: a press conference by Mgr van Bekkum, Archbishop of Ruteng (Indonesia), a lecture by Cardinal Lercaro to the Brazilian episcopate, of Mgr Jenny, Auxiliary of Cambrai, to French-speaking journalists.

Other events:
- The Secretariat for Christian Unity, presided over by Cardinal Bea, was, by the decision of the Pope, assimilated to a conciliar Commission, and consequently would be able to present the schemas it had prepared.

- On 13 November, Cardinal Cicognani announced to the Fathers that the Sovereign Pontiff had decided to introduce the name of St Joseph into the canon of the Mass.

14 November
In the course of the nineteenth General Congregation, Cardinal Ottaviani presented the five chapters of the Theological schema on the sources of Revelation: 1) The double source of revelation; 2) Inspiration and the literary genres in Scripture; 3–4. The Old and New Testament; 5) Holy Scripture in the Church.

This presentation was immediately followed by interventions on the schema as a whole. In the first place were heard some cardinals who outlined, in a general kind of way, a discussion that would reveal two main tendencies.

16 November
At the twentieth, twenty-second and twenty-third General Congregations, continuation of interventions on the schemas as a whole.

20 November
At the twenty-third General Congregation, presided over by Cardinal Frings, there was a vote on the appropriateness of interrupting the study of the schema. 1,368 Fathers voted in favour of interruption, 822 against. The vote was not without significance, but it could not be decisive because the two-thirds majority was not obtained.

21 November
Pope John XXIII made known to the Council his decision to adjourn the debate on the sources of Revelation, and to confide to a Joint Commission of some cardinals, some members of the Theological Commission and of the Secretariat for Unity, the task of producing another draft of the schema.

23 November
Cardinal Cento introduced the schema on 'The Means of Social Communication', and Mgr Stourm (France) read out the report presenting it.

26 November
End of the discussion about the Modern Means of Communication, with the unanimous consent of the assembly. At the end of the twenty-seventh General Congregation, presided over by Cardinal Tisserant, the 2,133 Fathers present began the study of the schema prepared by the Commission for the Eastern Churches on Unity.

27-28-29 November
The discussion of this schema was continued through the course of General Congregations, which also included several votes on the Modern Means of Communication and on the Liturgy.

1 December
On the proposition of Mgr Felici, the Fathers voted on the following text: 'as the examination of the Decree on the Unity of the Church has been concluded, the Council Fathers approve it as a document in which are gathered the common truths of the Faith, and as a mark of respect and goodwill towards our separated brothers in the East. However, in conformity with the comments and proposi-

tions formulated in the Council Hall, this decree should form a single document with the Decree on Ecumenism and the chapter on the same subject contained in the schema of the Dogmatic Constitution on the Church.' This text was adopted by 2,068 votes in favour, with 36 against.

1 December
The schema on the Church was introduced by Cardinal Ottaviani and presented by Mgr Franić (Yugoslavia).

3–4–5 and 6 December
Various interventions concerning the schema on the Church.

5 December
At the thirty-fourth General Congregation, presided over by Cardinal Alfrink, in the presence of 2,114 Fathers a booklet was distributed to the members of the Council containing a list of the various subjects which constituted the programme of Vatican II. The number of schemas was reduced to 20, although the Central Commission had accepted 73.

6 December
Mgr Felici communicated to the Council the regulations laid down by John XXIII for work in the interval between Sessions.

7 December
Allocution by his Holiness John XXIII for the end of the First Session.

8 December
Solemn closure of the First Session.

SECOND SESSION

1963
29 September
At 9.00 am, opening of the Second Session of Vatican II, in the basilica of St Peter. After Mass celebrated by Cardinal Tisserant, Dean of the Sacred College, and sung by the assembly, Paul VI pronounced his profession of faith; the new Fathers appointed since the end of the First Session did the same, through the mouth of Mgr Felici, Secretary General. The obedience of the cardinals. Paul VI pronounced, in Latin, a message which reaffirmed and made more precise the task of the Council and, at the same time, the programme of his pontificate.

2,427 Fathers had announced their participation in the Second Session: 75 cardinals, 2,228 archbishops and bishops, 59 prefects apostolic and 65 superiors general of Orders and Congregations.

30 September
Thirty-seventh General Congregation, under the direction of Cardinal Agagianian, 2,258 Fathers present. Mass celebrated in the Ambrosian rite by Mgr Colombo (Milan). After the address of a message to the Pope and indication of the practical implications of the new regulations, the opening of the debate on the schema *De Ecclesia*.
- Paul VI received the journalists.

1 October
Thirty-eighth General Congregation, under the direction of Cardinal Lercaro. 2,301 Fathers present. By a majority of 2,231 *placet*, 43 *non placet*, and 27 invalid votes, the assembly decided to 'retain the schema' *De Ecclesia*.
- Meeting of Non-Catholic Observers with the Secretariat for Unity.

2 October
Thirty-ninth General Congregation, under the direction of Cardinal Döpfner. Continuation of the debate about Chapter I of the schema *De Ecclesia*. Press conference of Fr Feifel, SJ, expert on non-Christian religions.

3 October
Fortieth General Congregation, under the direction of Cardinal Suenens. Continuation of the debate on Chapter I of the schema *De Ecclesia*.

4 October
Forty-first General Congregation. End of the debates on Chapter I of the schema *De Ecclesia*, and beginning of the discussion of Chapter II.

7 October
Forty-second General Congregation. Continuation of discussion of Chapter II of the schema *De Ecclesia*.

8 October
Forty-third General Congregation, under the direction of Cardinal Döpfner. Vote on four amendments to Chapter II of the *Schema on the Liturgy*: on the definition of the Mass (2,278 *placet*, 12 *non placet*, 8 null;) on the use of vernacular language (2,264, 14, 12); on the simplification of the ritual of the Mass (2,249, 31, 4); on the homily (2,263, 15, 7). Presentation of the work of the Liturgical Commission by Cardinal Lercaro (Italy) and Mgr Viana (Spain). Continuation of the discussion of Chapter II of the schema *De Ecclesia*.
- Paul VI appointed M. Veronese, former President of UNESCO and of the first two world congresses of the Lay Apostolate, as one of the Lay Auditors; M. Jean Guitton, accepted among the Lay Observers by John XXIII, chose the status of Lay Auditor.

9 October

Forty-fourth General Congregation, under the direction of Cardinal Suenens. Vote on four amendments to Chapter II of the *Schema on the Liturgy*. Continuation of the discussion of Chapter II of the schema *De Ecclesia*.

10 October

Forty-fifth General Congregation, under the direction of Cardinal Agagianian. Vote on nine amendments to Chapter II of the *schema on the Liturgy*. Continuation of the discussion of Chapter II of the schema *De Ecclesia*.
- First of a series of meetings of Superiors General of Religious Orders and Congregations.

11 October

Forty-sixth General Congregation, under the direction of Cardinal Lercaro. Continuation of the discussion of Chapter II of the schema *De Ecclesia*.
- At Mass, remembrance of the catastrophe of Vaiont, and distribution of Communion to the Lay Auditors present.
- Paul VI celebrated at St Mary Major the divine motherhood of Mary, and the first anniversary of the opening of the Council by John XXIII.

13 October

Beatification of John Népomucène Neumann.

14 October

Forty-seventh General Congregation, under the direction of Cardinal Döpfner. Vote on Chapter II of the *schema on the Liturgy* as a whole: 1,417 *placet*, 36 *non placet*, 781 *placet iuxta modum*, 8 null; the chapter was sent back to the Commission. Continuation of the discussion of Chapter II of the schema *De Ecclesia*.
- The six Eastern patriarchs took their seats at a table opposite the seats of the cardinals.

15 October

Forty-eighth General Congregation, under the direction of Cardinal Suenens. Vote on four amendments to Chapter III of the *Schema on the Liturgy*, presented by Mgr Hallinan (USA). Vote, by sitting or standing, on the closure of the discussion of Chapter II of the schema *De Ecclesia*.
- Paul VI appointed M. Emilio Inglesis as one of the Lay Auditors.

16 October

Forty-ninth General Congregation. Vote on four amendments to Chapter III of the *Schema on the Liturgy*. Despite the vote taken the previous day, prolongation of Chapter II of the schema *De Ecclesia* and opening of the debate on Chapter III.

17 October
Fiftieth General Congregation. Discussion of Chapter III of the schema *De Ecclesia*.
- Paul VI received the sixty-six Non-Catholic Observers, and gave an important discourse.

18 October
Fifty-first General Congregation, under the direction of Cardinal Döpfner. Discussion of Chapter II of the schema *De Ecclesia*.

20 October
Paul VI consecrated fourteen missionary bishops.

21 October
Fifty-second General Congregation, under the direction of Cardinal Döpfner. Presentation by Mgr Martin (Canada), of Chapter II of the *Schema on the Liturgy*, and the amendments which were to be put to the vote. Continuation of the discussion of Chapter III of the schema *De Ecclesia*.

22 October
Fifty-third General Congregation. Continuation of the debate on Chapter III of the schema *De Ecclesia*.

23 October
Fifty-fourth General Congregation. Continuation of the debate on Chapter III of the schema *De Ecclesia*.

24 October
Fifty-fifth General Congregation. Vote on Chapter IV of the *Schema on the Liturgy* (Divine Office): 1,683 *placet*, 505 *placet iuxta modum*, 43 *non placet*. Interventions by Cardinal König (Austria), in favour, and of Cardinal Santos (Philippines) against the integration of the *schema on the Virgin* into the schema *De Ecclesia*. Continuation and conclusion of the debate on Chapter III of the schema *De Ecclesia*.

25 October
Fifty-sixth General Congregation. Vote on the final amendments to Chapter V of the *Schema on the Liturgy*. Prolongation (in virtue of article 57 of the regulations) of the debate on Chapter III of the schema *De Ecclesia*, and the beginning of the debate on Chapter IV, on holiness in the Church.

27 October
Beatification of Fr Dominic of the Mother of God.

28 October
Commemoration of the election of John XXIII: celebration of Mass by Paul VI, and reading, in French, of a tribute to the instigator of the Council by Cardinal Suenens.

29 October
Fifty-seventh General Congregation. Vote on the integration of the *schema on the Virgin* into the schema *De Ecclesia:* 1,114 *placet*; 1,074 *non placet*. Vote on Chapter V of the *Schema on the Liturgy* (the liturgical year): 2,054 *placet*, 21 *non placet*, 16 *placet iuxta modum*. Continuation of the debate on Chapter IV of the schema *De Ecclesia.*

30 October
Fifty-eighth General Congregation. *Votes of orientation.* Continuation of the debate on Chapter IV of the schema *De Ecclesia.*

31 October
Fifty-ninth General Congregation. Conclusion of the debate on Chapter IV of the schema *De Ecclesia.*

3 November
Beatification of Leonardo Murialdo.

4 November
Celebration of the fourth centenary of the institution of seminaries by the Council of Trent.

5 November
Sixtieth General Congregation. Opening of the debate on the *schema on Bishops and the Government of Dioceses*, presented by Cardinal Marella (Curia) and Mgr Carli (Italy).

7 November
Sixty-first General Congregation. By a majority of more than seventy per cent, the Fathers decided to continue the examination of the current plan on *Bishops and the Government of Dioceses* and continued the discussion of Chapter I on the relations between bishops and the Roman Curia.

8 November
Sixty-second General Congregation. Distribution of Chapter IV of the schema *De oecumenismo*, on the attitude of Catholics with regard to the Jews. Continuation of the debate on Chapter I of the schema on *Bishops and the Government of Dioceses.*

9 November
Sixty-third General Congregation. Continuation of the debate on Chapter I of the schema on *Bishops and Dioceses*; opening of the discussion on Chapter II, on coadjutor and auxiliary bishops, introduced by a report from Mgr Carli (Italy).

11 November
Sixty-fourth General Congregation. Continuation of the discussion of Chapter II of the schema on *Bishops and Dioceses*. Clarification by Cardinal Döpfner of the implications of the vote on five questions: he indicated the path to be followed.

12 November
Sixty-fifth General Congregation. Conclusion of the discussion of Chapter II of the schema on *Bishops and Dioceses*, and beginning of that on Chapter III, on episcopal conferences. The Council decided to remit, without discussion, to the commission for the revision of Canon Law, the current Chapter V of the schema, which concerned the setting up and the territorial boundaries of parishes.

13 November
Sixty-sixth General Congregation. Continuation of the discussion on episcopal conferences. Mgr Carli again criticised the indicative vote about the five questions, and denied that the episcopal conference had its basis in collegiality.

14 November
Sixty-seventh General Congregation. Mgr Felici announced that the next Session of the Council would be programmed in such a way that the Fathers would be able to attend the Eucharistic Congress in Bombay (28 November—6 December 1964). Votes on the two chapters of the *schema on the Means of Social Communication*: Chapter I: 1,832 *placet*, 243 *placet iuxta modum*, 92 null; Chapter II: 1,893 *placet*, 125 *placet iuxta modum*, 103 null. Continuation of the discussion on episcopal conferences, and the beginning of the debate on Chapter IV of the schema in question, on the division and boundaries of dioceses.

16 November
Sixty-eighth General Congregation. Continuation and conclusion of the discussion on *Bishops and the Government of Dioceses*.

18 November
Sixty-ninth General Congregation. The assembly definitively approved (by 2,066 votes to 20, with 2 null ballots) the introduction and the first chapter of the *schema on the Liturgy*. Cardinal Cicognani (Curia) presented the *schema on Ecumenism*; Mgr Martin, Archbishop of Rouen (France), as rapporteur, explained the content of the first three chapters. General discussion of the schema as a whole.

19 November

Seventieth General Congregation. Cardinal Bea presented Chapter IV of the *schema on Ecumenism*, concerning the Jews; Mgr De Smedt, Bishop of Bruges, Chapter V, concerning religious freedom, followed by discussion of the schema as a whole.

20 November

Seventy-first General Congregation. Definitive vote on Chapter II of the *Schema on the Liturgy*, by 2,112 to 40. Continuation of the discussion of the *schema on Ecumenism* as a whole.

21 November

Seventy-second General Congregation. Definitive vote on Chapter III of the *Schema on the Liturgy*. Opening of the discussion on Chapter I of the *schema on Ecumenism*.

22 November

Seventy-third General Congregation. *The Council approved*, by 2,158 votes to 19, with one null ballot, the *Constitution on the Liturgy*, which was thus the first text definitively voted by the Second Vatican Council.

Some new interventions on the *schema on Ecumenism* in general.

25 November

Seventy-fourth General Congregation. *The Council approved the Decree on the Means of Social Communication*. Continuation of the discussion on Chapter I and the beginning of the discussion of Chapter II of the *schema on Ecumenism*.

26 November

Seventy-fifth General Congregation. Continuation of the discussion of Chapter I and II of the *schema on Ecumenism*.

27 November

Seventy-sixth General Congregation. End of the discussion of Chapter II and the beginning of the discussion of Chapter III of the *schema on Ecumenism*.

28 November

Seventy-seventh General Congregation. *Vote* for the enlargement of the conciliar Commissions. Continuation of the debate on the *De Revelatione*.

29 November

Seventy-eighth General Congregation. Deferment of the plan for a Message to Priests. Continuation of the debate on the *De Revelatione*.

2 December

Seventy-ninth General Congregation. Announcement of the adjournment of the Message to Priests. Continuation of the debate on Chapter III of the *schema on Ecumenism* and conclusion of the debate on the first three chapters. Presentation of the schema on the *Apostolate of the Laity*.

3 December

Ceremony commemorating the fourth centenary of the Council of Trent and reading of the motu proprio *Pastorale Munus*.

4 December

Public sitting for closure of the Second Session. Final *votes* on the *Constitution on the Liturgy* and the *Decree on the Means of Social Communication*. Promulgation of these texts by the Pope, who made an address.

THIRD SESSION

1964
14 September

At 9.00 am, opening of the Third Session in St Peter's Basilica. After Mass, concelebrated by the Pope and twenty-four bishops, the bishops who had been appointed since the closure of the Second Session pronounced their profession of faith, through the mouth of Mgr Felici, Secretary General. Paul VI gave an allocution in Latin focussing the attention of the Council on the problems of the episcopate.

15 September

Eightieth General Congregation. Cardinal Tisserant (President), Cardinal Agagianian (Moderator), and Mgr Felici (Secretary General) greeted the assembly and introduced the work with directives about procedure and appeals for discretion. Opening of the debate on Chapter VII of the *De Ecclesia*.

16 September

Eighty-first General Congregation. Conclusion of the debate on Chapter VII of the *De Ecclesia* and beginning of the debate on Chapter VIII of the same schema.

17 September

Eighty-second General Congregation. Announcement of the vote held the previous day on Chapter I of the *De Ecclesia*: 2,114 *placet*, 11 *non placet*, and 63 *placet iuxta modum*. Continuation of the debate on Chapter VIII of the *De Ecclesia*.

18 September

Eighty-third General Congregation. Conclusion of the debate on Chapter VIII of the *De Ecclesia*. Opening of the debate on the schema *on the Pastoral Office of Bishops*.

21 September
Eighty-fourth General Congregation. *Vote* on four amendments to Chapter III of the *De Ecclesia*. Continuation of the debate on the schema *on the Pastoral Office of Bishops*. Presentation of reports for and against the amendments suggested for Chapter III of the *De Ecclesia*.

22 September
Eighty-fifth General Congregation. *Vote* on eight amendments to Chapter III of the *De Ecclesia*. Continuation of the debate on the schema *on the Pastoral Office of Bishops*.

23 September
Paul VI brought into the basilica the head of St Andrew, which was to be restored to the Church of Patras; homily by Cardinal König.
- Eighty-sixth General Congregation. *Votes* on five amendments to Chapter III of the *De Ecclesia*. Conclusion of the debate *on the Pastoral Office of Bishops*. Beginning of the debate on *Religious Freedom*, introduced by Mgr De Smedt (Belgium).

24 September
Eighty-seventh General Congregation. *Votes* on six amendments to Chapter III of the *De Ecclesia*. Continuation of the debate on *Religious Freedom*.

25 September
Eighty-eighth General Congregation. *Vote* on six amendments to Chapter III of the *De Ecclesia*. Conclusion of the debate on *Religious Freedom*. Presentation of the *Declaration on Non-Christians and, in particular, the Jews*, by Cardinal Bea (Curia).

28 September
Eighty-ninth General Congregation. *Votes* on six amendments to Chapter III of the *De Ecclesia*. Conclusion of the debate on the *Declaration on Non-Christians and, in particular, the Jews*.

29 September
Ninetieth General Congregation. *Vote* on six amendments to Chapter III of the *De Ecclesia*. Continuation of the debate on *non-Christians and, in particular, the Jews*.

30 September
Ninety-first General Congregation. *Vote* on Chapter III and IV of the *De Ecclesia*. Beginning of the debate on the *De Revelatione*.

1 October
Ninety-second General Congregation. Continuation of the debate on the *De Revelatione*.

2 October
Ninety-third General Congregation. Continuation of the debate on the *De Revelatione*.

5 October
Ninety-fourth General Congregation. Four *votes* on the schema *De Œcumenismo*. Continuation of the debate on the *De Revelatione*.

6 October
Ninety-fifth General Congregation. Five *votes* on the schema *De Œcumenismo*. Introduction to debate on the schema on the *Apostolate of the Laity* by Cardinal Cento. Conclusion of the debate on the *De Revelatione*.

7 October
Ninety-sixth General Congregation. Four *votes* on the schema *De Œcumenismo*. Continuation of the debate on the schema on the *Apostolate of the Laity*.

8 October
Ninety-seventh General Congregation. One *vote* on the schema *De Œcumenismo*. Continuation of the debate on the schema on the *Apostolate of the Laity*.

9 October
Ninety-eighth General Congregation. Continuation of the debate on the schema on the *Apostolate of the Laity*.

12 October
Ninety-ninth General Congregation. Continuation of the debate on the schema on the *Apostolate of the Laity*.

13 October
One hundredth General Congregation. Conclusion of the debate on the *Apostolate of the Laity*. Opening of the debate on the schema *on Priests*, presented by Mgr Marty.

14 October
Hundred-and-first General Congregation. Continuation of the debate on *Priestly Life and Ministry*.

15 October
Hundred-and-second General Congregation. Conclusion of the debate on *Priestly Life and Ministry*. Opening of the debate on *the Eastern Churches*, presented by Mgr Bukatko.

October
Hundred-and-third General Congregation. Distribution of the instruction for the Liturgy. Continuation of the debate on *the Eastern Churches*.

19 October
Hundred-and-fourth General Congregation. *Votes* on the declaration *on Priests* and on the amendments to Chapter VII of the *De Ecclesia*. Continuation of the debate on *the Eastern Churches*.

20 October
Hundred-and-fifth General Congregation. *Votes* on *the Eastern Churches* and on Chapter VII of the *De Ecclesia* as a whole. Conclusion of the debate on *the Eastern Churches*. Opening of the debate on *schema XIII*, introduced by Mgr Guano (Italy).

21 October
Hundred-and-sixth General Congregation. *Votes* on *the Eastern Churches*. Continuation of the debate on *schema XIII*.

22 October
Hundred-and-seventh General Congregation. *Votes* on *the Eastern Churches*. Continuation of the debate on *schema XIII*.

23 October
Hundred-and-eighth General Congregation. Conclusion of the debate on *schema XIII* as a whole. *Vote* to take *schema XIII* into consideration. Beginning of the debate on the preamble and Chapter I of *schema XIII*.

26 October
Hundred-and-ninth General Congregation. Continuation of the debate on the preamble and Chapter I and II of *schema XIII*.

27 October
Hundred-and-tenth General Congregation. Continuation of the debate of Chapter II and III of *schema XIII*.

28 October
Hundred-and-eleventh General Congregation. Continuation of the debate on Chapter IV of *schema XIII*.

29 October
Hundred-and-twelfth General Congregation. *Vote* on Chapter VIII of the *De Ecclesia*. Continuation of the debate on Chapter IV of *schema XIII*.

30 October
Hundred-and-thirteenth General Congregation. *Vote* on the amended text of Chapters I and II of the *De Ecclesia*. Continuation of the debate on Chapter IV of *schema XIII*.

4 November
Hundred-and–fourteenth General Congregation. *Votes* on Chapter I of the schema *on the Pastoral Office of Bishops* as a whole, and the amendments to Chapter II. Continuation of the debate on Chapter IV of *schema XIII*.

5 November
Hundred-and-fifteenth General Congregation. *Votes* on the amendments to the schema *on the Pastoral Office of Bishops*. Continuation of the debate on Chapter IV of *schema XIII*.

6 November
Hundred-and-sixteenth General Congregation, under the presidency of the Pope. *Votes* on Chapter II of the schema *on the Pastoral Office of Bishops* as a whole, and on the amendments to Chapter III of the same schema. Beginning of the debate on *the Missions*, introduced by Cardinal Agagianian and Mgr Lokuang.

7 November
Hundred–and-seventeenth General Congregation. Continuation of the debate on *the Missions*.

9 November
Hundred-and-eighteenth General Congregation. Conclusion of the debate, and *vote* on *the Missions*. Continuation of the debate on Chapter IV of *schema XIII*.

10 November
Hundred-and-nineteenth General Congregation. *Vote* on the amended texts of the preamble and Chapter I of the *De Œcumenismo*. End of the debate on *schema XIII*. Opening of the debate on *Religious Life*, introduced by Mgr Shea.

11 November
Hundred-and-twentieth General Congregation. *Vote* on the amended text of Chapter II of the *De Œcumenismo*. Continuation of the debate *on Religious Life*.

Beginning of the debate on *Religious Life*.

12 November
Hundred-and-twenty-first General Congregation. Conclusion of the debate and *vote* on *Religious Life*. Opening of the debate on *Seminaries*.

14 November
Hundred-and-twenty-second General Congregation. *Votes* on Chapter III of the schema *De Œcumenismo* and on the Propositions on *Religious Life*. Continuation of the debate on *Seminaries*.

16 November
Hundred-and-twenty-third General Congregation. *Votes* on the Propositions on *Religious Life*. Continuation of the debate on *Seminaries*.

17 November
Hundred-and-twenty-fourth General Congregation. *Votes* on Chapter III, IV and V of the schema *De Ecclesia*, and on the Propositions on *Seminaries*, and beginning of the debate on *Christian Education*.

18 November
Hundred-and-twenty-fifth General Congregation. Continuation of the debate on *Christian Education*.

19 November
Hundred-and-twenty-sixth General Congregation. *Vote* on the schema *De Ecclesia* as a whole. Cardinal Tisserant announced the *adjournment* of the discussion and of the vote on *Religious Freedom*. Reaction. Conclusion of the debate on *Christian Education* and opening of the debate on *the Sacrament of Marriage*, introduced by Cardinal Aloïsi Masella and Mgr Schneider.

20 November
Hundred-and-twenty-seventh General Congregation. *Vote* on the *Eastern churches*, on the *De Œcumenismo*, on *Non-Christian Religions* and on *the Sacrament of Marriage*. Conclusion of the debate on *Marriage*.

21 November
Public sitting for the closure of the Third Session, under the presidency of the Pope who concelebrated Mass in honour of the Presentation of Mary in the

Temple, with twenty-four bishops representing the great Marian sanctuaries, for the pastors and faithful who were suffering for Christ. Final *votes* on the schema *De Ecclesia*, on the Decree concerning *the Eastern Catholic Churches* and on the schema *De Œcumenismo.* Promulgation of these texts by the Pope, who gave an address.

FOURTH SESSION

1965
14 September
Public sitting for the opening of the Fourth and last Session. Paul VI concelebrated Mass with twenty-six cardinals and bishops who were members of the Council of Presidents, of the Co-ordinating Commission and of the Secretariat, and gave an address, at the end of which he announced a synod of bishops. In the evening, a penitential procession from the basilica of Santa Croce to the basilica of St John Lateran.

15 September
Hundred-and-twenty-eighth General Congregation. Paul VI was present at the presentation by Cardinal Marella and the reading by Mgr Felici of the *Motu proprio, Apostolica solicitudo* instituting a synod of bishops. Reading of a telegram from Patriarch Athenagoras. Beginning of the debate on *Religious Freedom*, introduced by the report of Mgr De Smedt (Belgium).

16 September
Hundred-and-twenty-ninth General Congregation. Mgr Felici presented the agenda for the Session. Continuation of the debate on *Religious Freedom*.

17 September
Hundred-and-thirtieth General Congregation. Continuation of the debate on *Religious Freedom*.

20 September
Hundred-and-thirty-first General Congregation. Continuation of the debate on *Religious Freedom. Votes* on *Divine Revelation*.

21 September
Hundred-and-thirty-second General Congregation. Conclusion of the debate on *Religious Freedom. Vote* on giving consideration to the plan of the declaration on *Religious Freedom*: in favour 1,197, against 224, 1 null ballot. Beginning of the debate on *schema XIII,* presented by Mgr Garrone. *Votes* on *Divine Revelation*.

22 September
Hundred-and-thirty-third General Congregation. New interventions on *Religious Freedom*. Continuation of the debate on *schema XIII*. *Votes* on *Divine Revelation*.

23 September
Hundred-and thirty-fourth General Congregation. *Votes* on the *Apostolate of the Laity*. Continuation of the debate on *schema XIII*.

24 September
Hundred-and-thirty-fifth General Congregation. *Votes* on the *Apostolate of the Laity*. Continuation of the debate on *schema XIII*.

27 September
Hundred-and-thirty-sixth General Congregation. *Final votes* on the *Apostolate of the Laity*. Continuation of the debate on first part of *schema XIII*.

28 September
Hundred-and-thirty-seventh General Congregation. Continuation of the debate on the first part of *schema XIII*.

29 September
Hundred-and-thirty-eighth General Congregation. *Votes* on the *Pastoral Office of Bishops*. Continuation of the debate on the second part (some specific problems) of *schema XIII*.

30 September
Hundred-and-thirty-ninth General Congregation. *Votes* on the *Pastoral Office of Bishops*. Continuation of the debate on *schema XIII*.

1 October
Hundred-and-fortieth General Congregation. Continuation of the debate on *schema XIII*.

4 October
Hundred-and-forty-first General Congregation. Continuation of the debate on *schema XIII*.

5 October
Hundred-and forty-second General Congregation. Paul VI gave an account of his journey to the United Nations. Continuation of the debate on *schema XIII*.

6 October
Hundred-and-forty-third General Congregation. *Vote* on the *Pastoral Office of Bishops* and on *Religious Life*. Continuation of the debate on *schema XIII*.

7 October
Hundred-and-forty-fourth General Congregation. *Vote* on *Religious Life*. Conclusion of the debate on *schema XIII*. Beginning of the debate on *the Missions*, introduced by Fr Schütte.

8 October
Hundred-and-forty-fifth General Congregation. *Vote* on *Religious Life*. Continuation of the debate on *the Missions*. Resumption of the debate on *schema XIII*.

11 October
Hundred-and-forty-sixth General Congregation. Reading of a letter from the Pope about priestly celibacy. Continuation of the debate on *the Missions*.

12 October
Hundred-and-forty-seventh General Congregation. Conclusion of the debate on *the Missions*.

13 October
Hundred-and-forty-eighth General Congregation. *Votes* on S*eminaries*. Conclusion of the debate on *the Missions*. The schema on *the Missions* taken into account by 2,070 votes *against* 15. *Votes* on *Christian Education*. Presentation of the schema on *Priests* by Mgr Marty.

14 October
Hundred-and-forty-ninth General Congregation. *Votes* on *Non-Christian Religions*, introduced by Cardinal Bea, and on *Christian Education*. Debate on *Priests*.

15 October
Hundred-and-fiftieth General Congregation. *Vote* on *Non-Christian Religions*. Continuation of the debate on *Priests*.

16 October
Hundred-and-fifty-first General Congregation. Conclusion of the debate on *Priests*.

From 18 to 24 October
Suspension of General Congregations. Meetings of the Commissions for *Religious Freedom, Life and Ministry of Priests, the Missions* and *schema XIII*. Meeting of episcopal conferences consulted by Paul VI on the modification of the rules

about fasting and abstinence, indulgences, and mixed marriages. Meeting, on 21 October, of the presidents of episcopal conferences in the presence of the Pope, for the exchange of points of view on the matter of fasting and abstinence, following the report of Mgr Palazzini, Secretary to the Congregation for the Council. Public lectures by Cardinal Zoungrana (Upper Volta) on the missions, by Fr Arrupe, SJ, on culture, by Cardinal Alfrink (Netherlands) on peace. On 23 and 24 October, an international study session on the diaconate.

25 October
Hundred-and-fifty-second General Congregation. Resumption of the debate on *Priests*. Report of Mgr De Smedt on *Religious Freedom*.

26 October
Hundred-and-fifty-third General Congregation. Conclusion of the debate on *Priests*. *Votes* on *Religious Freedom*.

27 October
Hundred-and-fifty-fourth General Congregation. *Votes* on *Religious Freedom*. Intervention by Mgr Fals, parish priest of Sacred Heart, Philadelphia (USA) on *the Life and Ministry of Priests*.

28 October
Public sitting. Definitive votes on five texts to be promulgated immediately afterwards by Paul VI: the Decree *On the Pastoral Office of Bishops*, the Decree *On the Formation of Priests*, the Declaration *on Christian Education*, the Decree *On the Renewal and Adaptation of Religious Life*, the Declaration *On Non-Christian Religions*. Concelebrated Mass with Paul VI, who gave an address.

29 October
Hundred-and-fifty-fifth General Congregation. *Vote* on the text on *Religious Freedom* as a whole. *Votes* on the *schema on Revelation*, introduced by Cardinal Florit.

From 30 October to 7 November
Holidays for All Saints, except for the Commissions responsible for schemas that had to be revised.

9 November
Hundred-and-fifty-sixth General Congregation. Through a letter to Cardinal Tisserant, Paul VI announced the Council would close on 8 December. Presentation by Cardinal Cento and Mgr Sessolo, of a plan for the reform of the codification of *indulgences*.

10 November
Hundred and-fifty-seventh General Congregation. Final *vote* on *the Apostolate of the Laity,* approved by 2,201 against 2, with five null ballots. Report from Fr Schütte on the amended schema for *the Missions*. Communications about *indulgences.*

11 November
Hundred-and-fifty-eighth General Congregation. *Vote* on the schema for *the Missions*. Communications about *indulgences.*

12 November
Hundred-and-fifty-ninth General Congregation. Announcement by Mgr Felici about the private character of the lectures given at the *Domus Mariae*. Report by Mgr Marty on the amended schema on *the ministry of priests.*

13 November
Hundred-and-sixtieth General Congregation. *Votes* on *Priests*. Further communications about *indulgences* were to be made in writing.

15 November
Hundred-and-sixty-first General Congregation. Report by Mgr Garrone on the amended text of *schema XIII. Votes* on *schema XIII.*

16 November
Hundred-and-sixty-second General Congregation. *Votes* on *schema XIII.*

17 November
Hundred-and sixty-third General Congregation. *Votes* on *schema XIII.*

18 November
Public sitting. Paul VI concelebrated Mass with some theologians, promulgated the Dogmatic Constitution *on Divine Revelation* and the Decree on *the Apostolate of the Laity,* and announced the opening of the process for the beatification of Pius XII and John XXIII.

19 November
Hundred-and-sixty-fourth General Congregation. *Vote* on the *Declaration on Religious Freedom.*

From 20 to 29 November
Suspension of General Congregations; work in Commissions.

26 November
Paul VI paid a visit to the journalists at the Council Press Office.

30 November
Hundred-and-sixty-fifth General Congregation. *Vote* on the schema on *the Missions.*

2 December
Hundred-and-sixty-sixth General Congregation. *Vote* on the schema on *the Life and Ministry of Priests.*

4 December
Hundred-and-sixty-seventh General Congregation. *Votes* on *schema XIII.* Mgr Felici read out a message of thanks from the non-Catholic Observers. Distribution of gifts and souvenirs of the Council. In the afternoon the Pope, a number of bishops and the Non-Catholic Observers prayed together at St Paul Outside-the -Walls.

6 December
Hundred-and-sixty-eighth General Congregation. Final *votes* on *schema XIII.*

7 December
Public sitting. Paul VI concelebrated Mass with twenty-four presidents of episcopal conferences, promulgated the *Declaration on Religious Freedom*, the *Decree on the Missionary Activity of the Church*, the *Decree on the Life and Ministry of Priests* and the *Pastoral Constitution on the Church in the Modern World*, and gave an important homily. Mgr Willebrands read the Declaration and Cardinal Bea the Apostolic Brief lifting the anathemas between Rome and Constantinople.

8 December
Solemn ceremony of closure in St Peter's Square. Paul VI gave a homily; the Council addressed messages to people of all categories. Mgr Felici read out the Decree of closure of Vatican II.

CHRONOLOGICAL TABLES RECAPITULATING CONGAR'S PARTICIPATION IN THE COMPOSITION OF THE VARIOUS CONCILIAR SCHEMAS

In the following tables we recapitulate all the meetings in which Fr Congar participated during the preparatory period, the Sessions, and the intervals between the Sessions of the Council, for the purpose of composing the various schemata. As well as the official meetings of the various Commissions and sub-commissions, both before and during the Council, we have also included Fr Congar's participation in the 'workshops' organised by the French episcopate during the conciliar Sessions with the help of experts, as well as a certain number of informal group meetings whether of bishops and experts, or of experts alone. However, to avoid overloading these tables, we have omitted a number of very restricted team-meetings concerned with preparing or giving shape to work already done in official Commissions or sub-commissions. We have also omitted the innumerable lectures and chats given by Fr Congar to different groups of bishops on the conciliar themes and schemas, limiting ourselves to actual working meetings. In order to help the reader of the *Diaries* to situate Fr Congar's part in the general evolution of the Council, we have marked in bold character for each schema the debates and votes of the conciliar assembly which punctuated its development.

Preparatory schemas: Preparatory Theological Commission.
15 November 1960: Theological Preparatory Commission.
27 and 28 March 1961: informal meeting of the French members of the Preparatory Theological Commission with Mgr Dubois.
From 18 to 28 September 1961: Preparatory Theological Commission.
19 and 20 September 1961: sub-commission on *De Ecclesia*.
From 20 to 23 November 1961: Preparatory Theological Commission.
From 5 to 10 March 1962: Preparatory Theological Commission.
8 and 9 March 1962: sub-commission on *De Ecclesia*.

Dogmatic Constitution on the Church: *Lumen Gentium*
First Session
19 October 1962: meeting of French and German bishops and theologians, organised by Mgr Volk.

25 October 1962: meeting of theologians on the alternative schema *De Episcopis (De Ecclesia)* of G Philips.

6 November 1962: meeting of German theologians at Cardinal Frings', where Philips' *De Ecclesia* was addressed.

26 November 1962: meeting of the working group of French bishops (study of the schema on the Virgin Mary).

28 November 1962: meeting of representatives of the French bishops according to places of residence, then meeting of the whole French episcopate.

1 December 1962: working-group of French episcopate on the schema *De Ecclesia*.

From 1 to 7 December 1962: debate *in aula* on the schema *De Ecclesia*.

First Inter-session

12 and 13 January 1963: informal meeting organised by G Thils at Louvain with Mgr De Smedt and G Philips.

24 January 1963: informal meeting of some French bishops at Mont Sainte-Odile (Lower Rhine).

25 and 26 January 1963: meeting of experts organised by Mgr Volk at Mainz with regard to the German schema.

6 and 7 February 1963: meeting of the bishops of the Thirds Apostolic region at Angers.

From 2 to 11 March 1963: sub-commission of the Doctrinal Commission for the reworking of the *De Ecclesia*.

From 5 to 13 March 1963: Doctrinal Commission.

From 15 to 28 May 1963: Doctrinal Commission.

7 September 1963: meeting of experts organised by Cardinal Suenens at Malines in view of a new chapter on the People of God.

Second Session

1 and 8 October 1963: meetings with the Observers about the *De Ecclesia*.

From 30 September to 31 October 1963: debate *in aula* on the *De Ecclesia*.

30 October 1963: orientation votes on the Episcopate and the Diaconate.

From 2 October to 2 December 1963: meetings of the Doctrinal Commission.

11 October 1963: meeting of 'Conciliar Strategy' organised by Mgr Elchinger.

14 and 21 October 1963: French workshop on the priesthood.

16 and 24 October 1963: meeting of Spanish bishops and experts with representatives from other countries.

From 30 October to 3 December 1963: sub-commission for the drafting of a new chapter on the People of God.

Second Inter-session

From 30 January to 1 February 1964: Sub-commission for the chapter on the People Of God.
From 2 to 13 March 1964: doctrinal sub-commission.
From 1 to 6 June 1964: Doctrinal Commission.
3 June 1964: sub-commission on the question of Mary as mediator.
8 June 1964: examination of the chapter on the Church triumphant (the future Chapter VII) by some experts at Cardinal Browne's.

Third Session

19 September 1964: meeting of some thirty bishops and experts to finalise tactics regarding the *modi* for the *De Ecclesia*.
15 and 16 September 1964: debate *in aula* on Chapter VII of the *De Ecclesia*.
16 September 1964: vote on Chapter I.
17 and 18 September 1964: vote on Chapter II.
From 16 to 18 September 1964: debate *in aula* on Chapter VIII of the *De Ecclesia* on the Virgin Mary.
From 21 to 30 September 1964: votes on Chapter III.
22 September 1964: meeting with the Observers on Chapter VIII on the Virgin Mary.
30 September 1964: vote on Chapters IV, V and VI.
From 5 October to 6 November 1964: meetings of the Doctrinal Commission.
19 and 20 October 1964: vote on Chapter VII of the *De Ecclesia*.
29 October 1964: vote on Chapter VIII of the *De Ecclesia*.
30 October 1964: vote on the *modi* for Chapters I & II.
From 17 to 19 November 1964: votes on the *modi* for Chapters III to V, then on the *De Ecclesia* as a whole.
21 November 1964: solemn vote and promulgation in public sitting of the Dogmatic Constitution on the Church.

Dogmatic Constitution on Divine Revelation: *Dei Verbum*

First Session

19 October 1962: meeting of German and French bishops and theologians organised by Mgr Volk.
8 November 1962: meeting of bishops and theologians at the Biblical Institute.
11 November 1962: meeting of theologians at Mgr Volk's.
From 14 to 21 November 1962: debate *in aula* on the schema on the sources of Revelation.

20 November 1962: a majority of the Fathers voted for the interruption of the examination of the schema, but a two-thirds majority was not achieved.
21 November 1962: the Pope made known to the Council his decision to adjourn the debate and to appoint a Joint Commission for a new schema.
16 and 22 November 1962: working-group of French bishops on Tradition.

First Inter-session

4 March 1963: Joint Commission on *De Revelatione.*

Second Inter-session

2 and 7 March 1964: Doctrinal Commission.
11 March, then from 20 to 25 April 1964: sub-commission charged by the Doctrinal Commission with preparing a new *De Revelatione.*
From 1 to 5 June 1964: Doctrinal Commission.

Third Session

From 30 September to 6 October 1964: debate *in aula* on the new schema *De Revelatione.*
6 and 15 October 1964: meeting with the Observers.
From 20 to 22 October 1964: sub-commission on *De Revelatione* (dealing with amendments).
10 November 1964: Doctrinal Commission.

Fourth Session

From 20 to 22 September 1965: votes on the amended schema.
29 September, 4 and 6 October 1965: Doctrinal Commission (*expensio modorum*).
29 October 1965: votes on the *modi for* the schema.
18 November 1965: solemn vote and promulgation in public sitting of the Dogmatic Constitution on Divine Revelation.

Constitution on the Sacred Liturgy: *Sacrosanctum Concilium*

First Session

From 22 October to 13 November 1962: presentation and discussion of the schema on the Liturgy.
14 and 17 November 1962: votes on the schema.

Second Session

From 8 to 29 October 1963: votes on the amended schema.
11 October 1963: meeting of 'Conciliar Strategy' organised by Mgr Elchinger .
From 20 to 22 November 1963: final votes on the schema on the Liturgy.
4 December 1963: solemn vote and promulgation in public sitting of the Constitution on the Sacred Liturgy.

Pastoral Constitution on the Church in the World: *Gaudium et Spes.*

First Inter-session

From 17 to 20 May 1963: sub-commission (arising out of the Joint Commission for schema XVII), responsible for the preamble and Chapter I on the vocation of humankind.
From 20 to 25 May 1963: Joint Commission for schema XVII.
7, 8 and 17 September 1963: meetings of experts at Malines, organised by Cardinal Suenens, to take up again theological section of the schema.

Second Session

1 November 1963: informal meeting of experts about conscientious objection and peace.

Second Inter-session

4 and 9 March, 28 and 29 April, 4 and 6 June 1964: Meetings of the Joint Commission for schema XVII (now become schema XIII).
10 September 1964: informal meeting of bishops and experts to prepare the restricted session which was to follow.
From 10 to 12 September 1964: restricted session of the Joint Commission.
11 and 12 September 1964: theological sub-commission of the Joint Commission.

Third Session

8 October 1964: French workshop to study schema XIII.
13 October 1964: Joint Commission.

From 20 October to 10 November 1964: debate *in aula* **on schema XIII.**
26 October 1964: Doctrinal Commission.
16 November 1964: Joint Commission.
17 November 1964: central sub-commission of the Joint Commission.

Third Inter-session

From 31 January to 6 February 1965: session of the enlarged central sub-commission at Ariccia.
From 8 to 12 February 1965: Central sub-commission in Rome.
3 April 1965: Joint Commission.

Fourth Session

17 September 1965: meeting of 'Conciliar Strategy' (bishops and experts).
From 21 September to 7 October 1965: debate on schema XIII.
24 September 1965: meeting of 'Conciliar Strategy' (bishops and experts).
6 October 1965: Doctrinal Commission.
From 11 to 16 October 1965: sub-commission *De homine.*
16 October 1965: Joint Commission.
From 15 to 17 November 1965: report and vote on the amended text of schema XIII.

4 and 6 December 1965: votes on the *modi* and vote on schema XIII as a whole.
7 December 1965: solemn vote and promulgation in public sitting of the Pastoral Constitution on the Church in the World.

Decree on the Life and Ministry of Priests: *Presbyterorum Ordinis.*

Third Session

18 September 1964: workshop of French bishops on Priests.
From 13 to 15 October 1964: debate *in aula* on the schema on Priests.
19 October 1964: vote in favour of the reworking of the schema.
27 and 30 October 1, 4, 7 and 11 November 1964: meeting of experts to prepare a new schema.
9 and 12 November 1964: Commission for the Discipline of the Clergy and of the Christian people.

Third Inter-session

From 22 to 27 March 1965: group of experts from the Commission for the Discipline of the Clergy and of the Christian People.

Fourth Session

23 September 1965: workshop of French bishops on the *De Presbyteris.*
26 September 1965: sub-group of the French workshop.
30 September 1965: workshop of French bishops on Priesthood.

From 13 to 26 October 1965: report on the debate *in aula* on the schema on Priests.
From 20 to 30 October 1965: meetings of experts for the *De Presbyteris*.
26 October 1965: meeting with the Observers on the *De Presbyteris*
28 and 29 October 1965: Commission for the Discipline of the Clergy and the Christian People.
From 12 to 15 November 1965: report and vote on the amended schema on the Ministry of Priests.
From 17 to 21 November 1965: Meetings of experts on the *modi for* the schema.
2 December 1965: vote on the schema on the Ministry and Life of Priests.
7 December 1965: vote and promulgation in public sitting of the Decree on the Ministry and Life of Priests.

Decree on the Apostolate of the Laity: *Apostolicam actuositatem*.

Second session

22 January 1964: meeting of the bishops of the Apostolic Region of the East at Marienthal to discuss the schema.

Third Session

From 7 to 13 October 1964: debate on the schema on the Apostolate of the Laity.

Fourth Session

From 23 to 27 October 1965: votes on the amended schema.
9 and 10 November 1965: votes on the *modi* and on the schema as a whole.
18 November 1965: solemn vote and promulgation in public sitting of the Decree on the Apostolate of the Laity.

Decree on the Missionary Activity of the Church: *Ad Gentes*.

Third Session

From 6 to 9 November 1964: discussion *in aula* of the schema on the Missions.
9 November 1964: vote in favour of the reworking of the schema.

Third Inter-session

13 December 1964: meeting in Paris with Mgr Riobé and Fr X Seumois.
19 and 20 December 1964: meetings in Strasbourg with J Glazik, L Kaufmann and X Seumois.

From 12 to 15 January 1965: sub-commission (of the Commission for the Missions) charged with the drafting of a new schema, on the shores of Lake Nemi.
From 29 March to 2 April 1965: Commission for the Missions on the shores of Lake Nemi.

Fourth Session

18 September 1965: Commission for the Missions.
5 and 12 October 1965: meeting with the Observers.
From 7 to 13 October 1965: debate *in aula* on the new schema.
15 October 1965: Commission for the Missions.
From 19 to 21 October 1965: drafting sub-commission at Lake Nemi.
22 October 1965: drafting sub-commission for Chapter I.
27 October 1965: Commission for the Missions.
10 and 11 November 1965: presentation and vote on the amended schema for the Missions.
12 and 13 November 1965: drafting-group at Nemi for the *expensio modorum.*
17 November 1965: Commission for the Missions.
30 November 1965: votes on the *modi* and vote on the schema for the Missions as a whole.
7 December 1965: solemn vote and promulgation in public sitting of the Decree on the Missionary Activity of the Church.

Decree on Ecumenism: *Unitatis Redintegratio*

First Session

From 26 to 30 November 1962: presentation and discussion *in aula* of the schema on Unity, prepared by the Preparatory Commission for the Eastern Churches.
1 December 1962: vote in favour of a new schema.

Second Session

7 and 12 November 1963: French workshop on *De Oecumenismo.*
17 November 1963: meeting with Spanish bishops and experts at which the *De Oecumenismo* was discussed.
From 18 November to 2 December 1963: discussion of the schema on Ecumenism.

Second Inter-session

From 3 to 9 February 1964: session on the *De Oecumenismo* with the experts from the Secretariat for Christian unity.

From 5 to 8 October 1964: votes on the schema *De Oecumenismo*.
From 10 to 20 November 1964: votes on the *modi* and vote on the schema *De Oecumenismo* as a whole.
21 November 1964: solemn vote and promulgation in public sitting of the Decree on Ecumenism.

Declaration on Religious Freedom: *Dignitatis Humanae*

Second session

19 November 1963: presentation *in aula* of Chapter V of the schema on Ecumenism that dealt with religious freedom.
22 November 1963: French workshop on the chapter *De libertate religiosa*.

Third Session

From 23 to 28 September 1964: debate *in aula* on the Declaration on Religious Freedom.
19 November 1964: announcement of the adjournment of the discussion and of the vote on the revised schema.

Third Inter-session

From 19 to 27 February 1965: session of experts at the Secretariat for Christian Unity.
1 & 2 March 1965: plenary session of the Secretariat for Christian Unity.
From 3 to 11 May 1965: session at Secretariat for Christian Unity.

Fourth Session

From 15 to 22 September 1965: debate *in aula* on the schema.
21 September 1965: vote in favour of the schema as a basis for revision.
15 September 1965: meeting of the Secretariat for Unity.
28 September 1965: at the Secretariat for Unity: a meeting of sub-commission III, responsible for the revision of Nos 8–14 of the schema.
29 September and 1 October 1965: sub-commission responsible for the *De libertate* at the Secretariat for Unity.
From 6 to 10 October 1965: sub-commission responsible for the *De libertate*.
10 October 1965: session at the Secretariat for Unity on the *De libertate*.
26 and 27 October 1965: votes on the revised schema.
6 and 7 November 1965: meetings of experts for the *expensio modorum*.
8 November 1965: plenary meeting of the Secretariat for Unity.

19 November 1965: votes on the *modi* and vote on the Declaration on Religious Freedom as a whole.
7 December 1965: solemn vote and promulgation in public sitting of the Declaration on Religious Freedom.
Declaration of the relations of the Church with Non-Christian Religions: *Nostra Aetate*

Second session

19 November 63: presentation of Chapter IV of the schema on Ecumenism, dealing with Non-Christians and especially the Jews.

Second Inter-session

25 and 27 April 1964: meetings with Mgr Willerbrands and C Moeller at the Secretariat for Christian Unity to prepare a new text that would be a declaration about Jews and non-Christians.

Third Session

From 25 to 29 September 1964: presentation and discussion *in aula* of the Declaration on non-Christians and, in particular, the Jews.
6 October 1964: meeting with the Observers about the Declaration.
10 October 1964: meeting of the Secretariat for Christian Unity.
From 20 to 25 October 1964: working-group of the Secretariat for Christian Unity to revise the schema.
12 November 1964: examination of the schema by the Doctrinal Commission.
20 November 1964: vote on the revised schema on Non-Christian Religions.
Third inter-session

From 23 to 26 February 1965: session of experts at the Secretariat for Christian Unity.
3 May 1965: session at the Secretariat for Christian Unity.

Fourth Session

15 September 1965: meeting at the Secretariat for Christian Unity.
14 and 15 October 1965: votes on the *modi* and vote on the schema on Non-Christian Religions as a whole.
28 October 1965: solemn vote and promulgation in public sitting of the Declaration on the relation of the Church to Non-Christian Religions.

LATIN TITLES USED BY CONGAR FOR THE PREPARATORY SCHEMAS AND SOME OF THEIR CHAPTERS

We have put in bold character the titles of the preparatory schemas and, occasionally, some of their chapters in their final state.

Schema *De Ecclesia* (on the Church)
Prepared by the Preparatory Theological Commission

Chapter 1: *De Ecclesiae militantis natura*
De Ecclesiae natura (on the nature of the Church).

Chapter III: *De Episcopatu ut supremo gradu Sacramenti Ordinis et de Sacerdotio*
De Episocopatu (On the Episcopate).

Chapter IV: *De Episcopis residentialibus*
De Episcopis (On Bishops) / *De Sacra hierarchia* (On the sacred hierarchy).

Chapter V: *De statibus evangelicae acquirendae perfectionis*
De statibus perfectionis (The states of perfection).

Chapter VI: *De Laicis*
De Laicis (On the Laity).

Chapter VII: *De Ecclesiae magisterio*
De Magisterio (On the Magisterium).

Chapter IX: *De relationibus inter Ecclesiam et Statum*
De Ecclesia et Statu (On Church and State) / *De Ecclesia et Statu deque Tolerantia* (On Church and State and on tolerance).

Chapter X: *De necessitate ecclesia annuntiandi evangelicum omnibus gentibus et ubique terrarum*

De missionibus (On Missions) / *De officio predicandi* (On the office of preaching) / *De praedicatione Evangelii* (On the preaching of the Gospel).

Chapter XI: *De oecumenismo*
De oecumenismo or De Ecumenismo (On Ecumenism).

Schema *De Beata Maria Virgine Matre Dei et Matre hominum* (On the Blessed Virgin Mary, Mother of God and Mother of humankind)
Prepared by the Preparatory Theological Commission

De Beata Maria Virgine or *De Beata Virgine Maria* or *De B.V.M* or *De B Maria V.* (On the Blessed Virgin Mary).
De Virgine Maria (On the Virgin Mary).
Beata Virgine Maria (Blessed Virgin Mary).

Schema *De fontibus Revelationis* (On the sources of revelation)
Prepared by the Preparatory Theological Commission

De fontibus (On the sources).
De duobus fontibus (On the two sources).

Chapter I: *De duplici fonte Revelationis*
De duplici fonte (On a double source) / *De duobus fontibus* (On the two sources).

Chapter II: *De Scripturae inspiratione, inerrantia et compositione litteraria*
De inspiriatione et inerrantia (On the inspiration and inerrancy)

Schema *De deposito Fidei pure custodiendo* (On guarding the deposit of Faith in its purity)
Prepared by the Preparatory Theological Commission

De deposito fidei (On the deposit of faith).
De deposito (On the deposit).
De deposito pure custodiendo (On guarding the deposit in its purity).

Schema *De ordine morali* (On the moral order)
Prepared by the Preparatory Theological Commission

De re morali (On moral questions).

Schema *De castitate, matrimonio, familia, virginitate* (On chastity, marriage, the family, virginity)
Prepared by the Preparatory Theological Commission

De matrimonio (On marriage).
De familia (On the family).
De castitate et matrimonio (On chastity and marriage).
De castitate (On chastity).

Pars secunda: De matrimonio et familia
Chapter *De matrimonio* (On Marriage).
Chapter *De Matrimonio et familia* (On Marriage on the family).

Schema *De ordine sociali* (On the social order)
Prepared by the Preparatory Theological Commission

De ordine morali sociali (On the moral social order).

Schema *De Sacra Liturgia* (On the Sacred Liturgy)
Prepared by the Preparatory Theological Commission

De Liturgia (On the Liturgy).

Schema *De Verbo Dei* (On the Word of God)
Prepared for the Secretariat of Christian Unity

De Verbo Dei revelato (On revealed Word of God).

Schema *De Ecclesiae unitate* (On the unity of the Church)
Prepared by the Commission of Oriental Churches

De Ecclesiae unitate (On the Unity of the Church).
De unitate (On unity).
'Ut sint unam' ('That they may be one').

Schema *De Cura animarum* (On the care of souls)
Prepared by the Preparatory Commission for the discipline of clergy

LATIN TITLES USED BY CONGAR FOR THE CONCILIAR SCHEMAS AND CERTAIN OF THEIR CHAPTERS AND PARAGRAPHS

We have put in bold characters the titles of the conciliar texts and of their different elements in their final state.

LUMEN GENTIUM
Dogmatic Constitution on the Church
Prepared by the Doctrinal Commission

De Ecclesia (On the Church)

Alternative Schema of Philips from 1962–1963:
        Chapter *De membris* (On members);
        Chapter *De episcopis* (On bishops).

Chapter I: *De mysterio Ecclesiae* (On the mystery of the Church)
No. 7: *De corpore Christi mystico* (On the mystical body of Christ).
Chapter II: *De populo Dei* (On the people of God).
Chapter III: *De episcopis* (On bishops) / *De hierarchia* (On the hierarchy) / *De sacra hierarchia* (On the sacred hierarchy) / *De collegialitate* (On collegiality).
No. 28: De presbyteris (On priests).
Chapter IV: *De Laicis* (On the laity).
Chapters V and VI: *De Religiosis* (On religious) / *De vocatione ad sanctitatem* (On the vocation to holiness) / *De statibus perfectionis* (On the states of perfection) / *De sanctitate* (On holiness).
Chapter VII: *De indole eschatologica* (On the eschatological character [of the Church]).
Chapter VIII: *De Beata* or *De Beata Maria Virgine* or again *De B.M.V.* (On the Blessed Virgin Mary) / *De Beata Maria Virgine Matre Ecclesiae* or *De B.M.V. Matre Ecclesiae* (On the Blessed Virgin Mary Mother of the Church) / *De Maria Matre Ecclesiae* (On Mary Mother of the Church).

DEI VERBUM
Dogmatic Constitution on divine Revelation
Prepared by the Doctrinal Commission

De Revelatione (On Revelation).
De divina Revelatione (On divine Revelation).

Chapter I: *De ipsa Revelatione* (On Revelation in itself).
Chapter II: *De Traditione* (On Tradition).

SACROSANCTUM CONCILIUM
Constitution on the Holy Liturgy
Prepared by the Commission on the Liturgy

De Liturgia (On the Liturgy) / *De Sacra Liturgia* (On the Sacred Liturgy).

GADIUM ET SPES
Pastoral Constitution of the Church in the World
Prepared by the Joint Commission of the Doctrinal Commission and the
Commission for the Apostolate of the Laity

Schema XVII, later Schema XIII

De Ecclesiae principiis et actione ad bonum societatis promovendum (On the
principles and the action of the Church for promoting the good of society).
De praesentia Ecclesiae (On the presence of the Church).
De Ecclesia in mundo (On the Church in the world).
De Ecclesia in hoc mundo (On the Church in this world).

Foreword: *Proemium* (Preamble).
Preliminary Exposition: *Conspectus* (overall view) / *conspectus generalis*
(overall view)

First Part:
Chapter I: *De vocatione supernaturali hominis* (On the supernatural vocation of
the human being) / *De vocatione hominis* (On the vocation of the human being)
/ *De persona humana* (On the human person).
Chapter II: *De persona humana in societate* (On the human person in society).

Second Part:
Chapter I: *De Matrimonio et Familia* (On Marriage and the Family).
Chapter II: *De culturae progressu rite promovendo* (On the correct promotion of
culture), *De cultura* (On culture).

Chapter III: *De œconomia, et iustitia sociali* (On the economy and social justice).
Chapter V: *De communitate gentium et pace* or *De communitate gentium et de pace* (On the community of peoples and on peace).

CHRISTUS DOMINUS
Decree on the Pastoral Function of Bishops in the Church
Prepared by the Commission for Bishops and the Government of Dioceses.

De Episcopis et regimine diocesium (On bishops and the government of dioceses).
De regimine diocesium (On the government of dioceses).
De Episcopis et de diocesium regimine (On bishops and on government of dioceses).
De Episcopis (on bishops).
De munere episocopurm / De episcoporum munere (On the function of bishops).
De munere episcoporum in Ecclesia (On the function of bishops in the Church).
De pastorali episcoporum munere in Ecclesia (On the pastoral function of bishops in the Church).
De pastorali munere (On the pastoral function).
De episcoporum pastorali munere / De Episcoporum pastorali / De pastorali episcoporum munere (On the pastoral function of bishops).

PRESBYTERORIUM ORDINIS
Decree on the Ministry and the life of Priests
Prepared by the Commission for the Discipline of Clergy and of the Christian People

De *clericis* (On Clerics).
De sacerdotibus / De presbyteris (On Priests).
De sacerdotio (On Priesthood).
De presybterorum ministerio et vita (On the ministry and the life of priests).

OPTATAM TOTIUS
Decree on the Formation of Priests
Prepared by the Commission for Seminaries, Studies and Catholic Education

De seminariis (On seminaries).
De institutione sacerdotali (On priestly formation).

PERFECTAE CARITATIS
Decree on the Renewal and Adaptation of the Religious Life
Prepared by the Commission for Religious

De religiosis (On Religious).

APOSTOLICAM ACTUOSITATEM
Decree on the Apostolate of the Laity
Prepared by the Commission for the Apostolate of the Laity

De laicis (On the Laity)
De apostolatu laicorum (On the Apostolate of the Laity).

AD GENTES
Decree on the Missionary Activity of the Church
Prepared by the Commission for the Missions

De Missionibus (On Missions).
De activitate missionali Ecclesiae (On the missionary activity of the Church).
De missionali actitivitate or *De activitate missionali* (On missionary activity).

UNITATIS REDINGERATIO
Decree on Ecumenism
Prepared by the Secretariat for Christian Unity

De oecumenismo (On Ecumenism)
De unione fovenda inter Christianos (On the promotion of unity between Christians).

ORIENATALIUM ECCLESIARUM
Decree on the Eastern Catholic Churches
Prepared by the Commission for the Eastern Churches

De Ecclesiis orientalibus (On the Eastern Churches)

INTER MIRIFICA
Decree on the Means of Social Communication
Prepared by the Secretariat for the Press and the Means of Communication

De mediis cummunicationis inter homines (On the means of communication between people).

DIGNITATIS HUMANAE
Declaration on Religious Freedom
Prepared by the Secretariat for Christian Unity

De libertate religiosa (On Religious Freedom).
De libertate (On Freedom).

NOSTRA AETATE
Declaration on the relations of the Church with non-Christian religions
Prepared by the Secretariat for Christian Unity

De judaico populo (On the Jewish People).
Declaratio de Hebraeis et gentibus non Christianis (Declaration on the Jews and non-Christian peoples).
De Iudeis /Du Iudaeis (On the Jews).
De religionibus non Christianis (On non-Christian religions).
Declaratio de habitude Ecclesiae ad religiones non christianas (Declaration on the attitude of the Church to non-Christian religions).
De Ecclesiae habitudine ad religiones non Christianas / De habitudine Ecclesiae ad religiones non christianas (On the attitude of the Church to non-Christian religions).
De non christianis (On non-Christians).

GRAVISSIMUM EDUCATIONIS
Declaration on Christian education
Prepared by the Commission for Seminaries, Study and Catholic Education

De studiis et scholis (On universities and schools)
De scholis (On Schools).
De educatione christiana (On Christian education).

Votum *De matrimonii sacramento*
(On the Sacrament of Marriage)
Prepared by the Commission for the Discipline of Sacraments

De matrimonio (On Marriage)

NAMES COMMONLY USED
FOR COMMISSION IN THE *JOURNAL*

We have put in bold character the official name used in the notes of this edition, followed by the names used by Congar in the Journal when they are different, as well as their translation, when they are in Latin.

PREPARATORY COMMISSIONS

Preparatory Central Commission.
Central Commission.
Preparatory Theological Commission.
Theological Commission.
Preparatory Commission for the Eastern Churches.
Eastern Commission.
Preparatory Commission for the Discipline of the Sacraments.
Commission for the Sacraments.
Preparatory Commission for the Missions.
Preparatory Commission *De Missionibus.*
Preparatory Commission for the Liturgy.
Preparatory Liturgical Commission.

SECRETARIAT FOR CHRISTIAN UNITY

Secretariat for Unity.
Secretariat.
Bea Secretariat.

COMMISSIONS OF THE COUNCIL

Doctrinal Commission.
Theological Commission.
Commission *De fide et moribus* (On faith and morals).

Commission for Bishops and for the Government of Dioceses.
Commission *De regimine diocesium* (On the Government of Dioceses).
Commission *De episcopis* (On Bishops).
Commission for Eastern Churches.
Commission for the Eastern Churches.
Eastern Commission.
Commission for the Discipline of the Sacraments.
Commission for the Sacraments.
Commission for the Discipline of the Clergy and of the Christian Peoples.
Commission *De disciplina cleri* (On the discipline of the clergy).
Commission *De disciplina cleri et populi christiani* (On the discipline of the Clergy and of the Christian People).
Commission *Pro disciplina cleri* (For the Discipline of Clerics).
Commission for the discipline of Clerics and of the Christian People.
Commission of Clergy.

Commission for Religious.
Religious.

Commission for the Missions.

Commission for the Liturgy.
Liturgical Commission.

Commission for Seminaries, Studies and Catholic Education.
Commission for Studies.
Commission for Studies and the formation of priests.
Commission of Schools and Universities.

Commission for the Lay Apostolate.
Commission for the Laity.
Apostolate of Laity.
Commission of the Lay Apostolate.

GLOSSARY

1. Technical terms in use at the Council

Adsumus: Latin prayer recited at the beginning of each General Congregation.

Central Preparatory Commission: the Commission responsible for coordinating the work of the Preparatory Commissions of the Council.

Coetus internationalis patrum : a group of Council Fathers who formed the most radical section of the conciliar minority, and that was opposed, in particular, to episcopal collegiality and religious freedom.

Co-ordinating Commission: the Commission appointed by John XXIII at the end of the First Session to follow through and co-ordinate the work of the conciliar Commissions during the Inter-session: it was to become, *de facto*, one of the principal directing organs of the Council during and between the Sessions.

Council of Presidents: a directing organ of the Council, with the responsibility of presiding over the General Congregations. The establishment of the Co-ordinating Commission, and then of the Commission of Moderators was to reduce its importance.

Deicide: a word used of the Jewish People to attribute to it collective responsibility for the death of Christ (God incarnate).

Dutch Centre for Conciliar Documentation (DO-C): a centre established for the Council by various Catholic organisms in the Netherlands, with the object of organising lectures in Rome and making theological and historical documentation available. It was subsidised by the bishops of the Netherlands.

Experts of the Council: experts nominated by the pope: they were able to attend sessions of the conciliar Assembly and to be invited to participate in the work of the conciliar Commissions.

Father (Council Father): a voting member of the Council (usually a bishop, an abbot, or the head of a religious order). Congar also used the term 'Father' to refer to priests who were members of religious orders (apart from Benedictines, to whom he gave the prefix 'Dom'). He occasionally used 'Father' of priests who were not members of religious orders, but more normally gave these the prefix 'l'abbé' or 'Don' (if they were Italian). These distinctions have been maintained in the English translation. 'Fathers' is also used in the *Journal* to refer to the Fathers of the Church (i.e. Early Christian Writers).

General Congregation: a working session of the conciliar Fathers.

Guests of the Secretariat for Unity: Non-Catholic Christians personally invited by the pope to attend the Council and to contribute in this way to the ecumenical opening.

Lay Auditors at the Council: lay persons invited to attend the Council, beginning from the Second Session; they were able to attend sessions of the Council and to participate in the work of the conciliar Commissions.

Moderators (*moderatores*): the four cardinals appointed by Paul VI in September 1963 to see that the Council made proper progress; in part, they took over the task of the Council of Presidents and they were to be one of the principal directing organs of the Council.

Non-Catholic Observers: Delegates sent, at the invitation of the pope, by the various Churches and Ecclesial Communities separated from Rome, to witness the work of the Council and to contribute at it to the ecumenical opening.

Nota Bene (NB): the concluding lines of the *Nota explicativa praevia* which clarified that the Doctrinal Commission had not wanted to settle the question of the validity of ordinations in the Orthodox Churches.

***Nota praevia explicativa* (preliminary explanatory note)**: a note placed, at the request of the pope, at the beginning of the *Relatio* concerning the *modi* for Chapter III of the *De Ecclesia*, with the purpose of clarifying the interpretation of this chapter and of obtaining in this way a consensus among the conciliar Fathers with respect to episcopal collegiality.

Post-Conciliar Central Commission: the Commission responsible for co-ordinating the work of the Post-Conciliar Commissions.

Private Experts: experts invited as advisors by one or more of the conciliar Fathers.

Secretariat for Extraordinary Affairs: intended by John XXIII to be an organ of mediation, it was suppressed by Paul VI.

Theological note: the weight to be assigned to a theological proposition, especially as found in a conciliar or papal document, as to its bearing on revealed truth: e.g. infallible, certain, reformable etc. There are corresponding negative notes: e.g. heretical, temerarious, offensive to pious ears, etc.

Workshops: groups of bishops and experts established by the French episcopate to work on the questions or schemas dealt with by the Council.

2. (Mainly) Latin Words and Phrases

Animadversiones: observations (the term usually refers to the reactions of conciliar Fathers to a schema).

Aula: precinct (the term usually refers to St Peter's Basilica, in which the conciliar Assembly met).

Capella papale: a liturgical celebration at which the pope presides.

Caput: head; chapter.

Collegium: college.

Communicatio in sacris: participating in a sacramental celebration together with Non-Catholic Christians.

Curia, curial:the central administrative offices of the Roman Church. The term was also occasionally used by Congar to refer to the central administrative offices of the Dominican Order.

Deicida / deicidium: deicide (cf the Glossary).

Ecclesia: Church. {Congar used the Latin word in a pregnant sense, to indicate the real Church, as distinct from ecclesiastical epiphenomena}.

Effatum (effata): utterance (utterances), used by Congar of papal pronouncements.

Emendatio (emendationes): emendation(s):(the term usually refers to an important modification proposed for the text of a schema at first reading).

Ex sese: of himself, herself, itself, themselves: (the expression was used by the First Vatican Council to make clear that irreformable definitions promulgated by the pope are such by themselves and do not juridically require consent by the Church either before or after the event).

Expensio modorum: the examination of *modi* (the term covers the analysis of *modi* proposed for a schema and the detailed reply given to them; it indicates both the work of analysis and response and the written report submitted to the Council Fathers).

Faith and Order: a Commission of the World Council of Churches.

Flabella: large fans of ostrich feathers that formerly flanked the pope on solemn ceremonial occasions.

In aula: in the conciliar Assembly.

In genere: in general; on the whole.

Iuxta modum : subject to modification.

Mater Ecclesiae: Mother of the Church.

Mediatrix: Latin feminine of *mediator*.

Minutante (minutanti): person(s) employed in the Roman Congregations in the studying of dossiers and the preparation of proposals for action on them.

Modus (modi): modification(s). (The term usually refers to small modifications proposed for the text of a conciliar schema at the second reading).

Munus: office, function, duty.

Non placet: 'it does not please': the conventional formula for voting against a proposal.

Observatores: Observers (the term refers to the Non-Catholic Observers delegated by other Churches).

Partim, partim: 'partly, ... partly' (the formula '*partim ... partim*' was adopted, and then rejected, by the Fathers of the Council of Trent when speaking of truths of the Faith that are contained in Scripture and in Tradition).

Peritus (periti): expert(s) of the Council (the word usually indicates experts officially nominated by the pope and able to participate in the work of the conciliar Commissions).

Placet in genere: 'it pleases on the whole'.

Placet iuxta modum: 'it pleases subject to modification'. The conventional formula for casting a qualified vote in favour of a proposal.

Placet: 'it pleases'. The conventional formula for voting in favour of a proposal.

Populus Dei: The People of God.

Potestas: Power.

Presidium / praesidium: presidency (that is to say, usually, the Council of Presidents).

Proemium: preface.

Relatio (relationes): report(s): (the term usually indicates the presentation, in writing or in speech or both, of a schema or of a part of a schema).

Relatio generalis: general report: (the term usually indicates the presentation of a schema as a whole).

Relator (relatores): rapporteur(s): (the term usually indicates the member of a conciliar Commission charged with presenting a schema to the Fathers of the Council).

Schema, Schemata: Schema(s), position paper(s). The term can refer to any project of the Council at any stage of its development up until its promulgation.

Scrittore: scribe (the term is used of certain administrative officials in the Roman Curia).

Sedia gestatoria: an ostentatious sedan chair formally used by the popes on ceremonial occasions.

Socius (socii): companion(s) (in the Dominican Order, Priors Provincial may be accompanied by one or more of these, elected by their Provinces, when attending General Chapters; assistants to the Master of the Dominican Order are also so called).

Studium: a (Dominican) house of studies.

Synodos endemousa: a permanent synod: (in the Byzantine Church it refers to an advisory council of bishops attached to the Patriarch and regularly consulted by him. Cardinal Alfrink's proposal was somewhat different, inspired by the experience of the Central Preparatory Commission).

Veritas salutaris: saving truth.

Via media: middle road (between two extremes).

Votum (vota): a proposal (proposals) in writing, made at the Council by a Council Father or an expert.

3. Ecclesiastical Institutions

Angelicum: the ecclesiastical faculties conducted by the Dominicans in Rome; it became the Pontifical University of St Thomas Aquinas in 1963.

Antonianum: Pontifical Athenaeum conducted by the Franciscans in Rome.

Catholic Conference for Ecumenical Questions: a working group of Catholic ecumenists founded by J Willebrands and F Thijssen at the beginning of the

1950s, a number of whose members were later to be co-opted by the Secretariat for Christian Unity.

Chevetogne: Belgian Benedictine Abbey founded by Dom Lambert Beauduin, with the purpose of furthering rapprochement with Eastern Christians, it publications include the journal *Irénikon*.

École biblique et archéologique française de Jérusalem: a centre of research and training in biblical studies founded by Fr Marie-Joseph Lagrange, OP, and conducted by the Dominicans.

Faith and Order: Commission of the World Council of Churches responsible for doctrinal, and especially ecclesiological dialogue between the Churches.

Gregorianum: Pontifical University in Rome founded and conducted by the Jesuits.

Istina: Centre of Ecumenical Research founded by the Dominicans of the Province of France; its superior was Fr Christophe-Jean Dumont, OP. It published the journal *Istina*.

Lateran: Pontifical University associated with the Lateran Basilica in Rome.

Little Church: a Church that had its origins in the rejection of the Concordat between Pius VII and Bonaparte in 1801.

Pontifical Biblical Institute (Biblicum): Institute founded in 1909 within the Gregorianum for the promotion of biblical studies.

Pontifical Greek College: a Roman College for Byzantine-rite clerical students.

Propaganda (fide): Roman Congregation in charge of Catholic Churches in mission territories, now called the Congregation for the Evangelisation of Peoples.

Saint Jerome Abbey: Benedictine Abbey founded in Rome in 1933 by Pope Pius XI for the revision of the Vulgate text of the Bible.

Urbanianum: Pontifical University in Rome attached to the Congregation for the Propagation of the Faith (Propaganda).

4. Encyclicals

Divino afflante Spiritu: on biblical exegesis, published in 1943 by Pius XII.

Ecclesiam suam: on the Church and dialogue: published 6 August 1964 by Paul VI.

Humani generis: condemnation of some contemporary theological positions, published in 1950 by Pius XII.

Mater et Magistra: on social changes, published 15 May 1961 by John XXIII.

Mediator Dei: on the Liturgy, published in 1947 by Pius XII.

Mysterium fidei: on the Eucharist, published 3 September 1965 by Paul VI.

Mystici corporis: on the Church as the Mystical Body of Christ, published in 1943 by Pius XII.

Pacem in terris: on peace in the world, published 11 April 1963 by John XXIII.

5. Other

Constitutive Tradition: the concept of an oral tradition, deriving from Christ, and containing certain truths not to be found in the Gospels.

Denzinger: a well-known collection of documents of the Magisterium (chiefly of the Councils and the popes) that traditionally bears the name of its first editor, Heinrich Josef Denzinger.

EUR (Esposizione Universale di Roma): a modern quarter of the city of Rome, the origin of which goes back to the World Exposition of 1937.

Integrist, Integrism: a term used by Congar to refer to persons, groups, or currents of thought in French Catholicism which he considered reactionary (cf page xlvii).

Motu proprio: a pontifical act published by the pope 'of his own accord' as supreme legislator.

New Life: a Christian movement founded by former Rover Scouts in France.

Secretariat: when used without further qualification, this normally refers to the Secretariat for Christian Unity, though Congar sometimes uses it in other senses, e.g. of the secretarial offices of the Council.

Syllabus (of Errors): a catalogue of eighty errors thought to imperil Catholicism in modern society that accompanied the encyclical *Quanta cura* published in 1864 by Pope Pius IX.

Titular bishop: a bishop without a diocese, who is given the fictitious title of a diocese that no longer exists: they are mainly Apostolic Nuncios, auxiliary bishops, and bishops working in the Roman Curia.

PRINCIPAL WORKS BY CONGAR
MENTIONED IN THE *JOURNAL*

Yves Congar, *Chrétien désunis. Principes d'un 'oecuménisme' catholique*, Coll. 'Unam Sanctum', 1 (Paris: Cerf, 1937).

Yves Congar, *Leur résistance. Mémorial de officers évadés anciens de Colditz et de Lübeck morts pour la France. Témoignage d'Yves Congar* (Paris, 1948).

Yves, M.-J. Congar, *Vraie et fausse réforme dans l'Église*, Coll. 'Unam Sanctam', 20 (Paris: Cerf, 1950).

Yves, M.-J. Congar, *Jalons pour une théologie du laïcat*, Coll. 'Unam Sanctum, 23 (Paris: Cerf, 1953).

Yves, M.-J. Congar, 'Neuf cents ans après. Notes sur le "Schisme oriental"', in *1054–1954 – L'Église et les Églises – neuf siecles de douloureuse separation entre l'Orient et l'Occident* (Chevetogne, 1954), 3–95.

Yves Congar, *La Pentecôte – Chatres 1956* (Paris: Cerf, 1956).

Le Mystère du Temple ou l'Économie de la Présence de Dieu à sa creature de la Genèse à l'Apocalypse, Coll. 'Lectio Divina' (Paris: Cerf, 1958).

Yves, M.-J. Congar, *La Tradition et les traditions. Essai historique* (Paris: Fayard, 1960).

Yves, M.-J. Congar, *Aspects de l'oecuménisme* (Bruxelles: Éd de la Pensée Catholique, 1962).

Yves, M.-J. Congar, *La foi et la théologie*, Coll. 'Le Mystère Chrétien' (Tournai, Desclée, 1962).

Yves, M.-J. Congar, *Sacerdoce et laïcat devant leurs tâches d'évangelisation et de civilisation* (Paris: Cerf, 1962).

Yves, M.-J. Congar, *et al, L'Épiscopat et l'Église universelle*, Coll. 'Unam Sanctam', 39 (Paris: Cerf, 1962).

Yves, M.-J. Congar, *La Tradition et la vie de l'Église* (Paris: Fayard, 1963).

Yves, M.-J. Congar, *Pour une Église servante et pauvre* (Paris: Cerf, 1963).

Yves, M.-J. Congar, *La Concile au jour le jour* (Paris: Cerf, 1963).

Yves, M.-J. Congar, *La Tradition et les traditions. Essai théologique* (Paris: Fayard, 1963).

Yves, M.-J. Congar, *Sainte Église. Études et approaches ecclésiologiques*, Coll. 'Unam Sanctum', 41 (Paris: Cerf, 1963).

Yves, M.-J. Congar, *Le Concile au jour le jour. Deuxième session* (Paris: Cerf, 1964).

Yves Congar, Hans Küng et Daniel O'Hanlon (eds), *Discours au Concile Vatican II* (Paris: Cerf, 1964).

Yves, M.-J. Congar, *Chrétiens en dialogue. Contribution catholiques à l'Ecuménisme*, Coll. 'Unam Sanctam', 50 (Paris: Cerf, 1964).

Yves, M.-J. Congar, *et al, Église et pauvreté*, Coll. 'Unam Sanctun', 57 (Paris: Cerf, 1965).

Yves, M.-J. Congar, *Le Concile au jour le jour. Troisième session* (Paris: Cerf, 1965).

Yves, M.-J. Congar, *Jésus-Christ, notre Médiateur et notre Seigneur* (Paris: Cerf, 1966).

Yves, M.-J. Congar, *Le Concile au jour le jour. Quatrième session* (Paris: Cerf, 1966).

Yves, M.-J. Congar, *et al, L'Église de Vatican II*, Coll. 'Unam Sanctum', 51, A, B, C, (Paris: Cerf, 1966).

Yves, M.-J. Congar, *et al, Le diacre dans l'Égise et le monde d'auhourd'hui*, Coll. 'Unam Sanctum', 59 (Paris: Cerf, 1966).

Yves, M.-J. Congar, *Situation et tâches présentes de la théologie* (Paris: Cerf, 1967).

Yves Congar, *À mes frères*, Coll. ' Foi Vivante', 71 (Paris: Cerf, 1968).

Yves Congar, *L'Église une, sainte, catholique, et apsotolique*, 'Mysterium Salutis', 15 (Paris: Cerf, 1970).

Yves Congar, *Une vie pour la verite* (Le Centurion, 1975).

PLAN OF ROME

Some centres and meeting places
1. Room of the Dutch Doucmentation Centre (DO-C), place Navone
2. Italian Episcopal Conference, via Aurelia
3. Waldensian Faculty of Theology, via Cossa
4. Foyer Unitas, 30 via S. Maria dell'Anima
5. Domus Mariae, 481 via Aurelia
6. Abbey of Saint-Jerome, 21 via di Torre Rossa
7. Hotel Columbus, 33 via della Conciliazione
8. Domus Pacis, 94 via di Torre Rossa

Principal Institutes, Faculties and Universites
9. Pontifical Univerity of St Thomas (Angelicum), 1 salita del Grillo
10. Pontifical University Antonianum, 124 via Merulana
11. Sant' Anselmo, 19 via Porta Lavernale
12. Collegio San Bonaventura, 42 via S. Teodoro
13. Pontifical Salesian Athenaeum 42 via Marsala
14. College of Propaganda, via del Gianicolo
15. Faculty of Theology Marianum, 6 viale 30 aprile
16. Biblicum Institute 25 via della Pilotta
17. Institute of Sacred Music, 20a place Saint-Augustin
18. Oriental Institute, 7 via S. Maria Maggiore
19. Gregorianum, 4 place della Pilotta
20. Lateran University, 4 via S. Giovanni in Laterano

Organs of the Council and Roman Curia
21. Appartements of the Pope and the Secrétary of State
22. Aula of the Council
23. Palazzo of the la Chancellerie
24. Palazzo delle Congregazioni, place Pie XII
25. Eastern Congregation
26. Congrgation of Propaganda, 48 piazza di Spagna
27. Holy Office, 11 piazza del S. Uffizio
28. Saint-Martha, Cité du Vatican
29. Secretriat for Christain Unity, 64 via dei Corridori puis 1 via dell'Erba
30. Press and Information Office, 52-54 via della Conciliazione

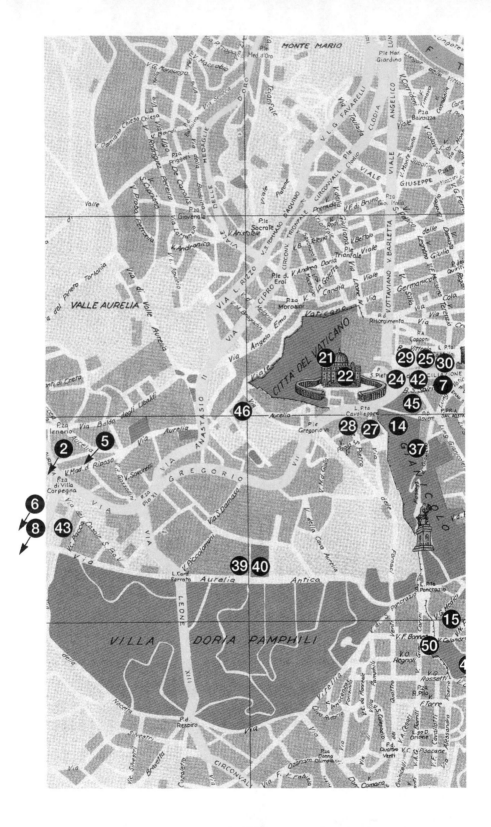

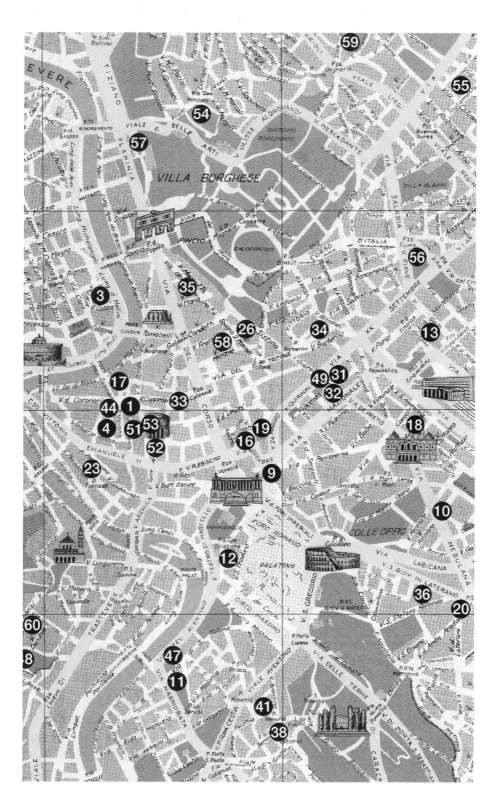

Residences and Meeting Places for Certain Groups of Council Fathers
31. Belguim College, 26 via del Quirinale
32. Canadian College, 117 via delle Quattro Fontane
33. Capranica College Capranica, 98 place Capranica
34. German-Hungarian College, 13 via S. Nicola da Tolentino
35. Greek Collège, 149 via del Babuino
36. Irish College, 7 via dei SS. Quattro
37. North American College, 14 via del Gianicolo
38. Dutch College, 1 via E. Rosa
39. Brazilian Collegio Pio, 527 via Aurelia
40. Latin American Collegio Pio, 511 via Aurelia
41. Polish College, 2a place Remuria
42. Portugues College, 12 via Banco S. Spirito
43. Spanish College, 2 via Torrerossa
44. German College de S. Maria dell'Anima, 20 via della Pace
45. General Curia of the Society of Jesus, Borgo S. Spirito
46. General Curia of the Friars Minor, 25 via S. Maria Mediatrice
47. Santa Sabina (General Curia of the Dominicans), 1 piazza Pietro d'Il-liria
48. General Curia of the Missionnaries of La Salette, 3 place Principessa di Sarsina
49. Procure Saint-Sulpice, 113 via delle Quattro Fontane
50. Salvator Mundi, 67 via della Mura Gianicolensi
51. Saint-Louis-des-Français, 5 via S. Giovanna d'Arco
52. French Seminary, 42 via S. Chiara

Résidences of some Ambasadorrs to the Holy See
53. Argentine Embassy , 37 place Saint-Louis-des-Français
54. Belgium Embassy , 4 via de Notaris
55. German Embassy, 56 via Bruxelles
56. French Embassy, Villa Bonaparte, 66a via XX Settembre
57. Italian Embassy, 166 via Flaminia
58. Spainish Embasy, 57 place d'Espagne
59. Viale Romania (Sisters of Saint-Thomas-de-Villeneuve), viale Romania
60. Via Ulisse Seni (Sisters of the Retreat of the Sacred Heart), 2 via Ulisse Seni

INDEX OF COUNCIL FATHERS

INDEX OF OTHER NAMES